Microsoft Press
Computer Dictionary

Third Edition

PUBLISHED BY
Microsoft Press
A Division of Microsoft Corporation
One Microsoft Way
Redmond, Washington 98052-6399

Library of Congress Cataloging-in-Publication Data
Microsoft Press Computer Dictionary. -- 3rd ed.
    p.   cm.
  ISBN 1-57231-446-X
   1. Computers--Dictionaries. 2. Microcomputers--Dictionaries.
 I. Microsoft Press.
 QA76.15.M54 1997
 004'.03--dc21   97-15489
                             CIP

Printed and bound in the United States of America.

1 2 3 4 5 6 7 8 9 QMQM 2 1 0 9 8 7

Distributed to the book trade in Canada by Macmillan of Canada, a division of Canada Publishing Corporation.

A CIP catalogue record for this book is available from the British Library.

Microsoft Press books are available through booksellers and distributors worldwide. For further information about international editions, contact your local Microsoft Corporation office. Or contact Microsoft Press International directly at fax (425) 936-7329.

Acquisitions Editor: Kim Fryer
Project Editor: Maureen Williams Zimmerman, Anne Taussig
Technical Editors: Dail Magee Jr., Gary Nelson, Jean Ross, Jim Fuchs, John Conrow, Kurt Meyer, Robert Lyon, Roslyn Lutsch

Contents

Introduction

The *Microsoft Press Computer Dictionary, Third Edition* is designed to be a comprehensive and authoritative source of definitions for computer-related terms and abbreviations. The dictionary includes terms drawn from a wide variety of topics:

Applications

    Databases
    Desktop Publishing
    Multimedia
    Spreadsheets
    Word Processing

Communication and Networks

    E-mail
    Intranet

Data and Data Storage

Games

Graphics

Hardware

    Architecture
    Chips, Cards, and Boards
    Computers
    Disks, Drives, and Other Media
    Peripherals
    Processors

History

Information Processing

    General Computing
    Input/Output
    Memory and Memory Management

Internet

    Protocols
    Security
    Tools (user and developer)
    World Wide Web

Organizations

Software Engineering

    Concepts
    Programming Languages
    Tools and Techniques

Standards

Systems and Environments

    Operating Systems

Although this book covers nearly every aspect of computing, it does not include entries on most companies or on most makes and models of computers, nor does it contain entries on most application software products. The few exceptions to this rule of thumb are key companies and products that have a historical or universal importance within the computing industry.

This dictionary emphasizes terminology that the average computer user will encounter in documentation, online help, computer manuals, marketing and sales materials, the popular media, and the computer trade press. Because most computer users operate personal computers and desktop systems at home, work, or both, the majority of the entries in this dictionary cover the terminology used in describing and working with these systems. However, some specialized or highly technical language is included that pertains to areas of industry, academia, software and hardware development, and research. These terms have been included because they have a bearing on more common computer terminology or because they are of historical significance.

Changes in the Third Edition

The third edition of the *Microsoft Press Computer Dictionary* has been revised and updated to reflect the many advances in the computer field and to include several areas that have come into prominence in the public eye, such as the Internet. Over 2,500 new entries have been added, covering the Internet, the World Wide Web, network computing, hardware and software advances, virtual reality, multimedia, and workgroup computing.

Existing entries from the second edition of the *Microsoft Press Computer Dictionary* have been updated to include changes in the field.

All entries have been styled in a more traditional dictionary format than in previous editions. Pronunciations and parts of speech are given for all terms. Entries that have more than one sense, or definition, are broken into numbered lists.

Order of Presentation

Entries are alphabetized by letter. Spaces are ignored, as are characters such as hyphens and slashes; for example, *Baudot code* falls between *baud* and *baud rate,* and *machine-independent* falls between *machine identification* and *machine instruction*. Numbers and symbols are located at the beginning of the book and are listed in ascending ASCII order. If an entry begins with a letter or letters but contains a number, it is listed alphabetically, according to the initial letter(s), and then according to ASCII order. Thus, *V20* precedes *V.2x,* and both precede *VAB*.

Entries

Entries are of two types: main entries, which contain full definitions, and synonymous cross-references, which contain *See* references to the appropriate main entries. Synonymous cross-references are generally secondary or less common ways of referring to a main entry. The definition at the main entry can be substituted as a definition for the synonymous cross-reference.

Format

Information in each main entry is presented in a consistent format: entry name in boldface, spelling variants (if any), pronunciation, part of speech, definition, illustration or table references (if any), acronym (if any), alternative names (if any), and cross-references (if any).

Main Entries

Entries that are acronyms or abbreviations for one or more words or concatenations of two or more words have those words spelled out at the beginning of the definition. The letters in these words or phrases that make up the acronym, abbreviation, or concatenation are in boldface.

When a main entry is spelled exactly the same as another main entry, the two entries are differentiated by the use of a superscript numeral after each term. These entries are called homographs, and they are generally different parts of speech. For example,

e-mail[1] (noun)
e-mail[2] (verb)

Spelling Variants

When a main entry has one or more variations in the way it is spelled, each spelling variant follows the main entry, after the word *or*.

Pronunciations

Pronunciation keys appear after all defined terms in the dictionary. Within the pronunciation keys, individual words are separated by word spaces, and syllables within each word are separated by stress marks or hyphens.

Variant Pronunciations

The *Microsoft Press Computer Dictionary, Third Edition* uses a generalized system for representing pronunciations, particularly for the vowels. There are many subtle variations, well known to phonologists in particular, in the ways Americans in different parts of the United States pronounce many vowels. However, most can recognize words that are pronounced slightly differently by others and should be able to interpret the broad category represented for each of the vowel sounds in this dictionary and apply it in their own regional variation or dialect. This dictionary represents only standard American pronunciations, but there are cases in which sufficient divergence in pronunciation exists, even within the United States, so some variant pronunciations have been included.

Variants are separated by commas, and the most common pronunciation may appear first. However, because there are many cases where two pronunciations are (at least roughly) equally widely used, the order in which they appear should not be interpreted to mean that the first one given is more "correct" or common than the other(s). Variants are shown on a word-by-word basis; for a multiword entry, pronunciation keys are given only for the word or words that have variant pronunciations.

For words that are spelled with the letters *wh*, the pronunciation is listed with two variants: one with a simple *w* (w) and one with the *hw* sound (hw).

Words that are spelled with either *au* or *aw* include a variant pronunciation with the letter *o* with a circumflex accent (ô), which represents the vowel sound some Americans (those who make a significant distinction between this sound and a "regular" short *o*) pronounce when they say the word *dawn*. In some parts of the country, this vowel sound is also used in words with other spellings, such as *coffee* or *talk*, but this seems to be a distinctly dialectical variation rather than a standard one. It is therefore very difficult for any individual to predict how any other might pronounce these particular words, so variants have not been included for them.

Stress

The syllable or syllables pronounced with the heaviest, or primary, stress in a term are followed by acute accents (´); those with lighter, or secondary, stress are followed by grave accents (`). For example, in the word *computer*, the second syllable is spoken more forcefully, or with more stress, than the first and third syllables and therefore is followed in the pronunciation key by an acute accent (kəm-pyōō´tər). In the word *engineering*, the third syllable is stressed most heavily, but the first syllable is stressed more than the second or fourth, so the first syllable is followed by a grave accent, indicating secondary stress (en`jə-nēr´ēng).

Special Characters and Diacritics

The dictionary's pronunciation schema keeps the use of technical phonetic characters to a minimum. Instead, a system that is more familiar to most Americans represents short vowels with plain letters (a, e, i, o, u) and long vowels with overbars (ā, ē, ī, ō, ōō). The ligatured *o*'s represent the vowel sounds in the words *foot* (ŏŏ) and *food* (ōō).

The letter *a* with an umlaut (ä) is included as an alternative to the short *o* (o). It is used when the vowel is represented orthographically by some letter or combination of letters other than the letter *o*, such as *a* (as in *father*), *au* (as in *caught*), or *aw* (as in *dawn*). This is done mainly to avoid confusing the reader visually with pronunciations such as won´dər for the word *wander.*

One other pair of alternative characters is used to represent a single vowel sound: the schwa (ə) and a short u (u). Traditionally, the schwa has been reserved for unstressed, or reduced, vowels, but in recent years it has become much more commonly used in dictionaries to also represent the short, stressed *u*. In this dictionary, the short *u* is used only in words that are spelled with the letter *u*, and the schwa is used for all other spellings except for "syllabic *l*'s," in which cases the vowel is dropped entirely, as in the word *little* (li´tl).

One other diacritic used in the pronunciations is a circumflex over the letter *a* (â). This is used instead of the short *e* only in combination with the letter *r*, to represent the vowel sound heard in words such as *air, software,* and *very.* This is done to avoid representations such as ker´ək-tər for the word *character,* which might lead some readers to believe that the sound should be pronounced as is the *er* in the word *her.*

Acronyms

When acronyms are pronounced as a series of sounded-out letters, capital letters are used to represent the pronunciation of the letters; for example, the pronunciation for the term *EPS* is E`P-S´, not ē`pē-es´. *Note:* Letter-by-letter pronunciations are included for all acronyms in the dictionary, even those that are pronounced as words by most people; for example, the pronunciation for the term *ASCII* includes both a´skē and A`S-C-I-I´.

Pronunciation Symbols

The following charts include the characters used for the pronunciations in the *Microsoft Press Computer Dictionary, Third Edition* (MPCD), the International Phonetic Alphabet (IPA) symbols to which those characters correspond, and some example words in which the letter or letters that represents each sound is underlined. No attempt has been made to repre-

sent foreign sounds as they are pronounced in their original language; only Americanized pronunciations are given for foreign words and names.

VOWELS

MPCD	IPA	Representative Words
a	æ	b<u>a</u>t
ā	e	<u>a</u>pe
ä	ɑ	f<u>a</u>ther
ô	ɔ	d<u>aw</u>n
är	ɔr	d<u>ar</u>t
âr	ɛr	h<u>air</u>
e	ɛ	l<u>e</u>t
ē	i	b<u>ee</u>, <u>e</u>qual
ēr	ir	h<u>ear</u>
i	ɪ	s<u>i</u>t
ī	aɪ	n<u>i</u>ce
īr	aɪr	w<u>ire</u>
o	ɑ	h<u>o</u>t
ō	o	<u>oa</u>ts, h<u>o</u>me
ôr	or	t<u>or</u>n
o͞o	U	b<u>oo</u>k
o͞or	Ur	t<u>our</u>
o͞o	u	b<u>oo</u>t, r<u>u</u>le
oi	ɔɪ	<u>oi</u>l, b<u>oy</u>
ou	aU	<u>ou</u>t
u	ʌ	c<u>u</u>p
ur	ɝ	p<u>ur</u>ge
ə	ə	<u>a</u>bout, it<u>e</u>m, ed<u>i</u>ble, gall<u>o</u>p
ər	ər	ev<u>er</u>

CONSONANTS

MPCD	IPA	Representative Words
b	b	<u>b</u>it
ch	ʧ	<u>ch</u>ild, rat<u>ch</u>et
d	d	<u>d</u>og
f	f	<u>f</u>ill, <u>ph</u>obia, lau<u>gh</u>
g	g	<u>g</u>old, <u>gh</u>ost
h	h	<u>h</u>ome
j	ʤ	<u>j</u>ail, led<u>ge</u>
k	k	<u>k</u>id, <u>c</u>ow, <u>ch</u>rome
l	l, ļ	<u>l</u>ive, doub<u>le</u>
m	m	<u>m</u>ap
n	n	<u>n</u>ot, <u>kn</u>ow

ng	ŋg , ŋ	fi<u>ng</u>er, si<u>ng</u>
p	p	<u>p</u>ine, a<u>pp</u>le
r	r	<u>r</u>at
s	s	<u>s</u>oon, <u>c</u>ell
sh	ʃ	<u>sh</u>oe, no<u>t</u>ion, <u>ch</u>arade
t	t	<u>tes</u>t
th	θ	<u>th</u>in
dh	ð	<u>th</u>en
v	v	<u>v</u>ine
w	w	<u>w</u>ine
hw	ʌʌ	<u>wh</u>ine
y	j	<u>y</u>et
z	z	<u>z</u>oom, bed<u>s</u>
zh	ʒ	plea<u>s</u>ure, colla<u>ge</u>

Parts of Speech

Entries are broken down into four parts of speech, in addition to prefixes, abbreviated as follows:

n.	noun
vb.	verb
adj.	adjective
adv.	adverb

Definitions

Each of the more than 7,300 entries is written in clear, standard English. Many go beyond a simple definition to provide additional detail and to put the term in context for a typical computer user. When an entry has more than one sense or definition, the definitions are presented in a numbered list, to make it easier to distinguish the particular, sometimes subtle, variations in meaning.

Illustration and Table References

Some entries have affiliated illustrations or tables that aid in defining the entry. In most cases, illustrations and tables appear on the same page as the entries to which they apply. In some instances, however, page layout requirements have forced them to a subsequent page. Entries with illustrations or tables usually have references at the end of the definition for an entry, in the following formats:

See the illustration.
See the table.

Acronyms

Some terminology in the computer field, particularly computer standards and Internet slang, can be shortened to form acronyms. Sometimes the acronym is the more common way to refer to the concept or object; in these cases, the acronym is the main entry. In other cases, the acronym is not as commonly used as the words or phrase for which it stands. In these cases, the words or phrase constitute the main entry. The acronym is given after the definition for these entries in the following format:

Acronym:

Alternative Names

Some items or concepts in the computer field can be referred to by more than one name. Generally, though, one way is preferred. The preferred terminology is the main entry. Alternative names are listed after any acronyms; otherwise they are listed after the definition in the following format:

Also called:

Cross-References

Cross-references are of three types: *See, See also,* and *Compare*. A *See* reference is used in an entry that is a synonymous cross-reference and simply points to another entry that contains the information sought. A *See also* reference points to one or more entries that contain additional or supplemental information about a topic and follows any acronyms or alternative names after the definition. A *Compare* reference points to an entry or entries that offer contrast and follows any *See also* references; otherwise it follows any acronyms or alternative names after the definition.

Future Printings and Editions

Every effort has been made to ensure the accuracy and completeness of this book. If you find an error, think that an entry does not contain enough information, or seek an entry that does not appear in this edition, please let us know. Address your letter to:

Dictionary Editor, Microsoft Press, One Microsoft Way, Redmond, WA 98052-8302. Or send e-mail to mspcd@microsoft.com.

Online Updates

Quarterly updates and revisions will be made to the *Microsoft Press Computer Dictionary, Third* *Edition,* on the Microsoft Press Web site. These updates are meant to supplement the content of this dictionary and keep it up to date in a field that is rapidly evolving. Click the update button in the electronic (CD-ROM) version of the dictionary or point your Web browser to http://mspress.microsoft.com/mspress/products/1031/ to access the update site for the dictionary.

$0.02 \mī˘ to͞o sents´\ *See* my two cents.

& \am´pər-sand`\ **1.** UNIX command suffix for running the preceding command as a background process. *See also* background[1]. **2.** A root user command suffix for starting a daemon that is to remain running after logout. *See also* daemon. **3.** The default character used to designate a character entity (special character) in an HTML or SGML document. *See also* HTML, SGML. **4.** In spreadsheet programs, an operator for inserting text into a formula specifying the relationship between cells.

* \stär´\ *See* asterisk.

. \stär`dot-stär´\ *See* star-dot-star.

.. \dot-dot´\ DOS and UNIX syntax for the parent directory. A single dot refers to the current directory.

/ \slash\ **1.** A character used to delimit parts of a directory path in UNIX and FTP or parts of an Internet address in Web browsers. **2.** A character used to flag switches or parameters that control the execution of a program invoked by a command-line interface. *See also* command-line interface.

// \dəb´l slash`\ Notation used with a colon to separate the URL protocol (such as http or ftp) from the URL host machine name, as in http://www.yahoo.com. *See also* URL.

: \kō´lən\ A symbol used after the protocol name in a URL. *See also* URL.

< > \an´ gl brak` əts\ **1.** A pair of symbols used to set off a tag in an HTML document. *See also* HTML. **2.** In an Internet Relay Chat (IRC) or multi-user dungeon (MUD), a set of symbols used to designate some action or reaction, as in <chuckle>. *See also* IRC, MUD. **3.** A pair of symbols used to set off a return address in an e-mail header.

> \rīt` an´gl brak`ət\ **1.** A symbol used in DOS and UNIX to direct the output resulting from some command into a file. **2.** A symbol commonly used in e-mail messages to designate text included from another message.

? \kwes´chən märk`\ *See* question mark.

@ \at\ The separator between account names and domain name in Internet e-mail addresses. When spoken, @ is read as "at." Therefore, user@host.com would be read as "user at host dot com."

**** \bak´slash\ *See* backslash.

0 wait state \zēr`-ō wāt´ stāt\ *n. See* zero wait state.

100BaseT \wən-hun`drəd-bās-T´\ *n.* An Ethernet standard for baseband local area networks using twisted-pair cable carrying 100 megabits per second (Mbps). *Also called* Fast Ethernet. *See also* Ethernet (definition 1).

101-key keyboard \wən`ō-wən`kē kē´bōrd\ *n.* A computer keyboard modeled after the enhanced keyboard; introduced by IBM for the IBM PC/AT. The 101-key keyboard and the enhanced keyboard are similar in the number and function of their keys; they may differ in the way the keys are laid out, the amount of tactile feedback expressed when a key is pressed, and the shape and feel of the keycaps. See the illustration on the next page. *See also* enhanced keyboard.

1024×768 \ten`twən-tē-fōr` bī-sev` ən-siks-tē-āt´\ *n.* A standard super VGA computer display having a resolution of 1,024 columns of pixels by 768 rows of pixels. *See also* SVGA.

10Base2 \ten`bās-to͞o´\ *n.* The Ethernet and IEEE 802.3 standard for baseband local area networks using a thin coaxial cable up to 200 meters long and carrying 10 megabits per second (Mbps) in a bus topology. A network node is connected to the cable by a BNC connector on the adapter card. *Also called* Cheapernet, thin Ethernet, ThinNet, ThinWire. *See also* BNC connector, bus network, coaxial cable, Ethernet (definition 1), IEEE 802 standards.

10Base5 \ten`bās-fīv´\ *n.* The Ethernet and IEEE 802.3 standard for baseband local area networks using a thick coaxial cable up to 500 meters long and carrying 10 megabits per second (Mbps) in a bus topology. A network node is equipped with a transceiver that plugs into a 15-pin AUI connector on the adapter card and taps into the cable. *Also called* thick Ethernet, ThickNet, ThickWire. *See also* coaxial cable, Ethernet (definition 1), IEEE 802 standards.

10BaseF \ten`bās-F´\ *n.* The Ethernet standard for baseband local area networks using fiber-optic cable carrying 10 megabits per second (Mbps) in a star topology. All nodes are connected to a repeater or to a central concentrator. A node is equipped with a fiber-optic transceiver that plugs into an AUI connector on the adapter card and attaches to the cable with an ST or SMA fiber-optic connector. The 10BaseF standard comprises 10BaseFB for a backbone, 10BaseFL for the link between the central concentrator and a station, and 10BaseFP for a star network. *See also* Ethernet (definition 1), fiber optics, star network.

10BaseT \ten`bās-T´\ *n.* The Ethernet standard for baseband local area networks using twisted-pair cable carrying 10 megabits per second (Mbps) in a star topology. All nodes are connected to a central hub known as a multiport repeater. *See also* Ethernet (definition 1), star network, twisted-pair cable.

12-hour clock \twelv`ou-ər klok´\ *n.* A clock that expresses the time within a 12-hour range, returning to 1:00 after 12:59 AM or PM. *Compare* 24-hour clock.

1.2M \wən`point-tōō´M´\ *adj.* Short for 1.2-megabyte. Refers to the capacity for high-density 5.25-inch floppy disks.

14.4 \fōr`tēn-fōr´\ *n.* A modem with a maximum data transfer rate of 14.4 kilobits per second (Kbps).

1.44M \wən`point-fōr`fōr-M´\ *adj.* Short for 1.44-megabyte. Refers to the capacity for high-density 3.5-inch floppy disks.

16-bit \siks-tēn´bit`\ *See* 8-bit, 16-bit, 32-bit, 64-bit.

16-bit application \siks-tēn`bit a-plə-kā´shən\ *n.* An application written to run on a computer with a 16-bit architecture or operating system, such as MS-DOS or Windows 3.*x*.

16-bit color \siks-tēn`bit kə´lər\ *adj.* Of, pertaining to, or characteristic of a display that can produce 2^{16} (65,536) distinct colors. *Compare* 24-bit color, 32-bit color.

16-bit machine \siks-tēn`bit mə-shēn´\ *n.* A computer that works with data in groups of 16 bits at a time. A computer may be considered a 16-bit machine either because its microprocessor operates internally on 16-bit words or because its data bus can transfer 16 bits at a time. The IBM PC/AT and similar models based on the Intel 80286 microprocessor are 16-bit machines in terms of both the word size of the microprocessor and the size of the data bus. The Apple Macintosh Plus and Macintosh SE use a microprocessor with a 32-bit word length (the Motorola 68000), but they have 16-bit data buses and are generally considered 16-bit machines.

1NF \wən`N-F´\ *n.* Short for first normal form. *See* normal form (definition 1).

101-key keyboard.

2000 time problem \to͞o-thouz`ənd tīm´ probləm\ *n.* A potential problem for computer programs when the year 2000 is reached, in that a variety of logic checks within programs may suddenly fail if they rely on two-digit year indicators. For example, suppose a computer does routine logic checks on whether report dates are valid, by checking if a report's date follows the date for a report the previous year. Such a check will fail when the report for year "00" (interpreted as year zero by the computer) follows year "99." In the past, before RAM became much cheaper, one way to conserve memory was to indicate years with only two digits, and this method of handling dates has remained at the core of much software. Other possible faults include unanticipated shortening of index numbers, stock numbers, and the like, when the digits for the year occur first, and are accidentally read as leading zeros, and so deleted. For example, ABC-97001, for part number 1 in 1997, could first become ABC-00001 and then get shortened to ABC-1, for part number 1 in year "00."

Since the internals of programs' construction are not generally visible, such problems may not be evident until programs start failing after 12:00 AM, January 1, 2000. It remains practically impossible to test all extant software for this problem, but, as a precaution, critical software can be tested using future dates.

24-bit color \twen`tē-fōr´bit kə´lər\ *n.* RGB color in which the level of each of the three primary colors in a pixel is represented by 8 bits of information. A 24-bit color image can contain over 16 million different colors. Not all computer monitors support 24-bit color. Those that do not may use 8-bit color (256 colors) or 16-bit color (65,536 colors). See the illustration. *Also called* true color. *See also* bit depth, pixel, RGB. *Compare* 16-bit color, 32-bit color.

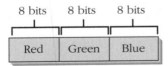

24-bit color. Eight bits are used to represent the level of each of the three primary colors in a 24-bit color pixel.

24-hour clock \twen`tē-fōr-ou`ər klok´\ *n.* A clock that expresses the time within a 24-hour range, from 0000 (midnight) to 2359 (one minute before the following midnight). *Compare* 12-hour clock.

256-bit \to͞o´fif-tē-siks´bit\ *adj.* Having a data path that is 256 bits wide.

286 \to͞o`ā-tē-siks´\ *n. See* 80286.

287 \to͞o`ā-tē-sev´ən\ *n. See* 80287.

28.8 \twen`tē-āt-āt´\ *n.* A modem with a maximum data transfer rate of 28.8 kilobits per second (Kbps).

2NF \to͞o´N-F´\ *n.* Short for second normal form. *See* normal form (definition 1).

2.PAK \to͞o´pak\ *n.* An artificial intelligence programming language.

32-bit \thər`tē-to͞o´bit\ *See* 8-bit, 16-bit, 32-bit, 64-bit.

32-bit application \thər`tē-to͞o´bit a-plə-kā´shən\ *n.* An application written to run on a computer with a 32-bit architecture or operating system, such as Mac OS or Windows 95.

32-bit clean \thər-tē-to͞o´bit klēn´\ *adj.* **1.** Refers to Macintosh hardware designed to run in 32-bit mode, which can address up to 1 gigabyte of physical RAM under System 7. This includes all present Macintosh computers; some older models used 16-bit addressing. **2.** Refers to software written for 32-bit operation.

32-bit color \thər-tē-to͞o´bit kə´lər\ *n.* RGB color that is similar to 24-bit color, with 8 additional bits used to allow for faster transfer of an image's color. *See also* bit depth. *Compare* 16-bit color, 24-bit color, RGB.

32-bit driver \thər-tē-to͞o´bit drī´vər\ *n.* A software subsystem that controls either a hardware device (device driver) or another software subsystem. The 32-bit versions of this software take full advantage of the instruction sets of the 486 and Pentium processors for improved speed. *See also* driver, instruction set.

32-bit machine \thər-tē-to͞o´bit mə-shēn´\ *n.* A computer that works with data in groups of 32 bits at a time. The Apple Macintosh II and higher models are 32-bit machines, in terms of both the word size of their microprocessors and the size of the data buses, as are computers based on the Intel 80386 and higher-level microprocessors.

32-bit operating system \thər-tē-tŏŏ`bit op´ər-ā-tēng si`stəm\ *n.* An operating system in which 4 bytes, or 32 bits, can be processed at one time. Windows NT, Linux, and OS/2 are examples. *See also* instruction set, protected mode.

34010, 34020 \thrē-fŏr-ō`wən-ō´ thrē-fŏr-ō`tŏŏ-ō´\ *n.* Graphics coprocessors from Texas Instruments (TI), used mainly in high-end PC graphics boards, which have become something of a de facto standard for programmable graphics processors. Although both chips use 32-bit registers, the 34010 uses a 16-bit data bus and the 34020 uses a 32-bit bus. The 34020 is compatible with the earlier 34010, and both chips work with TIGA (Texas Instruments Graphical Architecture), a TI standard that allows a single application driver to be used with all boards based on the standard. *See also* de facto standard, TIGA, video graphics board.

3.5-inch floppy disk \thrē`point-fīv-inch flop´ē disk\ *n. See* microfloppy disk.

360K \thrē`siks`tē-K´\ *adj.* Short for 360-kilobyte. The capacity for standard 5.25-inch floppy disks.

.386 \dot`thrē-ā`tē-siks´\ *n.* A file extension for virtual device drivers under Windows 3.1. *See also* virtual device driver.

386 \thrē`ā-tē-siks´\ *n. See* 80386DX.

386BSD \thrē`ā-tē-siks`B-S-D´\ *n.* A version of BSD UNIX, different from BSDI's BSD386. *See also* BSD UNIX.

386DX \thrē`ā-tē-siks`D-X´\ *n. See* 80386DX.

386SL \thrē`ā-tē-siks`S-L´\ *n. See* 80386SL.

386SX \thrē`ā-tē-siks`S-X´\ *n. See* 80386SX.

387 \thrē`ā-tē-sev´ən\ *n. See* 80387.

387SX \thrē`ā-tē-sev-ən-S-X´\ *n. See* 80387SX.

3-D \thrē-D´\ *adj.* **1.** Short for three-dimensional. Of, pertaining to, or being an object or image having or appearing to have all three spatial dimensions (length, width, and depth). **2.** Having the illusion of depth or varying distances, as in 3-D audio.

3-D array \thrē`D ər-ā´\ *n.* A matrix in which each element is uniquely identified by three distinct indexes. *See also* three-dimensional array.

3-D audio \thrē`D ä´dē-ō, ô´dē-ō\ *n.* Short for three-dimensional audio. Recorded as stereo sound, 3-D audio enables the listener to feel immersed in the sound and to determine its exact location (up, down, left, right, forward, or back-

ward). This technology is commonly used in video games and virtual-reality systems, as well as in some Internet applications. *Also called* 3-D sound, binaural sound.

3-D graphic \thrē`D graf´ik\ *n.* Any graphical image that depicts one or more objects in three dimensions—height, width, and depth. A 3-D graphic is rendered on a two-dimensional medium; the third dimension, depth, is indicated by means of perspective and by techniques such as shading or gradient use of color. See the illustration.

3-D graphic.

3-D metafile \thrē-D` met´ə-fīl\ *n.* A device-independent file for storing a 3-D display. *See also* metafile.

3DMF \thrē-D`M-F´\ *n. See* QuickDraw 3-D.

3-D model \thrē`D mod´əl\ *n. See* three-dimensional model.

3-D sound \thrē`D sound´\ *n. See* 3-D audio.

3GL \thrē`G-L´\ *n.* Short for third-generation language. A programming language one step above assembly language, characterized by being readable by humans. Some examples are C, Pascal, and Basic. *Also called* high-level language (HLL). *Compare* 4GL, assembly language. *See also* third-generation language.

3NF \thrē`N-F´\ *n.* Short for third normal form. *See* normal form (definition 1).

3Station \thrē´stā`shən\ *n.* The archetypal diskless workstation, developed by Bob Metcalfe at 3Com Corporation. *See also* diskless workstation.

400 \fōr`hun´dred\ *n.* HTTP status code—Bad Request. A Hypertext Transfer Protocol message from an HTTP server indicating that a client request cannot be completed because the syntax of the request is incorrect. *See also* HTTP server (definition 1), HTTP status codes.

401 \fōr`ō-wən´\ *n.* HTTP status code—Unauthorized. A Hypertext Transfer Protocol message from an HTTP server indicating that a client request cannot be completed because the transaction requires an Authorization header, which was not supplied. *See also* HTTP server (definition 1), HTTP status codes.

402 \fōr`ō-tōō´\ *n.* HTTP status code—Payment Required. A Hypertext Transfer Protocol message from an HTTP server indicating that a client request cannot be completed because the transaction requires a payment, and no ChargeTo header was supplied. *See also* HTTP server (definition 1), HTTP status codes.

403 \fōr`ō-thrē´\ *n.* HTTP status code—Forbidden. A Hypertext Transfer Protocol message from an HTTP server indicating that a client request cannot be completed because access is restricted. *See also* HTTP server (definition 1), HTTP status codes.

404 \fōr`ō-fōr´\ *n.* HTTP status code—Not Found. A Hypertext Transfer Protocol message from an HTTP server indicating that a client request cannot be completed because the server is unable to find an address that matches the URL requested. *See also* HTTP server (definition 1), HTTP status codes, URL.

486 \fōr`ā-tē-siks´\ *n. See* i486DX.

486DX \fōr`ā-tē-siks`D-X´\ *n. See* i486DX.

486SL \fōr`ā-tē-siks`S-L´\ *n. See* i486SL.

486SX \fōr`ā-tē-siks`S-X´\ *n. See* i486SX.

4GL \fōr`G-L´\ *n.* A programming language designed to mimic human language. The designation is often used to specify languages used with relational databases and is intended to imply that such languages are a step up from standard high-level programming languages such as C, Pascal, and COBOL. *See also* application development language, high-level language. *Compare* 3GL, assembly language.

4GL architecture \fōr`G-L är´kə-tek-chur\ *n. See* two-tier client/server.

4mm tape \fōr`mil-ə-mē-tər tāp´\ *n. See* digital audio tape.

4NF \fōr`N-F´\ *n.* Short for fourth normal form. *See* normal form (definition 1).

5.25-inch floppy disk \fīv`point-tōō-fīv-inch flop´ē disk\ *n. See* floppy disk.

56K \fif`tē-siks-K´\ *adj.* Having 56 kilobits per second (Kbps) available for traffic on a communications circuit. One voice channel can carry up to 64 Kbps (called a T0 carrier); 8 Kbps are used for signaling, leaving 56 Kbps available for traffic. *See also* T-carrier.

586 \fīv`ā-tē-siks´\ *n.* The unofficial name used by industry analysts and by the computer trade press to describe Intel's successor to the i486 microprocessor prior to its release. In the interest of using a name whose trademark could be more easily protected, however, Intel decided to name the microprocessor Pentium. *See also* Pentium.

5NF \fīv`N-F´\ *n.* Short for fifth normal form. *See* normal form (definition 1).

5x86 \fīv-X`ā-tē-siks´\ *n.* Cyrix Corporation's clone of the Intel Pentium CPU. *See also* 586, 6x86, central processing unit, clone, Pentium.

64-bit \siks-tē-fōr´bit`\ *See* 8-bit, 16-bit, 32-bit, 64-bit.

64-bit machine \siks-tē-fōr`bit mə-shēn´\ *n.* A computer that works with data in groups of 64 bits at a time. A computer may be considered a 64-bit machine either because its CPU operates internally on 64-bit words or because its data bus can transfer 64 bits at a time. A 64-bit CPU thus has a word size of 64 bits, or 8 bytes; a 64-bit data bus has 64 data lines, so it ferries information through the system in sets of 64 bits at a time. Examples of 64-bit architecture include the Alpha AXP from Digital Equipment Corporation, the Ultra workstation from Sun Microsystems, Inc., and the PowerPC 620 from Motorola and IBM.

6502 \siks`fīv-ō-tōō´\ *n.* The 8-bit microprocessor, developed by Rockwell International, that was used in the Apple II and Commodore 64 microcomputers.

65816 \siks-fīv-āt`wən-siks´\ *n.* A 16-bit microprocessor from Western Digital Design used in the Apple IIGS. It can emulate the 6502, providing compatibility with all old Apple II software. *See also* 6502.

6800 \siks-tē-āt`hun´drəd\ *n.* An 8-bit microprocessor developed by Motorola in the early 1970s. It failed to gain wide acceptance.

68000 \siks-tē-āt`thou´sənd\ *n.* The original microprocessor in the 680x0 family from Motorola, introduced in 1979 and used in the first Apple

Macintosh computers as well as the Apple Laser-Writer IISC and Hewlett-Packard's LaserJet printers. The 68000 has 32-bit internal registers but transfers data over a 16-bit data bus. With 24-bit physical addressing, the 68000 can address 16 megabytes of memory—16 times as much memory as does the Intel 8088 found in the IBM PC. In addition, the 68000's architecture, in which addressing is linear (as opposed to the 8088's segmented addressing) and in which all address registers work the same way and all data registers work the same way, makes programming more straightforward. *See also* linear addressing architecture, segmented addressing architecture.

68020 \siks-āt`ō-tōō-ō´\ *n.* A microprocessor in the 680x0 family from Motorola, introduced in 1984. This chip has 32-bit addressing and a 32-bit data bus and is available in speeds from 16 MHz to 33 MHz. The 68020 is found in the original Macintosh II and the LaserWriter IINT from Apple.

68030 \siks-āt`ō-thrē-ō´\ *n.* A microprocessor in the 680x0 microprocessor family from Motorola, introduced in 1987. This chip has 32-bit addressing and a 32-bit data bus and is available in speeds from 20 MHz to 50 MHz. The 68030 has built-in paged memory management, precluding the need for supplemental chips to provide that function.

68040 \siks-āt`ō-fōr-ō´\ *n.* A microprocessor in the 680x0 family from Motorola, introduced in 1990, with 32-bit addressing and a 32-bit data bus. The 68040 runs at 25 MHz and includes a built-in floating-point unit and memory management units, including independent 4-KB instruction and data caches, which eliminate the need for supplemental chips to provide these functions. In addition, the 68040 is capable of parallel instruction execution by means of multiple independent instruction pipelines, multiple internal buses, and separate caches for both data and instructions.

6845 \siks-āt`fōr-fīv´\ *n.* A programmable video controller from Motorola used in IBM's Monochrome Display Adapter (MDA) and Color/Graphics Adapter (CGA). The 6845 became such an integral part of the IBM PC and compatibles that later generations of video adapters, such as EGA and VGA, continue to support the operations of the 6845. *See also* CGA, EGA, MDA, VGA.

68881 \siks-āt`āt-ā-tē-wən´\ *n.* The floating-point coprocessor from Motorola for use with the 68000 and the 68020. The 68881 provides instructions for high-performance floating-point arithmetic, a set of floating-point data registers, and 22 built-in constants including π and powers of 10. The 68881 conforms to the ANSI/IEEE 754-1985 standard for binary floating-point arithmetic. The 68881 can produce a dramatic improvement in system performance when software takes advantage of it. *See also* floating-point processor.

68K \siks`tē-āt-K´\ *n. See* 68000.

6x86 \siks`X-ā-tē-siks´\ *n.* An 8086-compatible microprocessor designed by Cyrix Corporation. It is socket-compatible with some Pentium microprocessors from Intel and can be used in their place. *See also* 8086, microprocessor, Pentium.

7-bit ASCII \sev`ən-bit a´ skē, A`S-C-I-I´\ *n.* A 7-bit ASCII character set used for standard UNIX mail messages. The leftover eighth bit is a parity bit used for error correction. *See also* ASCII, parity bit.

7-track \sev´ən-trak`\ *n.* A tape storage scheme that places data on seven separate, parallel tracks on 1/2-inch reel-to-reel magnetic tape. This is an old recording format used with computers that transfer data 6 bits at a time. Data is recorded as 6 data bits and 1 parity bit. Some personal computers now use the 9-track tape storage scheme. *See also* 9-track.

80286 \āt`ō-tōō-ā-tē-siks´\ *n.* A 16-bit microprocessor from Intel, introduced in 1982 and included in the IBM PC/AT and compatible computers in 1984. The 80286 has 16-bit registers, transfers information over the data bus 16 bits at a time, and uses 24 bits to address memory locations. The 80286 operates in two modes: real mode, which is compatible with the 8086 and supports MS-DOS, and protected mode, which enables the CPU to access 16 megabytes of memory and protects the operating system from incorrect memory accesses by ill-behaved applications, which could crash a system in real mode. *Also called* 286. *See also* protected mode, real mode.

80287 \āt`ō-tōō-ā-tē-sev´ən\ *n.* A floating-point coprocessor from Intel for use with the 80286 family of microprocessors. Available in speeds from 6 MHz to 12 MHz, the 80287 offers the same mathematical capabilities that the 8087 coprocessor provides to an 8086-based system. Because the 80287 conforms to the 80286 memory management and protection schemes, it can be used in both the real and protected modes of the 80286. Also, if the computer manufacturer implements support for it in the motherboard design, the 80287 can be used in a system with an 80386 microprocessor. *See also* floating-point processor.

802.x standards \āt-ō-tōō-X´ stan`dərdz\ *n. See* IEEE 802 standards.

80386 \āt`ō-thrē-ā-tē-siks´\ *n. See* 80386DX.

80386DX \āt`ō-thrē-ā-tē-siks-D-X´\ *n.* A 32-bit microprocessor from Intel, introduced in 1985. The 80386 is a full 32-bit microprocessor; that is, it has 32-bit registers, it can transfer information over its data bus 32 bits at a time, and it can use 32 bits to address memory. Like the earlier 80286, the 80386 operates in two modes: real mode, which is compatible with the 8086 chip and supports MS-DOS, and protected mode, which allows the CPU to access 4 GB of memory directly, supports multitasking, and protects the operating system from crashing as a result of an incorrect memory access caused by an application program error. The 80386 also includes a virtual 8086 mode (also called virtual real mode), which appears to software as an 8086 but whose 1-MB effective address space can be located anywhere in physical memory under the same safeguards as in protected mode. The virtual 8086 mode is the basis for the MS-DOS prompt available inside Windows. *Also called* 386, 386DX, 80386. *See also* protected mode, real mode, virtual real mode.

80386SL \āt`ō-thrē`āt-siks`S-L´\ *n.* A microprocessor from Intel intended for use in laptop computers. The 80386SL has similar features to the 80386SX, but it also has capabilities for reducing its power consumption. In particular, the 80386SL can reduce its clock speed to zero when not in use and return to full speed, with the contents of all its registers intact, when called on to perform another task. *Also called* 386SL. *See also* 80386SX, green PC, i486SL.

80386SX \āt`ō-thrē-ā-tē-siks-S-X´\ *n.* A microprocessor from Intel, introduced in 1988 as a low-cost alternative to the 80386DX. The 80386SX is basically an 80386DX processor limited by a 16-bit

data bus. The 16-bit design allows 80386SX systems to be configured from less expensive AT-class parts, resulting in a much lower total system price. The 80386SX offers improved performance over the 80286 and access to software designed for the 80386DX. The 80386SX also offers 80386DX features such as multitasking and virtual 8086 mode. *Also called* 386SX. *See also* 80386DX.

80387 \āt`ō-thrē-ā-tē-sev´ən\ *n.* The floating-point coprocessor introduced by Intel for use with the 80386 microprocessors. Available in speeds from 16 MHz to 33 MHz, the 80387 offers the same mathematical capabilities that the 8087 provides for an 8086-based system, as well as transcendental operations for sine, cosine, tangent, arctangent, and logarithm calculations. The 80387 conforms to the ANSI/IEEE 754-1985 standard for binary floating-point arithmetic. The 80387 operates independently of the 80386's mode, and it performs as expected regardless of whether the 80386 is running in real, protected, or virtual 8086 mode. *Also called* 387. *See also* 80386DX, floating-point processor.

80387SX \āt`ō-thrē-ā-tē-sev`ən-S-X´\ *n.* The floating-point coprocessor from Intel for use with the 80386SX microprocessor. It provides the same capabilities that the 80387 does for an 80386-based system, but it is available only in a 16-MHz version. *Also called* 387SX. *See also* 80386SX, floating-point processor.

80486 \āt`ō-fōr-ā-tē-siks´\ *n. See* i486DX.

80486SL \ā`tē-fōr-ā`tē-siks`S-L´\ *n. See* i486SL.

80486SX \ā`tē-fōr-ā`tē-siks`S-X´\ *n. See* i486SX.

8080 \āt`ō-āt-ō´\ *n.* One of the first chips capable of serving as the basis of a personal computer, introduced by Intel in 1974 and used in the Altair 8800. The 8080 provided 8-bit data operations and 16-bit addressing and influenced the design of the Z80. Furthermore, the microprocessors of the 80x86 line, which serve as the foundation for the IBM PC and all its successors and compatibles, are all based on a set of registers organized similarly to the 8080's. *See also* Altair 8800, Z80.

8086 \āt`ō-āt-six´\ *n.* The original microprocessor in the 80x86 family from Intel, introduced in 1978. The 8086 has 16-bit registers, a 16-bit data bus, and 20-bit addressing, allowing access to 1 megabyte of memory. Its internal registers include a set that is organized in the same way as those of the 8080. Speeds range from 4.77 MHz to 10 MHz. *See also* 8080.

8087 \āt`ō-āt-sev´ən\ *n.* A floating-point coprocessor from Intel for use with the 8086/8088 and 80186/80188 microprocessors. Available in speeds from 5 MHz to 10 MHz, the 8087 offers instructions, not found in the 8086/8088 instruction sets, for performing arithmetic, trigonometric, exponential, and logarithmic operations on 16-, 32-, and 64-bit integers; 32-, 64-, and 80-bit floating-point numbers; and 18-digit BCD (binary-coded decimal) operands. With application software that takes advantage of these instructions, the 8087 can dramatically improve system performance. The 8087 conforms to the proposed IEEE 754 standard for binary floating-point arithmetic. *See also* 8086, 8088, floating-point processor.

8088 \āt`ō-āt-āt´\ *n.* The microprocessor on which the original IBM PC was based. Released by Intel in 1978, the 8088 is identical to the 8086 but transfers information 8 bits at a time (through an 8-bit data bus) rather than 16 bits at a time (through a 16-bit data bus). *See also* 8086, bus.

80-character line length \ā`tē-kâr-ək-tər līn´ length\ *n.* A standard line length for text mode displays. This length, found in the earliest IBM PCs and in professional terminals of the 1970s and 1980s, is a legacy of the punched card and of mainframe operating systems in which each line in a file as displayed on a terminal appeared to the computer as a card in a deck. Graphical user interfaces support longer or shorter lines depending on the fonts chosen. A message composed with longer lines using a graphical e-mail program appears broken up and difficult to read when viewed by a user with only a terminal emulation program and a shell account.

80x86 \ā`-tē-X`ā-tē-siks´\ *n. See* 8086.

82385 \ā-tē-tōō`thrē-ā-tē-fīv´\ *n.* A cache controller chip by Intel that allows modified cache blocks to be restored to main memory in parallel with cache accesses by the CPU (or DMA). *See also* cache, central processing unit, controller, direct memory access.

8.3 \āt`dot-thrē´\ *n.* The standard format for filenames in MS-DOS/Windows 3.*x*: a filename with eight or fewer characters, followed by a period

("dot"), followed by a three-character file extension. *Compare* long filenames.

8514/A \āt`fīv-wən`fōr-A´\ *n.* A graphics adapter introduced by IBM in April 1987 and withdrawn in October 1991. The 8514/A was designed to increase the capability of the VGA adapter in some of IBM's PS/2 computers from a resolution of 640 by 480 pixels with 16 simultaneous colors to a resolution of 1,024 by 768 pixels (almost quadrupling the amount of information displayed on the screen) with 256 simultaneous colors. The 8514/A worked only in Micro Channel Architecture–based PS/2 computers, and it used the interlacing method for display, which can cause a perceptible flicker at higher resolutions. Therefore, it never gained widespread popularity; the SVGA (Super VGA) adapter prevailed because it was designed to work with the more prevalent ISA and EISA bus architectures. *See also* EISA, interlacing, ISA, Micro Channel Architecture, noninterlaced, SVGA, VGA.

88000 \ā-tē-āt`thou´sənd\ *n.* A reduced instruction set computing (RISC) chip set from Motorola, introduced in 1988 and based on the Harvard architecture. The 20-MHz 88000 set includes one 88100 CPU and at least two 88200 CMMUs (cache memory management units)—one for data memory and one for instruction memory. The 88100 RISC CPU includes both integer and floating-point processors and has thirty-two 32-bit general-purpose registers, 21 control registers, and 32-bit data paths and addresses. The 88100 is capable of addressing 4 gigabytes of external data and 1 gigabyte of 32-bit instructions in memory space. Up to four chip sets can be set up to work with the same memory in a multiprocessing configuration. *See also* central processing unit, floating-point processor, Harvard architecture, RISC.

88100 \ā-tē-āt`wən-hun´drəd\ *n. See* 88000.

88200 \ā-tē-āt`tōō-hun´drəd\ *n. See* 88000.

8-bit, 16-bit, 32-bit, 64-bit \āt´bit siks-tēn´bit` thər-tē-tōō´bit` siks-tē-fōr´bit`\ *adj.* **1.** Capable of transferring 8, 16, 32, or 64 bits, respectively, on data bus lines. For example, the IBM Micro Channel Architecture includes one or more 32-bit data buses with additional 16-bit and 8-bit data lines. *See also* 16-bit machine, 32-bit machine, 64-bit machine, 8-bit machine. **2.** Capable of transferring 8, 16, 32, or 64 bits, respectively, on the data path of a video adapter. An n-bit video adapter can display up to 2^n colors. For example, an 8-bit video adapter is capable of displaying up to 256 colors; a 16-bit adapter can display up to 65,536 colors; and a 24-bit adapter can display over 16 million colors. (A 24-bit video adapter has a 32-bit data path, although the upper 8 bits are not used directly to generate color.) *See also* alpha channel.

8-bit machine \āt`bit mə-shēn´\ *n.* A computer that works with data in groups of 8 bits at a time. A computer may be considered an 8-bit machine either because its microprocessor operates internally on 8-bit words or because its data bus can transfer 8 bits at a time. The original IBM PC was based on a microprocessor (the 8088) that worked internally on 16-bit words but transferred them 8 bits at a time. Such machines are generally called 8-bit machines because the size of the data bus limits the machine's overall speed.

8mm tape \āt`mil-ə-mē-tər tāp´\ *n.* A tape cartridge format used for data backups, similar to that used for some video cameras except that the tape is rated for data storage. The capacity is 5 GB or more of (optionally compressed) data.

8-N-1 \āt`N-wən´\ *n.* Short for **8** bits, **N**o parity, **1** stop bit. Typical default settings for serial communications, such as modem transmissions.

9600 \nīn`tē-siks-hun´dred\ *n.* A modem with a maximum data transfer rate of 9,600 bits per second (bps).

9-track \nīn´trak\ *n.* A tape storage scheme that places data on nine separate parallel tracks (one track for each of 8 data bits of a byte and 1 parity bit) on 1/2-inch reel-to-reel magnetic tape. *See also* 7-track.

Å \ang´strəm\ *n. See* angstrom.

A: \A\ *n.* In Windows and some other operating systems, the identifier used for the first, or primary, floppy disk drive; unless otherwise specified by changing the CMOS startup instructions, this is the drive the operating system checks first for startup instructions.

ABC \A`B-C´\ *n.* **1.** Acronym for **A**tanasoff-**B**erry **C**omputer. The first electronic digital computer, created by John Atanasoff and Clifford Berry of Iowa State University in 1942. **2.** Acronym for **a**utomatic **b**rightness **c**ontrol. A circuit that changes the luminance of a monitor to compensate for ambient lighting conditions. **3.** An imperative language and programming environment from CWI, Netherlands. This interactive, structured, high-level language is easy to learn and use. It is not a systems-programming language, but it is good for teaching or prototyping.

.ab.ca \dot-A-B`dot-C-A´\ *n.* On the Internet, the major geographic domain specifying that an address is located in Alberta, Canada.

abend or **ABEND** \ab´end\ *n.* Short for **ab**normal **end**. The premature ending of a program because of program error or system failure. *See also* abort, crash[1].

ABI \A`B-I´\ *n. See* application binary interface.

ABIOS \A´bī¯ōs, A`B-I-O-S´\ *n.* Acronym for **A**dvanced **B**asic **I**nput/**O**utput **S**ystem. A set of input/output service routines designed to support multitasking and protected mode that were built into IBM PS/2 PCs. *See also* BIOS.

abnormal end \ab-nōr`məl end´\ *n. See* abend.

abort \ə-bōrt´\ *vb.* To terminate abruptly, often used in reference to a program or procedure in progress.

absolute address \ab`sə-lōōt a´dres, ə-dres´\ *n.* A means of specifying a precise memory location in a program by using its address (number) rather than an expression to calculate the address. *Also called* direct address, machine address, real address. *See also* absolute coding. *Compare* relative address, virtual address.

absolute coding \ab`sə-lōōt kō´dēng\ *n.* Program code that uses absolute addressing rather than indirect addressing. *See also* absolute address, indirect address.

absolute coordinates \ab`sə-lōōt cō-ōr´di-nəts\ *n.* Coordinates that are defined in terms of their distance from the origin, the point where the axes intersect. Graphs and computer graphics use absolute coordinates to locate points on a chart or display grid—for example, points in relation to the x- and y-axes on a graph or the x-, y-, and z-axes used to specify the location of a three-dimensional graphic object on the screen. See the illustration. *See also* Cartesian coordinates.

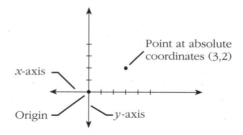

Absolute coordinates.

absolute path \ab-sə-lōōt´ path´\ *n.* A path specification to a file that begins from the topmost level of the identification of a disk drive (for example, C:\docs\work\contract.txt). *See also* path (definition 2). *Compare* relative path.

absolute pointing device \ab`sə-lōōt poin´tēng də-vīs`\ *n.* A mechanical or physical pointing device whose location is associated with the position of the on-screen cursor. For example, if the user of a graphics tablet places the pen on the upper right corner of the tablet, the cursor moves to the upper right corner of the screen or on-screen window associated with the pen. *See also* absolute coordinates, graphics tablet. *Compare* relative pointing device.

absolute value \ab`sə-lōōt val´yōō\ *n*. The magnitude of a number, irrespective of its sign (+ or –). An absolute value is always greater than or equal to zero. For example, 10 is the absolute value of 10 and of –10. Programming languages and spreadsheet programs commonly include functions that return the absolute value of a number.

abstract[1] \ab´strakt\ *adj*. **1.** In character recognition systems, of, pertaining to, or being a type of symbol that, unlike a letter or numeral, has no intrinsic meaning and must be defined before it can be interpreted. **2.** In programming, of, pertaining to, or being a data type defined by the operations that can be performed on objects of that type rather than by the properties of the objects themselves. *See also* abstract data type.

abstract[2] \ab´strakt\ *n*. In information processing and library science, a summary typically consisting of a paragraph or a few paragraphs at the beginning of an investigative document, such as a scientific paper.

abstract class \ab`strakt klas´\ *n*. In the C++ programming language, the opposite of a concrete class (one in which objects can be created). An abstract class is a class of which no objects can be created; rather, the class is used to define subclasses, and objects are created from the subclasses. *See also* object (definition 2).

abstract data type \ab-strakt` dā´tə tīp, dat´ə\ *n*. In programming, a data set defined by the programmer in terms of the information it can contain and the operations that can be performed with it. An abstract data type is more generalized than a data type constrained by the properties of the objects it contains—for example, the data type "pet" is more generalized than the data types "pet dog," "pet bird," and "pet fish." The standard example used in illustrating an abstract data type is the stack, a small portion of memory used to store information, generally on a temporary basis. As an abstract data type, the stack is simply a structure onto which values can be pushed (added) and from which they can be popped (removed). The type of value, such as integer, is irrelevant to the definition.

The way in which the program performs operations on abstract data types is encapsulated, or hidden, from the rest of the program. Encapsulation enables the programmer to change the definition of the data type or its operations without introducing errors to the existing code that uses the abstract data type. Abstract data types represent an intermediate step between traditional programming and object-oriented programming. *See also* data type, object-oriented programming.

abstract machine \ab`strakt mə-shēn´\ *n*. A design for a processor that is not meant for implementation but that represents a model for processing an intermediate language, called abstract machine language, used by an interpreter or compiler. Its instruction set can use instructions that more closely resemble the compiled language than the instructions used by an actual computer. It can also be used to make the implementation of the language more portable to other platforms.

abstract syntax \ab`strakt sin´taks\ *n*. A data structure description that is independent of hardware structures and encodings.

Abstract Syntax Notation One \ab`strakt sin`taks nō-tā`shən wən´\ *n*. The ISO standard notation for independent specification of data types and structures for syntax conversion. *Acronym*: ASN.1 (A`S-N-wən´). *See also* data type, ISO, syntax.

abstract syntax tree \ab`strakt sin´taks trē´\ *n*. A treelike representation of programs used in many integrated programming environments and structure-oriented editors.

A/B switch box \A-B` swich´ boks\ *n*. An enclosure that contains a two-position selector switch. When a user selects a switch setting, the signal passing through the box may be directed either from a single input to one of two outputs, or from the selected input to a single output. See the illustration on the next page. *See also* switch (definition 1).

AC \A-C´\ *n*. *See* alternating current.

AC adapter \A-C´ ə-dap`tər\ *n*. An external power supply that converts from a 110 VAC or 220 VAC domestic electric supply ("house current" or "main power") to low-voltage DC, which is required to operate solid-state electronic equipment (such as a laptop computer) that does not include an internal power supply. See the illustration on the next page.

A/B switch box.

AC adapter.

accelerator \ak-sel´ər-ā`tər\ *n.* **1.** In applications, a key or key combination used to perform a defined function. *Also called* shortcut key. **2.** In hardware, a device that speeds or enhances the operation of one or more subsystems, leading to improved program performance. *See also* accelerator card, Windows-based accelerator.

accelerator board \ak-sel´ər-ā-tər bōrd`\ *n.* *See* accelerator card.

accelerator card \ak-sel´ər-ā-tər kärd´\ *n.* A printed circuit board that replaces or augments the computer's main microprocessor, resulting in faster performance. *Also called* accelerator board. *See also* expansion board, graphics accelerator.

acceptable use policy \ak-sep`tə-bl yo͞os´ pol`ə-sē\ *n.* A statement issued by an Internet service provider or an online information service that indicates what activities users may or may not engage in while logged into the service. For example, some providers prohibit users from engaging in commercial activity on the network. *Acronym:* AUP (A`U-P´). *See also* ISP, online information service.

acceptance test \ak-sep´təns test`\ *n.* A formal evaluation of a hardware product performed by the customer, usually at the factory, to verify that the product is performing according to specifications.

access[1] \ak´ses\ *n.* **1.** The act of reading data from or writing data to memory. **2.** Connection to the Internet or other network or system.

access[2] \ak´ses\ *vb.* To gain entry to memory in order to read or write data.

access arm \ak´ses ärm`\ *n.* A mechanical arm that moves the read/write head(s) over the surface of a disk in a disk drive. See the illustration. *Also called* head arm.

Access arm

Access arm.

ACCESS.bus \ak`ses-dot-bus´\ *n.* A bidirectional bus for connecting peripherals to a PC. The ACCESS.bus can connect up to 125 low-speed peripherals, such as printers, modems, mice, and keyboards, to the system through a single, general-purpose port. Peripherals that support the ACCESS.bus provide a connector or port connection that is similar to a phone-jack connector and are daisy-chained together. However, the PC communicates directly with each peripheral and vice versa. Connecting an ACCESS.bus device (for example, a printer) to a system results in the system automatically identifying and configuring it for optimum performance. Peripherals can be connected while the computer is running *(hot plugging)* and are automatically assigned a unique address (auto-addressing). Developed by Digital Equipment Corporation, the ACCESS.bus competes with Intel's USB. *See also* bidirectional, bus, daisy chain, hot plugging, input/output port, peripheral. *Compare* USB.

access code \ak´ses kōd`\ *n. See* password.

access control \ak´ses kən-trōl`\ *n.* The mechanisms for limiting access to certain items of information or to certain controls based on users' identity and their membership in various predefined groups. Access control is typically used by system administrators for controlling user access to network resources, such as servers, directories, and files. *See also* access privileges, system administrator.

access control list \ak`ses kən-trōl´ list\ *n.* A list associated with a file that contains information about which users or groups have permission to access or modify the file. *Acronym:* ACL (A`C-L´).

accessibility \ak-ses`ə-bil´ə-tē\ *n.* The quality of a system incorporating hardware or software that makes it usable by people with one or more physical disabilities, such as restricted mobility, blindness, or deafness.

access mechanism \ak´ses mek`ə-niz-əm\ *n.* **1.** The disk drive components that move the read/write head(s) to the proper track of a magnetic disk or optical disc. **2.** A circuit that allows one part of a computer system to send signals to another part. *See also* disk controller. **3.** In programming, the means by which an application can read from or write to a resource. *Also called* access method.

access method \ak´ses meth`əd\ *n. See* access mechanism (definition 3).

access number \ak´ses num`bər\ *n.* The telephone number used by a subscriber to gain access to an online service.

accessory \ak-ses´ər-ē`\ *n. See* peripheral.

access path \ak´ses path`\ *n.* The route followed by an operating system to find the location of a stored file. The access path begins with a drive or volume (disk) designator, continues through a chain of directories and subdirectories, if any, and

ends with the filename. C:\books\diction\ start.exe is an example of an access path.

access privileges \ak´ses priv`ə-lə-jəz, priv`lə-jəz\ *n.* The type of operations permitted a given user for a certain system resource on a network or a file server. A variety of operations, such as the ability to access a server, view the contents of a directory, open or transfer files, and create, modify, or delete files or directories, can be allowed or disallowed by the system administrator. Assigning access privileges to users helps the system administrator to maintain security on the system, as well as the privacy of confidential information, and to allocate system resources, such as disk space. *See also* file protection, file server, permission, system administrator, write access.

access provider \ak´ses prə-vī`dər\ *n. See* ISP.

access rights \ak´ses rīts`\ *n.* The permission to view, enter, or modify a file, folder, or system.

access speed \ak´ses spēd`\ *n. See* access time.

access time \ak´ses tīm`\ *n.* **1.** The amount of time it takes for data to be delivered from memory to the processor after the address for the data has been selected. **2.** The time needed for a read/write head in a disk drive to locate a track on a disk. Access time is usually measured in milliseconds and is used as a performance measure for hard disks and CD-ROM drives. *See also* read/write head, seek time, settling time, wait state. *Compare* cycle time.

account \ə-kount´\ *n.* **1.** A record-keeping arrangement used by the vendor of an online service to identify a subscriber and to maintain a record of customer usage for billing purposes. **2.** A record kept by local area networks and multi-user operating systems for each authorized user of the system for identification, administration, and security purposes.

accounting file \ə-koun´tēng fīl`\ *n.* A file generated by a printer controller that keeps track of the number of pages printed per job as well as the user that requested the print job.

accounting machine \ə-koun´tēng mə-shēn`\ *n.* **1.** One of the earliest applications of automatic data processing, used in business accounting primarily during the 1940s and 1950s. The first accounting machines were nonelectronic and used punched cards and wires arranged in plug-board panels. **2.** A computer in which an accounting software package starts up whenever the machine is turned on, the computer thus becoming a dedicated machine with accounting as its sole function.

account policy \ə-kount´ pol`ə-sē\ *n.* **1.** On local area networks and multi-user operating systems, a set of rules governing whether a new user is allowed access to the system and whether an existing user's rights are expanded to include additional system resources. An account policy also generally states the rules with which the user must comply while using the system in order to maintain access privileges. **2.** In Windows NT, a set of rules controlling the use of passwords by the user accounts of a domain or of an individual computer. *See also* domain (definition 2).

ACCU \A`C-C-U´\ *n. See* Association of C and C++ Users.

accumulator \ə-kyōōm´yə-lā`tər\ *n.* A register used for logic or arithmetic, usually to count items or accumulate a sum.

accuracy \a´kyər-ə-sē`\ *n.* The degree to which the result of a calculation or measurement approximates the true value. *Compare* precision (definition 1).

ACIS \A`C-I-S´\ *n.* Acronym for **A**ndy, **C**harles, **I**an's **S**ystem. An object-oriented geometric modeling toolkit designed for use as a "geometry engine" within 3-D modeling applications. ACIS provides an open architecture framework for wire-frame, surface, and solid modeling from a common, unified data structure. ACIS is generally considered the de facto standard for solids modeling. ACIS is developed by Spatial Technology, Inc.

ACK \ak\ *n.* Short for **ack**nowledgment. A message sent by the receiving unit to the sending station or computer indicating either that the unit is ready to receive transmission or that a transmission was received without error. *Compare* NAK.

ACL \A`C-L´\ *n. See* access control list.

ACM \A`C-M´\ *n. See* Association for Computing Machinery.

acoustic coupler \ə-kōō`stik kəp´lər\ *n.* A communications device with a built-in insulated cradle into which a telephone handset is fitted to estab-

lish a connection between sending and receiving computers. *See also* modem.

Acrobat \a´krə-bat`\ *n.* A commercial program from Adobe that converts a fully formatted document created on a Windows, Macintosh, MS-DOS, or UNIX platform into a Portable Document Format (PDF) file that can be viewed on several different platforms. Acrobat enables users to send documents that contain distinctive typefaces, color, graphics, and photographs electronically to recipients, regardless of the application used to create the originals. Recipients need the Acrobat reader, which is available free, to view the files.

acronym \a´krə-nim`\ *n.* A word derived from the first letters or groups of letters in a multiword descriptive noun or other expression, often serving as a mnemonic, such as RAM (**r**andom **a**ccess **m**emory) and AUTOEXEC.BAT (**auto**matically **exec**uted **bat**ch file).

ACSE \A`C-S-E´\ *n. See* Association Control Service Element.

action statement \ak´shən stāt`mənt\ *n. See* statement.

activation record \ak`tə-vā´shən rek`ərd\ *n.* A data structure that represents the state of some construct (such as a procedure, function, block, expression, or module) of a running program. An activation record is useful for the run-time management of both data and sequencing. *See also* data structure.

active \ak´tiv\ *adj.* Pertaining to the device, program, file, or portion of the screen that is currently operational or subject to command operations. Usually the cursor or a highlighted section shows the active element on the display screen.

active cell \ak´tiv sel´\ *n.* The highlighted cell on a spreadsheet display that is the current focus of operation. See the illustration. *Also called* current cell, selected cell. *See also* range.

active content \ak`tiv kon´tent\ *n.* Material on a Web page that changes on the screen with time or in response to user action. Active content is implemented through ActiveX controls. *See also* ActiveX controls.

active file \ak`tiv fīl´\ *n.* The file affected by a current command—typically a data file.

Active Framework for Data Warehousing \ak`-tiv frām`wərk fər dā`tə wâr´hou-zēng, dat´ə\ *n.* A

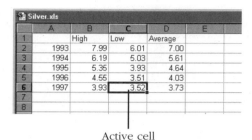

Active cell

Active cell.

data warehousing solution developed by Microsoft and Texas Instruments that represents Microsoft's standard for managing meta data. *Acronym:* AFDW (A`F-D-W´). *See also* ActiveX, meta data.

active hub \ak`tiv hub´\ *n.* The central computer that regenerates and retransmits all signals in an active star network. *See also* active star.

active-matrix display \ak`tiv-mā´triks dis-plā`\ *n.* A liquid crystal display (LCD) made from a large array of liquid crystal cells using active-matrix technology. The active matrix is a method of addressing an array of simple LC cells—one cell per pixel. In its simplest form there is one thin-film transistor (TFT) for each cell. Active-matrix displays are often used in laptop and notebook computers because of their thin width and are notable for their high-quality color displays, which are viewable from all angles, unlike passive-matrix displays. See the illustration. *Also called* TFT, TFT display, TFT LCD. *See also* liquid crystal display, TFT. *Compare* passive-matrix display.

ActiveMovie \ak`tiv-mōō´vē\ *n.* Cross-platform digital video technology developed by Microsoft for online and desktop multimedia.

active program \ak`tiv prō´gram\ *n.* The program currently in control of a microprocessor.

active star \ak`tiv stär´\ *n.* A form of the star network topology in which the central computer actively regenerates and retransmits all signals. *See also* star network.

active window \ak`tiv win´dō\ *n.* In an environment capable of displaying multiple on-screen windows, the window containing the display or document that will be affected by current cursor movements, commands, and text entry. *See also* graphical user interface. *Compare* inactive window.

ActiveX \ak`tiv-X´\ *n.* A set of technologies that enables software components to interact with one another in a networked environment, regardless of the language in which the components were created. ActiveX, which was developed as a proposed standard by Microsoft in the mid 1990s and is currently administered by the Open Group, is built on Microsoft's Component Object Model (COM). Currently, ActiveX is used primarily to develop interactive content for the World Wide Web, although it can be used in desktop applications and other programs. ActiveX controls can be embedded in Web pages to produce animation and other multimedia effects, interactive objects, and sophisticated applications. *See also* ActiveX controls, COM. *Compare* applet, plug-in (definition 2).

Active-matrix display.

ActiveX controls \ak`tiv-X´ kən-trōlz`\ *n.* Reusable software components that incorporate ActiveX technology. These components can be used to add specialized functionality, such as animation or pop-up menus, to Web pages, desktop applications, and software development tools. ActiveX controls can be written in a variety of programming languages, including C, C++, Visual Basic, and Java. *See also* ActiveX. *Compare* helper program.

activity ratio \ak-tiv´ə-tē rā`shō\ *n.* The number of records in use compared with the total number of records in a database file. *See also* database, record.

ACTOR \ak´tər\ *n.* An object-oriented language developed by The Whitewater Group, Ltd., designed primarily to facilitate Microsoft Windows programming. *See also* object-oriented programming.

actuator \ak´chōō-ā`tər\ *n.* A disk drive mechanism for moving the read/write head(s) to the location of the desired track on a disk. See the illustration. *See also* disk drive, stepper motor, voice coil.

.ad \dot`A-D´\ *n.* On the Internet, the major geographic domain specifying that an address is located in Andorra.

Ada \ā´də\ *n.* A high-level Pascal-based programming language designed under the direction of the U.S. Department of Defense (DoD) in the late 1970s and intended to be the primary language for DoD software development. Ada was named after Augusta Ada Byron, who assisted Charles Babbage in developing programs for his Analytical Engine, the first mechanical computer, in the nineteenth century. *See also* Pascal.

adapter or **adaptor** \ə-dap´tər`\ *n.* A printed circuit board that enables a personal computer to use a peripheral device, such as a CD-ROM drive, modem, or joystick, for which it does not already have the necessary connections, ports, or circuit boards. Commonly, a single adapter card can have more than one adapter on it. See the illustration. *Also called* interface card. *See also* controller, expansion board, network adapter, port, video adapter.

adaptive answering \ə-dap`tiv an´sər-ēng\ *n.* The ability of a modem to detect whether an incoming call is a fax or a data transmission and respond accordingly. *See also* modem.

Actuator.   A stepper motor actuator.

adaptive delta pulse code modulation \ə-dap`tiv del´tə puls` kōd´ moj-ə-lā´shən, mo-dyə-lā´shən\ *n.* A class of compression encoding and decoding algorithms used in audio compression and other data compression applications. These algorithms store digitally sampled signals as a series of changes in value, adapting the range of

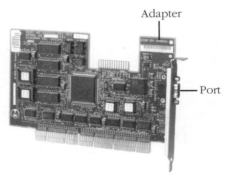

Adapter.

the change with each sample as needed, thus increasing the effective bit resolution of the data. *Acronym:* ADPCM (A`D-P-C-M´). *See also* pulse code modulation. *Compare* adaptive differential pulse code modulation.

adaptive differential pulse code modulation \ə-dap`tiv dif-ər-en`shəl puls` kōd´ moj-ə-lā´shən, mo-dyə-lā´shən\ *n.* A digital audio compression algorithm that stores a sample as the difference between a linear combination of previous samples and the actual sample, rather than the measurement itself. The linear combination formula is modified every few samples to minimize the dynamic range of the output signal, resulting in efficient storage. *See also* pulse code modulation. *Compare* adaptive delta pulse code modulation.

adaptive system \ə-dap`tiv si´stəm\ *n.* A system that is capable of altering its behavior based on certain features of its experience or environment. *See also* expert system.

ADB \A`D-B´\ *n. See* Apple Desktop Bus.

ADC \A`D-C´\ *n. See* analog-to-digital converter.

A-D converter \A-D´ kən-vər`tər\ *n. See* analog-to-digital converter.

adder \ad´ər\ *n.* **1.** A CPU (central processing unit) component that adds two numbers sent to it by processing instructions. *See also* central processing unit. **2.** A circuit that sums the amplitudes of two input signals. *See also* full adder, half adder.

add-in \ad´in\ *n. See* add-on.

addition record \ə-dish´ən rek`ərd\ *n.* **1.** A file that describes new record entries (such as a new customer, employee, or product) in a database so that they can later be scrutinized and posted. **2.** A record in a change file specifying a new entry. *See also* change file.

add-on \ad´on\ *n.* **1.** A hardware device, such as an expansion board or chip, that can be added to a computer to expand its capabilities. *Also called* add-in. *See also* open architecture (definition 2). **2.** A supplemental program that can extend the capabilities of an application program. *See also* utility program.

address[1] \a´dres, ə-dres´\ *n.* **1.** A number specifying a location in memory where data is stored. *See also* absolute address, address space, physical address, virtual address. **2.** A name or token spec-

ifying a particular site on the Internet or other network. **3.** A code used to specify an e-mail destination.

address[2] \a´dres, ə-dres´\ *vb.* To reference a particular storage location.

addressable cursor \ə-dres`ə-bl kur´sər\ *n.* A cursor programmed so that it can be moved to any location on the screen, as by means of the keyboard or a mouse.

address book \a´dres bŏŏk`, ə-dres´\ *n.* **1.** In an e-mail program, a reference section listing e-mail addresses and individuals' names. **2.** As a Web page, an informal e-mail or URL phone book. See the illustration.

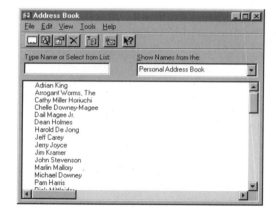

Address book.

address bus \a´dres bus`, ə-dres´\ *n.* A hardware path usually consisting of 20 to 64 separate lines used to carry the signals specifying a memory location. *See also* bus.

address decoder \a´dres dē-kō`dər, ə-dres´\ *n.* An electronic device that converts a numeric address so as to select a memory location on one or more RAM chips.

addressing \ə-dres´ēng, a´dres-ēng\ *n.* The process of assigning or referring to an address. In programming, the address is typically a value specifying a memory location. *See also* address[1].

address mapping table \a´dres map`ēng tā`bl, ə-dres´\ *n.* A table used by routers or Domain Name System (DNS) servers to resolve Internet Protocol (IP) addresses from a text entry such as a name.

Acronym: AMT (A`M-T´). *See also* DNS server, IP address, router.

address mark \a´dres märk`, ə-dres´\ *n. See* index mark.

address mask \a´dres mask`, ə-dres´\ *n.* A number that, when compared by the computer with a network address number, will block out all but the necessary information. For example, in a network that uses XXX.XXX.XXX.YYY and where all computers within the network use the same first address numbers, the mask will block out XXX.XXX.XXX and use only the significant numbers in the address, YYY. *See also* address[1] (definition 2).

address mode \a´dres mōd`, ə-dres´\ *n.* The method used to indicate an address in memory. *See also* absolute address, indexed address, paged address, relative address.

address modification \a´dres mod-ə-fə-kā`shən, ə-dres´\ *n.* The process of updating an address during computation.

address register \a´dres rej`ə-stər, ə-dres´\ *n.* A high-speed memory circuit that holds a memory address for the transfer of information.

address resolution \a´dres rez-ə-lōō´shən, ə-dres´\ *n.* The identification of a computer's hardware address by finding the corresponding match in an address mapping table. *See also* address mapping table.

Address Resolution Protocol \a`dres re-zə-lōō`-shən prō`tə-kol, ə-dres`\ *n. See* ARP.

address space \a´dres spās`, ə-dres´\ *n.* The total range of memory locations addressable by a computer.

address translation \a´dres tranz-lā`shən, ə-dres´\ *n.* The process of converting one kind of address to another, such as a virtual address to a physical address.

ADJ \A`D-J´\ *n.* Short for **adj**acent. A Boolean qualifier to indicate cases where two instances are adjacent to each other. In the case of a search string, "Microsoft ADJ Word" would return only instances where "Microsoft" and "Word" are adjacent in the string.

ADN \A`D-N´\ *n. See* Advanced Digital Network.

Adobe Type Manager \ə-dō`bē tīp´ man`ē-jər\ *n.* Software from Adobe Systems, Inc., that manages PostScript fonts on a system. *Acronym:* ATM (A`T-M´). *See also* PostScript.

ADP \A`D-P´\ *n. See* data processing.

ADPCM \A`D-P-C-M´\ *n. See* adaptive delta pulse code modulation.

ADSL \A`D-S-L´\ *n. See* asymmetric digital subscriber line.

Advanced Digital Network \əd-vansd` dij`i-təl net´wərk\ *n.* A dedicated line service capable of transmitting data, video, and other digital signals with exceptional reliability, offered as a premier service by communications companies. Usually Advanced Digital Network refers to speeds at or above 56 kilobits per second (Kbps). *See also* dedicated line.

Advanced Power Management \ad-vansd` pou´-ər man-əj-mənt\ *n.* An application programming interface developed by Microsoft and Intel to monitor and conserve power on a PC-based system, particularly a battery-powered laptop computer, by enabling programs to communicate their power requirements so that the system can route power away from unused hardware components. *Acronym:* APM (A`P-M´). *See also* application programming interface.

Advanced Program-to-Program Communication \ad-vansd` prō`gram-tə-prō`gram kə-myōō-nə-kā´shən\ *n. See* APPC.

Advanced Research Projects Agency Network \ad-vansd` rē`sərch proj`ekts ā`jən-sē net´wərk\ *n. See* ARPANET.

Advanced RISC \əd-vansd` risk´, R`-I-S-C´\ *n.* Short for **A**dvanced **r**educed **i**nstruction **s**et **c**omputing. A specification for a RISC microchip architecture and system environment designed by MIPS Computer Systems to provide binary compatibility among software applications. *See also* RISC.

Advanced RISC Computing Specification \ad-vansd` risk` kəm-pyōō´tēng spes-ə-fə-kā`shən, R-I-S-C`\ *n.* The minimum hardware requirements enabling a RISC-based system to comply with the Advanced Computing Environment standard. *See also* Advanced RISC.

Advanced SCSI Programming Interface \ad-vansd` skuz`ē prō-gram-ēng in´tər-fās, S-C-S-I`\ *n.* An interface specification developed by Adaptec, Inc., for sending commands to SCSI host adapters. The interface provides an abstraction layer that insulates the programmer from considerations of the particular host adapter used. *Acronym:* ASPI (A`S-P-I´, a´spē). *See also* adapter, SCSI.

.ae \dot`A-E´\ *n.* On the Internet, the major geographic domain specifying that an address is located in United Arab Emirates.

.af \dot`A-F´\ *n.* On the Internet, the major geographic domain specifying that an address is located in Afghanistan.

AFDW \A`F-D-W´\ *n. See* Active Framework for Data Warehousing.

AFIPS \ā´fips\ *n.* Acronym for **A**merican **F**ederation of **I**nformation **P**rocessing **S**ocieties. An organization formed in 1961 for the advancement of computing and information-related concerns. The U.S. representative of the International Federation of Information Processing, AFIPS was replaced by the Federation on Computing in the United States (FOCUS) in 1990.

AFK \A`F-K´\ *adv.* Acronym for **a**way **f**rom **k**eyboard. A phrase occasionally seen in live chat services on the Internet and online information services as an indication that one is momentarily unable to answer. *See also* chat[1] (definition 1).

.af.mil \dot-A-F`dot-mil´, dot-A-F`dot-M-I-L´\ *n.* On the Internet, the major geographic domain specifying that an address belongs to the United States Air Force.

AFS \A`F-S´\ *n.* Acronym for **A**ndrew **F**ile **S**ystem. Carnegie-Mellon's distributed file system for facilitating accessibility to remote files in large networks.

.ag \dot`A-G´\ *n.* On the Internet, the major geographic domain specifying that an address is located in Antigua and Barbuda.

agent \ā´jənt\ *n.* **1.** A program that performs a background task for a user and reports to the user when the task is done or some expected event has taken place. **2.** A program that searches through archives or other repositories of information on a topic specified by the user. Agents of this sort are used most often on the Internet and are generally dedicated to searching a single type of information repository, such as postings on Usenet groups. Spiders are a type of agent used on the Internet. *Also called* intelligent agent. *See also* spider. **3.** In client/server applications, a process that mediates between the client and the server. **4.** In Simple Network Management Protocol (SNMP), a program that monitors network traffic. *See also* SNMP.

.ai \dot`A-I´\ *n.* On the Internet, the major geographic domain specifying that an address is located in Anguilla.

AI \A-I´\ *n. See* artificial intelligence.

.aiff \dot`A-I-F-F´\ *n.* The file extension that identifies audio files in the sound format originally used on Apple and Silicon Graphics (SGI) computers.

AIFF \A`I-F-F´\ *n.* The sound format originally used on Apple and Silicon Graphics (SGI) computers. AIFF stores waveform files in an 8-bit monaural format. *See also* waveform.

AIX \A`I-X´\ *n.* Acronym for **A**dvanced **I**nteractive **Ex**ecutive. A version of the UNIX system provided by IBM for its UNIX workstations and its PCs.

.ak.us \dot-A-K`dot-U-S´\ *n.* On the Internet, the major geographic domain specifying that an address is located in Alaska, United States.

.al \dot`A-L´\ *n.* On the Internet, the major geographic domain specifying that an address is located in Albania.

alarm \ə-lärm´\ *n.* A visual or auditory signal from a computer alerting the user to an error or hazardous situation.

alert \ə-lərt´\ *n.* **1.** On the Macintosh and in many graphical user interfaces, an audible or visual alarm that signals an error or represents a warning of some sort. *See also* alert box. **2.** In programming, an asynchronous notification sent by one thread to another. The alert interrupts the recipient thread at defined points in its execution and causes it to execute an asynchronous procedure call. *See also* asynchronous procedure call, thread (definition 1).

alert box \ə-lərt´ boks`\ *n.* An on-screen box, in a graphical user interface, that is used to deliver a message or warning. An alert box from Windows. See the illustration. *Compare* dialog box.

Alert box.

ALGOL \al´gäl, al´gôl\ *n.* Short for **Algo**rithmic **L**anguage. The first structured procedural programming language, developed in the late 1950s and once widely used in Europe.

algorithm \al´gə-ridh`əm\ *n.* A finite sequence of steps for solving a logical or mathematical problem.

algorithmic language \al`gə-ridh`mik lang´wəj\ *n.* A programming language, such as Ada, Basic, C, or Pascal, that uses algorithms for problem solving.

alias \ā´lē-əs, āl´yəs\ *n.* **1.** An alternative label for some object, such as a file or data collection. **2.** A name used to direct e-mail messages to a person or group of people on a network. **3.** A false signal that results from the digitization of an analog audio sample.

aliasing \ā´lē-ə-sēng`, āl´yə-sēng`\ *n.* In computer graphics, the jagged appearance of curves or diagonal lines on a display screen, which is caused by low screen resolution. See the illustration.

Aliasing. The lower resolution of the image on the right reveals the aliasing effect.

aliasing bug \ā´lē-əs-ēng bug`, āl`yə-sēng\ *n.* A class of subtle programming errors that can arise in code that performs dynamic allocation. If several pointers address the same chunk of storage, the program may free the storage using one of the pointers, but then attempt to use another one (an alias), which would no longer be pointing to the desired data. This bug is avoidable by the use of allocation strategies that never use more than one copy of a pointer to allocated core memory, or by the use of higher-level languages, such as LISP, which employ a garbage collection feature. *Also called* stale pointer bug. *See also* alias, dynamic allocation, garbage collection.

align \ə-līn´\ *vb.* **1.** In an application such as a word processor, to position lines of type relative to some point, such as the page margin. The most common types of alignment are shown.

Left	Centered
aligned	centered
on the	around
left	a
edge	midpoint

Right	Decimal
aligned	.999
on the	10.99
right	100.999
edge	10.999

2. To adjust some device to position it within specified tolerances, such as the read/write head relative to a track on a disk. **3.** In data handling, to store multiple-byte data units so that the respective bytes fall in corresponding locations of memory.

alignment \ə-līn´mənt\ *n.* The arrangement of objects in fixed or predetermined positions, rows, or columns. For example, the Macintosh Finder can do automatic alignment of icons in a folder or on the desktop.

allocate \al´ə-kāt`\ *vb.* To reserve a resource, such as sufficient memory, for use by a program. *Compare* deallocate.

allocation \al`ə-kā´shən\ *n.* In operating systems, the process of reserving memory for use by a program.

allocation block size \al-ə-kā`shən blok´ sīz\ *n.* The size of an individual block on a storage medium, such as a hard drive, which is determined by factors such as total disk size and partitioning options.

allocation unit \al`ə-kā´shən yo͞o`nit\ *n.* See cluster.

all points addressable \äl´ points ə-dres`ə-bl\ *n.* The mode in computer graphics in which all pixels can be individually manipulated. *Acronym:* APA (A`P-A´). *See also* graphics mode.

Alpha \al´fə\ *n.* Digital Equipment Corporation's (DEC's) internal name for its 64-bit RISC-based microprocessor product introduced in February 1992 as the DECchip 21064. For trademark reasons, DEC has expanded the name to Alpha AXP, used as an adjective to describe the DECchip technology. The term *Alpha* is sometimes used in literature to describe the DECchip product, in such phrases as "Alpha-based computer." *See also* DECchip 21064.

alpha[1] \al´fə\ *adj.* Of or pertaining to software that is an alpha.

alpha[2] \al´fə\ *n.* A software product that has been completed and is ready for initial testing in a laboratory. *Compare* beta.

Alpha AXP \al´fə A`X-P`\ *adj.* Of, pertaining to, or characteristic of Digital Equipment Corporation's (DEC's) 64-bit RISC-based microprocessor technology implemented in its DECchip product. The designation AXP is used by DEC in its personal computer products to indicate that a product has a DECchip microprocessor. *See also* Alpha, DECchip 21064, RISC.

alphabet \al´fə-bet`\ *n.* **1.** The set of characters composed of the letters used in a written language. **2.** In communications and data processing, the subset of a complete character set, including letters, numerals, punctuation marks, and other common symbols as well as the codes used to represent them. *See also* ASCII, CCITT, character set, EBCDIC, ISO.

alphabetic \al`fə-bet´ik\ *adj.* Arranged in order according to the letters of the alphabet.

Alpha box \al´fə boks`\ *n.* A computer built around the DECchip 21064 processor (called Alpha). *See also* DECchip 21064.

alpha channel \al´fə chan`əl\ *n.* The high-order 8 bits of a 32-bit graphics pixel used to manipulate the remaining 24 bits for purposes of coloring or masking.

Alpha chip \al´fə chip`\ *n. See* DECchip 21064.

alphageometric \al`fə-jē`ə-me´trik\ *adj.* In reference to computer graphics, especially videotext and teletext systems, pertaining to or being a display method that uses codes for alphanumeric characters and creates graphics using geometric primitives. Shapes such as horizontal and vertical lines and corners are alphageometric. *See also* alphamosaic.

alphamosaic \al`fə-mō-zā´ik\ *adj.* In reference to computer graphics, especially videotext and teletext systems, pertaining to or being a display technique that uses codes for alphanumeric characters

and creates graphics using rectangular arrangements of elements to form a mosaic. *See also* alphageometric.

alphanumeric \al`fə-no͞o-mâr´ik, al`fə-nyo͞o-mâr´ik\ *adj.* Consisting of letters or digits, or both, and sometimes including control characters, space characters, and other special characters. *See also* ASCII, character set, EBCDIC.

alphanumeric display terminal \al`fə-no͞o-mâr`ik dis-plā´ tər`mə-nəl, al`fə-nyo͞o-mâr`ik\ *n.* A terminal capable of displaying characters but not graphics.

alphanumeric mode \al`fə-no͞o-mâr`ik mōd´, al`fə-nyo͞o-mâr`ik\ *n. See* text mode.

alphanumeric sort \al`fə-no͞o-mâr`ik sōrt´, al`fə-nyo͞o-mâr`ik\ *n.* A method of sorting data, such as a set of records, that typically uses the following order: punctuation marks, numerals, alphabetic characters (with capitals preceding lowercase letters), and any remaining symbols.

alpha test \al´fə test`\ *n.* The process of user testing that is carried out on a piece of alpha software.

Altair 8800 \al`târ ā`tē-āt-hun´drəd\ *n.* A small computer introduced in 1975 by Micro Instrumentation Telemetry Systems of New Mexico and sold primarily in kit form. The Altair was based on the 8-bit Intel 8080 microprocessor, had 256 bytes of random access memory, received input through a bank of switches on the front panel, and displayed output via a row of light-emitting diodes. Although it was short-lived, the Altair is considered the first successful personal computer, which was then called a home computer. See the illustration.

AltaVista \äl`tə-vi´stə\ *n.* A World Wide Web search site hosted by Digital Equipment Corporation. AltaVista may be found at URL http:// www.altavista.digital.com/.

alternate key \äl´tər-nət kē`\ *n.* **1.** Any candidate key in a database not designated as the primary key. **2.** *See* Alt key.

alternating current \äl`tər-nā`tēng kur´ənt\ *n.* Electric current that reverses its direction of flow (polarity) periodically according to a frequency measured in hertz, or cycles per second. *Acronym:* AC (A-C´). *Compare* direct current.

Alt key \ält´ kē`\ *n.* A key included on PC and other standard keyboards that is used in conjunction with another key to produce some special feature or function and is typically marked with the letters Alt.

alt. newsgroups \ält`dot no͞oz´gro͞ops\ *n.* Internet newsgroups that are part of the alt. ("alternative") hierarchy and have the prefix alt. Unlike the seven Usenet newsgroup hierarchies (comp., misc., news., rec., sci., soc., talk.) that require formal votes among users in the hierarchy before official newsgroups can be established, anybody can create an alt. newsgroup. Therefore, newsgroups devoted to discussions of obscure or bizarre topics are generally part of the alt. hierarchy.

ALU \A`L-U´\ *n. See* arithmetic logic unit.

AM \A´M\ *n. See* amplitude modulation.

.am \dot`A-M´\ *n.* On the Internet, the major geographic domain specifying that an address is located in Armenia.

American Federation of Information Processing Societies \ə-mâr`ə-kən fed-ər-ā`shən əv in-fər-mā´shən pro`se-sēng sə-sī´ə-tēz\ *n. See* AFIPS.

American National Standards Institute \ə-mâr`ə-kən nash`ə-nəl stan´dərdz in`stə-to͞ot\ *n. See* ANSI.

American Standard Code for Information Interchange \ə-mâr`i-kən stan`dərd kōd` fər in-fər-mā´shən in´tər-chānj\ *n. See* ASCII.

America Online \ə-mer`i-kə on-līn´\ *n.* An online information service, based in Vienna, Virginia, that provides e-mail, news, educational and entertainment services, and computer support by means of a graphical user interface. America Online is one of the largest American Internet access providers. *Acronym:* AOL (A`O-L´).

AMI BIOS \A`M-I` bī´ōs, am`ē, B`I-O-S´\ *n.* A ROM BIOS developed and marketed by American Megatrends, Inc. (AMI), for use in IBM-compatible computers. A popular feature is that its configuration software is stored in the ROM chip along with the BIOS routines, so the user does not need a separate configuration disk to modify system settings, such as amount of memory installed and number and types of disk drives. *See also* BIOS, Phoenix BIOS, ROM BIOS.

Amiga \ə-mē´gə\ *n.* A model of desktop computer introduced by Commodore in 1985. The Amiga was especially strong in its ability to support sound and video, which made it popular among broadcast and multimedia producers, but it was overshadowed by the IBM Personal Computer (and its clones) and the Apple Macintosh. The ownership of the Amiga design has been through the hands of several companies in the United States and Germany. See the illustration.

amp \amp\ *n. See* ampere.

ampere \am´pir, am´pâr\ *n.* Abbreviated a, A, amp. The basic unit of electric current. One ampere is equivalent to a flow of 1 coulomb per second.

Altair 8800.

Amiga.

amplitude \am´plə-tōōd`\ *n.* A measure of the strength of a signal, such as sound or voltage, determined by the distance from the baseline to the peak of the waveform. *See also* waveform.

amplitude modulation \am`plə-tōōd moj-ə-lā´shən, mod-yə-lā´shən\ *n.* A method of encoding information in a transmission, such as radio, using a carrier wave of constant frequency but of varying amplitude. See the illustration. *Acronym:* AM (A´M).

AMPS \A`M-P-S´\ *n.* Acronym for **A**dvanced **M**obile **P**hone **S**ervice. One of the original cellular phone services, relying on frequency-division multiplexing.

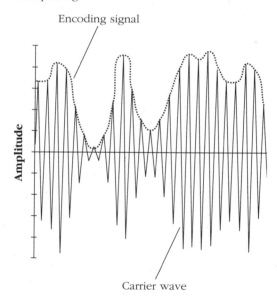

Amplitude modulation.

AMPS/NAMPS \amps`N´amps, A-M-P-S`N´A-M-P-S`\ *n. See* AMPS, NAMPS.

AMT \A`M-T´\ *n. See* address mapping table.

.an \dot`A-N´\ *n.* On the Internet, the major geographic domain specifying that an address is located in the Netherlands Antilles.

analog \an´ə-log`\ *adj.* Pertaining to or being a device or signal having the property of continuously varying in strength or quantity, such as voltage or audio. *Compare* digital (definition 2).

analog channel \an´ə-log chan`əl\ *n.* A communications channel, such as a voice-grade telephone line, carrying signals that vary continuously and can assume any value within a specified range.

analog computer \an´ə-log kəm-pyōō´tər\ *n.* A computer that measures data varying continuously in value, such as speed or temperature.

analog data \an´ə-log dā`tə, dat`ə\ *n.* Data that is represented by continuous variations in some physical property, such as voltage, frequency, or pressure. *Compare* digital data transmission.

analog display \an´ə-log dis-plā`\ *n.* A video display capable of depicting a continuous range of colors or shades rather than discrete values. *Compare* digital display.

analog line \an´ə-log līn`\ *n.* A communications line, such as a standard telephone line, that carries continuously varying signals.

analog signal generator \an`ə-log sig-nəl jen´ər-ā-tər\ *n.* A device that generates continuously variable signals and is sometimes used to activate an actuator in a disk drive. *See also* actuator.

analog-to-digital converter \an`ə-log-tə-dij`i-təl kən-vər´tər\ *n.* A device that converts a continuously varying (analog) signal, such as sound or voltage, from a monitoring instrument to binary code for use by a computer. See the illustration. *Acronym:* ADC (A`D-C´). *Also called* A-D converter. *See also* modem. *Compare* digital-to-analog converter.

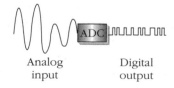

Analog input   Digital output

Analog-to-digital converter.

analysis \ə-nal´ə-sis`\ *n*. The evaluation of a situation or problem, including review from various aspects or points of view. In computing, analysis commonly involves such features as flow control, error control, and evaluation of efficiency. Often the overall problem is divided into smaller components that can be more easily dealt with. *See also* flow analysis, numerical analysis, systems analysis. *Compare* synthesis.

analysis graphics \ə-nal´ə-sis graf`iks\ *n*. *See* presentation graphics.

Analytical Engine \an`ə-lit`ə-kəl en´jən\ *n*. A mechanical calculating machine designed by British mathematician Charles Babbage in 1833 but never completed. It was the first general-purpose digital computer. *See also* Difference Engine.

anchor \an´kər\ *n*. **1.** A format code in a desktop publishing or word processing document that keeps an element in the document, such as a figure or a caption or label associated with the figure, in a certain position in the document. The anchored object is generally attached to another element in the document such as a piece of text (often a paragraph), a graphic, or a particular place in the document. As text and other objects are added to the document, the anchored object moves relative to the object to which it is anchored or remains stationary. **2.** A tag in an HTML document that defines a section of text, an icon, or other element as a link to another element in the document or to another document or file. **3.** *See* hyperlink.

ancillary equipment \an`sə-lâr-ē i-kwip´mənt\ *n*. *See* peripheral.

AND \and\ *n*. A logical operation combining the values of two bits (0, 1) or two Boolean values (false, true) that returns a value of 1 (true) if both input values are 1 (true) and returns a 0 (false) otherwise. The possible combinations are shown in the following table.

a	*b*	*a AND b*
0	0	0
0	1	0
1	0	0
1	1	1

AND gate \and´ gāt\ *n*. A digital circuit whose output is a value of 1 only when all input values are 1. See the illustration. *See also* truth table.

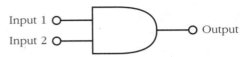

AND gate.   *The symbol for an AND gate as used in electronic schematics.*

Andrew File System \an`drōō fīl´ si`stəm\ *n*. *See* AFS.

angle bracket \ang´l brak`ət\ *n*. *See* < >.

angstrom \ang´strəm\ *n*. Abbreviated Å. A unit of measure equal to one 10-billionth (10^{-10}) of a meter or one 250-millionth of an inch. Light wavelength, for example, is commonly measured in angstroms.

animated cursors \an`ə-mā-təd kur´sərz\ *n*. A Windows 95 and Windows NT feature that allows a series of frames, one after another, to appear at the mouse pointer location instead of a single image, thus producing a short loop of animation. The animated cursors feature is designated by the .ani suffix.

animated GIF \an`ə-mā-təd gif´\ *n*. A series of graphic images in GIF format, displayed sequentially in a single location to give the appearance of a moving picture. *See also* GIF.

animation \an`ə-mā´shən\ *n*. The illusion of movement created by using a succession of static images. In computer graphics, the images can all be drawn separately, or starting and ending points can be drawn with the intervening images provided by software. *See also* 3-D graphic, surface modeling, tween, wire-frame model.

ANN \an, A`N-N´\ *n*. *See* artificial neural network.

annotation \an`ə-tā´shən\ *n*. A note or comment attached to some part of a document to provide related information. Some applications support voice annotations or annotations accessible by icons. *See also* comment.

annoybot \ə-noi´bot`\ *n*. A bot on an Internet Relay Chat (IRC) channel or multiuser dungeon (MUD) that interacts with the user in an obnoxious manner. *See also* bot, IRC, MUD.

anode \an´ōd\ *n.* In electronics, the positively charged terminal or electrode toward which electrons flow. *Compare* cathode.

anonymity \an`ə-nim´ə-tē\ *n.* The ability to send an e-mail message or an article to a newsgroup without one's identity becoming known. Ordinarily, the e-mail address of the sender appears automatically in a message's header, which is created by the client software. To achieve anonymity, a message must be sent through an anonymous remailer—which, however, maintains a record of the sender's identity to enable replies. *See also* anonymous remailer.

anonymous \ə-non´ə-məs`\ *n.* On the Internet, the standard login name used to obtain access to a public FTP file archive. *See also* anonymous FTP.

anonymous FTP \ə-non`ə-məs F`-T-P´\ *n.* The ability to access a remote computer system on which one does not have an account, via the Internet's File Transfer Protocol (FTP). Users have restricted access rights with anonymous FTP and usually can only copy files to or from a public directory, often named */pub,* on the remote system. Users can also typically use FTP commands, such as listing files and directories. When using anonymous FTP, the user accesses the remote computer system with an FTP program and generally uses *anonymous* or *ftp* as a logon name. The password is usually the user's e-mail address, although a user can often skip giving a password or give a false e-mail address. In other cases, the password can be the word *anonymous.* Many FTP sites do not permit anonymous FTP access in order to maintain security. Those that do permit anonymous FTP sometimes restrict users to only downloading files for the same reason. *See also* /pub, FTP[1] (definition 1), logon.

anonymous post \ə-non`ə-məs pōst´\ *n.* A message in a newsgroup or mailing list that cannot be traced to its originator. Generally this is accomplished by using an anonymous server for newsgroup posts or an anonymous remailer for e-mail. *See also* anonymous remailer.

anonymous remailer \ə-non`ə-məs rē-mā´lər\ *n.* An e-mail server that receives incoming messages, replaces the headers that identify the original sources of the messages, and sends the messages to their ultimate destinations. The purpose of an anonymous remailer is to hide the identities of the senders of the e-mail messages.

anonymous server \ə-non`ə-məs sər´vər\ *n.* **1.** The software used by an anonymous remailer. *See also* anonymous remailer. **2.** Software that provides anonymous FTP service. *See also* anonymous FTP. **3.** *See* anonymous remailer.

ANSI \an´sē\ *n.* Acronym for **A**merican **N**ational **S**tandards **I**nstitute. A voluntary, nonprofit organization of U.S. business and industry groups formed in 1918 for the development of trade and communication standards. ANSI is the American representative of the International Standards Organization and has developed recommendations for the use of programming languages including FORTRAN, C, and COBOL. *See also* ANSI C, ANSI.SYS, SCSI.

ANSI C \an´sē C´\ *n.* A version of the C programming language standardized by ANSI. *See also* ANSI, K&R C.

ANSI/SPARC \an´sē spärk`\ *n.* Acronym for **A**merican **N**ational **S**tandards **I**nstitute **S**tandards **P**lanning **a**nd **R**equirements **C**ommittee. The ANSI committee that, in the 1970s, proposed a generalized, three-schema architecture that is used as the foundation for some database management systems.

ANSI.SYS \an´sē-dot`sis´, an´sē-sis`\ *n.* An installable device driver for MS-DOS computers that uses ANSI commands (escape sequences) to enhance the user's control of the console. *See also* ANSI, driver, escape sequence, install.

answer mode \an´sər mōd`\ *n.* A setting that allows a modem to answer an incoming call automatically. It is used in all fax machines. *Also called* auto answer.

answer-only modem \an´sər ōn´lē mō´dəm\ *n.* A modem that can receive but not originate calls.

answer/originate modem \an´sər ə-rij´ə-nāt mō´dəm\ *n.* A modem that can both send and receive calls—the most common type of modem in use.

anti-aliasing \an`tī-a´lē-ə-seng, an`tē-, -āl´yə-seng\ *n.* A software technique for smoothing the jagged appearance of curved or diagonal lines caused by poor resolution on a display screen.

Methods of anti-aliasing include surrounding pixels with intermediate shades and manipulating the size and horizontal alignment of pixels. See the illustration. *See also* dithering. *Compare* aliasing.

Anti-aliasing. *The image on the right shows the result of anti-aliasing through the use of higher resolution.*

anti-glare \an`tī-glâr´, an`tē-\ *adj.* Pertaining to any measure taken to reduce reflections of external light on a monitor screen. The screen may be coated with a chemical (which may reduce its brightness), covered with a polarizing filter, or simply rotated so that external light is not reflected into the user's eye.

antistatic device \an`tē-stat´ic də-vīs`, an`-tī-\ *n.* A device designed to minimize shocks caused by the buildup of static electricity, which can disrupt computer equipment or cause data loss. An antistatic device may take the form of a floor mat, a wristband with a wire attached to the workstation, a spray, a lotion, or other special-purpose device. *See also* static, static electricity.

antivirus program \an`tī-vīr´us prō`gram, an`tē-\ *n.* A computer program that scans a computer's memory and mass storage to identify, isolate, and eliminate viruses, and that examines incoming files for viruses as the computer receives them.

any key \en`ē kē`\ *n.* Any random key on a computer keyboard. Some programs prompt the user to "press any key" to continue. It does not matter which key the user presses. There is no key on the keyboard called Any.

any-to-any connectivity \en`ē-too-en`ē kə-nek-tiv´ə-tē\ *n.* The property of an integrated computer network environment where it is possible to share data across multiple protocols, host types, and network topologies.

.ao \dot`A-O´\ *n.* On the Internet, the major geographic domain specifying that an address is located in Angola.

AOL \A`O-L´\ *n. See* America Online.

APA \A`P-A´\ *n. See* all points addressable.

APC \A`P-C´\ *n. See* asynchronous procedure call.

API \A`P-I´\ *n. See* application programming interface.

APL \A`P-L´\ *n.* Acronym for **A P**rogramming **L**anguage. A high-level language introduced in 1968 for scientific and mathematical applications. APL is a subprogram-based interpreted language that uses a large set of special characters and terse syntax and is available for use on PC-compatible machines. *See also* interpreted language.

APM \A`P-M´\ *n. See* Advanced Power Management.

app \ap\ *n. See* application.

APPC \A`P-P-C´\ *n.* Acronym for **A**dvanced **P**rogram-to-**P**rogram **C**ommunication. A protocol developed as part of IBM's Systems Network Architecture and designed to enable applications programs running on different computers to communicate and exchange data directly.

append \ə-pend´\ *vb.* To place or insert as an attachment by adding data to the end of a file or database or extending a character string. *See also* file, string. *Compare* truncate.

Apple Desktop Bus \ap`l desk`top bus´\ *n.* A serial communications pathway built into Apple Macintosh and Apple IIGS computers. Typically a flexible cord, it enables low-speed input devices, such as a keyboard or mouse, to communicate with the computer. The bus functions like a simple local area network that can connect up to 16 devices, such as light pens, trackballs, and graphics tablets, to the computer. Although there are only two external ports, more than two devices can be linked in a series called a daisy chain. *Acronym:* ADB (A`D-B´). *See also* bus, daisy chain, device driver, input/output port, serial communication.

AppleDraw \ap`l-drä`, ap`l-drô`\ *n.* A shareware drawing application for Macintosh computers.

Apple Events \ap`l ə-vents´, ē-vents´\ *n.* A feature added to Mac OS System 7 that enables one application to send a command, such as save or open, to another application. *See also* Mac OS.

Apple Extended Keyboard \ap`l eks-ten`dəd kē´bōrd\ *n.* A 105-key keyboard that works with the Macintosh SE, Macintosh II, and Apple IIGS computers. This keyboard marks Apple's first inclusion of function (F) keys, whose absence was long cited as a shortcoming of the Macintosh compared with IBM PCs and compatibles. This feature, along with other layout changes and the addition of new keys and lights, makes the Apple Extended Keyboard quite similar in form to the IBM enhanced keyboard. See the illustration. *See also* enhanced keyboard.

Apple II \ap`l too´\ *n.* The second computer introduced by the Apple Computer Corporation, in April 1977. The Apple II featured 4K dynamic RAM, expandable to 48K (with 16K chips), and used the 6502 microprocessor. The Apple II was the first computer to offer a TV video adapter as an optional alternative to a color computer monitor. It also featured sound and eight expansion slots. *See also* 6502.

Apple key \ap´l ke¯\ *n.* A key on Apple keyboards labeled with an outline of the Apple logo . On the Apple Extended Keyboard, this key is the same as the Command key, which functions similarly to the Control key on IBM and compatible keyboards. It is generally used in conjunction with a character key as a shortcut to making menu selections or starting a macro.

Apple Macintosh \ap´l mak´ən-tosh\ *n. See* Macintosh.

Apple Newton \ap´l noo´tən\ *n. See* Newton.

AppleScript \ap´l-skript`\ *n.* A script language used with Macintosh computers running under the System 7 operating system to execute commands and automate functions. *See also* script.

AppleShare \ap´l-shâr\ *n.* File server software that works with the Mac OS and allows one Macintosh computer to share files with another on the same network. *See also* file server, Mac OS.

applet \a´plət\ *n.* A small piece of code that can be transported over the Internet and executed on the recipient's machine. The term is especially used to refer to such programs as they are embedded in line as objects in HTML documents on the World Wide Web.

AppleTalk \ap´l täk`\ *n.* An inexpensive local area network developed by Apple that can be used by Apple and non-Apple computers to communicate and share resources such as printers and file servers. Non-Apple computers must be equipped with AppleTalk hardware and suitable software. The network uses a layered set of protocols similar to the ISO/OSI model and transfers information in the form of packets called frames. AppleTalk supports connections to other AppleTalk networks through devices known as bridges, and it supports connections to dissimilar networks through devices called gateways. *See also* bridge, frame (definition 2), gateway.

application \a`plə-kā´shən\ *n.* A program designed to assist in the performance of a specific task, such as word processing, accounting, or inventory management. *Compare* utility.

application binary interface \a-plə-kā`shən bī´-nər-ē in´tər-fās, bī`när-ē\ *n.* A set of instructions that specifies how an executable file interacts with the hardware and how information is stored. *Acronym:* ABI (A`B-I´). *Compare* application programming interface.

Apple Extended Keyboard.

application-centric \a`plə-kā`shən-sen´trik\ *adj.* Of, pertaining to, or characteristic of an operating system in which a user invokes an application to open or create documents (such as word processing files or spreadsheets). Command-line interfaces and some graphical user interfaces such as the Windows 3.*x* Program Manager are application-centric. *Compare* document-centric.

application developer \a-plə-kā`shən də-vel´ə-pər\ *n.* An individual who designs and analyzes the appearance and operation of an application program.

application development environment \a-plə-kā`shən də-vel´əp-mənt en-vī`rən-mənt, en-vī`ərn-mənt\ *n.* An integrated suite of programs for use by software developers. Typical components of application development environments include a compiler, file browsing system, debugger, and text editor for use in creating programs.

application development language \a-plə-kā`shən də-vel´əp-mənt lang`wəj\ *n.* A computer language designed for creating applications. The term is usually restricted to refer to languages with specific high-level constructs geared toward record design, form layout, database retrieval and update, and similar tasks. *See also* application, application generator, 4GL.

application development system \a-plə-kā`shən də-vel´əp-mənt sis`təm\ *n.* A programming environment designed for the development of an application, typically including a text editor, compiler, and linker, and often including a library of common software routines for use in the developed program.

application file \a`plə-kā`shən fīl´\ *n. See* program file.

application gateway \a-plə-kā`shən gāt`wā\ *n.* Software running on a machine that is intended to maintain security on a secluded network yet allow certain traffic to go between the private network and the outside world. *See also* firewall.

application generator \a-plə-kā`shən jen´ər-ā-tər\ *n.* Software for generating source or machine code for running an application based on a description of the desired functionality. Limited in scope, application generators are included with some database programs and use built-in instruc-

tion sets to generate program code. *See also* application.

application heap \a`plə-kā´shən hēp`\ *n.* A block of RAM used by an application to store its code, resources, records, document data, and other information. *See also* heap (definition 1), RAM.

application layer \a`plə-kā´shən lâr`, la`yər\ *n.* The highest layer of standards in the Open Systems Interconnection (OSI) model. The application layer contains signals that perform useful work for the user, such as file transfer or remote access to a computer, as opposed to lower levels, which control the exchange of data between transmitter and receiver. *See also* ISO/OSI model.

application processor \a`plə-kā´shən pros`e-sər\ *n.* A processor dedicated to a single application.

application program \a`plə-kā´shən prō`gram\ *n. See* application.

application programming interface \a-plə-kā`shən prō`gra-mēng in´tər-fās\ *or* **application program interface** \a-plə-kā`shən prō`gram in´tər-fās\ *n.* A set of routines used by an application program to direct the performance of procedures by the computer's operating system. *Acronym:* API (A`P-I´).

application shortcut key \a-plə-kā`shən shōrt´kut kē`\ *n.* A key or combination of keys that when pressed will quickly perform an action within an application that would normally require several user actions, such as menu selections. *Also called* keyboard shortcut.

application software \a-plə-kā`shən soft´-wâr\ *n. See* application.

application-specific integrated circuit \a-plə-kā`shən-spə-sif`ik in`tə-grā-təd sər´kət\ *n. See* gate array.

application suite \a-plə-kā`shən swēt`\ *n. See* suite (definition 1).

.aq \dot`A-Q´\ *n.* On the Internet, the major geographic domain specifying that an address is located in Antarctica.

.ar \dot`A-R´\ *n.* On the Internet, the major geographic domain specifying that an address is located in Argentina.

arbitration \är`bə-trā´shən\ *n.* A set of rules for resolving competing demands for a machine resource by multiple users or processes. *See also* contention.

.arc \dot-ärk´, -A`R-C`\ *n.* The file extension that identifies compressed archive files encoded using the Advanced RISC Computing Specification (ARC) format. *See also* compressed file.

arcade game \är-kād´ gām`\ *n.* **1.** A coin-operated computer game for one or more players that features high-quality screen graphics, sound, and rapid action. **2.** Any computer game designed to mimic the style of a coin-operated arcade game, such as games marketed for the home computer. *See also* computer game.

Archie \är´chē\ *n.* An Internet utility for finding files in public archives obtainable by anonymous FTP. The master Archie server at McGill University in Montreal downloads FTP indexes from participating FTP servers and merges them into a master list and sends updated copies of the master list to other Archie servers each day. Archie is a shortened form of *archive. See also* anonymous FTP, FTP[1] (definition 1). *Compare* Jughead, Veronica.

Archie client \är´chē klī`ənt\ *n. See* Archie.

Archie server \är´chē sər`vər\ *n.* On the Internet, a server that contains Archie indexes to the names and addresses of files in public FTP archives. *See also* Archie, FTP[1] (definition 1), server (definition 2).

architecture \är´kə-tek`chər\ *n.* **1.** The physical construction or design of a computer system and its components. *See also* cache, CISC, closed architecture, network architecture, open architecture, pipelining, RISC. **2.** The data-handling capacity of a microprocessor. **3.** The design of application software incorporating protocols and the means for expansion and interfacing with other programs.

archive[1] \är´kīv\ *n.* **1.** A tape or disk containing files copied from another storage device and used as backup storage. **2.** A compressed file. **3.** A file directory on the Internet that is available by File Transfer Protocol (FTP) or an Internet directory established for dissemination of stored files.

archive[2] \är´kīv\ *vb.* **1.** To copy files onto a tape or disk for long-term storage. **2.** To compress a file.

archive bit \är´kīv bit`\ *n.* A bit that is associated with a file and is used to indicate whether or not the file has been backed up. *See also* back up, bit.

archive file \är´kīv fīl`\ *n.* A file that contains a set of files, such as a program with its documentation and example input files, or collected postings from a newsgroup. On UNIX systems, archive files can be created using the tar program; they can then be compressed using compress or gzip. PKZIP under MS-DOS and Windows and StuffIt under Mac OS create archive files that are already compressed. *See also* compress[1], gzip, PKZIP, StuffIt, tar[1].

archive site \är´kīv sīt`\ *n.* A site on the Internet that stores files. The files are usually accessed through one of the following ways: downloaded through anonymous FTP, retrieved through Gopher, or viewed on the World Wide Web. *See also* anonymous FTP, Gopher.

area chart \âr´ē-ə chärt`\ *n.* A graphical presentation, such as of quarterly sales figures, that uses shading or coloring to emphasize the difference between the line representing one set of data points and the line representing a separate but related set of data points. See the illustration.

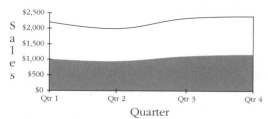

Quarterly Sales Summary

Area chart.

area search \âr´ē-ə sərch`\ *n.* In information management, the examination of a group of documents for the purpose of identifying those that are relevant to a particular subject or category.

arg \ärg\ *n. See* argument.

argument \är´gyə-mənt\ *n.* An independent variable, used with an operator or passed to a subprogram that uses the argument to carry out specific operations. *See also* algorithm, operator (definition 1), parameter, subprogram.

arithmetic[1] \âr-ith-met´ik\ *adj.* Pertaining to the mathematical operations of addition, subtraction, multiplication, and division.

arithmetic[2] \ər-ith´mə-tik\ *n.* The branch of mathematics dealing with the addition, subtraction, multiplication, and division of real numbers.

arithmetic expression \är`ith-met`ik eks-presh´-ən\ *n.* A series of elements, including data labels and constants as well as numbers, that are joined by arithmetic operators, such as + and −, and can be calculated to produce a value.

arithmetic logic unit \är-ith-met`ik loj´ik yoo`nit\ *n.* A component of a microprocessor chip used for arithmetic, comparative, and logical functions. *Acronym:* ALU (A`L-U´). *See also* gate (definition 1).

arithmetic operation \ə-rith´mə-tik op-ər-ā´shən, är-ith-met`ik\ *n.* Any of the standard calculations performed in arithmetic—addition, subtraction, multiplication, or division. The term is also used in reference to negative numbers and absolute values.

arithmetic operator \är-ith-met`ik op´ər-ā-tər\ *n.* An operator that performs an arithmetic operation: +, −, ×, or /. An arithmetic operator usually takes one or two arguments. *See also* argument, binary, logical operator, operator (definition 1), unary.

.arj \dot`A-R-J´\ *n.* The DOS file extension used with archive files created with the ARJ compression program.

.army.mil \dot-är´mē-dot-mil´, dot-är´mē-dot-M-I-L´\ *n.* On the Internet, the major geographic domain specifying that an address belongs to the United States Army.

ARP \A`R-P´, arp\ *n.* Acronym for **A**ddress **R**esolution **P**rotocol. A TCP/IP protocol for determining the hardware address (or physical address) of a node on a local area network connected to the Internet, when only the IP address (or logical address) is known. An ARP request is sent to the network, and the node that has the IP address responds with its hardware address. Although ARP technically refers only to finding the hardware address, and RARP (for Reversed ARP) refers to the reverse procedure, ARP is commonly used for both senses. *See also* IP address, TCP/IP.

ARPANET \är´pə-net`, A`R-P`A-N`E-T´\ *n.* A large wide area network created in the 1960s by the U.S. Department of Defense Advanced Research Projects Agency (ARPA, renamed DARPA in the 1970s) for the free exchange of information between universities and research organizations, although the military also used this network for communications. In the 1980s MILNET, a separate network, was spun off from ARPANET for use by the military. ARPANET was the network from which the Internet evolved. *See also* Internet, MILNET.

ARP request \ärp´ rə-kwest`, A-R-P´\ *n.* Short for **A**ddress **R**esolution **P**rotocol **request**. An ARP packet containing the Internet address of a host computer. The receiving computer responds with or passes along the corresponding Ethernet address. *See also* ARP, Ethernet, IP address, packet.

array \ər-ā´\ *n.* In programming, a list of data values, all of the same type, any element of which can be referenced by an expression consisting of the array name followed by an indexing expression. Arrays are part of the fundamentals of data structures, which, in turn, are a major fundamental of computer programming. *See also* array element, index, record[1], vector.

array element \ər-ā´ el`ə-mənt\ *n.* A data value in an array.

array processor \ər-ā´ pros`e-sər\ *n.* A group of interconnected, identical processors operating synchronously, often under the control of a central processor.

arrow key \är´ō kē`\ *n.* Any of four keys labeled with arrows pointing up, down, left, and right, used to move the cursor vertically or horizontally on the display screen or, in some programs, to extend the highlight. See the illustration.

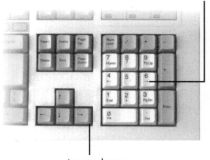

Arrow keys
(when Num Lock is off)

Arrow keys

Arrow key. When Num Lock is off, the arrow keys on the number keypad can be used.

article \är´tə-kəl\ *n.* A message that appears in an Internet newsgroup. *Also called* post. *See also* newsgroup.

artificial intelligence \är-tə-fish`əl in-tel´i-jəns\ *n.* The branch of computer science concerned with enabling computers to simulate such aspects of human intelligence as speech recognition, deduction, inference, creative response, the ability to learn from experience, and the ability to make inferences given incomplete information. Two common areas of artificial-intelligence research are expert systems and natural-language processing. *Acronym:* AI (A-I´). *See also* expert system, natural-language processing.

artificial life \är`tə-fish-əl līf´, är-tə-fish`əl\ *n.* The study of computer systems that simulate some aspects of the behavior of living organisms. Artificial life includes systems in which programs intended to perform some particular task compete for survival and reproduction based on their performance; the offspring can combine pieces of code and undergo random variations, and the programs so modified compete in turn, until an optimal solution is found.

artificial neural network \är-tə-fish`əl nər´əl net´wərk, nyər`əl\ *n.* A form of computer artificial intelligence that uses software based on concepts understood from biological neural networks to adaptively perform a task. *Acronym:* ANN (an, A`N-N´).

.ar.us \dot-A-R`dot-U-S´\ *n.* On the Internet, the major geographic domain specifying that an address is located in Arkansas, United States.

.as \dot`A-S´\ *n.* On the Internet, the major geographic domain specifying that an address is located in American Samoa.

.asc \dot`A-S-C´\ *n.* A filename extension most commonly indicating that the file contains ASCII text that can be processed by all types of word processing software, including MS-DOS Edit, Windows Notepad, Windows-95/NT WordPad, and Microsoft Word. Some systems may use this extension to indicate that a file contains image information. *See also* ASCII.

ascender \ə-sen´dər\ *n.* The portion of a lowercase letter that extends above the main body (x-height) of the letter. See the illustration. *See also* baseline, x-height. *Compare* descender.

ascending order \ə-sen`dēng ōr´dər\ *n.* The arrangement of a sequence of items from lowest to highest, such as from 1 to 10 or from A to Z.

Ascender.

The rules for determining ascending order in a particular application can be very complicated: capital letters before lowercase letters, extended ASCII characters in ASCII order, and so on.

ascending sort \ə-sen`dēng sōrt´\ *n.* A sort that results in the arrangement of items in ascending order. *See also* alphanumeric sort, ascending order. *Compare* descending sort.

ascii \a`skē, A`S-C`I-I´\ *n.* In an FTP client program, the command that instructs the FTP server to send or receive files as ASCII text. *See also* ASCII, FTP client. *Compare* binary[2].

ASCII \a`skē, A`S-C`I-I´\ *n.* Acronym for **A**merican **S**tandard **C**ode for **I**nformation **I**nterchange. A coding scheme using 7 or 8 bits that assigns numeric values to up to 256 characters, including letters, numerals, punctuation marks, control characters, and other symbols. ASCII was developed in 1968 to standardize data transmission among disparate hardware and software systems and is built into most minicomputers and all personal computers. *See also* ASCII file, character, character code, control character, extended ASCII. *Compare* EBCDIC.

ASCII character set \a`skē kâr´ək-tər set`, A`S-C-I-I´\ *n.* A standard 7-bit code for representing ASCII characters using binary values; code values range from 0 to 127. Most PC-based systems use an 8-bit extended ASCII code, with an extra 128 characters used to represent special symbols, foreign-language characters, and graphic symbols. The ASCII character set appears in Appendix A. *See also* ASCII, character, EBCDIC, extended ASCII.

ASCII EOL value \a`skē E`O-L´ val`yōō, A-S-C-I-I´\ *n.* The sequence of bytes that indicates the end of a line of text. For Windows and MS-DOS systems, this is the hexadecimal sequence 0D 0A or the decimal sequence 13 10. Data files imported from other kinds of computers may not display correctly if the software used is not capable of recognizing these differences and adjusting for them. *See also* ASCII, EOL.

ASCII file \a´skē fīl`, A`S-C-I-I`\ *n*. A document file in ASCII format, containing characters, spaces, punctuation, carriage returns, and sometimes tabs and an end-of-file marker, but no formatting information. *Also called* ASCII file, text file, text-only file. *See also* ASCII, text file. *Compare* binary file.

ASCII transfer \a´skē trans`fər, A`S-C-I-I`\ *n*. The preferred mode of electronic exchange for text files. In ASCII mode, character conversions to and from the network-standard character set are performed. *See also* ASCII. *Compare* binary transfer.

ASCIIZ string \a`skē-Z´ strēng, A`S-C-I-I-Z´\ *n*. In programming, an ASCII string terminated by the NULL character (a byte containing the character whose ASCII value is 0). *Also called* null-terminated string.

ASIC \A`S-I-C´\ *n*. Acronym for **a**pplication-**s**pecific **i**ntegrated **c**ircuit. *See* gate array.

ASN.1 \A`S-N-wən´\ *n*. *See* Abstract Syntax Notation One.

aspect ratio \a´spekt rā`shō\ *n*. In computer displays and graphics, the ratio of the width of an image or image area to its height. An aspect ratio of 2:1, for example, indicates that the image is twice as wide as it is high. The aspect ratio is an important factor in maintaining correct proportions when an image is printed, rescaled, or incorporated into another document.

ASPI \A`S-P-I´, a`spē\ *n*. *See* Advanced SCSI Programming Interface.

ASR \A`S-R´\ *n*. *See* automatic system reconfiguration.

assemble \ə-sem´bl\ *vb*. In programming, to convert an assembly language program to equivalent machine language instructions, called object code. *See also* assembler, assembly language, linker, object code.

assembler \ə-sem´blər\ *n*. A program that converts assembly language programs, which are understandable by humans, into executable machine language. *See also* assemble, assembly language, assembly listing, compiler (definition 2), machine code.

assembly language \ə-sem´blē lang´wəj\ *n*. A low-level programming language using abbreviations or mnemonic codes in which each statement corresponds to a single machine instruction. An assembly language is translated to machine language by the assembler and is specific to a given processor. Advantages of using an assembly language include increased execution speed and direct programmer interaction with system hardware. *See also* assembler, compiler, high-level language, low-level language, machine code.

assembly listing \ə-sem´blē li`stēng\ *n*. A file created by an assembler that includes the statements of an assembly language program, the machine language generated by the assembler, and a list of the symbols used in the program. *See also* assembler, assembly language.

assertion \ə-sər´shən\ *n*. A Boolean statement used in a program to test a condition that, if the program is operating correctly, should always evaluate as true; otherwise the program will typically terminate with an appropriate error message. Assertions are used for debugging programs and for documenting how a program should operate.

assignment operator \ə-sīn´mənt op`ər-ā-tər\ *n*. An operator used to assign a value to a variable or data structure. *See also* assignment statement, operator (definition 1).

assignment statement \ə-sīn´mənt stāt`mənt\ *n*. A programming language statement used to assign a value to a variable. It usually consists of three elements: an expression to be assigned, an assignment operator (typically a symbol such as = or :=), and a destination variable. On execution of the assignment statement, the expression is evaluated and the resulting value is stored in the specified destination. *See also* assignment operator, expression, variable.

associate \ə-sō´shē-āt`, ə-sō´sē-āt\ *vb*. To inform the operating system that a particular filename extension is linked to a specific application. When a file is opened that has an extension associated with a given application, the operating system automatically starts the application and loads the file.

Association Control Service Element \ə-sō-sē-ā`shən kən-trōl´ sər-vis el´ə-mənt\ *n*. An Open Systems Interconnection (OSI) method to establish a call between two applications by checking the identities and contexts of the application entities and performing an authentication security check. *Acronym:* ACSE (A`C-S-E´). *See also* ISO/OSI model.

Association for Computing Machinery \ə-sō-sē-ā`shən fər kəm-pyōō´tēng mə-shē`nər-ē\ *n*. A membership society founded in 1947 and devoted to the advancement of knowledge and technical proficiency of information processing professionals. *Acronym:* ACM (A`C-M´).

Association of C and C++ Users \ə-sō-sē-ā`shən əv C` and C-plus-plus´ yōō-zərz\ *n*. An organization of people interested in the programming language C and its variants. Members of the association include professional programmers, manufacturers and vendors of compilers, and non-professional programming enthusiasts. *Acronym:* ACCU (A`C-C-U´).

associative storage \ə-sō`shē-ā-tiv stōr´əj, ə-sō`sē-ā-tiv, ə-sō´shə-tiv\ *n*. A memory-based storage method in which data items are accessed not on the basis of a fixed address or location but by analysis of their content. *Also called* content-addressed storage.

associativity \ə-sō`shē-ā-tiv´ə-tē, ə-sō`sē-ə-tiv´ə-tē, ə-sō`shə-tiv´ə-tē\ *n*. *See* operator associativity.

asterisk \a´stər-isk\ *n*. **1.** The character (*) used in applications and programming languages to signify multiplication. **2.** In Windows, MS-DOS, OS/2, and other operating systems, a wildcard character that can be used in place of other characters, as in *.*, which represents any combination of filename and extension. *See also* question mark, star-dot-star, wildcard character. **3.** In the C and C++ programming languages, the character used to dereference a pointer to a class or structure. *See also* dereference, pointer (definition 1).

asymmetrical transmission \ā`si-me`trə-kəl tranz-mish´ən\ *n*. A form of transmission used by high-speed modems, typically those that operate at rates of 9,600 bps or more, that allows simultaneous incoming and outgoing transmission by dividing a telephone line bandwidth into two channels: one in the range of 300 to 450 bps and one at a speed of 9,600 bps or more.

asymmetric digital subscriber line \ā`si-me-trik dij`i-təl sub-skrī`bər līn`\ *n*. Technology and equipment allowing high-speed digital communication, including video signals, across an ordinary twisted-pair copper phone line, with speeds up to 9 megabits per second (9 Mbps) downstream (to the customer) and up to 800 kilobits per second (800 Kbps) upstream. *Acronym:* ADSL (A`D-S-L´). *Also called* asymmetric digital subscriber loop. *Compare* symmetric digital subscriber line.

asymmetric digital subscriber loop \ā`si-me-trik dij`i-təl sub-skrī`bər lōōp`\ *n*. *See* asymmetric digital subscriber line.

asynchronous device \ā-sēn`krə-nəs də-vīs´\ *n*. A device whose internal operations are not synchronized with the timing of any other part of the system.

asynchronous operation \ā-sēn`krə-nəs op`-ər-ā´shən\ *n*. An operation that proceeds independently of any timing mechanism, such as a clock. For example, two modems communicating asynchronously rely upon each sending the other start and stop signals in order to pace the exchange of information. *Compare* synchronous operation.

asynchronous procedure call \ā-sēn`krə-nəs prə-sē´jur käl\ *n*. A function call that executes separately from an executing program when a set of enabling conditions exist. After the conditions have been met, the operating system's kernel issues a software interrupt and directs the executing program to execute the call. *Acronym:* APC (A`P-C´). *See also* function call.

Asynchronous Protocol Specification \ā-sin`-krə-nəs prō`tə-kol spes`ə-fə-kā`shən\ *n*. The X.445 standard. *See* CCITT X Series.

Asynchronous Transfer Mode \ā-sēn`krə-nəs trans´fər mōd`\ *n*. *See* ATM (definition 1).

asynchronous transmission \ā-sēn`krə-nəs tranz-mish´ən\ *n*. In modem communication, a form of data transmission in which data is sent intermittently, one character at a time, rather than in a steady stream with characters separated by fixed time intervals. Asynchronous transmission relies on the use of a start bit and stop bit(s), in addition to the bits representing the character (and an optional parity bit), to distinguish separate characters. See the illustration on the next page.

.at \dot`A-T´\ *n*. On the Internet, the major geographic domain specifying that an address is located in Austria.

AT&T System V \A`T-ənd-T` si-stəm fīv´\ *n*. *See* System V.

ATA \A`T-A´\ *n*. Acronym for **A**dvanced **T**echnology **A**ttachment. ANSI group X3T10's official name

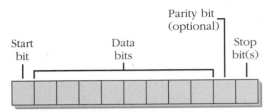

Asynchronous transmission. *The coding of a typical character sent in asynchronous transmission.*

for the disk drive interface standard commonly known as Integrated Drive Electronics (IDE). *Also called* AT Attachment.

ATA hard disk drive card \A`T-A` härd disk` drīv kärd`\ *n.* Expansion card used to control and interface with an ATA hard disk drive. These cards are usually ISA cards. *See also* ATA, ISA.

ATA/IDE hard disk drive \A-T-A`I-D-E` härd disk´ drīv`\ *n.* IDE (Integrated Drive Electronics—or numerous other interpretations) and ATA (AT Attachment) are one and the same thing: a disk drive implementation designed to integrate the controller onto the drive itself, thereby reducing interface costs and making firmware implementations easier.

ATAPI \A`T-A-P-I´\ *n.* The interface used by the IBM PC AT system for accessing CD-ROM devices.

AT Attachment \A-T´ ə-tach`mənt\ *n. See* ATA.

AT bus \A-T´ bus`\ *n.* The electric pathway used by IBM AT and compatible computers to connect the motherboard and peripheral devices. The AT bus supports 16 bits of data, whereas the original PC bus supports only 8 bits. *Also called* expansion bus. *See also* EISA, ISA, Micro Channel Architecture.

aTdHvAaNnKcSe \thanks` in əd-vans´\ *n. See* TIA.

ATDP \A`T-D-P´\ *n.* Acronym for **At**tention **D**ial **P**ulse, a command that initiates pulse (as opposed to touch-tone) dialing in Hayes and Hayes-compatible modems. *Compare* ATDT.

ATDT \A`T-D-T´\ *n.* Acronym for **At**tention **D**ial **T**one, a command that initiates touch-tone (as opposed to pulse) dialing in Hayes and Hayes-compatible modems. *Compare* ATDP.

.atl.ga.us \dot-A-T-L`dot-G-A`dot-U-S´\ *n.* On the Internet, the major geographic domain specifying that an address is located in Atlanta, Georgia, United States.

ATM \A`T-M´\ *n.* **1.** Acronym for **A**synchronous **T**ransfer **M**ode. A network technology capable of transmitting data, voice, video, and frame relay traffic in real time. Data, including frame relay data, is broken into packets containing 53 bytes each, which are switched between any two nodes in the system at rates ranging from 1.5 Mbps to 622 Mbps. ATM is defined in the broadband ISDN protocol at the levels corresponding to levels 1 and 2 of the ISO/OSI model. It is currently used in local area networks involving workstations and personal computers, but it is expected to be adopted by the telephone companies, which will be able to charge customers for the data they transmit rather than for their connect time. *See also* broadband, ISDN, ISO/OSI model. **2.** *See* Adobe Type Manager.

ATM Forum \A`T-M´ fōr`um\ *n.* Forum created in 1991 and including more than 750 companies related to communications and computing, as well as government agencies and research groups. The forum aims to promote Asynchronous Transfer Mode for data communication. *See also* ATM (definition 1).

atomic operation \ə-tom`ik op`ər-ā´shən\ *n.* An operation considered or guaranteed to be indivisible (by analogy with an atom of matter, once thought to be indivisible). Either the operation is uninterruptible or, if it is aborted, a mechanism is provided that ensures the return of the system to its state prior to initiation of the operation.

at sign \at´ sīn\ *n. See* @.

attach \ə-tach´\ *vb.* To include an external document as part of an e-mail message, using MIME or some other encoding application. Most modern e-mail clients have the ability to attach documents, as well as to decode attached documents that are received.

attached document \ə-tachd` do´kyə-mənt\ *n.* An ASCII text file or a binary file, such as a document created in a word processing system, that is included with an e-mail message as an attachment. The file is not part of the actual e-mail message, and it is generally encoded using uuencoding, MIME, or BinHex. Most e-mail programs automatically encode an attached document for transmission with a message. The recipient of the message must have an e-mail program capable of decoding the attached document or use a separate utility to decode it in order to read the document. *See also* ASCII, binary file, BinHex, MIME, uuencode.

attached processor \ə-tachd` pros´es-ər\ *n.* A secondary processor attached to a computer system, such as a keyboard or video subsystem processor.

attenuation \ə-ten`yo͞o-ā´shən\ *n.* The weakening of a transmitted signal, such as the distortion of a digital signal or the reduction in amplitude of an electrical signal, as it travels farther from its source. Attenuation is usually measured in decibels and is sometimes desirable, as when signal strength is reduced electronically, for example, by a radio volume control, to prevent overloading.

atto- \at´ō\ *prefix* Metric prefix meaning 10^{-18} (one quintillionth).

attribute \a´trə-byo͞ot`\ *n.* **1.** In a database record, the name or structure of a field. For example, the files LASTNAME, FIRSTNAME, and PHONE would be attributes of each record in a PHONELIST database. The size of a field or the type of information it contains would also be attributes of a database record. **2.** In screen displays, an element of additional information stored with each character in the video buffer of a video adapter running in character mode. Such attributes control the background and foreground colors of the character, underlining, and blinking. **3.** In markup languages such as SGML and HTML, a name-value pair within a tagged element that modifies certain features of that element. *See also* HTML, SGML.

ATX \A`T-X´\ *n.* A specification for PC motherboard architectures with built-in audio and video capabilities, introduced by Intel in 1995. ATX supports USB and full-length boards in all sockets. *See also* board, motherboard, specification, USB.

.au \dot`A-U´\ *n.* On the Internet, the major geographic domain specifying that an address is located in Australia.

audio \ä´dē-ō, ô´dē-ō\ *adj.* Relating to frequencies within the range of perception by the human ear—from about 15 to 20,000 hertz (cycles per second). *See also* audio response, synthesizer.

audio board \ä´dē-ō bōrd`, ô´dē-ō\ *n. See* audio card.

audio card \ä´dē-ō kärd`, ô´dē-ō\ *n.* An expansion card that converts analog audio signals from a microphone, audio tape, or other source to digital form that can be stored as a computer audio file, and converts computer audio files to electrical signals that can be played through a speaker. Output sounds can be routed through speakers or headphones. Input can be entered through a microphone connected to the computer. Most audio cards support MIDI. Audio cards enable sounds to be heard from CD-ROMs and other storage media or over the Internet. *Also called* audio board, sound board, sound card. *See also* MIDI.

audiocast \ä´dē-ō-kast`, ô´dē-ō-kast`\ *n.* The transmission of an audio signal using IP protocols. *See also* IP.

audio compression \ä´dē-ō kəm-presh`ən, ô´dē-ō\ *n.* A method of reducing the overall loudness of an audio signal. This is accomplished by limiting the amount of apparent distortion when the signal is played back through a speaker or transmitted through a communications link.

audio output \ä´dē-ō out´po͞ot, ô-dē-ō\ *n. See* audio response.

audio output port \ä´dē-ō out´po͞ot pōrt`, ô-dē-ō\ *n.* A circuit consisting of a digital-to-analog converter that transforms signals from the computer to audible tones. It is used in conjunction with an amplifier and speaker. *See also* digital-to-analog converter.

audio response \ä´dē-ō rə-spons`, ô´dē-ō\ *n.* Any sound produced by a computer; specifically, spoken output produced by a computer in response to some specific type of input. Such output may be generated using a combination of words from a digitized vocabulary or through the synthesis of words from tables of phonemes. *See also* frequency response, phoneme.

audiotex \ä´dē-ō-teks`, ô´dē-ō-\ *n.* An application allowing users to send and receive information by telephone. Users typically call an audiotex system and are presented with a series of choices or a series of questions through a voice mail system. When users select choices by pressing the buttons on the phone (rotary dial phones cannot be used for audiotex) or by speaking aloud, a database host responds by sending information to the voice mail system, which then converts the data to a spoken message for the user, or it responds by receiving and storing the information entered by the user. *Also called* audiotext. *See also* voice mail.

audiotext \ä´dē-ō-tekst`, ô´dē-ō-tekst`\ *n. See* audiotex.

Audio Video Interleaved \ä`dē-ō vid`ē-ō in´tər-lēvd, ô`dē-ō\ *n. See* AVI.

audiovisual \ä`dē-ō-vizh´ŏŏ-əl, ô`dē-ō-vizh´ŏŏ-əl\ *adj.* Relating to or being any material that uses a combination of sight and sound to present information.

audit \ä´dit, ô´dit\ *n.* In reference to computing, an examination of equipment, programs, activities, and procedures to determine how efficiently the overall system is performing, especially in terms of ensuring the integrity and security of data.

auditing \ä´di-tēng, ô´di-tēng\ *n.* The process an operating system uses to detect and record security-related events, such as an attempt to create, to access, or to delete objects such as files and directories. The records of such events are stored in a file known as a security log, whose contents are available only to those with the proper clearance. *See also* security log.

audit trail \ä´dit trāl`, ô´dit\ *n.* In reference to computing, a means of tracing all activities affecting a piece of information, such as a data record, from the time it is entered into a system to the time it is removed. An audit trail makes it possible to document, for example, who made changes to a particular record and when.

AUI cable \A`U-I´ kā-bl\ *n.* Short for **A**ttachment **U**nit **I**nterface **cable.** A transceiver cable used to connect a host adapter within a computer to an Ethernet (10Base5 or 10BaseF) network. *See also* 10Base5, 10BaseF, Ethernet (definition 1), transceiver cable.

AUP \A`U-P´\ *n. See* acceptable use policy.

authentication \ä-then`tə-kā´shən, ô-then`tə-kā´shən\ *n.* In a multiuser or network operating system, the process by which the system validates a user's logon information. A user's name and password are compared against an authorized list, and if the system detects a match, access is granted to the extent specified in the permission list for that user. *See also* logon, password, permission, user account, user name.

authoring language \ä´thər-ēng lang`wəj, ô´thər-ēng\ *n.* A computer language or application development system designed primarily for creating programs, databases, and materials for computer-aided instruction (CAI). A familiar example in relation to microcomputers is PILOT, a language used to create lessons. *See also* CAI, PILOT.

authoring system \ä´thər-ēng si`stəm, ô´thər-ēng\ *n.* Application software that enables the operator to create and format a document for a specific kind of computer environment. An authoring system, especially for multimedia work, often consists of several applications within the framework of a single, controlling application. *See also* authoring language.

authorization \ä`thər-ə-zā´shən, ô`thər-ə-zā´shən\ *n.* In reference to computing, especially remote computers on a network, the right granted an individual to use the system and the data stored on it. Authorization is typically set up by a system administrator and verified by the computer based on some form of user identification, such as a code number or password. *Also called* access privileges, permission. *See also* network, system administrator.

authorization code \ä`thər-ə-zā´shən kōd`, ô`thər-ə-zā´shən\ *n. See* password.

auto answer \ä´tō an`sər, ô´tō\ *n. See* answer mode.

AutoCorrect \ä´tō kər-ekt`, ô´tō kər-ekt`\ *n.* A function in Microsoft Word for Windows that automatically corrects errors and makes other substitutions as soon as a user types text. For example, AutoCorrect can be set up to fix misspellings, such as *teh* for *the,* or to change "straight" (" ") quotation marks to "smart" (" ") quotation marks. The user can select which AutoCorrect features to enable. *See also* smart quotes.

auto dial \ä´tō dīl`, ô´tō\ *n.* A feature enabling a modem to open a telephone line and initiate a call by transmitting a stored telephone number as a series of pulses or tones.

AUTOEXEC.BAT \ä´tō-eks-ek´dot-bat, ô´tō-, -B-A-T`\ *n.* A special-purpose batch file (set of commands) that is automatically carried out by the MS-DOS operating system when the computer is started or restarted. Created by the user or (in later versions of MS-DOS) by the operating system at system installation, the file contains basic startup commands that help configure the system to installed devices and to the user's preferences.

auto-key \ä´tō-kē`, ô´tō-\ *n. See* typematic.

automata theory \ä-tom´ə-tə thēr`ē, ô-tom´ə-tə, thē`ər-ē\ *n.* **1.** The study of computing processes and their capabilities and limitations; that is, how systems receive and process input and produce output. *See also* cellular automata. **2.** The study of the relationship between behavioral theories and the operation of automated devices.

automated office \ä`tə-mā-təd of´is, ô`tə-mā-təd\ *n.* A broad term used to refer to an office where work is carried out with the aid of computers, telecommunications facilities, and other electronic devices.

automatic answering \ä`tə-mat-ik an´sər-ēng, ô`tə-mat-ik\ *n. See* answer mode.

automatic data processing \ä`tə-mat-ik dā´tə pros´es-ēng, ô`tə-mat-ik, dat`ə\ *n. See* data processing.

automatic dialing \ä`tə-mat-ik dī´lēng, ô`tə-mat-ik\ *n. See* auto dial.

automatic error correction \ä`tə-mat-ik âr´ər kər-ek`shən, ô`tə-mat-ik\ *n.* A process that, upon detection of an internal processing or data transmission error, invokes a routine designed to correct the error or retry the operation.

Automatic Sequence Controlled Calculator \ä`tə-mat-ik sē`kwəns kən-trōld kal´kyə-lā-tər, ô`tə-mat-ik\ *n. See* Mark I.

automatic system reconfiguration \ä`tə-mat-ik si`stəm rē`kən-fi-gyər-ā´shən, ô`tə-mat-ik\ *n.* Automation of configuration by the system to accommodate some change in either the software or the hardware. *Acronym:* ASR (A`S-R´).

automonitor \ä`tō-mon´ə-tər, ô´tō-mon`ə-tər\ *n.* A process or system feature capable of assessing the status of its own internal environment.

AutoPlay \ä`tō-plā`, ô´tō-\ *n.* A feature in Windows 95 that allows it to automatically operate a CD-ROM. When a CD is inserted into a CD-ROM drive, Windows 95 looks for a file called AUTO-RUN.INF on the CD. If the file is found, Windows 95 will open it and carry out its instructions, which are usually to set up an application from the CD-ROM on the computer's hard disk or to start the

application once it has been installed. If an audio CD is inserted into the drive, Windows 95 will automatically launch the CD Player application and play it.

autopolling \ä`tō-pō`lēng, ô´tō-pō`lēng\ *n.* The process of periodically determining the status of each device in a set so that the active program can process the events generated by each device, such as whether a mouse button was pressed or whether new data is available at a serial port. This can be contrasted with event-driven processing, in which the operating system alerts a program or routine to the occurrence of an event by means of an interrupt or message rather than having to check each device in turn. *Also called* polling. *Compare* event-driven processing, interrupt-driven processing.

auto-repeat \ä`tō-rə-pēt`, ô´tō-rə-pēt`\ *n. See* typematic.

autorestart \ä`tō-rē´stärt, ô`tō-rē´stärt\ *n.* A process or system feature that can automatically restart the system after the occurrence of certain types of errors or a power system failure.

autosave \ä`tō-sāv`, ô´tō-sāv`\ *n.* A program feature that automatically saves an open file to a disk or other medium at defined intervals or after a certain number of keystrokes to ensure that changes to a document are periodically saved.

autosizing \ä`tō-sī´zēng, ô´tō-\ *n.* The ability of a monitor to accept signals at one resolution and display the image at a different resolution. A monitor capable of autosizing maintains the aspect ratio of an image but enlarges or reduces the image to fit in the space available. *See also* monitor, resolution (definition 1).

autostart routine \ä`tō-stärt rōō-tēn`, ô´tō-stärt\ *n.* A process by which a system or device is automatically prepared for operation with the occurrence of powering up, or turning the system on, or some other predetermined event. *See also* AUTOEXEC.BAT, autorestart, boot[2], power up.

autotrace \ä`tō-trās`, ô´tō-trās`\ *n.* A drawing program feature that draws lines along the edges of a bitmapped image to convert the image to an object-oriented one. *See also* bitmapped graphics, object-oriented graphics.

AUX \äks, ôks, A`U-X´\ *n.* The logical device name for auxiliary device; a name reserved by the MS-DOS operating system for the standard auxiliary device. AUX usually refers to a system's first serial port, also known as COM1.

A/UX \A`U-X´\ *n.* A version of the multiuser, multitasking UNIX operating system provided by Apple Computer for various Macintosh computers and based on the AT&T System V, release 2.2 of UNIX with some enhancements. A/UX incorporates a number of Apple features, including support for the Macintosh Toolbox, so that applications can provide users with the graphics-based interface characteristic of that computer. *See also* System V.

auxiliary equipment \äks-il`ē-âr-ē i-kwip´mənt, ôks-il`ē-âr-ē, äks-il`yər-ē, ôks-il`yər-ē\ *n. See* peripheral.

auxiliary storage \äks-il`ē-âr-ē stōr´əj, ôks-il`ē-âr-ē, äks-il`yər-ē, ôks-il`yər-ē\ *n.* Any storage medium, such as disk or tape, not directly accessed by a computer's microprocessor, as is random access memory (RAM). In current usage, such media are typically referred to as *storage* or *permanent storage,* and the RAM chips that the microprocessor uses directly for temporary storage are referred to as *memory.*

availability \ə-vā`lə-bil´ə-tē\ *n.* In processing, the accessibility of a computer system or resource, such as a printer, in terms of usage or of the percentage of the total amount of time the device is needed.

available time \ə-vā`lə-bl tīm´\ *n. See* uptime.

avatar \av`ə-tär´\ *n.* **1.** In virtual-reality environments such as certain types of Internet chat rooms, a graphical representation of a user. An avatar typically is a generic picture or animation of a human

of either gender, a photograph or caricature of the user, a picture or animation of an animal, or an object chosen by the user to depict his or her virtual-reality "identity." **2.** *See* superuser.

.avi \dot`A-V-I´\ *n.* The file extension that identifies an audiovisual interleaved data file in the Microsoft RIFF format.

AVI \A`V-I´\ *n.* Acronym for **A**udio **V**ideo **I**nterleaved. A Windows multimedia file format for sound and moving pictures that uses the Microsoft RIFF (Resource Interchange File Format) specification.

.aw \dot`A-W´\ *n.* On the Internet, the major geographic domain specifying that an address is located in Aruba.

axis \aks´is\ *n.* In a chart or other two-dimensional system using coordinates, the horizontal line (*x*-axis) or vertical line (*y*-axis) that serves as a reference for plotting points. In a three-dimensional coordinate system, a third line (*z*-axis) is used to represent depth. See the illustration. *See also* Cartesian coordinates.

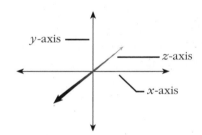

Axis.

.az \dot`A-Z´\ *n.* On the Internet, the major geographic domain specifying that an address is located in Azerbaijan.

b[1] \B\ *adj.* Short for **b**inary.

b[2] \B\ *n.* **1.** Short for **b**it. **2.** Short for **b**aud.

B \B\ *n.* Short for **b**yte.

B: \B\ *n.* **1.** Identifier for a second floppy disk drive on MS-DOS and other operating systems. **2.** Identifier for a single disk drive when used as the secondary drive.

.ba \dot`B-A´\ *n.* On the Internet, the major geographic domain specifying that an address is located in Bosnia and Herzegovina.

backbone \bak´bōn\ *n.* **1.** A network of communication transmission that carries major traffic between smaller networks. The backbones of the Internet, including communications carriers such as Sprint and MCI, can span thousands of miles using microwave relays and dedicated lines. **2.** The smaller networks (compared with the entire Internet) that perform the bulk of the packet switching of Internet communication. Today these smaller networks still consist of the networks that were originally developed to make up the Internet—the computer networks of the educational and research institutions of the United States—especially NSFnet, the computer network of the National Science Foundation in Oak Ridge, Tennessee. *See also* NSFnet, packet switching. **3.** The wires that carry major communications traffic within a network. In a local area network, a backbone may be a bus. *Also called* collapsed backbone.

backbone cabal \bak´bōn kə-bäl`, kə-bal`\ *n.* On the Internet, a term for the group of network administrators responsible for naming the hierarchy of Usenet newsgroups and devising the procedures for creating new newsgroups. The backbone cabal no longer exists.

back door \bak dōr´\ *n.* A means of gaining access to a program or system by bypassing its security controls. Programmers often build back doors into systems under development so that they can fix bugs. If the back door becomes known to anyone other than the programmer, or if it is not removed before the software is released, it becomes a security risk. *Also called* trapdoor.

back end \bak end´\ *n.* **1.** In a client/server application, the part of the program that runs on the server. *See also* client/server architecture. *Compare* front end. **2.** The part of a compiler that transforms source code (human-readable program statements) into object code (machine-readable code). *See also* compiler (definition 2), object code, source code.

back-end processor \bak`end pros´es-ər\ *n.* **1.** A slave processor that performs a specialized task such as providing rapid access to a database, freeing the main processor for other work. Such a task is considered "back-end" because it is subordinate to the computer's main function. **2.** A processor that manipulates data sent to it from another processor; for example, a high-speed graphics processor dedicated to painting images on a video display operates in response to commands passed "back" to it by the main processor. *Compare* coprocessor.

background[1] \bak´ground\ *adj.* In the context of processes or tasks that are part of an operating system or program, operating without interaction with the user while the user is working on another task. Background processes or tasks are assigned a lower priority in the microprocessor's allotment of time than foreground tasks and generally remain invisible to the user unless the user requests an update or brings the task to the foreground. Generally, only multitasking operating systems are able to support background processing. However, some operating systems that do not support multitasking may be able to perform one or more types of background tasks. For example, in the Apple Macintosh operating system running with multitasking turned off, the Background Printing option can be used to print documents while the user is doing other work. *See also* multi-tasking. *Compare* foreground[1].

background[2] \bak´ground\ *n.* **1.** The color against which characters and graphics are displayed, such as a white background for black characters. *Compare* foreground[2] (definition 1). **2.** The colors, textures, patterns, and pictures that comprise the surface of the desktop, upon which icons, buttons, menu bars, and toolbars are situated. *See also* wallpaper. **3.** The colors, textures, patterns, and pictures that comprise the surface of a Web page, upon which text, icons, graphics, buttons, and other items are situated. *See also* wallpaper. **4.** The condition of an open but currently inactive window in a windowing environment. *See also* inactive window. *Compare* foreground[2] (definition 2).

background noise \bak´ground noiz`\ *n.* The noise inherent in a line or circuit, independent of the presence of a signal. *See also* noise.

background printing \bak´ground prin`tēng\ *n.* The process of sending a document to a printer at the same time that the computer is performing one or more other tasks.

background processing \bak´ground pros`es-ēng\ *n.* The execution of certain operations by the operating system or a program during momentary lulls in the primary (foreground) task. An example of a background process is a word processor program printing a document during the time that occurs between the user's keystrokes. *See also* background[1].

background program \bak´ground prō-gram\ *n.* A program that can run or is running in the background. *See also* background[1].

background task \bak´ground task`\ *n.* *See* background[1].

back-lit display \bak`lit dis-plā´\ *n.* An LCD display that uses a light source behind the screen to enhance image sharpness and readability, especially in environments that are brightly lit.

back panel \bak` pan´əl\ *n.* The panel at the rear of a computer cabinet through which most of the connections to outside power sources and peripherals are made. See the illustration.

backplane \bak´plān\ *n.* A circuit board or framework that supports other circuit boards, devices, and the interconnections among devices, and pro-

Back panel.

vides power and data signals to supported devices.

backslash \bak´slash\ *n.* The character (\) used to separate directory names in MS-DOS path specifications. When used as a leading character, it means that the path specification begins from the topmost level for that disk drive. *See also* path (definition 5).

Backspace key \bak´spās kē`\ *n.* **1.** A key that, on IBM and compatible keyboards, moves the cursor to the left, one character at a time, usually erasing each character as it moves. **2.** On Macintosh keyboards, a key (called the Delete key on some Macintosh keyboards) that erases currently selected text or, if no text is selected, erases the character to the left of the insertion point (cursor).

backtracking \bak´trak`ēng\ *n.* The ability of an expert system to try alternative solutions in an attempt to find an answer. The various alternatives can be viewed as branches on a tree: in backtracking, the program follows one branch and, if it reaches the end without finding what it seeks, backs up and tries another branch.

backup \bak´up\ *n.* A duplicate copy of a program, a disk, or data, made either for archiving purposes or for safeguarding valuable files from loss should the active copy be damaged or destroyed. A backup is an "insurance" copy. Some application programs automatically make backup copies of data files, maintaining both the current version and the preceding version on disk. *Also called* backup copy, backup file.

back up \bak up´\ *vb.* **1.** To make a duplicate copy of a program, a disk, or data. *See also* backup. **2.** To return to a previous stable state, such as one in which a database is known to be complete and consistent.

backup and recovery \bak`up ənd ri-kəv´ər-ē\ *n.* A strategy available in many database management systems that allows a database to be restored to the latest complete unit of work (transaction) after a software or hardware error has rendered the database unusable. The process starts with the latest backup copy of the database. The transaction log, or change file, for the database is read, and each logged transaction is recovered through the last checkpoint on the log. *See also* backup, checkpoint, log (definition 1).

backup and restore \bak`up ənd ri-stōr´\ *n.* The process of maintaining backup files and putting them back onto the source medium if necessary.

backup copy \bak´up kop`ē\ *n. See* backup.

backup file \bak´up fīl`\ *n. See* backup.

Backus-Naur form \bak-us-nou´ər fōrm`\ *n.* A metalanguage used for defining the syntax of formal languages, both for the developer of the language and for the user. A language is defined by a set of statements, in each of which a language element known as a metavariable, written in angle brackets, is defined in terms of actual symbols (called terminals) and other metavariables (including itself if necessary). Shown below is the syntax of a number in Backus-Naur form. The symbol "::=" means "is defined as" and the "¦" symbol separates alternatives. *Acronym:* BNF (B`N-F´). *See also* metalanguage, normal form (definition 2).

```
<number>::=<unsigned number>¦
          <sign> <unsigned number>
<unsigned   number>::=<digit>¦<digit>
<unsigned
             number>.
<digit>::=0¦1¦2¦3¦4¦5¦6¦7¦8¦9
<sign>::=+¦-
```

backward chaining \ba`kwərd chā´nēng\ *n.* In expert systems, a form of problem solving that starts with a statement and a set of rules leading to the statement and then works backward, matching the rules with information from a database of facts until the statement can be either verified or proved wrong. *Compare* forward chaining.

bacterium \bak-tēr´ē-um`\ *n.* A type of computer virus that repeatedly replicates itself, eventually taking over the entire system. *See also* virus.

bad block \bad blok´\ *n.* **1.** A faulty memory location. A bad block is identified by the computer's memory controller in the self-test procedure when the computer is turned on or is rebooted. **2.** *See* bad sector.

bad sector \bad` sek´tər\ *n.* A disk sector that cannot be used for data storage, usually because of media damage or imperfections. Finding, marking, and avoiding bad sectors on a disk is one of the many tasks performed by a computer's operating system. A disk-formatting utility can also find and mark the bad sectors on a disk.

bad track \bad trak´\ *n.* A track on a hard disk or floppy disk that is identified as containing a faulty sector and consequently is bypassed by the operating system. *See also* bad sector.

.bak \dot-bak´\ *n.* An auxiliary file, created either automatically or upon command, that contains the second-most-recent version of a file and that bears the same filename, with the extension .bak. *See also* backup.

balanced line \bal`ənsd līn´\ *n.* A transmission line, such as twisted-pair cabling, that contains two conductors capable of carrying equal voltages and currents of opposite polarity and direction.

balloon help \bə-lōōn´ help`\ *n.* In the Mac OS 7.*x*, an on-screen help feature in the form of a cartoon dialog balloon. After activating this feature by clicking on the balloon icon on the toolbar, the user can position the cursor over an icon or other item, and a dialog balloon will appear that describes the function of the item. See the illustration.

Balloon help.

ball printer \bäl´ prin`tər\ *n.* An impact printer that uses a small ball-shaped print head that bears fully formed characters in raised relief on its surface. The printer rotates and tilts the ball to line up characters and then strikes the ball against a ribbon. This method was used in the IBM Selectric typewriter.

band \band\ *n.* **1.** In printing graphics, a rectangular portion of a graphic sent by the computer to a printer. The technique of dividing a graphic into bands prevents a printer from having to reconstruct an entire image in memory before printing it. **2.** In communications, a contiguous range of frequencies used for a particular purpose, such as radio or television broadcasts.

bandpass filter \band´pas fil`tər\ *n.* An electronic circuit that passes signals that are within a certain frequency range (band) but blocks or attenuates signals above or below the band. *See also* attenuation. *Compare* highpass filter, lowpass filter.

bandwidth \band´width\ *n.* **1.** The difference between the highest and lowest frequencies that an analog communications system can pass. For example, a telephone accommodates a bandwidth of 3,000 Hz: the difference between the lowest (300 Hz) and highest (3,300 Hz) frequencies it can carry. **2.** The data transfer capacity of a digital communications system.

bandwidth on demand \band`width on də-mand´\ *n.* In telecommunications, the capability of increasing throughput, in increments, as required by the channel to be serviced. *See also* bandwidth, channel (definition 2), throughput.

bank \bank\ *n.* **1.** Any group of similar electrical devices connected together for use as a single device. For example, transistors may be connected in a row/column array inside a chip to form memory, or several memory chips may be connected together to form a memory module such as a SIMM. See the illustration. *See also* SIMM. **2.** A section of memory, usually of a size convenient for a CPU to address. For example, an 8-bit processor can address 65,536 bytes of memory; therefore, a 64-kilobyte (64-KB) memory bank is the largest that the processor can address at once. To address another 64-KB bank of memory requires circuitry that fools the CPU into looking at a separate block

of memory. *See also* bank switching, page (definition 2).

Bank. A bank of soldered chips (top) and a bank of SIMMs (bottom).

bank switching \bank´ swich`ēng\ *n.* A method of expanding a computer's available random access memory (RAM) by switching between banks of RAM chips that share a range of memory addresses, which is set aside before switching begins. Only one bank is directly accessible at a time; when a bank is not active, it retains whatever is stored in it. Before another bank can be used, the operating system, driver, or program must explicitly issue a command to the hardware to make the switch. Because switching between banks takes time, memory-intensive operations take longer with bank-switched memory than with main memory. Bank-switched memory typically takes the form of an expansion card that plugs into a slot on the motherboard.

banner \ban´ər\ *n.* A section of a Web page containing an advertisement that is usually an inch or less tall and spans the width of the Web page. The banner contains a link to the advertiser's Web site. See the illustration. *See also* Web page, Web site.

Banner.

banner page \ban´ər pāj`\ *n.* **1.** The title page that may be added to printouts by most print spoolers. Such a page typically incorporates account ID information, job length, and print spooler information, and is used primarily to separate one print job from another. *See also* print spooler. **2.** In software, an initial screen used to identify a product and credit its producers.

bar chart \bär´ chärt\ *n.* A type of graphic in which data items are shown as rectangular bars. The bars may be displayed either vertically or horizontally and may be distinguished from one another by color or by some type of shading or pattern. Positive and negative values may be shown in relation to a zero baseline. Two types of bar charts are common: a standard bar chart, in which each value is represented by a separate bar, and a stacked bar chart, in which several data points are "stacked" to produce a single bar. See the illustration. *Also called* bar graph.

bar code \bär´ kōd\ *n.* The special identification code printed as a set of vertical bars of differing widths on books, grocery products, and other merchandise. Used for rapid, error-free input in such facilities as libraries, hospitals, and grocery stores, bar codes represent binary information that can be read by an optical scanner. The coding can include numbers, letters, or a combination of the two; some codes include built-in error checking and can be read in either direction.

bar code reader \bär´ kōd rē`dər\ *n. See* bar code scanner.

bar code scanner \bär´ kōd skan`ər\ *n.* An optical device that uses a laser beam to read and inter-

Vertical bar chart

Stacked bar chart

Bar chart.　　*Two common types of bar chart.*

pret bar codes, such as the Universal Product Codes found on grocery products and other retail items. *See also* bar code, Universal Product Code.

bare board \bâr bōrd´\ *n.* A circuit board with no chips on it; most commonly, a memory board not populated with memory chips.

bare bones[1] \bâr bōnz´\ *adj.* Purely functional; stripped or otherwise clean of features. Bare bones applications provide only the most basic functions necessary to perform a given task. By the same token, a bare bones computer provides a minimal amount of hardware or is sold at retail with no peripherals and just the operating system (and no other software).

bare bones[2] \bâr bōnz´\ *n.* **1.** An application that provides only the most basic functions necessary to perform a given task. **2.** A computer consisting only of motherboard (equipped with CPU and RAM), cabinet, power supply, floppy disk drive, and keyboard, to which the user must add hard disk, video adapter, monitor, and any other peripherals. *See also* motherboard, peripheral.

bar graph \bär´graf\ *n. See* bar chart.

base \bās\ *n.* **1.** In mathematics, a number that is raised to the power specified by an exponent. For example, in $2^3 = 2 \times 2 \times 2 = 8$, the base is 2. **2.** In mathematics, the number of digits in a particular numbering system. With microcomputers, four numbering systems are commonly used or referred to—binary, octal, decimal, and hexadecimal—and each is based on a different number of digits. The binary, or base-2, numbering system, which is used to discuss the states of a computer's logic, has two digits, 0 and 1. Octal, or base-8, has eight digits, 0 through 7. The familiar decimal, or base-10, numbering system has ten digits, 0 through 9. Hexadecimal, or base-16, has sixteen digits, 0 through 9 and A through F. When numbers are written in a particular base, the base is often subscripted and enclosed in parentheses after the number, as in $24\mathrm{AE}_{(16)} = 9{,}390$. *Also called* radix. *See also* binary[1], decimal, hexadecimal, octal. **3.** One of three terminals (emitter, base, and collector) in a bipolar transistor. The current through the base controls the current between the emitter and the collector. *See also* transistor. **4.** The insulating foundation of a printed circuit board. *See also* circuit board.

base 2 \bās tōō´\ *adj. See* binary.[1]

base 8 \bās āt´\ *adj. See* octal.

base 10 \bās ten´\ *adj. See* decimal.

base 16 \bās` siks-tēn´\ *adj. See* hexadecimal.

base address \bās´ a`dres, ə-dres`\ *n.* The part of a two-part memory address that remains constant and provides a reference point from which the location of a byte of data can be calculated. A base address is accompanied by an offset value that is added to the base to determine the exact location (the absolute address) of the information. The concept is similar to a street address system. For example, "2010 Main Street" consists of a base (the 2000 block of Main Street) plus an offset (10 from the beginning of the block). Base addresses are known as segment addresses in IBM PCs and compatibles; data in these computers is identified by its position as a relative offset from the start of the segment. *See also* absolute address, offset, relative address, segment.

baseband \bās´band\ *adj.* Of or relating to communications systems in which the medium of transmission (such as a wire or fiber-optic cable) carries a single message at a time in digital form. Baseband communication is found in local area networks such as Ethernet and Token Ring. *See also* Ethernet, fiber optics, Token Ring network. *Compare* broadband.

baseband network \bās´band net`wərk\ *n.* A type of local area network in which messages travel in digital form on a single transmission channel between machines connected by coaxial cable or twisted-pair wiring. Machines on a baseband network transmit only when the channel is not busy, although a technique called *time-division multiplexing* can enable channel sharing. Each message on a baseband network travels as a packet that contains information about the source and destination machines as well as message data. Baseband networks operate over short distances at speeds ranging from about 50 kilobits per second (50 Kbps) to 16 megabits per second (16 Mbps). Receiving, verifying, and converting a message, however, add considerably to the actual time, reducing throughput. The maximum recommended distance for such a network is about 2 miles, or considerably less if the network is heavily used. *See also* coaxial cable, multiplexing, packet (definition 2), throughput, time-division multiplexing, twisted-pair cable. *Compare* broadband network.

base class \bās´ klas\ *n.* In C++, a class from which other classes have been or can be derived by inheritance. *See also* class, derived class, inheritance, object-oriented programming.

baseline \bās´līn\ *n.* In the printing and display of characters on the screen, an imaginary horizontal line with which the base of each character, excluding descenders, is aligned. See the illustration. *See also* ascender, descender, font.

Descender   Baseline

Baseline.

base memory \bās´ mem`ər-ē\ *n. See* conventional memory.

base RAM \bās´ ram, R-A-M`\ *n. See* conventional memory.

Basic or **BASIC** \bā´sik, B`A-S-I-C´\ *n.* Acronym for **B**eginner's **A**ll-purpose **S**ymbolic **I**nstruction **C**ode, a high-level programming language developed in the mid-1960s by John Kemeny and Thomas Kurtz at Dartmouth College. It is widely considered one of the easiest programming languages to learn. *See also* True BASIC, Visual Basic.

Basic Rate Interface \bā`sik rāt in´tər-fās\ *n. See* BRI.

.bat \dot-bat´, -B`A-T´\ *n.* The file extension that identifies a batch program file. In MS-DOS, .bat files are executable files that contain calls to other program files. *See also* batch file.

batch \bach\ *n.* A group of documents or data records that are processed as a unit. *See also* batch job, batch processing.

batch file \bach´ fīl\ *n.* An ASCII text file containing a sequence of operating-system commands, possibly including parameters and operators supported by the batch command language. When the user types a batch filename at the command prompt, the commands are processed sequentially. *Also called* batch program. *See also* AUTOEXEC.BAT, .bat.

batch file transmission \bach` fīl tranz-mish´ən\ *n.* The transmission of multiple files as the result of a single command. *Acronym:* BFT (B`F-T´).

batch job \bach´ job\ *n.* A program or set of commands that runs without user interaction. *See also* batch processing.

batch processing \bach´ pros`es-ēng\ *n.* **1.** Execution of a batch file. *See also* batch file. **2.** The practice of acquiring programs and data sets from users, running them one or a few at a time, and then providing the results to the users. **3.** The practice of storing transactions for a period of time before they are posted to a master file, typically in a separate operation undertaken at night. *Compare* transaction processing.

batch program \bach´ prō`gram\ *n.* A program that executes without interacting with the user. *See also* batch file. *Compare* interactive program.

batch system \bach´ si`stəm\ *n.* A system that processes data in discrete groups of previously scheduled operations rather than interactively or in real time.

batch total \bach´ tō`təl\ *n.* A total calculated for an element common to a group (batch) of records, used as a control to verify that all information is accounted for and has been entered correctly. For example, the total of a day's sales can be used as a batch total to verify the records of all individual sales.

battery \bat´ər-ē`\ *n.* Two or more cells in a container that produces an electrical current when two electrodes within the container touch an electrolyte. In personal computers, batteries are used as an auxiliary source of power when the main power is shut off, as a power source for laptop and notebook computers (rechargeable batteries, such as nickel cadmium, nickel metal hydride, and lithium ion, are used), and as a method to keep the internal clock and the circuitry responsible for the part of RAM that stores important system information always powered up. *See also* lead ion battery, lithium ion battery, nickel cadmium battery, nickel metal hydride battery, RAM.

battery backup \bat`ər-ē bak´up\ *n.* **1.** A battery-operated power supply used as an auxiliary source of electricity in the event of a power failure. **2.** Any use of a battery to keep a circuit running when the main power is shut off, such as powering a computer's clock/calendar and the special RAM that stores important system information between sessions. *See also* UPS.

battery meter \bat´ər-ē mē`tər\ *n.* A device used to measure the current (capacity) of an electrical cell.

baud \bäd, bôd\ *n.* One signal change per second, a measure of data transmission speed. Named after the French engineer and telegrapher Jean-Maurice-Emile Baudot and originally used to measure the transmission speed of telegraph equipment, the term now most commonly refers to the data transmission speed of a modem. *See also* baud rate.

Baudot code \bō-dō´ kōd`\ *n.* A 5-bit coding scheme used principally for telex transmissions, originally developed for telegraphy by the French engineer and telegrapher Jean-Maurice-Emile Baudot. Sometimes it is equated, although inaccurately, with the International Alphabet Number 2 proposed by the Comité Consultatif International Télégraphique et Téléphonique (CCITT).

baud rate \bäd´ rāt, bôd´\ *n.* The speed at which a modem can transmit data. The baud rate is the number of events, or signal changes, that occur in one second—not the number of bits per second (bps) transmitted. In high-speed digital communications, one event can actually encode more than one bit, and modems are more accurately described in terms of bits per second than baud rate. For example, a so-called 9,600-baud modem actually operates at 2,400 baud but transmits 9,600 bits per second by encoding 4 bits per event $(2{,}400 \times 4 = 9{,}600)$ and thus is a 9,600-bps modem. *Compare* bit rate, transfer rate.

bay \bā\ *n.* A shelf or opening used for the installation of electronic equipment—for example, the space reserved for additional disk drives, CD-ROM drives, or other equipment in the cabinets of microcomputers. *See also* drive bay.

.bb \dot`B-B´\ *n.* On the Internet, the major geographic domain specifying that an address is located in Barbados.

BBL \B`B-L´\ *n.* Acronym for **b**e **b**ack **l**ater. An expression used commonly on live chat services on the Internet and online information services to indicate that a participant is temporarily leaving the discussion forum but intends to return at a later time. *See also* chat[1] (definition 1).

BBS \B`B-S´\ *n.* **1.** Acronym for **b**ulletin **b**oard **s**ystem. A computer system equipped with one or more modems or other means of network access that serves as an information and message-passing center for remote users. Often BBSs are focused on special interests, such as science fiction, movies, Windows software, or Macintosh systems, and can have free or fee-based access, or a combination. Users dial into a BBS with their modems and post messages to other BBS users in special areas devoted to a particular topic, in a manner reminiscent of the posting of notes on a cork bulletin board. Many BBSs also allow users to chat online with other users, send e-mail, download and upload files that include freeware and shareware software, and access the Internet. Many software and hardware companies run proprietary BBSs for customers that include sales information, technical support, and software upgrades and patches. **2.** Acronym for **b**e **b**ack **s**oon. A shorthand expression often seen in Internet discussion groups by a participant leaving the group who wishes to bid a temporary farewell to the rest of the group.

bcc \B`C-C´\ *n.* Acronym for **b**lind **c**ourtesy **c**opy. A feature of e-mail programs that allows a user to send a copy of an e-mail message to a recipient without notifying other recipients that this was done. Generally, the recipient's address is entered into a field called "bcc:" in the mail header. *Also called* blind carbon copy. *See also* e-mail[1] (definition 1), header (definition 1). *Compare* cc.

.bc.ca \dot-B-C`dot-C-A´\ *n.* On the Internet, the major geographic domain specifying that an address is located in British Columbia, Canada.

BCD \B`C-D´\ *n. See* binary-coded decimal.

BCNF \B`C-N-F´\ *n.* Acronym for **B**oyce-**C**odd **n**ormal **f**orm. *See* normal form (definition 1).

.bd \dot`B-D´\ *n.* On the Internet, the major geographic domain specifying that an address is located in Bangladesh.

.be \dot`B-E´\ *n.* On the Internet, the major geographic domain specifying that an address is located in Belgium.

bearer channel \bâr´ər chan`əl\ *n.* One of the 64-Kbps communications channels on an ISDN circuit. A BRI (Basic Rate Interface) ISDN line has 2 bearer channels and 1 data channel. A PRI (Primary Rate Interface) ISDN line has 23 bearer channels (in North America) or 30 bearer channels (in Europe) and 1 data channel. *See also* BRI, channel (definition 2), ISDN.

BeBox \bē´boks\ *n.* A high-performance multiprocessor computer (RISC-based PowerPC) made by Be, Inc., and loaded with Be's operating system, BeOS. Currently the BeBox is being marketed as a tool for software developers. *See also* BeOS, PowerPC, RISC.

beginning-of-file \bə-gin´ēng-əv-fīl`\ *n.* **1.** A code placed by a program before the first byte in a file, used by the computer's operating system to keep track of locations within a file with respect to the first byte (character) in it. **2.** The starting location of a file on a disk relative to the first storage location on the disk. A data directory or catalog contains this location. *Acronym:* BOF (B`O-F´, bof). *Compare* end-of-file.

Bell communications standards \bel` kə-myōo-nə-kā´shənz stan`dərdz\ *n.* A series of data transmission standards originated by AT&T during the late 1970s and early 1980s that, through wide acceptance in North America, became de facto standards for modems. Bell 103, now mostly obsolete, governed transmission at 300 bits per second (bps) with full-duplex, asynchronous communications over dial-up telephone lines using frequency-shift keying (FSK). Bell 212A governed modem operations at 1200 bps with full-duplex, asynchronous communications over dial-up telephone lines using phase-shift keying (PSK). An international set of transmission standards, known as the CCITT recommendations, has become generally accepted as the primary source of standardization, especially for communications at speeds greater than 1200 bps. *See also* CCITT V series, FSK, phase-shift keying.

Bell-compatible modem \bel`kəm-pat`ə-bl mō´dəm\ *n.* A modem that operates according to the Bell communications standards. *See also* Bell communications standards.

bells and whistles \belz` ənd wis´əlz, hwis´əlz\ *n.* Attractive features added to hardware or software beyond basic functionality, comparable to accessories, such as electric door locks and air conditioning, added to an automobile. Products, especially computer systems, without such adornments are sometimes called "plain vanilla."

benchmark[1] \bench´märk\ *n.* A test used to measure hardware or software performance. Benchmarks for hardware use programs that test the capabilities of the equipment—for example, the speed at which a CPU can execute instructions or handle floating-point numbers. Benchmarks for software determine the efficiency, accuracy, or speed of a program in performing a particular task, such as recalculating data in a spreadsheet. The same data is used with each program tested, so the resulting scores can be compared to see which programs perform well and in what areas. The design of fair benchmarks is something of an art, because various combinations of hardware and software can exhibit widely variable performance under different conditions. Often, after a benchmark has become a standard, developers try to optimize a product to run that benchmark faster than similar products run it in order to enhance sales. *See also* sieve of Eratosthenes.

benchmark[2] \bench´märk\ *vb.* To measure the performance of hardware or software.

benign virus \bə-nīn` vīr´us, bē-nīn`\ *n.* A program that exhibits properties of a virus, such as self-replication, but does not otherwise do harm to the computer systems that it infects.

BeOS \bē´O-S´\ *n.* Short for **Be o**perating **s**ystem. An object-oriented operating system by Be, Inc., designed for a BeBox or Power Macintosh system. This operating system supports symmetric multiprocessing, multitasking, and protected memory and is well suited for multimedia animation and communications. *See also* BeBox, multitasking, protected mode, symmetric multiprocessing.

Bernoulli box \bər-nōō´lē boks`\ *n.* A removable floppy disk drive for personal computers that uses a nonvolatile cartridge and has high storage capacity. Named after Daniel Bernoulli, an eighteenth-century physicist who first demonstrated the principle of aerodynamic lift, the Bernoulli box uses high speed to bend the flexible disk close to the read/write head in the disk drive. *See also* read/write head.

Bernoulli distribution \bər-nōō´lē di-strə-byōō´shən\ *n.* *See* binomial distribution.

Bernoulli process \bər-nōō´lē pros`es\ *n.* A mathematical process involving the Bernoulli trial, a repetition of an experiment in which there are only two possible outcomes, such as success and failure. This process is used mostly in statistical analysis. *See also* Bernoulli sampling process, binomial distribution.

Bernoulli sampling process \bər-nōō´lē sam´plēng pros`es\ *n.* In statistics, a sequence of *n* independent and identical trials of a random experiment, with each trial having one of two possible outcomes. *See also* Bernoulli process, binomial distribution.

best of breed \best` əv brēd´\ *adj.* A term used to describe a product that is the best in a particular category of products.

beta[1] \bā´tə\ *adj.* Of or relating to software or hardware that is a beta. *See also* beta[2]. *Compare* alpha[1].

beta[2] \bā´tə\ *n.* A new software or hardware product, or one that is being updated, that is ready to be released to users for beta testing. *See also* beta test.

beta site \bā´tə sīt`\ *n.* An individual or an organization that tests software before it is released to the public. The company producing the software usually selects these beta sites from a pool of established customers or volunteers. Most beta sites perform this service free of charge, often to get a first look at the software and to receive free copies of the software once it is released to the public.

beta test \bā´tə test`\ *n.* A test of software that is still under development, accomplished by having people actually use the software. In a beta test, a software product is sent to selected potential customers and influential end users (known as beta sites), who test its functionality and report any operational or utilization errors (bugs) found. The beta test is usually one of the last steps a software developer takes before releasing the product to market; however, if the beta sites indicate that the software has operational difficulties or an extraordinary number of bugs, the developer may conduct more beta tests before the software is released to customers.

betweening \bə-twē´nēng\ *n. See* tween.

Bézier curve \bez´ē-ā kurv\ *n.* A curve that is calculated mathematically to connect separate points into smooth, free-form curves and surfaces of the type needed for illustration programs and CAD models. Bézier curves need only a few points to define a large number of shapes—hence their usefulness over other mathematical methods for approximating a given shape. See the illustration. *See also* CAD.

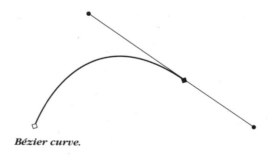

Bézier curve.

BFT \B`F-T´\ *n. See* batch file transmission, binary file transfer.

.bg \dot`B-G´\ *n.* On the Internet, the major geographic domain specifying that an address is located in Bulgaria.

BGP \B`G-P´\ *n. See* Border Gateway Protocol.

.bh \dot`B-H´\ *n.* On the Internet, the major geographic domain specifying that an address is located in Bahrain.

bias \bī əs\ *n.* **1.** A uniform or systematic deviation from a point of reference. **2.** In mathematics, an indication of the amount by which the average of a group of values deviates from a reference value. **3.** In electronics, a voltage applied to a transistor or other electronic device to establish a reference level for its operation. **4.** In communications, a type of distortion in the length of transmitted bits, caused by a lag that occurs as voltage builds up or falls off each time the signal changes from 0 to 1 or vice versa.

bidirectional \bī`dər-ek´shə-nəl\ *adj.* Operating in two directions. A bidirectional printer can print from left to right and from right to left; a bidirectional bus can transfer signals in both directions between two devices.

bidirectional parallel port \bī`dər-ek-shə-nəl pâr´ə-lel pōrt`\ *n.* An interface that supports two-way parallel communication between a device and a computer.

bidirectional printing \bī`dər-ek`shə-nəl prin´tēng\ *n.* The ability of an impact or ink-jet printer to print from left to right and from right to left. Bidirectional printing improves speed substantially because no time is wasted returning the print head to the beginning of the next line, but it may lower print quality.

bi-endian \bī`en´dē-ən\ *adj.* Of, pertaining to, or characteristic of processors and other chips that can be switched to work in big endian or little endian mode. The PowerPC chip has this ability, which allows it to run the little endian Windows NT or the big endian MacOS/PPC. *See also* big endian, little endian, PowerPC.

bifurcation \bī`fur-kā´shən\ *n.* A split that results in two possible outcomes, such as 1 and 0 or on and off.

Big Blue \big blōō´\ *n.* The International Business Machines (IBM) Corporation. This nickname comes from the corporate color used on IBM's early mainframes and still used in the company logo.

big endian \big`en´dē-ən\ *adj.* Storing numbers in such a way that the most significant byte is placed first. For example, given the hexadecimal number A02B, the big endian method would cause the number to be stored as A02B, and the little endian method would cause the number to be stored as 2BA0. The big endian method is used by Motorola microprocessors; Intel microprocessors use the little endian method. The term *big endian* is derived from Jonathan Swift's *Gulliver's Travels,* in which the Big-Endians were a group of people who opposed the emperor's decree that eggs should be broken at the small end before they were eaten. *Compare* little endian.

big red switch \big`red swich´\ *n.* The power on/off switch of a computer, thought of as a kind of interrupt of last resort. On the IBM PC and many other computers, it is indeed big and red. Using the switch is an interrupt of last resort because it deletes all the data in RAM and can also damage the hard drive. *Acronym:* BRS (B`R-S´).

billion \bil´yən\ *n.* **1.** In American usage (as is usual with microcomputers), a thousand million, or 10^9. Computer terminology uses the prefixes *giga-* for 1 billion and *nano-* for 1 billionth. **2.** In British usage, a million million, or 10^{12}, which is a *trillion* in American usage.

billisecond \bil´i-sek`ənd\ *n. See* nanosecond.

.bin \dot-bin´, dot`B-I-N´\ *n.* A filename extension for a file encoded with MacBinary. *See also* MacBinary.

binary[1] \bī´nər-ē`, bī´når`ē\ *adj.* Having two components, alternatives, or outcomes. The binary number system has 2 as its base, so values are expressed as combinations of two digits, 0 and 1. These two digits can represent the logical values *true* and *false* as well as numerals, and they can be represented in an electronic device by the two states *on* and *off,* recognized as two voltage levels. Therefore, the binary number system is at the heart of digital computing. Although ideal for computers, binary numbers are usually difficult for people to interpret because they are repetitive strings of 1s and 0s. To ease translation, programmers and others who habitually work with the computer's internal processing abilities use hexadecimal (base-16) or octal (base-8) numbers. Equivalents and conversion tables for binary, dec-

imal, hexadecimal, and octal are in Appendix E. *See also* base (definition 2), binary-coded decimal, binary number, bit, Boolean algebra, byte, cyclic binary code, digital computer, dyadic, logic circuit. *Compare* ASCII, decimal, hexadecimal, octal.

binary[2] \bī´nər-ē`, bī´når`ē\ *n.* In an FTP client program, the command that instructs the FTP server to send or receive files as binary data. *See also* FTP client, FTP server. *Compare* ascii.

binary chop \bī´nər-ē chop`, bī´når-ē\ *n. See* binary search.

binary-coded decimal \bī`nər-ē-kō`dəd des´ə-məl, bī´når-ē-\ *n.* A system for encoding decimal numbers in binary form to avoid rounding and conversion errors. In binary-coded decimal coding, each digit of a decimal number is coded separately as a binary numeral. Each of the decimal digits 0 through 9 is coded in 4 bits, and for ease of reading, each group of 4 bits is separated by a space. This format is also called 8-4-2-1, after the weights of the four bit positions, and uses the following codes: 0000 = 0; 0001 = 1; 0010 = 2; 0011 = 3; 0100 = 4; 0101 = 5; 0110 = 6; 0111 = 7; 1000 = 8; 1001 = 9. Thus, the decimal number 12 is 0001 0010 in binary-coded decimal notation. *Acronym:* BCD (B`C-D´). *See also* base (definition 2), binary number, binary[1], decimal, EBCDIC, packed decimal, round.

binary compatibility \bī´nər-ē kəm-pat`ə-bil´ə-tē, bī´når-ē\ *n.* Portability of executable programs (binary files) from one platform, or flavor of operating system, to another. *See also* flavor, portable (definition 1).

binary conversion \bī´nər-ē kən-vər´zhən, bī´når-ē\ *n.* The conversion of a number to or from the binary number system. Conversion tables are in Appendix E. *See also* binary[1].

binary device \bī´nər-ē də-vīs`, bī´når-ē\ *n.* Any device that processes information as a series of on/off or high/low electrical states. *See also* binary[1].

binary digit \bī´nər-ē dij´ət, bī´når-ē\ *n.* Either of the two digits in the binary number system, 0 and 1. *See also* bit.

binary file \bī´nər-ē fīl`, bī´når-ē\ *n.* A file consisting of a sequence of 8-bit data or executable code, as distinguished from files consisting of human-readable ASCII text. Binary files are usually in a form readable only by a program, often compressed or structured in a way that is easy for a particular program to read. *Compare* ASCII file.

binary file transfer \bī´nər-ē fīl trans´fər, bī´när-ē\ *n.* Transfer of a file containing arbitrary bytes or words, as opposed to a text file containing only printable characters (for example, ASCII characters with codes 10, 13, and 32–126). On modern operating systems a text file is simply a binary file that happens to contain only printable characters, but some older systems distinguish the two file types, requiring programs to handle them differently. *Acronym:* BFT (B`F-T´).

binary format \bī´nər-ē fōr´mat, bī´när-ē\ *n.* Any format that structures data in 8-bit form. Binary format is generally used to represent object code (program instructions translated into a machine-readable form) or data in a transmission stream. *See also* binary file.

binary notation \bī´nər-ē, nō-tā´shən, bī´när-ē\ *n.* Representation of numbers using the binary digits, 0 and 1. *Compare* floating-point notation.

binary number \bī´nər-ē num´bər, bī´när-ē\ *n.* A number expressed in binary form. Because binary numbers are based on powers of 2, they can be interpreted as follows:

Digit position and meaning:

$$2^6 \quad 2^5 \quad 2^4 \quad 2^3 \quad 2^2 \quad 2^1 \quad 2^0$$

Decimal value:

64 32 16 8 4 2 1

The binary number 1001101, for example, means

2^6	2^5	2^4	2^3	2^2	2^1	2^0
64	32	16	8	4	2	1
1	0	0	1	1	0	1

or the sum of

1	times 64	64
0	times 32	0
0	times 16	0
1	times 8	8
1	times 4	4
0	times 2	0
1	times 1	1

which is decimal 77. Equivalents and conversion tables are in Appendix E. *See also* binary[1].

binary search \bī´nər-ē sərch`, bī´när-ē\ *n.* A type of search algorithm that seeks an item, with a known name, in an ordered list by first comparing the sought item to the item at the middle of the list's order. The search then divides the list in two, determines in which half of the order the item should be, and repeats this process until the sought item is found. *Also called* binary chop, dichotomizing search. *See also* search algorithm. *Compare* hash search, linear search.

binary synchronous protocol \bī´nər-ē sin`-krə-nəs prō´tə-kol, bī´när-ē\ *n. See* BISYNC.

binary transfer \bī´nər-ē trans´fər, bī´när-ē\ *n.* The preferred mode of electronic exchange for executable files, application data files, and encrypted files. *Compare* ASCII transfer.

binary tree \bī´nər-ē trē´, bī´när-ē\ *n.* In programming, a specific type of tree data structure in which each node has at most two subtrees, one left and one right. Binary trees are often used for sorting information; each node of the binary search tree contains a key, with values less than that key added to one subtree and values greater than that key added to the other. See the illustration. *See also* binary search, tree.

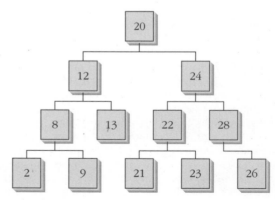

Binary tree.

binaural sound \bī´nōr´əl sound`, bin`ōr´əl\ *n. See* 3-D audio.

bind \bīnd\ *vb.* To associate two pieces of information with one another. The term is most often used with reference to associating a symbol (such as the name of a variable) with some descriptive information (such as a memory address, a data type, or an actual value). *See also* binding time, dynamic binding, static binding.

binding time \bīn´dēng tīm`\ *n.* The point in a program's use at which binding of information occurs, usually in reference to program elements being bound to their storage locations and values. The most common binding times are during compilation (compile-time binding), during linking (link-time binding), and during program execution (run-time binding). *See also* bind, compile-time binding, link-time binding, run-time binding.

BinHex[1] \bin´heks\ *n.* **1.** A code for converting binary data files into ASCII text so they can be transmitted via e-mail to another computer or in a newsgroup post. This method can be used when standard ASCII characters are needed for transmission, as they are on the Internet. BinHex is used most frequently by Mac users. *See also* MIME. **2.** An Apple Macintosh program for converting binary data files into ASCII text and vice versa using the BinHex code. *Compare* uudecode[1], uuencode[1].

BinHex[2] \bin´heks\ *vb.* To convert a binary file into printable 7-bit ASCII text or to convert the resulting ASCII text file back to binary format using the BinHex program. *Compare* uudecode[2], uuencode[2].

binomial distribution \bī-nō`mē-əl dis-trə-byoō´-shən\ *n.* In statistics, a list or a function that describes the probabilities of the possible values of a random variable chosen by means of a Bernoulli sampling process. A Bernoulli process has three characteristics: each trial has only two possible outcomes—success or failure; each trial is independent of all other trials; and the probability of success for each trial is constant. A binomial distribution can be used to calculate the probability of getting a specified number of successes in a Bernoulli process. For example, the binomial distribution can be used to calculate the probability of getting a 7 three times in 20 rolls of a pair of dice. *Also called* Bernoulli distribution.

bionics \bī-on´iks`\ *n.* The study of living organisms, their characteristics, and the ways they function, with a view toward creating hardware that can simulate or duplicate the activities of a biological system. *See also* cybernetics.

BIOS \bī´ōs, B`I-O-S´\ *n.* Acronym for **b**asic **i**nput/**o**utput **s**ystem. On PC-compatible computers, the set of essential software routines that test hardware at startup, start the operating system, and support the transfer of data among hardware devices. The BIOS is stored in read-only memory (ROM) so that it can be executed when the computer is turned on. Although critical to performance, the BIOS is usually invisible to computer users. *See also* AMI BIOS, CMOS setup, Phoenix BIOS, ROM BIOS. *Compare* Toolbox.

bipolar \bī`pō´lər\ *adj.* **1.** Having two opposite states, such as positive and negative. **2.** In information transfer and processing, pertaining to or characteristic of a signal in which opposite voltage polarities represent on and off, true and false, or some other pair of values. *See also* nonreturn to zero. *Compare* unipolar. **3.** In electronics, pertaining to or characteristic of a transistor having two types of charge carriers. *See also* transistor.

BIS \B`I-S´\ *n. See* business information system.

bistable \bī`stā´bl\ *adj.* Of, pertaining to, or characteristic of a system or device that has two possible states, such as on and off. *See also* flip-flop.

bistable circuit \bī-stā`bl sər´kət\ *n.* Any circuit that has only two stable states. The transition between them must be initiated from outside the circuit. A bistable circuit is capable of storing 1 bit of information.

bistable multivibrator \bī-stā`bl mul-tī-vī´brā-tər, mul-tē-vī´brā-tər\ *n. See* flip-flop.

BISYNC \bī´sēnk\ *n.* Short for **bi**nary **sync**hronous communications protocol. A communications standard developed by IBM. BISYNC transmissions are encoded in either ASCII or EBCDIC. Messages can be of any length and are sent in units called frames, optionally preceded by a message header. BISYNC uses synchronous transmission, in which message elements are separated by a specific time interval, so each frame is preceded and followed by special characters that enable the sending and receiving machines to synchronize their clocks. STX and ETX are control characters that mark the beginning and end of the message text; BCC is a set of characters used to verify the accuracy of transmission. See the illustration on the next page. *Also called* BSC.

bit \bit\ *n.* Short for **bi**nary digi**t**. The smallest unit of information handled by a computer. One bit expresses a 1 or a 0 in a binary numeral, or a true or false logical condition, and is represented physically by an element such as a high or low voltage at one point in a circuit or a small spot on a disk magnetized one way or the other. A single bit conveys little information a human would consider meaningful. A group of 8 bits, however, makes up a byte, which can be used to represent many types of information, such as a letter of the alphabet, a decimal digit, or other character. *See also* ASCII, binary[1], byte.

bit block \bit´ blok\ *n.* In computer graphics and display, a rectangular group of pixels treated as a unit. Bit blocks are so named because they are, literally, blocks of bits describing the pixels' display characteristics, such as color and intensity. Programmers use bit blocks and a technique called bit block transfer (bitblt) to display images rapidly on the screen and to animate them. *See also* bit block transfer.

bit block transfer \bit´ blok trans`fər\ *n.* Abbreviated bitblt. In graphics display and animation, a programming technique that manipulates blocks of bits in memory that represent the color and other attributes of a rectangular block of pixels forming a screen image. The image described can range in size from a cursor to a cartoon. Such a bit block is moved through a computer's video RAM as a unit so that its pixels can be rapidly displayed in a desired location on the screen. The bits can also be altered; for example, light and dark portions of an image can be reversed. Successive displays can thus be used to change the appearance of an image or to move it around on the screen.

Some computers contain special graphics hardware for manipulating bit blocks on the screen independently of the contents of the rest of the screen. This speeds the animation of small shapes, because a program need not constantly compare and redraw the background around the moving shape. *See also* sprite.

bitblt \bit´B-L-T´, bit´blit\ *n. See* bit block transfer.

bit bucket \bit´ buk`ət\ *n.* An imaginary location into which data can be discarded. A bit bucket is a null input/output device from which no data is read and to which data can be written without effect. The NUL device recognized by MS-DOS is a bit bucket. A directory listing, for example, simply disappears when sent to NUL.

bit density \bit´ den`sə-tē\ *n.* A measure of the amount of information per unit of linear distance or surface area in a storage medium or per unit of time in a communications pipeline.

bit depth \bit´ depth\ *n.* The number of bits per pixel allocated for storing indexed color information in a graphics file.

bit flipping \bit´ flip`ēng\ *n.* A process of inverting bits—changing 1s to 0s and vice versa. For example, in a graphics program, to invert a black-and-white bitmapped image (to change black to white and vice versa), the program could simply flip the bits that compose the bit map.

bit image \bit´ im`əj\ *n.* A sequential collection of bits that represents in memory an image to be displayed on the screen, particularly in systems having a graphical user interface. Each bit in a bit image corresponds to one pixel (dot) on the screen. The screen itself, for example, represents a single bit image; similarly, the dot patterns for all the characters in a font represent a bit image of the

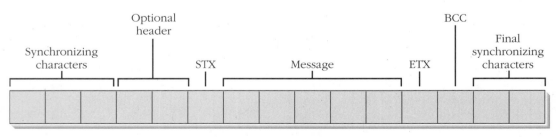

BISYNC. ***The structure of a BISYNC frame.***

font. In a black-and-white display each pixel is either white or black, so it can be represented by a single bit. The "pattern" of 0s and 1s in the bit image then determines the pattern of white and black dots forming an image on the screen. In a color display the corresponding description of on-screen bits is called a pixel image because more than one bit is needed to represent each pixel. *See also* bit map, pixel image.

bit manipulation \bit´ mə-ni-pyə-lā`shən\ *n.* An action intended to change only one or more individual bits within a byte or word. Manipulation of the entire byte or word is much more common and generally simpler. *See also* mask.

bit map or **bitmap** \bit´ map, bit´map\ *n.* A data structure in memory that represents information in the form of a collection of individual bits. A bit map is used to represent a bit image. Another use of a bit map in some systems is the representation of the blocks of storage on a disk, indicating whether each block is free (0) or in use (1). *See also* bit image, pixel image.

bitmapped font \bit´mapd font´\ *n.* A set of characters in a particular size and style in which each character is described as a unique bit map (pattern of dots). Macintosh screen fonts are examples of bitmapped fonts. See the illustration. *See also* downloadable font, outline font, TrueType. *Compare* PostScript font, vector font.

Bitmapped font. Each character is composed of a pattern of dots.

bitmapped graphics \bit`mapd graf´iks\ *n.* Computer graphics represented as arrays of bits in memory that represent the attributes of the individual pixels in an image (one bit per pixel in a black-and-white display, multiple bits per pixel in a color or gray-scale display). Bitmapped graphics are typical of paint programs, which treat images as collections of dots rather than as shapes. *See*

also bit image, bit map, pixel image. *Compare* object-oriented graphics.

BITNET \bit`net\ *n.* Acronym for **B**ecause **I**t's **T**ime **Net**work. A wide area network, founded in 1981 and operated by the Corporation for Research and Educational Networking (CREN) in Washington, D.C., used to provide e-mail and file transfer services between mainframe computers at educational and research institutions in North America, Europe, and Japan. BITNET uses the IBM Network Job Entry (NJE) protocol rather than TCP/IP, but it can exchange e-mail with the Internet. The listserv software for maintaining mailing lists was originated on BITNET.

bit. newsgroups \bit`dot-nōōz´grōōps\ *n.* A hierarchy of Internet newsgroups that mirror the content of some BITNET mailing lists. *See also* BITNET.

bit-oriented protocol \bit` or-ē-ent-əd prō´tə-kol´\ *n.* A communications protocol in which data is transmitted as a steady stream of bits rather than as a string of characters. Because the bits transmitted have no inherent meaning in terms of a particular character set (such as ASCII), a bit-oriented protocol uses special sequences of bits rather than reserved characters for control purposes. The HDLC (high-level data link control) defined by ISO is a bit-oriented protocol.

bit parallel \bit´ pār`ə-lel\ *adj.* Transmitting simultaneously all bits in a set (such as a byte) over separate wires in a cable. *See also* parallel transmission.

bit pattern \bit´ pat`ərn\ *n.* **1.** A combination of bits, often used to indicate the possible unique combinations of a specific number of bits. For example, a 3-bit pattern allows 8 possible combinations and an 8-bit pattern allows 256 combinations. **2.** A pattern of black and white pixels in a computer system capable of supporting bitmapped graphics. *See also* pixel.

bit plane \bit´ plān\ *n.* **1.** One of a set of bit maps that collectively make up a color image. Each bit plane contains the values for one bit of the set of bits that describe a pixel. One bit plane allows two colors (usually black and white) to be represented; two bit planes, four colors; three bit planes, eight colors; and so on. These sections of memory are called bit planes because they are treated as if they were separate layers that stack one upon another to form the complete image. By contrast, in a chunky pixel image, the bits describing a given pixel are stored contiguously within the same byte. The use of bit planes to represent colors is often associated with the use of a color look-up table, or color map, which is used to assign colors to particular bit patterns. Bit planes are used in the EGA and VGA in 16-color graphics modes; the four planes correspond to the 4 bits of the IRGB code. *See also* color look-up table, color map, EGA, IRGB, layering, VGA. *Compare* color bits. **2.** Rarely, one level of a set of superimposed images (such as circuit diagrams) to be displayed on the screen.

bit rate \bit´ rāt\ *n.* The speed at which binary digits are transmitted. *See also* transfer rate.

bit serial \bit´ sēr`ē-əl\ *n.* The transmission of bits in a byte one after another over a single wire. *See also* serial transmission.

bit slice microprocessor \bit` slīs mī`krō-pros´es-ər\ *n.* A building block for microprocessors that are custom-developed for specialized uses. These chips can be programmed to handle the same tasks as other CPUs but they operate on short units of information, such as 2 or 4 bits. They are combined into processors that handle the longer words.

bits per inch \bits` pər inch´\ *n.* A measure of data storage capacity; the number of bits that fit into an inch of space on a disk or a tape. On a disk, bits per inch are measured based on inches of circumference of a given track. *See also* packing density. *Acronym:* BPI (B`P-I´).

bits per second \bits` pər sek´ənd\ *n. See* bps.

bit stream \bit´ strēm\ *n.* **1.** A series of binary digits representing a flow of information transferred through a given medium. **2.** In synchronous communications, a continuous flow of data in which characters in the stream are separated from one another by the receiving station rather than by markers, such as start and stop bits, inserted into the data.

bit stuffing \bit´ stuf´ēng\ *n.* The practice of inserting extra bits into a stream of transmitted data. Bit stuffing is used to ensure that a special sequence of bits appears only at desired locations. For example, in the HDLC, SDLC, and X.25 communications protocols, six 1 bits in a row can

appear only at the beginning and end of a frame (block) of data, so bit stuffing is used to insert a 0 bit into the rest of the stream whenever five 1 bits appear in a row. The inserted 0 bits are removed by the receiving station to return the data to its original form. *See also* HDLC, SDLC, X.25.

bit transfer rate \bit` trans´fər rāt\ *n. See* transfer rate.

bit twiddler \bit´ twid`lər, twi´dl-ər\ *n.* Slang for someone devoted to computers, particularly one who likes to program in assembly language. *See also* hacker.

BIX \biks, B`I-X´\ *n.* Acronym for *B* YTE **I**nformation **Ex**change. An online service originated by *BYTE* magazine, now owned and operated by Delphi Internet Services Corporation. BIX offers e-mail, software downloads, and conferences relating to hardware and software.

biz. newsgroups \biz`dot nōōz´grōōps\ *n.* Usenet newsgroups that are part of the biz. hierarchy and have the prefix of biz. These newsgroups are devoted to discussions related to business. Unlike most other newsgroup hierarchies, biz. newsgroups permit users to post advertisement and other marketing material. *See also* newsgroup, traditional newsgroup hierarchy.

.bj \dot`B-J´\ *n.* On the Internet, the major geographic domain specifying that an address is located in Benin.

black box \blak boks´\ *n.* A unit of hardware or software whose internal structure is unknown but whose function is documented. The internal mechanics of the function do not matter to a designer who uses a black box to obtain that function. For example, a memory chip can be viewed as a black box. Many people use memory chips and design them into computers, but generally only memory chip designers need to understand their internal operation.

blackout \blak´out\ *n.* A condition in which the electricity level drops to zero; a complete loss of power. A number of factors cause a blackout, including natural disasters, such as a storm or an earthquake, or a failure in the power company's equipment, such as a transformer or a power line. A blackout might or might not damage a computer, depending on the state of the computer when the blackout occurs. As with switching a computer off before saving any data, a blackout will cause all unsaved data to be irretrievably lost. The most potentially damaging situation is one in which a blackout occurs while a disk drive is reading information from or writing information to a disk. The information being read or written will probably become corrupted, causing the loss of a small part of a file, an entire file, or the entire disk; the disk drive itself might suffer damage as a result of the sudden power loss. The only reliable means of preventing damage caused by a blackout is to use a battery-backed uninterruptible power supply (UPS). *See also* UPS. *Compare* brownout.

blank[1] \blānk\ *n*. The character entered by pressing the spacebar. *See also* space character.

blank[2] \blānk\ *vb*. To not show or not display an image on part or all of the screen.

blanking \blān´kēng\ *n*. The brief suppression of a display signal as the electron beam in a raster-scan video monitor is moved into position to display a new line. After tracing each scan line, the beam is at the right edge of the screen and must return to the left (horizontal retrace) to begin a new line. The display signal must be turned off during the time of the retrace (horizontal blanking interval) to avoid overwriting the line just displayed. Similarly, after tracing the bottom scan line, the electron beam moves to the top left corner (vertical retrace), and the beam must be turned off during the time of this retrace (vertical blanking interval) to avoid marking the screen with the retrace path.

blast \blast\ *vb*. *See* burn.

bleed \blēd\ *n*. In a printed document, any element that runs off the edge of the page or into the gutter. Bleeds are often used in books to mark important pages so they are easier to find. *See also* gutter.

blind carbon copy \blīnd` kär`bən kop´ē\ *n*. *See* bcc.

blind courtesy copy \blīnd` kər´tə-sē kop`ē\ *n*. *See* bcc.

blind search \blīnd sərch´\ *n*. A search for data in memory or on a storage device with no foreknowledge as to the data's order or location. *See also* linear search. *Compare* binary search, indexed search.

blink \blēnk\ *vb*. To flash on and off. Cursors, insertion points, menu choices, warning messages, and other displays on a computer screen that are intended to catch the eye are often made to blink. The rate of blinking in a graphical user interface can sometimes be controlled by the user.

blink speed \blēnk´ spēd\ *n*. The rate at which the cursor indicating the active insertion point in a text window, or other display element, flashes on and off.

blip \blip\ *n*. A small, optically sensed mark on a recording medium, such as microfilm, that is used for counting or other tracking purposes.

bloatware \blōt´wâr\ *n*. Software whose files occupy an extremely large amount of storage space on a user's hard disk, especially in comparison with previous versions of the same product.

block[1] \blok\ *n*. **1.** Generally, a contiguous collection of similar things that are handled together as a whole. **2.** A section of random access memory temporarily assigned (allocated) to a program by the operating system. **3.** A group of statements in a program that are treated as a unit. For example, if a stated condition is true, all of the statements in the block are executed, but none are executed if the condition is false. **4.** A unit of transmitted information consisting of identification codes, data, and error-checking codes. **5.** A collection of consecutive bytes of data that are read from or written to a device (such as a disk) as a group. **6.** A rectangular grid of pixels that are handled as a unit. **7.** A segment of text that can be selected and acted upon as a whole in an application.

block[2] \blok\ *vb*. **1.** To distribute a file over fixed-size blocks in storage. **2.** To prevent a signal from being transmitted. **3.** To select a segment of text, by using a mouse, menu selection, or cursor key, to be acted upon in some way, such as to format or to delete the segment.

block cipher \blok´ sī`fər\ *n*. A private key encryption method that encrypts data in blocks of a fixed size (usually 64 bits). The encrypted data block contains the same number of bits as the original. *See also* encryption, private key.

block cursor \blok´ kur`sər\ *n*. An on-screen cursor that has the same width and height in pixels as a text-mode character cell. A block cursor is used in text-based applications, especially as the mouse pointer when a mouse is installed in the system. *See also* character cell, cursor (definition 1), mouse pointer.

block device \blok´ də-vīs`\ *n.* A device, such as a disk drive, that moves information in blocks—groups of bytes—rather than one character (byte) at a time. *Compare* character device.

block diagram \blok´ dī`ə-gram\ *n.* A chart of a computer or other system in which labeled blocks represent principal components and lines and arrows between the blocks show the pathways and relationships among the components. A block diagram is an overall view of what a system consists of and how it works. To show the various components of such a system in more detail, different types of diagrams, such as flowcharts or schematics, are used. See the illustration. *Compare* bubble chart, flowchart.

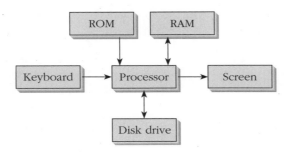

Block diagram.

block gap \blok´ gap\ *n.* The unused physical space that separates blocks of data or physical records on a tape or formatted sectors on a disk. *Also called* IBG, interblock gap.

block header \blok´ hed`ər\ *n.* Information that appears at the beginning of a block of data and serves such purposes as signaling the beginning of the block, identifying the block, providing error-checking information, and describing such characteristics as the block length and the type of data contained in the block. *See also* header (definition 2).

blocking factor \blok´ēng fak`tər\ *n.* **1.** The size of the chunks in which data is transferred to or from a block device such as a disk. If fewer bytes are requested, the disk drive will still read the whole block. Common blocking factors on personal computers are 128, 256, and 512 bytes.

2. The number of file records in one disk block. If the record length for a file is 170 bytes, a block on the disk contains 512 bytes, and records do not span blocks, then the blocking factor is 3, and each block contains 510 (170 × 3) bytes of data and 2 unused bytes.

block length \blok´ length\ *n.* The length, usually in bytes, of a block of data. Block length typically ranges from 512 bytes through 4,096 kilobytes (KB), depending on the purpose for which the block is used.

block move \blok´ mōōv\ *n.* Movement of a number of items of data together to a different location, as in reorganizing documents with a word processor or moving the contents of cell ranges in a spreadsheet. Most CPUs have instructions that easily support block moves.

block size \blok´ sīz\ *n.* The declared size of a block of data transferred internally within a computer, via FTP, or by modem. The size is usually chosen to make most efficient use of all the hardware devices involved. *See also* FTP[1] (definition 1).

block structure \blok´ struk`chur\ *n.* The organization of a program into groups of statements called *blocks,* which are treated as units. Programming languages such as Ada, C, and Pascal were designed around block structure. A block is a section of code surrounded by certain delimiters (such as BEGIN and END or { and }), which signify that the intervening code can be treated as a related group of statements. For example, in C, each function is a separate block. Block structure also limits the scope of constants, data types, and variables declared in a block to that block. *See also* function (definition 2), procedure, scope (definition 1).

block transfer \blok´ trans`fər\ *n.* The movement of data in discrete blocks (groups of bytes).

blow \blō\ *vb. See* burn.

blow up \blō up´\ *vb.* To terminate abnormally, as when a program crosses some computational or storage boundary and cannot handle the situation on the other side, as in, "I tried to draw outside the window, and the graphics routines blew up." *See also* abend, abort.

blue screen \blōō´ skrēn\ *n.* A technique used in film matte special effects, in which one image is superimposed on another image. Action or objects are filmed against a blue screen. The desired background is filmed separately, and the shot containing the action or objects is superimposed onto the background. The result is one image where the blue screen disappears.

.bm \dot`B-M´\ *n*. On the Internet, the major geographic domain specifying that an address is located in Bermuda.

.bmp \dot-B`M-P´\ *n*. The file extension that identifies raster graphics stored in bit map file format. *See also* bit map.

.bn \dot`B-N´\ *n*. On the Internet, the major geographic domain specifying that an address is located in Brunei Darussalam.

BNC connector \B-N-C´ kə-nek`tər\ *n*. A connector for coaxial cables that locks when one connector is inserted into another and rotated 90 degrees. BNC connectors are often used with closed-circuit television. See the illustration. *See also* coaxial cable.

BNC connector. Male (left) and female (right) BNC connectors.

.bo \dot`B-O´\ *n*. On the Internet, the major geographic domain specifying that an address is located in Bolivia.

board \bōrd\ *n*. An electronic module consisting of chips and other electronic components mounted on a flat, rigid substrate on which conductive paths are laid between the components. A personal computer contains a main board, called the motherboard, which usually has the microprocessor on it and slots into which other, smaller boards, called cards or adapters, can be plugged to expand the functionality of the main system, such as to connect to monitors, disk drives, or a network. *See also* adapter, card (definition 1), motherboard.

board computer \bōrd´ kəm-pyōō`tər\ *n*. *See* single-board.

board level \bōrd´ lev`əl\ *n*. A level of focus in troubleshooting and repair that involves tracking down a problem in a computer to a circuit board and replacing the board. This is in contrast to the component level, which involves repairing the board itself. In many cases board-level repairs are made in order to quickly restore the device to working condition; the boards replaced are then repaired and tested for use in later board-level repairs. *See also* circuit board.

body \bod´ē\ *n*. In e-mail and Internet newsgroups, the content of a message. The body of a message follows the header, which contains information about the sender, origin, and destination of the message. *See also* header (definition 1).

body face \bod´ē fās`\ *n*. A typeface suitable for the main text in a document rather than for headings and titles. Because of their readability, fonts having serifs, such as Times and Palatino, are good body faces, although sans serif faces can also be used as body text. *See also* sans serif, serif. *Compare* display face.

BOF \B`O-F´, bof\ *n*. **1.** Acronym for **b**irds **o**f a **f**eather. Meetings of special interest groups at trade shows, conferences, and conventions. BOF sessions provide an opportunity for people working on the same technology at different companies or research institutions to meet and exchange their experiences. **2.** *See* beginning-of-file.

boilerplate \boi´lər-plāt´\ *n*. Recyclable text; a piece of writing or code, such as an organization's mission statement or the graphics code that prints a software company's logo, which can be used over and over in many different documents. The size of boilerplate text can range from a paragraph or two to many pages. It is, essentially, generic composition that can be written once, saved on disk, and merged, either verbatim or with slight modification, into whatever documents or programs later require it.

boldface \bōld´fās\ *n*. A type style that makes the text to which it is applied appear darker and heavier than the surrounding text. Some applications allow the user to apply a "Bold" command to selected text; other programs require that special codes be embedded in the text before and after words that are to be printed in boldface. **This sentence appears in boldface.**

bomb[1] \bom\ *n.* A program planted surreptitiously, with intent to damage or destroy a system in some way—for example, to erase a hard disk or cause it to be unreadable to the operating system. *See also* Trojan horse, virus, worm.

bomb[2] \bom\ *vb.* To fail abruptly and completely, without giving the user a chance to recover from the problem short of restarting the program or system. *See also* abend, bug (definition 1), crash[2] (definition 1), hang.

bookmark \book´märk\ *n.* **1.** A marker inserted at a specific point in a document to which the user may wish to return for later reference. **2.** In Netscape Navigator, a link to a Web page or other URL that a user has stored in a local file in order to return to it later. See the illustration. *See also* Favorites folder, hotlist, URL.

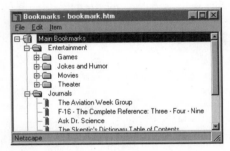

Bookmark.

bookmark file \book´märk fīl`\ *n.* **1.** A Netscape Navigator file containing the addresses of preferred Web sites. It is synonymous with the Favorites folder in Internet Explorer and the hotlist in Mosaic. *See also* Favorites folder, hotlist, Internet Explorer, Mosaic. **2.** A rendering of such a file in HTML format, generally posted on a Web page for the benefit of other people. *See also* HTML.

Boolean \boo´lē-ən`\ *adj.* Of, pertaining to, or characteristic of logical (true, false) values. Many languages directly support a Boolean data type, with predefined values for true and false; others use integer data types to implement Boolean values, usually (although not always) with 0 equaling false and "not 0" equaling true. *See also* Boolean algebra, Boolean operator.

Boolean algebra \boo`lē-ən al´jə-brə\ *n.* An algebra, fundamental to computer operations but developed in the mid-nineteenth century by English mathematician George Boole, for determining whether logical propositions are true or false rather than for determining the values of numerical expressions. In Boolean algebra, variables must have one of only two possible values, *true* or *false,* and relationships between these variables are expressed with logical operators, such as AND, OR, and NOT. Given these two-state variables and the relationships they can have to one another, Boolean algebra produces such propositions as $C = A$ AND B, which means that C is *true* if and only if both A is *true* and B is *true;* thus, it can be used to process information and to solve problems. Furthermore, Boolean logic can be readily applied to the electronic circuitry used in digital computing. Like the binary numbers 1 and 0, *true* and *false* are easily represented by two contrasting physical states of a circuit, such as voltages, and computer circuits known as logic gates control the flow of electricity (bits of data) so as to represent AND, OR, NOT, and other Boolean operators. Within a computer, these logic gates are combined, with the output from one becoming the input to another so that the final result (still nothing more than sets of 1s and 0s) is meaningful data, such as the sum of two numbers. See the illustration. *See also* adder (definition 1), binary[1], Boolean operator, gate (definition 1), logic circuit, truth table.

Boolean expression \boo`lē-ən eks-presh´ən\ *n.* An expression that yields a Boolean value *(true* or *false).* Such expressions can involve comparisons (testing values for equality or, for non-Boolean values, the < [less than] or > [greater than] relation) and logical combination (using Boolean operators such as AND, OR, and XOR) of Boolean expressions. *Also called* conditional expression, logical expression. *See also* Boolean, Boolean algebra, Boolean operator, relational operator.

Boolean logic \boo`lē-ən loj´ik\ *n. See* Boolean algebra.

Boolean operator \boo`lē-ən op´ər-ā-tər\ *n.* An operator designed to work with Boolean values. The four most common Boolean operators in programming use are AND (logical conjunction), OR (logical inclusion), XOR (exclusive OR), and NOT (logical negation). Boolean operators are often used as qualifiers in database searches—for example, *find all records where DEPARTMENT = "mar-* *keting" OR DEPARTMENT = "sales" AND SKILL =* *"word processing". Also called* logical operator. *See also* AND, exclusive OR, NOT, OR.

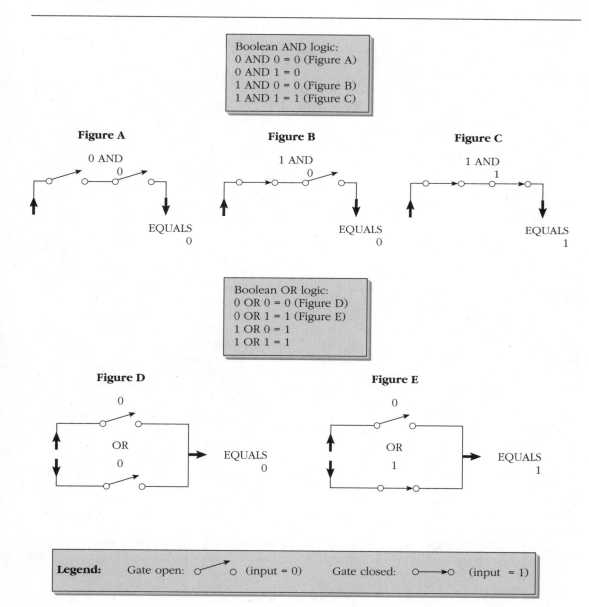

Boolean AND logic:
0 AND 0 = 0 (Figure A)
0 AND 1 = 0
1 AND 0 = 0 (Figure B)
1 AND 1 = 1 (Figure C)

Figure A   **Figure B**   **Figure C**

0 AND   1 AND   1 AND
0   0   1

EQUALS   EQUALS   EQUALS
0   0   1

Boolean OR logic:
0 OR 0 = 0 (Figure D)
0 OR 1 = 1 (Figure E)
1 OR 0 = 1
1 OR 1 = 1

Figure D   **Figure E**

0   0

OR   OR
0   EQUALS   1   EQUALS
               0   1

Legend: Gate open: ○——→○ (input = 0)   Gate closed: ○——→○ (input = 1)

Boolean algebra.   The ways in which circuits can simulate Boolean operations. The boxed tables show the possible results of various input combinations.

Boolean search \bōō`lē-ən sərch´\ *n.* A database search that uses Boolean operators. *See also* Boolean operator.

boot[1] \bōōt\ *n.* The process of starting or resetting a computer. When first turned on *(cold boot)* or reset *(warm boot),* the computer executes the software that loads and starts the computer's more complicated operating system and prepares it for use. Thus, the computer can be said to pull itself up by its own bootstraps. *Also called* bootstrap. *See also* BIOS, bootstrap loader, cold boot, warm boot.

boot[2] \bōōt\ *vb.* **1.** To start or reset a computer by turning the power on, by pressing a reset button on the computer case, or by issuing a software command to restart. *Also called* bootstrap, boot up. *See also* reboot. **2.** To execute the bootstrap loader program. *Also called* bootstrap. *See also* bootstrap loader.

bootable \bōō´tə-bl\ *adj.* Containing the system files necessary for booting a PC and running it. *See also* boot[2].

bootable disk \bōō`tə-bl disk´\ *n. See* boot disk.

boot block \bōōt´ blok\ *n.* A portion of a disk that contains the operating-system loader and other basic information that enables a computer to start up. *See also* block[1] (definition 5).

boot disk \bōōt´ disk\ *n.* A floppy disk that contains key system files from a PC-compatible operating system and that can boot, or start, the PC. A boot disk must be inserted in the primary floppy disk drive (usually drive A:) and is used when there is some problem with starting the PC from the hard disk, from which the computer generally boots. *Also called* bootable disk. *See also* A:, boot[2], boot drive, hard disk.

boot drive \bōōt´ drīv\ *n.* In a PC-compatible computer, the disk drive that the BIOS uses to automatically load the operating system when the computer is turned on. Generally, the default boot drive is the primary floppy disk drive A: in PC-compatible computers with MS-DOS, Windows 3.*x*, or Windows 95 operating systems. If a floppy disk is not found in that drive, the BIOS will check the primary hard disk next, which is drive C:. The BIOS for these operating systems can be reconfigured to search drive C: first by using the BIOS

setup program. *See also* A:, BIOS, disk drive, hard disk.

boot failure \bōōt´ fāl`yur\ *n.* The inability of a computer to locate or activate the operating system and thus boot, or start, the computer. *See also* boot[2].

boot loader \bōōt´ lō`dər\ *n. See* bootstrap loader.

BOOTP \bōōt´P\ *n. See* Boot Protocol.

boot partition \bōōt´ pär-tish`ən\ *n.* The partition on a hard disk that contains the operating system and support files that the system loads into memory when the computer is turned on or restarted.

Boot Protocol \bōōt´ prō`tə-kol\ *n.* A protocol described in RFCs 951 and 1084 and used for booting diskless workstations. *Also called* BOOTP. *See also* boot[2], RFC.

boot record \bōōt´ rek`ərd\ *n.* The section of a disk that contains the operating system.

boot sector \bōōt´ sek`tər\ *n.* The portion of a disk reserved for the bootstrap loader (the self-starting portion) of an operating system. The boot sector typically contains a short machine language program that loads the operating system.

bootstrap[1] \bōōt´strap\ *n. See* boot[1].

bootstrap[2] \bōōt´strap\ *vb. See* boot[2].

bootstrap loader \bōōt´strap lō`dər\ *n.* A program that is automatically run when a computer is switched on (booted). After first performing a few basic hardware tests, the bootstrap loader loads and passes control to a larger loader program, which typically then loads the operating system. The bootstrap loader typically resides in the computer's read-only memory (ROM).

boot up \bōōt up´\ *See* boot.

border \bōr´dər\ *n.* **1.** In programs and working environments that feature on-screen windows, the edge surrounding the user's workspace. Window borders provide a visible frame around a document or graphic. Depending on the program and its requirements, they can also represent an area in which the cursor or a mouse pointer takes on special characteristics. For example, clicking the mouse on a window border can enable the user to resize the window or split the window in two. **2.** In printing, a decorative line or pattern along one or more edges of a page or illustration.

Border Gateway Protocol \bōr`dər gāt`wā prō´-tə-kol\ *n.* A protocol used by NSFnet that is based on the External Gateway Protocol. *Acronym:* BGP (B`G-P´). *See also* External Gateway Protocol, NSF-net.

boss screen \bos´ skrēn\ *n.* A false display screen usually featuring business-related material that can be substituted for a game display when the boss walks by. Boss screens were popular with MS-DOS games, where it was difficult to switch to another application quickly. However, games designed for the Mac or Windows 95 generally don't need them because it is easy to switch to a different screen or application to hide the fact that one is playing a game.

bot \bot\ *n.* **1.** Short for ro**bot**. A displayed representation of a person or other entity whose actions are based on programming. **2.** A program that performs some task on a network, especially a task that is repetitive or time-consuming. **3.** On the Internet, a program that performs a repetitive or time-consuming task, such as searching Web sites and newsgroups for information and indexing them in a database or other record-keeping system (called *spiders*); automatically posting one or more articles to multiple newsgroups (often used in spamming and called *spambots*); and to keep IRC channels open. *Also called* Internet robot. *See also* IRC, newsgroup, spam, spambot, spider.

bottom-up design \bot`əm-up də-zīn´\ *n.* A program development design methodology in which the lower-level tasks of a program are defined first; the design of the higher-level functions proceeds from the design of the lower-level ones. *See also* bottom-up programming, top-down programming. *Compare* top-down design.

bottom-up programming \bot`əm-up prō´gram-ēng\ *n.* A programming technique in which lower-level functions are developed and tested first; higher-level functions are then built using the lower-level functions, and so on. Many program developers believe that the ideal combination is top-down design and bottom-up programming. *See also* top-down design. *Compare* object-oriented programming, top-down programming.

bounce \bouns\ *vb.* To return to the sender, used in reference to undeliverable e-mail.

BounceKeys \bouns´kēz\ *n.* A feature in Windows 95 that instructs the processor to ignore double strokes of the same key and other unintentional keystrokes.

bound[1] \bound\ *adj.* Limited in performance or speed; for example, an input/output-bound system is limited by the speed of its input and output devices (keyboard, disk drives, and so on), even though the processor or program is capable of performing at a higher rate.

bound[2] \bound\ *n.* The upper or lower limit in a permitted range of values.

bounding box \boun´dēng boks\ *n. See* graphic limits.

Bourne shell \bōrn´ shel\ *n.* The first major shell, or command interpreter, for UNIX and part of the AT&T System V release. The Bourne shell was developed at AT&T Bell Laboratories by Steve Bourne in 1979. While the Bourne shell lacks some features common in other UNIX shells, such as command-line editing and recall of previously issued commands, it is the one that the majority of shell scripts adhere to. *Also called* sh. *See also* shell[1], shell script, System V, UNIX. *Compare* C shell, Korn shell.

Boyce-Codd normal form \bois`kod nōr`məl fōrm´\ *n. See* normal form (definition 1).

bozo \bō´zō\ *n.* A slang term used frequently on the Internet, particularly in newsgroups, for a foolish or eccentric person.

bozo filter \bō´zō fil`tər\ *n.* On the Internet, slang for a feature in some e-mail clients and newsgroup readers or a separate utility that allows the user to block, or filter out, incoming e-mail messages or newsgroup articles from specified individuals. Generally these individuals are ones that the user does not want to hear from, such as bozos. *Also called* kill file. *See also* bozo.

BPI \B`P-I´\ *n. See* bits per inch, bytes per inch.

bps \B`P-S´\ *n.* Short for **b**its **p**er **s**econd. The speed at which a device such as a modem can transfer data. Speed in bps is not the same as baud rate. *See also* baud, baud rate.

.br \dot`B-R´\ *n.* On the Internet, the major geographic domain specifying that an address is located in Brazil.

braindamaged \brān´dam`əjd\ *adj.* Performing in an erratic or destructive manner. A braindamaged application or utility program is characterized by some or all of the following traits: a mysterious and unintuitive user interface, failure to respond predictably to commands, failure to release unused memory, failure to close open files, and use of "reserved" elements of the operating system that can result in a fatal error in a program or the operating system. Braindamaged programs are also often responsible for causing problems across local area networks. *Compare* kludge (definition 2).

brain dump \brān´ dump\ *n.* A large, unorganized mass of information, presented in response to a query via e-mail or a newsgroup article, that is difficult to digest or interpret.

branch \branch\ *n.* **1.** A node intermediate between the root and the leaves in some types of logical tree structure, such as the directory tree in Windows or a tape distribution organization. **2.** Any connection between two items such as blocks in a flowchart or nodes in a network. **3.** *See* branch instruction.

branch instruction \branch´ in-struk`shən\ *n.* An assembly- or machine-level instruction that transfers control to another instruction, usually based on some condition (that is, it transfers if a specific condition is true or false). Branch instructions are most often relative transfers, jumping forward or backward by a certain number of bytes of code. *See also* GOTO statement, jump instruction.

branchpoint \branch´point\ *n.* The location at which a given branch instruction occurs if the attendant condition (if any) is true. *See also* branch instruction.

branch prediction \branch´ prə-dik`shən\ *n.* A technique used in some processors with an instruction called prefetch to guess whether or not a branch will be taken in a program, and to fetch executable code from the appropriate location. When a branch instruction is executed, it and the next instruction executed are stored in a buffer. This information is used to predict which way the instruction will branch the next time it is executed. When the prediction is correct (as it is over 90 percent of the time), executing a branch does not cause a pipeline break, so the system is not slowed down by the need to retrieve the next instruction. *See also* branch instruction, buffer[1], central processing unit, pipeline processing.

BRB \B`R-B`\ Acronym for (I'll) **b**e **r**ight **b**ack. An expression used commonly on live chat services on the Internet and online information services by participants signaling their temporary departure from the group. *See also* chat[1] (definition 1).

breadboard \bred´bōrd\ *n.* A blank, perforated board used to support prototype electronic circuits. Experimenters would put components on one side of the board and run the leads through the perforations to be connected by wires running along the underside. Today a circuit designer's breadboard is made of plastic. Its holes are small and closely spaced to accommodate the pins of chips, and connections are made by metal strips plugged into the holes. See the illustration. *Compare* wire-wrapped circuits.

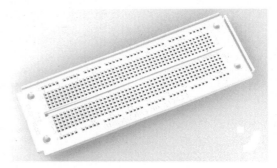

Breadboard.

break[1] \brāk\ *n.* **1.** Interruption of a program caused by the user pressing the Break key or its equivalent. **2.** Interruption of a communications transmission that occurs when the receiving station interrupts and takes over control of the line or when the transmitting station prematurely halts transmission.

break[2] \brāk\ *vb.* **1.** To interrupt execution at a given spot, usually for the purpose of debugging. *See also* breakpoint. **2.** To cause a routine, module, or program that had previously worked to cease working correctly.

Break key \brāk´ kē\ *n.* A key or combination of keys used to tell a computer to halt, or break out of, whatever it is doing. On IBM PCs and compatibles under DOS, pressing the Pause/Break or Scroll Lock/Break key while holding down the Ctrl key issues the break command (as does Ctrl-C).

On Macintosh computers, the key combination that sends a break code is Command-period.

breakout box \brāk´out boks`\ *n*. A small hardware device that can be attached between two devices normally connected by a cable (such as a computer and a modem) to display and, if necessary, change the activity through individual wires of the cable. See the illustration.

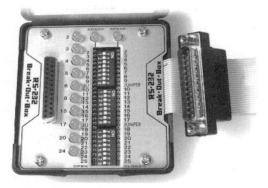

Breakout box.

breakpoint \brāk´point\ *n*. A location in a program at which execution is halted so that a programmer can examine the program's status, the contents of variables, and so on. A breakpoint is set and used within a debugger and is usually implemented by inserting at that point some kind of jump, call, or trap instruction that transfers control to the debugger. *See also* debug, debugger.

BRI \B`R-I´\ *n*. Acronym for **B**asic **R**ate **I**nterface. An ISDN subscriber service that uses two B (64 Kbps) channels and one D (64 Kbps) channel to transmit voice, video, and data signals. *See also* ISDN.

bridge \brij\ *n*. **1.** A device that connects networks using the same communications protocols so that information can be passed from one to the other. *Compare* gateway. **2.** A device that connects two local area networks, whether or not they use the same protocols. A bridge operates at the ISO/OSI data-link layer. *See also* data-link layer. *Compare* router.

bridge router \brij´ rou`tər, rōō`tər\ *n*. A device that supports the functions of both a bridge and router. A bridge router links two segments of a local or wide area network, passing packets of data between the segments as necessary, and uses Level 2 addresses for routing. *Also called* Brouter. *See also* bridge (definition 2), router.

bridgeware \brij´wâr\ *n*. Hardware or software designed to convert application programs or data files to a form that can be used by a different computer.

Briefcase \brēf´kās\ *n*. A system folder in Windows 95 used for synchronizing files between two computers, usually between desktop and laptop computers. The Briefcase can be transferred to another computer via disk, cable, or network. When files are transferred back to the original computer, the Briefcase updates all files to the most recent version.

brightness \brīt´nəs\ *n*. The perceived quality of radiance or luminosity of a visible object. Brightness is literally in the eye (and mind) of the beholder; a candle in the night appears brighter than the same candle under incandescent lights. Although its subjective value cannot be measured with physical instruments, brightness can be measured as luminance (radiant energy). The brightness component of a color is different from its color (the hue) and from the intensity of its color (the saturation). *See also* color model, HSB.

broadband \brod´band\ *adj*. Of or relating to communications systems in which the medium of transmission (such as a wire or fiber-optic cable) carries multiple messages at a time, each message modulated on its own carrier frequency by means of modems. Broadband communication is found in wide area networks. *Compare* baseband.

broadband modem \brod`band mō´dəm\ *n*. A modem for use on a broadband network. Broadband technology allows several networks to coexist on a single cable. Traffic from one network does not interfere with traffic from another, since the conversations happen on different frequencies, rather like the commercial radio system. *See also* broadband network.

broadband network \brod`band net´wərk\ *n*. A local area network on which transmissions travel as radio-frequency signals over separate inbound and outbound channels. Stations on a broadband network are connected by coaxial or fiber-optic cable, which can carry data, voice, and video simultaneously over multiple transmission channels that are distinguished by frequency. A broadband network is capable of high-speed operation (20 megabits or more), but it is more expensive than a baseband network and can be difficult to install. Such a network is based on the same technology used by cable television (CATV). *Also called* wideband transmission. *Compare* baseband network.

broadcast[1] \brod´kast\ *adj*. Sent to more than one recipient. In communications and on networks, a broadcast message is one distributed to all stations. *See also* e-mail[1] (definition 1).

broadcast[2] \brod´kast\ *n*. As in radio or television, a transmission sent to more than one recipient.

broadcast storm \brod´kast stõrm`\ *n*. A network broadcast that causes multiple hosts to respond simultaneously, overloading the network. A broadcast storm may occur when old TCP/IP routers are mixed with routers that support a new protocol. *Also called* network meltdown. *See also* communications protocol, router, TCP/IP.

Brouter \brou´tər, brōō´tər\ *See* bridge router.

brownout \broun´out\ *n*. A condition in which the electricity level is appreciably reduced for a sustained period of time. In contrast to a blackout, or total loss of power, a brownout continues the flow of electricity to all devices connected to electrical outlets, although at lower levels than the normally supplied levels (120 volts in the United States). A brownout can be extremely damaging to

sensitive electronic devices, such as computers, because the reduced and often fluctuating voltage levels can cause components to operate for extended periods of time outside the range they were designed to work in. On a computer, a brownout is characterized by a smaller, dimmer, and somewhat fluctuating display area on the monitor and potentially erratic behavior by the system unit. The only reliable means of preventing damage caused by a brownout condition is to use a battery-backed uninterruptible power supply (UPS). *See also* UPS. *Compare* blackout.

browse \brouz\ *vb*. To scan a database, a list of files, or the Internet, either for a particular item or for anything that seems to be of interest. Generally, browsing implies observing, rather than changing, information. In unauthorized computer hacking, browsing is a (presumably) nondestructive means of finding out about an unknown computer after illegally gaining entry.

browser \brou´zər\ *n*. *See* Web browser.

browser box \brou´zər boks`\ *n*. *See* Web TV.

BRS \B`R-S´\ *n*. *See* big red switch.

brush \brush\ *n*. A tool used in paint programs to sketch or fill in areas of a drawing with the color and pattern currently in use. Paint programs that offer a variety of brush shapes can produce brushstrokes of varying width and, in some cases, shadowing or calligraphic effects.

.bs \dot`B-S´\ *n*. On the Internet, the major geographic domain specifying that an address is located in the Bahamas.

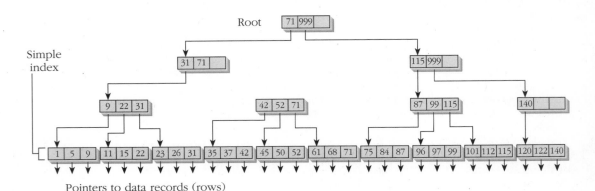

B-tree. A B-tree index structure.

BSC \B`S-C´\ *n. See* BISYNC.

BSD UNIX \B-S-D` yoō´niks\ *n.* Acronym for **B**erkeley **S**oftware **D**istribution **UNIX.** A UNIX version developed at the University of California at Berkeley, providing additional capabilities such as networking, extra peripheral support, and use of extended filenames. BSD UNIX was instrumental in gaining widespread acceptance of UNIX and in getting academic institutions connected to the Internet. BSD UNIX is now being developed by Berkeley Software Design, Inc. *See also* UNIX.

.bt \dot`B-T´\ *n.* On the Internet, the major geographic domain specifying that an address is located in Bhutan.

B-tree \B´trē\ *n.* A tree structure for storing database indexes. Each node in the tree contains a sorted list of key values and links that correspond to ranges of key values between the listed values. To find a specific data record given its key value, the program reads the first node, or root, from the disk and compares the desired key with the keys in the node to select a subrange of key values to search. It repeats the process with the node indicated by the corresponding link. At the lowest level, the links indicate the data records. The database system can thus rapidly skip down through the levels of the tree structure to find the simple index entries that contain the location of the desired records or rows. See the illustration.

BTW or **btw** \B`T-W´\ Acronym for **b**y **t**he **w**ay. An expression often used to preface remarks in e-mail and Internet newsgroup articles.

bubble chart \bub´l chärt`\ *n.* A chart in which annotated ovals (bubbles) representing categories, operations, or procedures are connected by lines or arrows that represent data flows or other relationships among the items represented by bubbles. In systems analysis, bubble charts, rather than block diagrams or flowcharts, are used to describe the connections between concepts or parts of a whole, without emphasizing a structural, sequential, or procedural relationship between the parts. See the illustration. *Compare* block diagram, flowchart.

bubble-jet printer \bub´l-jet prin´tər\ *n.* A form of nonimpact printer that uses a mechanism similar to that used by an ink-jet printer to shoot ink from nozzles to form characters on paper. A

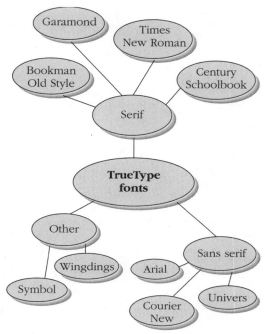

Bubble chart.

bubble-jet printer uses special heating elements to prepare the ink, whereas an ink-jet printer uses piezoelectric crystals. See the illustration. *See also* ink-jet printer, nonimpact printer. *Compare* laser printer.

Bubble-jet printer.

bubble memory \bub´1 mem`ər-ē\ *n.* Memory formed by a series of persistent magnetic "bubbles" in a thin film substrate. In contrast to ROM, information can be written to bubble memory. In contrast to RAM, data written to bubble memory remains there until it is changed, even when the computer is turned off. For this reason, bubble memory has had some application in environments in which a computer system must be able to recover with minimal data loss in the event of a power failure. The use of and demand for bubble memory has all but disappeared because of the introduction of flash memory, which is less expensive and easier to produce. *See also* flash memory, nonvolatile memory.

bubble sort \bub´1 sōrt`\ *n.* A sorting algorithm that starts at the end of a list with *n* elements and moves all the way through, testing the value of each adjacent pair of items and swapping them if they aren't in the right order. The entire process is then repeated for the remaining *n* − 1 items in the list, and so on, until the list is completely sorted, with the largest value at the end of the list. A bubble sort is so named because the "lightest" item in a list (the smallest) will figuratively "bubble up" to the top of the list first; then the next-lightest item bubbles up to its position, and so on. See the illustration. *Also called* exchange sort. *See also* algorithm, sort. *Compare* insertion sort, merge sort, quicksort.

List to be sorted

Compared last

3
4

Compared third

Compared second

2
5

Compared first

1

List after first pass	List after second pass
1	1
3	2
4	3
2	4
5	5

Bubble sort.

bubble storage \bub´1 stōr`əj\ *n. See* bubble memory.

bucket \buk´ət\ *n.* A region of memory that is addressable as an entity and can be used as a receptacle to hold data. *See also* bit bucket.

buffer[1] \buf´ər\ *n.* A region of memory reserved for use as an intermediate repository in which data is temporarily held while waiting to be transferred between two locations, as between an application's data area and an input/output device. A device or its adapter may in turn use a buffer to store data awaiting transfer to the computer or processing by the device.

buffer[2] \buf´ər\ *vb.* To use a region of memory to hold data that is waiting to be transferred, especially to or from input/output (I/O) devices such as disk drives and serial ports.

buffer pool \buf´ər pool`\ *n.* A group of memory or storage-device locations that are allocated for temporary storage, especially during transfer operations.

buffer storage \buf´ər stōr`əj\ *n.* **1.** The use of a special area in memory to hold data temporarily for processing until a program or operating system is ready to deal with it. **2.** An area of storage that is used to hold data to be passed between devices that are not synchronized or have different bit transfer rates.

bug \bug\ *n.* **1.** An error in coding or logic that causes a program to malfunction or to produce incorrect results. Minor bugs, such as a cursor that does not behave as expected, can be inconvenient or frustrating, but do not damage information. More severe bugs can require the user to restart the program or the computer, losing whatever previous work had not been saved. Worse yet are bugs that damage saved data without alerting the user. All such errors must be found and corrected by the process known as *debugging*. Because of the potential risk to important data, commercial application programs are tested and debugged as completely as possible before release. After the program becomes available, further minor bugs are corrected in the next update. A more severe bug can sometimes be fixed with a piece of software called a *patch*, which circumvents the problem or in some other way alleviates its effects. *See also* beta test, bomb[2], crash[2] (definition 1), debug, debugger, hang, inherent error, logic error, semantic error, syntax error. **2.** A recurring physical problem that prevents a system or set of components from working together properly. While the origin of this definition is in some dispute, computer folklore attributes the first use of bug in this sense to a problem in the Harvard Mark I or the Army/ University of Pennsylvania ENIAC that was traced to a moth caught between the contacts of a relay in the machine (although a moth is not entomologically a true bug).

buggy \bug´ē\ *adj.* Full of flaws, or bugs, in reference to software. *See also* bug (definition 1).

building-block principle \bil´dēng-blok prin`sə-pəl\ *n. See* modular design.

built-in check \bilt`in chek´\ *n. See* hardware check, power-on self test.

built-in font \bilt`in font´\ *n. See* internal font.

built-in groups \bilt`in gro͞ops´\ *n.* The default groups provided with Microsoft Windows NT and Windows NT Advanced Server. A group defines a collection of rights and permissions for the user accounts that are its members. Built-in groups are therefore a convenient means of providing access to commonly used resources. *See also* group[1].

bulk eraser \bulk´ ē-rā`sər\ *n.* A device for eliminating all information from a storage medium, such as a floppy disk or a tape, by generating a strong magnetic field that scrambles the alignment of the ferrous materials in the media that encode stored data.

bulk storage \bulk´ stōr`əj\ *n.* Any medium capable of containing large quantities of information, such as tape, fixed disk, or optical disc.

bullet \bo͞ol´ət, bul´ət\ *n.* A typographical symbol, such as a filled or empty circle, diamond, box, or asterisk, used to set off a small block of text or each item in a list. Round and square bullets are used to set off different levels of information. *See also* dingbat.

bulletin board system \bo͞ol´ə-tən bōrd si`stəm, bul´ə-tən\ *n. See* BBS.

bulletproof \bo͞ol´ət-pro͞of`, bul´ət-\ *adj.* Capable of overcoming hardware problems that, in another system, could lead to interruption of the task in progress.

bundle \bun´dl\ *vb.* To combine products for sale as a lot. Frequently, operating system software and some widely used applications are bundled with a computer system for sale.

bundled software \bun`dld soft´wâr\ *n.* **1.** Programs sold with a computer as part of a combined hardware/software package. **2.** Smaller programs sold with larger programs to increase the latter's functionality or attractiveness.

burn \burn\ *vb.* To write data electronically into a programmable read-only memory (PROM) chip by using a special programming device known variously as a PROM programmer, PROM blower, or PROM blaster. The term is also used in reference to creating read-only memory compact discs (CD-ROMs). *Also called* blast, blow. *See also* PROM.

burn in \burn in´\ *vb.* **1.** To keep a new system or device running continuously so that any weak elements or components will fail early and can be found and corrected before the system becomes an integral part of the user's work routine. Such a test is often performed at the factory before a device is shipped. **2.** To make a permanent change in the phosphor coating on the inside of a monitor screen by leaving the monitor on and keeping a bright, unchanging image on the screen for extended periods. Such an image will remain visible after the monitor is turned off. Burning in was a danger with older PC monitors; it is no longer a concern with most new PC monitors. *Also called* ghosting.

burst[1] \burst\ *n.* Transfer of a block of data all at one time without a break. Certain microprocessors and certain buses have features that support various types of burst transfers. *See also* burst speed (definition 1).

burst[2] \burst\ *vb.* To break fanfold continuous-feed paper apart at its perforations, resulting in a stack of separate sheets.

burster \bur´stər\ *n.* A device used to burst, or break apart at the perforations, fanfold continuous-feed paper.

burst mode \burst´ mōd\ *n.* A method of data transfer in which information is collected and sent as a unit in one high-speed transmission. In burst mode, an input/output device takes control of a multiplexer channel for the time required to send its data. In effect, the multiplexer, which normally merges input from several sources into a single high-speed data stream, becomes a channel dedicated to the needs of one device until the entire transmission has been sent. Burst mode is used both in communications and between devices in a computer system. *See also* burst[1].

burst rate \burst´ rāt\ *n*. *See* burst speed (definition 1).

burst speed \burst´ spēd\ *n*. **1.** The fastest speed at which a device can operate without interruption. For example, various communications devices (as on networks) can send data in bursts, and the speed of such equipment is sometimes measured as the burst speed (the speed of data transfer while the burst is being executed). *Also called* burst rate. **2.** The number of characters per second that a printer can print on one line without a carriage return or linefeed. Burst speed measures the actual speed of printing, without consideration of the time taken to advance paper or to move the print head back to the left margin. Almost always, the speed claimed by the manufacturer is the burst speed. By contrast, *throughput* is the number of characters per second when one or more entire pages of text are being printed and is a more practical measurement of printer speed in real-life situations.

bursty \bur´stē\ *adj*. Transmitting data in spurts, or bursts, rather than in a continuous stream.

bus \bus\ *n*. A set of hardware lines (conductors) used for data transfer among the components of a computer system. A bus is essentially a shared highway that connects different parts of the system—including the microprocessor, disk-drive controller, memory, and input/output ports—and enables them to transfer information. The bus consists of specialized groups of lines that carry different types of information. One group of lines carries data; another carries memory addresses (locations) where data items are to be found; yet another carries control signals. Buses are characterized by the number of bits they can transfer at a single time, equivalent to the number of wires within the bus. A computer with a 32-bit address bus and a 16-bit data bus, for example, can transfer 16 bits of data at a time from any of 2^{32} memory locations. Most microcomputers contain one or more expansion slots into which additional boards can be plugged to connect them to the bus.

bus enumerator \bus´ ə-n$\overline{oo}$´mər-ā-tər\ *n*. A device driver that identifies devices located on a specific bus and assigns a unique identification code to each device. The bus enumerator is responsible for loading information about the devices onto the hardware tree. *See also* bus, device driver, hardware tree.

bus extender \bus´ eks-ten`dər\ *n*. **1.** A device that expands the capacity of a bus. For example, IBM PC/AT computers used a bus extender to add onto the earlier PC bus and allow the use of 16-bit expansion boards in addition to 8-bit boards. *See also* bus. **2.** A special board used by engineers to raise an add-on board above the computer's cabinet, making it easier to work on the circuit board.

business graphics \biz´nəs graf´iks\ *n*. *See* presentation graphics.

business information system \biz`nəs in-fər-mā´shən si`stəm\ *n*. A combination of computers, printers, communications equipment, and other devices designed to handle data. A completely automated business information system receives, processes, and stores data; transfers information as needed; and produces reports or printouts on demand. *Acronym:* BIS (B`I-S´). *See also* management information system.

business software \biz´nəs soft`wâr\ *n*. Any computer application designed primarily for use in business, as opposed to scientific use or entertainment. In addition to the well-known areas of word processing, spreadsheets, databases, and communications, business software for microcomputers also encompasses such applications as accounting, payroll, financial planning, project management, decision and support systems, personnel record maintenance, and office management.

bus mouse \bus´ mous\ *n*. A mouse that attaches to the computer's bus through a special card or port rather than through a serial port. *See also* mouse. *Compare* serial mouse.

bus network \bus´ net`wərk\ *n*. A topology (configuration) for a local area network in which all nodes are connected to a main communications line (bus). On a bus network, each node monitors activity on the line. Messages are detected by all nodes but are accepted only by the node(s) to which they are addressed. A malfunctioning node ceases to communicate but does not disrupt operation (as it might on a ring network, in which messages are passed from one node to the next). To avoid collisions that occur when two or more nodes try to use the line at the same time, bus networks commonly rely on collision detection or token passing to regulate traffic. See the illustration. *See also* collision detection, contention, CSMA/CD, token bus network, token passing. *Compare* ring network, star network.

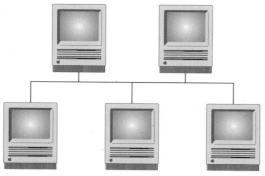

Bus network.   *A bus network configuration.*

bus system \bus´ si`stəm\ *n.* The interface circuitry that controls the operations of a bus and connects it with the rest of the computer system. *See also* bus.

bus topology \bus´ to-pol`ə-jē\ *n. See* bus network.

button \but´ən\ *n.* **1.** A graphic element in a dialog box that, when activated, performs a specified function. The user activates a button by clicking on it with a mouse or, if the button has the focus, by hitting the Return or Enter key. See the illustration. **2.** On a mouse, a movable piece that is pressed to activate some function. Older mouse models have only one button; newer models typically have two or more buttons.

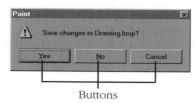

Button.

button bomb \but´ən bom`\ *n.* A button on Web pages with the image of a bomb.

button help \but´ən help`\ *n.* Help information displayed via the selection of buttons or icons. Applications such as the World Wide Web, multimedia kiosks, and computer-aided instruction often use button help icons to ease system navigation.

.bw \dot`B-W´\ *n.* On the Internet, the major geographic domain specifying that an address is located in Botswana.

bypass \bī´pas\ *n.* In telecommunications, the use of communication pathways other than the local telephone company, such as satellites and microwave systems.

byte \bīt\ *n.* Abbreviated B. Short for **b**inar**y te**rm. A unit of data, today almost always consisting of 8 bits. A byte can represent a single character, such as a letter, a digit, or a punctuation mark. Because a byte represents only a small amount of information, amounts of computer memory and storage are usually given in kilobytes (1,024 bytes), megabytes (1,048,576 bytes), or gigabytes (1,073,741,824 bytes). *See also* bit, gigabyte, kilobyte, megabyte. *Compare* octet, word.

bytecode \bīt´kōd\ *n.* An encoding of a computer program that a compiler produces when the original source code is processed. This encoding is in an abstract, processor-independent form that cannot be directly executed by most CPUs but is highly suitable for further analysis (for example, compiler optimization), for processing by interpreters (for example, executing Java applets within Web browsers), or for use in generation of binary instructions for the target computer's CPU. Intermediate bytecode production is a feature of the compilers for the Pascal and Java programming languages. *See also* compiler (definition 2), central processing unit, interpreter, Java, Java applet, Pascal.

***BYTE* Information Exchange** \bit` in-fər-mā´shən eks-chānj`\ *n. See* BIX.

byte-oriented protocol \bīt` ōr`ē-en-təd prō´tə-kol\ *n.* A communications protocol in which data is transmitted as a string of characters in a particular character set, such as ASCII, rather than as a stream of bits as in a bit-oriented protocol. To express control information, a byte-oriented protocol relies on control characters, most of which are defined by the coding scheme used. The asynchronous communications protocols commonly used with modems and IBM's BISYNC protocol are byte-oriented protocols. *Compare* bit-oriented protocol.

bytes per inch \bīts` pər inch´\ *n.* The number of bytes that fit into an inch of length on a disk track or a tape. *Acronym:* BPI (B`P-I´).

.bz \dot`B-Z´\ *n.* On the Internet, the major geographic domain specifying that an address is located in Belize.

C \C\ *n.* A programming language developed by Dennis Ritchie at Bell Laboratories in 1972. It is so named because its immediate predecessor was the B programming language. Although C is considered by many to be more a machine-independent assembly language than a high-level language, its close association with the UNIX operating system, its enormous popularity, and its standardization by the American National Standards Institute (ANSI) have made it perhaps the closest thing to a standard programming language in the microcomputer/workstation marketplace. C is a compiled language that contains a small set of built-in functions that are machine dependent. The rest of the C functions are machine independent and are contained in libraries that can be accessed from C programs. C programs are composed of one or more functions defined by the programmer; thus C is a structured programming language. *See also* C++, compiled language, library, Objective-C, structured programming.

C++ \C`plus-plus´\ *n.* An object-oriented version of the C programming language, developed by Bjarne Stroustrup in the early 1980s at Bell Laboratories and adopted by a number of vendors, including Apple Computer and Sun Microsystems, Inc. *See also* C, object-oriented programming, Objective-C.

C2 \C-tōō´\ *n.* The lowest level of security in the U.S. National Computer Security Center's hierarchy of criteria for trusted computer systems, requiring user logon with password and a mechanism for auditing. The C2 level is outlined in the Orange Book. *See also* Orange Book (definition 1).

.ca \dot`C-A´\ *n.* On the Internet, the major geographic domain specifying that an address is located in Canada.

.cab \dot-kab´\ *n.* File extension for cabinet files, which are multiple files compressed into one and extractable with the extract.exe utility. Such files

are frequently found on Microsoft software (for example, Windows 95) distribution disks.

cabinet \kab´ə-nət`\ *n.* The box in which the main components of a computer (CPU, the hard drive, floppy and CD-ROM drives, and expansion slots for peripheral devices, such as monitors) are located. See the illustration. *See also* CPU, expansion slot.

Cabinet.

cable \kā´bl\ *n.* A collection of wires shielded within a protective tube, used to connect peripheral devices to a computer. A mouse, a keyboard, and a printer might all be connected to a computer with cables. Printer cables typically implement a serial or a parallel path for data to travel along.

cable connector \kā´bl kə-nek`tər\ *n.* The connector on either end of a cable. *See also* DB connector, DIN connector, RS-232-C standard, RS-422/423/449.

cable matcher \kā´bl mach`ər\ *n.* A device that allows the use of a cable that has slightly different wire connections from those required by the device(s) to which it is attached.

cable modem \kā´bl mō`dəm\ *n.* A modem that sends and receives data through a coaxial cable television network instead of telephone lines, as with a conventional modem. Cable modems, which have speeds of 500 kilobits per second (Kbps), can generally transmit data faster than current conventional modems. *See also* coaxial cable, modem.

cabling diagram \kā´bə-lēng dī´ə-gram\ *n.* A plan that shows the path of cables that attach computer system components or peripherals. Cabling diagrams are particularly important for explaining the connection of disk drives to a disk controller.

cache \kash\ *n.* A special memory subsystem in which frequently used data values are duplicated for quick access. A memory cache stores the contents of frequently accessed RAM locations and the addresses where these data items are stored. When the processor references an address in memory, the cache checks to see whether it holds that address. If it does hold the address, the data is returned to the processor; if it does not, a regular memory access occurs. A cache is useful when RAM accesses are slow compared with the microprocessor speed, because cache memory is always faster than main RAM memory. *See also* disk cache, wait state.

cache card \kash´ kärd\ *n.* An expansion card that increases a system's cache memory. *See also* cache, expansion board.

cache memory \kash´ mem`ər-ē\ *n. See* cache.

CAD \kad, C`A-D´\ *n.* Acronym for **c**omputer-**a**ided **d**esign. A system of programs and workstations used in designing engineering, architectural, and scientific models ranging from simple tools to buildings, aircraft, integrated circuits, and molecules. Various CAD applications create objects in two or three dimensions, presenting the results as wire-frame "skeletons," as more substantial models with shaded surfaces, or as solid objects. Some programs can also rotate or resize models, show interior views, generate lists of materials required for construction, and perform other allied functions. CAD programs rely on mathematics, often requiring the computing power of a high-performance workstation. *See also* CAD/CAM, I-CASE.

CAD/CAM \kad´kam, C-A-D`C-A-M´\ *n.* Acronym for **c**omputer-**a**ided **d**esign/**c**omputer-**a**ided **m**anufacturing. The use of computers in both the design and manufacture of a product. With CAD/CAM, a product, such as a machine part, is designed with a CAD program and the finished design is translated into a set of instructions that

can be transmitted to and used by the machines dedicated to fabrication, assembly, and process control. *See also* CAD, I-CASE.

CADD \C`A-D-D´, kad-D´\ *n. See* computer-aided design and drafting.

caddy \kad´ē\ *n.* A plastic carrier that holds a CD-ROM and is inserted into a CD-ROM drive. Some personal computers, especially older models, have CD-ROM drives that require the use of a caddy. Most current CD-ROM drives do not require a caddy. See the illustration.

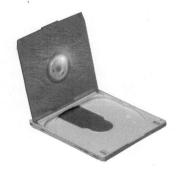

Caddy.

CAE \C`A-E´\ *n.* Acronym for **c**omputer-**a**ided **e**ngineering. An application that enables the user to perform engineering tests and analyses on designs created with a computer. In some instances, capabilities such as logic testing that are generally attributed to CAE applications are also part of CAD programs, so the distinction between CAD and CAE is not a hard-and-fast one. *See also* CAD, I-CASE.

CAI \C`A-I´\ *n.* Acronym for **c**omputer-**a**ided (or **c**omputer-**a**ssisted) **i**nstruction. An educational program designed to serve as a teaching tool. CAI programs typically use tutorials, drills, and question-and-answer sessions to present a topic and to test the student's comprehension. CAI programs are excellent aids for presenting factual material and for allowing students to pace their learning speed. Subjects and complexity range from beginning arithmetic to advanced mathematics, science, history, computer studies, and specialized topics. *See also* I-CASE. *Compare* CBT, CMI.

CAL \C`A-L´\ *n.* Acronym for **c**omputer-**a**ssisted (or **c**omputer-**a**ugmented) **l**earning. *See* CAI.

calculator \kal´kyə-lā`tər\ *n.* Broadly, any device that performs arithmetic operations on numbers. Sophisticated calculators can be programmed for certain functions and can store values in memory, but they differ from computers in several ways: they have a fixed set of commands, they do not recognize text, they cannot retrieve values stored in a data file, and they cannot find and use values generated by a program such as a spreadsheet.

calendar program \kal´ən-dər prō`gram\ *n.* An application program in the form of an electronic calendar, commonly used for highlighting dates and scheduling appointments. Some calendar programs resemble wall calendars, displaying dates in blocks labeled with the days of the week; others display dates day by day and enable the user to enter appointments, notes, and other memoranda. A day-of-the-week type of calendar program could, for example, be used to find out that Christmas 1999 will be on a Saturday. Depending on its capabilities, such a program might cover only the current century, or it might cover hundreds of years and even allow for the change (in 1582) from the Julian to the Gregorian calendar. A calendar/scheduler program might show blocks of dates or, like an appointment book, single days divided into hours or half hours, with room for notes. Some programs allow the user to set an alarm to go off at an important point in the schedule. Other programs can coordinate the calendars of different people on the same network, so that a person entering an appointment into his or her calendar also enters the appointment into a colleague's calendar.

.calgary.ca \dot-kal`gər-ē-dot-C-A-´\ *n.* On the Internet, the major geographic domain specifying that an address is located in Calgary, Alberta, Canada.

call[1] \käl\ *n.* In a program, an instruction or statement that transfers program execution to some section of code, such as a subroutine, to perform a specific task. Once the task is performed, program execution resumes at the calling point in the program. *See also* calling sequence.

call[2] \käl\ *vb.* **1.** To establish a connection through a telecommunications network. **2.** To transfer program execution to some section of code (usually a subroutine) while saving the nec-essary information to allow execution to resume at the calling point when the called section has completed execution. Some languages (such as FORTRAN) have an explicit CALL statement; others (such as C and Pascal) perform a call when the name of a procedure or function appears. In assembly language, there are various names for a CALL instruction. When a subroutine call occurs in any language, one or more values (known as arguments or parameters) are often passed to the subroutine, which can then use and sometimes modify these values. *See also* argument, parameter.

callback \käl`bak\ *n.* A user authentication scheme used by computers running dial-in services. A user dials in to a computer and types a logon ID and password. The computer breaks the connection and automatically calls the user back at a preauthorized number. This security measure usually prevents unauthorized access to an account even if an individual's logon ID and password have been stolen. *See also* authentication.

callback modem \käl`bak mō`dəm\ *n.* A modem that, instead of answering an incoming call, requires the caller to enter a touch-tone code and hang up so that the modem can return the call. When the modem receives the caller's code, it checks the code against a stored set of phone numbers. If the code matches an authorized number, the modem dials the number and then opens a connection for the original caller. Callback modems are used when communications lines must be available to outside users but data must be protected from unauthorized intruders.

calling sequence \käl´ēng se`kwəns\ *n.* In a program when a subroutine call occurs, an agreement between the calling routine and the called routine on how arguments will be passed and in what order, how values will be returned, and which routine will handle any necessary housekeeping (such as cleaning up the stack). The calling sequence becomes important when the calling and called routines were created with different compilers or if either was written in assembly language. Two common calling sequences are the C calling sequence and the Pascal calling sequence. In the C calling sequence, the calling routine pushes any arguments included in the call on the stack in reverse order (right to left) and performs any stack cleanup; this permits a varying number of arguments to be passed to a given routine. In the Pascal calling sequence, the calling routine pushes any included arguments on the stack in the order in which they appear (left to right), and the called routine is expected to clean up the stack. *See also* argument, call, stack.

CALL instruction \käl´ in-struk`shən\ *n.* A type of programming instruction that diverts program execution to a new area in memory (sequence of directives) and also allows eventual return to the original sequence of directives.

CALS \kalz, C`A-L-S´\ *n.* Acronym for **C**omputer-**A**ided **A**cquisition and **L**ogistics **S**upport. A Department of Defense standard for electronic exchange of data with commercial suppliers.

CAM \kam, C`A-M´\ *n.* **1.** Acronym for **c**omputer-**a**ided **m**anufacturing. The use of computers in automating the fabrication, assembly, and control aspects of manufacturing. CAM applies to the manufacture of products ranging from small-scale production to the use of robotics in full-scale assembly lines. CAM relates more to the use of specialized programs and equipment than it does to the use of microcomputers in a manufacturing environment. *See also* CAD/CAM, I-CASE. **2.** *See* Common Access Method.

camera-ready \kam´ər-ə-red`ē\ *adj.* In publishing, of or pertaining to the stage at which a document, with all typographic elements and graphics in place, is suitably prepared to be sent to a printing service. The printing service photographs the camera-ready copy and then uses the photograph to make plates for printing. Some applications are advertised as being able to bring documents to the camera-ready stage, eliminating the need for manual layout and pasteup of elements onto boards.

campuswide information system \kam`pus-wīd in-fər-mā´shən si`stəm\ *n.* Information and services distributed on a college or university campus through computer networks. Campuswide information system services typically include student and faculty directories, calendars of campus events, and access to databases. *Acronym:* CWIS (C`W-I-S´).

cancel \kan´səl\ *n.* A control character used in communication with printers and other comput-

ers, commonly designated as CAN. It usually means that the line of text being sent should be canceled. In ASCII, which is the basis of character sets used by most microcomputers, this is represented internally as character code 24.

cancelbot \kan´səl-bot`\ *n.* Short for **cancel** ro**bot**. A program that identifies articles in newsgroups based on a set of criteria and cancels the distribution of those articles. Although the criteria for cancellation is set by the owner of the cancelbot, most cancelbots exist to identify and eliminate spam messages posted to dozens or hundreds of newsgroups. *See also* spam.

cancel message \kan´səl mes`əj\ *n.* A message sent to Usenet news servers indicating that a certain article is to be canceled, or deleted, from the server. *See also* article, news server, Usenet.

candidate key \kan´də-dāt kē`\ *n.* A unique identifier for a tuple (row) within a relation (database table). The candidate key may be either simple (a single attribute) or composite (two or more attributes). By definition, every relation must have at least one candidate key, but it is possible for a relation to have more than one candidate key. If there is only one candidate key, it automatically becomes the primary key for the relation. If there are multiple candidate keys, the designer must designate one as the primary key. Any candidate key that is not the designated primary key is an alternate key. *See also* key (definition 2), primary key.

canned program \kand` prō´gram\ *n. See* canned software.

canned routine \kand` rōō-tēn´\ *n.* A previously written routine that is copied into a program and used as is, without modification. *See also* library routine.

canned software \kand` soft´wâr\ *n.* Off-the-shelf software, such as word processors and spreadsheet programs.

canonical form \kə-non`ə-kəl fōrm´\ *n.* In mathematics and programming, the standard or prototypical form of an expression or statement.

capacitance \kə-pas´ə-təns`\ *n.* The ability to store an electric charge. Capacitance is measured in farads. A capacitance of 1 farad will hold 1 coulomb of charge at a potential of 1 volt. In practical use, a farad is an extremely large amount of capacitance; typical capacitors have values of microfarads (10^{-6}) or picofarads (10^{-12}). *See also* capacitor.

capacitor \kə-pas´ə-tər`\ *n.* A circuit component that provides a known amount of capacitance (ability to store an electric charge). A capacitor typically consists of two conductive plates separated by an insulating (dielectric) material. If other factors remain constant, capacitance increases as the plates are made larger or brought closer together. A capacitor blocks direct current but passes alternating current to an extent that depends on its capacitance and on the frequency of the current. See the illustration. *See also* capacitance.

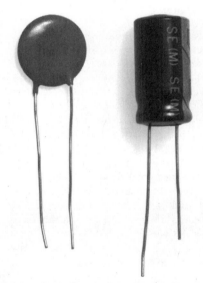

Capacitor. Two of several kinds of capacitors: ceramic disk (left) and electrolytic (right).

capacity \kə-pas´ə-tē`\ *n.* The amount of information a computer or an attached device can process or store. *See also* computer.

caps \kaps\ *n.* Short for **cap**ital letter**s**. *Compare* lowercase.

Caps Lock key \kaps´ lok kē`\ *n.* A toggle key that, when on, shifts the alphabetic characters on the keyboard to uppercase. The Caps Lock key does not affect numbers, punctuation marks, or other symbols.

capstan \kap´stən, kap´stan\ *n.* On a tape recorder, a polished metal post against which a turning rubber wheel (called a pinch roller) presses to move a length of magnetic tape placed between the wheel and the post. The capstan controls the speed of the tape as it moves past the recording head. See the illustration. *See also* pinch roller.

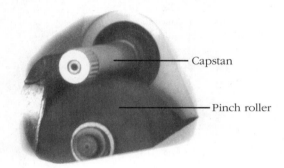

Capstan

Pinch roller

Capstan.

capture \kap´chur\ *vb.* In communications, to transfer received data into a file for archiving or later analysis.

capture board \kap´chur bōrd`\ *n. See* video capture card.

capture card \kap´chur kärd`\ *n. See* video capture card.

carbon copy \kär`bən kop´ē\ *n. See* cc.

carbon ribbon \kär´bən rib`ən\ *n.* A ribbon used with impact printers, especially daisy-wheel printers, and with typewriters for highest-quality output. A carbon ribbon is made of a thin strip of Mylar coated on one side with a carbon film. Characters printed with a carbon ribbon are extremely crisp and free from the fuzziness that can be associated with an inked cloth ribbon. *Also called* film ribbon, Mylar ribbon. *See also* daisy-wheel printer. *Compare* cloth ribbon.

card \kärd\ *n.* **1.** A printed circuit board or adapter that can be plugged into a computer to provide added functionality or new capability. These cards provide specialized services, such as mouse support and modem capabilities, that are not built into the computer. See the illustration. *See also* adapter, board, printed circuit board. **2.** In programs such as the HyperCard hypertext program, an on-screen representation of an index card on which information can be stored and "filed" (saved) for future reference. *See also* hypertext. **3.** A manila card about 3 inches high by 7 inches long on which 80 columns of data could be entered in the form of holes punched with a keypunch machine. The punched holes corresponded to numbers, letters, and other characters and could be read by a computer that used a punched-card reader. See the illustration. *Also called* punched card. *See also* card reader (definition 2).

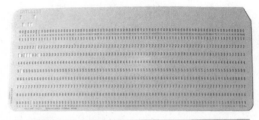

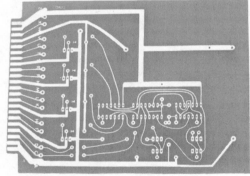

Card. Punched card (top) and printed circuit card (bottom).

card cage \kärd´ kāj\ *n.* An enclosure area for holding printed circuit boards (cards). Most computers have an area with protective metal and mounting brackets where cards are installed. The term originally came from an external box that held rack-mounted cards or peripherals and resembled a cage.

cardinal number \kär`də-nəl num´bər\ *n.* A number that indicates how many items there are in a set—for example, "There are 27 names on that list." *Compare* ordinal number.

card punch \kärd´ punch\ *n. See* keypunch.

card reader \kärd´ rē`dər\ *n.* **1.** An input device used chiefly for identification purposes that reads information that has been magnetically encoded, usually in two tracks, on a plastic card, such as a credit card or an employee badge. **2.** A mechanical apparatus that reads computer data from punched cards. No longer in widespread use, card readers allow computer data to be created offline and then input to the computer for processing. This need for offline data creation was because of limited CPU resources. Reading batches of punched cards was a better use of CPU time than waiting for a human operator to key data directly into the computer's memory. *Also called* punched-card reader.

caret \kâr´ət\ *n.* The small, upward-pointing symbol (∧) typically found over the 6 key on the top row of a microcomputer keyboard. In some programming languages, the caret is used as an exponentiation operator. For example, the expression 3 ∧ 2 represents the number 3 raised to the second power. The caret is also used to represent the Control key on the keyboard. For example, ∧Z means "hold the Control key down and press the Z key."

careware \kâr´wâr\ *n.* Software developed by an individual or a small group and distributed freely, with the proviso that users make a donation to a charity if they continue to use the software after trying it out. The charity is one usually designated by the software creator.

carpal tunnel syndrome \kär`pəl tun´əl sin`drōm\ *n.* A form of repetitive strain injury to the wrist and hand. Making the same small motions over and over can cause swelling and scarring of the soft tissue of the wrist, which then compresses the main nerve leading to the hand. Symptoms of carpal tunnel syndrome include pain and tingling in the fingers, and in advanced cases, carpal tunnel syndrome can lead to loss of functionality of the hands. Typing at a computer keyboard without proper wrist support is a common cause of carpal tunnel syndrome. *Acronym:* CTS (C`T-S´). *See also* repetitive strain injury, wrist support.

carriage \kâr´əj\ *n.* The assembly that holds the platen of a typewriter or a typewriterlike printer. On a standard typewriter, the platen and carriage move past a fixed position within the typewriter housing, where the keys strike the paper; the platen rotates to advance the paper held in the carriage. On most impact printers for computers, however, the print head moves back and forth across a platen, which rotates but does not move horizontally; in such machines, the assembly that carries the print head is often called the print-head carriage assembly. *See also* carriage return, platen.

carriage return \kâr´əj rə-turn`\ *n.* A control character that tells a computer or printer to return to the beginning of the current line. A carriage return is similar to the return on a typewriter but does not automatically advance to the beginning of a new line. For example, a carriage-return character alone, received at the end of the words This is a sample line of text would cause the cursor or printer to return to the first letter of the word *This*. In the ASCII character set, the carriage-return character has the decimal value of 13 (hexadecimal 0D).

carrier \kâr´ē-ər`\ *n.* **1.** In communications, a specified frequency that can be modulated to convey information. **2.** A company that provides telephone and other communications services to consumers.

Carrier Detect \kâr´ē-ər dē-tekt`\ *n. See* CD.

carrier frequency \kâr´ē-ər frē`kwən-sē\ *n.* A radio-frequency signal, such as those used with modems and on networks, used to transmit information. A carrier frequency is a signal that vibrates at a fixed number of cycles per second, or hertz (Hz), and is modulated (changed) in either frequency or amplitude to enable it to carry intelligible information.

carrier system \kâr´ē-ər si`stəm\ *n.* A communications method that uses different carrier frequencies to transfer information along multiple channels of a single path. Transmission involves modulating the signal on each frequency at the originating station and demodulating the signal at the receiving station.

carry \kâr´ē\ *n.* In arithmetic, the process of moving a digit to the next higher position when the sum of two numbers is greater than the largest digit in the number system being used. Computers, based on logic circuits, and often able to add all digits in two numbers simultaneously (do parallel addition), perform carries in several exotic ways. For example, they perform complete carries, in which one carry is allowed to propagate—that is, to generate other carries in other digit positions. They can also perform partial carries, in

which carries resulting from parallel addition are stored temporarily.

carry bit \kâr´ē bit\ *n.* The bit, associated with an adder circuit, that indicates that an addition operation has produced a carry (as in 9 + 7). *Also called* carry flag.

carry flag \kâr´ē flag\ *n. See* carry bit.

Cartesian coordinates \kär-tē´zhən kō-ōr`də-nəts\ *n.* Points on a plane (two dimensions) or in space (three dimensions) that are located by their positions in relation to intersecting axes; named after the French mathematician René Descartes, who introduced the system in the seventeenth century. In two dimensions, points are described by their positions in relation to the two familiar axes, x (usually horizontal) and y (usually vertical). In three dimensions, a third axis, z, is added to the x- and y-axes. See the illustration. *See also* x-y-z coordinate system. *Compare* polar coordinates.

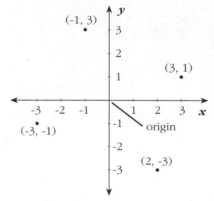

Cartesian coordinates.

Cartesian product \kär-tē´zhən prod`ukt\ *n. See* product (definition 1).

cartridge \kär´trij\ *n.* Any of various container devices that usually consist of some form of plastic housing. *See also* disk cartridge, ink cartridge, memory cartridge, ribbon cartridge, ROM cartridge, tape cartridge, toner cartridge.

cartridge font \kär´trij font`\ *n.* A font contained in a plug-in cartridge and used to add fonts to laser, ink-jet, or high-end dot-matrix printers. Cartridge fonts are distinguished both from internal fonts, which are contained in ROM in the printer and are always available, and from downloadable (soft) fonts, which reside on disk and which can be sent to the printer as needed. *See also* font cartridge. *Compare* internal font.

cascade \ka-skād´\ *n.* **1.** Additional elements displayed by a menu item or list box from which the user can choose in order to interact with other screen elements. See the illustration **2.** In newsgroup articles, the accumulation of quotation marks (often angle brackets) added by newsgroup readers each time an article is replied to. Most newsgroup readers will copy the original article in the body of the reply; after several replies, the original material will have several quotation marks. *See also* article, newsgroup, newsreader.

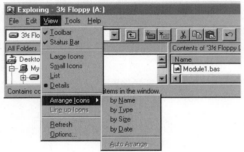

Cascade.

cascade connection \kas-kād´ kə-nek`shən\ *n.* *See* pipe (definition 1).

cascading menu \ka-skā`dēng men´yo͞o\ *n.* A hierarchical graphical menu system in which a side menu of subcategories is displayed when the pointer is placed on the main category.

Cascading Style Sheet mechanism \ka-skā`dēng stīl´ shēt mek`ə-ni-zəm\ *n.* *See* cascading style sheets.

cascading style sheets \ka-skā` dēng stīl´ shēts\ *n.* A Hypertext Markup Language (HTML) specification developed by the World Wide Web Consortium (W3C) that allows authors of HTML documents and users to attach style sheets to HTML documents. The style sheets include typographical information on how the page should appear, such as the font of the text in the page. This specification also directs the way in which the style sheets of the HTML document and the user's style will blend. Cascading style sheets have been proposed for the HTML 3.2 standard. *Also called* Cascading Style Sheet mechanism, CSS1. *See also* HTML, style sheet (definition 2).

cascading windows \ka-skā`dēng win´dōz\ *n.* A sequence of successive, overlapping windows in a graphical user interface, displayed so that the title bar of each is visible. *Also called* overlaid windows.

case \kās\ *n.* In text processing, an indication of whether one or more alphabetic characters are capitalized (uppercase) or not (lowercase). A case-sensitive program or routine distinguishes between uppercase and lowercase letters and treats the word *cat* as totally distinct from either *Cat* or *CAT*. A case-sensitive program that also separates capitalized and lowercased words would list *Arkansas* before *aardvark* or *antimony,* even though its alphabetic position follows both lowercased words.

CASE \kās\ *n.* Acronym for **c**omputer-**a**ided **s**oftware **e**ngineering. A comprehensive label for software designed to use computers in all phases of computer program development, from planning and modeling through coding and documentation. CASE represents a working environment consisting of programs and other development tools that help managers, systems analysts, programmers, and others to automate the design and implementation of programs and procedures for business, engineering, and scientific computer systems.

case-sensitive search \kās`sen-sə-tiv sərch´\ *n.* A search in a database in which capitalization of key words must exactly match the capitalization of words in the database. A case-sensitive search for "north and south" would fail to find a database entry for "North and South."

case sensitivity \kās´ sen-sə-tiv`ə-tē\ *n.* Discrimination between lowercase and uppercase characters in a program or a programming language. *See also* case.

case statement \kās´ stāt`mənt\ *n.* In programming languages such as Ada, Pascal, and C, a type of control statement that executes one of several sets of instructions based on some key value. Case statements are used in evaluating situations that can have a number of different results. "Case" in this sense refers to a refinement of a basic IF-THEN type of conditional statement (if A is true, then do B), but a case statement functions more like a series of nested IFs (if A, then do this; else if B, then do that; else . . .). In a case evaluation, a variable (such as a number or a string of characters) is compared against one after another of a series of constants assigned by the programmer. Each constant represents a different case and defines an action to be carried out. When the program finds a constant that matches the variable, it carries out whatever action is dictated by the case in which the match occurs. *See also* constant, control statement, variable.

cassette \kə-set´\ *n.* The unit consisting of both the plastic case and the magnetic tape it contains. Cassette tapes are used for backing up large amounts of computer data.

cassette tape \kə-set´ tāp`\ *n.* **1.** The tape within a cassette. **2.** The unit consisting of both the plastic cassette case and the tape it contains.

cast \kast\ *n.* A programmer-specified data conversion from one type to another, such as a conversion from integer to floating point. *Also called* coercion. *See also* data type.

CAT \kat, C`A-T´\ *n.* **1.** Acronym for **c**omputer-**a**ided **t**esting. A procedure used by engineers for checking or analyzing designs, especially those created with CAD programs. Computer-aided testing is also used by software developers for automated regression testing. **2.** Acronym for **c**omputer-**a**ssisted **t**eaching. *See* CAI. **3.** Acronym for **c**omputerized **a**xial **t**omography. A medical procedure in which a computer is used to generate a three-dimensional image of a body part from a series of X rays taken as cross sections along a single axis.

catalog \kat´ə-log`\ *n.* **1.** In a computer, a list containing specific information, such as name, length, type, and location of files or of storage space. **2.** In a database, the data dictionary. *See also* data dictionary.

catena \kə-tē´nə\ *n.* A series of items in a chained list—that is, a list in which one item points to the next in sequence. *See also* linked list.

cathode \kath´ōd\ *n.* **1.** The terminal or electrode that is negatively charged and from which electrons flow. **2.** The electron-emitting electrode in a vacuum tube. **3.** The negative terminal of a battery. *Compare* anode.

cathode-ray oscilloscope \kath`ōd-rā ə-sil´ə-skōp\ *n. See* oscilloscope.

cathode-ray tube \kath´ōd-rā tōōb`\ *n. See* CRT.

.ca.us \dot-C-A`dot-U-S´\ *n.* On the Internet, the major geographic domain specifying that an address is located in California, United States.

CBEMA \C`B-E`M-A´\ *n.* Acronym for **C**omputer and **B**usiness **E**quipment **M**anufacturers **A**ssociation. An organization of hardware vendors and manufacturers in the United States involved in standardizing information processing and related equipment.

CBL \C`B-L´\ *n.* Acronym for **c**omputer-**b**ased **l**earning. Applies to either computer-aided instruction (CAI), which focuses primarily on education, or computer-based training (CBT), which is application-specific or job-oriented teaching. *See also* CAI, CBT.

CBT \C`B-T´\ *n.* Acronym for **c**omputer-**b**ased **t**raining. The use of computers and specially developed tutorial programs for teaching. CBT uses color, graphics, and other attention-getting aids to help maintain interest, and it has both simple and sophisticated applications. A software developer, for example, might include a series of CBT lessons with an application to give new users a hands-on feel for the program; a consultant might use a longer and more detailed CBT program as a tool in a management-training seminar.

cc \C-C´\ *n.* Acronym for **c**ourtesy **c**opy. A directive to an e-mail program to send a complete copy of a given piece of mail to another individual. The use of cc mail addressing, as opposed to directly addressing the mail to a person, generally implies that the recipient is not required to take any action; the message is for informational purposes only. In a cc directive, the fact that this recipient received the mail is printed in the mail header and is thus known to all other recipients. *Also called* carbon copy. *See also* e-mail[1] (definition 1), header. *Compare* bcc.

.cc \dot`C-C´\ *n.* On the Internet, the major geographic domain specifying that an address is located in the Cocos Islands.

CCD \C`C-D´\ *n. See* charge-coupled device.

CCI \C`C-I´\ *n. See* Common Client Interface.

CCITT \C`C-I`T-T´\ *n.* Acronym for **C**omité **C**onsultatif **I**nternational **T**élégraphique et **T**éléphonique. Also known as the **I**nternational **T**elegraph and **T**elephone **C**onsultative **C**ommittee. An organization based in Geneva, Switzerland, and established as part of the United Nations International Telecommunications Union (ITU). Its functions have been taken over by the ITU. The ITU recommends use of communications standards that are recognized throughout the world. Protocols established by the ITU are applied to modems, networks, and facsimile transmission. *See also* CCITT Groups 1–4, CCITT V series, CCITT X series.

CCITT Groups 1–4 \C-C-I-T-T゛ grōōps wǝn-tǝ-fōr\ *n.* A set of four standards recommended by the Comité Consultatif International Télégraphique et Téléphonique (International Telegraph and Telephone Consultative Committee) for the encoding and transmission of images over fax machines. Groups 1 and 2 relate to analog devices and are generally out of use. Groups 3 and 4, which deal with digital devices, are outlined below. Group 3 is a widespread standard that supports standard images of 203 horizontal dots per inch (dpi) by 98 vertical dpi and fine images of 203 horizontal dpi by 198 vertical dpi; supports two methods of data compression, one (based on the Huffman code) reducing an image to 10 to 20 percent of the original, the second (READ, for relative element address designate) compressing images to 6 to 12 percent of the original; and provides for password protection and for polling so that a receiving machine can request transmission as appropriate. Group 4, a newer standard, supports images of up to 400 dpi; data compression based on a beginning row of white pixels (dots), with each succeeding line encoded as a series of changes from the line before, compressing images to 3 to 10 percent of the original; does not include error-correction information in the transmission; and requires an Integrated Services Digital Network (ISDN) phone line rather than a dial-up line.

CCITT V series \C゛C-I-T-T V´ sēr-ēz\ *n.* A set of recommendations developed by the Comité Consultatif International Télégraphique et Téléphonique (International Telegraph and Telephone Consultative Committee) for standardizing modem design and operations and adopted by the ITU-T and ISO. The complete series includes a number of recommendations covering signaling, coding, and circuit

characteristics, as well as modems. Those most relevant to computer users are briefly described below in terms of the modems they standardize:

V.21: 300-bps modems used with dial-up lines; full-duplex transmission. Not the same as Bell 103 (in North America).

V.22: 1,200-bps modems used with dial-up and leased lines; full-duplex transmission. Not the same as Bell 212A (in North America).

V.22bis: 2,400-bps modems used with dial-up and leased lines; full-duplex transmission.

V.23: 600/1,200-bps synchronous or asynchronous modems used with dial-up and leased lines; half-duplex transmission.

V.26: 2,400-bps modems used with four-wire leased lines; full-duplex transmission.

V.26bis: 1,200/2,400-bps modems used with dial-up lines; full-duplex transmission.

V.26ter: 2,400-bps modems used with dial-up and two-wire leased lines; DPSK modulation; fallback to 1,200 bps; echo canceling to remove phone-line echo; full-duplex transmission.

V.27: 4,800-bps modems used with leased lines; manual equalizer; full-duplex transmission.

V.27bis: 2,400/4,800-bps modems used with leased lines; automatic equalizer; full-duplex transmission.

V.27ter: 2,400/4,800-bps modems used with dial-up lines; full-duplex transmission.

V.29: 9,600-bps modems used with point-to-point leased circuits; half-duplex transmission or full-duplex transmission.

V.32: 9,600-bps modems used with dial-up lines; echo canceling to remove phone-line echo; full-duplex transmission.

V.32bis: 4,800/7,200/9,600/12,000/14,400-bps modems used with dial-up lines; echo canceling; full-duplex transmission.

V.33: 12,000/14,400-bps modems used with four-wire leased lines; synchronous; QAM modulation; time-division multiplexing; full-duplex transmission.

V.34: 28,800-bps modems; full-duplex transmission.

V.35: Group band modems, which combine the bandwidth of more than one telephone circuit.

CCITT X series \C-C-I-T-T-X´ sēr゛ēz\ *n.* A set of recommendations adopted by the International

Telecommunication Union Telecommunication Standardization Sector (ITU-T), formerly the CCITT, and ISO for standardizing equipment and protocols used in both public-access and private computer networks. Some of the recommendations in the X series include the following:

X.25 documents the interface required to connect a computer to a packet-switched network such as the Internet.

The X.200 series of recommendations documents the widely accepted seven-layer set of protocols known as the OSI (Open Systems Interconnection) model for standardizing computer-to-computer connections.

X.400 documents the format at the OSI application layer for e-mail messages over various network transports, including Ethernet, X.25, and TCP/IP. Gateways must be used to translate e-mail messages between the X.400 and Internet formats.

X.445, also known as the Asynchronous Protocol Specification, governs the transmission of X.400 messages over dial-up telephone lines.

X.500 documents protocols for client/server systems that maintain and access directories of users and resources in X.400 form.

ccNUMA \C`C-nōō´mə, C`C-N`U-M-A´\ *n.* Acronym for **C**ache-**C**oherent **N**on-**U**niform **M**emory **A**ccess. A technology that enables many symmetric multiprocessing systems to be connected by high-speed/wide-bandwidth interconnect hardware so that they function as one machine. *See also* symmetric multiprocessing.

CCP \C`C-P´\ *n.* Acronym for **C**ertificate in **C**omputer **P**rogramming. A senior-level programming credential awarded by the Institute for Certification of Computer Professionals to individuals who pass an extensive set of programming examinations.

cd \C-D´\ *n.* Acronym for **c**hange **d**irectory. In MS-DOS, UNIX, and FTP client programs, the command that changes the current directory to the directory whose path follows *cd* in the command. *See also* directory, path (definition 5).

CD \C-D´\ **1.** Acronym for **C**arrier **D**etect, a signal sent from a modem to the attached computer to indicate that the modem is on line. *See also* DCD. **2.** Acronym for **c**ompact **d**isc. *See* CD-I, CD-ROM, compact disc.

CD burner \C-D´ bur`nər\ *n. See* CD recorder.

CD-E \C`D-E´\ *n. See* compact disc–erasable.

cdev \C´dev, C`D-E-V´\ *n.* Short for **c**ontrol panel **dev**ice. A Macintosh utility that allows basic system settings to be customized. In Macintosh computers running System 6, a cdev is a utility program placed in the system folder. Keyboard and mouse cdevs are preinstalled. Other cdevs are provided with software packages and utilities. In System 7 cdevs are called control panels. *See also* control panel, system folder. *Compare* INIT.

CDFS \C`D-F-S´\ *n.* **1.** Acronym for **CD**-ROM **F**ile **S**ystem. A 32-bit protected-mode file system that controls access to the contents of CD-ROM drives in Windows 95. *See also* protected mode. **2.** A designation used with UNIX computers to indicate that a file system resides on a read-only removable medium (that is a CD-ROM). This usually implies that the compact disc is compliant with the ISO 9660 standard. CDFS is also used as a part of commands that mount media (hard drives, tape drives, remote networked drives, and CD-ROMs) for use on a computer. *See also* CD-ROM, ISO 9660.

CD-I \C`D-I´\ *n.* Acronym for **c**ompact **d**isc–**i**nteractive. A hardware and software standard for a form of optical disc technology that can combine audio, video, and text on high-capacity compact discs. CD-I includes such features as image display and resolution, animation, special effects, and audio. The standard covers methods of encoding, compressing, decompressing, and displaying stored information. *See also* CD-ROM.

CDMA \C`D-M-A´\ *n. See* Code Division Multiple Access.

CDP \C`D-P´\ *n.* Acronym for **C**ertificate in **D**ata **P**rocessing. A certificate awarded by the Institute for Certification of Computer Professionals to individuals who pass a set of examinations on computers and related areas, including programming, software, and systems analysis.

CDPD \C`D-P-D´\ *n. See* Cellular Digital Packet Data.

CD Plus \C-D` plus´\ *n.* A compact disc encoding format that allows mixing of audio recordings and computer data on the same CD, without the possibility of audio equipment becoming damaged by attempting to play the data sections.

CD-R \C`D-R´\ *n.* Acronym for **c**ompact **d**isc–**r**ecordable. A type of CD-ROM that can be written on a CD recorder and read on a CD-ROM drive. *See also* CD recorder, CD-ROM.

CD-R/E \C`D-R-E´\ *n. See* compact disc–recordable and erasable.

CD recorder \C-D´ rə-kōr`dər\ *n.* A device used to write CD-ROMs. Because a disc can be written only once on these machines, they are used most commonly to create CD-ROMs for data archives or to produce CD-ROM masters that can be duplicated for mass distribution. See the illustration. *Also called* CD-R machine, CD-ROM burner. *See also* CD-ROM.

CD recorder.

CD-R machine \C`D-R´ mə-shēn`\ *n. See* CD recorder.

CD-ROM \C`D-rom´, C`D-R-O-M´\ *n.* **1.** Acronym for **c**ompact **d**isc **r**ead-**o**nly **m**emory. A form of storage characterized by high capacity (roughly 650 megabytes) and the use of laser optics rather than magnetic means for reading data. Although CD-ROM drives are strictly read-only, they are similar to CD-R drives (write once, read many), optical WORM devices, and optical read-write drives. *See also* CD-I, CD-R, WORM. **2.** An individual compact disc designed for use with a computer and capable of storing up to 650 megabytes of data. *See also* compact disc, disc.

CD-ROM burner \C`D-rom´ bur`nər, C`D-R- O-M´\ *n. See* CD recorder.

CD-ROM drive \C`D-rom´ drīv`, C`D-R-O-M´\ *n.* A disk storage device that uses compact disc technology. *See also* CD-ROM, compact disc.

CD-ROM Extended Architecture \C`D-rom` eks-ten`dəd är´kə-tek`chur, C`D-R-O-M´\ *n. See* CD-ROM/XA.

CD-ROM File System \C`D-rom` fīl´ si`stəm, C`D-R-O-M´\ *n. See* CDFS (definition 1).

CD-ROM jukebox \C`D-rom` jōōk´boks, C`D-R-O-M´\ *n.* A CD-ROM player that can contain up to 200 CD-ROMs and is connected to a CD-ROM drive in a personal computer or workstation. A user can request data from any of the CD-ROMs in the jukebox, and the device will locate and play the disk that contains the data. While only one CD-ROM can be played at a time, if multiple CD-ROM jukeboxes are each connected to separate CD-ROM drives that are daisy-chained together to the computer, more than one CD-ROM can be used at a time. *See also* CD-ROM, CD-ROM drive, daisy chain.

CD-ROM/XA \C`D-rom`X-A´, C`D-R-O-M´\ *n.* Short for **CD-ROM E**xtended **A**rchitecture. An extended CD-ROM format developed by Philips, Sony, and Microsoft. CD-ROM/XA is consistent with the ISO 9660 (High Sierra) standard, with further specification of ADPCM (adaptive differential pulse code modulation) audio, images, and interleaved data. *See also* adaptive differential pulse code modulation, CD-ROM, High Sierra specification.

CD-RW \C`D-R-W´\ *n. See* compact disc–rewritable.

CDS \C`D-S´\ *n. See* Circuit Data Services.

CDV \C`D-V´\ *n.* **1.** Acronym for **c**ompressed **d**igital **v**ideo. The compression of video images for high-speed transmission. **2.** Acronym for **c**ompact **d**isc **v**ideo. A 5-inch videodisc. *See also* videodisc.

CD Video \C-D` vid´ē-ō\ *n. See* CDV (definition 2).

cell \sel\ *n.* **1.** The intersection of a row and a column in a spreadsheet. Each row and column in a spreadsheet is unique, so each cell can be uniquely identified—for example, cell B17, at the intersection of column B and row 17. Each cell is displayed as a rectangular space that can hold text, a value, or a formula. See the illustration. **2.** An addressable (named or numbered) storage unit for information. A binary cell, for example, is a storage unit that can hold 1 bit of information—that is, it can be either on or off.

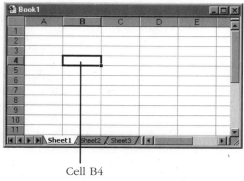

Cell B4

Cell.

cell animation or **cel animation** \sel´ an-ə-mā`shən\ *n.* A process performed by software that emulates traditional cell animation, which uses transparent celluloid sheets ("cells" or "cels" for short) to overlay active elements in an animation frame onto a static background. Computer cell animation is quite efficient because images can be quickly reproduced and manipulated. See the illustration.

cellular automata \sel`yōō-lər ô-tom´ə-tə\ *n.* In computer science, theoretical models of parallel computers. They enable the investigation of paral- lel computers without the need to actually build them. The cellular automaton is composed of a network of multiple cells, each representing a processor in the parallel computer. The cells must be identical, and they must have a finite amount of available memory. Each cell outputs a value calculated from the input values it receives from its neighboring cells, and all cells output their values simultaneously.

Cellular Digital Packet Data \sel`yə-lər dij`ə-təl pak`ət dā`tə, dat`ə\ *n.* A wireless standard provid- ing two-way, 19.2-Kbps packet data transmission over existing cellular telephone channels. *Acro- nym:* CDPD (C`D-P-D´). *See also* packet, wireless.

censorship \sen´sər-ship`\ *n.* The action of pre- venting material that a party considers objection- able from circulating within a system of communication over which that party has some power. The Internet as a whole is not censored, but some parts of it come under varying degrees of control. A news server, for example, often is set to exclude any or all of the alt. newsgroups, such as alt.sex.* or alt.music.white-power, which are unmoderated and tend to be controversial. A mod- erated newsgroup or mailing list may be consid- ered to be "censored" because the moderator will

Cell animation.

usually delete highly controversial and obscene content or content that is on a different topic from that followed by the newsgroup. Online services have identifiable owners, who often take some share of responsibility for what reaches their users' computer screens. In some countries, censorship of certain political or cultural Web sites is a matter of national policy.

censorware \sen´sər-wâr`\ *n.* Software that imposes restrictions on what Internet sites, newsgroups, or files may be accessed by the user.

center \sen´tər\ *vb.* To align characters around a point located in the middle of a line, page, or other defined area; in effect, to place text an equal distance from each margin or border. *See also* align (definition 1).

centi- \sen´ti-, sen´tə-\ *prefix* **1.** One hundred. **2.** One hundredth, as in *centimeter*—one hundredth of a meter.

centralized processing \sen`trə-līzd pros´es-ēng\ *n.* The location of computer processing facilities and operations in a single (centralized) place. *Compare* decentralized processing, distributed processing.

central office \sen`trəl of´is\ *n.* In communications, the switching center where interconnections between customers' communications lines are made.

central processing unit \sen`trəl pros´es-ēng yōō`-nit\ *n.* The computational and control unit of a computer. The central processing unit is the device that interprets and executes instructions. Mainframes and early minicomputers contained circuit boards full of integrated circuits that implemented the central processing unit. Single-chip central processing units, called *microprocessors,* made possible personal computers and workstations. Examples of single-chip central processing units are the Motorola 68000, 68020, and 68030 chips and the Intel 8080, 8086, 80286, 80386, and i486 chips. The central processing unit—or microprocessor, in the case of a microcomputer—has the ability to fetch, decode, and execute instructions and to transfer information to and from other resources over the computer's main data-transfer path, the bus. By definition, the central processing unit is the chip that functions as the "brain" of a computer. In some instances, however, the term encompasses both the processor and the computer's memory or, even more broadly, the main computer console (as opposed to peripheral equipment). *Acronym:* CPU (C`P-U´). *See also* microprocessor.

Centronics parallel interface \sen-tron`iks pâr`ə-lel in´tər-fās\ *n.* A de facto standard for parallel data exchange paths between computers and peripherals, originally developed by the printer manufacturer Centronics, Inc. The Centronics parallel interface provides eight parallel data lines plus additional lines for control and status information. *See also* parallel interface.

CERN \sərn, C`E-R-N´\ *n.* Acronym for **C**onseil **E**uropéen pour la **R**echerche **N**ucléaire (the European Laboratory for Particle Physics). CERN, a physics research center located in Geneva, Switzerland, is where the original development of the World Wide Web took place by Tim Berners-Lee in 1989 as a method to facilitate communication among members of the scientific community. *See also* NCSA (definition 1).

CERN server \sərn´ sər`vər, C`E-R-N´\ *n.* One of the first Hypertext Transfer Protocol (HTTP) servers, developed at CERN by Tim Berners-Lee. The CERN server is still in wide use and is free of charge. *See also* CERN, HTTP server (definition 1).

CERT \sərt, C`E-R-T´\ *n.* Acronym for **C**omputer **E**mergency **R**esponse **T**eam. An organization that provides a round-the-clock security consultation service for Internet users and provides advisories whenever new virus programs and other computer security threats are discovered.

certification \sər`tə-fə-kā´shən\ *n.* **1.** The act of awarding a document to demonstrate a computer professional's competence in a particular field. Some hardware and software suppliers, such as Microsoft and Novell, offer certification in the use of their products; other organizations, such as the Institute for Certification of Computer Professionals (ICCP) and the Computing Technology Industry Association (CompTIA), offer more general certification. **2.** The act of awarding a document to demonstrate that a hardware or software product meets some specification, such as being able to work with a certain other hardware or software product. **3.** The issuance of a notice that a user or site is trusted for the purpose of security and computer authentication. Often certification is used with Web sites.

.cf \dot`C-F´\ *n.* On the Internet, the major geographic domain specifying that an address is located in the Central African Republic.

.cg \dot`C-G´\ *n.* On the Internet, the major geographic domain specifying that an address is located in the Congo.

CGA \C`G-A´\ *n.* Acronym for **C**olor/**G**raphics **A**dapter. A video adapter board introduced by IBM in 1981. The CGA is capable of several character and graphics modes, including character modes of 40 or 80 horizontal characters (columns) by 25 vertical lines with 16 colors, and graphics modes of 640 horizontal pixels by 200 vertical pixels with 2 colors, or 320 horizontal pixels by 200 vertical pixels with 4 colors. *See also* graphics adapter, video adapter.

CGI \C`G-I´\ *n.* **1.** Acronym for **C**ommon **G**ateway **I**nterface. The specification that defines communications between information servers (such as HTTP servers) and resources on the server's host computer, such as databases and other programs. For example, when a user submits a form through a Web browser, the HTTP server executes a program (often called a CGI script) and passes the user's input information to that program via CGI. The program then returns information to the server via CGI. Use of CGI can make a Web page much more dynamic and add interactivity for the user. *See also* CGI script, HTTP server (definition 1). **2.** *See* Computer Graphics Interface.

cgi-bin \C`G-I´ bin\ *n.* Short for **C**ommon **G**ateway **I**nterface–**bin**aries. A file directory that holds external applications to be executed by HTTP servers via CGI. *See also* CGI (definition 1).

CGI script \C`G-I´ skript\ *n.* Short for **C**ommon **G**ateway **I**nterface **script**. An external application that is executed by an HTTP server machine in response to a request by a client, such as a Web browser. Generally, the CGI script is invoked when the user clicks on some element in a Web page, such as a link or an image. Communication between the CGI script and the server is carried out via the CGI specification. CGI scripts can be written in many programming languages, including C, C++, and Visual Basic. However, the most commonly used language for CGI scripts is Perl,

because it is a small but robust language and it is common on UNIX, which is the platform on which the majority of Web sites run. CGI scripts don't necessarily need to be scripts; they can also be batch programs or compiled programs. CGI scripts are used to provide interactivity in a Web page, including such features as providing a form that users can fill out, image maps that contain links to other Web pages or resources, and links that users can click on to send e-mail to a specified address. ActiveX controls and Java applets can provide much the same functionality as CGI scripts, through different means. *See also* CGI (definition 1), cgi-bin, image map, Perl. *Compare* ActiveX controls, Java applet.

CGM \C`G-M´\ *n. See* Computer Graphics Metafile.

.ch \dot`C-H´\ *n.* On the Internet, the major geographic domain specifying that an address is located in Switzerland.

chad \chad\ *n.* The paper removed when a hole is punched in a card, in a tape, or at the perforated edge of continuous-form paper—the computer equivalent of a doughnut hole.

chaining \chā´nēng\ *n.* In computers, the linking of two or more entities so that they are dependent upon one another for operation. In programming, two or more programs are said to be chained if the first program causes the second program to begin executing. In addition, program statements are said to be chained if each statement, except for the first, relies on the previous statement for input. With batch files, two or more batch files are said to be chained if the completion of the first batch file causes the second batch file to begin executing. With data storage, the term *chained* applies to two or more individual units of storage that are linked together. For example, a single file on a disk may actually be stored on several different sectors of the disk, each of which points to the next sector containing a piece of that file. These sectors are said to be chained together, or, more literally, to be a chain of clusters.

chain printer \chān´ prin`tər\ *n. See* line printer.

chalkware \chäk´wâr, chôk´wâr\ *n. See* vaporware.

Challenge Handshake Authentication Protocol \chal`ənj hand`shāk ə-then`-tə-kā´shən prō`tə-kol\ *n.* An authentication scheme used by

PPP servers to validate the identity of the originator of a connection, upon connection or any time later. *Acronym:* CHAP (chap, C`H-A-P´). *See also* authentication, PPP.

change file \chānj´ fīl\ *n.* A file that records transactional changes occurring in a database, providing a basis for updating a master file and establishing an audit trail. *Also called* transaction log. *See also* addition record.

channel \chan´əl\ *n.* **1.** A path or link through which information passes between two devices. A channel can be either internal or external to a microcomputer. *See also* bus. **2.** In communications, a medium for transferring information. Depending on its type, a communications channel can carry information (data, sound, and/or video) in either analog or digital form. A communications channel can be a physical link, such as the cable connecting two stations in a network, or it can consist of some electromagnetic transmission on one or more frequencies within a bandwidth in the electromagnetic spectrum, as in radio and television, or in optical, microwave, or voice-grade communication. *Also called* circuit, line. *See also* analog, band, bandwidth, digital (definition 2), electromagnetic spectrum, frequency.

channel access \chan´əl ak`ses\ *n.* **1.** A method used in networked systems to gain access to the data communication channel that links two or more computers. Common methods of channel access are contention, polling, and the token ring network. *See also* channel, contention, polling, token ring network. **2.** In wireless technology, an access method such as CDMA (Code Division Multiple Access). *See also* Code Division Multiple Access.

channel adapter \chan´əl ə-dap`tər\ *n.* A device that enables hardware using two different types of communications channels to communicate.

channel capacity \chan´əl kə-pas`ə-tē\ *n.* The speed at which a communications channel can transfer information, measured in bits per second (bps) or in baud.

channel hop \chan´əl hop`\ *vb.* To switch repeatedly from one IRC channel to another. *See also* IRC.

channel op \chan´əl op`\ *n.* Short for **channel operator.** A user on an IRC channel who has the privilege of expelling undesirable participants. *See also* IRC.

CHAP \chap, C`H-A-P´\ *n. See* Challenge Handshake Authentication Protocol.

character \kâr´ək-tər\ *n.* A letter, number, punctuation mark, or other symbol or control code that is represented to a computer by one unit— 1 byte—of information. A character is not necessarily visible, either on the screen or on paper; a space, for example, is as much a character as is the letter *a* or any of the digits 0 through 9. Because computers must manage not only so-called printable characters but also the look (formatting) and transfer of electronically stored information, a character can additionally indicate a carriage return or a paragraph mark in a word-processed document. It can be a signal to sound a beep, begin a new page, or mark the end of a file. *See also* ASCII, control character, EBCDIC.

character cell \kâr´ək-tər sel`\ *n.* A rectangular block of pixels that represents the space in which a given character is drawn on the screen. Computer displays use different numbers of pixels as character cells. Character cells are not always the same size for a given font, however; for proportionally spaced fonts, such as those commonly displayed on the Apple Macintosh, the height within a given font remains the same, but the width varies with each character.

character code \kâr´ək-tər kōd`\ *n.* A specific code that represents a particular character in a set, such as the ASCII character set. The character code for a given key depends on whether another key, such as Shift, is pressed at the same time. For example, pressing the A key alone normally generates the character code for a lowercase *a*. Pressing Shift plus the A key normally generates the character code for an uppercase *A*. *Compare* key code.

character definition table \kâr`ək-tər def-ə-nish´ən tā-bl\ *n.* A table of patterns that a computer can hold in memory and use as a reference for determining the arrangement of dots used to create and display bitmapped characters on the screen. *See also* bitmapped font.

character density \kâr´ək-tər den`sə-tē\ *n.* In printing or screen display, a measure of the number of characters per unit of area or of linear distance. *See also* pitch (definition 1).

character device \kâr´ək-tər də-vīs`\ *n*. **1.** A computer device, such as a keyboard or printer, that receives or transmits information as a stream of characters, one character at a time. The characters can be transferred either bit by bit (serial transmission) or byte by byte (parallel transmission) but are not moved from place to place in blocks (groups of bytes). *Compare* block device. **2.** In reference to video displays, a device that handles text but not graphics. *See also* text mode.

character generator \kâr´ək-tər jen`ər-ā-tər\ *n*. A program or a hardware device that translates a given character code, such as an ASCII code, into a matching pixel pattern for display on the screen. Such devices are typically limited in the number and range of styles of fonts they support, as compared to machines that support bitmapped characters. *Compare* bitmapped font.

character image \kâr´ək-tər im`əj\ *n*. A set of bits arranged in the shape of a character. Each character image exists within a rectangular grid, or *character rectangle,* that defines its height and width. *See also* bitmapped font.

characteristic \kâr`ək-tər-i´stik\ *n*. In mathematics, the exponent of a floating-point number (the portion following the *E* that indicates the position of the decimal point) or the integer portion of a logarithm. *See also* floating-point notation, logarithm.

character map \kâr´ək-tər map`\ *n*. In text-based computer graphics, a block of memory addresses that correspond to character spaces on a display screen. The memory allocated to each character space is used to hold the description of the character to be displayed in that space. *See also* alphageometric.

character mode \kâr´ək-tər mōd`\ *n*. *See* text mode.

character-oriented protocol \kâr`ək-tər-ōr-ē-en-təd prō´tə-kol\ *n*. *See* byte-oriented protocol.

character printer \kâr´ək-tər prin`tər\ *n*. **1.** A printer that operates by printing one character at a time, such as a standard dot-matrix printer or a daisy-wheel printer. *Compare* line printer, page printer. **2.** A printer that cannot print graphics, such as a daisy-wheel printer or even a dot-matrix or laser printer that lacks a graphics mode. Such a printer simply receives character codes from the controlling system and prints the appropriate characters. *Compare* graphics printer.

character recognition \kâr`ək-tər rek-əg-nish´ən\ *n*. The process of applying pattern-matching methods to character shapes that have been read into a computer to determine which alphanumeric characters or punctuation marks the shapes represent. Because different typefaces and text treatments, such as bold and italic, can make big differences in the way characters are shaped, character recognition can be prone to error. Some systems work only with known typefaces and sizes, with no text treatments. These systems achieve very high accuracy levels, but they can work only with text specifically printed for them. Other systems use extremely sophisticated pattern-matching techniques to learn new typefaces and sizes, achieving fairly good accuracy. *See also* magnetic-ink character recognition, optical character recognition, pattern recognition (definition 1).

character rectangle \kâr´ək-tər rek`tang-l\ *n*. The space taken up by the graphical representation (bit map) of a character. See the illustration. *See also* bit map.

Character rectangle.

character set \kâr´ək-tər set`\ *n*. A grouping of alphabetic, numeric, and other characters that have some relationship in common. For example, the standard ASCII character set includes letters, numbers, symbols, and control codes that make up the ASCII coding scheme.

characters per inch \kâr`ək-tərz pər inch`\ *n*. A measurement for the number of characters of a particular size and font that can fit into a line one inch long. This number is affected by two attributes of the type: its point size and the width of the letters in the particular font being measured. In monospace fonts, characters have a constant width; in proportional fonts, characters have varying widths. Thus, measurements of the number of characters per inch must be averaged. *Acronym:* cpi (C`P-I´). *See also* monospace font, pitch (definition 1), proportional font.

characters per second \kâr`ək-tərz pər sek´ənd\ *n.* **1.** A measure of the speed of a nonlaser printer, such as a dot-matrix or an ink-jet printer. **2.** A measure of the rate at which a device, such as a disk drive, can transfer data. In serial communications, the speed of a modem in bits per second can generally be divided by 10 for a rough determination of the number of characters per second transmitted. *Acronym:* CPS (C`P-S´).

character string \kâr´ək-tər strēng`\ *n.* A set of characters treated as a unit and interpreted by a computer as text rather than numbers. A character string can contain any sequence of elements from a given character set, such as letters, numbers, control characters, and extended ASCII characters. *Also called* string. *See also* ASCII, control character, extended ASCII.

character style \kâr´ək-tər stīl`\ *n.* Any attribute, such as boldface, italic, underline, or small caps, applied to a character. Depending on the operating system or program considered, the range of character styles of text might or might not include the font, which refers to the design of a group of characters in a given size. *See also* font family.

character user interface \kâr`ək-tər yo͞o`zər in´tər-fās\ *n.* A user interface that displays only text characters. *Acronym:* CUI (C`U-I´). *See also* user interface. *Compare* graphical user interface.

charge \chärj\ *n.* A property of subatomic particles, which can have either a negative charge or a positive charge. In electronics, a charge consists of either an excess of electrons (a negative charge) or a deficiency of electrons (a positive charge). The unit of charge is the *coulomb,* which corresponds to 6.28×10^{18} electrons.

charge-coupled device \chärj`kə-pld də-vīs´\ *n.* A device in which individual semiconductor components are connected so that the electrical charge at the output of one device provides the input to the next. The light-detecting component of digital cameras and many video cameras is a charge-coupled device. *Acronym:* CCD (C`C-D´).

chart \chärt\ *n.* A graphic or diagram that displays data or the relationships between sets of data in pictorial rather than numeric form.

chassis \chas´ē\ *n.* A metal frame on which electronic components, such as printed circuit boards, fans, and power supplies, are mounted.

chat[1] \chat\ *n.* **1.** Real-time conversation via computer. When a participant types a line of text and then presses the Enter key, that participant's words appear on the screens of the other participants, who can then respond in kind. Most online services support chat; on the Internet, IRC is the usual system. *See also* IRC. **2.** An Internet utility program that supports chat. IRC has largely superseded it.

chat[2] \chat\ *vb.* To carry on a real-time conversation with other users by computer. *See also* IRC.

Cheapernet \chē´pər-net`\ *n. See* 10Base2.

check bit \chek´ bit\ *n.* One of a set of bits that are added to a data message at its origin and scrutinized by the receiving process to determine whether an error has occurred during transmission. The simplest example is a parity bit. *See also* data integrity, parity bit.

check box \chek´ boks\ *n.* An interactive control often found in graphical user interfaces. Check boxes are used to enable or disable one or more features or options from a set. When an option is selected, an × or a check mark appears in the box. See the illustration. *See also* control (definition 2). *Compare* radio button.

check digit \chek´ dij`it\ *n.* A digit added to an account number or other identifying key value and then recomputed when the number is used. This process determines whether an error occurred when the number was entered. *See also* checksum.

checkpoint \chek´point\ *n.* **1.** A processing juncture at which the normal operation of a program or system is momentarily suspended in order to determine its environmental status. **2.** A file containing information that describes the state of the system (the environment) at a particular time.

checksum \chek´sum\ *n.* A calculated value that is used to test data for the presence of errors that can occur when data is transmitted or when it is written to disk. The checksum is calculated for a

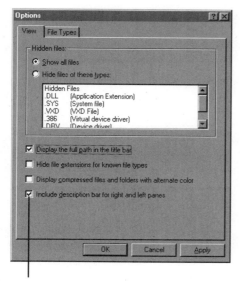

Check box

Check box.

given chunk of data by sequentially combining all the bytes of data with a series of arithmetic or logical operations. After the data is transmitted or stored, a new checksum is calculated in the same way using the (possibly faulty) transmitted or stored data. If the two checksums do not match, an error has occurred, and the data should be transmitted or stored again. Checksums cannot detect all errors, and they cannot be used to correct erroneous data. *See also* error-correction coding.

chiclet keyboard \chi´klət kē`bôrd\ *n.* A microcomputer keyboard used on the first version of the IBM PCjr home computer. Chiclet keys are small and square, resembling the chewing gum pieces, and they act like pushbuttons, without the resistance and clear feedback of traditional keys. They are also much smaller and typically are spread out, so touch typing is more difficult than on a conventional keyboard.

child \chīld\ *n.* **1.** A process initiated by another process (the parent). This initiating action is frequently called a *fork.* The parent process often sleeps (is suspended) until the child process stops executing. **2.** In a tree structure, the relationship of a node to its immediate predecessor. *See also* generation (definition 2), tree structure.

child directory \chīld´ dər-ek`tər-ē\ *n. See* subdirectory.

child menu \chīld´ men`yōō\ *n. See* submenu.

child process \chīld´ pros`es\ *n. See* child (definition 1).

chimes of doom \chīmz´ əv dōōm´\ *n.* In Macintosh computers, a series of chimes that sound as a result of serious system failure.

chip \chip\ *n. See* integrated circuit.

chip set \chip´ set\ *n.* A collection of chips designed to function as a unit in the performance of some common task. The term is most commonly used to refer to the set of integrated circuits, such as the programmable interrupt controller, that support a CPU together with the CPU itself. Often a chip set will fit on one chip. *See also* central processing unit, integrated circuit, programmable interrupt controller.

choke \chōk\ *n. See* inductor.

choose \chōōz\ *vb.* To pick a command or option from within a graphical user interface, as by clicking a button in a dialog box or pulling down a menu and then releasing the mouse button on one of its options. Although *select* is often used instead of *choose* to describe the same action, *choose* is the preferred term because *select* has specific connotations within computing. *See also* select.

Chooser \chōō´zər\ *n.* On the Apple Macintosh, a desk accessory that allows the user to select a printer or a device on a network, such as a file server or a printer.

Chooser extension \chōō´zər eks-ten`shən\ *n.* A program that adds items to the Macintosh Chooser desk accessory. At system startup, Chooser adds to its menu of options from the extensions available in the system extensions folder. For example, if you want to use a particular printer with your Mac OS, you must have the right Chooser extension for that printer in the extensions folder when the computer is turned on. *See also* Chooser, extension (definition 4).

chroma \krō´mə\ *n.* The quality of a color that combines hue and saturation. *See also* hue, saturation.

CHRP \C`H-R-P´\ *n. See* Common Hardware Reference Platform.

churn rate \churn´ rāt\ *n.* The rate of customer subscription turnover. In beeper, cell phone, and online businesses it is common for customers to drop their monthly subscriptions, creating a churn rate as high as 2 or 3 percent per month. High churn rates are costly to companies because attracting new subscribers through advertising and promotion is expensive.

.ci \dot`C-I´\ *n.* On the Internet, the major geographic domain specifying that an address is located in the Ivory Coast.

CIDR \C`I-D-R´\ *n. See* classless interdomain routing.

CIFS \C`I-F-S´\ *n. See* Common Internet File System.

CIM \C`I-M´\ *n.* **1.** Acronym for **c**omputer-**i**ntegrated **m**anufacturing. The use of computers, communication lines, and specialized software to automate both the managerial functions and the operational activities involved in the manufacturing process. A common database is used in all aspects of the process, from design through assembly, accounting, and resource management. Advanced CIM systems integrate computer-aided design and engineering (CAD/CAE), material requirements planning (MRP), and robotic assembly control to provide "paperless" management of the entire manufacturing process. **2.** Acronym for **c**omputer-**i**nput **m**icrofilm. A process in which information stored on microfilm is scanned and the data (both text and graphics) converted into codes that can be used and manipulated by a computer. Computer-input microfilm is similar to processes such as optical character recognition, in which images on paper are scanned and converted to text or graphics. *Compare* COM (definition 4).

.cincinnati.oh.us \dot-sin-sə-nat`ē-dot-O-H`dot-U-S´\ *n.* On the Internet, the major geographic domain specifying that an address is located in Cincinnati, Ohio, United States.

cipher \sī´fər\ *n.* **1.** A code. **2.** An encoded character. **3.** A zero.

circuit \sər´kət\ *n.* **1.** Any path that can carry electrical current. **2.** A combination of electrical components interconnected to perform a particular task. At one level, a computer consists of a single circuit; at another, it consists of hundreds of interconnected circuits.

circuit analyzer \sər´kət an-ə-lī´zər\ *n.* Any device for measuring one or more characteristics of an electrical circuit. Voltage, current, and resistance are the characteristics most commonly measured. Oscilloscopes are circuit analyzers.

circuit board \sər´kət bōrd`\ *n.* A flat piece of insulating material, such as epoxy or phenolic resin, on which electrical components are mounted and interconnected to form a circuit. Most modern circuit boards use patterns of copper foil to interconnect the components. The foil layers may be on one or both sides of the board and, in more advanced designs, in several layers within the board. A printed circuit board is one in which the pattern of copper foil is laid down by a printing process such as photolithography. See the illustration. *See also* board, printed circuit board.

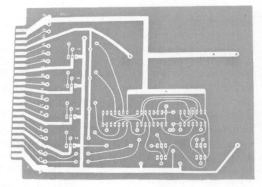

Circuit board.

circuit breaker \sər´kət brā´kər\ *n.* A switch that opens and cuts off the flow of current when the current exceeds a certain level. Circuit breakers are placed at critical points in circuits to protect against damage that could result from excessive current flow, which is typically caused by component failure. Circuit breakers are often used in place of fuses because they need only to be reset rather than replaced. *Compare* surge protector.

circuit card \sər´kət kärd\ *n. See* circuit board.

Circuit Data Services \sər´kət dā`tə sər´vi-səs, dat`ə\ *n.* A GTE service that uses circuit switching technology to provide fast data transfer using a laptop computer and cellular telephone. *Acronym:* CDS (C`D-S´). *See also* circuit switching.

circuit switching \sər´kət swich`ēng\ *n.* A method of opening communications lines, as through the telephone system, by creating a physical link between the initiating and receiving parties. In circuit switching, the connection is made at a switching center, which physically connects the two parties and maintains an open line between them for as long as needed. Circuit switching is typically used on the dial-up telephone network, and it is also used on a smaller scale in privately maintained communications networks. *Compare* message switching, packet switching.

circular list \sər`kyə-lər list´\ *n.* A linked or chained list in which processing continues through all items, as in a ring, and returns to the starting point, no matter where that point is located in the list. *See also* linked list.

CISC \sisk, C`I-S-C´\ *n.* Acronym for **c**omplex **i**nstruction **s**et **c**omputing. The implementation of complex instructions in a microprocessor design so that they can be invoked at the assembly language level. The instructions can be very powerful, allowing for complicated and flexible ways of calculating such elements as memory addresses. All this complexity, however, usually requires many clock cycles to execute each instruction. *Compare* RISC.

CIX \C`I-X´\ *n. See* Commercial Internet Exchange.

.ck \dot`C-K´\ *n.* On the Internet, the major geographic domain specifying that an address is located in the Cook Islands.

.cl \dot`C-L´\ *n.* On the Internet, the major geographic domain specifying that an address is located in Chile.

ClariNet \klar´ə-net\ *n.* A commercial service that distributes news articles from United Press International (UPI) and other news agencies in newsgroups that are part of the clari. hierarchy. Unlike most other newsgroups, access to the clari. newsgroups is restricted to Internet service providers who pay a subscription fee to ClariNet.

clari. newsgroups \klâr´i-dot nōōz`grōōps\ *n.* Internet newsgroups maintained by ClariNet Communications, Inc. ClariNet newsgroups contain news articles obtained from the Reuters and United Press International wire services, Sports-Ticker, Commerce Business Daily, and other sources. Unlike most other newsgroups, ClariNet groups are only accessible through Internet service providers who purchase the service. *See also* ClariNet, ISP, newsgroup.

class \klas\ *n.* In object-oriented programming, a generalized category that describes a group of more specific items, called *objects,* that can exist within it. A class is a descriptive tool used in a program to define a set of attributes or a set of services (actions available to other parts of the program) that characterize any member (object) of the class. Program classes are comparable in concept to the categories that people use to organize information about their world, such as *animal, vegetable,* and *mineral,* that define the types of entities they include and the ways those entities behave. The definition of classes in object-oriented programming is comparable to the definition of types in languages such as C and Pascal. *See also* object-oriented programming.

Class A network \klas` A` net´wərk\ *n.* An Internet network that can define a maximum of 16,777,215 hosts. Class A networks use the first byte of an IP address to designate the network, with the first (high-order) bit set to 0. The host is designated by the last 3 bytes. Class A addressing currently allows for a maximum of 128 networks. Class A networks are best suited for sites with few networks but numerous hosts and are usually designated for use by large government or educational institutions. *See also* host, IP address.

classless interdomain routing \klas`ləs in`tər-dō-mān´ rou`tēng, rōō`tēng\ *n.* An address scheme that uses aggregation strategies to minimize the size of top-level Internet routing tables. Routes are grouped with the objective of minimizing the quantity of information carried by core routers. The main requirement for this scheme is the use of routing protocols that support it, such as Border Gateway Protocol (BGP) Version 4 and RIP Version 2. *Acronym:* CIDR (C`I-D-R´). *See also* Border Gateway Protocol, communications protocol, RIP, router.

clean boot \klēn bōōt´\ *n.* Booting or starting a computer using the minimum system files in the operating system. The clean boot is used as a troubleshooting method for isolating problems associated with software that may be calling on the same system resources at the same time, causing conflicts that lower the performance of the system, make some programs inoperable, or crash the computer. *See also* boot[1], crash[2] (definition 1), operating system.

clean install \klēn` in-stäl´\ *n.* Reinstallation of software in a manner that ensures that no application or system files from a previous installation will remain. The procedure prevents "smart" installer programs from skipping file installations where a file already exists, which could potentially keep a problem from being removed.

clean interface \klēn` in´tər-fās\ *n.* A user interface with simple features and intuitive commands. *See also* user interface.

clean room \klēn´ ro͞om\ *n.* A room in which dust and other small particles are filtered from the air and in which protective clothing is worn to avoid contaminating electronic components and other delicate, sensitive equipment.

Clear key \klēr´ kē\ *n.* A key in the upper left corner of the numeric keypad on some keyboards. In many applications, it clears the currently selected menu choice or deletes the current selection.

Clear To Send \klēr` tə send´\ *n. See* CTS.

click \klik\ *vb.* To press and release a mouse button once without moving the mouse. Clicking is usually performed to select or deselect an item or to activate a program or program feature. *See also* right click. *Compare* double-click, drag.

clickable maps \klik`ə-bl maps´\ *n. See* image map.

click speed \klik´ spēd\ *n.* The maximum interval between the first and second time a user presses a button on a mouse or other pointing device that will still identify these actions as a double-click to the computer as opposed to two single-clicks. *See also* double-click, mouse, pointing device.

clickstream \klik´strēm\ *n.* The path a user takes while browsing a Web site. Each distinct selection made on a Web page adds one click to the stream. The further down the clickstream the user goes without finding the sought item, the more likely he or she is to depart to another Web site. Analysis of usage patterns helps Web site designers create user-friendly site structures, links, and search facilities. *See also* Web site.

client \klī´ənt\ *n.* **1.** In object-oriented programming, a member of a class (group) that uses the services of another class to which it is not related. *See also* inheritance (definition 1). **2.** A process, such as a program or task, that requests a service provided by another program—for example, a word processor that calls on a sort routine built into another program. The client process uses the requested service without having to "know" any working details about the other program or the service itself. *Compare* child (definition 1), descendant (definition 2). **3.** On a local area network or the Internet, a computer that accesses shared network resources provided by another computer (called a *server*). *See also* client/server architecture, server.

client error \klī´ənt âr`ər\ *n.* A problem reported by the Hypertext Transfer Protocol (HTTP) client module as the result of difficulty in interpreting a command or the inability to connect properly to a remote host.

client/server architecture \klī`ənt-sər-vər är´kə-tek-chur\ *n.* An arrangement used on local area networks that makes use of distributed intelligence to treat both the server and the individual workstations as intelligent, programmable devices, thus exploiting the full computing power of each. This is done by splitting the processing of an application between two distinct components: a "front-end" client and a "back-end" server. The client component is a complete, stand-alone personal computer (not a "dumb" terminal), and it offers the user its full range of power and features for running applications. The server component can be a personal computer, a minicomputer, or a mainframe that provides the traditional strengths offered by minicomputers and mainframes in a time-sharing environment: data management, information sharing between clients, and sophisticated network administration and security features. The client and server machines work together to accomplish the processing of the application being used. Not only does this increase the processing power available over older architectures but it also uses that power more efficiently. The client portion of the application is typically optimized for user interaction, whereas the server portion provides the centralized, multiuser functionality. *See also* distributed intelligence.

client-side image maps \klī`ənt-sīd im´əj maps\ *n.* A Web page user selection device whereby regions of an image can be clicked with the mouse to indicate user selections from a presented collection of options, comparable to clicking an icon of the desired item on a menu. Unlike the earliest Web implementation of image maps (circa 1993), client-side image maps do not transmit the mouse click coordinates to the Web server for processing, but perform the processing completely within the client program (i.e., Web browser) itself, generally improving the speed of response to the user. *See also* image map.

clip \klip\ *vb.* **1.** To cut off the portion of a displayed image that lies beyond a certain boundary, such as the edge of a window. Certain graphics programs also support clipping as a means of masking everything but a certain object so that painting tools, for example, can be applied to the object alone. **2.** To cut a photograph, drawing, or other illustrations from a clip art collection—either in a book or on a disk. *See also* clip art. **3.** To cut off the peaks of a signal in an electronic circuit.

clip art \klip´ärt\ *n.* A collection—either in a book or on a disk—of proprietary or public-domain photographs, diagrams, maps, drawings, and other such graphics that can be "clipped" from the collection and incorporated into other documents.

clipboard \klip´bōrd\ *n.* **1.** A special memory resource maintained by windowing operating systems. The clipboard stores a copy of the last information that was "copied" or "cut." A "paste" operation passes data from the clipboard to the current program. A clipboard allows information to be transferred from one program to another, provided the second program can read data generated by the first. Data copied using the clipboard is static and will not reflect later changes. *See also* cut and paste, DDE. *Compare* scrap. **2.** A computer that uses a pen as the primary input device. *See also* clipboard computer, pen computer.

clipboard computer \klip´bōrd kəm-pyōō`tər\ *n.* A portable computer whose overall appearance and operation resembles that of a traditional clipboard. A clipboard computer has an LCD or similar flat display and has a pen for user input instead of a keyboard, mouse, or other input device; the user operates it by touching the pen to the display.

Data entered in a clipboard computer is generally transferred to another computer via a cable or a modem. A clipboard computer is used as a traditional clipboard is used, as in field work, data collection, or meetings. *See also* pen computer, portable computer.

Clipper Chip \klip´ər chip`\ *n.* An integrated circuit that implements the SkipJack algorithm, an encryption algorithm created by the National Security Agency that encrypts 64-bit blocks of data with an 80-bit key. The Clipper is manufactured by the U.S. government to encrypt telephone data. It has the added feature that it can be decrypted by the U.S. government, which has tried unsuccessfully to make the chip compulsory in the United States. *See also* encryption.

clipping path \klip´ēng path`\ *n.* A polygon or curve that is used to mask an area in a document. Only what is inside the clipping path appears when the document is printed. *See also* PostScript.

clobber \klob´ər\ *vb.* To destroy data, generally by inadvertently writing other data over it.

clock \klok\ *n.* **1.** The electronic circuit in a computer that generates a steady stream of timing pulses—the digital signals that synchronize every operation. The system clock signal is precisely set by a quartz crystal, typically at a specific frequency between 1 and 50 megahertz. The clock rate of a computer is one of the prime determinants of its overall processing speed, and it can go as high as the other components of the computer allow. *Also called* system clock. **2.** The battery-backed circuit that keeps track of the time and date in a computer—not the same as the system clock. *Also called* clock/calendar.

clock/calendar \klok´kal`ən-dər\ *n.* An independent timekeeping circuit used within a microcomputer to maintain the correct time and calendar date. A clock/calendar circuit is battery powered, so it continues running even when the computer is turned off. The time and date kept by the clock/calendar can be used by the operating system (for example, to "stamp" files with the date and time of creation or revision) and by application programs (for example, to insert the date or time in a document). *Also called* clock, internal clock.

clock doubling \klok´ də`bl-ēng, də`blēng\ *n.* A technology employed by some Intel microprocessors that enables the chip to process data and instructions at twice the speed of the rest of the system. *See also* i486DX2.

clocking \klok´ēng\ *n. See* synchronization (definition 3).

clock pulse \klok´ puls\ *n.* An electronic pulse generated periodically by a crystal oscillator to synchronize the actions of a digital device.

clock rate \klok´ rāt\ *n.* The rate at which the clock in an electronic device, such as a computer, oscillates. The clock rate is normally given in hertz (Hz, one cycle per second), kilohertz (kHz, one thousand cycles per second), or megahertz (MHz, one million cycles per second). Clock rates in personal computers increased from about 5 MHz to about 50 MHz between 1981 and 1995. *Also called* clock speed, hertz time. *See also* clock (definition 1).

clock speed \klok´ spēd\ *n. See* clock rate.

clock tick \klok´ tik\ *n. See* CPU cycle (definition 2).

clone \klōn\ *n.* A copy; in microcomputer terminology, a look-alike, act-alike computer that contains the same microprocessor and runs the same programs as a better-known, more prestigious, and often more expensive machine.

close[1] \klōz\ *n.* An FTP command that instructs the client to close the current connection with a server. *See also* FTP[1] (definition 1), Web site.

close[2] \klōz\ *vb.* **1.** To end an application's relationship with an open file so that the application will no longer be able to access the file without opening it again. **2.** To end a computer's connection with another computer on a network.

close box \klōz´ boks\ *n.* In the Macintosh graphical user interface, a small box in the left corner of a window's title bar. Clicking on the box closes the window. *Compare* close button.

close button \klōz´ but`ən\ *n.* In the graphical user interface for Windows 95, Windows NT, and the X Window System, a square button in the right corner (left corner in X Windows) of a window's title bar with an × mark on it. Clicking on the button closes the window. *Also called* X button. *Compare* close box.

closed architecture \klōzd` är´kə-tek-chur\ *n.* **1.** Any computer design whose specifications are not freely available. Such proprietary specifica-

tions make it difficult or impossible for third-party vendors to create ancillary devices that work correctly with a closed-architecture machine; usually only its original maker can build peripherals and add-ons for such a machine. *Compare* open architecture (definition 1). **2.** A computer system that provides no expansion slots for adding new types of circuit boards within the system unit. The original Apple Macintosh was an example of a closed architecture. *Compare* open architecture (definition 2).

closed file \klōzd fīl´\ *n.* A file not being used by an application. An application must open such a file before reading or writing to it and must close it afterward. *Compare* open file.

closed shop \klōzd shop´\ *n.* A computer environment in which access to the computer is restricted to programmers and other specialists. *Compare* open shop.

closed system \klōzd` si´stəm\ *n. See* closed architecture (definition 2).

cloth ribbon \kloth` rib´ən\ *n.* An inked ribbon generally used with impact printers and typewriters. The print element strikes the ribbon and drives it against the paper so as to transfer ink; then the ribbon advances slightly to make fresh ink available. A cloth ribbon is wrapped onto a spool or loaded into a cartridge that is made to fit the printer used. Cloth ribbon, although adequate for most tasks, is sometimes replaced by film ribbon when the crispest possible output is called for. However, a cloth ribbon, which re-inks itself by capillary action, is usable for multiple impressions, unlike a film ribbon. *Compare* carbon ribbon.

cluster \klu´stər\ *n.* **1.** An aggregation, such as a group of data points on a graph. **2.** A communications computer and its associated terminals. **3.** In data storage, a disk-storage unit consisting of a fixed number of sectors (storage segments on the disk) that the operating system uses to read or write information; typically, a cluster consists of two to eight sectors, each of which holds a certain number of bytes (characters).

cluster controller \klu´stər kən-trō`lər\ *n.* An intermediary device that is situated between a computer and a group (cluster) of subsidiary devices, such as terminals on a network, and is used to control the cluster.

.cm \dot`C-M´\ *n.* On the Internet, the major geographic domain specifying that an address is located in Cameroon.

CMI \C`M-I´\ *n.* Acronym for **c**omputer-**m**anaged **i**nstruction. Any type of teaching that uses computers as educational tools. *See also* CAI, CBT.

CMOS \C`mos, C`M-O-S´\ *n.* **1.** Acronym for **c**omplementary **m**etal-**o**xide **s**emiconductor. A semiconductor technology in which pairs of metal-oxide semiconductor field effect transistors (MOSFETs), one N-type and the other P-type, are integrated on a single silicon chip. Generally used for RAM and switching applications, these devices have very high speed and extremely low power consumption. They are, however, easily damaged by static electricity. *See also* MOSFET, N-type semiconductor, P-type semiconductor. **2.** The battery-backed memory (presumably made with complementary metal-oxide semiconductor technology) used to store parameter values needed to boot IBM Personal Computers and compatibles, such as the type of disks and the amount of memory, as well as the clock/calendar time.

CMOS RAM \C`mos ram´, C`M-O-S`, R-A-M´\ *n.* Random access memory made using complementary metal-oxide semiconductor technology. CMOS chips consume extremely little power and have high tolerance for noise from the power supply. These characteristics make CMOS chips, including CMOS RAM chips, very useful in hardware components that are powered by batteries, such as most microcomputer clocks and certain types of scratch-pad RAM that are maintained by the operating system. *See also* CMOS (definition 1), parameter RAM, RAM.

CMOS setup \C`mos set´up, C`M-O-S`\ *n.* A system configuration utility, accessible at boot time, for setting up certain system options, such as the date and time, the kind of drives installed, and port configuration. *See also* CMOS (definition 2).

CMS \C`M-S´\ *n. See* color management system.

CMY \C`M-Y´\ *n.* Acronym for **c**yan-**m**agenta-**y**ellow. A model for describing colors that are produced by absorbing light, as by ink on paper, rather than by emitting light, as on a video monitor. The three kinds of cone cells in the eye respond to red, green, and blue light, which are absorbed (removed from white light) by cyan, magenta, and yellow pigments, respectively. Percentages of pigments in these subtractive primary colors can therefore be mixed to get the appearance of any desired color. Absence of any pigment leaves white unchanged; adding 100 percent of all three pigments turns white to black. *Compare* CMYK, RGB.

CMYK \C`M-Y-K´\ *n.* Acronym for **c**yan-**m**agenta-**y**ellow-blac**k**. A color model that is similar to the CMY color model but produces black with a separate black component rather than by adding 100 percent of cyan, magenta, and yellow. *See also* CMY.

.cn \dot`C-N´\ *n.* On the Internet, the major geographic domain specifying that an address is located in China.

.co \dot`C-O´\ *n.* On the Internet, the major geographic domain specifying that an address is located in Colombia.

coaxial cable \kō-aks`ē-əl kā´bl\ *n.* A two-conductor cable consisting of a center wire inside a grounded cylindrical shield, typically made of braided wire, that is insulated from the center wire. The shield prevents signals transmitted on the center wire from affecting nearby components and prevents external interference from affecting the signal carried on the center wire. See the illustration.

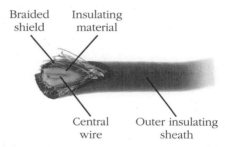

Braided shield   Insulating material

Central wire   Outer insulating sheath

Coaxial cable.

COBOL \kō´bol, C`O-B`O-L´\ *n.* Acronym for **Co**mmon **B**usiness-**O**riented **L**anguage. A verbose, English-like compiled programming language developed between 1959 and 1961 and still in widespread use today, especially in business applications typically run on mainframes. A COBOL program consists of an Identification Division, which specifies the name of the program and contains any other documentation the programmer wants to add; an Environment Division, which specifies the computer(s) being used and the files used in the program for input and output; a Data Division, which describes the format of the data structures used in the program; and a Procedure Division, which contains the procedures that dictate the actions of the program. *See also* compiled language.

cobweb site \kob´web sīt`\ *n.* A Web site that is far out of date. *See also* Web site.

CODASYL \kō´ də-sil`, C`O-D`A-S`Y-L´\ *n.* Acronym for **Co**nference on **Da**ta **Sy**stems **L**anguages. An organization founded by the U.S. Department of Defense. CODASYL is dedicated to the development of data-management systems and languages, among them the widely used COBOL business language.

code[1] \kōd\ *n.* **1.** Program instructions. Source code consists of human-readable statements written by a programmer in a programming language. Machine code consists of numerical instructions that the computer can recognize and execute and that were converted from source code. *See also* data, program. **2.** A system of symbols used to convert information from one form to another. A code for converting information in order to conceal it is often called a *cipher.* **3.** One of a set of symbols used to represent information.

code[2] \kōd\ *vb.* To write program instructions in a programming language. *See also* program.

codec \kō´dek\ *n.* **1.** Short for **co**der/**dec**oder. Hardware that can convert audio or video signals between analog and digital forms. **2.** Short for **co**mpressor/**dec**ompressor. Hardware or software that can compress and uncompress audio or video data. *See also* compress[2], uncompress. **3.** Hardware that combines the functions of definitions 1 and 2.

code conversion \kōd´ kən-vər`zhən\ *n.* **1.** The process of translating program instructions from one form into another. Code may be converted at the source-language level (for example, from C to Pascal), at the hardware-platform level (for example, from working on the IBM PC to working on the Apple Macintosh), or at the language level (for example, from source code in C to machine code). *See also* code[1] (definition 1). **2.** The process of transforming data from one representation to

another, such as from ASCII to EBCDIC or from two's complement to binary-coded decimal.

Code Division Multiple Access \kōd də-vizh`ən mul`tə-pl ak´ses\ *n.* A form of multiplexing in which the transmitter encodes the signal, using a pseudo-random sequence that the receiver also knows and can use to decode the received signal. Each different random sequence corresponds to a different communication channel. Motorola uses Code Division Multiple Access for digital cellular phones. *Acronym:* CDMA (C`D-M-A´). *Also called* spread spectrum. *See also* multiplexing, transmitter.

code page \kōd´ pāj\ *n.* In MS-DOS versions 3.3 and later, a table that relates the binary character codes used by a program to keys on the keyboard or to the appearance of characters on the display. Code pages are a means of providing support for character sets and keyboard layouts used in different countries. Devices such as the display and the keyboard can be configured to use a specific code page and to switch from one code page (such as United States) to another (such as Portugal) at the user's request.

coder \kō´dər\ *n. See* programmer.

code segment \kōd´ seg`mənt\ *n.* **1.** A memory segment containing program instructions. **2.** A named and segregated portion of a program's code typically performing a specific class of operations. Code segments in this sense are often loaded into memory as memory segments. The main program segment is kept in memory, and auxiliary segments are loaded only when they are required.

code snippet \kōd´ snip`ət\ *n.* **1.** In a graphical user interface, programming instructions embedded in a menu option or button defined by the user. The snippet—consisting of one or more lines of source code—determines what the option or button does when chosen or clicked on. **2.** A small piece of programming code that is part of a larger program. Usually the code snippet performs a specific function or task.

coding form \kō´dēng fōrm`\ *n.* A sheet of paper ruled with horizontal and vertical lines to aid in writing source code for older languages that have position-dependent syntax (such as FORTRAN). Most programmers now use graph paper if they use paper at all.

coercion \kō-ər´shən\ *n. See* cast.

coherence \kō-hēr´əns`\ *n.* **1.** In raster-scan technology, the assignment of the value of one pixel to the pixel next to it. **2.** In optics, the property of some electromagnetic waves of being in phase with one another, as in light from a laser.

cold boot \kōld´ bo͞ot\ *n.* A startup process that begins with turning on the computer's power. Typically, a cold boot involves some basic hardware checking by the system, after which the operating system is loaded from disk into memory. *See also* boot[1]. *Compare* warm boot.

cold fault \kōld´ fält, fôlt\ *n.* A fatal error that occurs immediately upon or shortly after startup as a result of the misalignment of components in the system. The process of running and shutting down any computer induces a series of thermal expansions and contractions in its internal components. Over time, these changes in the dimensions of components can create a microscopic crack in a chip or loosen a pin in a socket; thus, the system crashes when cold, but the problem seems to disappear after the machine is warm. For this reason some users leave the system unit (but not the monitor) of a computer running from day to day, rather than turning the machine on only when needed.

cold link \kōld´ lēnk\ *n.* A link established upon a request for data. Once the request is filled, the link is broken. The next time data is required, a link from the client to the server must be reestablished. In a client/server architecture cold links are useful when the linked item consists of a large amount of data. Dynamic Data Exchange (DDE), used in applications such as Microsoft Excel, uses cold links for data exchange. *See also* client/server architecture, DDE. *Compare* hot link.

cold start \kōld´ stärt\ *n. See* cold boot.

collaborative filtering \kə-lab`ər-ə-tiv fil´tər-ēng\ *n.* A means of deriving information from the experiences and opinions of a number of people. The term was coined by Doug Terry at Xerox PARC, who first used the technique by allowing users to annotate documents as they read them and to choose which documents to read next based not only on their content but also on what others wrote about them. A common use of collaborative filtering is the creation of lists of World Wide Web pages of interest to particular people; by documenting the experiences of several people, a list of interesting Web sites can be "filtered." Collaborative filtering is also used as a marketing research tool; by keeping a database of opinions and ratings regarding several products, researchers can predict which new products the people contributing to the database will like.

collapsed backbone \kə-lapsd` bak´bōn\ *n. See* backbone (definition 3).

collate \kō´lāt\ *vb.* In data handling, to merge items from two or more similar sets to create a combined set that maintains the order or sequence of items in the original sets.

collating sort \kō-lā´tēng sōrt`\ *n.* A sort that proceeds by continuous merging of two or more files to produce a certain sequence of records or data items.

collation sequence \kō-lā´shən sē`kwens\ *n.* The ordering relationship (sequence) among objects that is to be established by a collating sort. *See also* collating sort.

collector \kə-lek´tər`\ *n.* The region of a bipolar transistor into which charge carriers flow under normal operating conditions. The output of the transistor is usually taken from the collector. With respect to the base and emitter, the collector is positive in an NPN transistor and negative in a PNP transistor. *See also* NPN transistor, PNP transistor. *Compare* base (definition 3), emitter.

collision \kə-lizh´ən\ *n.* The result of two devices or network workstations trying to transmit signals at the exact same time on the same channel. The typical outcome is a garbled transmission.

collision detection \kə-lizh´ən də-tek`shən\ *n.* **1.** The process by which a node on a local area network monitors the communications line to determine when a collision has occurred; that is, when two nodes have attempted to transmit at the same time. Although network stations usually avoid collisions by monitoring the line and waiting for it to clear before transmitting, the method is not foolproof. When a collision does occur, the two nodes involved usually wait a random amount of time before attempting to retransmit. *See also* contention, CSMA/CD. **2.** The process by which a game or simulation program determines whether two objects on the screen are touching each other.

This is a time-consuming, often complicated procedure; some computers optimized for graphics and games, such as the Amiga, have special hardware built in specifically to detect collisions.

color \kə´lər\ *n*. In physics, the component of the human perception of light that depends on frequency. For light of a single frequency, color ranges from violet at the high-frequency end of the visible-light band (a small portion of the total electromagnetic spectrum) to red at the low-frequency end. In computer video, color is produced by a combination of hardware and software. Software manipulates combinations of bits that represent the distinct shades of color that are destined for particular positions on the screen (characters or individual dots, called pixels). The video adapter hardware translates these bits into electrical signals, which in turn control the brightnesses of different-colored phosphors at the corresponding positions on the screen of the monitor CRT. The user's eye unites the light from the phosphors to perceive a single color. *See also* color model, color monitor, CRT, HSB, monitor, RGB, video, video adapter.

color bits \kə´lər bits`\ *n*. A predetermined number of bits assigned to each displayable pixel that determine its color when it is displayed on a monitor. For example, two color bits are required for four colors; eight color bits are required for 256 colors. *See also* pixel image. *Compare* bit plane.

color box \kə´lər boks`\ *n*. In the Microsoft NT and Windows 95 Paint accessory, a graphic screen element in the form of a paint box that is used to select foreground and background colors.

color burst \kə´lər burst`\ *n*. A technique used to encode color in a composite video signal, originally developed so that black-and-white television monitors could display programs broadcast in color. The color burst consists of a combination of the red, green, and blue intensities (used by black-and-white displays) and two color-difference signals that determine separate red, green, and blue intensities (used by color displays). *See also* color look-up table.

color cycling \kə´lər sī´kl-ēng\ *n*. A technique used in computer graphics for changing the color of one or more pixels on the screen by changing the color palette used by the video adapter rather than by changing the color bits for each pixel. For example, to cause a red circle to fade away to a black background color, the program need only change the set of signal values corresponding to "red" in the video adapter's color look-up table, periodically making it darker until it matches the black background. At each step, the apparent color of the whole circle changes instantly; it appears to fade rather than to be painted over and over. The speed at which and the degree to which the circle fades are entirely up to the programmer.

Color/Graphics Adapter \kə-lər-graf´iks ə-dap`tər\ *n*. *See* CGA.

colorimeter \kəl`ər-im´i-tər\ *n*. A device that evaluates and identifies colors in terms of a standard set of synthesized colors.

color look-up table \kə´lər lŏŏk´up tā`bl\ *n*. A table stored in a computer's video adapter, containing the color signal values that correspond to the different colors that can be displayed on the computer's monitor. When color is displayed indirectly, a small number of color bits are stored for each pixel and are used to select a set of signal values from the color look-up table. *Also called* color map, color table, video look-up table. *See also* color bits, palette (definition 2), pixel.

color management \kə´lər man`əj-mənt\ *n*. In printing, the process of producing accurate, consistent color using any of a variety of output devices. Color management includes accurate conversion of RGB input from a scanner, camera, or monitor to CMYK output for a printer; application of a device profile for the printer or other output device on which the image will be reproduced; and allowance for environmental variations such as humidity and barometric pressure. *See also* CMYK, RGB.

color management system \kəl´ər man´əj-mənt si`stəm\ *n*. A technology developed by Kodak and licensed to many other software vendors that is designed to calibrate and match colors that appear on video monitors and computer monitors and those that appear in any printed form. *Acronym:* CMS (C`M-S´).

color map \kə´lər map´\ *n*. *See* color look-up table.

color model \kə´lər mod`əl\ *n*. Any method or convention for representing color in desktop publishing and graphic arts. In the graphic arts and printing fields, colors are often specified with the Pantone system. In computer graphics, colors can be described using any of several different color systems: HSB (hue, saturation, and brightness), CMY (cyan, magenta, and yellow), and RGB (red, green, and blue). *See also* CMY, HSB, Pantone Matching System, process color, RGB, spot color.

color monitor \kə`lər mon´i-tər\ *n*. A video display device designed to work with a video card or adapter to produce text or graphics images in color. A color monitor, unlike a monochrome display, has a screen coated internally with patterns of three phosphors that glow red, green, and blue when struck by an electron beam. To create colors such as yellow, pink, and orange, the three phosphors are lighted together in varying degrees. A video card that uses large groups of bits (6 or more) to describe colors and that generates analog (continuously variable) signals is capable of generating an enormous potential range of colors on a color monitor. *See also* color, color model, Cycolor.

color palette \kə`lər pal´it\ *n*. *See* palette (definition 1).

color plane \kə`lər plān`\ *n*. *See* bit plane.

color printer \kə`lər prin`tər\ *n*. A computer printer that can print full-color output. Most color printers can also produce black-and-white output.

color saturation \kə`lər sach-ər-ā`shən\ *n*. The amount of a hue contained in a color; the more saturation, the more intense the color. *See also* color model, HSB.

color scanner \kə`lər skan´ər\ *n*. A scanner that converts images to a digitized format and is able to interpret color. Depth of color depends on the scanner's bit depth—its ability to transform color into 8, 16, 24, or 32 bits. High-end color scanners, commonly used when output is to be printed, are able to encode information at a high resolution or number of dots per inch (dpi). Low-end color scanners encode information at a resolution of 72 dpi and are commonly used for computer screen images not intended for printing. See the illustration. *See also* resolution (definition 1), scanner.

color separation \kə`lər sep-ər-ā`shən\ *n*. **1.** The process of printing the colors in a document as separate output files, each of which is to be printed using a different-colored ink. There are

Color scanner.

two types of color separation: spot color separation and process color separation. *See also* color model, process color, spot color. **2.** One of the output files produced by a color document, to be printed in its own color of ink.

color table \kə`lər tā`bl\ *n*. *See* color look-up table.

.columbus.oh.us \dot-kə-lum`bus-dot-O-H`dot-U-S`\ *n*. On the Internet, the major geographic domain specifying that an address is located in Columbus, Ohio, United States.

column \kol`um\ *n*. **1.** A series of items arranged vertically within some type of framework—for example, a continuous series of cells running from top to bottom in a spreadsheet, a set of lines of specified width on a printed page, a vertical line of pixels on a video screen, or a set of values aligned vertically in a table or matrix. *Compare* row. **2.** In a relational database management system, the name for an attribute. The collection of column values that form the description of a particular entity is called a *tuple* or *row*. A column is equivalent to a field in a record in a nonrelational file system. *See also* entity, field (definition 1), row, table (definition 2).

column chart \kol`um chärt`\ *n*. A bar chart in which values are displayed and printed as vertical bars. See the illustration on the next page. *See also* bar chart.

.com \dot-kom´, -C`O-M´\ *n*. **1.** In the Internet's Domain Name System, the top-level domain that identifies addresses operated by commercial organizations. The domain name .com appears as a suffix at the end of the address. *See also* DNS (definition 1), domain (definition 3). *Compare* .edu, .gov, .mil, .net, .org. **2.** In MS-DOS, the file exten-

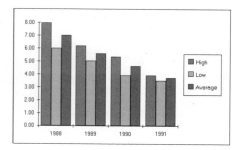

Column chart.

sion that identifies a command file. *See also* COM (definition 3).

COM \C`O-M´\ *n*. **1.** A name reserved by the MS-DOS operating system for serial communications ports. For example, if a modem is connected to one serial port and a serial printer to another, the devices are identified as COM1 and COM2 by the operating system. **2.** Acronym for **C**omponent **O**bject **M**odel. A specification developed by Microsoft for building software components that can be assembled into programs or add functionality to existing programs running on Microsoft Windows platforms. COM components can be written in a variety of languages, although most are written in C++, and can be unplugged from a program at run time without having to recompile the program. COM is the foundation of the OLE (object linking and embedding), ActiveX, and DirectX specifications. *See also* ActiveX, component (definition 2), DirectX, OLE. **3.** The extension reserved by MS-DOS for a type of executable binary (program) file limited to a single 64-kilobyte (KB) segment. COM files are often used for utility programs and short routines. They are not supported in OS/2. **4.** Acronym for **c**omputer-**o**utput **m**icrofilm. Microfilm that can record data from a computer.

COM1 \kom-wən´\ *n*. A serial communications port in Wintel systems. COM1 is usually specified by the I/O range 03F8H, is usually associated with interrupt request line IRQ4, and in many systems is used to connect an RS232 serial mouse. *See also* IRQ.

COM2 \kom-tōō´\ *n*. A serial communications port in Wintel systems. COM2 is usually specified by the I/O range 02F8H, is usually associated with interrupt request line IRQ3, and in many systems is used to connect a modem. *See also* IRQ.

COM3 \kom-thrē´\ *n*. A serial communications port in Wintel systems. COM3 is usually specified by the I/O range 03E8H, is usually associated with interrupt request line IRQ4, and in many systems is used as an alternative to COM1 or COM2 if the latter is being used by some other peripheral. *See also* IRQ.

combinatorial explosion \kom-bə-nə-tōr`ē-əl eks-plō´zhən\ *n*. A condition inherent in certain types of mathematical problems in which small increases in the problem's size (number of data items or parameters of the operation) lead to enormous increases in the time required to obtain a solution. *See also* combinatorics.

combinatorics \kom`bə-nə-tōr´iks\ *n*. A branch of mathematics related to probability and statistics, involving the study of counting, grouping, and arrangement of finite sets of elements. Combinatorics involves the two concepts of combinations and permutations. A combination is the grouping of elements taken from a larger set without regard to the order of the elements in each group; for example, taking two elements at a time from a set of four objects (A, B, C, and D) creates six combinations of objects: AB, AC, AD, BC, BD, and CD. A permutation is a grouping of elements taken from a larger set with regard to the order of the elements. For example, in making permutations of two objects from the same set of four objects, there would be four candidates to choose from for the first selection (A), and three left over to choose from for the second selection (B), or twelve permutations in all: AB, AC, AD, BA, BC, BD, CA, CB, CD, DA, DB, DC. *See also* combinatorial explosion.

COMDEX \kom´deks\ *n*. Any of a series of annual computer trade shows operated by Softbank COMDEX, Inc. One of these shows takes place in Las Vegas each November and is the largest computer trade show in the United States.

Comité Consultatif International Télégraphique et Téléphonique \kō-mē-tā` kōn-sōōl-tä-tēf` an-târ-nä-sē-ō-näl` tā`lā-grä-fēk` ā tā`lā-fō-nēk`\ *n*. *Also called* International Telegraph and Telephone Consultative Committee. *See* CCITT.

comma-delimited file \kom`ə-də-lim`ə-təd fīl´\ *n*. A data file consisting of fields and records, stored as text, in which the fields are separated from each other by commas. Use of comma-delimited files allows communication between database systems that use different formats. If the data in a field contains a comma, the field is further surrounded with quotation marks.

command \kə-mand´\ *n.* An instruction to a computer program that, when issued by the user, causes an action to be carried out. Commands are usually either typed at the keyboard or chosen from a menu.

command buffer \kə-mand´ buf`ər\ *n.* An area in memory in which commands entered by the user are kept. A command buffer can enable the user to repeat commands without retyping them completely, edit past commands to change some argument or correct a mistake, undo commands, or obtain a list of past commands. *See also* history, template (definition 4).

command button \kə-mand´ but`ən\ *n.* A control shaped like a pushbutton in a dialog box in a graphical user interface. By clicking a command button, the user causes the computer to perform some action, such as opening a file that has just been selected using the other controls in the dialog box.

COMMAND.COM \kə-mand´dot-kom`, kə-mand´-dot-C-O-M`\ *n.* The command interpreter for MS-DOS. *See also* command interpreter.

command-driven \kə-mand´driv`ən\ *adj.* Accepting commands in the form of code words or letters, which the user must learn. *Compare* menu-driven.

command-driven system \kə-mand´driv-ən si`stəm\ *n.* A system in which the user initiates operations by a command entered from the console. *Compare* graphical user interface.

command interpreter \kə-mand´ in-tər`prə-tər\ *n.* A program, usually part of the operating system, that accepts typed commands from the keyboard and performs tasks as directed. The command interpreter is responsible for loading applications and directing the flow of information between applications. In OS/2 and MS-DOS, the command interpreter also handles simple functions, such as moving and copying files and displaying disk directory information. *See also* shell[1].

Command key \kə-mand´ kē`\ *n.* On the original Macintosh keyboard, a key labeled with the spe-

cial symbol, sometimes called the propeller or puppy foot ⌘. This key is found on one or both sides of the Spacebar, depending on the version of the Apple keyboard. The key serves some of the same functions as the Control key on IBM keyboards. *See also* Control key.

command language \kə-mand´ lang`wəj\ *n.* The set of keywords and expressions that are accepted as valid by the command interpreter. *See also* command interpreter.

command line \kə-mand´ līn`\ *n.* A string of text written in the command language and passed to the command interpreter for execution. *See also* command language.

command-line interface \kə-mand`līn in´tər-fās\ *n.* A form of interface between the operating system and the user in which the user types commands, using a special command language. Although systems with command-line interfaces are usually considered more difficult to learn and use than those with graphical interfaces, command-based systems are usually programmable; this gives them flexibility unavailable in graphics-based systems that do not have a programming interface. *Compare* graphical user interface.

command mode \kə-mand´ mōd`\ *n.* A mode of operation in which a program waits for a command to be issued. *Compare* edit mode, insert mode.

command processing \kə-mand´ pros`es-ēng\ *n.* *See* command-driven system.

command processor \kə-mand´ pros`es-ər\ *n.* *See* command interpreter.

command shell \kə-mand´ shel\ *n.* *See* shell[1].

command state \kə-mand´ stāt`\ *n.* The state in which a modem accepts commands, such as a command to dial a telephone number. *Compare* online state.

comment \kom´ent\ *n.* Text embedded in a program for documentation purposes. Comments usually describe what the program does, who wrote it, why it was changed, and so on. Most programming languages have a syntax for creating comments so that they can be recognized and ignored by the compiler or assembler. *Also called* remark. *See also* comment out.

comment out \kom`ent out´\ *vb.* To disable one or more lines of code from a program temporarily by enclosing them within a comment statement. *See also* comment, conditional compilation, nest.

commerce server \kom´ərs sər`vər\ *n.* An HTTP server designed for conducting online business transactions. Data is transferred between the server and Web browser in an encrypted form to keep information such as credit card numbers reasonably secure. Commerce servers are typically used by online stores and companies that are set up for mail order business. The wares or services offered by the store or company are described and displayed in photographs on the store or company Web site, and users can order directly from the site, using their Web browser. A number of companies market commerce servers, including Netscape, Microsoft, and Quarterdeck. *See also* HTTP server (definition 1), Secure Sockets Layer, Web browser.

commercial access provider \kə-mər`shəl ak´ses prə-vī`dər\ *n. See* ISP.

Commercial Internet Exchange \kə-mər`shəl in´tər-net eks-chānj`\ *n.* A nonprofit trade organization of public Internet service providers. In addition to the usual representational and social activities, CIX also operates an Internet backbone router that is accessible to its members. *Acronym:* CIX (C`I-X´). *See also* backbone (definition 1), ISP, router.

Common Access Method \kom`ən ak´ses meth`əd\ *n.* A standard developed by Future Domain and other SCSI vendors allowing SCSI adapters to communicate with SCSI peripherals regardless of the particular hardware used. *See also* SCSI.

common carrier \kom`ən kâr´ē-ər\ *n.* A communications company (e.g., a telephone company) that provides service to the public and is regulated by governmental organizations.

Common Client Interface \kom`ən klī´ənt in´tər-fās\ *n.* A control interface begun with the X Windows version of NCSA Mosaic whereby other programs can control the local copy of a Web browser. The X Windows and Windows versions of NCSA Mosaic can communicate with other programs via TCP/IP. The Windows version is also capable of OLE communication. *Acronym:* CCI (C`C-I´). *See also* Mosaic, OLE, TCP/IP, X Window System.

Common Gateway Interface \kom`ən gāt`wā in´tər-fās\ *n. See* CGI (definition 1).

Common Hardware Reference Platform \kom`ən härd`wâr re´frəns plat`förm\ *n.* A specification describing a family of machines, based on the PowerPC processor, that are capable of booting multiple operating systems, including Mac OS, Windows NT, AIX, and Solaris. *Acronym:* CHRP (C`H-R-P´). *See also* PowerPC.

Common Internet File System \kom`ən in`tər-net fīl´ si`stəm\ *n.* A standard proposed by Microsoft that would compete directly with Sun Microsystems' Web Network File System. A system of file sharing of Internet or intranet files. *Acronym:* CIFS (C`I-F-S´).

Common LISP \kom`ən lisp´, L`I-S-P´\ *n.* Short for **Common Lis**t **P**rocessing. A formalized and standardized version of the LISP programming language. Because LISP is in the public domain, a number of different versions of the language have evolved, and Common LISP was made a standard to give programmers a definitive source for LISP. *See also* LISP, programming language, standard (definition 1).

Common Object Request Broker Architecture \kom`ən ob-jekt rə-kwest` brō-kər är´kə-tek-chur\ *n. See* CORBA.

Common User Access \kom`ən yo͞o-zər ak´ses\ *n.* A set of standards for management of user interfaces as part of IBM's Systems Application Architecture (SAA). Common User Access is designed to facilitate development of applications that are compatible and consistent across different platforms. *Acronym:* CUA (C`U-A´). *See also* standard (definition 1), user interface.

communications \kə-myo͞o-nə-kā´shənz\ *n.* The vast discipline encompassing the methods, mechanisms, and media involved in information transfer. In computer-related areas, communications involves data transfer from one computer to another through a communications medium, such as a telephone, microwave relay, satellite link, or physical cable. Two primary methods of computer communications exist: temporary connection of two computers through a switched network, such as the public telephone system, and permanent or semipermanent linking of multiple workstations or computers in a network. The line between the two is indistinct, however, because microcomputers equipped with modems are often used to access both privately owned and public-access network computers. *See also* asynchronous transmission, CCITT, channel (definition 2), communications protocol, IEEE, ISDN, ISO/OSI model, LAN, modem, network, synchronous transmission. *Compare* data transmission, telecommunications, teleprocess.

Communications Act of 1934 \kə-myōō-nə-kā´-shənz akt əv nīn`tēn-thər-tē-fōr´\ *n. See* FCC.

communications channel \kə-myōō-nə-kā´shənz chan`əl\ *n. See* channel (definition 2).

communications controller \kə-myōō-nə-kā´-shənz kən-trō`lər\ *n.* A device used as an intermediary in transferring communications to and from the host computer to which it is connected. By relieving the host computer of the actual tasks of sending, receiving, deciphering, and checking transmissions for errors, a communications controller helps to make efficient use of the host computer's processing time—time that might be better used for noncommunications tasks. A communications controller can be either a programmable machine in its own right or a nonprogrammable device designed to follow certain communications protocols. *See also* front-end processor (definition 2).

communications link \kə-myōō-nə-kā´shənz lēnk`\ *n.* The connection between computers that enables data transfer.

communications network \kə-myōō-nə-kā´shənz net`wərk\ *n. See* network.

communications parameter \kə-myōō-nə-kā´-shənz pər-am`ə-tər\ *n.* Any of several settings required in order to enable computers to communicate. In asynchronous communications, for example, modem speed, number of data bits and stop bits, and type of parity are parameters that must be set correctly to establish communication between two modems.

communications port \kə-myōō-nə-kā´shənz pōrt`\ *n. See* COM (definition 1).

communications program \kə-myōō-nə-kā´shənz prō`gram\ *n.* A software program that enables a computer to connect with another computer and to exchange information. For initiating communications, communications programs perform such tasks as maintaining communications parameters, storing and dialing phone numbers automatically,

recording and executing logon procedures, and repeatedly dialing busy lines. Once a connection is made, communications programs can also be instructed to save incoming messages on disk or to find and transmit disk files. During communication, these types of programs perform the major, and usually invisible, tasks of encoding data, coordinating transmissions to and from the distant computer, and checking incoming data for transmission errors.

communications protocol \kə-myōō-nə-kā´shənz prō`tə-kol\ *n.* A set of rules or standards designed to enable computers to connect with one another and to exchange information with as little error as possible. The protocol generally accepted for standardizing overall computer communications is a seven-layer set of hardware and software guidelines known as the OSI (Open Systems Interconnection) model. A somewhat different standard, widely used before the OSI model was developed, is IBM's SNA (Systems Network Architecture). The word *protocol* is often used, sometimes confusingly, in reference to a multitude of standards affecting different aspects of communication, such as file transfer (for example, XMODEM and ZMODEM), handshaking (for example, XON/XOFF), and network transmissions (for example, CSMA/CD). *See also* ISO/OSI model, SNA.

communications satellite \kə-myōō-nə-kā´shənz sat`ə-līt\ *n.* A satellite stationed in geosynchronous orbit that acts as a microwave relay station, receiving signals sent from a ground-based station (earth station), amplifying them, and retransmitting them on a different frequency to another ground-based station. Initially used for telephone and television signals, communications satellites can also be used for high-speed transmission of computer data. Two factors affecting the use of satellites with computers, however, are propagation delay (the time lag caused by the distance traveled by the signal) and security concerns. *See also* downlink, uplink.

communications server \kə-myōō-nə-kā´shənz sər`vər\ *n.* A gateway that translates packets on a local area network (LAN) into asynchronous signals, such as those used on telephone lines or in RS-232-C serial communications, and allows all nodes on the LAN access to its modems or

RS-232-C connections. *See also* gateway, RS-232-C standard.

communications slot \kə-myōō-nə-kā´shənz slot`\ *n.* On many models of the Apple Macintosh, a dedicated expansion slot for network interface cards. *Acronym:* CS (C-S´).

communications software \kə-myōō-nə-kā´shənz soft`wâr\ *n.* The software that controls the modem in response to user commands. Generally such software includes terminal emulation as well as file transfer facilities. *See also* modem, terminal emulation.

communications system \kə-myōō-nə-kā´shənz si`stəm\ *n.* The combination of hardware, software, and data transfer links that make up a communications facility.

Communications Terminal Protocol \kə-myōō-nə-kā´shənz tər´mə-nəl prō`tə-kol\ *n.* A terminal protocol that enables a user at a remote location to access a computer as if the remote computer were directly connected (hardwired) to the computer. *Acronym:* CTERM (C´tərm, C`T-E-R-M´).

compact disc \kom`pakt disk´\ *n.* **1.** An optical storage medium for digital data, usually audio. A compact disc is a nonmagnetic, polished metal disc with a protective plastic coating that can hold up to 74 minutes of high-fidelity recorded sound. The disk is read by an optical scanning mechanism that uses a high-intensity light source, such as a laser, and mirrors. See the illustration. *Acronym:* CD (C-D´). *Also called* optical disc. **2.** A technology that forms the basis of media such as CD-ROM, CD-ROM/XA, CD-I, CD-R, DVI, and PhotoCD. These media are all compact disc–based but store various types of digital information and have different read/write capabilities. Documentation for compact disc formats can be found in books designated by the color of their covers. For example, documentation for audio compact discs is found in the Red Book. *See also* CD-I, CD-R, CD-ROM, CD-ROM/XA, DVI, Green Book (definition 2), Orange Book (definition 2), PhotoCD, Red Book (definition 2).

compact disc–erasable \kom`pakt disk` ər-â´sə-bl\ *n.* A technological improvement in compact discs whereby information can be repeatedly changed on the CD. Contemporary CDs are "write once, read many," in that the information origi-

Compact disc.

nally written cannot be changed, but can only be appended to. *Acronym:* CD-E (C`D-E´).

compact disc–interactive \kom`pakt disk` in-tər-ak´tiv\ *n. See* CD-I.

compact disc player \kom`pakt disk´ plā-ər\ *n.* A device that reads the information stored on a compact disc. A compact disc player contains the optical equipment necessary for reading a disc's contents and the electronic circuitry for interpreting the data as it is read.

compact disc–recordable and erasable \kom`pakt disk` rə-kōr`də-bl ənd ər-ā´sə-bl\ *adj.* Of or pertaining to hardware and software for interfacing computers with both compact disc–recordable and compact disc–erasable devices. *See also* compact disc–recordable.

compact disc–rewritable \kom`pakt disk` rē-rī´tə-bl\ *n.* The technology, equipment, software, and media used in the production of multiple-write compact discs. *Acronym:* CD-RW (C`D-R-W´).

compaction \kəm-pak´shən\ *n.* The process of gathering and packing the currently allocated regions of memory or auxiliary storage into as small a space as possible, so as to create as much continuous free space as possible. *Compare* dispersion, file fragmentation (definition 1).

compact model \kom`pakt mod´əl\ *n.* A memory model of the Intel 80x86 processor family. The compact model allows only 64 kilobytes (KB) for the code of a program but up to 1 megabyte (MB) for the program's data. *See also* memory model.

comparator \kəm-pâr´-ə-tər\ *n.* A device for comparing two items to determine whether they are equal. In electronics, for example, a comparator is a circuit that compares two input voltages and indicates which is higher.

compare \kəm-pâr´\ *vb.* To check two items, such as words, files, or numeric values, so as to determine whether they are the same or different. In a program, the outcome of a compare operation often determines which of two or more actions is taken next.

compatibility \kəm-pat`ə-bil´ə-tē\ *n.* **1.** The degree to which a computer, an attached device, a data file, or a program can work with or understand the same commands, formats, or language as another. True compatibility means that any operational differences are invisible to people and programs alike. **2.** The extent to which two machines can work in harmony. Compatibility (or the lack thereof) between two machines indicates whether, and to what degree, the computers can communicate, share data, or run the same programs. For example, an Apple Macintosh and an IBM PC are generally incompatible because they cannot communicate freely or share data without the aid of hardware and/or software that functions as an intermediary or a converter. **3.** The extent to which a piece of hardware conforms to an accepted standard (for example, IBM-compatible or Hayes-compatible). In this sense, compatibility means that the hardware ideally operates in all respects like the standard on which it is based. **4.** In reference to software, harmony on a task-oriented level among computers and computer programs. Computers deemed software-compatible are those that can run programs originally designed for other makes or models. Software compatibility also refers to the extent to which programs can work together and share data. In another area, totally different programs, such as a word processor and a drawing program, are compatible with one another if each can incorporate images or files created using the other. All types of software compatibility become increasingly important as computer communications, networks, and program-to-program file transfers become near-essential aspects of microcomputer operation. *See also* downward compatibility, upward-compatible.

compatibility box \kəm-pat`ə-bil´ə-tē boks`\ *n.* *See* DOS box (definition 1).

compatibility mode \kəm-pat`ə-bil´ə-tē   mōd`\ *n.* A mode in which hardware or software in one system supports operations of software from another system. The term often refers to the ability of advanced operating systems designed for Intel microprocessors (for example, OS/2 and Windows NT) to run MS-DOS software or to the ability of some UNIX workstations and of some Apple Macintosh systems to run MS-DOS software.

compile \kəm-pīl´\ *vb.* To translate all the source code of a program from a high-level language into object code prior to execution of the program. Object code is executable machine code or a variation of machine code. More generally, *compiling* is sometimes used to describe translating any high-level symbolic description into a lower-level symbolic or machine-readable format. A program that performs this task is known as a *compiler. See also* compile time, compiler (definition 2), high-level language, machine code, source code. *Compare* interpret.

compile-and-go \kəm-pīl`ənd-gō´\ *adj.* Of, pertaining to, or characteristic of a development environment that automatically runs a program after compiling it. *See also* compile, execute.

compiled Basic \kəm-pīld` bā´sik, B-A-S-I-C´\ *n.* Any version of Basic that is translated into machine code prior to execution by a compiler. Basic has traditionally been an interpreted language (translated and executed statement by statement); because compiled Basic generally produces faster-executing programs, it is the technology of choice for professional Basic programmers. *See also* Basic, compiled language, interpreted language.

compiled language \kəm-pīld` lang´wəj\ *n.* A language that is translated into machine code prior to any execution, as opposed to an interpreted language, which is translated and executed statement by statement. *See also* compiler (definition 2). *Compare* interpreted language.

compiler \kəm-pī´lər\ *n.* **1.** Any program that transforms one set of symbols into another by following a set of syntactic and semantic rules. **2.** A program that translates all the source code of a program written in a high-level language into object code prior to execution of the program. *See also* assembler, compile, high-level language, interpreted language, language processor, object code.

compile time \kəm-pīl´ tīm`\ *n.* **1.** The amount of time required to perform a compilation of a program. Compile time can range from a fraction of a second to many hours, depending on the size and complexity of the program, the speed of the compiler, and the performance of the hardware. *See also* compiler (definition 2). **2.** The point at which a program is being compiled (i.e., most languages evaluate constant expressions at compile time but evaluate variable expressions at run time). *See also* link time, run time.

compile-time binding \kəm-pīl´tīm bīn`dēng\ *n.* Assignment of a meaning to an identifier (such as a function name or a constant) in a program at the time the program is compiled rather than at the time it is run. *Compare* run-time binding.

complement \kom´plə-ment`\ *n.* Loosely, a number that can be thought of as the "mirror image" of another number written to the same base, such as base 10 or base 2. Complements are commonly used to represent negative numbers. Two types of complements are encountered in computer-related contexts: radix-minus-1 complements and true complements. A radix-minus-1 complement is known in the decimal system as a nine's complement and in the binary system as a one's complement. True complements are known in the decimal system as ten's complement and in binary as two's complement—a form commonly used to represent negative numbers in processing. *See also* complementary operation, nine's complement, one's complement, ten's complement, two's complement.

complementary metal-oxide semiconductor \kom-plə-men`tər-ē met-əl-oks`īd sem´ī kən-duk`tər, sem´ē kən-duk`tər\ *n.* *See* CMOS.

complementary operation \kom-plə-men`tər-ē op`ər-ā´shən\ *n.* In Boolean logic, an operation that produces the opposite result from that of another operation performed on the same data. For example, if A is true, NOT A (its complement) is false. *See also* Boolean algebra.

completeness check \kəm-plēt´nəs chek`\ *n.* A survey to determine that all data required in a record is present. *Compare* consistency check.

complex instruction set computing \kom-pleks` in-struk`shən set kəm-pyōō´tēng\ *n.* *See* CISC.

complex number \kom`pleks num´bər\ *n.* A number of the form $a + bi,$ where a and b are real numbers and i is the square root of -1, called the imaginary unit. Complex numbers can be plotted as points on a two-dimensional plane called the complex plane. The a number is plotted along the plane's horizontal axis (the real axis), and the b number is plotted along the vertical axis (the imaginary axis). *Compare* real number.

comp. newsgroups \komp`dot nōōz`grōōps\ *n.* Usenet newsgroups that are part of the comp. hierarchy and have the prefix comp. These newsgroups are devoted to discussions of computer hardware, software, and other aspects of computer science. Comp. newsgroups are one of the seven original Usenet newsgroup hierarchies. The other six are misc., news., rec., sci., soc., and talk. *See also* newsgroup, traditional newsgroup hierarchy, Usenet.

component \kəm-pō´nənt\ *n.* **1.** A discrete part of a larger system or structure. **2.** An individual modular software routine that has been compiled and dynamically linked, and is ready to use with other components or programs. *See also* compile, component software, link (definition 1), program, routine.

Component Object Model \kəm-pō`nənt ob´jekt mod`əl\ *n.* *See* COM (definition 2).

component software \kəm-pō`nənt soft´wâr\ *n.* Modular software routines, or components, that can be combined with other components to form an overall program. A programmer can use and reuse an existing component and not have to understand its inner workings, just how to have another program or component call it and pass data to and from it. *Also called* componentware. *See also* component, program, routine.

componentware \kəm-pō´nənt-wâr`\ *n.* *See* component software.

COM port or **comm port** \kom´ pōrt\ *n.* Short for **com**munications **port**, the logical address assigned by MS-DOS (versions 3.3 and higher) and Microsoft Windows (including Windows 95 and Windows NT) to each of the four serial ports on an IBM Personal Computer or a PC compatible. COM ports also have come to be known as the actual serial ports on a PC's CPU where peripherals, such as printers, scanners, and external modems, are plugged in. See the illustration. *See also* COM (definition 1), input/ output port, serial port.

COM port.

composite display \kəm-poz´it di-splā`\ *n*. A display, characteristic of television monitors and some computer monitors, that is capable of extracting an image from a composite signal (also called an *NTSC signal*). A composite display signal carries on one wire not only the coded information required to form an image on the screen but also the pulses needed to synchronize horizontal and vertical scanning as the electron beam sweeps back and forth across the screen. Composite displays can be either monochrome or color. A composite color signal combines the three primary video colors (red, green, and blue) in a color burst component that determines the shade of color displayed on the screen. Composite color monitors are less readable than either monochrome monitors or the RGB color monitors that use separate signals (and wires) for the red, green, and blue components of the image. *See also* color burst, color monitor, monochrome display, NTSC, RGB monitor.

composite key \kəm-poz´it kē`\ *n*. A key whose definition consists of two or more fields in a file, columns in a table, or attributes in a relation.

composite video display \kəm-poz´it vid´ē-ō di-splā`\ *n*. A display that receives all encoded video information (including color, horizontal synchronization, and vertical synchronization) in one signal. A composite video signal under NTSC (National Television System Committee) standards is generally required for television sets and videotape recorders. *See also* NTSC. *Compare* RGB monitor.

compound statement \kom`pound stāt´mənt\ *n*. A single instruction composed of two or more individual instructions.

compress[1] \kəm-pres´\ *n*. A proprietary UNIX utility for reducing the size of data files. Files com-

pressed with this utility have the extension .Z added to their names.

compress[2] \kəm-pres´\ *vb*. To reduce the size of a set of data, such as a file or a communications message, so that it can be stored in less space or transmitted with less bandwidth. Data can be compressed by removing repeated patterns of bits and replacing them with some form of summary that takes up less space; restoring the repeated patterns decompresses the data. Lossless compression methods must be used for text, code, and numeric data files; lossy compression may be used for video and sound files. *See also* lossless compression, lossy compression.

compressed digital video \kəm-presd` dij`i-təl vid´ē-ō\ *n*. *See* CDV (definition 1).

compressed disk \kəm-presd` disk´\ *n*. A hard disk or floppy disk whose apparent capacity to hold data has been increased through the use of a compression utility, such as Stacker or Double Space. *See also* data compression.

compressed drive \kəm-presd` drīv´\ *n*. A hard disk whose apparent capacity has been increased through the use of a compression utility, such as Stacker or Double Space. *See also* compressed disk, data compression.

compressed file \kəm-presd` fīl´\ *n*. A file whose contents have been compressed by a special utility program so that it occupies less space on a disk or other storage device than in its uncompressed (normal) state. *See also* installation program, LHARC, PKUNZIP, PKZIP, utility program.

Compressed SLIP \kəm-presd` slip´, S-L-I-P´\ *n*. Short for **Compressed S**erial **L**ine **I**nternet **P**rotocol. A version of SLIP using compressed Internet address information, thereby making the protocol faster than SLIP. *Acronym:* CSLIP (C´slip, C`S-L-I-P´). *See also* SLIP.

compression \kəm-presh´ən`\ *n*. *See* data compression.

compressor \kəm-pres´ər`\ *n*. A device that limits some aspect of a transmitted signal, such as volume, in order to increase efficiency.

CompuServe \kom´pyōō-sərv`\ *n*. An online information service that provides information and communications capabilities, including Internet access. It is primarily known for its technical support forums for commercial hardware and software products and for being one of the first large commercial online services. CompuServe also operates various private network services.

computation-bound \kom-pyo͞o-tā´shən bound`\ *adj.* Of, pertaining to, or characteristic of a situation in which the performance of a computer is limited by the number of arithmetic operations the microprocessor must perform. When a system is computation-bound, the microprocessor is overloaded with calculations. *Also called* CPU-bound.

compute \kəm-pyo͞ot´\ *vb.* **1.** To perform calculations. **2.** To use a computer or cause it to do work.

computer \kəm-pyo͞o´tər\ *n.* Any machine that does three things: accepts structured input, processes it according to prescribed rules, and produces the results as output. Ways to categorize computers are described in the table. *See also* analog, digital (definition 2), integrated circuit, large-scale integration, very-large-scale integration.

computer-aided design \kəm-pyo͞o`tər-ā-dəd də-zīn´\ *n. See* CAD.

computer-aided design and drafting \kəm-pyo͞o`-tər-ā`dəd dē-sīn` ənd draf´tēng\ *n.* A system of hardware and software similar to CAD but with additional features related to engineering conventions, including the ability to display dimension specifications and other notes. *Acronym:* CADD (C`A-D-D´, kad-D´). *See also* CAD.

computer-aided design/computer-aided manufacturing \kəm-pyo͞o`tər-ā-dəd də-zīn` kəm-pyo͞o`tər-ā-dəd man-yə-fak´chur-ēng\ *n. See* CAD/CAM.

computer-aided engineering \kəm-pyo͞o`tər-ā-dəd en`jə-nēr´ēng\ *n. See* CAE.

computer-aided instruction \kəm-pyo͞o`tər-ā-dəd in-struk´shən\ *n. See* CAI.

computer-aided manufacturing \kəm-pyo͞o`tər-ā-dəd man`yə-fak´chur-ēng\ *n. See* CAM (definition 1).

computer-aided testing \kəm-pyo͞o`tər-ā-dəd te´stēng\ *n. See* CAT (definition 1).

Computer and Business Equipment Manufacturers Association \kəm-pyo͞o´tər and biz´nis ə-kwip`mənt man`yə-fak´chur-ərz ə-sō-sē-ā`shən\ *n. See* CBEMA.

computer art \kəm-pyo͞o´tər ärt`\ *n.* A broad term that can refer either to art created on a computer or to art generated by a computer, the difference being whether the artist is human or electronic. When created by human beings, computer art is done with painting programs that offer a range of line-drawing tools, brushes, shapes, patterns, and colors. Some programs also offer predrawn figures and animation capabilities.

computer-assisted diagnosis \kəm-pyo͞o`tər-ə-si`stəd dī-əg-nō´sis\ *n.* The use of computers by physicians in diagnosing patient conditions. Medi-

WAYS TO CATEGORIZE COMPUTERS

Class	Computers can be classified as supercomputers, mainframes, superminicomputers, minicomputers, workstations, or microcomputers. All other things (for example, the age of the machine) being equal, such a categorization provides some indication of the computer's speed, size, cost, and abilities.
Generation	First-generation computers of historic significance, such as UNIVAC, introduced in the early 1950s, were based on vacuum tubes. Second-generation computers, appearing in the early 1960s, were those in which transistors replaced vacuum tubes. Third-generation computers, dating from the 1960s, were those in which integrated circuits replaced transistors. Fourth-generation computers, appearing in the mid-1970s, are those, such as microcomputers, in which large-scale integration (LSI) enabled thousands of circuits to be incorporated on one chip. Fifth-generation computers are expected to combine very-large-scale integration (VLSI) with sophisticated approaches to computing, including artificial intelligence and true distributed processing.
Mode of processing	Computers are either analog or digital. Analog computers, generally used in scientific pursuits, represent values by continuously variable signals that can have any of an infinite number of values within a limited range at any particular time. Digital computers, the type most people think of as computers, represent values by discrete signals—the bits representing the binary digits 0 and 1.

cal application programs can help to determine the cause, symptoms, and treatment of a problem as well as to maintain a record of a patient's medical history and test results. *See also* expert system.

computer-assisted instruction \kəm-pyo͞o`tər-ə-si-stəd in-struk´shən\ *n. See* CAI.

computer-assisted learning \kəm-pyo͞o`tər-ə-si`stəd lər´nēng\ *n.* The use of computers and their multimedia abilities to present information for educational purposes.

computer-assisted teaching \kəm-pyo͞o`tər-ə-si-stəd tē´chēng\ *n. See* CAI.

computer-based learning \kəm-pyo͞o`tər-bāsd lər´nēng\ *n. See* CBL.

computer-based training \kəm-pyo͞o`tər-bāsd trā´nēng\ *n. See* CBT.

computer center \kəm-pyo͞o´tər sen`tər\ *n.* A centralized location that contains computers, such as mainframes or minicomputers, along with associated equipment for providing data processing services to a group of people.

computer conferencing \kəm-pyo͞o`tər kon´frən-sēng\ *n.* Person-to-person interaction through the use of computers located in different places but connected through communications facilities.

computer control console \kəm-pyo͞o`tər kən-trōl´ kon`sōl\ *n. See* system console.

computer crime \kəm-pyo͞o´tər krīm`\ *n.* The illegal use of a computer by an unauthorized individual, either for pleasure (as by a computer hacker) or for profit (as by a thief). *See also* hacker (definition 2).

computer-dependent \kəm-pyo͞o´tər də-pen`-dənt\ *adj. See* hardware-dependent.

Computer Emergency Response Team \kəm-pyo͞o`tər ē-mər`jən-sē rə-spons´ tēm\ *n. See* CERT.

computer engineering \kəm-pyo͞o´tər en-jə-nēr`ēng\ *n.* The discipline that involves the design and underlying philosophies involved in the development of computer hardware.

computer family \kəm-pyo͞o´tər fam`ə-lē\ *n.* A term commonly used to indicate a group of computers that are built around the same microprocessor or around a series of related microprocessors and that share significant design features. For example, the Apple Macintosh computers, from the original Macintosh (introduced in 1984) to the Quadra, represent a family designed by Apple

around the Motorola 68000, 68020, 68030, and 68040 microprocessors. Computer families tend to parallel microprocessor families, but this is not always the case. For instance, Macintoshes are no longer made with 680x0 processors, and the Macintosh family has "extended" to another generation: the Power Macs, based on the PowerPC microprocessor.

computer game \kəm-pyo͞o´tər gām`\ *n.* A class of computer program in which one or more users interact with the computer as a form of entertainment. Computer games run the gamut from simple alphabet games for toddlers to chess, treasure hunts, war games, and simulations of world events. The games are controlled from a keyboard or with a joystick or other device and are supplied on disks, on CD-ROMs, as game cartridges, or as arcade devices.

computer graphics \kəm-pyo͞o`tər graf´iks\ *n.* The display of "pictures," as opposed to only alphabetic and numeric characters, on a computer screen. Computer graphics encompasses different methods of generating, displaying, and storing information. Thus, computer graphics can refer to the creation of business charts and diagrams; the display of drawings, italic characters, and mouse pointers on the screen; or the way images are generated and displayed on the screen. *See also* graphics mode, presentation graphics, raster graphics, vector graphics.

Computer Graphics Interface \kəm-pyo͞o`tər graf´iks in´tər-fās\ *n.* A software standard applied to computer graphics devices, such as printers and plotters. Computer Graphics Interface is an offshoot of a widely recognized graphics standard called GKS (Graphical Kernel System), which provides applications programmers with standard methods of creating, manipulating, and displaying or printing computer graphics. *Acronym:* CGI (C`G-I´). *See also* Graphical Kernel System.

Computer Graphics Metafile \kəm-pyo͞o`tər graf´iks met`ə-fīl\ *n.* A software standard related to the widely recognized GKS (Graphical Kernel System) that provides applications programmers with a standard means of describing a graphic as a set of instructions for re-creating it. A graphics metafile can be stored on disk or sent to an output device; Computer Graphics Metafile provides a common language for describing such files in relation to the GKS standard. *Acronym:* CGM (C`G-M´). *See also* Graphical Kernel System.

computer-independent language \kəm-pyōō`tər-in-də-pen`dənt lang´wəj\ *n.* A computer language designed to be independent of any given hardware platform. Most high-level languages are intended to be computer-independent; actual implementations of the languages (in the form of compilers and interpreters) tend to have some hardware-specific features and aspects. *See also* computer language.

computer-input microfilm \kəm-pyōō`tər-in`pōōt mi´krō-film\ *n. See* CIM (definition 2).

computer instruction \kəm-pyōō´tər in-struk`shən\ *n.* **1.** An instruction that a computer can recognize and act on. *See also* machine instruction. **2.** The use of a computer in teaching. *See also* CAI.

computer-integrated manufacturing \kəm-pyōō`-tər-in-tə-grā-təd man-yə-fak´chur-ēng\ *n. See* CIM (definition 1).

computer interface unit \kəm-pyōō`tər in`tər-fās yōō`nit\ *n. See* interface (definition 3).

computerized axial tomography \kəm-pyōō`-tər-īzd ak`sē-əl tə-mo´grə-fē\ *n. See* CAT (definition 3).

computerized mail \kəm-pyōō`tər-īzd māl`\ *n. See* e-mail[1].

computer language \kəm-pyōō´tər lang`wəj\ *n.* An artificial language that specifies instructions to be executed on a computer. The term covers a wide spectrum, from binary-coded machine language to high-level languages. *See also* assembly language, high-level language, machine code.

computer letter \kəm-pyōō´tər let`ər\ *n. See* form letter.

computer literacy \kəm-pyōō`tər lit´ər-ə-sē\ *n.* Knowledge and an understanding of computers combined with the ability to use them effectively. On the least specialized level, computer literacy involves knowing how to turn on a computer, start and stop simple application programs, and save and print information. At higher levels, computer literacy becomes more detailed, involving the ability of power users to manipulate complex applications and, possibly, to program in languages such as Basic or C. At the highest levels, computer literacy leads to specialized technical knowledge of electronics and assembly language. *See also* power user.

computer-managed instruction \kəm-pyōō`tər-man`əjd in-struk`shən\ *n. See* CMI.

computer name \kəm-pyōō´tər nām`\ *n.* In computer networking, a name that uniquely identifies a computer to the network. A computer's name cannot be the same as any other computer or domain name on the network. It differs from a user name in that the computer name is used to identify a particular computer and all its shared resources to the rest of the system so that they can be accessed. *Compare* alias (definition 2), user name.

computer network \kəm-pyōō´tər net`wərk\ *n. See* network.

computer-output microfilm \kəm-pyōō`tər-out`pōōt mī´krō-film\ *n. See* COM (definition 4).

computerphile \kəm-pyōō´tər-fīl`\ *n.* A person who is immersed in the world of computing, who collects computers, or whose hobby involves computing.

computer power \kəm-pyōō´tər pou`ər\ *n.* The ability of a computer to perform work. If defined as the number of instructions the machine can carry out in a given time, computer power is measured in millions of instructions per second (MIPS) or millions of floating-point operations per second (MFLOPS). Power is measured in other ways too, depending on the needs or objectives of the person evaluating the machine. By users or purchasers of computers, power is often considered in terms of the machine's amount of random access memory (RAM), the speed at which the processor works, or the number of bits (8, 16, 32, and so on) handled by the computer at one time. Other factors enter into such an evaluation, however; two of the most important are how well the components of the computer work together and how well they are matched to the tasks required of them. For example, no matter how fast or powerful the computer, its speed will be hampered during operations involving the hard disk if the hard disk is slow (for example, with an access time of 65 milliseconds or higher). *See also* access time (definition 2), benchmark[1], MFLOPS, MIPS.

Computer Press Association \kəm-pyōō`tər pres´ ə-sō-sē-ā`shən\ *n.* A trade organization of journalists, broadcasters, and authors who write or report about computer technology and the computer industry.

Computer Professionals for Social Responsibility \kəm-pyōō`tər prə-fesh´ə-nəlz fər sō`shəl rə-spon-sə-bil´ə-tē\ *n. See* CPSR.

computer program \kəm-pyōō´tər prō`gram\ *n.* A set of instructions in some computer language intended to be executed on a computer so as to perform some task. The term usually implies a self-contained entity, as opposed to a routine or a library. *See also* computer language. *Compare* library (definition 1), routine.

computer-readable \kəm-pyōō`tər-rē´də-bl\ *adj.* Of, pertaining to, or characteristic of information that can be interpreted and acted on by a computer. Two types of information are referred to as computer-readable: bar codes, magnetic tape, magnetic-ink characters, and other formats that can be scanned in some way and read as data by a computer; and machine code, the form in which instructions and data reach the computer's microprocessor.

computer revolution \kəm-pyōō`tər rev-ə-lōō`-shən\ *n.* The societal and technological phenomenon involving the swift development and wide-spread use and acceptance of computers—specifically single-user personal computers. The impact of these machines is considered revolutionary for two reasons. First, their appearance and success were rapid. Second, and more important, their speed and accuracy produced a change in the ways in which information can be processed, stored, and transferred.

computer science \kəm-pyōō`tər sī´əns\ *n.* The study of computers, including their design, operation, and use in processing information. Computer science combines both theoretical and practical aspects of engineering, electronics, information theory, mathematics, logic, and human behavior. Aspects of computer science range from programming and computer architecture to artificial intelligence and robotics.

computer security \kəm-pyōō`tər sə-kyər´ə-tē\ *n.* The steps taken to protect a computer and the information it contains. On large systems or those handling financial or confidential data, computer security requires professional supervision that combines legal and technical expertise. On a microcomputer, data protection can be achieved by backing up and storing copies of files in a separate location, and the integrity of data on the computer can be maintained by assigning passwords to files, marking files "read-only" to avoid changes to them, physically locking a hard disk, storing sensitive information on floppy disks kept in locked cabinets, and installing special programs to protect against viruses. On a computer to which many people have access, security can be maintained by requiring personnel to use passwords and by granting only approved users access to sensitive information. *See also* bacterium, encryption, virus.

computer simulation \kəm-pyōō`tər sim-yə-lā´-shən\ *n. See* simulation.

computer system \kəm-pyōō`tər si`stəm\ *n.* The configuration that includes all functional components of a computer and its associated hardware. A basic microcomputer system includes a console, or system unit, with one or more disk drives, a monitor, and a keyboard. Additional hardware, called *peripherals,* can include such devices as a printer, a modem, and a mouse. Software is usually not considered part of a computer system, although the operating system that runs the hardware is known as system software.

computer telephone integration \kəm-pyōō`tər tel`ə-fōn in-tə-grā´shən\ *n.* A process allowing computer applications to answer incoming calls, provide database information on-screen at the same time the call comes in, automatically route and reroute calls by drag-and-drop, automatically dial and speed-dial outgoing calls from a computer-resident database, and identify incoming customer calls and transfer them to predetermined destinations. *See also* drag-and-drop.

computer typesetting \kəm-pyōō`tər tīp´set-ēng\ *n.* Typesetting operations that are partially or totally controlled by computers. Partial control can involve the transmittal of text directly from the source to the typesetter, without a paste-up stage. Full computerization can include the digitization of all graphics, which would then also be transmitted directly to the typesetter and regenerated without paste-up.

computer users' group \kəm-pyo͞o`tər yo͞o´zərz gro͞op\ *n. See* user group.

computer utility \kəm-pyo͞o`tər yo͞o-til´ə-tē\ *n. See* utility.

computer virus \kəm-pyo͞o´tər vīr-us\ *n. See* virus.

computer vision \kəm-pyo͞o`tər vizh´ən\ *n.* The processing of visual information by a computer. Computer vision is a form of artificial intelligence that creates a symbolic description of images that are generally input from a video camera or sensor in order to convert the images to digital form. Computer vision is often associated with robotics. *Acronym:* CV (C-V´). *See also* artificial intelligence, robotics.

COM recorder \kom´ rə-kōr`dər, C`O-M´\ *n.* Short for **c**omputer **o**utput **m**icrofilm **recorder**. A device that records computer information on microfilm.

CON \kon, C`O-N´\ *n.* The logical device name for *console;* reserved by the MS-DOS operating system for the keyboard and the screen. The input-only keyboard and the output-only screen together make up the console and represent the primary sources of input and output in an MS-DOS computer system.

concatenate \kən-kat´ə-nāt`\ *vb.* To join sequentially (for example, to combine the two strings "hello" and "there" into the single string "hello there"). *See also* character string.

concatenated data set \kon-kat`ə-nāt-əd da`tə set, dat´ə\ *n.* A group of separate sets of related data treated as a single unit for processing.

concentrator \kon´sən-trā`tər\ *n.* A communications device that combines signals from multiple sources, such as terminals on a network, into one or more signals before sending them to their destination. *Compare* multiplexer (definition 2).

conceptual schema \kən-sep`cho͞o-əl skē´mə\ *n.* In a database model that supports a three-schema architecture (such as that described by ANSI/X3/SPARC), a description of the information contents and structure of a database. A conceptual schema (also known as a *logical schema*) provides a model of the total database, thus acting as an intermediary between the two other types of schemas (internal and external) that deal with storing information and presenting it to the user. Schemas are generally defined using commands from a DDL (data definition language) supported by the database system. *See also* internal schema, schema.

concordance \kən-kōr´dəns`, kon-kōr´dəns`\ *n.* A list of words that appear in a document, along with the contexts of the appearances.

concurrent \kən-kur´ənt`, kon-kur´ənt`\ *adj.* Of, pertaining to, or characteristic of a computer operation in which two or more processes (programs) have access to the microprocessor's time and are therefore carried out nearly simultaneously. Because a microprocessor can work with much smaller units of time than people can perceive, concurrent processes appear to be occurring simultaneously but in reality are not.

concurrent execution \kən-kur`ənt eks-ə-kyo͞o´-shən, kon-kur`ənt\ *n.* The apparently simultaneous execution of two or more routines or programs. Concurrent execution can be accomplished on a single process or by using time-sharing techniques, such as dividing programs into different tasks or threads of execution, or by using multiple processors. *Also called* parallel execution. *See also* parallel algorithm, processor, sequential execution, task, thread (definition 1), time-sharing.

concurrent operation \kən-kur`ənt op`ər-ā´shən, kon-kur`ənt\ *n. See* concurrent.

concurrent processing \kən-kur`ənt pros´es-ēng, kon-kur`ənt\ *n. See* concurrent.

concurrent program execution \kən-kur`ənt prō´gram eks-ə-kyo͞o`shən, kon-kur`ənt\ *n. See* concurrent.

condensed \kən-densd´\ *adj.* Of, pertaining to, or characteristic of a font style, supported in some applications, that reduces the width of each character and then sets the characters closer together than their normal spacing. Many dot-matrix printers have a feature that causes the printer to reduce the width of each character and print them closer together, resulting in more characters fitting on a single line. *Compare* expanded.

condition \kən-dish´ən`\ *n.* The state of an expression or a variable (for example, when a result can be either true or false, or equal or not equal).

conditional \kən-dish´ə-nəl`\ *adj.* Of, pertaining to, or characteristic of an action or operation that takes place based on whether or not a certain condition is true. *See also* Boolean expression, conditional statement.

conditional branch \kən-dish´ə-nəl branch`\ *n.* In a program, a branch instruction that occurs when a particular condition code is true or false. The term is normally used in relation to low-level languages. *See also* branch instruction, condition code.

conditional compilation \kən-dish`ə-nəl kom-pə-lā´shən\ *n.* Selective compilation or translation of source code of a program based on certain conditions or flags; for example, sections of a program specified by the programmer might be compiled only if a DEBUG flag has been defined at compilation time. *See also* comment out.

conditional expression \kən-dish´ə-nəl eks-presh`ən\ *n. See* Boolean expression.

conditional jump \kən-dish´ə-nəl jump`\ *n.* In a program, a jump instruction that occurs when a particular condition code is true or false. The term is normally used in relation to low-level languages. *See also* condition code, jump instruction.

conditional statement \kən-dish´ə-nəl stāt´-mənt\ *n.* A programming-language statement that selects an execution path based on whether some condition is true or false (for example, the IF statement). *See also* case statement, conditional, IF statement, statement.

conditional transfer \kən-dish`ə-nəl trans´fər\ *n.* A transfer of the flow of execution to a given location in a program based on whether or not a particular condition is true. The term is usually used in relation to high-level languages. *See also* conditional statement.

condition code \kən-dish´ən kōd`\ *n.* One of a set of bits that are set *on* (1, or true) or *off* (0, or false) as the result of previous machine instructions. The term is used primarily in assembly or machine language situations. Condition codes are hardware-specific but usually include carry, overflow, zero result, and negative result codes. *See also* conditional branch.

conditioning \kən-dish´ə-nēng`\ *n.* The use of special equipment to improve the ability of a communications line to transmit data. Conditioning controls or compensates for signal attenuation, noise, and distortion. It can be used only on leased lines, where the path from sending to receiving computer is known in advance.

conductor \kən-duk´tər`\ *n.* A substance that conducts electricity well. Metals are good conductors, with silver and gold being among the best. The most commonly used conductor is copper. *Compare* insulator, semiconductor.

Conference on Data Systems Languages \kon´fər-əns on dā`tə si-stəmz lang`wə-jəz, kon´frəns, dat`ə\ *n. See* CODASYL.

CONFIG.SYS \kən-fig`-dot-S`Y-S´\ *n.* A special text file that controls certain aspects of operating-system behavior in MS-DOS and OS/2. Commands in the CONFIG.SYS file enable or disable system features, set limits on resources (for example, the maximum number of open files), and extend the operating system by loading device drivers that control hardware specific to an individual computer system.

configuration \kən-fi`gyər-ā´shən\ *n.* **1.** In reference to a single microcomputer, the sum of a system's internal and external components, including memory, disk drives, keyboard, video, and generally less critical add-on hardware, such as a mouse, modem, or printer. Software (the operating system and various device drivers), the user's choices established through configuration files such as the AUTOEXEC.BAT and CONFIG.SYS files on IBM PCs and compatibles, and sometimes hardware (switches and jumpers) are needed to "configure the configuration" to work correctly. Although system configuration can be changed, as by adding more memory or disk capacity, the basic structure of the system—its architecture—remains the same. *See also* AUTOEXEC.BAT, CONFIG.SYS. **2.** In relation to networks, the entire interconnected set of hardware, or the way in which a network is laid out—the manner in which elements are connected.

configuration file \kən-fi`gyər-ā´shən fīl`\ *n.* A file that contains machine-readable operating specifications for a piece of hardware or software or that contains information on another file or on a specific user, such as the user's logon ID.

connect charge \kə-nekt´ chärj`\ *n.* The amount of money a user must pay for connecting to a commercial communications system or service. Some services calculate the connect charge as a flat rate per billing period. Others charge a varying rate based on the type of service or the amount of information being accessed. Still others base their charges on the number of time units used, the time or distance involved per connection, the bandwidth of each connected session, or some combination of the preceding criteria. *See also* connect time.

connection \kə-nek´shən\ *n.* A physical link via wire, radio, fiber-optic cable, or other medium between two or more communications devices.

connectionless \kə-nek´shən-ləs\ *adj.* In communications, of, pertaining to, or characteristic of a method of data transmission that does not require a direct connection between two nodes on one or more networks. Connectionless communication is achieved by passing, or routing, data packets, each of which contains a source and destination address, through the nodes until the destination is reached. *See also* node (definition 2), packet (definition 2). *Compare* connection-oriented.

connection-oriented \kə-nek´shən-ōr`ē-ent-əd\ *adj.* In communications, of, pertaining to, or characteristic of a method of data transmission that requires a direct connection between two nodes on one or more networks. *Compare* connectionless.

connectivity \kə-nek`tiv´ə-tē\ *n.* **1.** The nature of the connection between a user's computer and another computer, such as a server or a host computer on the Internet or a network. This may describe the quality of the circuit or telephone line, the degree of freedom from noise, or the bandwidth of the communications devices. **2.** The ability of hardware devices or software packages to transmit data between other devices or packages. **3.** The ability of hardware devices, software packages, or a computer itself to work with network devices or with other hardware devices, software packages, or a computer over a network connection.

connectoid \kə-nek´toid`\ *n.* In Windows 95 and Windows NT, an icon representing a dial-up networking connection that will also execute a script for logging onto the network dialed.

connector \kə-nek´tər`\ *n.* **1.** In hardware, a coupler used to join cables or to join a cable to a device (for example, an RS-232-C connector used to join a modem cable to a computer). Most connector types are available in one of two genders—male or female. A male connector is characterized by one or more exposed pins; a female connector is characterized by one or more receptacles designed to accept the pins on the male connector. *See also* DB connector, DIN connector. **2.** In programming, a circular symbol used in a flowchart to indicate a break, as to another page.

connect time \kə-nekt´ tīm`\ *n.* The amount of time during which a user is actively connected to a remote computer. On commercial systems, the connect time is one means of calculating how much money the user must pay for using the system. *See also* connect charge.

consistency check \kən-si´stən-sē chek`\ *n.* A survey to verify that items of data conform to certain formats, bounds, and other parameters and are not internally contradictory. *Compare* completeness check.

console \kon´sōl\ *n.* A control unit, such as a terminal, through which a user communicates with a computer. In microcomputers, the console is the cabinet that houses the main components and controls of the system, sometimes including the screen, the keyboard, or both. With the MS-DOS operating system, the console is the primary input (keyboard) and primary output (screen) device, as evidenced by the device name CON. *See also* CON, system console.

constant \kon´stənt\ *n.* A named item that retains a consistent value throughout the execution of a program, as opposed to a variable, which can have its value changed during execution. *Compare* variable.

constant expression \kon`stənt eks-presh´ən\ *n.* An expression that is composed only of constants and, hence, whose value does not change during program execution. *Compare* variable expression.

constellation \kon`stə-lā´shən\ *n.* In communications, a pattern representing the possible states of a carrier wave, each of which is associated with a particular bit combination. A constellation shows the number of states that can be recognized as unique changes in a communications signal and thus the maximum number of bits that can be encoded in a single change (equivalent to 1 baud, or one event). See the illustration.

constraint \kən-strānt´\ *n.* In programming, a restriction on the solutions that are acceptable for a problem.

0111	0110	0010	0001
●	●	●	●
0100	0101	0011	0000
●	●	●	●
1100	1111	1001	1000
●	●	●	●
1101	1110	1010	1011
●	●	●	●

Constellation. A 16-point constellation and the possible bit combinations.

consultant \kən-sul´tənt\ *n*. A computer professional who deals with client firms as an independent contractor rather than as an employee. Consultants are often engaged to analyze user needs and develop system specifications.

contact manager \kon´takt man`ə-jər\ *n*. A type of specialized database that allows a user to maintain a record of personal communication with others. Contact managers are widely used by salespeople and others who want to keep track of conversations, e-mail, and other forms of communication with a large number of current and prospective customers or clients. *See also* database.

container \kən-tā´nər\ *n*. **1.** In OLE terminology, a file containing linked or embedded objects. *See also* OLE. **2.** In SGML, an element that has content as opposed to one consisting solely of the tag name and attributes. *See also* element (definition 2), SGML, tag (definition 3).

content \kon´tent\ *n*. **1.** The data that appears between the starting and ending tags of an element in an SGML or HTML document. The content of an element may consist of plain text or other elements. *See also* element (definition 2), HTML, SGML, tag (definition 3). **2.** The message body of a newsgroup article or e-mail message.

content-addressed storage \kon`tent-a`dresd stōr´əj, -ə-dresd`\ *n*. *See* associative storage.

contention \kən-ten´shən`\ *n*. On a network, competition among stations for the opportunity to use a communications line or network resource. In one sense, contention applies to a situation in which

two or more devices attempt to transmit at the same time, thus causing a collision on the line. In a somewhat different sense, contention also applies to a free-for-all method of controlling access to a communications line, in which the right to transmit is awarded to the station that wins control of the line. *See also* CSMA/CD. *Compare* token passing.

contents directory \kon´tents dər-ek`tər-ē\ *n*. A series of queues that contain the descriptors and addresses of routines located within a region of memory.

context-dependent \kon´tekst də-pen`dənt\ *adj*. Of, pertaining to, or characteristic of a process or a set of data characters whose meaning depends on the surrounding environment.

context-sensitive help \kon`tekst-sen`sə-tiv help´\ *n*. A form of assistance in which a program that provides on-screen help shows information to the user concerning the current command or operation being attempted.

context-sensitive menu \kon`tekst-sen`sə-tiv men´yōō\ *n*. A menu that highlights options as available or unavailable depending on the context in which the option is called. The menus on Windows' menu bar, for example, are context sensitive; options such as "copy" are grayed out if nothing is selected. See the illustration.

Context-sensitive menu. Paste is unavailable because nothing has been copied to the clipboard.

context switching \kon´tekst swich`ēng\ *n*. A type of multitasking; the act of turning the central processor's "attention" from one task to another, rather than allocating increments of time to each task in turn. *See also* multitasking, time slice.

contextual search \kən-teks`chōō-əl sərch´\ *n*. A search operation in which the user can direct a program to search specified files for a particular set of text characters.

contiguous \kən-ti´gyōō-əs\ *adj*. Having a shared boundary; being immediately adjacent. For example, contiguous sectors on a disk are data-storage segments physically located next to one another.

contiguous data structure \kən-ti`gyōō-əs dā´tə struk-chur, dat´ə\ *n.* A data structure, such as an array, that is stored in a consecutive set of memory locations. *See also* data structure. *Compare* noncontiguous data structure.

continuous carrier \kən-tin`yōō-əs kâr´ē-ər\ *n.* In communications, a carrier signal that remains on throughout the transmission, whether or not it is carrying information.

continuous-form paper \kən-tin`yōō-əs-fōrm pā´pər\ *n.* Paper in which each sheet is connected to the sheets before and after it, for use with most impact and ink-jet printers and some other printing devices designed with an appropriate paper-feed mechanism. The paper usually has holes punched along each side so that it can be pulled by a tractor-feed device. See the illustration. *See also* pin feed, sprocket feed, tractor feed.

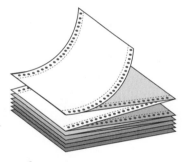

Continuous-form paper.

continuous processing \kən-tin`yōō-əs pros´es-ēng\ *n.* The processing of transactions as they are input to the system. *Compare* batch processing (definition 3).

continuous-tone image \kən-tin`yōō-əs-tōn im´-əj\ *n.* An image, such as a photograph, in which color or varying shades of gray are reproduced as gradients rather than as clustered or variably sized dots, as in traditional book or newspaper printing. Continuous-tone images can be viewed on an analog monitor (such as a television monitor), which accepts input as a continuously variable signal. They cannot be viewed on a digital monitor, which requires input broken into discrete units,

nor can they be printed in books or newspapers, which represent illustrations as groups of dots. *See also* scan (definition 2), video digitizer. *Compare* halftone.

continuous-tone printer \kən-tin´yōō-əs-tōn prin´tər\ *n.* A printer that produces an image using smoothly blended levels of continuous ink for gradations of gray or color. *Compare* dithering.

contouring \kon´tōōr-ēng`\ *n.* **1.** In computer graphics, such as CAD models, the representation of the surface of an object—its bumps and crannies. **2.** In image processing, the loss of detail that occurs in a shaded image when too few gradations of gray are used to reproduce a graphic, such as a photograph. In photography and graphic arts, this phenomenon is sometimes called *posterization*. See the illustration.

Contouring.　The left sphere is drawn with 32 gray levels; the transition from dark to light is smoother than in the right sphere, with 8 gray levels.

contrast \kon´trast\ *n.* **1.** The degree of difference between light and dark extremes of color on a monitor or on printed output. **2.** The control knob by which the contrast of a monitor is changed.

control \kən-trōl´\ *n.* **1.** Management of a computer and its processing abilities so as to maintain order as tasks and activities are carried out. Control applies to measures designed to ensure error-free actions carried out at the right time and in the right order relative to other data-handling or hardware-based activities. In reference to hardware, control of system operations can reside in a data pathway called a *control bus.* In reference to software, *control* refers to program instructions that manage data-handling tasks. **2.** In a graphical user interface, an object on the screen that can be manipulated by the user to perform an action. The most common controls are buttons, which allow the user to select options, and scroll bars, which allow the user to move through a document or position text in a window.

control break \kən-trōl´ brāk`\ *n.* A transition in control of the computer that typically gives control of the central processing unit (CPU) to the user console or to some other program.

Control-Break \kən-trōl´brāk`\ *n. See* Break key.

control bus \kən-trōl´ bus`\ *n.* The set of lines (conductors) within a computer that carry control signals between the central processing unit (CPU) and other devices. For example, a control bus line is used to indicate whether the CPU is attempting to read from memory or to write to it; another control bus line is used by memory to request an interrupt in case of a memory error.

control character \kən-trōl´ kâr`ək-tər\ *n.* **1.** Any of the first 32 characters in the ASCII character set (0 through 31 in decimal representation), each of which is defined as having a standard control function, such as carriage return, linefeed, or backspace. **2.** Any of the 26 characters Control-A through Control-Z (1 through 26 in decimal representation) that can be typed at the keyboard by holding the Control key down and typing the appropriate letter. The six remaining characters with control functions, such as Escape (ASCII 27), cannot be typed using the Control key. *Compare* control code.

control code \kən-trōl´ kōd`\ *n.* One or more nonprinting characters used by a computer program to control the actions of a device, used in printing, communications, and management of display screens. Control codes are mainly employed by programmers or by users to control a printer when an application program does not support the printer or one of its specialized features. In video, control codes are sent from a computer to a display unit to manipulate the appearance of text or a cursor on the screen. Popular video control code sets are ANSI and VT-100. *Also called* escape sequence, setup string. *See also* control character.

control console \kən-trōl´ kon`sōl\ *n. See* console.

control data \kən-trōl´ dā`tə, dat`ə\ *n.* Data that consists of information about timing and switching, used to synchronize and route other data or

to manage the operation of a device such as a bus or a port.

control flow \kən-trōl´ flō`\ *n.* The tracing of all possible execution paths in a program, often represented in the form of a diagram. See the illustration.

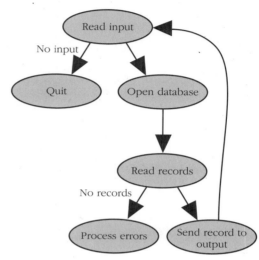

Control flow.

Control key \kən-trōl´ kē`\ *n.* A key that, when pressed in combination with another key, gives the other key an alternative meaning. In many application programs, Control (labeled CTRL or Ctrl on a PC keyboard) plus another key is used as a command for special functions. *See also* control character (definition 2).

controller \kən-trō´lər\ *n.* A device on which other devices rely for access to a computer subsystem. A disk controller, for example, controls access to one or more disk drives, managing physical and logical access to the drive or drives.

control logic \kən-trōl´ loj`ik\ *n.* The electronic circuitry that generates, interprets, and uses control data.

control panel \kən-trōl´ pan`əl\ *n.* In Windows and Macintosh systems, a utility that allows the user to control aspects of the operating system or hardware, such as system time and date, keyboard characteristics, and networking parameters.

control sequence \kən-trōl´ sē`kwens\ *n. See* control code.

control signal \kən-trōl´ sig`nəl\ *n.* An electronic signal used to control internal or external devices or processes.

control statement \kən-trōl´ stāt`mənt\ *n.* A statement that affects the flow of execution through a program. Control statements include conditional statements (CASE, IF-THEN-ELSE), iterative statements (DO, FOR, REPEAT, WHILE), and transfer statements (GOTO). *See also* conditional statement, iterative statement, statement, transfer statement.

control strip \kən-trōl´ strip`\ *n.* **1.** An equipment calibration tool used to determine the corrections needed to restore accuracy by comparing recorded data against known values. **2.** A utility that groups shortcuts to commonly used items or information, such as time, battery power level, desktop items, and programs, in an easily accessible place. *See also* shortcut.

control structure \kən-trōl´ struk`chur\ *n.* A portion of a program defined by the relationship between the statements, used in structured programming. There are three basic control structures: sequence, where one statement simply follows another; selection, where program flow depends on which criteria are met; and iteration, where an action is repeated until some condition occurs.

control unit \kən-trōl´ yo͞o`nit\ *n.* A device or circuit that performs an arbitrating or regulating function. For example, a memory controller chip controls access to a computer's memory and is the control unit for that memory.

control variable \kən-trōl´ vâr`ē-ə-bl\ *n.* In programming, the variable in a control statement that dictates the flow of execution. For example, the index variable in a FOR loop controls the number of times a group of statements are executed. *See also* control statement.

convention \kən-ven´shən\ *n.* Any standard that is used more or less universally in a given situation. Many conventions are applied to microcomputers. In programming, for example, a language such as C relies on formally accepted symbols and abbreviations that must be used in programs. Less formally, programmers usually adopt the convention of indenting subordinate instructions in a routine so that the structure of the program is more easily visualized. National and international committees often discuss and arbitrate conventions for programming languages, data structures, communication standards, and device characteristics. *See also* CCITT, ISO, NTSC, standard (definition 1).

conventional memory \kən-ven´shən-əl mem`-ər-ē\ *n.* The amount of RAM addressable by an IBM PC or compatible machine operating in real mode. This is typically 640 kilobytes (KB). Without the use of special techniques, conventional memory is the only kind of RAM accessible to MS-DOS programs. *See also* protected mode, real mode. *Compare* expanded memory, extended memory.

convergence \kən-vər´jəns`\ *n.* A coming together. Convergence can occur between different disciplines and technologies, as when telephone communications and computing converge in the field of telecommunications. It can also occur within a program, such as a spreadsheet, when a circular set of formulas are repeatedly recalculated (iterated), with the results of each iteration coming closer to a true solution.

conversational \kon`vər-sā´shə-nəl\ *adj.* Of, pertaining to, or characteristic of the mode of operation, typical of microcomputers, in which the computer user and the system engage in a dialogue of commands and system responses. *See also* interactive.

conversational interaction \kon-vər-sā`shə-nəl in-tər-ak´shən\ *n.* Interaction in which two or more parties alternately transmit and receive messages from each other. *See also* interactive processing.

conversational language \kon-vər-sā`shə-nəl lang´wəj\ *n.* Any programming language that allows the programmer to instruct the computer in a conversational mode, as opposed to more formal, structured languages. For example, in a COBOL program, in order to execute a procedure called CHECK 10 times, a program would use the following statement: PERFORM CHECK 10 TIMES.

conversational mode \kon`vər-sā´shə-nəl mōd`\ *n. See* conversational.

conversion \kən-vər´zhən\ *n.* The process of changing from one form or format to another;

where information is concerned, a changeover that affects form but not substance. Types of conversion include:

- Data conversion: Changing the way information is represented—for example, changing binary representation to decimal or hexadecimal.

- File conversion: Changing a file from one format to another. Another, more detailed, type of file conversion involves changing character coding from one standard to another, as in converting EBCDIC characters (which are used primarily with mainframe computers) to ASCII characters. *See also* ASCII, EBCDIC.

- Hardware conversion: Changing all or part of a computer system to work with new or different devices.

- Media conversion: Transferring data from one storage medium to another—for example, from disk to tape or from 3.5-inch Apple Macintosh disk to 5.25-inch MS-DOS disk.

- Software conversion: Changing or moving a program designed to run on one computer to run on another. Usually this involves detailed (professional) work on the program itself.

- System conversion: Changing from one operating system to another—for example, from MS-DOS to UNIX or OS/2.

conversion table \kən-vər´zhən tā`bl\ *n.* A table listing a set of characters or numbers and their equivalents in another coding scheme. Common examples of conversion tables include ASCII tables, which list characters and their ASCII values, and decimal-to-hexadecimal tables. Several conversion tables are in Appendixes A–E.

converter \kən-vər´tər`\ *n.* Any device that changes electrical signals or computer data from one form to another. For example, an analog-to-digital converter translates analog signals to digital signals.

cookbook[1] \ko͞ok´bo͞ok\ *adj.* Of, pertaining to, or characteristic of a book or manual that presents information using a step-by-step approach. For example, a cookbook approach to programming might present a series of sample programs that the reader could analyze and adapt to his or her own needs.

cookbook[2] \ko͞ok´bo͞ok\ *n.* A computer book or manual that presents information using a step-by-step approach. Most often, *cookbook* refers to a programming guide, but it can refer to a book that shows how to accomplish specialized tasks in an application.

cooked mode \ko͞okd´ mōd\ *n.* One of two forms (the other being raw mode) in which an operating system such as UNIX or MS-DOS "sees" the handle, or identifier, for a character-based device. If the handle is in cooked mode, the operating system stores each character in a buffer and gives special treatment to carriage returns, end-of-file markers, and linefeed and tab characters, sending a line of data to a device, such as the screen, only after it reads a carriage-return or end-of-file character. In cooked mode, characters read from standard input are often automatically echoed (displayed) on the screen. *Compare* raw mode.

cookie \ko͞ok´ē\ *n.* **1.** A block of data that a server returns to a client in response to a request from the client. **2.** On the World Wide Web, a block of data that a Web server stores on a client system. When a user returns to the same Web site, the browser sends a copy of the cookie back to the server. Cookies are used to identify users, to instruct the server to send a customized version of the requested Web page, to submit account information for the user, and for other administrative purposes. **3.** Originally an allusion to "fortune cookie," a UNIX program that outputs a different message, or "fortune," each time it is used. On some systems, the cookie program is run during user logon.

cookie filtering tool \ko͞ok´ē fil´tər-ēng to͞ol`\ *n.* A utility that prevents a cookie on a Web browser from relaying information about the user requesting access to a Web site. *See also* cookie (definition 2).

cooperative multitasking \kō-op`ər-ə-tiv mul´tē-ta-skēng, mul´tī-ta-skēng\ *n.* A type of multitasking in which one or more background tasks are given processing time during idle times in the foreground task only if the foreground task allows it. This is the primary mode of multitasking in the Macintosh operating system. *See also* background[1], context switching, foreground[1], multitasking, time slice. *Compare* preemptive multitasking.

cooperative processing \kō-op`ər-ə-tiv pros´es-ēng\ *n.* A mode of operation characteristic of distributed systems in which two or more computers, such as a mainframe and a microcomputer, can simultaneously carry out portions of the same program or work on the same data. *Compare* distributed processing.

coordinate \kō-ōr´də-nət\ *n.* Any element in a group of references to a particular location, such as the intersection of a certain row and column. In computer graphics and displays, coordinates specify such elements as points on a line, the corners of a square, or the location of a pixel on the screen. In other computer applications, coordinates specify cells on a spreadsheet, data points on a graph, locations in memory, and so on. *See also* Cartesian coordinates, polar coordinates.

coordinate dimensioning \kō-ōr`də-nət də-men´shə-nēng\ *n.* A form of spatial positioning in which a point is described, relative to a fixed reference, in terms of its distance and direction along predefined axes. *See also* Cartesian coordinates, three-dimensional model, two-dimensional model.

coordinated universal time format \kō-ōr`də-nā`təd yōō`nə-vər-səl tīm´ fōr`mat\ *n. See* Universal Time Coordinate.

coprocessor \kō`pros´es-ər\ *n.* A processor, distinct from the main microprocessor, that performs additional functions or assists the main microprocessor. The most common type of coprocessor is the floating-point coprocessor, also called a numeric or math coprocessor, which is designed to perform numeric calculations faster and better than the general-purpose microprocessors used in personal computers. *See also* floating-point processor.

copy \kop´ē\ *vb.* To duplicate information and reproduce it in another part of a document, in a different file or memory location, or in a different medium. A copy operation can affect data ranging from a single character to large segments of text, a graphics image, or one to many data files. Text and graphics, for example, can be copied to another part of a document, to the computer's memory (by means of a temporary storage facility such as the Microsoft Windows or Apple Macintosh Clipboard), or to a different file. Similarly, files can be copied from one disk or directory to another, and data can be copied from the screen to a printer or to a data file. In most cases, a copy procedure leaves the original information in place. *Compare* cut and paste, move.

copy disk \kop´ē disk`\ *n.* An MS-DOS command to duplicate the contents of a floppy disk on a second disk. *See also* floppy disk, MS-DOS.

copy holder \kop´ē hōl`dər\ *n.* An inclined clipboard or other such device designed to hold printed material so that it can be easily viewed by someone working at a computer keyboard.

copyleft \kop´ē-left`\ *n. See* General Public License.

copy program \kop´ē prō`gram\ *n.* **1.** A program designed to duplicate one or more files to another disk or directory. **2.** A program that disables or circumvents the copy-protection device on a computer program so that the software can be copied, often illegally, to another disk. *See also* copy protection.

copy protection \kop´ē prə-tek`shən\ *n.* A software "lock" placed on a computer program by its developer to prevent the product from being copied and distributed without approval or authorization.

copyright \kop´ē-rīt`\ *n.* A method of protecting the rights of an originator of a creative work, such as a text, a piece of music, a painting, or a computer program, through law. In many countries the originator of a work has copyright in the work as soon as it is fixed in a tangible medium (such as a piece of paper or a disk file); that rule applies in the United States for works created after 1977. Registration of a copyright, or the use of a copyright symbol, is not needed to create the copyright but does strengthen the originator's legal powers. Unauthorized copying and distribution of copyrighted material can lead to severe penalties, whether done for profit or not. Copyrights affect the computer community in three ways: the copyright protection of software, the copyright status of material (such as song lyrics) distributed over a network such as the Internet, and the copyright status of original material distributed over a network (such as a newsgroup post). The latter two involve electronic media that are arguably not tangible, and legislation protecting the information disseminated through electronic media is still evolving. *See also* fair use, General Public License.

CORBA \kōr´bə, C`O-R`B-A´\ *n.* Acronym for **C**ommon **O**bject **R**equest **B**roker **A**rchitecture. A specification developed by the Object Management Group in 1992 in which pieces of programs (objects) communicate with other objects in other programs, even if the two programs are written in different programming languages and are running on different platforms. A program makes its request for objects through an *object request broker,* or *ORB,* and thus does not need to know the structure of the program from where the object comes. CORBA is designed to work in object-oriented environments. *See also* object (definition 2), Object Management Group, object-oriented.

core \kōr\ *n.* One of the types of memory built into computers before random access memory (RAM) was available or affordable. Some people still use the term to refer to the main memory of any computer system, as in the phrase *core dump*—a listing of the raw contents of main memory at the moment of a system crash. *Compare* RAM.

core program \kōr´ prō`gram\ *n.* A program or program segment that is resident in random access memory (RAM).

coresident \kō`rez´ə-dənt\ *adj.* Of or pertaining to a condition in which two or more programs are loaded in memory at the same time.

corona wire \kər-ō´nə wīr`\ *n.* In laser printers, a wire though which high voltage is passed to ionize the air and transfer a uniform electrostatic charge to the photosensitive medium in preparation for the laser.

coroutine \kō´rōō-tēn`\ *n.* A routine that is in memory at the same time as, and frequently executed concurrently with, another.

corrective maintenance \kər-ek`tiv mān´tə-nəns\ *n.* The process of diagnosing and correcting computer problems after they occur. *Compare* preventive maintenance.

correspondence quality \kōr-ə-spon´dəns kwä`lə-tē\ *n. See* print quality.

corruption \kər-up´shən`\ *n.* A process wherein data in memory or on disk is unintentionally changed, with its meaning thereby altered or obliterated.

cost-benefit analysis \kost`ben´ə-fit ə-nal`ə-sis\ *n.* The comparison of benefits to costs for a particular item or action. Cost-benefit analysis is often used in MIS or IS departments to determine such things as whether purchasing a new computer system is a good investment or whether hiring more staff is necessary. *See also* IS, MIS.

coulomb \kōō´lom, kōō´lōm\ *n.* A unit of electrical charge equivalent to roughly 6.26×10^{18} electrons, with a negative charge being an excess of electrons and a positive charge being a deficiency of electrons.

counter \koun´tər\ *n.* **1.** In programming, a variable used to keep count of something. **2.** In electronics, a circuit that counts a specified number of pulses before generating an output. **3.** A device that keeps track of the number of visitors to a World Wide Web site.

counting loop \koun´tēng lōōp`\ *n.* In a program, a group of statements that are repeated, thereby incrementing a variable used as a counter (for example, a program might repeat a counting loop that adds 1 to its counter until the counter equals 10). *See also* loop[1] (definition 1).

country code \kən´trē kōd`\ *n. See* major geographic domain.

country-specific \kun`trē-spə-sif´ik\ *adj.* Of, pertaining to, or characteristic of hardware or software that uses characters or conventions unique to a particular country or group of countries. *Country-specific* does not necessarily refer to spoken languages, although it does allow for special characters (such as accent marks) that are language-specific. Generally, the features considered country-specific include keyboard layout (including special-character keys), time and date conventions, financial and monetary symbols, decimal notation (decimal point or comma), and alphabetic sorting order. Such features are handled either by a computer's operating system (for example, by the Keyboard and Country commands in MS-DOS) or by application programs that offer options for tailoring documents to a particular set of national or international conventions.

courseware \kōrs´wâr\ *n.* Software dedicated to education or training.

courtesy copy \kər´tə-sē kop`ē\ *n. See* cc.

CPA \C`P-A´\ *n. See* Computer Press Association.

cpi \C`P-I´\ *n. See* characters per inch.

CPM \C`P-M´\ *n. See* critical path method.

CP/M \C`P-M´\ *n.* Acronym for **C**ontrol **P**rogram/ **M**onitor. A line of operating systems from Digital Research, Inc., for microcomputers based on Intel microprocessors. The first system, CP/M-80, was the most popular operating system for 8080- and Z80-based microcomputers. Digital Research also developed CP/M-86 for 8086/8088-based computers, CP/M-Z8000 for Zilog Z8000-based computers, and CP/M-68K for Motorola 68000-based computers. When the IBM PC and MS-DOS were introduced, common use of CP/M by end users dwindled. DRI continues to enhance the CP/M line, supporting multitasking with the Concurrent CP/M and MP/M products. *See also* MP/M.

cps \C`P-S´\ *n. See* characters per second.

CPSR \C`P-S-R´\ *n.* Acronym for **C**omputer **P**rofessionals for **S**ocial **R**esponsibility. A public advocacy organization of computer professionals. CPSR was originally formed out of concern over the use of computer technology for military purposes but has extended its interest to such issues as civil liberties and the effect of computers on workers.

CPU \C`P-U´\ *n. See* central processing unit.

CPU-bound \C`P-U´bound\ *adj. See* computation-bound.

CPU cache \C`P-U´ kash\ *n.* A section of fast memory linking the central processing unit (CPU) and main memory that temporarily stores data and instructions the CPU needs to execute upcoming commands and programs. Considerably faster than main memory, the CPU cache contains data that is transferred in blocks, thereby speeding execution. The system anticipates the data it will need through algorithms. *Also called* cache memory, memory cache. *See also* cache, central processing unit, VCACHE.

CPU cycle \C`P-U´ sī-kl\ *n.* **1.** The smallest unit of time recognized by the central processing unit (CPU)—typically a few hundred-millionths of a second. **2.** The time required for the CPU to perform the simplest instruction, such as fetching the contents of a register or performing a no-operation instruction (NOP). *Also called* clock tick.

CPU fan \C-P-U´ fan`\ *n.* An electric fan usually placed directly on a central processing unit (CPU) or on the CPU's heat sink to help dissipate heat from the chip by circulating air around it. *See also* central processing unit, heat sink.

CPU speed \C-P-U´ spēd`\ *n.* A relative measure of the data-processing capacity of a particular central processing unit (CPU), usually measured in megahertz. *See also* central processing unit.

CPU time \C`P-U´ tīm\ *n.* In multiprocessing, the amount of time during which a particular process has active control of the central processing unit (CPU). *See also* central processing unit, multiprocessing.

.cr \dot`C-R´\ *n.* On the Internet, the major geographic domain specifying that an address is located in Costa Rica.

CR \C-R´\ *n. See* carriage return.

cracker \krak´ər\ *n.* A person who overcomes the security measures of a computer system and gains unauthorized access. The goal of some crackers is to obtain information illegally from a computer system or use computer resources. However, the goal of the majority is to merely break into the system. *See also* hacker (definition 2).

crash[1] \krash\ *n.* The failure of either a program or a disk drive. A program crash results in the loss of all unsaved data and can leave the operating system unstable enough to require restarting the computer. A disk drive crash, sometimes called a disk crash, leaves the drive inoperable and can cause loss of data. *See also* abend, head crash.

crash[2] \krash\ *vb.* **1.** For a system or program, to fail to function correctly, resulting in the suspension of operation. *See also* abend. **2.** For a magnetic head, to hit a recording medium, with possible damage to one or both.

crash recovery \krash´ rə-kəv`ər-ē\ *n.* The ability of a computer to resume operation after a disastrous failure, such as the failure of a hard drive. Ideally, recovery can occur without any loss of data, although usually some, if not all, data is lost. *See also* crash[1].

crawler \krä´lər, krô´lər\ *n. See* Web browser, spider.

Cray-1 \krā-wən´\ *n.* An early supercomputer developed in 1976 by Seymour Cray. Extremely powerful in its day, the 64-bit Cray-1 ran at 75 MHz and was capable of executing 160 million floating-point operations per second. *See also* supercomputer.

CRC \C`R-C´\ *n.* Acronym for **c**yclical (or **c**yclic) **r**edundancy **c**heck. A procedure used in checking for errors in data transmission. CRC error checking uses a complex calculation to generate a number based on the data transmitted. The sending device performs the calculation before transmission and sends its result to the receiving device. The receiving device repeats the same calculation after transmission. If both devices obtain the same result, it is assumed that the transmission was error-free. The procedure is known as a redundancy check because each transmission includes not only data but extra (redundant) error-checking values. Communications protocols such as XMODEM and Kermit use cyclical redundancy checking.

creator \krē-ā´tər\ *n.* On the Apple Macintosh, the program that creates a file. Files are linked to their creators by creator codes; this link enables the operating system to open the creator application when a document file is opened.

creeping featurism \krē`pēng fē´chur-iz-əm\ *n.* The process by which features are added to a new version of a program by software developers until the program becomes unduly cumbersome and difficult to use. Generally, creeping featurism occurs as developers attempt to enhance the competitiveness of the program with each new release by adding new features.

crippled version \krip`ld vər´zhən\ *n.* A scaled-down or functionally reduced version of hardware or software, distributed for demonstration purposes. *See also* demo.

critical error \krit`i-kəl âr´ər\ *n.* An error that suspends processing until the condition can be corrected either by software or by user intervention (for example, an attempt to read to a nonexistent disk, an out-of-paper condition on the printer, or a checksum fault in a data message).

critical-error handler \krit-i-kəl-âr´ər hand`lər\ *n.* A software routine that attempts to correct or achieve a graceful exit from a critical or threatening error. *See also* critical error, graceful exit.

critical path method \krit`i-kəl path´ meth`əd\ *n.* A means of evaluating and managing a large project by isolating tasks, milestone events, and schedules and by showing interrelationships among them. The critical path for which this method is named is a line connecting crucial events, any of which, if delayed, affects subsequent events and, ultimately, completion of the project. *Acronym:* CPM (C`P-M´).

crop \krop\ *vb.* In computer graphics, to cut off part of an image, such as unneeded sections of a graphic or extra white space around the borders. As in preparing photographs or illustrations for traditional printing, cropping is used to refine or clean up a graphic for placement in a document.

crop marks \krop´ märks\ *n.* **1.** Lines drawn at the edges of pages to mark where the paper will be cut to form pages in the final document. See the illustration. *See also* registration marks. **2.** Lines drawn on photographs or illustrations to indicate where they will be cropped, or cut. *See also* crop.

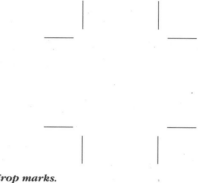

Crop marks.

cross-assembler \kros´ə-sem`blər\ *n.* An assembler that executes on one hardware platform but generates machine code for another. *See also* assembler, compiler, cross-compiler, cross development.

cross-check \kros´chek\ *vb.* To check the accuracy of a calculation by using another method to verify the result. *Compare* cross-foot.

cross-compiler \kros´kəm-pī`lər\ *n.* A compiler that executes on one hardware platform but generates object code for another. *See also* assembler, compiler, cross-assembler, cross development.

cross development \kros` də-vel´əp-mənt\ *n.* The use of one system to develop programs for a different type of system, often because the software development tools of the development system are superior to those of the target system.

cross-foot \kros´foot\ *vb.* To check the accuracy of a total, as on a ledger sheet, by adding across columns and down rows, all figures contributing to the total.

cross hairs \kros´ hârz\ *n*. Intersecting lines used by some computer input devices to locate a particular *x-y*-coordinate.

cross-hatching \kros´hach`ēng\ *n*. Shading made up of regularly spaced, intersecting lines. Cross-hatching is one of several methods for filling in areas of a graphic. See the illustration.

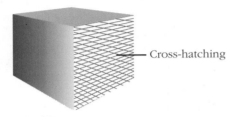

Cross-hatching.

cross-linked files \kros`lēnkd fīlz´\ *n*. In Windows 95, Windows 3.*x*, and MS-DOS, a file-storage error occurring when one or more sections, or *clusters,* of the hard drive or a floppy disk have been erroneously allocated to more than one file in the file allocation table. Like lost clusters, cross-linked files can result from the ungraceful exit (messy or abrupt termination) of an application program. *See also* file allocation table, lost cluster.

cross-platform \kros´plat´fōrm\ *adj*. Of, pertaining to, or characteristic of a software application or hardware device that can be run or operated on more than one system platform.

cross-post \cros´pōst\ *vb*. To copy a message or news article from one newsgroup, conference topic, e-mail system, or other communications channel to another—for example, from a Usenet newsgroup to a CompuServe forum or from e-mail to a newsgroup.

crosstalk \kros´täk\ *n*. Interference caused by a signal transferring from one circuit to another, as on a telephone line.

CRT \C`R-T´\ *n*. Acronym for **c**athode-**r**ay **t**ube. The basis of the television screen and the standard microcomputer display screen. A CRT display is built around a vacuum tube containing one or more electron guns whose electron beams rapidly sweep horizontally across the inside of the front surface of the tube, which is coated with a material that glows when irradiated. Each electron beam moves from left to right, top to bottom, one horizontal scan line at a time. To keep the screen image from flickering, the electron beam refreshes the screen 30 times or more per second. The clarity of the image is determined by the number of pixels on the screen. See the illustration. *See also* pixel, raster, resolution (definition 1).

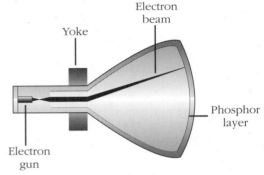

CRT. *Cutaway view of a CRT.*

CRT controller \C`R-T´ kən-trō`lər\ *n*. The part of a video adapter board that generates the video signal, including the horizontal and vertical synchronization signals. *See also* video adapter.

cruise \krōōz\ *vb*. See surf.

crunch \krunch\ *vb*. To process information. *See also* number crunching.

cryoelectronic \krī`ō-ə-lek-tron´ik\ *adj*. Involving the use of superconducting electronics kept in a cryogenic environment at very low temperatures.

cryptoanalysis \krip`tō-ə-nal´ə-sis\ *n*. The decoding of electronically encrypted information for the purpose of understanding encryption techniques. *See also* cryptography, encryption.

cryptography \krip-to´grə-fē`\ *n*. The use of codes to convert data so that only a specific recipient will be able to read it, using a key. The persistent problem of cryptography is that the key must be transmitted to the intended recipient and may be intercepted. Public key cryptography is a recent significant advance. *See also* code[1] (definition 2), encryption, PGP, private key, public key.

.cs \dot`C-S´\ *n*. On the Internet, the major geographic domain specifying that an address is located in the former Czechoslovakia.

C shell \C´shel\ *n*. One of the command-line interfaces available under UNIX. The C shell is very usable but is not on every system. *Compare* Bourne shell, Korn shell.

CSLIP \C´slip, C`S-L-I-P´\ *n*. *See* Compressed SLIP.

CSMA/CD \C`S-M-A`C-D´\ *n*. Acronym for **C**arrier **S**ense **M**ultiple **A**ccess with **C**ollision **D**etection. A network protocol for handling situations in which two or more nodes (stations) transmit at the same time, thus causing a collision. With CSMA/CD, each node on the network monitors the line and transmits when it senses that the line is not busy. If a collision occurs because another node is using the same opportunity to transmit, both nodes stop transmitting. To avoid another collision, both then wait for differing random amounts of time before attempting to transmit again. *Compare* token passing.

CSO \C`S-O´\ *n*. Acronym for **C**omputing **S**ervices **O**ffice. An Internet directory service that matches users' own names with e-mail addresses, generally at colleges and universities. The CSO service, which can be reached through Gopher, was originally developed at the Computing Services Office at the University of Illinois.

CSO name server \C-S-O` nām´ sər`vər\ *n*. A facility that provides e-mail directory information through the CSO system. *See also* CSO.

CSS \C`S-S´\ *n*. *See* cascading style sheets.

CSS1 \C`S-S-wən´\ *n*. *See* cascading style sheets.

CTERM \C´tərm, C`T-E-R-M´\ *n*. *See* Communications Terminal Protocol.

CTI \C`T-I´\ *n*. Acronym for **c**omputer-**t**elephony **i**ntegration. The practice of using a computer to control one or more telephone and communications functions.

CTL \kən-trōl´\ *n*. Short for **control**. *See* control character (definition 2), Control key.

CTRL or **Ctrl** \kən-trōl´\ Short for **control**. A designation used to label the Control key on computer keyboards. *See also* control character (definition 2), Control key.

Ctrl-Alt-Delete \kən-trōl`ält`də-lēt´\ *n*. A three-key combination used with IBM and compatible computers to restart (reboot) the machine. Pressing Ctrl-Alt-Delete (Control-Alt-Delete) causes a warm boot in MS-DOS—the computer restarts but does not go through all of the internal checks involved when power to the system is switched on (cold boot). In Windows 95 and Windows NT, Ctrl-Alt-Delete provides a dialog box from which the user may choose to shut down the computer or end any current tasks.

Ctrl-C \kən-trōl`C´\ *n*. **1.** In UNIX, the key combination used to break out of a running process. **2.** The keyboard shortcut recognized by many programs (as in Windows) as an instruction to copy the currently selected item.

Ctrl-S \kən-trōl`S´\ *n*. **1.** On systems in which a software handshake is used between terminals and a central computer, the key combination used to suspend output. Ctrl-Q will resume output after a Ctrl-S suspension. *See also* software handshake, XON/XOFF. **2.** A keyboard shortcut recognized by many programs as an instruction to save the current document or file.

CTS \C`T-S´\ *n*. Acronym for **C**lear **T**o **S**end. In serial communications, a signal sent, as from a modem to its computer, to indicate that transmission can proceed. CTS is a hardware signal sent over line 5 in RS-232-C connections. *Compare* RTS.

.cu \dot`C-U´\ *n*. On the Internet, the major geographic domain specifying that an address is located in Cuba.

CUA \C`U-A´\ *n*. *See* Common User Access.

CUI \C`U-I´\ *n*. *See* character user interface.

CUL8R \sē`yōō-lā´tər\ A fanciful shorthand notation meaning "See you later," sometimes seen in Internet discussion groups as a farewell by a participant temporarily leaving the group.

curly quotes \kur´lē kwōts`\ *n*. *See* smart quotes.

current \kur´ənt\ *n*. The flow of electric charge through a conductor, or the amount of such flow. Current is measured in amperes. *See also* ampere, coulomb. *Compare* volt.

current cell \kur`ənt sel´\ *n*. *See* active cell.

current directory \kur`ənt dər-ek´tər-ē\ *n*. The disk directory at the end of the active directory path—the directory that is searched first for a requested file, and the one in which a new file is stored unless another directory is specified. *See also* path (definition 2).

current drain \kur´ənt drān`\ *n*. **1.** The current taken from a voltage source by its load (the object receiving the current). *Also called* drain. **2.** The load itself. For example, a flashlight bulb takes current from the battery; this current is the drain on the battery, and the bulb itself may also be called the drain.

current location counter \kur`ənt lō-kā´shən koun`tər\ *n. See* program counter.

current-mode logic \kur`ənt-mōd loj´ik\ *n.* A type of circuit design in which the transistors operate in unsaturated (amplifying) mode.

cursor \kur´sər\ *n.* **1.** A special on-screen indicator, such as a blinking underline or rectangle, that marks the place at which a keystroke will appear when typed. **2.** In reference to digitizing tablets, the stylus (pointer or "pen"). **3.** In applications and operating systems that use a mouse, the arrow or other on-screen icon that moves with movements of the mouse.

cursor blink speed \kur`sər blink´ spēd`\ *n.* The rate at which a cursor on screen flashes on and off. *See also* cursor (definition 1).

cursor control \kur´sər kən-trōl`\ *n.* The ability of a computer user to move the cursor to a specified location on the screen. Keys dedicated to cursor control include the left, right, up, and down arrow keys and certain others, such as Backspace, Home, and End. Pointing devices such as the mouse can also control cursor movements, often helping the user move the cursor long distances from place to place in a document.

cursor key \kur´sər kē`\ *n. See* arrow key.

CUSeeMe \C-U`sē-mē´\ *n.* A video conferencing program developed at Cornell University. It was the first program to give Windows and Mac OS users the ability to engage in real-time video conferencing over the Internet, but it requires a lot of bandwidth (at least 128 Kbps speed) to function properly.

customize \ku´stə-mīz`\ *vb.* To modify or assemble hardware or software to suit the needs or preferences of the user. Traditionally, hardware customizing ranges from designing an electronic circuit for a particular customer to putting together a computer facility tailored to a customer's special need. Software customizing usually means modifying or designing software for a specific customer.

custom software \ku`stəm soft´wâr\ *n.* Any type of program developed for a particular client or to address a special need. Certain products, such as dBASE and Lotus 1-2-3, are designed to provide the flexibility and tools required for producing tailor-made applications. *See also* CASE.

cut \kut\ *vb.* To remove part of a document, usually placing it temporarily in memory so that the cut portion can be inserted (pasted) elsewhere. *Compare* delete.

cut and paste \kut` ənd pāst´\ *n.* A procedure in which the computer acts as an electronic combination of scissors and glue for reorganizing a document or for compiling a document from different sources. In cut and paste, the portion of a document to be moved is selected, removed to storage in memory or on disk, and then reinserted into the same or a different document.

.cv \dot`C-V´\ *n.* On the Internet, the major geographic domain specifying that an address is located in Cape Verde.

CV \C-V´\ *n. See* computer vision.

CWIS \C`W-I-S´\ *n. See* campuswide information system.

.cy \dot`C-Y´\ *n.* On the Internet, the major geographic domain specifying that an address is located in Cyprus.

cybercafe or **cyber café** \sī`bər-ka-fā´\ *n.* **1.** A coffee shop or restaurant that offers access to PCs or other terminals that are connected to the Internet, usually for a per-hour or per-minute fee. Users are encouraged to buy beverages or food to drink or eat while accessing the Internet. **2.** A virtual café on the Internet, generally used for social purposes. Users interact with each other by means of a chat program or by posting messages to one another through a bulletin board system, such as in a newsgroup or on a Web site.

cybercash \sī´bər-kash`\ *n. See* e-money.

cyberchat \sī´bər-chat`\ *n. See* IRC.

cybercop \sī´bər-kop`\ *n.* A person who investigates criminal acts committed online, especially fraud and harassment.

Cyberdog \sī´bər-dog`\ *n.* Apple's Internet suite for HTML browsing and e-mail, based on OpenDoc for easy integration with other applications. *See also* OpenDoc.

cybernaut \sī´bər-nät`, sī´bər-nôt`\ *n.* One who spends copious time online, exploring the Internet. *Also called* Internaut. *See also* cyberspace.

cybernetics \sī`bər-net´iks\ *n*. The study of control systems, such as the nervous system, in living organisms and the development of equivalent systems in electronic and mechanical devices. Cybernetics compares similarities and differences between living and nonliving systems (whether those systems comprise individuals, groups, or societies) and is based on theories of communication and control that can be applied to either or both. *See also* bionics.

cyberpunk \sī´bər-punk`\ *n*. **1.** A genre of near-future science fiction in which conflict and action take place in virtual-reality environments maintained on global computer networks in a worldwide culture of dystopian alienation. The prototypical cyberpunk novel is William Gibson's *Neuromancer* (1982). **2.** A category of popular culture that resembles the ethos of cyberpunk fiction. **3.** A person or fictional character who resembles the heroes of cyberpunk fiction.

cybersex \sī`bər-seks`\ *n*. Communication via electronic means, such as e-mail, chat, or newsgroups, for the purpose of sexual stimulation or gratification. *See also* chat[1] (definition 1), newsgroup.

cyberspace \sī´bər-spās`\ *n*. **1.** The advanced shared virtual-reality network imagined by William Gibson in his novel *Neuromancer* (1982). **2.** The universe of environments, such as the Internet, in which persons interact by means of connected computers. A defining characteristic of cyberspace is that communication is independent of physical distance.

cybrarian \sī-brâr´ē-ən\ *n*. Software used at some libraries that allows one to query a database through the use of an interactive search engine.

cycle power \sī´kl pou`ər\ *vb*. To turn the power to a machine off and back on in order to clear something out of memory or to reboot after a hung or crashed state.

cycle time \sī´kl tīm`\ *n*. The amount of time between a random access memory (RAM) access and the earliest time a new access can occur. *See also* access time (definition 1).

cyclical redundancy check \si`klə-kəl rə-dun´dən-sē chek`\ *n*. *See* CRC.

cyclic binary code \si´klik bī`nər-ē kōd\ *n*. A binary representation of numbers in which each number differs from the one that precedes it by one unit (bit), in one position. Cyclic binary numbers differ from "plain" binary numbers, even though both are based on two digits, 0 and 1. The numbers in the cyclic binary system represent a code, much like Morse code, whereas "plain" binary numbers represent actual values in the binary number system. Because sequential numbers differ by only 1 bit, cyclic binary is used to minimize errors in representing unit measurements.

Decimal	Cyclic binary	"Plain" binary
0	0000	0000
1	0001	0001
2	0011	0010
3	0010	0011
4	0110	0100
5	0111	0101
6	0101	0110
7	0100	0111
8	1100	1000
9	1101	1001

Cycolor \sī´kəl`ər\ *n*. A color printing process that uses a special film embedded with millions of capsules filled with cyan, magenta, and yellow dyes. When exposed to red, green, or blue light, the respective capsules become hard and unbreakable. The film is then pressed against specially treated paper, and the capsules that have not hardened in the previous process break, releasing their colors onto the paper. *See also* CMY.

.cz \dot`C-Z´\ *n*. On the Internet, the major geographic domain specifying that an address is located in the Czech Republic.

DA \D-A´\ *n. See* desk accessory.

DAC \D`A-C´\ *n. See* digital-to-analog converter.

daemon \dē´mən\ *n.* A program associated with UNIX systems that performs a housekeeping or maintenance utility function without being called by the user. A daemon sits in the background and is activated only when needed, for example, to correct an error from which another program cannot recover.

daisy chain \dā´zē chān`\ *n.* A set of devices connected in series. In order to eliminate conflicting requests to use the channel (bus) to which all the devices are connected, each device is given a different priority, or, as in the Apple Desktop Bus, each device monitors the channel and transmits only when the line is clear.

daisy wheel \dā´zē hwēl`, wēl`\ *n.* A print element consisting of a set of formed characters with each character mounted on a separate type bar, all radiating from a center hub. See the illustration. *See also* daisy-wheel printer, thimble, thimble printer.

daisy-wheel printer \dā´zē hwēl prin`tər, wēl\ *n.* A printer that uses a daisy-wheel type element. Daisy-wheel output is crisp and slightly imprinted, with fully formed characters resembling typewriter quality. Daisy-wheel printers were standard for high-quality printing until being superseded by laser printers. *See also* daisy wheel, thimble, thimble printer.

damping \dam´pēng\ *n.* A technique for preventing overshoot (exceeding the desired limit) in the response of a circuit or device.

DAP \D`A-P´, dap\ *n. See* Directory Access Protocol.

dark fiber \därk` fī´bər\ *n.* Unused capacity in fiber-optic communications.

Darlington circuit \där´lēng-tən sər`kət\ *n.* An amplifier circuit made of two transistors, often mounted in the same housing. The collectors of

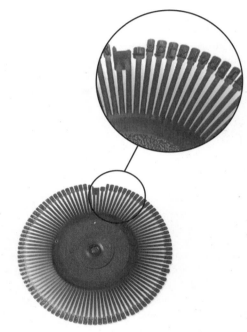

Daisy wheel. A section of the daisy wheel is enlarged to show detail.

the two transistors are connected, and the emitter of the first is connected to the base of the second. Darlington circuits provide high-gain amplification. *Also called* Darlington pair.

Darlington pair \där´lēng-tən pâr`\ *n. See* Darlington circuit.

DARPA \där´pə, D`A-R-P-A´\ *n. See* Defense Advanced Research Projects Agency.

DARPANET \där´pə-net`, D-A-R-P-A´net`\ *n.* Short for **D**efense **A**dvanced **R**esearch **P**rojects **A**gency **Net**work. *See* ARPANET.

DASD \D`A-S-D´, daz´dē\ *n.* Acronym for **d**irect **a**ccess **s**torage **d**evice. A data storage device by which information can be accessed directly, instead of by passing sequentially through all storage areas. For example, a disk drive is a DASD, but a tape unit is not, because, with a tape unit, the data is stored as a linear sequence. *See also* direct access. *Compare* sequential access.

.dat \dot-dat´, dot`D-A-T´\ *n.* A generic file extension for a data file.

DAT \dat, D`A-T´\ *n. See* digital audio tape, dynamic address translation.

data \dā´tə, dat´ə\ *n.* Plural of the Latin *datum,* meaning an item of information. In practice, *data* is often used for the singular as well as the plural form of the noun. *Compare* information.

data acquisition \dā´tə a-kwə-zi´shən, dat`ə\ *n.* The process of obtaining data from another source, usually one outside a specific system.

data aggregate \dā´tə a`grə-gət, dat´ə\ *n.* A collection of data records. It usually includes a description of the placement of the data blocks and their relation to the entire set.

data attribute \dā´tə a`tri-byo͞ot, dat´ə\ *n.* Structural information about data that describes its context and meaning.

data bank \dā´tə bank`, dat´ə\ *n.* Any substantial collection of data.

database \dā´tə-bās\ *n.* A file composed of records, each containing fields together with a set of operations for searching, sorting, recombining, and other functions.

database administrator \dā´tə-bās əd-min`-əs-trā-tər\ *n.* One who manages a database. The administrator determines the content, internal structure, and access strategy for a database, defines security and integrity, and monitors performance. *Acronym:* DBA (D`B-A´). *Also called* database manager.

database analyst \dā´tə-bās an`ə-list\ *n.* One who provides the analytic functions needed to design and maintain applications requiring a database.

database designer \dā´tə-bās də-zī´nər\ *n.* One who designs and implements functions required for applications that use a database.

database engine \dā´tə-bās en`jən\ *n.* The program module or modules that provide access to a database management system (DBMS).

database machine \dā´tə-bās mə-shēn`\ *n.* **1.** A peripheral that executes database tasks, thereby relieving the main computer from performing

them. **2.** A database server that performs only database tasks.

database management system \dā´tə-bās man´əj-mənt si`stəm\ *n.* A software interface between the database and the user. A database management system handles user requests for database actions and allows for control of security and data integrity requirements. *Acronym:* DBMS (D`B-M-S´). *Also called* database manager. *See also* database engine.

database manager \dā´tə-bās man`ə-jər\ *n. See* database administrator, database management system.

database publishing \dā´tə-bās pu`blə-shēng\ *n.* The use of desktop publishing or Internet technology to produce reports containing information obtained from a database.

database server \dā´tə-bās sər`vər\ *n.* A network node, or station, dedicated to storing and providing access to a shared database. *Also called* database machine.

database structure \dā´tə-bās struk`chur\ *n.* A general description of the format of records in a database, including the number of fields, specifications regarding the type of data that can be entered in each field, and the field names used.

data bit \dā´tə bit`, dat´ə\ *n.* In asynchronous communications, one of a group of from 5 to 8 bits that represents a single character of data for transmission. Data bits are preceded by a start bit and followed by an optional parity bit and one or more stop bits. *See also* asynchronous transmission, bit, communications parameter.

data buffer \dā´tə buf`ər, dat´ə\ *n.* An area in memory where data is temporarily stored while being moved from one location to another. *See also* buffer[1].

data bus \dā´tə bus`, dat´ə\ *n. See* bus.

data cable \dā´tə kā`bl, dat´ə\ *n.* Fiber-optic or wire cable used to transfer data from one device to another.

data capture \dā´tə kap`chur, dat´ə\ *n.* **1.** The collection of information at the time of a transaction. **2.** The process of saving on a storage medium a record of interchanges between a user and a remote information utility.

data carrier \dā´tə kâr`ē-er, dat´ə\ *n. See* carrier (definition 1).

Data Carrier Detected \dā`tə kâr`ē-er də-tek´təd, dat´ə\ *n. See* DCD.

data chaining \dā´tə chā`nēng, dat´ə\ *n.* The process of storing segments of data in noncontiguous locations while retaining the ability to reconnect them in the proper sequence.

data channel \dā´tə chan`əl, dat´ə\ *n. See* channel.

data collection \dā´tə kə-lek`shən, dat´ə\ *n.* **1.** The process of acquiring source documents or data. **2.** The grouping of data by means of classification, sorting, ordering, and other organizing methods.

datacom \dā´tə-kom`, dat´ə-kom`\ *n.* Short for **data com**munications. *See* communications.

data communications \dā´tə kə-myōō-nə-kā´shənz, dat´ə\ *n. See* communications.

data compaction \dā´tə kəm-pak`shən, dat´ə\ *n. See* data compression.

data compression \dā´tə kəm-presh`ən, dat´ə\ *n.* A means of reducing the amount of space or bandwidth needed to store or transmit a block of data, used in data communications, facsimile transmission, and CD-ROM publishing. *Also called* data compaction.

data conferencing \dā´tə kon`frən-sēng, dat´ə\ *n.* Simultaneous data communication among geographically separated participants in a meeting. Data conferencing involves whiteboards and other software that enable a single set of files at one location to be accessed and modified by all participants. See the illustration. *See also* desktop conferencing, whiteboard. *Compare* video conferencing.

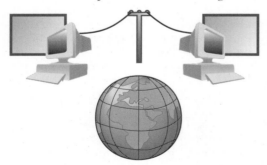

Data conferencing.

data control \dā´tə kən-trōl`, dat´ə\ *n.* The aspect of data management concerned with tracking how and by whom data is used, accessed, altered, owned, and reported on.

data corruption \dā´tə kər-up`shən, dat´ə\ *n. See* corruption.

data declaration \dā´tə de-klər-ā`shən, dat´ə\ *n.* A statement in a program that specifies the characteristics of a variable. The requirements for data declarations vary among different programming languages but can include such values as variable name, data type, initial value, and size specification. *See also* array, data type, record[1], variable.

data definition language \dā´tə def-ə-nish´ən lang-wəj, dat´ə\ *n.* A language that defines all attributes and properties of a database, especially record layouts, field definitions, key fields, file locations, and storage strategy. *Acronym:* DDL (D`D-L´).

data description language \dā´tə dəs-krip´shən lang-wəj, dat´ə\ *n.* A language designed specifically for declaring data structures and files. *See also* data definition language.

data dictionary \dā´tə dik`shə-nâr-ē, dat´ə\ *n.* A database containing data about all the databases in a database system. Data dictionaries store all the various schema and file specifications and their locations. They also contain information about which programs use which data and which users are interested in which reports.

data directory \dā´tə dər-ek`tər-ē, dat´ə\ *n. See* catalog, data dictionary.

data-driven processing \dā´tə-driv-ən pros´es-ēng, dat`ə-driv-ən\ *n.* A form of processing where the processor or program must wait for data to arrive before it can advance to the next step in a sequence.

data element \dā´tə el`ə-ment, dat´ə\ *n.* A single unit of data. *Also called* data item. *See also* data field.

data encryption \dā´tə en-krip`shən, dat´ə\ *n. See* encryption.

data encryption key \dā´tə en-krip´shən kē`, dat`ə\ *n.* A sequence of data that is used to encrypt and decrypt other data. *Acronym:* DEK (D`E-K´). *See also* decryption, encryption, key (definition 3).

data encryption standard \dā´tə en-krip´shən stan`dərd, dat´ə\ *n. See* DES.

data entry \dā´tə en´trē, dat´ə\ *n.* The process of writing new data to computer memory.

data/fax modem \dā´tə-faks´ mō`dəm, dat`ə\ *n*. A modem that can handle both serial data and facsimile images to either send or receive transmissions. See the illustration.

Data/fax modem.

data field \dā´tə fēld`, dat´ə\ *n*. A well-defined portion of a data record, such as a column in a database table.

data field masking \dā´tə fēld ma´skēng, dat`ə\ *n*. The process of filtering or selecting part of a data field to control the way it is returned and displayed.

data file \dā´tə fīl`, dat´ə\ *n*. A file consisting of data in the form of text, numbers, or graphics, as distinct from a program file of commands and instructions. *Compare* program file.

data flow or **dataflow** \dā´tə flō`, dat´ə\ *n*. **1.** The movement of data through a system, from entry to destination. **2.** In parallel processing, a design in which a calculation is made either when all necessary data is available (data-driven processing) or when other processors request the data (demand-driven processing). *See also* parallel processing.

data fork \dā´tə fôrk`, dat´ə\ *n*. In Macintosh files, the part of a stored document that contains user-supplied information, such as the text of a word-processing document. A Macintosh file can have a data fork, a resource fork (which contains information such as program code, font data, digitized sound, or icons), and a header. All three parts are used by the operating system in file management and storage. *See also* resource (definition 2), resource fork.

data format \dā´tə fôr´mat, dat´ə\ *n*. The structure applied to data by an application program to provide a context in which the data can be interpreted.

data frame \dā´tə frām`, dat´ə\ *n*. A packet of information transmitted as a unit on a network. Data frames are defined by the network's data-link layer and exist only on the wire between network nodes. *See also* data-link layer, frame (definition 2).

data glove \dā´tə gləv`, dat´ə\ *n*. A data input device or controller in the form of a glove fitted with sensors that convert movement of the hand and fingers into commands. *See also* virtual reality.

datagram \dā´tə-gram`, dat´ə-gram`\ *n*. One packet, or unit, of information, along with relevant delivery information such as the destination address, that is sent through a packet-switching network. *See also* packet switching.

data independence \dā´tə in-də-pen´dəns, dat´ə\ *n*. The separation of data in a database from the programs that manipulate it. Data independence makes stored data as accessible as possible.

data integrity \dā´tə in-te´grə-tē, dat´ə\ *n*. The accuracy of data and its conformity to its expected value, especially after being transmitted or processed.

data interchange format \dā´tə in´tər-chānj fôr-mat, dat´ə\ *n*. A format consisting of ASCII codes in which database, spreadsheet, and similar documents can be structured to facilitate their use by and transfer to other programs. *Acronym:* DIF (D`I-F´). *See also* ASCII.

data item \dā´tə ī´təm, dat´ə\ *n*. *See* data element.

data library \dā´tə lī`brâr-ē, dat´ə\ *n*. A cataloged collection of data files on disk or in another storage medium.

data link \dā´tə lēnk`, dat´ə\ *n*. A connection between any two devices capable of sending and receiving information, such as a computer and a printer or a main computer and a terminal. Sometimes the term is extended to include equipment, such as a modem, that enables transmission and receiving. Such devices follow protocols that govern data transmission. *See also* communications protocol, data-link layer, DCE, DTE.

data link escape \dā´tə lēnk` ə-skāp`, dat´ə\ *n*. In data transmission, a control character that changes the meaning of the characters immediately following it.

data-link layer \dā´tə-lēnk lâr`, dat´ə-, lā`ər\ *n*. The second of seven layers in the ISO/OSI model for standardizing computer-to-computer communications. The data-link layer is one layer above the physical layer. Its concern is packaging and addressing data and managing the flow of transmissions. It is the lowest of the three layers (data-link, network, and transport) involved in actually moving data between devices. *See also* ISO/OSI model.

data management \dā´tə man`əj-mənt, dat´ə\ *n.* The control of data from acquisition and input through processing, output, and storage. In microcomputers, hardware manages data by gathering it, moving it, and following instructions to process it. The operating system manages the hardware and ensures that the parts of the system work in harmony so that data is stored safely and accurately. Application programs manage data by receiving and processing input according to the user's commands, and sending results to an output device or to disk storage. The user also is responsible for data management by acquiring data, labeling and organizing disks, backing up data, archiving files, and removing unneeded material from the hard disk.

data manipulation \dā´tə mə-ni`pyə-lā`shən, dat´ə\ *n.* The processing of data by means of programs that accept user commands, offer ways to handle data, and tell the hardware what to do with the data.

data manipulation language \dā´tə mə-ni`pyə-lā`shən lang`wəj, dat´ə\ *n.* In database management systems, a language that is used to insert data in, update, and query a database. Data manipulation languages are often capable of performing mathematical and statistical calculations that facilitate generating reports. *Acronym:* DML (D`M-L´). *See also* structured query language.

data mart \dā´tə märt`, dat´ə\ *n.* A scaled-down version of a data warehouse that is tailored to contain only information likely to be used by the target group. *See also* data warehouse.

data medium \dā´tə mē`dē-um, dat´ə\ *n.* The physical material on which computer data is stored.

data migration \dā´tə mī-grā`shən, dat´ə\ *n.* **1.** The process of moving data from one repository or source, such as a database, to another, usually via automated scripts or programs. Often data migration involves transferring data from one type of computer system to another. **2.** In supercomputing applications, the process of storing large

amounts of data offline while making them appear to be online as disk-resident files.

data mining \dā´tə mī`nēng, dat´ə\ *n.* The process of identifying commercially useful patterns or relationships in databases or other computer repositories through the use of advanced statistical tools.

data model \dā´tə mod´əl, dat´ə\ *n.* A collection of related object types, operators, and integrity rules that form the abstract entity supported by a database management system (DBMS). Thus, one speaks of a relational DBMS, a network DBMS, and so on, depending on the type of data model a DBMS supports. In general, a DBMS supports only one data model as a practical rather than a theoretical restriction.

data network \dā´tə net`wərk, dat´ə\ *n.* A network designed for transferring data encoded as digital signals, as opposed to a voice network, which transmits analog signals.

data packet \dā´tə pak`ət, dat´ə\ *n. See* packet.

data point \dā´tə point`, dat´ə\ *n.* Any pair of numeric values plotted on a chart.

data processing \dā´tə pros´es-ēng, dat´ə\ *n.* **1.** The general work performed by computers. **2.** More specifically, the manipulation of data to transform it into some desired result. *Acronym:* DP (D-P´). *Also called* ADP, automatic data processing, EDP, electronic data processing. *See also* centralized processing, decentralized processing, distributed processing.

Data Processing Management Association \dā´tə pros`es-ēng man´əj-mənt ə-sō-sē-ā´shən, dat`ə\ *n. See* DPMA.

data protection \dā´tə pro-tek´shən, dat`ə\ *n.* The process of ensuring the preservation, integrity, and reliability of data. *See also* data integrity.

data rate \dā´tə rāt`, dat´ə\ *n.* The speed at which a circuit or communications line can transfer information, usually measured in bits per second (bps).

data record \dā´tə rek`ərd, dat´ə\ *n. See* record[1].

data reduction \dā´tə rə-duk`shən, dat´ə\ *n.* The process of converting raw data to a more useful form by scaling, smoothing, ordering, or other editing procedures.

data segment \dā´tə seg`mənt, dat´ə\ *n.* The portion of memory or auxiliary storage that contains the data used by a program.

data set \dā´tə set`, dat´ə\ *n*. **1.** A collection of related information made up of separate elements that can be treated as a unit in data handling. **2.** In communications, a modem. *See also* modem.

Data Set Ready \dā´tə set red`ē, dat´ə\ *n. See* DSR.

data sharing \dā´tə shâr`ēng, dat´ə\ *n*. The use of a single file by more than one person or computer. Data sharing can be done by physically transferring a file from one computer to another, or, more commonly, by networking and computer-to-computer communications.

data signal \dā´tə sig`nəl, dat´ə\ *n*. The information transmitted over a line or circuit. It consists of binary digits and can include actual information or messages and other elements such as control characters or error-checking codes.

data sink \dā´tə sēnk`, dat´ə\ *n*. **1.** Any recording medium where data can be stored until needed. **2.** In communications, the portion of a Data Terminal Equipment (DTE) device that receives transmitted data.

data source \dā´tə sōrs`, dat´ə\ *n*. **1.** The originator of computer data, frequently an analog or digital data collection device. **2.** In communications, the portion of a Data Terminal Equipment (DTE) device that sends data.

data stream \dā´tə strēm`, dat´ə\ *n*. An undifferentiated, byte-by-byte flow of data.

data structure \dā´tə struk`chur, dat´ə\ *n*. An organizational scheme, such as a record or array, that can be applied to data to facilitate interpreting the data or performing operations on it.

data switch \dā´tə swich`, dat´ə\ *n*. A device in a computer system that routes incoming data to various locations.

Data Terminal Ready \dā´tə tər-mə-nəl red´ē, dat`ə\ *n. See* DTR.

data traffic \dā´tə traf`ik, dat´ə\ *n*. The exchange of electronic messages—control and data—across a network. Traffic capacity is measured in bandwidth; traffic speed is measured in bits per unit of time.

data transfer \dā´tə trans`fər, dat´ə\ *n*. The movement of information from one location to another, either within a computer (as from a disk drive to memory), between a computer and an external device (as between a file server and a computer on a network), or between separate computers.

data transfer rate \dā´tə trans´fər rāt, dat`ə\ *n*. *See* data rate.

data transmission \dā´tə tranz-mish`ən, dat´ə\ *n*. The electronic transfer of information from a sending device to a receiving device.

data type \dā´tə tīp`, dat´ə\ *n*. In programming, a definition of a set of data that specifies the possible range of values of the set, the operations that can be performed on the values, and the way in which the values are stored in memory. Defining the data type allows a computer to manipulate the data appropriately. Data types are most often supported in high-level languages and often include types such as real, integer, floating point, character, Boolean, and pointer. How a language handles data typing is one of its major characteristics. *See also* cast, constant, enumerated data type, strong typing, type checking, user-defined data type, variable, weak typing.

data validation \dā´tə val`ə-dā`shən, dat´ə\ *n*. The process of testing the accuracy of data.

data value \dā´tə val´yōō, dat´ə\ *n*. The literal or interpreted meaning of a data item, such as an entry in a database, or a type, such as an integer, that can be used for a variable.

data warehouse \dā´tə wâr´hous, dat`ə\ *n*. A database, frequently very large, that can access all of a company's information. While the warehouse can be distributed over several computers and may contain several databases and information from numerous sources in a variety of formats, it should be accessible through a server. Thus, access to the warehouse is transparent to the user, who can use simple commands to retrieve and analyze all the information. The data warehouse also contains data about how the warehouse is organized, where the information can be found, and any connections between data. Frequently used for decision support within an organization, the data warehouse also allows the organization to organize its data, coordinate updates, and see relationships between information gathered from different parts of the organization. *See also* database, decision support system, server (definition 1), transparent (definition 1).

date stamping \dāt´ stam`pēng\ *n*. A software feature that automatically inserts the current date into a document.

datum \dā´tum\ *n.* Singular of *data;* a single item of information. *See also* data.

daughterboard \dä´tər-bōrd, dô´tər-bōrd\ *n.* A circuit board that attaches to another, such as the main system board (motherboard), to add extra capabilities. See the illustration. *See also* motherboard.

Daughterboard.

DAV connector \D-A-V´ kə-nek`tər\ *n. See* digital audio/video connector.

dB \des´ə-bəl, D-B´\ *n. See* decibel.

DB \D-B´\ *n. See* database.

DBA \D`B-A´\ *n. See* database administrator.

DB connector \D-B´ kə-nek`tər\ *n.* Any of various connectors that facilitate parallel input and output. The initials DB (for data bus) are followed by a number that indicates the number of lines (wires) within the connector. For example, a DB-9 connector supports up to nine lines, each of which can connect to a pin on the connector. See the illustration.

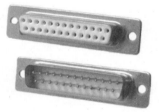

DB connector.   A female (top) and a male (bottom) DB connector.

.dbf \dot`D-B-F´\ *n.* A file extension for a dBASE database file.

DBMS \D`B-M-S´\ *n. See* database management system.

DC \D-C´\ *n. See* direct current.

DCA \D`C-A´\ *n.* **1.** Acronym for **D**ocument **C**ontent **A**rchitecture. A formatting guideline used in IBM's Systems Network Architecture (SNA) that enables the exchange of text-only documents between differing types of computers. DCA provides for two types of document formatting:

Revisable-Form-Text DCA (RFTDCA), which allows for modification of formatting, and Final-Form-Text DCA (FFTDCA), which cannot be modified. *See also* DIA, SNA. **2.** Acronym for **D**irectory **C**lient **A**gent. *See* DUA.

DCD \D´C-D´\ *n.* Acronym for **D**ata **C**arrier **D**etected. A signal in serial communications that is sent from a modem to its computer to indicate that the modem is ready for transmitting. *Also called* RLSD (Received Line Signal Detect). *See also* RS-232-C standard.

DCE \D´C-E´\ *n.* **1.** Acronym for **D**ata **C**ommunications **E**quipment. One of two types of hardware connected by an RS-232-C serial connection, the other being a Data Terminal Equipment (DTE) device. A DCE is an intermediary device that often transforms input from a DTE before sending it to a recipient. A modem, for example, is a DCE that modulates data from a microcomputer (DTE) and sends it along a telephone connection. *See also* RS-232-C standard. *Compare* DTE. **2.** *See* Distributed Computing Environment.

DCOM \D´kom, D´C-O-M´\ *n.* Acronym for **D**istributed **C**omponent **O**bject **M**odel. The version of Microsoft's Component Object Model (COM) specification that stipulates how components communicate over Windows-based networks. It permits the distribution of different components for a single application across two or more networked computers, running an application distributed across a network so that the distribution of components is not apparent to the user, and remotely displaying an application. *Also called* Distributed COM. *See also* COM (definition 2), component (definition 2).

DCTL \D´C-T-L´\ *n. See* direct-coupled transistor logic.

DDBMS \D`D-B´M-S´\ *n. See* distributed database management system.

DDC \D`D-C´\ *n.* Acronym for **D**isplay **D**ata **C**hannel. A VESA standard that allows software control of graphical computer monitors. Under DDC, monitor characteristics are provided to the graphics subsystem, which uses the data to configure the display and provide a bidirectional communication channel between the monitor and computer. *Also called* VESA DDC. *See also* VESA[2].

DDE \D`D-E´\ *n.* Acronym for **D**ynamic **D**ata **E**xchange. An interprocess communication method featured in Microsoft Windows and OS/2. DDE allows two or more programs that are running simultaneously to exchange data and commands. In Windows 3.1, DDE was largely supplanted by OLE, which is an extension of DDE. In Windows 95 and Windows NT, OLE and ActiveX are more commonly used. *See also* ActiveX, interprocess communication, OLE.

DDL \D`D-L´\ *n. See* data definition language.

.de \dot`D-E´\ *n.* On the Internet, the major geographic domain specifying that an address is located in Germany.

dead halt \ded hält´\ *n.* A machine stop with no hope of recovery by either the program or the operating system. The only choice after a dead halt is to reboot. *Also called* drop-dead halt. *See also* hang. *Compare* reboot.

dead key \ded´ kē\ *n.* A key used with another key to create an accented character. When pressed, a dead key produces no visible character (hence its name) but indicates that the accent mark it represents is to be combined with the next key pressed. *See also* key (definition 1).

dead-letter box \ded`let´ər boks`\ *n.* In e-mail or message systems, a file to which undeliverable messages are sent.

deadlock \ded´lok\ *n.* **1.** A situation that occurs when two programs or devices are each waiting for a response from the other before continuing. *Also called* deadly embrace. **2.** In operating systems, a situation in which two or more processes are prevented from continuing while each waits for resources to be freed by the continuation of the other.

deadly embrace \ded`lē em-brās´\ *n. See* deadlock (definition 1).

deallocate \dē-al´ə-kāt\ *vb.* To free previously allocated memory. *See also* pointer. *Compare* allocate.

deblock \dē-blok´\ *vb.* To remove one or more logical records (units of stored information) from a block. Application or database systems must often deblock information to make specific units of information available for processing. *Compare* block[2] (definition 1).

debug \dē-bug´\ *vb.* To detect, locate, and correct logical or syntactical errors in a program or malfunctions in hardware. In hardware contexts, the term *troubleshoot* is the term more often used, especially when the problem is a major one. *See also* bug, debugger.

debugger \dē-bug´ər\ *n.* A program designed to aid in debugging another program by allowing the programmer to step through the program, examine the data, and monitor conditions such as the values of variables. *See also* bug (definition 1), debug.

decay \də-kā´\ *n.* A decrease in the amplitude of a signal over time.

DECchip 21064 \D`E-C`chip tōō`wən-ō`siks-fōr´\ *n.* A Digital Equipment Corporation microprocessor introduced in February 1992. The DECchip 21064 is a 64-bit, RISC-based, superscalar, super-pipelined chip with 64-bit registers, a 64-bit data bus, a 64-bit address bus, and a 128-bit data path between the microprocessor and memory. It also has a built-in 8-KB instruction cache, a built-in 8-KB data cache, and a floating-point processor. The DECchip 21064 contains 1.7 million transistors and operates at 3.3 volts. The 200-MHz version runs at a peak rate of 400 MPS. The chip's architecture is SMP compliant, so that several chips can be used in a parallel (multiprocessor) configuration. *See also* floating-point processor, MIPS, pipelining (definition 1), RISC, superpipelining, superscalar.

deceleration time \dē-sel`ər-ā´shən tīm`\ *n.* The time required for an access arm to come to a stop as it approaches the desired portion of a disk. The faster the arm moves, the more momentum it gains and the greater the deceleration time.

decentralized processing \dē-sen`trə-līzd pros´es-ēng, dē´-sen-trə-līzd\ *n.* The distribution of computer processing facilities in more than one location. Decentralized processing is not the same as distributed processing, which assigns multiple computers to the same task to increase efficiency.

deci- \des´ə\ *prefix* Metric prefix meaning 10^{-1} (one tenth).

decibel \des´ə-bəl\ *n.* Abbreviated dB. One tenth of a bel (named after Alexander Graham Bell), a unit used in electronics and other fields to measure the strength of a sound or signal. Decibel measurements fall on a logarithmic scale and compare the measured quantity against a known reference. The following formula gives the number of decibels between two values:

$$dB = n \log (x/r)$$

where x is the measured quantity, r is the reference quantity, and n is 10 for voltage and current measurements and 20 for power measurements.

decimal \des´ə-məl, des´məl\ *n.* The base-10 numbering system. *See also* base (definition 2).

decision box \də-sizh´ən boks`\ *n.* A diamond-shaped flowchart symbol denoting a decision that results in a branching in the process being considered. See the illustration.

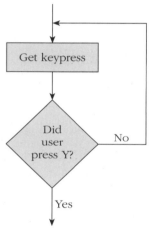

Decision box.

decision support system \də-sizh`ən su-pōrt´ si-stəm\ *n.* A set of programs and related data designed to help with analysis and decision making. A decision support system provides more help in formulating decisions than a management information system (MIS) or an executive information system (EIS). It includes a database, a body of knowledge about the subject area, a "language" used to formulate problems and questions, and a modeling program for testing alternative decisions. *Acronym:* DSS (D`S-S´). *Compare* executive information system, management information system.

decision table \də-sizh´ən tā`bl\ *n.* A tabular listing of possible conditions (inputs) and the desired result (output) corresponding to each condition. A decision table may be used in the preliminary analysis of program flow, or it may be converted and incorporated into the program itself.

decision tree \də-sizh´ən trē`\ *n.* Similar to a decision table, an analysis instrument where possible outcomes of some condition are represented as branches, which may in turn generate other branches. See the illustration. *See also* branch (definition 1), tree structure.

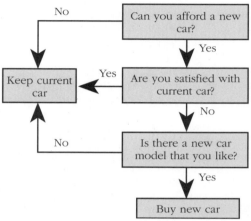

Decision tree.

deck \dek\ *n.* A storage device, such as a tape deck, or a group of such devices.

declaration \de`klər-ā´shən\ *n.* A binding of an identifier to the information that relates to it. For example, to make a declaration of a constant means to bind the name of the constant with its value. Declaration usually occurs in a program's source code; the actual binding can take place at compile time or run time. *See also* bind, constant, data declaration, data type, identifier, instruction, routine, type declaration, variable.

declarative markup language \də-klâr`ə-tiv mär´kup lang`wəj\ *n.* In text processing, a system of text-formatting codes that indicates only that a unit of text is a certain part of a document. Document formatting is then done by another program, called a parser. SGML and HTML are examples of declarative markup languages. *Acronym:* DML (D`M-L´). *See also* HTML, SGML.

declare \də-klâr´\ *vb.* To specify the name and type of a variable that will be used in a program. In most high-level programming languages, variables are declared at the beginning of sections of code. *See also* variable.

decoder \dē`kō´dər, də-kō´dər\ *n.* **1.** A device or program routine that converts coded data back to its original form. This can mean changing unreadable or encrypted codes into readable text or changing one code to another, although the latter type of decoding is usually referred to as conversion. *Compare* conversion. **2.** In electronics and hardware, a type of circuit that produces one or more selected output signals based on the combination of input signals it receives.

decollate \dē`kō´lāt\ *vb.* To separate copies in a multipart continuous paper form.

decompiler \dē´-kəm-pī´lər\ *n.* A program that attempts to generate high-level source code from assembly language code or machine code. This can be a difficult task, as some assembly language code has no corresponding high-level source code. *See also* disassembler. *Compare* compiler (definition 2).

decompress \dē`kəm-pres´\ *vb. See* uncompress.

.de.co.us \dot-D-E`dot-C-O-dot-U-S´\ *n.* On the Internet, the major geographic domain specifying that an address is located in Denver, Colorado, United States.

decrement[1] \de´krə-mənt\ *n.* The amount by which a number is decreased. *Compare* increment[1].

decrement[2] \de´krə-mənt\ *vb.* To decrease a number by a given amount. *Compare* increment[2].

decryption \dē-krip´shən\ *n.* The process of restoring encrypted data to its original form. *Compare* encryption.

DECstation \dek´stā`shən, D-E-C´\ *n.* **1.** A small computer system used primarily for word processing, introduced by Digital Equipment Corporation in 1978. **2.** One of a series of personal computers introduced by Digital Equipment Corporation in 1989. **3.** One of a series of single-user UNIX workstations introduced by Digital Equipment Corporation in 1989 and based on RISC processors. *See also* RISC.

dedicated \ded´ə-kā`təd\ *adj.* Of, pertaining to, or being a device, program, or procedure devoted to a single task or function.

dedicated channel \ded`ə-kā-təd chan´əl\ *n.* A communications link reserved for a particular use or a particular user.

dedicated line \ded`ə-kā-təd līn´\ *n.* **1.** A communications channel that permanently connects two or more locations. Dedicated lines are private or leased lines, rather than public ones. T1 lines, which are used by many organizations for Internet connectivity, are examples of dedicated lines. *Also called* leased line, private line. *Compare* switched line. **2.** A telephone line that is used for one purpose only, such as to receive or send faxes or to serve as a modem line.

deep copy \dēp´ kop`ē\ *n.* A copy of the contents of a data structure, including all its substructures.

deep hack \dēp hak´\ *n.* A state of total concentration on and preoccupation with a programming effort. *Also called* deep hack mode.

de facto standard \dē fak`tō stan´dərd\ *n.* A design, program, or language that has become so widely used and imitated that it has little competition, but whose status has not been officially recognized as standard by an organization such as the American National Standards Institute (ANSI) or the International Organization for Standardization (ISO). *See also* standard. *Compare* de jure standard.

default[1] \də-fält´, də-fôlt´, dē´fält, dē´fôlt\ *n.* A choice made by a program when the user does not specify an alternative. Defaults are built into a program when a value or option must be assumed for the program to function.

default[2] \də-fält´, də-fôlt´, dē´fält, dē´fôlt\ *vb.* In reference to programs, to make a choice when the user does not specify an alternative.

default button \də-fält´ but`ən, də-fôlt´, dē´fält, dē´fôlt\ *n.* The control that is automatically selected when a window is introduced by an application or operating system, typically activated by pressing the Enter key.

default drive \də-fält´ drīv´, də-fôlt´, dē´fält, dē´fôlt\ *n.* The disk drive that an operating system reads to and writes from when no alternative is specified.

default home page \də-fält` hōm´ pāj, də-fôlt`, dē`fält, dē`fôlt\ *n.* On a Web server, the file that is returned when a directory is referenced without a specific filename. This is specified by the Web server software and is typically the file called index.html or index.htm.

default printer \dəfält´ prin`tər, də-fôlt´, dē´fält, dē´fôlt\ *n.* The printer to which a computer sends documents for printing unless an alternative is specified.

Defense Advanced Research Projects Agency \də-fens` əd-vansd` rē´sərch proj`ekts ā`jən-sē\ *n.* The U.S. government agency that provided the original support for the development of the interconnected networks that later grew into the Internet. *Acronym:* DARPA (där´pə, D`A-R-P-A´). *See also* ARPANET.

deferred address \də-fərd` a´dres, ə-dres`\ *n.* An indirect address (memory location) whose calculation is delayed until a program is run. *See also* relative address.

deferred processing \də-fərd` pros´es-ēng\ *n.* Processing of data after it has been received and stored in blocks. *Compare* direct processing.

deflection coils \də-flek´shən koilz`\ *n. See* yoke.

deformation \def`ər-mā´shən\ *n.* In multimedia and computer-aided design applications, the process of altering a model via certain tools, such as stretch, shatter, bend, and twist. *See also* CAD, multimedia.

defragmentation \dē`frag mən-tā´ shən\ *n.* The process of rewriting parts of a file to contiguous sectors on a hard disk to increase the speed of access and retrieval. When files are updated, the computer tends to save these updates on the largest continuous space on the hard disk, which is often on a different sector than the other parts of the file. When files are thus "fragmented," the computer must search the hard disk each time the file is accessed to find all of the file's parts, which slows down response time. Windows 95 and Windows NT include defragmentation utilities (or *defraggers*) as part of the operating system. For the MAC OS, Windows 3.*x*, and DOS systems, defragmentation utilities must be purchased separately. *See also* optimization (definition 1). *Compare* fragmentation.

degausser \dē-gä´sər, dē-gô´sər\ *n.* A device used to remove magnetization from a video monitor or tape recorder head and to erase information from magnetic storage media, such as tapes and disks.

degradation \de`grə-dā´shən\ *n.* **1.** In communications, a deterioration of signal quality, as from line interference. **2.** In computer systems, a reduction in level of performance or service. Degradation in microcomputer performance is indicated

by slow response times or frequent pauses for disk access because memory is insufficient to hold an entire program plus the data the program is using.

deinstall \dē`in-stäl´\ *vb. See* uninstall.

dejagging \dē-jag´ēng\ *n.* Smoothing of the jagged, "stairstep" appearance of diagonal lines and curves in graphical images. *Also called* antialiasing. *Compare* aliasing.

de jure standard \də jōōr`ā stan´dərd\ *n.* A standard for hardware or software development that has been issued or approved through a formal process by a standards organization. *See also* standard. *Compare* de facto standard.

DEK \D`E-K´\ *n. See* data encryption key.

deka- \dek´ə\ *prefix* Metric prefix meaning 10^1 (a factor of 10).

delay distortion \də-lā´ di-stōr`shən\ *n. See* envelope delay.

delete \də-lēt´\ *vb.* To eliminate text, a file, or part of a document with the intention of removing the information permanently. There are several ways to delete. On-screen characters and parts of documents can be deleted with the Delete key, the Backspace key, or with a program's Delete command. Files can be deleted through a command to the operating system.

Delete key \də-lēt´ kē`\ *n.* **1.** On IBM and PC-compatible computers, a key whose function changes depending on the application program. Usually it erases the character under the cursor, although in some applications it can erase selected text or graphics. **2.** On Apple Macintosh computers, a key on the ADB and Extended keyboards that erases the character preceding the insertion point or erases highlighted text or graphics.

deletia \də-lē´shə\ *n.* Omitted material. The term is used in responses to Usenet or mailing list messages to indicate that some unnecessary material has been excluded from the incorporated message being answered.

delimit \di-lim´it\ *vb.* To set the limits of some entity, generally by using a special symbol called a delimiter. Programming languages typically delimit such variable-length elements as comments, strings, and program blocks. *See also* delimiter.

delimiter \di-lim´i-tər\ *n.* A special character that sets off, or separates, individual items in a program or set of data. In the following example, commas separate the fields in a database record (each non-numeric field is enclosed by double quotation marks).

"Jones", "718 Harbor Drive", "Bayview", "WA", 98077;

"Smith", "324 Marina Ave.", "Yelm", "WA", 98597;

See also delimit, field (definition 1), record[1].

Del key \də-lēt´ kē`\ *n. See* Delete key.

Delphi Information Service \del`fī in`fər-mā´shən sər`vəs\ *n.* An online information service and Internet access provider based in Boston.

demand-driven processing \də-mand`-driv-ən pros´es-ēng\ *n.* The processing of data immediately as it becomes available or ready. Such real-time processing avoids the need to store data that has not been processed. *Compare* data-driven processing.

demand paging \də-mand´ pā`jēng\ *n.* The most common implementation of virtual memory, in which pages of data are read into main memory from an auxiliary storage device only in response to interrupts that result when software requests a memory location that the system has saved to auxiliary storage and reused for other purposes. *See also* paging, swap (definition 2), virtual memory.

demo \dem´ō\ *n.* **1.** Short for **demo**nstration. A partial or limited version of a software package distributed free of charge for advertising purposes. Demos often consist of animated presentations that describe or demonstrate the program's features. *See also* crippled version. **2.** A computer in a store that is available for customers to test, to see if they wish to buy it.

demodulation \di-moj`ə-lā´shən, di-mo`dyə-lā´-shən\ *n.* In communications, the means by which a modem converts data from modulated carrier frequencies (waves that have been modified in such a way that variations in amplitude and frequency represent meaningful information) over a telephone line to the digital form needed by a computer, with as little distortion as possible. *Compare* modulation (definition 1).

demonstration program or **demo program** \dem`ən-strā´shən prō`gram\ *n.* **1.** A prototype that shows the on-screen look and sometimes the proposed capabilities of a program under development. *See also* prototyping. **2.** A scaled-down

version of a proprietary program offered as a marketing tool.

denizen \den´i-zən\ *n.* A participant in a Usenet newsgroup.

dependence \də-pen´dəns\ *n.* The state in which one entity relies upon specific hardware, software, or specific events for its own definition or functionality. *See also* context-dependent, dependent variable, device dependence, hardware-dependent, software-dependent.

dependent variable \də-pen`dənt vâr´ē-ə-bl\ *n.* A variable in a program whose value relies on the outcome of another operation.

depth queuing \depth´ kyo͞o`ēng\ *vb.* **1.** In computer graphics and modeling, giving a two-dimensional object a three-dimensional appearance through such techniques as shading and hidden-line removal. **2.** Drawing objects from background to foreground to ease in the task of hidden-line removal.

deque \dek\ *n.* Short for **d**ouble-**e**nded **que**ue. A form of the queue data structure that can have elements added to or removed from either end of the list. *See also* queue.

dequeue \dē-kyo͞o´\ *vb.* To remove from a queue. *See also* queue.

dereference \dē`ref´rəns\ *vb.* In programming, to access information at the address contained by a pointer. The syntax for dereferencing varies among computer languages. *See also* double-dereference, handle (definition 1), pointer.

derived class \dər-īvd` klas´\ *n.* In object-oriented programming, a class created from another class, called the base class. A derived class inherits all the features of its base class. It can then add data elements and routines, redefine routines from the base class, and restrict access to base-class features. *See also* base class, class, inheritance (definition 1), object-oriented programming.

derived font \dər-īvd` font´\ *n.* A font that has been scaled or modified from a previously existing font. For example, the Macintosh operating system can generate characters in font sizes other than the installed range of sizes. *See also* font. *Compare* intrinsic font.

derived relation \dər-īvd` rə-lā´shən\ *n.* A relation produced as the result of one or more relational-algebra operations on other relations. *See also* relational algebra, view[1] (definition 2).

DES \D`E-S`\ *n.* Acronym for **D**ata **E**ncryption **S**tandard. A specification for encryption of computer data developed by IBM and adopted by the U.S. government as a standard in 1976. DES uses a 56-bit key. *See also* encryption, key (definition 3).

descendant \də-sen´dənt`\ *n.* **1.** In object-oriented programming, a class (group) that is a more specialized form of another, higher-level class. *See also* class, object-oriented programming. **2.** In computing, a process (roughly, a program or task) that is called by another process and inherits certain of the originator's properties, such as open files. *See also* child (definition 1), inheritance (definition 2). *Compare* client (definition 2).

descender \də-sen´dər\ *n.* The portion of a lowercase letter that falls below the baseline. See the illustration. *See also* baseline, x-height. *Compare* ascender.

Descender   Baseline

Descender.

descending sort \də-sen`dēng sōrt´\ *n.* A sort that arranges items in descending order—for example, with Z preceding A and higher numbers preceding lower ones. *See also* alphanumeric sort. *Compare* ascending sort.

descriptor \dəs-krip´tər\ *n.* **1.** In information retrieval, a word, similar to an index entry in a book, that identifies a significant topic or element in a stored document or group of documents. It is used as a key in rapid search and retrieval of information. *See also* keyword (definition 1). **2.** In programming, a piece of stored information used to describe something else, often in terms of structure, content, or some other property. *Compare* identifier.

deselect \dē`se-lekt´\ *vb.* To reverse the action of selecting an option, a range of text, a collection of graphical objects, and so on. *Compare* select.

deserialize \dē-sēr´ē-ə-līz`\ *vb.* To change from serial (by bit) to parallel (by byte); to convert a single (serial) stream of bits to parallel streams representing the same information. *Compare* serialize.

design cycle \də-zīn´ sī`kl\ *n.* All the phases involved in developing and producing new hardware or software, including product specification, creation of prototypes, testing, debugging, and documentation.

desk accessory \desk` ak-ses´ər-ē\ *n.* A type of small program on Macintosh computers and in windowing programs for IBM and PC-compatible machines that acts as the electronic equivalent of a clock, calendar, calculator, or other small appliance found on a typical desktop. Desk accessories are conveniences that can be activated when needed and then either put away or moved to a small part of the screen. A special type of desk accessory, a control panel, provides the user with the ability to change the date and time as well as to control screen colors, mouse movements, and other parameters. *Acronym:* DA (D-A´). *Also called* desktop accessory. *See also* control panel.

desktop \desk´top\ *n.* An on-screen work area that uses icons and menus to simulate the top of a desk. A desktop is characteristic of the Apple Macintosh and of windowing programs such as Microsoft Windows. Its intent is to make a computer easier to use by enabling users to move pictures of objects and to start and stop tasks in much the same way as they would if they were working on a physical desktop. *See also* graphical user interface.

desktop accessory \desk`top ak-ses´ər-ē\ *n.* See desk accessory.

desktop computer \desk`top kəm-pyoo͞´tər\ *n.* A computer that fits conveniently on the surface of a business desk. Most personal computers as well as some workstations can be considered desktop computers. *Compare* portable computer.

desktop conferencing \desk`top kon´frən-sēng\ *n.* The use of computers for simultaneous communication among geographically separated participants in a meeting. This communication may include input to and display from application programs as well as audio and video communication. *See also* data conferencing, teleconferencing, video conferencing.

desktop enhancer \desk´top en-han`sər\ *n.* Software that adds functionality to a windows-based operating system such as Microsoft Windows or Mac OS—for example, an enhanced file browser, clipboard, or multimedia player.

Desktop file \desk´top fīl`\ *n.* A hidden file maintained on a particular volume (roughly equivalent to a disk) by the Macintosh operating system for storing information about the files on it, such as version data, lists of icons, and file references.

Desktop Management Interface \desk`top man`əj-mənt in´tər-fās\ *n. See* DMI.

desktop publishing \desk`top pu´bli-shēng\ *n.* The use of a computer and specialized software to combine text and graphics to create a document that can be printed on either a laser printer or a typesetting machine. Desktop publishing is a multiple-step process involving various types of software and equipment. The original text and illustrations are generally produced with software such as word processors and drawing and painting programs and with photograph-scanning equipment and digitizers. The finished product is then transferred to a page-makeup program, which is the software most people think of as the actual desktop publishing software. This type of program enables the user to lay out text and graphics on the screen and see what the results will be; for refining parts of the document, these programs often include word processing and graphics features in addition to layout capabilities. As a final step, the finished document is printed either on a laser printer or, for the best quality, by typesetting equipment.

desktop video \desk`top vid´ē-ō\ *n.* The use of a personal computer to display video images. The video images may be recorded on video tape or on a laser disc or may be live footage from a video camera. Live video images can be transmitted in digital form over a network in video conferencing. *Acronym:* DTV (D`T-V´).

destination \de`stə-nā´shən\ *n.* The location (drive, folder, or directory) to which a file is copied or moved. *Compare* source (definition 1).

destructive read \dis-truk´tiv rēd´\ *n.* An attribute of certain memory systems, notably core systems. In a destructive read of a memory location, the data is passed on to the processor, but the copy in memory is destroyed by the process of reading. Destructive memory systems require special logic to rewrite data back to a memory location after it is read. *Also called* destructive readout. *See also* core. *Compare* nondestructive readout.

detail file \dē´tāl fīl`\ *n. See* transaction file.

detection \də-tek´shən\ *n.* Discovery of a certain condition that affects a computer system or the data with which it works.

determinant \də-tər´mə-nənt`\ *n.* In database design theory, any attribute or combination of attributes on which any other attribute or combination of attributes is functionally dependent.

determinism \də-tər´mə-ni-zəm`\ *n.* In computing, the ability to predict an outcome or to know in advance how data will be manipulated by a processing system. A deterministic simulation, for example, is one in which a certain input always produces the same output.

developer's toolkit \də-vel`ə-pərz tōōl`kit\ *n.* A set of routines (usually in one or more libraries) designed to allow developers to more easily write programs for a given computer, operating system, or user interface. *See also* library (definition 1), toolbox.

development cycle \də-vel´əp-mənt sī`kl\ *n.* The process of application development from definition of requirements to finished product, including the following stages: analysis, design and prototyping, software coding and testing, and implementation.

device \də-vīs´\ *n.* A generic term for a computer subsystem. Printers, serial ports, and disk drives are often referred to as devices; such subsystems frequently require their own controlling software, called device drivers. *See also* device driver.

device address \də-vīs´ a`dres, ə-dres´\ *n.* A location within the address space of a computer's random access memory (RAM) that can be altered either by the microprocessor or by an external device. Device addresses are different from other locations in RAM, which can be altered only by the microprocessor. *See also* device, input/output, RAM.

device control character \də-vīs` kən-trōl´ kâr`ək-tər\ *n. See* control character.

device controller \də-vīs´ kən-trō`lər\ *n. See* input/output controller.

device dependence \də-vīs´ də-pen`dəns\ *n*. The requirement that a particular device be present or available for the use of a program, interface, or protocol. Device dependence in a program is often considered unfortunate because the program either is limited to one system or requires adjustments for every other type of system on which it is to run. *Compare* device independence.

device driver \də-vīs´ drī`vər\ *n*. A software component that permits a computer system to communicate with a device. In most cases, the driver also manipulates the hardware in order to transmit the data to the device. However, device drivers associated with application packages typically perform only the data translation; these higher-level drivers then rely on lower-level drivers to actually send the data to the device. Many devices, especially video adapters on PC-compatible computers, will not work properly—if at all—without the correct device drivers installed in the system.

device independence \də-vīs` in-də-pen´dəns\ *n*. A characteristic of a program, interface, or protocol that supports software operations that produce similar results on a wide variety of hardware. For example, the PostScript language is a device-independent page description language because programs issuing PostScript drawing and text commands need not be customized for each potential printer. *Compare* device dependence.

device-independent bitmap \də-vīs`in-də-pen`-dənt bit´map\ *n*. *See* DIB.

device manager \də-vīs´ man`ə-jər\ *n*. A software utility that allows viewing and changing hardware configuration settings, such as interrupts, base addresses, and serial communication parameters.

Device Manager \də-vīs´ man`ə-jər\ *n*. In Windows 95, a function within the System Properties utility that indicates device conflicts and other problems and allows a user to change the properties of the computer and each device attached to it. *See also* property, property sheet.

device name \də-vīs´ nām`\ *n*. The label by which a computer system component is identified by the operating system. MS-DOS, for example, uses the device name COM1 to identify the first serial communications port.

device resolution \də-vīs` rez`ə-lōō´shən\ *n*. *See* resolution (definition 1).

DFS \D`F-S´\ *n*. *See* distributed file system.

DGIS \D`G-I-S´\ *n*. Acronym for **D**irect **G**raphics **I**nterface **S**pecification. An interface developed by Graphics Software Systems. DGIS is firmware (generally implemented in ROM on a video adapter) that allows a program to display graphics on a video display through an extension to the IBM BIOS Interrupt 10H interface.

DHCP \D`H-C-P´\ *n*. Acronym for **D**ynamic **H**ost **C**onfiguration **P**rotocol. A TCP/IP protocol that enables a network connected to the Internet to assign a temporary IP address to a host automatically when the host connects to the network. *See also* IP address, TCP/IP. *Compare* dynamic SLIP.

Dhrystone \drī´stōn\ *n*. A general-performance benchmarking test, originally developed by Rheinhold Weicker in 1984 to measure and compare computer performance. The test reports general system performance in dhrystones per second. It is intended to replace the older and less reliable Whetstone benchmark. The Dhrystone benchmark, like most benchmarks, consists of standard code revised periodically to minimize unfair advantages to certain combinations of hardware, compiler, and environment. Dhrystone concentrates on string handling and uses no floating-point operations. Like most benchmarking tests, it is heavily influenced by hardware and software design, such as compiler and linker options, code optimizing, cache memory, wait states, and integer data types. *See also* benchmark[2]. *Compare* sieve of Eratosthenes, Whetstone.

DIA \D`I-A´\ *n*. Acronym for **D**ocument **I**nterchange **A**rchitecture. A document exchange guideline used in IBM's Systems Network Architecture (SNA). DIA specifies methods of organizing and addressing documents for transmission between computers of different sizes and models. DIA is supported by IBM's Advanced Program-to-Program Communication (APPC) and by Logical Unit (LU) 6.2, which establish the capabilities and types of interactions possible in an SNA environment. *See also* DCA (definition 1), SNA.

diacritical mark \dī-ə-krit´i-kəl märk`\ *n*. An accent mark above, below, or through a written character—for example, the acute (´) and grave (`) accents.

dialect \dī´ə-lekt`\ *n.* A variant of a language or protocol. For example, Transact-SQL is a dialect of structured query language (SQL).

dialog \dī´ə-log`\ *n.* **1.** In computing, the exchange of human input and machine responses that forms a "conversation" between an interactive computer and the person using it. **2.** The exchange of signals by computers communicating on a network.

dialog box \dī´ə-log boks`\ *n.* In a graphical user interface, a special window displayed by the system or application to solicit a response from the user. *See also* windowing environment. *Compare* integrator.

dial-up \dīl´up\ *adj.* Of, pertaining to, or being a connection that uses the public switched telephone network rather than a dedicated circuit or some other type of private network.

dial-up access \dīl´up ak`ses\ *n.* Connection to a data communications network through a public switched telecommunication network.

dial-up service \dīl´up sər`vəs\ *n.* A telephone connection provider for a local or worldwide public switched telephone network that provides Internet or intranet access, advertisement via a Web page, access to news services, or access to the stock market and other resources.

DIB \D`I-B´\ *n.* **1.** Acronym for **d**evice-**i**ndependent **b**it map. A file format designed to ensure that bitmapped graphics created using one application can be loaded and displayed in another application exactly the way they appeared in the originating application. *See also* bitmapped graphics. **2.** Acronym for **D**irectory **I**nformation **B**ase. A directory of user and resource names in an X.500 system. The DIB is maintained by a Directory Server Agent (DSA). *Also called* white pages.

DIBengine \D`I-B-en´jən\ *n.* Software, or a combination of hardware and software, that produces DIB files. *See also* DIB (definition 1).

dibit \dī´bit\ *n.* A set of 2 bits representing one of four possible combinations: 00, 01, 10, and 11. In communications, a dibit is a kind of transmission unit made possible by the modulation technique known as differential phase-shift keying, which encodes data by using four different states (phase shifts) in the transmission line to represent each of the four dibit combinations. *See also* phase-shift keying.

dichotomizing search \dī-kot`ə-mī-zēng sərch´\ *n. See* binary search.

DIF \D`I-F´\ *n. See* data interchange format.

difference \di´frəns, dif´ər-əns\ *n.* **1.** The amount by which two values differ. In electronics, differences in physical elements, such as waveforms or voltages, are used in the operation of circuits, amplifiers, multiplexers, communications equipment, and so on. **2.** In database management, it is an operator in relational algebra that is used in sorting record sets (tuples). For example, given two relational tables, A and B, that are union-compatible (contain the same number of fields, with corresponding fields containing the same types of values), the statement

DIFFERENCE A, B

builds a third relation containing all those records that appear in A but not in B. *See also* relational algebra, tuple. *Compare* intersect, union.

Difference Engine \dif´ər-əns en´jin, dif´rəns\ *n.* An early computerlike mechanical device designed by British mathematician and scientist Charles Babbage in the early 1820s. The Difference Engine was intended to be a machine with a 20-decimal capacity capable of solving mathematical problems. The concept of the Difference Engine was enhanced by Babbage in the 1830s in the design of his more famous Analytical Engine, a mechanical precursor of the electronic computer. *See also* Analytical Engine.

differential \dif´ər-en´shəl\ *adj.* In electronics, a reference to a type of circuit that makes use of the difference between two signals rather than the difference between one signal and some reference voltage.

differential phase-shift keying \dif-ər-en`shəl fāz´shift kē`ēng\ *n. See* phase-shift keying.

differentiator \dif´ər-en´shē-ā`tər\ *n.* A circuit whose output is the differential (first derivative) of the input signal. The differential measures how fast a value is changing, so the output of a differentiator is proportional to the instantaneous rate of change of the input signal. See the illustration on the next page. *Compare* integrator.

digest \dī´jest\ *n.* **1.** An article in a moderated newsgroup that summarizes multiple posts submitted to the moderator. *See also* moderator, newsgroup. **2.** A message in a mailing list that is sent to

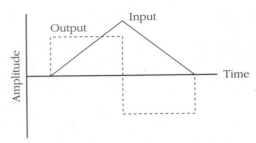

Differentiator.   An example of the action of a differentiator circuit.

subscribers in place of the multiple individual posts that the digest contains. If the mailing list is moderated, the digest may be edited. *See also* moderated.

digicash \dij`ikash´\ *n.* *See* e-money.

digit \dij´it\ *n.* One of the characters used to indicate a whole number (unit) in a numbering system. In any numbering system, the number of possible digits is equal to the base, or radix, used. For example, the decimal (base-10) system has 10 digits, 0 through 9; the binary (base-2) system has 2 digits, 0 and 1; and the hexadecimal (base-16) system has 16 digits, 0 through 9 and A through F.

digital \dij´i-təl\ *adj.* **1.** Related to digits or the way they are represented. **2.** In computing, analogous to *binary* because the computers familiar to most people process information coded as combinations of binary digits (bits). *Compare* analog.

digital audio disc \dij´i-təl ä´dē-ō disk`, ô´dē-ō\ *n.* *See* compact disc.

digital audio tape \dij´i-təl ä´dē-ō tāp, ô´dē-ō tāp\ *n.* A magnetic tape storage medium for recording digitally encoded audio information. *Acronym:* DAT (dat, D`A-T´).

digital audio/video connector \dij´i-təl ä`dē-ō-vid´ē-ō kə-nek`tər, ô´dē-ō\ *n.* An interface on some high-end video cards or TV tuner cards that allows the simultaneous transmission of digital audio and video signals. *Also called* DAV connector. *See also* interface (definition 3), video adapter.

digital camera \dij´i-təl kam´ər-ə, kam´rə\ *n.* A type of camera that stores photographed images electronically instead of on traditional film. A digital camera uses a CCD (charge-coupled device)

element to capture the image through the lens when the operator releases the shutter in the camera; circuitry within the camera then stores the image captured by the CCD in a storage medium such as solid-state memory or a hard disk. After the image has been captured, it is downloaded by cable to the computer using software supplied with the camera. Once stored in the computer, the image can be manipulated and processed much like the image from a scanner or related input device. *See also* charge-coupled device.

digital cash \dij-i-təl kash`\ *n.* *See* e-money.

digital communications \dij`i-təl kə-myoo-nə-kā´shənz\ *n.* Exchange of communications in which all information is transmitted in binary-encoded (digital) form.

digital computer \dij`i-təl kəm-pyoo´tər\ *n.* A computer in which operations are based on two or more discrete states. Binary digital computers are based on two states, logical "on" and "off," represented by two voltage levels, arrangements of which are used to represent all types of information—numbers, letters, graphics symbols, and program instructions. Within such a computer, the states of various circuit components change continuously to move, operate on, and save this information. *Compare* analog computer.

Digital Darkroom \dij`i-təl därk´room\ *n.* A Macintosh program developed by Silicon Beach Software for enhancement of black-and-white photographs or scanned images.

digital data transmission \dij`i-təl dā´tə tranz-mish`ən, dat´ə\ *n.* The transfer of information encoded as a series of bits rather than as a fluctuating (analog) signal in a communications channel.

digital display \dij`i-təl dis-plā´\ *n.* A video display capable of rendering only a fixed number of colors or gray shades. Examples of digital displays are IBM's Monochrome Display, Color/Graphics Display, and Enhanced Color Display. *See also* CGA, EGA, MDA. *Compare* analog display.

digital line \dij`i-təl līn´\ *n.* A communications line that carries information only in binary-encoded (digital) form. To minimize distortion and noise interference, a digital line uses repeaters to regenerate the signal periodically during transmission. *See also* repeater. *Compare* analog line.

digital linear tape \dij`i-təl lin`ē-ər tāp´\ *n*. A magnetic storage medium used to back up data. Digital linear tape allows for faster transfer of data compared with other tape technologies. *Acronym:* DLT (D`L-T´).

Digital Micromirror Display \dij`i-təl mī`krō-mēr-ər dis-plā´\ *n*. The circuit technology behind Texas Instruments' Digital Projection System. An array of individually addressable mirrors on a chip, each less than 0.002 mm wide, rotate to reflect light into the lens of the projection system, creating a bright, full-color display. Displays can be combined to create high-definition systems of 1,920 × 1,035 (1,987,200) pixels with 64 million colors. *Acronym:* DMD (D`M-D´).

digital photography \dij`i-təl fə-to´grə-fē\ *n*. Photography by means of a digital camera. Digital photography differs from conventional photography in that a digital camera does not use a silver halide–based film to capture an image. Instead, a digital camera captures and stores each image electronically. *See also* digital camera.

digital proof \dij`i-təl prōōf´\ *n*. *See* direct digital color proof.

digital recording \dij`i-təl rə-kōr´dēng\ *n*. The storage of information in binary-encoded (digital) format. Digital recording converts information—text, graphics, sound, or pictures—to strings of 1s and 0s that can be physically represented on a storage medium. Digital recording media include computer disks and tapes, optical (or compact) discs, and ROM cartridges of the type used for some software and many computer games.

digital signal \dij`i-təl sig´nəl\ *n*. A signal, such as one transmitted within or between computers, in which information is represented by discrete states—for example, high and low voltages—rather than by fluctuating levels in a continuous stream, as in an analog signal.

digital signal processor \dij`i-təl sig´nəl pros`es-ər\ *n*. An integrated circuit designed for high-speed data manipulation and used in audio, communications, image manipulation, and other data acquisition and data control applications. *Acronym:* DSP (D`S-P´).

digital signature \dij`i-təl sig´nə-chur\ *n*. A personal authentication method based on encryption and secret authorization codes used for "signing" electronic documents.

Digital Simultaneous Voice and Data \dij`i-təl sī`mul-tā`nē-əs vois and dā´tə, dat´ə\ *n*. A modem technology, patented by Multi-Tech Systems, Inc., that allows a single telephone line to be used for conversation together with data transfer. This is accomplished by switching to packet-mode communications when the need for voice transfer is detected; digitized voice packets are then transferred along with data and command packets. *Acronym:* DSVD (D`S-V-D´).

digital sort \dij`i-təl sōrt´\ *n*. A type of ordering process in which record numbers or their key values are sorted digit by digit, beginning with the least significant (rightmost) digit. *Also called* radix sort.

digital speech \dij`i-təl spēch´\ *n*. *See* speech synthesis.

digital subscriber line \dij`i-təl sub-skrī`bər lin`\ *n*. An ISDN BRI (Basic Rate Interface) line or channel. *Acronym:* DSL (D`S-L´). *See also* BRI, ISDN.

digital-to-analog converter \dij`i-təl-t<span>ōō</span>-an´ə-log kən-vər´-tər\ *n*. A device that translates digital data to an analog signal. A digital-to-analog converter takes a succession of discrete digital values as input and creates an analog signal whose amplitude corresponds, moment by moment, to each digital value. See the illustration. *Acronym:* DAC (D`A-C´). *Compare* analog-to-digital converter.

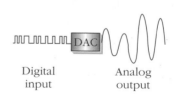

Digital input   Analog output

Digital-to-analog converter.

digital versatile disc \dij`i-təl vər´sə-təl disk`\ *n*. *See* digital video disc.

digital video disc \dij`i-təl vid´ē-ō disk`\ *n*. The next generation of optical disc storage technology. With digital video disc technology, video, audio, and computer data can be encoded onto a compact disc (CD). A digital video disc can store greater amounts of data than a traditional CD. A standard single-layer, single-sided digital video disc can store 4.7 GB of data; a two-layer standard increases the single-sided disc capacity to 8.5 GB. Digital video discs can be double-sided with a maximum storage of 17 GB per disc. A digital video disc player is needed to read digital video discs; this player is equipped to read older optical storage technologies. Advocates of the digital video disc intend to replace current digital storage formats, such as laser disc, CD-ROM, and audio CD, with the single digital format of the digital video disc. *Acronym:* DVD (D`-V-D´). *Also called* digital versatile disc. *See also* digital video disc–ROM.

digital video disc–erasable \dij`i-təl vid`ē-ō disk`ər-ā´sə-bl\ *n.* A proposed extension to the digital video disc recording format to allow multiple re-recording by a consumer. *Acronym:* DVD-E (D`-V-D-E´). *Also called* digital video disc–ROM.

digital video disc–recordable \dij`i-təl vid`ē-ō disk`rə-kōr´də-bl\ *n.* A proposed extension to the digital video disc recording format to allow one-time recording by a consumer. *Acronym:* DVD-R (D`-V-D-R´).

digital video disc–ROM \dij`i-təl vid`ē-ō disk rom´, R`O-M´\ *n.* A computer-readable version of a digital video disc containing either 4.7 or 8.5 GB of storage per side, the larger if 3M's dual-layer "2P" technology is used. *Acronym:* DVD-ROM (D`-V-D-rom´, -R-O-M´). *See also* digital video disc.

digital video–interactive \dij`i-təl vid`ē-ō-in-tər-ak´tiv\ *n.* A hardware/software system developed by RCA, General Electric, and Intel that implements compression of digital video and audio for microcomputer applications. *Acronym:* DV-I (D`-V-I´).

Digital Video Interface \dij`i-təl vid`ē-ō in´tər-fās\ *n. See* DVI.

digiterati \dij`i-tər-ä´tē\ *n.* The digital counterpart of literati, an undefined collection of individuals recognized as knowledgeable, hip, or up-to-date regarding all things digital.

digitize \dij´i-tīz`\ *vb.* To convert any continuously varying (analog) source of input, such as the lines in a drawing or a sound signal, to a series of discrete units represented in a computer by the binary digits 0 and 1. Analog-to-digital converters are commonly used to perform this translation. *See also* aliasing, analog-to-digital converter.

digitizing tablet \dij´i-tī-zēng ta`blət\ *n. See* graphics tablet.

DikuMUD \dī`kōō-mud´, dī`kōō-M-U-D´\ *n.* **1.** Multiuser dungeon (MUD) software developed by five individuals at the Computer Science Institute at Copenhagen University (whose acronym in Danish is DIKU). DikuMUD uses multimedia and is object-oriented, but the classes are hard-coded. The software is covered by a license agreement that forbids its distribution for money. *See also* MUD, multimedia, object-oriented. **2.** A game that uses the DikuMUD software.

dimensioning \di-men´shə-nēng`\ *n.* In CAD programs, a means of specifying and possibly controlling the measurements and spatial relationships of elements in a modeled object, such as using lines, arrows, and text (that is, measurements) to indicate the length, height, and thickness of each of the walls in a modeled room or house. *See also* CAD.

dimmed \dimd\ *adj.* Shown on the screen in gray characters instead of black characters on white or white characters on black. Menu options are dimmed in a graphical user interface to indicate that under current circumstances they are not available—for example, "Cut" when no text has been highlighted or "Paste" when there is no text in the clipboard.

DIN connector \D-I-N´ kə-nek`tər, din`\ *n.* A multipin connector conforming to the specification of the German national standards organization (Deutsch Industrie Norm). DIN connectors are used to link various components in personal computers. See the illustration.

DIN connector.

dingbat \dēng´bat\ *n.* A small graphical element used for decorative purposes in a document. Some fonts, such as Zapf Dingbats, are designed to present sets of dingbats. See the illustration. *See also* font. *Compare* bullet.

❀✿✤✥✦✧✩✪✫●○■□❐❑▲▼◆❖▶❚❙❘
✢✣✤✥❀✦✧★✩✪✬✭✮✯✰✱✲✳✴✵✶✷✸✹✺

Dingbat. *The top line shows the lowercase characters of the Zapf Dingbats font, and the bottom line shows the uppercase.*

diode \dī´ōd\ *n*. A device that passes current in only one direction. A diode is usually a semiconductor. See the illustration. *See also* semiconductor.

Diode. *The photos (top) show two of the many types of diode packages. The band on the right end of each indicates polarity. At bottom is a schematic representation of a diode.*

diode-transistor logic \dī´ōd tran-zi´stər loj`ik\ *n*. A type of circuit design that employs diodes, transistors, and resistors to perform logic functions. *Acronym:* DTL (D`T-L´).

DIP \dip, D`I-P´\ *n*. **1.** Acronym for **d**ual **i**n-line **p**ackage. A standard for packaging integrated circuits in which the microminiature electronic circuits etched on a silicon wafer are enclosed in a rectangular housing of plastic or ceramic and connected to downward-pointing pins protruding from the longer sides of the chip. Designed to facilitate circuit board manufacturing, this design does not work well for modern chips requiring very large numbers of connections. See the illustration. *Compare* leadless chip carrier, pin grid array, SIP, surface-mount technology. **2.** *See* document image processing.

dipole \dī´pōl\ *n*. A pair of opposite electric charges or magnetic poles of opposite sign separated by a small distance.

DIP switch \dip´ swich, D`I-P´\ *n*. One or more small rocker- or sliding-type switches contained in the plastic or ceramic housing of a dual in-line package (DIP) connected to a circuit board. Each switch on a DIP switch can be set to one of two positions, closed or open, to control options on the circuit board. See the illustration. *See also* DIP.

DIP. *Note the notch on one end of the DIP, which shows the location of the first and last pins.*

DIP switch. *Two types of DIP switch, slider (top) and rocker (bottom).*

dir \dər\ *n*. An MS-DOS command that instructs a computer to display a list of files and subdirectories in the current directory or folder. If the command is followed by a path, the computer displays a list of files and subdirectories in the specified directory or folder. See the illustration on the next page. *See also* command, MS-DOS, path (definition 2).

direct access \dər-ekt` ak´ses\ *n*. The ability of a computer to find and go straight to a particular storage location in memory or on disk to retrieve or store an item of information. Note that direct access is not the same as direct memory access (DMA), which is the ability to transfer information directly between an input/output channel and memory rather than taking the longer and more circuitous route of I/O channel to microprocessor to memory. *See also* random access. *Compare* direct memory access.

direct access storage device \dər-ekt` ak`ses stōr´əj də-vīs`\ *n. See* DASD.

direct address \dər-ekt` a´dres, ə-dres´\ *n. See* absolute address.

direct cable connection \dər-ekt` kā´bl kə-nek`shən\ *n.* A link between the I/O ports of two computers that uses a single cable rather than a modem or other active interface device. In most cases, a direct cable connection requires a null modem cable.

direct-connect modem \dər-ekt` kə-nekt mō´dəm\ *n.* A modem that uses standard telephone wire and connectors and plugs directly into a telephone jack, eliminating the need for an intermediary telephone. *Compare* acoustic coupler.

direct-coupled transistor logic \dər-ekt` kə-pld tranz-i´stər loj`ik\ *n.* A circuit design that uses transistors and resistors only, with the transistors directly connected to each other. This design was used in the earliest commercial integrated circuits. The switching speed and power consumption of such circuits are about average. *Acronym:* DCTL (D`C-T-L´).

direct current \dər-ekt` kur´ənt\ *n.* Electrical current whose direction of flow does not reverse. The current may stop or change amplitude, but it always flows in the same direction. *Acronym:* DC (D-C´). *Compare* alternating current.

direct digital color proof \dər-ekt` dij`i-təl kə`lər prŏŏf´\ *n.* A test sheet produced by a lower-cost output device, such as a color laser printer, to serve as an approximation of what the final image will look like when produced on professional-quality printing equipment. A direct digital color proof does not involve color separation, as in tra-

ditional proofs. Instead, a direct digital color proof is printed in all colors at one time on a single page, resulting in somewhat lower quality compared with traditional separation methods but having the advantages of increased speed and reduced cost. *Acronym:* DDCP (D`D-C-P´). *Also called* digital proof. *See also* color separation (definition 1).

Direct Graphics Interface Specification \dər-ekt` graf`iks in´tər-fās spes-ə-fə-kā`shən\ *n. See* DGIS.

DirectInput \dər-ekt` in´put\ *n.* An application programming interface for joysticks and similar pointing devices in Windows 95.

direction key \dər-ek´shən kē`\ *n. See* arrow key.

direct memory access \dər-ekt´ mem-ər-ē ak`ses\ *n.* Memory access that does not involve the microprocessor and is frequently used for data transfer directly between memory and an "intelligent" peripheral device, such as a disk drive. *Acronym:* DMA (D`M-A´).

directory \dər-ek´tər`ē\ *n.* A catalog for filenames and other directories stored on a disk. A directory is a way of organizing and grouping the files so that the user is not overwhelmed by a long list of them. The topmost directory is called the *root directory;* the directories within a directory are called *subdirectories.* Depending on how an operating system supports directories, filenames in a directory can be viewed and ordered in various ways—for example, alphabetically, by date, by size, or as icons in a graphical user interface.

```
Command Prompt                                              _ □ ×

C:\Christenson>dir
 Volume in drive C is NTFS Drive
 Volume Serial Number is A870-3BFD

 Directory of C:\Christenson

03/01/97  02:52p      <DIR>          .
03/01/97  02:52p      <DIR>          ..
03/01/97  02:53p               96,525 Carter Christenson.txt
03/01/97  02:53p               83,275 Cathy Christenson.txt
03/01/97  02:54p              117,203 Koltan Christenson.txt
03/01/97  02:52p               98,279 Mr. 02--Ken Christenson Jr.txt
             6 File(s)        395,282 bytes
                          659,172,352 bytes free

C:\Christenson>_
```

Dir.   An example of a directory list.

What the user views as a directory is supported in the operating system by tables of data, stored on the disk, that indicate characteristics and the location of each file. In the Macintosh and Windows 95 operating systems, directories are called *folders*.

Directory Access Protocol \dər-ek`tər-ē ak-ses prō´tə-kol\ *n*. The protocol that governs communications between X.500 clients and servers. *See also* CCITT X series.

Directory Client Agent \dər-ek`tər-ē klī´ənt ā`jənt\ *n. See* DUA.

Directory Information Base \dər-ek`tər-ē in-fər-mā´shən bās`\ *n. See* DIB (definition 2).

directory path \dər-ek´tər-ē path`\ *n. See* pathname.

directory replication \dər-ek`tər-ē re-plə-kā´shən\ *n*. The copying of a master set of directories from a server (called an *export server*) to specified servers or workstations (called *import computers*) in the same or other domains. Replication simplifies the task of maintaining identical sets of directories and files on multiple computers because only a single master copy of the data must be maintained. *See also* directory, server.

Directory Server Agent \dər-ek`tər-ē sər´vər ā`jənt\ *n. See* DSA.

directory service \dər-ek´tər-ē sər´vəs\ *n*. A service on a network that returns mail addresses of other users or enables a user to locate hosts and services.

Directory System Agent \dər-ek`tər-ē si´stəm ā`jənt\ *n. See* DSA.

directory tree \dər-ek´tər-ē trē`\ *n*. A graphic display listing the directories and subdirectories on a hard disk in tree form, with subdirectories shown as branches of the main directory. See the illustration. *See also* branch (definition 1), directory, tree structure.

Directory User Agent \dər-ek`tər-ē yoo´zər ā`jənt\ *n. See* DUA.

direct processing \dər-ekt` pros´e-sēng\ *n*. Processing of data as it is received by the system, as opposed to deferred processing, in which data is stored in blocks before processing. *Compare* deferred processing.

direct read after write \dər-ekt` rēd af-tər rīt´\ *n. See* DRAW.

Directory tree. *An example of a directory tree shown in Windows Explorer.*

direct read during write \dər-ekt` rēd dər-ēng rīt´\ *n. See* DRDW.

direct sequence \dər-ekt` sē´kwəns\ *n*. In spread spectrum communication, a form of modulation in which a carrier is modulated by a series of binary pulses. *See also* modulation (definition 1), spread spectrum.

direct view storage tube \dər-ekt` vyoo stōr´əj toob\ *n*. A type of cathode-ray tube (CRT) in which the screen can retain images for a long time and in which a beam of electrons from an electron gun can be moved arbitrarily across the screen surface (as opposed to a standard cathode-ray tube, in which the electron beam is moved in a specific pattern). This type of CRT is capable of displaying a precise, detailed image without requiring any screen refresh. However, once the image is drawn, it cannot be changed without a complete erasing of the screen. *Acronym:* DVST (D`V-S-T´). *Also called* storage tube. *Compare* CRT.

DirectX \dər-ekt`X´\ *n*. Windows 95 software that gives applications direct access to a computer's sound and graphics hardware.

dirty \dər´tē\ *adj*. Of, pertaining to, or characteristic of a communications line that is hampered by excessive noise, degrading the quality of the signal. *See also* noise (definition 2).

dirty bit \dər´tē bit`\ *n*. A bit used to mark modified data in a cache so that the modifications may be carried over to primary memory. *See also* bit, cache.

dirty power \dər´tē pou´ər\ *n*. A power source that can cause damage to electronic components, due to noise, voltage spikes, or incorrect voltage levels.

dirty ROM \dər`tē rom´, R-O-M´\ *n*. Short for **dirty read-only memory**. In the earlier versions of the Macintosh (Mac II, IIx, SE/30, and IIcx), a memory system that simulates a 32-bit system but is not a true (clean) 32-bit system. Among other flaws, a dirty ROM machine can access only 8 megabytes of memory under Mac OS System 7. System extensions such as MODE32 and the 32-bit enabler are available to allow a dirty ROM machine to function like a true, 32-bit clean machine.

disable \di-sā´bl`\ *vb*. To suppress something or to prevent it from happening. Disabling is a method of controlling system functions by disallowing certain activities. For example, a program might temporarily disable nonessential interrupts (requests for service from system devices) to prevent interruptions during a critical point in processing. *Compare* enable.

disabled folders \di-sā´bld fōl´dərz\ *n*. In the Mac OS, several folders in the System folder that contain system extensions, control panels, and other items that have been removed from the system by the extension manager. Items currently in disabled folders will not be installed upon system startup; they may, however, later be moved back to their regular folders automatically by the extension manager. *See also* extension manager, System folder.

disassembler \dis`ə-sem´blər\ *n*. A program that converts machine code to assembly language source code. Most debuggers have some kind of built-in disassembler that allows the programmer to view an executable program in terms of human-readable assembly language. *See also* decompiler. *Compare* assembler.

disassociate \dis`ə-sō´sē-āt\ *vb*. In Windows 95 and NT, to remove an association between a file and some application. *Compare* associate.

disaster dump \di-za´stər dump`\ *n*. A dump (transfer of memory contents to a printer or other output device) made when a program fails without hope of recovery.

disc \disk\ *n*. A round, flat piece of nonmagnetic, shiny metal encased in a plastic coating, designed to be read from and written to by optical (laser) technology. It is now standard practice to use the spelling *disc* for optical discs and *disk* in all other computer contexts, such as floppy disk, hard disk, and RAM disk. *See also* compact disc.

disconnect \dis`kə-nekt´\ *vb*. To break a communications link.

discrete \di-skrēt´\ *adj*. Separate; individual; identifiable as a unit. For example, bits are discrete elements of data processed by a computer.

discrete multitone \dis-krēt` mul´tē-tōn, mul´tī-tōn\ *n*. In telecommunications, a technology that uses digital signal processors to split available bandwidth into a number of subchannels, allowing over 6 Mbps of data to be carried over one copper twisted-pair wire. *Acronym:* DMT (D`M-T´).

discretionary hyphen \di-skresh`ə-nār`ē hī´fən\ *n*. *See* hyphen.

discussion group \di-skush´ən grōōp`\ *n*. Any of a variety of online forums in which people communicate about subjects of common interest. Forums for discussion groups include electronic mailing lists, Internet newsgroups, and IRC channels.

disk \disk\ *n*. A round, flat piece of flexible plastic (floppy disk) or inflexible metal (hard disk) coated with a magnetic material that can be electrically influenced to hold information recorded in digital (binary) form. In most computers a disk is the primary means of storing data on a permanent or semipermanent basis. Floppy disks are encased in a protective plastic jacket to protect them from damage and contamination. A hard disk is enclosed in a rigid case and can be exposed only in a dust-free environment. Types of disks used with microcomputers include floppy disks, microfloppy disks, hard disks, and removable cartridges that can be used with some hard disk drives and units, such as the Bernoulli box. *Compare* compact disc, disc.

disk access time \disk´ ak`ses tīm\ *n*. *See* access time (definition 2).

disk buffer \disk´ buf`ər\ *n*. A small amount of memory set aside for the purpose of storing data read from, or soon to be written to, a disk. Because disk devices are slow compared with the CPU, it is not efficient to access the disk for only one or two bytes of data. Instead, during a read, a large chunk of data is read and stored in the disk buffer. When the program wants information, it is copied from the buffer. Many requests for data can be satisfied by a single disk access. The same technique can be applied to disk writes. When the program has information to store, it writes it into the disk buffer area in memory. When the buffer has been filled, the entire contents of the buffer are written to the disk in a single operation.

disk cache \disk´ kash\ *n.* A portion of a computer's random access memory (RAM) set aside for temporarily holding information read from disk. A disk cache does not hold entire files, as does a RAM disk (a portion of memory that acts as if it were a disk drive). Instead, a disk cache is used to hold information that either has recently been requested from disk or has previously been written to disk. If the required information remains in a disk cache, access time is considerably faster than if the program must wait for the disk drive mechanism to fetch the information from disk. *See also* cache. *Compare* disk buffer.

disk cartridge \disk´ kär`trij\ *n.* A removable disk enclosed in a protective case. A disk cartridge can be used by certain types of hard disk drives and related devices, such as the external data storage units known as Bernoulli boxes.

disk controller \disk´ kən-trō`lər\ *n.* A special-purpose chip and associated circuitry that directs and controls reading from and writing to a computer's disk drive. A disk controller handles such tasks as positioning the read/write head, mediating between the drive and the microprocessor, and controlling the transfer of information to and from memory. Disk controllers are used with floppy disk drives and hard disks and can either be built into the system or be part of a card that plugs into an expansion slot.

disk copy \disk´ kop`ē\ *n.* The process of duplicating a source disk's data and the data's organizational structure onto a target disk. *See also* backup.

disk crash \disk´ krash\ *n.* The failure of a disk drive. *See also* crash[1].

disk directory \disk´ dər-ek`tər-ē\ *n.* An index of the files on a disk, analogous to a card catalog. A disk directory includes information about the files, such as their names, sizes, dates of creation, and physical locations on the disk. *See also* directory.

disk drive \disk´ drīv\ *n.* An electromechanical device that reads from and writes to disks. The main components of a disk drive include a spindle on which the disk is mounted, a drive motor that spins the disk when the drive is in operation, one or more read/write heads, a second motor that positions the read/write head(s) over the disk, and controller circuitry that synchronizes read/write activities and transfers information to and from the computer. Two types of disk drives are in common use: floppy disk drives and hard disk drives. Floppy disk drives are designed to accept removable disks in either 5.25-inch or 3.5-inch format; hard disk drives are faster, high-capacity storage units that are completely enclosed in a protective case. See the illustration.

Disk drive.   *A 3.5-inch floppy disk drive.*

disk driver \disk´ drī`vər\ *n.* A device driver that is added to a system to support a specific manufacturer's disk device. *See also* device driver.

disk duplexing \disk´ dōō`pleks-ēng\ *n. See* disk mirroring.

disk envelope \disk´ en`və-lōp, än`və-lōp\ *n.* The paper container that holds a 5.25-inch floppy disk and its attached jacket. The disk envelope protects exposed surfaces of the disk from dust and other foreign material that can scratch and otherwise damage the surface, resulting in the loss of recorded data. *See also* disk jacket.

diskette \dis-ket´\ *n. See* floppy disk.

disk interface \disk´ in`tər-fās\ *n.* **1.** The circuitry that connects a disk drive to a computer system. **2.** A standard for connecting disk drives and computers. The ST506 standard for connecting hard disks to computers is a disk interface standard.

disk jacket \disk´ jak`et\ *n.* The protective plastic sheath that covers a floppy disk.

diskless workstation \disk`ləs wərk´stā-shən\ *n.* A station on a computer network that is not equipped with a disk drive and that uses files stored in a file server. *See also* file server.

disk memory \disk´ mem`ər-ē\ *n*. *See* virtual memory.

disk mirroring \disk´ mēr`ər-ēng\ *n*. A technique in which all or part of a hard disk is duplicated onto one or more other hard disks, each of which ideally is attached to its own controller. With disk mirroring, any change made to the original disk is simultaneously made to the other disks, so that if the original disk becomes damaged or corrupted, the mirror disks will contain a current, undamaged collection of the data from the original disk. *Also called* disk duplexing. *See also* fault tolerance.

disk operating system \disk´ op`ər-ā-tēng si`stəm\ *n*. *See* DOS.

disk pack \disk´ pak\ *n*. A collection of disks in a protective container. Used primarily with mini-computers and mainframe computers, a disk pack is a removable medium, generally a stack of 14-inch disks in a plastic housing.

disk partition \disk´ pär-tish`ən\ *n*. A logical compartment on a physical disk drive. A single disk might have two or more logical disk parti-tions, each of which would be referenced with a different disk drive name. Multiple partitions are divided into a primary (boot) partition and one or more extended partitions.

disk server \disk´ sər`vər\ *n*. A node on a local area network that acts as a remote disk drive shared by network users. Unlike a file server, which performs the more sophisticated tasks of managing network requests for files, a disk server functions as a storage medium on which users can read and write files. A disk server can be divided into sections (volumes), each of which appears to be a separate disk. *Compare* file server.

disk striping \disk´ strī pēng\ *n*. The procedure of combining a set of same-size disk partitions that reside on separate disks (from 2 to 32 disks) into a single volume, forming a virtual "stripe" across the disks that the operating system recognizes as a single drive. Disk striping enables multiple I/O operations in the same volume to proceed concur-rently, thus offering enhanced performance. *See also* disk striping with parity, input/output.

disk striping with parity \disk` strī-pēng with pâr´ə-tē\ *n*. The technique of maintaining parity information across a disk stripe so that if one disk partition fails, the data on that disk can be re-created using the information stored across the remaining partitions in the disk stripe. *See also* disk striping, fault tolerance, parity.

disk unit \disk´ yōō`nit\ *n*. A disk drive or its housing.

dispatcher \di´spach`ər\ *n*. In some multitasking operating systems, the set of routines responsible for allocating central processing unit (CPU) time to various applications.

dispatch table \di´spach tā`bl\ *n*. A table of iden-tifiers and addresses for a certain class of routines such as interrupt handlers (routines carried out in response to certain signals or conditions). *Also called* interrupt vector table, jump table, vector table. *See also* interrupt handler.

disperse \di-spərs´\ *vb*. To break up and place in more than one location—for example, to disperse results among several sets of data or to disperse items (such as fields in records) so that they appear in more than one place in the output. *Com-pare* distribute.

dispersion \di-spər´shən, di-spər´zhən\ *n*. The degree to which, at any given time, data in a dis-tributed (interconnected) system of computers is stored at different locations or on different devices.

display \di-splā´\ *n*. The visual output device of a computer, which is commonly a CRT-based video display. With portable and notebook computers, the display is usually an LCD-based or a gas plasma–based flat-panel display. *See also* flat-panel display, liquid crystal display, video adapter, video display.

display adapter \di-splā´ ə-dap`tər\ *n*. *See* video adapter.

display attribute \di-splā´ a`tri-byōot\ *n*. A qual-ity assigned to a character or image displayed on the screen. Display attributes include such features as color, intensity, and blinking. Users of applica-tions can control display attributes when programs allow them to change color and other screen ele-ments.

display background \di-splā´ bak`ground\ *n*. In computer graphics, the portion of an on-screen image that remains static while other elements change; for example, window borders on a screen, or a palette of shapes or patterns in a drawing program.

display board \di-splā´ bōrd`\ *n. See* video adapter.

display card \di-splā´ kärd`\ *n. See* video adapter.

display cycle \di-splā´ sī`kl\ *n.* The complete set of events that must occur in order for a computer image to be displayed on the screen, including both the software creation of an image in a computer's video memory and the hardware operations required for accurate on-screen display. *See also* refresh cycle.

Display Data Channel \dis-plā´ dā`tə chan`əl, dat`ə\ *n. See* DDC.

display device \di-splā´ də-vīs`\ *n. See* display.

display element \di-splā´ el`ə-mənt\ *n. See* graphics primitive.

display entity \di-splā´ en`tə-tē\ *n. See* entity, graphics primitive.

display face \di-splā´ fās`\ *n.* A typeface suitable for headings and titles in documents, distinguished by its ability to stand out from other text on the page. Sans serif faces such as Helvetica and Avant Garde often work well as display faces. *See also* sans serif. *Compare* body face.

display frame \di-splā´ frām`\ *n.* One image in an animation sequence. *See also* frame (definition 3).

display image \di-splā´ im`əj\ *n.* The collection of elements displayed together at a single time on a computer screen.

display page \di-splā´ pāj`\ *n.* One screenful of display information stored in a computer's video memory. Computers can have enough video memory to hold more than one display page at a time. In such instances, programmers, especially those concerned with creating animation sequences, can update the screen rapidly by creating or modifying one display page while another is being viewed by the user. *See also* animation.

display port \dis-plā´ pōrt`\ *n.* An output port on a computer that provides a signal for a display device such as a video monitor.

Display PostScript \di-splā´ pōst`skript\ *n.* An extended version of the PostScript language, intended for device-independent imaging (including monitors and printers) in a multitasking environment. Display PostScript has been adopted by some hardware manufacturers as the standard imaging approach for both screens and printers. *See also* PostScript.

Display Power Management Signaling \dis-plā´ pou-ər man´əj-mənt sig`nə-lēng\ *n. See* DPMS.

display screen \di-splā´ skrēn`\ *n.* The part of a video unit on which images are shown. *See also* CRT.

display terminal \di-splā´ tər`mə-nəl\ *n. See* terminal (definition 1).

Distance Vector Multicast Routing Protocol \di`stəns vek`tər mul`tē-kast rou`tēng prō`tə-kol, mul`tī-kast, rōō`tēng\ *n.* An Internet routing protocol that provides an efficient mechanism for connectionless datagram delivery to a group of hosts across an Internet network. It is a distributed protocol that dynamically generates IP multicast delivery trees using a technique called Reverse Path Multicasting (RPM). *Acronym:* DVMRP (D`V-M-R-P´).

distortion \di-stōr´shən`\ *n.* An undesirable change in the waveform of a signal. Distortion can occur during signal transmission, as when a radio broadcast becomes garbled, or when a signal passes through a circuit, as when a stereo system is turned up too loud. Distortion often results in loss of information. It is mainly a problem in analog signals; digital signals are not affected by moderate distortion.

distribute \di-stri´byōōt`\ *vb.* To allocate among locations or facilities, as in a data-processing function that is performed by a collection of computers and other devices linked together by a network.

distributed bulletin board \dis-tri´byōō-təd bul´-ə-tin bōrd\ *n.* A collection of newsgroups distributed to all computers in a wide area network. *See also* newsgroup, Usenet.

Distributed COM \dis-tri´byōō-təd kom\ *n. See* DCOM.

Distributed Component Object Model \dis-tri´-byōō-təd kəm-pō`nənt ob`jekt mod`əl\ *n. See* DCOM.

distributed computing \dis-tri`byōō-təd kəm-pyōō´tēng\ *n. See* distributed processing.

Distributed Computing Environment \dis-tri´-byōō-təd kəm-pyōō´tēng en-vīr`ən-mənt, en-vī´ərn-mənt\ *n.* A set of standards from the Open Group (formerly the Open Software Foundation) for development of distributed applications that can operate on more than one platform. *Acronym:* DCE (D`C-E´). *See also* distributed processing.

distributed database \dis-tri`byōō-təd da´tə-bās\ *n.* A database implemented on a network. The component partitions are distributed over various nodes (stations) of the network. Depending on the specific update and retrieval traffic, distributing the database can significantly enhance overall performance. *See also* partition (definition 2).

distributed database management system \dis-tri`byōō-təd da´tə-bās man`əj-mənt si`stəm\ *n.* A database management system capable of managing a distributed database. *Acronym:* DDBMS (D`D-B`M-S´). *See also* distributed database.

distributed file system \dis-tri`byōō-təd　　fīl si`stəm\ *n.* A file management system in which files may be located on multiple computers connected over a local or wide area network.

distributed intelligence \dis-tri`byōō-təd in-tel´ə-jəns\ *n.* A system in which processing ability (intelligence) is distributed among multiple computers and other devices, each of which can work independently to some degree but can also communicate with the other devices to function as part of the larger system. *See also* distributed processing.

distributed network \dis-tri`byōō-təd net`wərk\ *n.* A network in which processing, storage, and other functions are handled by separate units (nodes) rather than by a single main computer.

distributed processing \dis-tri`byōō-təd pros´es-ēng\ *n.* A form of information processing in which work is performed by separate computers linked through a communications network. Distributed processing is usually categorized as either plain distributed processing or true distributed processing. Plain distributed processing shares the workload among computers that can communicate with one another. True distributed processing has separate computers perform different tasks in such a way that their combined work can contribute to a larger goal. The latter type of processing requires a highly structured environment that allows hardware and software to communicate, share resources, and exchange information freely.

Distributed System Object Model \dis-tri`byōō-təd si`stəm ob´jekt mod´əl\ *n.* IBM's System Object Model (SOM) in a shared environment, where binary class libraries can be shared between applications on networked computers or between applications on a given system. The Distributed System Object Model complements existing object-oriented languages by allowing SOM class libraries to be shared among applications written in different languages. *Acronym:* DSOM (D`S-O-M´). *See also* SOM (definition 1).

distributed transaction processing \dis-tri`byōō-təd tranz-ak´shən pros`es-ēng\ *n.* Transaction processing that is shared by one or more computers communicating over a network. *Acronym:* DTP (D`T-P´). *See also* distributed processing, transaction processing.

distribution list \dis-trə-byōō´shən list`\ *n.* A list of recipients on an e-mail mailing list. This can be in the form of either a mailing list program, such as LISTSERV, or an alias in an e-mail program for all recipients of an e-mail message. *See also* alias (definition 2), LISTSERV, mailing list.

distributive sort \di-stri´byə-tiv sōrt`\ *n.* An ordering process in which a list is separated into parts and then reassembled in a particular order. *See also* sort algorithm. *Compare* bubble sort, insertion sort, merge sort, quicksort.

dithering \didh´ər-ēng\ *n.* A technique used in computer graphics to create the illusion of varying shades of gray on a monochrome display or printer, or additional colors on a color display or printer. Dithering relies on treating areas of an image as groups of dots that are colored in different patterns. Akin to the print images called *halftones,* dithering takes advantage of the eye's tendency to blur spots of different colors by averaging their effects and merging them into a single perceived shade or color. Depending on the ratio of black dots to white dots within a given area, the overall effect is of a particular shade of gray. Dithering is used to add realism to computer graphics and to soften jagged edges in curves and diagonal lines at low resolutions. See the illustration. *See also* aliasing, halftone.

divergence \di-vər´jəns\ *n.* A moving apart or separation. On computer displays, divergence occurs when the red, green, and blue electron beams in a color monitor do not collectively light the same spot on the screen. Within a program, such as a spreadsheet, divergence can occur when

Not dithered　　　　Dithered

Dithering. A halftone image (left) and a dithered image (right), both at 72 cells per inch.

a circular set of formulas is repeatedly recalculated (iterated), with the results of each iteration moving further from a stable solution. *Compare* convergence.

divide overflow \di-vīd` ō´vər-flō\ *n. See* overflow error.

division by zero \di-vizh`ən bī zēr´ō\ *n.* An error condition caused by an attempt to divide a number by zero, which is mathematically undefined, or by a number that is sufficiently near to zero that the result is too large to be expressed by the machine. Computers do not allow division by zero, and software must provide some means of protecting the user from program failure on such attempts.

.dj \dot`D-J´\ *n.* On the Internet, the major geographic domain specifying that an address is located in Djibouti.

.dk \dot`D-K´\ *n.* On the Internet, the major geographic domain specifying that an address is located in Denmark.

.dl_ \dot`D-L´\ *n.* A file extension indicating a compressed .dll file, used in a Windows setup procedure. *See also* .dll.

DLC \D`L-C´\ *n.* Acronym for **D**ata **L**ink **C**ontrol. An error-correction protocol in the Systems Network Architecture (SNA) responsible for transmission of data between two nodes over a physical link. *See also* HDLC, SNA.

.dll \dot`D-L-L´\ *n.* A file extension for a dynamic-link library. *See also* dynamic-link library.

DLL \D`L-L´\ *n. See* dynamic-link library.

DLT \D`L-T´\ *n. See* digital linear tape.

DMA \D`M-A´\ *n. See* direct memory access.

DMD \D`M-D´\ *n. See* Digital Micromirror Display.

DMI \D`M-I´\ *n.* Acronym for **D**esktop **M**anagement **I**nterface. A system for managing the configurations and status of PCs on a network from a central computer. In DMI an agent program runs in the background on each machine and returns information or performs some action (as specified by a file on that machine) in response to a query received from the central computer. The actions to be performed by the agent may include watching for errors and reporting them to the central computer as they occur; for example, a printer may be set up to report to the central computer when paper runs out or jams. DMI was developed by the DMTF (Desktop Management Task Force), a consortium of computer equipment manufacturers, and competes with SNMP (although the two can coexist on the same system). *See also* agent (definition 1), DMTF. *Compare* SNMP.

DML \D`M-L´\ *n. See* data manipulation language.

DMT \D`M-T´\ *n. See* discrete multitone.

DMTF \D`M-T-F´\ *n.* Acronym for **D**esktop **M**anagement **T**ask **F**orce. A consortium formed in 1992 to develop standards for PC-based stand-alone and networked systems based on user and industry needs.

DNS \D`N-S´\ *n.* **1.** Acronym for **D**omain **N**ame **S**ystem. The system by which hosts on the Internet have both domain name addresses (such as bluestem.prairienet.org) and IP addresses (such as 192.17.3.4). The domain name address is used by human users and is automatically translated into the numerical IP address, which is used by the packet-routing software. *See also* domain name address, IP address. **2.** Acronym for **D**omain **N**ame **S**ervice. The Internet utility that implements the Domain Name System (see definition 1). DNS servers, also called *name servers*, maintain databases containing the addresses and are accessed transparently to the user.

DNS server \D`N-S´ sər`vər\ *n.* A computer that can answer Domain Name Service (DNS) queries. The DNS server keeps a database of host computers and their corresponding IP addresses. Presented with the name apex.com, for example, the DNS server would return the IP address of the hypothetical company Apex. *See also* DNS (definition 2), IP address.

.do \dot`D-O´\ *n*. On the Internet, the major geographic domain specifying that an address is located in the Dominican Republic.

.doc \dot-dok´, -D-O-C´\ *n*. A file extension that identifies document files formatted for a word processor. This is the default file extension for Microsoft Word document files.

dock \dok\ *vb*. **1.** To connect a laptop or notebook computer to a docking station. *See also* docking station, laptop, portable computer. **2.** To move a toolbar to the edge of an application window so that it attaches and becomes a feature of the application window.

docking mechanism \dok´ēng mek`ə-niz-əm\ *n*. The portion of a docking station that physically connects the portable computer with the station. *See also* docking station.

docking station \dok´ēng stā`shən\ *n*. A unit for housing a laptop or notebook computer that contains a power connection, expansion slots, and connections to peripherals, such as a monitor, printer, full-sized keyboard, and mouse. The purpose of a docking station is to turn the laptop or notebook computer into a desktop machine and allow users the convenience of using such peripherals as a monitor and a full-sized keyboard. See the illustration. *See also* expansion slot, laptop, peripheral, portable computer.

doctype \dok´tīp\ *n*. A declaration at the beginning of an SGML document that gives a public or system identifier for the document type definition (DTD) of the document. *See also* SGML.

document[1] \do´kyə-mənt`\ *n*. Any self-contained piece of work created with an application program and, if saved on disk, given a unique filename by which it can be retrieved. Documents are generally thought of as word-processed materials only. To a computer, however, data is nothing more than a collection of characters, so a spreadsheet or a graphic is as much a document as is a letter or report. In the Macintosh environment in particular, a document is any user-created work named and saved as a separate file.

document[2] \do´kyə-mənt`\ *vb*. To explain or annotate something, such as a program or a procedure.

documentation \do`kyə-mən-tā´shən\ *n*. The set of instructions shipped with a program or a piece of hardware. Documentation usually includes necessary information about the type of computer system required, setup instructions, and instructions on the use and maintenance of the product.

document-centric \do`kyə-mənt-sen´trik\ *adj*. Of, pertaining to, or characteristic of an operating system in which the user opens document files and thus automatically invokes the applications (such as word processors or spreadsheet programs) that process them. Many graphical user interfaces, such as the Macintosh Finder, as well as the World Wide Web, are document-centric. *Compare* application-centric.

Docking station.

Document Content Architecture \do´kyə-mənt kon`tent är´kə-tek-chur\ *n. See* DCA (definition 1).

document file \do´kyə-mənt fīl`\ *n.* A user-created file that represents the output of a program. *Also called* data file. *Compare* program file.

document image processing \do´kyə-mənt im´əj pros`es-ēng\ *n.* A system for storing and retrieving information for an enterprise in the form of bit-mapped images of paper documents input with a scanner rather than in the form of text and numeric files. Document image processing takes more memory than purely electronic data processing, but it more readily incorporates signatures, drawings, and photographs and can be more familiar to users without computer training. *See also* paperless office.

Document Interchange Architecture \do`kyə-mənt in´tər-chānj är`kə-tek-chur\ *n. See* DIA.

document management \do´kyə-mənt man´əj-mənt\ *n.* The full spectrum of electronic document creation and distribution within an organization.

document processing \do´kyə-mənt pros`es-ēng\ *n.* The act of retrieving and manipulating a document, In terms of the way a computer works, document processing involves three main steps: creating or retrieving a data file, using a program to manipulate the data in some way, and storing the modified file.

document reader \do´kyə-mənt rē´dər\ *n.* A device that scans printed text and uses character recognition to convert it to computer text files. *See also* character recognition.

document retrieval \do´kyə-mənt rə-trē´vəl\ *n.* A capability built into some application programs that enables the user to search for specific documents by specifying items of information, such as date, author, or previously assigned keywords. Document retrieval depends on an indexing scheme that the program maintains and uses. Depending on the program's capabilities, document retrieval might allow the user to specify more than one condition to refine a search.

document source \dok´yə-mənt sōrs`\ *n.* The plain-text HTML form of a World Wide Web document, with all tags and other markup displayed as such rather than being formatted. See the illustration. *Also called* source, source document. *See also* HTML.

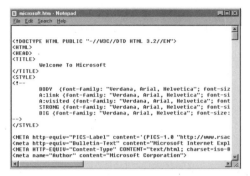

Document source.   HTML source code shown in Notepad.

Document Style Semantics and Specification Language \do´kyə-mənt stīl` se-man`tiks ənd spes`ə-fə-kā´shən lang`wəj\ *n.* An ISO standard under preparation addressing the semantics of high-quality composition in a manner independent of particular formatting systems or processes. It is intended as a complementary standard to SGML for the specification of semantics. *Acronym:* DSSSL (D`S-S-S-L´). *See also* ISO, SGML.

document window \do´kyə-mənt win`dō\ *n.* In windowing environments, such as the Apple Macintosh and Microsoft Windows, an on-screen window (enclosed work area) in which the user can create, view, or work on a document. See the illustration.

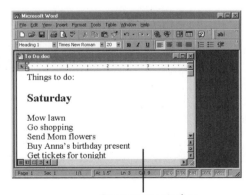

Document window

Document window.

DoD \D`O-D´\ *n. See* U.S. Department of Defense.

DO loop \dōō lōōp`, D-O´\ *n.* A control statement used in programs that executes a section of code a number of times until a specified condition is met. DO loops are found in FORTRAN and Basic, among other languages. *See also* iterative statement. *Compare* FOR loop.

domain \dō-mān´\ *n.* **1.** In database design and management, the set of valid values for a given attribute. For example, the domain for the attribute AREA-CODE might be the list of all valid three-digit numeric telephone area codes in the United States. *See also* attribute (definition 1). **2.** For Windows NT Advanced Server, a collection of computers that share a common domain database and security policy. Each domain has a unique name. **3.** In the Internet and other networks, the highest subdivision of a domain name in a network address, which identifies the type of entity owning the address (for example, .com for commercial users or .edu for educational institutions) or the geographical location of the address (for example, .fr for France or .sg for Singapore). The domain is the last part of the address (for example, www.acm.org). *See also* domain name.

domain name \dō-mān´ nām`\ *n.* An address of a network connection that identifies the owner of that address in a hierarchical format: *server.organization.type.* For example, www.whitehouse.gov identifies the Web server at the White House, which is part of the U.S. government.

domain name address \dō-mān` nām a´dres, ə-dres´\ *n.* The address of a device connected to the Internet or any other TCP/IP network, in the hierarchical system that uses words to identify servers, organizations, and types, such as www.logos.net. *See also* TCP/IP.

domain name server \dō-mān` nām sər´vər\ *n. See* DNS server.

Domain Name System \dō-mān` nām si´stəm\ *n. See* DNS (definition 1).

Domain Naming System \dō-mān´ nā`mēng si`stəm\ *n. See* DNS (definition 1).

dongle \dong´l\ *n. See* hardware key.

do-nothing instruction \dōō´nə-thēng in-struk`-shən\ *n. See* no-operation instruction.

dopant \dō´pənt\ *n.* An impurity that is added in small quantities to semiconductor material during the manufacture of diodes, transistors, and integrated circuits. The resistance of a semiconductor falls between the resistance of a conductor and the resistance of an insulator (hence its name); dopants are added to the semiconductor to increase its conductivity. The type and amount of dopant determine whether the semiconductor will be N-type (in which current is conducted by free electrons) or P-type (in which current is conducted by electron vacancies, called "holes"). Common dopants include arsenic, antimony, bismuth, and phosphorus. *See also* N-type semiconductor, P-type semiconductor.

DOS \dos, D`O-S´\ *n.* Acronym for **d**isk **o**perating **s**ystem. A generic term describing any operating system that is loaded from disk devices when the system is started or rebooted. The term originally differentiated between disk-based systems and primitive microcomputer operating systems that were memory-based or that supported only magnetic or paper tape. *See also* MS-DOS, PC-DOS.

DOS box \dos´ boks, D`O-S´\ *n.* **1.** An OS/2 process that supports the execution of MS-DOS programs. *Also called* compatibility box. **2.** A computer that uses the MS-DOS or PC-DOS operating system, as opposed to one that runs some other operating system, such as UNIX.

DOS extender \dos´ eks-ten`dər, D`O-S´\ *n.* A program designed to extend the 640 KB of conventional memory available for use by DOS and DOS-based applications. A DOS extender works by claiming a portion of reserved memory (memory used by other parts of the system, such as the video adapter, the ROM BIOS, and the I/O ports).

DOS prompt \dos´ prompt, D`O-S´\ *n.* The visual indication from the MS-DOS command processor that the operating system is ready to accept a new command. The default DOS prompt is a path followed by a greater-than sign (for example, C:>); the user can also design a custom prompt with the PROMPT command.

dot \dot\ *n.* **1.** In the UNIX, MS-DOS, OS/2, and other operating systems, the character that separates a filename from an extension as in TEXT.DOC (pronounced "text-dot-doc"). **2.** In computer graphics and printing, a small spot combined with others in a matrix of rows and columns to form a character or a graphic element in a drawing or design. The dots forming an image on the screen are called pixels. The resolution of a display or printing device is often expressed in dots per inch (dpi). Dots are not the same as spots, which are groups of dots used in the halftoning process. *See also* pixel, resolution (definition 1). *Compare* spot. **3.** In an Internet address, the character that separates the different parts of the domain name, such as the entity name from the domain. *See also* domain (definition 3), domain name.

dot address \dot´ a`dres, ə-dres´\ *n.* An IP address in dotted quad form. *See also* IP address.

dot-addressable mode \dot`ə-dres´ə-bl mōd`\ *n.* A mode of operation in which a computer program can address ("point to") individual dots on the screen or in a printed character. *See also* all points addressable.

dot com \dot kom´\ *n. See* .com (definition 1).

dot command \dot´ kə-mand`\ *n.* A formatting command typed into a document and preceded by a period (dot) to distinguish it from printable text. Text formatting programs such as the XENIX nroff editor and word processing programs such as WordStar use dot commands for formatting.

dot file \dot´ fīl\ *n.* A file under UNIX whose name begins with a period. Dot files do not appear in ordinary listings of the files in a directory. Dot files are often used to store program setup information for the particular user; for example, .newsrc in a user's account indicates to a newsreader which newsgroups the user subscribes to.

dot-matrix[1] \dot`mā´triks\ *adj.* Referring to video and print hardware that forms character and graphic images as patterns of dots.

dot matrix[2] \dot`mā´triks\ *n.* The rectangular grid, or matrix, of tiny "cells" in which dots are displayed or printed in the patterns required to form text characters, circles, squares, and other graphical images. Depending on the frame of reference, the size of a dot matrix varies from a few rows and columns to an invisible grid covering an entire display screen or printed page. *See also* dot-matrix printer, raster.

dot-matrix printer \dot-mā´triks prin`tər\ *n.* Any printer that produces characters made up of dots

using a wire-pin print head. The quality of output from a dot-matrix printer depends largely on the number of dots in the matrix, which might be low enough to show individual dots or might be high enough to approach the look of fully formed characters. Dot-matrix printers are often categorized by the number of pins in the print head—typically 9, 18, or 24. *Compare* daisy-wheel printer, laser printer.

dot pitch \dot´ pich\ *n.* **1.** In printers, the distance between dots in a dot-matrix. *See also* dot-matrix[2]. **2.** In video displays, a measure of image clarity. A video display's dot pitch is the vertical distance, expressed in millimeters, between like-colored pixels. A smaller dot pitch generally means a crisper image, although the difference between two displays can vary because some manufacturers use different methods to determine the dot pitch of their products. A display's dot pitch is an integral part of the product and so cannot be altered. *See also* CRT, display.

dots per inch \dots` pər inch´\ *n.* A measure of screen and printer resolution that is expressed as the number of dots that a device can print or display per linear inch. *Acronym:* dpi (D`P-I´).

double buffering \dəb´l buf´ər-ēng\ *n.* The use of two temporary storage areas (buffers) rather than one to hold information coming from and going to a particular input/output device. Because one buffer can be filled while the other is being emptied, double buffering increases transfer speed. *Also called* ping-pong buffer.

double-click \də`bl-klik´\ *vb.* To press and release a mouse button twice without moving the mouse. Double-clicking is a means of rapidly selecting and activating a program or program feature. *Compare* click, drag.

double dabble \də`bl dab´l\ *n.* A method of converting binary numbers to decimals by a process of doubling sums and adding successive bits: doubling the bit farthest to the left, adding the next bit and doubling the sum, adding the next bit and doubling the sum, and so on until the rightmost bit has been included in the total.

double-density disk \də`bl-den-sə-tē disk´\ *n.* A disk created to hold data at twice the density (bits per inch) of a previous generation of disks. Early IBM PC floppy disks held 180 KB of data. Double-density disks increased that capacity to 360 KB. Double-density disks use modified frequency modulation encoding for storing data. *See also* floppy disk, microfloppy disk, modified frequency modulation encoding. *Compare* high-density disk.

double-dereference \də`bl-dē-ref´ər-əns, -dē-ref´rəns\ *vb.* To dereference a pointer that is pointed to by another pointer; in other words, to access the information pointed to by a handle. *See also* dereference, handle (definition 1), pointer (definition 1).

double-precision \də´bl-prə-sizh´ən\ *adj.* Of, pertaining to, or characteristic of a number stored in twice the amount (two words—typically 8 bytes) of computer memory that is required for storing a less precise (single-precision) number. Double-precision numbers are commonly handled by a computer in floating-point form. *See also* floating-point number. *Compare* single-precision.

double-sided disk \də`bl-sī-dəd disk´\ *n.* A floppy disk that can hold data on both its top and bottom surfaces.

double-strike \də´bl-strīk`\ *n.* On an impact printer, such as a daisy-wheel printer, the process of printing twice over a word, producing text that appears darker and heavier, or bolder, than it normally appears. On dot-matrix printers, double striking with a slight offset can be used to fill in the space between the dots, producing smoother and darker characters.

double word \də`bl wərd´\ *n.* A unit of data consisting of two contiguous words (connected bytes, not text) that are handled together by a computer's microprocessor.

doubly linked list \də`blē lēnkd list´\ *n.* A series of nodes (items representing discrete segments of information) in which each node refers to both the next node and the preceding node. Because of these two-way references, a doubly linked list can be traversed both forward and backward, rather than in a forward direction only, as with a singly linked list.

down \doun\ *adj.* Not functioning, in reference to computers, printers, communications lines on networks, and other such hardware.

downlink \doun´lēnk\ *n.* The transmission of data from a communications satellite to an earth station.

download \doun´lōd\ *vb.* **1.** In communications, to transfer a copy of a file from a remote computer to the requesting computer by means of a modem or network. **2.** To send a block of data, such as a PostScript file, to a dependent device, such as a PostScript printer. *Compare* upload.

downloadable font \doun´lō-də-bl font`\ *n.* A set of characters stored on disk and sent (downloaded) to a printer's memory when needed for printing a document. Downloadable fonts are most commonly used with laser printers and other page printers, although many dot-matrix printers can accept some of them. *Also called* soft font.

downsizing \doun´sī`zēng\ *n.* In computing, the practice of moving from larger computer systems, such as mainframes and minicomputers, to smaller systems in an organization, generally to save costs and to update to newer software. The smaller systems are usually client/server systems composed of a combination of PCs, workstations, and some legacy system such as a mainframe, connected in one or more local area networks or wide area networks. *See also* client/server architecture, legacy system.

downstream \doun-strēm´\ *n.* The direction in which a news feed for a newsgroup is passed from one news server to the next. *See also* news feed, news server, newsgroup.

downtime \doun´tīm\ *n.* The amount or percentage of time a computer system or associated hardware remains nonfunctional. Although downtime can occur because hardware fails unexpectedly, it can also be a scheduled event, as when a network is shut down to allow time for maintenance.

downward compatibility \doun´wərd kəm-pat`ə-bil´ə-tē\ *n.* The capability of source code or programs developed on a more advanced system or compiler version to be executed or compiled by a less advanced (older) version. *Compare* upward-compatible.

DP \D-P´\ *n.* *See* data processing.

dpi \D`P-I´\ *n.* *See* dots per inch.

DPMA \D`P-M-A´\ *n.* Acronym for **D**ata **P**rocessing **M**anagement **A**ssociation. A trade organization of information systems (IS) professionals. DPMA was founded in 1951 as the National Machine Accountants Association.

DPMI \D`P-M-I´\ *n.* Acronym for **D**OS **P**rotected **M**ode **I**nterface. A software interface, originally developed for Microsoft Windows version 3.0, that enables MS-DOS–based application programs to run in the protected mode built into 80286 and higher microprocessors. In protected mode, the microprocessor can support multitasking and use of memory beyond 1 MB—capabilities otherwise unavailable to programs designed to run under MS-DOS. *See also* protected mode. *Compare* real mode, Virtual Control Program Interface.

DPMS \D`P-M-S´\ *n.* Acronym for VESA **D**isplay **P**ower **M**anagement **S**ignaling. A VESA standard for signals that put a video monitor into "standby" or "suspend" mode to reduce power consumption. *See also* green PC, VESA².

DPSK \D`P-S-K´\ *n.* Acronym for **d**ifferential **p**hase-**s**hift **k**eying. *See* phase-shift keying.

draft mode \draft´ mōd\ *n.* A high-speed, relatively low-quality print mode offered by most dot-matrix printers. *See also* dot-matrix printer, draft quality, print quality.

draft quality \draft´ kwäl`ə-tē\ *n.* A low grade of printing generated by the draft mode on dot-matrix printers. Draft quality varies among printers, ranging from suitable for most purposes to nearly useless. *See also* draft mode, print quality.

drag \drag\ *vb.* In graphical user interface environments, to move an image or a window from one place on the screen to another by "grabbing" it and pulling it to its new location using the mouse. The mouse pointer is positioned over the object, and the mouse button is pressed and held while the mouse is moved to the new location.

drag-and-drop \drag´ənd-drop`\ *vb.* To perform operations in a graphical user interface by dragging objects on the screen with the mouse. For example, to delete a document in the Mac OS, a user can drag the document icon across the screen and drop it on the trashcan icon. See the illustration. *See also* drag, graphical user interface.

drain \drān\ *n.* **1.** In a FET, the electrode toward which charge carriers (electrons or holes) move from the source under control of the gate. *See also* FET, gate (definition 2), MOSFET, source (definition 2). **2.** *See* current drain.

DRAM \D´ram\ *n. See* dynamic RAM.

DRAW \drä, drô, D`R-A-W´\ *n.* Acronym for **d**irect **r**ead **a**fter **w**rite. A technique used with optical discs to verify the accuracy of information imme-

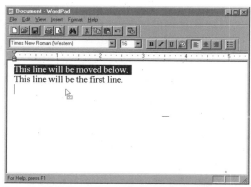

Drag-and-drop. *A text drag-and-drop operation in WordPad.*

diately after it has been recorded (written) on the disc. *Compare* DRDW.

drawing interchange format \drä`ēng in´tər-chānj fōr`mat, drô´ēng\ *n. See* DXF.

drawing program \drä´ēng prō`-gram, drô´ēng\ *n.* A program for manipulating object-oriented graphics, as opposed to manipulating pixel images. In a drawing program, for example, the user can manipulate an element, such as a line, a circle, or a block of text, as an independent object simply by selecting the object and moving it. *See also* object-oriented graphics, pixel image, vector graphics.

DRDW \D`R-D-W´\ *n.* Acronym for **d**irect **r**ead **d**uring **w**rite. A technique used with optical discs to verify the accuracy of information at the time it is being recorded on the disc. *Compare* DRAW.

dribbleware \drib´l-wâr`\ *n.* Updates, patches, and new drivers for a software product that are released one at a time, as they become available, rather than being issued together in a new version of the product. A company using the dribbleware technique may distribute new and replacement files on diskette or CD-ROM, or make them available for download through the Internet or a private network. *See also* driver, patch[1].

drift \drift\ *n.* The movement of charge carriers in a semiconductor caused by an applied voltage. The term is also used to refer to any slow, unwanted change in a parameter; for example, the value of a resistor might change, or drift, slightly as the resistor warms or cools.

drill down \dril doun´\ *vb.* To start at a top-level menu, directory, or Web page and pass through several intermediate menus, directories, or linked pages, until the file, page, menu command, or other item being sought is reached. Drilling down is common practice in searching for files or information on the Internet, where high-level Gopher menus and World Wide Web pages are frequently very general and become more specific at each lower level. See the illustration. *See also* Gopher, menu, Web page.

Drill down.

drive \drīv\ *n. See* disk drive.

drive bay \drīv´ bā\ *n.* A hollow, rectangular area in a computer chassis designed to hold a disk drive. A drive bay always has side walls, usually made of metal, that generally contain holes to facilitate installation of a disk drive. Some drive bays, such as those intended to hold hard disks, are not visible to the user. Most drives are located on the front of the chassis so that the user can interact with the drive.

drive letter \drīv´ let`ər\ *n.* The naming convention for disk drives on IBM and compatible computers. Drives are named by letter, beginning with A, followed by a colon.

drive mapping \drīv´ map`ēng\ *n.* The assignment of a letter or name to a disk drive so that the operating system or network server can identify and locate it. For example, in PCs, the primary drive mappings are A: and B: for floppy disk drives and C: for the hard disk. *See also* A:, disk drive, hard disk.

drive number \drīv´ num`bər\ *n.* The naming convention for Macintosh disk drives. For example, a two-drive system calls its drives 0 and 1.

driver \drī´vər\ *n.* A hardware device or a program that controls or regulates another device. A line driver, for example, boosts signals transmitted over a communications line. A device driver is a device-specific control program that enables a computer to work with a particular device, such as a printer or a disk drive. *See also* device driver.

DRO \D´R-O´\ *n.* Acronym for **d**estructive **r**ead-**o**ut. *See* destructive read.

drop cap \drop kap´\ *n.* A large capital letter at the beginning of a text block that occupies the vertical depth of two or more lines of regular text. See the illustration.

Asectetuer sed adipsicing elite in sed utm diam nonummy nibh wisi tincidunt eusismond ut laoreet dolore

Drop cap.

drop-dead halt \drop`ded hält´\ *n. See* dead halt.

drop-down menu \drop´doun men`yŏŏ\ *n.* A menu that drops from the menu bar when requested and remains open without further action until the user closes it or chooses a menu item. *Compare* pull-down menu.

drop in \drop in´\ *vb.* To read a spurious signal during a data read/write operation, producing erroneous data.

droplet \drop´lit\ *n.* **1.** An extension for Quark Express that allows files to be dragged onto a page from the finder. **2.** A feature from Frontier that allows scripts to be embedded within an application and run when the application is double-clicked. **3.** A general name for any AppleScript program that allows files to be dragged and dropped into it for processing. *See also* AppleScript.

drop out \drop out´\ *vb.* To lose the signal momentarily during a data read/write operation, thus producing erroneous data.

drum \drum\ *n.* A rotating cylinder used with some printers and plotters and (in the early days of mainframe computing) as a magnetic storage medium for data. In laser printers, a rotating drum is coated with a photoelectric material that retains a charge when struck by a laser beam. The electrically charged spots on the drum then attract toner particles that the drum transfers to the paper as the paper passes by.

drum plotter \drum´ plot`ər\ *n.* A plotter in which paper is wrapped around a large revolving drum, with a pen that moves back and forth at the uppermost point on the drum. The paper is rolled with the drum to align the correct point on the paper with the pen. Drums take up a fraction of the space required by flatbed plotters that can handle the same paper size. They also effectively have no limit on the length of the paper they can handle, which can be an advantage in some applications. *See also* plotter. *Compare* flatbed plotter, pinch-roller plotter.

drum scanner \drum´ skan`ər\ *n.* A type of scanner where the medium being scanned, such as a sheet of paper, is rotated around a stationary scan head. *See also* scanner. *Compare* feed scanner, flatbed scanner, handheld scanner.

.drv \dot`D-R-V´\ *n.* The file extension for a driver file. *See also* driver.

dry run \drī run´\ *n.* Running a program intended to have a dramatic effect, such as formatting a disk or printing a book, with the effect disabled, thus avoiding formatting a disk with data on it or wasting paper.

DSA \D`S-A´\ *n.* Acronym for **D**irectory **S**ystem **A**gent or **D**irectory **S**erver **A**gent. An X.500 server program that looks up the address of a user on the network when requested by a DUA (Directory User Agent). *See also* agent (definition 3), DUA, CCITTX series.

DSL \D`S-L´\ *n. See* digital subscriber line.

DSOM \D`S-O-M´\ *n. See* Distributed System Object Model.

DSP \D`S-P´\ *n. See* digital signal processor.

DSR \D`S-R´\ *n.* Acronym for **D**ata **S**et **R**eady. A signal used in serial communications sent, for example, by a modem to the computer to which it is attached, to indicate that it is ready to operate. DSR is a hardware signal sent over line 6 in RS-232-C connections. *See also* RS-232-C standard. *Compare* CTS.

DSS \D`S-S´\ *n. See* decision support system.

DSSSL \D`S-S-S-L´\ *n. See* Document Style Semantics and Specification Language.

DSVD \D`S-V-D´\ *n. See* Digital Simultaneous Voice and Data.

DTE \D`T-E´\ *n.* Acronym for **D**ata **T**erminal **E**quipment. In the RS-232-C hardware standard, any device, such as a microcomputer or a terminal, that has the ability to transmit information in digital form over a cable or a communications line. *See also* RS-232-C standard. *Compare* DCE.

DTL \D`T-L´\ *n. See* diode-transistor logic.

DTP \D`T-P´\ *n. See* desktop publishing, distributed transaction processing.

DTR \D`T-R´\ *n.* Acronym for **D**ata **T**erminal **R**eady. A signal used in serial communications sent, for example, by a computer to its modem to indicate that the computer is ready to accept incoming transmission. *See also* RS-232-C standard.

DTV \D`T-V´\ *n.* Acronym for **desk**top **v**ideo. The use of digital cameras over a network for video conferencing. *See also* video conferencing.

DUA \D`U-A´\ *n.* Acronym for **D**irectory **U**ser **A**gent. An X.500 client program that sends a request to a DSA for the address of a user on the network. *Also called* DCA, Directory Client Agent. *See also* agent (definition 3), DSA.

dual boot \doo`əl boot´\ *n.* A computer configuration that allows a user to boot one of a choice of two operating systems on a PC. Some possible dual boot combinations include Windows 95/Windows NT, Windows NT/OS/2, and Windows 95/Linux. Some operating systems, such as Windows 95 and OS/2, include a multiple boot option. Older operating systems, such as Windows 3.*x* and DOS, require the use of a boot utility to perform a dual boot. *See also* boot[1].

dual channel controller \doo`əl chan-əl kən-trō´lər\ *n.* A circuit or device that governs signal access to two pathways.

dual density \doo`əl den´sə-tē\ *adj.* Of, pertaining to, or characteristic of floppy disk drives that can read from and write to disks in more than one density format.

dual disk drive \doo`əl disk´ drīv\ *adj.* Of, pertaining to, or characteristic of a computer that has two floppy disk drives.

dual in-line package \doo`əl in`līn pak´əj\ *n. See* DIP (definition 1).

dual processors \doo`əl pros´es-ərz\ *n.* Two processors used in a computer to speed its operation—one processor to control memory and the bus, and another to manage input/output. Many personal computers use a second processor to perform floating-point mathematical operations. *See also* coprocessor, floating-point notation.

dual-scan display \doo`əl-skan dis-plā´\ *n.* A passive matrix LCD-type display used in laptop computers. The screen refresh rate is twice as fast in dual-scan displays as in standard passive matrix displays. Compared with active matrix displays, dual-scan displays are more economical in terms of power consumption but have less clarity and a smaller viewing angle. *See also* passive matrix display.

dual-sided disk drive \doo`əl sī`dəd disk´ drīv\ *n.* A disk drive that can read or write information to both the top and bottom sides of a double-sided disk. Dual-sided disk drives have two read/write heads, one for each disk surface.

dumb quotes \dum´ kwōts\ *n.* Quotation marks that have the same appearance (usually upright like the apostrophe ' and quotation marks " on a typewriter) whether they stand before or after the material being quoted. *Compare* smart quotes.

dumb terminal \dum´ tər`mə-nəl\ *n.* A terminal that does not contain an internal microprocessor. Dumb terminals are typically capable of displaying only characters and numbers and responding to simple control codes. *Compare* smart terminal.

dummy \dum´ē\ *n.* A placeholder, usually a character, a record, or a variable, that is used to reserve space until the intended item is available. *See also* stub.

dummy argument \dum´ē är`gyə-mənt\ *n.* In programming, an argument that does not convey any information into or out of the called routine and is usually used to hold a place for an argument that will be used in a future revision of the routine. *See also* argument.

dummy instruction \dum´ē in-struk`shən\ *n. See* no-operation instruction.

dummy module \dum´ē mä`jool, mod`yool\ *n.* A module, or group of routines, that performs no function but will do so in some future revision—essentially, a collection of dummy routines. *See also* dummy routine.

dummy routine \dum´ē roo-tēn´\ *n.* A routine that performs no action but that can be rewritten to do so at some future time. Top-down program development usually involves the creation of dummy routines that are turned into functional routines as development proceeds. *Also called* stub. *See also* dummy argument, dummy module, top-down programming.

duplex[1] \doo´pleks\ *adj.* Capable of carrying information in both directions over a communications channel. A system is full-duplex if it can carry information in both directions at once; it is half-duplex if it can carry information in only one direction at a time.

duplex[2] \doo´pleks\ *n.* **1.** Simultaneous communications, in both directions, between the sender and receiver. *Also called* duplex transmission, full-duplex transmission. *See also* half-duplex transmission. **2.** Photographic paper on which an image can be printed on both sides.

duplex channel \doo´pleks chan´əl\ *n.* A communications link that allows for duplex (two-way) transmission.

duplex printer \doo´pleks prin´tər\ *n.* A printer capable of printing on both sides of the page.

duplex system \doo´pleks si`stəm\ *n.* A system of two computers, one of which is active while the other remains on standby, ready to take over processing if the active machine malfunctions.

duplex transmission \doo´pleks tranz-mish´ən\ *n. See* duplex[2] (definition 1).

duplicate key \doo´plə-kət kē`\ *n.* A value assigned to an indexed field in one record in a database that duplicates a value assigned to the same field in another record in the database. For example, a key (or index) composed of ZIP-CODE would necessarily contain duplicate values if the file contained a number of addresses from a single Zip code. A field in which duplicate values are permitted cannot serve as a primary key because the primary key must be unique, but it can serve as a component of a composite primary key. *See also* field (definition 1), key (definition 2), primary key.

duplication check \doo`plə-kā´shən chek`\ *n.* **1.** A survey made to determine whether duplicate records or keys exist in a file. *See also* key (definition 2). **2.** The use of separate independent calculations to establish the accuracy of a result.

DVD \D`V-D´\ *n. See* digital video disc.

DVD-E \D`V-D-E´\ *n. See* digital video disc–erasable.

DVD-R \D`V-D-R´\ *n. See* digital video disc–recordable.

DVD-ROM \D`V-D-rom´, -R-O-M´\ *n. See* digital video disc–ROM.

DVI or **DV-I** \D`V-I´\ *n.* Acronym for **D**igital **V**ideo **I**nterface. A hardware-based compression/decompression technique for storing full-motion video, audio, graphics, and other data on a computer or on a CD-ROM. DVI technology was developed by RCA in 1987 and acquired by Intel in 1988. Intel has since developed a software version of DVI, called Indeo. *Also called* digital video–interactive.

DV-I \D`V-I´\ *n. See* digital video–interactive.

DVMRP \D`V-M-R-P´\ *n. See* Distance Vector Multicast Routing Protocol.

Dvorak keyboard \də-vōr´zhak   kē`bōrd,   də-vōr´zhäk, dē-vōr´ak\ *n.* A keyboard layout developed by August Dvorak and William L. Dealey in 1936 as an alternative to the overwhelmingly popular QWERTY keyboard. The Dvorak keyboard was designed to speed typing by placing the characters on the keyboard for easiest access to the most frequently typed letters. In addition, pairs of letters that often occur sequentially were separated so that the hands could alternate typing them. See the illustration. *See also* ergonomic keyboard, keyboard. *Compare* QWERTY keyboard.

Dvorak keyboard.

DVST \D`V-S-T´\ *n. See* direct view storage tube.

DXF \D`X-F´\ *n.* Short for drawing interchange format. A computer-aided design file format originally developed for use with the AutoCAD program to facilitate transfer of graphics files between different applications.

dyadic \dī-ad´ik`\ *adj.* Of, pertaining to, or characteristic of a pair—for example, a dyadic processor, which contains two processors controlled by the same operating system. The term is usually limited to describing a system with two microprocessors. Dyadic Boolean operations are those such as AND and OR in which the outcome depends on both values. *See also* Boolean algebra, operand. *Compare* unary.

dye-diffusion printer \dī`di-fyo͞o-zhən prin´tər\ *n. See* continuous-tone printer.

dye-polymer recording \dī`pol´-ə-mər rə-kōr´dēng\ *n.* A recording technology used with optical discs in which dye embedded in a plastic polymer coating on an optical disc is used to create minute bumps on the surface that can be read by a laser. Dye-polymer bumps can be flattened and re-created, thus making an optical disc rewritable.

dye-sublimation printer \dī`su-blə-mā`shən prin´tər\ *n. See* continuous-tone printer.

dynalink \dī´nə-lēnk`\ *n.* Short for **dyna**mic **link.** *See* dynamic-link library.

Dynaload drivers \dī`nə-lōd drī`vərz\ *n.* Device drivers that are supported by Dynaload. Dynaload is a command that can be run from a DOS prompt under IBM's PC DOS 7 and will load compliant device drivers without modification of the CONFIG.SYS file. *See also* CONFIG.SYS.

dynamic \dī-nam´ik`\ *adj.* Occurring immediately and concurrently. The term is used in describing both hardware and software; in both cases it describes some action or event that occurs when and as needed. In dynamic memory management, a program is able to negotiate with the operating system when it needs more memory.

dynamic address translation \dī-nam`ik a´dres tranz-lā`shən, ə-dres´\ *n.* On-the-fly conversion of memory-location references from relative addresses (such as "three units from the beginning of X") to absolute addresses (such as "location number 123") when a program is run. *Acronym:* DAT (dat, D`A-T´).

dynamic allocation \dī-nam`ik a-lə-kā`shən\ *n.* The allocation of memory during program execution according to current needs. Dynamic allocation almost always implies that dynamic deallocation is possible too, so data structures can be created and destroyed as required. *See also* allocate, deallocate. *Compare* static allocation.

dynamic binding \dī-nam`ik bīn`dēng\ *n.* Binding (converting symbolic addresses in the program to storage-related addresses) that occurs during program execution. The term often refers to object-oriented applications that determine, during run time, which software routines to call for particular data objects. *Also called* late binding. *Compare* static binding.

dynamic caching \dī-nam`ik kash`ēng\ *n.* A technique for storing recently used data in memory where cache size is based on how much memory is available rather than how much memory is assigned to the application currently running.

Dynamic Data Exchange \dī-nam`ik dā´tə ekschānj`, dat´ə\ *n. See* DDE.

dynamic dump \dī-nam`ik dump´\ *n.* A listing, either stored on disk or sent to a printer, of memory contents generated at the time of a break in the execution of a program—a useful tool for programmers interested in knowing what is happening at a certain point in the execution of a program.

Dynamic Host Configuration Protocol \dī-nam`ik hōst´ kən-fi-gyər-ā`shən prō`tə-kol\ *n. See* DHCP.

dynamic keys \dī-nam`ik kēz´\ *n.* An encryption technique in which messages are encrypted differently for each transmission based on different keys so that if a key is captured and decrypted, it would never be useful again. *See also* encryption, key (definition 3).

dynamic-link library \dī-nam`ik-lēnk lī´brär-ē\ *n.* A feature of the Microsoft Windows family of operating systems and OS/2 that allows executable routines to be stored separately as files with DLL extensions and to be loaded only when needed by a program. A dynamic-link library has several advantages. First, it does not consume any memory until it is used. Second, because a dynamic-link library is a separate file, a programmer can make corrections or improvements to only that module without affecting the operation of the calling program or any other dynamic-link library. Finally, a programmer can use the same dynamic-link library with other programs. *Acronym:* DLL (D`L-L´).

dynamic memory allocation \dī-nam`ik mem´ər-ē al-ə-kā`shən\ *n.* The allocation of memory to a process or program at run time. Dynamic memory is allocated from the system heap by the operating system upon request from the program.

dynamic page \dī-nam`ik pāj´\ *n.* An HTML document that contains animated GIFs, Java applets, or ActiveX controls. *See also* ActiveX controls, GIF, HTML, Java applet.

dynamic RAM \dī-nam`ik ram´, R-A-M´\ *n.* A form of semiconductor random access memory (RAM). Dynamic RAMs store information in integrated circuits containing capacitors. Because capacitors lose their charge over time, dynamic RAM boards must include logic to refresh (recharge) the RAM chips continuously. While a dynamic RAM is being refreshed, it cannot be read by the processor; if the processor must read the RAM while it is being refreshed, one or more wait states occur. Despite being slower, dynamic RAMs are more commonly used than RAMs because their circuitry is simpler and because they can hold up to four times as much data. *Acronym:* DRAM (dram, D´ram). *See also* RAM. *Compare* static RAM.

dynamic random access memory \dī-nam`ik ran`dəm ak-ses mem´ər-ē\ *n. See* dynamic RAM.

dynamic relocation \dī-nam`ik rē-lō-kā`shən\ *n.* The relocation in memory of data or of the code of a currently running program by an internal system routine. Dynamic relocation helps a computer use memory efficiently.

dynamic scheduling \dī-nam`ik skej`ə-lēng\ *n.* The management of concurrently running processes (programs), usually by the operating system.

dynamic SLIP \dī-nam`ik slip´, S`L-I-P´\ *n.* Short for **dynamic S**erial **L**ine **I**nternet **P**rotocol. Internet access under SLIP in which the user's IP address is not permanent but is reassigned from a pool each time the user connects. The number of IP addresses an Internet service provider needs to offer is reduced to the number of connections that can be in use at once, rather than the total number of subscribers. *See also* IP address, ISP, SLIP.

dynamic storage \dī-nam`ik stōr´əj\ *n.* **1.** Information storage systems whose contents will be lost if power is removed from the system. RAM (random access memory) systems are the most common form of dynamic storage, and both dynamic RAM (DRAM) and static RAM (SRAM) are considered forms of dynamic storage. *See also* dynamic RAM, static RAM. *Compare* permanent storage. **2.** In programming, blocks of memory that can be allocated, deallocated, or freely changed in size.

dynamic Web page \dī-nam`ik web´ pāj\ *n.* A Web page that has fixed form but variable content, allowing it to be tailored to a customer's search criteria.

.dz \dot`D-Z´\ *n.* On the Internet, the major geographic domain specifying that an address is located in Algeria.

e \E\ *n*. The symbol for the base of the natural logarithm, 2.71828. Introduced by Leonhard Euler in the mid-eighteenth century, *e* is a fundamental mathematical constant used in calculus, science, engineering, and programming languages, as in logarithmic and exponential functions in C and Basic.

E \E\ *prefix See* exa-.

early binding \ər`lē bīn´dēng\ *n. See* static binding.

EAROM \E`A´rom, E`A-R-O-M´\ *n*. Acronym for **e**lectrically **a**lterable **r**ead-**o**nly **m**emory. *See* EEPROM.

Easter egg \ē´stər eg`\ *n*. A hidden feature of a computer program. It may be a hidden command, an animation, a humorous message, or a list of credits for the people who developed the program. In order to display an Easter egg, a user often must enter an obscure series of keystrokes.

EBCDIC \eb´sē-dik`, E`B-C`D-I-C´\ *n*. Acronym for **E**xtended **B**inary **C**oded **D**ecimal **I**nterchange **C**ode. An IBM code that uses 8 bits to represent 256 possible characters (compared with unextended ASCII's 7 bits and 128 characters). It is used primarily in IBM mainframes, whereas personal computers use ASCII. *Compare* ASCII.

e-bomb \E´bom\ *n*. Short for **e**-mail **bomb.** A technique used by some hackers in which a target is put on a large number of mailing lists so that network traffic and storage are tied up by e-mail sent by other mailing list subscribers to the lists' recipients.

.ec \dot`E-C´\ *n*. On the Internet, the major geographic domain specifying that an address is located in Ecuador.

e-cash \E´kash\ *n. See* e-money.

ECC \E`C-C´\ *See* error-correcting code, error-correction coding.

echo[1] \ek´ō\ *n*. In communications, a signal transmitted back to the sender that is distinct from the original signal. Network connections can be tested by sending an echo back to the main computer.

echo[2] \ek´ō\ *vb*. To transmit a received signal back to the sender. Computer programs, such as MS-DOS and OS/2, can be commanded to echo input by displaying data on the screen as it is received from the keyboard. Data communications circuits may echo text back to the originating terminal to confirm that it has been received.

echo cancellation \ek´ō kan-sə-lā`shən\ *n*. A technique for eliminating unwanted incoming transmissions in a modem that are echoes of the modem's own transmission. The modem sends a modified, reversed version of its transmission on its receiving path, thus erasing echoes while leaving incoming data intact. Echo cancellation is standard in V.32 modems.

echo check \ek´ō chek`\ *n*. In communications, a method for verifying the accuracy of transmitted data by retransmitting it to the sender, which compares the echoed signal with the original.

echoplex \ek´ō-pleks`\ *n*. In communications, a technique for error detection. The receiving station retransmits data back to the sender's screen, where it can be displayed visually to check for accuracy.

echo suppressor \ek´ō su-pres`ər\ *n*. In communications, a method for preventing echoes in telephone lines. Echo suppressors inhibit signals from the listener to the speaker, creating a one-way channel. For modems that send and receive on the same frequency, the echo suppressor must be disabled to allow two-way transmission. This disabling produces the high-pitched tone heard in modem-to-modem connections.

ECL \E`C-L´\ *n. See* emitter-coupled logic.

ECMA \ek´mə, E`C-M-A´\ *n*. Acronym for **E**uropean **C**omputer **M**anufacturers **A**ssociation. An organization based in Geneva, Switzerland, whose American counterpart is CBEMA (Computer and

Business Equipment Manufacturers Association). Its standard, ECMA-101, is used for transmitting formatted text and graphical images while retaining their original formatting.

e-commerce \E´kom`ərs\ *n.* *See* electronic commerce.

e-credit \E´kred`it\ *n.* *See* electronic credit.

edge \ej\ *n.* **1.** In graphics, a border joining two polygons. **2.** In data structures, a link between two nodes on a tree or graph. *See also* graph, node (definition 3), tree.

edge connector \ej´ kə-nek`tər\ *n.* The set of wide, flat metallic contacts on an expansion board that is inserted into a personal computer's expansion slot or a ribbon cable's connector. It connects the board with the system's shared data pathway, or bus, by means of a series of printed lines that connect to the circuits on the board. The number and pattern of lines differ with the various types of connectors. See the illustration. *See also* expansion board, ribbon cable.

Edge connector. **Two types of edge connector: EISA (top) and 16-bit ISA (bottom).**

EDI \E`D-I´\ *n.* Acronym for **e**lectronic **d**ata **i**nterchange. A set of standards for controlling the transfer of business documents, such as purchase orders and invoices, between computers. The goal of EDI is the elimination of paperwork and increased response time. For EDI to be effective, users must

agree on certain standards for formatting and exchanging information, such as the X.400 protocol. *See also* CCITT X series, standard (definition 1).

edit \ed´it\ *vb.* **1.** To make a change to an existing file or document. Changes to the existing document are saved in memory or in a temporary file but are not added to the document until the program is instructed to save them. Editing programs typically provide safeguards against inadvertent changes, such as by requesting confirmation before saving under an existing filename, by allowing the user to assign a password to a file, or by giving the option of setting the file to read-only status. **2.** To run software that makes extensive, predictable changes to a file automatically, such as a linker or a filter for graphics.

editing keys \ed´ə-tēng kēz`\ *n.* A set of keys on some keyboards that assist in editing. Located between the main keyboard and the numeric keypad, editing keys consist of three pairs: Insert and Delete, Home and End, and Page Up and Page Down.

edit key \ed´it kē`\ *n.* In a software application, a predefined key or combination of keys that, when pressed, causes the application to enter edit mode.

edit mode \ed´it mōd`\ *n.* The mode of a program in which a user can make changes to a document, as by inserting or deleting data or text. *Compare* command mode.

editor \ed´ə-tər\ *n.* A program that creates files or makes changes to existing files. An editor is usually less powerful than a word processor, lacking the latter's capability for text formatting, such as use of italics. Text or full-screen editors allow the user to move through the document using direction arrows. In contrast, line editors require the user to indicate the line number on which text is to be edited. *See also* Edlin.

Edlin \ed´lin\ *n.* An outdated line-by-line text editor used in MS-DOS through version 5. Its OS/2 counterpart is SSE. *See also* editor.

.edmonton.ca \dot-ed`mən-tən-dot-C-A`\ *n.* On the Internet, the major geographic domain specifying that an address is located in Edmonton, Canada.

EDO DRAM \E`D-O D´ram, ē`dō dram´, D-R-A-M´\ *n.* Acronym for **e**xtended **d**ata **o**ut **d**ynamic **r**andom **a**ccess **m**emory. A type of memory that allows for faster read times than DRAM of comparable speed by allowing a new read cycle to begin while data is being read from a previous cycle. This allows for faster overall system performance. *Compare* dynamic RAM, EDO RAM.

EDO RAM \E`D-O´ ram`, R-A-M´\ *n.* Acronym for **e**xtended **d**ata **o**ut **r**andom **a**ccess **m**emory. A type of dynamic RAM that keeps data available for the CPU while the next memory access is being initialized, resulting in increased speed. Pentium-class computers using Intel's Triton chip set are designed to take advantage of EDO RAM. *See also* central processing unit, dynamic RAM. *Compare* EDO DRAM.

EDP \E`D-P´\ *n.* Acronym for **e**lectronic **d**ata **p**rocessing. *See* data processing.

.edu \dot-E`D-U´\ *n.* In the Internet's Domain Name System, the top-level domain that identifies addresses operated by four-year, degreed educational institutions. The domain name .edu appears as a suffix at the end of the address. In the United States, schools that offer kindergarten through high school classes use the top-level domain of .k12.us or just .us. *See also* .k12.us, .us, DNS (definition 1), domain (definition 3). *Compare* .com, .gov, .mil, .net, .org.

edutainment \ej`oo-tān´mənt, ed`yoo-tān´mənt\ *n.* Multimedia content in software, on CD-ROM, or on a Web site that purports to educate the user as well as entertain. *See also* multimedia.

.ee \dot`E-E´\ *n.* On the Internet, the major geographic domain specifying that an address is located in Estonia.

EEMS \E`E-M-S´\ *n.* Acronym for **E**nhanced **E**xpanded **M**emory **S**pecification. A superset of the original Expanded Memory Specification (EMS). Version 3.0 of EMS allowed only storage of data and supported 4-page frames. EEMS allowed up to 64 pages along with executable code to be stored in expanded memory. The features of EEMS were included in EMS version 4.0. *See also* EMS, page frame.

EEPROM \E`E´prom, E`E-P`R-O-M´\ *n.* Acronym for **e**lectrically **e**rasable **p**rogrammable **r**ead-**o**nly **m**emory. A type of EPROM that can be erased with an electrical signal. It is useful for stable storage for long periods without electricity while still allowing reprogramming. EEPROMs contain less

memory than RAM, take longer to reprogram, and can be reprogrammed only a limited number of times before wearing out. *See also* EPROM, ROM.

EFF \E`F-F´\ *n. See* Electronic Frontier Foundation.

e-form \E´fōrm\ *n.* Short for **e**lectronic **form.** An online document that contains blank spaces for a user to fill in with requested information and that can be submitted through a network to the organization requesting the information. On the Web, e-forms are often coded in CGI script and secured via encryption. *See also* CGI (definition 1).

.eg \dot`E-G´\ *n.* On the Internet, the major geographic domain specifying that an address is located in Egypt.

EGA \E`G-A´\ *n.* Acronym for **E**nhanced **G**raphics **A**dapter. An IBM video display standard introduced in 1984. It emulates the Color/Graphics Adapter (CGA) and the Monochrome Display Adapter (MDA) and provides medium-resolution text and graphics. It was superseded by Video Graphics Display (VGA).

EGP \E`G-P´\ *n. See* External Gateway Protocol.

.eh \dot`E-H´\ *n.* On the Internet, the major geographic domain specifying that an address is located in Western Sahara.

EIA \E`I-A´\ *n.* Acronym for **E**lectronic **I**ndustries **A**ssociation. An association based in Washington, D.C., with members from various electronics manufacturers. It sets standards for electronic components. RS-232-C, for example, is the EIA standard for connecting serial components. *See also* RS-232-C standard.

EIDE \E`I-D-E´\ *n. See* Enhanced IDE.

Eiffel \ī´fəl\ *n.* An object-oriented programming language developed by Bertrand Meyer in 1988. It runs on MS-DOS, OS/2, and UNIX. Its major design features are the ability to use modules in multiple programs and software extensibility.

EIS \E`I-S´\ *n. See* executive information system.

EISA \ē´sə, E`I-S-A´\ *n.* Acronym for **E**xtended **I**ndustry **S**tandard **A**rchitecture. A bus standard for the connection of add-on cards to a PC motherboard, such as video cards, internal modems, sound cards, drive controllers, and cards that support other peripherals. EISA was introduced in 1988 by a consortium of nine computer industry companies. The companies—AST Research, Compaq, Epson, Hewlett-Packard, NEC, Olivetti,

Tandy, Wyse, and Zenith—were referred to collectively as "the Gang of Nine." EISA maintains compatibility with the earlier Industry Standard Architecture (ISA) but provides for additional features introduced by IBM in its Micro Channel Architecture bus standard. EISA has a 32-bit data path, and it uses connectors that can accept ISA cards. However, EISA cards are compatible only with EISA systems. EISA can operate at much higher frequencies than the ISA bus and provides much faster data throughput than ISA. *See also* ISA, Micro Channel Architecture.

electroluminescent \ə-lek`trō-lōō-mə-nes´ənt\ *adj.* Giving off light when electric current is applied. Electroluminescent panels are used in portable computers to backlight the liquid crystal displays. A thin phosphor layer is sandwiched between two thin electrode panels, one of which is nearly transparent. *See also* liquid crystal display.

electroluminescent display \ə-lek`trō-lōō-mə-nes`ənt dis-plā´\ *n.* A type of flat-panel display used in laptops in which a thin phosphor layer is set between vertical and horizontal electrodes. These electrodes form *xy*-coordinates; when a vertical and a horizontal electrode are charged, the phosphor at their intersection emits light. Electroluminescent displays provide a sharp, clear image and a wide viewing angle. They were replaced by active matrix LCD screens. *See also* flat-panel display, liquid crystal display, passive-matrix display. *Compare* active-matrix display.

electrolysis \ə-lek`trol´ə-sis\ *n.* A process in which a chemical compound is broken down into its constituent parts by passing an electric current through it.

electromagnet \ə-lek´trō-mag`nət\ *n.* A device that creates a magnetic field when electric current passes through it. An electromagnet typically contains an iron or steel core with wire wrapped around it. Current is passed through the wire, producing a magnetic field. Electromagnets are used in disk drives to record data onto the disk surface.

electromagnetic radiation \ə-lek`trō-mag-net`ik rā-dē-ā´shən\ *n.* The propagation of a magnetic field through space. Radio waves, light, and X rays are examples of electromagnetic radiation, all traveling at the speed of light.

electromagnetic spectrum \ə-lek`trō-mag-net`ik spek´trum\ *n.* The range of frequencies of electromagnetic radiation. In theory, the spectrum's range is infinite. See the illustration.

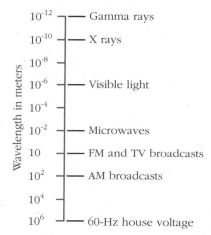

Electromagnetic spectrum.

electromotive force \ə-lek`trō-mō`tiv fōrs´\ *n.* The force that causes movement in charge carriers (the electrons) in a conductor. *Acronym:* EMF (E`M-F´). *Also called* potential, voltage. *See also* ampere, coulomb.

electron beam \ə-lek´tron bēm`\ *n.* A stream of electrons moving in one direction. An electron beam is used in a cathode-ray tube (CRT) to produce an image as it is passed across the phosphor coating inside the tube. *See also* CRT.

electron gun \ə-lek´tron gun`\ *n.* A device that produces an electron beam, typically found in television or computer monitors. *See also* CRT.

electronic bulletin board \ə-lek-tron`ik bul´ə-tən bōrd`\. *n.* See BBS (definition 1).

electronic cash \ə-lek-tron`ik kash´\ *n.* See e-money.

electronic circuit \ə-lek-tron`ik sər´kət\ *n.* See circuit.

electronic commerce \ə-lek-tron`ik kom´ərs\ *n.* Commercial activity that takes place by means of connected computers. Electronic commerce can occur between a user and a vendor through an online information service, the Internet, or a BBS, or between vendor and customer computers through electronic data interchange (EDI). *Also called* e-commerce. *See also* EDI.

electronic credit \ə-lek-tron`ik kred´it\ *n*. A form of electronic commerce involving credit card transactions carried out over the Internet. *Also called* e-credit. *See also* electronic commerce.

electronic data interchange \ə-lek-tron`ik dā´tə in-tər-chānj, dat´ə\ *n*. *See* EDI.

electronic data processing \ə-lek-tron`ik dā´tə pros-es-ēng, dat´ə\ *n*. *See* data processing.

electronic form \ə-lek-tron`ik fōrm´\ *n*. *See* e-form.

Electronic Frontier Foundation \ə-lek-tron`ik frən-tēr´ foun-dā`shən\ *n*. A public advocacy organization dedicated to the defense of civil liberties for computer users. The organization was founded in 1990 by Mitchell Kapor and John Perry Barlow as a response to U.S. Secret Service raids on hackers. *Acronym:* EFF (E`F-F´).

Electronic Industries Association \ə-lek-tron`ik in´dus-trēz ə-sō-sē-ā`shən\ *n*. *See* EIA.

electronic journal \ə-lek-tron`ik jər´nəl\ *n*. *See* journal.

electronic mail \ə-lek-tron`ik māl´\ *n*. *See* e-mail[1].

electronic mail services \ə-lek-tron`ik māl´ sər`və-səs\ *n*. Services that allow users, administrators, or daemons to send, receive, and process e-mail. *See also* daemon.

electronic mall \ə-lek-tron`ik mäl´\ *n*. A virtual collection of online businesses that affiliate with the intention of increasing the exposure of each business through the fellow businesses.

electronic money \ə-lek-tron`ik mən´ē\ *n*. *See* e-money.

electronic music \ə-lek-tron`ik myoo´zik\ *n*. Music created with computers and electronic devices. *See also* MIDI, synthesizer.

electronic office \ə-lek-tron`ik of´is\ *n*. A term used especially in the late 1970s to mid-1980s to refer to a hypothetical paperless work environment to be brought about by the use of computers and communications devices.

electronic photography \ə-lek-tron`ik fə-to´grə-fē\ *n*. *See* digital photography.

electronic publishing \ə-lek-tron`ik pu`bli-shēng\ *n*. A general term for distributing information via electronic media, such as communications networks or CD-ROM.

electronics \ə-lek-tron´iks\ *n*. The branch of physics dealing with electrons, electronic devices, and electrical circuits.

electronic software distribution \ə-lek-tron`ik soft´wâr dis-trə-byoo`shən\ *n*. A means of directly distributing software to users on line over the Internet. Electronic software distribution is analogous to direct-mail ordering. *Acronym:* ESD (E`S-D´).

electronic spreadsheet \ə-lek-tron`ik spred´shēt\ *n*. *See* spreadsheet program.

electronic storefront \ə-lek-tron`ik stōr´frənt\ *n*. A business that displays its merchandise on the Internet and has provisions for contact or online sales.

electronic text \ə-lek-tron`ik tekst´\ *n*. *See* e-text.

electron tube \ə-lek´tron toob`, tyoob´\ *n*. A device for switching and amplifying electronic signals. It consists of a sealed glass container with electronic elements, such as metallic plates and grids, inside. In most applications, tubes have been replaced by transistors, although they are still used in cathode-ray tubes and in some radio frequency circuits and audio amplifiers. *Also called* vacuum tube, valve. *See also* CRT.

electrophotographic printers \ə-lek`trō-fō-tə-graf`ik prin´tərz\ *n*. Printers in a category including laser, LED, LCD, and ion-deposition printers. In such a printer, a negative image is applied to an electrically charged, photosensitive drum. A photosensitive drum develops a pattern of electrostatic charge on its surface representing the photo negative of the image the drum will print. Powdered ink (toner) adheres to the charged areas of the drum, the drum presses the ink onto the paper, and then heat binds the toner to the paper. The printer types vary mainly in how they charge the drum. *See also* ion-deposition printer, laser printer, LCD printer, LED printer.

electrophotography \ə-lek`trō-fə-to´grə-fē\ *n*. The production of photographic images using electrostatic charges. This method is used in photocopiers and laser printers. *Also called* xerography. *See also* electrophotographic printers.

electroplating \ə-lek`trō-plā´tēng\ *n*. The use of electrolysis for depositing a thin layer of one material onto another material. *See also* electrolysis.

electrostatic \ə-lek`trō-stat´ik\ *adj*. Of or relating to electric charges that are not flowing along a conducting path. Electrostatic charges are used in copiers and laser printers to hold toner particles on a photoconducting drum and in flatbed plotters to hold the plot medium in place.

electrostatic discharge \ə-lek`trō-stat`ik dis´-chärj\ *n.* The discharge of static electricity from an outside source, such as human hands, into an integrated circuit, often resulting in damage to the circuit. *Acronym:* ESD (E`S-D´).

electrostatic plotter \ə-lek`trō-stat`ik plot´ər\ *n.* A plotter that creates an image from a dot pattern on specially coated paper. The paper is electrostatically charged and exposed to toner, which adheres to the dots. Electrostatic plotters can be up to 50 times faster than pen plotters but are more costly. Color models produce images through multiple passes with cyan, magenta, yellow, and black. *See also* plotter. *Compare* electrophotographic printers, pen plotter.

electrostatic printer \ə-lek`trō-stat`ik prin´tər\ *n.* *See* electrostatic plotter.

elegant \el´ə-gənt\ *adj.* Combining simplicity, terseness, efficiency, and subtlety. On the academic side of computer science, elegant design (say, of programs, algorithms, or hardware) is a priority, but in the frenetic pace of the computer industry, elegant design normally is sacrificed for the sake of speeding a product's development, frequently resulting in bugs that are difficult to correct.

element \el´ə-mənt\ *n.* **1.** Any stand-alone item within a broader context. For example, a data element is an item of data with the characteristics or properties of a larger set; a picture element (pixel) is one single dot on a computer screen or in a computer graphic; a print element is the part of a daisy-wheel printer that contains the embossed characters. *See also* daisy-wheel printer, data element, graphics primitive, pixel, thimble. **2.** In markup languages such as HTML and SGML, the combination of a set of tags, any content contained between the tags, and any attributes the tags may have. Elements can be nested, one within the other. *See also* attribute (definition 3), HTML, markup language, SGML.

elevator \el´ə-vā`tər\ *n.* The square box within a scroll bar that can be moved up and down to change the position of text or an image on the screen. See the illustration. *Also called* scroll box, thumb. *See also* scroll bar.

— Elevator

Elevator.

elevator seeking \el´ə-vā-tər sē`kēng\ *n.* A method of limiting hard disk access time in which multiple requests for data are prioritized based on the location of the data relative to the read/write head. This serves to minimize head movement. *See also* access time (definition 2), hard disk, read/write head.

elite \ē-lēt´, ā-lēt´, ə-lēt´\ *n.* **1.** A size of fixed-width type that prints 12 characters to the inch. **2.** A fixed-width font that may be available in various type sizes. *See also* monospace font.

ELIZA \ə-lī´zə\ *n.* A program, modeled on Rogerian psychotherapy, that conducts simulated conversations with humans by echoing responses and posing questions based on key words in earlier comments. It was created by Dr. Joseph Weizenbaum, who considered it a bit of a joke and was alarmed that people took it seriously.

ellipsis \ə-lip´sis\ *n.* A set of three dots (...) used to convey incompleteness. In many windowing applications, selection of a command that is followed by an ellipsis will produce a submenu or a dialog box. In programming and software manuals, an ellipsis in a syntax line indicates the repetition of certain elements. *See also* dialog box, syntax.

elm \elm\ *n.* Short for **el**ectronic **m**ail. A program for reading and composing e-mail on UNIX systems. The elm program has a full-screen editor, making it easier to use than the original mail program, but elm has largely been superseded by pine. *See also* e-mail[1]. *Compare* Eudora, pine.

e-mail[1] or **E-mail** or **email** \ē´māl\ *n.* **1.** The exchange of text messages and computer files over a communications network, such as a local area network or the Internet, usually between computers or terminals. **2.** An electronic text message.

e-mail[2] or **E-mail** or **email** \ē´māl\ *vb.* To send an e-mail message.

e-mail address \ē´māl a`dres, ə-dres`\ *n*. A string that identifies a user so that the user can receive Internet e-mail. An e-mail address typically consists of a name that identifies the user to the mail server, followed by an at sign (@) and the host name and domain name of the mail server. For example, if Anne E. Oldhacker has an account on the machine called baz at Foo Enterprises, she might have an e-mail address aeo@baz.foo.com, which would be pronounced "A E O at baz dot foo dot com."

e-mail filter \ē´māl fil`tər\ *n*. A feature in e-mail–reading software that automatically sorts incoming mail into different folders or mailboxes based on information contained in the message. For example, all incoming mail from a user's Uncle Joe might be placed in a folder labeled "Uncle Joe." Filters may also be used either to block or accept e-mail from designated sources.

embedded \em-bed´əd\ *adj*. In software, pertaining to code or a command that is built into its carrier. For example, application programs insert embedded printing commands into a document to control printing and formatting. Low-level assembly language is embedded in higher-level languages, such as C, to provide more capabilities or better efficiency.

embedded command \em-bed`əd kə-mand´\ *n*. A command placed in a text, graphics, or other document file, often used for printing or page-layout instructions. Such commands often do not appear on screen but can be displayed if needed. In transferring documents from one program to another, embedded commands can cause problems if the programs are incompatible.

embedded controller \em-bed`əd kən-trō´lər\ *n*. A processor-based controller circuit board that is built into the computer machinery. *See also* controller.

embedded hyperlink \em-bed`əd hī´pər-lēnk\ *n*. A link to a resource that is embedded within text or is associated with an image or an image map. *See also* hyperlink, image map.

embedded interface \em-bed`əd in´tər-fās\ *n*. An interface built into a hardware device's drive and controller board so that the device can be directly connected to the computer's system bus. *See also* controller, interface (definition 3). *Compare* ESDI, SCSI, ST506 interface.

em dash \em´ dash\ *n*. A punctuation mark (—) used to indicate a break or interruption in a sentence. It is named for the em, a typographical unit of measure that in some fonts equals the width of a capital M. *Compare* en dash, hyphen.

EMF \E`M-F´\ *n*. *See* electromotive force.

emitter \ə-mit´ər, ē-mit´ər\ *n*. In transistors, the region that serves as a source of charge carriers. *Compare* base (definition 3), collector.

emitter-coupled logic \ə-mit´ər-kup-ld loj´ik, ē-mit`ər-\ *n*. A circuit design in which the emitters of two transistors are connected to a resistor so that only one of the transistors switches at a time. The advantage of this design is very high switching speed. Its drawbacks are the high number of components required and susceptibility to noise. *Acronym:* ECL (E`C-L´).

EMM \E`M-M´\ *n*. *See* Expanded Memory Manager.

e-money or **emoney** \ē´mən-ē\ *n*. Short for **e**lectronic **money**. A generic name for the exchange of money through the Internet. *Also called* cybercash, digicash, digital cash, e-cash.

emotag \ē´mō-tag`\ *n*. In an e-mail message or newsgroup article, a letter, word, or phrase that is encased in angle brackets and that, like an emoticon, indicates the attitude the writer takes toward what he or she has written. Often emotags have opening and closing tags, similar to HTML tags, that enclose a phrase or one or more sentences. For example: <joke>You didn't think there would really be a joke here, did you?</joke>. Some emotags consist of a single tag, such as <grin>. *See also* emoticon, HTML.

emoticon \ə-mō´ti-kon`\ *n*. A string of text characters that, when viewed sideways, form a face expressing a particular emotion. An emoticon is often used in an e-mail message or newsgroup post as a comment on the text that precedes it. Common emoticons include :-) or :) (meaning "I'm smiling at the joke here"), ;-) ("I'm winking and grinning at the joke here"), :-(("I'm sad about this"), :-7 ("I'm speaking with tongue in cheek"), :D or :-D (big smile; "I'm overjoyed"), and :-O (either a yawn of boredom or a mouth open in amazement). *Compare* emotag.

EMS \E`M-S´\ *n*. Acronym for **E**xpanded **M**emory **S**pecification. A technique for adding memory to

PCs that allows for increasing memory beyond the Intel 80x86 microprocessor real-mode limit of 1 megabyte. In earlier versions of microprocessors, EMS bypassed this memory board limit with a number of 16-kilobyte banks of RAM that could be accessed by software. In later versions of Intel microprocessors, including the 80386 and 80486 models, EMS is converted from extended memory by software memory managers, such as EMM386 in MS-DOS 5. Now EMS is used mainly for older MS-DOS applications because Windows and other applications running in protected mode on 80386 and higher microprocessors are free of the 1-MB limit. *Also called* LIM EMS. *See also* expanded memory, protected mode. *Compare* conventional memory, extended memory.

em space \em´ spās\ *n.* A typographical unit of measure that is equal in width to the point size of a particular font. For many fonts, this is equal to the width of a capital M, from which the em space takes its name. *Compare* en space, fixed space, thin space.

emulate \e´myo͞o-lāt`\ *vb.* For a hardware or software system to behave in the same manner as another hardware or software system. In a network, for example, microcomputers often emulate mainframes or terminals so that two machines can communicate.

emulation \e`myə-lā´shən\ *n.* The process of a computer, device, or program imitating the function of another computer, device, or program.

emulator \e´myə-lā`tər\ *n.* Hardware or software designed to make one type of computer or component act as if it were another. By means of an emulator, a computer can run software written for another machine. In a network, microcomputers might emulate mainframes or terminals so that two machines can communicate.

emulsion laser storage \ē-mul`shən lā´zər stōr-`əj\ *n.* A method for recording data in film by selective heating with a laser beam.

enable \e-nā´bl\ *vb.* To activate or turn on. *Compare* disable.

encapsulate \en-kap`sə-lāt`\ *vb.* To treat a collection of structured information as a whole without affecting or taking notice of its internal structure. In communications, a message or packet constructed according to one protocol, such as a TCP/

IP packet, may be taken with its formatting data as an undifferentiated stream of bits that is then broken up and packaged according to a lower-level protocol (for example, as ATM packets) to be sent over a particular network; at the destination, the lower-level packets are assembled, re-creating the message as formatted for the encapsulated protocol. In object-oriented programming, the implementation details of a class are encapsulated in a separate file whose contents do not need to be known by a programmer using that class. *See also* ATM (definition 1), object-oriented programming, TCP/IP.

Encapsulated PostScript \en-kap`sə-lā-təd pōst´ skript\ *n. See* EPS.

encapsulated type \en-kap`sə-lā-təd tīp`\ *n. See* abstract data type.

encipher \en-sī´fər\ *vb. See* encryption.

encode \en-kōd´\ *vb.* **1.** In data security, to encrypt. *See also* encryption. **2.** In programming, to put something into code, which frequently involves changing the form—for example, changing a decimal number to binary-coded form. *See also* binary-coded decimal, EBCDIC.

encryption \en-krip´shən\ *n.* The process of encoding data to prevent unauthorized access, especially during transmission. Encryption is usually based on a key that is essential for decoding. The U.S. National Bureau of Standards created a complex encryption standard, Data Encryption Standard (DES), which provides almost unlimited ways to encrypt documents. *See also* DES.

encryption key \en-krip´shən kē\ *n.* A sequence of data that is used to encrypt other data and that, consequently, must be used for the data's decryption. *See also* decryption, encryption.

end-around carry \end`ə-round kâr´ē\ *n.* A special type of end-around shift operation on a binary value that treats the carry bit as an extra bit; that is, the carry bit is moved from one end of the value to the other. *See also* carry, end-around shift, shift.

end-around shift \end`ə-round shift`\ *n.* An operation performed on a binary value in which a bit is shifted out of one end and into the other end. For example, a right-end shift on the value 00101001 yields 10010100. *See also* shift.

en dash \en´ dash\ *n.* A punctuation mark (–) used to show ranges of dates and numbers, as in

1990–92, and in compound adjectives where one part is hyphenated or consists of two words, as in pre–Civil War. The en dash is named after a typographical unit of measure, the en space, which is half the width of an em space. *See also* em space. *Compare* em dash, hyphen.

End key \end´ kē\ *n.* A cursor-control key that moves the cursor to a certain position, usually to the end of a line, the end of a screen, or the end of a file, depending on the program.

endless loop \end`ləs lōōp´\ *n. See* infinite loop.

end mark \end´ märk\ *n.* A symbol that designates the end of some entity, such as a file or word processing document.

end-of-file \end`əv-fīl´\ *n.* A code placed by a program after the last byte of a file to tell the computer's operating system that no additional data follows. In ASCII, end-of-file is represented by the decimal value 26 (hexadecimal 1A) or the Ctrl-Z control character. *Acronym:* EOF (E`O-F´).

end-of-text \end`əv-tekst´\ *n.* In data transmission, a character used to mark the end of a text file. End-of-text does not necessarily signify the end of transmission; other information, such as error-checking or transmission control characters, can be included at the end of the file. In ASCII, end-of-text is represented by the decimal value 3 (hexadecimal 03). *Acronym:* ETX (E`T-X´).

end-of-transmission \end`əv-tranz-mish´ən\ *n.* A character representing the end of a transmission. In ASCII, the end-of-transmission character has the decimal value 4 (hexadecimal 04). *Acronym:* EOT (E`O-T´).

endpoint \end´point\ *n.* The beginning or end of a line segment.

end user \end´ yōō´zər\ *n.* The ultimate user of a computer or computer application in its finished, marketable form.

End-User License Agreement \end`yōō-zər lī´səns ə-grē`mənt\ *n.* A legal agreement between a software manufacturer and the software's purchaser with regard to terms of distribution, resale, and restricted use. *Acronym:* EULA (yōō´lə, E`U-L-A´).

Energy Star \en´ər-jē stär`\ *n.* A symbol affixed to systems and components that denotes lower power-consumption design. Energy Star is the name of an Environmental Protection Agency program that encourages PC manufacturers to build systems that are energy efficient. Requirements dictate that systems or monitors be capable of automatically entering a "sleep state" or a lower power-consumption state while the unit is inactive, where the low-power state is defined as 30 watts or less. Systems and monitors that comply with these guidelines are marked with an Energy Star sticker.

engine \en´jən\ *n.* A processor or portion of a program that determines how the program manages and manipulates data. The term *engine* is most often used in relation to a specific program; for example, a database engine contains the tools for manipulating a database. *Compare* back-end processor, front-end processor.

Enhanced Expanded Memory Specification \en-hansd` eks-pan`dəd mem´ər-ē spes`ə-fə-kā`shən\ *n. See* EEMS.

Enhanced Graphics Adapter \en-hansd` graf´iks ə-dap`tər\ *n. See* EGA.

Enhanced Graphics Display \en-hansd` graf´iks dis-plā`\ *n.* A PC video display capable of producing graphic images with resolutions ranging from 320 × 200 through 640 × 400 pixels, in color or in black and white. Resolution and color depth depend on the vertical and horizontal scanning frequencies of the display, the capabilities of the video display controller card, and available video RAM.

Enhanced IDE \en-hansd` I-D-E´\ *n.* Short for **Enhanced** I**ntegrated** D**rive** E**lectronics.** An extension of the IDE standard, Enhanced IDE is a hardware interface standard for disk drive designs that house control circuits in the drives themselves. It allows for standardized interfaces to the system bus while providing for advanced features, such as burst data transfer and direct data access. Enhanced IDE accommodates drives as large as 8.4 gigabytes (IDE supports up to 528 megabytes). It supports the ATA-2 interface, which permits transfer rates up to 13.3 megabytes per second (IDE permits up to 3.3 megabytes per second), and the ATAPI interface, which connects drives for CD-ROMs, optical discs and tapes, and multiple channels. Most PCs have Enhanced IDE drives, which are cheaper than SCSI drives and provide much of the same functionality. *Acronym:* EIDE (E`I-D-E´). *See also* IDE, SCSI.

enhanced keyboard \en-hansd` kē´bōrd\ *n.* An IBM 101/102-key keyboard that replaced the PC and AT keyboards. It features 12 function keys across the top (rather than 10 on the left side), extra Control and Alt keys, and a bank of cursor and editing keys between the main keyboard and number pad. It is similar to the Apple Extended Keyboard. See the illustration.

enhanced parallel port \en-hansd` pâr´ə-lel pōrt`\ *n.* A connection port for peripheral devices, most often used for printers, external disk drives, or tape drives. Enhanced parallel ports utilize high-speed circuits for faster data throughput. Data and communications control lines are wired in parallel; each data line corresponds to 1 data bit. Data is transferred across all lines in sync. *Acronym:* EPP (E`P-P´). *See also* input/output port.

enhanced serial port \en-hansd` sēr´ē-əl pōrt`\ *n.* A connection port for peripheral devices, commonly used for mice and external modems. Enhanced serial ports utilize 16550-type or newer high-speed UART circuits for faster data throughput. Data is transferred as a sequence of bits and bytes on a pair of lines, either synchronously (data flows in one direction only) or asynchronously (data flows each way in turn). *Acronym:* ESP (E`S-P´). *See also* input/output port, UART.

Enhanced Small Device Interface \en-hansd` smäl` də-vīs in´tər-fās\ *n. See* ESDI.

ENIAC \ē´nē-ak`, E`N-I-A-C´\ *n.* An 1,800-square-foot, 30-ton computer containing 17,468 vacuum tubes and 6,000 manual switches. Developed between 1942 and 1946 for the U.S. Army by J. Presper Eckert and John Mauchly at the University of Pennsylvania, ENIAC is considered to have been the first truly electronic computer. It remained in operation until 1955.

enlarge \en-lärj´\ *vb.* In Microsoft Windows and other graphical user interfaces, to increase the size of a window. *See also* maximize. *Compare* minimize, reduce.

E notation \E´ nō-tā`shən\ *n. See* floating-point notation.

ENQ \E`N-Q´\ *n. See* enquiry character.

enquiry character \en-kwīr´ē kâr`ək-tər, en´kwər-ē\ *n.* Abbreviated ENQ. In communications, a control code transmitted from one station to request a response from the receiving station. In ASCII, the enquiry character is designated by decimal value 5 (hexadecimal 05).

en space \en´ spās\ *n.* A typographical unit of measure that is equal in width to half the point size of a particular font. *Compare* em space, fixed space, thin space.

Enter key \en´tər kē`\ *n.* The key that is used at the end of a line or command to instruct the computer to process the command or text. In word processing programs, the Enter key is used at the end of a paragraph. *Also called* Return key.

enterprise computing \en´tər-prīz kəm-pyoō`-tēng\ *n.* In a large enterprise such as a corporation, the use of computers in a network or series of interconnected networks that generally encompass a variety of different platforms, operating

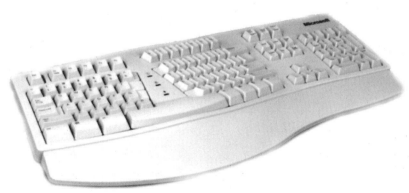

Enhanced keyboard.   The Microsoft Natural keyboard with enhanced features.

systems, protocols, and network architectures. *Also called* enterprise networking.

enterprise network \en´tər-prīz` net`wərk\ *n.* In a large enterprise such as a corporation, the network (or interconnected networks) of computer systems owned by the enterprise, which fills the enterprise's various computing needs. This network can span diverse geographical locations and usually encompasses a range of platforms, operating systems, protocols, and network architectures.

enterprise networking \en´tər-prīz   net`wər-kēng\ *n. See* enterprise computing.

entity \en´tə-tē`\ *n.* In computer-aided design and object-oriented design, an item that can be treated as a unit and, often, as a member of a particular category or type. *See also* CAD, object-oriented design.

entry \en´trē\ *n.* **1.** A unit of information treated as a whole by a computer program. **2.** The process of inputting information.

entry point \en´trē point`\ *n.* A place in a program where execution can begin.

enumerated data type \ə-nōo`mər-ā-təd dā´tə tīp, dat´ə\ *n.* A data type consisting of a sequence of named values given in a particular order.

envelope \en´və-lōp`, än´və-lōp\ *n.* **1.** In communications, a single unit of information that is grouped with other items, such as error-checking bits. **2.** The shape of a sound wave, caused by changes in amplitude. See the illustration.

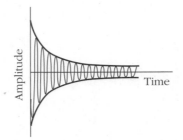

Envelope.

envelope delay \en´və-lōp də-lā`, än´və-lōp\ *n.* In communications, the difference in travel times of different frequencies in a signal. If the frequencies reach their destination at different times, signal distortion and errors can result. *Also called* delay distortion.

environment \en-vīr´ən-mənt`, en-vī´ərn-mənt`\ *n.* **1.** The configuration of resources available to the user. *Environment* refers to the hardware and the operating system running on it. For example, Microsoft Windows and Apple Macintosh are called windowing environments because they are based on screen regions called windows. **2.** In microcomputing, *environment* refers to a definition of the specifications, such as command path, that a program operates in.

EOF \E`O-F´\ *n. See* end-of-file.

EOL \E`O-L´\ *n.* Acronym for **e**nd **o**f **l**ine. A control (nonprinting) character that signals the end of a data line in a data file.

EOT \E`O-T´\ *n. See* end-of-transmission.

epitaxial layer \ep-ə-taks´ē-əl lâr`, lā`ər\ *n.* In semiconductors, a layer that has the same crystal orientation as the underlying layer.

EPP \E`P-P´\ *n. See* enhanced parallel port.

EPP IEEE standard \E`P-P` I-E-E-E´ stan`dərd\ *n.* An IEEE standard relating to the Enhanced Parallel Port (EPP) protocol. This protocol was originally developed by Intel, Xircom, and Zenith Data Systems as a means to provide a high-performance parallel port link that would still be compatible with the standard parallel port. This protocol capability was implemented by Intel in the 386SL chip set (82360 I/O chip), prior to the establishment of the IEEE 1284 committee and the associated standards work. The EPP protocol offered many advantages to parallel port peripheral manufacturers and was quickly adopted by many as an optional data transfer method. A loose association of about 80 interested manufacturers was formed to develop and promote the EPP protocol. This association became the EPP Committee and was instrumental in helping to get this protocol adopted as one of the IEEE 1284 advanced modes. *See also* communications protocol, IEEE, parallel port.

EPROM \E´prom, E`P-R-O-M´\ *n.* Acronym for **e**rasable **p**rogrammable **r**ead-**o**nly **m**emory. A nonvolatile memory chip that is programmed after it is manufactured. EPROMs can be reprogrammed by removing the protective cover from the top of the chip and exposing the chip to ultraviolet light. Though EPROMS are more expensive than PROM chips, they can be more cost-effective if many changes are required. *Also called* reprogrammable read-only memory (RPROM). *See also* EEPROM, PROM, ROM.

.eps \dot-E`P-S´\ *n.* The file extension that identifies Encapsulated PostScript files. *See also* EPS.

EPS \E`P-S´\ *n.* Acronym for **E**ncapsulated **P**ost**S**cript. A PostScript file format that can be used as an independent entity. The EPS image must be incorporated into the PostScript output of an application such as a desktop publisher. Many high-quality clip-art packages consist of such images. *See also* PostScript.

EPSF \E`P-S-F´\ *n.* Acronym for **E**ncapsulated **P**ost**S**cript **f**ile. *See* EPS.

equality \ē-kwäl´ə-tē´\ *n.* The property of being identical, used most often in reference to values and data structures.

equalization \ē`kwə-lə-zā´shən\ *n.* A form of conditioning used to compensate for signal distortion and delay on a communication channel. Equalization attempts to maintain the amplitude and phase characteristics of a signal so that it remains true to the original when it reaches the receiving device.

equation \ē-kwā´zhən\ *n.* A mathematical statement that indicates equality with the use of an equal sign (=) between two expressions. In programming languages, assignment statements are written in equation form. *See also* assignment statement.

.er \dot`E-R´\ *n.* On the Internet, the major geographic domain specifying that an address is located in Eritrea.

erasable programmable read-only memory \ər-ā`sə-bl prō-gram`ə-bl rēd`ōn-lē mem´ər-ē\ *n.* *See* EPROM.

erasable storage \ər-ā`sə-bl stōr´əj\ *n.* Storage media that can be used repeatedly because the user has the ability to erase whatever data was previously there. Most forms of magnetic storage, such as tape and disk, are erasable.

erase \ər-ās´, ēr-ās´\ *vb.* To remove data permanently from a storage medium. This is usually done by replacing existing data with zeros or meaningless text or, in magnetic media, by disturbing the magnetic particles' physical arrangement, either with the erase head or with a large magnet. *Erase* differs from *delete* in that *delete* merely tells the computer that data or a file is no

longer needed; the data remains stored and is recoverable until the operating system reuses the space containing the deleted file. *Erase,* on the other hand, removes data permanently. *See also* erase head. *Compare* delete.

erase head \ər-ās´ hed`\ *n.* The device in a magnetic tape machine that erases previously recorded information.

Eratosthenes' sieve \âr-ə-tos`thə-nēz siv´\ *n.* *See* sieve of Eratosthenes.

ergonomic keyboard \ər-gə-nom`ik kē´bōrd\ *n.* A keyboard designed to reduce the risk of wrist and hand injuries that result from prolonged use or repetitive movement. An ergonomic keyboard can include such features as alternative key layouts and palm rests. *See also* Dvorak keyboard, keyboard, Kinesis ergonomic keyboard.

ergonomics \er`gə-nom´iks\ *n.* The study of people (their physical characteristics and the ways they function) in relation to their working environment (the furnishings and machines they use). The goal of ergonomics is to incorporate comfort, efficiency, and safety into the design of keyboards, computer desks, chairs, and other items in the workplace.

error \âr´ər\ *n.* A value or condition that is not consistent with the true, specified, or expected value or condition. In computers, an error results when an event does not occur as expected or when impossible or illegal maneuvers are attempted. In data communications, an error occurs when there is a discrepancy between the transmitted and received data. *See also* critical error, error message, error rate, error ratio, fatal error, hard error, inherent error, intermittent error, logic error, machine error, overflow error, parity error, propagated error, read error, recoverable error, syntax error, system error, write error. *Compare* fault.

error analysis \âr´ər ə-nal´ə-sis\ *n.* The art and science of detecting errors in numeric calculations, especially in long and involved computations, where the possibility of errors increases.

error checking \âr´ər chek`ēng\ *n.* A method for detecting discrepancies between transmitted and received data during file transfer.

error control \âr´ər kən-trōl´\ *n.* **1.** The section of a program, procedure, or function that checks for errors such as type mismatches, overflows and underflows, dangling or illegal pointer references, and memory-use inconsistencies. **2.** The process of anticipating program errors during software development.

error-correcting code \âr`ər-kər-ek`tēng kōd´\ *n.* A code, designed for transmission of electronic data, that encodes data in such a way that transmission errors may be detected and corrected by examination of the encoded data on the receiving end. Error-correcting codes are used by most modems. *See also* modem.

error-correction coding   \âr`ər-kər-ek´shən kō`dēng\ *n.* A method for encoding that allows for detection and correction of errors that occur during transmission. Most error-correction codes are characterized by the maximum number of errors they can detect and by the maximum number of errors they can correct. *See also* error detection and correction. *Compare* error-detection coding.

error detection and correction \âr`ər də-tek`shən and kər-ek´shən\ *n.* A method for discovering and resolving errors during file transfer. Some programs only detect errors; others detect and attempt to fix them.

error-detection coding \âr`ər-də-tek´shən  kō`dēng\ *n.* A method of encoding data so that errors that occur during storage or transmission can be detected. Most error-detection codes are characterized by the maximum number of errors they can detect. *See also* checksum. *Compare* error-correction coding.

error file \âr´ər fīl`\ *n.* A file that records the time and type of data processing and transmission errors.

error handling \âr´ər han`də-lēng, hand`lēng\ *n.* The process of dealing with errors (or exceptions) as they arise during the running of a program. Some programming languages, such as C++, Ada, and Eiffel, have features that aid in error handling. *See also* bug (definition 1).

error message \âr´ər mes`əj\ *n.* A message from the system or program indicating that an error requiring resolution has occurred.

error rate \âr´ər rāt`\ *n.* In communications, the ratio of the number of bits or other elements that arrive incorrectly during transmission. For a 1,200-bps modem, a typical error rate would be 1 in every 200,000 bits. *See also* parity, parity bit, Xmodem, Ymodem.

error ratio \âr´ər rā`shō\ *n.* The ratio of errors to the number of units of data processed. *See also* error rate.

error trapping \âr´ər trap`ēng\ *n.* **1.** The process by which a program checks for errors during execution. **2.** The process of writing a function, program, or procedure such that it is capable of continuing execution despite an error condition.

.es \dot`E-S´\ *n.* On the Internet, the major geographic domain specifying that an address is located in Spain.

escape character \e-skāp´ kâr`ək-tər\ *n. See* ESC character.

escape code \e-skāp´ kōd`\ *n.* A character or sequence of characters that indicates that a following character in a data stream is not to be processed in the ordinary way. In the C programming language, the escape code is the backslash \, which has several uses, as shown by the statement

```
printf ("The backslash \"\\\" is the
escape code.\n");.
```

The last backslash, which is the next-to-last character in the string, indicates that the following *n* is not to be printed, but that the sequence \n represents the newline character. By contrast, the backslashes before the quotation marks indicate that the latter *are* to be printed, rather than marking the end of one string and the beginning of another; similarly, the backslash before a backslash indicates that the second backslash is to be printed, rather than serving as an escape code. The resulting output is *The backslash* "\" *is the escape code.*

Escape key \e-skāp´ kē`\ *n.* A key on a computer keyboard that sends the escape (ESC) character to the computer. In many applications, the Escape key moves the user back one level in the menu structure or exits the program. *See also* Clear key.

escape sequence \e-skāp´ sē`kwəns\ *n.* A sequence of characters that usually begins with the ESC character (ASCII 27, hexadecimal 1B), which is followed by one or more additional characters. An escape sequence escapes from the normal sequence of characters (such as text) and issues an instruction or command to a device or program.

ESC character \e-skāp´ kâr`ək-tər\ *n*. One of the 32 control codes defined in the ASCII character set. It usually indicates the beginning of an escape sequence (a string of characters that give instructions to a device such as a printer). It is represented internally as character code 27 (hexadecimal 1B). *Also called* escape character.

Esc key \e-skāp´ kē`\ *n*. *See* Escape key.

ESD \E`S-D´\ *n*. *See* electronic software distribution, electrostatic discharge.

ESDI \E`S-D-I´, ez´dē\ *n*. Acronym for **E**nhanced **S**mall **D**evice **I**nterface. A device that allows disks to communicate with computers at high speeds. ESDI drives typically transfer data at about 10 megabits per second, but they are capable of doubling that speed.

ESP \E`S-P´\ *n*. *See* enhanced serial port.

ESP IEEE standard \E`S-P` I-E-E-E´ stan`dərd\ *n*. Short for **E**ncapsulating **S**ecurity **P**ayload **IEEE standard**. A standard for providing integrity and confidentiality to IP (Internet Protocol) datagrams. In some circumstances, it can also provide authentication to IP datagrams. *See also* authentication, datagram, IEEE, IP.

.et \dot`E-T´\ *n*. On the Internet, the major geographic domain specifying that an address is located in Ethiopia.

e-text \E´tekst\ *n*. Short for **e**lectronic **text**. A book or other text-based work that is available on line in an electronic media format. An e-text can be read on line or downloaded to a user's computer for offline reading. *See also* ezine.

Ethernet \ē´thər-net`\ *n*. **1.** An IEEE 802.3 standard for contention networks. Ethernet uses a bus or star topology and relies on the form of access known as Carrier Sense Multiple Access with Collision Detection (CSMA/CD) to regulate communication line traffic. Network nodes are linked by coaxial cable, by fiber-optic cable, or by twisted-pair wiring. Data is transmitted in variable-length frames containing delivery and control information and up to 1,500 bytes of data. The Ethernet standard provides for baseband transmission at 10 megabits (10 million bits) per second. *See also* 10Base2, 10Base5, 10BaseF, 10BaseT, baseband, bus network, coaxial cable, contention, CSMA/CD, IEEE 802 standards, twisted-pair cable. **2.** A widely used local area network system developed by Xerox in 1976, from which the IEEE 802.3 standard was developed.

Ethernet/802.3 \ē´thər-net-āt`-ō-tōō` point-thrē´\ *n*. The IEEE standard for 10- or 100-Mbps transmissions over an Ethernet network. Ethernet/802.3 defines both hardware and data packet construction specifications.

E-time \ē´tīm\ *n*. *See* execution time.

etiquette \et´ə-kət\ *n*. *See* netiquette.

ETX \E`T-X´\ *n*. *See* end-of-text.

Eudora \yōō`dōr´ə\ *n*. An e-mail client program originally developed as freeware for Macintosh computers by Steve Dorner at the University of Illinois, now maintained in both freeware and commercial versions for both Macintosh and Microsoft Windows by Qualcomm, Inc.

EULA \yōō´lə, E`U-L-A´\ *n*. *See* End-User License Agreement.

European Computer Manufacturers Association \yər-ə-pē`ən kəm-pyōō`tər man´yu-fak´chur-ərz ə-sō-sē-ā`shən\ *n*. *See* ECMA.

European Laboratory for Particle Physics \yər-ə-pē`ən lab`rə-tōr`ē fōr pär`tə-kl fiz´iks\ *n*. *See* CERN.

evaluation \i-val`yōō-ā´shən\ *n*. The determination, by a program, of the value of an expression or the action that a program statement specifies. Evaluation can take place at compile time or at run time.

even parity \ē`vən pâr´ə-tē\ *n*. *See* parity.

event \ə-vent´, ē-vent´\ *n*. An action or occurrence, often generated by the user, to which a program might respond—for example, key presses, button clicks, or mouse movements. *See also* event-driven programming.

event-driven \ə-vent´ driv`ən, ē-vent´\ *adj*. Of, pertaining to, or being software that accomplishes its purpose by responding to externally caused events, such as the user pressing a key or clicking a button on a mouse. For example, an event-driven data entry form will allow the user to click on and edit any field at any time rather than forcing the user to step through a fixed sequence of prompts.

event-driven processing \ə-vent´ driv-ən pros´es-ēng, ē-vent´\ *n*. A program feature belonging to more advanced operating-system architectures such as the Apple Macintosh operating system,

Microsoft Windows, UNIX, and OS/2. In times past, programs were required to interrogate, and effectively anticipate, every device that was expected to interact with the program, such as the keyboard, mouse, printer, disk drive, and serial port. Often, unless sophisticated programming techniques were used, one of two events happening at the same instant would be lost. Event processing solves this problem through the creation and maintenance of an event queue. Most common events that occur are appended to the event queue for the program to process in turn; however, certain types of events can preempt others if they have a higher priority. An event can be of several types, depending on the specific operating system considered: pressing a mouse button or keyboard key, inserting a disk, clicking on a window, or receiving information from a device driver (as for managing the transfer of data from the serial port or from a network connection). *See also* autopolling, event, interrupt.

event-driven programming \ə-vent`driv-ən prō´-gram-ēng, ē-vent`\ *n.* A type of programming in which the program constantly evaluates and responds to sets of events, such as key presses or mouse movements. Event-driven programs are typical of Apple Macintosh computers, although most graphical interfaces, such as Microsoft Windows or the X Window System, also use such an approach. *See also* event.

exa- \eks´ə\ *prefix* Abbreviated E. A prefix meaning one quintillion (10^{18}). In computing, which is based on the binary (base-2) numbering system, exa- has a literal value of 1,152,921,504,606,846,976, which is the power of 2 (2^{60}) closest to one quintillion.

exabyte \eks´ə-bīt`\ *n.* Abbreviated EB. Roughly 1 quintillion bytes, or a billion billion bytes, or 1,152,921,504,606,846,976 bytes.

exception \eks-ep´shən\ *n.* In programming, a problem or change in conditions that causes the microprocessor to stop what it is doing and handle the situation in a separate routine. An exception is similar to an interrupt; both refer the microprocessor to a separate set of instructions. *See also* interrupt.

exception error 12 \eks-ep`shən âr-ər twelv´\ *n.* An error created in DOS environments caused by

a stack overflow. This problem may be corrected by modifying the CONFIG.SYS file and editing the STACKS= entries.

exception handling \eks-ep´shən han`-də-lēng, hand`lēng\ *n. See* error handling.

exchangeable disk \eks-chanj`ə-bl disk´\ *n. See* removable disk.

exchange sort \eks-chānj´ sôrt`\ *n. See* bubble sort.

exclusive NOR \eks-kloo`siv nôr´\ *n.* A two-state digital electronic circuit in which the output is driven high only if the inputs are all high or all low.

exclusive OR \eks-kloo`siv ôr´\ *n.* A Boolean operation that yields "true" if and only if one of its operands is true and the other is false, as shown in the table below. *Acronym:* EOR (E´ôr). *Also* called XOR. *See also* Boolean operator, truth table. Compare AND, OR.

a	*b*	*a XOR b*
0	0	0
0	1	1
1	0	1
1	1	0

.exe \dot`E-X-E´\ *n.* In MS-DOS, a filename extension that indicates that a file is an executable program. To run an executable program, the user types the filename without the .exe extension at the prompt and presses Enter. *See also* executable program.

executable[1] \eks´ə-kyoo´tə-bl\ *adj.* Of, pertaining to, or being a program file that can be run. Executable files have extensions such as .bat, .com, and .exe.

executable[2] \eks`ə-kyoo´tə-bl\ *n.* A program file that can be run, such as file0.bat, file1.exe, or file2.com.

executable program \eks`ə-kyoo`te-bl prō´gram\ *n.* A program that can be run. The term usually applies to a compiled program translated into machine code in a format that can be loaded into memory and run by a computer's processor. In interpreter languages, an executable program can be source code in the proper format. *See also* code (definition 1), compiler (definition 2), computer program, interpreter, source code.

execute \eks´ə-kyoot`\ *vb.* To perform an instruction. In programming, execution implies loading the machine code of the program into memory and then performing the instructions.

execution time \eks`ə-kyo͞o´shən tīm`\ *n*. The time, measured in clock ticks (pulses of a computer's internal timer), required by a microprocessor to decode and carry out an instruction after it is fetched from memory. *Also called* E-time. *See also* instruction time.

executive \egz-e´kyə-tiv`\ *n*. *See* operating system.

executive information system \egz-e`kyə-tiv infər-mā´shən si-stəm\ *n*. A set of tools designed to organize information into categories and reports. Because it emphasizes information, an executive information system differs from a decision support system (DSS), which is designed for analysis and decision making. *Acronym:* EIS (E`I-S´). *Compare* decision support system.

exerciser \eks´ər-sī`zər\ *n*. A program that exercises a piece of hardware or software by running it through a large set of operations.

exit \egz´it, eks´it\ *vb*. In a program, to move from the called routine back to the calling routine. A routine can have more than one exit point, thus allowing termination based on various conditions.

expanded \eks-pan´dəd\ *adj*. A font style that sets characters farther apart than the normal spacing. *Compare* condensed.

expanded memory \eks-pan`dəd mem´ər-ē\ *n*. A type of memory, up to 8 MB, that can be added to IBM PCs. Its use is defined by the Expanded Memory Specification (EMS). Expanded memory is not accessible to programs in MS-DOS, so the Expanded Memory Manager (EMM) maps pages (blocks) of bytes from expanded memory into page frames in accessible memory areas. *See also* EEMS, EMS, Expanded Memory Manager, page frame.

Expanded Memory Manager \eks-pan`dəd mem`ər-ē man´ə-jər\ *n*. A driver that implements the software portion of the Expanded Memory Specification (EMS) to make expanded memory in IBM and compatible PCs accessible. *Acronym:* EMM (E`M-M´). *See also* EMS, expanded memory, extended memory.

Expanded Memory Specification \eks-pan`dəd mem`ər-ē spes`-ə-fə-kā´shən\ *n*. *See* EMS.

expansion \eks-pan´shən\ *n*. A way of increasing a computer's capabilities by adding hardware that performs tasks that are not part of the basic system. Expansion is usually achieved by plugging printed circuit boards (expansion boards) into openings (expansion slots) inside the computer. *See also* expansion board, expansion slot, open architecture (definition 2), PC Card, PCMCIA slot.

expansion board \eks-pan´shən bōrd`\ *n*. A circuit board that is plugged into a computer's bus (main data transfer path) to add extra functions or resources to the computer. Typical expansion boards add memory, disk drive controllers, video support, parallel and serial ports, and internal modems. For laptops and other portable computers, expansion boards come in credit card–sized devices called PC Cards that plug into a slot in the side or back of the computer. See the illustration. *Also called* expansion board, extender board. *See also* expansion slot, PC Card, PCMCIA slot.

Expansion board.

expansion bus \eks-pan´shən bus`\ *n. See* AT bus.

expansion card \eks-pan´shən kärd`\ *n. See* expansion board.

expansion slot \eks-pan´shən slot`\ *n.* A socket in a computer, designed to hold expansion boards and connect them to the system bus (data pathway). Expansion slots are a means of adding or enhancing the computer's features and capabilities. In laptop and other portable computers, expansion slots come in the form of PCMCIA slots designed to accept PC Cards. See the illustration. *See also* expansion board, PC Card, PCMCIA slot.

expert system \eks`pərt si´stəm\ *n.* An application program that makes decisions or solves problems in a particular field, such as finance or medicine, by using knowledge and analytical rules defined by experts in the field. It uses two components, a knowledge base and an inference engine, to form conclusions. Additional tools include user interfaces and explanation facilities, which enable the system to justify or explain its conclusions as well as allowing developers to run checks on the operating system. *See also* artificial intelligence, inference engine, intelligent database, knowledge base.

expiration date \eks`pər-ā´shən dāt\ *n.* The date on which a shareware, beta, or trial version of a program stops functioning, pending purchase of the full version or the entry of an access code.

expire \eks-pīr´\ *vb.* To stop functioning in whole or in part. Beta versions of software are often programmed to expire when a new version is released. *See also* beta[2].

exploded view \eks-plō`dəd vyoo´\ *n.* A form of display that shows a structure with its parts separated but depicted in relation to each other. See the illustration.

Explorer \eks-plōr´ər\ *n. See* Internet Explorer, Windows Explorer.

exponent \eks`pō-nənt\ *n.* In mathematics, a number that shows how many times a number is used as a factor in a calculation; in other words, an exponent shows that number's power. Positive exponents, as in 2^3, indicate multiplication (2 times 2 times 2). Negative exponents, as in 2^{-3}, indicate division (1 divided by 2^3). Fractional exponents, as in $8^{1/3}$, indicate the root of a number (the cube root of 8).

exponential notation \eks`pə-nen`shəl nō-tā´shən\ *n. See* floating-point notation.

8-bit slot

16-bit slot

Expansion slot. Expansion slots on a motherboard.

exponentiation \eks`pə-nen`shē-ā´shən\ *n*. The operation in which a number is raised to a given power, as in 2^3. In computer programs and programming languages, exponentiation is often shown by a caret (^), as in 2^3.

export \eks´pōrt, eks-pōrt´\ *vb*. To move information from one system or program to another. Files that consist only of text can be exported in ASCII (plain text format). For files with graphics, however, the receiving system or program must offer some support for the exported file's format. *See also* EPS, PICT, TIFF. *Compare* import.

expression \eks-presh´ən\ *n*. A combination of symbols—identifiers, values, and operators—that yields a result upon evaluation. The resulting value can then be assigned to a variable, passed as an argument, tested in a control statement, or used in another expression.

extended ASCII \eks-ten`dəd a´skē, A`S-C-I-I´\ *n*. Any set of characters assigned to ASCII values between decimal 128 and 255 (hexadecimal 80 through FF). The specific characters assigned to the extended ASCII codes vary between computers and between programs, fonts, or graphics characters. Extended ASCII adds capability by allowing for 128 additional characters, such as accented letters, graphics characters, and special symbols. *See also* ASCII.

Extended Binary Coded Decimal Interchange Code \eks-ten`dəd bī`nər-ē kō-dəd des`ə-məl in´tər-chānj kōd\ *n*. *See* EBCDIC.

extended characters \eks-ten`dəd kâr´ək-tərz\ *n*. Any of the 128 additional characters in the extended ASCII (8-bit) character set. These characters include those used in several foreign languages, such as accent marks, and special symbols used for creating pictures. *See also* extended ASCII.

extended data out random access memory \eks-ten`dəd dā`tə out ran`dəm ak`ses mem´ərē, dat`ə\ *n*. *See* EDO RAM.

Extended Edition \eks-ten`dəd ə-dish´ən\ *n*. A version of OS/2 with built-in database and communications facilities, developed by IBM. *See also* OS/2.

eXtended Graphics Array \ek-sten`dəd graf´iks ər-ā´\ *n*. An advanced standard for graphics con-

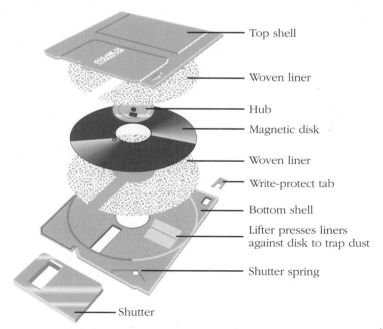

Top shell
Woven liner
Hub
Magnetic disk
Woven liner
Write-protect tab
Bottom shell
Lifter presses liners against disk to trap dust
Shutter spring
Shutter

Exploded view. An exploded view of a microfloppy disk.

troller and display mode design, introduced by IBM in 1990. This standard supports 640 × 480 resolution with 65,536 colors, or 1,024 × 768 resolution with 256 colors, and is used mainly on workstation-level systems. *Acronym:* XGA (X˘G-A´).

Extended Industry Standard Architecture \eks-ten`dəd in`du-strē stan-dərd är´kə-tek-chur\ *n. See* EISA.

extended memory \eks-ten`dəd mem´ər-ē\ *n.* System memory beyond 1 megabyte in computers based on the Intel 8086 processors. This memory is accessible only when an 80386 or higher-level processor is operating in protected mode or in emulation on the 80286. To use extended memory, MS-DOS programs need the aid of software that temporarily places the processor into protected mode or by the use of features in the 80386 or higher-level processors to remap portions of extended memory into conventional memory. Programs running under Microsoft Windows, OS/2, and other operating systems that run on Intel processors and use the protected mode of the 80386 and higher-level processors can access all system memory in the same way. *See also* EMS, extended memory specification, protected mode.

extended memory specification \eks-ten`dəd mem`ər-ē spes`-ə-fə-kā´shən\ *n.* A specification developed by Lotus, Intel, Microsoft, and AST Research that defines a software interface allowing real-mode applications to use extended memory and areas of memory not managed by MS-DOS. Memory is managed by an installable device driver, the Expanded Memory Manager (EMM). The application must use the driver to access the additional memory. *Acronym:* XMS (X˘M-S´). *See also* Expanded Memory Manager, extended memory.

extended VGA \eks-ten`dəd V-G-A´\ *n.* An enhanced set of Video Graphics Array (VGA) standards that is capable of displaying an image of from 800 × 600 pixels to 1600 × 1200 pixels and that can support a palette of up to 16.7 million (2^{24}) colors. This palette approaches the 19 million colors that a normal person can distinguish, so it is considered a digital standard for color realism that parallels analog television. *Also called* Super VGA, SVGA. *See also* analog-to-digital converter, CRT, VGA.

extender board \eks-ten´dər bōrd`\ *n. See* expansion board.

extensible language \eks-ten`sə-bl lang´wəj\ *n.* A computer language that allows the user to extend or modify the syntax and semantics of the language. In the strict sense, the term relates to only a few of the languages actually used, such as Forth, that allow the programmer to change the language itself. *See also* computer language, semantics (definition 1), syntax.

extension \eks`-ten´shən\ *n.* **1.** A set of characters added to a filename that serves to extend or clarify its meaning or to identify a file as a member of a category. An extension may be assigned by the user or by a program, as, for example, .com or .exe for executable programs that MS-DOS can load and run. **2.** A supplemental set of codes used to include additional characters in a particular character set. **3.** A program or program module that adds functionality to or extends the effectiveness of a program. **4.** On the Macintosh, a program that alters or augments the functionality of the operating system. There are two types: system extensions, such as QuickTime, and Chooser extensions, such as printer drivers. When a Macintosh is turned on, the extensions in the Extensions folder within the System folder are loaded into memory. *See also* Chooser extension, QuickTime, System folder.

extension manager \eks-ten´shən man`ə-jər\ *n.* On the Macintosh, a utility that allows the user to determine which extensions are loaded when the computer is turned on. *See also* extension (definition 4).

extent \eks-tent´\ *n.* On a disk or other direct-access storage device, a continuous block of storage space reserved by the operating system for a particular file or program.

external command \eks-tər`nəl kə-mand´\ *n.* A program included in an operating system that is loaded into memory and executed only when its name is entered at the system prompt. Although an external command is a program in its own right, it is called a command because it is included with the operating system. *See also* XCMD. *Compare* internal command.

external function \eks-tər`nəl funk´shən\ *n. See* XFCN.

External Gateway Protocol \eks-tər`nəl gāt´wā prō`tə-kol\ *n.* A protocol for distributing information regarding availability to the routers and gateways that interconnect networks. *Acronym:* EGP (E`G-P´). *See also* gateway, router.

external hard disk \eks-tər`nəl härd´ disk\ *n.* A free-standing hard disk with its own case and power supply, connected to the computer with a data cable and used mainly as a portable unit. *See also* hard disk.

external interrupt \eks-tər`nəl in´tər-upt\ *n.* A hardware interrupt generated by hardware elements external to the microprocessor. *See also* hardware interrupt, internal interrupt, interrupt.

external modem \eks-tər`nəl mō´dəm\ *n.* A stand-alone modem that is connected via cable to a computer's serial port. *See also* internal modem.

external reference \eks-tər`nəl ref´ər-əns, re´frəns\ *n.* A reference in a program or routine to some identifier, such as code or data, that is not declared within that program or routine. The term usually refers to an identifier declared in code that is separately compiled. *See also* compile.

external storage \eks-tər`nəl stōr´əj\ *n.* A storage medium for data, such as a disk or tape unit, that is external to a computer's memory.

external viewer \eks-tər`nəl vyo͞o´ər\ *n.* A separate application used to view documents that are of a type that cannot be handled by the current application. *See also* helper program.

extract \eks-trakt´\ *vb.* **1.** To remove or duplicate items from a larger group in a systematic manner. **2.** In programming, to derive one set of characters from another by using a mask (pattern) that determines which characters to remove.

extra-high-density floppy disk \eks`trə-hī-den`-sə-tē flop´ē disk\ *n.* A 3.5-inch floppy disk capable of holding 4 MB of data and requiring a special disk drive that has two heads rather than one. *See also* floppy disk.

extranet \eks´trə-net`\ *n.* An extension of a corporate intranet using World Wide Web technology to facilitate communication with the corporation's suppliers and customers. An extranet allows customers and suppliers to gain limited access to a company's intranet in order to enhance the speed and efficiency of their business relationship. *See also* intranet.

extrinsic semiconductor \eks-trin`zik sem´ē-kən-duk`tər, sem´ī-kən-duk`tər\ *n.* A semiconductor that conducts electricity due to a P-type or N-type impurity that allows electrons to flow under certain conditions, such as heat application, by forcing them to move out of their standard state to create a new band of electrons or electron gaps. *See also* N-type semiconductor, P-type semiconductor, semiconductor.

ezine \ē´zēn\ *n.* Short for **e**lectronic maga**zine.** A digital production available on the Internet, a BBS, or other online service, often free of charge.

F \F\ *n. See* farad.

F2F \F`too-F´\ *adv.* Short for face-to-face. In person, rather than over the Internet. The term is used in e-mail.

face \fās\ *n.* **1.** In geometry and computer graphics, one side of a solid object, such as a cube. **2.** In printing and typography, short for *typeface.*

face time \fās´ tīm\ *n.* Time spent dealing face-to-face with another person, rather than communicating electronically.

facsimile \fak`sim´ə-lē\ *n. See* fax.

factor \fak´tər\ *n.* In mathematics, an item that is multiplied in a multiplication problem; for example, 2 and 3 are factors in the problem 2 × 3. The prime factors of a number are a set of prime numbers that, when multiplied together, produce the number.

factorial \fak-tōr´-ē-əl\ *n.* Expressed as *n*! (*n* factorial), the result of multiplying the successive integers from 1 through *n*; *n*! equals $n \times (n - 1) \times (n - 2) \times \cdots \times 1$.

fail-safe system \fāl`sāf si´stəm\ *n.* A computer system designed to continue operating without loss of or damage to programs and data when part of the system breaks down or seriously malfunctions. *Compare* fail-soft system.

fail-soft system \fāl`soft si´stəm\ *n.* A computer system designed to fail gracefully over a period of time when an element of hardware or software malfunctions. A fail-soft system terminates nonessential functions and remains operating at a diminished capacity until the problem has been corrected. *Compare* fail-safe system.

failure \fāl´yur\ *n.* The inability of a computer system or related device to operate reliably or to operate at all. A common cause of system failure is loss of power, which can be minimized with a battery-powered backup source until all devices can be shut down. Within a system, electronic failures generally occur early in the life of a system or component and can often be produced by burning in the equipment (leaving it turned on constantly) for a few hours or days. Mechanical failures are difficult to predict but are most likely to affect devices, such as disk drives, that have moving parts.

failure rate \fāl´yur rāt`\ *n.* The number of failures in a specified time period. Failure rate is a means of measuring the reliability of a device, such as a hard disk. *See also* MTBF.

fair use \fâr yoos´\ *n.* A legal doctrine describing the boundaries of legitimate use of copyrighted software or other published material.

fallout \fäl´out\ *n.* Any failure of components that occurs while equipment is being burned in, especially when the test is done at the factory. *See also* burn in (definition 1).

family \fam´ə-lē, fam´lē\ *n.* A series of hardware or software products that have some properties in common, such as a series of personal computers from the same company, a series of CPU chips from the same manufacturer that all use the same instruction set, or a set of fonts that are intended to be used together, such as Times New Roman. *See also* central processing unit, font, instruction set.

fan[1] \fan\ *n.* The cooling mechanism built into computer cabinets, laser printers, and other such devices to prevent malfunction due to heat buildup. Fans are the main source of the continuous humming associated with computers and other hardware.

fan[2] \fan\ *vb.* To flip through a stack of printer paper to ensure that the pages are loose and will not stick together or jam the printer.

fanfold paper \fan´fōld pā`pər\ *n.* Paper with pin-feed holes on both margins designed to be fed into the tractor-feed mechanism of a printer, page by page, in a continuous, unbroken stream. *Also called* z-fold paper.

fan-in \fan´in\ *n*. The maximum number of signals that can be fed to a given electronic device, such as a logic gate, at one time without risking signal corruption. The fan-in rating of a device depends on its type and method of construction. *Compare* fan-out.

fan-out \fan´out\ *n*. The maximum number of electronic devices that can be fed by a given electronic device, such as a logic gate, at one time without the signal becoming too weak. The fan-out rating of a device depends on its type and method of construction. *Compare* fan-in.

fanzine \fan´zēn\ *n*. A magazine, distributed online or by mail, that is produced by and devoted to fans of a particular group, person, or activity. *See also* ezine.

FAQ \fak, F´A-Q´\ *n*. Acronym for **f**requently **a**sked **q**uestions. A document listing common questions and answers on a particular subject. FAQs are often posted on Internet newsgroups where new participants ask the same questions that regular readers have answered many times.

farad \fâr´ad\ *n*. Abbreviated F. The unit of capacitance (the ability to hold a charge). A 1-farad capacitor holds a charge of 1 coulomb with a potential difference of 1 volt between its plates. In practical use, a farad is an extremely large amount of capacitance; capacitance is usually expressed in terms of microfarads (10^{-6}) or picofarads (10^{-12}).

FARNET \fär´net, F-A-R´net`\ *See* Federation of American Research Networks.

Fast Ethernet \fast` ē´thər-net\ *n*. Ethernet capable of supporting 100 megabits per second. *See also* Ethernet (definition 1).

fast Fourier transform \fast fo͞or`ē-ā trans´fōrm\ *n*. A set of algorithms used to compute the discrete Fourier transform of a function, which in turn is used for solving series of equations, performing spectral analysis, and carrying out other signal-processing and signal generation tasks. *Acronym:* FFT (F´F-T´). *See also* Fourier transform.

fast infrared port \fast` in`frə-red pōrt´\ *n*. *See* FIR port.

fast packet \fast´ pak`et\ *n*. A standard for high-speed network technology that utilizes fast switching of fixed-length cells or packets for real-time transmission of data. *Also called* Asynchronous Transfer Mode, ATM. *See also* packet (definition 2), packet switching.

Fast SCSI \fast´ skuz`ē, S`C-S-I´\ *n*. A form of the SCSI-2 interface that can transfer data 8 bits at a time at up to 10 megabytes per second. The Fast SCSI connector has 50 pins. *Also called* Fast SCSI-2. *See also* SCSI, SCSI-2. *Compare* Fast/Wide SCSI, Wide SCSI.

Fast/Wide SCSI \fast`wīd skuz´ē, S`C-S-I´\ *n*. A form of the SCSI-2 interface that can transfer data 16 bits at a time at up to 20 megabytes per second. The Fast/Wide SCSI connector has 68 pins. *Also called* Fast/Wide SCSI-2. *See also* SCSI, SCSI-2. *Compare* Fast SCSI, Wide SCSI.

FAT \fat, F`A-T´\ *n*. *See* file allocation table.

fatal error \fā´təl âr`ər\ *n*. An error that causes the system or application program to crash—that is, to fail abruptly with no hope of recovery.

fat application \fat´ a-plə-kā`shən\ *n*. An application that can be used on both PowerPC processor–based Macintosh computers and 68K-based Macintosh computers.

fat binary \fat´ bī´nər-ē\ *n*. An application format that supports both PowerPC processor–based Macintosh computers and 68K-based Macintosh computers.

fatbits \fat´bits\ *n*. **1.** Originally (as FatBits), a feature of the Apple MacPaint program in which a small portion of a drawing can be enlarged and modified one pixel (FatBit) at a time. **2.** A similar feature in any program that allows pixel-by-pixel modification through a zoom feature.

fat client \fat` clī´ənt\ *n*. In a client/server architecture, a client machine that performs most or all of the processing, with little or none performed by the server. The client handles presentation and functions, and the server manages data and access to it. *See also* client (definition 3), client/server architecture, server (definition 2), thin server. *Compare* fat server, thin client.

FAT file system \fat` fīl´ si-stəm, F`A-T´\ *n*. The system used by MS-DOS to organize and manage files. The FAT (file allocation table) is a data structure that MS-DOS creates on the disk when the disk is formatted. When MS-DOS stores a file on a formatted disk, the operating system places information about the stored file in the FAT so that MS-DOS can retrieve the file later when requested.

The FAT is the only file system MS-DOS can use; OS/2, Windows NT, and Windows 95 operating systems can use the FAT file system in addition to their own file systems (HPFS, NTFS, and VFAT, respectively). *See also* file allocation table, HPFS, NTFS, OS/2, VFAT, Windows 95, Windows NT.

father \fä´dhər\ *n.* See generation (definition 1).

father file \fä´dhər fīl`\ *n.* A file that is the last previously valid set of a changing set of data. The father file is immediately preceded by a grandfather file and immediately succeeded by its son. The pairs *father* and *son, parent* and *child* (or *descendant*), and *independent* and *dependent* are synonymous. *See also* generation (definition 1).

fat server \fat` sər´vər\ *n.* In a client/server architecture, a server machine that performs most of the processing, with little or none performed by the client. Applications logic and data reside on the server, and presentation services are handled by the client. *See also* client (definition 3), client/server architecture, server (definition 2), thin client. *Compare* fat client, thin server.

fatware \fat´wâr\ *n.* Software that monopolizes hard disk space and power due to an overabundance of features or inefficient design. *Also called* bloatware.

fault \fält, fôlt\ *n.* A physical defect, such as a loose connection, that prevents a system or device from operating as it should.

fault tolerance \fält´ tol`ər-ens, fôlt´\ *n.* The ability of a computer or an operating system to respond to a catastrophic event or fault, such as a power outage or a hardware failure, in a way that ensures that no data is lost and any work in progress is not corrupted. This can be accomplished with a battery-backed power supply, backup hardware, provisions in the operating system, or any combination of these. In a fault-tolerant network, the system has the ability either to continue the system's operation without loss of data or to shut the system down and restart it, recovering all processing that was in progress when the fault occurred.

favorite \fä´vər-it`, fä´vrət\ *n.* In Microsoft Internet Explorer, a user-defined shortcut to a page on the World Wide Web, analogous to a bookmark in Netscape Navigator. *See also* Favorites folder, hotlist. *Compare* bookmark (definition 2).

Favorites folder \fä´vər-its fōl`dər, fä´vrəts\ *n.* In Microsoft Internet Explorer, a collection of shortcuts to Web sites that a user has selected for future reference. Other Web browsers refer to this collection by other names, such as bookmarks or hotlists. *See also* bookmark file (definition 1), Internet Explorer, URL. *Compare* bookmark (definition 2), hotlist.

fax \faks\ *n.* Short for facsimile. The transmission of text or graphics over telephone lines in digitized form. Conventional fax machines scan an original document, transmit an image of the document as a bit map, and reproduce the received image on a printer. Resolution and encoding are standardized in the CCITT Groups 1–4 recommendations. Fax images can also be sent and received by microcomputers equipped with fax hardware and software. *See also* CCITT Groups 1–4.

fax machine \faks´ mə-shēn`\ *n.* Short for facsimile machine. A device that scans pages, converts the images of those pages to a digital format consistent with the international facsimile standard, and transmits the image through a telephone line. A fax machine also receives such images and prints them on paper. See the illustration. *See also* scan (definition 2).

Fax machine.

fax modem \faks´ mō`dəm\ *n.* A modem that sends (and possibly receives) data encoded in a fax format (typically CCITT fax format), which a fax machine or another modem decodes and converts to an image. The image must already have been encoded on the host computer. Text and graphic documents can be converted into fax format by special software usually provided with the modem; paper documents must first be scanned in. Fax modems may be internal or external and may combine fax and conventional modem capabilities. See the illustration. *See also* fax, modem.

Fax modem.

fax on demand \faks` on də-mand´\ *n*. An automated system that makes information available for request by telephone. When a request is made, the system faxes the information to the telephone number given in the request. *Acronym:* FOD (F`O-D´).

fax program \faks´ prō`gram\ *n*. A computer application that allows the user to send, receive, and print fax transmissions. *See also* fax.

fax server \faks´ sər`vər\ *n*. A computer on a network capable of sending and receiving fax transmissions to and from other computers on the network. *See also* fax, server (definition 1).

FCB \F`C-B´\ *n*. *See* file control block.

FCC \F`C-C´\ *n*. Acronym for **F**ederal **C**ommunications **C**ommission. The U.S. agency created by the Communications Act of 1934, which regulates interstate and international wire, radio, and other broadcast transmissions, including telephone, telegraph, and telecommunications.

F connector \F´ kə-nek`tər\ *n*. A coaxial connector, used primarily in video applications, that requires a screw-on attachment. See the illustration.

F connector. Female (left) and male (right) F connectors.

FDDI \F`D-D-I´\ *n*. Acronym for **F**iber **D**istributed **D**ata **I**nterface. A standard developed by the American National Standards Institute (ANSI) for high-speed fiber-optic local area networks. FDDI provides specifications for transmission rates of 100 megabits (100 million bits) per second on networks based on the token ring standard. FDDI II, an extension of the FDDI standard, contains additional specifications for the real-time transmission of analog data in digitized form. *See also* token ring network.

FDHP \F`D-H-P´\ *n*. Acronym for **F**ull **D**uplex **H**andshaking **P**rotocol. A protocol used by duplex modems to determine the source type of the transmission and match it. *See also* duplex[1], handshake.

FDM \F`D-M´\ *n*. Acronym for **f**requency-**d**ivision **m**ultiplexing. A means of loading multiple transmission signals onto separate bands of a single communications channel so that all signals can be carried simultaneously. FDM is used in analog transmissions, as on a baseband network or in communications over a telephone line. In FDM the frequency range of the channel is divided into narrower bands, each of which can carry a different transmission signal. For example, FDM might divide a voice channel with a frequency range of 1,400 hertz (Hz) into four subchannels—820–990 Hz, 1,230–1,400 Hz, 1,640–1,810 Hz, and 2,050–2,220 Hz—with adjacent subchannels separated by a 240-Hz guard band to minimize interference.

feasibility study \fē`zə-bil´ə-tē stud`ē\ *n*. An evaluation of a prospective project for the purpose of determining whether or not the project should be undertaken. Feasibility studies normally consider the time, budget, and technology required for completion and are generally used in computing departments in large organizations.

feature \fē´chur\ *n*. A unique, attractive, or desirable property of a program or of a computer or other hardware.

feature extraction \fē´chur eks-trak`shən\ *n*. The selection of significant aspects of a computer image for use as guidelines in computerized pattern matching and image recognition. *See also* image processing.

Federal Communications Commission \fed`ər-əl kə-myōō-nə-kā´shənz kə-mish`ən\ *n*. *See* FCC.

Federal Information Processing Standards
\fed`ər-əl in-fər-mā´shən pros`es-ēng stan`dərdz\ *n.*
A system of standards, guidelines, and technical methods for information processing within the U.S. federal government. *Acronym:* FIPS (fips, F`I-P-S´).

Federal Internet Exchange \fed`ər-əl in´tər-net eks-chānj`\ *n. See* FIX.

federated database \fed`ər-ā-təd dā´tə-bās\ *n.* A database to which scientists contribute their findings and knowledge regarding a particular field or problem. A federated database is designed for scientific collaboration on problems of such scope that they are difficult or impossible for an individual to solve. *See also* database.

Federation of American Research Networks \fed-ər-ā`shən əv ə-mâr´ə-kən rē´sarch net`wərks\ *n.* A nonprofit association of internetworking technology companies in the United States that serves as a national advocate for internetworking, with a primary focus on the education, research, and related communities. *Acronym:* FARNET (fär´net, F`A-R´net). *See also* internetwork.

Federation on Computing in the United States \fed-ər-ā`shən on kəm-pyo͞o`tēng in dhə yo͞o-nī`təd stāts´\ *n.* The U.S. representative of the International Federation of Information Processing (IFIP). *Acronym:* FOCUS (fō´kus, F`O-C-U-S´). *See also* IFIP.

feed[1] \fēd\ *n. See* news feed.

feed[2] \fēd\ *vb.* **1.** To advance paper through a printer. **2.** To supply media to a recording device, as by inserting disks into a disk drive.

feedback \fēd´bak\ *n.* The return of a portion of system output as input to the same system. Often feedback is deliberately designed into a system, but sometimes it is unwanted. In electronics, feedback is used in monitoring, controlling, and amplifying circuitry.

feedback circuit \fēd´bak sər`kət\ *n.* Any circuit or system that returns (feeds back) a portion of its output to its input. A common example of a feedback system, although it is not completely electronic, is a thermostatically controlled household heating system. This self-limiting or self-correcting process is an example of negative feedback, in which changes in output are fed back to the source so that the change in the output is reversed.

In positive feedback, an increase in output is fed back to the source, increasing the output further, which creates a snowballing effect. An example of unwanted positive feedback is the "screech" that occurs when the microphone of a public address system is brought too close to its loudspeaker.

feed scanner \fēd´ skan`ər\ *n. See* sheet-fed scanner.

female connector \fē`māl kə-nek´tər\ *n.* A connector that has one or more receptacles for the insertion of pins. Female connector part numbers often include an *F* (female), an *S* (socket), a *J* (jack), or an *R* (receptacle). For example, a female DB-25 connector might be labeled DB-25S or DB-25F. (Note that although the letter *F* can denote a female connector, it does not have that meaning in *F connector,* which is a type of coaxial cable connector.) See the illustration. *Compare* male connector.

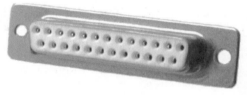

Female connector.

femto- \fem´tō\ *prefix* Metric prefix meaning 10^{-15} (one quadrillionth).

femtosecond \fem´tō-sek`ənd\ *n.* Abbreviated fs. One quadrillionth (10^{-15}) of a second.

FEP \F`E-P´\ *n. See* front-end processor.

ferric oxide \fâr`ik oks´īd\ *n.* The chemical substance Fe_2O_3, an oxide of iron used with a binding agent in the magnetic coating applied to disks and tapes for data storage.

ferric RAM \fâr´ik ram`, R-A-M´\ *n. See* FRAM.

ferromagnetic domain \fâr`ō-mag-net`ik dō-mān´\ *n. See* magnetic domain.

ferromagnetic material \fâr`ō-mag-net`ik mə-tēr´ē-əl\ *n.* A substance that can become highly magnetized. Ferrite and powdered iron are ferromagnetic materials commonly used in electronics, for example, as cores for inductors to increase their inductance and in the coating on floppy and hard disks and magnetic tape.

FET \fet, F`E-T´\ *n.* Acronym for **f**ield-**e**ffect **t**ransistor. A type of transistor in which the flow of current between the source and the drain is modulated by the electric field around the gate electrode. FETs are used as amplifiers, oscillators, and switches and are characterized by an extremely high input impedance (resistance) that makes them particularly suitable for amplification of very small signals. Types of FETs include the junction FET (illustrated) and the metal-oxide semiconductor FET (MOSFET). See the illustration. *See also* MOSFET.

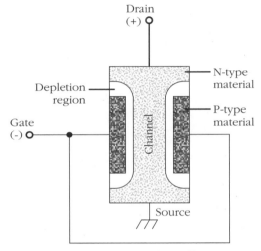

FET. *An N-channel junction field-effect transistor.*

fetch \fech\ *vb.* To retrieve an instruction or an item of data from memory and store it in a register. Fetching is part of the execution cycle of a microprocessor; first an instruction or item of data must be fetched from memory and loaded into a register, after which it can be executed (if it is an instruction) or acted upon (if it is data).

fetch time \fech´ tīm\ *n. See* instruction time.

FF \F-F´\ *n. See* form feed.

FFT \F´F-T´\ *n. See* fast Fourier transform.

FFTDCA \F´F-T´D-C-A´\ *n. See* Final-Form-Text DCA.

.fi \dot`F-I´\ *n.* On the Internet, the major geographic domain specifying that an address is located in Finland.

Fiber Distributed Data Interface \fī`bər distri`byōō-təd dā´tə in´tər-fās, dat`ə\ *n. See* FDDI.

fiber optics \fī`bər op´tiks\ *n.* A technology for the transmission of light beams along optical fibers. A light beam, such as that produced in a laser, can be modulated to carry information. Because light has a higher frequency on the electromagnetic spectrum than other types of radiation, such as radio waves, a single fiber-optic channel can carry significantly more information than most other means of information transmission. Optical fibers are thin strands of glass or other transparent material, with dozens or hundreds of strands housed in a single cable. Optical fibers are essentially immune to electromagnetic interference. *See also* optical fiber.

Fibonacci numbers \fib-ə-nä´chē num`bərz\ *n.* In mathematics, an infinite series in which each successive integer is the sum of the two integers that precede it—for example, 1, 1, 2, 3, 5, 8, 13, 21, 34, ... Fibonacci numbers are named for the thirteenth-century mathematician Leonardo of Pisa. In computing, Fibonacci numbers are used to speed binary searches by repeatedly dividing a set of data into groups in accordance with successively smaller pairs of numbers in the Fibonacci sequence. For example, a data set of 34 items would be divided into one group of 21 and another of 13. If the item being sought is in the group of 13, the group of 21 is discarded, and the group of 13 is divided into groups of 5 and 8; the search would continue until the item was located. The ratio of two successive terms in the Fibonacci sequence converges on the Golden Ratio, a "magic number" that seems to represent the proportions of an ideal rectangle. The number describes many things, from the curve of a nautilus shell to the proportions of playing cards or, intentionally, the Parthenon, in Athens, Greece. *See also* binary search.

fiche \fēsh\ *n. See* microfiche.

Fidonet \fī´dō-net`\ *n.* **1.** A protocol for sending e-mail, newsgroup postings, and files over telephone lines. The protocol originated on the Fido BBS, initiated in 1984 by Tom Jennings, and maintaining low costs has been a factor in its subsequent development. Fidonet can exchange e-mail with the Internet. **2.** The network of BBSs, private companies, NGOs (nongovernment organizations), and individuals that use the Fidonet protocol.

.fidonet.org \dot-fī˜dō-net-dot-ōrg´\ *n.* On the Internet, the major domain specifying that an address is located on Fidonet.

field \fēld\ *n.* **1.** A location in a record in which a particular type of data is stored. For example, EMPLOYEE-RECORD might contain fields to store Last-Name, First-Name, Address, City, State, Zip-Code, Hire-Date, Current-Salary, Title, Department, and so on. Individual fields are characterized by their maximum length and the type of data (for example, alphabetic, numeric, or financial) that can be placed in them. The facility for creating these specifications usually is contained in the data definition language (DDL). In relational database management systems, fields are called *columns.* **2.** A space in an on-screen form where the user can enter a specific item of information.

field-effect transistor \fēld`ə-fekt tranz-i´stər\ *n.* See FET.

field-programmable logic array \fēld`prō-gram-ə-bl loj´ik ər-ā`\ *n.* An integrated circuit containing an array of logic circuits in which the connections between the individual circuits, and thus the logic functions of the array, can be programmed after manufacture, typically at the time of installation in the field. Programming can be performed only once, typically by passing high current through fusible links on the chip. *Acronym:* FPLA (F`P-L-A´). *Also called* PLA, programmable logic array.

field separator \fēld´ sep`ər-ā-tər\ *n.* Any character that separates one field of data from another. *See also* delimiter, field (definition 1).

FIFO \fī´fō, F`I-F-O´\ *n.* See first in, first out.

fifth-generation computer \fifth`jen-ər-ā`shən kəm-pyōō´tər\ *n.* See computer.

fifth normal form \fifth` nōr`məl fōrm´\ *n.* Abbreviated 5NF. *See* normal form (definition 1).

file \fīl\ *n.* A complete, named collection of information, such as a program, a set of data used by a program, or a user-created document. A file is the basic unit of storage that enables a computer to distinguish one set of information from another. A file is the "glue" that binds a conglomeration of instructions, numbers, words, or images into a coherent unit that a user can retrieve, change, delete, save, or send to an output device.

file allocation table \fīl´ al-ə-kā`shən tā`bl\ *n.* A table or list maintained by some operating systems to manage disk space used for file storage. Files on a disk are stored, as space allows, in fixed-size groups of bytes (characters) rather than from beginning to end as contiguous strings of text or numbers. A single file can thus be scattered in pieces over many separate storage areas. A file allocation table maps available disk storage space so that it can mark flawed segments that should not be used and can find and link the pieces of a file. In MS-DOS, the file allocation table is commonly known as the FAT. *See also* FAT file system.

file attribute \fīl´ a`trə-byōōt\ *n.* A restrictive label attached to a file that describes and regulates its use—for example, hidden, system, read-only, archive, and so forth. In MS-DOS, this information is stored as part of the file's directory entry.

file backup \fīl´ bak`up\ *n.* See backup.

file compression \fīl´ kəm-presh`ən\ *n.* The process of reducing the size of a file for transmission or storage. *See also* data compression.

file control block \fīl´ kən-trōl` blok\ *n.* A small block of memory temporarily assigned by a computer's operating system to hold information about an opened file. A file control block typically contains such information as the file's identification, its location on disk, and a pointer that marks the user's current (or last) position in the file. *Acronym:* FCB (F`C-B´).

file conversion \fīl´ kən-vər`zhən\ *n.* The process of transforming the data in a file from one format to another without altering its contents—for example, converting a file from a word processor's format to its ASCII equivalent.

file extension \fīl´ eks-ten`shən\ *n.* See extension (definition 1).

file extent \fīl´ eks-tent`\ *n.* See extent.

file format \fīl´ fōr`mat\ *n.* The structure of a file that defines the way it is stored and laid out on the screen or in print. The format can be fairly simple and common, as are files stored as "plain" ASCII text, or it can be quite complex and include various types of control instructions and codes used by programs, printers, and other devices. Examples include RTF (Rich Text Format), DCA (Document Content Architecture), PICT, DIF (Data Interchange Format), DXF, TIFF (Tagged Image File Format), and EPSF (Encapsulated PostScript Format).

file fragmentation \fīl´ frag-mən-tā`shən\ *n.* **1.** The breaking apart of files into small, separate segments for storage on disk. The condition is a natural consequence of enlarging files and saving them on a crowded disk that no longer contains contiguous blocks of free space large enough to hold them. File fragmentation is not an integrity problem, although it can eventually slow read and write access times if the disk is very full and storage is badly fragmented. Software products are available for redistributing (optimizing) file storage to reduce fragmentation. **2.** In a database, a situation in which records are not stored in their optimal access sequence because of accumulated additions and deletions of records. Most database systems offer or contain utility programs that resequence records to improve efficiency of access and to aggregate free space occupied by deleted records.

file gap \fīl´ gap\ *n. See* block gap.

file handle \fīl´ han`dl\ *n.* In MS-DOS, OS/2, and Windows, a token (number) that the system uses to identify or refer to an open file or, sometimes, to a device.

file-handling routine \fīl´hand-lēng rōō-tēn`\ *n.* Any routine designed to assist in creating, opening, accessing, and closing files. Most high-level languages have built-in file-handling routines, although more sophisticated or complex file-handling routines in an application are often created by the programmer.

file header \fīl´ hed`ər\ *n. See* header (definition 2).

file layout \fīl´ lā`out\ *n.* In data storage, the organization of records within a file. Frequently, descriptions of the record structure are also included within the file layout.

file librarian \fīl´ lī-brār`ē-ən\ *n.* A person or process responsible for maintaining, archiving, copying, and providing access to a collection of data.

file maintenance \fīl´ mān`tə-nəns\ *n.* Broadly, the process of changing information in a file, altering a file's control information or structure, or copying and archiving files. A person using a terminal to enter data, the program accepting the data from the terminal and writing it to a data file, and a database administrator using a utility to alter the format of a database file are all forms of file maintenance.

file manager \fīl´ man`ə-jər\ *n.* A module of an operating system or environment that controls the physical placement of and access to a group of program files.

filename \fīl´nām\ *n.* The set of letters, numbers, and allowable symbols assigned to a file to distinguish it from all other files in a particular directory on a disk. A filename is the handle by which a computer user saves and requests a block of information. Both programs and data have filenames and often extensions that further identify the type or purpose of the file. Naming conventions, such as maximum length and allowable characters of a filename, vary from one operating system to another. *See also* directory, path (definition 5).

filename extension \fīl´nām eks-ten`shən\ *n. See* extension (definition 1).

file protection \fīl´ prə-tek`shən\ *n.* A process or device by which the existence and integrity of a file are maintained. Methods of file protection range from allowing read-only access and assigning passwords to covering the write-protect notch on a disk and locking away floppy disks holding sensitive files.

file recovery \fīl´ rə-kəv`ər-ē\ *n.* The process of reconstructing lost or unreadable files on disk. Files are lost when they are inadvertently deleted, when on-disk information about their storage is damaged, or when the disk is damaged. File recovery involves the use of utility programs that attempt to rebuild on-disk information about the storage locations of deleted files. Because deletion makes the file's disk space available but does not remove the data, data that has not yet been overwritten can be recovered. In the case of damaged files or disks, recovery programs read whatever raw data they can find, and save the data to a new disk or file in ASCII or numeric (binary or hexadecimal) form. In some instances, however, such reconstructed files contain so much extraneous or mixed information that they are unreadable. The best way to recover a file is to restore it from a backup copy.

file retrieval \fīl´ rə-trē`vəl\ *n.* The act of transferring a data file from a storage location to the machine where it is to be used.

file server \fīl´ sər`vər\ *n*. A file-storage device on a local area network that is accessible to all users on the network. Unlike a disk server, which appears to the user as a remote disk drive, a file server is a sophisticated device that not only stores files but manages them and maintains order as network users request files and make changes to them. To deal with the tasks of handling multiple— sometimes simultaneous—requests for files, a file server contains a processor and controlling software as well as a disk drive for storage. On local area networks, a file server is often a computer with a large hard disk that is dedicated only to the task of managing shared files. *Compare* disk server.

file sharing \fīl´ shâr`ēng\ *n*. The use of computer files on networks, wherein files are stored on a central computer or a server and are requested, reviewed, and modified by more than one individual. When a file is used with different programs or different computers, file sharing can require conversion to a mutually acceptable format. When a single file is shared by many people, access can be regulated through such means as password protection, security clearances, or file locking to prohibit changes to a file by more than one person at a time.

file size \fīl´ sīz\ *n*. The length of a file, typically given in bytes. A computer file stored on disk actually has two file sizes, logical size and physical size. The logical file size corresponds to the file's actual size—the number of bytes it contains. The physical size refers to the amount of storage space allotted to the file on disk. Because space is set aside for a file in blocks of bytes, the last characters in the file might not completely fill the block (allocation unit) reserved for them. When this happens, the physical size is larger than the logical size of the file.

filespec \fīl´spek\ *n*. *See* file specification (definition 1).

file specification \fīl` spes`ə-fə-kā´shən\ *n*. **1.** Abbreviated filespec. The path to a file, from a disk drive through a chain of directory files to the filename that serves to locate a particular file. **2.** A filename containing wildcard characters that indicate which files among a group of similarly named files are requested. **3.** A document that describes the organization of data within a file.

file structure \fīl´ struk`chur\ *n*. A description of a file or group of files that are to be treated together for some purpose. Such a description includes file layout and location for each file under consideration.

file system \fīl´ si`stəm\ *n*. In an operating system, the overall structure in which files are named, stored, and organized. A file system consists of files, directories, and the information needed to locate and access these items. The term can also refer to the portion of an operating system that translates requests for file operations from an application program into low-level, sector-oriented tasks that can be understood by the drivers controlling the disk drives. *See also* driver.

file transfer \fīl´ trans`fər\ *n*. The process of moving or transmitting a file from one location to another, as between two programs or over a network.

File Transfer Protocol \fīl` trans-fər prō´tə-kol\ *n*. *See* FTP[1] (definition 1).

file type \fīl´ tīp\ *n*. A designation of the operational or structural characteristics of a file. A file's type is often identified in the filename. With MS-DOS, a file's type is usually reflected in the filename extension. *See also* file format.

fill \fil\ *n*. In computer graphics, to "paint" the inside of an enclosed figure, such as a circle, with color or a pattern. The portion of the shape that can be colored or patterned is the fill area. Drawing programs commonly offer tools for creating filled or nonfilled shapes; the user can specify color or pattern.

film at 11 \film` at ə-lev´ən\ A phrase sometimes seen in newsgroups. An allusion to a brief newsbreak on TV that refers to a top news story that will be covered in full on the 11 o'clock news, it is used sarcastically to ridicule a previous article's lack of timeliness or newsworthiness. *See also* newsgroup.

film recorder \film` rə-kōr`dər\ *n*. A device for capturing on 35-mm film the images displayed on a computer screen.

film ribbon \film´ rib`ən\ *n*. *See* carbon ribbon.

filter \fil´tər\ *n*. **1.** A program or set of features within a program that reads its standard or designated input, transforms the input in some desired way, and then writes the output to its standard or designated output destination. A database filter, for example, might flag information of a certain age. **2.** In communications and electronics, hardware or software that selectively passes certain elements of a signal and eliminates or minimizes others. A filter on a communications network, for example, must be designed to transmit a certain frequency but attenuate (dampen) frequencies above it (a low-pass filter), those below it (a highpass filter), or those above and below it (a bandpass filter). **3.** A pattern or mask through which data is passed to weed out specified items. For instance, a filter used in e-mail or in retrieving newsgroup messages can allow users to filter out messages from other users. *See also* e-mail filter, mask. **4.** In computer graphics, a special effect or production effect that is applied to bitmapped images; for example, shifting pixels within an image, making elements of the image transparent, or distorting the image. Some filters are built into a graphics program, such as a paint program or an image editor. Others are separate software packages that plug into the graphics program. *See also* bitmapped graphics, image editor, paint program.

filtering program \fil´tər-ēng prō`gram\ *n.* A program that filters information and presents only results that match the qualifications defined in the program.

FilterKeys \fil´tər-kēz`\ *n.* A Windows 95 accessibility control panel feature that enables users with physical disabilities to use the keyboard. With FilterKeys, the system ignores brief and repeated keystrokes that result from slow or inaccurate finger movements. *See also* accessibility. *Compare* MouseKeys, ShowSounds, SoundSentry, StickyKeys, ToggleKeys.

Final-Form-Text DCA \fī`nəl-fōrm-tekst` D-C-A´\ *n.* A standard in Document Content Architecture (DCA) for storing documents in ready-to-print form for interchange between dissimilar programs. A related standard is Revisable-Form-Text DCA (RFTDCA). *Acronym:* FFTDCA (F`F-T`D-C-A´). *See also* DCA (definition 1). *Compare* Revisable-Form-Text DCA.

find \fīnd\ *vb. See* search[2].

Finder \fīn´dər\ *n.* The standard interface to the Macintosh operating system, allowing the user to view the contents of directories (folders); to move,

copy, and delete files; and to launch applications. Items in the system are often represented as icons, and a mouse or similar pointing device is used to manipulate these items. The Finder was the first commercially successful graphical user interface, and it helped launch a wave of interest in icon-based systems. *See also* MultiFinder.

finger[1] \fēng´ər\ *n.* An Internet utility, originally limited to UNIX but now available on many other platforms, that enables a user to obtain information on other users who may be at other sites (if those sites permit access by finger). Given an e-mail address, finger returns the user's full name, an indication of whether or not the user is currently logged on, and any other information the user has chosen to supply as a profile. Given a first or last name, finger returns the logon names of users whose first or last names match.

finger[2] \fēng´ər\ *vb.* To obtain information on a user by means of the finger program.

fingerprint reader \fēng´-ər-print rē`dər\ *n.* A scanner that reads human fingerprints for comparison to a database of stored fingerprint images.

FIPS \fips, F`I-P-S´\ *n. See* Federal Information Processing Standards.

firewall \fīr´wäl\ *n.* A security system intended to protect an organization's network against external threats, such as hackers, coming from another network, such as the Internet. A firewall prevents computers in the organization's network from communicating directly with computers external to the network and vice versa. Instead, all communication is routed through a proxy server outside of the organization's network, and the proxy server decides whether it is safe to let a particular message or file pass through to the organization's network.

firmware \fərm´wâr\ *n.* Software routines stored in read-only memory (ROM). Unlike random access memory (RAM), read-only memory stays intact even in the absence of electrical power. Startup routines and low-level input/output instructions are stored in firmware. It falls between software and hardware in terms of ease of modification. *See also* RAM, ROM.

FIR port \F`I-R´ pōrt\ *n.* Short for **f**ast **i**nf**r**ared **port**. A wireless I/O port, most common on a portable computer, that exchanges data with an external device using infrared light. *See also* infrared, input/output port.

FIRST \fərst, F`I-R-S-T`\ *n.* Acronym for **F**orum of **I**ncident **R**esponse and **S**ecurity **T**eams. An organization within the Internet Society (ISOC) that coordinates with CERT in order to encourage information sharing and a unified response to security threats. *See also* CERT, Internet Society.

first-generation computer \fərst-jen-ər-ā`shən kəm-pyo͞o´tər\ *n. See* computer.

first in, first out \fərst-in`fərst-out´\ *n.* A method of processing a queue, in which items are removed in the same order in which they were added—the first in is the first out. Such an order is typical of a list of documents waiting to be printed. *Acronym:* FIFO (fī´fō, F`I-F-O´). *See also* queue. *Compare* last in, first out.

first normal form \fərst` nōr-məl fōrm´\ *n. See* normal form (definition 1).

fitting \fit´ēng\ *n.* The calculation of a curve or other line that most closely approximates a set of data points or measurements. *See also* regression analysis.

FIX \fiks, F`I-X´\ *n.* Acronym for **F**ederal **I**nternet **Ex**change. A connection point between the U.S. government's various internets and the Internet. There are two Federal Internet Exchanges: FIX West, in Mountain View, California; and FIX East, in College Park, Maryland. Together, they link the backbones of MILNET, ESnet (the TCP/IP network of the Department of Energy), and NSInet (NASA Sciences Internet) with NSFnet. *See also* backbone (definition 1), MILNET, NSFnet, TCP/IP.

fixed disk \fiksd disk`\ *n. See* hard disk.

fixed-length field \fiksd`length fēld´\ *n.* In a record or in data storage, a field whose size in bytes is predetermined and constant. A fixed-length field always takes up the same amount of space on a disk, even when the amount of data stored in the field is small. *Compare* variable-length field.

fixed-pitch spacing \fikst`pich spā´sēng\ *n. See* monospacing.

fixed-point arithmetic \fiksd`point ər-ith´mə-tik\ *n.* Arithmetic performed on fixed-point numbers. *See also* fixed-point notation.

fixed-point notation \fiksd`point nō-tā´shən\ *n.* A numeric format in which the decimal point has

a specified position. Fixed-point numbers are a compromise between integral formats, which are compact and efficient, and floating-point numeric formats, which have a great range of values. Like floating-point numbers, fixed-point numbers can have a fractional part, but operations on fixed-point numbers usually take less time than floating-point operations. *See also* floating-point notation, integer.

fixed space \fiksd´ spās\ *n.* A set amount of horizontal space used to separate characters in text—often, the width of a numeral in a given font. *See also* em space, en space, thin space.

fixed spacing \fiksd` spā´sēng\ *n. See* monospacing.

fixed storage \fiksd` stōr´əj\ *n.* Any nonremovable storage, such as a large disk that is sealed permanently in its drive.

fixed-width font \fiksd`width font´\ *n. See* monospace font.

fixed-width spacing \fiksd`width spā´sēng\ *n. See* monospacing.

fixed-word-length computer \fiksd`wərd`length kəm-pyo͞o´tər\ *n.* A description that applies to almost all computers and refers to the uniform size of the data units, or words, that are processed by the microprocessor and shuttled through the system over the hardware lines composing the main data bus. Fixed-word-length computers, including IBM and Macintosh personal computers, commonly work with 2 or 4 bytes at a time.

.fj \dot`F-J´\ *n.* On the Internet, the major geographic domain specifying that an address is located in Fiji.

F keys \F´kēz\ *n. See* function key.

flag \flag\ *n.* **1.** Broadly, a marker of some type used by a computer in processing or interpreting information; a signal indicating the existence or status of a particular condition. Flags are used in such areas as communications, programming, and information processing. Depending on its use, a flag can be a code, embedded in data, that identifies some condition, or it can be one or more bits set internally by hardware or software to indicate an event of some type, such as an error or the result of comparing two values. **2.** In the HDLC communications protocol, a flag is the unique series of bits 01111110, used to start and end a transmission frame (message unit). *See also* HDLC.

flame[1] \flām\ *n.* An abusive or personally insulting e-mail message or newsgroup posting.

flame[2] \flām\ *vb.* **1.** To send an abusive or personally insulting e-mail message or newsgroup posting. **2.** To criticize personally by means of e-mail messages or newsgroup postings.

flame bait \flām´ bāt\ *n.* A posting to a mailing list, newsgroup, or other online conference that is likely to provoke flames, often because it expresses a controversial opinion on a highly emotional topic. *See also* flame[1], flame war. *Compare* troll.

flamefest \flām´fest\ *n.* A series of inflammatory messages or articles in a newsgroup or other online conference.

flamer \flā´mər\ *n.* A person who sends or posts abusive messages via e-mail, in newsgroups and other online forums, and in online chats. *See also* chat[1] (definition 1), newsgroup.

flame war \flām´ wōr\ *n.* A discussion in a mailing list, newsgroup, or other online conference that has turned into a protracted exchange of flames. *See also* flame[1].

flash memory \flash´ mem`ər-ē\ *n.* A type of nonvolatile memory. Flash memory is similar to EEPROM memory in function but it must be erased in blocks, whereas EEPROM can be erased one byte at a time. Because of its block-oriented nature, flash memory is commonly used as a supplement to or replacement for hard disks in portable computers. In this context, flash memory either is built into the unit or, more commonly, is available as a PC Card that can be plugged into a PCMCIA slot. A disadvantage of the block-oriented nature of flash memory is that it cannot be practically used as main memory (RAM) because a computer needs to be able to write to memory in single-byte increments. *See also* EEPROM, nonvolatile memory, PC Card, PCMCIA slot.

flash ROM \flash´ rom, R-O-M`\ *n. See* flash memory.

flat address space \flat` a´dres spās`, ə-dres´\ *n.* An address space in which each location in memory is specified by a unique number. (Memory addresses start at 0 and increase sequentially by 1.)

The Macintosh operating system, OS/2, and Windows NT use a flat address space. MS-DOS uses a segmented address space, in which a location must be accessed with a segment number and an offset number. *See also* segmentation. *Compare* segmented address space.

flatbed plotter \flat´bed plot`ər\ *n.* A plotter in which paper is held on a flat platform and a pen moves along both axes, traveling across the paper to draw an image. This method is slightly more accurate than that used by drum plotters, which move the paper under the pen, but requires more space. Flatbed plotters can also accept a wider variety of media, such as vellum and acetate, because the material does not need to be flexible. *See also* plotter. *Compare* drum plotter, pinch-roller plotter.

flatbed scanner \flat´bed skan`ər\ *n.* A scanner with a flat transparent surface that holds the image to be scanned, generally a book or other paper document. A scan head below the surface moves across the image. Some flatbed scanners can also reproduce transparent media, such as slides. See the illustration. *Compare* drum scanner, handheld scanner, sheet-fed scanner.

Flatbed scanner.

flat file \flat´ fīl\ *n.* A file consisting of records of a single record type in which there is no embedded structure information that governs relationships between records.

flat-file database \flat´fīl dā´tə-bās\ *n.* A database that takes the form of a table, where only one table can be used for each database. A flat-file database can only work with one file at a time. *Compare* relational database.

flat file directory \flat` fīl´ dər-ek`tər-ē\ *n.* A directory that cannot contain subdirectories but simply contains a list of filenames. *Compare* hierarchical file system.

flat file system \flat` fīl´ si`stəm\ *n*. A filing system with no hierarchical order in which no two files on a disk may have the same name, even if they exist in different directories. *Compare* hierarchical file system.

flat memory \flat` mem´ər-ē\ *n*. Memory that appears to a program as one large addressable space, whether consisting of RAM or virtual memory. The 68000 and VAX processors have flat memory; by contrast, 80x86 processors operating in real mode have segmented memory. *Also called* linear memory.

flat pack \flat´ pak\ *n*. An integrated circuit housed in a flat rectangular package with connecting leads along the edges of the package. The flat pack was a precursor of surface-mounted chip packaging. *See also* surface-mount technology. *Compare* DIP (definition 1).

flat-panel display \flat`pan-əl dis-plā´\ *n*. A video display with a shallow physical depth, based on technology other than the CRT (cathode-ray tube). Such displays are typically used in laptop computers. Common types of flat-panel displays are the electroluminescent display, the gas discharge display, and the LCD display.

flat screen \flat skrēn´\ *n*. *See* flat-panel display.

flavor \flā´vər\ *n*. One of several varieties of a system, having its own details of operation. UNIX in particular is found in distinct flavors, such as BSD UNIX or AT&T UNIX System V.

flexible disk \fleks`ə-bl disk´\ *n*. *See* floppy disk.

.fli \dot`F-L-I´\ *n*. The file extension that identifies animation files in the FLI file format.

flicker \flik´ər\ *n*. Rapid, visible fluctuation in a screen image, as on a television or computer monitor. Flicker occurs when the image is refreshed (updated) too infrequently or too slowly for the eye to perceive a steady level of brightness. In television and raster-scan displays, flicker is not noticeable when the refresh rate is 50 to 60 times per second. Interlaced displays, in which the odd-numbered scan lines are refreshed on one sweep and even-numbered lines on the other, achieve a flicker-free effective refresh rate of 50 to 60 times per second because the lines appear to merge, even though

each line is actually updated only 25 to 30 times per second.

flight simulator \flīt´ sim`yə-lā-tər\ *n*. A computer-generated recreation of the experience of flying. Sophisticated flight simulators costing hundreds of thousands of dollars can provide pilot training, simulating emergency situations without putting human crews and planes at risk. Flight simulator software running on personal computers simulates flight in a less realistic fashion; it provides entertainment and practice in navigation and instrument reading.

flip-flop \flip´flop\ *n*. A circuit that alternates between two possible states when a pulse is received at the input. For example, if the output of a flip-flop is high and a pulse is received at the input, the output "flips" to low; a second input pulse "flops" the output back to high, and so on. *Also called* bistable multivibrator.

flippy-floppy \flip´ē-flop`ē\ *n*. A 5.25-inch floppy disk that uses both sides for storage but is used in an older drive that can read only one side at a time. Thus, to access the opposite side, the disk must be physically removed from the drive and flipped over. Disk and disk-drive manufacturers discourage the practice of turning a double-sided disk into a flippy-floppy (by cutting an extra write-protect notch on the side opposite the original one), because the felt pad that rides on the disk surface opposite the single read/write head can damage data on that side of the disk. *See also* double-sided disk.

float \flōt\ *n*. The data type name used in some programming languages, notably C, to declare variables that can store floating-point numbers. *See also* data type, floating-point number, variable.

floating-point arithmetic \flō`tēng-point` ər-ith´mə-tik\ *n*. Arithmetic performed on floating-point numbers. *See also* floating-point notation, floating-point number.

floating-point constant \flō`tēng-point` kon´stənt\ *n*. A constant representing a real, or floating-point, value. *See also* constant, floating-point notation.

floating-point notation \flō`tēng-point` nō-tā´shən\ *n*. A numeric format that can be used to represent very large real numbers and very small real numbers. Floating-point numbers are stored in two parts, a mantissa and an exponent. The mantissa specifies the digits in the number, and the exponent specifies the magnitude of the number (the position of the decimal point). For example, the numbers 314,600,000 and 0.0000451 are expressed respectively as 3146E5 and 451E-7 in floating-point notation. Most microprocessors do not directly support floating-point arithmetic; consequently, floating-point calculations are performed either by using software or with a special floating-point processor. *Also called* exponential notation. *See also* fixed-point notation, floating-point processor, integer.

floating-point number \flō`tēng-point` num´bər\ *n.* A number represented by a mantissa and an exponent according to a given base. The mantissa is usually a value between 0 and 1. To find the value of a floating-point number, the base is raised to the power of the exponent, and the mantissa is multiplied by the result. Ordinary scientific notation uses floating-point numbers with 10 as the base. In a computer, the base for floating-point numbers is usually 2.

floating-point operation \flō`tēng-point` op-ər-ā´shən\ *n.* An arithmetic operation performed on data stored in floating-point notation. Floating-point operations are used wherever numbers may have either fractional or irrational parts, as in spreadsheets and computer-aided design (CAD). Therefore, one measure of a computer's power is how many millions of floating-point operations per second (MFLOPS or megaflops) it can perform. *Acronym:* FLOP (flop, F`L-O-P´). *Also called* floating-point operation. *See also* floating-point notation, MFLOPS.

floating-point processor \flō`tēng-point` pros´-es-ər\ *n.* A coprocessor for performing arithmetic on floating-point numbers. Adding a floating-point processor to a system can speed up the processing of math and graphics dramatically if the software is designed to recognize and use it. The i486DX and 68040 and higher microprocessors have built-in floating-point processors. *Also called* math coprocessor, numeric coprocessor. *See also* floating-point notation, floating-point number.

floating-point register \flō`tēng-point rej´ə-stər\ *n.* A register designed to store floating-point values. *See also* floating-point number, register.

FLOP \flop, F`L-O-P´\ *n. See* floating-point operation.

floppy disk \flop´ē disk`\ *n.* A round piece of flexible plastic film coated with ferric oxide particles that can hold a magnetic field. When placed inside a disk drive, the floppy disk rotates to bring different areas, or sectors, of the disk surface under the drive's read/write head, which can detect and alter the orientation of the particles' magnetic fields to represent binary 1s and 0s. A floppy disk 5.25 inches in diameter is encased in a flexible plastic jacket and has a large hole in the center, which fits around a spindle in the disk drive; such a disk can hold from a few hundred thousand to over one million bytes of data. A 3.5-inch disk encased in rigid plastic is also called a floppy disk or a microfloppy disk. In addition, 8-inch floppy disks were common in DEC and other minicomputer systems. *See also* 3.5-inch floppy disk, 5.25-inch floppy disk, microfloppy disk.

floppy disk controller \flop´ē disk kən-trō´lər\ *n. See* disk controller.

floppy disk drive \flop´e disk´ drīv`\ *n.* An electromechanical device that reads data from and writes data to floppy or microfloppy disks. *See also* floppy disk.

FLOPS \flops, F`L-O-P-S´\ *n.* Acronym for **fl**oating-point **o**perations **p**er **s**econd. A measure of the speed at which a computer can perform floating-point operations. *See also* floating-point operation, MFLOPS. *Compare* MIPS.

floptical \flop´tə-kəl\ *adj.* Using a combination of magnetic and optical technology to achieve a very high data density on special 3.5-inch disks. Data is written to and read from the disk magnetically, but the read/write head is positioned optically by means of a laser and grooves on the disk. The term was coined by and is a registered trademark of Insite Peripherals.

flow analysis \flō´ ə-nal`ə-sis\ *n.* A method of tracing the movement of different types of information through a computer system, especially with regard to security and the controls applied to ensure the integrity of the information. *See also* flowchart.

flowchart \flō´chärt\ *n.* A graphic map of the path of control or data through the operations in a program or an information-handling system. Symbols such as squares, diamonds, and ovals represent

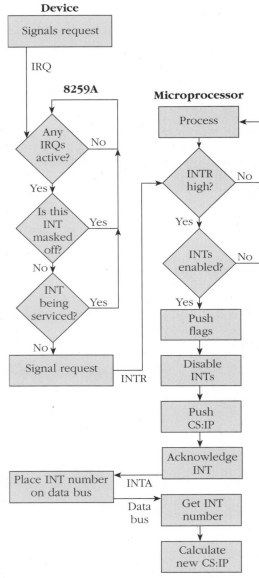

Flowchart.

various operations. These symbols are connected by lines and arrows to indicate the flow of data or control from one point to another. Flowcharts are used both as aids in showing the way a proposed program will work and as a means of understanding the operations of an existing program. See the illustration.

.fl.us \dot-F-L`dot-U-S´\ *n.* On the Internet, the major geographic domain specifying that an address is located in Florida, United States.

flush[1] \flush\ *adj.* Aligned in a certain way on the screen or on paper. Flush left, for example, means aligned on the left side; flush right means aligned on the right side. *See also* align (definition 1).

flush[2] \flush\ *vb.* To clear a portion of memory. For example, to flush a disk file buffer is to save its contents on disk and then clear the buffer for filling again.

flux \fluks\ *n.* **1.** The total strength of a magnetic, electric, or radiation field over a given area. **2.** A chemical used to aid the binding of solder to electrical conductors.

flux reversal \fluks´ rə-vər`səl\ *n.* The change in orientation of the minute magnetic particles on the surface of a disk or tape toward one of two magnetic poles. The two different alignments are used to represent binary 1 and binary 0 for data storage: a flux reversal typically represents a binary 1, and no reversal represents a binary 0.

.fm \dot`F-M´\ *n.* On the Internet, the major geographic domain specifying that an address is located in Micronesia.

FM \F-M´\ *n. See* frequency modulation.

FM encoding \F-M´ en-kō`dēng\ *n. See* frequency modulation encoding.

.fo \dot`F-O´\ *n.* On the Internet, the major geographic domain specifying that an address is located in the Faeroe Islands.

focus \fō´kus,\ *vb.* In television and raster-scan displays, to make an electron beam converge at a single point on the inner surface of the screen.

FOCUS \fō´kus, F`O-C-U-S´\ *n. See* Federation on Computing in the United States.

FOD \F`O-D´\ *n. See* fax on demand.

folder \fōl´dər\ *n.* In the Mac OS, Windows 95, and other operating systems, a container for programs and files in graphical user interfaces, symbolized on the screen by a graphical image (icon) of a file folder. This container is called a directory in other systems, such as MS-DOS and UNIX. A folder is a means of organizing programs and documents on a disk and can hold both files and additional folders. It first appeared commercially in Apple Computer's Lisa in 1983 and in the Apple Macintosh in 1984. *See also* directory.

folio \fō′lē-ō`\ *n.* A printed page number.

follow-up \fol′ō-up`\ *n.* A post to a newsgroup that replies to an article. The follow-up has the same subject line as the original article, with the prefix "Re:" attached. An article and all of its follow-ups, in the order they were received, constitute a thread, which a user can read together using a newsreader.

font \font\ *n.* A set of characters of the same typeface (such as Garamond), style (such as italic), and weight (such as bold). A font consists of all the characters available in a particular style and weight for a particular design; a typeface consists of the design itself. Fonts are used by computers for on-screen displays and by printers for hard-copy output. In both cases, the fonts are stored either as bit maps (patterns of dots) or as outlines (defined by a set of mathematical formulas). Even if the system cannot simulate different typefaces on the screen, application programs may be able to send information about typeface and style to a printer, which can then reproduce the font if a font description is available. *See also* bit map, font generator.

font card \font′ kärd\ *n. See* font cartridge, ROM card.

font cartridge \font′ kär`trij\ *n.* A plug-in unit available for some printers that contains fonts in several different styles and sizes. Font cartridges, like downloadable fonts, enable a printer to produce characters in sizes and styles other than those created by the fonts built into it. *Also called* font card. *See also* ROM cartridge.

Font/DA Mover \font`D-A′ mōō`vər\ *n.* An application for older Apple Macintosh systems that allows the user to install screen fonts and desk accessories.

font editor \font′ ed`ə-tər\ *n.* A utility program that enables the user to modify existing fonts or to create and save new ones. Such an application commonly works with a screen representation of the font, with a representation that can be downloaded to a PostScript or other printer, or with both. *See also* PostScript font, screen font.

font family \font′ fam`ə-lē\ *n.* The set of available fonts representing variations of a single typeface.

For example, Times Roman and Times Roman Italic are members of the same font family. When the user indicates "italic," the system selects the correct italic font for the font family, with its characteristic appearance. If there is no italic font in the family, the system simply slants, or "obliques," the corresponding roman character. *See also* italic, roman.

font generator \font′ jen`ər-ā-tər\ *n.* A program that transforms built-in character outlines into bit maps (patterns of dots) of the style and size required for a printed document. Font generators work by scaling a character outline to size; often they can also expand or compress the characters they generate. Some font generators store the resultant characters on disk; others send them directly to the printer.

font number \font′ num`bər\ *n.* The number by which an application or operating system internally identifies a given font. On the Apple Macintosh, for example, fonts can be identified by their exact names as well as their font numbers, and a font number can be changed if the font is installed in a system already having a font with that number. *See also* font.

font page \font′ pāj\ *n.* A portion of video memory reserved for holding programmer-specified character definition tables (sets of character patterns) used for displaying text on the screen on IBM Multi-Color Graphics Array video systems.

font size \font′ sīz\ *n.* The point size of a set of characters in a particular typeface. *See also* point[1] (definition 1).

font suitcase \font′ sōōt`kās\ *n.* A file on Macintosh computers that contains one or more fonts or desk accessories. Such files are indicated in early versions of the operating system with the icon of a suitcase marked with a capital A. From System 7.0 onward, this icon is used to denote individual fonts.

foo \fōō\ *n.* A string used by programmers in place of more specific information. Variables or functions in code examples intended to demonstrate syntax, as well as temporary scratch files, may all appear with the name *foo.* Likewise, a programmer may type *foo* to test a string input handler. If a second placeholder string is needed, it will often be *bar,* suggesting that the origin of both is the U.S. Army phrase FUBAR (an acronym which, in discreet language, represents Fouled Up Beyond All Recognition/Repair). However, other origins have been claimed. *Compare* fred (definition 2).

footer \foot´ər\ *n.* One or more identifying lines printed at the bottom of a page. A footer may contain a folio (page number), a date, the author's name, and the document title. *Also called* running foot. *Compare* header (definition 1).

footprint \foot´print\ *n.* The surface area occupied by a personal computer or other device.

force \fōrs\ *vb.* In programming, to perform a particular action that would normally not occur. The term is most often used in the context of forcing data to be within a particular range of values—for example, forcing a divisor to be nonzero. *See also* cast.

foreground[1] \fōr´ground\ *adj.* Currently having control of the system and responding to commands issued by the user. *See also* multitasking. *Compare* background[1].

foreground[2] \fōr´ground\ *n.* **1.** The color of displayed characters and graphics. *Compare* background[2] (definition 1). **2.** The condition of the program or document currently in control and affected by commands and data entry in a windowing environment. *Compare* background[2] (definition 4).

fork[1] \fōrk\ *n.* One of the two parts of a file recognized by the Mac OS. A Macintosh file has a data fork and a resource fork. Most or all of a typical user-produced document is in the data fork; the resource fork usually contains application-oriented information, such as fonts, dialog boxes, and menus. *See also* data fork, resource fork.

fork[2] \fōrk\ *vb.* To initiate a child process in a multitasking system after a parent process has been started. *See also* multitasking.

FOR loop \fōr´ loop\ *n.* A control statement that executes a section of code a specified number of times. Actual syntax and usage vary from language to language. In most cases, the value of an index variable moves through a range of values, being assigned a different (and usually consecutive) value each time the program moves through the section of code. *See also* iterative statement, loop[1] (definition 1). *Compare* DO loop.

form \fōrm\ *n.* **1.** A structured document with spaces reserved for entering information and often containing special coding as well. **2.** In some applications (especially databases), a structured window, box, or other self-contained presentation element with predefined areas for entering or changing information. A form is a visual "filter" for the underlying data it is presenting, generally offering the advantages of better data organization and greater ease of viewing. **3.** In optical media, a data storage format used in compact disc technology. **4.** In programming, a metalanguage (such as Backus-Naur form) used to describe the syntax of a language. *See also* Backus-Naur form.

formal language \fōr`məl lang´wəj\ *n.* A combination of syntax and semantics that completely defines a computer language. *See also* Backus-Naur form, semantics (definition 1), syntax.

formal logic \fōr´məl loj´ik\ *n.* A study of the logical expressions, sequences, and overall construction of a valid argument, without regard to the truth of the argument. Formal logic is used in proving program correctness.

format[1] \fōr´mat\ *n.* **1.** In general, the structure or appearance of a unit of data. **2.** The arrangement of data within a document file that typically permits the document to be read or written by a certain application. Many applications can store a file in a more generic format, such as plain ASCII text. **3.** The layout of data storage areas (tracks and sectors) on a disk. **4.** The order and types of fields in a database. **5.** The attributes of a cell in a spreadsheet, such as its being alphabetic or numeric, the number of digits, the use of commas, and the use of currency signs. **6.** The specifications for the placement of text on a page or in a paragraph.

format[2] \fōr´mat\ *vb.* **1.** To change the appearance of selected text or the contents of a selected cell in a spreadsheet. **2.** To prepare a disk for use by organizing its storage space into a collection of data "compartments," each of which can be located by the operating system so that data can be sorted and retrieved. When a previously used disk is formatted, any preexisting information on it is lost.

format bar \fōr´mat bär`\ *n.* A toolbar within an application used for modifying the format of the document being displayed, such as changing font size or type.

formatting \fŏr´mat`ēng\ *n.* **1.** The elements of style and presentation that are added to documents through the use of margins, indents, and different sizes, weights, and styles of type. **2.** The process of initializing a disk so that it can be used to store information. *See also* initialize.

form feed \fōrm´ fēd\ *n.* A printer command that tells a printer to move to the top of the next page. In the ASCII character set, the form-feed character has the decimal value 12 (hexadecimal 0C). Because its purpose is to begin printing on a new page, form feed is also known as the page-eject character. *Acronym:* FF (F-F´).

form letter \fōrm´ let`ər\ *n.* A letter created for printing and distribution to a group of people whose names and addresses are taken from a database and inserted by a mail-merge program into a single basic document. *See also* mail merge.

formula \fōr´myə-lə\ *n.* A mathematical statement that describes the actions to be performed on numeric values. A formula sets up a calculation without regard to the actual values it is to act upon, such as $A + B$, with A and B representing whatever values the user designates. Thus, a formula is unlike an arithmetic problem, such as $1 + 2$, which includes values and must be restated if any value is changed. Through formulas, users of applications such as spreadsheets gain the power to perform "what-if" calculations simply by changing selected values and having the program recalculate the results. Sophisticated programs include many built-in formulas for performing standard business and mathematical calculations.

Forth \fōrth\ *n.* A programming language originated by Charles Moore in the late 1960s. Moore chose the language's name, a shortened version of the word *fourth,* because he believed it was a fourth-generation language and his operating system would allow him to use only five letters for a program name. Forth is an interpreted, structured language that uses threading, which lets programmers easily extend the language and enables Forth to fit a great deal of functionality into limited space. Unlike most other programming languages, Forth uses postfix notation for its mathematical expressions and requires the programmer to work

with the program stack directly. *See also* 4GL, interpreted language, postfix notation, stack, threading.

FORTRAN or **Fortran** \fōr´tran\ *n.* Short for **for**mula **tran**slation. The first high-level computer language (developed over the period 1954–58 by John Backus) and the progenitor of many key high-level concepts, such as variables, expressions, statements, iterative and conditional statements, separately compiled subroutines, and formatted input/output. FORTRAN is a compiled, structured language. The name indicates its roots in science and engineering, where it is still used heavily, although the language itself has been expanded and improved vastly over the last 35 years to become a language that is useful in any field. *See also* compiled language, structured programming.

fortune cookie \fōr´chun kŏok`ē\ *n.* A proverb, prediction, joke, or other phrase chosen at random from a collection of such items and output to the screen by a program. Fortune cookies are sometimes displayed at logon and logoff times by UNIX systems.

forum \fōr´um\ *n.* A medium provided by an online service or BBS for users to carry on written discussions of a particular topic by posting messages and replying to them. On the Internet, the most widespread forums are the newsgroups in Usenet.

Forum of Incident Response and Security Teams \fōr`um əv in`sə-dənt rə-spons` and se-kyur´ə-tē tēmz`\ *n.* *See* FIRST.

forward \fōr´wərd\ *vb.* In e-mail, to send a received message, either modified or in its entirety, to a new recipient.

forward chaining \fōr`wərd chā´nēng\ *n.* In expert systems, a form of problem solving that starts with a set of rules and a database of facts and works to a conclusion based on facts that match all the premises set forth in the rules. *See also* expert system. *Compare* backward chaining.

forward error correction \fōr`wərd âr´ər kər-ek`shən\ *n.* In communications, a means of controlling errors by inserting extra (redundant) bits into a stream of data transmitted to another device. The redundant bits are used by the receiving device in detecting and, where possible, correcting errors in the data. *See also* error-correction coding.

forward pointer \fȯr`wərd poin´tər\ *n.* A pointer in a linked list that contains the address (location) of the next element in the list.

FOSDIC \foz´dik, F-O-S`D-I-C´\ *n.* Acronym for **f**ilm **o**ptical **s**ensing **d**evice for **i**nput to **c**omputers. A device used by the U.S. government to read documents on microfilm and store them digitally on magnetic tape or on a disk that can be accessed by a computer.

Fourier transform \fo͞or`ē-ā tranz`fȯrm\ *n.* A mathematical method, developed by the French mathematician Jean-Baptiste-Joseph Fourier (1768–1830), for signal processing and signal generation tasks such as spectral analysis and image processing. The Fourier transform converts a signal value that is a function of time, space, or both into a function of frequency. The inverse Fourier transform converts a function of frequencies into a function of time, space, or both. *See also* fast Fourier transform.

fourth-generation computer \fōrth`jen-ər-ā`shən kəm-pyo͞o´tər\ *n. See* computer.

fourth-generation language \fōrth`jen-ər-ā`shən lang`wəj\ *n. See* 4GL.

fourth normal form \fōrth nȯr`məl fōrm´\ *n.* Abbreviated 4NF. *See* normal form (definition 1).

FPD \F`P-D´\ *n. See* full-page display.

FPLA \F`P-L-A´\ *n. See* field-programmable logic array.

FPU \F`P-U´\ *n.* Acronym for **f**loating-**p**oint **u**nit. A circuit that performs floating-point calculations. *See also* circuit, floating-point operation.

.fr \dot`F-R´\ *n.* On the Internet, the major geographic domain specifying that an address is located in France.

fractal \frak´təl\ *n.* A word coined by mathematician Benoit Mandelbrot in 1975 to describe a class of shapes characterized by irregularity, but in a way that evokes a pattern. Computer graphics technicians often use fractals to generate nature-like images such as landscapes, clouds, and forests. The distinguishing characteristic of fractals is that they are "self-similar"; any piece of a fractal, when magnified, has the same character as the whole. The standard analogy is that of a coastline, which has a similar structure whether viewed on a

local or continental scale. Interestingly, it is often difficult to measure the length of the perimeter of such a shape exactly because the total distance measured depends on the size of the smallest element measured. For example, one could measure on a given coastline the perimeter of every peninsula and inlet, or at a higher magnification the perimeter of every small promontory and jetty, and so on. In fact, a given fractal may have a finite area but an infinite perimeter; such shapes are considered to have a fractional dimension—for example, between 1 (a line) and 2 (a plane)—hence the name fractal. See the illustration. *See also* cellular automata, graftal.

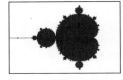

Fractal.   The first figure shows the classical Mandelbrot set; the three below it show successive magnifications of the lobe at the bottom of the first figure.

fractional T1 \frak`shə-nəl T-wən´\ *n.* A shared connection to a T1 line, in which only a fraction of the 24 T1 voice or data channels are used. *Acronym:* FT1 (F`T-wən´). *See also* T1.

FRAD \frad, F`R-A-D´\ *n. See* frame relay assembler/disassembler.

fragmentation \frag`mən-tā´shən\ *n.* The scattering of parts of the same disk file over different areas of the disk. Fragmentation occurs as files on a disk are deleted and new files are added. Such fragmentation slows disk access and degrades the overall performance of disk operations, although usually not severely. Utility programs are available for rearranging file storage on fragmented disks.

FRAM \F´ram, F`R-A-M´\ *n.* Acronym for **f**erromagnetic **r**andom **a**ccess **m**emory. A form of data storage technology in which data is recorded semipermanently on small cards or strips of material coated with a ferric oxide (iron-based) magnetic film. As with tape or disk, the data persists without power; as with semiconductor RAM, a computer can access the data in any order.

frame \frām\ *n.* **1.** In asynchronous serial communications, a unit of transmission that is sometimes measured in elapsed time and begins with the start bit that precedes a character and ends with the last stop bit that follows the character. **2.** In synchronous communications, a package of information transmitted as a single unit. Every frame follows the same basic organization and contains control information, such as synchronizing characters, station address, and an error-checking value, as well as a variable amount of data. For example, a frame used in the widely accepted HDLC and related SDLC protocols begins and ends with a unique flag (01111110). See the illustration. *See also* HDLC, SDLC. **3.** A single screen-sized image that can be displayed in sequence with other, slightly different, images to create animated drawings. **4.** The storage required to hold one screen-sized image of text, graphics, or both. **5.** A rectangular space containing, and defining the proportions of, a graphic. **6.** The part of an on-screen window (title bar and other elements) that is controlled by the operating system rather than by the application running in the window. **7.** A rectangular section of the page displayed by a Web browser that is a separate HTML document from the rest of the page. Web pages can have multiple frames, each of which is a separate document. Associated with each frame are the same capabilities as for an unframed Web page, including scrolling and linking to another frame or Web site; these capabilities can be used independently of other frames on the page. Frames, which were introduced in Netscape Navigator 2.0, are often used as a table of contents for one or more HTML documents on a Web site. Most current Web browsers support frames, although older ones do not. *See also* HTML document, Web browser.

Frame.   The fields in an HDLC-SDLC frame.

frame buffer \frām´ buf´ər\ *n.* A portion of a computer's display memory that holds the contents of a single screen image. *See also* video buffer.

frame grabber \frām´ grab`ər\ *n. See* video digitizer.

frame rate \frām´ rāt\ *n.* **1.** The speed at which full, single-screen images are transmitted to and displayed by a raster-scan monitor. Frame rate is calculated as the number of times per second (hertz) the electron beam sweeps the screen. **2.** In animation, the number of times per second an image is updated. When the frame rate exceeds about 14 frames per second, animation seems to blend into smooth motion. *See also* animation.

frame relay \frām´ rē`lā\ *n.* A packet-switching protocol for use on wide area networks. Frame relay transmits variable-length packets at up to 1.544 Mbps. It is a variant of X.25 but dispenses with some of X.25's error detection for the sake of speed. *See also* ATM (definition 1), X.25.

frame relay assembler/disassembler \frām`rē-lā ə-sem`blər-dis´ə-sem`blər\ *n.* A combination channel service unit/digital service unit (CSU/DSU) and router that connects an internal network to a frame relay connection. The device converts data (which may be in the form of IP packets or conform to some other network protocol) into packets for transmission over the frame relay network and converts such packets back to the original data. Since this type of connection is direct, without a firewall, other network protection is necessary. *Acronym:* FRAD (frad, F`R-A-D´). *See also* firewall, frame relay, IP.

frame source \frām´ sōrs\ *n.* In the HTML frames environment, a contents document that will look for the source document to display within a frame drawn by the local browser. *See also* HTML.

frames per second \frāmz` pər sek´ənd\ *n. See* frame rate.

framework \frām´wərk\ *n.* In object-oriented programming, a reusable basic design structure, consisting of abstract and concrete classes, that assists in building applications. *See also* abstract class, object-oriented programming.

FRC \F`R-C´\ *n. See* functional redundancy checking.

fred \fred\ *n.* **1.** An interface utility for X.500. *See also* CCITT X series. **2.** A placeholder string used by programmers in syntax examples to stand for a variable name. If a programmer has used *fred,* the next placeholder needed is likely to be *barney.* *Compare* foo.

free block \frē´ blok\ *n.* A region (block) of memory that is not currently being used.

FreeBSD \frē`B-S-D´\ *n.* A freely distributed version of BSD UNIX (Berkeley Software Distribution UNIX) for IBM and IBM-compatible PCs. *See also* BSD UNIX.

free-form language \frē`fōrm lang´wəj\ *n.* A language whose syntax is not constrained by the position of characters on a line. C and Pascal are free-form languages; FORTRAN is not.

freenet or **free-net** \frē`net\ *n.* A community-based computer BBS and Internet service provider, usually operated by volunteers and providing free access to subscribers in the community or access for a very small fee. Many freenets are operated by public libraries or universities. *See also* ISP.

.freenet.edu \dot-frē`net-dot-E-D-U´\ *n.* On the Internet, the major domain specifying that an address is located on a freenet. *See also* freenet.

free software \frē` soft´wâr\ *n.* Software, complete with source code, that is distributed freely to users who are in turn free to use, modify, and distribute it, provided that all alterations are clearly marked and that the name and copyright notice of the original author are not deleted or modified in any way. Unlike freeware, which a user might or might not have permission to modify, free software is protected by a license agreement. Free software is a concept pioneered by the Free Software Foundation in Cambridge, Massachusetts. *Compare* freeware, public-domain software, shareware.

Free Software Foundation \frē soft´wâr foun-dā`shən\ *n.* An advocacy organization founded by Richard Stallman, dedicated to eliminating restrictions on people's right to use, copy, modify, and redistribute computer programs for noncommercial purposes. The Free Software Foundation is the maintainer of GNU software, which is UNIX-like software that can be freely distributed. *See also* GNU.

free space \frē´ spās\ *n.* Space on a floppy disk or a hard drive not currently occupied by data. *See also* floppy disk, hard disk.

freeware \frē´wâr\ *n.* A computer program given away free of charge and often made available on the Internet or through user groups. An independent program developer might offer a product as freeware either for personal satisfaction or to assess its reception among interested users. Freeware developers often retain all rights to their software, and users are not necessarily free to copy or distribute it further. *Compare* free software, public-domain software, shareware.

freeze-frame video \frēz`frām vid´ē-ō\ *n.* Video in which the image changes only once every few seconds. *Compare* full-motion video.

frequency \frē´kwən-sē´\ *n.* The measure of how often a periodic event occurs, such as a signal going through a complete cycle. Frequency is usually measured in hertz (Hz), with 1 Hz equaling 1 occurrence (cycle) per second. In the United States, household electricity is alternating current with a frequency of 60 Hz. Frequency is also measured in kilohertz (kHz, or 1,000 Hz), megahertz (MHz, or 1,000 kHz), gigahertz (GHz, or 1,000 MHz), or terahertz (THz, or 1,000 GHz). See the illustration. *Compare* wavelength.

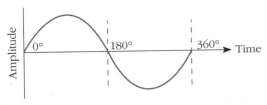

Frequency.

frequency counter \frē´kwən-sē koun`tər\ *n.* **1.** An item of engineering test equipment that measures and displays the frequencies of electronic signals. **2.** An electronic circuit, often found embedded in process-control computers, that counts the frequency of occurrence of an activity.

frequency-division multiplexing \frē`kwən-sē-də-vizh`ən mul´tē-pleks-ēng, mul´tī-pleks-ēng\ *n.* See FDM.

frequency hopping \frē´kwən-sē hop`ēng\ *n.* The switching of frequencies within a given bandwidth during a point-to-point transmission. Frequency hopping reduces the chance of unauthorized signal interception or the effects of single-frequency jamming.

frequency modulation \frē´kwən-sē mo-dyə-lā`shən, moj-ə-lā`shən\ *n*. A way of encoding information in an electrical signal by varying its frequency. The FM radio band uses frequency modulation, as does the audio portion of broadcast television. See the illustration. *Acronym:* FM (F-M´). *Compare* amplitude modulation.

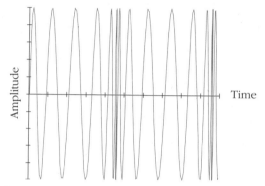

Frequency modulation.

frequency modulation encoding \frē`kwən-sē mo-dyə-lā`shən en-kō´dēng, moj-ə-lā`shən\ *n*. Abbreviated FM encoding. A method of storing information on a disk in which both data and additional synchronizing information, called clock pulses, are recorded on the surface. FM encoding is relatively inefficient because of the extra disk space required by the clock pulses. It has been generally superseded by a more efficient method called *modified* frequency modulation (MFM) encoding and by the complex but extremely efficient technique called run-length limited (RLL) encoding. *Compare* modified frequency modulation encoding, run-length limited encoding.

frequency response \frē´kwən-sē rə-spons`\ *n*. The range of frequencies an audio device can reproduce from its input signals. *See also* frequency.

frequency-shift keying \frē´kwən-sē-shift kē`ēng\ *n*. *See* FSK.

frequently asked questions \frē`kwənt-lē askd` kwes´chənz\ *n*. *See* FAQ.

friction feed \frik´shən fēd`\ *n*. A means of moving paper through a printer in which the paper is pinched either between the printer's platen and pressure rollers or (in printers that do not have a platen) between two sets of rollers. Friction feed is available on most printers, for use with paper that does not have pin-feed holes. In printers that have tractor feed as well as friction feed, the friction-feed mechanism should be left disengaged when the tractor is being used, to avoid unnecessary stress on the tractor gears. *See also* platen. *Compare* pin feed, tractor feed.

friendly \frend´lē\ *adj*. Referring to features built into hardware or software that make a computer or computer program easy to learn and easy to use. Friendliness is emphasized by most developers and sought after by most users. *See also* user-friendly.

fringeware \frinj´wâr\ *n*. Freeware whose reliability and value are questionable. *See also* freeware.

front end \frənt end`\ *n*. In applications, software or a feature of software that provides an interface to another application or tool. Front ends are often used to supply a common interface for a range of tools produced by a software manufacturer. A front end generally offers a more user-friendly interface than that of the application running "behind" it.

front-end processor \frənt`end pros´es-ər\ *n*. **1.** Generally, a computer or processing unit that produces and manipulates data before another processor receives it. *Compare* back-end processor (definition 2). **2.** In communications, a computer that is located between communications lines and a main (host) computer and is used to relieve the host of housekeeping chores related to communications; sometimes considered synonymous with communications controller. A front-end processor is dedicated entirely to handling transmitted information, including error detection and control; receipt, transmission, and possibly encoding of messages; and management of the lines running to and from other devices. *See also* communications controller.

front panel \frənt` pan´əl\ *n*. The faceplate of a computer cabinet through which the control knobs, switches, and lights are available to an operator. *See also* console.

fry \frī\ *vb*. To destroy a circuit board or another component of a computer by applying excessive voltage. Even when applied voltage is not excessive, an electronic component can become fried when it breaks down, conducting more current than its design permits.

fs \F-S´\ *n. See* femtosecond.

FSK \F`S-K´\ *n.* Acronym for **f**requency-**s**hift **key**ing. A simple form of modulation in which the digital values 0 and 1 are represented by two different frequencies. FSK was used by early modems running at 300 bits per second.

FT1 \F`T-wən´\ *n. See* fractional T1.

FTAM \F`T-A-M´\ *n.* Acronym for **F**ile-**T**ransfer **A**ccess and **M**anagement. A communications standard for transferring files between different makes and models of computer.

FTP[1] \F`T-P´\ *n.* **1.** Acronym for **F**ile **T**ransfer **P**rotocol, the protocol used for copying files to and from remote computer systems on a network using TCP/IP, such as the Internet. This protocol also allows users to use FTP commands to work with files, such as listing files and directories on the remote system. *See also* TCP/IP. **2.** A common logon ID for anonymous FTP.

FTP[2] \F`T-P´\ *vb.* To download files from or upload files to remote computer systems, via the Internet's File Transfer Protocol. The user needs an FTP client to transfer files to and from the remote system, which must have an FTP server. Generally, the user also needs to establish an account on the remote system to FTP files, although many FTP sites permit the use of anonymous FTP. *See also* FTP client, FTP server.

FTP client or **ftp client** \F-T-P´ klī`ənt\ *n.* A program that enables the user to upload and download files to and from an FTP site over a network, such as the Internet, using the File Transfer Protocol. *See also* FTP[1] (definition 1). *Compare* FTP server.

FTP commands \F-T-P´ kə-mandz`\ *n.* Commands that are part of the File Transfer Protocol. *See also* FTP[1] (definition 1).

FTP program or **ftp program** \F`T-P´ prō`gram\ *n. See* FTP client.

FTP server \F`T-P´ sər-vər\ *n.* A file server that uses the File Transfer Protocol to permit users to upload or download files through the Internet or any other TCP/IP network. *See also* file server, FTP[1] (definition 1), TCP/IP. *Compare* FTP client.

FTP site \F-T-P´ sīt`\ *n.* **1.** The collection of files and programs residing on an FTP server. *See also*

FTP server, FTP[1] (definition 1). **2.** *See* FTP server.

full adder \ful` ad´ər\ *n.* A logic circuit used in a computer to add binary digits. A full adder accepts three digital inputs (bits): 2 bits to be added and a carry bit from another digit position. It produces two outputs: a sum and a carry bit. Full adders are combined with two-input circuits called *half adders* to enable computers to add 4 or more bits at a time. *See also* carry bit, half adder.

full-duplex \ful`dōō´pleks\ *adj. See* duplex[1].

full-duplex transmission \ful`dōō´pleks tranz-mish´ən\ *n. See* duplex[2] (definition 1).

full justification \ful` ju`stə-fə-kā´shən\ *n.* In typesetting, word processing, and desktop publishing, the process of aligning text evenly along both the left and right margins of a column or page. See the illustration on the next page. *See also* justify (definition 2).

full-motion video \ful`mō-shən vid´ē-ō\ *n.* Digital video that is displayed at 30 frames per second (fps). *Compare* freeze-frame video.

full-motion video adapter \ful`mō`shən vid´ē-ō ə-dap`tər\ *n.* An expansion card for a computer that can convert motion video from devices such as a video cassette recorder to a digital format that a computer can use such as AVI, MPEG, or Motion JPEG. *See also* AVI, Motion JPEG, MPEG.

full name \ful nām´\ *n.* A user's complete name, usually consisting of last name, first name, and middle initial. The full name is often maintained by the operating system as part of the information that identifies and defines a user account. *See also* user account.

full-page display \ful-pāj´ dis-plā`\ *n.* A video display with sufficient size and resolution to show at least one 8½-by-11-inch image. Such displays are useful for desktop publishing applications. *Acronym:* FPD (F`P-D´). *See also* portrait monitor.

full path \ful path´\ *n.* A pathname containing all possible components of a pathname, including the drive, root directory, any subdirectories, and the file or object name. *See also* pathname, root directory, subdirectory. *Compare* relative path.

full pathname \ful` path´nām\ *n.* In a hierarchical filing system, a listing of the directories or folders that lead from the root directory of a disk drive to a particular file. For example, the MS-DOS full pathname c:\book\chapter\myfile.doc indicates that myfile.doc is located in a directory called *chapter,* which in turn is located in a directory called *book* in the root directory of the C: drive. *See also* path (definition 2).

full-screen \ful'skrēn\ *adj.* Capable of using or being displayed on the full area of a display screen. Applications running in windowing environments, although they might use the entire area of the screen, commonly allocate different areas to different windows, any of which can be enlarged to fill the entire screen.

full-text search \ful-tekst' sərch`\ *n.* A search for one or more documents, records, or strings based on all of the actual text data rather than on an index containing a limited set of keywords. For example, a full-text search can locate a document containing the words "albatrosses are clumsy on land" by searching files for just those words without the need of an index containing the keyword "albatross." *See also* index.

fully formed character \ful`ē fõrmd` kâr´ək-tər\ *n.* A character formed by striking an inked ribbon with a molded or cast piece of type in the manner of a typewriter. Impact printers that produce fully formed characters use letters attached to wheels (daisy wheels), balls, thimbles, bands, or chains, rather than dot-matrix wires. *See also* daisy wheel, near-letter-quality, thimble.

fully populated board \ful`ē po`pyə-lā-təd bõrd´\ *n.* A printed circuit board whose integrated circuit (IC) sockets are all occupied. Memory boards in particular may have fewer than the maximum possible number of memory chips, leaving some IC sockets empty. Such a board is said to be *partially populated.*

Lorem ipsum

Lorem ipsum dolor sit amet, consectetuer adipiscing elit, sed diam nonummy nibh euismod tincidunt ut laoreet dolore magna aliquam erat volutpat. Ut wisi enim ad minim veniam, quis nostrud exerci tation ullamcorper suscipit lobortis nisl ut aliquip ex ea commodo consequat.

Duis autem vel eum iriure dolor in hendrerit in vulputate velit esse molestie consequat, vel illum dolore eu feugiat nulla facilisis at vero eros et accumsan et iusto odio dignissim qui blandit praesent luptatum zzril delenit augue duis dolore te feugait nulla facilisi.

Lorem ipsum dolor sit amet, consectetuer adipiscing elit, sed diam nonummy nibh euismod tincidunt ut laoreet dolore magna aliquam erat volutpat.

Ut wisi enim ad minim veniam, quis nostrud exerci tation ullamcorper suscipit lobortis nisl ut aliquip ex ea commodo consequat.Duis autem vel eum iriure dolor in hendrerit in vulputate

Full justification.

function \funk´shən\ *n*. **1.** The purpose of, or the action carried out by, a program or routine. **2.** A general term for a subroutine. **3.** In some languages, such as Pascal, a subroutine that returns a value. *See also* function call, procedure, routine, subroutine.

functional design \funk`shə-nəl   də-zīn´\   *n*. The specification of the relationships between working parts of a computer system, including details of logical components and the way they work together. Functional design is shown graphically in a functional diagram, which uses special symbols to represent the elements of the system.

functional programming \funk`shə-nəl   prō´-gram-ēng\ *n*. A style of programming in which all facilities are provided as functions (subroutines), usually without side effects. Pure functional programming languages lack a traditional assignment statement; assignment is usually implemented by copy and modify operations. Functional programming is thought to offer advantages for parallel-processing computers. *See also* side effect.

functional redundancy checking \funk`shə-nəl rə-dun´dən-sē chek-ēng\ *n*. A method of preventing errors by having two processors execute the same instructions on the same data at the same time. If the results produced by the two processors do not agree, an error has occurred. The Intel Pentium and higher processors have built-in support for functional redundancy checking. *Acronym:* FRC (F`R-C´).

functional specification \funk`shə-nəl spes`ə-fə-kā´shən\ *n*. A description of the scope, objectives, and types of operations that are to be considered in the development of an information-handling system.

function call \funk´shən käl`\ *n*. A program's request for the services of a particular function. A function call is coded as the name of the function along with any parameters needed for the function to perform its task. The function itself can be a part of the program, be stored in another file and brought into the program when the program is compiled, or be a part of the operating system. *See also* function (definition 2).

function key \funk´shən kē`\ *n*. Any of the 10 or more keys labeled F1, F2, F3, and so on, that are placed along the left side or across the top of a keyboard (or both) and are used for special tasks by different programs. The meaning of a function key is defined by a program or, in some instances, by the user. Function keys are used in application programs or the operating system to provide either a shortcut for a series of common instructions (such as calling up a program's on-screen help facility) or a feature that is not otherwise available. *See also* key (definition 1). *Compare* Command key, Control key, Escape key.

function library \funk`shən lī´brär-ē\ *n*. A collection of routines compiled together. *See also* function (definition 2), library (definition 1), toolbox.

function overloading \funk`shən ō´vər-lō-dēng\ *n*. The capability of having several routines in a program with the same name. The different functions are distinguished by their parameter types, return value types, or both; the compiler automatically selects the correct version, based on parameter types and return types. For example, a program might have one trigonometric sine function that uses a floating-point parameter to represent an angle in radians, and another that uses an integer parameter to represent an angle in degrees. In such a program, sin(3.14159/2.0) would return the value 1.0 (because the sine of π/2 radians is 1), but sin(30) would return the value 0.5 (because the sine of 30 degrees is 0.5). *See also* operator overloading.

fuse \fyo͞oz\ *n*. A circuit element that burns out or breaks when the current passing through it exceeds a certain level. A fuse protects a circuit from damage caused by excess current. It performs the same function as a circuit breaker, but it cannot be reset, so it must be replaced if it breaks. A fuse consists of a short length of wire of a specific composition and thickness; the thicker the wire, the more current it can pass before the wire melts and breaks the circuit.

fusible link \fyo͞o`zə-bl lēnk´\ *n*. A circuit component, often part of an integrated circuit, that is designed to break, or burn like a fuse, when a relatively high current is applied. Rather than protecting against excessive current flow, fusible links allow intentional circuit modification in the field. Fusible links were used in PROM chips, and they form the foundation of a kind of integrated circuit known as a field-programmable logic array. One can customize such a circuit "in the field," after it has been made in the factory, by selectively programming high current through certain fusible links and breaking them. *See also* field-programmable logic array, PROM.

fuzzy logic \fuz`ē loj´ik\ *n.* A form of logic used in some expert systems and other artificial-intelligence applications in which variables can have degrees of truthfulness or falsehood represented by a range of values between 1 (true) and 0 (false). With fuzzy logic, the outcome of an operation can be expressed as a probability rather than as a certainty. For example, an outcome might be probably true, possibly true, possibly false, or probably false. *See also* expert system.

FWIW \F`W-I-W´\ *adv.* Acronym for **f**or **w**hat **i**t's **w**orth. An expression used in e-mail and newsgroups.

.fx \dot`F-X´\ *n.* On the Internet, the major geographic domain specifying that an address is located in metropolitan France.

FYI \F`Y-I´\ *n.* **1.** Acronym for **f**or **y**our **i**nformation. An expression used in e-mail and newsgroups to introduce information that is thought to be useful to the reader. **2.** An electronic document distributed through InterNIC like a request for comments (RFC), but intended to explain an Internet standard or feature for users rather than to define it for developers, as the RFC does. *See also* InterNIC. *Compare* RFC.

G \gig´ə, jig´ə\ *prefix See* giga-.

.ga \dot`G-A´\ *n.* On the Internet, the major geographic domain specifying that an address is located in Gabon.

GaAs \G`A-A-S´\ *n. See* gallium arsenide.

gain \gān\ *n.* The increase in the amplitude of a signal, as of voltage, current, or power, that is produced by a circuit. Gain can be expressed as a factor or in decibels. *See also* decibel.

gallium arsenide \gal´ē-əm är´sə-nīd\ *n.* A semiconductor compound used in place of silicon to make devices that perform faster, require less power, and are more tolerant of temperature changes and radiation than those made with silicon. *Also called* GaAs.

game \gām\ *n. See* computer game.

game card \gām´ kärd\ *n. See* ROM card.

game cartridge \gām´ kär`trij\ *n. See* ROM cartridge.

Game Control Adapter \gām` kən-trōl` ə-dap´tər\ *n.* In IBM personal computers and compatibles, a circuit that processes input signals at a game port. Devices such as joysticks and game paddles use potentiometers to represent their positions as varying voltage levels; the Game Control Adapter converts these levels to numbers using an analog-to-digital converter (ADC). *See also* analog-to-digital converter, game port, potentiometer.

game port \gām´ pōrt\ *n.* In IBM personal computers and compatibles, an I/O port for devices such as joysticks and game paddles. The game port is often included with other I/O ports on a single expansion card. *See also* Game Control Adapter.

game theory \gām´ thēr`ē, thē`ə-rē\ *n.* A mathematical theory, ascribed to John von Neumann, that considers strategy and probability in terms of competitive games in which all players have partial control and each seeks the most advantageous moves in relation to the others.

Gantt chart \gant´ chärt\ *n.* A bar chart that shows individual parts of a project as bars against a horizontal time scale. Gantt charts are used as a project-planning tool for developing schedules. Most project-planning software can produce Gantt charts.

gap \gap\ *n. See* inter-record gap.

garbage \gär`bəj\ *n.* Incorrect or corrupted data.

garbage collection \gär`bəj kə-lek´shən\ *n.* A process for automatic recovery of heap memory. Blocks of memory that had been allocated but are no longer in use are freed, and blocks of memory still in use may be moved to consolidate the free memory into larger blocks. *See also* heap (definition 1).

garbage in, garbage out \gär`bəj in´ gär`bəj out´\ *n.* A computing axiom meaning that if the data put into a process is incorrect, the data output by the process will also be incorrect. *Acronym:* GIGO (gī´gō, G`I-G-O´).

gas-discharge display \gas`dis´chärj di-splā`\ *n.* A type of flat-panel display, used on some portable computers, containing neon between a horizontal and a vertical set of electrodes. When one electrode in each set is charged, the neon glows (as in a neon lamp) where the two electrodes intersect, representing a pixel. *Also called* gas-plasma display. *See also* flat-panel display, pixel.

gas-plasma display \gas`pla´zmə di-splā`\ *n. See* gas-discharge display.

gate \gāt\ *n.* **1.** An electronic switch that is the elementary component of a digital circuit. It produces an electrical output signal that represents a binary 1 or 0 and is related to the states of one or more input signals by an operation of Boolean logic, such as AND, OR, or NOT. *Also called* logic gate. *See also* gate array. **2.** The input terminal of a field-effect transistor (FET). *Also called* gate electrode. *See also* drain (definition 1), FET, MOSFET, source (definition 2). **3.** A data structure used by 80386 and higher microprocessors to control access to privileged functions, to change data segments, or to switch tasks.

gate array \gāt´ ər-ā´\ *n.* A special type of chip that starts out as a nonspecific collection of logic gates. Late in the manufacturing process, a layer is added to connect the gates for a specific function. By changing the pattern of connections, the manufacturer can make the chip suitable for many needs. This process is very popular because it saves both design and manufacturing time. The drawback is that much of the chip goes unused. *Also called* application-specific integrated circuit, logic array.

gated \gā´təd\ *adj.* **1.** Transmitted through a gate to a subsequent electronic logic element. **2.** Transmitted through a gateway to a subsequent network or service. For example, a mailing list on BITNET may be gated to a newsgroup on the Internet.

gate electrode \gāt´ ə-lek`trōd\ *n. See* gate (definition 2).

gateway \gāt´wā\ *n.* A device that connects networks using different communications protocols so that information can be passed from one to the other. A gateway both transfers information and converts it to a form compatible with the protocols used by the receiving network. *Compare* bridge.

gating circuit \gā´tēng sər`kət\ *n.* An electronic switch whose output is either on or off, depending on the state of two or more inputs. For example, a gating circuit may be used to pass or not pass an input signal, depending on the states of one or more control signals. A gating circuit can be constructed from one or more logic gates. *See also* gate (definition 1).

.ga.us \dot-G-A`dot-U-S´\ *n.* On the Internet, the major geographic domain specifying that an address is located in Georgia, United States.

.gb \dot`G-B´\ *n.* On the Internet, the major geographic domain specifying that an address is located in Great Britain.

GB \gig´ə-bīt`, jig´ə-bīt`, G-B´\ *n. See* gigabyte.

Gbps \G`B-P-S´\ *n. See* gigabits per second.

.gd \dot`G-D´\ *n.* On the Internet, the major geographic domain specifying that an address is located in Grenada.

GDI \G`D-I´\ *n.* Acronym for **G**raphical **D**evice **I**nterface. In Microsoft Windows, a graphics display system used by applications to display or print bitmapped text (TrueType fonts), images, and other graphical elements. The GDI is responsible for drawing dialog boxes, buttons, and other elements in a consistent style on screen by calling the appropriate screen drivers and passing them the information on the item to be drawn. The GDI also works with GDI printers, which have limited ability to prepare a page for printing. Instead, the GDI handles that task by calling the appropriate printer drivers and moving the image or document directly to the printer, rather than reformatting the image or document in PostScript or another printer language. *See also* bitmapped font, dialog box, driver, PostScript.

.ge \dot`G-E´\ *n.* On the Internet, the major geographic domain specifying that an address is located in the republic of Georgia.

geek \gēk\ *n.* **1.** Generally, a person who enjoys cerebral activities (such as wordplay, computer programming, and use of the Internet) more than the mainstream population does. Geeks in this sense increasingly claim the word with pride, but it may give offense when used by others, suggesting inadequacy in normal social relationships. **2.** A computer expert or specialist. For issues of etiquette, see definition 1. *Compare* guru, techie.

gender bender \jen´dər ben`dər\ *n. See* gender changer.

gender changer \jen´dər chān`jər\ *n.* A device for joining two connectors that are either both male (having pins) or both female (having sockets). See the illustration. *Also called* gender bender.

Gender changer.

General Protection Fault \jen`ər-əl prə-tek´shən fält, fôlt\ *n.* The error condition that occurs in an 80386 or higher processor running in protected mode (such as Windows 3.1) when an application attempts to access memory outside of its authorized memory space or an invalid instruction is issued. *Acronym:* GPF (G`P-F´). *See also* protected mode.

General Public License \jen`ər-əl pu`blik lī´səns\ *n.* The agreement under which software, such as the GNU (GNU's Not UNIX) utilities, is distributed by the Free Software Foundation. Anyone who has a copy of such a program may redistribute it to another party and may charge for distribution and support services, but may not restrict the other party from doing the same. A user may modify the program, but if the modified version is distributed, it must be clearly identified as such and is also covered under the General Public License. A distributor must also either provide source code or indicate where source code can be obtained. *Also called* copyleft. *See also* free software, Free Software Foundation, GNU.

general-purpose computer \jen`ər-əl-pur-pəs kəm-pyōō´tər\ *n.* A computer that can perform any computational task. Each task depends on specific software.

general-purpose controller \jen`ər-əl-pur-pəs kən-trō´lər\ *n.* A controller that is designed for multiple uses. *See also* controller.

General-Purpose Interface Bus \jen`ər-əl-pur-pəs in´tər-fās bus\ *n.* A bus developed for the exchange of information between computers and industrial automation equipment. The electrical definition of this bus has been incorporated into an IEEE standard. *Acronym:* GPIB (G`P-I-B´). *See also* IEEE 488.

general-purpose language \jen`ər-əl-pur-pəs lang´-wəj\ *n.* A programming language, such as Ada, Basic, C, or Pascal, designed for a variety of applications and uses. By contrast, SQL is a language designed to be used only with databases.

general-purpose register \jen`ər-əl-pur-pəs rej´-ə-stər\ *n.* **1.** A register within a microprocessor that is available for any use rather than being reserved, like a segment selector or stack pointer, for a specific use by the processor design or operating system. **2.** Any digital circuit capable of storing binary data.

generation \jen`ər-ā´shən\ *n.* **1.** A concept used to distinguish stored versions of a set of files. The oldest is called the grandfather, the next oldest is the father, and the newest is the son. **2.** A concept used to distinguish among a process, another process that it initiates (its child), and the process that initiated it (its parent or the child's grandparent). *See also* process[1]. **3.** A category that distinguishes products, such as computers or programming languages, according to the technological advances they represent. *See also* computer.

generic icon \jə-nâr`ik ī´kon\ *n.* An icon on a Macintosh screen that identifies a file only as a document or an application. Ordinarily the icon for an application will be specific to that application, and the icon for a document will be specific to the application that opens it. If a generic icon appears instead, the information that the Macintosh Finder uses to identify the application has been damaged. *See also* Finder, icon, Macintosh.

GEnie \jē´nē\ *n.* Acronym for **G**eneral **E**lectric **n**etwork for **i**nformation **e**xchange. An online information service developed by General Electric (GE) Information Services. GEnie provides business information, forums, home shopping, and news and can exchange e-mail with the Internet.

geographic information system \jē-ə-graf`ik in-fər-mā´shən si`stəm\ *n.* An application or suite of applications for viewing and creating maps. Generally, geographic information systems contain a viewing system (sometimes allowing users to view maps with a Web browser), an environment for creating maps, and a server for managing maps and data for real-time online viewing. *Acronym:* GIS (G`I-S´).

geometry \jē-om´ə-trē`\ *n.* The branch of mathematics that deals with the construction, properties, and relationships of points, lines, angles, curves, and shapes. Geometry is an essential part of computer-aided design and graphics programs.

GeoPort \jē´ō-pōrt`\ *n.* A fast serial input/output port on a Macintosh Centris 660AV, Quadra 660AV, Quadra 840AV, or PowerMac computer. Any Macintosh-compatible serial device can be connected to a GeoPort, but with GeoPort-specific hardware and software the GeoPort can transmit data at up to 2 megabits per second (Mbps) and can handle voice, fax, data, and video transmission.

GEOS \jē´ōs, G`E-O-S´\ *n.* An operating system created by Geoworks (formerly Berkeley Softworks). GEOS is a compact, object-oriented GUI that can run on Apple, Commodore, and MS-DOS platforms.

geostationary \jē`ō-stā´shə-nâr-ē\ *adj. See* geosynchronous.

geosynchronous \jē`ō-sēn´krə-nəs\ *adj.* Completing one revolution in the same time that the earth completes one rotation, as a communications satellite. *Also called* geostationary.

germanium \jər-mā´nē-um\ *n.* A semiconductor element (atomic number 32) that is used in some transistors, diodes, and solar cells but has been replaced by silicon in most applications. Germanium has a lower bias voltage than silicon but is more sensitive to heat (as in soldering).

get \get\ *n.* An FTP command that instructs the server to transfer a specified file to the client. *See also* FTP client, FTP commands, FTP server.

.gf \dot`G-F´\ *n.* On the Internet, the major geographic domain specifying that an address is located in French Guiana.

GFLOP \G´flop, G`F-L-O-P´\ *See* gigaflops.

.gh \dot`G-H´\ *n.* On the Internet, the major geographic domain specifying that an address is located in Ghana.

ghost[1] \gōst\ *n.* A dim, secondary image that is displaced slightly from the primary image on a video display (due to signal reflection in transmission) or on a printout (due to unstable printing elements).

ghost[2] \gōst\ *vb.* **1.** To produce a duplicate, such as duplicating an application in memory. *See also* screen saver. **2.** To display an option on a menu or on a submenu in faint type to show that it cannot be selected at the present time.

ghosting \gō´stēng\ *n. See* burn in (definition 2).

.gi \dot`G-I´\ *n.* On the Internet, the major geographic domain specifying that an address is located in Gibraltar.

.gif \dot-gif´, -G`I-F´\ *n.* The file extension that identifies GIF bit map images. *See also* GIF.

GIF \gif\ *n.* **1.** Acronym for **G**raphics **I**nterchange **F**ormat. A graphics file format developed by CompuServe and used for transmitting raster images on the Internet. An image may contain up to 256 colors, including a transparent color. The size of the file

depends on the number of colors actually used. The LZW compression method is used to reduce the file size still further. *See also* raster graphics. **2.** A graphic stored as a file in the GIF format.

giga- \gig´ə, jig´ə\ *prefix* **1.** One billion (1,000 million, 10^9). **2.** In data storage, $1,024 \times 1,048,576$ (2^{30}) or $1,000 \times 1,048,576$. *See also* gigabyte, gigaflops, gigahertz, kilo-, mega-.

Gigabit Ethernet \gig´ə-bit ē´thər-net, jig´ə-bit\ *n.* The IEEE standard dubbed 802.3z, which includes support for transmission rates of 1,000 megabits per second (Mbps) over an Ethernet network. The usual Ethernet standard (802.3) supports only up to 100 Mbps. *Compare* Ethernet/802.3.

gigabits per second \gig`ə-bits pər sek´ənd, jig`ə-bits\ *n.* A measurement of data transfer speed, as on a network, in multiples of 1,073,741,824 (2^{30}) bits. *Acronym:* Gbps (G`B-P-S´).

gigabyte \gig´ə-bīt`, jig´ə-bīt`\ *n.* **1.** 1,024 megabytes ($1,024 \times 1,048,576$ [2^{30}] bytes). **2.** One thousand megabytes ($1,000 \times 1,048,576$ bytes). *Acronym:* GB (gig´ə-bīt`, jig´ə-bīt`, G-B´).

gigaflops \gig´ə-flops`, jig´ə-flops`\ *n.* A measure of computing performance: one billion (1,000 million) floating-point operations per second. *Acronym:* GFLOP (G´flop, G`F-L-O-P´). *See also* floating-point operation.

gigahertz \gig´ə-hərts`, jig´ə-hərts`\ *n.* Abbreviated GHz. A measure of frequency: one billion (1,000 million) cycles per second.

GIGO \gī´gō, G`I-G-O´\ *n. See* garbage in, garbage out.

GIS \G`I-S´\ *See* geographic information system.

GKS \G`K-S´\ *n. See* Graphical Kernel System.

.gl \dot`G-L´\ *n.* On the Internet, the major geographic domain specifying that an address is located in Greenland.

glare filter \glâr´ fil`tər\ *n.* A transparent mask placed over the screen of a video monitor to reduce or eliminate light reflected from its glass surface.

glitch \glich\ *n.* **1.** A problem, usually minor. **2.** A brief surge in electrical power.

global \glō´bəl\ *adj.* Pertaining to an entire document, file, or program rather than to a restricted segment of it. *Compare* local, local variable.

global group \glō´bəl grōōp`\ *n.* In Windows NT Advanced Server, a collection of user accounts within one domain that are granted permissions and rights to access resources, servers, and workstations outside of the group's own domain as well as within that domain. *See also* group, local group, Windows NT Advanced Server.

globally unique identifier \glō`bə-lē yo͞o-nēk´ ī-den´tə-fī-ər\ *n.* In the Component Object Model (COM), a 16-byte code that identifies an interface to an object across all computers and networks. Such an identifier is unique because it contains a time stamp and a code based on the network address hardwired on the host computer's LAN interface card. These identifiers are generated by a utility program. *Acronym:* GUID (go͞o´id, gwid).

global operation \glō`bəl op-ər-ā´shən\ *n.* An operation, such as a search and replace, that affects an entire document, program, or other object such as a disk.

global search and replace \glō`bəl sərch` ənd rə-plās´\ *n.* A search-and-replace operation that finds and changes all instances of the selected string throughout a document. *See also* search and replace.

Global System for Mobile Communications \glō`bəl si`stəm fər mō`bəl kə-myo͞o-nə-kā´shənz\ *n.* A digital cellular telephone standard in use in more than 60 countries, including much of Europe. Trial GSM systems have been set up in the United States. *Acronym:* GSM (G`S-M´).

global universal identification \glō`bəl yo͞o-nə-vər`səl ī-den-tə-fə-kā´shən\ *n.* An identification scheme in which only one name is associated with a particular object; this name is accepted across platforms and applications. *Acronym:* GUID (G`U-I-D). *See also* globally unique identifier.

global variable \glō`bəl vâr´ē-ə-bl\ *n.* A variable whose value can be accessed and modified by any statement in a program, not merely within a single routine in which it is defined. *See also* global. *Compare* local variable.

.gm \dot`G-M´\ *n.* On the Internet, the major geographic domain specifying that an address is located in Gambia.

.gn \dot`G-N´\ *n.* On the Internet, the major geographic domain specifying that an address is located in Guinea.

gnomon \nō´mon\ *n.* In computer graphics, a representation of the three-dimensional (*x-y-z*) axis system.

GNU \no͞o, G`N-U´\ *n.* Acronym for **G**NU's **N**ot UNIX. A collection of software based on the UNIX operating system maintained by the Free Software Foundation. GNU is distributed under the GNU General Public License, which requires that anyone who distributes GNU or a program based on GNU may charge only for distribution and support and must allow the user to modify and redistribute the code on the same terms. *See also* Free Software Foundation, General Public License. *Compare* Linux.

Good Times virus \go͞od´ tīmz vīr´us\ *n.* A purported e-mail virus alluded to in a warning that has been propagated widely across the Internet, as well as by fax and standard mail. The letter claims that reading an e-mail message with the subject "Good Times" will cause damage to the user's system. In fact, it is currently impossible to harm a system by reading an e-mail message, although it is possible to include a virus in a file that is attached to an e-mail message. Some consider the chain letter itself to be the "virus" that wastes Internet bandwidth and the reader's time. Information on such hoaxes and on real viruses can be obtained from CERT (http://www.cert.org/). *See also* urban legend, virus.

Gopher or **gopher** \gō´fər\ *n.* An Internet utility for finding textual information and presenting it to the user in the form of hierarchical menus, from which the user selects submenus or files that can be downloaded and displayed. One Gopher client may access all available Gopher servers, so the user accesses a common "Gopherspace." The name of the program is a three-way pun: it is designed to go for desired information; it tunnels through the Internet and digs the information up; and it was developed at the University of Minnesota (whose athletic teams are named the Golden Gophers). Gopher is being subsumed by the World Wide Web.

Gopher server \gō´fər sər`vər\ *n.* The software that provides menus and files to a Gopher user. *See also* Gopher.

Gopher site \gō´fər sīt`\ *n.* A computer on the Internet on which a Gopher server runs. *See also* Gopher, Gopher server.

Gopherspace \gō´fər-spās`\ *n.* The total set of information on the Internet that is accessible as menus and documents through Gopher. *See also* Gopher.

GOSIP \gos´ip, G`O-S-I-P´\ *n.* Acronym for **G**overnment **O**pen **S**ystems **I**nterconnection **P**rofile. A U.S. government requirement that all of its new network purchases comply with the ISO/OSI standards. GOSIP went into effect on August 15, 1990, but was never fully implemented and was replaced by POSIT.

GOTO statement \gō´tōō stāt`mənt\ *n.* A control statement used in programs to transfer execution to some other statement; the high-level equivalent of a branch or jump instruction. Use of GOTO statements is generally discouraged, because they make it difficult not only for a programmer to trace the logic of a program but also for a compiler to generate optimized code. *See also* branch instruction, jump instruction, spaghetti code.

.gov \dot-gəv´, -G`O-V´\ *n.* In the Internet's Domain Name System, the top-level domain that identifies addresses operated by government agencies. The domain name .gov appears as a suffix at the end of the address. In the United States, only nonmilitary federal government agencies may use the .gov domain. State governments in the United States use the top-level domain of .state.us, with .us preceded by the two-letter abbreviation for the state, or just .us; other regional governments in the United States are registered under the .us domain. *See also* DNS (definition 1), domain (definition 3), .state.us, .us. *Compare* .com, .edu, .mil, .net, .org.

.gov.ca \dot-gəv`dot-C-A´, dot-G-O-V`dot-C-A´\ *n.* On the Internet, the major domain specifying that an address belongs to the Canadian government.

Government Open Systems Interconnection Profile \gəv`ərn-mənt ō´pən si`stəmz in`tər-kə-nek´shən prō`fīl\ *n.* *See* GOSIP.

.gp \dot`G-P´\ *n.* On the Internet, the major geographic domain specifying that an address is located in Guadeloupe.

GPF \G`P-F´\ *n.* *See* General Protection Fault.

GPIB \G`P-I-B´\ *n.* *See* General-Purpose Interface Bus.

GPL \G`P-L´\ *n.* *See* General Public License.

.gq \dot`G-Q´\ *n.* On the Internet, the major geographic domain specifying that an address is located in Equatorial Guinea.

.gr \dot`G-R´\ *n.* On the Internet, the major geographic domain specifying that an address is located in Greece.

grabber \grab´ər\ *n.* **1.** A device for capturing graphical image data from a video camera or another full-motion video source and putting it into memory. *Also called* frame grabber, video digitizer. **2.** Any device for capturing data. **3.** Software that takes a "snapshot" of the currently displayed screen image by transferring a portion of video memory to a file on disk. **4.** In some graphics-based applications, a special type of mouse pointer.

graceful exit \grās`ful eks´it, egz´it\ *n.* The methodical termination of a process, even under error conditions, that allows the operating system or parent process to regain normal control, leaving the system in a state of equilibrium. This is expected behavior. *See also* fail-soft system.

grade \grād\ *n.* In communications, the range of frequencies available for transmission on a single channel. For example, voice-grade telephone frequencies range from about 300 hertz (Hz) through 3,400 Hz.

grade of service \grād` əv sər´vəs\ *n.* The probability that a user of a shared communications network, such as a public telephone system, will receive an "all channels busy" signal. The grade of service is used as a measure of the traffic-handling ability of the network and is usually applied to a specific period, such as the peak traffic hour. A grade of service of 0.002, for example, assumes that a user has a 99.8 percent chance that a call made during the specified period will reach its intended destination.

grafPort \graf´pōrt\ *n.* A structure used on the Apple Macintosh to define a graphics environment with its own pen size, font, fill patterns, and so on. Each window has a grafPort, and grafPorts can be used to send graphics to off-screen windows or files.

graftal \graf´təl\ *n.* One of a family of geometric forms, similar to fractals but easier to compute. Graftals are often used in the special-effects industry to create synthetic images of structures such as trees and plants. *See also* fractal.'

grammar checker \gram´ər chek`ər\ *n.* A software accessory that checks text for errors in grammatical construction.

grandfather \grand´fä`dhər\ *n. See* generation (definition 1).

grandfather/father/son \grand`fä-dhər-fä`dhər-sən´\ *adj. See* generation (definition 1).

grandparent \grand´pâr`ənt\ *n. See* generation (definition 2).

granularity \gran`yə-lâr´ə-tē\ *n.* A description, from "coarse" to "fine," of a computer activity or feature (such as screen resolution, searching and sorting, or time slice allocation) in terms of the size of the units it handles (pixels, sets of data, or time slices). The larger the pieces, the coarser the granularity.

graph \graf\ *n.* In programming, a data structure consisting of zero or more nodes and zero or more edges, which connect pairs of nodes. If any two nodes in a graph can be connected by a path along edges, the graph is said to be connected. A subgraph is a subset of the nodes and edges within a graph. A graph is directed (a digraph) if each edge links two nodes together only in one direction. A graph is weighted if each edge has some value associated with it. *See also* node (definition 3), tree.

Graphical Device Interface \graf´i-kəl də-vīs´ in´-tər-fās\ *n. See* GDI.

graphical interface \graf`i-kəl in´tər-fās\ *n. See* graphical user interface.

Graphical Kernel System \graf`i-kəl kər´nəl si`-stəm\ *n.* A computer graphics standard, recognized by ANSI and ISO, that specifies methods of describing, manipulating, storing, and transferring graphical images. It functions at the application level rather than the hardware level and deals with logical workstations (combinations of input and output devices such as keyboard, mouse, and monitor) rather than with individual devices. Graphical Kernel System was developed in 1978 to handle two-dimensional graphics; the later modification, GKS-3D, extended the standard to three-dimensional graphics. *Acronym:* GKS (G`K-S´). *See also* ANSI, ISO.

graphical user interface \graf`i-kəl yōō´zər in´-tər-fās`\ *n.* A type of environment that represents programs, files, and options by means of icons, menus, and dialog boxes on the screen. The user can select and activate these options by pointing and clicking with a mouse or, often, with the key-

board. A particular item (such as a scroll bar) works the same way to the user in all applications, because the graphical user interface provides standard software routines to handle these elements and report the user's actions (such as a mouse click on a particular icon or at a particular location in text, or a key press); applications call these routines with specific parameters rather than attempting to reproduce them from scratch. *Acronym:* GUI (gōō´ē).

graphic character \graf´ik kâr`ək-tər\ *n.* Any character that is represented by a visible symbol, such as an ASCII character. A graphic character is not the same as a graphics character. *Compare* graphics character.

graphic limits \graf´ik lim`its\ *n.* On a computer screen, the boundary of a graphical image in a graphics software program, including all the area enclosed within the graphic. In some graphics environments the limits of a graphic consist of the smallest rectangle that can completely enclose it, called its *bounding rectangle* or *bounding box.*

graphics accelerator \graf´iks ak-sel`ər-ā-tər\ *n.* A video adapter that contains a graphics coprocessor. A graphics accelerator can update the video display much more quickly than the CPU can, and it frees the CPU for other tasks. A graphics accelerator is a necessity for modern software such as graphical user interfaces and multimedia applications. *See also* graphics coprocessor, video adapter.

graphics adapter \graf´iks ə-dap´tər\ *n.* A video adapter capable of displaying graphics as well as alphanumeric characters. Almost all video adapters in common use today are graphics adapters.

graphics card \graf´iks kärd`\ *n. See* video adapter.

graphics character \graf´iks kâr`ək-tər\ *n.* A character that can be combined with others to create simple graphics, such as lines, boxes, and shaded or solid blocks. See the illustration. *Compare* graphic character.

Graphics Controller \graf´iks kən-trō`lər\ *n.* The part of the EGA and VGA video adapters that allows the computer to access the video buffer. *See also* EGA, VGA.

graphics coprocessor \graf´iks kō´pros-es-ər\ *n.* A specialized microprocessor, included in some video adapters, that can generate graphical images such as lines and filled areas in response to instructions from the CPU, freeing the CPU for other work.

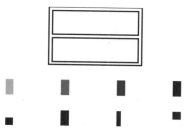

Graphics character. **Box built up from line graphics characters (top); shaded and solid blocks (bottom) from the IBM expanded character set.**

graphics data structure \graf´iks dā´tə struk`chur, dat´ə\ *n.* A data structure that is designed specifically for representing one or more elements of a graphical image.

graphics engine \graf´iks en`jən\ *n.* **1.** A display adapter that handles high-speed graphics-related processing, freeing the CPU for other tasks. *Also called* graphics accelerator, video accelerator. **2.** Software that, based on commands from an application, sends instructions for creating graphic images to the hardware that actually creates the images. Examples are Macintosh QuickDraw and Windows Graphics Device Interface (GDI).

Graphics Interchange Format \graf´iks in´tər-chānj fōr`mat\ *n. See* GIF.

graphics interface \graf´iks in`tər-fās\ *n. See* graphical user interface.

graphics mode \graf´iks mōd`\ *n.* **1.** On computers such as the IBM PC, the display mode in which lines and characters on the screen are drawn pixel by pixel. Because graphics mode creates images from individual dots on the screen, programs have more flexibility in creating images than they do in text (or character) mode. Thus, the computer is able to display a mouse pointer as an arrowhead or other shape rather than as a blinking square or rectangle, and it can display character attributes, such as boldface and italics, as they will appear in print rather than using conventions such as highlighting, underlining, or

alternate colors. *Compare* text mode. **2.** A particular set of color and resolution values, often related to a particular video adapter, such as VGA color with 16 colors and 640 × 480 pixels on the screen. *See also* high resolution, low resolution, resolution (definition 1).

graphics port \graf´iks pōrt`\ *n. See* grafPort.

graphics primitive \graf´iks prim`ə-tiv\ *n.* A drawing element, such as a text character, an arc, or a polygon, that is drawn and manipulated as a single unit and is combined with other primitives to create an image. *Compare* entity.

graphics printer \graf´iks prin`tər\ *n.* A printer, such as a laser, ink-jet, or dot-matrix impact printer, that can produce graphics formed pixel by pixel and not merely text characters. Nearly all printers presently used with personal computers are graphics printers; daisy-wheel printers are the exception. *Compare* character printer.

graphics processor \graf´iks pros`es-ər\ *n. See* graphics coprocessor.

graphics tablet \graf´iks ta`blət\ *n.* A device used to input graphics position information in engineering, design, and illustration applications. A flat rectangular plastic board is equipped with a puck or a pen (also called a stylus) and sensing electronics that report the position of the puck or stylus to the computer, which translates that data into a cursor position on the screen. See the illustration. *Also called* digitizing tablet. *See also* puck, stylus.

Graphics tablet.

graphics terminal \graf´iks tər`mə-nəl\ *n.* A terminal capable of displaying graphics as well as text. Such terminals usually interpret graphics control commands rather than receiving streams of already-processed pixels.

Gray code \grā´ kōd\ *n. See* cyclic binary code.

gray scale \grā´ skāl\ *n.* A sequence of shades ranging from black through white, used in computer graphics to add detail to images or to represent a color image on a monochrome output device. Like the number of colors in a color image, the number of shades of gray depends on the number of bits stored per pixel. Grays may be represented by actual gray shades, by halftone dots, or by dithering. *See also* dithering, halftone.

greater than \grā´tər dhan`\ *adj. See* relational operator.

greater than or equal to \grā`tər dhan ōr ē´kwəl too\ *adj. See* relational operator.

Great Renaming \grāt` rē-nā´mēng\ *n.* The changeover to the current system of Usenet hierarchies throughout the Internet. Before the Great Renaming, which took place in 1985, nonlocal newsgroup names had the form net.*; for example, a group that carried source code, formerly named net.sources, was renamed comp.sources.misc. *See also* local newsgroups, newsgroup, traditional newsgroup hierarchy, Usenet.

greeking \grē´kēng\ *n.* **1.** The use of gray bars or other graphics to represent lines of characters too small to be drawn legibly on a screen at the chosen resolution, such as when viewing the layout of a whole page or pair of facing pages. **2.** The use of nonsense words to represent the text of a document in design samples. A garbled Latin text beginning "Lorem ipsum dolor sit amet" is traditionally used for this purpose. Greeking does not involve substituting the Greek alphabet for the Roman one.

greek text \grēk tekst´\ *n. See* greeking.

Green Book \grēn´ book\ *n.* A specifications book written by the Sony and Philips Corporations, covering the CD-I (compact disc–interactive) technology. *See also* CD-I. *Compare* Orange Book (definition 2), Red Book (definition 2).

green PC \grēn` P-C´\ *n.* A computer system designed to conserve energy. For example, some computers shut off power to nonessential systems when no input has been detected for a certain amount of time, a condition known as *sleep mode.*

Green PCs may also be distinguished by the use of minimal packaging materials and replaceable components, such as toner cartridges, that are recyclable.

Gregorian calendar \gre-gōr´ē-ən kal´ən-dər\ *n.* The calendar used today in the Western world, introduced by Pope Gregory XIII in 1582 to replace the Julian calendar. To approximate better the length of the astronomical year (365.2422 days), years divisible by 100 are leap years only if they are also divisible by 400 (thus, 2000 will be a leap year, but 1900 was not). To correct the error accumulated since A.D. 1, 10 days were dropped from October 1582; however, Britain and the American colonies did not adopt the Gregorian calendar until 1752 and had to remove 11 days then. *Compare* Julian calendar.

grep[1] \grep, G`R-E-P´\ *n.* Acronym for **g**lobal **r**egular **e**xpression **p**rint. A UNIX command used to search a file or files by key word.

grep[2] \grep, G`R-E-P´\ *vb.* To search text, especially with the UNIX grep utility.

grid \grid\ *n.* Two sets of lines or linear elements at right angles to each other. A spreadsheet is a grid of rows and columns; a graphics screen is a grid of horizontal and vertical lines of pixels. In optical character recognition, a grid is used for measuring or specifying characters. *See also* Cartesian coordinates.

grok \grok\ *vb.* To understand deeply and appreciatively. The term comes from Robert A. Heinlein's novel *Stranger in a Strange Land,* where it is also a Martian word for "to drink" and implies the kind of devoted interest that a Martian—native of a dry planet—would have in water. Hackers often use it (for example, in Internet discussions) in reference to computer expertise. *See also* cyberpunk.

ground \ground\ *n.* A conducting path from an electric circuit to earth or to a conducting body serving in place of earth, usually used as a safety device. *See also* grounding.

grounding \groun´dēng\ *n.* The connection of sections of an electrical circuit to a common conductor, called the *ground,* which serves as the reference for the other voltages in the circuit. The ground conductor on installed circuit boards is usually connected to the chassis, or metal frame, holding the electronic parts; the chassis is in turn usually connected to the third (round) prong on the power plug, which connects to a ground circuit that is, in fact, connected to the earth. This is important to avoid creating a shock hazard.

group[1] \gro͞op\ *n.* A collection of elements that can be treated as a whole, such as a collection of records in a database report, or a collection of objects that can be moved and transformed as a single object in a drawing program. In various multiuser operating systems, a group is a set of user accounts, sometimes called *members;* privileges can be specified for the group, and each member will then have those privileges. *See also* built-in groups, global group, local group, user account.

group[2] \gro͞op\ *vb.* In a drawing program, to transform a number of objects into a group. *See also* drawing program.

groupware \gro͞op´wâr\ *n.* Software intended to enable a group of users on a network to collaborate on a particular project. Groupware may provide services for communication (such as e-mail), collaborative document development, scheduling, and tracking. Documents may include text, images, or other forms of information.

grovel \grov´əl\ *vb.* **1.** To search or do other work at great length without apparent progress. Some programs grovel over a whole input file before they begin to produce output. A programmer may have to grovel through manuals in search of documentation on a particular command, or through code in search of a bug. **2.** To post a plea for some favor to a newsgroup.

GSM \G`S-M´\ *n. See* Global System for Mobile Communications.

.gt \dot`G-T´\ *n.* On the Internet, the major geographic domain specifying that an address is located in Guatemala.

.gu \dot`G-U´\ *n.* On the Internet, the major geographic domain specifying that an address is located in Guam.

guest \gest\ *n.* A common name for a login account that can be accessed without a password. BBSs and service providers often maintain such an account so that prospective subscribers can sample the services offered.

GUI \go͞o´ē\ *n. See* graphical user interface.

GUID \G`U-I-D\ *n. See* globally unique identifier, global universal identification.

gunzip \G`un-zip´\ *n.* A GNU utility for decompressing files compressed with gzip. *See also* GNU, uncompress. *Compare* gzip.

guru \go͞o´ro͞o\ *n.* A technical expert who is available to help solve problems and to answer questions in an intelligible way. *See also* techie, wizard (definition 1).

gutter \gut´ər\ *n.* The blank space or inner margin between two facing pages of a bound document.

.gy \dot`G-Y´\ *n.* On the Internet, the major geographic domain specifying that an address is located in Guyana.

.gz \dot`G-Z´\ *n.* The file extension that identifies archive files that have been compressed with the UNIX gzip compression program. *See also* compressed file, gzip.

gzip \G´zip\ *n.* A GNU utility for compressing files. *See also* compress[2], GNU. *Compare* gunzip.

H \H\ *n. See* henry.

H.324 \H`thrē-tōō-fōr´\ *n.* An International Telecommunications Union standard for simultaneously transmitting video, data, and voice over POTS modem connections. *See also* POTS.

hack[1] \hak\ *n.* **1.** A modification to the code in a program, often made without taking the time to find an elegant solution. **2.** A sloppy job. *See also* kludge (definition 2), patch[2].

hack[2] \hak\ *vb.* **1.** To apply creative ingenuity to a problem or project. **2.** To alter the behavior of an application or an operating system by modifying its code rather than by running the program and selecting options.

hacker \hak´ər\ *n.* **1.** A computerphile; a person who is totally engrossed in computer technology and computer programming or who likes to examine the code of operating systems and other programs to see how they work. **2.** A person who uses computer expertise for illicit ends, such as by gaining access to computer systems without permission and tampering with programs and data. *Also called* cracker.

HAGO \H`A-G-O´\ Acronym for **h**ave **a g**ood **o**ne. An expression used to conclude e-mail messages or in signing off from IRC.

hairline \hâr´līn\ *n.* The smallest amount of visible space or the narrowest line that is displayable on a printed page. The size of a hairline depends on the materials, hardware, and software used or on the organizations involved. The United States Postal Service defines a hairline as 1/2 point (roughly 0.007 inch), whereas the Graphic Arts Technical Foundation (GATF) defines a hairline as 0.003 inch. *See also* point[1] (definition 1), rule (definition 1).

HAL \hal, H`A-L´\ *n. See* hardware abstraction layer.

half adder \haf´ ad`ər\ *n.* A logic circuit that can add two input data bits and produce a sum bit and a carry bit as output. A half adder cannot accept a carry bit from a previous addition; to add two input bits and a carry bit, a full adder is required. To add two multibit binary numbers, a computer uses a half adder and one or more full adders. *See also* carry bit, full adder.

half-card \haf´kärd\ *n. See* short card.

half-duplex \haf`dōō´pleks\ *adj.* Of or pertaining to two-way communication that takes place in only one direction at a time. For example, communication between people is half-duplex when one person listens and waits to speak until the other has finished speaking. *Compare* duplex[1].

half-duplex transmission \haf`dōō´pleks tranzmish´ən\ *n.* Two-way electronic communication that takes place in only one direction at a time. *Compare* duplex[2] (definition 1), simplex transmission.

half-height drive \haf´hīt drīv`\ *n.* Any of a generation of disk drives that are roughly one-half the height of the previous generation of drives.

half router \haf` rou´tər, rōō´tər\ *n.* A device that connects a local area network (LAN) to a communications line (such as one to the Internet) using a modem and controls the routing of data to individual stations on the LAN.

halftone \haf´tōn\ *n.* A printed reproduction of a photograph or other illustration, using evenly spaced spots of varying diameter to produce apparent shades of gray. The darker the shade at a particular point in the image, the larger the corresponding spot in the halftone. In traditional publishing, halftones are created by photographing an image through a screen. In desktop publishing, each halftone spot is represented by an area containing a number of dots printed by a laser printer or digital imagesetter. In both cases, the frequency of the halftone dots is measured in lines per inch. Higher printer resolution enables effective use of higher frequencies of halftone dots, enhancing image quality. *See also* dithering, gray scale, imagesetter, spot function.

half-word \haf´wərd\ *n.* Half the number of bits considered to be a word in a particular computer; if a word is 32 bits, a half-word will be 16 bits or 2 bytes. *See also* word.

hammer \ham´ər\ *n.* The part of an impact printer that strikes or causes another component to strike the ribbon to print a character on the paper. In a dot-matrix printer, the pins or wires are the hammers; in a daisy-wheel printer, the hammer strikes the daisy wheel.

Hamming code \ham´ēng kōd`\ *n.* A family of error-correction codes named for R. W. Hamming of Bell Labs. In one of the simplest Hamming codes, every 4 data bits are followed by 3 check bits, each computed from the 4 data bits. If any one of the 7 bits becomes altered, a simple computation can detect the error and determine which bit is altered. *See also* error-correction coding, forward error correction.

handheld computer \hand`held kəm-pyōō´tər\ *n.* A computer small enough to be held in one hand while being operated by the other hand. Handheld computers are commonly used in transportation and other field service industries. They are usually built to perform specific tasks. They often have restricted specialized keyboards rather than the standard QWERTY layout, smaller displays, input devices such as bar code readers, and communications devices for sending their data to a central computer; they rarely have disk drives. Their software is usually proprietary and stored in ROM. *See also* QWERTY keyboard, ROM. *Compare* handheld PC, PDA.

handheld PC \hand`held P-C´\ *n.* A computer that is small enough to fit in a jacket pocket and can run, for example, Microsoft Windows CE (a scaled-down version of Windows 95) and applications made for that operating system. See the illustration. *Acronym:* HPC (H`P-C´). *Compare* handheld computer, PDA.

handheld scanner \hand´held skan`ər\ *n.* A type of scanner used as follows: the user passes the scan head, contained within a handheld unit, over the medium being scanned, such as a piece of paper. *See also* scan head, scanner. *Compare* drum scanner, feed scanner, flatbed scanner.

Handheld PC.

handle \han´dl\ *n.* **1.** A pointer to a pointer; that is, a variable that contains the address of another variable, which in turn contains the address of the desired object. In certain operating systems, the handle points to a pointer stored in a fixed location in memory, whereas that pointer points to a movable block. If programs start from the handle whenever they access the block, the operating system can perform memory management tasks such as garbage collection without affecting the programs. *See also* pointer (definition 1). **2.** Any token that a program can use to identify and access an object such as a device, a file, a window, or a dialog box. **3.** One of several small squares displayed around a graphical object in a drawing program. The user can move or reshape the object by clicking on a handle and dragging. See the illustration.

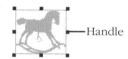
—Handle

Handle.   *A computer graphics handle.*

handler \han´dəl-ər, hand´lər\ *n.* **1.** A routine that manages a common and relatively simple condition or operation, such as error recovery or data movement. **2.** In some object-oriented programming languages that support messages, a subroutine that processes a particular message for a particular class of objects. *See also* message, object-oriented programming.

handshake \hand´shāk\ *n.* A series of signals acknowledging that communication or the transfer of information can take place between computers or other devices. A hardware handshake is an exchange of signals over specific wires (other than the data wires), in which each device indicates its readiness to send or receive data. A software handshake consists of signals transmitted over the same wires used to transfer data, as in modem-to-modem communications over telephone lines.

hands-on \handz´on\ *adj.* Involving interactive work with a computer or a computer program. A hands-on tutorial, for example, would teach a skill (such as the use of a program) by means of practice sessions and question-and-answer dialogues.

handwriting recognition \hand´rī`tēng rek-əg-nish`ən\ *n.* **1.** The ability of a computer to identify a user by recognizing features of handwriting, especially a signature. **2.** The ability of a computer to translate handwritten text into character data for input. This technology is still under considerable development, and most handwriting recognition programs require users to form letters and words in a very consistent and clear manner to work adequately. The development of handwriting recognition programs has been spurred by PDAs, which frequently have keyboards that are too small for data entry, and software designed for Asian markets that have languages with numerous characters, which makes keyboards a cumbersome method for entering text. *See also* PDA. *Compare* optical character recognition.

hang \hang\ *vb.* To stop responding. A hung program or computer system does not respond to user input, but the screen looks as if everything is running normally. The program or system might be waiting for something, for example, information from a network, or it might have terminated abnormally. It might resume running normally on its own, or the user might need to terminate and restart the program or reboot the computer. A hung computer system is said to be locked up. *See also* crash[2] (definition 1).

hanging indent \hang`ēng in´dent\ *n.* Placement of the beginning of the first line of a paragraph farther to the left than the subsequent lines. *Also called* outdent. *Compare* indent.

hard \härd\ *adj.* **1.** Permanent, fixed, or physically defined; unchangeable by the ordinary operation of a computer system. *See also* hard copy, hard error, hard return, hard-sectored disk. *Compare* soft (definition 1). **2.** Retaining magnetization even

in the absence of an external magnetic field. *Compare* soft (definition 2).

hard card \härd´ kärd\ *n.* A circuit board, carrying a hard disk and containing its controller, that plugs into an expansion slot and uses the expansion bus for power as well as for data and control signals. By contrast, a hard disk in a drive bay communicates with a separate controller card by a ribbon cable and has a direct cable to the computer's main power supply. *See also* controller, drive bay, expansion slot, ribbon cable.

hard-coded \härd`kō´dəd\ *adj.* **1.** Designed to handle a specific situation only. **2.** Depending on values embedded in the program code rather than on values that can be input and changed by the user.

hard copy \härd´ kop`ē\ *n.* Printed output on paper, film, or other permanent medium. *Compare* soft copy.

hard disk \härd´ disk\ *n.* A device containing one or more inflexible platters coated with material in which data can be recorded magnetically, together with their read/write heads, the head-positioning mechanism, and the spindle motor in a sealed case that protects against outside contaminants. The protected environment allows the head to fly 10 to 25 millionths of an inch above the surface of a platter rotating typically at 3,600 to 7,200 rpm; therefore, much more data can be stored and accessed much more quickly than on a floppy disk. Most hard disks contain from two to eight platters. See the illustration. *Also called* hard disk drive. *Compare* floppy disk.

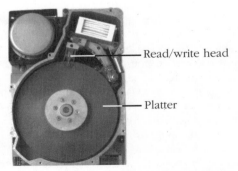

Read/write head

Platter

Hard disk. *The cover of this hard disk has been removed to reveal the components within.*

hard disk drive \härd disk´ drīv`\ *n. See* hard disk.

hard disk type \härd` disk´ tīp\ *n.* One or more numbers that inform a computer about the characteristics of a hard disk, such as the number of read/write heads and the number of cylinders the hard disk contains. The hard disk type numbers are usually marked on a label attached to the disk and must be input to the computer when the hard disk is installed, often by means of the computer's CMOS setup program. *See also* CMOS setup.

hard error \härd´ âr`ər\ *n.* **1.** An error caused by a hardware failure or by accessing incompatible hardware. *See also* hard failure. *Compare* soft error. **2.** An error that prevents a program from returning to normal operation. *See also* fatal error.

hard failure \härd´ fāl-yər\ *n.* A cessation of function from which no recovery is possible, usually requiring a call to a repair service to correct. *Also called* hardware failure.

hard hyphen \härd` hī´fən\ *n. See* hyphen.

hard return \härd` rə-tərn´\ *n.* A character input by the user to indicate that the current line of text is to end and a new line is to begin. In word processing programs that automatically break lines within the margins of a page, a hard return indicates the end of a paragraph. In text-entry programs that lack wordwrap, on the other hand, a hard return is required to end each line, and often two or more hard returns are needed to end a paragraph. *See also* wordwrap. *Compare* soft return.

hard-sectored disk \härd`sek-tərd disk´\ *n.* A floppy disk whose data sectors have been physically marked with punched holes that are detected by sensors in the drive to locate the beginning of each sector. *Compare* soft-sectored disk.

hard space \härd´ spās\ *n. See* nonbreaking space.

hardware \härd´wâr\ *n.* The physical components of a computer system, including any peripheral equipment such as printers, modems, and mouse devices. *Compare* firmware, software.

hardware abstraction layer \härd`wâr ab-strak´shən lâr`, lā`ər\ *n.* In advanced operating systems such as Windows NT, a layer in which assembly language code is isolated. A hardware abstraction layer functions similarly to an application programming interface (API) and is used by programmers to write device-independent applications. *Acronym:* HAL (hal, H`A-L´). *See also* application programing interface, device independence.

hardware check \härd´wâr chek`\ *n.* An automatic check performed by hardware to detect internal errors or problems.

hardware-dependent \härd´wâr-də-pen`dənt\ *adj.* Of or pertaining to programs, languages, or computer components and devices that are tied to a particular computer system or configuration. Assembly language, for example, is hardware-dependent because it is created for and works only with a particular make or model of microprocessor.

hardware failure \härd´wâr fāl`yər\ *n.* A malfunction of a physical component in a computer system, such as a disk head crash or memory error. *See also* hard failure.

hardware handshake \härd`wâr hand´shāk\ *n. See* handshake.

hardware interrupt \härd´wâr in`tər-upt\ *n.* A request for service from the central processing unit, generated either externally by a hardware device such as a disk drive or an input/output port, or internally by the CPU itself. External hardware interrupts are used for such situations as a character received from a port and needing to be processed, a disk drive ready to transfer a block of data, or a tick of the system timer. Internal hardware interrupts occur when a program attempts an impossible action such as accessing an unavailable address or dividing by zero. Hardware interrupts are assigned levels of importance or priority. The highest priority is given to a type of interrupt called a nonmaskable interrupt—one that indicates a serious error, such as a memory failure, that must be serviced immediately. *See also* external interrupt, interrupt.

hardware key \härd´wâr kē`\ *n.* **1.** A security device connected to an input/output port to permit the use of a particular software package on that computer. The use of the hardware key permits backup copying of software but prevents its unlicensed use on additional computers. *Also called* dongle. **2.** Any physical device used to secure a computer system from unauthorized access, such as the lock on the front of the cabinet of some personal computers.

hardware monitor \härd´wâr mon`ə-tər\ *n*. A separate board-level circuit used to oversee the performance of a hardware/software system. A hardware monitor can detect the cause of a fatal error such as a system crash, whereas a software monitor or debugger cannot. *Compare* debugger.

hardware profile \härd`wâr prō´fīl\ *n*. A set of data that describes the configuration and characteristics of a given piece of computer equipment. Such data is typically used to configure computers for use with peripheral devices.

hardware tree \härd´wâr trē`\ *n*. In Windows 95, a data structure containing information about the configuration and requirements of a system's hardware devices. Consisting of nodes that point to active devices, the hardware tree is dynamic and is reconstructed every time Windows 95 is started or refreshed. The hardware tree facilitates the Plug and Play capability of Windows 95.

hardwired \härd´wīrd\ *adj*. **1.** Built into a system using hardware such as logic circuits, rather than accomplished through programming. **2.** Physically connected to a system or a network, as by means of a network connector board and cable.

Harvard architecture \här`vərd är´kə-tek-chur\ *n*. A processor architecture that uses separate address buses for code and for data. This increases throughput by allowing the system to fetch instructions at the same time that it reads and writes data. This architecture also allows optimization of memory system design because instructions tend to be fetched sequentially, whereas data reads and writes are more random.

Harvard Mark I \här`vərd märk` wən´\ *n*. *See* Mark I.

hash[1] \hash\ *n*. In many FTP client programs, a command that instructs the FTP client to display a pound sign (#) each time it sends or receives a block of data. *See also* FTP client.

hash[2] \hash\ *vb*. To be mapped to a numerical value by a transformation known as a hashing function. Hashing is used to convert an identifier or key, meaningful to a user, into a value for the location of the corresponding data in a structure, such as a table. For example, given the key

MOUSE and a hashing function that added up the ASCII values of the characters, divided the total by 127, and took the remainder, MOUSE would hash to 12, and the data identified by MOUSE would be found among the items in entry 12 in the table.

hash coding \hash´ kō`dēng\ *n*. *See* hash[2].

hash search \hash´ sərch\ *n*. A search algorithm that uses hashing to find an element of a list. Hash searches are highly efficient because the hashing enables direct or almost direct access to the target element. *See also* binary search, hash[2], linear search, search algorithm.

hash total \hash´ tō`təl\ *n*. An error-checking value derived from the addition of a set of numbers taken from data (not necessarily numeric data) that is to be processed or manipulated in some way. After processing, the hash total is recalculated and compared with the original total. If the two do not match, the original data has been changed in some way.

Hayes-compatible \hāz´kəm-pat`ə-bl\ *adj*. Responding to the same set of commands as the modems manufactured by Hayes Microcomputer Products. This command set has become the de facto standard for microcomputer modems.

HDBMS \H`D-B`M-S´\ *n*. *See* hierarchical database management system.

HDF \H`D-F´\ *n*. *See* Hierarchical Data Format.

HDLC \H`D-L-C´\ *n*. Acronym for **H**igh-level **D**ata **L**ink **C**ontrol. A protocol for information transfer adopted by the ISO. HDLC is a bit-oriented, synchronous protocol that applies to the data-link (message-packaging) layer (layer 2 of the ISO/OSI model) for computer-microcomputer communications. Messages are transmitted in units called frames, which can contain differing amounts of data but which must be organized in a particular way. *See also* frame (definition 1), ISO/OSI model.

HDSL \H`D-S-L´\ *n*. *See* High-data-rate Digital Subscriber Line.

HDTV \H`D-T-V´\ *n*. Acronym for **h**igh-**d**efinition **tele**vision. A method of transmitting and receiving television signals that produces a picture with much greater resolution and clarity than does standard television technology.

head \hed\ *n*. The read/write mechanism in a disk or tape drive. It converts changes in the magnetic field of the material on the disk or tape surface to changing electrical signals and vice versa. Disk drives usually contain one head for each surface that can be read from and written to.

head arm \hed´ ärm\ *n. See* access arm.

head-cleaning device \hed´klē-nēng də-vīs`\ *n.* An apparatus for applying a small amount of cleaning fluid to a magnetic head to remove accumulated debris.

head crash \hed´ krash\ *n.* A hard disk failure in which a read/write head, normally supported on a cushion of air only millionths of an inch thick, comes into contact with the platter, damaging the magnetic coating in which data is recorded. Still more damage occurs when the head picks up material gouged out of the surface and pushes it. A head crash can be caused by mechanical failure or by heavy shaking of the disk drive. If the crash occurs on a directory track, the whole disk may become instantly unreadable.

header \hed´ər\ *n.* **1.** In word processing or printing, text that is to appear at the top of pages. A header might be specified for the first page, all pages after the first, even pages, or odd pages. It usually includes the page number and may also show the date or the title or other information about a document. *Also called* heading, running head. *Compare* footer. **2.** An information structure that precedes and identifies the information that follows, such as a block of bytes in communications, a file on a disk, a set of records in a database, or an executable program. **3.** One or more lines in a program that identify and describe for human readers the program, function, or procedure that follows.

header file \hed´ər fīl`\ *n.* A file that is identified to be included at the beginning of a program in a language such as C and that contains the definitions of data types and declarations of variables used by the functions in the program.

header label \hed´ər lā`bəl\ *n.* An initial structure, such as an opening record, in the linear organization of a file or communication that describes the length, type, and structure of the data that follows. *Compare* trailer label (definition 1).

header record \hed´ər rek`ərd\ *n.* The first record in a sequence of records.

heading \hed´eng\ *n. See* header (definition 1).

head-per-track disk drive \hed`pər-trak` disk´ drīv\ *n.* A disk drive that has one read/write head for every data track. Such a disk drive has a very low seek time because the heads do not have to move across the disk surface to the required track for reading and writing. Because read/write heads are expensive, this type of drive is uncommon.

head positioning \hed´ pə-zish`ə-nēng\ *n.* The process of moving the read/write head of a disk drive to the proper track for reading and writing.

head slot \hed´ slot\ *n.* The oblong opening in the jacket of a floppy disk that provides access to the magnetic surface of the disk for the read/write head. See the illustration.

Head slot

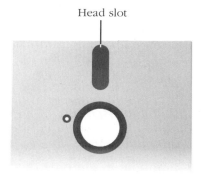

Head slot

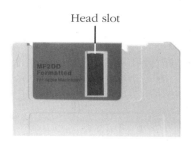

Head slot.   The head slots on a 5.25-inch disk (top) and a 3.5-inch disk (bottom). (The metal shutter on the 3.5-inch disk has been pulled back to show the head slot.)

head switching \hed´ swich`ēng\ *n.* The process of electrically switching among multiple read/write heads in a disk drive.

heap \hēp\ *n.* **1.** A portion of memory reserved for a program to use for the temporary storage of data structures whose existence or size cannot be determined until the program is running. To build and use such elements, programming languages such as C and Pascal include functions and procedures for requesting free memory from the heap, accessing it, and freeing it when it is no longer needed. In contrast to stack memory, heap memory blocks are not freed in reverse of the order in which they were allocated, so free blocks may be interspersed with blocks that are in use. As the program continues running, the blocks may have to be moved around so that small free blocks can be merged together into larger ones to meet the program's needs. *See also* garbage collection. *Compare* stack. **2.** A complete binary tree in which the value of any node is not exceeded by the value of either of its children. *See also* binary tree.

heap sort or **heapsort** \hēp´ sōrt\ *n.* A space-efficient sorting method that first arranges the key fields into a heap structure and then repeatedly removes the root of the heap, which must, by definition, have the largest key, and re-forms the heap. *See also* heap (definition 2).

heat pipe \hēt´ pīp\ *n.* A cooling device consisting of a sealed metal tube containing a liquid and a wick. The liquid evaporates at the hot end; the vapor spreads along the tube to the cold end, where it condenses onto the wick; the liquid flows back along the wick to the hot end by capillary action. Heat pipes have been used in Pentium-based laptop computers, which have high cooling requirements and little room for conventional heat sinks. *Compare* heat sink.

heat sink \hēt´ sink\ *n.* A device that absorbs and dissipates heat produced by an electrical component, such as an integrated circuit, to prevent overheating. Heat sinks are usually made of metal and often have fins that assist in transferring heat to the atmosphere. See the illustration. *Compare* heat pipe.

hecto- \hek´tō\ *prefix* Metric prefix meaning 10^2 (one hundred).

hello, world \hel-ō´ wərld`\ *n.* The output of the first program in Brian Kernighan and Dennis Ritchie's *The C Programming Language*. The program is traditionally the first test a C programmer makes in a new environment.

help \help\ *n.* **1.** The capability of many application programs to display advice or instructions for

Heat sink.

using their features when so requested by the user, as by a screen button or menu item or a function key. The user can access help without interrupting work in progress or leafing through a manual. Some help facilities are context-sensitive, meaning that the user receives information specific to the task or command being attempted. Although help facilities are not usually as extensive as manuals, they give the user a means of refreshing the memory and may also offer the more advanced user quick access to details on little-used program features. *Also called* online help. **2.** In many applications, a command that displays an explanation of another command that follows it. For instance, in many FTP programs, the command *help* can be followed by other commands, such as *cd* (change directory) or *ls* (list files and directories), to discover the purpose of these other commands.

Help \help\ *n.* An item on a menu bar in a graphical user interface that enables the user to access the help feature of the present application. *See also* graphical user interface, help (definition 1), menu bar.

help desk \help´ desk\ *n.* **1.** Technical support staff who help solve users' problems with hardware or software systems or refer such problems to those who can solve them. Help desks are typically run by larger organizations, such as corporations or universities, or vendors to corporations, to assist users in the organization. **2.** A software application for tracking problems with hardware and software and their solutions.

helper \hel´pər\ *n. See* helper application.

helper application \hel´pər a-plə-kā`shən\ *n.* An application intended to be launched by a Web browser when the browser downloads a file that it is not able to process itself. Examples of helper applications are sound and movie players. Helper applications generally must be obtained and installed by users; they usually are not included in the browser itself. Many current Web browsers no longer require helper applications for common multimedia file formats. *Also called* helper program. *Compare* ActiveX controls, plug-in (definition 2).

helper program \hel´pər prō`gram\ *n. See* helper application.

Help key \help´ kē\ *n.* A key on the keyboard that the user can press to request help. *See also* function key, help (definition 1).

help screen \help´ skrēn\ *n.* A screen of information that is displayed when the user requests help. *See also* help (definition 1).

henry \hen´rē\ *n.* Abbreviated H. The unit of inductance. A current changing at a rate of one ampere per second will generate one volt across an inductance of one henry. In practice, a henry is a very large unit; inductances measured in millihenries (mH = 10^{-3} H), microhenries (μH = 10^{-6} H), or nanohenries (nH = 10^{-9} H) are more commonly encountered. *See also* inductance.

Hercules Graphics Card \hər´kyə-lēz graf´iks kärd\ *n. See* HGC.

hertz \hərts\ *n.* Abbreviated Hz. The unit of frequency measurement; one cycle (of a periodic event such as a waveform) per second. Frequencies of interest in computers and electronic devices are often measured in kilohertz (kHz = 1,000 Hz = 10^3 Hz), megahertz (MHz = 1,000 kHz = 10^6 Hz), gigahertz (GHz = 1,000 MHz = 10^9 Hz), or terahertz (THz = 1,000 GHz = 10^{12} Hz).

hertz time \hərts´ tīm\ *n. See* clock rate.

heterogeneous environment \het-ər-ə-jē´nē-əs en-vīr´ən-mənt, en-vī´ərn-mənt\ *n.* A computing milieu, usually within an organization, in which hardware and software from two or more manufacturers are used. *Compare* homogeneous environment.

heuristic \hyər`i´stik\ *n.* An approach or algorithm that leads to a correct solution of a programming task by nonrigorous or self-learning means. One approach to programming is first to develop a heuristic and then to improve on it. The term comes from Greek *heuriskein* ("to discover, find out") and is related to "eureka" ("I have found it").

Hewlett-Packard Graphics Language \hyo͞o`lət-pak`ərd graf´iks lang-wəj\ *n. See* HPGL.

Hewlett-Packard Printer Control Language \hyo͞o`lit-pak`ərd prin´tər kən-trōl´ lang`wəj\ *n. See* Printer Control Language.

hex \heks\ *n. See* hexadecimal.

hexadecimal \heks`ə-des´ə-məl\ *adj.* Using 16 rather than 10 as the base for representing numbers by digits. The hexadecimal system uses the digits 0 through 9 and the letters A through F (uppercase or lowercase) to represent the decimal numbers 0 through 15. One hexadecimal digit is equivalent to 4 bits, and 1 byte can be expressed by two hexadecimal digits. For example, binary 0101 0011 corresponds to hexadecimal 53. To prevent confusion with decimal numbers, hexadecimal numbers in programs or documentation are usually followed by *H* or preceded by *&*, *$*, or *0x*. Thus, 10H = decimal 16; 100H = decimal 16^2 = decimal 256. Equivalents and conversion tables for binary, decimal, hexadecimal, and octal numbers are given in Appendix E. *Also called* hex.

hexadecimal conversion \heks`ə-des´ə-məl kən-vər´zhən\ *n.* Conversion of a number to or from the hexadecimal system. For conversion tables, *see* Appendix E.

HFS \H`F-S´\ *n. See* Hierarchical File System.

HGA \H`G-A´\ *n.* Acronym for **H**ercules **G**raphics **A**dapter. *See* HGC.

HGC \H`G-C´\ *n.* Acronym for **H**ercules **G**raphics **C**ard. A video adapter introduced in 1982 by Hercules Computer Technology for IBM Personal Computers and compatibles and now superseded by VGA and its successors. It offered a monochrome graphics mode with 720 × 348 pixels. *See also* VGA.

HGC Plus \H`G-C plus´\ *n.* A video adapter, introduced in 1986 by Hercules Computer Technology, that offered additional video buffer space to store 12 fonts of 256 characters each, which could be used for graphics characters.

HHOK \H`H-O-K´\ Acronym for **h**a, **h**a, **o**nly **k**idding. An indication of humor or facetiousness often used in e-mail and online communications.

hidden file \hid`ən fīl´\ *n.* A file that, in order to protect it from deletion or modification, is not shown in the normal listing of the files contained in a directory. Such a file is often used to store code or data critical to the operating system.

hidden line \hid`ən līn´\ *n.* In any application, such as a CAD program, that represents solid three-dimensional objects, a line in a drawing that would (or should) be hidden if the object were perceived as a solid construction. The process of removing such lines in an application is called hidden-line removal. *See also* CAD, hidden surface.

hidden surface \hid`ən sur´fəs\ *n.* A surface of a solid three-dimensional object, such as one represented in a CAD program, that would not be visible when the object is viewed from a particular angle—for example, the underside of the wing of an airplane viewed from the top. *See also* CAD, hidden line.

hide \hīd\ *vb.* To defer the display of an application's active window while leaving the application running. Windows that have been hidden are returned to active display by issuing the appropriate command to the operating system.

hierarchical \hī¯ər-är´ki-kəl, hīr-är`kə-kəl\ *adj.* Of, relating to, or organized as a hierarchy. *See also* hierarchy.

hierarchical computer network \hī-ər-är`ki-kəl kəm-pyo͞o´tər net`wərk, hīr-är`kə-kəl\ *n.* **1.** A network in which one host computer controls a number of smaller computers, which may in turn act as hosts to a group of PC workstations. **2.** A network in which control functions are organized according to a hierarchy and in which data processing tasks may be distributed.

hierarchical database \hī-ər-är`ki-kəl dā´tə-bās, hīr-är`kə-kəl\ *n.* A database in which records are grouped in such a way that their relationships form a branching, treelike structure. This type of database structure, most commonly used with databases for large computers, is well suited for organizing information that breaks down logically into successively greater levels of detail. The organization of records in a hierarchical database should reflect the most common of the most time-critical types of access expected.

hierarchical database management system \hī-ər-är`ki-kəl dā´tə-bās man´əj-mənt si`stəm, hīr-är`kə-kəl\ *n.* A database management system that supports a hierarchical model. *Acronym:* HDBMS (H¯D-B`M-S´). *See also* hierarchical model.

Hierarchical Data Format \hī-ər-är`ki-kəl dā´tə fōr`mat, hīr-är`kə-kəl, dat´ə\ *n.* A file format for storing multiple types of graphical and numerical data and transferring them between different types of machines, together with a library of functions for handling such files in a uniform way. NCSA developed and supports the file format and library and has placed them in the public domain. Hierachical Data Format files are supported on most common types of computers. The format can easily be extended to accommodate additional data models. The library functions have both FORTRAN and C interfaces. *Acronym:* HDF (H¯D-F´). *See also* NCSA (definition 1).

hierarchical file system \hī-ər-är`ki-kəl fīl´ sistəm, hīr-är`kə-kəl\ *n.* A system for organizing files on a disk in which files are contained in directories or folders, each of which can contain other directories as well as files. The main directory for the disk is called the root; the chain of directories from the root to a particular file is called the path. *See also* hierarchy, path (definition 2), root. *Compare* flat file system.

Hierarchical File System \hī-ər-är`ki-kəl fīl´ sistəm, hīr-är`kə-kəl\ *n.* A tree-structured file system used on the Apple Macintosh in which folders can be nested within other folders. *Acronym:* HFS (H¯F-S´). *See also* hierarchy, path (definition 2), root. *Compare* flat file system.

hierarchical menu \hī-ər-är`ki-kəl men´yo͞o, hīr-är`kə-kəl\ *n.* A menu that has one or more submenus. Such a menu/submenu arrangement is hierarchical because each level subsumes the next.

hierarchical model \hī¯ər-är`-ki-kəl mod´əl, hīr-är`kə-kəl\ *n.* A model used in database management in which each record may be the "parent" of one or more "child" records, which may or may not have the same structure as the parent; a record can have no more than one parent. Conceptually, therefore, a hierarchical model can be, and usually is, regarded as a tree. The individual records are not necessarily contained in the same file. *See also* tree.

hierarchy \hī¯ər-är`-kē\ *n.* A type of organization that, like a tree, branches into more specific units, each of which is "owned" by the higher-level unit immediately above. Hierarchies are characteristic of several aspects of computing because they provide organizational frameworks that can reflect logical links, or relationships, between separate records, files, or pieces of equipment. For example, hierarchies are used in organizing related files on a disk, related records in a database, and related (interconnected) devices on a network. In applications such as spreadsheets, hierarchies of a sort are used to establish the order of precedence in which arithmetic operations are to be performed by the computer. *See also* hierarchical file system.

High-bit-rate Digital Subscriber Line \hī-bit`rāt dij`i-təl sub-skrī´bər līn\ *n.* A protocol for digital transmission of data over standard copper telecommunications lines as opposed to fiber-optic lines. *Acronym:* HDSL (H`D-S-L´). *Also called* High-data-rate Digital Subscriber Line.

high byte \hī´ bīt\ *n.* The byte containing the most significant bits (bits 8 through 15) in a 2-byte grouping representing a 16-bit (bits 0 through 15) value. See the illustration. *See also* hexadecimal.

high-capacity CD-ROM \hī´kə-pas`ə-tē C-D-rom´, -R-O-M´\ *n. See* digital video disc.

High-data-rate Digital Subscriber Line \hī-dā`tə-rāt dij`i-təl sub-skrī´bər līn`, hī-dat`ə-rāt\ *n. See* High-bit-rate Digital Subscriber Line.

high-definition television \hī`def-ə-nish`ən tel´-ə-vizh`ən\ *n. See* HDTV.

high-density disk \hī`den-sə-tē disk´\ *n.* **1.** A 3.5-inch floppy disk that can hold 1.44 MB. *Compare* double-density disk. **2.** A 5.25-inch floppy disk that can hold 1.2 MB. *Compare* double-density disk.

high DOS memory \hī` dos´ mem`ər-ē, D-O-S´\ *n. See* high memory.

high-end \hī´end\ *adj.* A descriptive term for something that uses the latest technology to maximize performance. There is usually a direct correlation between high-end technology and higher prices.

High-level Data Link Control \hī`lev-əl dā`tə lēnk kən-trōl´, dat`ə\ *n. See* HDLC.

high-level language \hī`lev-əl lang´wəj\ *n.* A computer language that provides a level of abstraction from the underlying machine language. Statements in a high-level language generally use keywords similar to English and translate into more than one machine-language instruction. In practice, every computer language above assembly language is a high-level language. *Also called* high-order language. *Compare* assembly language.

highlight \hī´līt\ *vb.* To alter the appearance of displayed characters as a means of calling attention to them, as by displaying them in reverse video (light on dark rather than dark on light, and vice versa) or with greater intensity. Highlighting is used to indicate an item, such as an option on a menu or text in a word processor, that is to be acted on in some way. See the illustration on the next page.

high memory \hī´ mem`ər-ē\ *n.* **1.** Memory locations addressed by the largest numbers. **2.** In IBM PCs and compatibles, the range of addresses between 640 kilobytes and 1 megabyte, used primarily for the ROM BIOS and control hardware such as the video adapter and input/output ports. *Compare* low memory.

high memory area \hī` mem´ər-ē âr`ē-ə\ *n.* In IBM PCs and compatibles, the 64-kilobyte range of addresses immediately above 1 megabyte. By means of the file HIMEM.SYS, MS-DOS (versions 5.0 and later) can move portions of itself into the high memory area, thereby increasing the amount

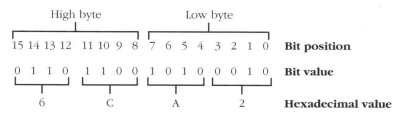

High byte.   The high byte is binary 01101100, or hexadecimal 6C, or decimal 108.

Highlighting

Highlighting.

of conventional memory available for applications. *Acronym:* HMA (H˙M-A´). *See also* conventional memory, expanded memory.

high-order \hī´ōr˙dər\ *adj.* Having the most weight or significance. The high-order term usually appears first or leftmost in writing systems based on the Roman alphabet or Arabic numerals. For example, in the 2-byte hex value 6CA2, the high-order byte 6C has a value by itself of decimal 108 but counts for $108 \times 256 = 27,648$ in the group, whereas the low-order byte A2 counts only for decimal 162. *Compare* low-order.

high-order language \hī˙ōr-dər lang´wəj\ *n. See* high-level language.

highpass filter \hī´pas fil`tər\ *n.* An electronic circuit that passes all frequencies in a signal that are above a specified frequency. *Compare* bandpass filter, lowpass filter.

High Performance File System \hī˜ pər-fōr`məns fīl´ si-stəm\ *n. See* HPFS.

High-Performance Parallel Interface \hī˜ pər-fōr-məns pâr`ə-lel in´tər-fās\ *n. See* HIPPI.

High Performance Serial Bus (1394) \hī˜ pər-fōr´məns sēr`ē-əl bus` thər`tēn-nīn-tē-fōr´\ *n.* A serial bus interface for both the PC and Macintosh that can support transmission speeds of 100, 200, or 400 Mbps and allows daisy-chaining of up to 63 devices in a branched form. Devices connected in such a way will be able to draw power directly through the interface.

high-persistence phosphor \hī˜ pər-si`stəns fos´-fər\ *n.* A phosphor that glows for a relatively long time after being struck by electrons. High-persistence phosphors are used in direct view storage tubes, but most CRTs (cathode-ray tubes) use phosphors of relatively low persistence so that their images can be changed quickly without "ghosts" of earlier images remaining on the screen. *See also* CRT, direct view storage tube.

high resolution \hī˜ rez-ə-lōo´shən\ *n.* The capability for reproducing text and graphics with relative clarity and fineness of detail. High resolution is achieved by using a large number of pixels (dots) to create an image in a given area. For screen displays, the resolution is stated in terms of the total number of pixels in the horizontal and vertical dimensions. For example, the VGA video adapter has a resolution of 640 by 480 pixels. In printing, resolution refers to the number of dots per inch (dpi) produced by the printer, such as 300 to 600 dpi for a desktop laser or ink-jet printer or 1,000 to 2,000 dpi for a production-quality imagesetter. *Also called* hi-res.

High Sierra specification \hī˜ sē-âr´ə spes-ə-fə-kā`shən\ *n.* An industrywide format specification for the logical structure, file structure, and record structures on a CD-ROM. The specification is named after a meeting on CD-ROM held near Lake Tahoe in November 1985. It served as the basis for the international standard, ISO 9660.

high tech \hī tek´\ *n.* **1.** Cutting-edge applied science and engineering, usually involving computers and electronics. **2.** Sophisticated, often complex, specialized technical innovation.

HIPPI \H˙I-P-P-I´, hip´ē\ *n.* Acronym for **High-Performance Parallel Interface.** An ANSI communications standard used with supercomputers.

hi-res \hī-rez´\ *n. See* high resolution.

histogram \hi´stə-gram`\ *n.* A chart consisting of horizontal or vertical bars, the widths or heights of which represent the values of certain data.

history \hi´stər-ē`\ *n.* A list of the user's actions within a program, such as commands entered in an operating system shell, menus passed through using Gopher, or links followed using a Web browser.

hit \hit\ *n.* **1.** A successful retrieval of data from a cache rather than from the slower hard disk or

RAM. *See also* cache, hard disk, RAM. **2.** A successful retrieval of a record matching a query in a database. *See also* query (definition 1), record[1]. **3.** Retrieval of a document, such as a home page, from a Web site.

.hk \dot`H-K´\ *n.* On the Internet, the major geographic domain specifying that an address is located in Hong Kong.

HKEY \H´kē\ *n.* Short for **h**andle **key.** In Windows 95, a handle to a Registry key in which configuration information is stored. Each key leads to subkeys containing configuration information that, in earlier versions of Windows, was stored in .ini files. For example, the handle key HKEY_CURRENT_USER\Control Panel leads to the subkey for the Windows Desktop. *See also* handle (definition 1).

HLS \H`L-S´\ *n.* Acronym for **h**ue-**l**ightness-**s**aturation. *See* HSB.

HMA \H`M-A´\ *n.* *See* high memory area.

.hn \dot`H-N´\ *n.* On the Internet, the major geographic domain specifying that an address is located in Honduras.

Hollerith tabulating/recording machine \hol`ər-ith ta`byə-lā-tēng-rə-kōr´dēng mə-shēn\ *n.* An electromechanical machine invented by Herman Hollerith in the late 1800s for processing data supplied in the form of holes punched at predetermined locations in cards. Contacts made through the holes completed electrical circuits, allowing signals to be passed to counting and tabulating devices. This machine is considered to have reduced the time required to finish the 1890 U.S. census by two-thirds. Such machines were manufactured in the early 1900s by Hollerith's Tabulating Machine Company, which eventually became the International Business Machines Corporation (IBM).

hologram \hol´ə-gram`\ *n.* A three-dimensional image record created by holography. The hologram consists of a light interference pattern preserved in a medium such as photographic film. When suitably illuminated, it produces an image that changes its appearance as the viewer changes viewing angle. *See also* holography.

holography \hə-lo´grə-fē\ *n.* A method of reproducing three-dimensional visual images by recording light interference patterns on a medium such as photographic film, creating a hologram.

holy war \hō´lē wōr`\ *n.* **1.** A widespread and acrimonious debate among computer professionals over some aspect of the computer field, such as the debate over use of the GOTO statement in programming or that over big-endian versus little-endian data storage. **2.** An argument in a mailing list, newsgroup, or other forum over some emotional and controversial topic, such as abortion or Northern Ireland. Introducing a holy war that is off the purported topic of the forum is considered a violation of netiquette.

home \hōm\ *n.* A beginning position, such as the top left corner of a character-based display, the left end of a line of text, cell A1 of a spreadsheet, or the top of a document.

homebrew \hōm´broo\ *n.* Hardware or software developed by an individual at home or by a company for its own use rather than as a commercial product, such as hardware developed by electronics hobbyists when microcomputers first appeared in the 1970s.

home computer \hōm` kəm-pyoo´tər\ *n.* A personal computer designed and priced for use in the home.

home directory \hōm` dər-ek´tər-ē\ *n.* A directory associated with a user account under UNIX. The home directory is the current directory when the user first logs in, and the user can return to it by entering the command *cd* (change directory) without a pathname. The user's files will ordinarily be stored in the home directory and its descendants.

homegrown software \hōm`grōn soft´wâr\ *n.* Software developed by an individual at home rather than in a professional environment. Most public-domain and shareware programs are created this way.

Home key \hōm´ kē\ *n.* A key, found on most keyboards, whose function usually involves sending the cursor to some type of home position in an application. *See also* home.

home office \hōm` of´əs\ *n.* **1.** An office set up within a residence. **2.** The main headquarters of a company.

home page \hōm´pāj\ *n.* **1.** A document intended to serve as a starting point in a hypertext system, especially the World Wide Web. A home page is called a *start page* in Microsoft Internet Explorer. **2.** An entry page for a set of Web pages and other files in a Web site.

home record \hōm´ rek`ərd\ *n. See* header record.

homogeneous environment \hō-mō-jē`nē-əs en-vīr´ən-mənt, en-vī´ərn-mənt\ *n.* A computing milieu, usually within an organization, in which only one manufacturer's hardware and one manufacturer's software are used. *Compare* heterogeneous environment.

homogeneous network \hō-mō-jē`nē-əs net´-wərk\ *n.* A network on which all the hosts are similar and only one protocol is used.

hook \hŏŏk\ *n.* A location in a routine or program in which the programmer can connect or insert other routines for the purpose of debugging or enhancing functionality.

horizontal blanking interval \hōr`ə-zon-təl blan´-kēng in-tər-vəl\ *n. See* blanking, horizontal retrace.

horizontal flyback \hōr`ə-zon-təl flī´bak\ *n. See* horizontal retrace.

horizontal market software \hōr-ə-zon`təl mär`-kət soft´wâr\ *n.* Application programs, such as word processors, that can be used in all types of business, as opposed to those geared for a certain industry.

horizontal retrace \hōr`ə-zon-təl rē´trās\ *n.* The movement of the electron beam in a raster-scan video display from the right end of one scan line to the left end (the beginning) of the next. During horizontal retrace, the electron beam is turned off, so the time required for the beam to move is called the horizontal blanking interval. *See also* blanking. *Compare* vertical retrace.

horizontal scrolling \hōr`ə-zon-təl skrō´lēng\ *n.* A feature of programs such as word processors and spreadsheets that enables the user to scroll left and right to display information beyond the horizontal limits of the screen (or window, in a graphical user interface).

horizontal synchronization \hōr`ə-zon-təl sēn`-krə-nə-zā´shən\ *n.* On raster displays, the timing produced by a signal that controls the sweep of the display's electron beam as it moves from left to right and back again to form an image line by line. The horizontal synchronization signal is usually

controlled by a circuit known as a phase-locked loop, which maintains a constant precise frequency so that a clear image is formed.

host \hōst\ *n.* The main computer in a system of computers or terminals connected by communications links.

host adapter \hōst´ ə-dap`tər\ *n.* A device for connecting a peripheral to the main computer, typically in the form of an expansion card. *Also called* controller, host bus adapter.

host bus adapter \hōst´ bus ə-dap`tər\ *n. See* host adapter.

host language \hōst´ lang`wəj\ *n.* **1.** The machine language of a CPU. **2.** A high-level language that is specifically supported by an operating system with its toolbox routines and native development systems.

host name \hōst´ nām\ *n.* The name of a specific server on a specific network within the Internet, leftmost in the complete host specification. For example, www.microsoft.com indicates the server called "www" within the network at Microsoft Corporation.

host not responding \hōst` not rə-spon´dēng\ *n.* An error message issued by an Internet client indicating that the computer to which a request has been sent is refusing the connection or is otherwise unavailable to respond to the request.

host timed out \hōst` tīmd out´\ *n.* An error condition that occurs when a remote system fails to respond within a reasonable amount of time (a few minutes) during an exchange of data over a TCP connection. This condition may mean that the remote system has crashed or been disconnected from the network. The error message the user sees may or may not be phrased in this manner. *See also* TCP. *Compare* host not responding.

host unreachable \hōst` un-rē´chə-bl\ *n.* An error condition that occurs when the particular computer to which the user wishes to connect over a TCP/IP network cannot be accessed on its LAN because it is either down or disconnected from the network. The error message the user sees may or may not be phrased in this manner. *See also* TCP/IP.

hot \hot\ *adj.* Of special or urgent interest, or deemed popular.

hot carrier diode \hot` kâr-ē-ər dī´ōd\ *n. See* Schottky diode.

hot docking \hot´ dok`ēng\ *n.* The process of attaching a laptop computer to a docking station while the computer is running, and automatically activating the docking station's video display and other functions. *See also* docking station, laptop.

hot insertion \hot` in-sər´shən\ *n.* The insertion of a device or card while there is power to the system. Many newer laptops allow for hot insertion of PCMCIA cards. High-end servers may also allow hot insertion to reduce downtimes.

HotJava \hot´jav`ə\ *n.* A Web browser developed by Sun Microsystems, Inc. that is optimized to run Java applications and applets embedded in Web pages. *See also* applet, Java, Java applet.

hot key[1] \hot´ kē\ *n.* A keystroke or combination of keystrokes that switches the user to a different program, often a terminate-and-stay-resident (TSR) program or the operating system user interface. *See also* TSR.

hot key[2] \hot´ kē\ *vb.* To transfer to a different program by pressing a hot key.

hot link \hot´ lēnk\ *n.* **1.** A connection between two programs that instructs the second program to make changes to data when changes occur in the first program. For example, a word processor or desktop publishing program could update a document based on information obtained from a database through a hot link. **2.** *See* hyperlink.

hotlist \hot´list\ *n.* A list of frequently accessed items, such as Web pages in a Web browser, from which the user can select one. The hotlist of Web pages is called the bookmark list in Netscape Navigator and Lynx and is called the Favorites folder in Microsoft Internet Explorer.

hot plugging \hot´ plug-ēng\ *n.* A feature that allows equipment to be connected to an active device, such as a computer, while the device is powered on.

hot spot \hot´ spot\ *n.* The position in a mouse pointer, such as the position at the tip of an arrow or the intersection of the lines in a cross, that marks the exact location that will be affected by a mouse action, such as a button press.

hot swapping \hot´ swä`pēng\ *n. See* hot plugging.

HotWired \hot´wīrd\ *n.* A Web site affiliated with *Wired* magazine that contains news, gossip, and other information about the culture of the Internet: http://www.hotwired.com/frontdoor/.

housekeeping \hous´kē`pēng\ *n.* Any of various routines, such as updating the clock or performing garbage collection, designed to keep the system, the environment within which a program runs, or the data structures within a program in good working order.

HPC \H`P-C`\ *n. See* handheld PC.

HPFS \H`P-F-S`\ *n.* Acronym for **H**igh **P**erformance **F**ile **S**ystem. A file system available with OS/2 versions 1.2 and later. *See also* FAT file system, NTFS.

HPGL \H`P-G-L´\ *n.* Acronym for **H**ewlett-**P**ackard **G**raphics **L**anguage. A language originally developed for images destined for plotters. An HPGL file consists of instructions that a program can use to reconstruct a graphical image.

HPIB \H`P-I-B´\ *n.* Acronym for **H**ewlett-**P**ackard **I**nterface **B**us. *See* general-purpose interface bus.

HPPCL \H`P-P-C-L´\ *n.* Acronym for **H**ewlett-**P**ackard **P**rinter **C**ontrol **L**anguage. *See* Printer Control Language.

HP/UX or **HP-UX** \H`P-U-X´\ *n.* Acronym for **H**ewlett-**P**ackard **UNIX.** A version of the UNIX operating system specifically designed to be run on Hewlett-Packard's workstations. *See also* UNIX.

.hqx \dot`H-Q-X´\ *n.* A file extension for a file encoded with BinHex. *See also* BinHex.

.hr \dot`H-R´\ *n.* On the Internet, the major geographic domain specifying that an address is located in Croatia.

HREF \H´ref\ Short for **h**ypertext **ref**erence. An attribute in an HTML document that defines a link to another document on the Web. *See also* HTML.

HSB \H`S-B´\ *n.* Acronym for **h**ue-**s**aturation-**b**rightness. A color model in which hue is the color itself as placed on a color wheel, where 0° is red, 60° is yellow, 120° is green, 180° is cyan, 240° is blue, and 300° is magenta; saturation is the percentage of the specified hue in the color; and brightness is the percentage of white in the color. *Also called* HLS, HSV, hue. *See also* color model. *Compare* CMY, RGB.

HSV \H`S-V´\ *n.* Acronym for **h**ue-**s**aturation-**v**alue. *See* HSB.

H-sync \H´sēnk\ *n. See* horizontal synchronization.

.ht \dot`H-T´\ *n.* On the Internet, the major geographic domain specifying that an address is located in Haiti.

.htm \dot`H-T-M´\ *n.* The MS-DOS/Windows 3.*x* file extension that identifies Hypertext Markup Language (HTML) files, most commonly used as Web pages. Because MS-DOS and Windows 3.*x* cannot recognize file extensions longer than three letters, the .html extension is truncated to three letters in those environments. *See also* HTML.

.html \dot`H-T-M-L´\ *n.* The file extension that identifies Hypertext Markup Language (HTML) files, most commonly used as Web pages. *See also* HTML.

HTML \H`T-M-L´\ *n.* Acronym for **H**yper**t**ext **M**arkup **L**anguage. The markup language used for documents on the World Wide Web. HTML is an application of SGML that uses tags to mark elements, such as text and graphics, in a document to indicate how Web browsers should display these elements to the user and should respond to user actions such as activation of a link by means of a key press or mouse click. HTML 2.0, defined by the Internet Engineering Task Force (IETF), includes features of HTML common to all Web browsers as of 1995 and was the first version of HTML widely used on the World Wide Web. Future HTML development will be carried out by the World Wide Web Consortium (W3C). HTML 3.2, the latest proposed standard, incorporates features widely implemented as of early 1996. Most Web browsers, notably Netscape Navigator and Internet Explorer, recognize HTML tags beyond those included in the present standard. *See also* .htm, .html, SGML, tag (definition 3), Web browser.

HTML+ \H`T-M-L-plus´\ *n.* An unofficial specification for enhancements to the original HTML, such as forms and tables. HTML+ was not adopted as a standard but influenced the HTML 2.0 and HTML 3.2 standards. *See also* HTML.

HTML 2.0 \H`T-M-L` tōō`point-O´\ *n.* A revised version of the HTML specification that added the capability for forms and eliminated certain little-used tags. Produced as an Internet Draft in mid-1994, HTML 2.0 represented common practice among browser developers at the time. It was standardized as an RFC in November 1995. *See also* HTML, HTML 3.0, HTML 3.2, HTML+, RFC.

HTML 3.0 \H`T-M-L` thrē`point-O´\ *n.* A revised version of the HTML specification. Its primary enhancement to HTML 2.0 is the support of tables. HTML 3.0 was never standardized or fully implemented by a major browser developer. *See also* HTML, HTML 2.0, HTML 3.2, HTML+.

HTML 3.2 \H`T-M-L` thrē`point-tōō´\ *n.* A World Wide Web Consortium (W3C) recommendation for an HTML standard that supersedes the proposed HTML 3.0 standard and adds features to HTML 2.0 such as applets, sub- and superscripts, tables, and text flow around images. *See also* HTML, HTML 2.0, HTML 3.0.

HTML document \H`T-M-L` dok´yə-mənt\ *n.* **1.** A hypertext document that has been coded with HTML. **2.** *See* Web page.

HTML editor \H`T-M-L´ ed`ə-tər\ *n.* A software program used to create and modify HTML documents (Web pages). Most HTML editors include a method for inserting HTML tags without actually having to type out each tag. A number of HTML editors will also automatically reformat a document with HTML tags, based on formatting codes used by the word processing program in which the document was created. *See also* tag (definition 3), Web page.

HTML page \H`T-M-L´ pāj\ *n. See* Web page.

HTML tag \H`T-M-L´ tag`\ *n. See* tag (definition 3).

HTML validation service \H`T-M-L` val-ə-dā´shən sər`vis\ *n.* A service used to confirm that a Web page uses valid HTML according to the latest standard and/or that its hyperlinks are valid. An HTML validation service can catch small syntactical errors in HTML coding as well as deviations from the HTML standards. *See also* HTML.

HTTP \H`T-T-P´\ *n.* Acronym for **H**yper**t**ext **T**ransfer **P**rotocol. The client/server protocol used to access information on the World Wide Web. *See also* URL.

HTTPd \H`T-T-P-D´\ *n.* Short for **H**yper**t**ext **T**ransfer **P**rotocol **D**aemon. A small, fast HTTP server available free from NCSA. *See also* HTTP server, NCSA (definition 1).

HTTP Next Generation \H`T-T-P` nekst` jen`ər-ā´shən\ *n. See* HTTP-NG.

HTTP-NG \H`T-T-P`N-G´\ *n.* Acronym for **H**yper-**t**ext **T**ransfer **P**rotocol **N**ext **G**eneration. A standard under development by the World Wide Web Consortium (W3C) for improving performance and enabling the addition of features such as security. Whereas the current version of HTTP establishes a connection each time a request is made, HTTP-NG will set up one connection (which consists of separate channels for control information and data) for an entire session between a particular client and a particular server.

HTTPS \H`T-T-P-S´\ *n.* Web server software for Windows NT. Developed by the European Microsoft Windows NT Academic Centre (EMWAC) at the University of Edinburgh, Scotland, it is available for download from the Internet and offers such features as WAIS search capability. *See also* HTTP server, WAIS.

HTTP server \H`T-T-P´ sər`vər\ *n.* **1.** Server software that uses HTTP to serve up HTML documents and any associated files and scripts when requested by a client, such as a Web browser. The connection between client and server is usually broken after the requested document or file has been served. HTTP servers are used on Web and Intranet sites. *Also called* Web server. *See also* HTML, HTTP, server (definition 2). **2.** Any machine on which an HTTP server program is running.

HTTP status codes \H`T-T-P` stat´us kōdz`, stā´tus\ *n.* Three-digit codes sent by an HTTP server that indicate the results of a request for data. Codes beginning with 1 respond to requests that the client may not have finished sending; with 2, successful requests; with 3, further action that the client must take; with 4, requests that failed because of client error; and with 5, requests that failed because of server error. *See also* 400, 401, 402, 403, 404, HTTP.

.hu \dot`H-U´\ *n.* On the Internet, the major geographic domain specifying that an address is located in Hungary.

hub \hub\ *n.* In a network, a device joining communication lines at a central location, providing a common connection to all devices on the network. The term is an analogy to the hub of a wheel. *See also* active hub, switching hub.

hue \hyoō\ *n.* In the HSB color model, one of the three characteristics used to describe a color. Hue is the attribute that most readily distinguishes one color from other colors. It depends on the frequency of a light wave in the visible spectrum. *See also* color model, HSB. *Compare* brightness, saturation (definition 2).

Huffman coding \huf´mən kō`dēng\ *n.* A method of compressing a given set of data based on the relative frequency of the individual elements. The more often a given element, such as a letter, occurs, the shorter, in bits, is its corresponding code. It was one of the earliest data compression codes and, with modifications, remains one of the most widely used codes for a large variety of message types.

human engineering \hyoō`mən en-jə-nēr´ēng\ *n.* The designing of machines and associated products to suit the needs of humans. *See also* ergonomics.

human-machine interface \hyoō`mən-mə-shēn` in`tər-fās\ *n.* The boundary at which people make contact with and use machines; when applied to programs and operating systems, it is more widely known as the user interface.

hung \hung\ *adj. See* hang.

hybrid circuit \hī`brid sər`kət\ *n.* A circuit in which fundamentally different types of components are used to perform similar functions, such as a stereo amplifier that uses both tubes and transistors.

hybrid computer \hī`brid kəm-pyoō´tər\ *n.* A computer that contains both digital and analog circuits.

hybrid microcircuit \hī`brid mī´krō-sər-kət\ *n.* A microelectronic circuit that combines individual microminiaturized components and integrated components.

HyperCard \hī´pər-kärd`\ *n.* An information-management software tool, designed for the Apple Macintosh, that implements many hypertext concepts. A HyperCard document consists of a series of cards, collected into a stack. Each card can contain text, graphical images, sound, buttons that enable travel from card to card, and other controls. Programs and routines can be coded as scripts in an object-oriented language called HyperTalk or developed as external code resources (XCMDs and XFCNs). *See also* hypertext, object-oriented programming, XCMD, XFCN.

hyperlink \hī´pər-lēnk`\ *n*. A connection between an element in a hypertext document, such as a word, phrase, symbol, or image, and a different element in the document, another hypertext document, a file, or a script. The user activates the link by clicking on the linked element, which is usually underlined or in a color different from the rest of the document to indicate that the element is linked. Hyperlinks are indicated in a hypertext document through tags in markup languages such as SGML and HTML. These tags are generally not visible to the user. *Also called* hot link, hypertext link. *See also* anchor (definition 2), HTML, hypermedia, hypertext, URL.

hypermedia \hī´pər-mē`dē-ə\ *n*. The integration of any combination of text, graphics, sound, and video into a primarily associative system of information storage and retrieval in which users jump from subject to related subject in searching for information. Hypermedia attempts to offer a working and learning environment that parallels human thinking—that is, one in which the user can make associations between topics, rather than move sequentially from one to the next, as in an alphabetic list. For example, a hypermedia presentation on navigation might include links to astronomy, bird migration, geography, satellites, and radar. If the information is primarily in text form, it is regarded as hypertext; if video, music, animation, or other elements are included, the information is regarded as hypermedia. *See also* hypertext.

hyperspace \hī´pər-spās`\ *n*. The set of all documents that can be accessed by following hyperlinks in the World Wide Web. *Compare* cyber-space (definition 2), Gopherspace.

HyperTalk \hī´pər-täk\ *n*. The programming language used to manipulate HyperCard stacks. *See also* HyperCard.

hypertext \hī´pər-tekst\ *n*. Text linked together in a complex, nonsequential web of associations in which the user can browse through related topics. For example, in an article with the word *iron,* traveling among the links to *iron* might lead the user to the periodic table of the elements or a map of the migration of metallurgy in Iron Age Europe. The term *hypertext* was coined in 1965 to ¹escribe documents presented by a computer that express the nonlinear structure of ideas as opposed to the linear format of books, film, and speech. The term *hypermedia,* more recently introduced, is nearly synonymous but emphasizes the nontextual element, such as animation, recorded sound, and video. *See also* HyperCard, hypermedia.

hypertext link \hī´pər-tekst lēnk`\ *n. See* hyperlink.

Hypertext Markup Language \hī´pər-tekst märk´up lang`wəj\ *n. See* HTML.

Hypertext Transfer Protocol \hī´pər-tekst trans´fər prō`tə-kol\ *n. See* HTTP.

Hypertext Transfer Protocol Daemon \hī´pər-tekst trans`fər prō`tə-kol dē`mən\ *n. See* HTTPd.

Hypertext Transfer Protocol Next Generation \hī´pər-tekst trans`fər prō`tə-kol nekst` jen-ər-ā´shən\ *n. See* HTTP-NG.

HyperWave \hī´pər-wāv`\ *n*. A World Wide Web server that specializes in database manipulation and multimedia.

hyphen \hī´fən\ *n*. A punctuation mark (-) used to break a word between syllables at the end of a line or to separate the parts of a compound word. Word processing programs with sophisticated hyphenation capabilities recognize three types of hyphens: normal, optional, and nonbreaking. Normal hyphens, also called *required* or *hard hyphens,* are part of a word's spelling and are always visible, as in *long-term*. Optional hyphens, also called *discretionary* or *soft hyphens,* appear only when a word is broken between syllables at the end of a line; they are usually supplied by the word processing program itself. Nonbreaking hyphens are always visible, like normal hyphens, but they do not allow a line break. *See also* hyphenation program.

hyphenation program \hī-fə-nā´shən prō`gram\ *n*. A program (often included as part of a word processing application) that introduces optional hyphens at line breaks. A good hyphenation program will avoid ending more than three lines in a row with hyphens and will prompt the user for confirmation or tag ambiguous breaks, as in the word *desert* (did the army de-sert in the des-ert?). *See also* hyphen.

hysteresis \hī`stər-ē´sis\ *n*. The tendency of a system, a device, or a circuit to behave differently depending on the direction of change of an input parameter. For example, a household thermostat might turn on at 68 degrees when the house is cooling down, but turn off at 72 degrees when the house is warming up. Hysteresis is important in many devices, especially those employing magnetic fields, such as transformers and read/write heads.

HYTELNET \hī´tel´net, H´Y-tel´net\ *n.* A menu-driven index of Internet resources that are accessible via telnet, including library catalogs, databases and bibliographies, bulletin boards, and network information services. HYTELNET can operate through a client program on a computer connected to the Internet, or through the World Wide Web.

Hz \hərts\ *n.* Abbreviation for hertz.

I2O \I´too-O´\ *n.* Short for **I**ntelligent **I**nput/**O**utput. A specification for I/O device driver architecture that is independent of both the device being controlled and the host operating system. *See also* driver, input/output device.

i486DX \I´fōr-ā-tē-siks`D-X´\ *n.* An Intel microprocessor introduced in 1989. In addition to the features of the 80386 (32-bit registers, 32-bit data bus, and 32-bit addressing), the i486DX has a built-in cache controller, a built-in floating-point coprocessor, provisions for multiprocessing, and a pipelined execution scheme. *Also called* 486, 80486. *See also* pipelining (definition 1).

i486DX2 \I´fōr-ā-tē-siks`D-X-too´\ *n.* An Intel microprocessor introduced in 1992 as an upgrade to certain i486DX processors. The i486DX2 processes data and instructions at twice the system clock frequency. The increased operating speed leads to the generation of much more heat than in an i486DX, so a heat sink is often installed on the chip. *Also called* 486DX, 80486. *See also* heat sink, i486DX, microprocessor. *Compare* Over-Drive.

i486SL \I´fōr-ā-tē-siks`S-L´\ *n.* A low-power-consumption version of Intel's i486DX microprocessor designed primarily for laptop computers. The i486SL operates at a voltage of 3.3 volts rather than 5 volts, can shadow memory, and has a System Management Mode (SMM) in which the microprocessor can slow or halt some system components when the system is not performing CPU-intensive tasks, thus prolonging battery life. *See also* i486DX, shadow memory.

i486SX \I´fōr-ā-tē-siks`S-X´\ *n.* An Intel microprocessor introduced in 1991 as a lower-cost alternative to the i486DX. It runs at slower clock speeds and has no floating-point processor. *Also called* 486, 80486. *See also* 80386DX, 80386SX. *Compare* i486DX.

IAB \I´A-B´\ *See* Internet Architecture Board.

IAC \I´ak, I´A-C´\ Acronym for **I**nformation **A**nalysis **C**enter. One of several organizations chartered by the United States Department of Defense to facilitate the use of existing scientific and technical information. IACs establish and maintain comprehensive knowledge bases, including historical, technical, and scientific data, and also develop and maintain analytical tools and techniques for their use.

IANA \I´A-N-A´\ *See* Internet Assigned Numbers Authority.

I-beam \I´bēm\ *n.* A mouse cursor used by many applications, such as word processors, when in text-editing mode. The I-beam cursor indicates sections of the document where text can be inserted, deleted, changed, or moved. The cursor is named for its I shape. *Also called* I-beam pointer. *See also* cursor (definition 3), mouse.

I-beam pointer \I´bēm poin`tər\ *n. See* I-beam.

IBG \I´B-G´\ *n.* Acronym for **i**nter**b**lock **g**ap. *See* inter-record gap.

IBM AT \I-B-M` A-T´\ *n.* A class of personal computers introduced in 1984 and conforming to IBM's PC/AT (Advanced Technology) specification. The first AT was based on the Intel 80286 processor and dramatically outperformed its predecessor, the XT, in speed. *See also* 80286.

IBM PC \I-B-M` P-C´\ *n.* Short for **IBM P**ersonal **C**omputer. A class of personal computers introduced in 1981 and conforming to IBM's PC specification. The first PC was based on the Intel 8088 processor. For a number of years, the IBM PC was the de facto standard in the computing industry for PCs, and clones, or PCs that conformed to the IBM specification, have been called *PC-compatible*. See the illustration. *See also* PC-compatible, Wintel.

IBM PC-compatible \I-B-M` P-C`kəm-pat´ə-bl\ *adj. See* PC-compatible.

IC \I-C´\ *n. See* integrated circuit.

IBM PC.

I-CASE \I´kās, I´C-A-S-E`\ *n.* Acronym for **I**ntegrated **C**omputer-**A**ided **S**oftware **E**ngineering. Software that performs a wide variety of software engineering functions, such as program design, coding, and testing parts or all of the completed program.

ICM \I´C-M´\ *n. See* image color matching.

ICMP \I´C-M-P`\ *n.* Acronym for **I**nternet **C**ontrol **M**essage **P**rotocol. A network-layer (ISO/OSI level 3) Internet protocol that provides error correction and other information relevant to IP packet processing. For example, it can let the IP software on one machine inform another machine about an unreachable destination. *See also* communications protocol, IP, ISO/OSI model, packet (definition 1).

icon \ī´kon\ *n.* A small image displayed on the screen to represent an object that can be manipulated by the user. By serving as visual mnemonics and allowing the user to control certain computer actions without having to remember commands or type them at the keyboard, icons are a significant factor in the user-friendliness of graphical user interfaces. See the illustration. *See also* graphical user interface.

Recycle Bin

Icon.

iconic interface \ī-kon`ik in´tər-fās\ *n.* A user interface that is based on icons rather than on typed commands. *See also* graphical user interface, icon.

icon parade \ī´kon pər-ād`\ *n.* The sequence of icons that appears during the boot-up of a Macintosh computer.

.id \dot`I-D´\ *n.* On the Internet, the major geographic domain specifying that an address is located in Indonesia.

IDE \I´D-E´\ *n.* **1.** Acronym for **I**ntegrated **D**evice **E**lectronics. A type of disk-drive interface in which the controller electronics reside on the drive itself, eliminating the need for a separate adapter card. The IDE interface is compatible with the controller used by IBM in the PC/AT computer but offers advantages such as look-ahead caching. **2.** *See* integrated development environment.

identifier \ī-den´tə-fī`ər, ə-den´tə-fī`ər\ *n.* Any text string used as a label, such as the name of a procedure or a variable in a program or the name attached to a hard disk or floppy disk. *Compare* descriptor.

idle \ī´dl\ *adj.* **1.** Operational but not in use. **2.** Waiting for a command.

idle character \ī´dl kâr`ək-tər\ *n.* In communications, a control character transmitted when no other information is available or ready to be sent. *See also* SYN.

idle interrupt \ī´dl in`tər-upt\ *n.* An interrupt that occurs when a device or process becomes idle.

idle state \ī´dl stāt`\ *n.* The condition in which a device is operating but is not being used.

IDSL \I´D-S-L´\ *n.* Acronym for **I**nternet **d**igital **s**ubscriber **l**ine. A high-speed digital communications service that provides Internet access as fast as 1.1 Mbps (megabits per second) over standard telephone lines. IDSL uses a hybrid of ISDN and digital subscriber line technology. *See also* digital subscriber line, ISDN.

.ie \dot`I-E´\ *n.* On the Internet, the major geographic domain specifying that an address is located in Ireland.

IE \I-E´\ *n.* **1.** Acronym for **i**nformation **e**ngineering. A methodology for developing and maintaining information-processing systems, including computer systems and networks, within an organization. **2.** *See* Internet Explorer.

IEEE \I´E-E-E´, I´trip-l-E´\ *n.* Acronym for **I**nstitute of **E**lectrical and **E**lectronics **E**ngineers. An organization of engineering and electronics professionals notable for developing standards for hardware and software.

IEEE 488 \ΓE-E-E` fōr-āt-āt´, Γtrip-l-E´\ *n*. The electrical definition of the General-Purpose Interface Bus (GPIB), specifying the data and control lines and the voltage and current levels for the bus. *See also* General-Purpose Interface Bus.

IEEE 696/S-100 \ΓE-E-E` siks-nīn-siks`S`wən-hun´-drəd, Γtrip-l-E´\ *n*. The electrical definition of the S-100 bus, used in early personal computer systems that used microprocessors such as the 8080, Z-80, and 6800. The S-100 bus, based on the architecture of the Altair 8800, was extremely popular with early computer enthusiasts because it permitted a wide range of expansion boards. *See also* Altair 8800, S-100 bus.

IEEE 802 standards \ΓE-E-E` āt-ō-tōō´ stan`dərdz, Γtrip-l-E´\ *n*. A set of standards developed by the IEEE to define methods of access and control on local area networks. The IEEE 802 standards correspond to the physical and data-link layers of the ISO Open Systems Interconnection model, but they divide the data-link layer into two sublayers. The logical link control (LLC) sublayer applies to all IEEE 802 standards and covers station-to-station connections, generation of message frames, and error control. The media access control (MAC) sublayer, dealing with network access and collision detection, differs from one IEEE 802 standard to another: IEEE 802.3 is used for bus networks that use CSMA/CD, both broadband and baseband, and the baseband version is based on the Ethernet standard. IEEE 802.4 is used for bus networks that use token passing, and IEEE 802.5 is used for ring networks that use token passing (token ring networks). In addition, IEEE 802.6 is an emerging standard for metropolitan area networks, which transmit data, voice, and video over distances of more than five kilometers. See the illustration. *See also* bus network, ISO/OSI model, ring network, token passing, token ring network.

IEPG \ΓE-P-G´\ *n*. Acronym for **I**nternet **E**ngineering and **P**lanning **G**roup. A collaborative group of Internet service providers whose goal is to promote the Internet and coordinate technical efforts on it.

IESG \ΓE-S-G´\ *See* Internet Engineering Steering Group.

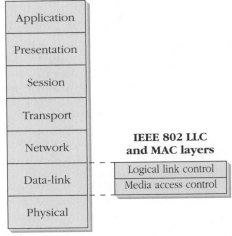

ISO/OSI model

| Application |
| Presentation |
| Session |
| Transport |
| Network |
| Data-link |
| Physical |

IEEE 802 LLC and MAC layers

| Logical link control |
| Media access control |

IEEE 802 standards. *ISO/OSI model with IEEE 802 LLC and MAC layers shown.*

IETF \ΓE-T-F´\ *n*. Acronym for **I**nternet **E**ngineering **T**ask **F**orce. The organization that is charged with studying technical problems facing the Internet and proposing solutions to the IAB. The IETF is managed by the IESG. *See also* Internet Engineering Steering Group.

.iff \dot`I-F-F´\ *n*. The file extension that identifies files in the IFF (Interchange File Format) format. IFF was most commonly used on the Amiga platform, where it constituted almost any kind of data. On other platforms, IFF is mostly used to store image and sound files.

IFF \ΓF-F´\ *n*. Acronym for **I**nterchange **F**ile Format. *See* .iff.

IFIP \Γfip, ΓF-I-P´\ *n*. Acronym for **I**nternational **F**ederation of **I**nformation **P**rocessing. An organization of societies, representing over 40 member nations, that serves information-processing professionals. The United States is represented by the Federation on Computing in the United States (FOCUS). *See also* AFIPS, FOCUS.

IFS \ΓF-S´\ *n*. *See* Installable File System Manager.

IF statement \if´ stāt`mənt\ *n*. A control statement that executes a block of code if a Boolean expression evaluates to true. Most programming languages also support an ELSE clause, which specifies code that is to be executed only if the

Boolean expression evaluates to false. *See also* conditional.

IGES \ΓG-E-S´\ *n.* *See* Initial Graphics Exchange Specification.

IGMP \ΓG-M-P´\ *See* Internet Group Membership Protocol.

IGP \ΓG-P´\ *n.* Acronym for **I**nterior **G**ateway **P**rotocol. A protocol that governs the transmission of routing information.

IGRP \ΓG-R-P´\ *n.* Acronym for **I**nterior **G**ateway **R**outing **P**rotocol. A protocol developed by Cisco Systems that allows coordination between the routing of a number of gateways. Goals of IGRP include stable routing in large networks, fast response to changes in network topology, and low overhead. *See also* communications protocol, gateway, topology.

IIL \ΓI-L´\ or **I²L** \Γtoo-L´\ *n.* *See* integrated injection logic.

IIS \ΓI-S´\ *See* Internet Information Server.

.il \dot`I-L´\ *n.* On the Internet, the major geographic domain specifying that an address is located in Israel.

illegal \i-lē´gəl\ *adj.* Not allowed, or leading to invalid results. For example, an illegal character in a word processing program would be one that the program cannot recognize; an illegal operation might be impossible for a program or system because of built-in constraints. *Compare* invalid.

illuminance \i-loo´mə-nəns`\ *n.* **1.** The amount of light falling on, or illuminating, a surface area. **2.** A measure of illumination (such as watts per square meter) used in reference to devices such as televisions and computer displays. *Compare* luminance.

.il.us \dot-I-L`dot-U-S´\ *n.* On the Internet, the major geographic domain specifying that an address is located in Illinois, United States.

.image \dot`im´əj\ *n.* A file extension for a Macintosh Disk Image, a storage type often used on Apple's FTP software download sites.

image \im´əj\ *n.* **1.** A stored description of a graphic picture, either as a set of brightness and color values of pixels or as a set of instructions for reproducing the picture. *See also* bit map, pixel map. **2.** A duplicate, copy, or representation of all or part of a hard or floppy disk, a section of memory or hard drive, a file, a program, or data. For example, a RAM disk can hold an image of all or part of a disk in main memory; a virtual RAM program can create an image of some portion of the computer's main memory on disk. *See also* RAM disk.

image color matching \im`əj kə´lər mach`ēng\ *n.* The process of image output correction to match the same colors as were scanned or input.

image compression \im´əj kəm-presh`ən\ *n.* The use of a data compression technique on a graphical image. Uncompressed graphics files tend to use up large amounts of storage, so image compression is useful to conserve space. *See also* compressed file, data compression, video compression.

image editing \im´əj ed`ə-tēng\ *n.* The process of changing or modifying a bitmapped image, usually with an image editor.

image editor \im´əj ed`ə-tər\ *n.* An application program that allows users to modify the appearance of a bitmapped image, such as scanned photos, by using filters and other functions. Creation of new images is generally accomplished in a paint or drawing program. *See also* bitmapped graphics, filter (definition 4), paint program.

image enhancement \im´əj en-hans`mənt\ *n.* The process of improving the quality of a graphic image, either automatically by software or manually by a user through a paint or drawing program. *See also* anti-aliasing, image processing.

image map \im´əj map`\ *n.* An image that contains more than one hyperlink on a Web page. Clicking on different parts of the image links the user to other resources on another part of the Web page, a different Web page, or a file. Often an image map, which can be a photograph, drawing, or a composite of several different drawings or photographs, is used as a map to the resources found on a particular Web site. Image maps are created with CGI scripts. *Also called* clickable maps. *See also* CGI script, hyperlink, Web page.

image processing \im´əj pros`es-ēng\ *n.* The analysis, manipulation, storage, and display of graphical images from sources such as photographs, drawings, and video. Image processing spans a sequence of three steps. The input step (image capture and digitizing) converts the differences in coloring and shading in the picture into binary values that a computer can process. The processing step can include image enhancement and data compression. The output step consists of the display or printing of the processed image. Image processing is used in such applications as television and film, medicine, satellite weather mapping, machine vision, and computer-based pattern recognition. *See also* image enhancement, video digitizer.

imagesetter \im´əj-set`ər\ *n.* A typesetting device that can transfer camera-ready text and artwork from computer files directly onto paper or film. Imagesetters print at high resolution (commonly above 1,000 dpi) and are usually PostScript-compatible.

imaginary number \i-maj`ə-nâr-ē num´bər\ *n.* A number that must be expressed as the product of a real number and i, where $i^2 = -1$. The sum of an imaginary number and a real number is a complex number. Although imaginary numbers are not directly encountered in the universe (as in "1.544i megabits per second"), some pairs of quantities, especially in electrical engineering, behave mathematically like the real and imaginary parts of complex numbers. *Compare* complex number, real number.

imaging \im´ə-jēng\ *n.* The processes involved in the capture, storage, display, and printing of graphical images.

IMAP4 \Ī´map-fōr´, Ī`M-A-P-fōr´\ *n.* Acronym for **I**nternet **M**essage **A**ccess **P**rotocol **4**. The latest version of IMAP, a method for an e-mail program to gain access to e-mail and bulletin-board messages stored on a mail server. Unlike POP, IMAP allows a user to retrieve messages efficiently from more than one computer. *See also* POP3, Post Office Protocol.

IMHO \Ī`M-H-O´\ Acronym for **i**n **m**y **h**umble **o**pinion. IMHO, used in e-mail and in online forums, flags a statement that the writer wants to present as a personal opinion rather than as a statement of fact.

Imitation Game \im-ə-tā´shən gām`\ *n. See* Turing test.

immediate access \i-mē`dē-ət ak´ses\ *n. See* direct access, random access.

immediate operand \i-mē`dē-ət op´ər-and\ *n.* A data value, used in the execution of an assembly language instruction, that is contained in the instruction itself rather than pointed to by an address in the instruction.

immediate printing \i-mē`dē-ət prin´tēng\ *n.* A process in which text and printing commands are sent directly to the printer without being stored as a printing file and without the use of an intermediate page-composition procedure or a file containing printer setup commands.

IMO \Ī`M-O´\ Acronym for **i**n **m**y **o**pinion. A shorthand phrase used often in e-mail and Internet news and discussion groups to indicate an author's admission that a statement he or she has just made is not strictly a fact.

impact printer \im´pakt prin`tər\ *n.* A printer, such as a wire-pin dot-matrix printer or a daisy-wheel printer, that drives an inked ribbon mechanically against the paper to form marks. *See also* daisy-wheel printer, dot-matrix printer. *Compare* nonimpact printer.

impedance \im-pē´dəns\ *n.* Opposition to the flow of alternating current. Impedance has two aspects: resistance, which impedes both direct and alternating current and is always greater than zero; and reactance, which impedes alternating current only, varies with frequency, and can be positive or negative.

import \im-pōrt´, im´pōrt\ *vb.* To bring information from one system or program into another. The system or program receiving the data must somehow support the internal format or structure of the data. Conventions such as the TIFF (Tagged Image File Format) and PICT formats (for graphics files) make importing easier. *See also* PICT, TIFF. *Compare* export.

.in \dot`I-N´\ *n.* On the Internet, the major geographic domain specifying that an address is located in India.

inactive window \in`ak-tiv win´dō, i-nak`tiv\ *n.* In an environment capable of displaying multiple on-screen windows, any window other than the one currently being used for work. An inactive window can be partially or entirely hidden behind another window, and it remains inactive until the user selects it. See the illustration. *Compare* active window.

in-band signaling \in`band sig´nə-lēng\ *n.* Transmission within the voice or data-handling frequencies of a communication channel.

Inactive window

Inactive window.

in-betweening \in`bə-twē´nēng\ *n. See* tween.

Inbox \in´boks\ *n.* In many e-mail applications, the default mailbox where the program stores incoming messages. *See also* e-mail, mailbox. *Compare* Outbox.

incident light \in´sə-dənt līt´\ *n.* The light that strikes a surface in computer graphics. *See also* illuminance.

INCLUDE directive \in-klood´ dər-ek`tiv\ *n.* A statement within a source-code file that causes another source-code file to be read in at that spot, either during compilation or during execution. It enables a programmer to break up a program into smaller files and enables multiple programs to use the same files.

inclusive OR \in-kloo`siv ōr´\ *n. See* OR.

increment[1] \in´krə-mənt\ *n.* A scalar or unit amount by which the value of an object such as a number, a pointer within an array, or a screen position designation is increased. *Compare* decrement[1].

increment[2] \in´krə-mənt\ *vb.* To increase a number by a given amount. For example, if a variable has the value 10 and is incremented successively by 2, it takes the values 12, 14, 16, 18, and so on. *Compare* decrement[2].

indent[1] \in-dent´\ *n.* **1.** Displacement of the left or right edge of a block of text in relation to the margin or to other blocks of text. **2.** Displacement of the beginning of the first line of a paragraph relative to the other lines in the paragraph. *Compare* hanging indent.

indent[2] \in-dent´\ *vb.* To displace the left or right edge of a text item, such as a block or a line, relative to the margin or to another text item.

independent content provider \in-də-pen`dənt kon´tent prə-vī`dər\ *n.* A business or organization that supplies information to an online information service, such as America Online, for resale to the information service's customers. *See also* online information service.

independent software vendor \in`də-pen`dənt soft´wâr ven`dər\ *n.* A third-party software developer; an individual or an organization that independently creates computer software. *Acronym:* ISV (Ī`S-V´).

index[1] \in´deks\ *n.* **1.** A listing of keywords and associated data that point to the location of more comprehensive information, such as files and records on a disk or record keys in a database. **2.** In programming, a scalar value that allows direct access into a multi-element data structure such as an array without the need for a sequential search through the collection of elements. *See also* array, element (definition 1), hash, list.

index[2] \in´deks\ *vb.* **1.** In data storage and retrieval, to create and use a list or table that contains reference information pointing to stored data. **2.** In a database, to find data by using keys such as words or field names to locate records. **3.** In indexed file storage, to find files stored on disk by using an index of file locations (addresses). **4.** In programming and information processing, to locate information stored in a table by adding an offset amount, called the index, to the base address of the table.

indexed address \in`deksd a´dres, ə-dres´\ *n.* The location in memory of a particular item of data within a collection of items, such as an entry in a table. An indexed address is calculated by starting with a base address and adding to it a value stored in a register called an index register.

indexed search \in`deksd sərch´\ *n.* A search for an item of data that uses an index to reduce the amount of time required.

indexed sequential access method \in`deksd si-kwen`shəl ak´ses meth`əd\ *n.* A scheme for decreasing the time necessary to locate a data record within a large database, given a key value that identifies the record. A smaller index file is used to store the keys along with pointers that locate the corresponding records in the large main database file. Given a key, first the index file is searched for the key and then the associated pointer is used to access the remaining data of the record in the main file. *Acronym:* ISAM (Iʹ-S-A-Mʹ, Iʹsam).

index hole \inʹdeks hōl`\ *n.* The small round hole near the large round spindle opening at the center of a 5.25-inch floppy disk. The index hole marks the location of the first data sector, enabling a computer to synchronize its read/write operations with the disk's rotation. See the illustration.

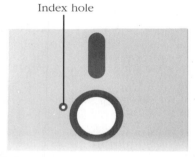

Index hole

Index hole.

index mark \inʹdeks märk`\ *n.* **1.** A magnetic indicator signal placed on a soft-sectored disk during formatting to mark the logical start of each track. **2.** A visual information locator, such as a line, on a microfiche.

indicator \inʹdə-kā`tər\ *n.* A dial or light that displays information about the status of a device, such as a light connected to a disk drive that glows when the disk is being accessed.

indirect address \in`dər-ekt aʹdres, ə-dresʹ\ *n.* *See* relative address.

inductance \in-dukʹtəns\ *n.* The ability to store energy in the form of a magnetic field. Any length of wire has some inductance, and coiling the wire, especially around a ferromagnetic core, increases the inductance. The unit of inductance is the henry. *Compare* capacitance, induction.

induction \in-dukʹshən\ *n.* The creation of a voltage or current in a material by means of electric or magnetic fields, as in the secondary winding of a transformer when exposed to the changing magnetic field caused by an alternating current in the primary winding. *See also* impedance. *Compare* inductance.

inductor \in-dukʹtər\ *n.* A component designed to have a specific amount of inductance. An inductor

passes direct current but impedes alternating current to a degree dependent on its frequency. An inductor usually consists of a length of wire coiled in a cylindrical or toroidal (doughnut-shaped) form, sometimes with a ferromagnetic core. See the illustration. *Also called* choke.

Inductor.   *One of several kinds of inductors.*

Industry Standard Architecture \in`dus-trē stan`dərd ar`kə-tek-chur\ *n. See* ISA.

INET \Iʹnet, Iʹ-N-E-Tʹ\ *n.* **1.** Short for **Internet. 2.** An annual conference held by the Internet Society.

.inf \dot-infʹ, dot`I-N-Fʹ\ *n.* The file extension for device information files, files containing scripts used to control hardware operations.

infection \in-fekʹshən\ *n.* The presence of a virus or Trojan horse in a computer system. *See also* Trojan horse, virus, worm.

infer \in-fərʹ\ *vb.* To formulate a conclusion based on specific information, either by applying the rules of formal logic or by generalizing from a set of observations. For example, from the facts that birds have feathers and that canaries are birds, one can infer (draw the inference) that canaries have feathers.

inference engine \inʹfər-əns en`jən\ *n.* The processing portion of an expert system. It matches input propositions with facts and rules contained in a knowledge base and then derives a conclusion, on which the expert system then acts.

inference programming \inʹfər-əns prō`gram-ēng\ *n.* A method of programming (as in Prolog) in which programs yield results based on logical inference from a set of facts and rules. *See also* Prolog.

infinite loop \in`fə-nət lōōpʹ\ *n.* **1.** A loop that, because of semantic or logic errors, can never terminate through normal means. **2.** A loop that is intentionally written with no explicit termination condition but will terminate as a result of side effects or direct intervention. *See also* loop[1] (definition 1), side effect.

infix notation \in´fiks nō-tā`shən\ *n.* A notation, used for writing expressions, in which binary operators appear between their arguments, as in 2 + 4. Unary operators usually appear before their arguments, as in −1. *See also* operator precedence, postfix notation, prefix notation, unary operator.

infobahn \in´fō-bän`\ *n.* The Internet. *Infobahn* is a mixture of the terms *information* and *Autobahn,* a German highway known for the high speeds at which drivers can legally travel. *Also called* Information Highway, Information Superhighway, the Net.

information \in`fər-mā´shən\ *n.* The meaning of data as it is intended to be interpreted by people. Data consists of facts, which become information when they are seen in context and convey meaning to people. Computers process data without any understanding of what the data represents.

Information Analysis Center \in-fər-mā`shən ə-nal´ə-sis sen`tər\ *n. See* IAC.

information center \in-fər-mā`shən sen`tər\ *n.* **1.** A large computer center and its associated offices; the hub of an information management and dispersal facility in an organization. **2.** A specialized type of computer system dedicated to information retrieval and decision-support functions. The information in such a system is usually read-only and consists of data extracted or downloaded from other production systems.

information engineering \in-fər-mā`shən en-jə-nēr´ēng\ *n. See* IE (definition 1).

information explosion \in-fər-mā´shən eks-plō`-zhən\ *n.* **1.** The current period in human history, in which the possession and dissemination of information has supplanted mechanization or industrialization as a driving force in society. **2.** The rapid growth in the amount of information available today. *Also called* information revolution.

information hiding \in-fər-mā´shən hī`dēng\ *n.* A design practice in which implementation details for both data structures and algorithms within a module or subroutine are hidden from routines using that module or subroutine, so as to ensure that those routines do not depend on some particular detail of the implementation. In theory, information hiding allows the module or subroutine to be changed without breaking the routines that use it. *See also* break, module, routine, subroutine.

Information Highway or **information highway** \in`fər-mā-shən hī´wā\ *n. See* Information Superhighway.

information kiosk \in`fər-mā´shən kē`osk\ *n. See* kiosk.

information management \in-fər-mā´shən man´-əj-mənt\ *n.* The process of defining, evaluating, safeguarding, and distributing data within an organization or a system.

information packet \in`fər-mā´shən pak`ət\ *n. See* packet.

information processing \in-fər-mā`shən pros´es-ēng\ *n.* The acquisition, storage, manipulation, and presentation of data, particularly by electronic means.

information resource management \in-fər-mā`-shən rē´sōrs man`əj-mənt\ *n.* The process of managing the resources for the collection, storage, and manipulation of data within an organization or system.

information retrieval \in-fər-mā`shən rē-trē´vəl\ *n.* The process of finding, organizing, and displaying information, particularly by electronic means.

information revolution \in-fər-mā`shən rev-ə-loo`shən\ *n. See* information explosion.

information science \in-fər-mā`shən sī´əns\ *n.* The study of how information is collected, organized, handled, and communicated. *See also* information theory.

Information Services \in`fər-mā-shən sər´və-sez\ *n.* The formal name for a company's data processing department. *Acronym:* IS (I-S´). *Also called* Data Processing, Information Processing, Information Systems, Information Technology, Management Information Services, Management Information Systems.

Information Superhighway \in-fər-mā`shən soo´-pər-hī`wā\ *n.* The existing Internet and its general infrastructure, including private networks, online services, and so on. *See also* National Information Infrastructure.

Information Systems \in-fər-mā`shən si´stəmz\ *n. See* Information Services.

Information Technology \in-fər-mā`shən   tek-nol´ə-jē\ *n. See* Information Services.

information theory \in-fər-mā´shən thēr`ē, thē`-ə-rē\ *n.* A mathematical discipline founded in 1948 that deals with the characteristics and the transmission of information. Information theory was originally applied to communications engineering but has proved relevant to other fields, including computing. It focuses on such aspects of communication as amount of data, transmission rate, channel capacity, and accuracy of transmission, whether over cables or within society.

information warehouse \in`fər-mā`shən wâr´-hous\ *n.* The total of an organization's data resources on all computers.

information warfare \in`fər-mā`shən wōr`fâr\ *n.* Attacks on the computer operations on which an enemy country's economic life or safety depends. Possible examples of information warfare include crashing air traffic control systems or massively corrupting stock exchange records.

infrared \in`frə-red´\ *adj.* Having a frequency in the electromagnetic spectrum in the range just below that of red light. Objects radiate infrared in proportion to their temperature. Infrared radiation is traditionally divided into four somewhat arbitrary categories based on its wavelength. *Acronym:* IR (I-R´).

near infrared	750–1,500 nanometers (nm)
middle infrared	1,500–6,000 nm
far infrared	6,000–40,000 nm
far-far infrared	40,000 nm–1 millimeter (mm)

Infrared Data Association \in`frə-red` dā`tə ə-sō-sē-ā`shən, dat´ə\ *n.* The industry organization of computer, component, and telecommunications vendors who have established the standards for infrared communication between computers and peripheral devices such as printers. *Acronym:* IrDA (ər´də, I`R-D-A´).

infrared port \in`frə-red´ pōrt\ *n.* An optical port on a computer for interfacing with an infrared-capable device. Communication is achieved without physical connection through cables. Currently, the devices must be only a few feet apart, and the ports aligned with one another for communication to occur. Infrared ports can be found on some lap-tops, notebooks, and printers. *See also* cable, infrared, input/output port.

inherent error \in-hâr`ənt âr´ər\ *n.* An error in assumptions, design, logic, algorithms, or any combination thereof that causes a program to work improperly, regardless of how well written it is. For example, a serial communications program that is written to use a parallel port contains an inherent error. *See also* logic, semantics (definition 1), syntax.

inherit \in-hâr´ət\ *vb.* To acquire the characteristics of another class, in object-oriented programming. The inherited characteristics may be enhanced, restricted, or modified. *See also* class.

inheritance \in-hâr´ət-əns\ *n.* **1.** The transfer of the characteristics of a class in object-oriented programming to other classes derived from it. For example, if "vegetable" is a class, the classes "legume" and "root" can be derived from it, and each will inherit the properties of the "vegetable" class: name, growing season, and so on. *See also* class, object-oriented programming. **2.** The transfer of certain properties, such as open files, from a parent program or process to another program or process that the parent causes to run. *See also* child (definition 1).

inheritance code \in-hâr´ə-təns kōd`\ *n.* A set of structural and procedural attributes belonging to an object that have been passed on to it by the class or object from which it was derived. *See also* object-oriented programming.

inhibit \in-hib´it\ *vb.* To prevent an occurrence. For example, to inhibit interrupts from an external device means to prevent the external device from sending any interrupts.

.ini \dot-I`N-I´\ *n.* In DOS and Windows 3.*x*, the file extension that identifies an initialization file, which contains user preferences and startup information about an application program.

INIT \i-nit´\ *n.* On older Macintosh computers, a system extension that is loaded into memory at startup time. *See also* extension (definition 4). *Compare* cdev.

Initial Graphics Exchange Specification \ə-nish`əl graf`iks eks-chānj´ spes-ə-fə-kā`shən\ *n.* A standard file format for computer graphics, supported by the American National Standards Institute (ANSI), that is particularly suitable for describing models created with computer-aided design (CAD) programs. It includes a wide variety of basic geometric forms (primitives) and, in keeping with CAD objectives, offers methods for describing and annotating drawings and engineering diagrams. *Acronym:* IGES (Ī´G-E-S´). *See also* ANSI.

initialization \ə-nish`ə-lə-zā´shən\ *n.* The process of assigning initial values to variables and data structures in a program.

initialization string \i-nish´əl-ə-zā´shən strēng`\ *n.* A sequence of commands sent to a device, especially a modem, to configure it and prepare it for use. In the case of a modem, the initialization string consists of a string of characters.

initialize \ə-nish´ə-līz`\ *vb.* **1.** To prepare a storage medium, such as a disk or a tape, for use. This may involve testing the medium's surface, writing startup information, and setting up the file system's index to storage locations. **2.** To assign a beginning value to a variable. **3.** To start up a computer. *See also* cold boot, startup.

initializer \ə-nish´ə-lī`zər\ *n.* An expression whose value is the first (initial) value of a variable. *See also* expression.

initial program load \ə-nish`əl prō´gram lōd`\ *n.* The process of copying an operating system into memory when a system is booted. *Acronym:* IPL (Ī´-P-L´). *See also* boot, startup.

initiator \ə-nish´ē-ā`tər\ *n.* The device in a SCSI connection that issues commands. The device that receives the commands is the target. *See also* SCSI, target.

ink cartridge \ēnk´ kär`trij\ *n.* A disposable module that contains ink and is typically used in an ink-jet printer. *See also* ink-jet printer.

ink-jet printer \ēnk´jet prin`tər\ *n.* A nonimpact printer in which liquid ink is vibrated or heated into a mist and sprayed through tiny holes in the print head to form characters or graphics on the paper. Ink-jet printers are competitive with some laser printers in price and print quality if not in speed. However, the ink, which must be highly soluble to avoid clogging the nozzles in the print head, produces fuzzy-looking output on some papers and smears if touched or dampened shortly after printing. *See also* nonimpact printer, print head.

inline \in`līn\ *adj.* **1.** In programming, referring to a function call replaced with an instance of the function's body. Actual arguments are substituted for formal parameters. An inline function is usually done as a compile-time transformation to increase the efficiency of the program. *Also called* unfold, unroll. **2.** In HTML code, referring to graphics displayed along with HTML-formatted text. Inline images placed in the line of HTML text use the tag <IMG>. Text within an inline image can be aligned to the top, bottom, or middle of a specific image.

inline code \in`līn kōd´\ *n.* Assembly language or machine language instructions embedded within high-level source code. The form it takes varies considerably from compiler to compiler, if it is supported at all.

inline graphics \in`līn graf´iks\ *n.* Graphics files that are embedded in an HTML document or Web page and viewable by a Web browser or other program that recognizes HTML. By avoiding the need for separate file opening operations, inline graphics can speed the access and loading of an HTML document. *Also called* inline image.

inline image \in`līn im´əj\ *n.* An image that is embedded within the text of a document. Inline images are common on Web pages. *See also* inline graphics.

inline processing \in`līn pros´es-ēng\ *n.* Operation on a segment of low-level program code, called inline code, to optimize execution speed or storage requirements. *See also* inline code.

inline subroutine \in`līn sub´rōō-tēn\ *n.* A subroutine whose code is copied at each place in a program at which it is called, rather than kept in one place to which execution is transferred. Inline subroutines improve execution speed, but they also increase code size. Inline subroutines obey the same syntactical and semantic rules as ordinary subroutines.

inner join \in`ər join´\ *n.* An operator in relational algebra, often implemented in database management. The inner join produces a relation (table) that contains all possible ordered concatenations (joinings) of records from two existing tables that meet certain specified criteria on the data values. It is thus equivalent to a product followed by a select applied to the resulting table. *Compare* outer join.

inoculate \i-no´kyə-lāt`\ *vb.* To protect a program against virus infection by recording characteristic information about it. For example, checksums on the code can be recomputed and compared with the stored original checksums each time the program is run; if any have changed, the program file is corrupt and may be infected. *See also* checksum, virus.

input[1] \in´pŏŏt\ *n.* Information entered into a computer or program for processing, as from a keyboard or from a file stored on a disk drive.

input[2] \in´pŏŏt\ *vb.* To enter information into a computer for processing.

input area \in´pŏŏt âr`ē-ə\ *n. See* input buffer.

input-bound \in´pŏŏt-bound`\ *adj. See* input/output-bound.

input buffer \in´pŏŏt buf`ər\ *n.* A portion of computer memory set aside for temporary storage of information arriving for processing. *See also* buffer[1].

input channel \in´pŏŏt chan`əl\ *n. See* input/output channel.

input device \in´put də-vīs`\ *n.* A peripheral device whose purpose is to allow the user to give input to a computer system. Examples of input devices are keyboards, mice, joysticks, and styluses. *See also* peripheral.

input driver \in´pŏŏt drī`vər\ *n. See* device driver.

input/output \in`pŏŏt-out´pŏŏt\ *n.* The complementary tasks of gathering data for a computer or a program to work with, and of making the results of the computer's activities available to the user or to other computer processes. Gathering data is usually done with input devices such as the keyboard and the mouse, as well as disk files, while the output is usually made available to the user via the display and the printer and via disk files or communications ports for the computer. *Acronym:* I/O (I-O´).

input/output area \in`pŏŏt-out´pŏŏt âr`ē-ə\ *n. See* input/output buffer.

input/output-bound \in`pŏŏt-out´pŏŏt-bound`\ *adj.* Characterized by the need to spend lengthy amounts of time waiting for input and output of data that is processed much more rapidly. For example, if the processor is capable of making rapid changes to a large database stored on a disk faster than the drive mechanism can perform the read and write operations, the computer is input/output-bound. A computer may be simply input-

bound or output-bound if only input or only output limits the speed at which the processor accepts and processes data. *Also called* I/O-bound.

input/output buffer \in`pŏŏt-out´pŏŏt buf`ər\ *n.* A portion of computer memory reserved for temporary storage of incoming and outgoing data. Because input/output devices can often write to a buffer without intervention from the CPU, a program can continue execution while the buffer fills, thus speeding program execution. *See also* buffer[1].

input/output bus \in`pŏŏt-out´pŏŏt bus`\ *n.* A hardware path used inside a computer for transferring information to and from the processor and various input and output devices. *See also* bus.

input/output channel \in`pŏŏt-out´pŏŏt chan`əl\ *n.* A hardware path from the CPU to the input/output bus. *See also* bus.

input/output controller \in`pŏŏt-out´pŏŏt kən-trō`lər\ *n.* Circuitry that monitors operations and performs tasks related to receiving input and transferring output at an input or output device or port, thus providing the processor with a consistent means of communication (input/output interface) with the device and also freeing the processor's time for other work. For example, when a read or write operation is performed on a disk, the drive's controller carries out the high-speed, electronically sophisticated tasks involved in positioning the read-write heads, locating specific storage areas on the spinning disk, reading from and writing to the disk surface, and even checking for errors. Most controllers require software that enables the computer to receive and process the data the controller makes available. *Also called* device controller, I/O controller.

input/output device \in`pŏŏt-out´pŏŏt də-vīs`\ *n.* A piece of hardware that can be used both for providing data to a computer and for receiving data from it, depending on the current situation. A disk drive is an example of an input/output device. Some devices, such as a keyboard or a mouse, can be used only for input and are also called input devices. Other devices, such as printers, can be used only for output and are also called output devices. Most devices require installation of software routines called device drivers to enable the computer to transmit and receive data to and from them.

input/output interface \in`poot-out`poot in´tər-fās\ *n. See* input/output controller.

input/output port \in`poot-out´poot pōrt`\ *n.* A channel through which data is transferred between an input or output device and the processor. The port appears to the CPU as one or more memory addresses that it can use to send or receive data. Specialized hardware, such as in an add-on circuit board, places data from the device in the memory addresses and sends data from the memory addresses to the device. Ports may also be dedicated solely to input or to output.

input/output processor \in`poot-out´poot pros`-es-ər\ *n.* Hardware designed to handle input and output operations to relieve the burden on the main processing unit. For example, a digital signal processor can perform time-intensive, complicated analysis and synthesis of sound patterns without CPU overhead. *See also* front-end processor (definition 1).

input/output statement \in`poot-out´poot stāt`-mənt\ *n.* A program instruction that causes data to be transferred between memory and an input or output device.

input port \in´poot pōrt`\ *n. See* input/output port.

input stream \in´poot strēm`\ *n.* A flow of information used in a program as a sequence of bytes that are associated with a particular task or destination. Input streams include series of characters read from the keyboard to memory and blocks of data read from disk files. *Compare* output stream.

inquiry \in´kwər-ē\ *n.* A request for information. *See also* query.

INS \Ī`N-S´\ *n. See* WINS.

insertion point \in-sər´shən point`\ *n.* A blinking vertical bar on the screen, such as in graphical user interfaces, that marks the location at which inserted text will appear. *See also* cursor (definition 1).

insertion sort \in-sər´shən sōrt`\ *n.* A list-sorting algorithm that starts with a list that contains one item and builds an ever-larger sorted list by inserting the items to be sorted one at a time into their correct positions on that list. Insertion sorts are inefficient when used with arrays, because of constant shuffling of items, but are ideally suited for sorting linked lists. *See also* sort algorithm. *Compare* bubble sort, quicksort.

Insert key \in´sərt kē`\ *n.* A key on the keyboard, labeled "Insert" or "Ins," whose usual function is to toggle a program's editing setting between an insert mode and an overwrite mode, although it may perform different functions in different applications. *Also called* Ins key.

insert mode \in´sərt mōd`\ *n.* A mode of operation in which a character typed into a document or at a command line pushes subsequent existing characters further to the right on the screen rather than overwriting them. Insert mode is the opposite of overwrite mode, in which new characters replace subsequent existing characters. The key or key combination used to change from one mode to the other varies among programs, but the Insert key is most often used. *Compare* overwrite mode.

Ins key \in´sərt kē`\ *n. See* Insert key.

install \in-stäl´\ *vb.* **1.** To set in place and prepare for operation. Operating systems and application programs commonly include a disk-based installation program that does most of the work of setting up the program to work with the computer, printer, and other devices. Often such a program can check for devices attached to the system, request the user to choose from sets of options, create a place for the program on the hard disk, and modify system startup files as necessary. **2.** To transfer one of a limited number of copies of a program to a disk from a copy-protected program disk; a special procedure is needed because the normal method of copying the program has been disabled.

installable device driver \in-stäl`ə-bl də-vīs´ drī`-vər\ *n.* A device driver that can be embedded within an operating system, usually in order to override an existing, less-functional service.

Installable File System Manager \in-stä`lə-bl fīl´ si-stəm man`ə-jər\ *n.* In Windows 95, the part of the file system architecture responsible for arbitrating access to the different file system components. *Acronym:* IFS (Ī`F-S´).

installation program \in`stə-lā´shən prō`gram\ *n.* A program whose function is to install another program, either on a storage medium or in memory. An installation program might be used to guide a user through the often complex process of setting up an application for a particular combination of machine, printer, and monitor. Installation programs are necessary for copy-protected applications, which cannot be copied by normal operating-system commands. They typically limit the number of copies that can be installed.

Installer \in-stä´lər\ *n*. A program, provided with the Apple Macintosh operating system, that allows the user to install system upgrades and make bootable (system) disks.

instance \in´stəns\ *n*. An object, in object-oriented programming, in relation to the class to which it belongs. For example, an object *myList* that belongs to a class *List* is an instance of the class *List*. *See also* class, instance variable, instantiate, object (definition 2).

instance variable \in´stəns vâr`ē-ə-bl\ *n*. A variable associated with an instance of a class (an object). If a class defines a certain variable, each instance of the class has its own copy of that variable. *See also* class, instance, object (definition 2), object-oriented programming.

instantiate \in-stan´shē-āt\ *vb*. To create an instance of a class. *See also* class, instance, object (definition 2).

instruction \in-struk´shən\ *n*. An action statement in any computer language, most often in machine or assembly language. Most programs consist of two types of statements: declarations and instructions. *See also* declaration, statement.

instruction code \in-struk´shən kōd`\ *n*. *See* operation code.

instruction counter \in-struk´shən coun`tər\ *n*. *See* instruction register.

instruction cycle \in-struk´shən sī`kl\ *n*. The cycle in which a processor retrieves an instruction from memory, decodes it, and carries it out. The time required for an instruction cycle is the sum of the instruction (fetch) time and the execution (translate and execute) time and is measured by the number of clock ticks (pulses of a processor's internal timer) consumed.

instruction mix \in-struk´shən miks`\ *n*. The assortment of types of instructions contained in a program, such as assignment instructions, mathematical instructions (floating-point or integer), control instructions, and indexing instructions. Knowledge of instruction mixes is important to designers of CPUs because it tells them which instructions should be shortened to yield the great-

est speed, and to designers of benchmarks because it enables them to make the benchmarks relevant to real tasks.

instruction pointer \in-struk´shən poin`tər\ *n*. *See* program counter.

instruction register \in-struk´shən rej`ə-stər\ *n*. A register in a central processing unit that holds the address of the next instruction to be executed.

instruction set \in-struk´shən set`\ *n*. The set of machine instructions that a processor recognizes and can execute. *See also* assembler, microcode.

instruction time \in-struk´shən tīm`\ *n*. The number of clock ticks (pulses of a computer's internal timer) required to retrieve an instruction from memory. Instruction time is the first part of an instruction cycle; the second part is the execution (translate and execute) time. *Also called* I-time.

instruction word \in-struk´shən wərd`\ *n*. **1.** The length of a machine language instruction. **2.** A machine language instruction containing an operation code identifying the type of instruction, possibly one or more operands specifying data to be affected or its address, and possibly bits used for indexing or other purposes. *See also* assembler, machine code.

insulator \in´sə-lā`tər\ *n*. **1.** Any material that is a very poor conductor of electricity, such as rubber, glass, or ceramic. *Also called* nonconductor. *Compare* conductor, semiconductor. **2.** A device used to separate elements of electrical circuits and prevent current from taking unwanted paths, such as the stacks of ceramic disks that suspend high-voltage power lines from transmission towers.

integer \in´tə-jər\ *n*. **1.** A positive or negative "whole" number, such as 37, −50, or 764. **2.** A data type representing whole numbers. Calculations involving only integers are much faster than calculations involving floating-point numbers, so integers are widely used in programming for counting and numbering purposes. Integers can be signed (positive or negative) or unsigned (positive). They can also be described as long or short, depending on the number of bytes needed to store them. Short integers cover a smaller range of numbers (for example, −32,768 through 32,767) than do long integers (for example, −2,147,483,648 through 2,147,483,647). *Also called* integral number. *See also* floating-point notation.

integral modem \in`tə-grəl mō´dəm\ *n*. A modem that is built into a computer, as opposed to an internal modem, which is a modem on an expansion card that can be removed. *See also* external modem, internal modem, modem.

integral number \in`tə-grəl num`bər\ *n*. *See* integer (definition 2).

integrated circuit \in`tə-grā-təd sər`kət\ *n*. A device consisting of a number of connected circuit elements, such as transistors and resistors, fabricated on a single chip of silicon crystal or other semiconductor material. Integrated circuits are categorized by the number of elements they contain. *Acronym:* IC (I-C´). *Also called* chip. *See also* central processing unit.

small-scale integration (SSI)	fewer than 10
medium-scale integration (MSI)	10–100
large-scale integration (LSI)	100–5,000
very-large-scale integration (VLSI)	5,000–50,000
super-large-scale integration (SLSI)	50,000–100,000
ultra-large-scale integration (ULSI)	more than 100,000

integrated development environment \in`tə-grā-təd də-vel´əp-mənt en-vīr`ən-mənt, en-vī´ərn-mənt\ *n*. A set of integrated tools for developing software. The tools are generally run from one user interface and consist of a compiler, an editor, and a debugger, among others. *Acronym:* IDE (I`D-E´).

Integrated Device Electronics \in`tə-grā-təd də-vīs` ə-lek-tron´iks\ *n*. *See* IDE (definition 1).

integrated injection logic \in`tə-grā-təd in-jek´-shən lo`ik\ *n*. A type of circuit design that uses both NPN and PNP transistors and does not require other components, such as resistors. Such circuits are moderately fast, consume little power, and can be manufactured in very small sizes. *Acronym:* I²L (I`t$\overline{oo}$-L´), IIL (I`I-L´). *Also called* merged transistor logic. *See also* NPN transistor, PNP transistor.

Integrated Services Digital Network \in`tə-grā-təd sər`və-səz dij`ə-təl net´wərk\ *n*. *See* ISDN.

integrated software \in`tə-grā-təd soft´wâr\ *n*. A program that combines several applications, such as word processing, database management, and spreadsheets, in a single package. Such software

is "integrated" in two ways: it can transfer data from one of its applications to another, helping users coordinate tasks and merge information created with the different software tools; and it provides the user with a consistent interface for choosing commands, managing files, and otherwise interacting with the programs so that the user will not have to master several, often very different, programs. The applications in an integrated software package are often not, however, designed to offer as much capability as single applications, nor does integrated software necessarily include all the applications needed in a particular environment.

integration \in`tə-grā´shən\ *n*. **1.** In computing, the combining of different activities, programs, or hardware components into a functional unit. *See also* integral modem, integrated software, ISDN. **2.** In electronics, the process of packing multiple electronic circuit elements on a single chip. *See also* integrated circuit. **3.** In mathematics, specifically calculus, a procedure performed on an equation and related to finding the area under a given curve or the volume within a given shape.

integrator \in`tə-grā`tər\ *n*. A circuit whose output represents the integral, with respect to time, of the input signal—that is, its total accumulated value over time. See the illustration. *Compare* differentiator.

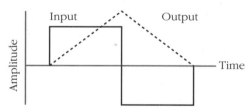

Integrator. ***An example of the action of an integrator circuit.***

integrity \in-te´grə-tē\ *n*. The completeness and accuracy of data stored in a computer, especially after it has been manipulated in some way. *See also* data integrity.

intelligence \in-tel´ə-jəns\ *n*. **1.** The ability of hardware to process information. A device without intelligence is said to be dumb; for example, a dumb terminal connected to a computer can receive input and display output but cannot process information independently. **2.** The ability of a program to monitor its environment and initiate appropriate actions to achieve a desired state. For example, a program waiting for data to be read from disk might switch to another task in the meantime. **3.** The ability of a program to simulate human thought. *See also* artificial intelligence. **4.** The ability of a machine such as a robot to respond appropriately to changing stimuli (input).

intelligent \in`tel´ə-jənt\ *adj.* Of, pertaining to, or characteristic of a device partially or totally controlled by one or more processors integral to the device.

intelligent agent \in-tel`ə-jənt ā´jənt\ *n. See* agent (definition 2).

intelligent cable \in-tel`ə-jənt kā´bl\ *n.* A cable that incorporates circuitry to do more than simply pass signals from one end of the cable to the other, such as to determine the characteristics of the connector into which it is plugged. *Also called* smart cable.

intelligent database \in-tel`ə-jənt dā´tə-bās\ *n.* A database that manipulates stored information in a way that people find logical, natural, and easy to use. An intelligent database conducts searches relying not only on traditional data-finding routines but also on predetermined rules governing associations, relationships, and even inferences regarding the data. *See also* database.

Intelligent Input/Output \in-tel`ə-jənt in`pōot out´pōot\ *n. See* I2O.

intelligent terminal \in-tel`ə-jənt tər´mə-nəl\ *n.* A terminal with its own memory, processor, and firmware that can perform certain functions independent of its host computer, most often the rerouting of incoming data to a printer or video screen.

Intelligent Transportation Infrastructure \in-tel`ə-jənt trans-pər-tā`shən in`frə-struk´chur\ *n.* A system of automated urban and suburban highway and mass transit control and management services proposed in 1996 by U.S. Secretary of Transportation Federico Peña. *Acronym:* ITI (I´T-I´).

Intensity Red Green Blue \in-ten`sə-tē red` grēn blōō´\ *n. See* IRGB.

interactive \in`tər-ak´tiv\ *adj.* Characterized by conversational exchange of input and output, as

when a user enters a question or command and the system immediately responds. The interactivity of microcomputers is one of the features that makes them approachable and easy to use.

interactive fiction \in`tər-ak`tiv fik´shən\ *n.* A type of computer game in which the user participates in a story by giving commands to the system. The commands given by the user determine, to some extent, the events that occur during the story. Typically the story involves a goal that must be achieved, and the puzzle is to determine the correct sequence of actions that will lead to the accomplishment of that goal.

interactive graphics \in`tər-ak`tiv graf´iks\ *n.* A form of user interface in which the user can change and control graphic displays, often with the help of a pointing device such as a mouse or a joystick. Interactive graphics interfaces occur in a range of computer products from games to computer-aided design (CAD) systems.

interactive processing \in`tər-ak`tiv pros´es-ēng\ *n.* Processing that involves the more or less continuous participation of the user. Such a command/response mode is characteristic of microcomputers. *Compare* batch processing (definition 2).

interactive program \in`tər-ak`tiv prō´gram\ *n.* A program that exchanges output and input with the user, who typically views a display of some sort and uses an input device, such as a keyboard, mouse, or joystick, to provide responses to the program. A computer game is an interactive program. *Compare* batch program.

interactive session \in`tər-ak`tiv sesh´ən\ *n.* A processing session in which the user can more or less continuously intervene and control the activities of the computer. *Compare* batch processing (definition 2).

interactive television \in`tər-ak`tiv tel´ə-vizh`ən\ *n.* A video technology in which a viewer interacts with the television programming. Typical uses of interactive television include Internet access, video on demand, and video conferencing. *See also* video conferencing.

interactive video \in`tər-ak`tiv vid´ē-ō\ *n.* The use of computer-controlled video, in the form of a CD-ROM or videodisc, for interactive education or entertainment. *See also* CD-ROM, interactive, interactive television, videodisc.

interapplication communication \in`tər-a-plə-kā`shən kə-myōō-nə-kā´shən\ *n.* The process of one program sending messages to another program. For example, some e-mail programs allow users to click on a URL within the message. After the user clicks on the URL, a browser will automatically launch and access the URL.

interblock gap \in`tər-blok gap´\ *n. See* interrecord gap.

Interchange File Format \in`tər-chānj fīl´ fōr-mat\ *n. See* .iff.

Interchange Format \in`tər-chānj fōr`mat\ *n. See* Rich Text Format.

interface \in´tər-fās`\ *n.* **1.** The point at which a connection is made between two elements so that they can work with each other. **2.** Software that enables a program to work with the user (the user interface, which can be a command-line interface, menu-driven, or a graphical user interface), with another program such as the operating system, or with the computer's hardware. **3.** A card, plug, or other device that connects pieces of hardware with the computer so that information can be moved from place to place. For example, standardized interfaces such as RS-232-C standard and SCSI enable communications between computers and printers or disks. *See also* RS-232-C standard, SCSI. **4.** A networking or communications standard, such as the ISO/OSI model, that defines ways for different systems to connect and communicate.

interface adapter \in´tər-fās ə-dap`tər\ *n. See* network adapter.

interface card \in´tər-fās kärd`\ *n. See* adapter.

interference \in`tər-fēr´əns\ *n.* **1.** Noise or other external signals that affect the performance of a communications channel. **2.** Electromagnetic signals that can disturb radio or television reception. The signals can be generated naturally, as in lightning, or by electronic devices, such as computers.

Interior Gateway Protocol \in-tēr`ē-ər gāt`wā prō`tə-kol\ *n. See* IGP.

Interior Gateway Routing Protocol \in-tēr`ē-ər gāt`wā rōō`tēng prō`tə-kol, rout´ēng\ *n. See* IGRP.

interlacing \in`tər-lā`sēng\ *n.* A technique used in some raster-scan video displays in which the electron beam refreshes (updates) all odd-numbered scan lines in one vertical sweep of the screen and all even-numbered scan lines in the next sweep. Because of the screen phosphor's ability to maintain an image for a short time before fading and the tendency of the human eye to average or blend subtle differences in light intensity, the human viewer sees a complete display, but the amount of information carried by the display signal and the number of lines that must be displayed per sweep are halved. *Compare* noninterlaced.

interleave \in´tər-lēv\ *vb.* To arrange the sectors on a hard disk in such a way that after one sector is read; the next sector in numeric sequence will arrive at the head when the computer is ready to accept it rather than before, which would make the computer wait a whole revolution of the platter for the sector to come back. Interleaving is set by the format utility that initializes a disk for use with a given computer.

interleaved memory \in`tər-lēvd mem´ər-ē\ *n.* A method of organizing the addresses in RAM memory in order to reduce wait states. In interleaved memory, adjacent locations are stored in different rows of chips so that after accessing a byte, the processor does not have to wait an entire memory cycle before accessing the next byte. *See also* access time (definition 1), wait state.

interlock \in´tər-lok\ *vb.* To prevent a device from acting while the current operation is in progress.

intermediate language \in`tər-mē`dē-ət lang´wəj\ *n.* A computer language used as an intermediate step between the original source language, usually a high-level language, and the target language, usually machine code. Some high-level compilers use assembly language as an intermediate language. *See also* compiler (definition 2), object code.

intermittent \in`tər-mit´ənt\ *adj.* Pertaining to something, such as a signal or connection, that is not unbroken but occurs at periodic or occasional intervals.

intermittent error \in`tər-mit`ənt âr´ər\ *n.* An error that recurs at unpredictable times.

internal clock \in-tər`nəl klok´\ *n. See* clock/calendar.

internal command \in-tər`nəl kə-mand´\ *n.* A routine that is loaded into memory along with the operating system and resides there for as long as the computer is on. *Compare* external command.

internal font \in-tər`nəl font´\ *n.* A font that is already loaded in a printer's memory (ROM) when the printer is shipped. *Compare* downloadable font, font cartridge.

internal interrupt \in-tər`nəl in´tər-upt\ *n.* An interrupt generated by the processor itself in response to certain predefined situations, such as an attempt to divide by zero or an arithmetic value exceeding the number of bits allowed for it. *See also* interrupt. *Compare* external interrupt.

internal memory \in-tər`nəl mem´ər-ē\ *n. See* primary storage.

internal modem \in-tər`nəl mō´dəm\ *n.* A modem constructed on an expansion card to be installed in one of the expansion slots inside a computer. *Compare* external modem, integral modem.

internal schema \in-tər`nəl skē´mə\ *n.* A view of information about the physical files composing a database, including filenames, file locations, accessing methodology, and actual or potential data derivations, in a database model such as that described by ANSI/X3/SPARC, that supports a three-schema architecture. The internal schema corresponds to the schema in systems based on CODASYL/DBTG. In a distributed database, there may be a different internal schema at each location. *See also* conceptual schema, schema.

internal sort \in-tər`nəl sōrt´\ *n.* **1.** A sorting operation that takes place on files completely or largely held in memory rather than on disk during the process. **2.** A sorting procedure that produces sorted subgroups of records that will be subsequently merged into one list.

International Federation of Information Processing \in-tər-nash`ə-nəl fed-ər-ā`shən əv in-fər-mā`shən pros´es-ēng\ *n. See* IFIP.

International Organization for Standardization \in-tər-nash`ə-nəl ōr-gə-nə-zā`shən fōr stan`dər-də-zā´shən\ *n. See* ISO.

International Telecommunications Union \in-tər-nash`ə-nəl tel`ə-kə-myōō-nə-kā´shənz yōōn-`yən\ *n.* An intergovernmental organization responsible for making recommendations and standardization regarding telephone and data communications systems for public and private

telecommunication organizations. The ITU was founded in 1865 and became an agency of the United Nations in 1947. The ITU was formerly known as CCITT (Comité Consultatif International Télégraphique et Téléphonique) and changed its name to ITU in March 1993. They may be contacted at International Telecommunications Union, Information Services Department, Place des Nations, 1211 Geneva 20, Switzerland. Telephone: +41 (22) 730 5554. Fax: +41 (22) 730 5337. E-mail: helpdesk@itu.ch, teledoc@itu.arcom.ch. *Acronym:* ITU (I`T-U´).

International Telegraph and Telephone Consultative Committee \in`tər-nash`ə-nəl tel`ə-graf and tel`ə-fōn kən-sul`tə-tiv kə-mit`ē, kon´sul-tā-tiv\ *n. See* CCITT.

Internaut \in´tər-nät`, in´tər-nôt`\ *n. See* cybernaut.

internet \in´tər-net\ *n.* Short for internetwork. A set of computer networks that may be dissimilar and are joined together by means of gateways that handle data transfer and conversion of messages from the sending networks' protocols to those of the receiving network.

Internet \in´tər-net\ *n.* The worldwide collection of networks and gateways that use the TCP/IP suite of protocols to communicate with one another. At the heart of the Internet is a backbone of high-speed data communication lines between major nodes or host computers, consisting of thousands of commercial, government, educational, and other computer systems, that route data and messages. One or more Internet nodes can go off line without endangering the Internet as a whole or causing communications on the Internet to stop, because no single computer or network controls it. The genesis of the Internet was a decentralized network called ARPANET created by the Department of Defense in 1969 to facilitate communications in the event of a nuclear attack. Eventually other networks, including BITNET, Usenet, UUCP, and NSFnet, were connected to ARPANET. Currently, the Internet offers a range of services to users, such as FTP, e-mail, the World Wide Web, Usenet news, Gopher, IRC, telnet, and others. *Also called* the Net. *See also* BITNET, FTP[1] (definition 1), Gopher, IRC, NSFnet, telnet[1], Usenet, UUCP, World Wide Web.

Internet access \in´tər-net ak`ses\ *n.* **1.** The capability of a user to connect to the Internet. This is generally accomplished through one of two ways. The first is through a dialing up of an Internet service provider or an online information services provider via a modem connected to the user's computer. This method is the one used by the majority of home computer users. The second way is through a dedicated line, such as a T1 carrier, that is connected to a local area network, to which, in turn, the user's computer is connected. The dedicated line solution is used by larger organizations, such as corporations, which either have their own node on the Internet or connect to an Internet service provider that is a node. A third way that is emerging is for users to use set-top boxes with their TVs. Generally, however, this will give a user access only to documents on the World-Wide Web. *See also* dedicated line (definition 1), ISP, LAN, modem, node (definition 2), set-top box. **2.** The capability of an online information service to exchange data with the Internet, such as e-mail, or to offer Internet services to users, such as newsgroups, FTP, and the World Wide Web. Most online information services offer Internet access to their users. *See also* FTP[1] (definition 1), online information service.

Internet access device \in`tər-net ak´ses də-vīs`\ *n.* A communications and signal-routing mechanism, possibly incorporating usage tracking and billing features, for use in connecting multiple remote users to the Internet.

Internet access provider \in`tər-net ak´ses prə-vī`dər\ *n. See* ISP.

Internet account \in`tər-net ə-kount`\ *n.* A generic term for a registered username at an Internet Service Provider (ISP). An Internet account is accessed via username and password. Services such as dial-in PPP Internet access and e-mail are provided by ISPs to Internet account owners.

Internet address \in´tər-net a`dres, ə-dres`\ *n. See* domain name address, e-mail address, IP address.

Internet appliance \in´tər-net ə-plī`əns\ *n. See* set-top box.

Internet Architecture Board \in`tər-net är´kə-tek-chur bōrd`\ *n.* The body of the Internet Society (ISOC) responsible for overall architectural considerations regarding the Internet. The IAB also serves to adjudicate disputes in the standards process. *Acronym:* IAB (Ī´A-B´). *See also* Internet Society.

Internet Assigned Numbers Authority \in`tər-net ə-sīnd` num`bərz ə-thôr`ə-tē\ *n.* A unit of the Internet Architecture Board that registers and controls the assignment of various Internet-related numerical designations, such as IP port, protocol, and enterprise numbers. *Acronym:* IANA (Ī´A-N-A´).

Internet backbone \in`tər-net bak`bōn\ *n.* One of several high-speed networks connecting many local and regional networks, with at least one connection point where it exchanges packets with other Internet backbones. Historically, the NSFnet (predecessor to the modern Internet) was the backbone to the entire Internet in the United States. This backbone linked the supercomputing centers that the National Science Foundation (NSF) runs. Today, different providers have their own backbones so that the backbone for the supercomputing centers is independent of backbones for commercial Internet providers such as MCI and Sprint. *See also* backbone.

Internet broadcasting \in`tər-net brod´ka-stēng\ *n.* Broadcasting of audio, or audio plus video, signals across the Internet. Internet broadcasting includes conventional over-the-air broadcast stations that transmit their signals into the Internet as well as Internet-only stations. Listeners use audio Internet software, such as RealAudio. One method of Internet broadcasting is MBONE. *See also* MBONE, RealAudio.

Internet Control Message Protocol \in`tər-net kən-trōl´ mes`əj prō`tə-kol\ *n. See* ICMP.

Internet Draft \in´tər-net draft`\ *n.* A document produced by the IETF (Internet Engineering Task Force) for purposes of discussing a possible change in standards that govern the Internet. An Internet Draft is subject to revision or replacement at any time; if not replaced or revised, the Internet Draft is valid for no more than six months. An Internet Draft, if accepted, may be developed into an RFC. *See also* IETF, RFC.

Internet Engineering and Planning Group \in`tər-net en-jə-nēr´ēng ənd plan`ēng grōōp\ *n. See* IEPG.

Internet Engineering Steering Group \in`tər-net en-jə-nēr`ēng stēr´ēng gro͞op\ *n.* The group within the Internet Society (ISOC) that, along with the Internet Architecture Board (IAB), reviews the standards proposed by the Internet Engineering Task Force (IETF). *Acronym:* IESG (I`E-S-G´).

Internet Engineering Task Force \in`tər-net en`jə-nēr`ēng task` fōrs\ *n. See* IETF.

Internet Explorer \in`tər-net eks-plōr´ər\ *n.* Microsoft's Web browser, introduced in October 1995. Internet Explorer is now available in Windows and Macintosh versions. Later versions provide the ability to incorporate advanced design and animation features into Web pages and recognize ActiveX controls and Java applets. *See also* ActiveX controls, Java applet, Web browser.

Internet gateway \in`tər-net gāt`wā\ *n.* A device that provides the connection between the Internet backbone and another network, such as a LAN (local area network). Usually the device is a computer dedicated to the task or a router. The gateway generally performs protocol conversion between the Internet backbone and the network, data translation or conversion, and message handling. A gateway is considered a node on the Internet. *See also* gateway, Internet backbone, node (definition 2), router.

Internet Group Membership Protocol \in`tər-net gro͞op` mem´bər-ship prō`tə-kol\ *n.* A protocol used by IP hosts to report their host group memberships to any immediately neighboring multicast routers. *Acronym:* IGMP (I`G-M-P´).

Internet Information Server \in`tər-net in`fər-mā´shən sər`vər\ *n.* Microsoft's brand of Web server software, utilizing Hypertext Transfer Protocol to deliver World Wide Web documents. It incorporates various functions for security, allows for CGI programs, and also provides for Gopher and FTP servers.

Internet Naming Service \in`tər-net nā´mēng sər`vis\ *n. See* WINS.

Internet Protocol \in`tər-net prō`tə-kol\ *n. See* IP.

Internet Protocol next generation \in`tər-net prō`tə-kol nekst` jen-ər-ā´shən\ *n. See* IPng.

Internet Relay Chat \in`tər-net rē´lā chat`\ *n. See* IRC.

Internet Research Steering Group \in`tər-net rē`sərch stēr´ēng gro͞op\ *n.* The governing body of the Internet Research Task Force (IRTF). *Acronym:* IRSG (I`R-S-G´).

Internet Research Task Force \in`tər-net rē`sərch task´ fōrs\ *n.* A volunteer organization that makes long-term recommendations concerning the Internet to the Internet Architecture Board. *Acronym:* IRTF (I`R-T-F´). *See also* Internet Society.

Internet robot \in`tər-net rō`bot\ *n. See* spider.

Internet security \in`tər-net se-kyər´ə-tē\ *n.* A broad topic dealing with all aspects of data authentication, privacy, integrity, and verification for transactions over the Internet. For example, credit card purchases made via a World Wide Web browser require attention to Internet security issues to ensure that the credit card number is not intercepted by an intruder or copied from the server where the number is stored, and to verify that the credit card number is actually sent by the person who claims to be sending it.

Internet Server Application Programming Interface \in`tər-net sər-vər a-plə-kā`shən prō`gram-ēng in`tər-fās\ *n. See* ISAPI.

Internet service provider \in`tər-net sər´vəs prə-vī`dər\ *n. See* ISP.

Internet Society \in`tər-net sə-sī`ə-tē\ *n.* An international organization, comprising individuals, companies, foundations, and government agencies, that promotes the use, maintenance, and development of the Internet. The Internet Architecture Board (IAB) is a body within the Internet Society. In addition, the Internet Society publishes the *Internet Society News* and produces the annual INET conference. *Acronym:* ISOC (ī´sok, I`S-O-C´). *See also* INET (definition 2), Internet Architecture Board.

Internet Software Consortium \in`tər-net soft´wâr kən-sōr`shē-əm, kən-sōr`shəm\ *n.* A nonprofit organization that develops software that is available for free, via the World Wide Web or FTP, as well as development of Internet standards such as the Dynamic Host Configuration Protocol (DHCP). *See also* DHCP.

Internet Talk Radio \in`tər-net täk rā´dē-ō\ *n.* Audio programs similar to radio broadcasts but distributed over the Internet in the form of files that can be downloaded via FTP. Internet Talk Radio programs, prepared at the National Press Building in Washington, D.C., are 30 minutes to 1 hour in length; a 30-minute program requires about 15 MB of disk space. Features include the Internet Hall of Flame and the Geek of the Week. *Acronym:* ITR (Ī´T-R´).

Internet telephone \in`tər-net tel´ə-fōn\ *n.* Point-to-point voice communication that uses the Internet instead of the public-switched telecommunications network to connect the calling and called parties. Both the sending and the receiving party need a computer, a modem, an Internet connection, and an Internet telephone software package to make and receive calls.

Internet television \in`tər-net tel´ə-vizh-ən\ *n.* The transmission of television audio and video signals over the Internet.

internetwork \in`tər-net´wərk\ *adj.* Of or pertaining to communications between connected networks. Often used to refer to communication between one local area network and another over the Internet or another wide-area network. *See also* LAN, wide area network.

Internetwork Packet Exchange \in`tər-net-wərk pak´ət eks-chānj`\ *n. See* IPX.

Internet Worm \in`tər-net wərm`\ *n.* A string of self-replicating computer code that was distributed through the Internet in November 1988. In a single night, it overloaded and shut down a large portion of the computers connected to the Internet at that time by replicating itself over and over on each computer it accessed, exploiting a bug in UNIX systems. Intended as a prank, the Internet Worm was written by a student at Cornell University. *See also* back door, worm.

InterNIC \in`tər-nik`, in`tər-N-I-C´\ *n.* Short for NSFnet (**Inter**net) **N**etwork **I**nformation **C**enter. The organization that is charged with registering domain names and IP addresses as well as distributing information about the Internet. InterNIC was formed in 1993 as a consortium involving the U.S. National Science Foundation, AT&T, General Atomics, and Network Solutions Inc. (Herndon, Va.). The latter partner administers InterNIC Registration Services, which assigns Internet names and addresses. InterNIC can be reached by e-mail at info@internic.net or on the Web at http://www.internic.net/.

interoperability \in`tər-op`ər-ə-bil´ə-tē\ *n.* Referring to components of computer systems that are able to function in different environments. For

example, Microsoft's NT operating system is interoperable on Intel, DEC Alpha, and other CPUs. Another example is the SCSI standard for disk drives and other peripheral devices that allows them to interoperate with different operating systems. With software, interoperability occurs when programs are able to share data and resources. Microsoft Word, for example, is able to read files created by Microsoft Excel.

interpolate \in-tər´pə-lāt\ *vb.* To estimate intermediate values between two known values in a sequence.

interpret \in-tər´prət\ *vb.* **1.** To translate a statement or instruction into executable form and then execute it. **2.** To execute a program by translating one statement at a time into executable form and executing it before translating the next statement, rather than by translating the program completely into executable code (compiling it) before executing it separately. *See also* interpreter. *Compare* compile.

interpreted language \in-tər`prə-təd lang´wəj\ *n.* A language in which programs are translated into executable form and executed one statement at a time rather than being translated completely (compiled) before execution. Basic, LISP, and APL are generally interpreted languages, although Basic can also be compiled. *See also* compiler. *Compare* compiled language.

interpreter \in-tər´prə-tər\ *n.* A program that translates and then executes each statement in a program written in an interpreted language. *See also* compiler, interpreted language, language processor.

interprocess communication \in`tər-pros`es kə-myo͞o-nə-kā´shən\ *n.* The ability of one task or process to communicate with another in a multitasking operating system. Common methods include pipes, semaphores, shared memory, queues, signals, and mailboxes. *Acronym:* IPC (Ī´P-C´).

inter-record gap \in`tər-ek`ərd gap´\ *n.* An unused space between data blocks stored on a disk or tape. Because the speed of disks and tapes fluctuates slightly during operation of the drives, a new data block may not occupy the exact space occupied by the old block it overwrites. The inter-record gap prevents the new block from overwriting part of adjacent blocks in such a case. *Acronym:* IRG (I´R-G´). *Also called* gap, interblock gap.

interrogate \in-târ´ə-gāt\ *vb.* To query with the expectation of an immediate response. For example, a computer may interrogate an attached terminal to determine the terminal's status (readiness to transmit or receive).

interrupt \in´tər-upt\ *n.* A request for attention from the processor. When the processor receives an interrupt, it suspends its current operations, saves the status of its work, and transfers control to a special routine known as an interrupt handler, which contains the instructions for dealing with the particular situation that caused the interrupt. Interrupts can be generated by various hardware devices to request service or report problems, or by the processor itself in response to program errors or requests for operating-system services. Interrupts are the processor's way of communicating with the other elements that make up a computer system. A hierarchy of interrupt priorities determines which interrupt request will be handled first if more than one request is made. A program can temporarily disable some interrupts if it needs the full attention of the processor to complete a particular task. *See also* exception, external interrupt, hardware interrupt, internal interrupt, software interrupt.

interrupt-driven processing \in`tər-upt-driv-ən pros´es-ēng\ *n.* Processing that takes place only when requested by means of an interrupt. After the required task has been completed, the CPU is free to perform other tasks until the next interrupt occurs. Interrupt-driven processing is usually employed for responding to events such as a key pressed by the user or a floppy disk drive that has become ready to transfer data. *See also* interrupt. *Compare* autopolling.

interrupt handler \in´tər-upt hand`lər\ *n.* A special routine that is executed when a specific interrupt occurs. Interrupts from different causes have different handlers to carry out the corresponding tasks, such as updating the system clock or reading the keyboard. A table stored in low memory contains pointers, sometimes called vectors, that direct the processor to the various interrupt handlers. Programmers can create interrupt handlers to replace or supplement existing handlers, such

as by making a clicking sound each time the keyboard is pressed.

interrupt priority \in´tər-upt prī-ōr´ə-tē\ *n. See* interrupt.

interrupt request line \in`tər-upt rē-kwest´ līn\ *n.* A hardware line over which a device such as an input/output port, the keyboard, or a disk drive can send interrupts (requests for service) to the CPU. Interrupt request lines are built into the computer's internal hardware and are assigned different levels of priority so that the CPU can determine the sources and relative importance of incoming service requests. They are of concern mainly to programmers dealing with low-level operations close to the hardware. *Acronym:* IRQ (I´R-Q´).

interrupt vector \in`tər-upt vek´tər\ *n.* A memory location that contains the address of the interrupt handler routine that is to be called when a specific interrupt occurs. *See also* interrupt.

interrupt vector table \in`tər-upt vek´tər tā`bl\ *n. See* dispatch table.

intersect \in`tər-sekt´\ *n.* An operator in relational algebra, used in database management. Given two relations (tables), A and B, that have corresponding fields (columns) containing the same types of values (that is, they are union-compatible), then INTERSECT A, B builds a third relation containing only those tuples (rows) that appear in both A and B. *See also* tuple.

intranet \in´trə-net´\ *n.* A network designed for information processing within a company or organization. Its uses include such services as document distribution, software distribution, access to databases, and training. An intranet is so called because it usually employs applications associated with the Internet, such as Web pages, Web browsers, FTP sites, e-mail, newsgroups, and mailing lists, accessible only to those within the company or organization.

intraware \in´trə-wâr`\ *n.* Groupware or middleware for use on a company's private intranet. Intraware packages typically contain e-mail, database, workflow, and browser applications. *See also* groupware, intranet, middleware.

intrinsic font \in-trin´zik font`\ *n.* A font (type size and design) for which a bit image (an exact pattern) exists that can be used as is, without such modification as scaling. *Compare* derived font.

intruder \in-trōōˊdər`\ *n.* An unauthorized user or unauthorized program, generally considered to have malicious intent, on a computer or computer network. *See also* bacterium, cracker, Trojan horse, virus.

.in.us \dot-I-N`dot-U-Sˊ\ *n.* On the Internet, the major geographic domain specifying that an address is located in Indiana, United States.

invalid \in-valˊid`\ *adj.* Erroneous or unrecognizable because of a flaw in reasoning or an error in input. Invalid results, for example, might occur if the logic in a program is faulty. *Compare* illegal.

inverse video \in-vərs` vidˊē-ō\ *n. See* reverse video.

invert \in-vərtˊ\ *vb.* **1.** To reverse something or change it to its opposite. For example, to invert the colors on a monochrome display means to change light to dark and dark to light. See the illustration. **2.** In a digital electrical signal, to replace a high level by a low level and vice versa. This type of operation is the electronic equivalent of a Boolean NOT operation.

Normal   Inverted

Invert. An example showing the effects of inverting the colors on a monochrome display.

inverted file \in-vər`təd fīlˊ\ *n. See* inverted list.

inverted list \in-vər`təd listˊ\ *n.* A method for creating alternative locators for sets of information. For example, in a file containing data about cars, records 3, 7, 19, 24, and 32 might contain the value "Red" in the field COLOR. An inverted list (or index) on the field COLOR would contain a record for "Red" followed by the locator numbers 3, 7, 19, 24, and 32. *See also* field, record. *Compare* linked list.

inverted-list database \in-vər`təd-list daˊtə-bās\ *n.* A database similar to a relational database but with several differences that make it much more difficult for the database management system to ensure data consistency, integrity, and security than with a relational system.

- The rows (records or tuples) of an inverted-list table are ordered in a specific physical sequence, independent of any orderings that may be imposed by means of indexes.

- The total database can also be ordered, with specified logical merge criteria being imposed between tables.

- Any number of search keys, either simple or composite, can be defined. Unlike the keys of a relational system, these search keys are arbitrary fields or combinations of fields.

- No integrity or uniqueness constraints are enforced.

- Neither the indexes nor the tables are transparent to the user.

Compare relational database.

inverted structure \in-vər`təd strukˊchər\ *n.* A file structure in which record keys are stored and manipulated separately from the records themselves.

inverter \in-vərˊtər\ *n.* **1.** A logic circuit that inverts (reverses) the signal input to it—for example, inverting a high input to a low output. **2.** A device that converts direct current (DC) to alternating current (AC).

invoke \in-vōkˊ\ *vb.* To call or activate; used in reference to commands and subroutines.

I/O \I-Oˊ\ *n. See* input/output.

I/O-bound \I-Oˊbound`\ *adj. See* input/output-bound.

I/O controller \I-Oˊ kən-tro`lər\ *n. See* input/output controller.

I/O device \I-Oˊ də-vīs`\ *n. See* input/output device.

ion-deposition printer \ī`on-dep-ə-zishˊən prin`tər\ *n.* A page printer in which the image is formed in electrostatic charges on a drum that picks up toner and transfers it to the paper, as in a laser, LED, or LCD printer, but the drum is charged using a beam of ions rather than light. These printers, used mainly in high-volume data-processing environments, typically operate at speeds from 30 to 90 pages per minute. In ion-deposition printers, toner is typically fused to paper by a method that is fast and does not require heat but leaves the paper a little glossy, making it unsuitable for business correspondence. In addition, ion-deposition printers tend to produce thick, slightly fuzzy characters; the technology is also more expensive than that of a laser printer. *See also* electrophotographic printers, nonimpact printer, page printer. *Compare* laser printer, LCD printer, LED printer.

I/O port \I-O´ pōrt`\ *n. See* input/output port.

I/O processor \I-O´ pros`es-ər\ *n. See* input/output processor.

IO.SYS \ī´ō-sis`, I-O`dot-S-Y-S'´\ *n.* One of two hidden system files installed on an MS-DOS startup disk. IO.SYS in IBM releases of MS-DOS (called IBMBIO.COM) contains device drivers for peripherals such as the display, keyboard, floppy disk drive, hard disk drive, serial port, and real-time clock. *See also* MSDOS.SYS.

IP \I-P´\ *n.* Acronym for **I**nternet **P**rotocol. The protocol within TCP/IP that governs the breakup of data messages into packets, the routing of the packets from sender to destination network and station, and the reassembly of the packets into the original data messages at the destination. IP corresponds to the network layer in the ISO/OSI model. *See also* ISO/OSI model, TCP/IP. *Compare* TCP.

IP address \I-P´ a`dres, ə-dres`\ *n.* Short for **I**nternet **P**rotocol **address.** A 32-bit (4-byte) binary number that uniquely identifies a host (computer) connected to the Internet to other Internet hosts, for the purposes of communication through the transfer of packets. An IP address is expressed in "dotted quad" format, consisting of the decimal values of its 4 bytes, separated with periods; for example, 127.0.0.1. The first 1, 2, or 3 bytes of the IP address, assigned by InterNIC Registration Services, identify the network the host is connected to; the remaining bits identify the host itself. The 32 bits of all 4 bytes together can signify almost 2^{32}, or roughly 4 billion, hosts. (A few small ranges within that set of numbers are not used.) *See also* host, InterNIC, IP, packet (definition 2). *Compare* domain name.

IPC \I-P-C´\ *n. See* interprocess communication.

IPL \I-P-L´\ *n. See* initial program load.

IP multicasting \I-P´ mul`tē-kas´tēng, mul`tī-kas´tēng\ *n.* Short for **I**nternet **P**rotocol **multicasting.** The extension of local area network multicasting technology to a TCP/IP network. Hosts send and receive multicast datagrams, the destina-

tion fields of which specify IP host group addresses rather than individual IP addresses. A host indicates that it is a member of a group by means of the Internet Group Management Protocol. *See also* datagram, Internet Group Membership Protocol, IP, MBONE, multicasting.

IPng \I´pēng, I-P-N-G´\ Acronym for **I**nternet **P**rotocol **n**ext **g**eneration. A version of Internet Protocol (IP) developed by the Internet Engineering Task Force (IETF). Improvements over the original Internet Protocol include better security and an increased IP address size of 16 bytes. *See also* IETF, IP, IP address.

IP spoofing \I-P´ spoo`fēng\ *n.* The act of inserting a false sender IP address into an Internet transmission in order to gain unauthorized access to a computer system. *See also* IP address, spoofing.

IP switching \I-P´ swich`ēng\ *n.* A technology developed by Ipsilon Networks (Sunnyvale, Calif.) that enables a sequence of IP packets with a common destination to be transmitted over a high-speed, high-bandwidth Asynchronous Transfer Mode (ATM) connection.

IPv6 \I-P-V-siks´\ *n.* Short for **I**nternet **P**rotocol **v**ersion **6**. A proposed next generation for the Internet Protocol, currently version 4, which was introduced in September 1995 by the Internet Engineering Task Force and formerly known as IPng. *See also* IP, IPng.

IPX \I-P-X´\ *n.* Acronym for **I**nternetwork **P**acket **Ex**change. The protocol in Novell NetWare that governs addressing and routing of packets within and between LANs. IPX packets can be encapsulated in Ethernet packets or Token Ring frames. IPX operates at ISO/OSI levels 3 and 4 but does not perform all the functions at those levels. In particular, IPX does not guarantee that a message will be complete (no lost packets); SPX has that job. *See also* Ethernet (definition 1), packet, Token Ring network. *Compare* SPX (definition 1).

IPX/SPX \I-P-X-S-P-X\ *n.* The network and transport level protocols used by Novell NetWare, which together correspond to the combination of TCP and IP in the TCP/IP protocol suite. *See also* IPX, SPX (definition 1).

.iq \dot`I-Q´\ *n.* On the Internet, the major geographic domain specifying that an address is located in Iraq.

.ir \dot`I-R´\ *n.* On the Internet, the major geographic domain specifying that an address is located in Iran.

IR \I-R´\ *n. See* infrared.

IRC \I`R-C´\ *n.* Acronym for **I**nternet **R**elay **C**hat. A service that enables an Internet user to participate in a conversation on line in real time with other users. An IRC channel, maintained by an IRC server, transmits the text typed by each user who has joined the channel to all other users who have joined the channel. Generally, a channel is dedicated to a particular topic, which may be reflected in the channel's name. An IRC client shows the names of currently active channels, enables the user to join a channel, and then displays the other participants' words on individual lines so that the user can respond. IRC was invented in 1988 by Jarkko Oikarinen of Finland. *See also* channel (definition 2), server (definition 2).

IrDA \ər´də, I`R-D-A´\ *See* Infrared Data Association.

IRG \I`R-G´\ *n. See* inter-record gap.

IRGB \I`R-G-B´\ *n.* Acronym for **I**ntensity **R**ed **G**reen **B**lue. A type of color encoding originally used in IBM's Color/Graphics Adapter (CGA) and continued in the EGA (Enhanced Graphics Adapter) and VGA (Video Graphics Array). The standard 3-bit RGB color encoding (specifying eight colors) is supplemented by a fourth bit (called Intensity) that uniformly increases the intensity of the red, green, and blue signals, resulting in a total of 16 colors. *See also* RGB.

IRL \I`R-L´\ *n.* Acronym for **i**n **r**eal **l**ife. An expression used by many online users to denote life outside the computer realm, especially in conjunction with virtual worlds such as online talkers, IRC, MUDs, and virtual reality. *See also* IRC, MUD, talker, virtual reality.

IRQ \I`R-Q´\ *n.* Acronym for **i**nterrupt **req**uest. One of a set of possible hardware interrupts, identified by a number, on a Wintel computer. The number of the IRQ determines which interrupt handler will be used. In the AT bus, ISA, and EISA, 15 IRQs are available; in Micro Channel Architecture, 255 IRQs are available; each device's IRQ is hardwired or set by a jumper or DIP switch. The VL bus and the PCI local bus have their own interrupt systems, which they translate to IRQ numbers. *See also* AT bus, DIP switch, EISA, interrupt, IRQ conflict, ISA, jumper, Micro Channel Architecture, PCI local bus, VL bus.

IRQ conflict \I`R-Q´ kon`flikt\ *n.* The condition on a Wintel computer in which two different peripheral devices use the same IRQ to request service from the central processing unit (CPU). An IRQ conflict will prevent the system from working correctly; for example, the CPU may respond to an interrupt from a serial mouse by executing an interrupt handler for interrupts generated by a modem. IRQ conflicts can be prevented by the use of Plug and Play hardware and software. *See also* interrupt handler, IRQ, Plug and Play.

irrational number \ēr-ash`ə-nəl num`bər\ *n.* A real number that cannot be expressed as the ratio of two integers. Examples of irrational numbers are the square root of 3, pi, and *e. See also* integer, real number.

IRSG \I`R-S-G´\ *See* Internet Research Steering Group.

IRTF \I`R-T-F´\ *See* Internet Research Task Force.

.is \dot`I-S´\ *n.* On the Internet, the major geographic domain specifying that an address is located in Iceland.

IS \I-S´\ *See* Information Services.

ISA \I`S-A´, ī´sə\ *n.* Acronym for **I**ndustry **S**tandard **A**rchitecture. A bus design specification that allows components to be added as cards plugged into standard expansion slots in IBM Personal Computers and compatibles. Originally introduced in the IBM PC/XT with an 8-bit data path, ISA was expanded in 1984, when IBM introduced the PC/AT, to permit a 16-bit data path. A 16-bit ISA slot actually consists of two separate 8-bit slots mounted end-to-end so that a single 16-bit card plugs into both slots. An 8-bit expansion card can be inserted and used in a 16-bit slot (it occupies only one of the two slots), but a 16-bit expansion card cannot be used in an 8-bit slot. *See also* EISA, Micro Channel Architecture.

ISAM \I`S-A-M´, I´sam\ *n. See* indexed sequential access method.

ISAPI \I`S-A-P-I´\ *n.* Acronym for **I**nternet **S**erver **A**pplication **P**rogramming **I**nterface. An easy-to-use, high-performance interface for back-end applications for Microsoft's Internet Information Server (IIS). ISAPI has its own dynamic-link library, which offers significant performance advantages over the CGI (Common Gateway Interface) specification. *See also* API, dynamic-link library, Internet Information Server. *Compare* CGI.

ISA slot \ī´sə slot`, I`S A´\ *n.* A connection socket for a peripheral designed according to the ISA (Industry Standard Architecture) standard, which applies to the bus developed for use in the 80286 (IBM PC/AT) motherboard. *See also* ISA.

ISC \I`S-C´\ *n. See* Internet Software Consortium.

ISDN \I`S-D-N´\ *n.* Acronym for **I**ntegrated **S**ervices **D**igital **N**etwork. A worldwide digital communications network evolving from existing telephone services. The goal of ISDN is to replace the current telephone network, which requires digital-to-analog conversions, with facilities totally devoted to digital switching and transmission, yet advanced enough to replace traditionally analog forms of data, ranging from voice to computer transmissions, music, and video. ISDN is built on two main types of communications channels: a B channel, which carries data at a rate of 64 Kbps (kilobits per second), and a D channel, which carries control information at either 16 or 64 Kbps. Computers and other devices connect to ISDN lines through simple, standardized interfaces. When fully implemented (possibly around the turn of the century), ISDN is expected to provide users with faster, more extensive communications services. *See also* channel (definition 2).

ISDN terminal adapter \I`S-D-N` tər´mə-nəl ə-dap`tər\ *n.* The hardware interface between a computer and an ISDN line. *See also* ISDN.

ISIS or **IS-IS** \ī´sis, I`S-I-S´\ *n.* Acronym for **I**ntelligent **S**cheduling and **I**nformation **S**ystem. A toolkit designed to help prevent and eliminate faults in manufacturing systems. Developed in 1980 at Cornell University, ISIS is now available commercially.

ISO \ī´sō, I`S-O´\ *n.* Short for **I**nternational **O**rganization for **S**tandardization (often incorrectly identified as an acronym for International Standards Organization), an international association of countries, each of which is represented by its leading standard-setting organization—for example, ANSI (American National Standards Institute) for the United States. The ISO works to establish global standards for communications and information exchange. Primary among its accomplishments is the widely accepted ISO/OSI model, which defines standards for the interaction of computers connected` by communications networks. *ISO* is not an acronym; rather, it is derived from the Greek word *isos,* which means "equal" and is the root of the prefix "iso-."

ISO 9660 \ī´sō nīn`tē-siks-siks´tē, I`S-O´\ *n.* An international format standard for CD-ROM adopted by the ISO that follows the recommendations embodied in the High Sierra specification, with some modifications. *See also* High Sierra specification.

ISOC \ī´sok, I`S-O-C´\ *n. See* Internet Society.

isometric view \ī`sə-me`trik vyo͞o´\ *n.* A display method for three-dimensional objects in which every edge has the correct length for the scale of the drawing and in which all parallel lines appear parallel. An isometric view of a cube, for example, shows the faces in symmetrical relation to one another and the height and width of each face evenly proportioned; the faces do not appear to taper with distance as they do when the cube is drawn in perspective. See the illustration. *Compare* perspective view.

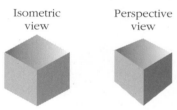

Isometric view   Perspective view

Isometric view.   A cube in isometric view and in perspective view.

ISO/OSI model \I-S-O`O-S-I´ mod`əl\ *n.* Short for **I**nternational **O**rganization for **S**tandardization **O**pen **S**ystems **I**nterconnection **model.** A layered architecture (plan) that standardizes levels of service and types of interaction for computers exchanging information through a communications network. The ISO/OSI model separates computer-to-computer communications into seven layers, or levels, each building upon the standards contained in the levels below it. The lowest of the seven layers deals solely with hardware links; the highest deals with software interactions at the application-program level.

ISO/OSI MODEL

ISO/OSI layer	Focus
Application (highest level)	Program-to-program transfer of information
Presentation	Text formatting and display, code conversion
Session	Establishing, maintaining, and coordinating communication
Transport	Accurate delivery, service quality
Network	Transport routes, message handling and transfer
Data-link	Coding, addressing, and transmitting information
Physical	Hardware connections

ISP \Ī´S-P´\ *n.* Acronym for **I**nternet **s**ervice **p**rovider. A business that supplies Internet connectivity services to individuals, businesses, and other organizations. Some ISPs are large national or multinational corporations that offer access in many locations, while others are limited to a single city or region. *Also called* access provider, service provider.

ISV \Ī´S-V´\ *n. See* independent software vendor.

.it \dot`I-T´\ *n.* On the Internet, the major geographic domain specifying that an address is located in Italy.

italic \i-tal´ik, ī-tal´ik\ *n.* A type style in which the characters are evenly slanted toward the right. *This sentence is in italics.* Italics are commonly used for emphasis, foreign-language words and phrases, titles of literary and other works, technical terms, and citations. *See also* font family. *Compare* roman.

iterate \it´ər-āt`\ *vb.* To execute one or more statements or instructions repeatedly. Statements or instructions so executed are said to be in a loop. *See also* iterative statement, loop.

iterative statement \it´ər-ə-tiv stāt`mənt\ *n.* A statement in a program that causes the program to repeat one or more statements. Examples of iterative statements in Basic are FOR, DO, REPEAT..UNTIL, and DO..WHILE. *See also* control statement.

ITI \Ī´T-I´\ *See* Intelligent Transportation Infrastructure.

I-time \I´tīm\ *n. See* instruction time.

ITR \Ī´T-R´\ *n. See* Internet Talk Radio.

ITU \Ī´T-U´\ *n. See* International Telecommunications Union.

IVUE \I´vyoo\ *n.* A proprietary image format (from Live Pictures) that allows files to be adjusted to screen resolution at any zoom level.

i-way \I´wā\ *n. See* Information Superhighway.

J \J\ *n.* A high-level programming language created by the developer of APL, Kenneth Iverson. J is a successor language to APL that may be run on many platforms, including DOS, Windows, OS/2, and Macintosh. Like APL, J is used primarily by mathematicians. *See also* APL.

jabber \jab´ər\ *n.* A continuous stream of random data transmitted over a network as the result of some malfunction.

jack \jak\ *n.* A connector designed to receive a plug. A jack is commonly used in making audio and video connections.

jacket \jak´ət\ *n. See* disk jacket.

jack in \jak` in´\ *vb.* **1.** To log on to a computer. **2.** To connect to a network or BBS, especially for purposes of entering an IRC or a virtual reality simulation, such as a MUD (to leave is to *jack out*). *See also* IRC, MUD.

Jacquard loom \jak`ərd lo͞om´\ *n.* The first machine that used punched cards to control its operation. In this loom, developed in 1801 by French inventor Joseph-Marie Jacquard, up to 24,000 cards were placed on a rolling drum. Where a hole was punched on a card, one of a set of rods could pass through and select a particular thread to be woven into the pattern. Jacquard was awarded a medal by the Emperor Napoleon for his invention. Later in the nineteenth century, punched cards were used in Charles Babbage's computer-like Analytical Engine and in Herman Hollerith's statistical tabulating machine. *See also* Analytical Engine, Hollerith tabulating/recording machine.

jaggies \jag´ēz\ *n.* The "stairsteps" that appear in diagonal lines and curves drawn at low resolutions in computer graphics. *Also called* aliasing.

Janet \jan´ət\ *n.* Short for the **J**oint **A**cademic **Net**work. A wide area network in the United Kingdom that serves as the principal backbone for the Internet in that country. *See also* backbone (definition 1).

Java \jä´və\ *n.* An object-oriented programming language, developed by Sun Microsystems, Inc. Similar to C++, Java is smaller, more portable, and easier to use than C++ because it is more robust and it manages memory on its own. Java was also designed to be secure and platform-neutral (meaning that it can be run on any platform) through the fact that Java programs are compiled into byte-codes, which are similar to machine code and are not specific to any platform. This makes it a useful language for programming Web applications, since users access the Web from many types of computers. Currently, the most widespread use of Java is in programming small applications, or applets, for the World Wide Web. *See also* byte-code, Java applet, object-oriented programming.

Java applet \jä´və a`plət\ *n.* A Java class that is loaded and run by an already-running Java application such as a Web browser or an applet viewer. Java applets can be downloaded and run by any Web browser capable of interpreting Java, such as Internet Explorer, Netscape Navigator, and Hot-Java. Java applets are frequently used to add multimedia effects and interactivity to Web pages, such as background music, real-time video displays, animations, calculators, and interactive games. Applets can be activated automatically when a user views a page, or they may require some action on the part of the user, such as clicking on an icon in the Web page. *See also* applet, Java.

Java chip \jä´və chip`\ *n.* An implementation on a single integrated circuit of the virtual machine specified for execution of the Java programming language. Such chips, which are being developed by Sun Microsystems, Inc., could be used in very small devices and as controllers for appliances. *See also* integrated circuit, Java, virtual machine.

Java-compliant browser \jä´və kəm-plī´ənt brou´-zər\ *n.* A Web browser with support for the Java programming language built into it. Most current Web browsers are Java-compliant. *See also* Java, Web browser.

Java Developer's Kit \jä`və də-vel´ə-pərz kit`\ *n.* A set of software tools developed by Sun Microsystems, Inc., for writing Java applets or applications. The kit, which is distributed free, includes a Java compiler, interpreter, debugger, viewer for applets, and documentation. *Acronym:* JDK (J`D-K´). *See also* applet, Java, Java applet.

Java Management Application Programming Interface \jä`və man`əj-mənt a-plə-kā`shən prō`gram-ēng in´tər-fās\ *n.* A set of application programming interface specifications, proposed by Sun Microsystems, Inc., to enable the Java language to be used for network management. *Acronym:* JMAPI (J´map`ē, J`M-A-P-I´). *See also* application programming interface, Java.

JavaScript \jä´və-skript`\ *n.* A scripting language developed by Netscape Communications and Sun Microsystems, Inc. that is loosely related to Java. JavaScript, however, is not a true object-oriented language, and it is limited in performance compared with Java because it is not compiled. Basic online applications and functions can be added to Web pages with JavaScript, but the number and complexity of available application programming interface functions are fewer than those available with Java. JavaScript code, which is included in a Web page along with the HTML code, is generally considered easier to write than Java, especially for novice programmers. A JavaScript-compliant Web browser, such as Netscape Navigator, is necessary to run JavaScript code. *See also* application programming interface, HTML, scripting language. *Compare* Java.

Java terminal \jä´və tər`mə-nəl\ *n.* A type of personal computer with a reduced number of components that is built primarily to provide an access terminal to the Web, including downloadable Java applets. Typically, such machines will not have locally addressable hard disks or installable programs but will obtain any necessary materials, including Java applets, for the user from somewhere on the network. Centrally obtained software is generally less expensive to administer but usually requires some download delay before usage may begin. Java terminals, currently under

development by Sun Microsystems, Inc., are similar in concept to NetPCs. *See also* Java, Java applet, network computer. *Compare* NetPC.

JCL \J`C-L´\ *n.* Acronym for **J**ob **C**ontrol **L**anguage. A command language used in IBM OS/360 mainframe systems. JCL is used to launch applications and specifies information on running time, program size, and the program files used for each application. *See also* command language.

JDK \J`D-K´\ *n. See* Java Developer's Kit.

jewel box \joo´əl boks, jool´\ *n.* A clear plastic container used to package and store a compact disc. See the illustration. *Also called* jewel case.

Jewel box.

.jfif \dot`J-F-I-F´\ *n.* The file extension that identifies graphic image files in the JPEG File Interchange Format. *See also* JPEG.

JIT \J`I-T´\ *n. See* just-in-time.

jitter \jit´ər\ *n.* **1.** Small vibrations or fluctuations in a displayed video image caused by irregularities in the display signal. Jitter is often visible in the form of horizontal lines that are of the same thickness as scan lines. **2.** A rough appearance in a fax caused by dots that are incorrectly recorded during the scanning process and thus wrongly positioned in the output. **3.** In digital communication, distortion caused by lack of synchronization of signals.

.jm \dot`J-M´\ *n.* On the Internet, the major geographic domain specifying that an address is located in Jamaica.

JMAPI \J´map`ē, J`M-A-P-I´\ *n. See* Java Management Application Programming Interface.

.jo \dot`J-O´\ *n.* On the Internet, the major geographic domain specifying that an address is located in Jordan.

job \job\ *n.* A specified amount of processing performed as a unit by a computer. On early

mainframe computers, data was submitted in batches, often on punched cards, for processing by different programs; work was therefore scheduled and carried out in separate jobs, or operations.

Job Control Language \job´ kən-trōl` lang`wəj\ *n. See* JCL.

job processing \job´ pros`es-ēng\ *n.* A computing method in which a series of jobs, each consisting of one or more tasks grouped together as a computationally coherent whole, is processed sequentially. *See also* batch processing (definition 2).

job queue \job´ kyōō`\ *n.* A list of programs or tasks waiting for execution by a computer. Jobs in the queue are often ordered according to some basis of priority. *See also* queue.

join \join\ *n.* **1.** A database table operation that creates a resultant entry in another table for each entry in the one table whose key field matches that of an entry in the other. *See also* inner join. **2.** A multiprocessing command that causes a child process to return control to its parent. *See also* child (definition 1), multiprocessing.

Joint Photographic Experts Group \joint` fō`tə-graf`ik eks´pərts grōōp`\ *n. See* JPEG (definition 1).

Joliet \jō`lē-et`\ *n.* An extension to the ISO 9660 (1988) standard developed to include long filenames or filenames outside the 8.3 convention. This format is used in some new CD-ROMs for operating systems, such as Windows 95, that can handle such filenames. *See also* 8.3, ISO 9660, long filenames.

Josephson junction \jō´zəf-sən junk`shən\ *n.* A cryoelectronic device that can attain extremely high circuit-switching speeds. In the Josephson effect, when two superconducting materials are in close proximity but are separated by an insulator, electric current can jump or tunnel through the gap.

journal \jər´nəl\ *n.* A computer-based log or record of transactions that take place in a computer or across a network. A journal could be used, for example, to record message transfers on a communications network, to keep track of system activities that alter the contents of a database, or to maintain a record of files that have been archived for storage or deleted from the system. A

journal is often kept as a means of reconstructing events or sets of data should they become lost or damaged. *See also* audit trail.

joystick \joi´stik`\ *n.* A pointing device used mainly but not exclusively for computer games. A joystick has a base, on which control buttons can be mounted, and a vertical stem, which the user can move in any direction to control the movement of an object on the screen; the stem may also have control buttons. The buttons activate various software features, generally producing on-screen events. A joystick is usually used as a relative pointing device, moving an object on the screen when the stem is moved and stopping the movement when the stem is released. In industrial control applications, the joystick can also be used as an absolute pointing device, with each position of the stem mapped to a specific location on the screen. See the illustration. *See also* absolute pointing device, relative pointing device.

Joystick.

.jp \dot`J-P`\ *n.* On the Internet, the major geographic domain specifying that an address is located in Japan.

.jpeg \dot`J´peg, dot`J-P-E-G`\ *n.* The file extension that identifies graphic images files in the JPEG format. *See also* JPEG.

JPEG \J`peg\ *n.* **1.** Acronym for **J**oint **P**hotographic **E**xperts **G**roup. An ISO/ITU standard for storing images in compressed form using a discrete cosine transform. JPEG trades off compression against loss; it can achieve a compression ratio of 100:1 with significant loss and possibly 20:1 with little noticeable loss. **2.** A graphic stored as a file in the JPEG format.

.jpg \dot-J`P-G`\ *n*. The file extension that identifies graphic images encoded in the JPEG File Interchange Format, as originally specified by the Joint Photographic Experts Group (JPEG). Inline graphics on World Wide Web pages are often .jpg files, such as coolgraphic.jpg. *See also* JPEG (definition 2).

Jughead \jug´hed\ *n*. Acronym for **J**onzy's **U**niversal **G**opher **H**ierarchy **E**xcavation **a**nd **D**isplay. An Internet service that enables a user to locate directories in Gopherspace through a keyword search. A Jughead server indexes keywords appearing in directory titles in top-level Gopher menus but does not index the files within the directories. To access Jughead, users must point their Gopher clients to a Jughead server. *See also* Gopher, Gopherspace. *Compare* Archie, Veronica.

jukebox \jook´boks\ *n*. Software that is designed to play a list of sound files in a user-specified order reminiscent of jukeboxes used to play vinyl records. *See also* CD-ROM jukebox.

Julian calendar \joo`lē-ən kal´ən-dər\ *n*. The calendar introduced by Julius Caesar in 46 B.C. to replace the lunar calendar. The Julian calendar provided for a year of 365 days with a leap year every 4 years, or an average year length of 365.25 days. Because the solar year is slightly shorter, the Julian calendar gradually moved out of phase with the seasons and was superseded by the Gregorian calendar, introduced by Pope Gregory XIII. *Compare* Gregorian calendar.

Julian date \joo´lē-ən dāt`\ *n*. **1.** A date expressed as the number of days elapsed since January 1, 4713 B.C. (on the Julian calendar)—for example, 2,450,000 for October 9, 1995 (Gregorian). Julian dates are useful for finding elapsed times between events that may be many years apart, as in astronomy. The starting point is the beginning of the Julian Period, defined in 1583 by Joseph Scaliger as the coincidence of several cycles based on the Julian calendar. *Acronym:* JD (J-D´). *See also* Gregorian calendar, Julian calendar. **2.** Often (but incorrectly), a date expressed as the year and the number of days elapsed since the beginning of the year—for example, 91.13 for January 13, 1991.

jumper \jum´pər\ *n*. A small plug or wire that can be connected between different points in an electronic circuit in order to alter an aspect of a hardware configuration. See the illustration. *Compare* DIP switch.

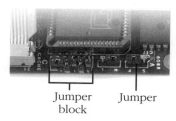

Jumper block   Jumper

Jumper. *A group of jumpers is referred to as a jumper block.*

jump instruction \jump´ in-struk`shən\ *n*. An instruction that transfers the flow of execution from one statement or instruction to another. *See also* GOTO statement, transfer statement.

jump table \jump´ tā`bl\ *n*. *See* dispatch table.

junction \junk´shən\ *n*. **1.** Any point at which two or more electrical components are connected. **2.** The contact between two types of semiconductors, such as N-type and P-type semiconductors. *See also* N-type semiconductor, P-type semiconductor, semiconductor.

justify \jus´tə-fī`\ *vb*. **1.** To align vertically. **2.** To align lines of text evenly along both the left and right margins of a column by inserting extra space between the words in each line. If the spacing is excessive, it can be reduced by rewriting or by hyphenating words at the ends of lines. *See also* align (definition 1). *Compare* rag.

just-in-time \just`in-tīm´\ *adj*. **1.** Describing a system of inventory control and industrial production management based on the Japanese *kanban* system. Under a just-in-time system, workers receive materials from suppliers "just in time" for scheduled manufacturing to take place. Line workers generally signal that they require materials by means of a card or a computerized request system. *Acronym:* JIT (J`I-T´). **2.** Describes a compiler that compiles Java on the fly. *See also* Java, on the fly.

K[1] \K, kil´ō-bīt`\ *n.* Short for **k**ilobyte.

K[2] \K, kil´ō\ *prefix See* kilo-.

K&R C \K`ənd-R C´\ *n.* Short for (Brian W.) **Ker**-nighan and (Dennis M.) **R**itchie **C**. The version of the C programming language, defined by those two authors, that was the informal C standard until a more formal standard was developed by an ANSI committee. *See also* C.

.k12.us \dot-K-twelv`dot-U-S´\ *n.* On the Internet, the major geographic domain specifying that an address is a U.S. K–12 (kindergarten through high school) educational site.

Kb \kil´ə-bit`, K-B´\ *n. See* kilobit.

KB \kil´ə-bīt`, K-B´\ *n. See* kilobyte.

Kbit \K´bit, kil´ə-bit`\ *n. See* kilobit.

Kbps \K`B-P-S´\ *n. See* kilobits per second.

Kbyte \K´bīt, kil´ə-bīt`\ *n. See* kilobyte.

kc \K-C´\ *n. See* kilocycle.

.ke \dot`K-E´\ *n.* On the Internet, the major geographic domain specifying that an address is located in Kenya.

Kerberos or **kerberos** \kər´bər-os`\ *n.* A network authentication protocol developed by MIT. Kerberos authenticates the identity of users attempting to log on to a network and encrypts their communications through secret-key cryptography. A free implementation of Kerberos is available from MIT (http://web.mit.edu/kerberos/www/), although it is also available in many commercial products. *See also* authentication, cryptography.

Kermit \kər´mit\ *n.* A file transfer protocol used in asynchronous communications between computers. Kermit is a very flexible protocol used in many software packages designed for communications over telephone lines. *Compare* Xmodem, Ymodem, Zmodem.

kern \kərn\ *vb.* To alter selectively the distance between pairs of letters for readability and to make the type spacing more balanced and proportional. See the illustration.

kernel \kər´nəl\ *n.* The core of an operating system—the portion of the system that manages memory, files, and peripheral devices; maintains the time and date; launches applications; and allocates system resources.

key \kē\ *n.* **1.** On a keyboard, the combination of a plastic keycap, a tension mechanism that suspends the keycap but allows it to be pressed down, and an electronic mechanism that records the key press and key release. **2.** In database management, an identifier for a record or group of records in a datafile. *See also* B-tree, hash[2], index[1] (definition 1), inverted list, key field. **3.** The code for deciphering encrypted data. **4.** A metal object used with a physical lock to disable a computer system.

keyboard \kē´bōrd\ *n.* A set of switches that resembles a typewriter keyboard and that conveys information from a user to a computer or data communications circuit. *See also* Alt key, Apple key, arrow key, Backspace key, Break key, Caps Lock key, character code, Clear key, Command key, control character, Control key, Delete key, Dvorak keyboard, End key, enhanced keyboard, Enter key, ergonomic keyboard, Escape key, function key, Help key, Home key, Insert key, keyboard buffer, keyboard controller, keyboard enhancer, keycap, key code, Num Lock key, numeric keypad, Option key, original Macintosh keyboard, Page Down key, Page Up key, Pause key, PC/XT keyboard, Power-on key, Print Screen

AWAKE
AWAKE

Kern. **The first three letters of the second example are kerned.**

key, QWERTY keyboard, Return key, scan code, Scroll Lock key, Shift key, Sys Req key, Tab key.

keyboard buffer \kē´bōrd buf´ər\ *n.* A small amount of system memory that stores the most recently typed characters. This buffer is used to store typed characters that have not yet been processed. *Also called* type-ahead buffer.

keyboard controller \kē´bōrd kən-trō`lər\ *n.* A microprocessor installed in a keyboard whose primary function is to wait for and report on keystrokes.

keyboard enhancer \kē´bōrd en-han`sər\ *n.* A program that monitors keystrokes as they are typed and that can be used to redefine the meaning of certain keys or key combinations. Keyboard enhancers are used to create and store macros—sets of keystrokes, mouse actions, menu selections, or other instructions—that are then assigned to keys. *Also called* macro program.

keyboard layout \kē´bōrd lā`out\ *n.* The key arrangement used for a particular keyboard, including such factors as the number of keys (101 is the current standard) and the configuration of the keys (QWERTY is the United States standard). Some proprietary systems use different layouts, and many allow you to map the keys to characters according to your preferences.

keyboard processor \kē´bōrd pros`es-ər\ *n. See* keyboard controller.

keyboard repeat \kē´bōrd rē-pēt´\ *n. See* typematic.

keyboard shortcut \kē´bōrd shōrt´kut\ *n. See* application shortcut key.

keyboard template \kē´bōrd tem`plāt, tem`plət\ *n.* A piece of plastic or heavy paper that fits over or around part of the keyboard, such as the function keys, and has information printed on it about the meanings of the keys.

keycap \kē´kap\ *n.* The plastic piece identifying a key on a keyboard.

key code \kē´ kōd\ *n.* A unique code number assigned to a particular key on a computer keyboard, used to tell the computer which key has been pressed or released. A key code is a special identifier for the key itself and is always the same for a particular key, regardless of the letter, number, or symbol on the key or the character generated by the key. *Compare* character code, scan code.

key escrow \kē` es´krō\ *n.* An encryption method in which a key is provided to a third party approved by a government agency so that any encrypted message can be read by the government. *See also* encryption. *Compare* key recovery.

key field \kē´ fēld\ *n.* A field in a record structure or an attribute of a relational table that has been designated to be part of a key. Any field can be keyed, or indexed, to improve or simplify the performance of retrieval and/or update operations. *See also* attribute (definition 1), field (definition 1), primary key.

key-frame \kē´frām\ *adj.* Describing animation in which starting and ending positions of an object are given, and all frames in between are interpolated by a computer to produce smooth automated animation. Most ray-traced computer animation is created using this technique. *See also* ray tracing.

key in \kē in´\ *vb.* To enter information into a computer by typing it on the computer's keyboard.

keypad \kē´pad\ *n. See* numeric keypad.

keypunch \kē´punch\ *n.* A keyboard-activated device used to punch holes in predetermined locations on paper cards roughly the size of a business envelope. It was used to provide programs and data to early computing systems.

key recovery \kē´ re-kə`vər-ē\ *n.* A private key encryption method that enables an authorized party (such as a government agency), using special software, to recover the key from the encrypted data. Under current law, any encryption software exported from the United States after 1998 must implement key recovery. This requirement supplants an earlier proposed requirement that encryption software for export implement key escrow. *See also* encryption, private key. *Compare* key escrow.

key sort \kē´ sōrt\ *n. See* tag sort.

keystroke \kē´strōk\ *n.* The act of pressing a key on a keyboard to enter a character or initiate a command in a program. The efficiency and ease of use of certain applications is often measured in terms of how many keystrokes it takes to perform common operations. *See also* command, key (definition 1), keyboard.

keyword \kē´wərd\ *n.* **1.** A characteristic word, phrase, or code that is stored in a key field and is used to conduct sorting or searching operations on records. *See also* key field. **2.** Any of the set of words that composes a given programming language or set of operating-system routines. *See also* reserved word.

keyword-in-context \kē`wərd-in-kon´tekst\ *n.* An automatic search methodology that creates indexes of document text or titles. Each keyword is stored in the resulting index along with some surrounding text, usually the word or phrase that precedes or follows the keyword in the text or title. *Acronym:* KWIC (kwik, K`W-I-C´).

.kh \dot`K-H´\ *n.* On the Internet, the major geographic domain specifying that an address is located in Cambodia.

Khornerstone \kōr´nər-stōn`\ *n.* A benchmark of floating-point calculation performance used to test UNIX workstations. *See also* benchmark[1], Dhrystone, floating-point operation, Whetstone.

kHz \kil´ə-hərts\ *n. See* kilohertz.

.ki \dot`K-I´\ *n.* On the Internet, the major geographic domain specifying that an address is located in Kiribati.

kill \kil\ *vb.* **1.** To stop or abort a process in a program or operating system. **2.** In file management, to erase a file, often without hope of reversing the action.

killer app \kil`ər ap´\ *n.* **1.** An application of such popularity and widespread standardization that it fuels sales of the hardware platform or operating system for which it was written. *See also* application. **2.** An application that supplants its competition. *See also* application.

kill file \kil´ fīl\ *n. See* bozo filter.

kilo- \kil´ō, kē´lō\ *prefix* **1.** Metric prefix meaning 10^3 (one thousand). **2.** In computer-related terms, a prefix meaning 2^{10} (1,024).

kilobaud \kil´ə-bäd, kil´ə-bôd\ *n.* A unit of measure of the transmission capacity of a communications channel, equal to 2^{10} (1,024) baud. *See also* baud.

kilobit \kil´ə-bit`\ *n.* Abbreviated Kb or Kbit. A data unit equal to 1,024 bits.

kilobits per second \kil`ə-bits pər sek´ənd\ *n.* Abbreviated Kbps. Data transfer speed, as on a network, measured in multiples of 1,024 bits per second.

kilobyte \kil´ə-bīt`\ *n.* Abbreviated K, KB, or Kbyte. A data unit of 1,024 bytes. *See also* kilo-.

kilocycle \kil´ə-sī`kl\ *n.* Abbreviated kc. A unit of measurement representing 1,000 cycles, generally meaning 1,000 cycles per second. *See also* kilohertz.

kilohertz \kil´ə-hərts\ *n.* Abbreviated kHz. A measure of frequency equivalent to 1,000 hertz, or 1,000 cycles per second. *See also* hertz.

Kinesis ergonomic keyboard \kə-nē`səs ər-gə-nom`ik kē´bōrd\ *n.* A keyboard designed ergonomically to eliminate repetitive strain injuries. *See also* ergonomic keyboard, repetitive strain injury.

kiosk \kē´osk\ *n.* A freestanding computer or terminal that provides information to the public, usually through a multimedia display.

kludge \klōōj\ *n.* **1.** A short-term or makeshift hardware construction. **2.** A program characterized by a lack of design or forethought, as if written in a hurry to satisfy an immediate need. A kludge basically operates properly, but its construction or design is severely lacking in elegance or logical efficiency. *See also* braindamaged, hack[1] (definition 1), spaghetti code.

knockout \nok´out\ *n.* **1.** In multicolor printing, the process of removing from one image the overlapping parts of a graphic or text that are to be printed in a different color so that ink colors will not mix. See the illustration. *See also* spot color. *Compare* overprint. **2.** In hardware, a section of a panel that can be removed to make space for a switch or other component.

Overprint

Knockout

Knockout. A knockout allows an overlapping image to print in the correct color.

knowbot \nō´bot\ *n*. Short for **know**ledge ro**bot**. An artificial-intelligence program that follows a set of predetermined rules to perform work, such as searching for files or looking for documents that contain specific pieces of information on a network, such as the Internet. *See also* bot (definition 2).

knowledge acquisition \nol`əj a`kwə-zish´ən\ *n*. The process of translating knowledge from one or more human experts into a form of representation usable by a computer, for the purpose of developing an expert system. *See also* expert system.

knowledge base \nol´əj bās`\ *n*. A form of database used in expert systems that contains the accumulated body of knowledge of human specialists in a particular field. The reasoning ability or problem-solving approach that a specialist would use is contained in the inference engine, which forms another crucial part of an expert system. *See also* expert system, inference engine.

knowledge-based system \nol`əj-bāsd si´stəm\ *n*. *See* expert system.

knowledge domain \nol`əj dō-mān`\ *n*. The specific area of expertise to which an expert system is devoted. *See also* expert system.

knowledge engineer \nol`əj en-jə-nēr´\ *n*. A computer scientist who builds an expert system by acquiring the needed knowledge and translating it into a program. *See also* expert system.

knowledge representation \nol`əj re-prə-zən-tā´shən\ *n*. The methodology that forms the basis for the decision-making structure in an expert system, usually taking the form of if-then rules. *See also* expert system.

Korn shell \kōrn´ shel\ *n*. A command-line interface, available under UNIX, that combines features of the Bourne and C shells. The Korn shell is fully compatible with the Bourne shell but also offers the history and command-line editing capability of the C shell. *See also* command-line interface, shell[1], UNIX. *Compare* Bourne shell, C shell.

.kp \dot`K-P´\ *n*. On the Internet, the major geographic domain specifying that an address is located in North Korea.

.kr \dot`K-R´\ *n*. On the Internet, the major geographic domain specifying that an address is located in South Korea.

KSR terminal \K`S-R´ tər`mə-nəl\ *n*. Short for **k**eyboard **s**end/**r**eceive **terminal.** A type of terminal that accepts input from a keyboard only and uses an internal printer rather than a screen to display the keyboard input and the output received from the sending terminal. *See also* TTY.

.kw \dot`K-W´\ *n*. On the Internet, the major geographic domain specifying that an address is located in Kuwait.

KWIC \kwik, K`W-I-C´\ *n*. *See* keyword-in-context.

.ky \dot`K-Y´\ *n*. On the Internet, the major geographic domain specifying that an address is located in the Cayman Islands.

.kz \dot`K-Z´\ *n*. On the Internet, the major geographic domain specifying that an address is located in Kazakhstan.

L1 cache \L-wən´ kash`\ *n.* A memory cache built into i486 and higher-level processors. The L1 cache, typically containing 8 KB, can be read in a single clock cycle, so it is tried first. The i486 contains one L1 cache; the Pentium contains two, one for code and one for data. *Also called* level 1 cache, on-chip cache. *See also* cache, i486DX, Pentium. *Compare* L2 cache.

L2 cache \L-too´ kash`\ *n.* A memory cache consisting of static RAM on a motherboard that uses an i486 or higher-level processor. The L2 cache, which typically contains 128 KB to 1 MB, is faster than the system DRAM but slower than the L1 cache built into the CPU chip. *Also called* level 2 cache. *See also* cache, dynamic RAM, i486DX, static RAM. *Compare* L1 cache.

L8R \lā´tər\ *adv.* Abbreviation for "later." As in "See you later," an expression often used in e-mail or Usenet groups as a closing remark.

.la \dot`L-A´\ *n.* On the Internet, the major geographic domain specifying that an address is located in Laos.

label \lā´bəl\ *n.* An identifier. A label can be a physical item, such as a stick-on tag used to identify disks and other computer equipment, or an electronic label added to floppy disks or hard disks. It can also be a word, symbol, or other group of characters used to identify a file, a storage medium, an element defined in a computer program, or a specific item in a document such as a spreadsheet or a chart. *See also* identifier.

label prefix \lā´bəl prē`fiks\ *n.* In a spreadsheet, a character at the beginning of a cell entry that identifies the entry to the program as a label.

lag \lag\ *n.* The time difference between two events. In electronics, a lag is a delay between a change in input and a change in output. On computer displays, a lag is a fading brightness left on the phosphor coating of the screen after an image changes. *See also* persistence.

LAN \lan\ *n.* Acronym for **l**ocal **a**rea **n**etwork. A group of computers and other devices dispersed over a relatively limited area and connected by a communications link that enables any device to interact with any other on the network. LANs commonly include microcomputers and shared resources such as laser printers and large hard disks. The devices on a LAN are known as nodes, and the nodes are connected by cables through which messages are transmitted. *See also* baseband network, broadband network, bus network, collision detection, communications protocol, contention, CSMA/CD, network, ring network, star network, token bus network, token passing, token ring network. *Compare* wide area network.

landscape mode \land´skāp mōd`\ *n.* A horizontal print orientation in which text or images are printed "sideways"—that is, the width of the image on the page is greater than the height. See the illustration. *Compare* portrait mode.

Lorem ipsum solebat somnus complexus est. Africanus se ostendit es forma quae mihi imagine elus quam ex isso erat notior. Quem ubi agnovi, quidem cohorrui. Quaesivi tamen vivertne ipse et Paulus pater et ali quos nos extintos.

Landscape mode.

landscape monitor \land´skāp mon`ə-tər\ *n.* A monitor that is wider than it is high. Landscape monitors are usually about 33 percent wider than they are high—roughly the same proportion as a television screen. *Compare* full-page display, portrait monitor.

language-description language \lang`wəj-də-skrip`shən lang´wəj\ *n. See* metalanguage.

language processor \lang´wəj pros`es-ər\ *n.* A hardware device or a software program designed to accept instructions written in a particular language and translate them into machine code. *See also* compiler (definition 2), interpreter.

language translation program \lang`wəj tranz-lā´shən prō`gram\ *n.* A program that translates statements written in one language into another language (usually from one high-level language into another). *See also* high-level language.

LAN Manager \lan´ man´ə-jər\ *n.* A local area network technology developed by Microsoft Corporation and distributed by Microsoft, IBM (as IBM LAN Server), and other original equipment manufacturers. LAN Manager connects computers running the MS-DOS, OS/2, or UNIX operating system and allows users to share files and system resources and to run distributed applications using a client/server architecture. *See also* client/server architecture, LAN.

laptop \lap´top\ *n.* A small, portable personal computer that runs on either batteries or AC power, designed for use during travel. Laptops have flat LCD or plasma screens and small keyboards. Most can run the same software as their desktop counterparts and can accept similar peripherals, such as sound cards, internal or external modems, and floppy disks and CD-ROM drives. Some laptops are designed to be plugged into a docking station, effectively making them desktop computers. Most have connectors for plugging in external keyboards and full-sized monitors. Older laptops weighed as much as 15 pounds; current laptops can weigh as little as 5 pounds, without peripherals such as floppy disk or CD-ROM drives. While *notebook* is the current term for ultralight portable computers, these machines are also commonly referred to as laptops. *See also* portable computer. *Compare* subnotebook computer.

large model \lärj` mod´əl\ *n.* A memory model of the Intel 80x86 processor family. The large model allows both code and data to exceed 64 kilobytes, but the total of both must generally be less than 1 megabyte. Each data structure must be less than 64 kilobytes in size. *See also* memory model.

large-scale integration \lärj`skāl` in-tə-grā´shən\ *n.* A term describing the concentration of between 100 and 5,000 circuit elements on a single chip. *Acronym:* LSI (L`S-I´). *See also* integrated circuit. *Compare* medium-scale integration, small-scale integration, super-large-scale integration, ultra-large-scale integration, very-large-scale integration.

laser or **LASER** \lā´zər\ *n.* Acronym for **l**ight **a**mplification by **s**timulated **e**mission of **r**adiation. A device that uses certain quantum effects to produce coherent light, which travels with greater efficiency than noncoherent light because the beam diverges only slightly as it travels. Lasers are used in computer technology to transmit data through fiber-optic cables, to read and write data on CD-ROMs, and to place an image on a photosensitive drum in laser printers.

laser engine \lā´zər en`jən\ *n. See* printer engine.

laser printer \lā´zər prin`tər\ *n.* An electrophotographic printer that is based on the technology used by photocopiers. A focused laser beam and a rotating mirror are used to draw an image of the desired page on a photosensitive drum. This image is converted on the drum into an electrostatic charge, which attracts and holds toner. A piece of electrostatically charged paper is rolled against the drum, which pulls the toner away from the drum and onto the paper. Heat is then applied to fuse the toner to the paper. Finally, the electrical charge is removed from the drum, and the excess toner is collected. By omitting the final step and repeating only the toner-application and paper-handling steps, the printer can make multiple copies. The only serious drawback of a laser printer is that it offers less paper-handling flexibility than do dot-matrix printers. Both multipart forms and wide-carriage printing, for example, are better handled by line printers, dot-matrix printers, or daisy-wheel printers. *See also* electrophotographic printers, nonimpact printer, page printer. *Compare* daisy-wheel printer, dot-matrix printer, ion-deposition printer, LCD printer, LED printer.

laser storage \lā´zər stōr`əj\ *n.* The use of optical read/write technology with metallic discs for information storage. *See also* compact disc.

LaserWriter 35 \lā`zər rī`tər thər`tē-fīv´\ *n.* The standard set of 35 PostScript fonts for the Apple LaserWriter family of laser printers. *See also* laser printer, PostScript font.

last in, first out \last in` fərst out´\ *n.* A method of processing a queue in which items are removed in inverse order relative to the order in which they were added—that is, the last in is the first out. *Acronym:* LIFO (lī´fō, L`I-F-O´). *See also* stack. *Compare* first in, first out.

latch \lach\ *n.* A circuit or circuit element used to maintain a particular state, such as on or off, or logical true or false. A latch changes state only in response to a particular input. *See also* flip-flop.

late binding \lāt´ bīn`dēng\ *n. See* dynamic binding.

latency \lā´tən-sē\ *n.* The time required for a signal to travel from one point on a network to another. *See also* ping[1] (definition 1).

LaTeX[1] or **L^AT_EX** \lä-tek´\ *n.* A document preparation system based on TeX, developed by Leslie Lamport. By using simple, intuitive commands for text elements such as headers, LaTeX lets the user focus more on document content than document appearance. *See also* header (definition 1), TeX.

LaTeX[2] \lä-tek´\ *vb.* To process a LaTeX file. *See also* LaTeX[1].

launch \länch, lônch\ *vb.* To activate an application program (especially on the Macintosh) from the operating system's user interface.

Launcher \län´chər, lôn´chər\ *n.* In Mac OS, a program that organizes frequently used applications and programs and that allows the user to execute them with a single mouse click.

.la.us \dot-L-A`dot-U-S´\ *n.* On the Internet, the major geographic domain specifying that an address is located in Louisiana, United States.

layer \lâr, lā´ər\ *n.* **1.** The protocol or protocols operating at a particular level within a protocol suite, such as IP within the TCP/IP suite. Each layer is responsible for providing specific services or functions for computers exchanging information over a communications network (such as the layers outlined in the ISO/OSI model shown in the table) and information is passed from one layer to the next. Although different suites have varying numbers of levels, generally the highest layer deals with software interactions at the application level, and the lowest governs hardware-level connections between different computers. *See also* ISO/OSI model, protocol stack, TCP/IP. **2.** In communications and distributed processing, a set of rules and standards that handles a particular class of events.

ISO/OSI MODEL

ISO/OSI layer	Focus
Application (highest level)	Program-to-program transfer of information
Presentation	Text formatting and display, code conversion
Session	Establishing, maintaining, and coordinating communication
Transport	Accurate delivery, service quality
Network	Transport routes, message handling and transfer
Data-link	Coding, addressing, and transmitting information
Physical	Hardware connections

layered interface \lârd` in´tər-fās, lā`ərd\ *n.* In programming, one or more levels of routines lying between an application and the computing hardware and separating activities according to the type of task the activities are designed to carry out. Ultimately, such an interface makes it easier to adapt a program to different types of equipment. See the illustration.

layering \lâr´ēng, lā´ər-ēng\ *n.* In computer graphics, the grouping of logically related elements in a drawing. Layering enables a program user to view, and work on independently, portions of a graphic instead of the entire drawing.

layout \lā´out\ *n.* **1.** The overall plan or design of a document system. *See also* page layout. **2.** In programming, the order and sequence of input and output. **3.** In computer design, the arrangement of circuits and other components of the system.

lazy evaluation \lā´zē ə-val-yə-wā´shən\ *n.* A programming mechanism that allows an evaluation action to be performed only when needed and only to a certain extent. Lazy evaluation allows a program to handle data objects such as extremely large tables and lists in a timely and effective manner.

.lb \dot`L-B´\ *n*. On the Internet, the major geographic domain specifying that an address is located in Lebanon.

.lc \dot`L-C´\ *n*. On the Internet, the major geographic domain specifying that an address is located in Saint Lucia.

LCC \L`C-C´\ *n*. *See* leadless chip carrier.

lcd \L`C-D´\ *n*. In some FTP clients, the command that changes the current directory on the local system. *See also* FTP client.

LCD \L`C-D´\ *n*. *See* liquid crystal display.

LCD printer \L`C-D´ prin`tər\ *n*. Short for **l**iquid **c**rystal **d**isplay **printer**. An electrophotographic printer similar to a laser printer and often incorrectly labeled as one. LCD printers use a bright light source, typically a halogen lamp. *Also called* liquid crystal shutter printer. *See also* electrophotographic printers, nonimpact printer, page printer. *Compare* ion-deposition printer, laser printer, LED printer.

LCD projector \L-C-D´ prə-jek`tər\ *n*. Short for **l**iquid **c**rystal **d**isplay **projector.** A device that casts an image of a computer's video output from a liquid crystal display onto a screen. *See also* liquid crystal display.

LDAP \L`D-A-P´\ *n*. *See* Lightweight Directory Access Protocol.

lead[1] \lēd\ *n*. In electronics, the metallic connector of certain components such as resistors and capacitors.

lead[2] \led\ *n*. In typography, the amount of vertical space between two lines of text.

leader \lē´dər\ *n*. A row of dots, hyphens, or other such characters used to lead the eye across a printed page to related information. Leaders can be created by many word processors and other programs.

leading \led´ēng\ *n*. The space, expressed in points, between lines of type, measured from the baseline (bottom) of one line to the baseline of the next. The term is derived from the traditional typesetting practice of inserting a thin bar of lead between lines of metal type. See the illustration on the next page. *See also* point[1] (definition 1).

leading edge \lē`dēng ej´\ *n*. The initial part of an electronic signal. If a digital signal switches from

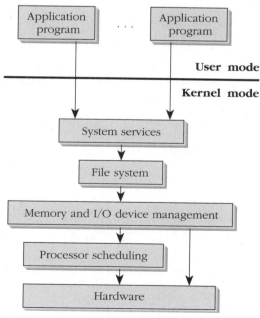

Layered interface.

off to on and then back to off, the transition from off to on is the leading edge of the signal.

leading zero \lē`dēng zēr-ō\ *n.* A zero that precedes the most significant (leftmost) digit of a number. One or more leading zeros may be used as fill characters in a field containing numeric input. Leading zeros have no significance in the value of a number.

lead ion battery \led` ī´on bat`ər-ē\ *n.* An energy storage device that is based on the conversion of chemical to electrical energy as ions flow from one terminal to another through an acid medium in which lead and copper are suspended. This type of battery is used in laptop and notebook computers.

leadless chip carrier \lēd`ləs chip´ kâr-ē-ər\ *n.* A method of mounting chips on boards. A leadless chip carrier has contacts, rather than leglike pins, for connecting it to the board. The chip simply rests in a socket that has contacts on its base for completing the connection, and the chip is clamped in place so that the contacts are secure. *Acronym:* LCC (L`C-C´). *See also* PLCC. *Compare* DIP (definition 1), pin grid array.

leaf \lēf\ *n.* Any node (location) in a tree structure that is at the farthest distance from the root (primary node), no matter which path is followed. Thus, in any tree, a leaf is a node at the end of a branch—one that has no descendants. *See also* root, subtree, tree.

leapfrog test \lēp´frog test`\ *n.* A diagnostic routine, used for testing disk or tape storage, that repeatedly copies itself onto the storage medium.

leased line \lēsd līn´\ *n. See* dedicated line (definition 1).

least significant bit \lēst` sig`nif´ə-kənt bit`\ *n.* In a sequence of one or more bytes, the low-order (usually rightmost) bit of a binary number. *Acronym:* LSB (L`S-B´). *See also* low-order. *Compare* most significant bit.

least significant character \lēst` sig-nif´ə-kənt kâr´ək-tər\ *n.* The low-order, or rightmost, charac-

ter in a string. *Acronym:* LSC (L`S-C´). *See also* low-order. *Compare* most significant character.

least significant digit \lēst sig-nif´ə-kənt dij´ət\ *n.* The low-order, or rightmost, digit in the normal representation of a number. *Acronym:* LSD (L`S-D´). *See also* low-order. *Compare* most significant digit.

LED \L`E-D´\ *n. See* light-emitting diode.

LED printer \L`E-D´ prin´tər\ *n.* Short for **l**ight-**e**mitting **d**iode **printer**. An electrophotographic printer similar to LCD and laser printers. The significant difference between LED and laser or LCD printers is in the light source; LED printers use an array of light-emitting diodes. *See also* electrophotographic printers, light-emitting diode, nonimpact printer, page printer. *Compare* ion-deposition printer, laser printer, LCD printer.

left justification \left ju-stə-fə-kā´shən\ *n.* In typesetting, word processing, and desktop publishing, the process of aligning text evenly along the left margin of a column or page. The right edge of the text is ragged. *See also* justify (definition 1), rag. *Compare* full justification, right justification.

left-justify \left`-ju´stə-fī\ *vb.* To justify, as text, along the left. *See also* justify (definition 1), rag. *Compare* right-justify.

legacy \leg´ə-sē\ *adj.* Of or pertaining to documents or data that existed prior to a certain time. The designation refers particularly to a change in process or technique that requires translating old data files to a new system.

legacy data \leg´ə-sē dā`tə, dat`ə\ *n.* Data acquired by an organization that was compiled by another organization. The acquiring organization thus receives the existing information as a "legacy" from the information's prior owner.

legacy system \leg´ə-sē si`stəm\ *n.* A computer, software program, network, or other computer equipment that remains in use after a business or organization installs new systems. Compatibility with legacy systems is an important consideration

---

Leading ⭥ A generous amount of space between lines of type is called open leading. ⟩ Baselines

Leading.   *Ordinary text is typically set with leading one or two points greater than the point size of the type.*

when a new version is installed. For example, will a new spreadsheet software release be able to read the existing business records without expensive and time-consuming conversion to a new format? Many legacy systems are based on mainframe computers, which are being slowly replaced in many organizations by client/server architectures. *See also* mainframe computer. *Compare* client/server architecture.

legend \lej´ənd\ *n.* Text that describes or explains a graphic, usually printed below the graphic. On a graph or map, the legend is the key to the patterns or the symbols used.

Lempel Ziv algorithm \lem`pəl ziv` al´gə-ridh-əm\ *n.* A mathematical algorithm designed to reduce a data file's size without sacrificing its integrity. *See also* .lzh.

length \length\ *n.* The number of linear units of storage space occupied by an object, such as a file on disk or a data structure in a program, typically measured in bits, bytes, or blocks.

less than \les´ dhan\ *adj. See* relational operator.

less than or equal to \les` dhan ōr ē´kwəl tōō\ *adj. See* relational operator.

letterbomb \let´ər-bom`\ *n.* An e-mail message that is intended to impair the recipient's computer use. Some sequences of control characters can lock up a terminal, files attached to the message may contain viruses or Trojan horses, and a sufficiently large message can overflow a mailbox or crash a system. *See also* control character, e-mail[1] (definition 1), mailbox, Trojan horse, virus.

letter quality \let`ər kwä´lə-tē\ *adj.* Pertaining to or being a level of print quality on dot-matrix printers that is better than draft quality. As the name implies, letter quality is supposed to be crisp and dark enough for use in business letters. *See also* print quality. *Compare* draft quality, near-letter-quality.

letter-quality printer \let`ər kwä-lə-tē prin´tər\ *n.* Any printer that produces output high enough in quality to be acceptable for business letters. *See also* daisy-wheel printer, laser printer.

level 1 cache \lev`əl wən´ kash`\ *n. See* L1 cache.

level 2 cache \lev`əl tōō´ kash`\ *n. See* L2 cache.

lexicographic sort \leks`ə-kə-graf`ik sōrt´\ *n.* A sort that arranges items in the order in which they would appear if listed in a dictionary. A lexico-graphic sort puts numbers, for instance, where they would be if they were spelled out; for example, 567 would fall in the F's. *Compare* alphanumeric sort.

lexicon \leks´ə-kon`\ *n.* **1.** The words of a language and their definitions. **2.** In programming, the identifiers, keywords, constants, and other elements of a language that make up its "vocabulary." The ways in which these vocabulary elements can be put together is the syntax of the language. *Compare* syntax.

LF \L-F´\ *n. See* linefeed.

LHARC \L`H-A`R-C´\ *n.* A freeware file-compression utility program developed by Haruyasu Yoshizaki and introduced in 1988. With LHARC, the contents of one or more files can be compressed into a singular, smaller file, with the extension .lha. A copy of the program is required to uncompress these files. LHARC can also embed a small program with the compressed information and save everything in a single file, called a self-extracting archive, with an .exe extension. As a result, the recipient of the compressed file does not need a separate utility program to uncompress the file. *See also* freeware, PKZIP, utility program.

.li \dot`L-I´\ *n.* On the Internet, the major geographic domain specifying that an address is located in Liechtenstein.

library \lī´brär`ē, lī´brər-ē\ *n.* **1.** In programming, a collection of routines stored in a file. Each set of instructions in a library has a name, and each performs a different task. **2.** A collection of software or data files.

library routine \lī´brär`ē rōō-tēn`, lī´brər-ē\ *n.* In programming, a routine stored in a collection of routines (a library) that can be used by any program that can link into the library. *See also* function library, library (definition 1).

.lib.us \dot-līb`dot-U-S´, dot-L-I-B`dot-U-S´\ *n.* On the Internet, the major geographic domain specifying that an address belongs to a library in the United States.

license agreement \lī´sens ə-grē`mənt\ *n.* A legal contract between a software provider and a user specifying the rights of the user regarding the software. Usually the license agreement is in effect with retail software once the user opens the software package.

licensing key \lī´sən-sēng kē`\ *n*. A short character string that serves as a password during the installation of licensed commercial software. The use of licensing keys is a security device aimed at reducing illegal duplication of licensed software.

LIFO \lī´fō, L`I-F-O´\ *n*. *See* last in, first out.

light-emitting diode \līt`ə-mit-ēng dī´ōd\ *n*. A semiconductor device that converts electrical energy into light, used, for example, for the activity lights on computer disk drives. Light-emitting diodes work on the principle of electroluminescence and are highly efficient, producing little heat for the amount of light output. See the illustration. *Acronym:* LED (L`E-D´).

Light-emitting diode. Two of several types of LED, jumbo and miniature. Note that one lead is shorter than the other to indicate polarity.

light guide \līt´ gīd\ *n*. A structure, such as a fiber-optic filament, designed to transmit light over distances with minimal attenuation or loss.

light pen \līt´ pen\ *n*. An input device consisting of a stylus that is connected to a computer's monitor. The user points at the screen with the stylus and selects items or chooses commands either by pressing a clip on the side of the light pen or by pressing the light pen against the surface of the screen (the equivalent of performing a mouse click). *See also* absolute pointing device. *Compare* touch screen.

light source \līt´ sōrs\ *n*. **1.** The device that provides the luminescence (for example, a bulb or laser) in any technology based on the use and interpretation of light, such as a scanner or CRT. **2.** In computer graphics, the imaginary location of a source of light, which determines the shading in an image.

lightwave system \līt´wāv si`stəm\ *n*. A system that transmits information by means of light.

Lightweight Directory Access Protocol \līt`wāt dər-ek`tər-ē ak´ses prō`tə-kol\ *n*. A network protocol designed to work on TCP/IP stacks to extract information from a hierarchical directory such as X.500. This gives users a single tool to comb through data to find a particular piece of information, such as a user name, e-mail address, security certificate, or other contact information. *Acronym:* LDAP (L`D-A-P´). *See also* CCITT X series.

Lightweight Internet Person Schema \līt`wāt in`tər-net pər´sən skē`mə\ *n*. In Lightweight Directory Access Protocol directories, a specification for the retrieval of such information as names and e-mail addresses. *Acronym:* LIPS (L`I-P-S´). *See also* Lightweight Directory Access Protocol.

LIM EMS \lim` E-M-S´, L-I-M`\ *n*. Acronym for **L**otus/**I**ntel/**M**icrosoft **E**xpanded **M**emory **S**pecification. *See* EMS.

limit check \lim´ət chek`\ *n*. In programming, a test that checks specified information to verify that it is within acceptable limits. *See also* array.

limiting operation \lim-ə-tēng op-ər-ā´shən\ *n*. Any routine or operation that constrains the performance of a larger process in which it is included; a bottleneck.

line \līn\ *n*. **1.** Any wire or wires, such as power lines and telephone lines, used to transmit electrical power or signals. **2.** In communications, a connection, usually a physical wire or other cable, between sending and receiving (or calling and called) devices, including telephones, computers, and terminals. **3.** In word processing, a string of characters displayed or printed in a single horizontal row. **4.** In programming, a statement (instruction) that occupies one line of the program. In this context, the common reference is to a "program line" or a "line of code."

line adapter \līn´ ə-dap`tər\ *n*. A device, such as a modem or network card, that connects a computer to a communications line and converts a signal to an acceptable form for transmission.

line analyzer \līn´ an`ə-lī-zər\ *n*. A monitoring device used to verify the integrity of a communications line and to assist in troubleshooting.

linear \lin´ē-ər\ *adj*. **1.** Having the characteristics of a line. **2.** Proceeding sequentially. For example, a linear search is one that moves from A to B to C. **3.** In mathematics and electronics, having a direct and proportional relationship among characteristics or variables. For example, the output of a linear amplifier is directly proportional to the input. *See also* linear programming.

linear addressing architecture \lin`ē-ər ə-dres`-ēng är´kə-tek-chur, a`dres-ēng är´kə-tek-chur\ *n.* An architecture that allows a microprocessor to access any individual memory location by means of a single address value. Thus, each memory location within the entire range of addressable memory has a unique, specified address. *See also* flat address space, segmented address space.

linear inferences per second \lin`ē-ər in`fər-ən-səz pər sek´ənd\ *n. See* LIPS (definition 2).

linear list \lin`ē-ər list´\ *n.* A simple ordered list of elements in which each element except the first immediately succeeds one other element, and each except the last immediately precedes one other. *Compare* linked list.

linear memory \lin`ē-ər mem´ər-ē\ *n. See* flat memory.

linear programming \lin`ē-ər prō´gram-ēng\ *n.* The process of creating programs that find optimal solutions for systems of equations (composed of linear functions) in which the terms given are not sufficient to derive a straightforward solution.

linear search \lin`ē-ər sərch´\ *n.* A simple, though inefficient, search algorithm that operates by sequentially examining each element in a list until the target element is found or the last item has been completely processed. Linear searches are primarily used for very short lists. *Also called* sequential search. *See also* search algorithm. *Compare* binary search, hash search.

linear structure \lin`ē-ər struk´chur\ *n.* A structure in which items are organized according to strict rules of precedence. In a linear structure, two conditions apply: if X precedes Y and Y precedes Z, then X precedes Z; and if X precedes Y and X precedes Z, then either Y precedes Z or Z precedes Y.

line-based browser \lin`bāsd brou´zər\ *n.* A Web browser whose display is based on text rather than graphics. A popular line-based browser is Lynx. *See also* Lynx, Web browser.

line cap \lin´ kap\ *n.* The way in which a line segment is terminated when the segment is printed, especially on a PostScript-compatible printer. See the illustration. *See also* line join.

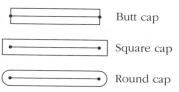

Butt cap

Square cap

Round cap

Line cap. The dots represent the mathematical endpoints of a specified line.

line chart \lin´ chärt\ *n.* A business graphic in which values from one or more sets of data are connected by lines. See the illustration.

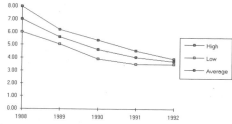

Line chart.

line concentration \lin´ kon-sən-trä`shən\ *n.* The funneling of multiple input channels into a smaller number of output channels. *See also* concentrator.

line conditioning \lin´ kən-dish`ə-nēng\ *n. See* conditioning.

line drawing \lin´ drä`ēng, drô`ēng\ *n.* A drawing made up of solid lines without shading or other features that suggest mass or contouring.

line driver \lin´ drī`vər\ *n.* A device used to increase transmission distance by amplifying a signal before placing it on the line or passing it along the line. *See also* short-haul.

line editor \lin´ ed`ə-tər\ *n.* A text-editing program that numbers each line of text, working with the document on a line-by-line rather than on a word-by-word basis. *See also* editor.

linefeed \lin´fēd\ *n.* A control character that tells a computer or printer to advance one line below the current line without moving the position of the cursor or print head. *Acronym:* LF (L-F´).

line join \līn´ join\ *n.* The way in which two line segments are connected when they are printed, especially on a PostScript-compatible printer. See the illustration. *See also* line cap.

Miter join

Round join

Beveled join

Line join.   Three styles of line join.

line level \līn´ lev`əl\ *n.* The strength of a communications signal at a given point on the line, measured in decibels (a multiple of the base-10 logarithm of the ratio between two values) or nepers (the natural logarithm of the ratio between two values).

line load \līn´ lōd\ *n.* **1.** In communications, a measure of the usage of a communications line expressed as a percentage of the maximum capacity of the circuit. **2.** In electronics, the amount of current carried by a line.

line noise \līn´ noiz\ *n.* Spurious signals in a communications channel that interfere with the exchange of information. In an analog circuit, line noise may take the form of a pure audio tone, static, or signals leaked from another circuit. In a digital circuit, line noise is any signal that makes it difficult or impossible for the device at the receiving end of the circuit to interpret the transmitted signal accurately. *See also* channel.

line number \līn´ num`bər\ *n.* **1.** A number assigned by a line editor to a line of text and used to refer to that line for purposes of viewing, editing, or printing. The line numbers are sequential. *See also* line editor. **2.** In communications, an identifying number assigned to a communications channel.

line printer \līn´ prin`tər\ *n.* Any printer that prints one line at a time as opposed to one character at a time (as with many dot-matrix printers) or one page at a time (as with some dot-matrix and most laser printers). Line printers typically produce the familiar 11-by-17-inch "computer" print-

outs. They are high-speed devices and are often used with mainframes, minicomputers, or networked machines rather than with single-user systems.

line regulator \līn´ re`gyə-lā-tər\ *n.* See voltage regulator.

line segment \līn´ seg`mənt\ *n.* A portion of a line, defined by its beginning and ending points.

lines of code \līnz` əv kōd´\ *n.* A measure of program length. Depending on circumstances, a line of code can be each line in the program (including blank lines and comments), each line containing actual code, or each statement. *See also* statement.

line spacing \līn´ spā`sēng\ *n.* See leading.

line speed \līn´ spēd\ *n.* See baud rate, data rate.

lines per minute \līnz` pər min´ut\ *n.* A measurement of printer speed, the number of lines of characters printed in one minute. *Acronym:* LPM (L`P-M´).

line style \līn´ stīl\ *n.* In desktop publishing, printing, and high-end word processing, the form and quality of a line, such as a dotted line, a double line, or a hairline. *See also* hairline.

line surge \līn´ surj\ *n.* A sudden, transient increase in the voltage or current carried by a line. A nearby lightning strike, for example, can cause a surge in power lines that can damage electrical equipment. Delicate types of equipment such as computers are often protected from line surges by surge suppressors placed in the power lines.

line voltage \līn´ vōl`təj\ *n.* The voltage present in a power line. In North America, line voltage is approximately 115 volts alternating current (VAC).

line width \līn´ width\ *n.* The length of a line of type measured from the left margin to the right margin on a piece of paper or on a computer screen. On a typewriter, line width is usually measured in terms of the number of monospace alphanumeric characters that can fit on the line; on a computer monitor or printer, line width is normally measured in inches, centimeters, points, or picas. *See also* pica (definition 2), point[1] (definition 1).

linguistics \lēng-wi´stiks\ *n.* The analytic study of human language. Close ties exist between linguistics and computer science because of the mutual interest in grammar, syntax, semantics, formal language theory, and natural-language processing.

link \lēnk\ *vb.* **1.** To produce an executable program from compiled modules (programs, routines, or libraries) by merging the object code (assembly language object code, executable machine code, or a variation of machine code) of the program and resolving interconnecting references (such as a library routine called by a program). *See also* linker. **2.** To connect two elements in a data structure by using index variables or pointer variables. *See also* index (definition 1), pointer (definition 1).

linkage editor \lēnk´əj ed`ə-tər\ *n.* *See* linker.

link edit \lēnk´ ed`it\ *vb.* *See* link (definition 1).

linked list \lēnkt list´\ *n.* In programming, a list of nodes or elements of a data structure connected by pointers. A singly linked list has one pointer in each node pointing to the next node in the list; a doubly linked list has two pointers in each node pointing to the next and previous nodes. In a circular list, the first and last nodes of the list are linked together. *See also* array, key (definition 2), list, node (definition 1), pointer (definition 1). *Compare* linear list.

linker \lēnk´ər\ *n.* A program that links compiled modules and data files to create an executable program. A linker can also have other functions, such as creating libraries. *See also* library, link (definition 1), program creation.

link time \lēnk´ tīm\ *n.* **1.** The length of time required to link a program. *See also* link (definition 1). **2.** The period during which a program is being linked. *See also* compile time (definition 2), link (definition 1), run time (definition 1).

link-time binding \lēnk´tīm bīn`dēng\ *n.* Assignment of a meaning to an identifier (such as a subroutine label) in a program at the time that various files of compiled code are linked together to form an executable program, rather than when the source code is compiled or when the program is run. *Compare* compile-time binding, run-time binding.

Linotronic \lī`nə-tron´ik\ *n.* Any in the series of high-quality typesetting devices known as Linotronic laser imagesetters, which can print at resolutions such as 1,270 and 2,540 dots per inch (dpi). These devices are commonly attached to PostScript raster image processors (RIPs) so that desktop publishing applications can typeset directly

from a microcomputer. *See also* imagesetter, PostScript, raster image processor.

Linpack \lin´-pak\ *n.* A benchmarking routine that solves 100 simultaneous equations in a test of CPU, floating-point processor, and memory access speeds. *See also* benchmark[2], central processing unit, floating-point processor.

Linux \lē´nuks, lin´uks\ *n.* A version of the UNIX System V Release 3.0 kernel developed for PCs with 80386 and higher-level microprocessors. Developed by Linus Torvalds of Sweden (for whom it is named) along with numerous collaborators worldwide, Linux is distributed free with source code through BBSs and the Internet, although some companies distribute it as part of a commercial package with Linux-compatible utilities. The Linux kernel works with the GNU utilities developed by the Free Software Foundation, which did not produce a kernel. *See also* free software, GNU, kernel, UNIX.

LIPS \L`I-P-S´\ *n.* **1.** Acronym for **L**anguage **I**ndependent **P**rogram **S**ubtitling. A system developed by the GIST group (C-DAC, India) and used by Indian Television for nationwide broadcast of programs with multilingual subtitles in teletext mode. This system was judged the best design in the VLSI design contest in the VLSI '93 International Conference. Three versions of this application-specific integrated circuit (ASIC) with different features were implemented in Xilinx 3K and 4K series FPLAs. *See also* field-programmable logic array, gate array, very-large-scale integration. **2.** Acronym for **l**inear **i**nferences **p**er **s**econd. A measure of speed for some types of artificial-intelligence machines and expert systems. *See also* artificial intelligence, expert system. **3.** *See* Lightweight Internet Person Schema.

liquid crystal display \li`kwid kri´stəl di-splā`\ *n.* A type of display that uses a liquid compound having a polar molecular structure, sandwiched between two transparent electrodes. When an electric field is applied, the molecules align with the field, forming a crystalline arrangement that polarizes the light passing through it. A polarized filter laminated over the electrodes blocks polarized light. In this way, a grid of electrodes can selectively "turn on" a cell, or a pixel, containing the liquid crystal material, turning it dark. In some types of liquid crystal displays, an electroluminescent panel is placed behind the screen to illuminate it. Other types of liquid crystal displays are capable of reproducing color. *Acronym:* LCD (L`C-D´).

liquid crystal display printer \li`kwid kri-stəl di-splā´ prin-tər\ *n. See* LCD printer.

liquid crystal shutter printer \li`kwid　　kri-stəl shut´ər prin-tər\ *n. See* LCD printer.

LISP \lisp, L`I-S-P´\ *n.* Short for **Lis**t **P**rocessing. A list-oriented programming language developed in 1959–60 by John McCarthy and used primarily to manipulate lists of data. LISP is heavily used in research and academic circles and is considered the standard language for artificial-intelligence research. *See also* artificial intelligence. *Compare* Prolog.

list \list\ *n.* A multi-element data structure that has a linear (first, second, third, . . .) organization but that allows elements to be added or removed in any order. Queues, deques, and stacks are simply lists with restrictions on adding and removing elements. *See also* deque, element (definition 1), linked list, queue, stack.

list box \list´ boks\ *n.* A control in Microsoft Windows that enables the user to choose one option from a list of possibilities. The list box appears as a box, displaying the currently selected option, next to a button marked with a down-arrow. When the user clicks on the button, the list appears. The list has a scroll bar if there are more options than the list has room to show.

listing \li´stēng\ *n.* A printed copy of program source code. Some compilers and assemblers produce optional assembly listings during compilation or assembly. Such listings of code often have additional information such as line numbers, nested block depth, and cross-reference tables. *See also* assembly listing.

list processing \list´ pros`es-ēng\ *n.* The maintenance and manipulation of multi-element data structures. This involves adding and deleting elements, writing data into elements, and traversing the list. List processing is the basis of the artificial-intelligence programming language LISP. *See also* LISP, list, node (definition 1).

LISTSERV \list´sərv\ *n.* One of the most popular commercial mailing list managers, marketed by L-SOFT International in versions for BITNET, UNIX, and Windows. *See also* mailing list, mailing list manager.

literal \lit´ər-əl\ *n.* A value, used in a program, that is expressed as itself rather than as a variable's value or the result of an expression. Examples are the numbers 25 and 32.1, the character *a*, the string *Hello*, and the Boolean value TRUE. *See also* constant, variable.

lithium ion battery \lith`ē-um ī´on bat`ər-ē\ *n.* An energy storage device based on the conversion of chemical to electrical energy in "dry" chemical cells. Despite the higher cost, the laptop industry is quickly adopting lithium ion batteries because of their increased storage capacity over both nickel cadmium and nickel metal hydride batteries, in response to the demand for greater power brought on by higher processor speeds and the use of devices such as CD-ROM drives. *Compare* nickel cadmium battery, nickel metal hydride battery.

little endian \lit´l en´dē-ən\ *adj.* Of, pertaining to, or being a method of storing a number so that the least significant byte appears first in the number. For example, given the hexadecimal number A02B, the little endian method would cause the number to be stored as 2BA0. The little endian method is used by Intel microprocessors. *Also called* reverse byte ordering. *Compare* big endian.

live \līv\ *adj.* **1.** Of or relating to real-world data or a program working with it, as opposed to test data. **2.** Of or relating to audio or video that is transmitted from one site to another as it is being produced, as opposed to being recorded before broadcast time. *See also* synchronous transmission. **3.** Capable of being manipulated by a user to cause changes in a document or part of a document.

Live3D \līv`thrē-D´\ *n.* A Netscape proprietary Virtual Reality Modeling Language (VRML) plug-in for Web browsers that allows users to view and interact with a virtual-reality world. *See also* VRML.

liveware \līv´wâr\ *n.* A slang term for people, to distinguish them from hardware, software, and firmware. *Also called* wetware.

.lk \dot`L-K´\ *n.* On the Internet, the major geographic domain specifying that an address is located in Sri Lanka.

LLC \L`L-C´\ *n. See* IEEE 802 standards.

load[1] \lōd\ *n.* **1.** The total computing burden a system carries at one time. **2.** In electronics, the amount of current drawn by a device. **3.** In communications, the amount of traffic on a line.

load[2] \lōd\ *vb.* To place information from storage into memory for processing, if it is data, or for execution, if it is program code.

load-and-go \lōd`ənd-gō´\ *adj.* In reference to a routine, able to begin execution immediately, once loaded. The term is commonly used in reference to compilers and the machine code they generate.

loaded line \lō`dəd līn´\ *n.* A transmission cable fitted with loading coils, usually spaced about a mile apart, that reduce amplitude distortion in a signal by adding inductance (resistance to changes in current flow) to the line. Loaded lines minimize distortion within the range of frequencies affected by the loading coils, but the coils also reduce the bandwidth available for transmission.

loader \lō´dər\ *n.* A utility that loads the executable code of a program into memory for execution. On most microcomputers, the loader is an invisible part of the operating system and is automatically invoked when a program is run. *See also* load module, loader routine.

loader routine \lō´dər rōō-tēn`\ *n.* A routine that loads executable code into memory and executes it. A loader routine can be part of an operating system or it can be part of the program itself. *See also* loader, overlay[1] (definition 1).

load module \lōd´ moj`ōōl, mo`dyōōl\ *n.* An executable unit of code loaded into memory by the loader. A program consists of one or more load modules, each of which can be loaded and executed independently. *See also* loader.

load point \lōd´ point\ *n.* The beginning of the valid data area on a magnetic tape.

load sharing \lōd´ shâr`ēng\ *n.* A method of managing one or more tasks, jobs, or processes by scheduling and simultaneously executing portions of them on two or more microprocessors.

local \lō´kəl\ *adj.* Close at hand or restricted to a particular area. More specifically, in communications, a local device is one that can be accessed directly rather than by means of a communications line. In information processing, a local operation is one performed by the computer at hand rather than by a remote computer. In programming, a local variable is a variable that is restricted in scope, that is, used in only one part (subprogram, procedure, or function) of a program. *Compare* remote.

local area network \lō`kəl âr`ē-ə net´wərk\ *n. See* LAN.

local bus \lō`kəl bus´\ *n.* A PC architecture designed to speed up system performance by allowing some expansion boards to communicate directly with the microprocessor, bypassing the normal system bus entirely. *See also* PCI local bus, VL bus.

local bypass \lō`kəl bī´pas\ *n.* A telephone connection used by some businesses that links separate buildings but bypasses the telephone company.

local group \lō`kəl grōōp´\ *n.* **1.** In Windows NT, a group that is granted permissions and rights to only those resources on the workstation on which the group resides. Local groups provide a convenient means of allowing users both inside and outside the workstation to use resources found only on the workstation containing the local group. *See also* group[1]. **2.** In Windows NT Advanced Server, a group that is granted permissions and rights to only the resources on the servers of its own domain. Local groups in this context provide a convenient means of allowing users from both inside and outside the domain to use resources found only on the servers of the domain. *See also* global group, group[1].

localhost \lō´kəl-hōst`\ *n.* The name that is used to represent the same computer on which a TCP/IP message originates. An IP packet sent to localhost has the IP address 127.0.0.1 and does not actually go out to the Internet. *See also* IP address, packet (definition 1), TCP/IP.

localization \lō`kə-lə-zā´shən\ *n.* The process of altering a program so that it is appropriate for the area in which it is used. For example, the developers of a word processing program must localize the sorting tables in the program for different countries or languages because the correct order of characters in one language might be incorrect in another.

local loop \lō`kəl lōōp´\ *n.* A telephone connection that runs from the subscriber to the local telephone exchange.

local memory \lō`kəl mem´ər-ē\ *n.* In multiprocessor systems, the memory on the same card or high-speed bus as a particular processor. Typically, memory that is local to one processor cannot be accessed by another without some form of permission.

local newsgroups \lō`kəl nōōz´grōōps\ *n.* Newsgroups that are targeted toward a geographically limited area such as a city or educational institution. Posts to these newsgroups contain information that is specific to the area, concerning such topics as events, meetings, and sales. *See also* newsgroup.

local reboot \lō`kəl rē´bōōt\ *n.* A reboot of the machine that one is directly working on, rather than a remote host. *See also* reboot.

LocalTalk \lō`kəl-täk´\ *n.* An inexpensive cabling scheme used by AppleTalk networks to connect Apple Macintosh computers, printers, and other peripheral devices. *See also* AppleTalk.

local variable \lō`kəl vâr´ē-ə-bl\ *n.* A program variable whose scope is limited to a given block of code, usually a subroutine. *See also* scope (definition 1). *Compare* global variable.

location \lō-kā´shən`\ *n. See* address[1] (definition 1).

lock \lok\ *n.* **1.** A software security feature that requires a key or dongle in order for the application to run correctly. *See also* dongle. **2.** A mechanical device on some removable storage medium (for example, the write-protect notch on a floppy disk) that prevents the contents from being overwritten. *See also* write-protect notch.

locked file \lokd fīl´\ *n.* **1.** A file on which one or more of the usual types of manipulative operation cannot be performed—typically, one that cannot be altered by additions or deletions. **2.** A file that cannot be deleted or moved or whose name cannot be changed.

locked volume \lokd` vol´yōōm\ *n.* On the Apple Macintosh, a volume (storage device, such as a disk) that cannot be written to. The volume can be locked either physically or through software.

lockout \lok´out\ *n.* The act of denying access to a given resource (file, memory location, I/O port), usually to ensure that only one program at a time uses that resource.

lock up \lok´ up\ *n.* A condition in which processing appears to be completely suspended and in which the program in control of the system will accept no input. *See also* crash[1].

log \log\ *n.* **1.** A record of transactions or activities that take place on a computer system. **2.** *See* logarithm.

logarithm \log´ər-idh`əm\ *n.* Abbreviated log. In mathematics, the power to which a base must be raised to equal a given number. For example, for the base 10, the logarithm of 16 is (approximately) 1.2041 because $10^{1.2041}$ equals (approximately) 16. Both natural logarithms (to the base *e,* which is approximately 2.71828) and common logarithms (to the base 10) are used in programming. Languages such as C and Basic include functions for calculating natural logarithms.

logic \loj´ik\ *n.* In programming, the assertions, assumptions, and operations that define what a given program does. Defining the logic of a program is often the first step in developing the program's source code. *See also* formal logic.

logical \loj´ə-kəl\ *adj.* **1.** Based on true and false alternatives as opposed to arithmetic calculation of numeric values. For example, a logical expression is one that, when evaluated, has a single outcome, either true or false. *See also* Boolean algebra. *Compare* fuzzy logic. **2.** Of or pertaining to a conceptual piece of equipment or frame of reference, regardless of how it may be realized physically. *Compare* physical.

logical decision \loj`ə-kəl də-sizh´ən\ *n.* Any decision that can have one of two outcomes (true/false, yes/no, and so on). *Compare* fuzzy logic.

logical device \loj`ə-kəl də-vīs´\ *n.* A device named by the logic of a software system, regardless of its physical relationship to the system. For example, a single floppy disk drive can simultaneously be, to the MS-DOS operating system, both logical drive A and drive B.

logical drive \loj`ə-kəl drīv´\ *n. See* logical device.

logical error \loj`ə-kəl âr´ər\ *n. See* logic error.

logical expression \loj`ə-kəl eks-presh´ən\ *n. See* Boolean expression.

logical file \loj`ə-kəl fīl`\ *n.* A file as seen from a conceptual standpoint, without reference to and as distinct from its physical realization in memory or storage. For example, a logical file might consist of a contiguous series of records, whereas the file might be physically stored in small pieces scattered over the surface of a disk or even on several disks. A logical file might also consist of some subset of columns (fields) and rows (records) extracted from a database. In this case, the logical file (or view) is only that information required by a particular application program or user.

logical link control \loj`i-kəl lēnk´ kən-trōl\ *n.* *See* IEEE 802 standards.

logical operator \loj´ə-kəl op´ər-ā`tər\ *n.* An operator that manipulates binary values at the bit level. In some programming languages, logical operators are identical to Boolean operators, which manipulate true and false values. *See also* Boolean operator, mask.

logical record \loj`ə-kəl rek´ərd\ *n.* Any unit of information that can be handled by an application program. A logical record can be a collection of distinct fields or columns from a database file or a single line in a text file. *See also* logical file.

logical schema \loj´ə-kəl skē´mə\ *n.* *See* conceptual schema.

logic analyzer \loj´ik an`ə-lī-zər\ *n.* A hardware device that facilitates sophisticated low-level debugging of programs. Typical features include the ability to monitor bus signals during execution, to halt execution when a given memory location is read or written to, and to trace back through some number of instructions when execution is halted for any reason. *See also* debugger.

logic array \loj´ik ər-ā`\ *n.* *See* gate array.

logic board \loj´ik bōrd`\ *n.* Another name for motherboard or processor board. The term was used in conjunction with older computers to distinguish the video board *(analog board)* from the motherboard. *See also* motherboard.

logic bomb \loj´ik bom`\ *n.* A logic error in a program that manifests itself only under certain conditions, usually when least expected or desired. The term *bomb* implies an error that causes the program to fail spectacularly. *See also* logic error.

logic chip \loj´ik chip`\ *n.* An integrated circuit that processes information, as opposed to simply storing it. A logic chip is made up of logic circuits.

logic circuit \loj´ik sər`kət\ *n.* An electronic circuit that processes information by performing a logical operation on it. A logic circuit is a combination of logic gates. It produces output based on the rules of logic it is designed to follow for the electrical signals it receives as input. *See also* gate (definition 1).

logic diagram \loj´ik dī`ə-gram\ *n.* A schematic that shows the connections between computer logic circuits and specifies the expected outputs resulting from a specific set of inputs.

logic error \loj´ik âr`ər\ *n.* An error, such as a faulty algorithm, that causes a program to produce incorrect results but does not prevent the program from running. Consequently, a logic error is often very difficult to find. *See also* logic, semantics, syntax.

logic gate \loj´ik gāt`\ *n.* *See* gate (definition 1).

logic operation \loj´ik op-ər-ā`shən\ *n.* An expression that uses logical values and operators; a bit-level manipulation of binary values. *See also* Boolean operator.

logic programming \loj´ik prō`gram-ēng\ *n.* A style of programming, best exemplified by Prolog, in which a program consists of facts and relationships from which the programming language is expected to draw conclusions. *See also* Prolog.

logic-seeking printer \loj´ik sē-kēng prin´tər\ *n.* Any printer with built-in intelligence that lets it look ahead of the current print position and move the print head directly to the next area to be printed, thus saving time in printing pages that are filled with spaces.

logic symbol \loj´ik sim`bəl\ *n.* A symbol that represents a logical operator such as AND or OR. For example, the symbol + in Boolean algebra represents logical OR, as in A + B (read, "A or B," not "A plus B").

logic tree \loj´ik trē`\ *n.* A logic specification method that uses a branching representation. Each of the tree's forks represents a decision point; the ends of the branches denote actions to be taken.

login \log´in\ *n.* *See* logon.

log in \log in´\ *vb.* *See* log on.

Logo \lō´gō\ *n.* A programming language with features that are heavily drawn from LISP. Logo is often used to teach programming to children and was developed originally by Seymour Papert at

MIT in 1968. Logo is considered an educational language, although some firms have sought to make it more widely accepted in the programming community. *See also* LISP, turtle, turtle graphics.

logoff \log´of\ *n*. The process of terminating a session with a computer accessed through a communications line. *Also called* logout.

log off \log of´\ *vb*. To terminate a session with a computer accessed through a communications line—usually a computer that is both distant and open to many users. *Also called* log out. *Compare* log on.

logon \log´on\ *n*. The process of identifying oneself to a computer after connecting to it over a communications line. *Also called* login.

log on \log on´\ *vb*. To identify oneself to a computer after connecting to it over a communications line. During the procedure, the computer usually requests the user's name and password. *Also called* log in. *Compare* log off.

logout \log´out\ *n*. See logoff.

log out \log out´\ *vb*. See log off.

LOL \L`O-L´\ Acronym for laughing out loud. An interjection used in e-mail, online forums, and chat services to express appreciation of a joke or other humorous occurrence.

long filenames \long` fīl´nāmz\ *n*. A feature of most current PC operating systems, notably Windows 95, Windows NT, and OS/2, that allows a user to assign a plain-text name to a file, rather than limiting possible names to just a few characters. Names can be over 200 characters long, include upper and lowercase letters, and have spaces between characters. *Compare* 8.3.

long-haul \long´häl, -hôl\ *adj*. Of, pertaining to, or being a type of modem that is able to transmit over long distances. *Compare* short-haul.

longitudinal redundancy check \lon`jə-tōō´də-nəl rē-dun´dən-sē chek`\ *n*. See LRC.

look and feel \look` ənd fēl´\ *n*. A general term referring to the appearance and functionality of hardware or software. The phrase is often used comparatively, as in "Windows NT has the same look and feel as Windows 95."

lookup \look´up\ *n*. A function, often built into spreadsheet programs, in which a previously constructed table of values called a lookup table is searched for a desired item of information. A lookup table consists of rows and columns of data. A lookup function examines the table either horizontally or vertically and then retrieves the data that corresponds to the argument specified as part of the lookup function.

loop[1] \loop\ *n*. **1.** A set of statements in a program executed repeatedly, either a fixed number of times or until some condition is true or false. *See also* DO loop, FOR loop, infinite loop, iterative statement. **2.** A pair of wires that runs between a telephone central office and customer premises.

loop[2] \loop\ *vb*. To execute a group of statements repeatedly.

loop check \loop´ chek\ *n*. See echo check.

loop configuration \loop´ kən-fi-gyər-ā`shən\ *n*. A communications link in which multiple stations are joined to a communications line that runs in a closed loop. Generally, data sent by one station is received and retransmitted in turn by each station on the loop. The process continues until the data reaches its final destination. See the illustration. *See also* ring network.

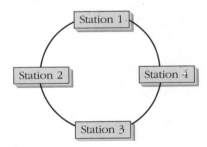

Loop configuration.

loophole \loop´hōl\ *n*. In programming, a logical failure to account for all possible situations. *See also* bug (definition 1), logic error.

loop invariant \loop` in-vâr´ē-ənt\ *n*. A condition that remains true while a loop iterates.

loop structure \loop´ struk`chur\ *n*. See iterative statement.

lo-res \lō-rez´\ *adj*. See low resolution.

loss balancing \los´ bal`ən-sēng\ *n*. Amplification of a signal or value to compensate for loss during a transmission or translation of a value.

lossless compression \los`ləs kəm-presh´ən\ *n*. The process of compressing a file such that, after being compressed and decompressed, it matches its original format bit for bit. Text, code, and numeric data files must be compressed using a lossless method; such methods can typically reduce a file to 40 percent of its original size. *Compare* lossy compression.

lossy compression \los`ē kəm-presh´ən\ *n.* The process of compressing a file such that some data is lost after the file is compressed and decompressed. Video and sound files often contain more information than is apparent to the viewer or listener; a lossy compression method, which does not preserve that excess information, can reduce such data to as little as 5 percent of its original size. *Compare* lossless compression.

lost cluster \lost` klu´stər\ *n.* A cluster (disk storage unit) marked by the operating system as being in use but not representing any part of any chain of stored segments of a file. A lost cluster usually represents debris resulting from incomplete data "housekeeping," as might result from the ungraceful exit (messy or abrupt termination) of an application program.

lowercase \lō`ər-kās´\ *adj.* In reference to letters, not capital—for example, *a, b, c. Compare* uppercase.

low frequency \lō` frē´kwən-sē\ *n.* The portion of the electromagnetic spectrum between 30 kilohertz (kHz) and 300 kHz. This range of frequencies is used for several types of radio communication, including the longwave broadcast band in Europe and Asia.

low-level language \lō`lev-əl lang´wəj\ *n.* A language that is machine dependent or that offers few control instructions and data types. Each statement in a program written in a low-level language usually corresponds to one machine instruction. *See also* assembly language. *Compare* high-level language.

low memory \lō` mem´ər-ē\ *n.* Memory locations addressed by the lowest numbers. In the IBM PC, which has an address space of 1 megabyte, the first 640 kilobytes are referred to as low memory. Low memory is reserved for RAM, which is shared by MS-DOS and application programs. *Compare* high memory.

low-order \lō´ōr`dər\ *adj.* Carrying the least weight or significance; typically, the rightmost element in a group. For example, the rightmost bit in

a group of bits is the low-order bit. *Compare* high-order.

lowpass filter \lō´pas fil`tər\ *n.* An electronic circuit that allows all frequencies below a specified frequency to pass through it. *Compare* bandpass filter, highpass filter.

low resolution \lō` rez`ə-lōō´shən\ *adj.* Abbreviated lo-res. Appearing in relatively coarse detail, used in reference to text and graphics in raster-oriented computer displays and printing. Low-resolution printing is comparable to draft-quality dot-matrix output printed at 125 dots per inch or less. *See also* resolution. *Compare* high resolution.

LPM \L`P-M´\ *n. See* lines per minute.

LPMUD \L-P`mud´, L`P-M-U-D´\ *n.* A type of multiuser dungeon (MUD), typically combat related, that contains its own object-oriented programming language for the creation of new areas and objects in the virtual world. *See also* MUD.

LPT \L`P-T´\ *n.* Logical device name for a line printer, a name reserved by the MS-DOS operating system for up to three parallel printer ports designated LPT1, LPT2, and LPT3. The first port, LPT1, is usually the same as the primary MS-DOS hardcopy output device PRN (the logical device name for the printer). The letters LPT were originally used to stand for *line print terminal.*

.lr \dot`L-R´\ *n.* On the Internet, the major geographic domain specifying that an address is located in Liberia.

LRC \L`R-C´\ *n.* Acronym for **l**ongitudinal **r**edundancy **c**heck. A procedure used to check the accuracy of data stored on magnetic tape or transmitted over a communications line. *See also* parity bit. *Compare* VRC.

.ls \dot`L-S´\ *n.* On the Internet, the major geographic domain specifying that an address is located in Lesotho.

ls \L-S´\ *n.* A UNIX command that instructs the server to return a list of files and subdirectories in the current directory or the directory specified in the command. Because many FTP sites are built on UNIX systems, this command can also be used on those sites. *See also* FTP site, UNIX.

LS-120 \L`S-wən-twen´tē\ *n.* A floppy disk drive that is capable of storing 120 MB of data on a single 3.5-inch floppy disk. LS-120 drives are also compatible with other floppy disk formats.

LSB \L`S-B´\ *n. See* least significant bit.

LSC \L`S-C´\ *n. See* least significant character.

LSD \L`S-D´\ *n. See* least significant digit.

LSI \L`S-I´\ *n. See* large-scale integration.

.lt \dot`L-T´\ *n.* On the Internet, the major geographic domain specifying that an address is located in Lithuania.

.lu \dot`L-U´\ *n.* On the Internet, the major geographic domain specifying that an address is located in Luxembourg.

LU \L-U´\ *n.* Acronym for **l**ogical **u**nit. In an IBM SNA network, a point denoting the beginning or end of a communications session. *See also* SNA.

luggable computer \lug`ə-bl kəm-pyoo´tər\ *n.* The first portable computers, produced in the early to mid-1980s. These early units, all of which had built-in CRT-based displays, weighed over 20 pounds and were the size of a medium suitcase—hence their name. *See also* portable computer.

luminance \loo´mə-nəns`\ *n.* **1.** A measure of the amount of light radiated by a given source, such as a computer display screen. **2.** The perceived brightness component of a given color, as opposed to its hue or its saturation. *See also* HSB. *Compare* illuminance.

luminance decay \loo`mə-nəns dē-kā´\ *n. See* persistence.

lurk \lurk\ *vb.* To receive and read articles or messages in a newsgroup or other online conference without contributing anything to the ongoing exchange.

lurker \lur´kər\ *n.* A person who lurks in a newsgroup or other online conference. *See also* lurk. *Compare* netizen.

.lv \dot`L-V´\ *n.* On the Internet, the major geographic domain specifying that an address is located in Latvia.

.ly \dot`L-Y´\ *n.* On the Internet, the major geographic domain specifying that an address is located in Libya.

Lynx \lēnks\ *n.* A text-only Web browser program for UNIX platforms.

.lzh \dot-L`Z-H´\ *n.* The file extension that identifies archive files compressed with the Lempel Ziv and Haruyasu algorithm. *See also* compressed file, Lempel Ziv algorithm, LHARC.

LZW compression \L`Z-W´ kəm-presh-ən\ *n.* A compression algorithm that makes use of repeating strings of data in its compression of character streams into code streams. It is also the basis of GIF compression. *See also* GIF.

m \mil´ə\ *n. See* milli-.

M \M, meg´ə\ *n. See* mega-.

.ma \dot`M-A´\ *n.* On the Internet, the major geographic domain specifying that an address is located in Morocco.

Mac \mak\ *n. See* Macintosh.

MAC \M`A-C´\ *n.* Acronym for **m**edia **a**ccess **c**ontrol. *See* IEEE 802 standards.

Mac- \mək, mak\ *prefix* A prefix used to indicate a software product's applicability for the Apple Macintosh computer, as in MacDraw.

MacBinary \mak`bī´nər-ē, mak`bī´när-ē\ *n.* A file transfer protocol used to preserve coding for Macintosh-produced files stored in non-Macintosh computers, containing the file's resource fork, data fork, and Finder information block. *See also* data fork, Finder, resource fork.

Mac clone \mak´ klōn\ *n.* A computer licensed and built to run the Macintosh operating system. Power Computing was named as the first licensee of the Macintosh OS in December 1994. *See also* Macintosh.

Mach \mäk\ *n.* A variant of the UNIX operating system developed at Carnegie-Mellon University. Mach was designed to support advanced features such as multitasking and multiprocessing. *See also* UNIX.

machine address \mə-shēn´ a`dres, ə-dres`\ *n. See* absolute address.

machine code \mə-shēn´ kōd`\ *n.* The ultimate result of the compilation of assembly language or any high-level language such as C or Pascal: sequences of 1s and 0s that are loaded and executed by a microprocessor. Machine code is the only language computers understand; all other programming languages represent ways of structuring human language so that humans can get computers to perform specific tasks. *Also called* machine language. *See also* compiler (definition 2).

machine cycle \mə-shēn´ sī`kl\ *n.* **1.** The time required for the fastest operation (usually a NOP, or no-op, which does nothing) a microprocessor can perform. **2.** The steps taken for each machine instruction. These steps are, typically, fetch the instruction, decode it, execute it, and perform any necessary storing.

machine-dependent \mə-shēn´də-pen`dənt\ *adj.* Of, pertaining to, or being a program or a piece of hardware that is linked to a particular type of computer because it makes use of specific or unique features of the equipment and that cannot easily be used with another computer, if at all. *Compare* machine-independent.

machine error \mə-shēn´ âr`ər\ *n.* A hardware error. Probably the most common type of machine error involves media, such as an error in reading a hard disk.

machine identification \mə-shēn` ī-den`tə-fə-kā´shən\ *n.* A code by which an executing program can determine the identity and characteristics of the computer and other devices with which it is operating.

machine-independent \mə-shēn` in-də-pen´dənt\ *adj.* Of, pertaining to, or being a program or piece of hardware that can be used on more than one type of computer with little or no modification. *Compare* machine-dependent.

machine instruction \mə-shēn´ in-struk`shən\ *n.* An instruction (action statement) in machine code that can be directly executed by a processor or microprocessor. *See also* instruction, statement.

machine language \mə-shēn´ lang`wəj\ *n. See* machine code.

machine-readable \mə-shēn´rē`də-bl\ *adj.* **1.** Presented in a form that a computer can interpret and use as input. For example, bar codes that can be scanned and used directly as computer input contain machine-readable information. **2.** Coded in the binary form used by computers and stored on a suitable medium such as magnetic tape. *See also* optical character recognition.

Macintosh \mak´ən-tosh\ *n*. A popular series of personal computers introduced by the Apple Computer Corporation in January 1984. The Macintosh was one of the earliest personal computers to incorporate a graphical user interface and the first to use 3.5-inch floppy disks. It was also the first to use the 32-bit Motorola 68000 microprocessor. Despite its user-friendly features, the Macintosh has lost market share during the 1990s, losing ground to PC-compatible computers, but still enjoys widespread use in desktop publishing and graphics-related applications. See the illustration. *Also called* Mac. *See also* graphical user interface, PC-compatible.

Macintosh Application Environment \mak`ən-tosh a-plə-kā´shən en-vīr`ən-mənt, en-vī`ərn-mənt\ *n*. A system shell for open RISC-based systems that provides a Macintosh interface within an X Window System window. The Macintosh Application Environment is compatible with both Mac and UNIX and will support all off-the-shelf products for the Macintosh. *Acronym:* MAE (M`A-E´). *See also* RISC, X Window System.

Macintosh File System \mak`ən-tosh fīl´ si-stəm\ *n*. The early, flat file system used on the Macintosh before the Hierarchical File System was introduced. *Acronym:* MFS (M`F-S´). *See also* flat file system. *Compare* Hierarchical File System.

Mac OS \mak` O-S´\ *n*. Short for **Mac**intosh **o**perating **s**ystem. The name given to the Macintosh operating system, beginning with version 7.5 in September 1994, when Apple started licensing the software to other computer manufacturers. *See also* Macintosh.

macro \ma´krō\ *n*. **1.** In applications, a set of keystrokes and instructions recorded and saved under a short key code or macro name. When the key code is typed or the macro name is used, the program carries out the instructions of the macro. Users can create a macro to save time by replacing an often-used, sometimes lengthy, series of strokes with a shorter version. **2.** In programming languages, such as C or assembly language, a name that defines a set of instructions that are substituted for the macro name wherever the name appears in a program (a process called *macro expansion*) when the program is compiled or assembled. Macros are similar to functions in that

Macintosh.

they can take arguments and in that they are calls to lengthier sets of instructions. Unlike functions, macros are replaced by the actual instructions they represent when the program is prepared for execution; function instructions are copied into a program only once. *Compare* function (definition 2).

macro assembler \ma´krō ə-sem`blər\ *n.* An assembler that can perform macro substitution and expansion. The programmer can define a macro that consists of several statements and then use the macro name later in the program, thus avoiding having to rewrite the statements. For example, the following macro, called *swap,* exchanges the values of two variables:

```
.macro swap,2
      ldx %1
      ldy %2
      stx %2
      sty %1
.endm
```

After defining swap, the programmer can then insert an instruction such as "swap a, b" in the assembly language program. While assembling, the assembler replaces the instruction with the statements within the macro that swap the values of the variables *a* and *b.*

macro expansion \ma´krō eks-pan`shən\ *n.* The act of replacing a macro with its defined equivalent. *Also called* macro substitution. *See also* macro, macro assembler, macro processor.

macro instruction \ma´krō in-struk`shən\ *n.* An instruction used to manage macro definitions. *See also* macro language.

macro language \ma´krō lang`wəj\ *n.* The collection of macro instructions recognized by a given macro processor. *See also* macro instruction, macro processor.

macro processor \ma´krō pros´es-ər\ *n.* A program that performs macro expansion. All programs that support macros have some form of macro processor, but these differ from program to program and in the macro language they support. *See also* macro, macro expansion, macro instruction.

macro program \ma´krō pro`gram\ *n. See* keyboard enhancer.

macro recorder \ma´krō rə-kōr´dər\ *n.* A program that records and stores keyboard macros. *See also* macro (definition 1).

macro substitution \ma´krō sub-stə-tōō`shən\ *n. See* macro expansion.

macro virus \ma´krō vīr`us\ *n.* A virus that is written in a macro language associated with an application. The macro virus is carried by a document file used with that application and executes when the document is opened.

MacTCP \mak`T-C-P´\ *n.* A Macintosh extension that allows Macintosh computers to use TCP/IP. *See also* TCP/IP.

MAE \M´A-E´\ *n. See* Macintosh Application Environment, Metropolitan Area Exchange.

magnetic bubble \mag-net´ik bub´l\ *n.* A movable magnetic domain in a thin-film substrate. In bubble memory, magnetic bubbles representing bits circulate past circuits that can read and write them. High costs and relatively long access times have relegated magnetic bubbles to specialized applications. *See also* bubble memory, magnetic domain. *Compare* core, RAM.

magnetic disk \mag-net´ik disk´\ *n.* A computer disk enclosed in a protective case (hard disk) or jacket (floppy disk) and coated with a magnetic material that enables data to be stored in the form of changes in magnetic polarity (with one polarity representing a binary 1 and the other a 0) on many small sections (magnetic domains) of the disk surface. Magnetic disks should be protected from exposure to sources of magnetism, which can damage or destroy the information they hold. *See also* disk, floppy disk, hard disk. *Compare* compact disc, magneto-optic disc.

magnetic domain \mag-net´ik dō-mān´\ *n.* A region of a ferromagnetic material in which the individual atomic or molecular magnetic particles are aligned in the same direction. *Also called* ferromagnetic domain.

magnetic field \mag-net´ik fēld´\ *n.* The space around a magnetic object in which magnetic force acts. A magnetic field is conceived of as consisting of flux lines that originate at the north magnetic pole and terminate at the south magnetic pole.

magnetic head \mag-net´ik hed´\ *n. See* head.

magnetic-ink character recognition \mag-net´-ik-ēnk kâr´ək-tər rek-əg-nish`ən\ *n.* A form of character recognition that reads text printed with magnetically charged ink, determining the shapes of characters by sensing the magnetic charge in the ink. Once the shapes have been determined, character recognition methods are used to translate the shapes into computer text. A familiar use of this form of character recognition is to identify bank checks. *Acronym:* MICR (mī´kər, M`I-C-R´). *See also* character recognition. *Compare* optical character recognition.

magnetic oxide \mag-net`ik oks´īd\ *n. See* ferric oxide.

magnetic storage \mag-net`ik stōr´əj\ *n.* A generic term for non-internal-memory computer data storage involving a magnetic medium, such as disk or tape.

magnetic tape \mag-net`ik tāp´\ *n. See* tape (definition 1).

magneto-optical recording   \mag-nē`tō-op-tə-kəl rə-kōr´dēng, mag-net`ō-\ *n.* A type of recording technology used with optical discs in which a laser beam heats a small portion of the magnetic material covering the disc. The heating enables a weak magnetic field to change the orientation of the portion, thus recording onto the disc. This technique can also be used to erase the disc, making the disc rewritable.

magneto-optic disc \mag-nē`tō-op-tik disk´, mag-net`ō-\ *n.* An erasable or semi-erasable storage disc, similar to a CD-ROM disc and of very high capacity, in which a laser beam is used to heat the recording surface to a point at which tiny regions on the surface can be magnetically aligned to store bits of data. *See also* CD-ROM, magneto-optical recording.

magnitude \mag´nə-tōod`\ *n.* The size of a number, regardless of its sign (+ or –). For example, 16 and –16 have the same magnitude. *See also* absolute value.

mailbomb[1] \māl´bom\ *n.* An excessively large amount of e-mail data (a very large number of messages or one very large message) sent to a user's e-mail address in an attempt to make the user's mailer program crash or to prevent the user from receiving further legitimate messages. *See also* e-mail[1] (definition 1). *Compare* letterbomb.

mailbomb[2] \māl´bom\ *vb.* To send a mailbomb to a user. One person might mailbomb a user with a single enormous message; a large number of users might mailbomb an unpopular person by simultaneously sending messages of normal size.

mailbot \māl´bot\ *n.* A program that automatically responds to e-mail messages or performs actions based on commands within the messages. A mailing list manager is one example. *See also* mailing list manager.

mailbox \māl´boks\ *n.* A disk storage area assigned to a network user for receipt of e-mail messages. *See also* e-mail[1] (definition 1).

mail digest \māl` dī´jest\ *n. See* digest (definition 2).

mailer-daemon \mā´lər-dē`mən\ *n.* A program used to transport e-mail between hosts on a network. *See also* daemon.

mail filter \māl´ fil`tər\ *n. See* e-mail filter.

mail header \māl´ hed`ər\ *n.* A block of text at the top of an e-mail message containing such information as the addresses of the sender and recipient(s), the date and time sent, the address to which a reply is to be sent, and the subject. The mail header is used by an e-mail client or program. *See also* e-mail[1] (definition 1).

mailing list \mā´lēng list`\ *n.* A list of names and e-mail addresses that are grouped under a single name. When a user places the name of the mailing list in a mail client's To: field, the client sends the message to the machine where the mailing list resides, and that machine automatically sends the message to all the addresses on the list (possibly allowing a moderator to edit it first). *See also* LISTSERV, mailing list manager, Majordomo, moderator.

mailing list manager \mā´lēng list man`ə-jər\ *n.* Software that maintains an Internet or intranet mailing list. The mailing list manager accepts messages posted by subscribers; sends copies of the messages (which may be edited by a moderator) to all the subscribers; and accepts and processes user requests, such as to subscribe or to unsubscribe to the mailing list. The most commonly used mailing list managers are LISTSERV and Majordomo. *See also* LISTSERV, mailing list, Majordomo, moderator.

mail merge \māl´ mərj\ *n.* A mass-mail facility that takes names, addresses, and sometimes pertinent facts about recipients and merges the information into a form letter or another such basic document.

mail reflector \māl´ rə-flek`tər\ *n.* A newsgroup that consists simply of the messages posted to a mailing list translated into newsgroup format.

mailto \māl´tōō\ *n.* A protocol designator used in the HREF of a hyperlink that enables a user to send e-mail to someone. For instance, Anne E. Oldhacker has the e-mail address aeo@baz.foo.com and an HTML document contains the code <A HREF="mailto:aeo@baz.foo.com">E-mail Anne! </A>. If a user clicks on the hyperlink "E-mail Anne!" the user's e-mail application is launched and the user can send e-mail to her without knowing her actual e-mail address. *See also* e-mail[1] (definition 1), HTML, hyperlink.

mainboard \mān´bōrd\ *n. See* motherboard.

main body \mān` bod´ē\ *n.* The set of statements in a computer program at which execution of the program begins and that invokes the subroutines of the program. *Also called* subroutine.

mainframe computer \mān`frām kəm-pyōō´tər\ *n.* A high-level computer designed for the most intensive computational tasks. Mainframe computers are often shared by multiple users connected to the computer by terminals. *See also* computer, supercomputer.

main function \mān` funk´shən\ *n.* The main body of a program written in a computer language that uses sets of functions to create an entire program. For example, the C language requires each program to contain a function called *main,* which C uses as the starting point of execution. *See also* main body.

main loop \mān lōōp´\ *n.* A loop in the main body of a program that performs the principal function of the program over and over until termination is somehow signaled. In event-driven programs, this loop checks for events received from the operating system and handles them appropriately. *See also* event-driven programming, main body.

main memory \mān` mem´ər-ē\ *n. See* primary storage.

main segment \mān` seg´mənt\ *n.* On the Macintosh, the principal code segment of a program, which must remain loaded throughout the execution of the program.

maintenance \mān´tə-nəns\ *n.* The process of taking measures to ensure that a hardware, software, or database system is functioning properly and is up to date.

Majordomo \mā´jər-dō´mō\ *n.* The name of a popular software program that manages and sup-

ports Internet mailing lists. *See also* mailing list, mailing list manager.

major geographic domain \mā`jər gē-ə-graf´ik dō-mān´\ *n.* A two-character sequence in an Internet domain name address that indicates the country in which a host is located. The major geographic domain is the last part of the domain name address, following the subdomain and domain codes; for example, uiuc.edu.us indicates a host at the University of Illinois in the United States, whereas cam.ac.uk indicates a host at the University of Cambridge in the United Kingdom. The code .us, which indicates a domain in the United States, is usually omitted. *Also called* country code. *See also* DNS (definition 1), domain name address.

major key \mā`jər kē´\ *n. See* primary key.

male connector \māl` kə-nek´tər\ *n.* A type of connector that has pins for insertion into receptacles. Male connector part numbers often include an *M* (male) or *P* (plug). For example, a male DB-25 connector might be labeled *DB-25M* or *DB-25P.* See the illustration. *Compare* female connector.

Male connector.

MAN \man, M`A-N´\ *n.* Acronym for **m**etropolitan **a**rea **n**etwork. A high-speed network that can carry voice, data, and images at up to 200 Mbps or faster over distances of up to 75 km. Based on the network architecture, the transmission speed can be higher for shorter distances. A MAN, which can include one or more LANs as well as telecommunications equipment such as microwave and satellite relay stations, is smaller than a wide area network but generally operates at a higher speed. *Compare* LAN, wide area network.

management information service \man`əj-mənt in-fər-mā´shən sər-vəs\ *n.* A department within an organization that functions as a clearing-house for information. *Acronym:* MIS (M`I-S´).

Management Information Services \man`əj-mənt in-fər-mā´shən sər´və-səs\ *n. See* Information Services.

management information system \man`əj-mənt in-fər-mā´shən si-stəm\ *n.* A computer-based system for processing and organizing information so as to provide various levels of management within an organization with accurate and timely information needed for supervising activities, tracking progress, making decisions, and isolating and solving problems. *Acronym:* MIS (M`I-S´).

Management Information Systems \man`əj-mənt in-fər-mā`shən si´stəmz\ *n. See* Information Services.

manager \man´ə-jər\ *n.* Any program that is designed to perform a certain set of housekeeping tasks related to computer operation, such as the maintenance of files. On the Apple Macintosh, Manager (with a capital M) is used in the names of various separate portions of the computer's operating system that handle input, output, and internal functions (e.g., File Manager and Memory Manager).

Manchester coding \man´che-stər kō`dēng\ *n.* A method of encoding data used in communications, such as on some LANs, that combines both data and timing signals in a stream of transmitted bits. *See also* phase encoding.

Mandelbrot set \man´dəl-brot set`\ *n. See* fractal.

man-machine interface \man`mə-shēn` in´tər-fās\ *n.* The set of commands, displays, controls, and hardware devices enabling the human user and the computer system to exchange information. *See also* user interface.

man pages \man´ pāj-əz\ *n.* Online documentation for UNIX commands and programs and the UNIX library routines available for use in C programs. These documents, also found in the *UNIX Programmer's Manual,* can be displayed on a user's terminal or printed using the command *man.*

mantissa \man`tis´ə\ *n.* **1.** In calculations that have logarithms, the positive decimal fraction of a common (base-10) logarithm. For example, the common logarithm of 16 is 1.2041; the characteristic, or whole-number portion, of the logarithm is 1 (the logarithm of 10), and the mantissa, or fractional portion, is .2041 (the logarithm of 1.6). *See also* characteristic, logarithm. **2.** In floating-point notation, the portion expressing the significant digits of a number. For example, the floating-point representation of 640,000 is 6.4E+05. The mantissa is 6.4; the exponent (E+05) shows

the power of 10 to which 6.4 is raised. *See also* floating-point notation.

map[1] \map\ *n.* Any representation of the structure of an object. For example, a memory map describes the layout of objects in an area of memory, and a symbol map lists the associations between symbol names and memory addresses in a program. *See also* image map.

map[2] \map\ *vb.* To translate one value into another. For example, in computer graphics one might map a three-dimensional image onto a sphere. In reference to virtual memory systems, a computer might translate (map) a virtual address into a physical address. *See also* virtual memory.

MAPI \ma´pē, M`A-P-I´\ *n.* Acronym for **M**essaging **A**pplication **P**rogramming **I**nterface. The Microsoft interface specification that allows different messaging and workgroup applications (including e-mail, voice mail, and fax) to work through a single client, such as the Exchange client included with Windows 95 and Windows NT. *See also* application programming interface.

mapped drives \mapd drīvz`\ *n.* **1.** In the Windows environment, network drives that have been assigned local drive letters and are locally accessible. **2.** Under UNIX, disk drives that have been defined to the system and can be made active.

margin \mär´jən\ *n.* In printing, those portions of a page—top, bottom, and sides—outside the main body of text.

mark \märk\ *n.* **1.** In applications and data storage, a symbol or other device used to distinguish one item from others like it. **2.** In digital transmission, the state of a communications line (positive or negative) corresponding to a binary 1. In asynchronous serial communications, a mark condition is the continuous transmission of binary 1s to indicate when the line is idle (not carrying information). In asynchronous error checking, setting the parity bit to 1 in each group of transmitted bits is known as mark parity. *See also* parity. *Compare* space. **3.** In optical sensing, a pencil line, as on a voting form or an IQ test, that can be recognized by an optical reader.

marker \mär´kər\ *n.* **1.** Part of a data communications signal that enables the communications equipment to recognize the structure of the message. Examples are the start and stop bits that frame a byte in asynchronous serial communications. **2.** A symbol that indicates a particular location on a display surface.

Mark I \märk wən´\ *n.* **1.** An electromechanical calculating machine designed in the late 1930s and early 1940s by Howard Aiken of Harvard University and built by IBM. *Also called* Automatic Sequence Controlled Calculator, Harvard Mark I. **2.** The first fully electronic stored-program computer, designed and built at Manchester University in England. It successfully executed its first program in June 1948. **3.** The first commercial computer, which was based on the Manchester Mark I and released in 1951.

markup language \mär´kup lang`wəj\ *n.* A set of codes in a text file that instruct a computer how to format it on a printer or video display or how to index and link its contents. Examples of markup languages are Hypertext Markup Language (HTML), which is used in Web pages, and Standard Generalized Markup Language (SGML), which is used for typesetting and desktop publishing purposes and in electronic documents. Markup languages of this sort are designed to enable documents and other files to be platform-independent and highly portable between applications. *See also* HTML, SGML.

marquee \mär-kē´\ *n.* A nonstandard HTML extension that causes scrolling text to appear as part of a Web page. Currently, marquees are viewable only with Internet Explorer. *See also* HTML, Internet Explorer, Web page.

mask \mask\ *n.* A binary value used to selectively screen out or let through certain bits in a data value. Masking is performed by using a logical operator (AND, OR, XOR, NOT) to combine the mask and the data value. For example, the mask 00111111, when used with the AND operator, removes (masks off) the two uppermost bits in a data value but does not affect the rest of the value. *See also* logical operator, mask bit.

11010101	Data value
AND 00111111	Mask
00010101	Resulting value

Mask. ***An example of a masking operation using the logical operator AND.***

maskable interrupt \ma`skə-bl in´tər-upt\ *n.* A hardware interrupt that can be temporarily disabled (masked) when a program needs the full attention of the microprocessor. *See also* external interrupt, hardware interrupt, interrupt. *Compare* nonmaskable interrupt.

mask bit \mask´ bit\ *n.* A given bit within a mask whose function is to screen out or let through the corresponding bit in a data value when the mask is used in an expression with a logical operator. *See also* mask.

masking \ma´skēng\ *n.* The process of using the *mask* operation to perform operations on bits, bytes, or words of data. *See also* mask.

mask off \mask of´\ *vb.* To use a mask to remove bits from a byte of data. *See also* mask.

massively parallel processing \mas`iv-lē pâr`ə-lel pros´es-ēng\ *n.* A computer architecture in which each of a large number of processors has its own RAM, which contains a copy of the operating system, a copy of the application code, and its own part of the data, on which that processor works independently of the others. *Acronym:* MPP (M`P-P´). *Compare* SMP.

massively parallel processor \mas`iv-lē pâr`ə-lel pros´es-ər\ *n.* A computer designed to perform massively parallel processing.

mass storage \mas` stōr´əj\ *n.* A generic term for disk, tape, or optical disc storage of computer data, so called for the large masses of data that can be stored in comparison with computer memory capacity. *Compare* memory.

master file \ma`stər fīl´\ *n.* In a set of database files, the file containing more or less permanent descriptive information about the principal subjects of the database, summary data, and one or more critical key fields. For example, customers' names, account numbers, addresses, and credit terms might be stored in a master file. *Compare* transaction file.

master key \ma´stər kē´\ *n.* The server-based component of software or data protection. In some systems, data or applications are stored on a server and must be downloaded to the local machine for use. When a client requests the data, it presents a session key. If the session key supplied matches the master key, the key server sends the requested packet. *See also* client (definition 3), server (definition 2).

master record \mas`tər rek´ərd\ *n*. A record in a master file; typically, the descriptive and summary data related to the item that is the subject of the record. *See also* master file.

master/slave arrangement \ma`stər-slāv´ ər-ānj`-mənt\ *n*. A system in which one device, called the master, controls another device, called the slave. For example, a computer can control devices connected to it.

matching \mach´ēng\ *n*. The process of testing whether two data items are identical or of finding a data item that is identical to a key. *See also* pattern recognition.

math coprocessor \math` kō´pros-es-ər\ *n*. *See* floating-point processor.

mathematical expression \math-ə-mat`ə-kəl eks-presh´ən\ *n*. An expression that uses numeric values, such as integers, fixed-point numbers, and floating-point numbers, and operators, such as addition, subtraction, multiplication, and division. *See also* expression.

mathematical function \math-ə-mat`ə-kəl funk´-shən\ *n*. A function in a program that performs a set of mathematical operations on one or more values or expressions and that returns a numeric value.

mathematical model \math-ə-mat`ə-kəl mod´əl\ *n*. The mathematical assumptions, expressions, and equations that underlie a given program. Mathematical models are used to model "real-world" physical systems such as planets in orbit around a star or resource production and consumption within a closed system.

matrix \mā´triks\ *n*. An arrangement of rows and columns used for organizing related items, such as numbers, dots, spreadsheet cells, or circuit elements. Matrices are used in mathematics for manipulating rectangular sets of numbers. In computing and computer applications, matrices are used for the similar purpose of arranging sets of data in table form, as in spreadsheets and lookup tables. In hardware, matrices of dots are used in creating characters on the screen as well as in print (as by dot-matrix printers). In electronics, matrices of diodes or transistors are used to create networks of logic circuits for such purposes as

encoding, decoding, or converting information. *See also* grid.

matrix line printer \mā´triks līn´ prin`tər\ *n*. *See* line printer.

.ma.us \dot-M-A` dot-U-S´\ *n*. On the Internet, the major geographic domain specifying that an address is located in Massachusetts, United States.

maximize \maks´ə-mīz`\ *vb*. In a graphical user interface, to cause a window to expand to fill all of the space available within a larger window or on the screen. *See also* enlarge, graphical user interface, Maximize button, window. *Compare* minimize, reduce.

Maximize button \maks´ə-mīz but`ən\ *n*. In Windows 3.*x*, Windows 95, and Windows NT, a button in the upper right-hand corner of a window that, when clicked, maximizes a window to fill all of the space available within a larger window or on the screen. *See also* graphical user interface, window. *Compare* Minimize button.

Mb \meg´ə-bit`\ *n*. *See* megabit.

MB \meg´ə-bīt`\ *n*. *See* megabyte.

.mb.ca \dot-M-B` dot-C-A´\ *n*. On the Internet, the major geographic domain specifying that an address is located in Manitoba, Canada.

MBONE or **Mbone** \M´bōn\ *n*. Short for **m**ulticast back**bone**. A small set of Internet sites, each of which can transmit real-time audio and video simultaneously to all the others. MBONE sites are equipped with special software to send and receive packets at high speed using the IP one-to-many multicasting protocol. The MBONE has been used for video conferencing and even for a Rolling Stones concert in 1994. *See also* RealAudio.

Mbps \M´B-P-S`\ *n*. Short for **m**ega**b**its **p**er **s**econd. One million bits per second.

.mc \dot`M-C´\ *n*. On the Internet, the major geographic domain specifying that an address is located in Monaco.

MC \meg´ə-sī`kl, M-C´\ *n*. *See* megacycle.

MC68000 \M-C`siks`tē-āt-thou´zənd\ *n*. *See* 68000.

MC68020 \M-C`siks`āt-ō-tōō´ō´\ *n*. *See* 68020.

MC68030 \M-C`siks`āt-ō-thrē-ō´\ *n*. *See* 68030.

MC68040 \M-C`siks`āt-ō-fōr-ō´\ *n*. *See* 68040.

MC68881 \M-C`siks`āt-āt-āt-wən`\ *n*. *See* 68881.

MCF \M´C-F´\ *n*. *See* Meta-Content Format.

MCGA \M´C-G-A´\ *n*. Acronym for **M**ulti-**C**olor **G**raphics **A**rray. A video adapter included in the

IBM PS/2 Models 25 and 30. The MCGA is capable of emulating the CGA (Color/Graphics Adapter) and provides two additional graphics modes: the first mode has 640 horizontal pixels by 480 vertical pixels with 2 colors chosen from a palette of 262,144 colors; the second has 320 horizontal pixels by 200 vertical pixels with 256 colors chosen from a palette of 262,144 colors. *See also* graphics mode (definition 2).

MCI \M`C-I´\ *n.* **1.** Acronym for **M**edia **C**ontrol **I**nterface. Part of the Windows application programming interface that enables a program to control multimedia devices. **2.** A major long-distance telephone service carrier, originally Microwave Communications, Inc.

.md \dot`M-D´\ *n.* On the Internet, the major geographic domain specifying that an address is located in the Republic of Moldova.

MDA \M`D-A´\ *n.* Acronym for **M**onochrome **D**isplay **A**dapter. The video adapter introduced with the earliest model of the IBM PC in 1981. MDA is capable of only one video mode: a character mode with 25 lines of 80 characters each, with underlining, blinking, and high-intensity characters. IBM did not use the name *Monochrome Display Adapter* or the acronym *MDA*.

MDI \M`D-I´\ *n.* Acronym for **m**ultiple-**d**ocument **i**nterface. A user interface in an application that allows the user to have more than one document open at the same time. *See also* user interface.

MDIS \M`D-I-S´\ *n.* *See* Metadata Interchange Specification.

.md.us \dot-M-D`dot-U-S´\ *n.* On the Internet, the major geographic domain specifying that an address is located in Maryland, United States.

mean time between failures \mēn` tīm` bə-twēn fāl´yərz\ *n.* *See* MTBF.

mean time to repair \mēn` tīm` tə ri-pār´\ *n.* *See* MTTR.

mechanical mouse \mə-kan`i-kəl mous´\ *n.* A type of mouse in which the motion of a ball on the bottom of the mouse is translated into directional signals. As the user moves the mouse, the ball rolls, turning a pair of wheels mounted at right angles inside the mouse that have conductive markings on their surfaces. Because the markings permit an electric current to flow, a set of conductive brushes that ride on the surface of the conduc-

tive wheels can detect these conductive markings. The electronics in the mouse translate these electrical movement signals into mouse-movement information that can be used by the computer. *See also* mouse, trackball. *Compare* optical mouse, optomechanical mouse.

media \mē´dē-ə\ *n.* The physical material, such as paper, disk, and tape, used for storing computer-based information. *Media* is plural; *medium* is singular.

media access control \mē`dē-ə ak´ses kən-trōl`\ *n.* *See* IEEE 802 standards.

Media Control Interface \mē`dē-ə kən-trōl in´tər-fās\ *n.* *See* MCI (definition 1).

media eraser \mē´dē-ə i-rā`sər\ *n.* A device that removes or obliterates data from a storage medium on a wholesale basis, usually by writing meaningless data (such as zeros) over it. *See also* bulk eraser.

media filter \mē`dē-ə fil`tər\ *n.* **1.** A device used with local area networks (LANs) as an adapter between two different types of media. For example, an RJ-45 connector might be used between coaxial cable and unshielded twisted pair (UTP) cables. Media filters are similar in function to transceivers. As with many components to LANs, manufacturers often choose different names for similar products, so a LAN expert is needed to decide what media filters are required for a particular LAN. *See also* coaxial cable, connector (definition 1), LAN, transceiver, UTP. **2.** A device added to data networks to filter out electronic noise from the environment. For example, a media filter might be added to an Ethernet network based on coaxial cabling to prevent data loss from interference by nearby electronic equipment. *See also* coaxial cable, Ethernet (definition 1).

medium[1] \mē´dē-um\ *adj.* Of or relating to the middle part of a range of possible values.

medium[2] \mē´dē-um\ *n.* **1.** A substance in which signals can be transmitted, such as a wire or fiber-optic cable. **2.** *See* media.

medium model \mē´dē-um mod`əl\ *n.* A memory model of the Intel 80x86 processor family. The medium model allows only 64 kilobytes for data but generally up to 1 megabyte for code. *See also* memory model.

medium-scale integration \mē`dē-um-skāl in-tə-grā´shən\ *n.* The concentration of between 10 and 100 circuit elements on a single chip. *Acronym:* MSI (M`S-I´). *See also* integrated circuit.

meg \meg\ *n. See* megabyte.

mega- \meg´ə\ *prefix* Abbreviated M. One million (10^6). In computing, which is based on the binary (base-2) numbering system, *mega-* has a literal value of 1,048,576, which is the power of 2 (2^{20}) closest to one million.

megabit \meg´ə-bit`\ *n.* Abbreviated Mb or Mbit. Usually 1,048,576 bits (2^{20}); sometimes interpreted as 1 million bits.

megabyte \meg´ə-bīt`\ *n.* Abbreviated MB. Usually 1,048,576 bytes (2^{20}); sometimes interpreted as 1 million bytes.

megacycle \meg´ə-sī`kl\ *n.* Abbreviated MC. A term for 1 million cycles—usually used to mean 1 million cycles per second. *See also* megahertz.

megaflops \meg´ə-flops`\ *n. See* MFLOPS.

megahertz \meg´ə-hərts`\ *n.* Abbreviated MHz. A measure of frequency equivalent to 1 million cycles per second.

megapel display \meg´ə-pel di-splā`\ *n. See* megapixel display.

megapixel display \meg`ə-piks`əl di-splā´\ *n.* A video display capable of displaying at least 1 million pixels. For example, a video display with a screen size of 1,024 horizontal pixels and 1,024 vertical pixels is a megapixel display. *Also called* megapel display.

member \mem´bər\ *n.* **1.** In object-oriented programming, a variable or routine that is part of a class. *See also* C++, class. **2.** A value that is part of a set data structure. *See also* set[2] (definition 1).

membrane keyboard \mem´brān kē`bōrd\ *n.* A keyboard in which an unbroken plastic or rubber shell (a membrane) covers keys that have little or no travel (movement). Rather than using normal, full-travel keys, membrane keyboards use pressure-sensitive areas that are sometimes, but not always, defined by small bumps under the membrane.

memo field \mem´ō fēld`\ *n.* A field in a database file that can contain unstructured text.

memory \mem´ər-ē\ *n.* A device where information can be stored and retrieved. In the most general sense, memory can refer to external storage such as disk drives or tape drives; in common usage, it refers only to the fast semiconductor storage (RAM) directly connected to the processor. *See also* core, EEPROM, EPROM, flash memory, PROM, RAM, ROM. *Compare* bubble memory, mass storage.

memory bank \mem´ər-ē bank`\ *n.* The physical location on a motherboard where a memory module can be inserted. *See also* bank (definition 1).

memory cache \mem´ər-ē kash`\ *n. See* CPU cache.

memory card \mem´ər-ē kärd`\ *n.* A memory module that is used to extend RAM storage capacity or in place of a hard disk in a portable computer, such as a laptop, notebook, or handheld PC. The module is usually the size of a credit card and can be plugged into a PCMCIA-compliant portable computer. The module can be composed of EPROM, RAM, or ROM chips or flash memory. *Also called* RAM card, ROM card. *See also* EPROM, flash memory, handheld PC, hard disk, module (definition 2), PCMCIA, RAM, ROM.

memory cartridge \mem´ər-ē kär`trij\ *n.* A plug-in module containing RAM (random access memory) chips that can be used to store data or programs. Memory cartridges are used primarily in portable computers as smaller, lighter (but more expensive) substitutes for disk drives. Memory cartridges typically use either a nonvolatile form of RAM, which does not lose its contents when power is turned off, or battery-backed RAM, which maintains its contents by drawing current from a rechargeable battery within the cartridge. *Also called* RAM cartridge. *See also* memory card, RAM. *Compare* ROM cartridge.

memory cell \mem´ər-ē sel`\ *n.* An electronic circuit that stores one bit of data. *See also* bit.

memory chip \mem´ər-ē chip`\ *n.* An integrated circuit devoted to memory storage. The memory storage can be *volatile* and hold data temporarily, such as RAM, or *nonvolatile* and hold data permanently, such as ROM, EPROM, EEPROM, or PROM. *See also* EEPROM, EPROM, integrated circuit, nonvolatile memory, PROM, RAM, volatile memory.

memory management \mem´ər-ē man`əj-mənt\ *n.* **1.** In operating systems for personal computers, procedures for optimizing the use of RAM (random access memory). These procedures include selectively storing data, monitoring it carefully, and freeing memory when the data is no longer needed. Most current operating systems optimize RAM usage on their own; some older operating systems, such as early versions of MS-DOS, required the use of third-party utilities to optimize RAM usage and necessitated that the user be more knowledgeable about how the operating system and applications used memory. *See also* memory management unit, RAM. **2.** In programming, the process of ensuring that a program releases each chunk of memory when it is no longer needed. In some languages, such as C and C++, the programmer must keep track of memory usage by the program. Java, a newer language, automatically frees any chunk of memory that is not in use. *See also* C, C++, garbage collection, Java.

memory management program \mem´ər-ē man`-əj-mənt prō`gram\ *n.* **1.** A program used to store data and programs in system memory, monitor their use, and reassign the freed space following their execution. **2.** A program that uses hard disk space as an extension of the random access memory (RAM).

memory management unit \mem´ər-ē man´əj-mənt yōō`nit\ *n.* The hardware that supports the mapping of virtual memory addresses to physical memory addresses. In some systems, such as those based on the 68020, the memory management unit is separate from the processor. In most modern microcomputers, however, the memory management unit is built into the CPU chip. In some systems, the memory management unit provides interfacing between the microprocessor and memory. This type of memory management unit is typically responsible for address multiplexing and, in the case of DRAMs, the refresh cycle. *Acronym:* MMU (M`M-U´). *See also* physical address, refresh cycle, virtual address.

memory model \mem´ər-ē mod`əl\ *n.* The approach used to address the code and the data that are used in a computer program. The memory model dictates how much memory can be used in a program for code and how much for data. Most computers with a flat address space support only a single memory model. Computers with a segmented address space usually support multiple memory models. *See also* compact model, flat

address space, large model, medium model, segmented address space, small model, tiny model.

memory-resident \mem`ər-ē-rez´ə-dənt\ *adj.* Permanently located in a computer's memory, rather than swapped in and out of memory as needed. *See also* memory, TSR.

memory size \mem´ər-ē sīz`\ *n.* The memory capacity of a computer, usually measured in megabytes. *See also* megabyte, memory.

memory typewriter \mem`ər-ē tīp´rī-tər\ *n.* An electric typewriter with internal memory and typically a one-line liquid crystal display for viewing the contents of that memory. Memory typewriters can usually hold one page of text at a time, to which small modifications can be made. Memory typewriters usually do not retain the contents of memory when power is turned off.

menu \men´yōō\ *n.* A list of options from which a user can make a selection in order to perform a desired action, such as choosing a command or applying a particular format to part of a document. Many application programs, especially those that offer a graphical interface, use menus as a means of providing the user with an easily learned, easy-to-use alternative to memorizing program commands and their appropriate usage. See the illustration.

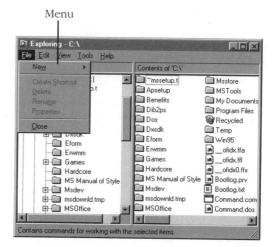

Menu.

menu bar \men´yōō bär`\ *n.* A rectangular bar displayed in an application program's on-screen window, often at the top, from which menus can be selected by the user. Names of available menus are displayed in the menu bar; choosing one with the keyboard or with a mouse causes the list of options in that menu to be displayed. See the illustration.

Menu bar

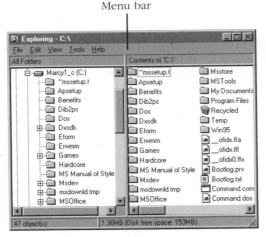

Menu bar.

menu-driven \men´yoo-driv`ən\ *adj.* Using menus to present choices of commands and available options. Menu-driven programs are usually considered friendlier and easier to learn than programs with a command-line interface. *Compare* command-line interface.

menu item \men´yoo ī`təm\ *n.* A choice on a menu, selectable by either the keyboard or a mouse. In some instances, a menu item that is not available (that is, not appropriate) for a given situation is "grayed" (dimmed in comparison to the valid menu choices). See the illustration.

merge \mərj\ *vb.* To combine two or more items, such as lists, in an ordered way and without changing the basic structure of either. *Compare* concatenate.

merged transistor logic \mərjd` tran-zi´stər loj`ik\ *n. See* integrated injection logic.

merge sort \mərj´ sōrt\ *n.* A sorting technique that combines several sorted (input) lists into a single sorted (output) list. *See also* bubble sort, insertion sort, quicksort, sort algorithm.

mesa \mā´sə\ *n.* An area of a germanium or silicon wafer that was protected during the etching process and is therefore higher than the surrounding etched areas. *See also* photolithography.

mesh network \mesh´ net`wərk\ *n.* A communications network having two or more paths to any node.

message \mes´əj\ *n.* **1.** In communications, a unit of information transmitted electronically from one device to another. A message can contain one or more blocks of text as well as beginning and ending characters, control characters, a software-generated header (destination address, type of message, and other such information), and error-checking or synchronizing information. A message can be routed directly from sender to receiver through a physical link, or it can be passed, either whole or in parts, through a switching system that routes it from one intermediate station to another. *See also* asynchronous transmission, block (definition 4), control character (definition 1), frame (definition 1), frame (definition 2), header (definition 2), message switching, network, packet (definition 1), packet switching, synchronous transmission. **2.** In software, a piece of information passed from the application or operating system to the user to suggest an action, indicate a condition, or inform that an event has occurred. **3.** In message-based operating environ-

Menu item

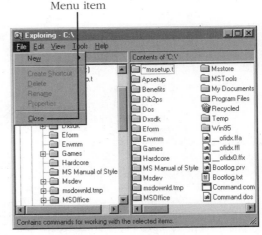

Menu item.

ments, such as Microsoft Windows, a unit of information passed among running programs, certain devices in the system, and the operating environment itself.

message header \mes´əj hed`ər\ *n.* A sequence of bits or bytes at the beginning of a message that usually provides a timing sequence and specifies such aspects of the message structure as its length, data format, and block identification number. *See also* header (definition 2).

message of the day \mes`əj əv dhə dā´\ *n.* A daily bulletin for users of a network, multiuser computer, or other shared system. In most cases, users are shown the message of the day when they log into the system. *Acronym:* MOTD (M`O-T-D´).

message queue \mes´əj kyo͞o`\ *n.* An ordered list of messages awaiting transmission, from which they are taken up on a first in, first out (FIFO) basis.

message reflection \mes´əj rə-flek`shən\ *n.* In object-oriented programming environments, such as Visual C++, OLE, and ActiveX, a function that allows a control to handle its own message. *See also* ActiveX controls, control (definition 2), OCX, VBX.

Message Security Protocol \mes`əj se-kyər`i-tē prō´tə-kol\ *n.* A protocol for Internet messages that is based on the use of encryption and verification to ensure security. It also allows for permissions at the server level for delivery or rejection of e-mail. *Acronym:* MSP (M`S-P´).

message switching \mes´əj swich`ēng\ *n.* A technique used on some communications networks in which a message, with appropriate address information, is routed through one or more intermediate switching stations before being sent to its destination. On a typical message-switching network, a central computer receives messages, stores them (usually briefly), determines their destination addresses, and then delivers them. Message switching enables a network both to regulate traffic and to use communications lines efficiently. *Compare* circuit switching, packet switching.

messaging \mes´ə-jēng\ *n.* The use of computers and data communication equipment to convey messages from one person to another, as by e-mail, voice mail, or fax.

messaging application \mes´ə-jēng a-plə-kā`shən\ *n.* An application that enables users to send messages (such as e-mail or fax) to each other.

Messaging Application Programming Interface \mes`ə-jēng a-plə-kā-shən prō´gram-ēng in`tər-fās\ *n. See* MAPI.

messaging client \mes´ə-jēng klī`ənt\ *n.* An application program that enables its user to send or receive messages (such as e-mail or fax) to and from other users with the help of a remote server.

metacharacter \met´ə-kâr`ək-tər\ *n.* A character embedded in a program source or a data stream that conveys information about other characters, rather than itself representing a character. A simple example is the backslash (\) character, which, when used in strings in the C programming language, indicates that the letter following the backslash is part of an escape sequence that enables C to display a nongraphic character. *See also* escape character.

metacompiler \met´ə-kəm-pī`lər\ *n.* A compiler that produces compilers. The UNIX utility *yacc* (Yet Another Compiler-Compiler) is a metacompiler. If it is given a language specification, yacc produces a compiler for that language. *See also* compiler (definition 2).

Meta-Content Format \met´ə-kon´tent fōr`mat\ *n.* An open format for describing information about content of a structured body of data such as a Web page, a set of files on a Windows desktop, or a relational database. Meta-Content Format might be used for indexes, data dictionaries, or price lists. *Acronym:* MCF (M`C-F´).

meta data or **metadata** \met´ə dā`tə, dat`ə\ *n.* Data about data. For example, the title, subject, author, and size of a file constitute meta data about the file. *See also* data dictionary, repository.

Metadata Interchange Specification \met`ə-dā`tə in´tər-chānj spes-ə-fə-kā`shən\ *n.* A set of specifications dealing with the exchanging, sharing, and managing of meta data. *Acronym:* MDIS (M`D-I-S´). *See also* meta data.

metafile \met´ə-fīl`\ *n.* A file that contains or defines other files. Many operating systems use metafiles to contain directory information about other files on a given storage device.

metalanguage \met´ə-lang`wəj\ *n.* A language used to describe other languages. Backus-Naur form (BNF) is a metalanguage commonly used to define programming languages. *Also called* language-description language. *See also* Backus-Naur form.

metal-oxide semiconductor \met`əl-oks`īd sem´ī-kən-duk`tər, sem´ē-kən-duk`tər\ *n. See* MOS.

metal-oxide semiconductor field-effect transistor \met`əl-oks`īd sem´ī-kən-duk`tər fēld´ə-fekt tranz-i`stər, sem´ē-kən-duk`tər\ *n. See* MOSFET.

metaoperating system \met`ə-op´ər-ā-tēng si`stəm\ *n.* An operating system under which several other operating systems are active. *Also called* supervisor.

method \meth´əd\ *n.* In object-oriented programming, a process performed by an object when it receives a message. *See also* object (definition 2), object-oriented programming.

Metropolitan Area Exchange \me`trə-pol´ə-tən âr`ē-ə eks-chānj´\ *n.* An interconnection point for Internet access providers within a metropolitan area. Data sent between participants in a Metropolitan Area Exchange can pass directly from one network to another without passing through a major backbone. *Acronym:* MAE (M`A-E´). *See also* backbone (definition 1), ISP.

metropolitan area network \me-trə-pol`ə-tən âr`ē-ə net´wərk\ *n. See* MAN.

MFLOPS \M´flops, M-F-L`O-P-S´\ *n.* Short for **m**illion **fl**oating-point **o**perations **p**er **s**econd. A measure of computing speed. *Also called* megaflops.

MFM encoding \M-F-M´ en-kō`dēng\ *n. See* modified frequency modulation encoding.

MFS \M`F-S´\ *n. See* Macintosh File System.

.mg \dot`M-G´\ *n.* On the Internet, the major geographic domain specifying that an address is located in Madagascar.

mget \M´get\ *n.* Short for **m**ultiple **get**. A command in most FTP clients with which a user can request the transfer of several files at once. *See also* FTP[1] (definition 1).

.mh \dot`M-H´\ *n.* On the Internet, the major geographic domain specifying that an address is located in the Marshall Islands.

MHz \meg´ə-hərtz\ *n. See* megahertz.

MI \M-I´\ *n. See* multiple inheritance.

MICR \mī´kər, M`I-C-R´\ *n. See* magnetic-ink character recognition.

micro- \mī´krō\ *prefix* **1.** In nonexact measurements, small or compact, as in *microprocessor* or *microcomputer*. **2.** Metric prefix meaning 10^{-6} (one millionth).

Micro Channel Architecture \mī´krō chan`əl ärk´ə-tek-chur\ *n.* The design of the bus in IBM PS/2 computers (except Models 25 and 30). The Micro Channel is electrically and physically incompatible with the IBM PC/AT bus. Unlike the PC/AT bus, the Micro Channel functions as either a 16-bit or a 32-bit bus. The Micro Channel can also be driven independently by multiple bus master processors.

microchip \mī´krō-chip`\ *n. See* integrated circuit.

microcircuit \mī´krō-sər`kət\ *n.* A miniaturized electronic circuit etched on a semiconductor chip. A microcircuit is made up of interconnected transistors, resistors, and other components. However, it is fabricated as a unit rather than as a set of vacuum tubes, discrete transistors, or other elements that have to be wired together. *See also* integrated circuit.

microcode \mī´krō-kōd`\ *n.* Very low-level code that defines how a processor operates. Microcode is even lower in level than machine code; it specifies what the processor does when it executes a machine-code instruction. *See also* machine code, microprogramming.

microcomputer \mī´krō-kəm-pyo͞o`tər\ *n.* A computer built around a single-chip microprocessor. Less powerful than minicomputers and mainframes, microcomputers have nevertheless evolved into very powerful machines capable of complex tasks. Technology has progressed so quickly that state-of-the-art microcomputers are as powerful as mainframe computers of only a few years ago, at a fraction of the cost. *See also* computer.

microelectronics \mī´krō-i-lek-tron´iks\ *n.* The technology of constructing electronic circuits and devices in very small packages. The most significant advance in microelectronics technology has been the integrated circuit. Circuits that 40 years ago required a roomful of power-hungry vacuum tubes can now be fabricated on a silicon chip smaller than a postage stamp and require only a few milliwatts of power. *See also* integrated circuit.

microfiche \mī´krō-fēsh`\ *n.* A small sheet of film, about 4 by 6 inches, used for recording photographically reduced images, such as document pages, in rows and columns forming a grid pattern. The resulting images are too small to read with the naked eye, and a microfiche reader is required to view the documents. *Compare* microfilm.

microfilm \mī´krō-film`\ *n.* A thin strip of film stored on a roll and used to record sequential data images. As with microfiche, a special device magnifies the images so that they can be read. *See also* CIM (definition 2), COM (definition 4). *Compare* microfiche.

microfloppy disk \mī`krō-flop´ē disk\ *n.* A 3.5-inch floppy disk of the type used with the Apple Macintosh and with IBM and compatible microcomputers. A microfloppy disk is a round piece of polyester film coated with ferric oxide and encased in a rigid plastic shell equipped with a sliding metal cover. On the Macintosh, a single-sided microfloppy disk can hold 400 kilobytes (KB); a double-sided (standard) disk can hold 800 KB; and a double-sided high-density disk can hold 1.44 megabytes (MB). On IBM and compatible machines, a microfloppy can hold either 720 KB or 1.44 MB of information. *See also* floppy disk.

microform \mī´krō-fōrm`\ *n.* The medium, such as microfilm or microfiche, on which a photographically reduced image, called a *microimage,* is stored. A microimage usually represents text, such as archived documents. *See also* microfiche, microfilm.

micrographics \mī`krō-graf´iks\ *n.* The techniques and methods for recording data on microfilm. *See also* microform.

microimage \mī´krō-im`əj\ *n.* A photographically reduced image, usually stored on microfilm or microfiche, that is too small to be read without magnification. *See also* microform, micrographics.

microinstruction \mī´krō-in-struk`shən\ *n.* An instruction that is part of the microcode. *See also* microcode.

microjustification \mī`krō-ju-stə-fə-kā´shən\ *n.* *See* microspace justification.

microkernel \mī´krō-kər`nəl\ *n.* **1.** In programming, the strictly hardware-dependent part of an operating system that is intended to be portable from one type of computer to another. The microkernel provides a hardware-independent interface to the rest of the operating system, so only the microkernel needs to be rewritten to port the operating system to a different platform. *See also* kernel, operating system. **2.** A kernel that has been designed with only the basic features and typically in a modular fashion.

micrologic \mī´krō-loj`ik\ *n.* A set of instructions, stored in binary form, or a set of electronic logic circuits that defines and governs the operation within a microprocessor.

microminiature \mī`krō-min´ə-chur\ *n.* An extremely small circuit or other electronic component, especially one that is a refinement of an already miniaturized element.

microphone \mī´krə-fōn`\ *n.* **1.** A device that converts sound waves into analog electrical signals. Additional hardware can convert the microphone's output into digital data that a computer can process; for example, to record multimedia documents or analyze the sound signal. **2.** A communications program that runs on the Apple Macintosh computer.

microprocessor \mī`krō-pros´es-ər\ *n.* A central processing unit (CPU) on a single chip. A modern microprocessor can have over 1 million transistors in an integrated-circuit package that is roughly 1 inch square. Microprocessors are at the heart of all personal computers. When memory and power are added to a microprocessor, all the pieces, excluding peripherals, required for a computer are present. The most popular lines of microprocessors today are the 680x0 family from Motorola, which powers the Apple Macintosh line, and the 80x86 family from Intel, which is at the core of all IBM PC–compatible and PS/2 computers. *See also* 6502, 65816, 6800, 68000, 68020, 68030, 68040, 80286, 80386DX, 80386SX, 8080, 8086, 8088, 88000, DECchip 21064, i486DX, i486DX2, i486SL, i486SX, Pentium, Pentium Pro, PowerPC, SPARC, Z80.

microprogramming \mī`krō-prō´gram-ēng\ *n.* The writing of microcode for a processor. Some systems, chiefly minicomputers and mainframes,

allow modification of microcode for an installed processor. *See also* microcode.

microsecond \mī´krō-sek`ənd\ *n.* Abbreviated μs. One millionth (10^{-6}) of a second.

Microsoft DOS \mī´krō-soft dos´, D-O-S´\ *n. See* MS-DOS.

Microsoft Internet Explorer \mī´krō-soft in`tər-net eks-plōr´ər\ *n. See* Internet Explorer.

Microsoft Network \mī´krō-soft` net´wərk\ *n. See* The Microsoft Network.

Microsoft Windows \mī´krō-soft win´dōz\ *n. See* Windows.

Microsoft Windows 95 \mī´krō-soft win`dōz nīn-tē-fīv´\ *n. See* Windows 95.

microspace justification \mī´krō-spās ju-stə-fə-kā´shən\ *n.* The addition of thin spaces between characters within words to fill out a line for justification, instead of relying only on adding space between words. Good microspace justification gives justified text a more polished, professional look; excessive microspace justification causes words to lose visual coherence. *Also called* micro-justification. *See also* justify (definition 2), micro-spacing.

microspacing \mī´krō-spā`sēng\ *n.* In printing, the process of adjusting character placement by very small increments.

microtransaction \mī´krō-tranz-ak`shən\ *n.* A business transaction that involves a very small amount of money, typically under about $5. *See also* millicent technology.

microwave relay \mī´krō-wāv rē`lā\ *n.* A communications link that uses point-to-point radio transmissions at frequencies higher than approximately 1 gigahertz (1,000 megahertz).

middleware \mid´l-wâr`\ *n.* **1.** Software that sits between two or more types of software and translates information between them. Middleware can cover a broad spectrum of software and generally sits between an application and an operating system, a network operating system, or a database management system. Examples of middleware include CORBA and other object broker programs and network control programs. *See also* CORBA. **2.** Software that provides a common application programming interface (API). Applications written using that API will run in the same computer systems as the middleware. An example of this type

of middleware is ODBC, which has a common API for many types of databases. *See also* application programming interface, ODBC. **3.** Software development tools that enable users to create simple programs by selecting existing services and linking them with a scripting language. *See also* scripting language.

MIDI \mid´ē, M´I-D-I´\ *n.* Acronym for **M**usical **I**nstrument **D**igital **I**nterface. A serial interface standard that allows for the connection of music synthesizers, musical instruments, and computers. The MIDI standard is based partly on hardware and partly on a description of the way in which music and sound are encoded and communicated between MIDI devices. The information transmitted between MIDI devices is in a form called a *MIDI message,* which encodes aspects of sound such as pitch and volume as 8-bit bytes of digital information. MIDI devices can be used for creating, recording, and playing back music. Using MIDI, computers, synthesizers, and sequencers can communicate with each other, either keeping time or actually controlling the music created by other connected equipment. *See also* synthesizer.

midrange computer \mid´rānj kəm-pyo͞o´tər\ *n.* A medium-size computer. The term is used interchangeably with *minicomputer,* except midrange computers do not include single-user workstations. *See also* minicomputer.

migration \mī-grā´shən\ *n.* The process of making existing applications and data work on a different computer or operating system.

.mil \dot-mil´, -M´I-L´\ *n.* In the Internet's Domain Name System, the top-level domain that identifies addresses operated by U.S. military organizations. The .mil designation appears at the end of the address. *See also* DNS (definition 1), domain (definition 3). *Compare* .com, .edu, .gov, .net, .org.

Military Network \mil`ə-târ-ē net´wərk\ *n. See* MILNET.

milli- \mil´ə\ *prefix* Abbreviated m. Metric prefix meaning 10^{-3} (one thousandth).

millicent technology \mil`ə-sent tek-nol´ə-jē\ *n.* A set of protocols for small-scale commercial transactions over the Internet, developed by Digital Equipment Corporation. Millicent technology is intended to handle purchases of items of information at prices less than a cent.

millions of instructions per second \mil`yənz əv in-struk`shənz pər sek´ənd\ *n.* See MIPS.

millisecond \mil´ə-sek`ənd\ *n.* Abbreviated ms or msec. One thousandth of a second.

millivolt \mil´ə-vōlt\ *n.* Abbreviated mV. One thousandth of a volt.

MILNET \mil´net\ *n.* Short for **Mil**itary **Net**work. A wide area network that represents the military side of the original ARPANET. MILNET carries nonclassified U.S. military traffic. *See also* ARPANET. *Compare* NSFnet.

MIMD \M`I-M-D´\ *n.* Acronym for **m**ultiple **i**nstruction, **m**ultiple **d**ata stream processing. A category of computer architecture engaged in parallel processing in which central processing units independently fetch instructions and operate on data. *See also* architecture (definition 1), central processing unit, instruction, parallel processing. *Compare* SIMD.

MIME \mīm, M`I-M-E´\ *n.* Acronym for **M**ultipurpose **I**nternet **M**ail **E**xtensions. A standard that extends the Simple Mail Transfer Protocol (SMTP) to permit data, such as video, sound, and binary files, to be transmitted by Internet e-mail without having to be translated into ASCII format first. This is accomplished by the use of MIME types, which describe the contents of a document. A MIME-compliant application sending a file, such as some e-mail programs, assigns a MIME type to the file. The receiving application, which must also be MIME-compliant, refers to a standardized list of documents that are organized into MIME types and subtypes to interpret the content of the file. For instance, one MIME type is *text,* and it has a number of subtypes, including *plain* and *html.* A MIME type of *text/html* refers to a file that contains text written in HTML. MIME is part of HTTP, and both Web browsers and HTTP servers use MIME to interpret e-mail files they send and receive. *See also* HTTP, HTTP server, Simple Mail Transfer Protocol, Web browser. *Compare* BinHex[1] (definition 1).

miniaturization \min`ə-chər-i-zā´shən\ *n.* In the development of integrated circuits, the process of reducing the size and increasing the density of transistors and other elements on a semiconductor chip. Besides providing the benefits of small size, miniaturization of electronic circuits lowers power requirements, reduces heat, and shortens delays in the propagation of signals from one circuit element to the next. *See also* integrated circuit, integration (definition 2).

minicomputer \min`ē-kəm-pyo͞o`tər\ *n.* A midlevel computer built to perform complex computations while dealing efficiently with a high level of input and output from users connected via terminals. Minicomputers also frequently connect to other minicomputers on a network and distribute processing among all the attached machines. Minicomputers are used heavily in transaction-processing applications and as interfaces between mainframe computer systems and wide area networks. *See also* computer, mainframe computer, microcomputer, supercomputer, wide area network. *Compare* midrange computer, workstation (definition 2).

mini-driver architecture \min`ē-drī-vər är´kə-tek-chur\ *n.* An architecture in Windows 3.1 and Windows 95 that uses a relatively small and simple driver, containing any additional instructions needed by a specific hardware device, to interface with the universal driver for that class of devices. *See also* driver.

minifloppy \min`ē-flop´ē\ *n.* A 5.25-inch floppy disk. *See also* floppy disk.

minimize \min´ə-mīz`\ *vb.* In a graphical user interface, to hide a window without shutting down the program responsible for the window. Usually an icon, button, or name for the window is placed on the desktop; when the user clicks on the button, icon, or name, the window is restored to its previous size. *See also* graphical user interface, Minimize button, taskbar, window. *Compare* maximize.

Minimize button \min´ə-mīz but`ən\ *n.* In Windows 3.*x*, Windows 95, and Windows NT, a button in the upper right-hand corner of a window that when clicked hides the window. In Windows 3.*x* and Windows NT 3.5 and lower, an icon appears on the desktop that represents the window; in Windows 95 and Windows NT 4.0, the name of the window appears on the taskbar at the bottom of the desktop screen. When the icon or the name is clicked, the window is restored to its previous size. *See also* graphical user interface, taskbar, window.

miniport drivers \min´ē-pōrt drī´vərz\ *n*. Drivers containing device-specific information that communicate with non-device-specific port drivers, which in turn communicate with the system. *See also* driver.

minitower \min´ē-tou`ər\ *n*. A vertical floor-standing computer cabinet that is about half the height (13 inches) of a tower case (24 inches). *See also* tower.

minor key \mī´nər kē`\ *n*. *See* alternate key (definition 1).

MIP mapping \M-I-P´ map`ēng\ *n*. Short for **m**ultum **i**n **p**arvo (Latin, "much in little") **mapping**. A form of mapping in which the appearance of a bit-mapped image is precalculated from a distance and used in a texture mapper. This allows for smoother texture-mapped images calculated in the distance, since pixel conversion may alter colors relative to human perception.

MIPS \mips, M`I-P-S´\ *n*. Acronym for **m**illions of **i**nstructions **p**er **s**econd. A common measure of processor speed. *See also* central processing unit, MFLOPS.

mirror image \mēr`ər im´əj\ *n*. An image that is an exact duplicate of the original with the exception that one dimension is reversed. For example, "<" and ">" are mirror images.

mirroring \mēr´ər-ēng`\ *n*. In computer graphics, the ability to display a mirror image of a graphic—a duplicate rotated or reflected relative to some reference such as an axis of symmetry. See the illustration.

mirror site \mēr´ər sīt`\ *n*. A file server that contains a duplicate set of files to the set on a popular server. Mirror sites exist to spread the distribution burden over more than one server or to eliminate the need to use high-demand international circuits.

MIS \M`I-S´\ *n*. *See* management information service, management information system.

misc. newsgroups \mis`dot nōōz´grōōps\ *n*. Usenet newsgroups that are part of the misc. hierarchy and have the prefix misc. These newsgroups cover topics that do not fit into the other standard Usenet hierarchies (comp., news., rec., sci., soc., talk.). *See also* newsgroup, traditional newsgroup hierarchy, Usenet.

.mi.us \dot-M-I`dot-U-S´\ *n*. On the Internet, the major geographic domain specifying that an address is located in Michigan, United States.

mixed cell reference \miksd` sel´ re`frəns\ *n*. In spreadsheets, a cell reference (the address of a cell needed to solve a formula) in which either the row or the column is relative (automatically changed when the formula is copied or moved to another cell) while the other is absolute (not changed when the formula is copied or moved). *See also* cell (definition 1).

.mk \dot`M-K´\ *n*. On the Internet, the major geographic domain specifying that an address is located in Macedonia.

.ml \dot`M-L´\ *n*. On the Internet, the major geographic domain specifying that an address is located in Mali.

.mm \dot`M-M´\ *n*. On the Internet, the major geographic domain specifying that an address is located in Myanmar.

MMU \M`M-U´\ *n*. *See* memory management unit.

 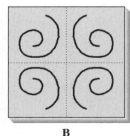 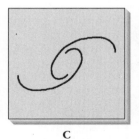 

A	B	C	D

Mirroring.   (A) Twofold symmetry with vertical axis; (B) fourfold symmetry with vertical and horizontal axes; (C) twofold radial symmetry; (D) threefold radial symmetry.

MMX \M´M-X´\ *n.* Short for **M**ulti**m**edia **Ex**tensions. An enhancement to the architecture of Intel Pentium processors that improves the performance of multimedia and communications applications.

.mn \dot`M-N´\ *n.* On the Internet, the major geographic domain specifying that an address is located in Mongolia.

mnemonic \nē-mon´ik`\ *n.* A word, rhyme, or other memory aid used to associate a complex or lengthy set of information with something that is simple and easy to remember. Mnemonics are widely used in computing. Programming languages other than machine language, for example, are known as *symbolic languages* because they use short mnemonics, such as *ADD* (for *addition*) and *def* (for *define*) to represent instructions and operations. Similarly, operating systems and applications based on typed commands use mnemonics to represent instructions to the program. MS-DOS, for example, uses *dir* (for *directory*) to request a list of files.

MNP10 \M`N-P-ten´\ *n.* Short for **M**icrocom **N**etworking **P**rotocol, Class **10.** An industry-standard communication protocol used for modem connections over analog cellular telephone connections. The most recent version of MNP10 is MNP 10EC (EC stands for Enhanced Cellular). *See also* communications protocol.

.mn.us \dot-M-N`dot-U-S´\ *n.* On the Internet, the major geographic domain specifying that an address is located in Minnesota, United States.

.mo \dot`M-O´\ *n.* On the Internet, the major geographic domain specifying that an address is located in Macau.

mobile computing \mō`bəl kəm-pyōō´tēng\ *n.* The process of using a computer while traveling. Mobile computing usually requires a portable computer that is battery powered, rather than a desktop system.

mode \mōd\ *n.* The operational state of a computer or a program. For example, edit mode is the state in which a program accepts changes to a file. *See also* address mode, compatibility mode, safe mode, video mode, virtual real mode.

modec \mō´dek\ *n.* In telecommunications, a device that generates analog modem signals digitally. The term *modec* is a combination of the terms *modem* and *codec*. *See also* codec (definition 1), modem.

model \mod´əl\ *n.* A mathematical or graphical representation of a real-world situation or object—for example, a mathematical model of the distribution of matter in the universe, a spreadsheet (numeric) model of business operations, or a graphical model of a molecule. Models can generally be changed or manipulated so that their creators can see how the real version might be affected by modifications or varying conditions. *See also* modeling, simulation.

modeling \mod´əl-ēng`\ *n.* **1.** The use of computers to describe the behavior of a system. Spreadsheet programs, for example, can be used to manipulate financial data, representing the health and activity of a company; to develop business plans and projections; or to evaluate the impact of proposed changes on the company's operations and financial status. *See also* simulation, spreadsheet program. **2.** The use of computers to describe physical objects and the spatial relationships among them mathematically. CAD programs, for example, are used to create on-screen representations of such physical objects as tools, office buildings, complex molecules, and automobiles. These models use equations to create lines, curves, and other shapes and to place those shapes accurately in relation to each other and to the two-dimensional or three-dimensional space in which they are drawn. *See also* CAD, rendering, solid model, surface modeling, three-dimensional model, two-dimensional model, wire-frame model.

modem \mō´dəm\ *n.* Short for **mo**dulator/**dem**odulator. A communications device that enables a computer to transmit information over a standard telephone line. Because a computer is digital (works with discrete electrical signals representing binary 1 and binary 0) and a telephone line is analog (carries a signal that can have any of a large number of variations), modems are needed to convert digital to analog and vice versa. When transmitting, modems impose (modulate) a computer's digital signals onto a continuous carrier frequency on the telephone line. When receiving, modems sift out (demodulate) the information from the carrier and transfer it in digital form to the computer. Sophisticated modems are also capable of such functions as automatic dialing, answering, and redialing in addition to transmitting and receiving. Without appropriate communications software, however, modems cannot perform any useful work. *See also* baud rate.

modem bank \mō´dəm bank`\ *n.* A collection of modems connected to a server maintained by an ISP or the operator of a BBS or remote-access LAN. Most modem banks are configured to allow a remote user to dial a single phone number that routes calls to an available phone number on the bank. *See also* BBS (definition 1), ISP, LAN.

modem eliminator \mō`dəm i-lim´ə-nā-tər\ *n.* A device that enables two computers to communicate without modems. *See also* null modem.

modem port \mō´dəm pōrt`\ *n.* A serial port used for connecting an external modem to a personal computer. *See also* modem, serial port.

modem ready \mō`dəm red´ē\ *n. See* MR.

moderated \mod´ər-ā`təd\ *adj.* Subjected to review by a moderator, who may remove irrelevant or inflammatory articles or messages before redistributing them through a newsgroup, mailing list, or other messaging system.

moderated discussion \mod´ər-āt-əd di-skush´ən\ *n.* Communication taking place on a mailing list, newsgroup, or other online forum that is edited by a moderator. When one submits a message to a moderated discussion, the moderator decides if the message is relevant to the discussion topic. If so, it is forwarded to the discussion group. The content of a moderated discussion is often perceived as more valuable than that of an unmoderated one because the information has been read and approved by a "gatekeeper," who has (presumably) filtered out irrelevant submissions. Some moderators also filter submissions for obscene or pornographic material or material that is potentially offensive. *See also* mailing list, moderator, newsgroup.

moderator \mod´ər-ā`tər\ *n.* In some Internet newsgroups and mailing lists, a person through whom all messages are filtered before they are distributed to the members of the newsgroup or list. The moderator discards or edits any messages that are not considered appropriate. *See also* mailing list, newsgroup.

modified frequency modulation encoding \mod`ə-fīd frē`kwən-sē moj`ə-lā´shən en-kō`dēng, mo`dyə-lā´shən\ *n.* Abbreviated MFM encoding. A widely used method of storing data on disks. MFM encoding is based on an earlier technique called frequency modulation encoding but improves on its efficiency by reducing the need for synchronizing information and by basing the magnetic coding of each bit on the status of the previously recorded bit. MFM encoding stores more information on a disk than does frequency modulation encoding and is used on many hard disks. It is not, however, as efficient a space saver as the technique known as *run-length limited encoding,* or RLL. *Compare* frequency modulation encoding, run-length limited encoding.

modifier key \mod´ə-fī-ər kē`\ *n.* A key on the keyboard that, when held down while another key is pressed, changes the meaning of the keystroke. *See also* Alt key, Command key, Control key, Shift key.

modify structure \mod´ə-fī struk`chur\ *n.* An operator available in some database management systems that permits fields (columns) to be added or deleted without the need to rebuild the entire database.

MO disk \M-O´ disk`\ *n. See* magneto-optic disc.

MO disk drive \M-O` disk´ drīv\ *n. See* magneto-optic disc.

Modula-2 \moj`ə-lə-tōō´, mo`dyə-lə-\ *n.* A modular high-level language designed in 1980 by Niklaus Wirth. Derived from Pascal, Modula-2 is noted for its emphasis on modular programming, its early support for data abstraction, and its lack of standard functions and procedures. *See also* modular programming.

modular design \moj´ə-lər də-zīn´, mo`dyə-lər\ *n.* An approach to designing hardware or software. In modular design, a project is broken into smaller units, or modules, each of which can be developed, tested, and finished independently before being combined with the others in the final product. Each unit is designed to perform a particular task or function and can thus become part of a "library" of modules that can often be reused in other products having similar requirements. In programming, for example, one module might consist of instructions for moving the cursor in a window on the screen. Because it is deliberately designed as a stand-alone unit that can work with other sections of the program, the same module might be able to perform the same task in another program as well, thus saving time in development and testing.

modular jack \mo`dyə-lər jak´, moj`ə-lər\ *n*. *See* phone connector.

modular programming \moj`ə-lər prō´gram-ēng, mo`dyə-lər\ *n*. An approach to programming in which the program is broken into several independently compiled modules. Each module exports specified elements (constants, data types, variables, functions, procedures); all other elements remain private to the module. Other modules can use only the exported elements. Modules clarify and regularize the interfaces among the major parts of a program. Thus, they facilitate group programming efforts and promote reliable programming practices. Modular programming is a precursor of object-oriented programming. *See also* module (definition 1), object-oriented programming.

modulate \moj´ə-lāt`, mo´dyə-lāt`\ *vb*. To change some aspect of a signal intentionally, usually for the purpose of transmitting information.

modulation \moj`ə-lā´shən, mo`dyə-lā´shən\ *n*. **1.** The process of changing or regulating the characteristics of a carrier wave vibrating at a certain amplitude (height) and frequency (timing) so that the variations represent meaningful information. **2.** In computer communications, the means by which a modem converts digital information sent by a computer to the audio form that it sends over a telephone line.

module \moj´o͞ol, mo´dyo͞ol\ *n*. **1.** In programming, a collection of routines and data structures that performs a particular task or implements a particular abstract data type. Modules usually consist of two parts: an interface, which lists the constants, data types, variables, and routines that can be accessed by other modules or routines, and an implementation, which is private (accessible only to the module) and which contains the source code that actually implements the routines in the module. *See also* abstract data type, information hiding, Modula-2, modular programming. **2.** In hardware, a self-contained component that can provide a complete function to a system and can

be interchanged with other modules that provide similar functions. *See also* memory card, SIMM.

modulo \moj´ə-lō, mod´yə-lō`\ *n*. An arithmetic operation whose result is the remainder of a division operation. For example, 17 *modulo* 3 = 2 because 17 divided by 3 yields a remainder of 2. Modulo operations are used in programming.

moiré \mwär-ā´\ *n*. A visible wavy distortion or flickering in an image that is displayed or printed with an inappropriate resolution. Several parameters affect moiré patterns, including the size and resolution of the image, resolution of the output device, and halftone screen angle. See the illustration.

Moiré.

molecular beam epitaxy \mə-le`kyə-lər bēm ep´ə-tak-sē\ *n*. A process used in the fabrication of semiconductor devices, such as integrated circuits. A device employing molecular beam epitaxy creates thin layers of semiconducting material by vaporizing the material and then directing a beam of molecules at the substrate on which the layer is to be formed. This technique allows very precise and very thin layers to be created.

monadic \mə-na´dik`\ *adj*. *See* unary.

monitor \mon´i-tər\ *n*. The device on which images generated by the computer's video adapter are displayed. The term *monitor* usually refers to a video display and its housing. The monitor is attached to the video adapter by a cable. *See also* CRT.

monochrome \mon´ə-krōm`\ *adj*. Of, pertaining to, or being a monitor that displays images in only one color—black on white (as on early monochrome Macintosh screens) or amber or green on black (as on early IBM and other monochrome monitors). The term is also applied to a monitor that displays only variable levels of a single color, such as a gray-scale monitor.

monochrome adapter \mon`ə-krōm ə-dap´tər\ *n*. A video adapter capable of generating a video signal for one foreground color or sometimes for a range of intensities in a single color, as for a gray-scale monitor.

monochrome display \mon´ə-krōm di-splā`\ *n.*
1. A video display capable of rendering only one
color. The color displayed depends on the phosphor of the display (often green or amber). **2.** A
display capable of rendering a range of intensities
in only one color, as in a gray-scale monitor.

Monochrome Display Adapter \mon`ə-krōm di-
splā´ ə-dap-tər\ *n. See* MDA.

monochrome graphics adapter   \mon`ə-krōm
graf´iks ə-dap-tər\ *n. See* HGC.

monochrome monitor \mon´ə-krōm mon´ə-tər\
n. See monochrome display.

monographics adapter \mon`ə-graf´iks ə-dap-
tər\ *n.* Any video adapter that can display only
monochrome text and graphics; any video adapter
functionally compatible with the Hercules Graphics Card (HGC). *See also* HGC.

monospace font \mon´ō-spās font`\ *n.* A font
(set of characters in a particular style and size),
similar to that used on a typewriter, in which each
character occupies the same amount of horizontal
space regardless of its width—an *i,* for example,
taking as much room as an *m.*

```
This is a sentence in a monospace font.
```

Also called fixed-width font. *See also* monospacing. *Compare* proportional font.

monospacing \mon´ō-spā`sēng\ *n.* A form of
print and display spacing in which each character
occupies the same amount of horizontal space on
the line, regardless of whether the character is
wide (such as *m*) or narrow (such as *l*). *Also called*
fixed spacing, fixed-pitch spacing, fixed-width
spacing. *See also* monospace font. *Compare* proportional spacing.

Monte Carlo method \mon`tē kär´lō meth`əd\ *n.*
A mathematical technique that uses repeated calculations and random numbers to find an approximate solution to a complex problem. The Monte
Carlo method, named for its relationship to games
of chance played in the casinos at Monte Carlo,
Monaco, can be used in situations in which it is
possible to calculate the probability of a particular
event occurring but not to factor in the complex
effects of many other contributing factors.

.montreal.ca \dot-mon-trē-äl`dot-C-A´\ *n.* On the
Internet, the major geographic domain specifying
that an address is located in Montreal, Canada.

MOO \mōō, M`O-O´\ *n.* Short for **M**UD, **o**bject
oriented. A form of multiuser dungeon (MUD) that
contains an object-oriented language with which
users can create areas and objects within the
MOO. Generally, MOOs are more focused on
communications and programming and less on
games than MUDs are. *See also* MUD.

.moov \dot-mōōv´, dot`M-O-O-V´\ *n.* A file exten-
sion indicating a QuickTime MooV video file for a
Macintosh computer. *See also* MooV.

MooV \mōō´V\ *n.* The file format for QuickTime
movies that stores synchronized tracks for control,
video, audio, and text. *See also* QuickTime.

morphing \mōr´fēng\ *n.* Short for meta**mor-
ph**osing. A process by which one image is grad-
ually transformed into another, creating the
illusion of a metamorphosis occurring in a short
time. A common motion picture special-effects
technique, morphing is available in many
advanced computer animation packages. *See also*
tween.

MOS \mos, M`O-S´\ *n.* Acronym for **m**etal-**o**xide
semiconductor. An integrated-circuit technology
in which field-effect transistors (FETs) are made
with an insulating layer of silicon dioxide
between a metal gate electrode and a semiconductor channel. MOS designs are widely used
both in discrete components and in integrated circuits. MOS integrated circuits have the advantages
of high component density, high speed, and low
power consumption. MOS devices are easily damaged by static electricity, so before they are
inserted in a circuit they should be kept with their
connectors embedded in conducting foam to prevent the buildup of static charges. *See also* FET,
MOSFET.

Mosaic \mō-zā´ik\ *n.* The first popular graphical
World Wide Web browser. Released on the Internet in early 1993 by the National Center for Supercomputing Applications (NCSA) at the University
of Illinois at Urbana-Champaign, Mosaic is available as freeware and shareware for Windows,
Macintosh, and X Window systems. Mosaic is distinguished from other early Web browsers by its
ease of use and its addition of inline images to
Web documents. *Also called* NCSA Mosaic.

MOSFET \mos´fet, M-O-S`F-E-T´\ *n.* Acronym for
metal-**o**xide **s**emiconductor **f**ield-**e**ffect **t**ransistor.

A common type of field-effect transistor in which a layer of silicon dioxide insulates the metal gate from the semiconductor current channel. MOSFETs have extremely high input impedance and therefore require almost no driving power. They are used in many audio applications, including high-gain amplifier circuits. Like all metal-oxide semiconductor (MOS) devices, MOSFETs are easily damaged by static electricity. See the illustration. *See also* FET, MOS.

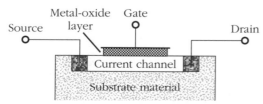

MOSFET.   *A schematic cross section of a MOSFET transistor.*

most significant bit \mōst` sig-nif´ə-kənt bit´\ *n.* In a sequence of one or more bytes, the highest-order bit of a binary number, not including the sign bit. *Acronym:* MSB (M`S-B´). *See also* high-order. *Compare* least significant bit.

most significant character \mōst` sig-nif´ə-kənt kâr´ək-tər\ *n.* The high-order, or leftmost, character in a string. *Acronym:* MSC (M`S-C´). *See also* high-order. *Compare* least significant character.

most significant digit \mōst` sig-nif´ə-kənt dij´-ət\ *n.* In a sequence of one or more digits, the highest-order digit, which is the leftmost digit. In *456.78*, *4* is the most significant digit. *Acronym:* MSD (M`S-D´). *Compare* least significant digit.

MOTD \M`O-T-D´\ *n. See* message of the day.

motherboard \mədh´ər-bōrd`\ *n.* The main circuit board containing the primary components of a computer system. This board contains the processor, main memory, support circuitry, and bus controller and connector. Other boards, including expansion memory and input/output boards, may attach to the motherboard via the bus connector. See the illustration. *See also* expansion slot. *Compare* daughterboard.

Motion JPEG \mō`shən J´peg, J`P-E-G´\ *n.* A standard for storing motion video, proposed by the Joint Photographic Experts Group (JPEG), that uses JPEG image compression for each frame. *See*

Motherboard.

also JPEG (definition 1). *Compare* MPEG (definition 1).

mount \mount\ *vb.* To make a physical disk or tape accessible to a computer's file system. The term is most commonly used to describe accessing disks in Apple Macintosh and UNIX-based computers.

mouse \mous\ *n.* A common pointing device. The basic features of a mouse are a flat-bottomed casing designed to be gripped by one hand; one or more buttons on the top; a multidirectional detection device (usually a ball) on the bottom; and a cable connecting the mouse to the computer. By moving the mouse on a surface (such as a desktop), the user typically controls an on-screen cursor. A mouse is a relative pointing device because there are no defined limits to the mouse's movement and because its placement on a surface does not map directly to a specific screen location. To select items or choose commands on the screen, the user presses one of the mouse's buttons, producing a "mouse click." See the illustration on the next page. *See also* bus mouse, mechanical mouse, optical mouse, optomechanical mouse, relative pointing device, serial mouse. *Compare* trackball.

MouseKeys \mous´kēz\ *n.* A feature in Microsoft Windows that allows a user to use the numeric keyboard to move the mouse pointer. MouseKeys is primarily intended for people who may have physical limitations that make it difficult to move a conventional mouse. *See also* mouse.

mouse pad \mous´ pad\ *n.* A surface on which a mouse can be moved, typically a rectangular rubber pad covered with fabric, providing more

Mouse.   Two types of mouse: for the Apple Macintosh (left) and for IBM PCs and compatibles (right).

traction than a wooden or glass desktop or table-top. *See also* mouse.

mouse pointer \mous´ poin`tər\ *n.* An on-screen element whose location changes as the user moves the mouse. Depending on the location of the mouse pointer and the operation of the program with which it is working, the area of the screen where the mouse pointer appears serves as the target for an action when the user presses one of the mouse buttons. *See also* block cursor, cursor (definition 3).

mouse port \mous´ pōrt\ *n.* **1.** In many PC-compatible computers, a dedicated connector where a mouse or other pointing device plugs into the computer. If a mouse port is not available, a serial port can be used to connect the mouse to the computer. *See also* connector, mouse, pointing device, serial port. **2.** In a Macintosh, the Apple Desktop Bus port. *See also* Apple Desktop Bus.

mouse scaling \mous´ skā`lēng\ *n. See* mouse sensitivity.

mouse sensitivity \mous` sen-sə-tiv´ə-tē\ *n.* The relationship of mouse movement to screen cursor movement. A more sensitive mouse signals to the computer more "mouse moves" per inch of physical mouse movement than does a less sensitive mouse. Increasing the sensitivity of the program or mouse driver can result in smaller cursor moves for a given mouse move, making it easier for the user to position the cursor precisely. High sensitivity is good for exacting work, such as CAD/CAM and graphic art; low sensitivity is good for tasks in which getting around the screen quickly is important and for applications such as Web browsers,

word processors, and spreadsheets, in which the cursor is used mostly to select buttons or text. *Also called* mouse scaling, mouse tracking.

mouse tracking \mous´ trak`ēng\ *n. See* mouse sensitivity.

mouse trails \mous´ trālz\ *n.* The creation of a shadowlike trail following the mouse pointer on screen in order to make it easier to see. Mouse trails are useful for laptops and notebooks, particularly ones with passive matrix displays or older models with monochrome screens. The relatively low resolution and contrast of these screens made it easy to lose sight of a small mouse pointer. See the illustration. *See also* mouse pointer, submarining.

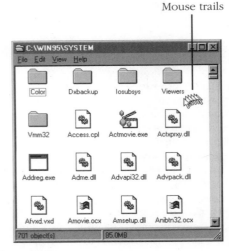

Mouse trails

Mouse trails.

.mov \dot`M-O-V´\ *n.* A filename extension for a movie file in Apple's QuickTime format. *See also* QuickTime.

move \m$\overline{oo}$v\ *n.* A command or instruction to transfer information from one location to another. Depending on the operation involved, a move can affect data in a computer's memory or it can affect text or a graphical image in a data file. In programming, for example, a move instruction might transfer a single value from one memory location to another. In applications, on the other hand, a move command might relocate a paragraph of text or all or part of a graphic from one place in a document to another. Unlike a copy procedure, which duplicates information, a move indicates that information either is or can be deleted from its original location. *Compare* copy.

.movie \dot`mōō´vē\ *n. See* .mov.

Moving Pictures Experts Group \mōōv´ing pik`-churz eks´pərts grōōp`\ *n. See* MPEG (definition 1).

Mozilla \mō`zil´ə\ *n.* A nickname for the Netscape Navigator Web browser, coined by the Netscape Corporation. *See also* Mosaic, Netscape Navigator.

MPC \M`P-C´\ *n. See* Multimedia PC.

.mpeg \dot`M´peg, dot`M-P-E-G´\ *n.* The file extension that identifies graphic image files in the MPEG format specified by the Moving Pictures Experts Group. *See also* MPEG.

MPEG \M´peg, M`P-E-G´\ *n.* **1.** Acronym for **M**oving **P**ictures **E**xperts **G**roup. A set of standards for audio and video compression established by the Joint ISO/IEC Technical Committee on Information Technology. The MPEG standard has different types that have been designed to work in different situations. *Compare* Motion JPEG. **2.** A video/audio file in the MPEG format. Such files generally have the extension .mpg. *See also* JPEG. *Compare* Motion JPEG.

MPEG-1 \M`peg-wən´, M`P-E-G-\ *n.* The original MPEG standard for storing and retrieving video and audio information, designed for CD-ROM technology. MPEG-1 defines a medium bandwidth of up to 1.5 Mbps, two audio channels, and non-interlaced video. *See also* MPEG (definition 1). *Compare* MPEG-2, MPEG-3, MPEG-4.

MPEG-2 \M`peg-tōō´, M`P-E-G-\ *n.* An extension of the MPEG-1 standard designed for broadcast television, including HDTV. MPEG-2 defines a higher bandwidth of up to 40 Mbps, five audio channels, a wider range of frame sizes, and inter-laced video. *See also* HDTV, MPEG (definition 1). *Compare* MPEG-1, MPEG-3, MPEG-4.

MPEG-3 \M`peg-thrē´, M`P-E-G-\ *n.* Initially an MPEG standard designed for HDTV (high-definition television), but it was found that MPEG-2 could be used instead. Therefore, this standard no longer exists. *See also* HDTV, MPEG (definition 1). *Compare* MPEG-1, MPEG-2, MPEG-4.

MPEG-4 \M`peg-for´, M`P-E-G-\ *n.* A standard currently under development designed for video-phones and multimedia applications. MPEG-4 provides a lower bandwidth of up to 64 Kbps. *See*

also MPEG (definition 1). *Compare* MPEG-1, MPEG-2, MPEG-3.

.mpg \dot-M`P-G-´\ *n.* A file extension that identifies encoded data streams that contain compressed audio and video information, using the format specified by the Moving Pictures Experts Group (MPEG). *See also* MPEG (definition 1).

MP/M \M`P-M´\ *n.* Acronym for **M**ulti-tasking **P**rogram for **M**icrocomputers. A multitasking, multiuser version of the CP/M operating system. *See also* CP/M.

MPOA \M`P-O-A´\ *n.* Acronym for **M**ulti-**P**rotocol **O**ver **A**TM. A specification established by the ATM Forum (an industry group of Asynchronous Transfer Mode users and vendors) to integrate ATM into existing Ethernet, token ring, and TCP/IP networks. *See also* ATM (definition 1).

MPP \M`P-P´\ *n. See* massively parallel processing, massively parallel processor.

MPPP \M`P-P-P´\ *n. See* Multilink Point-to-Point Protocol.

MPR II \M`P-R tōō´\ *n.* A standard for limiting magnetic and electric field emissions from video monitors, including VLF radiation. MPR II is a voluntary standard developed by the Swedish Board for Measurement and Testing in 1987 and updated in 1990. *See also* VLF radiation.

mput \M`pōot\ *n.* In many FTP clients, the command that instructs the local client to transmit multiple files to the remote server.

.mq \dot`M-Q´\ *n.* On the Internet, the major geographic domain specifying that an address is located in Martinique.

.mr \dot`M-R´\ *n.* On the Internet, the major geographic domain specifying that an address is located in Mauritania.

MR \M-R´\ *n.* Acronym for **m**odem **r**eady. A light on the front panel of a modem indicating that the modem is ready.

.ms \dot`M-S´\ *n.* On the Internet, the major geographic domain specifying that an address is located in Montserrat.

ms \mil´ə-sek-`ənd\ *n. See* millisecond.

MSB \M`S-B´\ *n. See* most significant bit.

MSC \M`S-C´\ *n. See* most significant character.

MSD \M`S-D´\ *n. See* most significant digit.

MS-DOS \M`S-dos´, M`S-D-O-S´\ *n.* Short for **M**icro**s**oft **D**isk **O**perating **S**ystem. A single-tasking, single-user operating system with a command-line interface, released in 1981, for IBM PCs and compatibles. MS-DOS, like other operating systems, oversees operations such as disk input and output, video support, keyboard control, and many internal functions related to program execution and file maintenance.

MS-DOS mode \M`S dos´ mōd, D-O-S´\ *n.* A shell in which the MS-DOS environment is emulated in 32-bit systems such as Windows 95. *See also* MS-DOS, shell[1].

MS-DOS shell \M`S dos´ shel, D-O-S´\ *n.* A shell environment based on a command line prompt that allows a user to interact with MS-DOS or an MS-DOS-emulating operating system.

MSDOS.SYS \M`S-dos`dot-sis´, M`S-D-O-S´dot-S-Y-S´\ *n.* One of two hidden system files installed on an MS-DOS startup disk. MSDOS.SYS, called IBMDOS.SYS in IBM releases of MS-DOS, contains the software that makes up the heart (kernel) of the operating system. *See also* IO.SYS.

msec \mil´ə-sek`ənd\ *n. See* millisecond.

MSI \M`S-I´\ *n. See* medium-scale integration.

MSN \M`S-N´\ *n. See* The Microsoft Network.

MSP \M`S-P´\ *n. See* Message Security Protocol.

.ms.us \dot-M-S`dot-U-S´\ *n.* On the Internet, the major geographic domain specifying that an address is located in Mississippi, United States.

MS-Windows \M`S-win´dōz\ *n. See* Windows.

.mt \dot`M-T´\ *n.* On the Internet, the major geographic domain specifying that an address is located in Malta.

MTBF \M`T-B-F´\ *n.* Acronym for **m**ean **t**ime **b**etween **f**ailures. The average time interval, usually expressed in thousands or tens of thousands of hours (sometimes called *power-on hours* or *POH*), that will elapse before a hardware component fails and requires service.

MTTR \M`T-T-R´\ *n.* Acronym for **m**ean **t**ime **t**o **r**epair. The average time interval, usually expressed in hours, that it takes to repair a failed component.

.mu \dot`M-U´\ *n.* On the Internet, the major geographic domain specifying that an address is located in Mauritius.

MUD, Object-Oriented \mud´ ob´jekt ōr`ē-entəd, M`U-D´\ *n. See* MOO.

MUD \mud, M`U-D´\ *n.* Acronym for **m**ulti**u**ser **d**ungeon. A virtual environment on the Internet in which multiple users simultaneously participate in a role-playing game and interact with each other in real time. *Also called* multiuser simulation environment.

Multibus \mul´tī-bus`, mul´tē-bus`\ *n.* A computer expansion bus designed by Intel Corporation that is used extensively by designers of high-performance workstations. A high-bandwidth bus (capable of extremely fast data transmission), Multibus also allows multiple bus masters. *See also* bus.

multicast backbone \mul´tē-kast bak`bōn, mul´tī-kast\ *n. See* MBONE.

multicasting \mul´tē-kas`tēng, mul´tī-kas`tēng\ *n.* The process of sending a message simultaneously to more than one destination on a network.

Multi-Color Graphics Array \mul´tī-kə-lər graf´iks ər-ā`, mul´tē-kə-lər\ *n. See* MCGA.

multi-element \mul´tē-el´ə-mənt, mul´tī-el´ə-mənt\ *adj.* Consisting of multiple data elements that all have the same format for storing the same kind of information. The data elements may be simple variables, as in an array of integer variables, or they may be more complicated data structures, as in an array of employee records each of which contains fields for an employee's name, Social Security number, pay rate, and so on.

multifile sorting \mul´tī-fīl sōr´tēng, mul´tē-fīl\ *n.* The process of sorting a body of data that resides in more than one file.

MultiFinder \mul´tī-fīn`dər, mul´tē-fīn`dər\ *n.* A version of the Apple Macintosh Finder that provides support for multitasking. The primary use of MultiFinder is to allow multiple applications to be simultaneously resident in memory. A single mouse click switches between applications, and information from one application can be copied to another. If the active application allows true multitasking, background tasks can be processed. *See also* Finder.

multifunction board \mul´tī-funk-shən bōrd´, mul´tē-funk-shən\ *n.* A computer add-in board that provides more than one function. Multifunction boards for personal computers frequently offer additional memory, serial/parallel ports, and a clock/calendar.

multilayer \mul´tī-lâr, mul´tē-lâr, mul´tī-lā`ər, mul´tē-lā`ər\ *adj.* **1.** In board design, of or pertaining to a printed circuit board consisting of two or more layers of board material. Each separate layer has its own metallic tracings to provide electrical connections between various electronic components and to provide connections to the other layers. The layers are laminated together to produce a single circuit board to which the components, such as integrated circuits, resistors, and capacitors, are attached. Multilayer design allows many more discrete paths between components than single-layer boards do. **2.** In computer-aided design (CAD), of or pertaining to drawings, such as electronic circuits, that are built up using multiple layers, each with a different level of detail or a different object, so that distinct parts of the drawing can be easily manipulated, overlaid, or peeled off.

Multilink Point-to-Point Protocol \mul`tē-lēnk point`tə-point` prō´tə-kol, mul`tī-lēnk\ *n.* An Internet protocol that allows computers to establish multiple physical links to combine their bandwidths. This technology creates a virtual link with more capacity than a single physical link. *Acronym:* MPPP (M`P-P-P´). *See also* PPP.

multimedia \mul`tī-mē´dē-ə, mul`tē-mē-mē´dē-ə\ *n.* The combination of sound, graphics, animation, and video. In the world of computers, multimedia is a subset of hypermedia, which combines the aforementioned elements with hypertext. *See also* hypermedia, hypertext.

Multimedia Extensions \mul`tē-mē´dē-ə eks-ten`shənz, mul`tī-mē´dē-ə\ *n. See* MMX.

Multimedia PC \mul`tē-mē´dē-ə P-C´, mul`tī-mē´dē-ə\ *n.* Software and hardware standards set forth by the Multimedia PC Marketing Council, which sets minimum standards for a PC's sound, video, and CD-ROM playing capabilities. *Acronym:* MPC (M`P-C´).

Multimedia Personal Computer \mul`tē-mē´dē-ə pər`sə-nəl kəm-pyōō´tər, mul`tī-mē´dē-ə\ *n. See* Multimedia PC.

multinode computer \mul`tē-nōd kəm-pyōō´tər, mul`tī-nōd\ *n.* A computer that uses multiple processors to share in the computation of a complex task. *See also* central processing unit, parallel processing.

multipart forms \mul`tī-pärt fōrmz´, mul`tē-pärt\ *n.* Computer printer paper arranged in sets with carbon paper between the sheets (or with a chemical coating that emulates carbon on the back of each sheet except the last) to produce copies of output from impact printers. Multipart forms are designated by the number of copies in a set, such as two-part, three-part, and so on.

multipass sort \mul`tī-pas sōrt´, mul`tē-pas\ *n.* A sorting operation that, usually because of the sorting algorithm being used, requires two or more passes through the data before completion. *See also* bubble sort, insertion sort, Shell sort, sort algorithm.

multiple-document interface \mul`tə-pl-do`kyə-mənt in´tər-fās\ *n. See* MDI.

multiple inheritance \mul`tə-pl in-hâr´ə-təns\ *n.* A feature of some object-oriented programming languages that allows a new class to be derived from several existing classes. Multiple inheritance both extends and combines existing types. *Acronym:* MI (M-I´). *See also* class, inherit, type.

multiple instruction, multiple data streams \mul`tə-pl in-struk`shən mul`tə-pl dā´tə strēmz, dat´ə\ *n. See* MIMD.

multiple-pass printing \mul`tə-pl-pas prin´tēng\ *n.* A form of dot-matrix printing in which the print head makes more than one pass across the page for each printed line, printing each line a second time exactly on top of the first pass. Multiple-pass printing can be used with dot-matrix printers to darken the print and smooth out errors in alignment. On better printers, a second pass might occur after the paper is moved up slightly, so that the dots in the characters overlap to create a crisper, darker image.

multiple recipients \mul`tə-pl rə-sip´ē-ənts\ *n.* **1.** The capability of sending e-mail to more than one user at a time by listing more than one e-mail address on a line. Delimiters such as commas or semicolons are used to separate the e-mail addresses. *See also* e-mail[1] (definition 1), mailing list. **2.** The subscribers on a mailing list. A message sent to the list is addressed to the "multiple recipients of" the list.

multiple regression \mul`tə-pl ri-gresh´ən\ *n.* A statistical technique that seeks to describe the behavior of a so-called "dependent" variable in terms of the observed behavior of numerous other, "independent" variables thought to affect it.

For each independent variable, a regression analysis can determine the correlation coefficient of the independent variable—that is, the degree to which variations in the independent variable cause changes in the dependent variable. *See also* dependent variable.

multiple-user system \mul`tə-pl-yo͞o`zər si´stəm\ *n. See* multiuser system.

multiplexer \mul´tə-pleks`ər\ *n.* **1.** A hardware circuit for selecting a single output from multiple inputs. **2.** A device for funneling several different streams of data over a common communications line. Multiplexers are used either to attach many communications lines to a smaller number of communications ports or to attach a large number of communications ports to a smaller number of communications lines. *Acronym:* MUX (M`U-X´, muks).

multiplexer channel \mul`tə-pleks`ər chan`əl\ *n.* One of the inputs to a multiplexer. *See also* multiplexer (definition 1).

multiplexing \mul´tə-pleks`ēng\ *n.* A technique used in communications and input/output operations for transmitting a number of separate signals simultaneously over a single channel or line. To maintain the integrity of each signal on the channel, multiplexing can separate the signals by time, space, or frequency. The device used to combine the signals is a *multiplexer. See also* FDM, space-division multiplexing, time-division multiplexing.

multiplicand \mul`tə-pli-kand`\ *n.* In arithmetic, the number that is multiplied by another number (the multiplier). In mathematics, the multiplicand and the multiplier are interchangeable, depending on how the problem is stated, because the result is the same if the two are reversed—for example, 2×3 and 3×2. In arithmetic performed by computers, however, the multiplicand is different from the multiplier because computer multiplication is usually performed as addition. Therefore, 2×3 means "add 2 three times," whereas 3×2 means "add 3 two times." *See also* factor. *Compare* multiplier (definition 1).

multiplier \mul´tə-pli͞¯`ər\ *n.* **1.** In arithmetic, the number that indicates how many times another number (the multiplicand) is multiplied. *See also* factor. *Compare* multiplicand. **2.** In computing, an

electronic device independent of the central processing unit (CPU) that performs multiplication by adding the multiplicand according to the value of the digits in the multiplier.

multipoint configuration \mul`tī-point kən-fi-gyər-ā´shən, mul`tē-point\ *n.* A communications link in which multiple stations are connected sequentially to the same communications line. Typically, the communications line is controlled by a primary station, such as a computer, and the stations attached to the line are secondary. See the illustration.

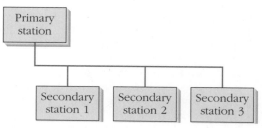

Multipoint configuration.

multiprocessing \mul`tī-pros´es-ēng, mul`tē-pros´es-ēng\ *n.* A mode of operation in which two or more connected and roughly equal processing units each carry out one or more processes (programs or sets of instructions) in tandem. In multiprocessing, each processing unit works on a different set of instructions or on different parts of the same process. The objective is increased speed or computing power, the same as in parallel processing and in the use of special units called *coprocessors. Compare* coprocessor, parallel processing.

Multi-Protocol Over ATM \mul`tē-prō`tə-kol ōvər A`T-M´, mul`tī-prō`tə-kol\ *n. See* MPOA.

Multipurpose Internet Mail Extensions \mul`tē-pur-pəs in`tər-net māl´ eks-ten`shənz, mul`tī-pur´pəs\ *n. See* MIME.

multiscan monitor \mul`tē-skan mon´ə-tər, mul`tī-skan\ *n.* A computer monitor capable of operating at different scanning frequencies to accommodate different screen resolutions.

multisync monitor \mul`tī-sēnk mon´ə-ter, mul`tē-sēnk\ *n.* A monitor capable of responding to a wide range of horizontal and vertical synchronization rates. Such a monitor can be used with a variety of different video adapters because it can automatically adjust itself to the synchronization rates of the video signal.

multisystem network \mul`tī-si-stəm net´wərk, mul`tē-si-stəm\ *n.* A communications network in which two or more host computers can be accessed by network users.

multitasking \mul´tī-task`ēng, mul´tē-task`ēng\ *n.* A mode of operation offered by an operating system in which a computer works on more than one task at a time. *See also* background[1], context switching, cooperative multitasking, foreground[1], time slice.

multithreaded application \mul`tē-thred-əd a-plə-kā´shən, mul`tī-thred-əd\ *n.* A program capable of running more than one program thread simultaneously. *See also* multithreading (definition 1), thread (definition 1).

multithreading \mul´tī-thred`ēng, mul´tē-thred`-ēng\ *n.* **1.** The running of several processes in rapid sequence (multitasking) within a single program. *See also* thread (definition 1). **2.** In data manipulation, a technique in which nodes in a tree data structure contain pointers to higher nodes to make traversal of the structure more efficient. *See also* thread (definition 2).

multiuser \mul´tē-yo͞o`zər, mul´tī-yo͞o`zər\ *n. See* multiuser system.

multiuser dungeon \mul´tē-yo͞o`zər dun`jən, mul`tē-yo͞o`zər\ *n. See* MUD.

multiuser simulation environment \mul`tē-yo͞o-zər sim-yə-lā´shən en-vīr`ən-mənt, mul`tē-yo͞o`zər, en-vī´ərn-mənt\ *n. See* MUD.

multiuser system \mul`tī-yo͞o´zər si`stəm, mul`tē-yo͞o´zər\ *n.* Any computer system that can be used by more than one person. Although a microcomputer shared by several people can be considered a multiuser system, the term is generally reserved for machines that can be accessed simultaneously by several people through communications facilities or via network terminals. *Compare* single-user computer.

multum in parvo mapping \mul`tum in pär`vō map`ēng\ *n. See* MIP mapping.

MUMPS \mumps, M`U-M-P-S´\ *n.* Acronym for **M**ass(achusetts) **U**tility **M**ulti**P**rogramming **S**ystem. An advanced, high-level programming language

and integrated database developed in 1966 at Massachusetts General Hospital and used widely by health care businesses. A unique feature of MUMPS is its ability to store both data and program fragments in its database.

MUSE \myo͞oz, M`U-S-E´\ *n.* Short for **m**ulti**us**er **s**imulation **e**nvironment. *See* MUD.

Musical Instrument Digital Interface \myo͞o`zi-kəl in`stru-mənt dij`i-təl in´tər-fās\ *n. See* MIDI.

mutual exclusion \myo͞o`cho͞o-əl eks-klo͞o´zhən\ *n.* A programming technique that ensures that only one program or routine at a time can access some resource, such as a memory location, an I/O port, or a file, often through the use of semaphores, which are flags used in programs to coordinate the activities of more than one program or routine. *See also* semaphore.

MUX \M`U-X´, muks\ *n. See* multiplexer (definition 2).

.mv \dot`M-V´\ *n.* On the Internet, the major geographic domain specifying that an address is located in the Maldive Islands.

.mw \dot`M-W´\ *n.* On the Internet, the major geographic domain specifying that an address is located in Malawi.

.mx \dot`M-X´\ *n.* On the Internet, the major geographic domain specifying that an address is located in Mexico.

.my \dot`M-Y´\ *n.* On the Internet, the major geographic domain specifying that an address is located in Malaysia.

My Briefcase \mī` brēf`kās\ *n.* A Windows 95 utility, helpful for workers away from the office, that manages the updating of modified files once the remote user's computer is connected back on the office network.

Mylar \mī`lär\ *n.* A polyester film product created by DuPont, often used as the base for magnetically coated storage media (disks and tape) and for carbon ribbons used with impact printers.

Mylar ribbon \mī`lär rib´ən\ *n. See* carbon ribbon.

MYOB \M`Y-O-B´\ Acronym for **M**ind **y**our **o**wn **b**usiness. An expression used in e-mail and newsgroups.

my two cents \mī` to͞o sents´\ *n.* An expression used informally in newsgroup articles and, less frequently, e-mail messages or mailing lists, to indicate that the message is the writer's contribution to an ongoing discussion. *Also called* $0.02. *See also* mailing list, newsgroup.

.mz \dot`M-Z´\ *n*. On the Internet, the major geographic domain specifying that an address is located in Mozambique.

n \N\ *prefix See* nano-.

.na \dot`N-A´\ *n.* On the Internet, the major geographic domain specifying that an address is located in Namibia.

NAK \nak, N`A-K´\ *n.* Acronym for **n**egative **ac**knowledgment. A control code, ASCII character 21 (hexadecimal 15), transmitted to a sending station or computer by the receiving unit as a signal that transmitted information has arrived incorrectly. *Compare* ACK.

Name Binding Protocol \nām` bīn`dēng prō´tə-kol\ *n. See* NBP.

named anchor \nāmd` an`kər\ *n.* In HTML, a tag within a document that can act as a destination for a hyperlink. Named anchors are useful because they allow a link to a specific location within a document. *Also called* named target. *See also* anchor (definition 2), HTML, hyperlink.

named target \nāmd` tär´gət\ *n. See* named anchor.

name server \nām´ sər`vər\ *n. See* CSO name server, DNS server.

name-value pair \nām`val´yoo pâr\ *n.* **1.** In the Perl programming language, a data set in which the data is associated with a name. *See also* Perl. **2.** In CGI programming, one of the data items collected from an HTML form by the browser and passed through the server to a CGI script for processing. *See also* CGI, CGI script, HTML.

NAMPS \namps, N`A-M-P-S´\ *n.* Acronym for **N**arrow-band **A**nalog **M**obile **P**hone **S**ervice. A standard proposed by Motorola Corporation that combines the current AMPS cellular telephone standard with digital signaling information, resulting in higher performance and increased capabilities. *See also* AMPS.

nano- \nan´ō\ *prefix* Abbreviated n. Metric prefix meaning 10^{-9} (one billionth).

nanosecond \nan´ō-sek`ənd\ *n.* One billionth of a second. A nanosecond is a time measure used to represent computing speed, particularly the speed at which electrical signals travel through circuits within the computer. *Acronym:* ns (N-S´).

NAP \N`A-P´\ *n. See* National Attachment Point.

narrowband \när´ō-band`\ *n.* A bandwidth set aside by the FCC for mobile or portable radio services, such as advanced two-way paging systems, including transmission rates between 50 bps and 64 Kbps. Narrowband formerly referred to the bandwidth from 50 to 150 bps. *See also* bandwidth, FCC. *Compare* broadband.

Narrow SCSI \när´ō skuz´ē, S`C-U-S-I´\ *n.* A SCSI or SCSI-2 interface that can transfer data only 8 bits at a time. *See also* SCSI, SCSI-2. *Compare* Fast/Wide SCSI, Wide SCSI.

NAT \N`A-T´\ *n.* Acronym for **n**etwork **a**ddress **t**ranslation. The process of converting between IP addresses used within an intranet or other private network (called a *stub domain*) and Internet IP addresses. This approach makes it possible to use a large number of addresses within the stub domain without depleting the limited number of available numeric Internet IP addresses. *See also* intranet, IP address.

National Attachment Point \nash`ə-nəl ə-tach´-mənt point`\ *n.* One of the four exchange points for Internet traffic sponsored by the National Science Foundation. Internet service providers connect with one of the National Attachment Points in order to exchange data with other providers. The four National Attachment Points are located in the San Francisco Bay area (operated by Pacific Bell), Chicago (operated by Ameritech), New York (operated by Sprint), and Washington, D.C. (operated by MFS). *Acronym:* NAP (N`A-P´).

National Center for Supercomputing Applications \nash`ən-əl sen`tər for soo`pər-kəm-pyoo´tēng a`plə-kā´shənz\ *n. See* NCSA (definition 1).

National Information Infrastructure \nash`ə-nəl in-fər-mā`shən in`frə-struk`chur\ *n.* A future high-bandwidth wide area network proposed by the U.S. government to carry data, fax, video, and voice transmissions to users throughout the United States. The network is to be developed mostly by private carriers; the government anticipates that the principal motive will be to deliver movies to homes on demand. Many of the proposed services are or will soon become available on the Internet itself. *Acronym:* NII (N`I-I´). *See also* Information Superhighway. *Compare* Internet.

National Science Foundation \nash`ə-nəl sī´əns foun-dā`shən\ *n.* A U.S. government agency intended to promote scientific research by funding both research projects and projects that facilitate scientific communication, such as NSFnet, the former backbone of the Internet. *See also* backbone (definition 1), NSFnet.

National Television System Committee \nash`-ə-nəl tel´ə-vizh`ən si`stəm kə-mit`ē\ *n.* *See* NTSC.

native \nā´tiv\ *adj.* Of, pertaining to, or characteristic of something that is in its original form. For example, many applications are able to work with files in a number of formats; the format the application uses internally is its native file format. Files in other formats must be converted to the application's native format before they can be processed by the application.

native application \nā`tiv a`plə-kā´shən\ *n.* A program that is designed specifically for a particular type of microprocessor, that is, a program that is binary compatible with a processor. A native application generally will run much faster than a non-native application, which must be run with the help of an emulator program. *See also* binary compatibility, emulator.

native code \nā`tiv kōd´\ *n.* Code specific to a particular machine or processor.

native compiler \nā`tiv kəm-pī´lər\ *n.* A compiler that produces machine code for the computer on which it is running, as opposed to a cross-compiler, which produces code for another type of computer. Most compilers are native compilers. *See also* compiler (definition 2), cross-compiler.

native file format \nā`tiv fīl´ fōr-mat\ *n.* The format an application uses internally to process data. The application must convert files in other formats

to the native format before it can work with them. For example, a word processor might recognize text files in ASCII text format, but it will convert them to its own native format before it displays them.

native language \nā´tiv lang´wəj\ *n.* *See* host language.

natural language \nach´ər-əl lang´wəj\ *n.* A language spoken or written by humans, as opposed to a programming language or a machine language. Understanding natural language and approximating it in a computer environment is one goal of research in artificial intelligence.

natural-language processing \nach`ər-əl-lang`-wəj pros´əs-ēng\ *n.* A field of computer science and linguistics that studies computer systems that can recognize and react to human language, either spoken or written. *See also* artificial intelligence. *Compare* speech recognition.

natural language query \na`chur-əl lang´wəj kwēr´ē, kwâr´ē\ *n.* A query to a database system that is composed in a subset of a natural language, such as English or Japanese. The query must conform to some restrictive syntax rules so that the system can parse it. *See also* parse, syntax.

natural-language recognition \nach`ər-əl-lang`-wəj rek-əg-nish´ən\ *n.* *See* speech recognition.

natural language support \nach´ur-əl lang´wəj su-pōrt`\ *n.* A voice recognition system that allows the user to use verbal commands in his or her own language to direct a computer's actions. *Acronym:* NLS (N`L-S´).

natural number \nach`ər-əl num´bər\ *n.* An integer, or whole number, that is equal to or greater than zero. *See also* integer (definition 1).

navigation bar \nav`ə-gā´shən bär`\ *n.* On a Web page, a grouping of hyperlinks for getting around in that particular Web site. *See also* hyperlink.

navigation keys \nav-ə-gā´shən kēz`\ *n.* The keys on a keyboard controlling cursor movement, including the four arrow keys and the Backspace, End, Home, Page Down, and Page Up keys. *See also* arrow key, Backspace key, End key, Home key, Page Down key, Page Up key.

Navigator \nav´ə-gā`tər\ *n.* *See* Netscape Navigator.

.navy.mil \dot-nā`vē-dot-mil´, dot-nā`vē-dot-M-I-L´\ *n.* On the Internet, the major geographic domain specifying that an address belongs to the U.S. Navy.

.nb.ca \dot-N-B`dot-C-A´\ *n.* On the Internet, the major geographic domain specifying that an address is located in New Brunswick, Canada.

NBP \N`B-P´\ *n.* Acronym for **N**ame **B**inding **P**rotocol. A protocol used on AppleTalk local area networks to translate between node names (known to users) and numeric AppleTalk addresses. NBP operates at the transport level (level 4 of the ISO/OSI model). *See also* AppleTalk, communications protocol, ISO/OSI model.

.nc \dot`N-C´\ *n.* On the Internet, the major geographic domain specifying that an address is located in New Caledonia.

NC \N-C´\ *n. See* network computer.

N-channel MOS \en`chan-əl mos´, M-O-S´\ *n. See* NMOS.

NCR paper \N`C-R´ pā-pər\ *n.* Short for **n**o **c**arbon **r**equired **paper**. A special paper used for multipart forms. NCR paper is impregnated with a chemical that darkens it when pressure is applied. *See also* multipart forms.

NCSA \N`C-S-A´\ *n.* **1.** Acronym for **N**ational **C**enter for **S**upercomputing **A**pplications. A research center located at the University of Illinois at Urbana-Champaign. NCSA was founded in 1985 as a part of the National Science Foundation, specializing in scientific visualization tasks, but is best known as the home of NCSA Mosaic, the first graphical Web browser, and of NCSA Telnet. *See also* Mosaic, NCSA Telnet. **2.** Acronym for **N**ational **C**omputer **S**ecurity **A**ssociation. An education and information organization concerned with computer security issues. Founded in 1989 and based in Carlisle, Pennsylvania, NCSA supplies books on computer security and hosts an annual conference.

NCSA Mosaic \N`C-S-A` mō-zā´ik\ *n. See* Mosaic.

NCSA server \N`C-S-A´ sər-vər\ *n.* The HTTP server developed by the National Center for Supercomputing Applications of the University of Illinois. This server and the CERN server were the first HTTP servers developed for the World Wide Web and are available free through downloading. *See also* HTTP server (definition 1), NCSA (definition 1). *Compare* CERN server.

NCSA Telnet \N`C-S-A` tel´net\ *n.* A freeware telnet client program developed and distributed by the National Center for Supercomputing Applications. *See also* client (definition 2), NCSA (definition 1).

.nc.us \dot-N-C`dot-U-S´\ *n.* On the Internet, the major geographic domain specifying that an address is located in North Carolina, United States.

NDMP \N`D-M-P´\ *n.* Acronym for **N**etwork **D**ata **M**anagement **P**rotocol. An open protocol for network-based backups of file servers that allows platform-independent data storage. *See also* backup, communications protocol, file server.

NDR \N`D-R´\ *n. See* nondestructive readout.

NDRO \N`D-R-O´\ *n. See* nondestructive readout.

.ne \dot`N-E´\ *n.* On the Internet, the major geographic domain specifying that an address is located in Niger.

near-letter-quality \nēr`let-ər-kwä´lə-tē\ *adj.* A print mode on high-end dot-matrix printers that produces clearer, darker characters than normal (draft-quality) printing. Near-letter-quality printing, although it is sharper than plain dot-matrix printing, is not as legible as output from a fully-formed-character printer, such as a daisy-wheel printer. *Acronym:* NLQ (N`L-Q´). *See also* print quality. *Compare* draft quality, letter quality.

negation \ne-gā´shən\ *n.* The conversion of a two-state (binary) signal or bit pattern to its opposite state—for example, the conversion of 1001 to 0110.

negative acknowledgment \neg`ə-tiv ak-nol´əj-mənt\ *n. See* NAK.

negative entry \neg`ə-tiv en´trē\ *n.* The act of assigning a negative sign to a number that has been entered into a calculator, thereby transforming the number to a negative number.

nest \nest\ *vb.* To embed one construct inside another. For example, a database may contain a nested table (a table within a table), a program may contain a nested procedure (a procedure declared within a procedure), and a data structure may include a nested record (a record containing a field that is itself a record).

nested transaction \ne`stəd tranz-ak´shən\ *n.* In programming, an operation or sequence of operations taking place within a larger transaction. A nested transaction can be aborted without requiring abortion of the larger transaction. *Also called* subtransaction. *See also* nest.

.net \dot-net´, -N`E-T´\ *n.* In the Internet's Domain Name System, the top-level domain that identifies addresses of network providers. The designation .net appears at the end of the address. *See also* DNS (definition 1), domain (definition 3). *Compare* .com, .edu, .gov, .mil, .org.

net. \net´dot\ *prefix* A prefix used to describe people and institutions on the Internet. For example, a very well respected person might be described as a net.god.

Net \net\ *n.* **1.** Short for Inter**net**. **2.** Short for Use**net**.

net address \net´ a`dres, ə-dres`\ *n.* **1.** A World Wide Web address (URL). *See also* URL. **2.** An e-mail address. **3.** The DNS name or IP address of a machine. *See also* DNS (definition 1), IP address.

NetBEUI \net`B-E-U-I´\ *n.* Short for **NetB**IOS **E**nhanced **U**ser **I**nterface. An enhanced NetBIOS protocol for network operating systems, originated by IBM for the LAN Manager server and now used with many other networks. *See also* LAN Manager, NetBIOS.

NetBIOS \net`bī´ōs, net`B-I-O-S´\ *n.* An application programming interface (API) that can be used by application programs on a local area network consisting of IBM and compatible microcomputers running MS-DOS, OS/2, or some version of UNIX. Primarily of interest to programmers, NetBIOS provides application programs with a uniform set of commands for requesting the lower-level network services required to conduct sessions between nodes on a network and to transmit information back and forth. *See also* application programming interface.

NetBIOS Enhanced User Interface \net`bī´ōs en-hansd` yo͞o`zər in´tər-fās, net´B-I-O-S`\ *n. See* NetBEUI.

NetBSD \net`B-S-D´\ *n.* A free version of the BSD UNIX operating system developed as a result of a volunteer effort. NetBSD is highly interoperable, runs on many hardware platforms, and is nearly POSIX compliant. *See also* BSD UNIX, POSIX.

net.god \net`dot-god´\ *n.* A highly respected person within the Internet community.

nethead \net´hed\ *n.* **1.** A person who uses the Internet as if addicted to it. **2.** A Grateful Dead fan who participates in the rec.music.gdead newsgroup or some other forum dedicated to that band.

netiquette \net´ə-kit`, net´ə-kət\ *n.* Short for **net**work e**tiquette**. Principles of courtesy observed in sending electronic messages, such as e-mail and Usenet postings. The consequences of violating netiquette include being flamed and having one's name placed in the bozo filter of one's intended audience. Disapproved behavior includes gratuitous personal insults; posting of large amounts of irrelevant material; giving away the plot of a movie, television show, or novel without warning; posting offensive material without encrypting it; and excessive cross-posting of a message to multiple groups without regard to whether the group members are likely to find it interesting. *See also* bozo filter, flame[2].

netizen \net´i-zən\ *n.* A person who participates in online communication through the Internet and other networks, especially conference and chat services, such as Internet news or Fidonet. *Compare* lurker.

NetPC \net`P-C´\ *n.* A computer platform specification created by Microsoft and Intel in 1996 for systems that use Windows NT server based application programs, rather than applications located on the client computer.

net.personality \net`dot-pər-sə-nal´ə-tē\ *n.* A slang term for a person who has attained some degree of celebrity on the Internet.

net.police \net´dot-pə-lēs`\ *n.* Persons (usually self-appointed) who try to enforce their understanding of the "rules" that apply to conduct on the Internet. Their activities may be directed toward users who violate the rules of netiquette, spammers who send unsolicited advertising as e-mail or to newsgroups, or even people who post "politically incorrect" comments to newsgroups or mailing lists. *See also* netiquette, spam.

Netscape Navigator \net`skāp nav´ə-gā`tər\ *n.* The most widely used family of Web browser programs, made by Netscape Corporation. Versions of Netscape Navigator are available for the Windows 3.1, Windows 95, Windows NT, and Macintosh platforms, and for many varieties of UNIX. Netscape Navigator, which is based on NCSA's Mosaic Web browser, was one of the first commercially available Web browsers. *See also* Mosaic, Web browser.

Netscape Server Application Programming Interface \net-skāp sər-vər a-plə-kā`shən prō-gram-ēng in´tər-fās\ *n. See* NSAPI.

Netspeak \net´spēk\ *n.* The set of conventions for writing English in e-mail, IRCs, and newsgroups. Netspeak is characterized by acronyms (such as IMHO or ROFL) and clarifying devices such as emotags and emoticons. Use of Netspeak should be governed by netiquette. *See also* emotag, emoticon, IMHO, IRC, netiquette, ROFL.

Net surfing \net´ sur´fēng\ *n.* The practice of exploring the Internet without a specific goal in mind. The concept of Net surfing is similar to (and probably derived from) "channel surfing" in reference to watching television.

net-top box \net´top boks`\ *n.* A type of personal computer with a reduced number of components that is built primarily to provide a low-cost access terminal to the various services available on the Internet, such as e-mail, Web access, and telnet connectivity. These machines, which are under development, will not have locally addressable hard disks or installable programs, but will obtain any necessary materials for the user from somewhere on a network to which the net-top box is connected. *Compare* Java terminal, NetPC.

Net TV \net` ´T-V´\ *n. See* Internet television.

NetWare \net´wâr\ *n.* Novell's LAN operating system. NetWare runs on many different hardware platforms and network configurations.

network \net´wərk\ *n.* A group of computers and associated devices that are connected by communications facilities. A network can involve permanent connections, such as cables, or temporary connections made through telephone or other communication links. A network can be as small as a local area network consisting of a few computers, printers, and other devices, or it can consist of many small and large computers distributed over a vast geographic area.

network adapter \net´wərk ə-dap`tər\ *n.* An expansion card or other device used to connect a computer to a local area network.

network address translation \net`wərk a´dres tranz-lā`shən, ə-dres`\ *n. See* NAT.

network administrator \net`wərk əd-min´ə-strā-tər\ *n.* The person in charge of operations on a computer network. The duties of a network administrator can be broad and might include such tasks as installing new workstations and other devices, adding and removing individuals from the list of authorized users, archiving files, overseeing password protection and other security measures, monitoring usage of shared resources, and handling malfunctioning equipment. *See also* system administrator.

network architecture \net`wərk är´kə-tek-chər\ *n.* The underlying structure of a computer network, including hardware, functional layers, interfaces, and protocols, used to establish communication and ensure the reliable transfer of information. Network architectures are designed to provide both philosophical and physical standards for the complexities of establishing communications links and transferring information without conflict. Various network architectures exist, including the internationally accepted seven-layer ISO Open Systems Interconnection (OSI) model and IBM's Systems Network Architecture (SNA). *See also* ISO/OSI model, SNA.

network card \net´wərk kärd`\ *n. See* network adapter.

network computer \net´wərk kəm-pyōō`tər\ *n.* A computer having the hardware and software necessary for it to be connected to a network. *Acronym:* NC (N-C´).

network control program \net`wərk kən-trōl´ prō-gram\ *n.* In a communications network that includes a mainframe computer, a program that usually resides in a communications controller and takes over communications tasks such as routing, error control, line control, and polling (checking terminals for transmissions), leaving the main computer free for other functions. *See also* communications controller.

network database \net`wərk dā´tə-bās\ *n.* **1.** A database that runs in a network. **2.** A database containing the address of other users in the network. **3.** In information management, a type of database in which data records can be related to one another in more than one way. A network database is similar to a hierarchical database in the sense that it contains a progression from one record to another. It differs in being less rigidly structured: any single record can point to more than one other record and, conversely, can be pointed to by one or more records. In effect, a network database allows more than one path between any two records, whereas a hierarchical database allows only one, from parent (higher-level record) to child (lower-level record). *Compare* hierarchical database, relational database.

Network Data Management Protocol \net`wərk dā`tə man´əj-mənt prō`tə-kol, dat`ə\ *n. See* NDMP.

network device driver \net`wərk də-vīs´ drī`vər\ *n.* Software that coordinates communication between the network adapter card and the computer's hardware and other software, controlling the physical function of the network adapter card.

network directory \net`wərk dər-ek´tər-ē\ *n.* On a local area network, a directory on a disk that is located on a computer other than the one the user is operating. A network directory differs from a network drive in that the user has access to only that directory. Whether the rest of the disk is accessible to the user depends on whether he or she has been granted access rights by the network administrator. On the Apple Macintosh, a network directory is referred to as a shared folder. *Also called* networked directory, shared directory. *See also* network drive, shared folder.

network drive \net`wərk drīv´\ *n.* On a local area network, a disk drive whose disk is available to other computers on the network. Access to a network drive might not be allowed to all users of the network; many operating systems contain security provisions that enable a network administrator to grant or deny access to part or all of a network drive. *Also called* networked drive. *See also* network directory.

networked directory \net`wərkd dər-ek´tər-ē\ *n. See* network directory.

networked drive \net`wərkd drīv´\ *n. See* network drive.

Network File System \net`wərk fīl´ si`stəm\ *n.* A distributed file system developed by Sun Microsystems, Inc. that allows users of Windows NT and UNIX workstations to access remote files and directories on a network as if they were local. *Acronym:* NFS (N`F-S´).

network information center \net`wərk in-fər-mā´shən sen`tər\ *n. See* NIC (definition 2).

network interface card \net`wərk in`tər-fās kärd`\ *n. See* network adapter.

network latency \net`wərk lā`tən-sē\ *n.* The time it takes for information to be transferred between computers in a network.

network layer \net`wərk lâr, lā´ər\ *n.* The third of the seven layers in the ISO/OSI model for standardizing computer-to-computer communications. The network layer is one level above the data-link layer and ensures that information arrives at its intended destination. It is the middle of the three layers (data-link, network, and transport) concerned with the actual movement of information from one device to another. *See also* ISO/OSI model.

network meltdown \net´wərk melt´doun\ *n. See* broadcast storm.

network model \net´wərk mod`əl\ *n.* A database structure, or layout, similar to a hierarchical model, except that records can have multiple parent records as well as multiple child records. A database management system that supports a network model can be used to simulate a hierarchical model. *See also* CODASYL, network database (definition 3). *Compare* hierarchical model.

network modem \net`wərk mō´dəm\ *n.* A modem that is shared by users of a network, for calling an online service provider, an ISP, a service bureau, or other online source. *See also* ISP, modem, online information service, service bureau (definition 2).

network news \net`wərk nōōz´\ *n.* The newsgroups on the Internet, especially those in the Usenet hierarchy.

Network News Transfer Protocol \net`wərk nōōz´ trans`fər prō`tə-kol\ *n. See* NNTP.

network operating system \net`wərk op´ər-ā-tēng si`stem\ *n.* An operating system installed on a server in a local area network that coordinates the activities of providing services to the computers and other devices attached to the network. Unlike a single-user operating system, a network operating system must acknowledge and respond to requests from many workstations, managing such details as network access and communications, resource allocation and sharing, data protection, and error control.

network operation center \net`wərk op-ər-ā´-shən sen`tər\ *n.* The office in an enterprise that is responsible for maintaining network integrity and improving network efficiency while reducing system downtime. *Acronym:* NOC (N`O-C´).

network OS \net`wərk O-S´\ *n. See* network operating system.

network protocol \net`wərk prō´tə-kol\ *n.* A set of rules and parameters that define and enable communication through a network.

network server \net´wərk sər`vər\ *n. See* server.

network services \net`wərk sər`vi-səz\ *n.* **1.** In a corporate environment, the division that maintains the network and the computers. **2.** In a Windows environment, extensions to the operating system that allow it to perform network functions such as network printing and file sharing.

network software \net`wərk soft`wâr\ *n.* Software including a component that facilitates connection to or participation in a network.

network structure \net´wərk struk`chər\ *n.* The record organization used in a particular network model.

Network Terminator 1 \net`wərk tər`mə-nā-tər wən`\ *n.* An ISDN device that acts as interface between an ISDN telephone line and one or more terminal adapters or terminal devices such as an ISDN telephone. *Acronym:* NT-1 (N`T-wən´). *See also* ISDN, ISDN terminal adapter.

Network Time Protocol \net`wərk tīm´ prō´tə-kol\ *n.* An Internet protocol used to synchronize the clocks in computers connected to the Internet. *Acronym:* NTP (N`T-P´). *See also* communications protocol.

network topology \net´wərk to-pol`ə-jē\ *n. See* topology.

neural network \nər`əl net´wərk, nyər`əl\ *n.* A type of artificial-intelligence system modeled after the neurons (nerve cells) in a biological nervous system and intended to simulate the way a brain processes information, learns, and remembers. A neural network is designed as an interconnected system of processing elements, each with a limited number of inputs and an output. These processing elements are able to "learn" by receiving weighted inputs that, with adjustment, time, and repetition, can be made to produce appropriate outputs. Neural networks are used in areas such as pattern recognition, speech analysis, and speech synthesis. *See also* artificial intelligence, pattern recognition (definition 1).

.ne.us \dot-N-E`dot-U-S´\ *n.* On the Internet, the major geographic domain specifying that an address is located in Nebraska, United States.

newbie \nōō´bē\ *n.* **1.** An inexperienced user on the Internet. **2.** In a particularly derogatory sense, an inexperienced Usenet user who asks for information that is readily available in the FAQ. *See also* FAQ.

newline character \nōō´līn kâr`ək-tər, nyōō´līn\ *n.* A control character that causes the cursor on a display or the printing mechanism on a printer to move to the beginning of the next line. It is functionally equivalent to a combination of the carriage return (CR) and linefeed (LF) characters. *Acronym:* NL (N-L´). *See also* carriage return, linefeed.

news.announce.newusers \nōōz`dot-ə-nouns`-dot-nōō-yōō´zərz\ *n.* A newsgroup that contains general information for new users about using Internet newsgroups for new users.

news feed or **newsfeed** \nōōz´fēd\ *n.* Deliveries, exchanges, or distributions of newsgroup articles to and from news servers. News feeds are accomplished through cooperating news servers, which communicate via NNTP through network connections. *Also called* feed. *See also* news server, newsgroup, NNTP.

newsgroup \nōōz´grōōp\ *n.* A forum on the Internet for threaded discussions on a specified range of subjects. A newsgroup consists of articles and follow-up posts. An article with all of its follow-up posts—all of which are (supposed to be) related to the specific subject named in the original article's subject line—constitutes a thread. Each newsgroup has a name that consists of a series of words, separated by periods, indicating the newsgroup's subject in terms of increasingly narrow categories, such as rec.crafts.textiles.needlework. Some newsgroups can be read and posted to only on one site; others, such as those in the seven Usenet hierarchies or those in ClariNet, circulate throughout the Internet. *See also* article, bit. newsgroups, ClariNet, follow-up, Great Renaming, local newsgroups, mail reflector, threaded discussion, traditional newsgroup hierarchy, Usenet. *Compare* mailing list.

newsmaster \nōōz′ma`stər\ *n.* The person in charge of maintaining the Internet news server at a particular host. Sending e-mail to "newsmaster@domain.name" is the standard way to reach a given newsmaster.

news. newsgroups \nōōz`dot-nōōz′grōōps\ *n.* Usenet newsgroups that are part of the news. hierarchy and begin with "news." These newsgroups cover topics that deal with Usenet itself, such as Usenet policy and the creation of new Usenet newsgroups. *See also* newsgroup, traditional newsgroup hierarchy, Usenet. *Compare* comp. newsgroups, misc. newsgroups, rec. newsgroups, sci. newsgroups, soc. newsgroups, talk. newsgroups.

.newsrc \dot-N`E-W`S-R-C′\ *n.* The file extension that identifies a setup file for UNIX-based newsreaders. The setup file typically contains a current list of newsgroups that the user subscribes to and the articles in each newsgroup that the user has already read. *See also* newsreader, setup (definition 2).

newsreader \nōōz′rē`dər\ *n.* A Usenet client program that enables a user to subscribe to Usenet newsgroups, read articles, post follow-ups, reply by e-mail, and post articles. Many Web browsers also provide these functions. *See also* article, e-mail[1] (definition 1), follow-up, newsgroup, Usenet, Web browser.

news server \nōōz′ sər`vər\ *n.* A computer or program that exchanges Internet newsgroups with newsreader clients and other servers. *See also* newsgroup, newsreader.

Newton \nōō′tən\ *adj.* Pertaining to the Apple Newton MessagePad personal digital assistant (PDA). *See also* PDA.

Newton OS \nōō`tən O-S′\ *n.* The operating system that controls the Apple Newton MessagePad personal digital assistant (PDA). *See also* PDA.

NeXT \nekst\ *n.* A product of NeXT Computer, Inc. (later NeXT Software, Inc.), a computer manufacturer and software developer founded in 1985 by Steven Jobs. NeXT was purchased by Apple Computer in 1997.

.nf \dot`N-F′\ *n.* On the Internet, the major geographic domain specifying that an address is located on Norfolk Island.

.nf.ca \dot-N-F`dot-C-A′\ *n.* On the Internet, the major geographic domain specifying that an address is located in Newfoundland, Canada.

NFS \N`F-S′\ *n. See* Network File System.

.ng \dot`N-G′\ *n.* On the Internet, the major geographic domain specifying that an address is located in Nigeria.

.nh.us \dot-N-H`dot-U-S′\ *n.* On the Internet, the major geographic domain specifying that an address is located in New Hampshire, United States.

.ni \dot`N-I′\ *n.* On the Internet, the major geographic domain specifying that an address is located in Nicaragua.

nibble or **nybble** \nib′l\ *n.* Half a byte (4 bits). *Compare* quadbit.

NIC \N`I-C′\ *n.* **1.** Acronym for **n**etwork **i**nterface **c**ard. *See* network adapter. **2.** Acronym for **n**etwork **i**nformation **c**enter. An organization that provides information about a network and other support to users of the network. The principal NIC for the Internet is InterNIC. Intranets and other private networks may have their own NICs. *See also* InterNIC.

NiCad battery \nik`ad bat′ər-ē\ *n. See* nickel cadmium battery.

nickel cadmium battery \nik`əl kad`mē-um bat′ər-ē\ *n.* A rechargeable battery that uses an alkaline electrolyte. Nickel cadmium batteries typically have a longer operating life and storage life than similar lead-acid batteries. *Also called* NiCad battery. *Compare* lead ion battery, lithium ion battery, nickel metal hydride battery.

nickel metal hydride battery \nik`əl met`əl hī′drīd bat`ər-ē\ *n.* A rechargeable battery that offers longer life and superior performance compared with similar nickel cadmium or other alkaline batteries. *Also called* NiMH battery. *Compare* lead ion battery, lithium ion battery, nickel cadmium battery.

nickname \nik′nām\ *n.* A name used in the destination field of an e-mail editor in place of one or more complete network addresses. For example "Fred" might be a nickname for fred@history.washington.edu. If the nickname has been established within the program, a user need only type "Fred" instead of the entire address, or perhaps "history faculty" instead of all the individual faculty addresses. *See also* alias (definition 2).

NII \N`I-I´\ *n. See* National Information Infrastructure.

nil pointer \nil´ poin`tər\ *n. See* null pointer.

NiMH battery \N`I-M-H` bat´ər-ē\ *n. See* nickel metal hydride battery.

nine's complement \nīnz` kom`plə-mənt\ *n.* A number in the base-10 (decimal) system that is the complement of another number. It is derived by subtracting each digit of the number to be complemented from 1 less than the base. For example, the nine's complement of 64 is 35—the number derived by subtracting 6 from 9 and 4 from 9. *See also* complement.

NIS \N`I-S´\ *n.* Acronym for **N**etwork **I**nformation **S**ervice. *See* Yellow Pages (definition 1).

nixpub \niks´pub\ *n.* A list of ISPs, available in the newsgroups comp.bbs.misc and alt.bbs and at ftp://VFL.Paramax.COM:/pub/pubnetc/nixpub.long. *See also* ISP.

.nl \dot`N-L´\ *n.* On the Internet, the major geographic domain specifying that an address is located in the Netherlands.

NL \N-L´\ *n. See* newline character.

NLQ \N`L-Q´\ *n. See* near-letter-quality.

NLS \N`L-S´\ *n. See* natural language support.

NMI \N`M-I´\ *n. See* nonmaskable interrupt.

NMOS or **N-MOS** \N´mos, N`M-O-S´\ *n.* Acronym for **N**-channel **m**etal-**o**xide **s**emiconductor. A semiconductor technology in which the conduction channel in MOSFETs is formed by the movement of electrons rather than holes (electron "vacancies" created as electrons move from atom to atom). Because electrons move faster than holes, NMOS is faster than PMOS, although it is more difficult and more expensive to fabricate. *See also* MOS, MOSFET, N-type semiconductor. *Compare* CMOS, PMOS.

NNTP \N`N-T-P´\ *n.* Acronym for **N**etwork **N**ews **T**ransfer **P**rotocol. The Internet protocol that governs the transmission of newsgroups.

.no \dot`N-O´\ *n.* On the Internet, the major geographic domain specifying that an address is located in Norway.

NOC \N`O-C´\ *n. See* network operation center.

node \nōd\ *n.* **1.** A junction of some type. **2.** In local area networks, a device that is connected to the network and is capable of communicating with other network devices. **3.** In tree structures, a location on the tree that can have links to one or more nodes below it. Some authors make a distinction between node and element, with an element being a given data type and a node comprising one or more elements as well as any supporting data structures. *See also* element (definition 1), graph, pointer (definition 1), queue, stack, tree.

noise \noiz\ *n.* **1.** Any interference that affects the operation of a device. **2.** Unwanted electrical signals, produced either naturally or by the circuitry, that degrade the quality or performance of a communications channel. *See also* distortion.

nonbreaking space \non`brā-kēng spās´\ *n.* A character that replaces the standard space character in order to keep two words together on one line rather than allowing a line to break between them.

nonconductor \non`kən-duk´tər\ *n. See* insulator.

noncontiguous data structure \non`kən-ti`gyōō-əs dā´tə struk`chər, dat´ə\ *n.* In programming, a data structure whose elements are not stored contiguously in memory. Data structures such as graphs and trees, whose elements are connected by pointers, are noncontiguous data structures. *Compare* contiguous data structure.

nondestructive readout \non`də-struk`tiv rē´-dout\ *n.* A reading operation that does not destroy the data read, either because the storage technology is capable of retaining the data or because the reading operation is accompanied by a data refresh (update) function. *Acronym:* NDR (N`D-R´), NDRO (N`D-R-O´). *Compare* destructive read.

nonexecutable statement \non`eks-ə-kyōō`tə-bl stāt´mənt\ *n.* **1.** A program statement that cannot be executed because it lies outside the flow of execution through the program. For example, a statement immediately following a *return()* statement but before the end of the block in C is nonexecutable. **2.** A type definition, variable declaration, preprocessor command, comment, or other statement in a program that is not translated into executable machine code.

nonimpact printer \non`im-pakt prin´tər\ *n.* Any printer that makes marks on the paper without striking it mechanically. The most common types are ink-jet, thermal, and laser printers. *See also* ink-jet printer, laser printer, thermal printer. *Compare* impact printer.

noninterlaced \non`in´tər-lāsd\ *adj.* A display method on raster-scan monitors in which the electron beam scans each line of the screen once during each refresh cycle. *Compare* interlacing.

nonmaskable interrupt \non`mas-kə-bl in´tər-upt\ *n.* A hardware interrupt that bypasses and takes priority over interrupt requests generated by software and by the keyboard and other such devices. A nonmaskable interrupt cannot be overruled (masked) by another service request and is issued to the microprocessor only in disastrous circumstances, such as severe memory errors or impending power failures. *Acronym:* NMI (N`M-I´). *Compare* maskable interrupt.

nonprocedural language \non`prə-sē-jər-əl lang´-wəj\ *n.* A programming language that does not follow the procedural paradigm of executing statements, subroutine calls, and control structures sequentially but instead describes a set of facts and relationships and then is queried for specific results. *Compare* procedural language.

nonreturn to zero \non`rə-tərn tə zēr´ō\ *n.* **1.** In data transmission, a method of encoding data in which the signal representing binary digits alternates between positive and negative voltage when there is a change in digits from 1 to 0 or vice versa. In other words, the signal does not return to a zero, or neutral, level after transmission of each bit. Timing is used to distinguish one bit from the next. **2.** In the recording of data on a magnetic surface, a method in which one magnetic state represents a 1 and, usually, the opposite state represents a 0. *Acronym:* NRZ (N`R-Z´).

nontrivial \non`triv´ē-əl\ *adj.* Being either difficult or particularly meaningful. For example, a complicated programmed procedure to handle a difficult problem would represent a nontrivial solution.

nonuniform memory architecture \non`yōō´-nə-fôrm mem`ər-ē är´kə-tek-chur\ *n.* A system architecture designed for Sequent's Non-Uniform Access Memory, a type of distributed shared memory using a number of shared memory segments instead of a single centralized physical memory. *Acronym:* NUMA (nōō´mə, N`U-M-A´).

nonvolatile memory \non`vol´ə-təl mem´ər-ē\ *n.* A storage system that does not lose data when power is removed from it. Intended to refer to core memory, ROM, EPROM, flash memory, bubble memory, or battery-backed CMOS RAM, the term is occasionally used in reference to disk subsystems as well. *See also* bubble memory, CMOS RAM, core, EPROM, flash memory, ROM.

NO-OP \nō´op, N`O-O-P´\ *n. See* no-operation instruction.

no-operation instruction \nō´op-ər-ā´shən in-struk`shən\ *n.* A machine instruction that has no results other than to cause the processor to use up clock cycles. Such instructions are useful in certain situations, such as padding out timing loops or forcing subsequent instructions to align on certain memory boundaries. *Acronym:* NO-OP (nō´op, N`O-O-P´), NOP (nō´op, N`O-P´). *See also* machine instruction.

NOP \nō´op, N`O-P´\ *n. See* no-operation instruction.

normal distribution \nôr`məl dis`trə-byōō´shən\ *n.* In statistics, a type of function that describes the probabilities of the possible values of a random variable. The function, whose graph is the familiar bell-shaped curve, can be used to determine the probability that the value of the variable will fall within a particular interval of values.

normal form \nôr`məl fôrm´\ *n.* **1.** In a relational database, a set of guidelines for structuring information to avoid redundancy and inconsistency and to promote efficient use of resources. A table in first normal form adheres to the first guideline, one in second normal form adheres to the first two guidelines, and so forth. **2.** In programming, the metalanguage sometimes called the Backus normal form (Backus-Naur form), a language used for describing the syntax of other languages—specifically, ALGOL 60, for which it was invented. *See also* Backus-Naur form.

normal hyphen \nôr`məl hī´fən\ *n. See* hyphen.

normalize \nôr`mə-līz`\ *vb.* **1.** In programming, to adjust the fixed-point and exponent portions of a floating-point number to bring the fixed-point portions within a specific range. **2.** In database management, to apply a body of techniques to a relational database in order to minimize the inclusion of duplication information. Normalization greatly simplifies query and update management, including security and integrity considerations, although at the expense of creating a larger number of tables. *See also* normal form (definition 1).

NOS \N`O-S´\ *n. See* network operating system.

NOT \not\ *n.* An operator that performs Boolean or logical negation. *See also* Boolean operator, logical operator.

notation \nō`tā´shən\ *n.* In programming, the set of symbols and formats used to describe the elements of programming, mathematics, or a scientific field. A language's syntax is defined in part by notation. *See also* syntax.

notebook computer \nōt´bŏŏk kəm-pyōō`tər\ *n. See* portable computer.

Novell NetWare \nō-vel` net-wâr´\ *n.* A family of local area network operating system products produced by Novell, Inc. Designed to run on IBM PCs and Apple Macintoshes, Novell NetWare allows users to share files and system resources such as hard disks and printers. *See also* network operating system.

.np \dot`N-P´\ *n.* On the Internet, the major geographic domain specifying that an address is located in Nepal.

NPN transistor \N`P-N` tranz-i´stər\ *n.* A type of transistor in which a base of P-type material is sandwiched between an emitter and a collector of N-type material. The base, emitter, and collector are the three terminals through which current flows. In an NPN transistor, electrons represent the majority of the charge carriers, and they flow from the emitter to the collector. See the illustration. *See also* N-type semiconductor, P-type semiconductor. *Compare* PNP transistor.

.nr \dot`N-R´\ *n.* On the Internet, the major geographic domain specifying that an address is located in Nauru.

NRZ \N`R-Z´\ *n. See* nonreturn to zero.

ns \N-S´\ *n. See* nanosecond.

NSAPI \N`S-A-P-I´\ *n.* Acronym for **N**etscape **S**erver **A**pplication **P**rogramming **I**nterface. A specification for interfaces between the Netscape HTTP server and other application programs. NSAPI can be used to provide access to application programs from a Web browser through a Web server. *See also* HTTP server (definition 1), Web browser.

.ns.ca \dot-N-S`dot-C-A´\ *n.* On the Internet, the major geographic domain specifying that an address is located in Nova Scotia, Canada.

NSF \N`S-F´\ *n. See* National Science Foundation.

NSFnet \N`S-F´net\ *n.* A wide area network, developed by the National Science Foundation to replace ARPANET for civilian purposes, that served as a major backbone for the Internet until mid-1995. Backbone services in the United States for the Internet are now provided by commercial carriers. *See also* ARPANET, backbone (definition 1).

NT \N-T´\ *n. See* Windows NT.

NT-1 \N`T-wən´\ *n. See* Network Terminator 1.

.nt.ca \dot-N-T`dot-C-A´\ *n.* On the Internet, the major geographic domain specifying that an address is located in the Northwest Territories, Canada.

NT file system \N`T fīl´ si-stəm\ *n. See* NTFS.

NTFS \N`T-F-S´\ *n.* Acronym for **NT f**ile **s**ystem. An advanced file system designed for use specifically with the Windows NT operating system. It

Internal diagram

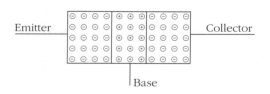

Emitter   Collector

Base

Schematic diagram

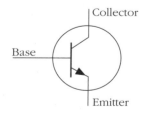

Collector

Base

Emitter

NPN transistor.

supports long filenames, full security access control, file system recovery, extremely large storage media, and various features for the Windows NT POSIX subsystem. It also supports object-oriented applications by treating all files as objects with user-defined and system-defined attributes. *See also* FAT file system, HPFS, POSIX.

NTP \N`T-P´\ *n*. Acronym for **N**etwork **T**ime **P**rotocol. A protocol used for synchronizing the system time on a computer to that of a server or other reference source such as a radio, satellite receiver, or modem. NTP provides time accuracy within a millisecond on local area networks and a few tens of milliseconds on wide area networks. NTP configurations may utilize redundant servers, diverse network paths, and cryptographic authentication to achieve high accuracy and reliability.

NTSC \N`T-S-C´\ *n*. Acronym for **N**ational **T**elevision **S**ystem (later changed to Standards) **C**ommittee. The standards-setting body for television and video in the United States. It is the sponsor of the NTSC standard for encoding color, a coding system compatible with black-and-white signals and the system used for color broadcasting in the United States.

N-type semiconductor \N`tīp sem´ē-kən-duk-tər, sem´ī-kən-duk-tər\ *n*. Semiconductor material in which electrical conduction is carried by electrons, in contrast to P-type semiconductors, in which conduction is carried by holes—that is, electron "vacancies." N-type semiconductors are created by adding a dopant with an excess of electrons during the manufacturing process. *See also* semiconductor. *Compare* P-type semiconductor.

.nu \dot`N-U´\ *n*. On the Internet, the major geographic domain specifying that an address is located in Niue.

NuBus \nōō´bus\ *n*. A high-performance expansion bus used in Apple Macintosh computers, offering high bandwidth and multiple bus controllers. Invented at the Massachusetts Institute of Technology (MIT), NuBus was eventually licensed to Texas Instruments and other companies. *See also* bus.

nuke \nōōk\ *vb*. **1.** To erase a file, directory, or entire hard disk. **2.** To stop a process in an operating system, an application, or a program. *Also called* kill.

NUL \nul\ *n*. **1.** A character code with a null value; literally, a character meaning "nothing." Although it is real in the sense of being recognizable, occupying space internally in the computer, and being sent or received as a character, a NUL character displays nothing, takes no space on the screen or on paper, and causes no specific action when sent to a printer. In ASCII, NUL is represented by the character code 0. *See also* ASCII. **2.** A "device," recognized by the operating system, that can be addressed like a physical output device (such as a printer) but that discards any information sent to it.

null character \nul´ kâr`ək-tər\ *n*. *See* NUL (definition 1).

null cycle \nul´ sī`kl\ *n*. The shortest amount of time required for execution of a program; the time needed to cycle through the program without requiring it to process new data or loop through sets of instructions.

null modem \nul´ mō`dəm\ *n*. A way of connecting two computers via a cable that enables them to communicate without the use of modems. A null modem cable accomplishes this by crossing the sending and receiving wires so that the wire used for transmitting by one device is used for receiving by the other and vice versa. See the illustration.

null modem cable \nul` mō-dəm kā`bl\ *n*. A serial data cable used to connect two personal computers, without a modem or other DCE device in between, through the computers' serial ports. Because both computers use the same pins to send data, a null modem cable connects the output pins in one computer's serial port to the input pins in the other. A null modem cable is used to transfer data between two personal computers in close proximity. See the illustration. *See also* serial port.

Null modem cable.

null pointer \nul´ poin`tər\ *n.* A pointer to nothing—usually a standardized memory address, such as 0. A null pointer usually marks the last of a linear sequence of pointers or indicates that a data search operation has come up empty. *Also called* nil pointer. *See also* pointer (definition 1).

null string \nul´ strēng\ *n.* A string containing no characters; a string whose length is zero. *See also* string.

null-terminated string \nul´tər-mə-nā-təd strēng`\ *n. See* ASCIIZ string.

NUMA \nōō´mə, N`U-M-A´\ *n. See* nonuniform memory architecture.

number cruncher \num´bər krun`chər\ *n.* **1.** A computer that is able to quickly perform large amounts of mathematical computations. **2.** A powerful workstation. **3.** A program whose main task is to perform mathematical computations, for example, a statistical program. **4.** A person who uses a computer to analyze numbers.

number crunching \num´bər krun`chēng\ *vb.* The calculation of large amounts of numeric data. Number crunching can be repetitive, mathematically complex, or both, and it generally involves far more internal processing than input or output functions. Numeric coprocessors greatly enhance the ability of computers to perform these tasks.

numerical analysis \nōō-mâr`ə-kəl ə-nal´ə-sis\ *n.* The branch of mathematics devoted to finding ways to solve abstract mathematical problems and finding concrete or approximate solutions for them.

numeric coprocessor \nōō-mâr`ik co´pros-es-ər\ *n. See* floating-point processor.

numeric keypad \nōō-mâr`ik kē´pad\ *n.* A calculator-style block of keys, usually at the right side of a keyboard, that can be used to enter numbers. In addition to keys for the digits 0 through 9 and keys for indicating addition, subtraction, multiplication, and division, a numeric keypad often includes an Enter key (usually not the same as the Enter or Return key on the main part of the keyboard). On Apple keyboards, the numeric keypad also includes a Clear key that usually functions like the Backspace key for deleting characters. In addition, many of the keys can serve dual purposes, such as cursor movement, scrolling, or editing tasks, depending on the status of the Num Lock key. See the illustration on the next page. *See also* Num Lock key.

Num Lock key \num´lok kē´\ *n.* Short for **Num**eric **Lock key**. A toggle key that, when turned on, activates the numeric keypad so that its keys can be used for calculator-style data entry. When the Num Lock key is toggled off, most of

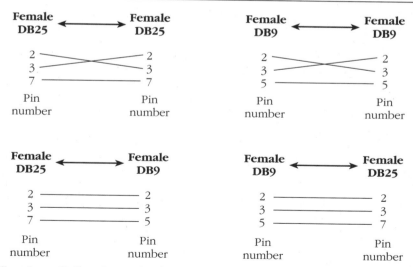

Null modem. ***Null modem cable-wiring schematics for IBM PC–compatible computers.***

Numeric keypad.

the numeric keypad keys are used for cursor movement and on-screen scrolling. *See also* numeric keypad.

nybble \nib´l\ *n. See* nibble.

.nyc.ny.us \dot-N-Y-C`dot-N-Y`dot-U-S´\ *n.* On the Internet, the major geographic domain specifying that an address is located in New York City, New York, United States.

.ny.us \dot-N-Y`dot-U-S´\ *n.* On the Internet, the major geographic domain specifying that an address is located in New York, United States.

.nz \dot`N-Z´\ *n.* On the Internet, the major geographic domain specifying that an address is located in New Zealand.

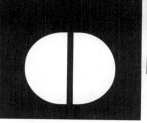

object \ob´jekt\ *n.* **1.** Short for object code (machine-readable code). **2.** In object-oriented programming, a variable comprising both routines and data that is treated as a discrete entity. *See also* abstract data type, module (definition 1), object-oriented programming. **3.** In graphics, a distinct entity. For example, a bouncing ball might be an object in a graphics program.

object code \ob´jekt kōd´\ *n.* The code, generated by a compiler or an assembler, that was translated from the source code of a program. The term most commonly refers to machine code that can be directly executed by the system's central processing unit (CPU), but it can also be assembly language source code or a variation of machine code. *See also* central processing unit.

object computer \ob´jekt kəm-pyōō´tər\ *n.* The computer that is the target of a specific communications attempt.

object database \ob´jekt dā´tə-bās\ *n. See* object-oriented database.

Object Database Management Group \ob´jəkt dā´tə-bās man´əj-mənt grōōp´\ *n.* An organization that promotes standards for object databases and defines interfaces to object databases. *Acronym:* ODMG (O`D-M-G´). *See also* Object Management Group.

object file \ob´jekt fīl´\ *n.* A file containing object code, usually the output of a compiler or an assembler and the input for a linker. *See also* assembler, compiler (definition 2), linker, object code.

Objective-C \əb-jek`tiv-C´\ *n.* An object-oriented version of the C language developed in 1984 by Brad Cox. It is most widely known for being the standard development language for the NeXT operating system. *See also* object-oriented programming.

object linking and embedding \ob`jekt lēnk`ēng and em-bed´ēng\ *n. See* OLE.

Object Management Architecture \ob`jekt man`əj-mənt är´kə-tek-chur\ *n. See* OMA.

Object Management Group \ob`jekt man´əj-mənt grōōp`\ *n.* An international organization that endorses open standards for object-oriented applications. It also defines the Object Management Architecture (OMA), a standard object model for distributed environments. The Object Management Group was founded in 1989. *Acronym:* OMG (O`M-G´). *See also* object model (definition 3), OMA, open standard.

object model \ob´jekt mod`əl\ *n.* **1.** The structural foundation for an object-oriented language, such as C++. This foundation includes such principles as abstraction, concurrency, encapsulation, hierarchy, persistence, polymorphism, and typing. *See also* abstract data type, object (definition 2), object-oriented programming, polymorphism. **2.** The structural foundation for an object-oriented design. *See also* object-oriented design. **3.** The structural foundation for an object-oriented application.

object module \ob´jekt moj`ōōl, mod`yōōl\ *n.* In programming, the object-code (compiled) version of a source-code file that is usually a collection of routines and is ready to be linked with other object modules. *See also* linker, module (definition 1), object code.

object-oriented \ob´jekt-ōr`ē-en-təd\ *adj.* Of, pertaining to, or being a system or language that supports the use of objects. *See also* object (definition 2).

object-oriented analysis \ob`jekt-ōr-ē-ent-əd ə-nal´ə-sis\ *n.* A procedure that identifies the component objects and system requirements of a system or process that involves computers and describes how they interact to perform specific tasks. The reuse of existing solutions is an objective of this sort of analysis. Object-oriented analysis generally precedes object-oriented design or object-oriented programming when a new object-oriented computer system or new software is developed. *See also* object (definition 2), object-oriented design, object-oriented programming.

object-oriented database \ob`jekt-ōr-ē-ent-əd dā´tə-bās\ *n.* A flexible database that supports the use of abstract data types, objects, and classes and that can store a wide range of data, often including sound, video, and graphics, in addition to text and numbers. Some object-oriented databases allow data retrieval procedures and rules for processing data to be stored along with the data or in place of the data. This allows the data to be stored in areas other than in the physical database, which is often desirable when the data files are large, such as those for video files. *Acronym:* OODB (O`O-D-B´). *See also* abstract data type, class, object (definition 2). *Compare* relational database.

object-oriented design \ob`jekt-ōr-ē-en-təd də-zīn´\ *n.* A modular approach to creating a software product or computer system, in which the modules (objects) can be easily and affordably adapted to meet new needs. Object-oriented design generally comes after object-oriented analysis of the product or system and before any actual programming. *See also* object (definition 2), object-oriented analysis.

object-oriented graphics \ob`jekt-ōr-ē-en-təd graf´iks\ *n.* Computer graphics that are based on the use of graphics primitives, such as lines, curves, circles, and squares. Object-oriented graphics, used in applications such as computer-aided design and drawing and illustration programs, describe an image mathematically as a set of instructions for creating the objects in the image. This approach contrasts with the use of bit-mapped graphics, in which a graphic is represented as a group of black-and-white or colored dots arranged in a certain pattern. Object-oriented graphics enable the user to manipulate objects as units. Because objects are described mathematically, object-oriented graphics can be layered, rotated, and magnified relatively easily. *Also called* structured graphics. *See also* graphics primitive. *Compare* bitmapped graphics, paint program.

object-oriented interface \ob`jekt-ōr-ē-en-təd in´tər-fās\ *n.* A user interface in which elements of the system are represented by visible screen entities, such as icons, that are used to manipulate the

system elements. Object-oriented display interfaces do not necessarily imply any relation to object-oriented programming. *See also* object-oriented graphics.

object-oriented operating system \ob`jekt-ōr-ē-en-təd op´ər-ā-tēng si`-stəm\ *n.* An operating system based on objects and designed in a way that facilitates software development by third parties, using an object-oriented design. *See also* object (definition 2), object-oriented design.

object-oriented programming \ob`jekt-ōr-ē-en-təd prō´gram`ēng\ *n.* A programming paradigm in which a program is viewed as a collection of discrete objects that are self-contained collections of data structures and routines that interact with other objects. *Acronym:* OOP (ōōp, O`O-P´). *See also* C++, object (definition 2), Objective-C.

object-relational server \ob`jekt-rə-lā`shə-nəl sər´vər\ *n.* A database server that supports object-oriented management of complex data types in a relational database. *See also* database server, relational database.

object request broker \ob`jekt rə-kwest´ brō-kər\ *n. See* ORB.

object wrapper \ob´jəkt rap`ər\ *n.* In object-oriented applications, a means of encapsulating a set of services provided by a non-object-oriented application so that the encapsulated services can be treated as an object. *See also* object (definition 2).

oblique \ō-blēk´\ *adj.* Describing a style of text created by slanting a roman font to simulate italics when a true italic font isn't available on the computer or printer. *See also* font, italic, roman.

OC3 \O`C-thrē´\ *n.* Short for **o**ptical **c**arrier **3.** One of several optical signal circuits used in the SONET high-speed fiber-optic data transmission system. OC3 carries a signal of 155.52 Mbps, the minimum transmission speed for which SONET and the European standard, SDH, are fully interoperable. *See also* SONET.

OCR \O`C-R´\ *n. See* optical character recognition.

octal \ok´təl\ *n.* The base-8 number system consisting of the digits 0 through 7, from the Latin *octo,* meaning "eight." The octal system is used in programming as a compact means of representing binary numbers. See Appendix E. *See also* base (definition 2).

octet \ok-tet´\ *n*. A unit of data that consists of exactly 8 bits, regardless of the number of bits a computer uses to represent a small amount of information such as a character. *Compare* byte.

OCX \O`C-X´\ *n*. Short for **OLE c**ustom control. A software module based on OLE and COM technologies that, when called by an application, produces a control that adds some desired feature to the application. OCX technology is portable across platforms, works on both 16-bit and 32-bit operating systems, and can be used with many applications. It is the successor to VBX (Visual Basic custom control) technology, which supported only Visual Basic applications, and is the basis for ActiveX controls. OCXs can be written in a variety of languages, although Visual C++ is most commonly used. Developed by Microsoft, OCX technology is covered in the 1996 OLE Controls specification (OCX 96). *See also* ActiveX controls, COM (definition 2), control (definition 2), OLE, VBX, Visual Basic.

ODBC \O`D-B-C´\ *n*. Acronym for **o**pen **d**ata**b**ase **c**onnectivity. In the Microsoft WOSA structure, an interface providing a common language for Windows applications to gain access to a database on a network. *See also* WOSA.

ODBMG \O`D-B-M-G´\ *See* Object Database Management Group.

odd parity \od` pâr´ə-tē\ *n*. *See* parity.

OEM \O`E-M´\ *n*. *See* original equipment manufacturer.

OFC \O`F-C´\ *n*. *See* Open Financial Connectivity.

office automation \of`is ä-tə-mā´shən, ô-tə-mā´-shən\ *n*. The use of electronic and communications devices, such as computers, modems, and fax machines and any associated software, to perform office functions mechanically rather than manually.

offline \of´līn\ *adj*. **1.** In reference to a computing device or a program, unable to communicate with or be controlled by a computer. *Compare* online (definition 1). **2.** In reference to one or more computers, being disconnected from a network. *Compare* online (definition 2).

offline navigator \of´līn nav´ə-gā-tər\ *n*. Software designed to download e-mail, Web pages, or newsgroup articles or postings from other online forums and save them locally to a disk, where they can be browsed without the user paying the cost of idle time while being connected to the Internet or an online information service. *Also called* offline reader.

offline reader \of´līn rē´dər\ *n*. *See* offline navigator.

offline storage \of´līn stōr´əj\ *n*. A storage resource, such as a disk, that is not currently available to the system.

offload \of´lōd\ *vb*. To assume part of the processing demand from another device. For example, some LAN-attached gateways can offload TCP/IP processing from the host machine, thereby freeing up significant processing capacity in the CPU. *See also* central processing unit, gateway, host, TCP/IP.

offset \of´set\ *n*. In relative addressing methods, a number that tells how far from a starting point a particular item is located. *See also* relative address.

off-the-shelf \of`dhə-shelf´\ *adj*. Ready-to-use; packaged. The term can refer to hardware or software.

ohm \ōm\ *n*. The unit of measure for electrical resistance. A resistance of 1 ohm will pass 1 ampere of current when a voltage of 1 volt is applied.

.oh.us \dot-O-H`dot-U-S´\ *n*. On the Internet, the major geographic domain specifying that an address is located in Ohio, United States.

.ok.us \dot-O-K`dot-U-S´\ *n*. On the Internet, the major geographic domain specifying that an address is located in Oklahoma, United States.

OLAP \ō´lap, O`L-A-P´\ *n*. *See* OLAP database.

OLAP database \ō`lap dā´tə-bās, O-L-A-P´\ *n*. Short for **on**line **a**nalytical **p**rocessing **database**. A relational database system capable of handling queries more complex than those handled by standard relational databases, through multidimensional access to data (viewing the data by several different criteria), intensive calculation capability, and specialized indexing techniques. *See also* database, query (definition 1), relational database.

OLE \ō-lā´, O`L-E´\ *n*. Acronym for **o**bject **l**inking and **e**mbedding. A technology for transferring and sharing information among applications. When an object, such as an image file created with a paint program, is linked to a compound document, such as a spreadsheet or a document created with a word processing program, the document contains only a reference to the object; any changes made to the contents of a linked object will be seen in the compound document. When an object is embedded in a compound document, the document contains a copy of the object; any changes made to the contents of the original object will not be seen in the compound document unless the embedded object is updated.

OLTP \O`L-T-P´\ *n.* Acronym for **on**line **t**ransaction **p**rocessing. A system for processing transactions as soon as the computer receives them and updating master files immediately in a database management system. OLTP is useful in financial record keeping and inventory tracking. *See also* database management system, transaction processing. *Compare* batch processing (definition 3).

.om \dot`O-M´\ *n.* On the Internet, the major geographic domain specifying that an address is located in Oman.

OM-1 \O`M-wən´\ *n. See* OpenMPEG Consortium.

OMA \O`M-A´\ *n.* Acronym for **O**bject **M**anagement **A**rchitecture. A definition developed by the Object Management Group (OMG) for object-oriented distributed processing. OMA includes the Common Object Request Broker Architecture (CORBA). *See also* CORBA, Object Management Group.

on-board computer \on`bōrd kəm-pyōō´tər\ *n.* A computer that resides within another device.

.on.ca \dot-O-N`dot-C-A´\ *n.* On the Internet, the major geographic domain specifying that an address is located in Ontario, Canada.

on-chip cache \on`chip kash´\ *n. See* L1 cache.

one's complement \wənz´ kom`plə-mənt\ *n.* A number in the binary (base-2) system that is the complement of another number. *See also* complement.

one-off \wən of´\ *n.* **1.** A product that is produced one at a time, instead of being mass produced. **2.** A CD-ROM created on a CD-R machine, which can create only one copy of a CD-ROM at a time.

one-pass compiler \wən`pas kəm-pī´lər\ *n.* A compiler that needs to read through a source file only once to produce the object code. The syntax of some languages makes it impossible to write a one-pass compiler for those languages. *See also* compiler (definition 2).

online \on`līn\ *adj.* **1.** In reference to a computing device or a program, activated and ready for operation; capable of communicating with or being controlled by a computer. *Compare* offline (definition 1). **2.** In reference to one or more computers, connected to a network. *Compare* offline (definition 2). **3.** In reference to a user, currently connected to the Internet, an online service, or a BBS or using a modem to connect to another modem. **4.** In reference to a user, being able to connect to the Internet, an online service, or BBS by virtue of having an account that gives one access.

online analytical processing \on`līn an-ə-lit`ə-kəl pros´es-ēng\ *n. See* OLAP database.

online community \on`līn kə-myōō´nə-tē\ *n.* **1.** All users of the Internet and World Wide Web collectively. **2.** A local community that places political forums online for the discussion of local government or issues of public concern. **3.** Members of a specific newsgroup, mailing list, MUD, BBS, or other online forum or group. *See also* BBS (definition 1), mailing list, MUD, newsgroup.

online help \on`līn help´\ *n. See* help.

online information service \on`līn in-fər-mā´shən sər-vəs\ *n.* A business that provides access to databases, file archives, conferences, chat groups, and other forms of information through dial-up, or dedicated communications links, or through the Internet. Most online information services also offer access to the Internet connections along with their own proprietary services. The largest consumer online information services in the United States are America Online, CompuServe, and The Microsoft Network.

online service \on`līn sər´vəs\ *n. See* online information service.

online state \on`līn stāt´\ *n.* The state of a modem when it is communicating with another modem. *Compare* command state.

online transaction processing \on`līn tranz-ak´shən pros`ə-sēng\ *n. See* OLTP.

on the fly \on` dhə flī´\ *adv.* Doing a task or process as needed without suspending or disturbing normal operations. For example, it is often said that an HTML document can be edited on the fly because its content can be revised without the need to completely shut down or recreate the Web site on which it resides. *See also* HTML document, Web site.

OO \O-O´\ *adj. See* object-oriented.

OOP \ōōp, O´O-P´\ *n. See* object-oriented programming.

opcode \op´kōd\ *n. See* operation code.

open[1] \ō´pən\ *adj.* Of, pertaining to, or providing accessibility. For example, an open file is one that can be used because a program has issued an "open file" command to the operating system.

open[2] \ō´pən\ *vb.* To make an object, such as a file, accessible.

open architecture \ō´pən är´kə-tek`chur\ *n.* **1.** Any computer or peripheral design that has published specifications. A published specification lets third parties develop add-on hardware for a computer or device. *Compare* closed architecture (definition 1). **2.** A design that provides for expansion slots on the motherboard, thereby allowing the addition of boards to enhance or customize a system. *Compare* closed architecture (definition 2).

OpenDoc \ō´pən-dok`\ *n.* An object-oriented application programming interface (API) that enables multiple independent programs (component software) on several platforms to work together on a single document (compound document). Similar to OLE, OpenDoc allows images, sound, video, other documents, and other files to be embedded or linked to the document. OpenDoc is supported by an alliance that includes Apple, IBM, the Object Management Group, and the X Consortium. *See also* application programming interface, component software. *Compare* ActiveX, OLE.

open file \ō´pən fīl`\ *n.* A file that can be read from, written to, or both. A program must first open a file before the file's contents can be used, and it must close the file when done. *See also* open[2].

Open Financial Connectivity \ō´pən fə-nan`shəl kə-nek-tiv´ə-tē\ *n.* The Microsoft specification for an interface between electronic banking services and Microsoft Money personal finance software. *Acronym:* OFC (O`F-C´).

Open Group \ō´pən grōōp`\ *n.* A consortium of computer hardware and software manufacturers and users from industry, government, and academia that is dedicated to the advancement of

multivendor information systems. The Open Group was formed in 1996 as a consolidation of the Open Software Foundation and X/Open Company Limited.

OpenMPEG Consortium \ō´pən-M´peg kən-sōr`shum, M´P-E-G´, kən-sōr`shē-um\ *n.* An international organization of hardware and software developers for promoting the use of the MPEG standards. *Acronym:* OM-1 (O´M-wən´). *See also* MPEG.

open shop \ō´pən shop´\ *n.* A computer facility that is open to users and not restricted to programmers or other personnel. An open shop is one in which people can work on or attempt to solve computer problems on their own rather than handing them over to a specialist.

Open Shortest Path First \ō´pən shōr´təst path fərst´\ *n. See* OSPF.

Open Software Foundation \ō´pən soft´wâr foun-dā`shən\ *n. See* OSF.

open standard \ō´pən stan´dərd\ *n.* A publicly available set of specifications describing the characteristics of a hardware device or software program. Open standards are published to encourage interoperability and thereby help popularize new technologies. *See also* standard (definition 2).

open system \ō´pən si´stəm\ *n.* **1.** In communications, a computer network designed to incorporate all devices—regardless of the manufacturer or model—that can use the same communications facilities and protocols. **2.** In reference to computer hardware or software, a system that can accept add-ons produced by third-party suppliers. *See also* open architecture (definition 1).

Open Systems Interconnection model \ō´pən si´stəms in-tər-kə-nek´shən mod`əl\ *n. See* ISO/OSI model.

operand \op´ər-and`\ *n.* The object of a mathematical operation or a computer instruction.

operating system \op´ər-ā-tēng si´stəm\ *n.* The software that controls the allocation and usage of hardware resources such as memory, central processing unit (CPU) time, disk space, and peripheral devices. The operating system is the foundation on which applications are built. Popular operating systems include Windows 95, Windows NT, Mac OS, and UNIX. *Acronym:* OS (O-S´). *Also called* executive.

operation \op`ər-ā´shən\ *n.* **1.** A specific action carried out by a computer in the process of executing a program. **2.** In mathematics, an action performed on a set of entities that produces a new entity. Examples of mathematical operations are addition and subtraction.

operation code \op`ər-ā´shən kōd`\ *n.* The portion of a machine language or assembly language instruction that specifies the type of instruction and the structure of the data on which it operates. *Also called* opcode. *See also* assembly language, machine code.

operations research \op`ər-ā´shənz rē`sərch\ *n.* The use of mathematical and scientific approaches to analyze and improve efficiency in business, management, government, and other areas. Developed around the beginning of World War II, operations research was initially used to improve military operations during the war. The practice later spread to business and industry as a means of breaking down systems and procedures and studying their parts and interactions to improve overall performance. Operations research involves use of the critical path method, statistics, probability, and information theory.

operator \op´ər-ā`tər\ *n.* **1.** In mathematics and in programming and computer applications, a symbol or other character indicating an operation that acts on one or more elements. *See also* binary[1], unary. **2.** A person who controls a machine or system, such as a computer or telephone switchboard.

operator associativity \op`ər-ā-tər ə-sō`sē-ə-tiv´ə-tē, ə-sō`shə-tiv´ə-tē\ *n.* A characteristic of operators that determines the order of evaluation in an expression when adjacent operators have equal precedence. The two possibilities are left to right and right to left. The associativity for most operators is left to right. *See also* expression, operator (definition 1), operator precedence.

operator overloading \op`ər-ā-tər ō´vər-lō-dēng\ *n.* The assignment of more than one function to a particular operator, with the implication that the operation performed will vary depending on the data type (operands) involved. Some languages, such as Ada and C++, specifically allow for operator overloading. *See also* Ada, C++, function overloading, operator (definition 1).

operator precedence \op`ər-ā-tər pres´ə-dens\ *n.* The priority of the various operators when more than one is used in an expression. In the absence of parentheses, operations with higher precedence are performed first. *See also* expression, operator (definition 1), operator associativity.

optical character recognition \op`tə-kəl kâr´ək-tər rek-əg-nish`ən\ *n.* The process in which an electronic device examines printed characters on paper and determines their shapes by detecting patterns of dark and light. Once the scanner or reader has determined the shapes, character recognition methods—pattern matching with stored sets of characters—are used to translate the shapes into computer text. *Acronym:* OCR (O`C-R´). *See also* character recognition. *Compare* magnetic-ink character recognition.

optical communications \op`tə-kəl kə-myōō-nə-kā´shənz\ *n.* The use of light and of light-transmitting technology, such as optical fibers and lasers, in sending and receiving data, images, or sound.

optical disc \op´tə-kəl disk\ *n. See* compact disc.

optical drive \op´tə-kəl drīv`\ *n.* A disk drive that reads and often can write data on optical (compact) discs. Examples of optical drives include CD-ROM drives and WORM disk drives. See the illustration. *See also* CD-ROM drive, compact disc, WORM.

Optical drive.

optical fiber \op`tə-kəl fī´bər\ *n.* A thin strand of transparent material used to carry optical signals. Optical fibers are constructed from special kinds of glass and plastic, and they are designed so that a beam of light introduced at one end will remain within the fiber, reflecting off the inner surfaces as it travels down the length of the fiber. Optical fibers are inexpensive, compact, and lightweight and are often packaged many hundred to a single cable. *See also* fiber optics.

optical mouse \op`tə-kəl mous´\ *n.* A type of mouse that uses a pair of light-emitting diodes (LEDs) and a special reflective grid pad to detect motion. The two lights are of different colors, and the special mouse pad has a grid of lines in the same colors, one color for vertical lines and another for horizontal lines. Light detectors paired with the LEDs sense when a colored light passes over a line of the same color, indicating the direction of movement. *See also* mouse. *Compare* mechanical mouse, optomechanical mouse.

optical reader \op`tə-kəl rē´dər\ *n.* A device that reads text from printed paper by detecting the pattern of light and dark on a page and then applying optical character recognition methods to identify the characters. *See also* optical character recognition.

optical recognition \op`tə-kəl rek-əg-nish´ən\ *n.* *See* optical character recognition.

optical scanner \op`tə-kəl skan´ər\ *n.* An input device that uses light-sensing equipment to scan paper or another medium, translating the pattern of light and dark or color into a digital signal that can be manipulated by either optical character recognition software or graphics software. Scanners have different methods for holding the input medium, including flatbed, whereby the medium is held on a piece of glass; sheet-fed, whereby sheets of paper are pulled over a stationary scanning mechanism; handheld, whereby the user moves the device over the document to be scanned; and overhead, whereby the document is placed face up on a stationary bed below a small tower, which moves across the page. *Compare* magnetic-ink character recognition, spatial digitizer.

optimization \op`tə-mə-zā´shən\ *n.* **1.** In programming, the process of producing more efficient (smaller or faster) programs through selection and design of data structures, algorithms, and instruction sequences. **2.** The process of a compiler or assembler in producing efficient executable code. *See also* optimizing compiler.

optimizer \op`tə-mī´zər\ *n.* A program or device that improves the performance of a computer, network, or other device or system. For example, a disk optimizer program reduces file access time.

optimizing compiler \op`tə-mī-zēng kəm-pī´lər\ *n.* A compiler that analyzes its output (assembly language or machine code) to produce more efficient (smaller or faster) instruction sequences.

optional hyphen \op`shə-nəl hī´fən\ *n.* *See* hyphen.

Option key \op´shən kē`\ *n.* A key on Apple Macintosh keyboards that, when pressed in combination with another key, produces special characters—graphics, such as boxes; international characters, such as currency symbols; and special punctuation marks, such as en dashes and em dashes. The Option key serves a purpose similar to that of the Control key or the Alt key on IBM and compatible keyboards in that it changes the meaning of the key with which it is used.

Options \op´shənz\ *n.* *See* Preferences.

optoelectronics \op`tō-ə-lek-tron´iks\ *n.* The branch of electronics in which the properties and behavior of light are studied. Optoelectronics deals with electronic devices that generate, sense, transmit, and modulate electromagnetic radiation in the infrared, visible, and ultraviolet portions of the electromagnetic spectrum.

optomechanical mouse \op`tō-mə-kan`ə-kəl mous´\ *n.* A type of mouse in which motion is translated into directional signals through a combination of optical and mechanical means. The optical portion includes pairs of light-emitting diodes (LEDs) and matching sensors; the mechanical portion consists of rotating wheels with cutout slits. When the mouse is moved, the wheels turn and the light from the LEDs either passes through the slits and strikes a light sensor or is blocked by the solid portions of the wheels. These changes in light contact are detected by the pairs of sensors and interpreted as indications of movement. Because the sensors are slightly out of phase with one another, the direction of movement is determined based on which sensor is the first to regain light contact. Because it uses optical equipment instead of mechanical parts, an optomechanical mouse eliminates the need for many of the wear-related repairs and maintenance necessary with purely mechanical mice, but it does not require the special operating surfaces associated with optical mice. See the illustration. *See also* mouse. *Compare* mechanical mouse, optical mouse.

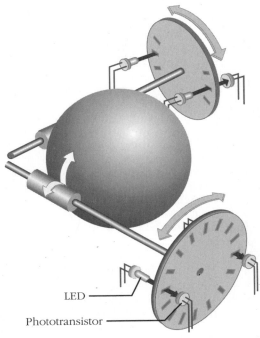

LED
Phototransistor

Optomechanical mouse. ***The interior of an opto-mechanical mouse.***

OR \ôr\ *n.* A logical operation for combining two bits (0 or 1) or two Boolean values (false or true). If one or both values are 1 (true), it returns the value 1 (true).

a	b	a OR b
0	0	0
0	1	1
1	0	1
1	1	1

Orange Book \ôr´ənj bŏŏk`\ *n.* **1.** A U.S. Department of Defense standards document entitled "Trusted Computer System Evaluation Criteria, DOD standard 5200.28-STD, December, 1985," which defines a system of ratings from A1 (most secure) to D (least secure), indicating the ability of a computer system to protect sensitive information. *Compare* Red Book (definition 1). **2.** A specifications book written by the Sony and Philips Corporations, covering the compact disc write-once formats (CD-R, PhotoCD). *See also* CD-R, ISO 9660, PhotoCD. *Compare* Green Book, Red Book (definition 2).

ORB \ôrb, O`R-B´\ *n.* Acronym for **o**bject **r**equest **b**roker. In client/server applications, an interface to which the client makes a request for an object. The ORB directs the request to the server containing the object and then returns the resulting values to the client. *See also* client (definition 1), CORBA.

order[1] \ôr´dər\ *n.* **1.** In computing, the relative significance of a digit or byte. *High-order* refers to the most significant (usually leftmost) digit or byte; *low-order* refers to the least significant (usually rightmost) digit or byte. **2.** The magnitude of a database in terms of the number of fields it contains. **3.** The sequence in which arithmetic operations are performed.

order[2] \ôr´dər\ *vb.* To arrange in a sequence, such as alphabetic or numeric.

ordinal number \ôr´də-nəl num´bər\ *n.* A number whose form indicates position in an ordered sequence of items, such as first, third, or twentieth. *Compare* cardinal number.

.org \dot-ôrg´, -O`R-G´\ *n.* In the Internet's Domain Name System, the top-level domain that identifies addresses operated by organizations that do not fit any of the other standard domains. For instance, the Public Broadcasting System (PBS) is neither a commercial, for-profit corporation (.com) nor an educational institution with enrolled students (.edu), so it has the Internet address pbs.org. The designation .org appears at the end of the address. *See also* DNS (definition 1), domain (definition 3). *Compare* .com, .edu, .gov, .mil, .net.

orientation \ôr´ē-ən-tā´shən\ *n. See* landscape mode, portrait mode.

original equipment manufacturer \ər-ij`ən-əl ə-kwip´mənt man`yə-fak`chur-ər\ *n.* The maker of a piece of equipment. In making computers and related equipment, manufacturers of original equipment typically purchase components from other manufacturers of original equipment, integrate them into their own products, and then sell the products to the public. *Acronym:* OEM (O`E-M´). *Compare* value-added reseller.

original Macintosh keyboard \ər-ij`ən-əl mak`ən-tosh kē´bōrd\ *n.* The keyboard supplied as standard equipment with the 128-KB Apple Macintosh and the Mac 512K. The original Macintosh keyboard is small and has no numeric keypad or function keys. Also, because the overall design goal was that the Macintosh should feel familiar, the only elements of this 58-key keyboard that differ from a typewriter keyboard are the Option keys at both ends of the bottom row, the Command key to the left of the Spacebar, and the Enter key to the right of the Spacebar. See the illustration.

orphan \ôr´fən\ *n.* The first line of a paragraph printed alone at the bottom of a page or column of text, or the last line of a paragraph printed alone at the top of a page or column. Orphans are visually unattractive and thus undesirable in printed materials. *Compare* widow.

orphan file \or´fən fïl`\ *n.* A file that remains on a system after it has ceased to be of use. For example, a file may be created to support a particular application but may remain after the application has been removed.

.or.us \dot-O-R`dot-U-S´\ *n.* On the Internet, the major geographic domain specifying that an address is located in Oregon, United States.

OS \O-S´\ *n. See* operating system.

OS/2 \O`S-tōō´\ *n.* A protected-mode, virtual-memory, multitasking operating system for personal computers based on the Intel 80286, 80386, i486, and Pentium processors. OS/2 can run most MS-DOS applications and can read all MS-DOS disks. Important OS/2 subsystems include Presentation Manager, which provides a graphical user interface, and LAN Manager, which provides networking facilities. OS/2 was initially developed as

a joint project of Microsoft and IBM but is now an IBM product. *See also* protected mode, virtual memory.

oscillation \os`ə-lā´shən\ *n.* A periodic change or alternation. In electronics, oscillation refers to a periodic change in an electrical signal.

oscillator \os`ə-lā´tər\ *n.* An electronic circuit that produces a periodically varying output at a controlled frequency. Oscillators, an important type of electronic circuit, can be designed to provide a constant or an adjustable output. Some oscillator circuits use a quartz crystal to generate a stable frequency. Personal computers use an oscillator circuit to provide the "clock" frequency—typically 1 to 200 megahertz (MHz)—that drives the processor and other circuits.

oscilloscope \ə-sil´ə-skōp`\ *n.* A test and measurement instrument that provides a visual display for an electrical signal. Most commonly, oscilloscopes are used to create a display of voltage over time. *Also called* cathode-ray oscilloscope.

OSF \O´S-F´\ *n.* Acronym for **O**pen **S**oftware **F**oundation. A nonprofit consortium of firms (including DEC, Hewlett-Packard, and IBM), formed in 1988, that promotes standards and specifications for programs operating under UNIX and licenses software (as source code) to its members. OSF's products include the Distributed Computing Environment, the graphical user interface Motif, and the OSF/1 operating system (a variant of UNIX).

OSI \O`S-I´\ *n. See* ISO/OSI model.

OSPF \O´S-P-F´\ *n.* Acronym for **O**pen **S**hortest **P**ath **F**irst. A routing protocol for IP networks, such as the Internet, that allows a router to calculate the shortest path to each node for sending messages.

Original Macintosh keyboard.

The router sends information on the nodes it is linked to, called link-state advertisements, to other routers on the network to accumulate link-state information to make its calculations. *See also* communications protocol, node (definition 2), path (definition 1), router.

OTOH \O`T-O-H`\ *n.* Acronym for **o**n **t**he **o**ther **h**and. A shorthand expression often used in e-mail, Internet news, and discussion groups.

Outbox \out´boks\ *n.* In many e-mail applications, the default mailbox where the program stores outgoing messages. *See also* e-mail[1] (definition 1), mailbox. *Compare* Inbox.

outdent \out´dent\ *n. See* hanging indent.

outer join \out´ər join`\ *n.* In database management, an operator in relational algebra. An outer join performs an extended join operation in which the tuples (rows) in one relation (table) that have no counterpart in the second relation appear in the resulting relation concatenated with all null values. *Compare* inner join.

outline font \out´līn font`\ *n.* A font (type design) stored in a computer or printer as a set of outlines for drawing each of the alphabetic and other characters in a character set. Outline fonts are templates rather than actual patterns of dots and are scaled up or down to match a particular type size. Such fonts are most often used for printing, as is the case with most PostScript fonts on a PostScript-compatible laser printer and TrueType fonts. *Compare* bitmapped font, screen font, stroke font.

out-of-band signaling \out`əv-band sig´nə-lēng\ *n.* Transmission of some signals, such as control information, on frequencies outside of the bandwidth available for voice or data transfer on a communications channel.

output[1] \out´po͞ot\ *n.* The results of processing, whether sent to the screen or printer, stored on disk as a file, or sent to another computer in a network.

output[2] \out´po͞ot\ *vb.* To send out data by a computer or sound by a speaker.

output area \out´po͞ot âr`ē-ə\ *n. See* output buffer.

output-bound \out´po͞ot-bound`\ *n. See* input/output-bound.

output buffer \out´po͞ot buf`ər\ *n.* A portion of memory set aside for temporary storage of infor-

mation, leaving main memory for storage, display, printing, or transmission. *See also* buffer[1].

output channel \out´po͞ot chan`əl\ *n. See* channel (definition 1), input/output channel.

output stream \out´po͞ot strēm`\ *n.* A flow of information that leaves a computer system and is associated with a particular task or destination. In programming, an output stream can be a series of characters sent from the computer's memory to a display or to a disk file. *Compare* input stream.

outsourcing \out´sōr`sēng\ *n.* The assignment of tasks to independent contractors, such as individual consultants or service bureaus. Tasks such as data entry and programming are often performed via outsourcing.

OverDrive \ō´vər-drīv`\ *n.* A type of microprocessor from Intel designed to replace a computer's existing i486SX or i486DX microprocessor. The OverDrive is functionally identical to Intel's i486DX2 microprocessor, but it is an end-user product, whereas the i486DX2 is sold only to computer manufacturers who build it into their own systems. Upgrading a system with an OverDrive processor differs from system to system, and some systems might not even support an OverDrive processor. *See also* i486DX, i486SL, i486SX, microprocessor. *Compare* i486DX2.

overflow \ō´vər-flō`\ *n.* **1.** Generally, the condition that occurs when data resulting from input or processing requires more bits than have been provided in hardware or software to store the data. Examples of overflow include a floating-point operation whose result is too large for the number of bits allowed for the exponent, a string that exceeds the bounds of the array allocated for it, and an integer operation whose result contains too many bits for the register into which it is to be stored. *See also* overflow error. *Compare* underflow. **2.** The part of a data item that cannot be stored because the data exceeds the capacity of the available data structure.

overflow error \ō´vər-flō âr`ər\ *n.* An error that arises when a number, often the result of an arithmetic operation, is too large to be contained in the data structure that a program provides for it.

overhead \ō´vər-hed`\ *n.* Work or information that provides support—possibly critical support—for a computing process but is not an intrinsic part of the operation or data. Overhead often adds to processing time but is generally necessary.

overlaid windows \o`vər-lād win´dōz\ *n. See* cascading windows.

overlay[1] \ō´vər-lā`\ *n.* **1.** A section of a program designed to reside on a designated storage device, such as a disk, and to be loaded into memory when needed, usually overwriting one or more overlays already in memory. Use of overlays allows large programs to fit into a limited amount of memory, but at the cost of speed. **2.** A printed form positioned over a screen, tablet, or keyboard for identification of particular features. *See also* keyboard template.

overlay[2] \ō´vər-lā`\ *vb.* **1.** In computer graphics, to superimpose one graphic image over another. **2.** In video, to superimpose a graphic image generated on a computer over video signals, either live or recorded.

overprint \ō´vər-print´\ *vb.* The process of printing an element of one color over one of another color without removing, or knocking out, the material underneath. *Compare* knockout (definition 1).

override \ō´vər-rīd´\ *vb.* To prevent something from happening in a program or in an operating system or to initiate another response. For example, a user can often override and thus abort a lengthy sorting procedure in a database program by pressing the Escape key.

overrun \ō´vər-run`\ *n.* In information transfer, an error that occurs when a device receiving data cannot handle or make use of the information as rapidly as it arrives. *See also* input/output-bound.

overscan \ō´vər-skan`\ *n.* The part of a video signal sent to a raster display that controls the area outside the rectangle containing visual information. The overscan area is sometimes colored to form a border around the screen. See the illustration.

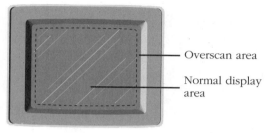

Overscan area

Normal display area

Overscan.

overshoot \ō`vər-shoot´\ *n.* The phenomenon in which a system suffers from a time delay in responding to input and continues to change state even after it has reached the desired state. This situation requires that correcting input be made so that the system reaches the desired state. For example, the arm carrying the heads in a hard disk drive might move slightly past the desired track before it stops, requiring another signal to pull it back.

overstrike \ō´vər-strīk´\ *vb.* To type or print one character directly over another so that the two occupy the same space on the page or screen.

overtype mode \ō´vər-tīp mōd`\ *n. See* overwrite mode.

overwrite mode \ō´vər-rīt mōd`\ *n.* A text-entry mode in which newly typed characters replace existing characters under or to the left of the cursor insertion point. *Also called* overtype mode, typeover mode. *Compare* insert mode.

P \pet´ə\ *prefix See* peta-.

P5 \P-fīv´\ *n.* Intel Corporation's internal working name for the Pentium microprocessor. Although it was not intended to be used publicly, the name P5 leaked out to the computer-industry trade press and was commonly used to reference the microprocessor before it was released. *See also* 586, Pentium.

.pa \dot`P-A´\ *n.* On the Internet, the major geographic domain specifying that an address is located in Panama.

pack \pak\ *vb.* To store information in a more compact form. Packing eliminates unnecessary spaces and other such characters and may use other special methods of compressing data as well. It is used by some programs to minimize storage requirements.

package \pak´əj\ *n.* **1.** A computer application consisting of one or more programs created to perform a particular type of work—for example, an accounting package or a spreadsheet package. **2.** In electronics, the housing in which an electronic component is packaged. *See also* DIP.

packaged software \pak`əjd soft´wâr\ *n.* A software program sold through a retail distributor, as opposed to custom software. *Compare* canned software.

packed decimal \pakd` des´ə-məl\ *adj.* A method of encoding decimal numbers in binary form that maximizes storage space by using each byte to represent two decimal digits. When signed decimal numbers are stored in packed decimal format, the sign appears in the rightmost four bits of the rightmost (least significant) byte.

packet \pak´ət\ *n.* **1.** A unit of information transmitted as a whole from one device to another on a network. **2.** In packet-switching networks, a transmission unit of fixed maximum size that consists of binary digits representing both data and a header containing an identification number, source and destination addresses, and sometimes error-control data. *See also* packet switching.

packet assembler/disassembler \pak`ət ə-sem´-blər-dis´ə-sem-blər\ *n.* An interface between non-packet-switching equipment and a packet-switching network. *Acronym:* PAD (P`A-D´).

packet filtering \pak´ət fil`tər-ēng\ *n.* The process of controlling network access based on IP addresses. Firewalls will often incorporate filters that allow or deny users the ability to enter or leave a local area network. Packet filtering is also used to accept or reject packets such as e-mail, based on the origin of the packet to ensure security on a private network. *See also* firewall, IP address, packet (definition 1).

Packet Internet Groper \pak`ət in´tər-net grō´-pər\ *n. See* ping[1] (definition 1).

packet switching \pak´ət swich`ēng\ *n.* A message-delivery technique in which small units of information (packets) are relayed through stations in a computer network along the best route available between the source and the destination. A packet-switching network handles information in small units, breaking long messages into multiple packets before routing. Although each packet may travel along a different path, and the packets composing a message may arrive at different times or out of sequence, the receiving computer reassembles the original message correctly. Packet-switching networks are considered to be fast and efficient. To manage the tasks of routing traffic and assembling/disassembling packets, such a network requires some "intelligence" from the computers and software that control delivery. The Internet is an example of a packet-switching network. Standards for packet switching on networks are documented in the CCITT recommendation X.25.

packing density \pak´ēng den`sə-tē\ *n.* The number of storage units per length or area of a storage device. Bits per inch is one measure of packing density.

PackIT \pak´it\ *n.* A file format used on the Apple Macintosh to represent collections of Mac files, possibly Huffman compressed. *See also* Huffman coding, Macintosh.

PAD \P`A-D´\ *n.* See packet assembler/disassembler.

pad character \pad´ kâr`ək-tər\ *n.* In data input and storage, an extra character inserted as filler to use up surplus space in a predefined block of a specified length, such as a fixed-length field.

padding \pad´ēng\ *n.* In data storage, the addition of one or more bits, usually zeros, to a block of data in order to fill it, to force the actual data bits into a certain position, or to prevent the data from duplicating a bit pattern that has an established meaning, such as an embedded command.

paddle \pad´l\ *n.* An early type of input device often used with computer games especially for side-to-side or up-and-down movements of an on-screen object. A paddle is less sophisticated than a joystick because it only permits the user, by turning a dial, to specify movement along a single axis. The paddle got its name because its most popular use was to control the on-screen paddles in the simple early video games, such as Pong. See the illustration.

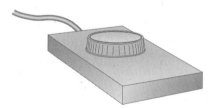

Paddle.

paddle switch \pad´l swich`\ *n.* Any switch that has a wide handle. The large on/off switch on many IBM personal computers is one type of paddle switch. See the illustration.

page \pāj\ *n.* **1.** In word processing, the text and display elements to be printed on one side of a sheet of paper, subject to formatting specifications such as depth, margin size, and number of columns. **2.** A fixed-size block of memory. When used in the context of a paging memory system, a

Paddle switch.

page is a block of memory whose physical address can be changed via mapping hardware. *See also* EMS, memory management unit, virtual memory. **3.** In computer graphics, a portion of display memory that contains one complete full-screen image; the internal representation of a screenful of information.

page break \pāj´ brāk\ *n.* The point at which the flow of text in a document moves to the top of a new page. Most word processors automatically place page breaks when the material on the page reaches a specified maximum. By contrast, a "hard" or "manual" page break is a command or code inserted by the user to force a page break at a specific place in the text. *See also* form feed.

paged address \pājd´ a´dres, ə-dres´\ *n.* In the 80386, i486, and Pentium paged-memory architecture, an address in memory created by combining the processes of segment translation and page translation. In the paged-memory scheme, which requires that the microprocessor's paging feature be enabled, logical addresses are transformed into physical addresses in two steps: segment translation and page translation. The first step, segment translation, converts a logical to a linear address—an address that refers indirectly to a physical address. After the linear address is obtained, the microprocessor's paging hardware converts the linear address to a physical address by specifying a page table (an array of 32-bit page specifiers), a page (a 4-KB unit of contiguous addresses within physical memory) within that table, and an offset within that page. This information collectively refers to a physical address.

page-description language \pāj-də-skrip`shən lang´wəj\ *n.* A programming language, such as PostScript, that is used to describe output to a printer or a display device, which then uses the instructions from the page-description language to construct text and graphics to create the required page image. Page-description languages are like other computer languages, with logical program flow allowing for sophisticated manipulation of the output. A page-description language, like a blueprint, sets out specifications (as for fonts and type sizes) but leaves the work of drawing characters and graphics to the output device itself. Because this approach delegates the detail work to the device that produces the output, a page-description language is machine-independent. These abilities come at a price, however. Page-description languages require printers with processing power and memory comparable to, and often exceeding, that of personal computers. *Acronym:* PDL (P`D-L´). *See also* PostScript.

paged memory management unit \pājd` mem-ər-ē man´əj-mənt yo͞o-nət\ *n.* A hardware unit that performs tasks related to accessing and managing memory used by different applications or by virtual-memory operating systems. *Acronym:* PMMU (P`M-M-U´).

Page Down key \pāj doun´ kē`\ *n.* A standard key (often labeled "PgDn") on most computer keyboards whose specific meaning is different in different programs. In many cases, it moves the cursor down to the top of the next page or a specific number of lines. See the illustration.

Page Down key.

page fault \pāj´ fält, fôlt\ *n.* The interrupt that occurs when software attempts to read from or write to a virtual memory location that is marked "not present." The mapping hardware of a virtual memory system maintains status information about every page in the virtual address space. A page either is mapped onto a physical address or

is not present in physical memory. When a read or write to an unmapped virtual address is detected, the memory management hardware generates the page fault interrupt. The operating system must respond to the page fault by swapping in the data for the page and updating the status information in the memory management unit. *See also* page (definition 2), swap (definition 2), virtual memory.

page frame \pāj´ frām\ *n.* A physical address to which a page of virtual memory may be mapped. In a system with 4,096-byte pages, page frame 0 corresponds to physical addresses 0 through 4,095. *See also* paging, virtual memory.

page-image buffer \pāj`im-əj buf´ər\ *n.* Memory in a page printer used to hold the bit map (image) of a page as the printer's raster image processor builds the page and as the printer produces the page. *See also* page printer, raster image processor.

page-image file \pāj` im-əj fīl´\ *n.* A file containing the necessary code for a printer or other display device to create the page or screen image. *See also* PostScript.

page layout \pāj´ lā`out\ *n.* In desktop publishing, the process of arranging text and graphics on the pages of a document. Page-layout programs excel in text placement and management of special effects applied to text. Although page-layout programs are generally slower than word-processing programs, they can perform such advanced tasks as flowing text into complex multicolumn page designs, printing documents in signatures, managing color separations, and supporting sophisticated kerning and hyphenation.

page makeup \pāj´ mā`kup\ *n.* The assembling of graphics and text on a page in preparation for printing.

page mode RAM \pāj´ mōd ram`, R-A-M´\ *n.* A specially designed dynamic RAM that supports access to sequential memory locations with a reduced cycle time. This is especially attractive in video RAM, where each location is accessed in ascending order to create the screen image. Page mode RAM can also improve the execution speed of code because code tends to execute sequentially through memory. *See also* cycle time, dynamic RAM.

page orientation \pāj´ ōr-ē-ən-tā`shən\ *n. See* landscape mode, portrait mode.

page printer \pāj´ prin`tər\ *n.* Any printer, such as a laser printer, that prints an entire page at once. Because page printers must store the entire page in memory before printing, they require relatively large amounts of memory. *Compare* line printer.

page reader \pāj´ rē`dər\ *n. See* document reader.

page setup \pāj´ set`up\ *n.* A set of choices that affect how a file is printed on the page. Page setup might reflect the size of paper going into the printer, the page margins, the specific pages in the document to be printed, whether the image is to be reduced or enlarged when printed, and whether another file is to be printed immediately after the first file is printed.

pages per minute \pā´jəz pər min´ət\ *n.* Abbreviated PPM or ppm. A rating of a printer's output capacity, that is, the number of printed pages the printer can produce in one minute. A printer's PPM rating is usually provided by the manufacturer and is based on a "normal" page. Pages with excessive graphics or fonts may reduce a printer's PPM rate dramatically.

Page Up key \pāj up´ kē`\ *n.* A standard key (often labeled "PgUp") on most computer keyboards whose specific meaning is different in different programs. In many cases, it moves the cursor up to the top of the previous page or a specific number of lines. See the illustration.

Page Up key.

pagination \paj`ə-nā´shun\ *n.* **1.** The process of dividing a document into pages for printing. **2.** The process of adding page numbers, as in a running head.

paging \pā´jēng\ *n.* A technique for implementing virtual memory. The virtual address space is divided into a number of fixed-size blocks called pages, each of which can be mapped onto any of the physical addresses available on the system. Special memory management hardware (MMU or PMMU) performs the address translation from virtual addresses to physical addresses. *See also* memory management unit, paged memory management unit, virtual memory.

paint[1] \pānt\ *n.* A color and pattern used with graphics programs to fill areas of a drawing, applied with tools such as a paintbrush or a spraycan.

paint[2] \pānt\ *vb.* To fill a portion of a drawing with paint.

paintbrush \pānt´brush\ *n.* An artist's tool in a paint program or another graphics application for applying a streak of solid color to an image. The user can usually select the width of the streak. *See also* paint program. *Compare* spraycan.

paint program \pānt´ prō`gram\ *n.* An application program that creates graphics as bit maps. A paint program, because it treats a drawing as a group of dots, is particularly appropriate for freehand drawing. Such a program commonly provides tools for images requiring lines, curves, and geometric shapes but does not treat any shape as an entity that can be moved or modified as a discrete object without losing its identity. See the illustration. *Compare* drawing program.

Paint program.

palette \pal´ət\ *n.* **1.** In paint programs, a collection of drawing tools, such as patterns, colors, brush shapes, and different line widths, from which the user can choose. **2.** A subset of the color look-up table that establishes the colors that can be displayed on the screen at a particular time. The number of colors in a palette is determined by the number of bits used to represent a pixel. *See also* color bits, color look-up table, pixel.

palmtop \pälm´top, päm´top\ *n.* A portable personal computer whose size enables it to be held in one hand while it is operated with the other hand. A major difference between palmtop computers and laptop computers is that palmtops are usually powered by off-the-shelf batteries such as AA cells. Palmtop computers typically do not have disk drives; rather, their programs are stored in ROM and are loaded into RAM when they are switched on. More recent palmtop computers are equipped with PCMCIA slots to provide wider flexibility and greater capability. *See also* handheld PC, PCMCIA slot, portable computer. *Compare* laptop.

PAM \pam, P`A-M`\ *n. See* pulse amplitude modulation.

panning \pan´ēng\ *n.* In computer graphics, a display method in which a viewing window on the screen scans horizontally or vertically, like a camera, to bring offscreen extensions of the current image smoothly into view. See the illustration.

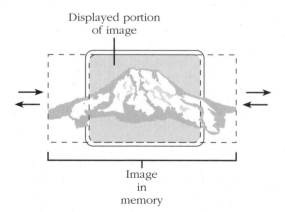

Displayed portion
of image

Image
in
memory

Panning.

Pantone Matching System \pan`tōn mach´ēng si`stəm\ *n.* In graphic arts and printing, a standard system of ink color specification consisting of a swatch book in which each of about 500 colors is

assigned a number. *Acronym:* PMS (P`M-S´). *See also* color model.

PAP \pap, P`A-P`\ *n.* **1.** Acronym for **P**assword **A**uthentication **P**rotocol. A method for verifying the identity of a user attempting to log on to a Point-to-Point Protocol (PPP) server. PAP is used if a more rigorous method, such as the Challenge Handshake Authentication Protocol (CHAP), is not available or if the user name and password that the user submitted to PAP must be sent to another program without encryption. **2.** Acronym for **P**rinter **A**ccess **P**rotocol. The protocol in Apple-Talk networks that governs communication between computers and printers.

paper feed \pā´pər fēd`\ *n.* A mechanism that moves paper through a printer. In laser printers and other page printers, the paper feed is usually a series of rollers that firmly grip and align the paper. In dot-matrix printers, the paper feed is usually a pin feed or tractor feed, in which small pins drag or push paper that has detachable edges punched with sprocket holes. Friction feed is another type of paper feed, in which the paper is gripped between the platen and pressure rollers and pulled by rotation of the platen.

paperless office \pā´pər-ləs of´əs\ *n.* The idealized office in which information is entirely stored, manipulated, and transferred electronically rather than on paper.

paper-white \pā´pər-hwīt`, pā´pər-wīt`\ *adj.* Of, pertaining to, or being a type of monochrome computer monitor whose default operating colors are black text on a white background. Paper-white monitors are popular in desktop publishing and word processing environments because the monitor most closely resembles a white sheet of paper printed with black characters.

paper-white monitor \pā´pər-hwīt mon`ə-tər, pā´pər-wīt\ *n.* A display monitor in which text and graphics characters are displayed in black against a white background to resemble the appearance of a printed page. Some manufacturers use the name to refer to a background that is tinted in a manner corresponding to bonded paper.

paradigm \pâr´ə-dīm`\ *n.* An archetypical example or pattern that provides a model for a process or system.

paragraph \pâr´ə-graf´\ *n.* **1.** In word processing, any part of a document preceded by one paragraph mark and ending with another. To the program, a paragraph represents a unit of information that can be selected as a whole or given formatting distinct from the surrounding paragraphs. **2.** On IBM and other computers built around the Intel 8088 or 8086 microprocessor, a 16-byte section of memory beginning at a location (address) that can be divided evenly by 16 (hexadecimal 10).

parallel \pâr´ə-lel`\ *adj.* **1.** Of or relating to electronic circuits in which the corresponding terminals of two or more components are connected. **2.** In geometry and graphics, of, relating to, or being lines that run side by side in the same direction in the same plane without intersecting. **3.** In data communications, of, relating to, or being information that is sent in groups of bits over multiple wires, one wire for each bit in a group. *See also* parallel interface. *Compare* serial. **4.** In data handling, of or relating to handling more than one event at a time, with each event having its own portion of the system's resources. *See also* parallel processing.

parallel access \pâr´ə-lel ak´ses\ *n.* The ability to store or retrieve all of the bits composing a single unit of information, such as a byte or a word (usually two bytes), at the same time. *Also called* simultaneous access.

parallel adder \pâr´ə-lel ad´ər\ *n.* A logic device that processes the addition of several (typically 4, 8, or 16) binary inputs simultaneously rather than sequentially, as is the case with half adders and full adders. Parallel adders speed processing because they require fewer steps to produce the result. *Compare* full adder, half adder.

parallel algorithm \pâr´ə-lel al´gər-idh-əm\ *n.* An algorithm in which more than one portion of the algorithm can be followed at one time. Parallel algorithms are usually used in multiprocessing environments. *Compare* sequential algorithm.

parallel circuit \pâr´ə-lel sər`kət\ *n.* A circuit in which the corresponding leads of two or more of the circuit components are connected. In a parallel circuit, there are two or more separate pathways between points. The individual components in a parallel circuit all receive the same voltage but share the current load. See the illustration. *Compare* series circuit.

Parallel circuit.

parallel computer \pâr´ə-lel kəm-pyo͞o´tər\ *n.* A computer that uses several processors that work concurrently. Software written for parallel computers can increase the amount of work done in a specific amount of time by dividing a computing task among several simultaneously functioning processors. *See also* parallel processing.

parallel computing \pâr´ə-lel kəm-pyo͞o´tēng\ *n.* The use of multiple computers or processors to solve a problem or perform a function. *See also* array processor, massively parallel processing, pipeline processing, SMP.

parallel database \pâr´ə-lel dā´tə-bās\ *n.* A database system involving the concurrent use of two or more processors or operating system processes to service database management requests such as SQL queries and updates, transaction logging, I/O handling, and data buffering. A parallel database is capable of performing a large number of simultaneous tasks across multiple processors and storage devices, providing quick access to databases containing many gigabytes of data.

Parallel Data Structure \pâr´ə-lel dā´tə struk`chur\ *n.* *See* PDS (definition 2).

parallel execution \pâr´ə-lel eks-ə-kyo͞o´shən\ *n.* *See* concurrent execution.

parallel interface \pâr´ə-lel in´tər-fās\ *n.* The specification of a data transmission scheme that sends multiple data and control bits simultaneously over wires connected in parallel. The most common parallel interface is the Centronics interface. *See also* Centronics parallel interface. *Compare* serial interface.

parallel port \pâr´ə-lel pōrt`\ *n.* The input/output connector for a parallel interface device. *See also* input/output port.

parallel printer \pâr´ə-lel prin`tər\ *n.* A printer that is connected to the computer via a parallel interface. In general, a parallel connection can move data between devices faster than a serial connection can. The parallel interface is preferred in the IBM PC world because its cabling is more standardized than that of the serial interface and because the MS-DOS operating system assumes that the system printer is attached to the parallel port. *See also* parallel interface. *Compare* serial printer.

parallel processing \pâr`ə-lel pros´es-ēng\ *n*. A method of processing that can run only on a computer that contains two or more processors running simultaneously. Parallel processing differs from multiprocessing in the way a task is distributed over the available processors. In multiprocessing, a process might be divided up into sequential blocks, with one processor managing access to a database, another analyzing the data, and a third handling graphical output to the screen. Programmers working with systems that perform parallel processing must find ways to divide a task so that it is more or less evenly distributed among the processors available. *Compare* coprocessor, multiprocessing.

parallel server \pâr`ə-lel sər`vər\ *n*. A computer system that implements some form of parallel processing to improve its performance as a server. *See also* SMP server.

parallel transmission \pâr`ə-lel tranz-mish´ən\ *n*. The simultaneous transmission of a group of bits over separate wires. With microcomputers, parallel transmission refers to the transmission of 1 byte (8 bits). The standard connection for parallel transmission is known as the Centronics interface. *See also* Centronics parallel interface. *Compare* serial transmission.

parameter \pər-am´ə-tər`\ *n*. In programming, a value that is given to a variable, either at the beginning of an operation or before an expression is evaluated by a program. Until the operation is completed, a parameter is effectively treated as a constant value by the program. A parameter can be text, a number, or an argument name assigned to a value that is passed from one routine to another. Parameters are used as a means of customizing program operation. *See also* argument, pass by address, pass by value, routine.

parameter-driven \pər-am´ə-tər-driv`ən\ *adj*. Of, pertaining to, or being a program or an operation whose character or outcome is determined by the values of the parameters that are assigned to it.

parameter passing \pər-am´ə-tər pas`ēng\ *n*. In programming, the substitution of an actual parameter value for a formal parameter when a procedure or function call is processed.

parameter RAM \pər-am`ə-tər ram´, R-A-M´\ *n*. A few bytes of battery-backed CMOS RAM on the motherboards of Apple Macintosh computers. Information about the configuration of the system is stored in parameter RAM. *Acronym:* PRAM (P´ram, P`R-A-M´, pram). *See also* CMOS RAM. *Compare* CMOS (definition 2).

PARC \pärk, P`A-R-C´\ *n. See* Xerox PARC.

parent/child \pâr`ənt-chīld´\ *adj*. **1.** Pertaining to or constituting a relationship between processes in a multitasking environment in which the parent process calls the child process and most often suspends its own operation until the child process aborts or is completed. **2.** Pertaining to or constituting a relationship between nodes in a tree data structure in which the parent is one step closer to the root (that is, one level higher) than the child.

parity \pâr`ə-tē\ *n*. The quality of sameness or equivalence, in the case of computers usually referring to an error-checking procedure in which the number of 1s must always be the same—either even or odd—for each group of bits transmitted without error. If parity is checked on a per-character basis, the method is called vertical redundancy checking, or VRC; if checked on a block-by-block basis, the method is called longitudinal redundancy checking, or LRC. In typical modem-to-modem communications, parity is one of the parameters that must be agreed upon by sending and receiving parties before transmission can take place. Types of parity are shown in the following table. *See also* parity bit, parity check, parity error.

Type	Description
Even parity	The number of 1s in each successfully transmitted set of bits must be an even number.
Odd parity	The number of 1s in each successfully transmitted set of bits must be an odd number.
No parity	No parity bit is used.
Space parity	A parity bit is used and is always set to 0.
Mark parity	A parity bit is used and is always set to 1.

parity bit \pâr´ə-tē bit`\ *n.* An extra bit used in checking for errors in groups of data bits transferred within or between computer systems. With microcomputers, the term is frequently encountered in modem-to-modem communications, in which a parity bit is often used to check the accuracy with which each character is transmitted, and in RAM, where a parity bit is often used to check the accuracy with which each byte is stored.

parity check \pâr´ə-tē chek`\ *n.* The use of parity to check the accuracy of transmitted data. *See also* parity, parity bit.

parity error \pâr`ə-tē âr´ər\ *n.* An error in parity that indicates an error in transmitted data or in data stored in memory. If a parity error occurs in communications, all or part of a message must be retransmitted; if a parity error occurs in RAM, the computer usually halts. *See also* parity, parity bit.

park \pärk\ *vb.* To position the read/write head over a portion of a disk that stores no data (and therefore can never be damaged) or beyond the surface of the disk, prior to shutting down the drive, especially in preparation for moving it. Parking can be performed manually, automatically, or, most typically, by a disk utility program.

parse \pärs\ *vb.* To break input into smaller chunks so that a program can act upon the information.

partition \pär-ti´shən`\ *n.* **1.** A logically distinct portion of memory or a storage device that functions as though it were a physically separate unit. **2.** In database programming, a subset of a database table or file.

Pascal \pa-skal´\ *n.* A concise procedural language designed between 1967 and 1971 by Niklaus Wirth. Pascal, a compiled, structured language built upon ALGOL, simplifies syntax while adding data types and structures such as subranges, enumerated data types, files, records, and sets. *See also* ALGOL, compiled language. *Compare* C.

pass[1] \pas\ *n.* In programming, the carrying out of one complete sequence of events.

pass[2] \pas\ *vb.* To forward a piece of data from one part of a program to another. *See also* pass by address, pass by value.

pass by address \pas` bī a´dres, ə-dres`\ *n.* A means of passing an argument or parameter to a subroutine. The calling routine passes the address (memory location) of the parameter to the called routine, which can then use the address to retrieve or modify the value of the parameter. *Also called* pass by reference. *See also* argument, call[1]. *Compare* pass by value.

pass by reference \pas` bī ref´ər-əns, ref´rəns\ *n.* *See* pass by address.

pass by value \pas` bī val´yōō\ *n.* A means of passing an argument or a parameter to a subroutine. A copy of the value of the argument is created and passed to the called routine. When this method is used, the called routine can modify the copy of the argument, but it cannot modify the original argument. *See also* argument, call[1]. *Compare* pass by address.

passive-matrix display \pas`iv-mā´triks dis-plā`\ *n.* An inexpensive, low-resolution liquid crystal display (LCD) made from a large array of liquid crystal cells that are controlled by transistors outside of the display screen. One transistor controls an entire row or column of pixels. Passive-matrix displays are commonly used in portable computers, such as laptops and notebooks, because of their thin width. While these displays have good contrast for monochrome screens, the resolution is weaker for color screens. These displays are also difficult to view from any angle other than straight on, unlike active-matrix displays. However, computers with passive-matrix displays are considerably cheaper than those with active-matrix screens. See the illustration on the next page. *Also called* dual-scan display. *See also* liquid crystal display, transistor. *Compare* active-matrix display.

password \pas´wərd\ *n.* A security measure used to restrict access to computer systems and sensitive files. A password is a unique string of characters that a user types in as an identification code. The system compares the code against a stored list of authorized passwords and users. If the code is legitimate, the system allows the user access at whatever security level has been approved for the owner of the password.

Password Authentication Protocol \pas`wərd ä-then-tə-kā´shən prō`tə-kol, ô-then-tə-kā´shən\ *n.* *See* PAP (definition 1).

password protection \pas`wərd prō-tek´shən\ *n.* The use of passwords as a means of allowing only authorized users access to a computer system or its files.

paste \pāst\ *vb.* To insert text or a graphic that has been cut or copied from one document into a different location in the same or a different document. *See also* cut, cut and paste.

patch[1] \pach\ *n.* A piece of object code that is inserted in an executable program as a temporary fix of a bug.

patch[2] \pach\ *vb.* In programming, to repair a deficiency in the functionality of an existing routine or program, generally in response to an unforeseen need or set of operating circumstances. Patching is a common means of adding a feature or a function to a program until the next version of the software is released. *Compare* hack (definition 2), kludge (definition 2).

path \path\ *n.* **1.** In communications, a link between two nodes in a network. **2.** A route through a structured collection of information, as in a database, a program, or files stored on disk.

3. In programming, the sequence of instructions a computer carries out in executing a routine. **4.** In information processing, such as the theory underlying expert (deductive) systems, a logical course through the branches of a tree of inferences leading to a conclusion. **5.** In file storage, the route followed by the operating system through the directories in finding, sorting, and retrieving files on a disk. **6.** In graphics, an accumulation of line segments or curves to be filled or drawn. See the illustration.

path menu \path´ men`yoo\ *n.* In windows environments, the menu or drop box used to enter the universal naming convention path to a shared network resource.

pathname \path´nām\ *n.* In a hierarchical filing system, a listing of the directories or folders that lead from the current directory to a file. *Also called* directory path.

pattern recognition \pat´ərn rek-əg-nish`ən\ *n.* **1.** A broad technology describing the ability of a

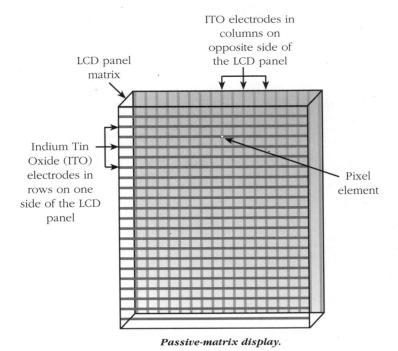

LCD panel matrix

ITO electrodes in columns on opposite side of the LCD panel

Indium Tin Oxide (ITO) electrodes in rows on one side of the LCD panel

Pixel element

Passive-matrix display.

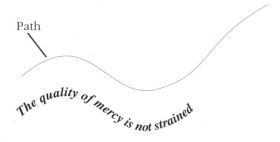

Path

The quality of mercy is not strained

Path.

computer to identify patterns. The term usually refers to computer recognition of visual images or sound patterns that have been converted to arrays of numbers. **2.** The recognition of purely mathematical or textual patterns.

Pause key \päz´ kē, pôz`\ *n.* **1.** A key on a keyboard that temporarily stops the operation of a program or a command. The Pause key is used, for example, to halt scrolling so that a multiscreen listing or document can be read. **2.** Any key that creates a pause in an operation. For example, many game programs have a Pause key, often simply the P key, that temporarily suspends the game.

PBX \P`B-X´\ *n.* Acronym for **P**rivate **B**ranch E**x**change. An automatic telephone switching system that enables users within an organization to place calls to each other without going through the public telephone network. Users can also place calls to outside numbers.

PC \P-C´\ *n.* **1.** A microcomputer that conforms to the standard developed by IBM for personal computers, which uses a microprocessor in the Intel 80x86 family (or compatible) and can execute the BIOS. *See also* 8086, BIOS, clone, IBM PC. **2.** A computer in IBM's Personal Computer line. *Also called* IBM PC. *See also* PC-compatible (definition 1). **3.** *See* personal computer.

PCB \P`C-B´\ *n. See* printed circuit board.

PC board \P-C´ bōrd`\ *n. See* printed circuit board.

PC Card \P-C´ kärd`\ *n.* A trademark of the Personal Computer Memory Card International Association (PCMCIA) that is used to describe add-in cards that conform to the PCMCIA specification. A PC Card is a removable device, approximately the same size as a credit card, that is designed to plug

into a PCMCIA slot. Release 1 of the PCMCIA specification, introduced in June 1990, specified a Type I card that is 3.3 millimeters thick and is intended to be used primarily as a memory-related peripheral. Release 2 of the PCMCIA specification, introduced in September 1991, specifies both a 5-millimeter-thick Type II card and a 10.5-millimeter-thick Type III card. Type II cards accommodate devices such as modem, fax, and network cards. Type III cards accommodate devices that require more space, such as wireless communications devices and rotating storage media (such as hard disks). *See also* PCMCIA, PCMCIA slot.

PC Card slot \P-C´ kärd´ slot`\ *n. See* PCMCIA slot.

PC-compatible \P-C´ kəm-pat´ə-bl\ *adj.* **1.** Conforming to IBM PC/XT and PC/AT hardware and software specifications, which have been the de facto standard in the computing industry for personal computers that use the Intel 80x86 family or compatible chips. Most PC-compatible computers today are developed outside of IBM; they are still sometimes referred to as clones. *Also called* IBM PC. *See also* 8086, clone, de facto standard, IBM AT. **2.** *See* Wintel.

PC-DOS \P-C`dos´, -D-O-S´\ *n.* Acronym for **P**ersonal **C**omputer **D**isk **O**perating **S**ystem. The version of MS-DOS sold by IBM. MS-DOS and PC-DOS are virtually identical, although filenames of utility programs sometimes differ in the two versions. *See also* MS-DOS.

P-channel MOS \P-chan`əl mos´, M-O-S´\ *n. See* PMOS.

PCI \P`C-I´\ *n. See* PCI local bus.

PCI local bus \P`C-I lō`kəl bus´\ *n.* Short for **P**eripheral **C**omponent **I**nterconnect **local bus.** A specification introduced by Intel Corporation that defines a local bus system that allows up to 10 PCI-compliant expansion cards to be installed in the computer. A PCI local bus system requires the presence of a PCI controller card, which must be installed in one of the PCI-compliant slots. Optionally, an expansion bus controller for the system's ISA, EISA, or Micro Channel Architecture slots can be installed as well, providing increased synchronization over all the system's bus-installed resources. The PCI controller can exchange data with the system's CPU either 32 bits or 64 bits at a time, depending on the implementation, and it allows intelligent, PCI-compliant adapters to perform tasks concurrently with the CPU using a technique called bus mastering. The PCI specification allows for multiplexing, a technique that permits more than one electrical signal to be present on the bus at one time. *See also* local bus. *Compare* VL bus.

PCL \P`C-L´\ *n. See* Printer Control Language.

PCM \P`C-M´\ *n. See* pulse code modulation.

PCMCIA \P`C-M`C-I-A´\ *n.* Acronym for **P**ersonal **C**omputer **M**emory **C**ard **I**nternational **A**ssociation. A group of manufacturers and vendors formed to promote a common standard for PC Card–based peripherals and the slot designed to hold them, primarily on laptop, palmtop, and other portable computers, as well as for intelligent electronic devices. PCMCIA is also the name of the standard for PC Cards, first introduced in 1990 as release 1. *See also* PC Card, PCMCIA slot.

PCMCIA card \P`C-M`C-I-A´ kärd`\ *n. See* PC card.

PCMCIA connector \P`C-M`C-I-A´ kə-nek`tər\ *n.* The 68-pin female connector inside a PCMCIA slot designed to hold the 68-pin male connector on a PC Card. *See also* PC Card, PCMCIA slot.

PCMCIA slot \P`C-M`C-I-A´ slot`\ *n.* An opening in the housing of a computer, peripheral, or other intelligent electronic device designed to hold a PC Card. *Also called* PC Card slot. *See also* PC Card, PCMCIA connector.

PC memory card \P-C` mem´ər-ē kärd`\ *n.* **1.** An add-in circuit card that increases the amount of RAM in a system. *See also* memory card. **2.** A Type I PC Card as specified by PCMCIA. In this context,

such a card consists of conventional static RAM chips powered by a small battery and is designed to provide additional RAM to the system. *See also* PC Card. *Compare* flash memory.

p-code \P´kōd\ *n. See* pseudocode.

PCT \P`C-T´\ *n.* Acronym for **p**rogram **c**omprehension **t**ool. A software engineering tool that facilitates the process of understanding the structure and/or functionality of computer programs.

.pcx \dot-P`C-X´\ *n.* The file extension that identifies bitmapped images in the PC Paintbrush file format.

PC/XT \P`C-X-T´\ *n.* The original IBM Personal Computer, introduced in 1981, which used the Intel 8088 CPU. *See also* IBM PC.

PC/XT keyboard \P`C-X-T´ kē`bōrd\ *n.* The original keyboard for the IBM Personal Computer. Strong, reliable, and equipped with 83 keys, the PC/XT keyboard offers a typist an audible click. See the illustration. *See also* IBM PC, PC/XT.

PDA \P`D-A´\ *n.* Acronym for **P**ersonal **D**igital **A**ssistant. A lightweight palmtop computer designed to provide specific functions like personal organization (calendar, note taking, database, calculator, and so on) as well as communications. More advanced models also offer multimedia features. Many PDA devices rely on a pen or other pointing device for input instead of a keyboard or mouse, although some offer a keyboard too small for touch typing to use in conjunction with a pen or pointing device. For data storage, a PDA relies on flash memory instead of power-hungry disk drives. *See also* firmware, flash memory, PC Card, pen computer.

PDC \P`D-C´\ *n. See* Primary Domain Controller.

PC/XT keyboard.

PD-CD drive \P`D-C-D´ drīv\ *n.* Short for **p**hase change rewritable **d**isc–compact **d**isc **drive.** A storage device that combines a CD-ROM drive and a phase change rewritable disc (PD) drive, which can store up to 650 megabytes of data on cartridges of rewritable optical discs. *See also* phase-change recording.

PDD \P`D-D´\ *n.* Acronym for **P**ortable **D**igital **D**ocument. A graphics file created from a document by QuickDraw GX under Mac OS. PDDs are stored in a form that is independent of printer resolution; they print at the highest resolution available on the printer used; and they can contain the original fonts used in the document. Therefore, a PDD can be printed by a computer other than the one on which it was created.

.pdf \dot`P-D-F´\ *n.* The file extension that identifies documents encoded in the Portable Document Format developed by Adobe Systems. In order to display or print a .pdf file, the user should obtain the freeware Adobe Acrobat Reader. *See also* Acrobat, Portable Document Format.

PDL \P`D-L´\ *n. See* page-description language.

PDM \P`D-M´\ *n. See* pulse duration modulation.

PDO \P`D-O´\ *n. See* Portable Distributed Objects.

PDS \P`D-S´\ *n.* **1.** Acronym for **P**rocessor **D**irect **S**lot. An expansion slot in Macintosh computers that is connected directly to the CPU signals. There are several kinds of PDS slots with different numbers of pins and different sets of signals, depending on which CPU is used in a particular computer. **2.** Acronym for **P**arallel **D**ata **S**tructure. A hidden file, located in the root directory of a disk that is shared under AppleShare, that contains access privilege information for folders.

.pe \dot`P-E´\ *n.* On the Internet, the major geographic domain specifying that an address is located in Peru.

.pe.ca \dot-P-E`dot-C-A´\ *n.* On the Internet, the major geographic domain specifying that an address is located on Prince Edward Island, Canada.

peek \pēk\ *vb.* **1.** To read a byte from an absolute memory location. Peek commands are often found in programming languages such as Basic that do not normally allow access to specific memory locations. **2.** To look at the next character in a buffer associated with an input device without actually removing the character from the buffer.

peer \pēr\ *n.* Any of the devices on a layered communications network that operate on the same protocol level. *See also* network architecture.

peer-to-peer architecture \pēr`tə-pēr` är´kə-tek-chur\ *n.* A network of two or more computers that use the same program or type of program to communicate and share data. Each computer, or *peer,* is considered equal in terms of responsibilities and each acts as a server to the others in the network. Unlike a client/server architecture, a dedicated file server is not required. However, network performance is generally not as good as under client/server, especially under heavy loads. *Also called* peer-to-peer network. *See also* peer, peer-to-peer communications, server. *Compare* client/server architecture.

peer-to-peer communications \pēr`-tə-pēr` kə-myōō-nə-kā´shənz\ *n.* Interaction between devices that operate on the same communications level on a network based on a layered architecture. *See also* network architecture.

peer-to-peer network \pēr`tə-pēr` net´wərk\ *n. See* peer-to-peer architecture.

pel \pel\ *n.* Short for **p**icture **el**ement. *See* pixel.

PEM \P`E-M´\ *n. See* Privacy-Enhanced Mail.

pen \pen\ *n. See* light pen, stylus.

pen-based computing \pen`bāsd kəm-pyōō´tēng\ *n.* The process of entering handwritten symbols into a computer via a stylus and pressure-sensitive pad. *See also* pen computer.

pen computer \pen´ kəm-pyōō`tər\ *n.* Any of a class of computers whose primary input device is a pen (stylus) instead of a keyboard. A pen computer is usually a smaller, handheld device and has a flat semiconductor-based display such as an LCD display. It requires either a special operating system designed to work with the pen input device or a proprietary operating system designed to work with a specific-purpose device. The pen computer is the primary model for an emerging class of computers known as personal digital assistants (PDAs). *See also* clipboard computer, PC Card, PDA.

pen plotter \pen´ plot`ər\ *n.* A traditional graphics plotter that uses pens to draw on paper. Pen plotters use one or more colored pens, either fiber-tipped pens or, for highest-quality output, drafting pens. *See also* plotter. *Compare* electrostatic plotter.

Pentium \pen´tē-um\ *n.* A microprocessor introduced by Intel Corporation in March 1993 as the successor to the i486. The Pentium is a superscalar, CISC-based microprocessor containing 3.3 million transistors. The Pentium has a 32-bit address bus, a 64-bit data bus, a built-in floating-point unit and memory management unit, two built-in 8-KB L1 caches, and a System Management Mode (SMM), which provides the microprocessor with the ability to slow or halt some system components when the system is idle or performing non-CPU-intensive tasks, thereby lessening power consumption. The Pentium also employs *branch prediction,* resulting in faster system performance. In addition, the Pentium has some built-in features to ensure data integrity, and it supports functional redundancy checking (FRC). *See also* branch prediction, CISC, functional redundancy checking, i486DX, L1 cache, microprocessor, P5, superscalar. *Compare* Pentium Pro (definition 1).

Pentium Pro \pen`tē-um prō´\ *n.* **1.** Intel's 150–200 MHz family of 32-bit processors, released in November 1995. The Pentium Pro is considered the next generation of processors in the 8086 family, following the Pentium, and is designed for running 32-bit operating systems and applications. *See also* 32-bit application, 32-bit operating system, 8086, microprocessor, Pentium. **2.** A PC that has a Pentium Pro processor.

Pentium upgradable \pen`tē-um up-grā´də-bl\ *n.* **1.** An i486 motherboard capable of being adapted to run a Pentium-class processor. *See also* i486DX, microprocessor, motherboard, Pentium. **2.** A 486 PC that can be upgraded to Pentium class by adding a Pentium processor. *See also* i486DX.

perfboard \pərf´bōrd\ *n.* Short for **perf**orated fiber **board.** *See* breadboard.

performance monitor \pər-fōr´məns mon´ə-tər\ *n.* A process or program that appraises and records status information about various system devices and other processes.

period \pēr´ē-əd`\ *n.* The length of time required for an oscillation to complete one full cycle. For an oscillating electrical signal, the period is the time between waveform repetitions. If f is the frequency of oscillation in hertz, and t is the period in seconds, then $t = 1/f$. See the illustration.

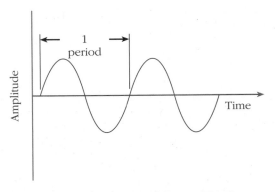

Period. **The period of an oscillating signal.**

peripheral \pər-if´ər-əl\ *n.* In computing, a device, such as a disk drive, printer, modem, or joystick, that is connected to a computer and is controlled by the computer's microprocessor. *Also called* peripheral device. *See also* console.

Peripheral Component Interconnect \pər-if´ər-əl kəm-pō`nənt in`tər-kə-nekt´\ *n. See* PCI local bus.

peripheral device \pər-if´ər-əl dē-vīs´\ *n. See* peripheral.

peripheral power supply \pər-if`ər-əl pou´ər su-plī´\ *n.* An auxiliary source of electricity used by a computer or a device as a backup in case of a power failure. *Acronym:* PPS (P`P-S´).

Perl \pərl\ *n.* Acronym for **P**ractical **E**xtraction and **R**eport **L**anguage. An interpreted language, based on C and several UNIX utilities. Perl has powerful string-handling features for extracting information from text files. Perl can assemble a string and send it to the shell as a command; hence, it is often used for system administration tasks. A program in Perl is known as a script. Perl was devised by Larry Wall at NASA's Jet Propulsion Laboratory.

permanent storage \pər´mə-nənt stōr´əj\ *n.* A recording medium that retains the data recorded on it for long periods of time without power. Ink on paper is by far the most widely used permanent storage, but data can be transferred from paper to a computer only with difficulty. Typically, some form of magnetic medium, such as floppy disk or tape, is preferable. Magnetic media are generally accepted as permanent, even though the magnetic fields that encode data in the media tend to fade eventually (in five years or more). *See also* nonvolatile memory.

permanent swap file \pər`mə-nənt swäp´ fīl\ *n.* In Windows, a file composed of contiguous disk sectors used for virtual memory operations. *See also* swap file, virtual memory.

permanent virtual circuit \pər`mə-nənt vər`-chōō-əl sər´kət\ *n. See* PVC.

permission \pər-mish´ən\ *n.* In a networked or multiuser computer environment, the ability of a particular user to access a particular resource by means of his or her user account. Permissions are granted by the system administrator or other authorized person; these permissions are stored in the system (often in a file called a *permissions log*) and are checked when a user attempts to access a resource.

perpendicular recording \pər-pən-dik`yə-lər rə-kōr´dēng\ *n.* A method of increasing storage capacity on magnetic media by aligning the magnetic dipoles, whose orientation determines bit values, in a direction that is perpendicular to the recording surface. *Also called* vertical recording.

persistence \pər-si´stəns\ *n.* A characteristic of some light-emitting materials, such as the phosphors used in CRTs, that causes an image to be retained for a short while after being irradiated, as by an electron beam in a CRT. The decay in persistence is sometimes called *luminance decay.*

persistent data \pər-si`stənt dā´tə, dat´ə\ *n.* Data that is stored in a database or on tape so that it is retained by the computer between sessions.

persistent link \pər-si`stənt lēnk´\ *n. See* hot link (definition 1).

persistent storage \pər-si`stənt stōr´əj\ *n.* Memory that remains intact when the power to a device is turned off, such as ROM. *See also* memory.

personal computer \pər`sə-nəl kəm-pyōō´tər\ *n.* A computer designed for use by one person at a time. Personal computers do not need to share the processing, disk, and printer resources of another computer. IBM PC-compatible computers and Apple Macintoshes are both examples of personal computers. *Acronym:* PC (P-C´).

Personal Computer \pər`sə-nəl kəm-pyōō´tər\ *n. See* IBM PC.

Personal Computer Memory Card International Association \pər`sən-əl kəm-pyōō-tər mem`ər-ē kärd in-tər-nash`ə-nəl ə-sō`sē-ā´shən\ *n. See* PCMCIA.

personal digital assistant \pər`sə-nəl dij`i-təl ə-si´stənt\ *n. See* PDA.

personal finance manager \pər`sə-nəl fī´nans man`ə-jər\ *n.* A software application designed to assist the user in performing simple financial accounting tasks, such as balancing checkbooks and paying bills.

personal information manager \pər`sə-nəl in-fər-mā´shən man`ə-jər\ *n. See* PIM.

perspective view \pər-spek`tiv vyōō´\ *n.* In computer graphics, a display method that shows objects in three dimensions (height, width, and depth), with the depth aspect rendered according to the desired perspective. An advantage of perspective view is that it presents a more accurate representation of what the human eye perceives. *Compare* isometric view.

peta- \pet´ə\ *prefix* Abbreviated P. Denotes 1 quadrillion (10^{15}). In computing, which is based on the binary (base-2) numbering system, *peta-* has a literal value of 1,125,899,906,842,624, which is the power of 2 (2^{50}) closest to 1 quadrillion.

petabyte \pet´ə-bīt\ *n.* Abbreviated PB. Either 1 quadrillion bytes or 1,125,899,906,842,624 bytes.

.pg \dot`P-G´\ *n.* On the Internet, the major geographic domain specifying that an address is located in Papua New Guinea.

PGA \P`G-A´\ *n. See* pin grid array, Professional Graphics Adapter.

PgDn key \pāj-doun´ kē`\ *n. See* Page Down key.

PGP \P`G-P´\ *n.* Acronym for **P**retty **G**ood **P**rivacy. A program for public key encryption, using the RSA algorithm, developed by Philip Zimmermann. PGP software is available in unsupported free versions and supported commercial versions. *See also* privacy, public key encryption, RSA encryption.

PgUp key \pāj-up´ kē`\ *n. See* Page Up key.

.ph \dot`P-H´\ *n.* On the Internet, the major geographic domain specifying that an address is located in the Philippines.

phase \fāz\ *n.* A relative measurement that describes the temporal relationship between two signals that have the same frequency. Phase is measured in degrees, with one full oscillation cycle having 360 degrees. The phase of one signal can lead or follow the other by 0 through 180 degrees. See the illustration.

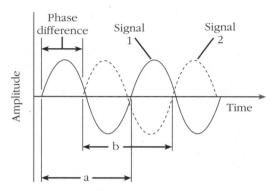

Phase. *The ratio of* **a** *to* **b** *is the phase difference, expressed in degrees.*

phase-change recording \fāz´chānj rə-kōr`dēng\ *n.* In optical media, a recording technique that uses a laser beam focused on a microscopic portion of metallic crystal to alter the reflectiveness of its structure in such a way that the change can be read as a 0 bit or 1 bit, depending on whether the resulting structure reflects or absorbs the laser light. *See also* PD-CD drive.

phase encoding \fāz´ en-kō`dēng\ *n.* **1.** The process of placing digital information on an analog carrier wave while periodically changing the phase of the carrier, in order to increase the bit density of the transmission. *See also* Manchester coding, phase. **2.** A recording technique used with magnetic storage devices in which each data-holding unit is divided into two parts, each of which is magnetized so that it is opposite in polarity to the other.

phase-locked \fāz´lokd\ *adj.* Of, pertaining to, or characteristic of the relationship between two signals whose phases relative to each other are kept constant by a controlling mechanism, such as an electronic device.

phase modulation \fāz´ moj-ə-lā`shən, mo-dyə-lā`shən\ *n.* A method of imposing information onto a waveform signal by shifting the phase of the wave to represent information, such as the binary digits 0 and 1. See the illustration. *See also* phase-shift keying.

phase-shift keying \fāz´shift kē`ēng\ *n.* A communications method used by modems to encode data that relies on phase shifts in a carrier wave to represent digital information. In its simplest form, phase-shift keying allows the phase of the carrier wave to be in either of two states: shifted 0 degrees or shifted 180 degrees, effectively reversing the phase of the wave. This straightforward phase-shift keying, however, is useful only when each phase can be measured against an unchanging reference value, so a more sophisticated technique called *differential phase-shift keying,* or *DPSK,* is used in many modems. In differential phase-shift keying, the phase of the carrier wave is shifted to represent

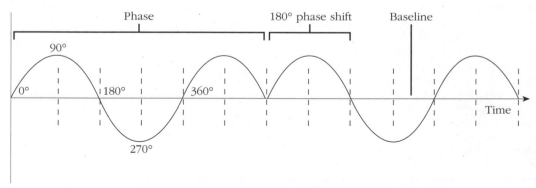

Phase modulation. *A phase shift of 180 degrees.*

more than two possible states, and each state is interpreted as a relative change from the state preceding it. No reference values or timing considerations are required, and because more than two states are possible, more than one binary digit can represent each state. *Acronym:* PSK (P`S-K´). *See also* phase modulation.

Phoenix BIOS \fē`niks bī´ōs, B-I-O-S´\ *n.* An IBM-compatible ROM BIOS manufactured by Phoenix Technologies, Ltd. A popular ROM BIOS in many so-called PC "clone" computers, the Phoenix BIOS was an early leader among the IBM-compatible computers shortly after they began to appear in the marketplace. *See also* BIOS, ROM BIOS. *Compare* AMI BIOS.

phone connector \fōn´ kə-nek`tər\ *n.* An attachment, usually an RJ-11 connector, used to join a telephone line to a device such as a modem. See the illustration.

Phone connector.

phoneme \fō´nēm\ *n.* In linguistics, the smallest unit of speech that distinguishes one word sound from another. Phonemes are the elements on which computer speech is based.

phono connector \fō´nō kə-nek`tər\ *n.* An attachment used to connect a device, such as a microphone or a pair of headphones, to a piece of audio equipment or to a computer peripheral or adapter with audio capability. See the illustration.

Phono connector.

phosphor \fos´fōr\ *n.* Any substance capable of emitting light when struck by radiation. The inside surface of a CRT screen is coated with a phosphor that, when excited by an electron beam, displays an image on the screen. *See also* persistence.

PhotoCD \fō`tō-C-D´\ *n.* A digitizing system from Kodak that allows 35mm film pictures, negatives,

slides, and scanned images to be stored on a compact disc. Images are stored in a file format called Kodak PhotoCD IMAGE PAC File Format, or PCD. Many photography or film development businesses offer this service. Images stored on a PhotoCD can usually be viewed by any computer with CD-ROM capabilities and the software required to read PCD. Such images can also be viewed using one of a variety of players designed to display images stored on CDs.

photo cell \fō´tō sel`\ *n. See* photoelectric device.

photocomposition \fō`tō-kom-pə-zish´ən\ *n.* In traditional typesetting, the use of photographic and electronic equipment in laying out and producing a printed page. In desktop publishing, phototypesetters are used to accomplish the same ends. *See also* phototypesetter. *Compare* imagesetter.

photoconductor \fō`tō-kən-duk`tər\ *n.* A material that exhibits increased conductivity when it is exposed to a source of light. Photoconductors are used in photodetectors, which are used in fiber optics to register light and convert it into electrical pulses. *See also* fiber optics.

photo editor \fō´tō ed`ə-tər\ *n.* A graphics application used to manipulate an image, such as a scanned photograph, digitally.

photoelectric device \fō`tō-i-lek´trik də-vīs`\ *n.* A device that uses light to create or modulate an electric signal. A photoelectric device uses semiconductor material and falls in one of two categories. In one type (photocell), light falling on the semiconductor generates an electrical current. In another type of device (photosensor), light changes the resistance of the semiconductor material, modulating an applied voltage.

photolithography \fō`tō-li-thō´grə-fē\ *n.* A technique used in the fabrication of integrated circuits. The circuit pattern is drawn, photographed, and reduced to a negative having the desired final size. This negative is called the *photomask*. Light is passed through the photomask onto a wafer made of semiconductor material that has been coated with a photoresistive material. Where light strikes the photoresistive material, its composition is changed. In the next step, the photoresistive material not affected by light is washed off. Finally, the semiconductor material is exposed to an etching solution that eats away the surface not protected by the photoresistive material, creating the desired circuit pattern on the surface of the wafer. *See also* photomask, photoresist.

photomask \fō´tō-mask`\ *n.* A photographic negative image of a circuit pattern used in fabrication of integrated circuits. *See also* photolithography.

photorealism \fō`tō-rē´ə-liz`əm\ *n.* The process of creating images that are as close to photographic or "real-life" quality as possible. In computer graphics, photorealism requires powerful computers and highly sophisticated software and is heavily mathematical. *See also* ray tracing.

photoresist \fō`tō-rē-zist`\ *n.* A compound that is used in photolithographic fabrication of integrated circuits and printed circuit boards. When exposed to ultraviolet light through a photomask, the photoresistive material exposed to the light polymerizes (hardens); the areas not exposed can be washed away, leaving the pattern of traces on the substrate. Subsequent etching removes areas not protected by the polymerized photoresist.

photosensor \fō`tō-sen`sər\ *n. See* photoelectric device.

phototypesetter \fō`tō-tīp´set-ər\ *n.* A printer similar to a laser printer but capable of resolutions over 2,000 dots per inch. Phototypesetters apply light directly to a photographic film or photosensitive paper. *See also* photocomposition. *Compare* imagesetter.

photovoltaic cell \fō`tō-vōl-tā´ik sel´\ *n. See* solar cell.

phreak[1] \frēk\ *n.* A person who breaks into, or *cracks,* telephone networks or other secured systems. In the 1970s, the telephone system used audible tones as switching signals, and *phone phreaks* used homebrew hardware to match the tones and steal long-distance service. *See also* homebrew. *Compare* cracker, hacker (definition 2).

phreak[2] \frēk\ *vb.* To break into, or *crack,* phone networks or computer systems. *See also* homebrew. *Compare* hack.

physical \fiz´i-kəl`\ *adj.* In computing, of, pertaining to, or characteristic of a real, as opposed to a conceptual, piece of equipment or frame of reference. *Compare* logical (definition 2).

physical address \fiz`i-kəl a´dres, ə-dres´\ *n.* An address that corresponds to a hardware memory location. In simple processors such as the 8088 and the 68000, every address is a physical address. In processors supporting virtual memory, programs reference virtual addresses, which are then mapped by memory management hardware onto physical addresses. *See also* memory management unit, paging, virtual memory.

physical-image file \fiz`i-kəl-im´əj fīl\ *n.* A hard disk copy of the material to be recorded onto a CD-ROM. Creating a complete copy precludes problems in writing the CD-ROM because of delays in assembling the material from a scattered group of files. *See also* CD-ROM. *Compare* virtual-image file.

physical layer \fiz´i-kəl lâr`, lā`ər\ *n.* The first, or lowest, of the seven layers in the International Organization for Standardization's Open Systems Interconnection (OSI) model for standardizing computer-to-computer communications. The physical layer is totally hardware-oriented and deals with all aspects of establishing and maintaining a physical link between communicating computers. Among specifications covered on the physical layer are cabling, electrical signals, and mechanical connections. *See also* ISO/OSI model.

physical memory \fiz´i-kəl mem´ər-ē\ *n.* Memory actually present in the system, as opposed to virtual memory. A computer might have only 4 megabytes of physical RAM but support a virtual memory capacity of 20 MB. *Compare* virtual memory.

physical storage \fiz`i-kəl stōr´əj\ *n. See* real storage.

PIC \P`I-C´\ *n. See* programmable interrupt controller.

pica \pī´kə\ *n.* **1.** With reference to typewriters, a fixed-width type font that fits 10 characters to the linear inch. *See also* pitch (definition 1). **2.** As used by typographers, a unit of measure equal to 12 points or approximately 1/6 inch. *See also* point[1] (definition 1).

pico- \pē`kō\ *prefix* Abbreviated p. Denotes one trillionth (10^{-12}), or, in the British numbering system, one million millionth.

picoJava \pē`kō-jä`və\ *n.* A microprocessor developed by Sun Microsystems, Inc., that executes Java code. *See also* Java.

picosecond \pē´kō-sek`ənd\ *n.* Abbreviated psec. One trillionth of a second.

PICS \piks, P`I-C-S`\ *n.* Acronym for **P**latform for **I**nternet **C**ontent **S**election. A standard for enabling users to filter their Web access automatically using software (such as Internet Explorer 3.0) that detects codes for ratings in the sites' HTML files. In addition to filtering out undesirable material, PICS can be used to screen sites according to whether they contain material of interest. Several rating systems, emphasizing different sets of criteria, are in use.

.pict \dot-pikt´\ *n.* The file extension that identifies graphic images in the Macintosh PICT format. *See also* PICT.

PICT \pikt\ *n.* A file-format standard for encoding graphical images, both object-oriented and bitmapped. The PICT file format was first used in Apple Macintosh applications, but many IBM PC-compatible applications can read the format too. *See also* bitmapped graphics, object-oriented graphics.

picture element \pik´chur el`ə-mənt\ *n. See* pixel.

pie chart \pī´chärt\ *n.* A type of graph that presents values as percentages (slices) of a whole (a pie).

piezoelectric \pē-ā`zō-ə-lek´trik, pē-āt`sō-ə-lek´trik\ *adj.* Of, pertaining to, or characteristic of crystals that can convert between mechanical and electrical energy. An electric potential applied to a piezoelectric crystal causes a small change in the shape of the crystal. Likewise, physical pressure applied to the crystal creates an electrical potential difference between the surfaces of the crystal.

piggyback board \pig´ē-bak bōrd`\ *n.* A printed circuit board that plugs into another circuit board to enhance its capabilities. A piggyback board is sometimes used to replace a single chip, in which case the chip is removed and the piggyback board is inserted into the empty socket. *See also* daughterboard.

PILOT \pī´lət, P`IL`O-T`\ *n.* Acronym for **P**rogrammed **I**nquiry, **L**earning **o**r **T**eaching. A programming language developed in 1976 by John A. Starkweather and designed primarily for creating applications for computer-aided instruction.

PIM \P`I-M´\ *n.* Acronym for **p**ersonal **i**nformation **m**anager. An application that usually includes an address book and organizes unrelated informa-

tion, such as notes, appointments, and names, in a useful way.

pin \pin\ *n.* A slender prong. Pins are commonly encountered as the contacts protruding from a male connector. Connectors are often identified by the number of pins they have. Other types of pins are the spidery, leglike metal appendages that connect computer chips to sockets on a circuit board or directly to the circuit board. See the illustration.

Pin

Pin

Pin. *A 14-pin DIP (top) and a 5-pin DIN (bottom).*

PIN \pin\ *n.* Acronym for **p**ersonal **i**dentification **n**umber. A unique code number assigned, as with automatic teller machine cards, to the authorized user.

pinch roller \pinch´ rō´lər\ *n.* A small cylindrical pulley that presses magnetic tape against the drive's capstan to move the tape over the tape machine's heads. See the illustration. *See also* capstan.

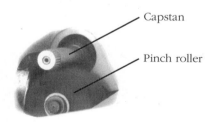

Capstan

Pinch roller

Pinch roller.

pinch-roller plotter \pinch´rō-lər plot`ər\ *n.* A type of plotter, intermediate between drum and flatbed types, that uses hard rubber or metal wheels to hold the paper against the main roller. *See also* plotter. *Compare* drum plotter, flatbed plotter.

pin-compatible \pin´kəm-pat`ə-bl\ *adj.* Having pins that are equivalent to the pins on another chip or device. A chip, for example, might have different internal circuitry from that used in another chip, but if the two chips use the same pins for input and output of identical signals, they are pin-compatible. *Compare* plug-compatible.

pine \pīn\ *n.* Acronym for **p**ine **i**s **n**ot **e**lm, or for **P**rogram for **I**nternet **N**ews and **E**-mail. One of the most commonly encountered programs for reading and composing e-mail on character-based UNIX systems. The pine program was developed as an improved version of elm at the University of Washington. *Compare* elm.

pin feed \pin´ fēd\ *n.* A method of feeding paper through a printer in which small pins, mounted on rollers on the ends of the platen, engage holes near the edges of continuous-form paper. See the illustration. *See also* continuous-form paper, paper feed. *Compare* tractor feed.

ping[1] \ping\ *n.* **1.** Acronym for **P**acket **In**ternet **G**roper. A protocol for testing whether a particular computer is connected to the Internet by sending a packet to its IP address and waiting for a response. The name actually comes from submarine active sonar, where a sound signal— called a "ping"—is broadcast, and surrounding objects are revealed by their reflections of the sound. **2.** A UNIX utility that implements the ping protocol.

ping[2] \ping\ *vb.* **1.** To test whether a computer is connected to the Internet using the ping utility. **2.** To test which users on a mailing list are current by sending e-mail to the list asking for a response.

Ping of Death \pēng` əv deth´\ *n.* A form of Internet vandalism that entails sending a packet that is substantially larger than the usual 64 bytes over the Internet via the ping protocol to a remote computer. The size of the packet causes the computer to crash or reboot. *See also* packet (definition 2), ping[1] (definition 1).

ping pong \pēng´ pong\ *n.* **1.** In communications, a technique that changes the direction of transmission so that the sender becomes the receiver and vice versa. **2.** In information processing and transfer, the technique of using two temporary storage areas (buffers) rather than one to hold both input and output.

ping-pong buffer \pēng´pong buf`ər\ *n.* A double buffer in which each part is alternately filled and flushed, resulting in a more or less continuous stream of input and output data. *See also* ping pong (definition 2).

pin grid array \pin´ grid ər-ā`\ *n.* A method of mounting chips on boards, preferred for chips with a very large number of pins. Pin grid array packages have pins protruding from the bottom surface of the chip, as opposed to dual in-line packages and leaderless chip carrier packages, which have pins protruding from the edges. See the illustration. *Acronym:* PGA (P`G-A´). *Compare* DIP, leadless chip carrier.

pinout \pin´out\ *n.* A description or diagram of the pins of a chip or connector. *See also* pin.

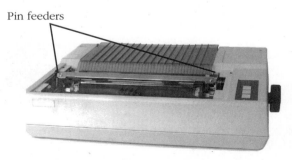

Pin feeders

Pin feed. Pin feeders on a dot-matrix printer.

Pin grid array. The pin grid array on the back of a Pentium chip.

pipe \pīp\ *n.* **1.** A portion of memory that can be used by one process to pass information along to another. Essentially, a pipe works like its name-sake: it connects two processes so that the output of one can be used as the input to the other. *See also* input stream, output stream. **2.** The vertical line character (|) that appears on a PC keyboard as the shift character on the backslash (\) key. **3.** In UNIX, a command function that transfers the output of one command to the input of a second command.

pipeline processing \pīp´līn pros`es-ēng\ *n.* A method of processing on a computer that allows fast parallel processing of data. This is accomplished by overlapping operations using a *pipe,* or a portion of memory that passes information from one process to another. *See also* parallel processing, pipe (definition 1), pipelining (definition 3).

pipelining \pīp´lī¯nēng\ *n.* **1.** A method of fetching and decoding instructions (preprocessing) in which, at any given time, several program instructions are in various stages of being fetched or decoded. Ideally, pipelining speeds execution time by ensuring that the microprocessor does not have to wait for instructions; when it completes execution of one instruction, the next is ready and waiting. *See also* superpipelining. **2.** In parallel processing, a method in which instructions are passed from one processing unit to another, as on an assembly line, and each unit is specialized for performing a particular type of operation. **3.** The use of pipes in passing the output of one task as input to another until a desired sequence of tasks has been carried out. *See also* pipe (definition 1), pour.

piracy \pīr´ə-sē\ *n.* **1.** The theft of a computer design or program. **2.** Unauthorized distribution and use of a computer program.

.pit \dot-pit´, dot`P-I-T´\ *n.* A file extension for an archive file compressed with PackIT. *See also* PackIT.

pitch \pich\ *n.* **1.** A measure, generally used with monospace fonts, that describes the number of characters that fit in a horizontal inch. *See also* characters per inch. *Compare* point[1] (definition 1). **2.** *See* screen pitch.

pixel \piks´əl\ *n.* Short for picture (**pix**) **el**ement. One spot in a rectilinear grid of thousands of such spots that are individually "painted" to form an image produced on the screen by a computer or on paper by a printer. A pixel is the smallest element that display or print hardware and software can manipulate in creating letters, numbers, or graphics. See the illustrations. *Also called* pel.

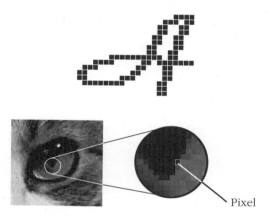

Pixel

Pixel. The letter A (top) is actually made up of a pattern of pixels in a grid, as is the cat's eye (bottom).

pixel image \piks´əl im`əj\ *n.* The representation of a color graphic in a computer's memory. A pixel image is similar to a bit image, which also describes a screen graphic, but a pixel image has an added dimension, sometimes called depth, that describes the number of bits in memory assigned to each on-screen pixel.

pixel map \piks´əl map`\ *n.* A data structure that describes the pixel image of a graphic, including such features as color, image, resolution, dimensions, storage format, and number of bits used to describe each pixel. *See also* pixel, pixel image.

PJ/NF \P`J-N-F´\ *n.* Acronym for **p**rojection-**j**oin **n**ormal **f**orm. *See* normal form (definition 1).

.pk \dot`P-K´\ *n.* On the Internet, the major geographic domain specifying that an address is located in Pakistan.

PKUNZIP \P`K-un-zip´\ *n.* A shareware utility program that uncompresses files compressed by the PKZIP shareware utility program. PKUNZIP is generally made available with PKZIP; distribution of PKUNZIP for commercial purposes is not permitted without obtaining permission from its publisher, PKware, Inc. *See also* PKZIP.

PKZIP \P`K-zip´\ *n.* A widely used shareware utility program for compressing files. Developed by PKware, Inc., in 1989 and available from a wide variety of sources, PKZIP can combine one or more files into a compressed output file having the extension .zip. A companion utility program, PKUNZIP, is required to uncompress the compressed files. *See also* PKUNZIP, shareware, utility program.

.pl \dot`P-L´\ *n.* On the Internet, the major geographic domain specifying that an address is located in Poland.

PLA \P`L-A´\ *n.* Acronym for **p**rogrammable **l**ogic **a**rray. *See* field-programmable logic array.

Plain Old Telephone Service \plān` old tel´ə-fōn sər-vəs\ *n.* *See* POTS.

plaintext \plān´tekst\ *n.* **1.** Nonencrypted or decrypted text. *See also* decryption, encryption. **2.** A file that is stored as plain ASCII data.

plain vanilla \plān´ və-nil`ə\ *adj.* Ordinary; the standard version of hardware or software without any enhancements. For example, a plain vanilla modem might have data transfer capability but no fax or voice features.

.plan \dot-plan´\ *n.* A file in a UNIX user's home directory that is displayed when other users finger that account. Users can enter information into .plan files at their discretion to provide information in addition to that normally displayed by the finger command. *See also* finger.

planar \plā´nər\ *adj.* **1.** In computer graphics, lying within a plane. **2.** In the fabrication of semiconductor materials, maintaining the original flat surface of the silicon wafer throughout processing, while the chemicals that make up the elements

that control the flow of current are diffused into (and beneath) the surface.

planar transistor \plā`nər tran-zis´tər\ *n.* A special form of transistor that is fabricated with all three elements (collector, emitter, and base) on a single layer of semiconductor material. The structure of a planar transistor permits it to dissipate relatively large amounts of heat, making this design suitable for power transistors. See the illustration.

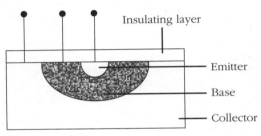

Planar transistor.

plasma display \plaz´mə dis-plā`\ *n.* *See* gas-discharge display.

plastic leadless chip carrier \plas`tik lēd`-ləs chip´ kâr-ē-ər\ *n.* *See* PLCC.

platen \plat´ən\ *n.* The cylinder in most impact printers and typewriters, around which the paper wraps and against which the print mechanism strikes the paper. The paper bail, a spring-loaded bar with small rollers, holds the paper smoothly against the platen just above the print mechanism. See the illustration.

platform \plat´fōrm\ *n.* **1.** The foundation technology of a computer system. Because computers are layered devices composed of a chip-level hardware layer, a firmware and operating-system layer, and an applications program layer, the bottommost layer of a machine is often called a platform. **2.** In everyday usage, the type of computer or operating system being used.

Platform for Internet Content Selection \plat`-fōrm fər in`tər-net kon´tent sə-lek`shən\ *n.* *See* PICS.

platter \plat´ər\ *n.* One of the individual metal data storage disks within a hard disk drive. Most hard disks have from two to eight platters. See the illustration. *See also* hard disk.

Platter. Two platters mounted on a hub.

PL/C \P`L-C´\ *n.* A version of the PL/I programming language developed at Cornell University and used on mainframe computers. *See also* PL/I.

PLCC \P`L-C-C´\ *n.* Acronym for **p**lastic **l**eadless **c**hip **c**arrier. An inexpensive variation of the leadless chip carrier (LCC) method of mounting chips on boards. Although the two carriers are similar in appearance, PLCCs are physically incompatible with leadless chip carriers, which are made from a ceramic material. See the illustration. *See also* leadless chip carrier.

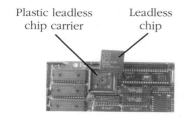

PLCC.

PLD \P`L-D´\ *n. See* programmable logic device.

PL/I \P`L-wən´\ *n.* Acronym for **P**rogramming **L**anguage **I** (One). A programming language developed by IBM (1964–1969), designed to bring together the key features of FORTRAN, COBOL, and ALGOL while introducing such new concepts as condition-based error handling and multitasking. The result of this effort was a compiled, structured language that was so complex that it never gained widespread acceptance. Nevertheless, PL/I is still used in some academic and research environments. *See also* ALGOL, COBOL, compiled language, FORTRAN.

PL/M \P`L-M´\ *n.* Acronym for **P**rogramming **L**anguage for **M**icrocomputers. A programming language derived from PL/I and developed in the early 1970s by Intel Corporation for microprocessors. PL/M was used primarily for the creation of operating systems. *See also* PL/I.

plot \plot\ *vb.* To create a graphic or a diagram by connecting points representing variables (values) that are defined by their positions in relation to a horizontal (x) axis and a vertical (y) axis (and sometimes a depth, or z, axis).

plotter \plot´ər\ *n.* Any device used to draw charts, diagrams, and other line-based graphics. Plotters use either pens or electrostatic charges and toner. Pen plotters draw on paper or transparencies with one or more colored pens. Electrostatic plotters "draw" a pattern on electrostatically charged dots on the paper and then apply toner and fuse it in place. Plotters use three basic types of paper handling: flatbed, drum, and pinch roller. Flatbed plotters hold the paper still and move the pen along both x and y axes. Drum plotters roll the paper over a cylinder. The pen moves along one axis while the drum, with the paper attached, moves along the other. Pinch-roller plotters are a hybrid of the two, in which the pen moves only along one axis

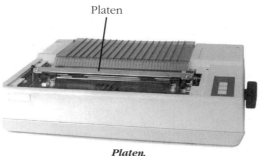

Platen.

while the paper is moved back and forth by small rollers.

Plug and Play \plug` ənd plā´\ *n.* A set of specifications developed by Intel that allows a PC to configure itself automatically to work with peripherals such as monitors, modems, and printers. A user can "plug" in a peripheral and "play" it without manually configuring the system. A Plug and Play PC requires both a BIOS that supports Plug and Play and a Plug and Play expansion card. *See also* BIOS, expansion board, peripheral.

plugboard \plug´bōrd\ *n.* A board that permits users to control the operation of a device by plugging cables into sockets.

plug-compatible \plug´kəm-pat`ə-bl\ *adj.* Equipped with connectors that are equivalent both in structure and in usage. For example, most modems having DB-25 connectors on their rear panels are plug-compatible; that is, one can be replaced by another without the cable having to be rewired. *Compare* pin-compatible.

plug-in \plug´in\ *n.* **1.** A small software program that plugs into a larger application to provide added functionality. **2.** A software component that plugs into the Netscape Navigator. Plug-ins permit the Web browser to access and execute files embedded in HTML documents that are in formats the browser normally would not recognize, such as many animation, video, and audio files. Most plug-ins are developed by software companies who have proprietary software in which the embedded files are created. *Compare* helper application.

.pm \dot`P-M´\ *n.* On the Internet, the major geographic domain specifying that an address is located in St. Pierre and Miquelon.

p-machine \P´mə-shēn`\ *n. See* pseudomachine.

PMMU \P`M-M-U´\ *n. See* paged memory management unit.

PMOS \P´mos\ *n.* Acronym for **P**-channel **m**etal-**o**xide **s**emiconductor. A MOSFET semiconductor technology in which the conduction channel is formed by the movement of holes (electron "vacancies" created as electrons move from atom to atom) rather than electrons. Because holes move more slowly than electrons do, PMOS is slower than NMOS, but it is also easier and less expensive to fabricate. *See also* MOS, MOSFET, P-type semiconductor. *Compare* CMOS, NMOS.

PMS \P`M-S´\ *n. See* Pantone Matching System.

.pn \dot`P-N´\ *n.* On the Internet, the major geographic domain specifying that an address is located in Pitcairn Island.

PNG \P`N-G´\ *n. See* Portable Network Graphics.

PNP \P`N-P´\ *n. See* Plug and Play, PNP transistor.

PNP transistor \P`N-P` tranz-i´stər\ *n.* A type of bipolar transistor in which a base of N-type material is sandwiched between an emitter and a collector of P-type material. The base, emitter, and collector are the three terminals of the transistor through which current flows. In a PNP transistor, holes (electron "vacancies") are the majority of the charge carriers, and they flow from the emitter to the collector. See the illustration. *See also* N-type semiconductor, P-type semiconductor. *Compare* NPN transistor.

point[1] \point\ *n.* **1.** A unit of measure used in printing, equal to approximately 1/72 of an inch. Character height and the amount of space (leading) between lines of text are usually specified in points. **2.** A single pixel on the screen, identified

Internal diagram

Schematic diagram

Emitter

Collector

Base

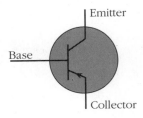

Emitter

Base

Collector

PNP transistor.

by its row and column numbers. **3.** A location in a geometric form, represented by two or more numbers that constitute its coordinates.

point[2] \point\ *vb.* To move an arrow or other such indicator to a particular item or position on the screen by using direction keys or by maneuvering a pointing device such as a mouse.

point-and-click \point´ənd-klik`\ *adj.* Enabling a user to select data and activate programs by using a mouse or other pointing device to move a cursor to a desired location ("point") and pressing a button on the mouse or other pointing device ("click").

PointCast \point´kast\ *n.* An Internet service that delivers and displays a personalized set of news articles to individual users. Unlike the World Wide Web and other Internet applications, PointCast is a *push* technology, where the server automatically uploads data without a specific command from the client. *See also* server (definition 2).

point chart \point´ chärt\ *n. See* scatter diagram.

point diagram \point´ dī´ə-gram\ *n. See* scatter diagram.

pointer \poin´tər\ *n.* **1.** In programming and information processing, a variable that contains the memory location (address) of some data rather than the data itself. *See also* address[1] (definition 1), handle (definition 1), reference[1]. **2.** *See* mouse pointer.

pointing device \poin´tēng də-vīs`\ *n.* An input device used to control an on-screen cursor for such actions as "pressing" on-screen buttons in dialog boxes, choosing menu items, and selecting ranges of cells in spreadsheets or groups of words in a document. A pointing device is often used to create drawings or graphical shapes. The most common pointing device is the mouse, which was popularized by its use with the Apple Macintosh. Other pointing devices include graphics tablets, styluses, light pens, joysticks, pucks, and trackballs. *See also* graphics tablet, joystick, light pen, mouse, puck, stylus, trackball.

point listing \point´ li`stēng\ *n.* A database of popular Web sites categorized by topics of interest and often rated by design and content.

point of presence \point´ əv prez´əns\ *n.* **1.** A point in a wide area network to which a user can connect with a local telephone call. **2.** A point at which a long distance telephone carrier connects to a local telephone exchange or to an individual user. *Acronym:* POP (pop).

point of sale \point` əv sāl`\ *n. See* POS.

point-to-point configuration \point`tə-point` kən-fi`gyur-ā´shən\ *n.* A communications link in which dedicated links exist between individual origins and destinations, as opposed to a point-to-multipoint configuration, in which the same signal goes to many destinations (such as a cable TV system), or a switched configuration, in which the signal moves from the origin to a switch that routes the signal to one of several possible destinations.

Point-to-Point Protocol \point`tōō-point` prō´tə-kol\ *n. See* PPP.

Point-to-Point Tunneling Protocol \point`tə-point` tun´əl-ēng prō´tə-kol\ *n.* A specification for virtual private networks in which some nodes of a local area network are connected through the Internet. *Acronym:* PPTP (P`P-T-P´). *See also* virtual network.

Poisson distribution \pwo-sōn´ dis-trə-byōō`shən\ *n.* A mathematical curve often used in statistics and simulation to represent the likelihood of some event occurring, such as the arrival of a customer in a queue, when the average likelihood is known. This distribution, named after the French mathematician S. D. Poisson, is simpler to calculate than the normal and binomial distributions. *See also* binomial distribution, normal distribution.

poke \pōk\ *vb.* To store a byte into an absolute memory location. PEEK (read a byte from memory) and POKE commands are often found in programming languages, such as Basic, that do not normally allow access to specific memory locations.

polar coordinates \pō`lər kō-ōr´də-nəts\ *n.* Coordinates of the form (r, θ) used to locate a point in two dimensions (on a plane). The polar coordinate r is the length of the line that starts at the origin and ends at the point, and θ (Greek theta) is the angle between that line and the positive x-axis. *Compare* Cartesian coordinates.

polarity \pō-lâr´ə-tē, pə-lâr´ə-tē\ *n.* The sign of the potential (voltage) difference between two points in a circuit. When a potential difference exists between two points, one point has a positive polarity and the other a negative polarity. Electrons flow from negative to positive; by convention, however, "current" is considered to flow from positive to negative.

polarized component \pō`lər-īzd kəm-pō´nent\ *n.* A circuit component that must be installed with its leads in a particular orientation with respect to the polarity of the circuit. Diodes, rectifiers, and some capacitors are examples of polarized components.

polarizing filter \pō`lər-ī-zēng fil´tər\ *n.* A transparent piece of glass or plastic that polarizes the light passing through it; that is, it allows only waves vibrating in a certain direction to pass through. Polarizing filters are often used to reduce glare on monitor screens. *See also* glare filter.

Polish notation \pō´lish nō-tā`shən\ *n. See* prefix notation.

polling \pō´lēng\ *n. See* autopolling.

polling cycle \pō´lēng sī`kl\ *n.* The time and sequence required for a program to poll each of its devices or network nodes. *See also* autopolling.

polygon \pol´ē-gon`\ *n.* Any two-dimensional closed shape composed of three or more line segments, such as a hexagon, an octagon, or a triangle. Computer users encounter polygons in graphics programs.

polyline \pol´ē-līn`\ *n.* An open shape consisting of multiple connected segments. Polylines are used in CAD and other graphics programs. *See also* CAD.

polymorphism \pol`ē-mōr´fiz-əm\ *n.* In an object-oriented programming language, the ability to redefine a routine in a derived class (a class that inherited its data structures and routines from another class). Polymorphism allows the programmer to define a base class that includes routines that perform standard operations on groups of related objects, without regard to the exact type of each object. The programmer then redefines the routines in the derived class for each type, taking into account the characteristics of the object. *See also* class, derived class, object (definition 2), object-oriented programming.

Pong \pong\ *n.* The first commercial video game, a table tennis simulation, created by Nolan Bushnell of Atari in 1972.

pop \pop\ *vb.* To fetch the top (most recently added) element of a stack, removing that element from the stack in the process. *Compare* push (definition 1).

POP \pop\ *n. See* point of presence, Post Office Protocol.

POP3 \P`O-P-thrē´\ *n.* Acronym for **P**ost **O**ffice **P**rotocol **3**. This is the current version of the Post Office Protocol standard in common use on TCP/IP networks. *See also* Post Office Protocol, TCP/IP.

populate \pop´yə-lāt\ *vb.* **1.** To put chips in the sockets of a circuit board. **2.** To import prepared data into a database from a file using a software procedure rather than by having a human operator enter individual records.

pop-up Help \pop´up help`\ *n.* An online help system whose messages appear as pop-up windows when the user clicks on a topic or area of the screen about which help is desired. Typically, a special form of click, such as clicking the right mouse button or Option-clicking, will activate pop-up Help, if it is available. *See also* balloon help.

pop-up menu or **popup menu** \pop´up men`-yōō\ *n.* In a graphical user interface, a menu that appears on-screen when a user selects a certain item. Pop-up menus can appear anywhere on the screen and generally disappear when the user selects an item in the menu. See the illustration. *Also called* popup. *Compare* drop-down menu, pull-down menu.

Pop-up menu.

pop-up messages \pop´up mes`ə-jəz\ *n.* The messages that appear when pop-up Help is used.

pop-up window \pop´up win`dō\ *n.* A window that appears when an option is selected. Typically, the window remains visible until the mouse button is released. See the illustration.

port[1] \pōrt\ *n. See* input/output port, port number.

Pop-up window.

port[2] \pōrt\ *vb.* **1.** To change a program in order to be able to run it on a different computer. **2.** To move documents, graphics, and other files from one computer to another.

portable \pōr´tə-bl\ *adj.* **1.** Capable of running on more than one computer system or under more than one operating system. Highly portable software can be moved to other systems with little effort, moderately portable software can be moved only with substantial effort, and nonportable software can be moved only with effort similar to or greater than the effort of writing the original program. **2.** Light enough, rugged enough, and free enough of encumbering external connections to be carried by a user.

portable computer \pōr´tə-bl kəm-pyōō´tər\ *n.* Any computer designed to be moved easily. Portable computers can be characterized by size and weight as in the table below.

Portable Digital Document \pōr´tə-bl dij´i-təl do´-kyə-mənt\ *n. See* PDD.

Portable Distributed Objects \pōr´tə-bl dis-trib´-yə-təd ob´jekts\ *n.* Software from NeXT, running under UNIX, that supports an object model in which objects to be stored at various locations on a network can be accessed as though they were at a single location. *Acronym:* PDO (P´D-O´).

Portable Document Format \pōr´tə-bl do´kyə-mənt fōr´mat\ *n.* The Adobe specification for electronic documents that use the Adobe Acrobat family of servers and readers. *Acronym:* PDF (P´D-F´). *See also* Acrobat, .pdf.

portable language \pōr´tə-bl lang´wəj\ *n.* A language that runs in the same way on different systems and therefore can be used for developing software for all of them. C, FORTRAN, and Ada are portable languages because their implementations on different systems are highly uniform; assembly language is extremely nonportable.

Portable Network Graphics \pōr´tə-bl net´wərk graf´iks\ *n.* A file format for bitmapped graphic images, designed to be a replacement for the GIF format, without the legal restrictions associated with GIF. *Acronym:* PNG (P´N-G´). *See also* GIF.

port enumerator \pōrt´ ə-nōō´mər-ā´tər\ *n.* In Windows, part of the Plug and Play system that detects I/O ports and reports them to the configuration manager. *See also* Plug and Play.

port expander \pōrt´ eks-pan´dər\ *n.* A hardware mechanism used for connecting several devices to

PORTABLE COMPUTERS

Type	Approximate weight	Power source	Comments
Transportable	15–30 lb.	House current	Sometimes called luggable; usually has floppy and hard drives; standard CRT screen.
Laptop	8–15 lb.	House current or batteries	Can be held on the lap; usually has a floppy drive; uses flat LCD or plasma screen.
Ultralight	2–8 lb.	Batteries or transformer pack	Easy to carry in a briefcase; sometimes uses RAM drive or EPROM instead of floppy or hard drive; thinner models are known as notebook computers.
Handheld	Less than 2 lb.	Batteries or transformer pack	Also called palmtop; can be held in one hand.

a single port. Although several devices might be connected, only one can use the port at any given moment.

port number \pōrt´ num`bər\ *n*. A number that enables IP packets to be sent to a particular process on a computer connected to the Internet. Some port numbers, called "well-known" port numbers, are permanently assigned; for example, e-mail data under SMTP goes to port number 25. A process such as a telnet session receives an "ephemeral" port number when it starts; data for that session goes to that port number, and the port number goes out of use when the session ends. A total of 65,535 port numbers are available for use with TCP, and the same number are available for UDP. *See also* IP, Simple Mail Transfer Protocol, socket (definition 1), TCP, UDP. *Compare* IP address.

portrait mode \pōr´trət mōd`\ *n*. A vertical print orientation in which a document is printed across the narrower dimension of a rectangular sheet of paper. This is the print mode typical of most letters, reports, and other such documents. See the illustration. *Compare* landscape mode.

> Lorem ipsum sobat somnus complexus est. Ridicanus se ostendit es forma quae mihi imagine elus quam ex isso erat notior. Quem ubi agnovi, quidem cohorrui. Quaesivi tamen viverte ipse et Paulus pater et ali quos nos extintos.

Portrait mode.

portrait monitor \pōr´trət mon`i-tər\ *n*. A monitor with a screen shape higher than it is wide. The proportions (but not necessarily the size) of the screen are usually the same as for a sheet of 8½-by-11-inch paper. See the illustration. *Compare* landscape monitor.

POS \P`O-S`\ *n*. Acronym for **p**oint **o**f **s**ale. The place in a store at which goods are paid for. Com-

Portrait monitor.

puterized transaction systems, such as those in use at automated supermarkets, use scanners for reading tags and bar codes, electronic cash registers, and other special devices to record purchases at this point.

POSIT \poz´it, P`O-S-I-T`\ *n*. Acronym for **P**rofiles for **O**pen **S**ystems **I**nternetworking **T**echnology. A set of nonmandatory standards for U.S. government network equipment. POSIT, which recognizes the prevalence of TCP/IP, is the successor to GOSIP. *See also* GOSIP, TCP/IP.

positional notation \pə-zish`ə-nəl nō-tā´shən\ *n*. In mathematics, a form of notation whose meaning relies in part on the relative location of the elements involved. For example, common numeric notation is positional notation. In the decimal number 34, the position of the numeral 3 signifies three 10s and the position of the numeral 4 signifies four 1s.

POSIX \pō´siks, P`O-S`I-X`\ *n*. Acronym for **P**ortable **O**perating **S**ystem **I**nterface for UNI**X**. An IEEE standard that defines a set of operating-system services. Programs that adhere to the POSIX standard can be easily ported from one system to another. POSIX was based on UNIX system services, but it was created in a way that allows it to be implemented by other operating systems.

post \pōst\ *vb*. To submit an article in a newsgroup or other online conference. The term is derived from the "posting" of a notice on a physical bulletin board. *See also* newsgroup.

POST \pōst\ *n*. *See* power-on self test.

posterization \pō`stər-ə-zā´shən\ *n*. *See* contouring.

postfix notation \pōst`fiks nō-tā´shən\ *n*. A form of algebraic notation in which the operators appear after the operands. *Also called* reverse Polish notation. *Compare* infix notation, prefix notation.

postmaster \pōst´ma`stər\ *n*. The logon name (and therefore the e-mail address) of an account that is responsible for maintaining e-mail services on a mail server. When an account holder is having trouble with e-mail, a message to "postmaster" or "postmaster@machine.org.domain.name" will usually reach a human who can solve the problem.

Post Office Protocol \pōst` of-əs prō´tə-kol\ *n*. A protocol for servers on the Internet that receive, store, and transmit e-mail and for clients on computers that connect to the servers to download and upload e-mail. *Acronym:* POP (pop).

postprocessor \pōst´pros`es-ər\ *n*. A device or a software routine, such as a linker, that operates on data manipulated first by another processor. *See also* back-end processor (definition 2). *Compare* preprocessor.

PostScript \pōst´skript\ *n*. A page-description language from Adobe Systems that offers flexible font capability and high-quality graphics. The most well-known page-description language, PostScript uses English-like commands to control page layout and to load and scale outline fonts. Adobe Systems is also responsible for Display PostScript, a graphics language for computer displays that gives users of both PostScript and Display PostScript absolute WYSIWYG (what-you-see-is-what-you-get), which is difficult when different methods are used for displaying and printing. *See also* outline font, page-description language.

PostScript font \pōst´skript font`\ *n*. A font defined in terms of the PostScript page-description language rules and intended to be printed on a PostScript-compatible printer. PostScript fonts are distinguished from bitmapped fonts by their smoothness, detail, and faithfulness to standards of quality established in the typographic industry. *See also* PostScript. *Compare* screen font.

pot \pot\ *n*. *See* potentiometer.

potential \pə-ten´shəl\ *n*. *See* electromotive force.

potentiometer \pə-ten`shē-om´ə-tər\ *n*. A circuit element that can be adjusted to provide varying amounts of resistance. The twist-knob and slider-type volume controls on many radios and television sets are potentiometers. See the illustration. *Also called* pot.

POTS \P`O-T-S´\ *n*. Acronym for **P**lain **O**ld **T**elephone **S**ervice. Basic dial telephone connections to the public switched network, without any added features or functions. A POTS line is nothing but a phone line connected to a simple desktop telephone instrument.

pour \pōr\ *vb*. To send a file or the output from a program to another file or to a device using a pipe. *See also* pipe (definition 1).

power \pou´ər\ *n*. **1.** In mathematics, the number of times a value is multiplied by itself—for example, 10 to the third power means 10 times 10 times 10. **2.** In computing, the electricity used to run a computer. **3.** The speed at which a computer performs and the availability of various features. *See also* computer power.

PowerBook \pou´ər-book`\ *n*. Any of several computers in the family of portable Macintosh computers made by Apple.

Potentiometer.　Four types of potentiometer, from left: standard, trim, thumbwheel, and slider.

power down \pou`ər doun´\ *vb.* To shut down (a computer); to turn off the power.

power failure \pou´ər fāl`yur\ *n.* Loss of electricity, which causes a loss of unsaved data in a computer's random access memory (RAM) if no backup power supply is connected to the machine. *Compare* surge.

Power Mac \pou´ər mak`\ *n. See* Power Macintosh.

Power Macintosh \pou`ər mak´ən-tosh\ *n.* An Apple Macintosh computer based on the PowerPC processor. The first Power Macintoshes, 6100/60, 7100/66, and 8100/80, were unveiled in March 1994. See the illustration. *Also called* Power Mac. *See also* PowerPC.

Power Macintosh.

Power-on key \pou-ər-on´ kē`\ *n.* A special key on the Apple ADB and Extended keyboards used for turning on a Macintosh II. The Power-on key is marked with a left-pointing triangle and is used in lieu of the on/off switch. There is no Power-off key; the system is shut down by choosing the Shut Down command from the Special menu.

power-on self test \pou`ər-on` self test´\ *n.* A set of routines stored in a computer's read-only memory (ROM) that tests various system components such as RAM, the disk drives, and the keyboard to see if they are properly connected and operating. If problems are found, these routines alert the user by sounding a series of beeps or displaying a message, often accompanied by a diagnostic numeric value, to the standard output or standard error device (usually the screen). If the power-on self test is successful, it passes control to the system's bootstrap loader. *Acronym:* POST (pōst). *See also* bootstrap loader.

PowerPC \pou`ər-P-C´\ *n.* A microprocessor architecture developed in 1992 by Motorola and IBM, with some participation by Apple. A PowerPC microprocessor is RISC-based and superscalar, with a 64-bit data bus and a 32-bit address bus. It also has separate data and instruction caches, although the size of each varies by implementation. All PowerPC microprocessors have multiple integer and floating-point units, and all have an operating voltage of 3.3 volts, except for the 601, which operates at 3.6 volts. The operating speed and number of instructions executed per clock cycle varies with the implementation. The 601 is available in an 80-MHz or 100-MHz version and executes three instructions per clock cycle. The 603, available in 80-MHz, 100-MHz, and 200-MHz versions, executes three instructions per clock cycle. The 604, available in 100-MHz, 120-MHz, and 133-MHz versions, executes four instructions per clock cycle. The 620, available in a 133-MHz version, also executes four instructions per clock cycle. PowerPC is a registered trademark of IBM. *See also* microprocessor, RISC.

PowerPC Platform \pou`ər-P-C´ plat-fōrm\ *n.* A platform developed by IBM, Apple, and Motorola based on the 601 and later chips. This platform supports the use of multiple operating systems such as Mac OS, Windows NT, and AIX as well as software designed for those individual operating systems. *Acronym:* PPCP (P`P-C-P´).

PowerPC Reference Platform \pou`ər P-C` re´-frəns plat`fōrm\ *n.* An open system standard developed by IBM. IBM's goal in designing the PowerPC Reference Platform was to ensure compatibility among PowerPC systems built by different companies. Apple's PowerPC Macintoshes are not yet compliant with the PowerPC Reference Platform, but future versions are expected to be. *Acronym:* PReP (prep, P`R-E-P´). *See also* Common Hardware Reference Platform, open system, PowerPC.

power supply \pou´ər su-plī´\ *n.* An electrical device that transforms standard wall outlet electricity (115–120 VAC in the United States) into the lower voltages (typically 5 to 12 volts DC) required by computer systems. Personal computer power supplies are rated by wattage; they usually range from about 90 watts at the low end to 250 watts at the high end.

power surge \pou´ər surj\ *n.* *See* surge.

power up \pou`ər up´\ *vb.* To start up a computer; to begin a cold boot procedure; to turn on the power.

power user \pou´ər yoo`zər\ *n.* A person adept with computers, particularly on an applications-oriented level rather than on a programming level. A power user is someone who knows a considerable amount about computers and is comfortable enough with applications to be able to work with their most sophisticated features.

PPCP \P`P-C-P´\ *n.* *See* Power PC Platform.

PPM \P`P-M´\ *n.* *See* pages per minute, pulse position modulation.

PPP \P`P-P´\ *n.* Acronym for **P**oint-to-**P**oint **P**rotocol. A data link protocol developed by the Internet Engineering Task Force in 1991 for dial-up telephone connections, such as between a computer and the Internet. PPP provides greater protection for data integrity and security than does SLIP, at a cost of greater overhead. *Compare* SLIP.

PPS \P`P-S´\ *n.* *See* peripheral power supply.

PPTP \P`P-T-P´\ *n.* *See* Point-to-Point Tunneling Protocol.

.pr \dot`P-R´\ *n.* On the Internet, the major geographic domain specifying that an address is located in Puerto Rico.

PRAM \pram, P´ram, P`R-A-M´\ *n.* Short for **p**arameter **RAM**. A portion of RAM in Macintosh computers that contains configuration information such as the date and time, desktop pattern, and other control panel settings. *See also* RAM.

P-rating \P´rā`tēng\ *n.* Short for **p**erformance **rating**. A microprocessor rating system by IBM, Cyrix, and others, based on throughput in realistic applications. Formerly, microprocessor clock speed was widely used as a method of rating, but it does not account for differing chip architectures or different types of work people do with comput-

ers. *See also* central processing unit, clock (definition 1), microprocessor.

precedence \pres´ə-dəns`\ *n.* In applications, the order in which values in a mathematical expression are calculated. In general, application programs perform multiplication and division first, followed by addition and subtraction. Sets of parentheses can be placed around expressions to control the order in which they are calculated. *See also* operator associativity, operator precedence.

precision \prə-sizh´ən\ *n.* **1.** The extent of detail used in expressing a number. For example, 3.14159265 gives more precision—more detail—about the value of pi than does 3.14. Precision is related to, but different from, accuracy. Precision indicates degree of detail; accuracy indicates correctness. The number 2.83845 is also more precise than 3.14, but it is less accurate for pi. *Compare* accuracy. **2.** In programming, numeric values are often referred to as single-precision or double-precision values. The difference between the two is in the amount of storage space allotted to the value. *See also* double-precision, single-precision.

precompiler \prē`kəm-pī´lər\ *n.* A program that reads in a source file and makes certain changes in order to prepare the source file for compilation. *Also called* preprocessor. *See also* compiler (definition 2).

preemptive multitasking \prē-emp`tiv mul´tī-ta-skēng, mul´tē-ta-skēng\ *n.* A form of multitasking in which the operating system periodically interrupts the execution of a program and passes control of the system to another waiting program. Preemptive multitasking prevents any one program from monopolizing the system. *Also called* time-slice multitasking. *See also* multitasking.

Preferences \pref´rən-səz\ *n.* A menu choice in many graphical user interface applications that allows the user to specify how the application will act each time it is used. For example, in a word processing application the user may be allowed to specify whether the ruler will appear, whether the document will appear in the same way as it will print (including margins), and other choices. *Also called* Options, Prefs.

prefix notation \prē´fiks nō-tā`shən\ *n.* A form of algebraic notation, developed in 1929 by Jan Lukasiewicz, a Polish logician, in which the operators appear before the operands. For example, the expression $(a + b) * (c - d)$ would be written in prefix notation as $* + a\ b - c\ d$. *Also called* Polish notation. *See also* infix notation, postfix notation.

Prefs \prefs\ *n. See* Preferences.

PReP \prep, P`R-E-P`\ *n. See* Power PC Reference Platform.

preprocessor \prē`pros´es-ər\ *n.* A device or routine that performs preliminary operations on input before passing it on for further processing. *See also* front-end processor (definition 1). *Compare* postprocessor.

presentation graphics \prē-zən-tā´shən graf`iks, prez-ən-tā´shən\ *n.* The representation of business information, such as sales figures and stock prices, in chart form rather than as lists of numbers. Presentation graphics are used to give viewers an immediate grasp of business statistics and their significance. Common examples are area charts, bar charts, line charts, and pie charts. *Also called* business graphics.

presentation layer \prē-zən-tā´shən lâr`, prez-ən-tā´shən, lā`ər\ *n.* The sixth of the seven layers in the International Organization for Standardization's Open Systems Interconnection (ISO/OSI) model for standardizing computer-to-computer communications. The presentation layer is responsible for formatting information so that it can be displayed or printed. This task generally includes interpreting codes (such as tabs) related to presentation, but it can also include converting encryption and other codes and translating different character sets. *See also* ISO/OSI model.

Presentation Manager \prē-zən-tā´shən man`ə-jər, prez-ən-tā´shən\ *n.* The graphical user interface provided with OS/2 versions 1.1 and later. The Presentation Manager derives from the MS-DOS–based Windows environment and provides similar capabilities. The user sees a graphical, window-oriented interface, and the programmer uses a standard set of routines for handling screen, keyboard, mouse, and printer input and output, no matter what hardware is attached to the system. *See also* OS/2, Windows.

pressure-sensitive \presh´ər-sen`sə-tiv\ *adj.* Of or pertaining to a device in which pressing on a thin surface produces an electrical connection and causes an event to be registered by the computer. Pressure-sensitive devices include touch-sensitive drawing pens, membrane keyboards, and some touch screens. *See also* touch screen.

Pretty Good Privacy \prit`ē gŏod prī´və-sē\ *n. See* PGP.

pretty print \prit´ē print`\ *n.* A feature of some editors used in programming that formats code so that it is easier to read and understand when printed. For example, a pretty-print feature might insert blank lines to set off modules or indent nested routines to make them easier to spot. *See also* code[1] (definition 1), editor, module (definition 1), routine.

preventive maintenance \prə-ven`tiv mān´tə-nəns\ *n.* Routine servicing of hardware intended to keep equipment in good operating condition and to find and correct problems before they develop into severe malfunctions.

preview \prē´vyōō\ *n.* In word processors and other applications, the feature that formats a document for printing but displays it on the video monitor rather than sending it directly to the printer.

primary channel \prī´mâr-ē chan´əl\ *n.* The data-transmission channel in a communications device, such as a modem. *Compare* secondary channel.

Primary Domain Controller \prī´mâr-ē dō-mān´ kən-trō`lər\ *n.* **1.** In Windows NT, a database providing a centralized administration site for resources and user accounts. The database allows users to log onto the domain, rather than onto a specific host machine. A separate account database keeps track of the machines in the domain and allocates the domain's resources to users. **2.** In any local area network, the server that maintains the master copy of the domain's user accounts database and that validates logon requests. *Acronym:* PDC (P`D-C´).

primary key \prī´mâr-ē kē`\ *n.* In databases, the key field that serves as the unique identifier of a specific tuple (row) in a relation (database table). *Also called* major key. *See also* alternate key (definition 1), candidate key. *Compare* secondary key.

primary storage \prī´mâr-ē stōr´əj\ *n.* Random access memory (RAM); the main general-purpose storage region to which the microprocessor has direct access. A computer's other storage options, such as disks and tape, are called *secondary storage* or (sometimes) *backing storage*.

primitive \prim´ə-tiv\ *n.* **1.** In computer graphics, a shape, such as a line, circle, curve, or polygon, that can be drawn, stored, and manipulated as a discrete entity by a graphics program. A primitive is one of the elements from which a large graphic design is created. **2.** In programming, a fundamental element in a language that can be used to create larger procedures that do the work a programmer wants to do.

print \print\ *vb.* In computing, to send information to a printer. The word is also sometimes used in the sense of "show me" or "copy this." For example, the PRINT statement in Basic causes output to be displayed (printed) on the screen. Similarly, an application program that can be told to "print" a file to disk interprets the command as an instruction to route output to a disk file instead of to a printer.

print buffer \print´ buf˄ər\ *n.* A section of memory to which print output can be sent for temporary storage until the printer is ready to handle it. A print buffer can exist in a computer's random access memory (RAM), in the printer, in a separate unit between the computer and the printer, or on disk. Regardless of its location, the function of a print buffer is to free the computer for other tasks by taking print output at high speed from the computer and passing it along at the much slower rate required by the printer. Print buffers vary in sophistication: some simply hold the next few characters to be printed, and others can queue, reprint, or delete documents sent for printing.

printed circuit board \prin˄təd sər´kət bõrd\ *n.* A flat board made of nonconducting material, such as plastic or fiberglass, on which chips and other electronic components are mounted, usually in predrilled holes designed to hold them. The component holes are connected electrically by predefined conductive metal pathways that are printed on the surface of the board. The metal leads protruding from the electronic components are soldered to the conductive metal pathways to form a connection. A printed circuit board should be held by the edges and protected from dirt and static electricity to avoid damage. See the illustration. *Acronym:* PCB (P`C-B´).

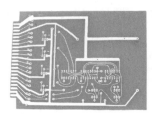

Printed circuit board.

printer \prin´tər\ *n.* A computer peripheral that puts text or a computer-generated image on paper or on another medium, such as a transparency film. Printers can be categorized in any of several ways. The most common distinction is impact versus nonimpact. Impact printers physically strike the paper and are exemplified by pin dot-matrix printers and daisy-wheel printers; nonimpact printers include every other type of print mechanism, including laser, ink-jet, and thermal printers. Other possible methods of categorizing printers include (but are not limited to) the following:

■ Print technology: Chief among these are pin dot-matrix, ink-jet, laser, thermal, and (although somewhat outdated) daisy-wheel or thimble printers. Pin dot-matrix printers can be further classified by the number of pins in the print head: 9, 18, 24, and so on.

■ Character formation: Fully formed characters made of continuous lines (such as those produced by a daisy-wheel printer) versus dot-matrix characters composed of patterns of dots (such as those produced by standard dot-matrix, ink-jet, and thermal printers). Laser printers, while technically dot-matrix, are generally considered to produce fully formed characters because their output is very clear and the dots are extremely small and closely spaced.

■ Method of transmission: Parallel (byte-by-byte transmission) versus serial (bit-by-bit transmission). These categories refer to the means by which output is sent to the printer rather than to any mechanical distinctions. Many printers are available in either parallel or serial versions, and still other printers offer both choices, yielding greater flexibility in installation options.

■ Method of printing: Character by character, line by line, or page by page. Character printers include standard dot-matrix, ink-jet, thermal, and daisy-wheel printers. Line printers include the band, chain, and drum printers that are commonly associated with large computer installations or networks. Page printers include the electro-photographic printers, such as laser printers.

■ Print capability: Text-only versus text-and-graphics. Text-only printers, including most daisy-wheel and thimble printers and some dot-matrix and laser printers, can reproduce only characters for which they have matching patterns, such as embossed type, or internal character maps. Text-and-graphics printers—dot-matrix, ink-jet, laser, and others—can reproduce all manner of images by "drawing" each as a pattern of dots.

■ Print quality: Draft versus near-letter quality versus letter quality.

See also ball printer, character printer, color printer, daisy-wheel printer, dot-matrix printer, draft quality, electrophotographic printers, graphics printer, impact printer, ink-jet printer, ion-deposition printer, laser printer, LCD printer, LED printer, letter quality, line printer, near-letter-quality, nonimpact printer, page printer, parallel printer, serial printer, thermal printer, thermal wax-transfer printer, thimble printer.

Printer Access Protocol \prin`tər ak`ses prō´tə-kol\ *n*. See PAP (definition 2).

Printer Control Language \prin´tər kən-trōl` lang`wəj\ *n*. A printer control language from Hewlett-Packard, used in its LaserJet, DeskJet, and RuggedWriter printer lines. Because of the LaserJet's dominance in the laser printer market, Printer Control Language has become a de facto standard. *Acronym:* PCL (P`C-L´). *Also called* Hewlett-Packard Printer Control Language.

printer controller \prin´tər kən-trō`lər\ *n*. The processing hardware in a printer, especially in a page printer. It includes the raster image processor, the memory, and any general-purpose microprocessors. A printer controller can also reside in a personal computer, attached via a high-speed cable to a printer that simply carries out its instructions. *Compare* printer engine.

printer driver \prin´tər drī`vər\ *n*. A software program designed to enable other programs to work with a particular printer without concerning themselves with the specifics of the printer's hardware and internal "language." Application programs can communicate properly with a variety of printers by using printer drivers, which handle all of the subtleties of each printer so that the application program doesn't have to. Today graphical user interfaces offer their own printer drivers, eliminating the need for an application that runs under the interface to have its own printer driver.

printer engine \prin´tər en`jən\ *n*. The part of a page printer, such as a laser printer, that actually performs the printing. Most printer engines are self-contained, replaceable cartridges. The engine is distinct from the printer controller, which includes all the processing hardware in the printer. The most widely used printer engines are manufactured by Canon. *Compare* printer controller.

printer file \prin´tər fīl` \ *n*. Output that would normally be destined for the printer but has been diverted to a computer file instead. A printer file is created for any of several reasons. For example, it allows output to be transferred to another program or to another computer. It also allows additional copies to be made at any time by simply copying the print image to the printer. Occasionally, the term *printer file* is used, incorrectly, to refer to the printer driver.

printer font \prin´tər font` \ *n*. A font residing in or intended for a printer. A printer font can be internal, downloaded, or on a font cartridge. *Compare* screen font.

printer port \prin´tər pōrt` \ *n*. A port through which a printer can be connected to a personal computer. On PC-compatible machines, printer ports are usually parallel ports and are identified in the operating system by the logical device name LPT. On many newer PCs, the parallel port on the case of the CPU has a printer icon beside it to identify it as a printer port. Serial ports can also be used for some printers (logical device name COM), although configuration is generally required. On Macintoshes, printer ports are usually serial ports and are also used to connect Macs to an AppleTalk network. *See also* AppleTalk, central processing unit, logical device, parallel port, serial port.

print head \print´ hed\ *n.* The part of a printer that mechanically controls the imprinting of characters on paper. See the illustration.

Pins

Print head. A 9-pin print head from a dot-matrix printer.

print job \print´ job\ *n.* A single batch of characters printed as a unit. A print job usually consists of a single document, which can be one page or hundreds of pages long. To avoid having to print individual documents separately, some software can group multiple documents into a single print job. *See also* print spooler.

print mode \print´ mōd\ *n.* A general term for the format of print output by a printer. Print modes range from portrait or landscape orientation of the paper to letter quality and size of the print. Dot-matrix printers support two print modes: draft and letter quality (LQ) or near-letter-quality (NLQ). Some printers can interpret both plain text (ASCII) and a page definition language such as PostScript. *See also* PostScript, printer.

printout \prin´tout\ *n. See* hard copy.

print quality \print´ kwä-lə-tē\ *n.* The quality and clarity of characters produced by a printer. Print quality varies with the type of printer; in general, dot-matrix printers produce lower-quality output than laser printers. The printer mode can also affect quality. *See also* resolution (definition 1).

print queue \print´ kyoo\ *n.* A buffer for documents and images waiting to be printed. When an application places a document in a print queue, it is held in a special part of the computer's memory, where it waits until the printer is ready to receive it.

Print Screen key \print´ skrēn kē\ *n.* A key on IBM PC and compatible keyboards that normally

causes the computer to send a character-based "picture" of the screen contents to the printer. The print screen feature works only when the display is in text mode or CGA graphics mode (the lowest-resolution color and graphics mode available on IBM compatibles). It will not work properly in other graphics modes. Some programs use the Print Screen key to capture a screen image and record it as a file on disk. These programs can typically work in any graphics mode and record the file as a graphics image. When the user is working directly with the MS-DOS operating system, and with some programs, the combination Control-Print Screen toggles the printer on or off. With printing turned on, the system sends every character to the printer as well as to the screen. The Print Screen key on the Apple Extended Keyboard is included for compatibility with operating systems such as MS-DOS. *Also called* PrtSc key.

print server \print´ sər`vər\ *n.* A workstation that is dedicated to managing printers on a network. The print server can be any station on the network.

print spooler \print´ spoo`lər\ *n.* Computer software that intercepts a print job on its way to the printer and sends it to disk or memory instead, where the print job is held until the printer is ready for it. The term *spooler* is an acronym created from "**s**imultaneous **p**eripheral **o**perations **o**n **l**ine."

print to file \print` tə fīl´\ *n.* A command in many applications that instructs the program to format a document for printing and store the formatted document as a file rather than sending it to a printer.

print wheel \print´ hwēl, wēl\ *n. See* daisy wheel.

priority \prī-ôr´-ə-tē\ *n.* Precedence in receiving the attention of the microprocessor and the use of system resources. Within a computer, unseen and unnoticed levels of priority are the means by which many different types of potential clashes and disruptions are avoided. Similarly, tasks running on a computer can be assigned priorities that determine when and for how long they receive time from the microprocessor. On networks, stations can be assigned priorities that determine when and how often they can control the communications line, and messages can be assigned priorities that indicate how soon they must be transmitted. *See also* interrupt.

Priority Frame \prī-ōr´ə-tē frām`\ *n.* A telecommunications protocol developed by Infonet and Northern Telecom, Inc., designed to carry data, facsimile, and voice information.

privacy \prī´və-sē\ *n.* The concept that a user's data, such as stored files and e-mail, is not to be examined by anyone else without that user's permission. A right to privacy is not generally recognized on the Internet. Federal law protects only e-mail in transit or in temporary storage, and only against access by Federal agencies. Employers often claim a right to inspect any data on their systems. To obtain privacy, the user must take active measures such as encryption. *See also* encryption, PGP, Privacy Enhanced Mail. *Compare* security.

Privacy Enhanced Mail \prī´və-sē   en-hansd` māl´\ *n.* An Internet standard for e-mail systems that use encryption techniques to ensure the privacy and security of messages. *Acronym:* PEM (P`E-M´). *See also* encryption, standard. *Compare* PGP.

Private Branch Exchange \prī`vət branch´ eks-chānj`\ *n. See* PBX.

private channel \prī`vət chan´əl\ *n.* In Internet relay chat (IRC), a channel reserved for the use of a certain group of people. Private channel names are hidden from view by the public at large. *Also called* secret channel. *See also* IRC.

Private Communications Technology \prī`vət kə-myo͞o`nə-kā`shənz tek-nol`ə-jē\ *n.* A specification designed to secure general-purpose business and personal communications on the Internet, and including features such as privacy, authentication, and mutual identification.

private folders \prī`vət fōl´dərz\ *n.* In a shared network environment, those folders on a user's computer that are not currently accessible by other users on the network. *Compare* public folders.

private key \prī´vət kē`\ *n.* One of two keys in public key encryption. The user keeps the private key secret and uses it to encrypt digital signatures and to decrypt received messages. *See also* public key encryption. *Compare* public key.

private line \prī`vət līn´\ *n. See* dedicated line (definition 1).

privatization \prī`və-tə-zā´shən\ *n.* Generally, the process of turning something over from gov-

ernment to commercial industry control. In the context of computer science and the Internet, the term refers to the government's turning over of various Internet backbones to private industry. For example, control of NSFnet was passed from the government to private business in 1992.

privileged instruction \priv`ə-ləjd in-struk´shən\ *n.* An instruction (usually a machine instruction) that can be executed only by the operating system. Privileged instructions exist because the operating system needs to perform certain operations that applications should not be allowed to perform; therefore, only the operating-system routines have the necessary privilege to execute these particular instructions.

privileged mode \priv´ə-ləjd mōd`\ *n.* A mode of execution, supported by the protected mode of the Intel 80286 and higher microprocessors, in which software can carry out restricted operations that manipulate critical components of the system, such as memory and input/output ports (channels). Application programs cannot be executed in privileged mode; the heart (kernel) of the OS/2 operating system can be, as can the programs (device drivers) that control devices attached to the system.

privileges \priv´ə-lə-jəz, priv´lə-jəz\ *n. See* access privileges.

PRN \P`R-N´\ *n.* The logical device name for *printer.* A name reserved by the MS-DOS operating system for the standard print device. PRN usually refers to a system's first parallel port, also known as LPT1.

probability \prob`ə-bil´ə-tē\ *n.* The likelihood that an event will happen, which can often be estimated mathematically. In mathematics, statistics and probability theory are related fields. In computing, probability is used to determine the likelihood of failure or error in a system or device.

problem solving \pro´bləm sol`vēng\ *n.* **1.** The process of devising and implementing a strategy for finding a solution or for transforming a less desirable condition into a more desirable one. **2.** An aspect of artificial intelligence wherein the task of problem solving is performed solely by a program. *See also* artificial intelligence.

procedural language \prə-sē`jər-əl lang`wəj\ *n.* A programming language in which the basic programming element is the procedure (a named sequence of statements, such as a routine, subroutine, or function). The most widely used high-level languages (C, Pascal, Basic, FORTRAN, COBOL, Ada) are all procedural languages. *See also* procedure. *Compare* nonprocedural language.

procedural rendering \prə-sē`jər-əl ren´dər-ēng\ *n.* The rendering of a two-dimensional image from three-dimensional coordinates with texturing according to user-specified conditions, such as direction and degree of lighting.

procedure \prə-sē´jər\ *n.* In a program, a named sequence of statements, often with associated constants, data types, and variables, that usually performs a single task. A procedure can usually be called (executed) by other procedures, as well as by the main body of the program. Some languages distinguish between a procedure and a function, with the latter (the function) returning a value. *See also* function, parameter, procedural language, routine, subroutine.

procedure call \prə-sē´jər käl`\ *n.* In programming, an instruction that causes a procedure to be executed. A procedure call can be located in another procedure or in the main body of the program. *See also* procedure.

process[1] \pros´es\ *n.* A program or part of a program; a coherent sequence of steps undertaken by a program.

process[2] \pros´es\ *vb.* To manipulate data with a program.

process-bound \pros´es-bound`\ *adj.* Limited in performance by processing requirements. *See also* computation-bound.

process color \pros´es kəl`ər\ *n.* A method of handling color in a document in which each block of color is separated into its subtractive primary color components for printing: cyan, magenta, and yellow (as well as black). All other colors are created by blending layers of various sizes of halftone spots printed in cyan, magenta, and yellow to create the image. *See also* color model, color separation (definition 1). *Compare* spot color.

processing \pros´es-ēng\ *n.* The manipulation of data within a computer system. Processing is the vital step between receiving data (input) and producing results (output)—the task for which computers are designed.

processor \pros´es-ər\ *n. See* central processing unit, microprocessor.

Processor Direct Slot \pros`es-ər-dər-ekt` slot´\ *n.* See PDS (definition 1).

Prodigy Information Service \prod`ə-jē in-fər-mā´shən sər´vəs\ *n.* An online information service founded by IBM and Sears. Like its competitors America Online and CompuServe, Prodigy offers access to databases and file libraries, online chat, special interest groups, e-mail, and Internet connectivity. *Also called* Prodigy.

product \prod´ukt\ *n.* **1.** An operator in the relational algebra used in database management that, when applied to two existing relations (tables), results in the creation of a new table containing all possible ordered concatenations (combinations) of tuples (rows) from the first relation with tuples from the second. The number of rows in the resulting relation is the product of the number of rows in the two source relations. *Also called* Cartesian product. *Compare* inner join. **2.** In mathematics, the result of multiplying two or more numbers. **3.** In the most general sense, an entity conceived and developed for the purpose of competing in a commercial market. Although computers are products, the term is more commonly applied to software, peripherals, and accessories in the computing arena.

production system \prə-duk´shən si`stəm\ *n.* In expert systems, an approach to problem solving based on an "IF this, THEN that" approach that uses a set of rules, a database of information, and a "rule interpreter" to match premises with facts and form a conclusion. Production systems are also known as rule-based systems or inference systems. *See also* expert system.

Professional Graphics Adapter \prə-fesh`ə-nəl graf´iks ə-dap`tər\ *n.* A video adapter introduced by IBM, primarily for CAD applications. The Professional Graphics Adapter is capable of displaying 256 colors, with a horizontal resolution of 640 pixels and a vertical resolution of 480 pixels. *Acronym:* PGA (P`G-A´).

Professional Graphics Display \prə-fesh`ə-nəl graf´iks dis-plā`\ *n.* An analog display introduced by IBM, intended for use with their Professional Graphics Adapter. *See also* Professional Graphics Adapter.

profile \prō´fīl\ *vb*. To analyze a program to determine how much time is spent in different parts of the program during execution.

Profiles for Open Systems Internetworking Technology \prō`fīlz fər ō`pən si`stəmz in`tər-net´wər-kēng tek-nol`ə-jē\ *n*. *See* POSIT.

program \prō´gram\ *n*. A sequence of instructions that can be executed by a computer. The term can refer to the original source code or to the executable (machine language) version. *Also called* software. *See also* program creation, routine, statement.

program card \prō´gram kärd`\ *n*. *See* PC Card, ROM card.

program cartridge \prō´gram kär`trij\ *n*. *See* ROM cartridge.

program counter \prō´gram koun`tər\ *n*. A register (small, high-speed memory circuit within a microprocessor) that contains the address (location) of the instruction to be executed next in the program sequence.

program creation \prō´gram krē-ā`shən\ *n*. The process of producing an executable file. Traditionally, program creation comprises three steps: (1) compiling the high-level source code into assembly language source code; (2) assembling the assembly language source code into machine-code object files; and (3) linking the machine-code object files with various data files, run-time files, and library files into an executable file. Some compilers go directly from high-level source to machine-code object, and some integrated development environments compress all three steps into a single command. *See also* assembler, compiler (definition 2), linker, program.

program file \prō´gram fīl`\ *n*. A disk file that contains the executable portion(s) of a computer program. Depending on its size and complexity, an application or other program, such as an operating system, can be stored in several different files, each containing the instructions necessary for some part of the program's overall functioning. *Compare* document file.

program generator \prō´gram jen`ər-ā-tər\ *n*. A program that creates other programs (usually in source code) based on a set of specifications and relationships given by the user. Program generators are often used to simplify the task of creating an application. *See also* 4GL, application generator.

program listing \prō´gram li`stēng\ *n*. A copy, usually on paper, of the source code of a program. Some compilers can generate program listings with line numbers, cross-references, and so on.

program logic \prō´gram loj`ik\ *n*. The logic behind the design and construction of a program—that is, the reasons it works the way it does. *See also* logic error.

programmable \prō-gram´ə-bl`\ *adj*. Capable of accepting instructions for performing a task or an operation. Being programmable is a characteristic of computers.

programmable function key \prō-gram`ə-bl funk´-shən kē`\ *n*. Any of several, sometimes unlabeled, keys on some third-party keyboards that allow the user to "play back" previously stored key combinations or sequences of keystrokes called *macros*. The same effect can be achieved with a standard keyboard and a keyboard enhancer, the latter of which intercepts the keyboard codes and substitutes modified values; but programmable function keys accomplish this without requiring RAM-resident software. *Compare* keyboard enhancer.

programmable interrupt controller \prō-gram`-ə-bl in`tər-upt kən-trō`lər\ *n*. An Intel chip that handles interrupt requests (IRQs). IBM AT machines use two programmable interrupt controllers to accommodate a maximum of 15 IRQs. The programmable interrupt controller has been replaced by the advanced programmable interrupt controller (APIC), which supports multiprocessing. *Acronym:* PIC (P`I-C´). *See also* IBM AT, IRQ.

programmable logic array \prō-gram`ə-bl loj´ik ər-ā`\ *n*. *See* field-programmable logic array.

programmable logic device \prō-gram`ə-bl loj´-ik də-vīs`\ *n*. A logic chip that is programmed by the customer rather than by the manufacturer. Like a gate array, a programmable logic device consists of a collection of logic gates; unlike a gate array, a programmable logic device need not have its programming completed as part of the manufacturing process. *Acronym:* PLD (P`L-D´). *See also* logic chip. *Compare* gate array.

programmable read-only memory \prō-gram`-ə-bl rēd`ōn`lē mem´ər-ē\ *n*. *See* PROM.

program maintenance \prō´gram mān`tə-nəns\ *n.* The process of supporting, debugging, and upgrading a program in response to feedback from individual or corporate users or the marketplace in general.

programmatic interface \prō-grə-mat´ik in´tər-fās\ *n.* **1.** A user interface dependent on user commands or on a special programming language, as contrasted with a graphical user interface. UNIX and MS-DOS have programmatic interfaces; the Apple Macintosh and Microsoft Windows have graphical user interfaces. *See also* command-line interface, graphical user interface, iconic interface. **2.** The set of functions any operating system makes available to a programmer developing an application. *See also* application programming interface.

Programmed Inquiry, Learning or Teaching \prō`gramd in´kwər-ē lər`nēng ōr tē´chēng\ *n.* *See* PILOT.

programmer \prō´gram-ər\ *n.* **1.** An individual who writes and debugs computer programs. Depending on the size of the project and the work environment, a programmer might work alone or as part of a team, be involved in part or all of the process from design through completion, or write all or a portion of the program. *See also* program. **2.** In hardware, a device used to program read-only memory chips. *See also* PROM, ROM (definition 2).

programmer's switch \prō´gram-ərz swich`\ *n.* A pair of buttons on Macintosh computers that enable the user to reboot the system or to enter a command-line interface at a low level of the operating system. Originally, only programmers testing software were expected to need those functions, so early models of the Macintosh hid the buttons inside the cabinet and supplied a plastic clip that could be attached so that the programmer could push them. In many later models the buttons are built into the cabinet; the button to reboot the system is marked with a triangle pointing leftward, and the other button is marked with a circle.

programming \prō´gram-ēng\ *n.* The art and science of creating computer programs. Programming begins with knowledge of one or more programming languages, such as Basic, C, Pascal, or assembly language. Knowledge of a language alone does not make a good program. Much more can be involved, such as expertise in the theory of algorithms, user interface design, and characteristics of hardware devices. Computers are rigorously logical machines, and programming requires a similarly logical approach to designing, writing (coding), testing, and debugging a program. Low-level languages, such as assembly language, also require familiarity with the capabilities of a microprocessor and the basic instructions built into it. In the modular approach advocated by many programmers, a project is broken into smaller, more manageable modules—stand-alone functional units that can be designed, written, tested, and debugged separately before being incorporated into the larger program. *See also* algorithm, kludge (definition 2), modular design, object-oriented programming, spaghetti code, structured programming.

programming language \prō´gram-ēng lang`wəj\ *n.* Any artificial language that can be used to define a sequence of instructions that can ultimately be processed and executed by the computer. Defining what is or is not a programming language can be tricky, but general usage implies that the translation process—from the source code expressed using the programming language to the machine code that the computer needs to work with—be automated by means of another program, such as a compiler. Thus, English and other natural languages are ruled out, although some subsets of English are used and understood by some fourth-generation languages. *See also* 4GL, compiler (definition 2), natural language, program.

Programming Language I \prō`gram-ēng lang`wəj wən´\ *n.* *See* PL/I.

program specification \prō´gram spes-ə-fə-kā`-shən\ *n.* In software development, a statement of the goals and requirements of a project, as well as the relation of the project to other projects.

program state \prō´gram stāt`\ *n.* The condition of a program (stack contents, memory contents, instruction being executed) at a given moment.

program statement \prō´gram stāt`mənt\ *n.* The statement defining the name, briefly describing the operation, and possibly giving other information about a program. Some languages, such as Pascal, have an explicit program statement; others do not, or they use other forms (such as the `main( )` function in C).

project \prə-jekt´\ *n.* An operator in the relational algebra used in database management. Given relation (table) A, the *project* operator builds a new relation containing only a specified set of attributes (columns) of A.

Project Gutenberg \proj`ekt gōō´tən-bərg\ *n.* A project that makes the texts of books that are in the public domain available over the Internet. The files for the books are in plain ASCII, to make them accessible to as many people as possible. Project Gutenberg, based at the University of Illinois at Urbana-Champaign, can be reached at mrcnext.cso.uiuc.edu via FTP or through the Web page http://www.promo.net/pg/. *See also* ASCII.

projection-join normal form \prə-jek`shən-join nōr-məl fōrm´\ *n. See* normal form (definition 1).

project life cycle \proj`ekt līf´ sī-kl\ *n.* A sequence of preplanned stages for taking a project from beginning to end.

project management \proj`ekt man´əj-mənt\ *n.* The process of planning, monitoring, and controlling the course and development of a particular undertaking.

Prolog \prō´log\ *n.* Short for **Pro**gramming in **Log**ic. A language designed for logic programming. Prolog evolved during the 1970s in Europe (primarily France and Scotland), and the first Prolog compiler was developed in 1972 by Philippe Roussel, at the University of Marseilles. The language has subsequently attained wide use in the field of artificial intelligence. Prolog is a compiled language that works with the logical relationship between pieces of data rather than mathematical relationships. *See also* artificial intelligence.

PROM \prom, P´rom, P`R-O-M´\ *n.* Acronym for **p**rogrammable **r**ead-**o**nly **m**emory. A type of read-only memory (ROM) that allows data to be written into the device with hardware called a PROM programmer. After a PROM has been programmed, it is dedicated to that data, and it cannot be reprogrammed. *See also* EEPROM, EPROM, ROM (definition 2).

PROM blaster \prom´ bla`stər, P´rom, P`R-O-M´\ *n. See* PROM programmer.

PROM blower \prom´ blō´ər, P´rom, P`R-O-M´\ *n. See* PROM programmer.

promiscuous-mode transfer \ prə-mis`kyōō-əs-mōd` trans´fər\ *n.* In network communications, a trans-fer of data in which a node accepts all packets regardless of their destination address.

PROM programmer \prom´ prō`gram-ər, P´rom, P`R-O-M´\ *n.* A hardware device that records instructions or data on a PROM (programmable read-only memory) chip or an EPROM (erasable programmable read-only memory) chip. *Also called* PROM blaster, PROM blower. *See also* EPROM, PROM.

prompt \prompt\ *n.* **1.** In command-driven systems, one or more symbols that indicate where users are to enter commands. For instance, in MS-DOS, the prompt is generally a drive letter followed by a "greater than" symbol (C>). In UNIX, it is usually %. *See also* command-driven system, DOS prompt. **2.** Displayed text indicating that a computer program is waiting for input from the user.

propagated error \prop`ə-gā-təd âr´ər\ *n.* An error used as input to another operation, thus producing another error.

propagation \prop`ə-gā´shən\ *n.* Travel of a signal, such as an Internet packet, from its source to one or more destinations. Propagation of messages over different paths with different lengths can cause messages to appear at a user's computer with varying delivery times. *See also* propagation delay.

propagation delay \prop`ə-gā´shən də-lā´\ *n.* The time needed by a communications signal to travel between two points; in satellite links, a noticeable delay of between one-quarter second and one-half second, caused by the signal traveling through space.

property \prop´ər-tē\ *n.* In Windows 95, a characteristic or parameter of an object or device. Properties of a file, for example, include type, size, and creation date and can be identified by accessing the file's property sheet. *See also* property sheet.

property sheet \prop´ər-tē shēt`\ *n.* A type of dialog box in Windows 95, accessed by choosing Properties in the File menu or by right-clicking on an object and selecting Properties, that lists the attributes or settings of an object such as a file, application, or hardware device. A property sheet presents the user with a tabbed, index-card-like selection of property pages, each of which features standard dialog-style controls for customizing parameters.

proportional font \prə-pōr´shən-əl font`\ *n.* A set of characters in a particular style and size in which a variable amount of horizontal space is allotted to each letter or number. In a proportional font, the letter *i*, for example, is allowed less space than the letter *m. Compare* monospace font.

proportional spacing \prə-pōr`shən-əl spā´sēng\ *n.* A form of character spacing in which the horizontal space each character occupies is proportional to the width of the character. The letter *w*, for example, takes up more space than the letter *i. Compare* monospacing.

proprietary \prə-prī´ə-târ-ē\ *adj.* Of, pertaining to, or characteristic of something that is privately owned. Generally, the term refers to technology that has been developed by a particular corporation or entity, with specifications that are considered by the owner to be trade secrets. Proprietary technology may be legally used only by a person or entity purchasing an explicit license. Also, other companies are unable to duplicate the technology, both legally and because its specifications have not been divulged by the owner. *Compare* public domain.

proprietary software \prə-prī`ə-târ-ē soft´wār\ *n.* A program owned or copyrighted by an individual or a business and available for use only through purchase or by permission of the owner. *Compare* public-domain software.

protected mode \prə-tek´təd mōd`\ *n.* An operating mode of the Intel 80286 and higher microprocessors that supports larger address spaces and more advanced features than real mode. When started in protected mode, these CPUs provide hardware support for multitasking, data security, and virtual memory. The Windows NT and OS/2 operating systems run in protected mode, as do most versions of UNIX for these microprocessors. *Compare* real mode.

protocol \prō´tə-kol`\ *n. See* communications protocol.

protocol layer \prō´tə-kol lā`ər, lâr`\ *n. See* layer.

protocol stack \prō´tə-kol stak`\ *n.* The set of protocols that work together on different levels to enable communication on a network. For example, TCP/IP, the protocol stack on the Internet, incorporates more than 100 standards including FTP, IP, SMTP, TCP, and Telnet. *Also called* protocol suite. *See also* ISO/OSI model.

protocol suite \prō´tə-kol swēt`\ *n. See* protocol stack.

prototyping \prō´tə-tī`pēng\ *n.* The creation of a working model of a new computer system or program for testing and refinement. Prototyping is used in the development of both new hardware and software systems and new systems of information management. Tools used in the former include both hardware and support software; tools used in the latter can include databases, screen mockups, and simulations that, in some cases, can be developed into a final product.

proxy \proks´ē\ *n. See* proxy server.

proxy server \proks´ē sər`vər\ *n.* A firewall component that manages Internet traffic to and from a local area network (LAN) and can provide other features, such as document caching and access control. A proxy server can improve performance by supplying frequently requested data, such as a popular Web page, and can filter and discard requests that the owner does not consider appropriate, such as requests for unauthorized access to proprietary files. *See also* firewall.

PrtSc key \print´ skrēn kē`\ *n. See* Print Screen key.

.ps \dot`P-S´\ *n.* The file extension that identifies PostScript printer files. *See also* PostScript.

PS/2 bus \P`S-tōō´ bus\ *n. See* Micro Channel Architecture.

psec \pī´kō-sek`ənd\ *n. See* picosecond.

pseudocode \sōō´dō-kōd`\ *n.* **1.** Abbreviated p-code. A machine language for a nonexistent processor (a pseudomachine). Such code is executed by a software interpreter. The major advantage of p-code is that it is portable to all computers for which a p-code interpreter exists. The p-code approach has been tried several times in the microcomputer industry, with mixed success. The best known attempt was the UCSD p-System. *See also* pseudomachine, UCSD p-System. **2.** Any informal, transparent notation in which a program or algorithm description is written. Many programmers write their programs first in a pseudocode that looks much like a mixture of English and their favorite programming language, such as C or Pascal, and then translate it line by line into the actual language being used.

pseudo compiler \sōō´dō kəm-pī´lər\ *n.* A compiler that generates a pseudolanguage. *See also* pseudolanguage.

pseudocomputer \sōō´dō kəm-pyōō´tər\ *n. See* pseudomachine.

pseudolanguage \sōō´dō-lang´wəj\ *n.* A nonexistent programming language—that is, one for which no implementation exists. The term can refer either to the machine language for a nonexistent processor or to a high-level language for which no compiler exists. *See also* pseudocode.

pseudomachine \sōō´dō-mə-shēn´\ *n.* Abbreviated p-machine. A processor that doesn't actually exist in hardware but that is emulated in software. A program written for the pseudomachine can run on several platforms without having to be recompiled. *See also* pseudocode, UCSD p-System.

pseudo-operation \sōō´dō-op-ər-ā´shən\   *n.* Abbreviated pseudo-op. In programming, a program instruction that conveys information to an assembler or compiler but is not translated into a machine language instruction—for example, an instruction that establishes the value of a constant or the manner in which Boolean (logical) expressions are to be evaluated.

PSK \P`S-K´\ *n. See* phase-shift keying.

PSN \P`S-N´\ *n.* Acronym for **p**acket-**s**witching **n**etwork. *See* packet switching.

p-system \P´si`stəm\ *n.* An operating system based on a pseudomachine implemented in software. A program written for the p-system is more portable than one written for a machine-dependent operating system. *See also* UCSD p-System.

.pt \dot`P-T´\ *n.* On the Internet, the major geographic domain specifying that an address is located in Portugal.

P-type semiconductor \P`tīp sem´ē-kən-duk-tər, sem´ī-kən-duk-tər\ *n.* Semiconductor material in which electrical conduction is carried by holes ("vacancies" left by electrons). Whether a semiconductor is N-type or P-type depends on the kind of dopant added during manufacture. A dopant with a shortage of electrons results in a P-type semiconductor. *Compare* N-type semiconductor.

/pub \slash-pub´\ *n.* Short for **pub**lic. A directory in an anonymous FTP archive that is accessible by the public and that generally contains files available for free download. *See also* anonymous FTP.

pub \pub\ *n. See* /pub.

public directory \pu`blik dər-ek´tər-ē\ *n.* A directory on an FTP server that is accessible by anonymous users for the purpose of retrieving or storing files. Often the directory is called /pub. *See also* anonymous FTP, FTP (definition 1), FTP server, /pub.

public domain \pu`blik dō-mān´\ *n.* The set of all creative works, such as books, music, or software, that are not covered by copyright or other property protection. Works in the public domain can be freely copied, modified, and otherwise used in any manner for any purpose. Much of the information, texts, and software on the Internet is in the public domain, but putting a copyrighted work on the Internet does not put it in the public domain. *Compare* proprietary.

public-domain software \pu`blik-dō-mān soft´-wār\ *n.* A program donated for public use by its owner or developer and freely available for copying and distribution. *Compare* free software, freeware, proprietary software, shareware.

public files \pu`blik fīlz´\ *n.* Files with no access restrictions.

public folders \pu`blik fōl´dərz\ *n.* The folders that are made accessible on a particular machine or by a particular user in a shared networking environment. *Compare* private folders.

public key \pu`blik kē\ *n.* One of two keys in public key encryption. The user releases this key to the public, who can use it for encrypting messages to be sent to the user and for decrypting the user's digital signature. *See also* public key encryption. *Compare* private key.

public key cryptography \pu`blik kē krip-to´grə-fē\ *n. See* public key encryption.

public key encryption \pu`blik kē´ en-krip`shən\ *n.* An asymmetric scheme that uses a pair of keys for encryption: the public key encrypts data, and a corresponding secret key decrypts it. For digital signatures, the process is reversed: the sender uses the secret key to create a unique electronic number that can be read by anyone possessing the corresponding public key, which verifies that the message is truly from the sender. *See also* private key, public key.

public rights \pu`blik rīts´\ *n.* In the context of the Internet, the extent to which members of the public are permitted to use (and to place) information on the Internet under intellectual property law. *See also* fair use, public domain, public-domain software.

puck \puk\ *n.* A pointing device used with a graphics tablet. A puck, which is often used in engineering applications, is a mouselike device with buttons for selecting items or choosing commands and a clear plastic section extending from one end with cross hairs printed on it. The intersection of the cross hairs on the puck points to a location on the graphics tablet, which in turn is mapped to a specific location on the screen. Because the puck's cross hairs are on a transparent surface, a user can easily trace a drawing by placing it between the graphics tablet and the puck and moving the cross hairs over the lines of the drawing. See the illustration. *See also* graphics tablet, stylus.

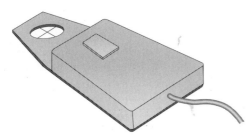

Puck.

pull \pul\ *vb.* **1.** The process of retrieving data from a network server. *Compare* push (definition 2). **2.** *See* pop.

pull-down menu \pul´doun men`yōo\ *n.* A menu that is pulled down from the menu bar and that remains available as long as the user holds it open. *Compare* drop-down menu.

pulse \puls\ *n.* A transient signal, usually brief and with a discrete onset and offset.

pulse amplitude modulation \puls` am`plə-tōod mo-dyə-lā´shən, moj`ə-lā´shən\ *n.* A method of encoding information in a signal by varying the amplitude of pulses. The unmodu-

lated signal consists of a continuous train of pulses of constant frequency, duration, and amplitude. During modulation the pulse amplitudes are changed to reflect the information being encoded. See the illustration. *Acronym:* PAM (pam, P`A-M´). *Compare* pulse code modulation, pulse duration modulation, pulse position modulation.

Pulse amplitude modulation.

pulse code modulation \puls` kōd` mo-dyə-lā´shən, moj`ə-lā´shən\ *n.* A method of encoding information in a signal by varying the amplitude of pulses. Unlike pulse amplitude modulation (PAM), in which pulse amplitude can vary continuously, pulse code modulation limits pulse amplitudes to several predefined values. Because the signal is discrete, or digital, rather than analog, pulse code modulation is more immune to noise than PAM. *Acronym:* PCM (P`C-M´). *Compare* pulse amplitude modulation, pulse duration modulation, pulse position modulation.

pulse duration modulation \puls` dur-ā´shən mo-dyə-lā´shən, moj`ə-lā´shən\ *n.* A method of encoding information in a signal by varying the duration of pulses. The unmodulated signal consists of a continuous train of pulses of constant frequency, duration, and amplitude. During modulation, the pulse durations are changed to

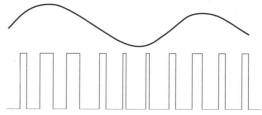

Pulse duration modulation.

reflect the information being encoded. See the illustration. *Acronym:* PDM (P`D-M´). *Also called* pulse length modulation, pulse width modulation.

pulse length modulation \puls´ length mo-dyə-lā`shən, moj-ə-lā`shən\ *n.* See pulse duration modulation.

pulse position modulation \puls pə-zish´ən mo-dyə-lā`shən, moj-ə-lā`shən\ *n.* A method of encoding information in a signal by varying the position of pulses. The unmodulated signal consists of a continuous train of pulses of constant frequency, duration, and amplitude. During modulation the pulse positions are changed to reflect the information being encoded. See the illustration. *Acronym:* PPM (P`P-M´). *Compare* pulse amplitude modulation, pulse code modulation, pulse duration modulation.

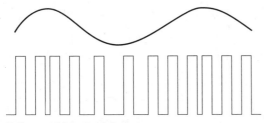

Pulse position modulation.

pulse width modulation \puls width´ mo-dyə-lā`shən, moj-ə-lā`shən\ *n.* *See* pulse duration modulation.

punched card \punchd kärd´\ *n.* An outdated computer-input medium made of stiff paper that stores data bits in columns containing patterns of punched holes. The method for creating the patterns used for different byte values is called Hollerith coding. See the illustration. *See also* Hollerith tabulating/recording machine.

Punched card.

punched-card reader \punchd`kärd´ rē`dər\ *n.* *See* card reader.

pure procedure \pyo͞or` prə-sē´jur\ *n.* Any procedure that modifies only data that is dynamically allocated (usually on the stack). A pure procedure cannot modify either global data or its own code. This restriction allows a pure procedure to be called simultaneously by separate tasks. *See also* reentrant code.

purge \purj\ *vb.* To eliminate old or unneeded information systematically; to clean up, as files.

push \po͝osh\ *vb.* **1.** To add a new element to a stack, a data structure generally used to temporarily hold pieces of data being transferred or the partial result of an arithmetic operation. *See also* stack. *Compare* pop. **2.** In networks and the Internet, to send data or a program from a server to a client at the instigation of the server. *Compare* pull (definition 1).

put \po͝ot\ *vb.* In programming, to write data, typically to a file; in particular, to write a very small unit of data, such as a character.

PVC \P`V-C´\ *n.* Acronym for **p**ermanent **v**irtual **c**ircuit. A permanent logical connection between two nodes on a packet-switching network. The PVC appears as a dedicated line to the nodes, but the data can be transmitted on a common carrier. *See also* common carrier, node (definition 2), packet switching, virtual private network. *Compare* SVC.

.pw \dot`P-W´\ *n.* On the Internet, the major geographic domain specifying that an address is located in Palau.

pwd \P`W-D´\ *n.* Acronym for **p**rint **w**orking **d**irectory. The UNIX command for displaying the current directory.

PWM \P`W-M´\ *n.* Acronym for **p**ulse **w**idth **m**odulation. *See* pulse duration modulation.

.py \dot`P-Y´\ *n.* On the Internet, the major geographic domain specifying that an address is located in Paraguay.

Python \pī´thon\ *n.* A portable, interpreted, object-oriented programming language developed and freely distributed by its developer. Python runs on many platforms, including UNIX, Windows, OS/2, and Macintosh, and is used for writing TCP/IP applications.

.qa \dot`Q-A´\ *n.* On the Internet, the major geographic domain specifying that an address is located in Qatar.

QAM \Q`A-M´, kwäm\ *n.* *See* quadrature amplitude modulation, queued access method.

QBE \Q`B-E´\ *n.* *See* query by example.

.qc.ca \dot-Q-C`dot-C-A´\ *n.* On the Internet, the major geographic domain specifying that an address is located in the province of Quebec, Canada.

.qt \dot`Q-T´\ *n.* A file extension used to identify multimedia files that use the QuickTime format. *See also* QuickTime.

quadbit \kwäd´bit\ *n.* A set of 4 bits representing one of 16 possible combinations. In communications, quadbits are a means of increasing transmission rates by encoding 4 bits at a time, instead of 1 or 2. The 16 quadbits are 0000, 0001, 0010, 0011, 0100, 0101, 0110, 0111, 1000, 1001, 1010, 1011, 1100, 1101, 1110, and 1111. *Compare* nibble.

quadrature amplitude modulation \kwä`drə-chər am`plə-tōōd moj`ə-lā´shən, mod`yə-lā´shən\ *n.* In communications, an encoding method that combines amplitude modulation and phase modulation to create a constellation of signal points, each representing one unique combination of bits that can be identified with one possible state that the carrier wave can be in. *Acronym:* QAM (Q`A-M´, kwäm). *See also* amplitude modulation, constellation, phase-shift keying, trellis-coded modulation.

quadrature encoding \kwä`drə-chər en-kō´dēng\ *n.* The most common method used to determine in which direction a mouse is moving. In mechanical mice, movement of the mouse ball is translated into horizontal or vertical movement by a pair of turning disks, one disk for horizontal movement and one disk for vertical movement, each of which makes and breaks contact with two sensors located on it. The two sensors are placed out of phase with each other, and the mouse notes which sensor receives contact first. The phrase *quadrature encoding* comes from the fact that each sensor sends a square-wave signal 90 degrees out of phase with the other. If the first signal occurs before the second, the mouse is assumed to have been moved in one direction; if the second signal occurs before the first, the mouse is assumed to have been moved in the opposite direction. *See also* mechanical mouse, mouse, optomechanical mouse.

quality assurance \kwä`lə-tē ə-shər´əns\ *n.* A system of procedures carried out to ensure that a product or a system adheres or conforms to established standards. *Also called* quality control.

quantity \kwän´tə-tē\ *n.* A number—positive or negative, whole or fractional—that is used to indicate a value.

quantize \kwän´tīz\ *vb.* To divide an element into separate, distinct units (quanta) and to assign a value to each resulting unit, especially in the domain of time. *Compare* digitize.

quantum \kwän´tum\ *n.* **1.** In communications, the unit resulting from division of a signal by quantization. **2.** A portion of time allotted on a time-sharing system. *Compare* time slice. **3.** An amount of something; as, in physics, a unit of radiant energy.

quartz crystal \kwōrts` kri´stəl\ *n.* A precisely shaped and precisely sized piece of the mineral quartz, used for its piezoelectric properties. When a voltage is applied to a quartz crystal, it vibrates at a frequency determined by its size and shape. Quartz crystals are commonly used to control the frequency of oscillator circuits such as the clocks in microcomputers. *See also* piezoelectric.

quasi-language \kwä`zē-lang´wəj, kwä`zī-\ *n.* A derogatory term for any programming language that, because of deficiencies, is not suitable for any serious work.

query \kwēr´ē, kwâr´ē\ *n*. **1.** The process of extracting data from a database and presenting it for use. **2.** A specific set of instructions for extracting particular data repetitively.

query by example \kwēr`ē bī ig-zam´pl, kwâr`ē\ *n*. A simple-to-use query language implemented on several relational database management systems. Using query by example, the user specifies fields to be displayed, intertable linkages, and retrieval criteria directly onto forms displayed on the screen. These forms are a direct pictorial representation of the table and row structures that make up the database. Thus, the construction of a query becomes a simple "checkoff" procedure from the viewpoint of the user. *Acronym:* QBE (Q`B-E´).

query language \kwēr´ē lang`wəj, kwâr´ē\ *n*. A subset of the data manipulation language; specifically, that portion relating to the retrieval and display of data from a database. It is sometimes used loosely to refer to the entire data manipulation language. *See also* data manipulation language.

question mark \kwes´chən märk`\ *n*. In some operating systems and applications, a wildcard character often used to represent any other single character. The question mark is one of two wildcard characters supported by the MS-DOS, Windows NT, and OS/2 operating systems. *See also* asterisk.

queue \kyo͞o\ *n*. A multi-element data structure from which (by strict definition) elements can be removed only in the same order in which they were inserted; that is, it follows a first in, first out (FIFO) constraint. There are also several types of queues in which removal is based on factors other than order of insertion—for example, some priority value assigned to each element. *See also* deque, element (definition 1). *Compare* stack.

queued access method \kyo͞od ak´ses meth`əd\ *n*. A programming technique that minimizes input/output delays by synchronizing the transfer of information between the program and the computer's input and output devices. *Acronym:* QAM (Q`A-M´, kwäm).

QuickDraw \kwik´drä, drô\ *n*. On the Apple Macintosh, the built-in group of routines within the operating system that control the display of graphics and text. Application programs call QuickDraw for on-screen displays. *See also* Toolbox.

QuickDraw 3-D \kwik`drä thrē-D´, kwik`drô\ *n*. A version of the Macintosh QuickDraw library that includes routines for doing 3-D graphics calculations. *See also* QuickDraw.

quicksort \kwik´sōrt\ *n*. An efficient sort algorithm, described by C.A.R. Hoare in 1962, in which the essential strategy is to "divide and conquer." A quicksort begins by scanning the list to be sorted for a median value. This value, called the *pivot,* is then moved to its final position in the list. Next, all items in the list whose values are less than the pivot value are moved to one side of the list, and the items with values greater than the pivot value are moved to the other side. Each resulting side is sorted the same way, until a fully sorted list results. *See also* sort algorithm. *Compare* bubble sort, insertion sort, merge sort.

QuickTime \kwik´tīm\ *n*. The multimedia extensions to the Apple Macintosh System 7 software, also available for Windows. QuickTime can synchronize up to 32 tracks of sounds, video images, or MIDI or other control output.

Quick Viewers \kwik´ vyo͞o`ərz\ *n*. A set of file viewers supplied with Windows 95.

quit[1] \kwit\ *n*. **1.** An FTP command that instructs the server to drop the current connection with the client from which it received the command. **2.** A command in many applications for exiting the program.

quit[2] \kwit\ *vb*. **1.** To stop in an orderly manner. **2.** To execute the normal shutdown of a program and return control to the operating system. *Compare* abort, bomb[2], crash[2] (definition 1), hang.

QWERTY keyboard \kwer´tē kē`bōrd\ *n*. A keyboard layout named for the six leftmost characters in the top row of alphabetic characters on most keyboards—the standard layout of most typewriters and computer keyboards. *Compare* Dvorak keyboard, ergonomic keyboard.

R&D \R`ənd-D´\ *n.* Acronym for **r**esearch and **d**evelopment.

race condition \rās´ kən-dish`ən\ *n.* **1.** A condition in which a feedback circuit interacts with internal circuit processes in a way that produces chaotic output behavior. **2.** A condition in which data propagates rapidly through a logic circuit far ahead of the clock signal intended to control its passage.

rack-mounted \rak´moun`təd\ *adj.* Built for installation in a metal frame or cabinet of standard width (typically 19 inches or 23 inches) and mounting arrangements.

RAD \rad, R`A-D´\ *n.* Acronym for **r**apid **a**pplication **d**evelopment. A method of building computer systems in which the system is programmed and implemented in segments, rather than waiting until the entire project is completed for implementation. Developed by programmer James Martin, RAD uses such tools as CASE and visual programming. *See also* CASE, visual programming.

radian \rā´dē-ən\ *n.* The angle between two radii of a circle such that the length of the arc between them is equal to the radius. The circumference of a circle is equal to 2π times the radius, so one radian contains $360/(2\pi) = 180/\pi$ = approximately 57.2958 degrees. Conversely, multiplying the number of degrees by $\pi/180$ gives the number of radians; 360 degrees equals 2π radians. See the illustration.

radio \rā´dē-ō`\ *n.* **1.** Electromagnetic waves longer than about 0.3 mm (frequencies lower than about 1 THz). Radio is used to transmit a wide variety of signals, using various frequency ranges and

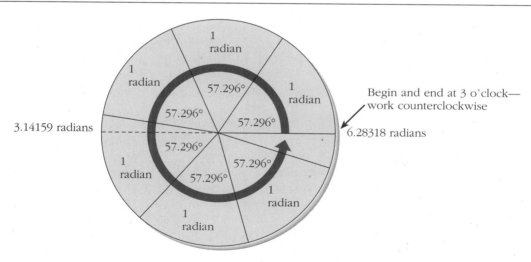

Radians = (3.14159 **x** (angle of degree)) ÷ 180
1 degree = 0.017453 radian

Radian.

types of modulation, such as AM and FM broadcasts, microwave relays, and television broadcasts. *See also* hertz, radio frequency. **2.** Audio signals transmitted over the Internet of quality comparable to those broadcast by commercial radio stations. *See also* Internet Talk Radio, MBONE, RealAudio.

radio button \rā´dē-ō but`ən\ *n.* In graphical user interfaces, a means of selecting one of several options, usually within a dialog box. A radio button appears as a small circle that, when selected, has a smaller, filled circle inside it. Radio buttons act like the station selector buttons on a car radio. Selecting one button in a set deselects the previously selected button, so one and only one of the options in the set can be selected at any given time. In contrast, check boxes are used when more than one option in the set can be selected at the same time. See the illustration. *Compare* check box.

Radio buttons

Radio button.

radio clock \rā´dē-ō klok`\ *n.* A device that receives a broadcast containing a standard time signal. Radio clocks are used in network communications to synchronize the host's hardware clock to the Universal Time Coordinate format in accordance with the Network Time Protocol (NTP). *See also* NTP, Universal Time Coordinate. ·

radio frequency \rā´dē-ō frē`kwən-sē\ *n.* Abbreviated RF. The portion of the electromagnetic spectrum with frequencies between 3 kilohertz and 300 gigahertz. This corresponds to wavelengths between 30 kilometers and 0.3 millimeter. *See also* radio (definition 1).

radio frequency interference \rā´dē-ō frē`kwen-sē in-tər-fēr´əns\ *n. See* RFI.

RADIUS \rā´dē-us`, R`A-D-I`U-S´\ *n.* Acronym for **R**emote **A**uthentication **D**ial-**I**n **U**ser **S**ervice protocol. A proposed Internet protocol in which an authentication server provides authorization and

authentication information to a network server to which a user is attempting to link. *See also* authentication, communications protocol, server (definition 2).

radix \rā´diks\ *n.* The base of a number system—for example, 2 in the binary system, 10 in the decimal system, 8 in the octal system, and 16 in the hexadecimal system. *See also* base (definition 2).

radix-minus-1 complement \rā`diks-mī-nus-wən´ kom`plə-mənt\ *n.* In a system for representing numbers using a fixed number of possible digits (radix) and a fixed number of positions for them, the number obtained from another number by subtracting each of the digits of the other number from the largest possible digit (equal to the radix minus 1). For example, in a system of five-digit decimal numbers, the radix-minus-1 complement of 1,234 is 98,765. Adding any number to its radix-minus-1 complement produces the largest possible number in the system (in the example, 99,999). Adding another 1 to this number produces, in our example, 100,000—but since only the lower five digits are used, the result is zero. Thus, the negative of any number in the system is its radix-minus-1 complement plus 1, because $-a + a = 0$. In the binary system, the radix-minus-1 complement is the one's complement, which is easily formed electronically by inverting all bits.

radix point \rā´diks point`\ *n.* The period or other character that separates the integer portion of a number from the fractional portion. In the decimal system, the radix point is the decimal point, as in the number 1.33.

radix sort \rā´diks sōrt`\ *n. See* digital sort.

radix sorting algorithm \rā`diks sōr-tēng al´gər-idh-əm\ *n.* A sorting algorithm that sorts by grouping elements according to successive parts of their keys. A simple example is sorting a list of numbers in the range 0–999. First the list is sorted by the hundreds digit into a set of (up to) 10 lists; then each list, one at a time, is sorted into a set of (up to) 10 lists based on the tens digit; and finally, each of those lists is sorted by the ones digit. This algorithm is usually most efficient when the sorting is done using binary values, which simplifies comparisons (is a given bit on or off?) and reduces the number of lists (each pass produces at most two lists).

rag \rag\ *n.* Irregularity along the left or right edge of a set of lines of text on a printed page. Rag complements justification, in which one or both edges of the text form a straight vertical line. See the illustration. *See also* justify, ragged left, ragged right.

Ragged right	Justified	Ragged left

Rag.

ragged left \rag`əd left´\ *adj.* Of, relating to, or being lines of text whose left ends are not vertically aligned but form an irregular edge. Text may be right-justified and have a ragged left margin. Ragged-left text is used infrequently—typically, for visual effect in advertisements. *See also* rag, right-justify.

ragged right \rag`əd rīt´\ *adj.* Of, relating to, or being lines of text whose right ends are not vertically aligned but form an irregular edge. Letters and other word-processed documents are commonly left-justified, with ragged-right margins. *See also* left-justify, rag.

RAID \rād, R`A-I-D´\ *n.* Acronym for **r**edundant **a**rray of **i**ndependent **d**isks (formerly called **r**edundant **a**rray of **i**nexpensive **d**isks). A data storage method in which data, along with information used for error correction, such as parity bits or Hamming codes, is distributed among two or more hard disk drives in order to improve performance and reliability. The hard disk array is governed by array management software and a disk controller, which handles the error correction. RAID is generally used on network servers. Several defined levels of RAID offer differing trade-offs among access speed, reliability, and cost. *See also* disk controller, error-correction coding, Hamming code, hard disk, parity bit, server (definition 1).

RAID array \rād´ ə-rā`, R`A-I-D´\ *n. See* RAID.

RAM \ram, R`A-M´\ *n.* Acronym for **r**andom **a**ccess **m**emory. Semiconductor-based memory that can be read and written by the central processing unit (CPU) or other hardware devices. The storage locations can be accessed in any order. Note that the various types of ROM memory are capable of random access but cannot be written to. The term *RAM,* however, is generally understood to refer to volatile memory that can be written to as well as read. *Compare* core, EPROM, flash memory, PROM, ROM (definition 2).

RAM cache \ram´ kash, R`A-M´\ *n.* Cache memory that is used by the system to store and retrieve data from the RAM. Frequently accessed segments of data may be stored in the cache for quicker access compared with secondary storage devices such as disks. *See also* cache, RAM.

RAM card \ram´ kärd, R`A-M´\ *n.* An add-in circuit board containing RAM memory and the interface logic necessary to decode memory addresses.

RAM cartridge \ram´ kär`trij, R`A-M´\ *n. See* memory cartridge.

RAM chip \ram´ chip, R`A-M´\ *n.* A semiconductor storage device. RAM chips can be either dynamic or static memory. *See also* dynamic RAM, RAM, static RAM.

RAM compression \ram´ kəm-presh`ən, R-A-M´\ *n.* Short for **r**andom **a**ccess **m**emory **compression.** This technology was an attempt by a number of software vendors to solve the problem of running out of global memory under Windows 3.*x*. Compression of the usual contents of RAM may lessen the system's need to read or write to virtual (hard disk–based) memory and thus speed up the system, as virtual memory is much slower than physical RAM. Because of the falling prices of RAM and the introduction of Windows 95 and Windows NT, which handle RAM more effectively, RAM compression is generally used only on older PCs. *See also* compression, RAM, Windows, Windows 95.

RAMDAC \ram´dak, R-A-M`D-A-C´\ *n.* Acronym for **r**andom **a**ccess **m**emory **d**igital-to-**a**nalog **c**onverter. A chip built into some VGA and SVGA video adapters that translates the digital representation of a pixel into the analog information needed by the monitor to display it. The presence of a RAMDAC chip generally enhances overall video performance. *See also* SVGA, VGA.

RAM disk \ram´ disk, R`A-M´\ *n.* Short for **r**andom **a**ccess **m**emory **disk.** A simulated disk drive whose data is actually stored in RAM memory. A special program allows the operating system to read from and write to the simulated device as if it were a disk drive. RAM disks are extremely fast, but they require that system memory be given up for their use. Also, RAM disks usually use volatile memory, so the data stored on them disappears when power is turned off. Many portables offer RAM disks that use battery-backed CMOS RAM to avoid this problem. *See also* CMOS RAM. *Compare* disk cache.

RAM refresh \ram´ rē-fresh`, R`A-M´\ *n. See* refresh (definition 2).

RAM resident \ram´ rez`ə-dənt, R-A-M´\ *adj. See* memory-resident.

RAM-resident program \ram`rez-ə-dent　prō´-gram, R`A-M´\ *n. See* terminate-and-stay-resident program.

random access \ran`dəm ak´ses\ *n.* The ability of a computer to find and go directly to a particular storage location without having to search sequentially from the beginning location. The human equivalent of random access would be the ability to find a desired address in an address book without having to proceed sequentially through all the addresses. A computer's semiconductor memory (both RAM and ROM) provides random access. Certain types of files stored on disk under some operating systems also allow random access. Such files are best used for data in which each record has no intrinsic relationship to what comes physically before or after it, as in a client list or an inventory. *Also called* direct access. *See also* RAM, ROM. *Compare* indexed sequential access method, sequential access.

random access memory \ran`dəm ak-ses mem´-ər-ē\ *n. See* RAM.

random noise \ran`dəm noiz´\ *n.* A signal in which there is no relationship between amplitude and time and in which many frequencies occur randomly, without pattern or predictability.

random number generation \ran`dəm num`bər jen-ər-ā`shən\ *n.* Production of an unpredictable sequence of numbers in which no number is any more likely to occur at a given time or place in the sequence than any other. Truly random number generation is generally viewed as impossible. The

process used in computers would be more properly called "pseudorandom number generation."

range \rānj\ *n.* **1.** A block of cells selected for similar treatment in a spreadsheet. A range of cells can extend across a row, down a column, or over a combination of the two, but all cells in the range must be contiguous, sharing at least one common border. Ranges allow the user to affect many cells with a single command—for example, to format them similarly, enter the same data into all of them, give them a name in common and treat them as a unit, or select and incorporate them into a formula. **2.** In more general usage, the spread between specified low and high values. Range checking is an important method of validating data entered into an application.

range check \rānj´ chek\ *n.* In programming, a limit check of both the upper and lower limits of a value, thus determining whether the value lies within an acceptable range. *See also* limit check.

RARP \R`A-R-P´\ *n.* Acronym for **R**everse **A**ddress **R**esolution **P**rotocol. A TCP/IP protocol for determining the IP address (or logical address) of a node on a local area network connected to the Internet, when only the hardware address (or physical address) is known. While RARP refers only to finding the IP address and ARP technically refers to the opposite procedure, ARP is commonly used for both senses. *See also* ARP.

RAS \R`A-S´\ *n. See* remote access server, Remote Access Service.

raster \ra´stər\ *n.* A rectangular pattern of lines; on a video display, the horizontal scan lines from which the term *raster scan* is derived.

raster display \ra´stər dis-plā´\ *n.* A video monitor (typically a CRT) that displays an image on the screen as a series of horizontal scan lines from top to bottom. Each scan line consists of pixels that can be illuminated and colored individually. Television screens and most computer monitors are raster displays. *See also* CRT, pixel. *Compare* vector display.

raster graphics \ra´stər graf`iks\ *n.* A method of generating graphics that treats an image as a collection of small, independently controlled dots (pixels) arranged in rows and columns. *Compare* vector graphics.

raster image \ra´stər im`əj\ *n.* A display image formed by patterns of light and dark or differently colored pixels in a rectangular array. *See also* raster graphics.

raster image processor \ra`stər im-əj pros´es-ər\ *n.* A device, consisting of hardware and software, that converts vector graphics or text into a raster (bitmapped) image. Raster image processors are used in page printers, phototypesetters, and electrostatic plotters. They compute the brightness and color value of each pixel on the page so that the resulting pattern of pixels re-creates the vector graphics and text originally described. *Acronym:* RIP (rip, R`I-P´).

rasterization \ra`stər-ə-zā´shən\ *n.* The conversion of vector graphics (images described in terms of mathematical elements, such as points and lines) to equivalent images composed of pixel patterns that can be stored and manipulated as sets of bits. *See also* pixel.

raster-scan display \ra´stər-skan dis-plā´\ *n. See* raster display.

raw data \rô´ dā´tə, dat´ə\ *n.* **1.** Unprocessed, typically unformatted, data, such as a stream of bits that has not been filtered for commands or special characters. *See also* raw mode. *Compare* cooked mode. **2.** Information that has been collected but not evaluated.

raw mode \rô´ mōd\ *n.* A way in which the UNIX and MS-DOS operating systems "see" a character-based device. If the identifier for the device indicates raw mode, the operating system does not filter input characters or give special treatment to carriage returns, end-of-file markers, and linefeed and tab characters. *Compare* cooked mode.

ray tracing \rā´ trā`sēng\ *n.* A sophisticated and complex method of producing high-quality computer graphics. Ray tracing calculates the color and intensity of each pixel in an image by tracing single rays of light backward and determining how they were affected on their way from a defined source of light illuminating the objects in the image. Ray tracing is demanding in terms of processing capability because the computer must account for reflection, refraction, and absorption of individual rays, as well as for the brightness, transparency level, and reflectivity of each object

and the positions of the viewer and the light source.

RCA connector \R`C-A´ kə-nek`tər\ *n.* A connector used for attaching audio and video devices, such as stereo equipment or a composite video monitor, to a computer's video adapter. See the illustration. *See also* composite video display. *Compare* phono connector.

RCA connector. A female version (left) and a male version (right).

RDBMS \R`D-B-M-S´\ *n.* Acronym for **r**elational **d**ata**b**ase **m**anagement **s**ystem. *See* relational database.

RDO \R`D-O´\ *n. See* Remote Data Objects.

read[1] \rēd\ *n.* The action of transferring data from an input source into a computer's memory or from memory into the central processing unit (CPU). *Compare* write[1].

read[2] \rēd\ *vb.* To transfer data from an external source, such as from a disk or the keyboard, into memory or from memory into the central processing unit (CPU). *Compare* write[2].

reader \rē´dər\ *n. See* card reader.

read error \rēd´ âr`ər\ *n.* An error encountered while a computer is in the process of obtaining information from storage or from another source of input. *Compare* write error.

README \rēd´mē\ *n.* A file containing information that the user either needs or will find informative and that might not have been included in the documentation. README files are placed on disk in plain-text form (without extraneous or program-specific characters) so that they can be read easily by a variety of word processing programs.

read notification \rēd´ nō-tə-fə-kā`shən\ *n.* An e-mail feature providing feedback to the sender that a message has been read by the recipient. See the illustration on the next page.

read-only \rēd`ōn´lē\ *adj.* Capable of being retrieved (read) but not changed (written). A read-only file or document can be displayed or printed

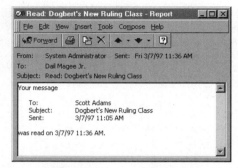

Read notification.

but not altered in any way; read-only memory (ROM) holds programs that cannot be changed; a read-only storage medium, such as CD-ROM, can be played back but cannot be used for recording information. *Compare* read/write.

read-only attribute \rēd`ōn-lē a´tri-byoōt\ *n.* In Windows and OS/2, a file attribute, stored with a file's directory, indicating whether or not a file may be changed or erased. When the read-only attribute is off, the file can be modified or deleted; when it is on, the file can only be displayed.

read-only memory \rēd`ōn-lē mem´ər-ē\ *n. See* ROM.

read-only terminal \rēd`ōn-lē tər´mə-nəl\ *n. See* RO terminal.

read/write \rēd-rīt´\ *adj.* Abbreviated R/W. Able to be both read from and written to. *Compare* read-only.

read/write channel \rēd-rīt´ chan`əl\ *n. See* input/output channel.

read/write head \rēd-rīt´ hed`\ *n. See* head.

read/write memory \rēd-rīt´ mem`ər-ē\ *n.* Memory that can be both read from and written to (modified). Semiconductor RAM and core memory are typical read/write memory systems. *Compare* ROM (definition 2).

real address \rēl` a´dres, ə-dres´\ *n.* An absolute (machine) address specifying a physical location in memory. *See also* physical address. *Compare* relative address, virtual address.

RealAudio \rēl`ä´dē-ō, rēl`ô´dē-ō\ *n.* Web software that streams prerecorded or live audio to a client, such as a Web browser, by decompressing it on the fly so that it can be played back to the Web browser user in real time.

reallocate \rē-al´ə-kāt`\ *n.* A function in C that allows the programmer to request a larger portion of heap memory than was previously assigned to a particular pointer. *See also* dynamic memory allocation, heap (definition 1).

real mode \rēl´ mōd`\ *n.* An operating mode in the Intel 80x86 family of microprocessors. In real mode, the processor can execute only one program at a time. It can access no more than about 1 MB of memory, but it can freely access system memory and input/output devices. Real mode is the only mode possible in the 8086 processor and is the only operating mode supported by MS-DOS. In contrast, the protected mode offered in the 80286 and higher microprocessors provides the memory management and memory protection needed for multitasking environments such as Windows. *See also* 8086, privileged mode. *Compare* protected mode, virtual real mode.

real-mode mapper \rēl`mōd map´ər\ *n.* An enhancement for Windows 3.*x* systems that allows 32-bit file system access. The real-mode mapper provides a 32-bit disk access interface to the DOS device driver chain. *Acronym:* RMM (R`M-M´).

real number \rēl` num´bər\ *n.* **1.** A number that can be represented in a number system with a given base, such as the decimal system, by a finite or infinite sequence of digits and a radix point. For example, 1.1 is a real number, as is 0.33333…. *See also* irrational number. *Compare* complex number, imaginary number. **2.** A data type, in a programming language such as Pascal, that is used for storing, to some limit of precision, values that include both integer and fractional parts. *See also* double-precision, single-precision. *Compare* floating-point number, integer.

Real Soon Now \rē`əl soōn´ nou, rēl`\ *adv.* Soon, but not really expected to be as soon as claimed. One might say, for example, that a commercial program will have some desired feature Real Soon Now if several versions ago the vendor knew of the need for the feature and has done nothing. *Acronym:* RSN (R`S-N´).

real storage \rēl` stōr´əj\ *n.* The amount of RAM memory in a system, as distinguished from virtual memory. *Also called* physical memory, physical storage. *See also* virtual memory.

real-time \rēl´tīm\ *adj.* Of or relating to a time frame imposed by external constraints. Real-time operations are those in which the machine's activities match the human perception of time or those in which computer operations proceed at the same rate as a physical or external process. Real-time operations are characteristic of aircraft guidance systems, transaction-processing systems, scientific applications, and other areas in which a computer must respond to situations as they occur (for example, animating a graphic in a flight simulator or making corrections based on measurements).

real-time animation \rēl`-tīm an-ə-mā´shən\ *n.* Computer animation in which images are computed and updated on the screen at the same rate at which the objects simulated might move in the real world. Real-time animation allows dynamic involvement by the user because the computer can accept and incorporate keystrokes or controller movements as it is drawing the next image in the animation sequence. Arcade-style animation (such as in a flight simulator program) makes use of real-time animation in translating game plays into on-screen actions. In contrast, in animation done in virtual time, image frames are first calculated and stored and later replayed at a higher rate to achieve smoother movement. *See also* animation, bit block.

real-time clock \rēl`-tīm klok´\ *n. See* clock (definition 2).

real-time conferencing \rēl`tīm kon´frən-sēng\ *n. See* teleconferencing.

real-time operating system \rēl`tīm op´ər-ā-tēng si`stəm\ *n.* An operating system designed or optimized for the needs of a process-control environment. *See also* real-time system.

real-time system \rēl`tīm si`stəm\ *n.* A computer and/or a software system that reacts to events before the events become obsolete. For example, airline collision avoidance systems must process radar input, detect a possible collision, and warn air traffic controllers or pilots while they still have time to react.

reboot \rē-bo͞ot´\ *vb.* To restart a computer by reloading the operating system. *See also* boot[2], cold boot, warm boot.

receipt notification \rə-sēt´ nō-tə-fə-kā`shən\ *n.* An e-mail feature providing feedback to the sender that a message has been received by the recipient. See the illustration.

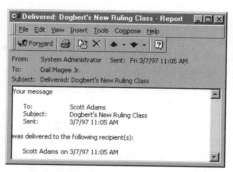

Receipt notification.

receive \rə-sēv´\ *vb.* To accept data from an external communications system, such as a local area network (LAN) or a telephone line, and store the data as a file.

Receive Data \rə-sēv` dā´tə, dat´ə\ *n. See* RXD.

rec. newsgroups \rek´dot-no͞oz`gro͞ops\ *n.* Usenet newsgroups that are part of the rec. hierarchy and whose names have the prefix "rec." These newsgroups cover topics devoted to discussions of recreational activities, hobbies, and the arts. *See also* newsgroup, traditional newsgroup hierarchy, Usenet. *Compare* comp. newsgroups, misc. newsgroups, news. newsgroups, sci. newsgroups, soc. newsgroups, talk. newsgroups.

recompile \rē`kəm-pīl´\ *vb.* To compile a program again, usually because of changes that needed to be made in the source code in response to error messages generated by the compiler. *See also* compile.

record[1] \rek´ərd\ *n.* A data structure that is a collection of fields (elements), each with its own name and type. Unlike an array, whose elements all represent the same type of information and are accessed using an index, the elements of a record represent different types of information and are accessed by name. A record can be accessed as a collective unit of elements, or the elements can be accessed individually. *See also* array, data structure, type[1] (definition 1).

record[2] \rə-kōrd´\ *vb.* To retain information, usually in a file.

record format \rek´ərd fōr`mat\ *n. See* record structure.

record head \rə-kōrd´ hed`\ *n.* The device in a tape machine that places data on the tape. In some tape machines, the record head is combined with the read head.

record layout \rek´ərd lā`out\ *n.* The organization of data fields within a record. *See also* record[1].

record length \rek´ərd length`\ *n.* The amount of storage space required to contain a record, typically given in bytes. *See also* record[1].

record locking \rek´ərd lok`ēng\ *n.* A strategy employed in distributed processing and other multiuser situations to prevent more than one user at a time from writing data to a record. *See also* record[1].

record number \rek´ərd num`bər\ *n.* A unique number assigned to a record in a database in order to identify it. A record number can identify an existing record by its position (for example, the tenth record from the beginning of a database), or it can be assigned to the record to serve as a key (for example, the number 00742 assigned to the tenth record from the beginning of the database). *See also* record[1].

record structure \rek´ərd struk`chur\ *n.* An ordered list of the fields that compose a record, together with a definition of the domain (acceptable values) of each field. *See also* record[1].

recover \rə-kəv´ər\ *vb.* **1.** To return to a stable condition after some error has occurred. A program recovers from an error by stabilizing itself and resuming execution of instructions without user intervention. **2.** To put back into a stable condition. A computer user may be able to recover lost or damaged data by using a program to search for and salvage whatever information remains in storage. A database may be recovered by restoring its integrity after some problem has damaged it, such as abnormal termination of the database management program.

recoverable error \rə-kəv´ər-ə-bl âr´ər\ *n.* An error that can be successfully managed by software. For example, when the user enters a number when a letter is required, the program can simply display an error message and prompt the user again.

recovery \rə-kəv´ər-ē`\ *n.* The restoration of lost data or the reconciliation of conflicting or erroneous data, after a system failure. Recovery is often achieved using a disk or tape backup and system logs. *See also* backup.

Recreational Software Advisory Council \re-krē-ā`shə-nəl soft`wâr ad-vī´zər-ē koun`səl\ *n.* An independent, nonprofit organization established in the fall of 1994 by a group of six trade organizations, led by the Software Publishers Association. The Council's goal was to create a new, objective content-labeling rating system for recreational software and other media such as the Internet. *Acronym:* RSAC (R´sak, R`S-A-C´).

rectifier \rek´tə-fī`ər\ *n.* A circuit component that passes current flowing in one direction but stops current flowing in the other direction. Rectifiers are used to convert alternating current to direct current.

recto \rek´tō\ *n.* The right-hand page of two facing pages. A recto is characteristically an odd-numbered page. *Compare* verso.

recursion \rə-kur´zhən\ *n.* The ability of a routine to call itself. Recursion enables certain algorithms to be implemented with small, simple routines, but it does not guarantee speed or efficiency. Erroneous use of recursion can cause a program to run out of stack space during execution, causing the program, and sometimes the entire system, to crash. *See also* call[1] (definition 2), routine.

Recycle Bin \rē-sī´kl bin`\ *n.* A folder in Windows 95, represented by an icon on the screen resembling a basket decorated with the recycling logo. To remove a file, the user drags its icon to the Recycle Bin. However, a file in the Recycle Bin is not actually deleted from the disk until the user opens the Recycle Bin, selects the file, and presses the Del key; until then, the user can retrieve it. *Compare* Trash.

Red Book \red´ book\ *n.* **1.** The standards documents of the U.S. National Security Agency entitled "Trusted Network Interpretation of the Trusted Computer System Evaluation Criteria (NCSC-TG-005)" and "Trusted Network Interpretation (NCS-TG-011)." These documents define a system of ratings from A1 (most secure) to D (nonsecure), indicating the ability of a computer network to protect sensitive information. *Compare* Orange Book (definition 1). **2.** A specifications book written by the Sony and Philips corporations and endorsed by ISO, covering audio compact discs. *Compare* Green Book, Orange Book (definition 2). **3.** Telecommunications standards published by the CCITT.

red-green-blue \red`grēn-bloō´\ *n. See* RGB.

redirection \rē`dər-ek´shən\ *n.* The process of writing to or reading from a file or device different from the one that would normally be the target or the source. For example, the MS-DOS or OS/2 command *dir >prn* redirects a directory listing from the screen to the printer. *Compare* pipe.

redlining \red´lī-nēng\ *n.* A feature of a word processing application that marks changes, additions, or deletions made to a document by a co-author or editor. The purpose of redlining is to produce a record of the changes made to a document during the course of its development.

redraw \rē´drä, rē´drô\ *n. See* refresh (definition 1).

reduce \rə-doōs´, rē-doōs´\ *vb.* In a graphical user interface, to decrease the size of a window. A user can reduce a window either by clicking on the appropriate button in the title bar or by clicking the mouse on the border of the window and dragging the border toward the middle of the window. *See also* maximize, minimize.

reduced instruction set computing \rə-doōsd in-struk`shən set kəm-pyoō´tēng\ *n. See* RISC.

redundancy check \rə-dun´dən-sē chek`\ *n. See* CRC, LRC.

redundant code \rə-dun`dənt kōd´\ *n.* Code that duplicates a function performed elsewhere—for example, code to sort a list that has already been sorted.

reengineer \rē´en-jə-nēr´\ *vb.* To rethink and redefine processes and procedures. In the context of computer systems, to reengineer means to change the way work is done in order to maximize the benefits of new technology.

reengineering \rē`en-jə-nēr´ēng\ *vb.* **1.** With regard to software, changing existing software to strengthen desirable characteristics and remove weaknesses. **2.** With regard to corporate management, using information technology principles to address the challenges posed by a global economy and to consolidate management of a rapidly expanding work force.

reentrant code \rē-en´trənt kōd`\ *n.* Code written so that it can be shared by several programs at the same time. When a program is executing reentrant code, another program can interrupt the execution and can then start or continue execution of that same code. Many operating-system routines are written to be reentrant so that only one copy needs to reside in memory to serve all executing applications. *See also* relocatable code.

reference[1] \ref´ər-əns`, re´frəns\ *n.* A data type in the C++ programming language. A reference must be initialized with a variable name. The reference then becomes an alias for that variable but actually stores the address of the variable.

reference[2] \ref´ər-əns`, re´frəns\ *vb.* To access a variable, such as an element in an array or a field in a record.

Reference.COM \re`frəns-dot-kom´\ *n.* An Internet search engine that indexes more than 150,000 Usenet newsgroups, mailing lists, and Web forums, located at www.reference.com.

reference parameter \ref´ər-əns   pər-am`ə-tər, re´frəns\ *n.* A parameter in which the address of a variable, rather than the explicit value, is passed to the called routine. *See also* parameter.

reflecting software \rə-flek`tēng soft´wâr\ *n. See* reflector.

reflective liquid-crystal display \rə-flek`tiv   li-kwid-kri´stəl dis-plā´\ *n.* A liquid crystal display that is not equipped with edge or back lighting to enhance readability but rather depends on reflecting ambient light, making it difficult to read in brightly lit environments such as the outdoors. *Also called* reflective LCD.

reflective routing \rə-flek`tiv rou´tēng, roō´tēng\ *n.* In wide area networks, the process of using a reflector to distribute data, thereby reducing the load of the network server. *See also* reflector.

reflector \rə-flek´tər\ *n.* A program that sends messages to a number of users upon receipt of a signal from a single user. A common type of reflector is an e-mail reflector, which forwards any e-mail sent to it to the multiple recipients currently on its list. *See also* multiple recipients. *Compare* mail reflector.

reformat \rē`fōr´mat\ *vb.* **1.** In applications, to change the look of a document by altering stylistic details, such as font, layout, indention, and alignment. **2.** In data storage, to prepare for reuse a disk that already contains programs or data, effectively destroying the existing contents.

refresh \rə-fresh´\ *vb.* **1.** To retrace a video screen at frequent intervals, even if the image does not change, so as to keep the phosphors irradiated. **2.** To recharge dynamic random access memory chips (DRAMs) so that they continue to retain the information stored in them. Circuitry on the memory board automatically performs this function. *See also* refresh cycle.

refreshable \rə-fresh´ə-bl\ *adj.* In programming, referring to a program module capable of being replaced in memory without affecting processing of the program or the information being used by the program.

refresh cycle \rə-fresh´ sī`kl\ *n.* The process in which controller circuitry provides repeated electric pulses to dynamic random access memory chips in order to renew the stored electric charges in those locations that contain binary 1. Each pulse is one refresh cycle. Without constant refreshing, dynamic semiconductor RAM loses any information stored in it—as it does when the computer is turned off or when the power fails. *See also* dynamic RAM, static RAM.

refresh rate \rə-fresh´ rāt`\ *n.* In reference to video hardware, the frequency with which the entire screen is redrawn to maintain a constant, flicker-free image. On TV screens and raster-scan monitors, the electron beam that lights the phosphor coating on the inner surface of the screen typically refreshes the entire image area at a rate of about 60 hertz, or 60 times per second. (Interlaced monitors, which redraw alternate lines during each sweep of the electron beam, actually refresh any particular line only 30 times per second. Because odd and even lines are refreshed on successive sweeps, however, the effective refresh rate is 60 times per second.)

REGEDIT \rej´ed`it\ *n. See* Registry Editor.

regenerate \rē-jen´ər-āt\ *vb. See* rewrite.

regeneration buffer \rē-jen-ər-ā´shən buf`ər\ *n. See* video buffer.

regenerator \rē-jen´ər-ā`tər\ *n. See* repeater.

region \rē´jən\ *n.* **1.** An area dedicated to or reserved for a particular purpose. **2.** In video programming, a contiguous group of pixels that are treated as a unit. On the Apple Macintosh, for example, a region is an area in a grafPort that can be defined and manipulated as an entity. The vis-

ible working area within a window is an example of a region. *See also* grafPort.

region fill \rē´jən fil\ *n.* In computer graphics, the technique of filling a defined region on the screen with a selected color, pattern, or other attribute. *See also* region.

register \rej´i-stər\ *n.* A set of bits of high-speed memory within a microprocessor or other electronic device, used to hold data for a particular purpose. Each register in a central processing unit is referred to in assembly language programs by a name such as *AX* (the register that contains the results of arithmetic operations in an Intel 80x86 processor) or *SP* (the register that contains the memory address of the top of the stack in various processors).

registration \rej`ə-strā´shən\ *n.* The process of precisely aligning elements or superimposing layers in a document or a graphic so that everything will print in the correct relative position. *See also* registration marks.

registration marks \rej-ə-strā´shən märks`\ *n.* Marks placed on a page so that in printing, the elements or layers in a document can be arranged correctly with respect to each other. Each element to be assembled contains its own registration marks; when the marks are precisely superimposed, the elements are in the correct position. See the illustration.

Registration marks.

Registry or **registry** \rej´is-trē`\ *n.* A central hierarchical database in Windows 95 and Windows NT used to store information necessary to configure the system for one or more users, applications, and hardware devices. The Registry contains information that Windows 95 and Windows NT continually reference during operation, such as profiles for each user, the applications installed on the computer and the types of documents each can create, property sheet settings for folders and application icons, what hardware exists on the system, and which ports are being used. The Registry replaces most of the text-based .ini files used in Windows 3.*x* and MS-DOS configuration files, such as AUTOEXEC.BAT and CONFIG.SYS. Although the Windows 95 Registry is similar to the one in Windows NT, there are some differences, such as how they are stored on disk. *Also called* System Registry. *See also* hierarchical database, .ini, input/output port, property sheet, Registry Editor.

Registry Editor \rej´is-trē ed`i-tər\ *n.* An application under Windows 95 that allows the user to edit the entries in the Registry. See the illustration. *Acronym:* REGEDIT (rej´ed`it). *See also* Registry.

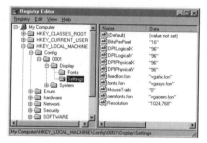

Registry Editor.

regression analysis \ri-gresh´ən ə-nal´ə-sis\ *n.* In statistics, an analysis of the degree to which variations in an independent variable affect a dependent variable (a variable whose value depends on the value of another variable). *See also* multiple regression.

regression testing \ri-gresh´ən te`stēng\ *n.* Complete retesting of a modified program, rather than a test of only the modified routines, to ensure that no errors have been introduced with the modifications.

relation \rə-lā´shən\ *n.* A structure composed of attributes (individual characteristics, such as name or address, corresponding to the columns in a table) and tuples (sets of attribute values describing particular entities, such as customers, corresponding to the rows in a table). Within a relation, tuples cannot be repeated; each must be unique. Further, tuples are unordered within a relation; interchanging two tuples does not change the relation. Finally, if relational theory is to be applicable,

the domain of each attribute must be atomic—that is, a simple value, rather than a structure such as an array or a record. A relation in which the domains of all attributes are atomic is said to be normalized or in first normal form. *See also* normal form (definition 1).

relational algebra \rə-lā`shən-əl al´jə-brə\ *n.* A collection of rules and operators that permit relations (tables) to be manipulated. Relational algebra is usually described as having the following operators: SELECT, PROJECT, PRODUCT, UNION, INTERSECT, DIFFERENCE, JOIN (or INNER JOIN), and DIVIDE. In a relational database, relational algebra is used to develop procedures to build new relations based on the existing relations.

relational calculus \rə-lā`shən-əl kal´kyə-lus\ *n.* In database management, a nonprocedural method for manipulating relations (tables). There are two families of relational calculus: domain calculus and tuple calculus. The two families of relational calculus are mathematically equivalent to each other and to relational algebra. Using either family, one can formulate a description of a desired relation, based on the existing relations in the database.

relational database \rə-lā`shən-əl dā´tə-bās\ *n.* A database or database management system that stores information in tables—rows and columns of data—and conducts searches by using data in specified columns of one table to find additional data in another table. In a relational database, the rows of a table represent records (collections of information about separate items) and the columns represent fields (particular attributes of a record). In conducting searches, a relational database matches information from a field in one table with information in a corresponding field of another table to produce a third table that combines requested data from both tables. For example, if one table contains the fields EMPLOYEE-ID, LAST-NAME, FIRST-NAME, and HIRE-DATE, and another contains the fields DEPT, EMPLOYEE-ID, and SALARY, a relational database can match the EMPLOYEE-ID fields in the two tables to find such information as the names of all employees earning a certain salary or the departments of all employees hired after a certain date. In other words, a relational database uses matching values in two tables to relate information in one to information in the other. Microcomputer database products typically are relational databases. *Compare* flat-file database, inverted-list database.

relational database management system \rə-lā`shən-əl dā`tə-bās man´əj-mənt si`stəm\ *n. See* relational database.

relational expression \rə-lā`shən-əl eks-presh´ən\ *n.* An expression that uses a relational operator such as "less than" or "greater than" to compare two or more expressions. A relational expression resolves to a Boolean (true/false) value. *See also* Boolean, relational operator.

relational model \rə-lā`shən-əl mod´əl\ *n.* A data model in which the data is organized in relations (tables). This is the model implemented in most modern database management systems.

relational operator \rə-lā`shən-əl op´ər-ā-tər\ *n.* An operator that allows the programmer to compare two (or more) values or expressions. Typical relational operators are greater than (>), equal to (=), less than (<), not equal to (<>), greater than or equal to (>=), and less than or equal to (<=). *See also* relational expression.

relational structure \rə-lā`shən-əl struk´chur\ *n.* The record organization used in the implementation of a relational model.

relative address \rel`ə-tiv a´dres, ə-dres´\ *n.* A location, as in a computer's memory, that is specified in terms of its distance (displacement or offset) from a starting point (base address). A relative address is typically computed by adding an offset to the base—in everyday terms, this is similar to creating the address 2001 Main Street, in which the base is the 2000 block of Main Street and the offset is 1, which specifies the first house from the beginning of the block. *Also called* indirect address.

relative coordinates \rel`ə-tiv kō-ōr´də-nəts\ *n.* Coordinates that are defined in terms of their distance from a given starting point, rather than from the origin (intersection of two axes). For example, from a starting point on the screen, a square defined by relative coordinates can be drawn as a series of lines, each representing a displacement in distance and direction from the end of the preceding point. The entire square can be redrawn at another location simply by changing the coordi-

nates of the starting point rather than by recalculating the coordinates of each corner with reference to the origin. See the illustration. *Compare* absolute coordinates.

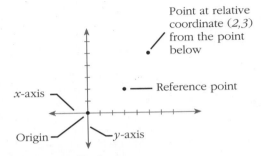

Relative coordinates.

relative movement \rel`ə-tiv mo͞ov´mənt\ *n.* **1.** Motion whose distance and direction are relative to a starting point. For example, when a mouse pointer is moved on the screen, the coordinates of its new position are relative to the previous location of the pointer. *See also* relative coordinates, relative pointing device. **2.** In computer graphics and cinematography, the movement of one object in relation to another, such as the movement of horse A from the perspective of horse B on a racetrack.

relative path \rel`ə-tiv path´\ *n.* A path that is implied by the current working directory. When a user enters a command that refers to a file, if the full pathname is not entered, the current working directory becomes the relative path of the file referred to. *Compare* full path.

relative pointing device \rel`ə-tiv poin´tēng də-vīs\ *n.* A cursor-control device, such as a mouse or a trackball, in which the movement of an on-screen cursor is linked to the movement of the device but not to the position of the device. For example, if a user picks up a mouse and puts it down in a different location on a desk, the position of the on-screen cursor does not change because no movement (rolling) is detected. When the user rolls the mouse again, the cursor moves to reflect the mouse movement against the surface of the desk. Relative pointing devices differ from absolute pointing devices, such as graphics tablets, in which the device's location within a defined area is always associated with a pre-defined on-screen position. *See also* relative coordinates, relative movement. *Compare* absolute pointing device.

relative URL \rel`ə-tiv U-R-Lˊ\ *n.* Short for **relative uniform resource locator.** A form of URL in which the domain and some or all directory names are omitted, leaving only the document name and extension (and perhaps a partial list of directory names). The indicated file is found in a location relative to the pathname of the current document. *Acronym:* RELURL (R`-E-L-U-R-Lˊ). *See also* file extension, URL.

relay \rēˊlā\ *n.* A switch activated by an electrical signal. A relay allows another signal to be controlled without the need for human action to route the other signal to the control point, and it also allows a relatively low-power signal to control a high-power signal.

release[1] \rə-lēsˊ\ *n.* **1.** A particular version of a piece of software, most commonly associated with the most recent version (as in "the latest release"). Some companies use the term *release* as an integral part of the product name (as in *Lotus 1-2-3 Release 2.2*). **2.** A version of a product that is available in general distribution. *Compare* beta[2].

release[2] \rə-lēsˊ\ *vb.* **1.** To relinquish control of a block of memory, a device, or another system resource to the operating system. **2.** To formally make a product available to the marketplace.

reliability \rə-lī`ə-bilˊə-tē\ *n.* The likelihood of a computer system or device continuing to function over a given period of time and under specified conditions. Reliability is measured by different performance indexes. For example, the reliability of a hard disk is often given as mean time between failures (MTBF): the average length of time the disk can be expected to function without failing. *See also* MTBF, MTTR.

reload \rē-lōdˊ\ *vb.* **1.** To load a program into memory from a storage device again in order to run it, because the system has crashed or the program's operation was otherwise interrupted. **2.** To retrieve a new copy of the Web page currently visible in a Web browser.

relocatable address \rē-lō-kā`tə-bl aˊdres, ə-dresˊ\ *n.* In programming, an address that is to be adjusted to reflect the actual place in memory into

which a program is loaded for execution. In "Get the byte located 12 bytes from this instruction," the address is relocatable; in "Get the byte located at address 255," the address is not relocatable. This convention is comparable to describing the "address" of a parked car as "level 2, row G" on one day and "level 5, row B" on another.

relocatable code \rē-lō-kā`tə-bl kōdˊ\ *n.* A program written in such a way that it can be loaded into any part of available memory rather than having to be placed in one specific location. In relocatable code, address references that depend on the program's physical location in memory are calculated at run time so that program instructions can be carried out correctly. *See also* reentrant code.

relocate \rē`lō-kātˊ\ *n.* To move programs and blocks of memory about within available space so as to use memory resources flexibly and efficiently. A relocatable program can be loaded by the operating system into any part of available memory rather than into only one specific area. A relocatable block of memory is a portion of memory that can be moved around by the operating system as required; for example, the system might collect several available, relocatable blocks of memory to form one larger block of the size requested for use by a program.

RELURL \R`E-L-U-R-Lˊ\ *n. See* relative URL.

remark \rə-märkˊ\ *n. See* comment, REM statement.

remote \rə-mōtˊ\ *adj.* Not in the immediate vicinity, as a computer or other device located in another place (room, building, or city) and accessible through some type of cable or communications link.

remote access \rə-mōt` akˊses\ *n.* The use of a remote computer.

Remote Authentication Dial-In User Service \rə-mōt` ä-then-tə-kā`shən dīlˊin y o͞o`zər sərˊvəs, ô-then-tə-kā`shən\ *n. See* RADIUS.

remote access server \rə-mōt` akˊses sərˊvər\ *n.* A host on a local area network that is equipped with modems to enable users to connect to the network over telephone lines. *Acronym:* RAS (R`A-Sˊ).

Remote Access Service \rə-mōt` akˊses sər`vis\ *n.* Windows software that allows a user to gain remote access to the network server via a modem. *Acronym:* RAS (R`A-S´). *See also* remote access.

remote administration \rə-mōt` əd-min-ə-strā´-shən\ *n.* The performance of system administration–related tasks via access from another machine in a network.

remote communications \rə-mōt` kə-myōō-nə-kā´shənz\ *n.* Interaction with a remote computer through a telephone connection or another communications line.

remote computer system \rə-mōt` kəm-pyōō´tər si`stəm\ *n. See* remote system.

Remote Data Objects \rə-mōt` dā`tə ob`jekts, dat´ə\ *n.* An object-oriented data access tool featured in the Enterprise Edition of Visual Basic 4.0. Remote Data Objects have no native file format of their own; they can be used only with databases complying with the most recent ODBC standards. This feature is popular for its speed and minimal coding requirements. *Acronym:* RDO (R`D-O´). *See also* ODBC, Visual Basic.

remote login \rə-mōt` log´in, rē-mōt`\ *n.* The action of logging in to a computer at a distant location by means of a data communications connection with the computer that one is presently using. After remote login, the user's own computer behaves like a terminal connected to the remote system. On the Internet, remote login is done primarily by rlogin and telnet. *See also* rlogin[1] (definition 1), telnet[1].

remote procedure call \rə-mōt` prə-sē´jur käl, rē-mōt`\ *n.* In programming, a call by one program to a second program on a remote system. The second program generally performs a task and returns the results of that task to the first program. *Acronym:* RPC (R`P-C´).

remote system \rə-mōt` si´stəm, rē-mōt`\ *n.* The computer or network that a remote user is accessing via a modem. *See also* remote access. *Compare* remote terminal.

remote terminal \rə-mōt` tər´mə-nəl, rē-mōt`\ *n.* A terminal that is located at a site removed from the computer to which it is attached. Remote terminals rely on modems and telephone lines to communicate with the host computer. *See also* remote access. *Compare* remote system.

removable disk \rə-mōōv´ə-bl disk`\ *n.* A disk that can be removed from a disk drive. Floppy

disks are removable; hard disks usually are not. *Also called* exchangeable disk.

REM statement \rem´ stāt`mənt\ *n.* Short for **rem**ark **statement.** A statement in the Basic programming language and the MS-DOS and OS/2 batch file languages that is used to add comments to a program or batch file. Any statement beginning with the word *REM* is ignored by the interpreter or compiler or the command processor. *See also* comment.

rename \rē-nām´\ *n.* A command in most file transfer protocol (FTP) clients and in many other systems that allows the user to assign a new name to a file or files.

render \ren´dər\ *vb.* To produce a graphic image from a data file on an output device such as a video display or printer.

rendering \ren´dər-ēng\ *n.* The creation of an image containing geometric models, using color and shading to give the image a realistic look. Usually part of a geometric modeling package such as a CAD program, rendering uses mathematics to describe the location of a light source in relation to the object and to calculate the way in which the light would create highlights, shading, and variations in color. Realism can range from opaque, shaded polygons to images approximating photographs in their complexity. *See also* ray tracing.

repaginate \rē`paj´ə-nāt\ *vb.* To recalculate the page breaks in a document.

Repeat \rə-pēt´\ *n.* A command in Microsoft Word that causes all information contained in either the last command dialog box or the last uninterrupted editing session to be repeated.

repeat counter \rə-pēt´ koun`tər\ *n.* A loop counter; typically, a register that holds a number representing how many times a repetitive process has been or is to be executed.

repeater \rə-pē´tər\ *n.* A device used on communications circuits that decreases distortion by amplifying or regenerating a signal so that it can be transmitted onward in its original strength and form. On a network, a repeater connects two networks or two network segments at the physical layer of the ISO/OSI model and regenerates the signal.

repeating Ethernet \rə-pē`tēng ē´thər-net\ *n. See* repeater.

repeat key \rə-pēt´ kē`\ *n.* On some keyboards, a key that must be held down at the same time as a character key to cause the character key's key code to be sent repeatedly. On most computer keyboards, however, a repeat key is not needed because a key automatically repeats if held down for longer than a brief delay. *Compare* typematic.

RepeatKeys \rə-pēt´ kēz`\ *n.* A feature of Windows 95 that allows a user to adjust or disable the typematic keyboard feature so as to accommodate users with restricted mobility, who may activate typematic by accident because they have trouble lifting their fingers from the keys. *See also* typematic. *Compare* BounceKeys, FilterKeys, MouseKeys, ShowSounds, SoundSentry, StickyKeys, ToggleKeys.

repetitive strain injury \rə-pet´ə-tiv strān in´jur-ē\ *n.* An occupational disorder of the tendons, ligaments, and nerves caused by the cumulative effects of prolonged repetitious movements. Repetitive strain injuries are appearing with increasing frequency among office workers who spend long hours typing at computerized workstations that are not equipped with safeguards such as wrist supports. *Acronym:* RSI (R`S-I´). *See also* carpal tunnel syndrome, wrist support.

replace \rə-plās´\ *vb.* To put new data in the place of other data, usually after conducting a search for the data to be replaced. Text-based applications such as word processors typically include search-and-replace commands. In such operations, both old and new data must be specified, and search-and-replace procedures may or may not be sensitive to uppercase and lowercase, depending on the application program. *See also* search[1], search and replace.

replication \re`plə-kā´shən\ *n.* In a distributed database management system, the process of copying the database (or parts of it) to the other parts of the network. Replication allows distributed database systems to remain synchronized. *See also* distributed database, distributed database management system.

report \rə-pōrt´\ *n.* The presentation of information about a given topic, typically in printed form. Reports prepared with computers and appropriate software can include text, graphics, and charts. Database programs can include special software for creating report forms and generating reports.

Desktop publishing software and laser printers or typesetting equipment can be used to produce publication-quality output.

report generator \rə-pōrt´ jen`ər-ā-tər\ *n.* An application, commonly part of a database management program, that uses a report "form" created by the user to lay out and print the contents of a database. A report generator is used to select specific record fields or ranges of records, to make the output attractive and to specify such features as headings, running heads, page numbers, and fonts.

report writer \rə-pōrt´ rī`tər\ *n. See* report generator.

repository \rə-poz´ə-tōr`ē\ *n.* **1.** A collection of information about a computing system. **2.** A superset of a data dictionary. *See also* data dictionary.

reprogrammable PROM \rē-prō-gram`ə-bl prom´, P´rom, P`R-O-M´\ *n. See* EPROM.

reprogrammable read-only memory \rē`prō-gram`ə-bl rēd`ōn-lē mem´ər-ē\ *n. See* EPROM.

Request for Comments \rə-kwest` fōr kom´ents\ *n. See* RFC.

Request for Discussion \rə-kwest` fōr di-skush´ən\ *n.* A formal proposal for a discussion concerning the addition of a newsgroup to the Usenet hierarchy, the first step in a process that ends with a call for votes. *Acronym:* RFD (R`F-D´). *See also* traditional newsgroup hierarchy, Usenet.

Request to Send \rə-kwest` tə send´\ *n. See* RTS.

required hyphen \rə-kwīrd` hī´fən\ *n. See* hyphen.

Research Libraries Information Network \rē`sərch lī`brâr-ēz in-fər-mā´shən net`wərk\ *n.* The combined online catalog of the Research Libraries Group, which includes many of the major research libraries in the United States. *Acronym:* RLIN (R´lin, R`L-I-N´).

reserve \rə-zərv´\ *n.* A command that allocates contiguous disk space for the device instance's workspace. Digital video devices recognize this command.

reserve accumulator \rə-zərv` ə-kyo͞o´myə-lā-tər\ *n.* An auxiliary storage register generally used to store the intermediate results of an extended calculation.

reserved character \rə-zərvd` kâr´ək-tər\ *n.* A keyboard character that has a special meaning to a program and, as a result, normally cannot be used in assigning names to files, documents, and other user-generated tools, such as macros. Characters commonly reserved for special uses include the asterisk (*), forward slash (/), backslash (\), question mark (?), and vertical bar (|).

reserved memory \re-zərvd˘ mem´ər-ē\ *n. See* UMA.

reserved word \rə-zərvd˘ wərd´\ *n.* A word that has special meaning to a program or in a programming language. Reserved words usually include those used for control statements (IF, FOR, END), data declarations, and the like. A reserved word can be used only in certain predefined circumstances; it cannot be used in naming documents, files, labels, variables, or user-generated tools such as macros.

reset button \rē´set but`ən\ *n.* A device that restarts a computer without turning off its power. *Compare* big red switch.

resident font \rez`ə-dənt font´\ *n. See* internal font.

resident program \rez`ə-dənt prō´gram\ *n. See* TSR.

resistance \rə-zi´stəns\ *n.* The ability to impede (resist) the flow of electric current. With the exception of superconductors, all substances have a greater or lesser degree of resistance. Substances with very low resistance, such as metals, conduct electricity well and are called *conductors.* Substances with very high resistance, such as glass and rubber, conduct electricity poorly and are called *nonconductors* or *insulators.*

resistor \rə-zi´stər\ *n.* A circuit component designed to provide a specific amount of resistance to current flow. See the illustration.

Bands

Resistor. The bands indicate the resistance in ohms, as well as tolerance (the margin of error from the amount of resistance indicated by the bands).

resize \rē-sīz´\ *vb.* To make an object or space larger or smaller. *Also called* scale.

resolution \rez`ə-loo´shən\ *n.* **1.** The fineness of detail attained by a printer or a monitor in producing an image. For printers that form characters from small, closely spaced dots, resolution is measured in dots per inch, or dpi, and ranges from about 125 dpi for low-quality dot-matrix printers to about 600 dpi for some laser and ink-jet printers (typesetting equipment can print at resolutions of over 1,000 dpi). For a video display, the number of pixels is determined by the graphics mode and video adapter, but the size of the display depends on the size and adjustment of the monitor; hence the resolution of a video display is taken as the total number of pixels displayed horizontally and vertically. See the following table. *See also* high resolution, low resolution. **2.** The process of translation between a domain name address and an IP address. *See also* DNS.

resolve \rə-zolv´\ *vb.* **1.** To match one piece of information to another in a database or lookup table. **2.** To find a setting in which no hardware conflicts occur. **3.** To convert a logical address to a physical address or vice versa.

resource \rē´sōrs, rə-sōrs´\ *n.* **1.** Any part of a computer system or a network, such as a disk drive, printer, or memory, that can be allotted to a program or a process while it is running. **2.** An item of data or code that can be used by more than one program or in more than one place in a program, such as a dialog box, a sound effect, or a font in a windowing environment. Many features in a program can be altered by adding or replacing resources without the necessity of recompiling the program from source code. Resources can also be copied and pasted from one program into another, typically by a specialized utility program called a *resource editor.*

resource allocation \rē´sōrs a-lə-kā`shən\ *n.* The process of distributing a computer system's facilities to different components of a job in order to perform the job.

resource data \rē´sōrs dā`tə, rə-sōrs´, dat`ə\ *n.* The data structures, templates, definition procedures, management routines, icon maps, and so forth associated with a particular resource, such as a menu, window, or dialog box. *See also* resource (definition 2), resource fork.

resource file \rē´sōrs fīl`, rə-sōrs´\ *n.* A file that consists of resource data and the resource map that indexes it. *See also* resource (definition 2), resource fork.

resource fork \rē´sōrs fōrk`, rə-sōrs´\ *n.* One of the two forks of an Apple Macintosh file (the other being the *data fork*). The resource fork of a program file contains reusable items of information that the program can use during the course of execution, such as fonts, icons, windows, dialog boxes, menus, and the program code itself. A user-created document typically stores its data in the data fork, but it can also use its resource fork for storing items that might be used more than once in the document. For example, in a HyperCard stack, the data that constitutes each card, or record, in the stack is stored in the data fork; digitized sounds and icons that might be used more than once are stored in the resource fork. The use of such resources makes program development easier because resources can be developed and altered independently of the program code. *See also* HyperCard, resource (definition 2). *Compare* data fork.

resource ID \rē´sōrs I-D`, rə-sōrs´\ *n.* A number that identifies a particular resource within a given resource type on the Apple Macintosh—for example, a particular menu among many resources of type MENU that a program might use. *See also* resource (definition 2).

Resource Reservation Setup Protocol \rē´sōrs rez-ər-vā`shən set´up prō´tə-kol\ *n.* A communications protocol designed to allow for "bandwidth on demand." A remote receiver requests that a certain amount of bandwidth be reserved by the server for a data stream; the server sends back a message (similar to the RSVP sent in reply to an invitation) indicating whether or not the request has been granted. *Acronym:* RRSP (R`R-S-P´), RSVP (R`S-V-P´).

resource type \rē´sōrs tīp`, rə-sōrs´\ *n.* One of numerous classes of structural and procedural resources in the Macintosh operating system, such as code, fonts, windows, dialog boxes, templates, icons, patterns, strings, drivers, cursors, color tables, and menus. Resource types have characteristic identifying labels, such as CODE for blocks of program instructions, FONT for fonts, CURS for mouse cursors, and so on. *See also* resource (definition 2), resource fork.

response time \rə-spons´ tīm`\ *n.* **1.** The time, often an average, that elapses between the issuance of a request and the provision of the data requested (or notification of inability to provide it). **2.** The time required for a memory circuit or storage device to furnish data requested by the central processing unit (CPU).

restart \rē-stärt´\ *vb.* See reboot.

restore[1] \rə-stōr´, rē-stōr´\ *n.* The act of restoring a file or files. *See also* backup, recovery.

COMMON SCREEN RESOLUTIONS FOR PERSONAL COMPUTERS

IBM Personal Computers and compatibles

Monochrome Display Adapter (MDA)	720 pixels across by 350 pixels down
Color/Graphics Adapter (CGA)	640 pixels across by 200 pixels down
Enhanced Graphics Adapter (EGA)	640 pixels across by 350 pixels down
Professional Graphics Adapter (PGA)	640 pixels across by 480 pixels down
Multi-Color Graphics Array (MCGA)	640 pixels across by 480 pixels down
Video Graphics Array (VGA)	720 pixels across by 400 pixels down in text mode, 640 pixels across by 480 pixels down in graphics mode
eXtended Graphics Array (XGA)	1,024 pixels across by 768 pixels down
Super Video Graphics Array (SVGA)	1,024 pixels across by 768 pixels down, or 1,280 pixels across by 1,024 pixels down

Apple Macintosh

Macintosh Classic	512 pixels across by 342 pixels down
Macintosh II family	640 pixels across by 480 pixels down on Apple's 12-inch black-and-white and 13-inch color monitors

restore[2] \rə-stōr´, rē-stōr´\ *vb.* To copy files from a backup storage device to their normal location, especially if the files are being copied to replace files that were accidentally lost or deleted.

restricted function \rə-strik`təd funk´shən\ *n.* A function or an operation that can be executed only under certain circumstances, especially when the central processing unit (CPU) is in privileged mode. *See also* privileged mode.

Restructured Extended Executor \rē-struk`-churd eks-ten`dəd eks´ə-kyōō`tər\ *n. See* REXX.

retrace \rē´trās\ *n.* The path followed by the electron beam in a raster-scan computer monitor as it returns either from the right to the left edge of the screen or from the bottom to the top of the screen. The retrace positions the electron beam for its next sweep across or down the screen; during this interval, the beam is briefly turned off to avoid drawing an unwanted line on the screen. Retracing occurs many times each second and uses tightly synchronized signals to ensure that the electron beam is turned off and on during the retrace. *See also* blanking, horizontal retrace, raster display, vertical retrace.

retrieve \rə-trēv´\ *vb.* To obtain a specific requested item or set of data by locating it and returning it to a program or to the user. Computers can retrieve information from any source of storage—disks, tapes, or memory.

return \rə-turn´\ *vb.* **1.** To transfer control of the system from a called routine or program back to the calling routine or program. Some languages support an explicit *return* or *exit* statement; others allow return only at the end (last statement) of the called routine or program. *See also* call[2] (definition 2). **2.** To report the outcome of a called routine to the calling routine or program.

return code \rə-turn´ kōd`\ *n.* In programming, a code that is used to report the outcome of a procedure or to influence subsequent events when a routine or process terminates (returns) and passes control of the system to another routine. Return codes can, for example, indicate whether an operation was successful or not and can thus be used to determine what is to be done next.

return from the dead \rə-turn` frəm dhə ded´\ *vb.* To regain access to the Internet after having been disconnected.

Return key \rə-turn´ kē`\ *n.* A key on a keyboard that is used to terminate input of a field or record or to execute the default action of a dialog box. On IBM Personal Computers and compatibles, this key is called ENTER. The corresponding key on a typewriter causes the carriage holding the paper to return to the starting position to begin a new line; hence the name. *See also* Enter key.

return to zero \rə-turn` tə zēr´ō\ *n.* Abbreviated RZ. A method of recording on magnetic media in which the reference condition, or "neutral" state, is the absence of magnetization. *Compare* nonreturn to zero.

reusability \rē-yōō`zə-bil´ə-tē\ *n.* The ability of code or a design to be usable again in another application or system.

Reverse Address Recognition Protocol \rə-vərs` a`dres rek`əg-nish´ən prō`tə-kol, ə-dres`\ *n. See* RARP.

Reverse ARP \re-vərs` arp´, A-R-P´\ *n. See* RARP.

reverse byte ordering \rə-vərs` bīt´ ōr-dər-ēng\ *n. See* little endian.

reverse engineering \rə-vərs` en-jə-nēr´ēng\ *n.* A method of analyzing a product in which the finished item is studied to determine its makeup or component parts—for example, studying a completed ROM chip to determine its programming or studying a new computer system to learn about its design. For computer software, "reverse engineering" typically involves decompilation of a substantial portion of the object code and studying the resulting decompiled code.

reverse path forwarding \rə-vərs` path fōr´wər-dēng\ *n.* A technique that makes routing decisions through a TCP/IP network by using the source address of a datagram rather than the destination address. Reverse path forwarding is used in broadcast and multicast applications because it reduces redundant transmissions to multiple recipients. *Acronym:* RPF (R`P-F´). *See also* datagram, TCP/IP.

reverse Polish notation \rə-vərs` pō´lish nō-tā`-shən\ *n. See* postfix notation.

reverse video \rə-vərs´ vid`ē-ō\ *n.* The reversal of light and dark in the display of selected characters on a video screen. For example, if text is normally displayed as white characters on a black background, reverse video presents text as black letters on a white background. Programmers commonly use reverse video as a means of highlighting text or special items (such as menu choices or the cursor) on the screen.

revert \rə-vərt´\ *vb.* To return to the last saved version of a document. Choosing this command tells the application to abandon all changes made in a document since the last time it was saved.

Revisable-Form-Text DCA \rə-vī´zə-bl-fōrm-tekst` D-C-A´\ *n.* A standard within Document Content Architecture (DCA) for storing documents in such a way that the formatting can be changed by the receiver. A related standard is Final-Form-Text DCA. *Acronym:* RFTDCA (R`F-T´D-C-A´). *See also* DCA. *Compare* Final-Form-Text DCA.

rewind \rē-wīnd´\ *vb.* To wind a magnetic tape spool or cassette to its beginning.

rewritable digital video disc \rē-rī´tə-bl dij`i-təl vid´ē-ō disk\ *n.* Technology for recording data on discs that have the same storage capacity as digital video discs (DVDs) but can be rewritten like the compact disc–rewritable (CD-RW) devices. *See also* digital video disc, PD-CD drive.

rewrite \rē-rīt´\ *vb.* To write again, especially in situations where information is not permanently recorded, such as RAM or a video display. *Also called* refresh, regenerate. *See also* dynamic RAM.

REXX \reks, R`E-X-X´\ *n.* Acronym for **R**estructured **Ex**tended **Ex**ecutor. A structured programming language used on IBM mainframes and with OS/2 Version 2.0. REXX programs invoke application programs and operating system commands.

RF \R-F´\ *n. See* radio frequency.

RFC \R`F-C´\ *n.* Acronym for **R**equest **f**or **C**omments. A document in which a standard, a protocol, or other information pertaining to the operation of the Internet is published. The RFC is actually issued, under the control of the IAB, *after* discussion and serves as the standard. RFCs can be obtained from sources such as InterNIC.

RFD \R`F-D´\ *n. See* Request for Discussion.

RFI \R`F-I´\ *n.* Acronym for **r**adio **f**requency **i**nterference. Noise introduced into an electronic circuit, such as a radio or television, by electromagnetic radiation produced by another circuit, such as a computer.

RF shielding \R-F´ shēl`dēng\ *n.* A structure, generally sheet metal or metallic foil, designed to prevent the passage of radio frequency (RF)

electromagnetic radiation. RF shielding is intended to keep RF radiation either inside a device or out of a device. Without proper RF shielding, devices that use or emit RF radiation can interfere with each other; for example, running an electric mixer might cause interference on a television. Computers generate RF radiation and, to meet Federal Communications Commission (FCC) standards, must be properly shielded to prevent this RF radiation from leaking out. The metal case of a PC provides most of the needed RF shielding. Devices meeting FCC type A standards are suitable for business use. Devices meeting the more stringent FCC type B standards are suitable for home use. *See also* radio frequency, RFI.

RFTDCA \R`F-T´D-C-A´\ *n. See* Revisable-Form-Text DCA.

RGB \R`G-B´\ *n.* Acronym for **r**ed-**g**reen-**b**lue. A model for describing colors that are produced by emitting light, as on a video monitor, rather than by absorbing it, as with ink on paper. The three kinds of cone cells in the eye respond to red, green, and blue light, respectively, so percentages of these additive primary colors can be mixed to get the appearance of any desired color. Adding no color produces black; adding 100 percent of all three colors results in white. *See also* CMYK, RGB monitor. *Compare* CMY.

RGB display \R-G-B´ dis-plā`\ *n. See* RGB monitor.

RGB monitor \R-G-B` mon´ə-tər\ *n.* A color monitor that receives its signals for red, green, and blue levels over separate lines. An RGB monitor generally produces sharper and cleaner images than those produced by a composite monitor, which receives levels for all three colors over a single line. *See also* RGB. *Compare* composite video display.

ribbon cable \rib´ən kā`bl\ *n.* A flat cable containing up to 100 parallel wires for data and control lines. For example, ribbon cables are used inside a computer's case to connect the disk drives to their controllers. See the illustration on the next page.

ribbon cartridge \rib´ən kär`trij\ *n.* A disposable module containing an inked fabric ribbon or a carbon-coated plastic film ribbon. Many impact printers use ribbon cartridges to make ribbon changing easier and cleaner.

Rich Text Format \rich tekst´ fōr`mat\ *n.* An adaptation of DCA (Document Content Architec-

Ribbon cable.

ing new nodes can be difficult. See the illustration. *See also* token passing, token ring network. *Compare* bus network, star network.

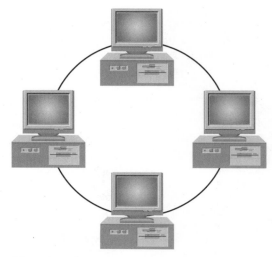

Ring network.

ture) that is used for transferring formatted text documents between applications, even those applications running on different platforms, such as between IBM and compatibles and Apple Macintoshes. *Acronym:* RTF (R`T-F´). *See also* DCA.

right click \rīt´ klik\ *vb.* To make a selection using the button on the right side of a mouse or other pointing device. Doing so in the Windows 95 environment typically brings up a pop-up menu with options applicable to the object over which the cursor is positioned. *See also* mouse, pointing device.

right justification \rīt` ju-stə-fi-kā´shən\ *n.* In typesetting, word processing, and desktop publishing, the process of aligning text evenly along the right margins of a column or page. The left edge of the text is ragged. *See also* justify (definition 1), rag. *Compare* full justification, left justification.

right-justify \rīt`ju´stə-fī\ *vb.* To align lines of text and other display elements so that the right edges form a smooth line. *See also* align (definition 1), rag. *Compare* left-justify.

rigid disk \rij´id disk`\ *n. See* hard disk.

ring network \rēng´ net`wərk\ *n.* A local area network in which devices (nodes) are connected in a closed loop, or ring. Messages in a ring network pass around the ring from node to node in one direction. When a node receives a message, it examines the destination address attached to the message. If the address is the same as the node's, the node accepts the message; otherwise, it regenerates the signal and passes the message along to the next node in the ring. Such regeneration allows a ring network to cover larger distances than star and bus networks. The ring can also be designed to bypass any malfunctioning or failed node. Because of the closed loop, however, add-

RIP \rip, R`I-P´\ *n. See* raster image processor.

RISC \risk, R`I-S-C´\ *n.* Acronym for **r**educed **i**nstruction **s**et **c**omputing. A microprocessor design that focuses on rapid and efficient processing of a relatively small set of simple instructions that comprises most of the instructions a computer decodes and executes. RISC architecture optimizes each of these instructions so that it can be carried out very rapidly—usually within a single clock cycle. RISC chips thus execute simple instructions more quickly than general-purpose CISC (complex instruction set computing) microprocessors, which are designed to handle a much wider array of instructions. They are, however, slower than CISC chips at executing complex instructions, which must be broken down into many machine instructions that RISC microprocessors can perform. Families of RISC chips include Sun Microsystems' SPARC, Motorola's 88000, Intel's i860, and the PowerPC developed by Apple, IBM, and Motorola. *See also* architecture, SPARC. *Compare* CISC.

Rivest-Shamir-Adleman encryption \riv`əst-shə-mēr`-ā´dəl-mən en-krip`shən\ *n. See* RSA encryption.

RJ-11 connector \R`J-ə-lev´ən kə-nek`tər\ *n. See* phone connector.

RJ-11 jack \R`J-ə-lev´ən jak\ *n. See* phone connector.

RLIN \R´lin, R`L-I-N´\ *n. See* Research Libraries Information Network.

RLL encoding \R`L-L´ en-kō-dēng\ *n. See* run-length limited encoding.

rlogin[1] \R`log´in\ *n.* **1.** A protocol used to log in to a networked computer in which the local system automatically supplies the user's login name. *See also* communications protocol, logon. *Compare* telnet[1]. **2.** A UNIX command in BSD UNIX that enables a user to log in to a remote computer on a network using the rlogin protocol. *See also* BSD UNIX.

rlogin[2] \R`log´in\ *vb.* To connect to a networked computer using the rlogin protocol.

RLSD \R`L-S-D´\ *n.* Acronym for **R**eceived **L**ine **S**ignal **D**etect. *See* DCD.

RMM \R`M-M´\ *n. See* real-mode mapper.

.ro \dot`R-O´\ *n.* On the Internet, the major geographic domain specifying that an address is located in Romania.

robopost \rō`bō-pōst`\ *vb.* To post articles to newsgroups automatically, usually by means of a bot. *See also* bot (definition 3), newsgroup, post.

robot \rō´bot\ *n.* **1.** A machine that can sense and react to input and cause changes in its surroundings with some degree of intelligence, ideally without human supervision. Although robots are often designed to mimic human movements in carrying out their work, they are seldom human-like in appearance. Robots are commonly used in manufacturing products such as automobiles and computers. *See also* robotics. **2.** *See* bot, spider.

robotics \rō-bot´iks\ *n.* The branch of engineering devoted to the creation and training of robots. Roboticists work within a wide range of fields, such as mechanical and electronic engineering, cybernetics, bionics, and artificial intelligence, all toward the end of endowing their creations with as much sensory awareness, physical dexterity, independence, and flexibility as possible. *See also* artificial intelligence, bionics, cybernetics.

robust \rō-bust´\ *adj.* Able to function or to continue functioning well in unexpected situations.

ROFL \R`O-F-L´\ Acronym for **r**olling **o**n the **f**loor, **l**aughing. An expression, used mostly in newsgroups and online conferences, to indicate one's appreciation of a joke or other humorous circumstance. *Also called* ROTFL.

role-playing game \rōl´plā-ēng gām`\ *n.* A game that is played online such as a MUD, in which participants take on the identities of characters that interact with each other. Often these games have a fantasy or science fiction setting and have a set of rules that all players need to follow. *See also* MUD.

rollback \rōl´bak\ *n.* A return to a previous stable condition, as when the contents of a hard disk are restored from a backup after a destructive hard disk error.

ROM \rom, R`O-M´\ *n.* **1.** Acronym for **r**ead-**o**nly **m**emory. A semiconductor circuit into which code or data is permanently installed by the manufacturing process. The use of this technology is economically viable only if the chips are produced in large quantities; experimental designs or small volumes are best handled using PROM or EPROM. **2.** Acronym for **r**ead-**o**nly **m**emory. Any semiconductor circuit serving as a memory that contains instructions or data that can be read but not modified (whether placed there by manufacturing or by a programming process, as in PROM and EPROM). *See also* EEPROM, EPROM, PROM.

roman \rō´mən\ *adj.* Having upright rather than slanted characters in a typeface. *See also* font family. *Compare* italic.

ROM Basic \rom` bā´sik, R-O-M´\ *n.* A Basic interpreter stored in ROM (read-only memory) so that the user can start programming after simply turning on the machine without having to load Basic from a disk or tape. ROM Basic was a feature of many early home computers.

ROM BIOS \rom` bī´ōs, R-O-M´\ *n.* Acronym for **r**ead-**o**nly **m**emory **b**asic **i**nput/**o**utput **s**ystem. *See* BIOS.

ROM card \rom´ kärd, R`O-M´\ *n.* A plug-in module that contains one or more printer fonts, programs, or games or other information stored in ROM (read-only memory). A typical ROM card is about the size of a credit card and several times thicker. It stores information directly in integrated circuit boards. *Also called* font card, game card. *See also* ROM (definition 1), ROM cartridge.

ROM cartridge \rom´ kär`trij, R-O-M´\ *n.* A plug-in module that contains one or more printer fonts, programs, games, or other information stored in ROM (read-only memory) chips on a board enclosed in a plastic case with a connector exposed at one end so that it can easily plug into a printer, computer, game system, or other device. For example, a cartridge that plugs into a game system is a ROM cartridge. *Also called* game cartridge. *See also* ROM (definition 1), ROM card.

ROM emulator \rom´ em`yə-lā-tər, R-O-M´\ *n.* A special circuit containing RAM memory that is connected to a target computer in place of the target computer's ROM chips. A separate computer writes the contents into the RAM, and then the target computer reads the RAM as if it were ROM. ROM emulators are used to debug ROM-resident software without the high cost and delay of manufacturing chips. Even though the use of a ROM emulator is more expensive than programming an EPROM, it is often preferred today because its contents can be changed much more quickly than those of an EPROM. *Also called* ROM simulator. *See also* EEPROM, EPROM, ROM (definition 1).

ROM simulator \rom´ sim`yə-lā-tər, R`O-M´\ *n.* See ROM emulator.

root \root\ *n.* The main or uppermost level in a hierarchically organized set of information. The root is the point from which subsets branch in a logical sequence that moves from a broad focus to narrower perspectives. *See also* leaf, tree.

root account \root´ ə-kount`, root´\ *n.* On UNIX systems, the account having control over the operation of a computer. The system administrator uses this account for system maintenance. *Also called* superuser. *See also* system administrator.

root directory \root´ dər-ek`tər-ē\ *n.* The point of entry into the directory tree in a disk-based hierarchical directory structure. Branching from this root are various directories and subdirectories, each of which can contain one or more files and subdirectories of its own. For example, in the MS-DOS operating system the root directory is identified by a name consisting of a single backslash character (\). Beneath the root are other directories, which may contain further directories, and so on. See the illustration.

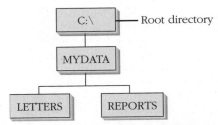

Root directory. *The structure of a hierarchical directory; the root is identified by the backslash.*

root name \root´ nām, root´\ *n.* In MS-DOS and Windows, the first part of a filename. In MS-DOS and earlier versions of Windows, the maximum length of the root name was eight characters; in Windows NT and later versions of Windows, the root name may be as long as 255 characters. *See also* 8.3, extension (definition 1), filename, long filenames.

ROT13 encryption \R`O-T´thər-tēn´ en-krip`shən\ *n.* A simple encryption method in which each letter is replaced with the letter of the alphabet 13 letters after the original letter, so that A is replaced by N, and so forth; N, in turn, is replaced by A, and Z is replaced by M. ROT13 encryption is not used to protect messages against unauthorized readers; rather, it is used in newsgroups to encode messages that a user may not want to read, such as sexual jokes or spoilers. Some newsreaders can automatically perform ROT13 encryption and decryption at the touch of a key.

rotate \rō´tāt\ *vb.* **1.** To turn a model or other graphical image so that it is viewed at a different angle. **2.** To move bits in a register to the left or to the right. The bit that moves out of the end position rotates to the newly vacated position at the opposite end of the register. *Compare* shift.

rotational delay \rō-tā`shə-nəl də-lā´\ *n.* The time required for a desired disk sector to rotate to the read/write head. *Also called* rotational latency.

rotational latency \rō-tā`shən-əl lā´tən-sē\ *n.* See rotational delay.

RO terminal \R-O´ tər`mə-nəl\ *n.* Short for **read-only terminal.** A terminal that can receive data but cannot send data. Nearly all printers can be classified as RO terminals.

ROTFL \R`O-T-F-L´\ See ROFL.

round \round\ *vb.* To shorten the fractional part of a number, usually increasing the last remaining (rightmost) digit or not, according to whether the deleted portion was over or under 5. For example, 0.3333 rounded to two decimal places is 0.33, and 0.6666 is 0.67. Computer programs often round numbers, sometimes causing confusion when the resulting values do not add up "correctly." Percentages in a spreadsheet can thus total 99 percent or 101 percent because of rounding.

round robin \round` rob´in\ *n.* A sequential, cyclical allocation of resources to more than one process or device.

routable protocol \rou´tə-bl pro`tə-kol, rōō´tə-bl\ *n.* A communications protocol that is used to route data from one network to another by means of a network address and a device address. TCP/IP is an example of a routable protocol.

router \rou´tər\ *n.* An intermediary device on a communications network that expedites message delivery. On a single network linking many computers through a mesh of possible connections, a router receives transmitted messages and forwards them to their correct destinations over the most efficient available route. On an interconnected set of local area networks (LANs) using the same communications protocols, a router serves the somewhat different function of acting as a link between LANs, enabling messages to be sent from one to another. *See also* bridge, gateway.

routine \rōō-tēn´\ *n.* Any section of code that can be invoked (executed) within a program. A routine usually has a name (identifier) associated with it and is executed by referencing that name. Related terms (which may or may not be exact synonyms, depending on the context) are *function, procedure,* and *subroutine. See also* function (definition 3), procedure, subroutine.

row \rō\ *n.* A series of items arranged horizontally within some type of framework—for example, a continuous series of cells running from left to right in a spreadsheet; a horizontal line of pixels on a video screen; or a set of data values aligned horizontally in a table. *Compare* column.

RPC \R`P-C´\ *n. See* remote procedure call.

RPF \R`P-F´\ *n. See* reverse path forwarding.

RPN \R`P-N´\ *n.* Acronym for **r**everse **P**olish **n**otation. *See* postfix notation.

RPROM \R´prom, R`P´rom, R`P-R`O-M´\ *n.* Short for **r**eprogrammable **PROM.** *See* EPROM.

RRSP \R`R-S-P´\ *n. See* Resource Reservation Setup Protocol.

RS-232-C standard \R`S-tōō-thrē-tōō-C´ stan´-dərd\ *n.* An accepted industry standard for serial communications connections. Adopted by the Electrical Industries Association, this Recommended Standard (RS) defines the specific lines and signal characteristics used by serial communications controllers to standardize the transmission of serial data between devices. The letter *C* denotes that the current version of the standard is the third in a series. *See also* CTS, DSR, DTR, RTS, RXD, TXD.

RS-422/423/449 \R`S-fōr-tōō-tōō` fōr-tōō-thrē`fōr-fōr-nīn´\ *n.* Standards for serial communications with transmission distances over 50 feet. RS-449 incorporates RS-422 and RS-423. Macintosh serial ports are RS-422 ports. *See also* RS-232-C standard.

RSAC \R´sak, R`S-A-C´\ *n. See* Recreational Software Advisory Council.

RSA encryption \R-S-A´ en-krip`shən\ *n.* Short for **R**ivest-**S**hamir-**A**dleman **encryption.** The patented public key encryption algorithm, introduced by Ronald Rivest, Adi Shamir, and Leonard Adleman in 1978, on which the PGP (Pretty Good Privacy) encryption program is based. *See also* PGP, public key encryption.

RSI \R`S-I´\ *n. See* repetitive strain injury.

RSN \R`S-N´\ *See* Real Soon Now.

RSVP \R`S-V-P´\ *n. See* Resource Reservation Setup Protocol.

RTF \R`T-F´\ *n. See* Rich Text Format.

RTFM \R`T-F-M´\ Acronym for **r**ead **t**he **f**laming (or **f**riendly) **m**anual. A common answer to a question in an Internet newsgroup or product support conference that is adequately explained in the instruction manual. *Also called* RTM.

RTM \R`T-M´\ Acronym for **r**ead **t**he **m**anual. *See* RTFM.

RTS \R`T-S´\ *n.* Acronym for **R**equest **t**o **S**end. A signal sent, as from a computer to its modem, to request permission to transmit; the signal is often used in serial communications. RTS is a hardware signal sent over pin 4 in RS-232-C connections. *See also* RS-232-C standard. *Compare* CTS.

.ru \dot`R-U´\ *n*. On the Internet, the major geographic domain specifying that an address is located in the Russian Federation.

rubber banding \rub´ər ban`dēng\ *n*. In computer graphics, changing the shape of an object made up of connected lines by "grabbing" a point on an anchored line and "pulling" it to the new location.

rudder control \rud´ər kən-trōl`\ *n*. A device, consisting of a pair of pedals, that enables a user to input rudder movements in a flight simulation program. The rudder control is used along with a joystick (which controls the simulated ailerons and elevators) and possibly a throttle control.

rule \rōōl\ *n*. **1.** A line printed above, below, or to the side of some element, either to set that item off from the remainder of the page or to improve the look of the page. Footnotes, for example, often appear below a short rule that sets them off from the main text on the page. The thickness of a rule is typically measured in points. (A point is approximately 1/72 inch.) *See also* point[1] (definition 1). **2.** In expert systems, a statement that can be used to verify premises and to enable a conclusion to be drawn. *See also* expert system.

rule-based system \rōōl`bāsd si´stəm\ *n*. *See* expert system, production system.

ruler \rōō´lər\ *n*. In some application programs, such as word processors, an on-screen scale marked off in inches or other units of measure and used to show line widths, tab settings, paragraph indents, and so on. In programs in which the ruler is "live," the on-screen ruler can be used with the mouse or with the keyboard to set, adjust, or remove tab stops and other settings. See the illustration.

Ruler

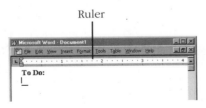

Ruler.

run \run\ *vb*. To execute a program.

run around \run` ə-round´\ *vb*. In page composition, to position text so that it flows around an illustration or other display.

run-length limited encoding \run`length lim´ə-təd en-kō´dēng\ *n*. Abbreviated RLL encoding. A fast and highly efficient method of storing data on a disk (usually a hard disk) in which patterns in the bits representing information are translated into codes rather than being stored literally bit by bit and character by character. In RLL encoding, changes in magnetic flux are based on the number of zeros that occur in sequence. This scheme allows data to be stored with fewer changes in magnetic flux than would otherwise be needed for the number of data bits involved and results in considerably higher storage capacity than is possible with older technologies, such as frequency modulation (FM) and modified frequency modulation (MFM) encoding. *Compare* frequency modulation encoding, modified frequency modulation encoding.

running foot \run`ēng fōōt´\ *n*. One or more lines of text in the bottom margin area of a page, composed of one or more elements such as the page number, the name of the chapter, the date, and so on. *Also called* footer.

running head \run`ēng hed´\ *n*. One or more lines of text in the top margin area of a page, composed of one or more elements such as the page number, the name of the chapter, the date, and so on. *Also called* header.

run time \run´ tīm\ *n*. **1.** The time period during which a program is running. *See also* compile time, dynamic allocation, dynamic binding, link time. **2.** The amount of time needed to execute a given program.

run-time \run´tīm\ *adj*. Occurring after a program has begun to be executed, such as evaluation of variable expressions and dynamic allocation of memory.

run-time binding \run´tīm bīn`dēng\ *n*. Assignment of a meaning to an identifier (such as a variable) in a program at the time the program is executed rather than at the time the program is compiled. *Compare* compile-time binding, link-time binding.

run-time error \run´tīm âr`ər\ *n*. A software error that occurs while a program is being executed, as detected by a compiler or other supervisory program.

run-time library \run´tīm lī`brâr-ē\ *n.* A file containing one or more prewritten routines to perform specific, commonly used functions. A run-time library, used primarily in high-level languages such as C, saves the programmer from having to rewrite those routines.

run-time version \run´tīm vər`zhən\ *n.* **1.** Program code that is ready to be executed. Generally, this code has been compiled and can operate without error under most user command sequences and over most ranges of data sets. **2.** A special release that provides the computer user with some, but not all, of the capabilities available in the full-fledged software package.

.rw \dot`R-W´\ *n.* On the Internet, the major geographic domain specifying that an address is located in Rwanda.

R/W \R-W´\ *adj. See* read/write.

RXD \R`X-D´\ *n.* Short for Receive (**rx**) **D**ata. A line used to carry received serial data from one device to another, such as from a modem to a computer. Pin 3 is the RXD line in RS-232-C connections. *See also* RS-232-C standard. *Compare* TXD.

RZ \R-Z´\ *n. See* return to zero.

S-100 bus \S`wən-hun´dred bus`\ *n.* A 100-pin bus specification used in the design of computers built around the Intel 8080 and Zilog Z-80 microprocessors. System designs using the Motorola 6800, 68000, and Intel iAPx86 family of microprocessors have also been built around the S-100 bus. S-100 computers were extremely popular with early computer enthusiasts. They had an open architecture, which permitted the configuration of systems with a wide range of add-on expansion boards.

.sa \dot`S-A´\ *n.* On the Internet, the major geographic domain specifying that an address is located in Saudi Arabia.

SAA \S`A-A´\ *n.* Acronym for **S**ystems **A**pplication **A**rchitecture. An IBM-developed standard for the appearance and operation of application software that will give programs written for all IBM computers—mainframe computers, minicomputers, and personal computers—a similar look and feel. SAA defines how an application interfaces with both the user and the supporting operating system. True SAA-compliant applications are compatible at the source level (before being compiled) with any SAA-compliant operating system—provided the system is capable of furnishing all the services required by the application.

Sad Mac \sad´ mak\ *n.* An error indication that occurs on Apple Macintosh computers when the system fails the initial diagnostic test. A Sad Mac is a picture of a Macintosh with a frowning face and X's for eyes, with an error code beneath the picture.

safe mode \sāf´ mōd\ *n.* In some versions of Windows, such as Windows 95, a boot mode in which most drivers and peripherals are disconnected to allow the user to correct some problem with the system. This will occur if the system was not shut down properly or if the system failed to complete a boot-up. *See also* boot[1].

sampling \sam´pl-ēng, sam´plēng\ *vb.* **1.** In statistics, gathering data from a representative subset of a larger group (called a population)—for example, determining a country's presumed voting pattern by polling a demographic cross section of voters. Other uses of this type of sampling might include checking the accuracy and efficiency of computerized transactions by reviewing every hundredth transaction or predicting traffic volumes by measuring traffic flow in a few strategic streets. There are many statistical procedures for estimating how accurately a given sample reflects the behavior of a group as a whole. **2.** The conversion of analog signals to a digital format; samples are taken at periodic intervals to measure and record some parameter, such as a signal from a temperature sensor or a microphone. Analog-to-digital converters are used in computers to sample analog signals as voltages and convert them to the binary form a computer can process. The two primary characteristics of this type of sampling are the sampling rate (usually expressed in samples per second) and the sampling precision (expressed in bits; 8-bit samples, for instance, can measure an input voltage accurate to 1/256 of the measured range).

sampling rate \sam´plēng rāt`\ *n.* The frequency with which samples of a physical variable, such as sound, are taken. The higher the sampling rate (that is, the more samples taken per unit of time), the more closely the digitized result resembles the original. *See also* sampling (definition 2).

sampling synthesizer \sam`plēng sin´thə-sī-zər\ *n.* A device designed to reproduce sounds, at differing frequencies, based on a digitized sound stored in read-only memory. For example, a recorded piano note, digitized and stored in memory, is used by the synthesizer to create other pianolike notes.

sans serif \san` sâr´if\ *adj.* Literally, "without stroke"; describes any typeface in which the characters have no serifs (the short lines or orna-ments at the upper and lower ends of the strokes). A sans serif typeface usually possesses a more straightforward, geometric appearance than a typeface with serifs and typically lacks the contrast between thick and thin strokes found in serif faces. Sans serif typefaces are used more frequently in display type, such as headlines, than in blocks of text. *Compare* serif[1].

SAP \S`A-P´\ *n. See* Service Advertising Protocol.

SAPI \S`A-P-I´\ *n.* Acronym for **S**peech **A**pplication **P**rogramming **I**nterface. A feature in Windows 95 and Windows NT that allows applications to include speech recognition or convert text to speech. *Also called* Speech API. *See also* speech recognition.

satellite \sat´ə-līt`\ *n. See* communications satellite.

satellite computer \sat´ə-līt kəm-pyōō`tər\ *n.* A computer that is connected to another computer, with which it interacts over a communications link. As its name indicates, a satellite computer is of lesser "stature" than the main, or host, computer; the host controls either the satellite itself or the tasks the satellite performs. *See also* remote communications.

saturated mode \sach´ər-ā-təd mōd`\ *n.* The state in which a switching device or amplifier is passing the maximum possible current. A device is in saturated mode when increasing the control signal does not result in output of additional current.

saturation \sach`ər-ā´shən\ *n.* **1.** In a switching device or amplifier, the fully conducting state. At saturation, the device is passing the maximum possible current. The term is most commonly used with reference to circuits containing bipolar or field-effect transistors. **2.** In color graphics and printing, the amount of color in a specified hue, often specified as a percentage. *See also* HSB.

save \sāv\ *vb.* To write data (typically a file) to a storage medium, such as a disk or tape.

.sb \dot`S-B´\ *n.* On the Internet, the major geographic domain specifying that an address is located in the Solomon Islands.

.sc \dot`S-C´\ *n.* On the Internet, the major geographic domain specifying that an address is located in Seychelles.

scalable \skā´lə-bl`\ *adj.* Of or relating to the characteristic of a piece of hardware or software that makes it possible for it to expand to meet future needs. For example, a scalable network allows the network administrator to add many additional nodes without the need to redesign the basic system.

scalable font \skā´lə-bl font´\ *n.* Any font that can be scaled to produce characters in varying sizes. Examples of scalable fonts are screen fonts in a graphical user interface, stroke fonts (such as Courier) and outline fonts common to most Post-Script printers, TrueType fonts, and the method for screen font definition used in Macintosh System 7. In contrast, most text-based interfaces and printing devices (such as daisy-wheel printers) offer text in only one size. *See also* outline font, PostScript font, screen font, stroke font, TrueType.

scalable parallel processing \skā´lə-bl pâr´ə-lel pros´es-ēng\ *n.* Multiprocessing architectures in which additional processors and additional users can easily be added without excessive increases in complexity and loss of performance. *Acronym:* SPP (S`P-P´).

Scalable Processor Architecture \skā`lə-bl pros-es-er är´kə-tek-chur\ *n. See* SPARC.

scalar \skā´lər\ *n.* A factor, coefficient, or variable consisting of a single value (as opposed to a record, an array, or some other complex data structure). *Compare* vector.

scalar data type \skā´lər dā´tə tīp, dat´ə\ *n.* A data type defined as having a predictable and enumerable sequence of values that can be compared for greater-than/less-than relationships. Scalar data types include integers, characters, user-defined enumerated data types, and (in most implementations) Boolean values. Some debate exists as to whether or not floating-point numbers can be considered a scalar data type; although they can be ordered, enumeration is often questionable because of rounding and conversion errors. *See also* Boolean expression, enumerated data type, floating-point number.

scalar processor \skā´lər pros`es-er\ *n.* A processor designed for high-speed computation of scalar values. A scalar value can be represented by a single number.

scalar variable \skā´lər vâr´ē-ə-bl\ *n. See* scalar.

scale[1] \skāl\ *n.* A horizontal or vertical line on a graph that shows minimum, maximum, and interval values for the data plotted.

scale[2] \skāl\ *vb.* **1.** To enlarge or reduce a graphic display, such as a drawing or a proportional character font, by adjusting its size proportionally. **2.** To alter the way in which values are represented so as to bring them into a different range—for example, to change linear feet to quarter inches on a blueprint drawing of a house. **3.** In programming, to determine the number of digits occupied by fixed-point or floating-point numbers. *See also* fixed-point notation, floating-point number.

scaling \skā´lēng\ *n.* In computer graphics, the process of enlarging or reducing a graphical image—scaling a font to a desired size or scaling a model created with a CAD program, for example. *See also* CAD.

scan \skan\ *vb.* **1.** In television and computer display technologies, to move an electron beam across the inner surface of the screen, one line at a time, to light the phosphors that create a displayed image. **2.** In facsimile and other optical technologies, to move a light-sensitive device across an image-bearing surface such as a page of text, converting the light and dark areas on the surface to binary digits that can be interpreted by a computer.

scan code \skan´ kōd\ *n.* A code number transmitted to an IBM or compatible computer whenever a key is pressed or released. Each key on the keyboard has a unique scan code. This code is not the same as the ASCII code for the letter, number, or symbol shown on the key; it is a special identifier for the key itself and is always the same for a particular key. When a key is pressed, the scan code is transmitted to the computer, where a portion of the ROM BIOS (read-only memory basic input/output system) dedicated to the keyboard translates the scan code into its ASCII equivalent. Because a single key can generate more than one character (lowercase *a* and uppercase *A,* for example), the ROM BIOS also keeps track of the status of keys that change the keyboard state, such as the Shift key, and takes them into account when translating a scan code. *Compare* key code.

scan head \skan´ hed\ *n.* An optical device found in scanners and fax machines that moves across the subject being scanned, converts light and dark areas to electrical signals, and sends those signals to the scanning system for processing.

scan line \skan´ līn\ *n.* **1.** One of many horizontal lines of a graphics display screen, such as a television or raster-scan monitor. **2.** A single row of pixels read by a scanning device.

scanner \skan´ər\ *n.* An optical input device that uses light-sensing equipment to capture an image on paper or some other subject. The image is translated into a digital signal that can then be manipulated by optical character recognition (OCR) software or graphics software. Scanners come in a number of types, including flatbed (scan head passes over a stationary subject), feed (subject is pulled across a stationary scan head), drum (subject is rotated around a stationary scan head), and hand-held (user passes device over a stationary subject).

scan rate \skan´ rāt\ *n. See* refresh rate.

scatter diagram \skat´ər dī´ə-gram\ *n.* A graph consisting of points whose coordinates represent values of data, often used to illustrate a correlation between one or more variables and a test group. See the illustration. *Also called* point chart, point diagram.

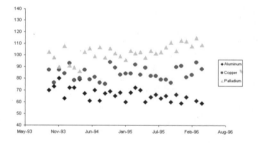

Scatter diagram.

schedule \skej´o͞o-əl, skej´o͞ol\ *vb.* To program a computer to perform a specified action at a specified time and date.

scheduler \sked´jə-lər\ *n.* An operating-system process that starts and ends tasks (programs), manages concurrently running processes, and allocates system resources. *Also called* dispatcher.

scheduling algorithm \skej´ə-lēng al`gə-ridh-əm\ *n.* An algorithm that governs the proper timing of a sequence of events in an operating system or application. For example, an effective motion graphics scheduling algorithm would be able to retrieve the graphic objects, process them, and display them without causing stutter or disruptions. *See also* algorithm.

schema \skē´mə\ *n.* A description of a database to a database management system (DBMS) in the language provided by the DBMS. A schema defines aspects of the database, such as attributes (fields) and domains and parameters of the attributes.

schematic \ski-mat´ik\ *n.* A diagram that shows a circuit's components and the connections between them using lines and a set of standard symbols to represent various electronic components. See the illustration.

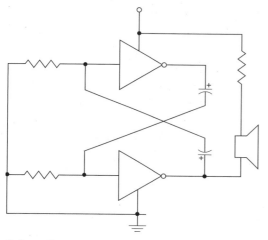

Schematic.

Schottky diode \shot´kē dī´od\ *n.* A type of diode (device that passes current in one direction) in which a semiconductor layer and a metal layer are brought into contact. It is characterized by very fast switching speeds. *Also called* hot carrier diode, Schottky barrier diode.

scientific notation \sī´ən-tif´ik nō-tā´shən\ *n.* A floating-point method of representing a number, especially a very large or very small one, in which numbers are expressed as products consisting of a number between 1 and 10 multiplied by a power of 10. *See also* floating-point notation.

sci. newsgroups \sī´dot-nōōz´grōōps\ *n.* Usenet newsgroups that are part of the sci. hierarchy and begin with "sci." These newsgroups are devoted to discussions of scientific research and applications, except computer science, which is discussed in the comp. newsgroups. *See also* newsgroup, traditional newsgroup hierarchy, Usenet. *Compare* comp. newsgroups, misc. newsgroups, news. newsgroups, rec. newsgroups, soc. newsgroups, talk. newsgroups.

scissoring \siz´ər-ēng\ *n.* See clip.

scope \skōp\ *n.* **1.** In programming, the extent to which an identifier, such as a constant, data type, variable, or routine, can be referenced within a program. Scope can be global or local. Scope can also be affected by redefining identifiers, such as by giving the same name to both a global variable and a local variable. *See also* block[1] (definition 3), global, local. **2.** In electronics, slang for oscilloscope. *See also* oscilloscope.

SCR \S`C-R´\ *n.* See silicon-controlled rectifier.

scrambler \skram´blər\ *n.* A device or program that reorders a signal sequence in order to render it indecipherable. *See also* encryption.

scrap \skrap\ *n.* An application or system file maintained for storing data that has been marked for movement, copying, or deletion. *See also* clipboard (definition 1).

scrapbook \skrap´bŏŏk\ *n.* **1.** A file in which a series of text and graphical images can be saved for subsequent use. **2.** A Macintosh system file that can hold a number of text and graphical images for later use. *Compare* clipboard (definition 1).

scratch[1] \skrach\ *n.* A memory region or file used by a program or operating system to hold work in progress temporarily. Created and maintained usually without the end user's knowledge, the scratch is needed only until the current session is terminated, at which time the data is saved or discarded. *Also called* scratch file. *See also* temporary file. *Compare* scrap.

scratch[2] \skrach\ *vb.* To erase or discard data.

scratch file \skrach´ fīl\ *n.* See scratch[1].

scratchpad \skrach´pad\ *n.* **1.** A temporary storage area used by a program or operating system for calculations, data, and other work in progress. *See also* scratch[1], temporary file. **2.** A high-speed memory circuit used to hold small items of data for rapid retrieval. *See also* cache.

scratchpad memory \skrach`pad mem´ər-ē\ *n.* See cache.

scratchpad RAM \skrach´pad ram`, R-A-M`\ *n.* Memory used by a central processing unit (CPU) for temporary data storage. *Also called* scratchpad, scratchpad memory. *See also* central processing unit, register.

screen angle \skrēn´ ang`l\ *n.* The angle at which the dots in a halftone screen are printed. A correct angle will minimize blur and other undesirable effects, such as moiré patterns. *See also* color separation (definition 1), halftone, moiré.

screen buffer \skrēn´ buf`ər\ *n. See* video buffer.

screen dump \skrēn´ dump\ *n.* A duplicate of a screen image; essentially, a "snapshot" of the screen that is either sent to a printer or saved as a file.

screen flicker \skrēn´ flik`ər\ *n. See* flicker.

screen font \skrēn´ font\ *n.* A typeface designed for display on a computer monitor screen. Screen fonts often have accompanying PostScript fonts for printing to PostScript-compatible printers. *See also* derived font, intrinsic font. *Compare* PostScript font, printer font.

screen frequency \skrēn´ frē`kwən-sē\ *n. See* halftone.

screen grabber \skrēn´ grab`ər\ *n. See* grabber (definition 3).

screen name \skrēn´ nām\ *n.* A name under which an America Online user is known. The screen name may be the same as the user's real name. *See also* America Online.

screen phone \skrēn´ fōn\ *n.* A type of Internet appliance combining a telephone with an LCD display screen, a digital fax modem, and a computer keyboard, with ports for a mouse, printer, and other peripheral devices. Screen phones can be used as regular telephones for voice communications and can also be used as terminals to gain access to the Internet and other online services.

screen pitch \skrēn´ pich\ *n.* A measurement of a computer monitor's screen density, representing the distance between phosphors on the display. The lower the number, the more detail can be displayed clearly. For example, a .28-dot-pitch screen has better resolution than one with .32. See the illustration. *See also* phosphor.

screen saver \skrēn´ sā`vər\ *n.* A utility that causes a monitor to blank out or display a certain image after a specified amount of time passes without the keyboard being touched or the mouse being moved. Touching a key or moving the

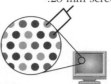

.28 mm screen pitch

Screen pitch.

mouse deactivates the screen saver. Screen savers were originally used to prevent images from becoming permanently etched on a monitor's screen. Although modern monitors are not susceptible to this problem, screen savers remain popular for their decorative and entertainment value. See the illustration.

Screen saver.

screen shot \skrēn´ shot\ *n.* An image that shows all or part of a computer display. The illustration shown here as well as the illustrations in this dictionary for the entries *alert box, cell,* and *menu bar,* for example, are screen shots.

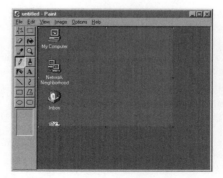

Screen shot.

script \skript\ *n.* A program consisting of a set of instructions to an application or utility program.

The instructions usually use the rules and syntax of the application or utility. *See also* macro.

scripting language \skrip´tēng lang`wəj\ *n.* A simple programming language designed to perform special or limited tasks, sometimes associated with a particular application or function. An example of a scripting language is Perl. *See also* Perl, script.

scroll \skrōl\ *vb.* To move a document or other data in a window in order to view a particular portion of the document. Scrolling may be controlled by the mouse, arrow keys, or other keys on the keyboard. *See also* scroll bar.

scroll arrow \skrōl´ âr`ō\ *n. See* scroll bar.

scroll bar \skrōl´ bär\ *n.* In some graphical user interfaces, a vertical or horizontal bar at the side or bottom of a display area that can be used with a mouse for moving around in that area. Scroll bars often have four active areas: two scroll arrows for moving line by line, a sliding scroll box for moving to an arbitrary location in the display area, and gray areas for moving in increments of one window at a time. See the illustration.

scroll box \skrōl´ boks\ *n. See* elevator.

Scroll Lock key \skrōl´ lok kē`\ *n.* On the IBM PC/XT and AT and compatible keyboards, a key on the top row of the numeric keypad that controls the effect of the cursor control keys and sometimes prevents the screen from scrolling. On the enhanced and Macintosh keyboards, this key is to the right of the function keys on the top row. Many modern applications ignore the Scroll Lock setting.

SCSI \skuz´ē, S`C-S-I´\ *n.* Acronym for **S**mall **C**omputer **S**ystem **I**nterface, a standard high-speed parallel interface defined by the X3T9.2 committee of the American National Standards Institute (ANSI).

A SCSI interface is used to connect microcomputers to SCSI peripheral devices, such as many hard disks and printers, and to other computers and local area networks. *Compare* ESDI, IDE.

SCSI-1 \skuz´ē-wən´, S-C-S-I´wən´\ *n. See* SCSI.

SCSI-2 \skuz´ē-tōō´, S-C-S-I´-tōō´\ *n.* An enhanced ANSI standard for SCSI (Small Computer System Interface) buses. Compared with the original SCSI standard (now called SCSI-1), which can transfer data 8 bits at a time at up to 5 MB per second, SCSI-2 offers increased data width, increased speed, or both. A SCSI-2 disk drive or host adapter can work with SCSI-1 equipment at the older equipment's maximum speed. *See also* Fast SCSI, Fast/Wide SCSI, SCSI, Wide SCSI. *Compare* UltraSCSI.

SCSI bus \skuz´ē bus, S`C-S-I´\ *n.* A parallel bus that carries data and control signals from SCSI devices to a SCSI controller. *See also* bus, controller, SCSI device.

SCSI chain \skuz´ē chān`, S`C-S-I´\ *n.* A set of devices on a SCSI bus. Each device (except the host adapter and the last device) is connected to two other devices by two cables, forming a daisy chain. *See also* daisy chain, SCSI.

SCSI connector \skuz´ē kə-nek`tər, S`C-S-I´\ *n.* A cable connector used to connect a SCSI device to a SCSI bus. See the illustration on the next page. *See also* bus, connector (definition 1), SCSI device.

SCSI device \skuz´ē də-vīs`, S`C-S-I´\ *n.* A peripheral device that uses the SCSI standard to exchange data and control signals with a computer's CPU. *See also* peripheral, SCSI.

SCSI ID \skuz´ē I-D´ S-C-S-I´\ *n.* The unique identity of a SCSI device. Each device connected to a SCSI bus must have a different SCSI ID. A maxi-

Scroll bars

Scroll bar.

SCSI connector.

mum of eight SCSI IDs can be used on the same SCSI bus. *See also* bus, SCSI device.

SCSI network \skuz´ē net`wərk, S`C-S-I´\ *n.* A set of devices on a SCSI bus, which acts like a local area network. *See also* SCSI.

SCSI port \skuz´ē pōrt`, S`C-S-I´\ *n.* **1.** A SCSI host adapter within a computer, which provides a logical connection between the computer and all of the devices on the SCSI bus. *See also* SCSI. **2.** A connector on a device for a SCSI bus cable. *See also* SCSI.

scuzzy \skuz´ē\ *n. See* SCSI.

.sd \dot`S-D´\ *n.* On the Internet, the major geographic domain specifying that an address is located in Sudan.

SDK \S`D-K´\ *n.* Acronym for **s**oftware **d**eveloper's **k**it. *See* developer's toolkit.

SDLC \S`D-L-C´\ *n.* Acronym for **S**ynchronous **D**ata **L**ink **C**ontrol, the data transmission protocol most widely used by networks conforming to IBM's Systems Network Architecture (SNA). SDLC is similar to the HDLC (High-level Data Link Control) protocol developed by the International Organization for Standardization (ISO). *See also* HDLC.

SDM \S`D-M´\ *n. See* space-division multiplexing.

SDRAM \S`D´ram, S`D-R-A-M´\ *n. See* synchronous DRAM.

SDSL \S`D-S-L´\ *n. See* symmetric digital subscriber line.

.se \dot`S-E´\ *n.* On the Internet, the major geographic domain specifying that an address is located in Sweden.

.sea \dot`S-E-A´\ *n.* A file extension for a self-extracting Macintosh archive compressed with StuffIt. *See also* self-extracting archive.

seamless integration \sēm`ləs in-tə-grā´shən\ *n.* The favorable result that occurs when a new hardware component or program blends smoothly into the overall operation of the system. It is usually the result of thoughtful design and programming.

search[1] \sərch\ *n.* The process of seeking a particular file or specific data. A search is carried out by a program through comparison or calculation to determine whether a match to some pattern exists or whether some other criteria have been met. *See also* binary search, hash search, linear search, search and replace, wildcard character.

search[2] \sərch\ *vb.* **1.** To look for the location of a file. **2.** To seek specific data within a file or data structure. *See also* replace.

search algorithm \sərch´ al`gər-idh-əm\ *n.* An algorithm designed to locate a certain element, called the target, in a data structure. *See also* algorithm, binary search, hash search, linear search.

search and replace \sərch` ənd rə-plās´\ *n.* A common process in applications such as word processors in which the user specifies two strings of characters. The process finds instances of the first string and replaces them with the second string.

search criteria \sərch´ krī-tēr`ē-ə\ *n.* The terms or conditions that a search engine uses to find items in a database. *See also* search engine.

search engine \sərch´ en`jən\ *n.* **1.** A program that searches for key words in documents or in a database. **2.** On the Internet, a program that searches for keywords in files and documents found on the World Wide Web, newsgroups, Gopher menus, and FTP archives. Some search engines are used for a single Internet site, such as a dedicated search engine for a Web site. Others search across many sites, using such agents as spiders to gather lists of available files and documents and store these lists in databases that users can search by keyword. Examples of the latter type of search engine are Lycos, AliWeb, and Excite. Most search engines reside on a server. *See also* agent (definition 2), FTP, Gopher, newsgroup, spider, World Wide Web.

search key \sərch´ kē\ *n.* **1.** The particular field (or column) of the records to be searched in a database. *See also* primary key, secondary key. **2.** The value that is to be searched for in a document or any collection of data.

search string \sərch´ strēng\ *n.* The string of characters to be matched in a search—typically (but not necessarily) a text string.

seat[1] \sēt\ *n.* One workstation or computer, in the context of software licensing on a per-seat basis. *See also* license agreement, workstation (definition 1).

seat[2] \sēt\ *vb.* To insert a piece of hardware fully and position it correctly in a computer or affiliated equipment, as in seating a single inline memory module (SIMM) in its socket.

secondary channel \sek`ən-dâr-ē chan´əl\ *n.* A transmission channel in a communications system that carries testing and diagnostic information rather than actual data. *Compare* primary channel.

secondary key \sek`ən-dâr-ē kē`\ *n.* A field that is to be sorted or searched within a subset of the records having identical primary key values. *See also* alternate key (definition 1), candidate key. *Compare* primary key.

secondary service provider \sek´ən-dâr-ē sər´vis prə-vī`dər\ *n.* An Internet service provider that provides a Web presence but not direct connectivity. *See also* ISP.

secondary storage \sek`ən-dâr´ē stōr´əj\ *n.* Any data storage medium other than a computer's random access memory (RAM)—typically tape or disk. *Compare* primary storage.

second normal form \sek`ənd nōr´məl fōrm`\ *n.* *See* normal form (definition 1).

secret channel \sē`krət chan´əl\ *n.* *See* private channel.

sector \sek´tər\ *n.* A portion of the data storage area on a disk. A disk is divided into sides (top and bottom), tracks (rings on each surface), and sectors (sections of each ring). Sectors are the smallest physical storage units on a disk and are of fixed size; typically, they are capable of holding 512 bytes of information apiece. See the illustration.

sector interleave \sek´tər in`tər-lēv\ *n.* *See* interleave.

sector map \sek´tər map`\ *n.* **1.** A map that indicates the unusable sectors on a disk. **2.** A table used to translate the sector numbers that are requested by the operating system into physical

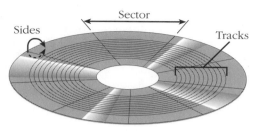

Sector.

sector numbers. The sector map represents a different method of performing sector interleaving. When a sector map is used, the sectors are formatted on the disk in sequential order. The mapping enables the system to read sectors in a nonsequential order. For example, using a 3-to-1 sector interleaving map, a system request for sectors 1 through 4 will result in the disk driver reading physical sectors 1, 4, 7, and 10. *See also* interleave.

secure channel \se-kyər` chan´əl\ *n.* A communications link that has been protected against unauthorized access, operation, or use by means of isolation from the public network, encryption, or other forms of control. *See also* encryption.

Secure Electronics Transactions protocol \sə-kyər` ə-lek-tron´iks tranz-ak`shənz prō`tə-kol\ *n.* Protocol for conducting secure transactions on the Internet, the result of a joint effort by GTE, IBM, MasterCard, Microsoft, Netscape, SAIC, Terisa Systems, VeriSign, and Visa. *Acronym:* SET (S`E-T´).

Secure Hash Algorithm \sə-kyər` hash` al´gə-ridh`əm, se-kyoor´\ *n.* *See* SHA.

Secure HTTP \se-kyər` H`T-T-P´\ *n.* *See* S-HTTP.

Secure Hypertext Transfer Protocol \se-kyər` hī`pər-tekst trans`fər pro`tə-kol\ *n.* *See* S-HTTP.

Secure/Multipurpose Internet Mail Extensions \se-kyər` mul`tē-pur-pəs in`tər-net māl´ eks-ten`shənz, mul`tī-pur-pəs\ *n.* *See* S/MIME.

secure site \sə-kyər` sīt`\ *n.* A Web site having the capability of providing secure transactions, ensuring that credit card numbers and other personal information will not be accessible to unauthorized parties.

Secure Sockets Layer \se-kyər` sok´əts lā`ər, lâr`\ *n.* A proposed open standard developed by Netscape Communications for establishing a secure communications channel to prevent the interception of critical information, such as credit card numbers. The primary purpose of Secure Sockets Layer is to enable secure electronic financial transactions on the World Wide Web, although it is designed to work with other Internet services as well. This technology, which uses public key encryption, is incorporated into the Netscape Navigator Web browser and Netscape's commerce servers. *Acronym:* SSL (S`S-L´). *See also* commerce server, open standard, public key encryption. *Compare* S-HTTP.

Secure Transaction Technology \se-kyər` tranz-ak`shən tek-nol´ə-jē\ *n.* The use of the Secure Sockets Layer (SSL), Secure HTTP (S-HTTP), or both in online transactions, such as form transmission or credit card purchases. *Acronym:* STT (S`T-T´). *See also* Secure Sockets Layer, S-HTTP.

secure wide area network \se-kyər` wīd` âr´ē-ə net´wərk\ *n.* A set of computers that communicate over a public network, such as the Internet, but use security measures, such as encryption, authentication, and authorization, to prevent their communications from being intercepted and understood by unauthorized users. *Acronym:* S/WAN (swän, S´wan, S`-W-A-N´). *See also* authentication, authorization, encryption, virtual private network (definition 1).

security \se-kyər´ə-tē\ *n.* Protection of a computer system and its data from harm or loss. A major focus of computer security, especially on systems that are accessed by many people or through communications lines, is the prevention of system access by unauthorized individuals.

security kernel \se-kyər´ə-tē ker`nəl\ *n.* An operating-system kernel that is protected from unauthorized use. *See also* kernel.

security log \se-kyər´ə-tē log`\ *n.* A log, generated by a firewall or other security device, that lists events that could affect security, such as access attempts or commands, and the names of the users involved. *See also* firewall, log (definition 1).

seed \sēd\ *n.* A starting value used in generating a sequence of random or pseudorandom numbers. *See also* random number generation.

seek \sēk\ *n.* The process of moving the read/write head in a disk drive to the proper site, typically for a read or write operation.

seek time \sēk´ tīm\ *n.* The time required to move a disk drive's read/write head to a specific location on a disk. *See also* access time (definition 2).

segment \seg´mənt\ *n.* A section of a program that, when compiled, occupies a contiguous address space and that is usually position independent; that is, it can be loaded anywhere in memory. With Intel-based microcomputers, a native-mode segment is a logical reference to a 64-KB contiguous portion of RAM in which the individual bytes are accessed by means of an offset value. Collectively, the segment:offset values reference a single physical location in RAM. *See also* overlay[1] (definition 1), real mode, segmentation.

segmentation \seg`mən-tā´shən\ *n.* The act of breaking up a program into several sections, or segments. *See also* segment.

segmented addressing architecture \seg`men-təd a´dres-ēng är`kə-tek-chur, ə-dres´ēng\ *n.* A memory-access technique typified by Intel 80x86 processors. Memory is divided into 64-KB segments in this architecture for addressing locations under the 16-bit address scheme; 32-bit schemes can address memory in segments as large as 4 GB. *Also called* segmented instruction addressing, segmented memory architecture. *Compare* linear addressing architecture.

segmented address space \seg`men-təd a´dres spās`, ə-dres´\ *n.* An address space that is logically divided into chunks called segments. To address a given location, a program must specify both a segment and an offset within that segment. (The offset is a value that references a specific point within the segment, based on the beginning of the segment.) Because segments may overlap, addresses are not unique; there are many logical ways to access a given physical location. The Intel 80x86 real-mode architecture is segmented; most other microprocessor architectures are flat. *See also* segment. *Compare* flat address space.

segmented instruction addressing \seg`men-təd in-struk´shən ə-dres`ēng, a`dres-ēng\ *n. See* segmented addressing architecture.

segmented memory architecture \seg`men-təd mem-ər-ē är`kə-tek-chur\ *n. See* segmented addressing architecture.

select \sə-lekt´\ *vb.* **1.** In general computer use, to specify a block of data or text on screen by highlighting it or otherwise marking it with the intent of performing some operation on it. **2.** In database management, to choose records according to a specified set of criteria. *See also* sort. **3.** In information processing, to choose from a number of options or alternatives, such as subroutines or input/output channels.

selected cell \sə-lek`təd sel´\ *n. See* active cell.

selection \sə-lek´shən\ *n.* **1.** In applications, the highlighted portion of an on-screen document. **2.** In communications, the initial contact made between a computer and a remote station receiving a message. **3.** In programming, a conditional branch. *See also* conditional branch.

selective calling \sə-lek´tiv kä´lēng\ *n.* The capability of a station on a communications line to designate the station that is to receive a transmission.

selector channel \sə-lek´tər chan`əl\ *n.* An input/output data transfer line used by one high-speed device at a time.

selector pen \se-lek´tər pen`\ *n. See* light pen.

self-adapting \self`ə-dap´tēng\ *adj.* The ability of systems, devices, or processes to adjust their operational behavior to environmental conditions.

self-checking digit \self`chek-ēng dij´ət\ *n.* A digit, appended to a number during its encoding, whose function is to confirm the accuracy of the encoding. *See also* checksum, parity bit.

self-clocking \self`klok´ēng\ *n.* A process in which timing signals are inserted into a data stream rather than being provided by an external source, such as in phase encoding.

self-documenting code \self`dok`yə-men-tēng kōd´\ *n.* Program source code that, through its use of a high-level language and descriptive identifi-ers, can be understood by other programmers without the need for additional comments.

self-extracting archive \self`eks-trak`tēng är´kīv\ *n. See* self-extracting file.

self-extracting file \self`eks-trak`tēng fīl´\ *n.* An executable program file that contains one or more compressed text or data files. When a user runs the program, it uncompresses the compressed files and stores them on the user's hard drive. See the illustration.

self-modifying code \self`mod`ə-fī-ēng kōd´\ *n.* Program code, usually object code generated by a compiler or assembler, that modifies itself during instruction by writing new operation codes, addresses, or data values over existing instructions. *See also* pure procedure.

self-monitoring analysis and reporting technology system \self`mon`i-tər-ēng ə-nal´ə-sis and rə-pōr`tēng tek-nol´ə-jē si`stəm\ *n. See* SMART system.

self-organizing map \self`ōr`gə-nī-zēng map´\ *n. See* SOM (definition 2).

self-test \self-test`\ *n.* A set of one or more diagnostic tests that a computer or peripheral device (such as a printer) performs on itself. *See also* power-on self test.

self-validating code \self`val`ə-dā-tēng kōd´\ *n.* Program code that can test itself to verify that it behaves correctly, usually by feeding itself a set of standard input values and testing the results against a set of expected output values.

semantic error \sə-man`tik âr´ər\ *n.* An error in meaning; a statement in a program that is syntactically correct (legal) but functionally incorrect. *See also* logic, semantics (definition 1), syntax.

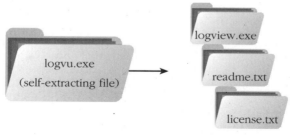

Self-extracting file.

semantics \sə-man´tiks\ *n.* **1.** In programming, the relationship between words or symbols and their intended meanings. Programming languages are subject to certain semantic rules; thus, a program statement can be syntactically correct but semantically incorrect; that is, a statement can be written in an acceptable form and still convey the wrong meaning. *See also* syntax. **2.** In artificial-intelligence research, the capacity of a network to represent relationships among objects, ideas, or situations in a humanlike way. See the illustration. *Compare* syntax.

```
CANARY — is a — BIRD
                 |
                has
                 |
              FEATHERS
```

Semantics.

semaphore \sem´ə-fōr´\ *n.* In programming, a signal—a flag variable—used to govern access to shared system resources. A semaphore indicates to other potential users that a file or other resource is in use and prevents access by more than one user. *See also* flag (definition 1).

semiconductor \sem´ē-kən-duk-tər,　sem´ī-kən-duk-tər\ *n.* A substance, commonly silicon or germanium, whose ability to conduct electricity falls between that of a conductor and that of a nonconductor (insulator). The term is used loosely to refer to electronic components made from semiconductor materials.

send \send\ *n.* To transmit a message or file through a communications channel.

send statement \send´ stāt´mənt\ *n.* In SLIP and PPP scripting languages, a statement that tells the program that dials an Internet service provider's number (a *dialer program*) to send certain characters. *See also* ISP, PPP, scripting language, SLIP.

sensor \sen´sər\ *n.* A device that detects or measures something by converting nonelectrical energy to electrical energy. A photocell, for example, detects or measures light by converting it to electrical energy. *See also* transducer.

sensor glove \sen´sər gləv´\ *n.* A hand-worn computer input device for virtual-reality environments. The glove translates finger movements by the user to commands for manipulating objects in the environment. *Also called* data glove. *See also* virtual reality.

SEPP \S`E-P-P´\ *n.* Acronym for **S**oftware **E**ngineering for **P**arallel **P**rocessing. A project of nine European universities and research institutions to develop tools for the development of parallel application programs for distributed memory multiprocessors.

sequence \sē´kwəns\ *n.* An ordered arrangement, as in a set of numbers, such as the Fibonacci sequence. *See also* Fibonacci numbers.

sequence check \sē´kwəns chek\ *n.* A process that verifies that data or records conform to a particular order. *Compare* completeness check, consistency check, duplication check.

Sequenced Packet Exchange \sē`kwensd pak´ət əks-chānj`\ *n.* See SPX (definition 1).

sequential access \si-kwen`shəl ak´ses\ *n.* A method of storing or retrieving information that requires the program to start reading at the beginning and continue until it finds the desired data. Sequential access is best used for files in which each piece of information is related to the information that comes before it, such as mailing list files and word processing documents. *Also called* serial access. *See also* indexed sequential access method. *Compare* random access.

sequential algorithm \si-kwen`shəl al´gə-ridh`əm\ *n.* An algorithm in which each step must occur in a particular order. *See also* algorithm. *Compare* parallel algorithm.

sequential execution \si-kwen`shəl eks`ə-kyōō´-shən\ *n.* The act of executing routines or programs in a linear sequence. *Compare* concurrent execution.

sequential logic element \si-kwen`shəl loj´ik el`ə-mənt\ *n.* A logic circuit element that has at least one input and one output and in which the output signal depends on the present and past states of the input signal or signals.

sequential processing \si-kwen`shəl pros´es-ēng\ *n.* **1.** The processing of items of information in the order in which they are stored or input. **2.** The execution of one instruction, routine, or task followed by the execution of the next in line. *Compare* multiprocessing, parallel processing, pipelining (definition 1).

sequential search \si-kwen`shəl sərch´\ *n. See* linear search.

serial \sēr´ē-əl`\ *adj.* One by one. For example, in serial transmission, information is transferred one bit at a time; a serial computer has only one arithmetic logic unit, which must execute the whole program one step at a time. *Compare* parallel (definition 3).

serial access \sēr`ē-əl ak´ses\ *n. See* sequential access.

serial adder \sēr`ē-əl ad´ər\ *n.* A circuit that adds two numbers one bit position (one digit place) at a time.

serial communication \sēr`ē-əl kə-myŌŌ`nə-kā´-shən\ *n.* The exchange of information between computers or between computers and peripheral devices one bit at a time over a single channel. Serial communications can be synchronous or asynchronous. Both sender and receiver must use the same baud rate, parity, and control information. *See also* baud rate, parity, start bit, stop bit.

Serial Infrared \sēr`ē-əl in´frə-red\ *n.* A system developed by Hewlett-Packard for transmitting data between two devices up to 1 meter apart using an infrared light beam. Infrared ports on the receiving and the sending devices must be aligned. Generally, Serial Infrared is used with laptops and many notebook computers, as well as with peripherals such as printers. *Acronym:* SIR (S`I-R´). *See also* infrared port.

serial interface \sēr`ē-əl in´tər-fās\ *n.* A data transmission scheme in which data and control bits are sent sequentially over a single channel. In reference to a serial input/output connection, the term usually implies the use of an RS-232 or RS-422 interface. *See also* RS-232-C standard, RS-422/423/449. *Compare* parallel interface.

serialize \sēr´ē-ə-līz\ *vb.* To change from parallel transmission (byte by byte) to serial transmission (bit by bit). *Compare* deserialize.

SerialKeys \sēr´ē-əl-kēz`\ *n.* A feature of Windows 95 that, in conjunction with a communications aid interface device, allows keystrokes and mouse controls to be accepted through a computer's serial port.

Serial Line Internet Protocol \sēr`ē-əl līn in´tər-net prō-tə-kol\ *n. See* SLIP.

serial mouse \sēr`ē-əl mous`\ *n.* A pointing device that attaches to the computer through a standard serial port. *See also* mouse. *Compare* bus mouse.

serial port \sēr`ē-əl pōrt`\ *n.* An input/output location (channel) that sends and receives data to and from a computer's central processing unit or a communications device one bit at a time. Serial ports are used for serial data communication and as interfaces with some peripheral devices, such as mice and printers.

serial port adapter \sēr`ē-əl pōrt ə-dap´tər\ *n.* An interface card or device that either provides a serial port or converts a serial port to another use. *See also* adapter, serial port.

serial printer \sēr`ē-əl prin´tər\ *n.* A printer connected to the computer via a serial interface (commonly RS-232-C or compatible). Connectors for this type of printer vary widely, which is one reason they are less popular than parallel printers among those who use IBM and IBM-compatible PCs. Serial printers are standard for Apple computers. *See also* DB connector, serial, serial transmission. *Compare* parallel printer.

serial processing \sēr`ē-əl pros´es-ēng\ *n. See* sequential processing (definition 2).

Serial Storage Architecture \sēr`ē-əl stōr`əj är´kə-tek-chur\ *n. See* SSA.

serial transmission \sēr`ē-əl tranz-mish´ən\ *n.* The transfer of discrete signals one after another. In communications and data transfer, serial transmission involves sending information over a single line one bit at a time, as in modem-to-modem connections. *Compare* parallel transmission.

series circuit \sēr´ēz sər`kət\ *n.* A circuit in which two or more components are linked in series. All the current passes through each component in a series circuit, but the voltage is divided among the components. See the illustration. *Compare* parallel circuit.

Series circuit.

serif[1] \sâr´if\ *adj.* Marked by the use of serifs. For example, Goudy is a serif typeface, whereas Helvetica is a sans serif typeface. See the illustration on the next page. *See also* serif[2]. *Compare* sans serif.

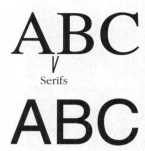

Serifs

Serif. A serif typeface (top) and a sans serif type-face (bottom).

serif² \sâr´if\ *n.* Any of the short lines or orna-ments at the ends of the strokes that form a type-face character.

server \sər´vər\ *n.* **1.** On a local area network (LAN), a computer running administrative soft-ware that controls access to the network and its resources, such as printers and disk drives, and provides resources to computers functioning as workstations on the network. **2.** On the Internet or other network, a computer or program that responds to commands from a client. For example, a file server may contain an archive of data or pro-gram files; when a client submits a request for a file, the server transfers a copy of the file to the cli-ent. *See also* client/server architecture. *Compare* client (definition 3).

server-based application \sər´vər-bāsd a-plə-kā´-shən\ *n.* A program that is shared over a network. The program is stored on the network server and can be used at more than one client machine at a time.

server cluster \sər´vər klu`stər\ *n.* A group of independent computers that work together as a single system. A server cluster presents the ap-pearance of a single server to a client.

server error \sər´vər âr`ər\ *n.* A failure to com-plete a request for information through HTTP that results from an error at the server rather than an error by the client or the user. Server errors are indicated by HTTP status codes beginning with 5. *See also* HTTP, HTTP status codes.

server push-pull \sər`vər po͞osh`pul´, po͞ol´\ *n.* A combination of Web client/server techniques indi-vidually called "server push" and "client pull." In server push, the server loads data to the client, but

the data connection stays open. This allows the server to continue sending data to the browser as necessary. In client pull, the server loads data to the client, but the data connection does not stay open. The server sends an HTML directive to the browser telling it to reopen the connection after a certain interval to get more data or possibly to open a new URL. See the illustration. *See also* HTML, server (definition 2), URL.

Server push   **Client pull**

Server push-pull.

server-side includes \sər`vər-sīd in-klo͞odz´\ *n.* A mechanism for including dynamic text in World Wide Web documents. Server-side includes are special command codes that are recognized and interpreted by the server; their output is placed in the document body before the document is sent to the browser. Server-side includes can be used, for example, to include the date/time stamp in the text of the file. *See also* server (definition 2).

service \sər´vəs\ *n.* **1.** A customer-based or user-oriented function, such as technical support or network provision. **2.** In reference to program-ming and software, a program or routine that pro-vides support to other programs, particularly at a low (close to the hardware) level. *See also* utility.

Service Advertising Protocol \sər`vəs ad`vər-tī-zēng prō´tə-kol\ *n.* A method used by a service-providing node in a network (such as a file server or application server) to notify other nodes on the network that it is available for access. When a server boots, it uses the protocol to advertise its service; when the same server goes offline, it uses the protocol to announce that it is no longer avail-able. *Acronym:* SAP (S`A-P´). *See also* server (defi-nition 1).

service bureau \sər´vis byər`ō\ *n.* **1.** A company that provides various services related to publish-ing, such as prepress production, desktop publishing, typesetting, imagesetting, and optical scanning of graphics. **2.** An organization that provides data processing services and access to software packages for a fee.

service provider \sər´vəs prə-vī´dər\ *n. See* ISP.

servo \sər´vō\ *n.* The part of a servomechanism, controlled by the servomechanism's feedback circuit, that produces the final mechanical output. *Also called* servomotor. *See also* servomechanism.

servomechanism \sər´vō-mek`ə-niz-əm\ *n.* A control system in which the final output is mechanical movement. A servomechanism uses feedback to control the position, velocity, or acceleration of a mechanical component. *Also called* servo system.

servomotor \sər´vō-mō`tər\ *n. See* servo.

servo system \sər´vō si`stəm\ *n. See* servomechanism.

session \sesh´ən\ *n.* **1.** The time during which a program is running. In most interactive programs, a session is the time during which the program accepts input and processes information. **2.** In communications, the time during which two computers maintain a connection. **3.** A specific protocol layer in the ISO/OSI networking model that manages communication between remote users or processes. *See also* ISO/OSI model, session layer.

session layer \sesh´ən lâr`, lā`ər\ *n.* The fifth of seven layers in the ISO/OSI networking model. The session layer handles the details that must be agreed on by the two communicating devices. *See also* ISO/OSI model.

set[1] \set\ *n.* In printing and display, a group of related characters, such as a character set. *See also* character set.

set[2] \set\ *vb.* **1.** To change the value of a bit to 1. **2.** To establish a particular condition, such as setting tab stops, setting a counter to 0, or setting a breakpoint. *See also* breakpoint.

SET protocol \S`E-T´ pro-tə-kol\ *n. See* Secure Electronics Transactions protocol.

settling time \set`ə-leng tīm´, set`lēng\ *n.* The time required for a disk drive's read/write head to stabilize over a new location on the disk after being moved.

set-top box \set´top boks`\ *n.* A device that converts a cable TV signal to an input signal to the TV set. Set-top boxes can be used to access the World Wide Web.

setup \set´up\ *n.* **1.** A computer along with all its devices. **2.** The procedures involved in preparing a software program or application to operate within a computer.

setup program \set´up prō`gram\ *n.* **1.** A built-in BIOS program for reconfiguring system parameters to accommodate a new disk drive. *See also* BIOS. **2.** *See* installation program.

setup string \set´up strēng`\ *n. See* control code.

setup wizard \set´up wiz`ərd\ *n.* In Microsoft Windows, a structured series of questions and options that leads a user through the process of installing a new program. See the illustration.

Setup wizard.

seven-segment display \sev`ən-seg`mənt dis-plā´\ *n.* A light-emitting diode (LED) display or liquid crystal display (LCD) that can show any of the 10 decimal digits. The seven segments are the seven bars that form a numeral 8 as in a calculator display.

sex changer \seks´ chān`jər\ *n. See* gender changer.

.sf.ca.us \dot-S-F`dot-C-A`dot-U-S´\ *n.* On the Internet, the major geographic domain specifying that an address is located in San Francisco, California, United States.

sfil \S´fīl\ *n.* The file type of a Macintosh System 7 sound file.

.sg \dot`S-G´\ *n.* On the Internet, the major geographic domain specifying that an address is located in Singapore.

.sgm \dot`S-G-M´\ *n.* The MS-DOS/Windows 3.*x* file extension that identifies files encoded in Standard Generalized Markup Language (SGML). Because MS-DOS and Windows 3.*x* cannot recognize file extensions longer than three letters, the .sgml extension is truncated to three letters in those environments. *See also* SGML.

.sgml \dot`S-G-M-L´\ *n.* The file extension that identifies files encoded in Standard Generalized Markup Language. *See also* SGML.

SGML \S`G-M-L´\ *n.* Acronym for **S**tandard **G**eneralized **M**arkup **L**anguage. An information management standard adopted by the International Organization for Standardization (ISO) in 1986 as a means of providing platform- and application-independent documents that retain formatting, indexing, and linked information. SGML provides a grammarlike mechanism for users to define the structure of their documents and the tags they will use to denote the structure in individual documents. *See also* ISO.

.sh \dot`S-H´\ *n.* On the Internet, the major geographic domain specifying that an address is located in Saint Helena.

sh \S´-H´\ *n.* *See* Bourne shell.

SHA \S`H-A´\ *n.* Acronym for **S**ecure **H**ash **A**lgorithm. A technique that computes a 160-bit condensed representation of a message or data file, called a *message digest.* The SHA is used by the sender and the receiver of a message in computing and verifying a digital signature, for security purposes. *See also* algorithm, digital signature.

shade[1] \shād\ *n.* A particular color variation produced by mixing black with a pure color. *See also* brightness, IRGB.

shade[2] \shād\ *vb.* To give added dimension to an image by including changes in appearance caused by light and shadow. *See also* color model.

shadow memory \shad´ō mem`ər-ē\ *n.* A technique employed by the BIOS in some 80x86-based computers to copy the system's ROM BIOS routines into an unused section of RAM during the computer's startup process. This helps boost system performance by diverting system requests for the BIOS routines to their "shadow" copies. *Also called* shadow RAM, shadow ROM.

shadow print \shad´ō print`\ *n.* A style applied to text in which a duplicate of each character is shifted, typically down and to the right, to create a shadow effect. See the illustration.

shadow RAM \shad´ō ram`, R-A-M`\ *n.* *See* shadow memory.

shadow ROM \shad´ō rom`, R-O-M`\ *n.* *See* shadow memory.

Shadows

Shadows

Shadow print.

share \shâr\ *vb.* To make files, directories, or folders accessible to other users over a network.

shared directory \shârd` dər-ek´tər-ē\ *n.* *See* network directory.

shared folder \shârd` fōl´dər\ *n.* On a Macintosh computer connected to a network and running System 6.0 or higher, a folder that a user has made available to others on the network. A shared folder is analogous to a network directory on a PC. *See also* network directory.

shared logic \shârd` loj´ik\ *n.* The use, by multiple circuits or software routines, of common circuits or routines to implement an operation.

shared memory \shârd` mem´ər-ē\ *n.* **1.** Memory accessed by more than one program in a multitasking environment. **2.** A portion of memory used by parallel-processor computer systems to exchange information. *See also* parallel processing.

shared network directory \shârd` net`wərk dər-ek´tər-ē\ *n.* *See* network directory.

shared printer \shârd´ prin`tər\ *n.* A printer that receives input from more than one computer.

shared resource \shârd` rē´sōrs, rə-sōrs´\ *n.* **1.** Any device, data, or program used by more than one device or program. **2.** In Windows NT, any resource made available to network users, such as directories, files, and printers.

shareware \shâr´wâr\ *n.* Copyrighted software that is distributed on a try-before-you-buy basis. Users who want to continue using the program after the trial period are encouraged to send a payment to the program's author. *Compare* free software, freeware, public-domain software.

sharpness \shärp´nəs\ *n.* *See* resolution (definition 1).

sheet-fed scanner \shēt`fed skan´ər\ *n.* A scanner with a single-sheet feed mechanism, in which sheets of paper are pulled in by the scanner and scanned as they pass over a stationary scanning mechanism. Sheet-fed scanners allow for automatic scanning of multiple-sheet documents. *See also* scanner. *Compare* drum scanner, flatbed scanner, handheld scanner.

sheet feeder \shēt´ fē`dər\ *n.* A device that accepts a stack of paper and feeds it to a printer one page at a time.

shelfware \shelf´wâr\ *n.* Software that has been unsold or unused for a long time, and so has remained on a retailer's or user's shelf.

shell[1] \shel\ *n.* A piece of software, usually a separate program, that provides direct communication between the user and the operating system. Examples of shells are Macintosh Finder and the MS-DOS command interface program COMMAND.COM. *See also* Bourne shell, C shell, Finder, Korn shell. *Compare* kernel.

shell[2] \shel\ *vb. See* shell out.

shell account \shel´ ə-kount`\ *n.* A computer service that permits a user to enter operating-system commands on the service provider's system through a command-line interface (usually one of the UNIX shells) rather than having to access the Internet through a graphical user interface. Shell accounts can provide Internet access through character-based tools, such as Lynx for browsing the World Wide Web. *See also* shell[1].

shell archive \shel´ är`kīv\ *n.* In UNIX and GNU, a collection of compressed files that has been prepared for transmission by an e-mail service using the shar command.

shell out \shel out´\ *vb.* To obtain temporary access to the operating-system shell without having to shut down the current application and return to that application after performing the desired shell function. Many UNIX programs allow the user to shell out; the user can do the same in windowing environments by switching to the main system window.

shell script \shel´ skript\ *n.* A script executed by the command interpreter (shell) of an operating system. The term generally refers to scripts executed by the Bourne, C, and Korn shells on UNIX platforms. *Also called* batch file. *See also* batch file, script, shell[1].

Shell sort \shel´ sōrt\ *n.* A programming algorithm used for ordering data. Named after its inventor, Donald Shell, it is faster than the bubble sort and the insertion sort. *See also* algorithm. *Compare* bubble sort, insertion sort.

shift \shift\ *vb.* In programming, to move the bit values one position to the left or right in a register or memory location. *See also* end-around shift. *Compare* rotate (definition 2).

Shift+click or **Shift click** \shift-klik´\ *vb.* To click the mouse button while holding down the Shift key. Shift+clicking performs different operations in different applications, but its most common use in Windows is to allow users to select multiple items in a list, for example, to select a number of files for deletion or copying.

Shift key \shift´ kē\ *n.* A keyboard key that, when pressed in combination with another key, gives that key an alternative meaning; for example, producing an uppercase character when a letter key is pressed. The Shift key is also used in various key combinations to create nonstandard characters or to perform special operations. The term is adapted from usage in relation to manual typewriters, in which the key physically shifted the carriage to print an alternative character. *See also* Caps Lock key.

Shift-PrtSc \shift`print´skrēn\ *n. See* Print Screen key.

shift register \shift´ rej`ə-stər\ *n.* A circuit in which all bits are shifted one position at each clock cycle. It can be either linear (a bit is inserted at one end and "lost" at the other during each cycle) or it can be *cyclic* or *looped* (the "lost" bit is inserted back at the beginning). *See also* register, shift.

Shockwave \shok´wāv\ *n.* A format for multimedia audio and video services within HTML documents, created by Macromedia, which markets a family of Shockwave servers and plug-in programs for Web browsers. *See also* HTML.

short card \shōrt´ kärd\ *n.* A printed circuit board that is half as long as a standard-size circuit board. See the illustration on the next page. *Also called* half-card. *See also* printed circuit board.

short-circuit evaluation \shōrt`sər`kət i-val-yoo̅-ā`shən\ *n.* A form of expression evaluation that guarantees that Boolean expressions will be evaluated only far enough to determine their value. *See also* AND, Boolean operator, OR.

shortcut \shōrt´kut\ *n.* In Windows 95, an icon on the desktop that a user can double-click on to immediately access a program, a text or data file, or a Web page. See the illustration. *See also* symbolic link.

Shortcut.

shortcut key \shōrt´kut kē\ *n. See* accelerator.

short-haul \shōrt´häl, shōrt´hôl\ *adj.* Of or pertaining to a communications device that transmits a signal over a communications line for a distance less than approximately 20 miles. *Compare* long-haul.

shout \shout\ *vb.* To use ALL CAPITAL LETTERS for emphasis in e-mail or a newsgroup article. Excessive shouting is considered a violation of netiquette. A word can be more acceptably emphasized by placing it between *asterisks* or _underscores_. *See also* netiquette.

shovelware \shə´vəl-wâr`\ *n.* A commercially sold CD-ROM containing a miscellaneous assortment of software, graphic images, text, or other data that could otherwise be obtained at little or no cost, such as freeware or shareware from the Internet and BBSs or public-domain clip art. *See also* BBS (definition 1), freeware, shareware.

ShowSounds \shō´soundz\ *n.* In Windows 95, a global flag that instructs application programs to provide some kind of visual indication that the program is generating a sound in order to alert users with hearing impairments or those in a noisy location such as a factory floor.

shrink-wrapped \shrēnk´rapd\ *adj.* Boxed and sealed in clear plastic film for commercial distribution. Use of the term implies a final version of a product as opposed to a beta version. *See also* beta[1].

SHTML \S`H-T-M-L´\ *n.* Acronym for **s**erver-parsed **HTML**. Hypertext Markup Language (HTML) text that contains embedded server-side include commands. SHTML documents are fully read, parsed, and modified by the server before being passed to the browser. *See also* HTML, server-side includes.

S-HTTP \S`H-T-T-P´\ *n.* Acronym for **S**ecure **H**ypertext **T**ransfer **P**rotocol. A proposed extension to HTTP that supports various encryption and authentication measures to keep all transactions secure from end to end.

shut down \shut doun´\ *vb.* To close a program or operating system in a manner ensuring that no data is lost.

Short card. A short card (top) and a standard-length card (bottom).

.si \dot`S-I´\ *n.* On the Internet, the major geographic domain specifying that an address is located in Slovenia.

sibling \si´blēng\ *n.* A process or node in a data tree that is descended from the same immediate ancestor(s) as other processes or nodes. *See also* generation (definition 2), node (definition 3).

sideband \sīd´band\ *n.* The upper or lower portion of a modulated carrier wave. One portion can be processed while the other is used to carry separate data, a technique that doubles the amount of information that can be carried over a single line. See the illustration.

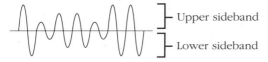

Upper sideband
Lower sideband

Sideband.

sidebar \sīd´bär\ *n.* A block of text placed to the side of the main body of text in a document, often set off by a border or other graphic element.

side effect \sīd´ ə-fekt´\ *n.* Any change of state caused by a subroutine, such as a routine that reads a value from a file and advances the current file position.

side head \sīd´ hed\ *n.* A heading placed in the margin of a printed document and top-aligned with the body text, rather than being vertically aligned with text, as is a normal head.

sieve of Eratosthenes \siv` əv âr-ə-tos´thə-nēz\ *n.* An algorithm for finding prime numbers. It is often used as a benchmark in testing the speed of a computer or programming language. *See also* benchmark[1].

.sig \dot-sig´, dot`S-I-G´\ *n.* A file extension for a signature file for e-mail or Internet newsgroup use. The contents of this file are automatically appended to e-mail correspondence or newsgroup articles by their respective client software. *See also* signature file.

SIG \sig, S`I-G´\ *n.* Acronym for **s**pecial **i**nterest **g**roup. An e-mail online discussion group or a group of users who meet and share information, especially one of the groups supported by the Association for Computing Machinery (ACM), such as SIGGRAPH for computer graphics.

SIGGRAPH \sig´graf, S`I-G`G-R`A-P-H´\ *n.* Short for **S**pecial **I**nterest **G**roup on **C**omputer **Graph**ics, a part of the Association for Computing Machinery (ACM).

sign \sīn\ *n.* The character used to indicate a positive or negative number. In assembly-level programming, the sign is indicated by the sign bit accompanying the number. *See also* sign bit.

signal \sig´nəl\ *n.* **1.** Any electrical quantity, such as voltage, current, or frequency, that can be used to transmit information. **2.** A beep or tone from a computer's speaker or a prompt displayed on screen that tells a user that the computer is ready to receive input.

signal converter \sig´nəl kən-vər`tər\ *n.* A device or circuit that converts a signal from one form to another, such as analog to digital, or pulse code modulation to frequency modulation.

signal-to-noise ratio \sig`nəl-tə-noiz´ rā-shō\ *n.* Abbreviated S/N. The amount of power, measured in decibels, by which the signal exceeds the amount of channel noise at the same point in transmission. *See also* noise (definition 2).

signature \sig´nə-chur\ *n.* **1.** A sequence of data used for identification, such as text appended to an e-mail message or fax. **2.** A unique number built into hardware or software for authentication purposes.

signature block \sig´nə-chur blok`\ *n.* A block of text that an e-mail client or a newsreader automatically places at the end of every message or article before the message or article is transmitted. Signature blocks typically contain the name, e-mail address, and affiliation of the person who created the message or article.

signature file \sig´nə-chur fīl`\ *n. See* .sig.

sign bit \sīn´ bit\ *n.* The most significant, or leftmost, bit of a number field, usually set to 1 if the number is negative.

sign extension \sīn´ eks-ten`shən\ *n. See* sign bit.

significant digits \sig-nif´ə-kənt dij´əts\ *n.* The sequence from the first nonzero digit to the last digit in a number (the last nonzero digit in an integer), used to express the number's precision (for example, 12,300 has three significant digits, and 0.000120300 has six). *See also* floating-point notation.

sign off \sīn of´\ *vb. See* log off.

sign on \sīn on´\ *vb. See* log on.

sign propagation \sīn´ prop-ə-gā`shən\ *n. See* sign bit.

silica gel \sil´i-kə jel`\ *n.* A desiccant (moisture-absorbent substance) often packaged with optical or electronic equipment.

silicon \sil´i-kon`\ *n.* A semiconductor used in many devices, especially microchips. Silicon, with atomic number 14 and atomic weight 28, is the second most common element in nature.

silicon chip \sil´i-kon chip`\ *n.* An integrated circuit that uses silicon as its semiconductor material.

silicon-controlled rectifier \sil`i-kon-kən-trōld rek´tə-fī-yər\ *n.* A semiconductor rectifier whose conductance can be controlled by a gate signal. *Acronym:* SCR (S`C-R´). *See also* gate (definition 1), rectifier.

silicon dioxide \sil´i-kon dī-oks´īd\ *n.* An insulator used to form thin insulating layers in some types of semiconductors; also the primary component of glass.

silicone \sil´i-kōn\ *n.* A polymer in which silicon and oxygen are major components. Silicone is an excellent electrical insulator and conducts heat well.

silicon foundry \sil´i-kon foun`drē\ *n.* A factory or machine used to create wafers of crystalline silicon.

silicon-on-sapphire \sil`i-kon-on-saf´īr\ *n.* A method of fabricating semiconductors in which the semiconductor devices are formed in a thin single layer of silicon that has been grown on an insulating substrate of synthetic sapphire. *Acronym:* SOS (S`O-S´).

Silicon Valley \sil`i-kon val´ē\ *n.* The region of California south of San Francisco Bay, otherwise known as the Santa Clara Valley, roughly extending from Palo Alto to San Jose. Silicon Valley is a major center of electronics and computer research, development, and manufacturing. See the illustration.

Silicon Valley.

SIM \S`I-M´\ *n. See* Society for Information Management.

SIMD \S`I-M-D´\ *n.* Acronym for **s**ingle-**i**nstruction, **m**ultiple-**d**ata stream processing. A category of parallel-processor computer architecture in which one instruction processor fetches instructions and distributes orders to several other processors. See the illustration. *See also* parallel processing. *Compare* MIMD.

SIMM \sim, S`I-M-M´\ *n.* Acronym for **s**ingle **i**nline **m**emory **m**odule. A small circuit board designed to accommodate surface-mount memory chips. See the illustration.

SIMM.

Simple Mail Transfer Protocol \sim`pl māl` trans-fər prō´tə-kol\ *n.* A TCP/IP protocol for sending messages from one computer to another on a network. This protocol is used on the Internet to route e-mail.

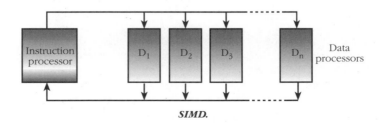

SIMD.

Acronym: SMTP (S`M-T-P´). *See also* communications protocol, TCP/IP. *Compare* CCITT X series, Post Office Protocol.

Simple Network Management Protocol \sim`pl net`wərk man´əj-mənt prō`tə-kol\ *n. See* SNMP.

simplex transmission \sim´pleks tranz-mish`ən\ *n.* Communication that takes place only from sender to receiver. *Compare* duplex[2] (definition 1), half-duplex transmission.

simulation \sim`yə-lā´shən\ *n.* The imitation of a physical process or object by a program that causes a computer to respond mathematically to data and changing conditions as though it were the process or object itself. *See also* emulator, modeling (definition 1).

simultaneous access \sī`mul-tā-nē-əs ak´ses\ *n. See* parallel access.

simultaneous processing \sī`mul-tā-nē-əs pros´-es-ēng\ *n.* **1.** True multiple-processor operation in which more than one task can be processed at a time. *See also* multiprocessing, parallel processing. **2.** Loosely, concurrent operation in which more than one task is processed by dividing processor time among the tasks. *See also* concurrent, multitasking.

sine wave \sīn´ wāv\ *n.* A uniform, periodic wave often generated by an object that vibrates at a single frequency. See the illustration. *Compare* square wave.

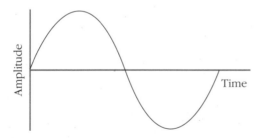

Sine wave.

single-board \sēng´l-bōrd`\ *adj.* Of or pertaining to a computer that occupies only one circuit board, usually with no capacity for additional boards.

single-density \sēng´l-den`sə-tē\ *adj.* Of or pertaining to a disk that is certified only for use with frequency modulation (FM) recording. A single-

density disk can store much less data than a disk using modified FM encoding or run-length limited encoding. *See also* modified frequency modulation encoding, run-length limited encoding.

single inline memory module \sēng`l in`līn mem´ər-ē moj`ool, mo`dyool\ *n. See* SIMM.

single inline package \sēng`l in`līn pak`əj\ *n. See* SIP.

single inline pinned package \sēn`gl in´līn pind pak`əj\ *n. See* SIP.

single-instruction, multiple-data stream processing \sēn`gl-in-struk´shən mul`tə-pl-dā´tə strēm pros-es-ēng, dat´ə\ *n. See* SIMD.

single-precision \sēng´l-prə-sizh`ən\ *adj.* Of or pertaining to a floating-point number having the least precision among two or more options commonly offered by a programming language, such as single-precision versus double-precision. *See also* floating-point notation, precision (definition 2). *Compare* double-precision.

single-sided \sēng´l-sī`dəd\ *adj.* Of or pertaining to a floppy disk in which data can be stored on only one side.

single step \sēng´l step\ *vb.* To execute a program one step at a time, usually within the context of a debugger. *See also* debugger.

single threading \sēng`l thred´ēng\ *n.* **1.** Within a program, the running of a single process at a time. **2.** A condition in which each leaf node of a tree data structure contains a pointer to its parent. *See also* node (definition 3), pointer (definition 1), threading.

single-user computer \sēng`l-yōō-zər kəm-pyōō´tər\ *n.* A computer designed for use by a single individual; a personal computer. *Compare* multiuser system.

sink \sēnk\ *n.* A device or part of a device that receives something from another device. *See also* data sink, heat sink.

SIP \sip, S`I-P´\ *n.* Acronym for **s**ingle **i**nline **p**ackage. A type of housing for an electronic component in which all leads (connections) protrude from one side of the package. See the illustration on the next page. *Also called* single inline pinned package. *Compare* DIP.

SIPP \sip, S`I-P-P´\ *n.* Acronym for **s**ingle **i**nline **p**inned **p**ackage. *See* SIP.

SIR \S`I-R´\ *n. See* Serial Infrared.

SIP.

.sit \dot-sit´, dot`S-I-T´\ *n.* The file extension for a Macintosh file compressed with StuffIt. *See also* StuffIt.

site \sīt\ *n. See* Web site.

site license \sīt´ lī`səns\ *n.* A purchase agreement for using multiple copies of the same software at a business or institution, usually at a volume discount.

size box \sīz´ boks\ *n.* A control in the upper right corner of the frame of a window on the Macintosh screen. When the user clicks on the size box, the window toggles between the size the user has set for it by dragging and the maximum size. *Compare* Maximize button.

.sj \dot`S-J´\ *n.* On the Internet, the major geographic domain specifying that an address is located on the Svalbard and Jan Mayen Islands.

.sk \dot`S-K´\ *n.* On the Internet, the major geographic domain specifying that an address is located in the Slovak Republic.

skew \skyōō\ *n.* The difference between what is and what should be—for example, the misalignment of a page that prevents accurate reproduction, or the difference between input and output when circuits do not respond evenly to a propagated signal.

Skutch box \skuch´ boks\ *n.* A slang term for a device manufactured by Skutch Electronics, Inc., that simulates the functioning of a telephone line with a good connection. Telephone line simulators are used to test telecommunications systems and devices.

.sl \dot`S-L´\ *n.* On the Internet, the major geographic domain specifying that an address is located in Sierra Leone.

slave \slāv\ *n.* Any device, including a computer, that is controlled by another computer, referred to as the master. *See also* master/slave arrangement.

sleep[1] \slēp\ *n.* **1.** In a multiprocessing environment, a temporary state of suspension during which a process remains in memory so that some event, such as an interrupt or call from another process, can "awaken" it. **2.** In programming, a state of suspension caused by a loop statement that creates an intentional delay.

sleep[2] \slēp\ *vb.* To suspend operation without terminating.

sleeve \slēv\ *n. See* disk envelope.

slice \slīs\ *n. See* time slice.

SLIP \slip, S`L-I-P´\ *n.* Acronym for **S**erial **L**ine **I**nternet **P**rotocol. A data link protocol that allows transmission of IP data packets over dial-up telephone connections, thus enabling a computer or a local area network to be connected to the Internet or some other network. *See also* data link, IP. *Compare* PPP.

SLIP emulator \slip´ em`yə-lā-tər, S`L-I-P´\ *n.* Software that mimics a SLIP connection in UNIX shell accounts that do not offer a direct SLIP connection. Many Internet service providers (ISPs) are UNIX based and offer shell accounts to users for Internet access. Like a SLIP connection, the SLIP emulator allows the user to avoid dealing with the ISP's UNIX environment directly when accessing the Internet and to use Internet applications such as graphical Web browsers. *See also* ISP, shell account, SLIP.

slot \slot\ *n. See* expansion slot.

slotted-ring network \slot`əd-rēng net´wərk\ *n.* A ring network allowing data to be transmitted between data stations in one direction. A slotted-ring network transfers data in predefined time slots (fixed-length portions of a data frame) in the transmission stream over one transmission medium. *See also* data frame, ring network. *Compare* token ring network.

SlowKeys \slō´kēz\ *n.* An accessibility feature built into Macintosh computers and available for DOS and Windows that allows the user to add a delay to the keyboard so that a key must be held down for a certain amount of time before it is accepted. This feature facilitates the use of the keyboard by individuals with poor motor control who might accidentally bump keys when moving around the keyboard.

SLSI \S`L-S-I´\ *n. See* super-large-scale integration.

.sm \dot`S-M´\ *n.* On the Internet, the major geographic domain specifying that an address is located in San Marino.

small caps \smäl kaps´\ *n.* A font of capital letters that are smaller than the standard capital letters in that typeface. THIS TEXT IS IN SMALL CAPS.

Small Computer System Interface \smäl` kəm-pyōō`tər si`stəm in`tər-fās\ *n. See* SCSI.

small model \smäl` mod´əl\ *n.* A memory model of the Intel 80x86 processor family that allows only 64 kilobytes (KB) for code and 64 KB for data. *See also* memory model.

small-scale integration \smäl`skāl in`tə-grā´shən\ *n.* A concentration of fewer than 10 components on a single chip. *Acronym:* SSI (S`S-I´). *See also* integrated circuit.

Smalltalk \smäl´täk\ *n.* An object-oriented language and development system developed at Xerox Palo Alto Research Center (PARC) in 1980. Smalltalk pioneered many language and user interface concepts that are now widely used in other environments, such as the concept of an object that contains data and routines and on-screen icons that the user can choose to make the computer perform certain tasks. *See also* object-oriented programming.

smart \smärt\ *adj.* A synonym for intelligent. *See* intelligence.

smart cable \smärt´ kā`bl\ *n. See* intelligent cable.

smart card \smärt´ kärd\ *n.* **1.** In computers and electronics, a circuit board with built-in logic or firmware that gives it some kind of independent decision-making ability. **2.** In banking and finance, a credit card that contains an integrated circuit that gives it a limited amount of "intelligence" and memory.

smart linkage \smärt` lēnk´əj\ *n.* A feature of programming languages that guarantees that routines will always be called with correct parameter types. *See also* link (definition 1).

smart quotes \smärt´ kwōts\ *n.* In word processors, a function that automatically converts the ditto marks (") produced by most computer keyboards to the inverted commas (" and ") used in typeset text.

SMART system \smärt´ si`stəm, S`M-A-R-T´\ *n.* Short for **s**elf-**m**onitoring **a**nalysis and **r**eporting **t**echnology **system**. A system by which technology is used to monitor and predict device performance and reliability. A SMART system employs various diagnostic tests to detect problems with devices, with the object of increasing productivity and protecting data.

smart terminal \smärt` tər´mə-nəl\ *n.* A terminal that contains a microprocessor and random access memory (RAM) and that does some rudimentary processing without intervention from the host computer. *Compare* dumb terminal.

SMDS \S`M-D-S´\ *n.* Acronym for **S**witched **M**ulti-megabit **D**ata **S**ervices. A very high-speed, switched data transport service that connects local area networks and wide area networks through the public telephone network.

smiley \smī´lē\ *n. See* emoticon.

S/MIME \S´mīm, S`-M-I-M-E´\ *n.* Acronym for **S**ecure/**M**ultipurpose **I**nternet **M**ail **E**xtensions. An Internet e-mail security standard that makes use of public key encryption. *See also* public key encryption.

SMIS \S`M-I-S´\ *n.* Acronym for **S**ociety for **M**anagement **I**nformation **S**ystems. *See* Society for Information Management.

smoke test \smōk´ test\ *n.* The testing of a piece of hardware after assembly or repairs by turning it on. The device fails the test if it produces smoke, explodes, or has some other unexpected violent or dramatic reaction, even if it appears to work.

smooth \smōōdh\ *vb.* **1.** To eliminate irregularities in statistical data by some process such as continuous averaging or by removing random (irrelevant) values. **2.** In graphics, to remove jagged edges from a figure or line. *See also* anti-aliasing.

SMP \S`M-P´\ *n.* Acronym for **s**ymmetric **m**ulti**p**rocessing. A computer architecture in which multiple processors share the same memory, which contains one copy of the operating system, one copy of any applications that are in use, and one copy of the data. Because the operating system divides the workload into tasks and assigns those tasks to whatever processors are free, SMP reduces transaction time. *See also* architecture, multiprocessing.

SMP server \S`M-P´ sər-vər\ *n.* Short for **s**ymmetric **m**ultiprocessing **server**. A computer that is designed with the SMP architecture to improve its performance as a server in client/server applications. *See also* SMP.

SMT \S`M-T´\ *n. See* surface-mount technology.

SMTP \S`M-T-P´\ *n. See* Simple Mail Transfer Protocol.

.sn \dot`S-N´\ *n.* On the Internet, the major geographic domain specifying that an address is located in Senegal.

SNA \S`N-A´\ *n.* Acronym for **S**ystems **N**etwork **A**rchitecture. A widely used communications framework developed by IBM to define network functions and establish standards for enabling computers to exchange and process data. See the illustration.

**ISO Open Systems
Interconnection**

SNA

Function management	Application
Data flow control	Presentation
Transmission control	Session
Path control	Transport
	Network
Data-link control	Data-link
	Physical

SNA. Comparable (not compatible) layers in the SNA and ISO/OSI architectures.

snail mail \snāl´ māl\ *n.* A popular phrase on the Internet for referring to mail services provided by the U.S. Postal Service and similar agencies in other countries. The term has its origins in the fact that regular postal mail is slow compared with e-mail.

snap-in \snap´in\ *n. See* plug-in.

snapshot \snap´shot\ *n.* A copy of main memory or video memory at a given instant, sent to the printer or hard disk. *Also called* snapshot dump. *See also* screen dump.

snapshot program \snap´shot prō`gram\ *n.* A program that performs a trace by taking a snapshot of certain chunks of memory at specified times.

.snd \dot`S-N-D´\ *n.* A file extension for a type of interchangeable sound file format used on Sun,

NeXT, and Silicon Graphics computers, consisting of raw audio data preceded by a text identifier.

sneakernet \snē´kər-net`\ *n.* Transfer of data between computers that are not networked together. The files must be written onto floppy disks on the source machine, and a person must physically transport the disks to the destination machine.

SNMP \S`N-M-P´\ *n.* Acronym for **S**imple **N**etwork **M**anagement **P**rotocol. The network management protocol of TCP/IP. In SNMP, agents, which can be hardware as well as software, monitor the activity in the various devices on the network and report to the network console workstation. Control information about each device is maintained in a structure known as a management information block. *See also* agent (definition 4), TCP/IP.

SNOBOL \snō´bōl, S`N-O-B`O-L´\ *n.* Acronym for **Stri**n**g-O**riented Sym**bol**ic Language. A string- and text-processing language developed between 1962 and 1967 by Ralph Griswold, David Farber, and I. Polonsky at AT&T Bell Laboratories. *See also* string.

snow \snō\ *n.* **1.** In television, temporary distortion of a displayed image caused by interference, usually in a weak signal, that takes the form of random white spots. **2.** In computer displays, a specific type of distortion characterized by the blinking on and off of random pixels that occurs when the microprocessor and the display hardware interfere with each other by attempting to use the computer's video memory at the same time.

.so \dot`S-O´\ *n.* On the Internet, the major geographic domain specifying that an address is located in Somalia.

Society for Information Management \sə-sī`i-tē fər in`fər-mā´shən man´əj-mənt\ *n.* A professional society based in Chicago for information systems executives, formerly the Society for Management Information Systems. *Acronym:* SIM (S`I-M´).

Society for Management Information Systems \sə-sī`i-tē fər man`əj-mənt in-fər-mā´shən si`-stəmz\ *n. See* Society for Information Management.

socket \sok´ət\ *n.* **1.** An identifier for a particular service on a particular node on a network. The socket consists of a node address and a port number, which identifies the service. For example, port 80 on an Internet node indicates a Web server. *See also* port number. **2.** The receptacle part of a connector, which receives a plug. *See also* female connector.

soc. newsgroups \sōsh`dot nōōz´grōōps\ *n.* Usenet newsgroups that are part of the soc. hierarchy and have the prefix soc. These newsgroups are devoted to discussions of current events and social issues. Soc. newsgroups are one of the seven original Usenet newsgroup hierarchies. The other six are comp., misc., news., rec., sci., and talk. *See also* newsgroup, traditional newsgroup hierarchy, Usenet.

soft \soft\ *adj.* **1.** In computing, temporary or changeable. For example, a soft error is a problem from which the system can recover, and a soft patch is a temporary program fix that holds only while the program is running. *Compare* hard (definition 1). **2.** In electronics, characterized by magnetic materials that do not retain their magnetism when a magnetic field is removed. *Compare* hard (definition 2).

soft boot \soft´ bōōt\ *n. See* warm boot.

soft copy \soft´ kop`ē\ *n.* The temporary images presented on a computer display screen. *Compare* hard copy.

soft error \soft´ âr`ər\ *n.* An error from which a program or operating system is able to recover. *Compare* hard error.

soft font \soft font´\ *n. See* downloadable font.

soft hyphen \soft` hī´fən\ *n. See* hyphen.

soft link \soft´ lēnk\ *n. See* symbolic link.

softmodem \soft´mō`dəm\ *n. See* software-based modem.

soft patch \soft pach´\ *n.* A fix or modification performed only while the code being patched is loaded into memory, so that the executable or object file is not modified in any way. *See also* patch[1].

soft return \soft` rə-turn´\ *n.* A line break inserted in a document by a word processor when the next word in the current line of text would cause the line to overflow into the margin—a movable line break. *See also* wordwrap. *Compare* hard return.

soft-sectored disk \soft`sek-tərd disk´\ *n.* A disk, especially a floppy disk, whose sectors have been marked with recorded data marks rather than

punched holes. *See also* index hole. *Compare* hard-sectored disk.

software \soft´wâr\ *n.* Computer programs; instructions that make hardware work. Two main types of software are system software (operating systems), which controls the workings of the computer, and applications, such as word processing programs, spreadsheets, and databases, which perform the tasks for which people use computers. Two additional categories, which are neither system nor application software but contain elements of both, are network software, which enables groups of computers to communicate, and language software, which provides programmers with the tools they need to write programs. In addition to these task-based categories, several types of software are described based on their method of distribution. These include packaged software (canned programs), sold primarily through retail outlets; freeware and public domain software, which are distributed free of charge; shareware, which is also distributed free of charge, although users are requested to pay a small registration fee for continued use of the program; and vaporware, software that is announced by a company or individuals but either never makes it to market or is very late. *See also* application, canned software, freeware, network software, operating system, shareware, system software, vaporware. *Compare* firmware, hardware, liveware.

software-based modem \soft`wâr-bāsd mō´dəm\ *n.* A modem that uses a general-purpose, reprogrammable digital signal processor chip and RAM-based program memory rather than a dedicated chip with the modem functions burned into the silicon. A software-based modem can be reconfigured to update and change the modem's features and functions.

software-dependent \soft´wâr-də-pen`dənt\ *adj.* Of, pertaining to, or being a computer or device that is tied to a particular program or set of programs developed for it.

software engineering \soft´wâr en-jə-nēr`ēng\ *n.* The design and development of software. *See also* programming.

software handshake \soft`wâr hand´shāk\ *n.* A handshake that consists of signals transmitted over the same wires used to transfer the data, as in modem-to-modem communications over telephone lines, rather than signals transmitted over special wires. *See also* hándshake.

software house \soft`wâr hous`\ *n.* An organization that develops and supports software for its customers.

software IC \soft`wâr I-C´\ *n. See* software integrated circuit.

software integrated circuit \soft`wâr in`tə-grā-təd sər´kət\ *n.* Abbreviated software IC. An existing software module that can be designed into a program, much as an integrated circuit can be designed into a logic board. *See also* abstract data type, module (definition 1), object-oriented programming.

software interrupt \soft`wâr in´tər-upt\ *n.* A program-generated interrupt that stops current processing in order to request a service provided by an interrupt handler (a separate set of instructions designed to perform the task required). *Also called* trap.

software package \soft´wâr pak`əj\ *n.* A program sold to the public, ready to run and containing all necessary components and documentation.

software piracy \soft`wâr pīr´ə-sē\ *n. See* piracy.

software portability \soft`wâr pōr-tə-bil´ə-tē\ *n. See* portable (definition 1).

software program \soft´wâr prō`gram\ *n. See* application.

software protection \soft`wâr prə-tek´shən\ *n. See* copy protection.

software publisher \soft´wâr pu`bli-shər\ *n.* A business engaged in the development and distribution of computer software.

software publishing \soft`wâr pub`li-shēng\ *n.* The design, development, and distribution of non-custom software packages.

software stack \soft´wâr stak`\ *n. See* stack.

software suite \soft´wâr swēt`\ *n. See* suite (definition 1).

software tools \soft´wâr tōōlz`\ *n.* Programs, utilities, libraries, and other aids, such as editors, compilers, and debuggers, that can be used to develop programs.

solar cell \sō´lər sel`\ *n.* A photoelectric device that produces electrical power when exposed to light. *Also called* photovoltaic cell.

Solaris \sō`lâr´əs\ *n.* A distributed UNIX-based computing environment created by Sun Microsys-

tems, Inc., widely used as a server operating system. Versions of Solaris exist for SPARC computers, 386 and higher Intel platforms, and the PowerPC.

solenoid \sō`lə-noid`\ *n.* An electromagnetic device that converts electrical energy to mechanical movement, typically consisting of an electromagnet with a movable rod through the center. See the illustration.

Solenoid.

solid ink \sol`id ēnk´\ *n.* Ink manufactured in the form of solid sticks resembling crayons, for use in solid-ink printers. *See also* solid-ink printer.

solid-ink printer \sol`id-ēnk prin´tər\ *n.* A computer printer using solid ink sticks. The ink sticks are heated until they melt, and the molten ink is sprayed onto the page, where it cools and solidifies. *See also* solid ink.

solid model \sol`id mod´əl\ *n.* A geometric shape or construction that has continuity in length, width, and depth and is treated by a program as if it had both surface and internal substance. *Compare* surface modeling, wire-frame model.

solid-state device \sol`id-stāt də-vīs´\ *n.* A circuit component whose properties depend on the electrical or magnetic characteristics of a solid substance (as opposed to a gas or vacuum). Transistors, diodes, and integrated circuits are solid-state devices.

solid-state disk drive \sol`id-stāt disk´ drīv\ *n.* A mass storage device that holds data in RAM rather than in magnetic storage. *See also* magnetic storage, RAM.

solid-state memory \sol`id-stāt mem´ər-ē\ *n.* Computer memory that stores information in solid-state devices.

solid-state relay \sol`id-stāt rē`lā\ *n.* A relay that depends on solid-state components, rather than mechanical components, to open and close a circuit.

SOM \S`O-M´\ *n.* **1.** Acronym for **S**ystem **O**bject **M**odel. A language-independent architecture from IBM that implements the CORBA standard. *See* *also* CORBA, OMA. **2.** Acronym for **s**elf-**o**rganizing **m**ap. A form of neural network in which neurons and their connections are added automatically as needed to develop the desired mapping from input to output.

SONET \son´ət, S`O-N-E-T´\ *n.* Acronym for **S**ynchronous **O**ptical **Net**work. A category of fiber-optic communication standards that permits extremely high-speed transmission (51.84 Mbps to 2.48 Gbps).

sort \sōrt\ *vb.* To organize data, typically a set of records, in a particular order. Programs and programming algorithms for sorting vary in performance and application. *See also* bubble sort, distributive sort, insertion sort, merge sort, quicksort.

sort algorithm \sōrt´ al`gər-idh-əm\ *n.* An algorithm that puts a collection of data elements into some sequenced order, sometimes based on one or more key values in each element. *See also* algorithm, bubble sort, distributive sort, insertion sort, merge sort, quicksort.

sorter \sōr´tər\ *n.* A program or routine that sorts data. *See also* sort.

sort field \sōrt´ fēld\ *n. See* sort key.

sort key \sōrt´ kē\ *n.* A field (commonly called a key) whose entries are sorted to produce a desired arrangement of the records containing the field. *See also* field (definition 1), primary key, secondary key.

SOS \S`O-S´\ *n. See* silicon-on-sapphire.

sound board \sound´ bōrd\ *n. See* sound card.

sound buffer \sound´ buf`ər\ *n.* A region of memory used to store the bit image of a sequence of sounds to be sent to a computer's speaker(s).

sound card \sound´ kärd\ *n.* A type of expansion board on PC-compatible computers that allows the playback and recording of sound, such as from a WAV or MIDI file or a music CD-ROM. Most PCs sold at retail include a sound card. *Also called* sound board. *See also* expansion board, MIDI, WAV.

sound clip \sound´ klip\ *n.* A file that contains a short audio item, usually an excerpt from a longer recording.

sound editor \sound´ ed`i-tər\ *n.* A program that allows the user to create and manipulate sound files.

sound generator \sound` jen´ər-ā-tər\ *n.* A chip or chip-level circuit that can produce electronic signals that can drive a speaker and synthesize sound.

sound hood \sound´ho͞od\ *n.* A five-sided box, lined with soundproofing material, that is placed over a loud printer to muffle its noise.

SoundSentry \sound´sen`trē\ *n.* An optional Windows 95 feature for users with hearing impairments or users who operate a computer in a noisy environment that instructs Windows to produce a visual cue such as a screen flash or a blinking title bar whenever a system beep occurs.

source \sōrs\ *n.* **1.** In information processing, a disk, file, document, or other collection of information from which data is taken or moved. *Compare* destination. **2.** In a FET, the electrode toward which charge carriers (electrons or holes) move from the source under control of the gate. *See also* CMOS (definition 1), drain (definition 1), FET, gate (definition 2), MOSFET, NMOS, PMOS.

source code \sōrs´ kōd\ *n.* Human-readable program statements written in a high-level or assembly language that are not directly readable by a computer. *Compare* object code.

source computer \sōrs´ kəm-pyo͞o´tər\ *n.* **1.** A computer on which a program is compiled. *Compare* object computer. **2.** A computer from which data is transferred to another computer.

source data \sōrs` dā´tə, dat´ə\ *n.* The original data on which a computer application is based.

source data acquisition \sōrs` dā-tə a-kwə-zish´ən, dat-ə\ *n.* The process of sensing, as with a bar code reader or other scanning device, or receiving source data. *See also* source data.

source data capture \sōrs` dā-tə kap´chur, dat-ə\ *n. See* source data acquisition.

source directory \sōrs´ də-rek`tə-rē\ *n.* During a file copy operation, the directory in which the original versions of the files are located.

source disk \sōrs´ disk\ *n.* Any disk from which data will be read, as during a copy operation or when an application is loaded from a disk into memory. *Compare* target disk.

source document \sōrs´ do`kyə-mənt\ *n.* The original document from which data is taken.

source drive \sōrs´ drīv\ *n.* The disk drive from which files are being copied during a copy operation.

source file \sōrs´ fīl\ *n*. In MS-DOS and Windows commands that involve the copying of data or program instructions, the file containing the data or instructions that are copied.

source language \sōrs´ lang`wəj\ *n*. The programming language in which the source code for a program is written. *See also* programming language, source code.

source program \sōrs´ prō`gram\ *n*. The source code version of a program. *See also* source code. *Compare* executable program.

source statement \sōrs´ stāt`mənt\ *n*. A single statement in the source code of a program. *See also* source code, statement.

Spacebar \spās´bär\ *n*. A long key occupying much of the bottom row of most keyboards that sends a space character to the computer.

space character \spās` kâr´ək-tər\ *n*. A character that is entered by pressing the Spacebar on the keyboard and that typically appears on the screen as a blank space.

space-division   multiplexing \spās`də-vizh-ən mul´tē-pleks-ēng, mul´tī-pleks-ēng\ *n*. The first automated form of communications multiplexing, which replaced the human-operated switchboard. Space-division multiplexing was replaced by frequency-division multiplexing (FDM), which was in turn replaced by time-division multiplexing (TDM). *Acronym:* SDM (S`D-M´). *See also* FDM, multiplexing, time-division multiplexing.

spaghetti code \spə-get´ē kōd`\ *n*. Code that results in convoluted program flow, usually because of excessive or inappropriate use of GOTO or JUMP statements. *See also* GOTO statement, jump instruction.

spam \spam\ *n*. An unsolicited e-mail message sent to many recipients at one time, or a news article posted simultaneously to many newsgroups. Spam is the electronic equivalent of junk mail. In most cases, the content of a spam message or article is not relevant to the topic of the newsgroup or the interests of the recipient; spam is an abuse of the Internet in order to distribute a message (usually commercial or religious) to a huge number of people at minimal cost.

spambot \spam´bot\ *n*. A program or device that automatically posts large amounts of repetitive or otherwise inappropriate material to newsgroups on the Internet. *See also* bot (definition 3), robopost, spam.

span \span\ *n*. *See* range.

SPARC \spärk, S`P-A-R-C´\ *n*. Acronym for **S**calable **P**rocessor **Arc**hitecture. A RISC (reduced instruction set computing) microprocessor specification from Sun Microsystems, Inc. *See also* RISC.

sparse array \spärs` ər-ā´\ *n*. An array (arrangement of items) in which many of the entries are identical, commonly zero. It is not possible to define precisely when an array is sparse, but it is clear that at some point, usually when about one third of the array consists of identical entries, it becomes worthwhile to redefine the array. *See also* array.

spatial data management \spā`shəl dā´tə man`-əj-mənt, dat´ə\ *n*. The representation of data as a collection of objects in space, particularly as icons on a screen, in order to make the data easier to comprehend and manipulate.

spatial digitizer \spā`shəl dij´i-tī-zər\ *n*. A three-dimensional scanner most often used in medical and geographical work. *Compare* optical scanner.

spec \spek\ *n*. *See* specification.

special character \spe`shəl kâr´ək-tər\ *n*. Any character that is not alphabetic, numeric, or the space character (for example, a punctuation character). *See also* reserved character, wildcard character.

special interest group \spe`shəl in´trəst grōōp`, in`tər-est´\ *n*. *See* SIG.

special-purpose   language \spe`shəl-pur-pəs lang´wəj\ *n*. A programming language whose syntax and semantics are best suited for a given field or approach. *See also* Prolog.

specification \spes´ə-fə-kā´shən\ *n*. **1.** A detailed description of something. **2.** In relation to computer hardware, an item of information about the computer's components, capabilities, and features. **3.** In relation to software, a description of the operating environment and proposed features of a new program. **4.** In information processing, a description of the data records, programs, and procedures involved in a particular task.

spectral color \spek`trəl kə´lər\ *n*. In video, the hue represented by a single wavelength in the visible spectrum. *See also* color model.

spectral response \spek`trəl rə-spons´\ *n*. In relation to sensing devices, the relationship between the device's sensitivity and the frequency of the detected energy.

spectrum \spek´trum\ *n.* The range of frequencies of a particular type of radiation. *See also* electromagnetic spectrum.

Speech API \spēch` A-P-I´\ *n. See* SAPI.

Speech Application Programming Interface \spēch` a-plə-kā`shən prō-gram-ēng in´tər-fās\ *n. See* SAPI.

speech recognition \spēch´ rek-əg-nish`ən\ *n.* The ability of a computer to understand the spoken word for the purpose of receiving commands and data input from the speaker. Systems have been developed that can recognize limited vocabularies as spoken by specific individuals, but developing a system that deals with a variety of speech patterns and accents, as well as with the various ways in which a request or a statement can be made, has so far proved to be a daunting task for systems designers. *See also* artificial intelligence, neural network.

Speech Recognition API \spēch` rek-əg-nish`ən A-P-I´\ *n. See* SRAPI.

Speech Recognition Application Programming Interface \spēch` rek-əg-nish`ən a-plə-kā`shən prō´gram-ēng in´tər-fās\ *n. See* SRAPI.

speech synthesis \spēch` sin´thə-sis\ *n.* The ability of a computer to produce "spoken" words either by splicing together prerecorded words or by programming the computer to produce the sounds that make up spoken words. *See also* artificial intelligence, neural network.

spelling checker \spel´ēng chek`ər\ *n.* An application that employs a disk-based dictionary to check for misspellings in a document. *Also called* spell checker.

spew \spyo͞o\ *vb.* On the Internet, to post an excessive number of e-mail messages or newsgroup articles.

spider \spī´dər\ *n.* An automated program that searches the Internet for new Web documents and places their addresses and content-related information in a database, which can be accessed with a search engine. Spiders are generally considered to be a type of bot, or Internet robot. *See also* bot (definition 3), search engine (definition 2).

spike \spīk\ *n.* A transient electrical signal of very short duration and usually high amplitude. *Compare* surge.

spindle \spin´dl\ *n.* An axle for mounting a disk or reel of magnetic tape.

spline \splīn\ *n.* In computer graphics, a curve calculated by a mathematical function that connects separate points with a high degree of smoothness. See the illustration. *See also* Bézier curve.

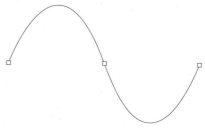

Spline.

split screen \split skrēn´\ *n.* A display method in which a program can divide the display area into two or more sections, which can contain different files or show different parts of the same file. See the illustration.

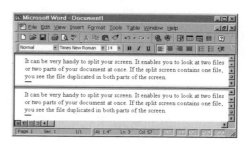

Split screen.

spoiler \spoi´lər\ *n.* A post to a newsgroup or mailing list that reveals what is intended to be a surprise, such as a plot twist in a film or television episode or the solution to a game. The subject line should contain the word *spoiler,* but netiquette requires that the sender further protect readers who do not or cannot scan posts for subject lines in advance by encrypting the post, putting one or more screenfuls of white space above the text, or both. *See also* netiquette.

spoofing \spōō´fēng\ *n.* The practice of making a transmission appear to come from an authorized user. For example, in IP spoofing, a transmission is given the IP address of an authorized user in order to obtain access to a computer or network. *See also* IP address.

spool \spool\ *vb.* To store a data document in a queue, where it awaits its turn to be printed. *See also* print spooler.

spot \spot\ *n.* A "composite dot" produced through the halftone creation process on a PostScript printer that consists of a group of dots arranged in a pattern reflecting the gray level of a particular pixel. *See also* gray scale, halftone. *Compare* dot (definition 2).

spot color \spot´ kə`lər\ *n.* A method of handling color in a document in which a particular color of ink is specified and each page having elements in that color is printed as a separate layer. The printer then prints one layer for each spot color in the document. *See also* color model, color separation (definition 1), Pantone Matching System. *Compare* process color.

spot function \spot´ funk`shən\ *n.* The PostScript procedure used to create a given type of screen in a halftone. *See also* halftone, PostScript, spot.

SPP \S`P-P´\ *n. See* scalable parallel processing.

spraycan \sprā´kan\ *n.* An artist's tool in Paintbrush or another graphics application for applying a pattern of dots to an image. See the illustration.

Spraycan.

spreadsheet program \spred´shēt prō`gram\ *n.* An application commonly used for budgets, forecasting, and other finance-related tasks that organizes data values using cells, where the relationships between cells are defined by formulas. A change to one cell produces changes to related cells. Spreadsheet programs usually provide graphing capabilities for output and a variety of formatting options for text, numeric values, and graph features. *See also* cell (definition 1).

spread spectrum \spred´ spek`trum\ *adj.* Of or pertaining to a system of secure radio communication in which the content of a transmission is broken into split-second pieces, which are transmitted over separate frequencies. When a receiver identifies a spread spectrum signal, it reassembles it to its original form. Spread spectrum was invented by the actress Hedy Lamarr in 1940, but it was not used until 1962.

sprite \sprīt\ *n.* In computer graphics, a small image that can be moved on the screen independently of other images in the background. Sprites are widely used in animation sequences and video games. *See also* object (definition 3).

sprocket feed \sprok´ət fēd`\ *n.* A paper feed in which pins engage holes in the paper to move it through a printer. Pin feed and tractor feed are both sprocket feeds. *See also* paper feed, pin feed, tractor feed.

SPX \S`P-X´\ *n.* **1.** Acronym for **S**equenced **P**acket **Ex**change. The transport level (ISO/OSI level 4) protocol used by Novell NetWare. SPX uses IPX to transfer the packets, but SPX ensures that messages are complete. *See also* ISO/OSI model. *Compare* IPX. **2.** Acronym for **si**m**p**le**x**. *See* simplex transmission.

SQL \sē´kwəl, S`Q-L´\ *n. See* structured query language.

square wave \skwâr wāv´\ *n.* A blocklike waveform that is generated by a source that changes instantly between alternate states, usually at a single frequency. See the illustration. *Compare* sine wave.

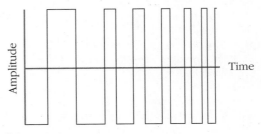

Square wave.

.sr \dot`S-R´\ *n.* On the Internet, the major geographic domain specifying that an address is located in Surinam.

SRAM \S´ram, S`R-A-M´\ *n. See* static RAM.

SRAPI \S`R-A-P-I´\ *n.* Acronym for **S**peech **R**ecognition **A**pplication **P**rogramming **I**nterface. A cross-platform application programming interface for speech recognition and text-to-speech functions supported by a consortium of developers including Novell, IBM, Intel, and Philips Dictation Systems. *See also* application programming interface, speech recognition.

SSA \S`S-A´\ *n.* Acronym for **S**erial **S**torage **A**rchitecture. An interface specification from IBM in which devices are arranged in a ring topology. In SSA, which is compatible with SCSI devices, data can be transferred at up to 20 megabytes per second in each direction. *See also* SCSI device.

SSD \S`S-D´\ *n.* Acronym for **s**olid-**s**tate **d**isk. *See* solid-state disk drive.

SSI \S`S-I´\ *n. See* small-scale integration.

SSL \S`S-L´\ *n. See* Secure Sockets Layer.

.st \dot`S-T´\ *n.* On the Internet, the major geographic domain specifying that an address is located in Sao Tomé and Principe.

ST506 interface \S`T-fīv`ō-siks in´tər-fās\ *n.* The hardware signal specification developed by Seagate Technologies for hard-disk-drive controllers and connectors. The ST506/412 version of this interface has become a de facto standard.

stack \stak\ *n.* A region of reserved memory in which programs store status data such as procedure and function call addresses, passed parameters, and sometimes local variables. *See also* pop, push (definition 1). *Compare* heap (definition 1).

stack pointer \stak´ poin`tər\ *n.* A register that contains the current address of the top element of the stack. *See also* pointer (definition 1), stack.

stackware \stak´wâr\ *n.* A HyperCard application consisting of a HyperCard data stack and Hyper-Card programming. *See also* HyperCard.

stairstepping \stâr´step`ēng\ *n.* A rough outline like the steps of a stair in a graphic line or curve that should be smooth. *Also called* aliasing, jaggies.

stale link \stāl lēnk´\ *n.* A hyperlink to an HTML document that has been deleted or moved, rendering the hyperlink useless. *See also* HTML document, hyperlink.

stale pointer bug *See* aliasing bug.

stand-alone \stand´ə-lōn`\ *adj.* Of, pertaining to, or being a device that does not require support from another device or system, for example, a computer that is not connected to a network.

standard \stan´dərd\ *n.* **1.** A de jure technical guideline advocated by a recognized noncommercial or government organization that is used to establish uniformity in an area of hardware or software development. The standard is the result of a formal process, based on specifications drafted by a cooperative group or committee after an intensive study of existing methods, approaches, and technological trends and developments. The proposed standard is later ratified or approved by a recognized organization and adopted over time by consensus as products based on the standard become increasingly prevalent in the market. Standards of this type are numerous, including the ASCII character set, the RS-232-C standard, the SCSI interface, and ANSI-standard programming languages, such as C and FORTRAN. *See also* ANSI, convention, RS-232-C standard, SCSI. **2.** A de facto technical guideline for hardware or software development that occurs when a product or philosophy is developed by a single company and, through success and imitation, becomes so widely used that deviation from the norm causes compatibility problems or limits marketability. This type of highly informal standard setting is exemplified by Hayes-compatible modems and IBM PC–compatible computers. *See also* compatibility (definition 3).

standard deviation \stan´dərd dē-vē-ā´shən\ *n.* In statistics, a measure of the dispersion of a group of measurements relative to the mean (average) of that group. Each score's difference from the mean is squared, and the standard deviation is defined as the square root of the average of these squared values.

standard disclaimer \stan`dərd dis-klā´mər\ *n.* A phrase placed in an e-mail message or news article that is intended to replace the statement required by some businesses and institutions that the contents of the message or article do not necessarily represent the opinions or policies of the organization from whose e-mail system the message originated.

standard function \stan`dərd funk´shən\ *n.* A function that is always available within a particular programming language. *See also* function (definition 1).

Standard Generalized Markup Language \stan`dərd jen`ər-ə-līzd märk´up lang`wəj\ *n. See* SGML.

star-dot-star \stär`dot-stär´\ *n.* A file specification (*.*) using the asterisk wildcard, which means "any combination of filename and extension" in operating systems such as MS-DOS. *See also* asterisk (definition 2), wildcard character.

star network \stär´ net`wərk\ *n.* A local area network (LAN) in which each device (node) is connected to a central computer in a star-shaped configuration (topology); commonly, a network consisting of a central computer (the hub) surrounded by terminals. See the illustration. *Compare* bus network, ring network.

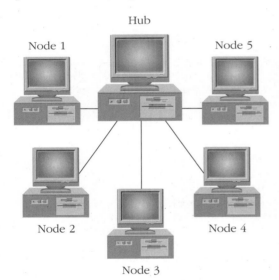

Hub

Node 1

Node 5

Node 2

Node 4

Node 3

Star network.

start bit \stärt´ bit\ *n.* In asynchronous transmission, the bit that signals the beginning of a character. *See also* asynchronous transmission.

Start button \stärt´ but`ən\ *n.* In Microsoft Windows 95, the control on the desktop task bar that opens the main menu. See the illustration.

Start button.

starting point \stär´tēng point`\ *n.* A World Wide Web document designed to help users begin navigating the Web. A starting point often contains tools such as search engines and hyperlinks to selected Web sites. *See also* hyperlink, search engine (definition 2), World Wide Web.

start page \stärt´ pāj\ *n. See* home page (definition 2).

start/stop transmission \stärt`stop `tranz-mish´-ən\ *n. See* asynchronous transmission.

startup \stärt´up\ *n. See* boot[1].

startup application \stärt`up a`plə-kā`shən\ *n.* On the Macintosh, the application that takes control of the system when the computer is turned on.

STARTUP.CMD \stärt`up-dot`C-M-D´\ *n.* A special-purpose batch file stored in the root directory of the startup disk in OS/2—the OS/2 equivalent of an MS-DOS AUTOEXEC.BAT file.

startup disk \stärt´up disk\ *n. See* system disk.

startup ROM \stärt´up rom`, R-O-M`\ *n.* The bootstrap instructions coded into a computer's ROM (read-only memory) and executed at startup. The startup ROM routines enable a computer to check itself and its devices (such as the keyboard and disk drives), prepare itself for operation, and run a short program to load an operating-system loader program. *See also* boot[1], power-on self test.

startup screen \stärt´up skrēn`\ *n.* A text or graphics display that appears on the screen when a program is started (run). Startup screens usually contain information about the software's version and often contain a product or corporate logo. See the illustration.

Startup screen.

state \stāt\ *n. See* status.

stateful \stāt´ful\ *adj.* Of or pertaining to a system or process that monitors all details of the state of an activity in which it participates. For example, stateful handling of messages takes account of their content. *Compare* stateless.

stateless \stāt´ləs\ *adj.* Of or pertaining to a system or process that participates in an activity without monitoring all details of its state. For example, stateless handling of messages might take account of only their sources and destinations but not their content. *Compare* stateful.

statement \stāt´mənt\ *n.* The smallest executable entity within a programming language.

state-of-the-art \stāt´əv-dhē-ärt´\ *adj.* Up to date; at the forefront of current hardware or software technology.

.state.us \dot-stāt`dot-U-S´\ *n.* On the Internet, the major geographic domain specifying that an address belongs to a state government in the United States.

static[1] \stat´ik\ *adj.* In information processing, fixed or predetermined. For example, a static memory buffer remains invariant in size throughout program execution. The opposite condition is *dynamic,* or ever-changing.

static[2] \stat´ik\ *n.* In communications, a crackling noise caused by electrical interference with a transmitted signal. *See also* noise (definition 2).

static allocation \stat`ik al-ə-kā´shən\ *n.* Apportionment of memory that occurs once, usually when the program starts. The memory remains allocated during the program's execution and is not deallocated until the program is finished. *See also* allocate, deallocate. *Compare* dynamic allocation.

static binding \stat`ik bīn´dēng\ *n.* Binding (converting symbolic addresses in the program to storage-related addresses) that occurs during program compilation or linkage. *Also called* early binding. *Compare* dynamic binding.

static electricity \stat`ik ə-lek-tris´ə-tē, ē-lek-tris´ə-tē\ *n.* An electrical charge accumulated in an object. Although generally harmless to humans, the discharge of static electricity through an electronic circuit can cause severe damage to the circuit.

static RAM \stat`ik ram´, R-A-M´\ *n.* A form of semiconductor memory (RAM) based on the logic circuit known as a flip-flop, which retains information as long as there is enough power to run the device. Static RAMs are usually reserved for use in caches. *Acronym:* SRAM (S´ram, S`R-A-M´). *See also* cache, RAM. *Compare* dynamic RAM.

stationery[1] \stā´shə-nâr`ē\ *adj.* Describing a type of document that, when opened by the user, is duplicated by the system; the copy is opened for the user's modification while the original document remains intact. Stationery documents can be used as document templates or boilerplates. *See also* boilerplate, template (definition 5).

stationery[2] \stā´shə-nâr`ē\ *n.* A stationery document. *See also* stationery[1].

statistical multiplexer \stə-tis`tə-kəl mul´ti-pleks-ər\ *n.* A multiplexing device that adds "intelligence" to time-division multiplexing by using buffering (temporary storage) and a microprocessor to combine transmission streams into a single signal and to allocate available bandwidth dynamically. *Also called* stat mux. *See also* dynamic allocation, multiplexing, time-division multiplexing.

statistics \stə-ti´stiks\ *n.* The branch of mathematics that deals with the relationships among groups of measurements and with the relevance of similarities and differences in those relationships. *See also* binomial distribution, Monte Carlo method, probability, regression analysis, standard deviation, stochastic.

stat mux \stat´muks\ *n. See* statistical multiplexer.

status \stat´us, stā´tus\ *n.* The condition at a particular time of any of numerous elements of computing—a device, a communications channel, a network station, a program, a bit, or other element—used to report on or to control computer operations.

status bar \stat´us bär`, stā´tus\ *n.* In Microsoft Windows, a space at the bottom of many program windows that contains a short text message about the current condition of the program. Some programs also display an explanation of the currently selected menu command in the status bar. See the illustration.

Status bar.

status codes \stat´us kōdz`, stā´tus\ *n.* Strings of digits or other characters that indicate the success or failure of some attempted action. Status codes were commonly used to report the results of early computer programs, but most software today uses words or graphics. Internet users, especially those with UNIX shell accounts, are likely to encounter status codes while using the Web or FTP. *See also* HTTP status codes.

step-frame \step´frām\ *n*. The process of capturing video images one frame at a time. This process is used by computers that are too slow to capture analog video images in real time.

stepper motor \step´ər mō´tər\ *n*. A mechanical device that rotates only a fixed distance each time it receives an electrical pulse.

step-rate time \step`rāt tīm´\ *n*. The time required to move a disk actuator arm from one track to the next. *See also* actuator, stepper motor.

StickyKeys \stik´ē-kēz`\ *n*. An accessibility feature built into Macintosh computers and available for Windows and DOS that causes modifier keys such as Shift, Control, or Alt to "stay on" after they are pressed, eliminating the need to press multiple keys simultaneously. This feature facilitates the use of modifier keys by users who are unable to hold down one key while pressing another.

stochastic \stə-kas´tik`\ *adj*. Based on random occurrences. For example, a stochastic model describes a system by taking into account chance events as well as planned events.

stop bit \stop´ bit\ *n*. In asynchronous transmission, a bit that signals the end of a character. In early electromechanical teleprinters, the stop bit provided time for the receiving mechanism to coast back to the idle position and, depending on the mechanism, had a duration of 1, 1.5, or 2 data bits. *See also* asynchronous transmission.

storage \stōr´əj\ *n*. In computing, any device in or on which information can be kept. Microcomputers have two main types of storage: random access memory (RAM) and disk drives and other external storage media. Other types of storage include read-only memory (ROM) and buffers.

storage device \stōr´əj də-vīs`\ *n*. An apparatus for recording computer data in permanent or semipermanent form. When a distinction is made between primary (main) storage devices and secondary (auxiliary) storage devices, the former refers to random access memory (RAM) and the latter refers to disk drives and other external devices.

storage location \stōr´əj lō-kā`shən\ *n*. The position at which a particular item can be found—either an addressed location or a uniquely identified location on a disk, tape, or similar medium.

storage media \stōr´əj mē`dē-ə\ *n*. The various types of physical material on which data bits are written and stored, such as floppy disks, hard disks, tape, and optical discs.

storage tube \stōr´əj tōōb`\ *n*. *See* direct view storage tube.

store-and-forward \stōr`ənd-fōr´wərd\ *n*. A message-passing technique used on communications networks in which a message is held temporarily at a collecting station before being forwarded to its destination.

stored program concept \stōrd prō´gram kon`sept\ *n*. A system architecture scheme, credited largely to the mathematician John von Neumann, in which both programs and data are in direct-access storage (random access memory, or RAM), thereby allowing code and data to be treated interchangeably. *See also* von Neumann architecture.

storefront \stōr´frənt\ *n*. *See* virtual storefront.

STP \S`T-P´\ *n*. Acronym for **s**hielded **t**wisted **p**air. A cable consisting of one or more twisted pairs of wires and a sheath of foil and copper braid. The twists protect the pairs from interference by each other, and the shielding protects the pairs from interference from outside. Therefore, STP cable can be used for high-speed transmission over long distances. *See also* twisted-pair cable. *Compare* UTP.

straight-line code \strāt´līn kōd`\ *n*. Program code that follows a direct sequence of statements rather than skipping ahead or jumping back via transfer statements such as GOTO and JUMP. *See also* GOTO statement, jump instruction. *Compare* spaghetti code.

stream cipher \strēm´ sī´fər\ *n*. A method for encrypting a data sequence of unlimited length using a key of fixed length. *See also* key (definition 3). *Compare* block cipher.

streaming \strē´mēng\ *n*. In magnetic tape storage devices, a low-cost technique to control the motion of the tape by removing tape buffers. Although streaming tape compromises start/stop performance, it achieves highly reliable storage and retrieval of data, and is useful when a steady supply of data is required by a particular application or computer.

streaming tape \strē´mēng tāp`\ *n. See* tape (definition 1).

stream-oriented file \strēm`ōr`ē-ent-əd fīl´\ *n.* A file used to store a fairly continuous series of bits, bytes, or other small, structurally uniform units.

street price \strēt´ prīs\ *n.* The actual retail or mail-order price of a consumer hardware or software product. In most cases, the street price is somewhat lower than the "suggested retail price."

stress test \stres´ test\ *n.* A test of a software or hardware system's functional limits, performed by subjecting the system to extreme conditions, such as peak volumes of data or extremes in temperature.

strikethrough \strīk´thrōō\ *n.* One or more lines drawn through a selected range of text, usually to show deletion or the intent to delete, as in ~~strikethrough~~.

string \strēng\ *n.* A data structure composed of a sequence of characters usually representing human-readable text.

string variable \strēng` vâr´ē-ə-bl\ *n.* An arbitrary name assigned by the programmer to a string of alphanumeric characters and used to reference that entire string. *See also* string.

strobe \strōb\ *n.* A timing signal that initiates and coordinates the passage of data, typically through an input/output (I/O) device interface, such as a keyboard or printer.

stroke \strōk\ *n.* **1.** In data entry, a keystroke—a signal to the computer that a key has been pressed. **2.** In typography, a line representing part of a letter. **3.** In paint programs, a "swipe" of the brush made with the mouse or keyboard in creating a graphic. **4.** In display technology, a line created as a vector (a path between two coordinates) on a vector graphics display (as opposed to a line of pixels drawn dot by dot on a raster graphics display).

stroke font \strōk´ font\ *n.* A font printed by drawing a combination of lines rather than by filling a shape, as with an outline font. *Compare* outline font.

stroke weight \strōk´ wāt\ *n.* The width, or thickness, of the lines (strokes) that make up a character. *See also* font.

stroke writer \strōk´ rī´tər\ *n.* In video, a display unit that draws characters and graphic images as sets of strokes—lines or curves connecting points—rather than as sets of dots, as on a typical raster-scan monitor. *See also* vector graphics.

strong typing \strong` tī´pēng\ *n.* A characteristic of a programming language that does not allow the program to change the data type of a variable during program execution. *See also* data type, variable. *Compare* weak typing.

structure \struk´chur\ *n.* **1.** The design and composition of a program, including program flow, hierarchy, and modularity. **2.** A collection of data elements. *See also* data structure.

structured graphics \struk`churd graf´iks\ *n. See* object-oriented graphics.

structured programming \struk`churd prō´gram-ēng\ *n.* Programming that produces programs with clean flow, clear design, and a degree of modularity or hierarchical structure. *See also* modular programming, object-oriented programming. *Compare* spaghetti code.

structured query language \struk`churd kwēr´ē lang-wəj, kwâr´ē\ *n.* A database sublanguage used in querying, updating, and managing relational databases—the de facto standard for database products. *Acronym:* SQL (sē´kwəl, S`Q-L´).

structured walkthrough \struk´churd wäk`thrōō\ *n.* **1.** A meeting of programmers working on different aspects of a software development project, in which the programmers attempt to coordinate the various segments of the overall project. The goals, requirements, and components of the project are systematically reviewed in order to minimize the error rate of the software under development. **2.** A method for examining a computer system, including its design and implementation, in a systematic fashion.

STT \S`T-T´\ *n. See* Secure Transaction Technology.

stub \stub\ *n.* A routine that contains no executable code and that generally consists of comments describing what will eventually be there; it is used as a placeholder for a routine to be written later. *Also called* dummy routine. *See also* top-down programming.

StuffIt \stuf´it\ *n.* A file compression program originally written for the Apple Macintosh, used for storing a file on one or more disks. Originally shareware, StuffIt is now a commercial product for Macs and PCs that supports multiple compression techniques and allows file viewing. StuffIt files can be uncompressed using a freeware program, StuffIt Expander.

style sheet \stīl´ shēt\ *n.* **1.** A file of instructions used to apply character, paragraph, and page layout formats in word processing and desktop publishing. **2.** A text file containing code to apply semantics such as page layout specifications to an HTML document. *See also* HTML document, semantics (definition 1).

stylus \stī´lus\ *n.* A pointing device used with a graphics tablet, usually attached to the tablet with a cord. See the illustration. *Also called* pen. *See also* graphics tablet, puck.

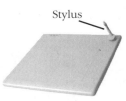
Stylus

Stylus. A stylus on a graphics tablet.

.su \dot`S-U´\ *n.* On the Internet, the major geographic domain specifying that an address is located in the former USSR.

subcommand \sub´kə-mand`\ *n.* A command in a submenu (a menu that appears when a user selects an option in a higher-level menu). See the illustration.

Subcommand.

subdirectory \sub´dər-ek`tər-ē\ *n.* A directory (logical grouping of related files) within another directory.

subject drift \sub´jəkt drift`\ *n. See* topic drift.

subject tree \sub´jəkt trē`\ *n.* A type of World Wide Web index that is organized by subject categories, many of which are broken down into subcategories, or "branches." The lowest level of the tree consists of links to specific Web pages. An example of a World Wide Web subject tree is Yahoo! *See also* Yahoo!

submarining \sub`mər-ē´nēng\ *n.* A phenomenon that occurs when some part of a screen display moves more quickly than the screen can show. The object (such as the mouse pointer) disappears from the screen and reappears where it comes to rest, just as a submarine resurfaces after a dive. Submarining is especially a problem with the slowly responding passive-matrix LCD displays on many laptop computers.

submenu \sub´men`yōō\ *n.* A menu that appears as the result of the selection of an item on another, higher-level menu.

subnet \sub´net\ *n.* A network that is a component of a larger network.

subnet mask \sub´net mask`\ *n. See* address mask.

subnotebook computer \sub`nōt`bŏŏk kəm-pyōō´tər\ *n.* A portable computer that is smaller and lighter than a conventional laptop computer.

subportable \sub-pōr´tə-bl\ *n. See* subnotebook computer.

subprogram \sub`prō´gram\ *n.* A term used in some languages for *routine* (procedure or function) because the structure and syntax of a subprogram closely model those of a program. *See also* program, routine.

subroutine \sub´rōō-tēn`\ *n.* A common term for *routine,* likely to be used in reference to shorter, general, frequently called routines. *See also* procedure, routine.

subschema \sub´skē`mə\ *n.* The definition of a user view of the database (in CODASYL/DBTG systems only), roughly equivalent to the external schema of an ANSI/X3/SPARC database management system or to a view in a relational database management system. *See also* schema.

subscribe \sub-skrīb´\ *vb.* **1.** To add a newsgroup to the list of such groups from which a user receives all new articles. **2.** To add a name to a LISTSERV distribution list. *See also* LISTSERV.

subscript \sub´skript\ *n.* **1.** One or more characters printed slightly below the baseline of surrounding text. *See also* baseline. *Compare* superscript. **2.** In programming, one or more numbers or variables that identify the location of an element in an array. *See also* array, index (definition 2).

substrate \sub´strāt\ *n.* The inactive supporting material used in a manufacturing process. In circuit boards, it is the base to which the traces (foil areas) are attached. In tapes and disks, it is the material on which the magnetic particles are fused.

substring \sub´strēng\ *n.* A sequential section of a string. *See also* string.

subtransaction \sub´tranz-ak`shən\ *n. See* nested transaction.

subtree \sub´trē\ *n.* Any node within a tree, along with any selection of connected descendant nodes. *See also* node (definition 3), tree.

suitcase \soot´kās\ *n.* A file on Macintosh computers that contains one or more fonts or desk accessories. In early versions of the operating system, such files are indicated with the icon of a suitcase. *See also* font suitcase.

suite \swēt\ *n.* A set of application programs sold as a package, usually at a lower price than that of the individual applications sold separately. A suite for office work, for example, might contain a word processing program, a spreadsheet, a database management program, and a communications program. *See* protocol stack.

summarize \sum´ər-īz`\ *vb.* To post the results of a survey or vote in short form to a newsgroup or mailing list after collecting the results by e-mail.

SunOS \sun`O-S´\ *n.* Short for **Sun O**perating **S**ystem. A variety of the UNIX operating system used on workstations from Sun Microsystems, Inc.

supercomputer \soo´pər-kəm-pyoo`tər\ *n.* A large, extremely fast, and expensive computer used for complex or sophisticated calculations. *See also* computer.

superconductor \soo´pər-kən-duk`tər\ *n.* A substance that has no resistance to the flow of electricity.

SuperDrive \soo´pər-drīv`\ *n.* An Apple 3.5-inch disk drive that can read and write in both Apple Macintosh (400K and 800K) and MS-DOS/Windows (720K and 1.44-MB) formats.

super-large-scale integration \soo`pər-lärj`skāl in-tə-grā´shən\ *n.* A reference to the density with which components (transistors and other elements) are packed onto an integrated circuit and to the fineness of the connections between them, generally considered to encompass the range from 50,000 to 100,000 circuit components. *Acronym:* SLSI (S`L-S-I´). *See also* integrated circuit. *Compare* large-scale integration,

medium-scale integration, small-scale integration, ultra-large-scale integration, very-large-scale integration.

superminicomputer \soo`pər-min´ē-kəm-pyoo`-tər\ *n. See* computer.

superpipelining \soo`pər-pī´plī-nēng\ *n.* A method of preprocessing used by some microprocessors in which two or more of a microprocessor's execution stages (fetch, decode, execute, and write-back) are divided into two or more pipelined stages, resulting in higher performance. *See also* DECchip 21064, pipelining (definition 1).

superscalar \soo´pər-skā`lər\ *adj.* Of, pertaining to, or being a microprocessor architecture that enables the microprocessor to execute multiple instructions per clock cycle. *See also* CISC, RISC.

superscript \soo´pər-skript`\ *n.* A character printed slightly above the surrounding text, usually in smaller type. *Compare* subscript (definition 1).

superserver \soo´pər-sər`vər\ *n.* A network server with especially high capabilities for speed and data storage. *See also* server.

superuser \soo´pər-yoo`zər\ *n.* A UNIX user account with root (i.e., unrestricted) access privileges, usually that of a system administrator. *See also* root account, system administrator, user account.

super VAR \soo´pər V-A-R´\ *n.* Short for **super v**alue-**a**dded **r**eseller. A large value-added reseller. *See also* value-added reseller.

super VGA \soo`pər V-G-A´\ *n. See* SVGA.

supervisor \soo´pər-vī`zər\ *n.* **1.** An operating system. **2.** A meta-operating system under which several operating systems are active. *See also* meta-operating system.

supervisor state \soo´pər-vī-zər stāt`\ *n.* The most privileged of the modes in which a Motorola 680x0 microprocessor can operate. Every operation of which the microprocessor is capable can be executed in the supervisor state. *See also* privileged mode. *Compare* user state.

support[1] \su-pōrt´\ *n.* Assistance, such as technical advice provided to customers.

support[2] \su-pōrt´\ *vb.* To work with another program or product; for example, an application might support file transfers from another program.

surf \surf\ *vb.* To browse among collections of information on the Internet, in newsgroups, in Gopherspace, and especially on the World Wide Web. As in channel surfing while watching television, users ride the wave of what interests them, jumping from topic to topic or from one Internet site to another. *Also called* cruise.

surface modeling \sur´fəs mod`əl-ēng\ *n.* A display method used by some CAD programs that gives on-screen constructions the appearance of solidity. *See also* CAD. *Compare* solid model, wireframe model.

surface-mount technology \sur`fəs-mount teknol´ə-jē\ *n.* A method of manufacturing printed circuit boards in which chips are fixed directly to the surface of the board instead of being soldered into holes predrilled to hold them. Its advantages are compactness, resistance to vibration, and the capacity for dense interconnections on both sides of the board. *Acronym:* SMT (S`M-T´). *Compare* DIP, leadless chip carrier, pin grid array.

surge \surj\ *n.* A sudden—and possibly damaging—increase in line voltage. *See also* surge protector, voltage regulator. *Compare* power failure.

surge protector \surj´ prə-tek`tər\ *n.* A device that prevents surges from reaching a computer or other kinds of electronic equipment. *Also called* surge suppressor. *See also* surge, transient suppressor.

surge suppressor \surj´ su-pres`ər\ *n. See* surge protector.

suspend \su-spend´\ *vb.* To halt a process temporarily. *See also* sleep[2].

Suspend command \su-spend´ kə-mand`\ *n.* A power management feature of Windows 95 for portable computers. Clicking on the Suspend command in the Start menu allows the user to temporarily suspend operations of the machine (enter "Suspend mode") without turning the power off, saving battery power without having to restart applications or reload data.

sustained transfer rate \su-stānd` trans´fər rāt`\ *n.* A measure of the speed at which data can be transferred to a storage device such as a disk or a tape. The sustained transfer rate is the data transfer speed that can be kept up by the device for an extended period of time.

.sv \dot`S-V´\ *n.* On the Internet, the major geographic domain specifying that an address is located in El Salvador.

SVC \S`V-C´\ *n.* Acronym for **s**witched **v**irtual **ci**rcuit. A logical connection between two nodes on a packet-switching network that is established only when data is to be transmitted. *See also* node (definition 1), packet switching. *Compare* PVC.

SVGA \S`V-G-A´\ *n.* Acronym for **S**uper **V**ideo **G**raphics **A**rray. A video standard established by the Video Electronics Standards Association (VESA) in 1989 to provide high-resolution color display on IBM-compatible computers. Although SVGA is a standard, compatibility problems can occur with the video BIOS. *See also* BIOS, video adapter.

S-video connector \S`vid-ē-ō kə-nek´tər\ *n.* A hardware interface for video devices that handles chrominance (color) and luminance (black and white) separately. An S-video connector is capable of providing a sharper image than those achieved with systems using RCA-type, or composite, connectors.

S/WAN \swän, S´wan, S`-W-A-N´\ *n. See* secure wide area network.

swap \swäp\ *vb.* **1.** To exchange one item for another, as in swapping floppy disks in and out of a single drive. **2.** To move segments of programs or data between memory and disk storage. *See also* virtual memory.

swap file \swäp´ fil\ *n.* A hidden file on the hard drive that Windows uses to hold parts of programs and data files that do not fit in memory. The operating system moves data from the swap file to memory as needed and moves data out of memory to the swap file to make room for new data. The swap file is a form of virtual memory. *See also* memory, virtual memory.

swim \swim\ *n.* A condition in which images slowly move about the positions they are supposed to occupy on screen.

switch \swich\ *n.* **1.** A circuit element that has two states: on and off. **2.** A control device that allows the user to choose one of two or more possible states. **3.** In communications, a computer or electromechanical device that controls routing and operation of a signal path. **4.** In operating systems such as MS-DOS, an argument used to control the execution of a command or an application, typically starting with a slash character (/).

switched Ethernet \swichd` ē´thər-net\ *n*. An Ethernet network run through a high-speed switch instead of an Ethernet hub. A switched Ethernet involves dedicated bandwidth of 10 Mbps between stations rather than a shared medium. *See also* Ethernet (definition 1), switch (definition 3).

switched line \swichd līn´\ *n*. A standard dial-up telephone connection; the type of line established when a call is routed through a switching station. *Compare* leased line.

Switched Multimegabit Data Services \swichd` mul-tē-meg`ə-bit dā-tə sər´və-səs, mul-tī-meg`ə-bit, dat-ə\ *n*. *See* SMDS.

switched network \swichd` net´wōrk\ *n*. A communications network that uses switching to establish a connection between parties, such as the dial-up telephone system.

switched virtual circuit \swichd` vər`chōō-əl sər´-kət\ *n*. *See* SVC.

Switcher \swich´ər\ *n*. A special Macintosh utility that allowed more than one program to be resident in memory at one time. Switcher was made obsolete by MultiFinder. *See also* MultiFinder.

switching \swich´ēng\ *n*. A communications method that uses temporary rather than permanent connections to establish a link or to route information between two parties. In the dial-up telephone network, for example, a caller's line goes to a switching center, where the actual connection is made to the called party. In computer networks, message switching and packet switching allow any two parties to exchange information. In both instances, messages are routed (switched) through intermediary stations that together serve to connect the sender and the receiver.

switching hub \swich´ēng hub`\ *n*. A central device (switch) that connects separate communication lines in a network and routes messages and packets among the computers on the network. The switch functions as a hub, or PBX, for the network. *See also* hub, packet (definition 1), PBX, switch (definition 3), switched Ethernet, switched network.

switching speed \swich´ēng spēd`\ *n*. In a packet-switching telecommunications technology,

such as ATM, the speed at which data packets are sent through the network. Switching speed is generally measured in kilobits or megabits per second. *See also* ATM (definition 1), packet switching.

.sy \dot`S-Y´\ *n*. On the Internet, the major geographic domain specifying that an address is located in Syria.

SYLK file \silk´ fīl, S`Y-L-K´\ *n*. Short for **sy**mbolic **link file**. A file constructed with a proprietary Microsoft format, used primarily for exchanging spreadsheet data in such a way that formatting information and intercellular data value relationships are preserved.

symbol \sim´bəl\ *n*. In programming, a name that represents a register, an absolute value, or a memory address (relative or absolute). *See also* identifier, operator (definition 1).

symbol font \sim´bəl font`\ *n*. A special font or typeface that replaces the characters normally accessible from the keyboard with alternative characters used as symbols, such as scientific, linguistic, or foreign-alphabet characters.

symbolic address \sim-bol`ik a´dres, ə-dres´\ *n*. A memory address that can be referred to in a program by name rather than by number.

symbolic coding \sim-bol`ik kō´dēng\ *n*. The expression of an algorithm in words, decimal numbers, and symbols rather than in binary numbers, so that a person can read and understand it. Symbolic coding is used in high-level programming languages. *See also* algorithm, high-level language.

symbolic language \sim-bol`ik lang´wəj\ *n*. A computer language that uses symbols such as keywords, variables, and operators to form instructions. All computer languages except machine language are symbolic.

symbolic link \sim-bol`ik lēnk´\ *n*. A disk directory entry that takes the place of a directory entry for a file but is actually a reference to a file in a different directory. *Also called* alias, shortcut, soft link, symlink.

symbolic logic \sim-bol`ik loj´ik\ *n*. A representation of the laws of reasoning, so named because symbols rather than natural-language expressions are used to state propositions and relationships. *See also* logic.

symbol set \sim´bəl set`\ *n.* Any collection of symbols legitimized by a data-coding system, such as extended ASCII, or a programming language.

symbol table \sim´bəl tā`bl\ *n.* A list of all identifiers encountered when a program is compiled (or assembled), their locations in the program, and their attributes, such as variable, routine, and so on. *See also* compile, identifier, linker, module (definition 1), object code.

symlink \sim´lēnk\ *n. See* symbolic link.

symmetric digital subscriber line \si-me´trik dij´i-təl sub-skrī´bər līn\ *n.* A digital telecommunications technology that allows data transmission at speeds up to 384 Kbps in both directions through copper wire. *Acronym:* SDSL (S`D-S-L´). *Compare* asymmetric digital subscriber line.

symmetric multiprocessing \si-me´trik mul`tē-pros´es-ēng, mul`tī-pros´es-ēng\ *n. See* SMP.

symmetric multiprocessing server \si-me´trik mul-tē-pros´es-ēng sər`vər, mul-tī-pros´es-ēng\ *n. See* SMP server.

SYN \S`Y-N´\ *n.* Short for **syn**chronous idle character. A character used in synchronous (timed) communications that enables the sending and receiving devices to maintain the same timing. *Also called* sync character.

sync character \sēnk´ kâr`ək-tər\ *n. See* SYN.

synchronization \sēn`krə-nə-zā´shən\ *n.* **1.** In networking, a communications transmission in which multibyte packets of data are sent and received at a fixed rate. *See also* packet (definition 1). **2.** In networking, the matching of timing between computers on the network. All of the computers are generally assigned identical times to facilitate and coordinate communications. **3.** In a computer, the matching of timing between components of the computer so that all are coordinated. For instance, operations performed by the operating system are generally synchronized with the signals of the machine's internal clock. *See also* clock (definition 1), operating system. **4.** In application or database files, version comparisons of copies of the files to ensure they contain the same data. **5.** In multimedia, precise real-time processing. Audio and video are transmitted over a network in synchronization so that they can be played back together without delayed responses. *See also* real-time.

synchronization signal \sēn`krə-nə-zā´shən sig`-nəl\ *n. See* sync signal.

synchronize \sēn`krə-nīz´\ *vb.* To cause to occur at the same time.

Synchronous Data Link Control \sēn`krə-nəs da´tə lēnk kən-trōl`, dat´ə\ *n. See* SDLC.

synchronous DRAM \sēn`krə-nəs D´ram, D`R-A-M´\ *n.* A form of dynamic random access memory (DRAM) that can run at higher clock speeds than conventional DRAM by employing a bursting technique in which the DRAM predicts the address of the next memory location to be accessed. *Acronym:* SDRAM (S`D´ram, S`D-R-A-M´). *See also* dynamic RAM.

synchronous idle character \sēn`krə-nəs ī´dl kâr´ək-tər\ *n. See* SYN.

synchronous operation \sēn`krə-nəs op-ər-ā´shən\ *n.* **1.** Any procedure under the control of a clock or timing mechanism. *Compare* asynchronous operation. **2.** In communications and bus operation, data transfer accompanied by clock pulses either embedded in the data stream or provided simultaneously on a separate line.

synchronous protocol \sēn`krə-nəs prō´tə-kol\ *n.* A set of guidelines developed to standardize synchronous communications between computers, usually based on either bit stream transmission or recognized character codes. Examples include the character-oriented binary synchronous (BISYNC) protocol and the bit-oriented High-level Data Link Control (HDLC) and Synchronous Data Link Control (SDLC) protocols. *See also* BISYNC, HDLC, SDLC.

synchronous transmission \sēn`krə-nəs tranz-mish´ən\ *n.* Data transfer in which information is transmitted in blocks (frames) of bits separated by equal time intervals. *Compare* asynchronous transmission.

synchronous UART \sēn`krə-nəs U´ärt, U`A-R-T´\ *n.* A universal asynchronous receiver/transmitter (UART) that supports synchronous serial transmission, where the sender and receiver share a timing signal. *See also* UART.

sync signal \sēnk´ sig´nəl\ *n.* Short for **sync**hronization **signal**. The part of a raster-display video signal that denotes the end of each scan line (the horizontal sync signal) and the end of the last scan line (the vertical sync signal).

synonym \sin´ə-nim`\ *n*. **1.** A word that is an equivalent of another word. The verbs *type* and *keyboard* are synonyms. **2.** In hashing, one of two distinct keys that produce the same hash address. *See also* hash[2].

syntax \sin´taks\ *n*. The grammar of a language; the rules governing the structure and content of statements. *See also* logic, programming language, syntax error. *Compare* semantics (definition 1).

syntax checker \sin´taks chek`ər\ *n*. A program for identifying errors in syntax for a programming language. *See also* syntax, syntax error.

syntax error \sin´taks âr`ər\ *n*. An error resulting from a statement that violates one or more of the grammatical rules of a language and is thus not "legal." *See also* logic, semantics (definition 1), syntax.

synthesis \sin´thə-sis`\ *n*. The combining of separate elements to form a coherent whole, or the result of such a combining (for example, combining digital pulses to replicate a sound, or combining digitized words to synthesize human speech). *See also* speech synthesis.

synthesizer \sin´thə-sī`zər\ *n*. A computer peripheral, chip, or stand-alone system that generates sound from digital instructions rather than through manipulation of physical equipment or recorded sound. *See also* MIDI.

.sys \dot-sis`\ *n*. A file extension for system configuration files.

sysadmin \sis´əd-min`\ *n*. The usual logon name or e-mail address for the system administrator of a UNIX-based system. *See also* system administrator.

sysgen \sis´jen\ *n*. *See* system generation.

sysop \sis´op\ *n*. Short for **sys**tem **op**erator. The overseer of a BBS or a small multiuser computer system.

Sys Req key \sis` rek kē´\ *n*. Short for **Sys**tem **Req**uest **key**. A key on some IBM and compatible keyboards that is intended to provide the same function as the Sys Req key on an IBM mainframe computer terminal: to reset the keyboard or to change from one session to another.

system \si´stəm\ *n*. Any collection of component elements that work together to perform a task. Examples are a hardware system consisting of a microprocessor, its allied chips and circuitry, input and output devices, and peripheral devices; an operating system consisting of a set of programs and data files; or a database management system used to process specific kinds of information.

system administrator \si`stəm ad-min´ə-strā-tər\ *n*. The person responsible for administering use of a multiuser computer system, communications system, or both. A system administrator performs such duties as assigning user accounts and passwords, establishing security access levels, allocating storage space, and watching for unauthorized access to prevent virus or Trojan horse programs from entering the system. *Also called* sysadmin. *See also* Trojan horse, virus. *Compare* sysop.

system board \si´stəm bōrd`\ *n*. *See* motherboard.

system clock \si´stəm klok\ *n*. *See* clock (definition 1).

system console \si´stəm kon´sōl\ *n*. The control center of a computer system, primarily with reference to mainframe and minicomputers. In networked or distributed systems, one workstation is designated as the system administrator's; this workstation is analogous to the LAN system console. *See also* console, LAN.

system development \si`stəm də-vel´əp-mənt\ *n*. The process of defining, designing, testing, and implementing a new system.

system disk \si´stəm disk`\ *n*. A disk that contains an operating system and can be used to boot a computer. *Also called* startup disk. *See also* boot[2], operating system.

system error \si´stəm âr`ər\ *n*. A software condition that renders the operating system incapable of continuing to function normally. This type of error usually requires rebooting the system.

system failure \si´stəm fāl`yər\ *n*. The inability of a computer to continue functioning, usually caused by software rather than hardware.

System file \si´stəm fīl`\ *n*. A resource file on the Macintosh that contains the resources needed by the operating system, such as fonts, icons, and default dialog boxes.

System folder \si´stəm fōl`dər\ *n*. The Macintosh file folder (directory) that contains the System file and other vital files, such as Finder, device drivers, INIT files, and control panel files. *See also* control panel, Finder, INIT, System file.

system font \si´stəm font`\ *n.* On the Macintosh and in some PC applications, the font used by the computer for on-screen text, such as menu titles and items (but not on-screen text within a word processor or other application). *See also* font.

system generation \si´stəm jen`ər-ā-shən\ *n.* The process of configuring and installing system software for a particular set of hardware components. Complex operating systems such as UNIX are shipped with device drivers and utilities that are often not relevant to a particular hardware configuration; putting together only the necessary components, as well as specifying important system characteristics, is part of the system generation process. *Also called* sysgen.

system heap \si´stəm hēp`\ *n. See* heap (definition 1).

system life cycle \si´stəm līf´ sī-kl\ *n.* An information system's useful life. At the end of a system's life cycle it is not feasible to repair or expand it, so it must be replaced.

System Object Model \si´stəm ob´jekt mod`əl\ *n. See* SOM (definition 1).

system operator \si´stəm op´ər-ā-tər\ *n. See* sysop.

system prompt \si´stəm prompt`\ *n. See* prompt (definition 1).

system recovery \si´stəm rə-kəv´ər-ē\ *n.* Processing that takes place after a system failure in order to restore a system to normal operation. System recovery takes place after the operating system is initiated. It sometimes requires that tasks in process during the failure be backed out of and that structures in memory during the failure be reconstructed.

System Registry \si´stəm rej´əs-trē\ *n. See* Registry.

System Request key \si´stəm rə-kwest´ kē`\ *n. See* Sys Req key.

system resource \si´stəm rē´sōrs\ *n.* On the Macintosh, any of numerous routines, definitions, and data fragments that are stored in the Macintosh System file, such as floating-point arithmetic routines, font definitions, and peripheral drivers. *See also* resource (definition 2).

systems analysis \si´stəmz ə-nal´ə-səs\ *n.* The examination of a system or problem with the goal of either improving an existing system or designing and implementing a new one. As a science, systems analysis is related to cybernetics, a branch of engineering that studies the behavior of systems.

systems analyst \si´stəmz an´ə-list\ *n.* A person who works on designing and developing systems. Systems analysts generally combine technical, managerial, and human-relations activities in order to complete their analyses.

Systems Application Architecture \si´stəmz ə-plə-kā´shən är`kə-tek-chur\ *n. See* SAA.

systems integration \si´stəmz in-tə-grā´shən\ *n.* The development of a computer system for a particular customer by combining products from different original equipment manufacturers (OEMs).

Systems Network Architecture \si´stəmz net´wərk är`kə-tek-chur\ *n. See* SNA.

system software \si´stəm soft´wâr\ *n.* The collection of programs and data that make up and relate to the operating system. *Compare* application.

systems programming \si´stəmz prō´gram-ēng\ *n.* The development or maintenance of programs designed to execute as part of an operating system, such as I/O routines, user interfaces, command-line interpreters, and task-scheduling and memory management routines.

system support \si´stəm su-pōrt´\ *n.* The provision of services and material resources for the use, maintenance, and improvement of an implemented system.

system timer \si´stəm tī´mər\ *n. See* clock (definition 1).

system unit \si´stəm yōō`nit\ *n. See* console.

System V \si´stəm fīv´\ *n.* A version of the UNIX system provided by AT&T and others. It is both a standard (principally controlled by AT&T) and a set of commercial products. *See also* UNIX.

.sz \dot`S-Z´\ *n.* On the Internet, the major geographic domain specifying that an address is located in Swaziland.

T \T\ *prefix See* tera-.

T1 or **T-1** \T-wən´\ *n.* A T-carrier that can handle 1.544 Mbps or 24 voice channels. Although originally designed by AT&T to carry voice calls, this high-bandwidth telephone line can also transmit text and images. T1 lines are commonly used by larger organizations for Internet connectivity. *See also* T-carrier. *Compare* fractional T1, T2, T3, T4.

T.120 standard \T`-wən-twen´tē stan`dərd\ *n.* A family of International Telecommunications Union (ITU) specifications for multipoint data communications services within computer applications, such as conferencing and multipoint file transfer.

T2 or **T-2** \T-too´\ *n.* A T-carrier that can handle 6.312 Mbps (megabits per second) or 96 voice channels. *See also* T-carrier. *Compare* T1, T3, T4.

T3 or **T-3** \T-thrē´\ *n.* A T-carrier that can handle 44.736 Mbps (megabits per second) or 672 voice channels. *See also* T-carrier. *Compare* T1, T2, T4.

T4 or **T-4** \T-fōr´\ *n.* A T-carrier that can handle 274.176 Mbps or 4,032 voice channels. *See also* T-carrier. *Compare* T1, T2, T3.

tab character \tab´ kâr`ek-tər\ *n.* A character used to align lines and columns on screen and in print. Although a tab is visually indistinguishable from a series of blank spaces in most programs, the tab character and the space character are different to a computer. A tab is a single character and therefore can be added, deleted, or overtyped with a single keystroke. The ASCII coding scheme includes two codes for tab characters: a horizontal tab for spacing across the screen or page and a vertical tab for spacing down the screen or page. *See also* Tab key.

Tab key \tab´ kē\ *n.* A key, often labeled with both a left-pointing and a right-pointing arrow, that traditionally (as in word processing) is used to insert tab characters into a document. In other applications, such as menu-driven programs, the Tab key is often used to move the on-screen high-light from place to place. Many database and spreadsheet programs allow the user to press the Tab key to move around within a record or between cells. The word *tab* is short for "tabulator," which was the name given to this key on typewriters, where it was used in creating tables. *See also* tab character.

table \tā´bl\ *n.* **1.** In programming, a data structure usually consisting of a list of entries, each entry being identified by a unique key and containing a set of related values. A table is often implemented as an array of records, a linked list, or (in more primitive languages) several arrays of different data types, all using a common indexing scheme. *See also* array, list, record[1]. **2.** In relational databases, a data structure characterized by rows and columns, with data occupying or potentially occupying each cell formed by a row-column intersection. The table is the underlying structure of a relation. *See also* relational database. **3.** In word processing, desktop publishing, and in HTML documents, a block of text formatted in aligned rows and columns.

table lookup \tā´bl look`up\ *n.* The process of using a known value to search for data in a previously constructed table of values—for example, using a purchase price to search a tax table for the appropriate sales tax. *See also* lookup.

tablet \tab´lət\ *n. See* graphics tablet.

tabulate \tab´yə-lāt`\ *vb.* **1.** To total a row or column of numbers. **2.** To arrange information in table form.

TACACS \T`A-C-A-C-S´\ *n.* Acronym for **T**erminal **A**ccess **C**ontroller **A**ccess **C**ontrol **S**ystem. A network access technique in which users log into a single centralized server that contains a database of authorized accounts. After the access server authenticates the user, it forwards the login information to the data server requested by the user. *See also* authentication, server (definition 2).

tag \tag\ *n.* **1.** In programming, one or more characters containing information about a file, record type, or other structure. **2.** In certain types of data files, a key or an address that identifies a record and its storage location in another file. *See also* tag sort. **3.** In markup languages such as SGML and HTML, a code that identifies an element in a document, such as a heading or a paragraph, for the purposes of formatting, indexing, and linking information in the document. In both SGML and HTML, a tag is generally a pair of angle brackets that contain one or more letters and numbers. Usually one pair of angle brackets is placed before an element, and another pair is placed after, to indicate where the element begins and ends. For example, in HTML, <IT>hello world</IT> indicates that the phrase "hello world" should be italicized. *See also* <>, element, emotag, HTML, SGML.

Tagged Image File Format \tagd` im´əj fīl´ fōr`mat\ *n. See* TIFF.

tag sort \tag´ sōrt\ *n.* A sort performed on one or several key fields for the purpose of establishing the order of their associated records. *Also called* key sort.

tag switching \tag´ swich`ēng\ *n.* A multilayer Internet switching technology developed by Cisco Systems that integrates routing and switching.

talk[1] \täk\ *n.* The UNIX command that, when followed by another user's name and address, is used to generate a request for a synchronous chat session on the Internet. *See also* chat[1] (definition 1).

talk[2] \täk\ *vb. See* chat[2].

talker \tä´kər\ *n.* An Internet-based synchronous communication mechanism most commonly used to support multiuser chat functions. Such systems typically provide specific commands for movement through separate *rooms,* or chat areas, and allow users to communicate with other users in real time through text messages, indicate simple gestures, use a bulletin board system (BBS) for posting comments, and send internal e-mail. *See also* BBS (definition 1), chat[1] (definition 1).

talk. newsgroups \täk`dot nōōz´grōops\ *n.* Usenet newsgroups that are part of the talk. hierarchy and have the prefix talk. as part of their names. These newsgroups are devoted to debate and discussion of controversial topics. Talk. newsgroups are one of the seven original Usenet newsgroup hierarchies. The other six are comp. misc., news., rec., sci., and soc. *See also* newsgroup, traditional newsgroup hierarchy, Usenet.

tandem processors \tan`dəm　pros´əs-ərz\ *n.* Multiple processors wired so that the failure of one processor transfers central processing unit (CPU) operation to another processor. Using tandem processors is part of the strategy for implementing fault-tolerant computer systems. *See also* central processing unit.

TANSTAAFL \tan´staf`l, T`A-N-S-T-A-A-F-L´\ *n.* Acronym for "There **a**in't **n**o **s**uch **t**hing **a**s **a** **f**ree **l**unch." An expression used on the Internet in e-mail, chat sessions, mailing lists, newsgroups, and other online forums. *See also* chat[1] (definition 1), e-mail[1] (definition 1), mailing list, newsgroup.

tap \tap\ *n.* A device that can be attached to an Ethernet bus to enable a computer to be connected.

tape \tāp\ *n.* **1.** A thin strip of polyester film coated with magnetic material that permits the recording of data. Because tape is a continuous length of data storage material and because the read/write head cannot "jump" to a desired point on the tape without the tape first being advanced to that point, tape must be read or written sequentially, not randomly (as can be done on a floppy disk or a hard disk). **2.** A storage medium consisting of a thin strip of paper used to store information in the form of sequences of punched holes, chemical impregnation, or magnetic ink imprinting.

tape cartridge \tāp´ kär`trij\ *n.* A module that resembles an audio cassette and contains magnetic tape that can be written on and read from by a tape drive. Tape cartridges are primarily used to back up hard disks. See the illustration. *See also* tape (definition 1).

Tape cartridge.

tape drive \tāp´ drīv\ *n.* A device for reading and writing tapes. *See also* tape (definition 1).

tape dump \tāp´ dump\ *n.* The process of simply printing the data contained on a tape cartridge without performing any report formatting. *See also* tape cartridge.

tape tree \tāp´ trē\ *n.* A means of audiotape distribution, used in Usenet music newsgroups and mailing lists, in which a recording is copied and sent to a number of *branch* participants, who in turn send copies to their *children,* or *leaves. See also* branch (definition 1), child (definition 2), leaf, tree structure. *Compare* vine.

TAPI \tap´ē, T´A-P-I´\ *n.* Acronym for **T**elephony **A**pplication **P**rogramming **I**nterface. In the Windows Open Systems Architecture (WOSA), a programming interface that gives Windows client applications access to a server's voice services. TAPI facilitates interoperability between personal computers and telephone equipment. *Also called* Telephony API. *See also* application programming interface, WOSA. *Compare* TSAPI.

.tar \dot-tär´, -T´A-R´\ *n.* The file extension that identifies uncompressed UNIX archives in the format produced by the tar program.

tar[1] \tär\ *n.* Acronym for **t**ape **ar**chive. A UNIX utility for making a single file out of a set of files that a user wishes to store together. The resulting file has the extension .tar. Unlike PKZIP, tar does not compress files, so compress or gzip is usually run on the .tar file to produce a file with extensions .tar.gz or .tar.Z. *See also* compress[1], gzip, PKZIP. *Compare* untar[1].

tar[2] \tär\ *vb.* To make a single file out of a set of files using the tar utility. *See also* compress, PKZIP. *Compare* untar[2].

target \tär´gət\ *n.* Loosely, the objective of a computer command or operation. Examples are a computer that is to run a program translated for its use, a "foreign" language (for another computer) into which a program is to be translated, or a group of people for whom a particular product is designed. In MS-DOS usage, the target is often the disk referred to by prompts in a copy operation (for example, "insert *target* diskette"). In terms of

the SCSI (small computer system interface) connection, the target is the device that receives commands. *See also* SCSI, target computer, target disk, target language.

target computer \tär´gət kəm-pyōō´tər\ *n.* The computer that receives data from a communications device, a hardware add-in, or a software package.

target disk \tär´gət disk`\ *n.* The disk to which data is to be written, as in a copy operation. *See also* target. *Compare* source disk.

target language \tär´gət lang`wəj\ *n.* The language into which source code is compiled or assembled. *See also* assembler, compiler (definition 2), cross-compiler.

task \task\ *n.* A stand-alone application or a subprogram that is run as an independent entity.

taskbar \task`bär\ *n.* A graphic toolbar used in Windows 95 to select, via the mouse, one of a number of active applications. See the illustration. *See also* task button, toolbar.

task button \task´ but`ən\ *n.* In Windows 95, a button that appears on the taskbar on the screen when an application is run. By clicking on the button, the user can switch from another application to the application corresponding to the button. *See also* taskbar.

task management \task´ man`əj-mənt\ *n.* The operating-system process of tracking the progress of and providing necessary resources for separate tasks that are running on a computer, especially in a multitasking environment.

task swapping \task´ swä`pēng\ *n.* The process of switching from one application to another by saving the data for the application presently running in the foreground to a storage device and loading the other application. *See also* foreground[2] (definition 2), task.

task switching \task´ swich`ēng\ *n.* The act of moving from one program to another without shutting down the first program. Task switching is a single act, as compared to multitasking, in which the central processing unit rapidly switches back

Taskbar.

and forth between two or more programs. *See also* task, task swapping. *Compare* multitasking.

TB \T-B´\ *n. See* terabyte.

.tc \dot`T-C´\ *n.* On the Internet, the major geographic domain specifying that an address is located on the Turks and Caicos Islands.

T-carrier \T´kâr`ē-ər\ *n.* A long-distance, digital communications line provided by a common carrier. Multiplexers at either end merge several voice channels and digital data streams for transmission and separate them when received. T-carrier service, introduced by AT&T in 1993, is defined at several capacity levels: T1, T2, T3, T4. In addition to voice communication, T-carriers are used for Internet connectivity. *See also* T1, T2, T3, T4.

Tcl/Tk \tik`l-T-K´\ *n.* Acronym for **T**ool **C**ommand **L**anguage/**T**ool **K**it. A programming system that includes a scripting language (Tcl) and a graphical user interface toolkit (Tk). The Tcl language issues commands to interactive programs, such as text editors, debuggers, and shells, which tie together complex data structures into scripts. *See also* graphical user interface, script, scripting language.

TCM \T`C-M´\ *n. See* trellis-coded modulation.

TCP \T`C-P´\ *n.* Acronym for **T**ransmission **C**ontrol **P**rotocol. The protocol within TCP/IP that governs the breakup of data messages into packets to be sent via IP, and the reassembly and verification of the complete messages from packets received by IP. TCP corresponds to the transport layer in the ISO/OSI model. *See also* ISO/OSI model, packet, TCP/IP. *Compare* IP.

TCP/IP \T`C-P`I-P´\ *n.* Acronym for **T**ransmission **C**ontrol **P**rotocol/**I**nternet **P**rotocol. A protocol developed by the Department of Defense for communications between computers. It is built into the UNIX system and has become the de facto standard for data transmission over networks, including the Internet.

TCP/IP stack \T`C-P-I-P´ stak`\ *n.* The set of TCP/IP protocols. *See also* protocol stack, TCP/IP.

.td \dot`T-D´\ *n.* On the Internet, the major geographic domain specifying that an address is located in Chad.

TDM \T`D-M´\ *n. See* time-division multiplexing.

tear-off \ter´of\ *adj.* Capable of being dragged from an original position in a graphical user interface and placed where the user desires. For exam-

ple, many graphics applications feature tear-off menus of tool palettes that can be dragged to locations other than the menu bar.

techie \tek´ē\ *n.* A technically oriented person. Typically, a techie is the person on whom a user calls when something breaks or the user cannot understand a technical problem. A techie may be an engineer or a technician, but not all engineers are techies. *See also* guru.

technical author \tek´ni-kəl ä`thər, ô`thər\ *n. See* tech writer.

technology \tek-nol´ə-jē\ *n.* The application of science and engineering to the development of machines and procedures in order to enhance or improve human conditions, or at least to improve human efficiency in some respect. *See also* high tech.

technophile \tek´nə-fīl`\ *n.* Someone who is enthusiastic about emerging technology. *Compare* computerphile.

tech writer \tek´ rī`tər\ *n.* Short for technical writer. One who writes the documentation material for a hardware or software product. *Also called* technical author. *See also* documentation.

telco \tel´kō\ *n.* Short for **tel**ephone **co**mpany. A term generally used in reference to a telephone company's provision of Internet services.

telecommunications \tel`ə-kə-myoo`nə-kā´-shənz\ *n.* The transmission and reception of information of any type, including data, television pictures, sound, and facsimiles, using electrical or optical signals sent over wires or fibers or through the air.

telecommute \tel´ə-kə-myoot´\ *vb.* To work in one location (often at home) and communicate with a main office at a different location through a personal computer equipped with a modem and communications software.

teleconferencing \tel´ə-kon`frən-sēng\ *n.* The use of audio, video, or computer equipment linked through a communications system to enable geographically separated individuals to participate in a meeting or discussion. *See also* video conferencing.

telecopy \tel´ə-kop`ē\ *vb. See* fax.

telematics \tel`ə-mat´iks\ *n.* In communications technology, the linking of computers and telecommunications.

telephony \tə-lef´ə-nē`, tel´ə-fō`nē\ *n.* Telephone technology; the conversion of sound into electrical signals, its transmission to another location, and its reconversion to sound, with or without the use of connecting wires.

Telephony API \tə-lef´ə-nē A-P-I´\ *n. See* TAPI.

telephony device \tə-lef´ə-nē də-vīs`\ *n.* A mechanism designed to translate sound into electrical signals, transmit them, and then convert them back to sound.

teleprocess \tel`ə-pros´es\ *vb.* To use a terminal or computer and communications equipment to access computers and computer files located elsewhere. *Teleprocess* is a term originated by IBM. *See also* distributed processing, remote access.

Telescript \tel´ə-skript`\ *n.* A communications-oriented programming language, released in 1994 by General Magic, that was designed to address the need for cross-platform, network-independent messaging and abstraction of complex network protocols. *See also* communications protocol.

teletext \tel´ə-tekst\ *n.* All-text information broadcast by a television station to a subscriber's television set.

Teletype \tel´ə-tīp`\ *n.* The Teletype Corporation, developer of the teletypewriter (TTY) and various other printers used with computers and communications systems. *See also* TTY.

teletype mode \tel´ə-tīp mōd`\ *n.* A mode of operation in which a computer or an application limits its actions to those characteristic of a teletypewriter (TTY). On the display, for example, teletype mode means that only alphanumeric characters can be shown, and they are simply "typed" on the screen, one letter after the other, and cannot be placed in any desired position. *See also* Teletype, TTY.

teletypewriter \tel´ə-tī´prī-tər\ *n. See* TTY.

telnet[1] \tel´net\ *n.* A client program that implements the Telnet protocol.

telnet[2] \tel´net\ *vb.* To access a remote computer over the Internet using the Telnet protocol. *See also* telnet[1].

Telnet \tel´net\ *n.* A protocol that enables an Internet user to log on to and enter commands on a remote computer linked to the Internet, as if the user were using a text-based terminal directly attached to that computer. Telnet is part of the TCP/IP suite of protocols.

template \tem´plət, tem´plāt\ *n.* **1.** In an application package, an overlay for the keyboard that identifies special keys and key combinations. **2.** In image processing, a pattern that can be used to identify or match a scanned image. **3.** In spreadsheet programs, a predesigned spreadsheet that contains formulas, labels, and other elements. **4.** In MS-DOS, a small portion of memory that holds the most recently typed MS-DOS command. **5.** In word processing and desktop publishing programs, a predesigned document that contains formatting and, in many cases, generic text.

temporary file \tem´pər-âr-ē fīl`\ *n.* A file created either in memory or on disk, by the operating system or some other program, to be used during a session and then discarded. *Also called* temp file. *See also* scratch[1].

temporary storage \tem`pər-âr-ē stōr´əj\ *n.* A region in memory or on a storage device that is temporarily allocated for use in storing intermediate data in a computational, sorting, or transfer operation.

ten's complement \tenz´ kom`plə-mənt\ *n.* A number in the base-10 system that is the true complement of another number and is derived either by subtracting each digit from 1 less than the base and adding 1 to the result or by subtracting each number from the next higher power of the base. For example, the ten's complement of 25 is 75, and it can be derived either by subtracting each digit from 9, which is 1 less than the base (9 − 2 = 7, 9 − 5 = 4) and then adding 1 (74 + 1 = 75) or by subtracting 25 from the next higher power of 10, which is 100 (100 − 25 = 75). *See also* complement. *Compare* nine's complement.

tera- \târ´ə\ *prefix* Abbreviated T. A prefix meaning 10^{12}: 1 trillion in the American numbering system, 1 million million in British numbering. *See also* terabyte.

terabyte \târ´ə-bīt`\ *n.* Abbreviated TB. A measurement used for high-capacity data storage. One terabyte equals 2^{40}, or 1,099,511,627,776, bytes, although it is commonly interpreted as simply one trillion bytes.

teraflops \târ´ə-flops`\ *n.* One trillion floating-point operations (FLOPS) per second. Teraflops serves as a benchmark for larger computers that measures the number of floating-point operations they can perform in a set amount of time. *Also called* TFLOPS. *See also* FLOPS.

terminal \tər´mə-nəl\ *n.* **1.** A device consisting of a video adapter, a monitor, and a keyboard. The adapter and monitor and, sometimes, the keyboard are usually combined in a single unit. A terminal does little or no computer processing on its own; instead, it is connected to a computer with a communications link over a cable. Terminals are used primarily in multiuser systems and today are not often found on single-user personal computers. *See also* dumb terminal, smart terminal, terminal emulation. **2.** In electronics, a point that can be physically linked to something else, usually by a wire, to form an electrical connection.

Terminal Access Controller Access Control System \tər`mə-nəl ak`ses kən-trō-lər ak`ses kən-trōl´si-stəm\ *n. See* TACACS.

terminal emulation \tər´mə-nəl em-yə-lā`shən\ *n.* The imitation of a terminal by using software that conforms to a standard, such as the ANSI standard for terminal emulation. Terminal-emulation software is used to make a microcomputer act as if it were a particular type of terminal while it is communicating with another computer, such as a mainframe. *See also* VT-52, VT-100, VT-200.

terminal server \tər´mə-nəl sər`vər\ *n.* In a local area network, a computer or a controller that allows terminals, microcomputers, and other devices to connect to a network or host computer, or to devices attached to that particular computer. See the illustration. *See also* controller, LAN, microcomputer, terminal.

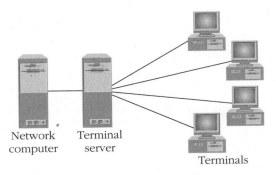

Terminal server.

terminal session \tər´mə-nəl sesh`ən\ *n.* The period of time spent actively using a terminal. *See also* session.

terminal strip \tər´mə-nəl strip`\ *n.* A usually long and narrow assembly containing one or more electrical connectors. Commonly, terminal strips consist of screws on which bare wires are wrapped before the screws are tightened; for example, some consumer-grade stereo receiver/amplifiers incorporate a set of terminal strips on the rear panel for attaching speaker wires to the unit. See the illustration.

Terminal strip.

terminate \tər´mə-nāt`\ *vb.* **1.** With reference to software, to end a process or program. Abnormal termination occurs in response to user intervention or because of a hardware or software error. **2.** With reference to hardware, to install a plug, jack, or other connector at the end of a wire or cable.

terminate-and-stay-resident program \tər-mə-nāt-ənd-stā-rez´ə-dənt prō`gram\ *n. See* TSR.

terminator \tər´mə-nā`tər\ *n.* **1.** A character that indicates the end of a string, such as the null character in an ASCIIZ string. *See also* ASCII, ASCIIZ string. **2.** An item of hardware that must be installed in the last device in a daisy chain or bus network, such as Ethernet or SCSI. *See also* terminator cap.

terminator cap \tər´mə-nā-tər kap`\ *n.* A special connector that must be attached to each end of an Ethernet bus. If one or both terminator caps are missing, the Ethernet network will not work.

ternary \tər´nər-ē`\ *adj.* In programming, of, pertaining to, or characteristic of an element with three possible values, a condition that has three possible states, or a base-3 number system. *Compare* binary[1], unary.

test \test\ *vb.* To check program correctness by trying out various sequences and input values. *See also* debug, test data.

test automation software \test ôt`ə-mā´shən soft`-wâr\ *n.* A program that automatically enters a predetermined set of characters or user commands in order to test new or modified versions of software applications.

test data \test´ dā¯tə, dat`ə\ *n.* A set of values used to test proper functioning of a program. Reasons for choosing particular test data include verifying known output (anticipated output) and pushing boundary conditions that might cause the program to fail.

test post \test´ pōst\ *n.* A newsgroup article that contains no actual message but is used simply as a means of checking the connection. *See also* article, newsgroup.

TeX or **T$_E$X** \tek\ *n.* A text-formatting software system created by mathematician and computer scientist Donald Knuth for producing typeset-quality scientific, mathematical, or other complex technical documents from plain ASCII text input. Implementations of TeX for UNIX systems, MS-DOS and Windows, and the Apple Macintosh are available free over the Internet (ftp://ftp.tex.ac.uk/tex-archive/) or in commercial distributions (which often include enhancements). Commands in the input file produce format elements and special symbols; for example, ${\pi}r^2$ produces the expression πr^2. TeX is extensible through macros, and macro files are available for a wide variety of applications. *See also* LaTeX[1].

Texas Instruments Graphics Architecture \teks`əs in`strə-mənts graf´iks är`kə-tek-chur\ *n. See* TIGA.

text \tekst\ *n.* **1.** Data that consists of characters representing the words and symbols of human speech; usually, characters coded according to the ASCII standard, which assigns numeric values to numbers, letters, and certain symbols. **2.** In word processing and desktop publishing, the main portion of a document, as opposed to headlines, tables, figures, footnotes, and other elements.

text box \tekst´ boks\ *n.* In a dialog box or HTML form, a box in which the user may enter text.

TextEdit \tekst´ed`ət\ *n.* A standard set of routines in the Macintosh operating system that are available to programs for controlling the way text is displayed. *See also* Toolbox.

text editor \tekst´ ed`ə-tər\ *n. See* editor.

text entry \tekst´ en`trē\ *n.* The inputting of text characters by means of a keyboard.

text file \tekst´ fīl\ *n.* A file composed of text characters. A text file can be a word-processing file or a "plain" ASCII file encoded in a format practically all computers can use. *See also* ASCII file, text (definition 1).

text mode \tekst´ mōd\ *n.* A display mode in which the monitor can display letters, numbers, and other text characters but no graphical images or WYSIWYG ("what-you-see-is-what-you-get") character formatting (italics, superscript, and so on). *Also called* alphanumeric mode, character mode. *Compare* graphics mode.

text-only file \tekst` ōn´lē fīl`\ *n. See* ASCII file.

text-to-speech \tekst`tə-spēch´\ *n.* The conversion of text-based data into voice output by speech synthesis devices to allow users to gain access to information by telephone or to allow blind or illiterate people to use computers.

texture \teks´chur\ *n.* In computer graphics, shading or other attributes added to the "surface" of a graphical image to give it the illusion of a physical substance. For example, a surface could be made to appear reflective to simulate metal or glass, or a scanned image of wood grain could be applied to a shape intended to simulate an object made of wood.

.tf \dot`T-F´\ *n.* On the Internet, the major geographic domain specifying that an address is located in the Southern French Territories.

TFLOPS \T´flops, T-F-L-O`P-S´\ *n. See* teraflops.

TFT \T`F-T´\ *n.* Acronym for **t**hin **f**ilm **t**ransistor. A transistor created using thin film methodology. *See also* active matrix display, thin film, transistor.

TFT display \T`F-T´ dis-plā´\ *n. See* active matrix display.

TFT LCD \T-F-T` L-C-D´\ *n. See* active matrix display.

.tg \dot`T-G´\ *n.* On the Internet, the major geographic domain specifying that an address is located in Togo.

TGA \T`G-A´\ *n.* **1.** Short for **Tar**ga. A raster graphics file format from Truevision, Inc., that handles 16-, 24-, and 32-bit color. *See also* 16-bit color, 24-bit color, 32-bit color, raster graphics, video graphics board. **2.** The brand name of a series of high-resolution video graphics boards.

.th \dot`T-H´\ *n.* On the Internet, the major geographic domain specifying that an address is located in Thailand.

The Microsoft Network \dhə mī`krə-soft net´wərk\ *n.* Microsoft Corporation's feature-rich online service, launched with the introduction of Windows 95 in August 1995. *Acronym:* MSN (M`S-N´).

thermal printer \thər´məl prin`tər\ *n.* A nonimpact printer that uses heat to generate an image on specially treated paper. The printer uses pins to produce an image, but rather than striking the pins against a ribbon to mark the paper as does a wire-pin dot-matrix printer, it heats the pins and brings them into gentle contact with the paper. The special coating on the paper discolors when it is heated.

thermal transfer printer \thər`məl trans´fər prin`tər\ *n. See* thermal wax-transfer printer.

thermal wax printer \thər`məl waks´ prin`tər\ *n. See* thermal wax-transfer printer.

thermal wax-transfer printer \thər`məl waks´-trans-fər prin`tər\ *n.* A special type of nonimpact printer that uses heat to melt colored wax onto paper to create an image. Like a standard thermal printer, it uses pins to apply the heat. Rather than making contact with coated paper, however, the pins touch a wide ribbon saturated with different colored waxes. The wax melts under the pins and adheres to the paper.

thesaurus \thə-sōr´us`\ *n.* **1.** A book of words and their synonyms. **2.** In microcomputer applications, both a file of synonyms stored on disk and the program used to search the file.

The World—Public Access UNIX \dhə wərld´ pub`lik ak`ses yo͞o´ niks\ *n.* One of the oldest public access Internet service providers, based in Boston. In 1990, The World began offering full dial-up Internet access to the public. Other services include World Wide Web access, Usenet, SLIP/PPP support, telnet, FTP, IRC, Gopher, and e-mail. In 1995, The World began supporting local dial-up access via UUNET. *See also* ISP.

thick Ethernet \thik` ē´thər-net\ *n. See* 10Base5, Ethernet.

thick film \thik´ film\ *adj.* A term describing a method used in the manufacture of integrated circuits. Thick film technology uses a stencil-like technique called *photosilkscreening* to deposit

multiple layers of special inks or pastes on a ceramic substrate. The inks or pastes can be conducting, insulating, or resistive. The passive components (wires, resistors, and capacitors) of the integrated circuits are formed by depositing a series of films of different characteristics and patterns. *Compare* thin film.

ThickNet \thik´net\ *n. See* 10Base5.

ThickWire \thik´wīr\ *n. See* 10Base5.

thimble \thim´bl\ *n.* A type element, similar to a daisy wheel, that bears a full character set, with each character on a separate type bar. As with a daisy wheel, the spokes, or type bars, radiate out from a central hub. On a thimble print element, however, each type bar is bent 90 degrees at its halfway point, so the type bars stick straight up with the type facing away from the hub. *See also* thimble printer. *Compare* daisy wheel, daisy-wheel printer.

thimble printer \thim´bl prin`tər\ *n.* A printer that uses a thimble print element, best known in a line of printers from NEC. Because these printers use fully formed characters like those on a typewriter, they generate letter-quality output that is indistinguishable from that of a typewriter. This includes the slight impression created by the type hitting the paper hard through the ribbon, which distinguishes this type of printout from that of laser printers. *See also* thimble. *Compare* daisy-wheel printer.

thin client \thin´ klī`ənt\ *n.* In a client/server architecture, a client computer that performs little or no data processing. The processing is instead performed by the server. *See also* client/server architecture, fat server, thin server. *Compare* fat client.

thin Ethernet \thin` ē´thər-net\ *n. See* 10Base2, Ethernet.

thin film \thin´ film\ *adj.* A method used in the fabrication of integrated circuits. Thin film technology operates on the same basic principles as thick film technology. Rather than using inks or pastes, however, thin film technology uses metals and metal oxides that are "evaporated" and then deposited on the substrate in the desired pattern to form the integrated circuit's passive components (wires, resistors, and capacitors). *See also* molecular beam epitaxy. *Compare* thick film.

thin film transistor \thin`film tranz-i`stər\ *n. See* TFT.

ThinNet \thin´net\ *n. See* 10Base2.

thin server \thin´ sər`vər\ *n.* A client/server architecture in which most of an application is run on the client machine, which is called a fat client, with occasional data operations on a remote server. Such a configuration yields good client performance, but complicates administrative tasks, such as software upgrades. *See also* client/server architecture, fat client, thin client. *Compare* fat server.

thin space \thin´ spās\ *n.* An amount of horizontal space in a font, equal to one-quarter the point size of the font. For example, a thin space in a 12-point font is 3 points wide. *See also* point[1] (definition 1). *Compare* em space, en space, fixed space.

thin system \thin´ si`stəm\ *n. See* thin server.

ThinWire \thin´wīr\ *n. See* 10Base2.

third-generation computer \thərd`jen-ər-ā`shən kəm-pyo͞o´tər\ *n.* Any of the computers produced from the mid-1960s to the 1970s that were based on integrated circuits rather than on separately wired transistors. *See also* computer.

third-generation language \thərd`jen-ər-ā`shən lang´wəj\ *n.* A high-level programming language that was designed to run on the third generation of computer processors, built on integrated circuit technology roughly from 1965 to 1970. C, FORTRAN, Basic, and Pascal are examples of third-generation languages still in use today. *Acronym:* 3GL (thrē`G-L´). *See also* 3GL, central processing unit, high-level language, integrated circuit. *Compare* 4GL, low-level language.

third normal form \thərd´ nōr´məl fōrm\ *n. See* normal form (definition 1).

third party \thərd` pär´tē\ *n.* A company that manufactures and sells accessories or peripherals for use with a major manufacturer's computer or peripheral, usually without any involvement from the major manufacturer.

thrashing \thrash´ēng\ *n.* The state of a virtual memory system that is spending almost all its time swapping pages in and out of memory rather than executing applications. *See also* swap (definition 2), virtual memory.

thread \thred\ *n.* **1.** In programming, a process that is part of a larger process or program. **2.** In a tree data structure, a pointer that identifies the par-

ent node and is used to facilitate traversal of the tree. **3.** In electronic mail and Internet newsgroups, a series of messages and replies related to a specific topic.

threaded discussion \thred`əd di-skush´ən\ *n.* In a newsgroup or other online forum, a series of messages or articles in which replies to an article are nested directly under it, instead of the articles being arranged in chronological or alphabetical order. *See also* newsgroup, thread (definition 3).

threaded newsreader \thred`əd no͞oz´rē-dər\ *n.* A newsreader that displays posts in newsgroups as threads. Replies to a post appear directly after the original post, rather than in chronological or any other order. *See also* newsreader, post, thread (definition 3).

threaded tree \thred`əd trē´\ *n.* A tree in which the leaf (end) nodes contain pointers to some of the nodes from which they arise. The pointers facilitate searching the tree for information. *See also* thread (definition 2).

threading \thred´ēng\ *n.* A technique used by certain interpretive languages, such as many Forth implementations, to speed execution. The references to other support routines in each threaded support routine, such as a predefined word in Forth, are replaced by pointers to those routines. *See also* Forth, thread (definition 1).

three-dimensional array \thrē`də-men`shə-nəl ər-ā´\ *n.* An ordered arrangement of information in which three numbers (integers) are used to locate a particular item. A three-dimensional array treats data as if it were laid out in rows, columns, and layers. *See also* 3-D array, array, two-dimensional array.

three-dimensional model \thrē`də-men`shə-nəl mod´əl\ *n.* A computer simulation of a physical object in which length, width, and depth are real attributes—a model, with x-, y-, and z-axes, that can be rotated for viewing from different angles.

three-tier client/server \thrē`tēr klī`ənt-sər´vər\ *n.* A client/server architecture in which software systems are structured into three tiers or layers: the user interface layer, the business logic layer, and the database layer. Layers may have one or more components. For example, there can be one or more user interfaces in the top tier, each user interface may communicate with more than one application in the middle tier at the same time, and the applications in the middle tier may use more than one database at a time. Components in a tier may run on a computer that is separate from the other tiers, communicating with the other components over a network. *See also* client/server architecture. *Compare* two-tier client/server.

throttle control \throt´l kən-trōl´\ *n.* A device that enables the user of a flight simulator or game to control simulated engine power. The throttle control is used along with a joystick (which controls the simulated ailerons and elevators) and possibly a rudder control.

throughput \throo´poot\ *n.* A measure of the data transfer rate through a typically complex communications system or of the data processing rate in a computer system.

thumb \thum\ *n. See* elevator.

thumbnail \thum´nāl\ *n.* A miniature version of an image or electronic version of a page that is generally used to allow quick browsing through multiple images or pages. For example, Web pages often contain thumbnails of images (which can be loaded much more quickly by the Web browser than the full-size image). Many of these thumbnails can be clicked on to load the complete version of the image. See the illustration.

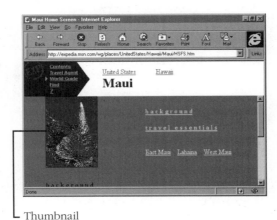
└ Thumbnail

Thumbnail.

thumbwheel \thum´hwēl, thum´wēl\ *n.* A wheel embedded in a case so that only a portion of the outside rim is revealed. When rolled with the thumb, the wheel can control an on-screen element such as a pointer or a cursor. Thumbwheels are used with three-dimensional joysticks and trackballs to control the depth aspect of the pointer or cursor. *See also* joystick, relative pointing device, trackball.

TIA \T´I-A´\ *n.* Acronym for **t**hanks **i**n **a**dvance. On the Internet, a popular sign-off to a request of some sort. *Also called* aTdHvAaNnKcSe.

tick \tik\ *n.* **1.** A regular, rapidly recurring signal emitted by a clocking circuit; also, the interrupt generated by this signal. **2.** In some microcomputer systems, notably Macintosh, one sixtieth of a second, the basic time unit used by the internal clock that is accessible by programs.

tiebreaker \tī´brā-kər´\ *n.* A circuit that arbitrates competing circuits and resolves bottlenecks by giving priority to one circuit at a time.

tie line \tī´ līn\ *n.* A private line leased from a communications carrier and often used to link two or more points in an organization.

.tif \dot-tif´, -T´I-F´\ *n.* The file extension that identifies bitmap images in Tagged Image File Format (TIFF). *See also* TIFF.

TIFF or **TIF** \tif\ *n.* Acronym for **T**agged **I**mage **F**ile **F**ormat or **T**ag **I**mage **F**ile **F**ormat. A standard file format commonly used for scanning, storage, and interchange of gray-scale graphic images. TIFF may be the only format available for older programs (such as older versions of MacPaint), but most modern programs are able to save images in a variety of other formats, such as GIF or JPEG. *See also* gray scale. *Compare* GIF, JPEG.

TIGA \tī´gə, T´I-G-A´\ *n.* Acronym for **T**exas **I**nstruments **G**raphics **A**rchitecture. A video adapter architecture based on the Texas Instruments 340x0 graphics processor.

tightly coupled \tīt´lē kəp´ld\ *adj.* **1.** Refers to two computing processes whose successful completion and individual performance rates are highly interdependent. **2.** Of, pertaining to, or characteristic of a relationship of interdependency between computers, as in multiprocessing.

tile \tīl\ *vb.* **1.** In computer-graphics programming, to fill adjacent blocks of pixels on the screen with a design or pattern without allowing any blocks to overlap. **2.** To fill the space on a monitor or within a smaller area with multiple copies of the same graphic image. See the illustration. **3.** In an environment with multiple windows, to rearrange and resize all open windows so that they appear fully on the screen without any overlap.

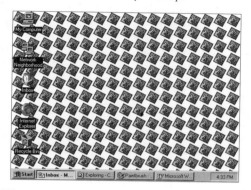

Tile.

time and date \tīm` ənd dāt´\ *n.* In computing, the timekeeping and datekeeping functions maintained by the computer's operating system, used most visibly as a means of "stamping" files with the date and time of creation or last revision.

time-division multiplexing \tīm`də-vizh-ən mul´ti-pleks-ēng\ *n.* A form of multiplexing in which transmission time is broken into segments, each of which carries one element of one signal. *See also* statistical multiplexer. *Compare* FDM.

time out or **timeout** or **time-out** \tīm out´\ *n.* An event that indicates that a predetermined amount of time has elapsed without some other expected event taking place. The time-out event is used to interrupt the process that had been waiting for the other expected event. For example, a dial-up remote system might allow the user 60 seconds to log in after making a connection. If the user fails to enter a valid login name and password within this time, the computer breaks the connection, thus protecting itself against crackers as well as freeing a phone line that may have gone dead.

timer \tī´mər\ *n.* A register (high-speed memory circuit) or a special circuit, chip, or software routine used to measure time intervals. A timer is not the same as the system clock, although its pulses can be derived from the system clock frequency. *See also* time and date. *Compare* clock (definition 1), clock/calendar.

time-sharing \tīm´shâr`ēng\ *n.* The use of a computer system by more than one individual at the same time. Time-sharing runs separate programs concurrently by interleaving portions of processing time allotted to each program (user). *See also* quantum (definition 2), time slice.

time slice \tīm´ slīs\ *n.* A brief period of time during which a particular task is given control of the microprocessor in a time-sharing multitasking environment. *See also* multitasking, preemptive multitasking. *Compare* quantum (definition 2).

time-slice multitasking \tīm`slīs mul´tē-ta-skēng, mul´tī-ta-skēng\ *n. See* preemptive multitasking.

Time to Live \tīm` tōō liv´\ *n.* A header field for a packet sent over the Internet indicating how long the packet should be held. *Acronym:* TTL (T`-T-L´). *See also* header (definition 2), packet (definition 1).

timing signals \tī´mēng sig`nəlz\ *n.* **1.** Any of several types of signals used to coordinate activities within a computer system. **2.** A signal used to coordinate data transfer operations.

tiny model \tī´nē mod´əl\ *n.* A memory model in the Intel 80x86 processor family. The tiny model allows a combined total of only 64 kilobytes (KB) for code and for data. *See also* 8086, memory model.

title bar \tī´tl bär´\ *n.* In a graphical user interface, a horizontal space at the top of a window that contains the name of the window. Most title bars also contain boxes or buttons for closing and resizing the window. Clicking on the title bar allows the user to move the entire window.

.tj \dot`T-J´\ *n.* On the Internet, the major geographic domain specifying that an address is located in Tajikistan.

.tk \dot`T-K´\ *n.* On the Internet, the major geographic domain specifying that an address is located in Tokelau.

TLA \T`L-A´\ *n.* Acronym for **t**hree-**l**etter **a**cronym. An ironic term, usually used in jest on the Internet in e-mail, newsgroups, and other online forums, referring to the large number of acronyms in computer terminology, particularly those consisting of three letters.

.tm \dot`T-M´\ *n.* On the Internet, the major geographic domain specifying that an address is located in Turkmenistan.

TMS34010 \T-M-S`thrē´-fōr-ō`wən-ō´\ *n. See* 34010, 34020.

.tn \dot`T-N´\ *n.* On the Internet, the major geographic domain specifying that an address is located in Tunisia.

.to \dot`T-O´\ *n.* On the Internet, the major geographic domain specifying that an address is located in Tonga.

TOF \T´O-F´, tof\ *n. See* top-of-file.

toggle[1] \tog´l\ *n.* An electronic device with two states or a program option that can be turned on or off using the same action, such as a mouse click.

toggle[2] \tog´l\ *vb.* To switch back and forth between two states. For example, the Num Lock key on an IBM-style keyboard toggles the numeric keypad between numbers and cursor movement.

ToggleKeys \tog´l-kēz`\ *n.* A feature of Windows 95 that sounds high and low beeps when one of the toggle keys (Caps Lock, Num Lock, or Scroll Lock) is turned on or off. *See also* typematic. *Compare* BounceKeys, FilterKeys, MouseKeys, ShowSounds, SoundSentry, StickyKeys, ToggleKeys.

token \tō´kən\ *n.* **1.** A unique structured data object or message that circulates continuously among the nodes of a token ring and describes the current state of the network. Before any node can send a message, it must first wait to control the token. *See also* token bus network, token passing, token ring network. **2.** Any nonreducible textual element in data that is being parsed—for example, the use in a program of a variable name, a reserved word, or an operator. Storing tokens as short codes shortens program files and speeds execution. *See also* Basic, parse.

token bus network \tō´kən bus net`wərk\ *n.* A local area network formed in a bus topology (stations connected to a single, shared data highway) that uses token passing as a means of regulating traffic on the line. On a token bus network, a token governing the right to transmit is passed from one station to another, and each station holds the token for a brief time, during which it alone can transmit information. The token is transferred in order of priority from an "upstream" station to the next "downstream" station, which might or might not be the next station on the bus. In essence, the token "circles" through the network in a logical ring rather than a physical one. Token bus networks are defined in the IEEE 802.4 standards. *See also* bus network, IEEE 802 standards, token passing. *Compare* token ring network.

token passing \tō´kən pas`ēng\ *n.* A method of controlling access on local area networks through the use of a special signal, called a *token,* that determines which station is allowed to transmit. The token, which is actually a short message, is passed from station to station around the network. Only the station with the token can transmit information. *See also* token bus network, token ring network. *Compare* collision detection, contention, CSMA/CD.

token ring network \tō´kən rēng net´wərk\ *n.* A local area network formed in a ring (closed loop) topology that uses token passing as a means of regulating traffic on the line. On a token ring network, a token governing the right to transmit is passed from one station to the next in a physical circle. If a station has information to transmit, it "seizes" the token, marks it as being in use, and inserts the information. The "busy" token, plus message, is then passed around the circle, copied when it arrives at its destination, and eventually returned to the sender. The sender removes the attached message and then passes the freed token to the next station in line. Token ring networks are defined in the IEEE 802.5 standards. *See also* IEEE 802 standards, ring network, token passing. *Compare* token bus network.

Token Ring network \tō´kən rēng net´wərk\ *n.* A token-passing, ring-shaped local area network developed by IBM that operates at 4 megabits (4 million bits) per second. With standard telephone wiring, the Token Ring network can connect up to 72 devices; with shielded twisted-pair (STP) wiring, the network supports up to 260 devices. Although it is based on a ring (closed loop) topology, the Token Ring network uses star-shaped clusters of up to eight workstations connected to a wiring concentrator (Multistation Access Unit, or MSAU), which, in turn, is connected to the main ring. The Token Ring network is designed to accommodate microcomputers, minicomputers, and mainframes; it follows the IEEE 802.5 standards for token ring networks. See the illustration. *See also* ring network, STP, token passing.

tone \tōn\ *n.* **1.** A particular tint of a color. *Also called* shade, value. *See also* brightness, color

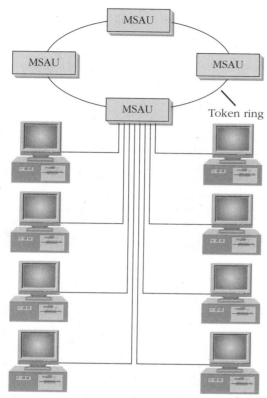

Token Ring network.　An IBM Token Ring configuration with MSAUs.

model. **2.** One sound or signal of a particular frequency.

toner \tō´nər\ *n.* Powdered pigment that is used in office copiers and in laser, LED, and LCD printers. *See also* electrophotographic printers.

toner cartridge \tō´nər kär`trij\ *n.* A disposable container that holds toner for a laser printer or other page printer. Some types of toner cartridge contain toner only; however, the most popular printer engines pack all expendables, including toner and the photosensitive drum, in a single cartridge. Toner cartridges are interchangeable among printers that use the same engine.

toolbar \tōōl´bär\ *n.* In an application in a graphical user interface, a row, column, or block of on-screen buttons or icons. When these buttons or icons are clicked on with the mouse, macros or certain functions of the application are activated. For example, word processors often feature toolbars with buttons for changing text to italic, boldface, and other styles. Toolbars often can be customized by the user and usually can be moved around on the screen according to the user's preference. See the illustration. *See also* graphical user interface. *Compare* menu bar, palette (definition 1), taskbar, title bar.

Toolbar.

toolbox \tōōl´boks\ *n.* A set of predefined (and usually precompiled) routines a programmer can use in writing a program for a particular machine, environment, or application. *Also called* toolkit. *See also* library (definition 1).

Toolbox \tōōl´boks\ *n.* A set of routines stored mostly in the read-only memory of a Macintosh that provides application programmers with the tools needed to support the graphical interface characteristic of the computer. *Also called* User Interface Toolbox.

Tool Command Language/Tool Kit \tōōl` kə-mand lang`wəj tōōl´ kit\ *n. See* Tcl/Tk.

toolkit \tōōl´kit\ *n. See* toolbox.

top-down design \top-doun` də-zīn´\ *n.* A program design methodology that starts with defining program functionality at the highest level (a series of tasks) and then breaks down each task into lower-level tasks, and so on. *See also* bottom-up programming, top-down programming. *Compare* bottom-up design.

top-down programming \top-doun` prō´gram-ēng\ *n.* An approach to programming that implements a program in top-down fashion. Typically, this is done by writing a main body with calls to several major routines (implemented as stubs). Each routine is then coded, calling other, lower-level, routines (also done initially as stubs). *See also* bottom-up design, stub, top-down design. *Compare* bottom-up programming.

topic drift \top´ik drift`\ *n.* The tendency of an online discussion to move from its original subject to other related or unrelated subjects. For example, someone in a conference devoted to television may ask about a news program; then somebody else may say something about a story on that program about food poisoning, which leads somebody else to start a general discussion on the advantages of organic fruits and vegetables.

topic group \top´ik gro͞op`\ *n*. An online discussion area for participants with a common interest in a particular subject.

top-level domain \top`lev-əl dō-mān´\ *n*. In the domain-name system of Internet addresses, any of the broadest category of names, under which all domain names fit. Top-level domains for sites in the United States include .com, .edu, .gov, .net, and .org. *See also* DNS (definition 1), major geographic domain.

top-of-file \top`əv-fīl´\ *n*. **1.** The beginning of a file. **2.** A symbol used by a program to mark the beginning of a file—the first character in the file or, in an indexed (ordered) database, the first indexed record. *See also* beginning-of-file. *Acronym:* TOF (T`O-F´, tof).

topology \to-pol´ə-jē\ *n*. The configuration formed by the connections between devices on a local area network (LAN) or between two or more LANs. *See also* bus network, LAN, ring network, star network, token ring network, tree network.

.tor.ca \dot-T-O-R`dot-C-A´\ *n*. On the Internet, the major geographic domain specifying that an address is located in Toronto, Canada.

total bypass \tō`təl bī´pas\ *n*. A communications network that uses satellite transmission to bypass both local and long-distance telephone links.

touch pad \tuch´ pad\ *n*. A variety of graphics tablet that uses pressure sensors, rather than the electromagnetics used in more expensive high-resolution tablets, to track the position of a device on its surface. *See also* absolute pointing device, graphics tablet.

touch screen \tuch´ skrēn\ *n*. A computer screen designed or modified to recognize the location of a touch on its surface. By touching the screen, the user can make a selection or move a cursor. The simplest type of touch screen is made up of a grid of sensing lines, which determine the location of a touch by matching vertical and horizontal contacts. Another, more accurate type uses an electrically charged surface and sensors around the

outer edges of the screen to detect the amount of electrical disruption and pinpoint exactly where contact has been made. A third type has infrared light-emitting diodes (LEDs) and sensors around the outer edges of the screen. These LEDs and sensors create an invisible infrared grid, which the user's finger interrupts, in front of the screen. *Compare* light pen.

touch-sensitive display \təch`sen`sə-tiv dis-plā´\ *n*. *See* touch screen.

touch-sensitive tablet \tuch`sen-sə-tiv ta´blət\ *n*. *See* touch pad.

tower \tou´ər\ *n*. A microcomputer system in which the cabinet for the central processing unit (CPU) is tall, narrow, and deep rather than short, wide, and deep. The motherboard is usually vertical, and the disk drives are often perpendicular to the motherboard. A tower cabinet is at least 24 inches tall. See the illustration. *See also* cabinet, microcomputer, motherboard. *Compare* minitower.

Tower.

.tp \dot`T-P´\ *n*. On the Internet, the major geographic domain specifying that an address is located in East Timor.

TP \T-P´\ *n*. *See* transaction processing.

TPC \T`P-C´\ *n*. *See* Transaction Processing Council.

TPC-D \T`P-C-D´\ *n*. Acronym for **T**ransaction **P**rocessing **C**ouncil Benchmark **D.** A benchmark standard that addresses a broad range of decision support applications working with complex data structures. *See also* Transaction Processing Council.

TP monitor \T-P´ mon`ə-tər\ *n.* Short for **tele**processing **monitor** or **t**ransaction **p**rocessing **monitor.** A program that controls the transfer of data between terminals (or clients) and a mainframe (or one or more servers) so as to provide a consistent environment for one or more online transaction processing (OLTP) applications. A TP monitor may also control the appearance of the screen displays and check input data for proper format. *See also* client (definition 3), mainframe computer, OLTP, server (definition 1).

.tr \dot`T-R´\ *n.* On the Internet, the major geographic domain specifying that an address is located in Turkey.

trace \trās\ *vb.* To execute a program in such a way that the sequence of statements being executed can be observed. *See also* debugger, single step.

track[1] \trak\ *n.* One of numerous circular data storage areas on a floppy disk or a hard drive, comparable to a groove on a record but not spiral. Tracks, composed of sectors, are recorded on a disk by an operating system during a disk format operation. On other storage media, such as tape, a track runs parallel to the edge of the medium. See the illustration.

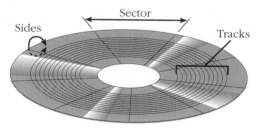

Track.

track[2] \trak\ *vb.* **1.** To follow a path. **2.** In data management, to follow the flow of information through a manual or an automated system. **3.** In data storage and retrieval, to follow and read from a recording channel on a disk or a magnetic tape. **4.** In computer graphics, to cause a displayed symbol, such as a pointer, to match on the screen the movements of a mouse or another pointing device.

trackball \trak´bäl\ *n.* A pointing device that consists of a ball resting on two rollers at right angles to each other, which translate the ball's motion into vertical and horizontal movement on the screen. A trackball also typically has one or more buttons to initiate other actions. A trackball's housing is stationary; its ball is rolled with the hand. See the illustration. *Compare* mechanical mouse.

Trackball.

trackpad \trak´pad\ *n.* A pointing device consisting of a small, flat pad that is sensitive to touch. Users move the mouse cursor on screen by touching the trackpad and moving their fingers across the trackpad's surface. Such devices are most commonly installed on laptop computers. *See also* pointing device.

tracks per inch \traks` pər inch´\ *n.* The density with which concentric tracks (data storage rings) are recorded or can be recorded in an inch of radius on a disk. The greater the density (the more tracks per inch), the more information a disk can hold. *Acronym:* TPI (T`P-I´).

tractor feed \trak´tər fēd`\ *n.* A method of feeding paper through a printer using pins mounted on rotating belts. The pins engage holes near the edges of continuous-form paper and either push or pull the paper through. See the illustration on the next page. *See also* continuous-form paper. *Compare* pin feed.

trademark \trād´märk\ *n.* A word, phrase, symbol, or design (or some combination thereof) used to identify a proprietary product, often accompanied by the symbol ™ or ®.

trade show \trād´ shō\ *n.* A multivendor sales event or exposition that showcases companies' products.

Tractor feeders

Tractor feed. Tractor feeders on a dot-matrix printer.

traditional newsgroup hierarchy \trə-dish`ə-nəl nōōz`grōōp hī´ər-är-kē, hīr´är-kē\ *n.* The seven standard newsgroup categories in Usenet: comp., misc., news., rec., sci., soc., and talk. Newsgroups can be added within the traditional hierarchy only following a formal voting process. *See also* comp. newsgroups, misc. newsgroups, newsgroup, news. newsgroups, rec. newsgroups, Request for Discussion, sci. newsgroups, soc. newsgroups, talk. newsgroups, Usenet. *Compare* alt. newsgroup.

traffic \traf´ik\ *n.* The load carried by a communications link or channel.

trailer \trā´lər\ *n.* Information, typically occupying several bytes, at the tail end of a block (section) of transmitted data and often containing a checksum or other error-checking data useful for confirming the accuracy and status of the transmission. *See also* checksum. *Compare* header (definition 2).

trailer label \trā´lər lā`bəl\ *n.* **1.** A small block of information used in tape processing that marks the end of a file or the end of the tape and that can contain other information, such as the number of records in the file or files on the tape. *Compare* header label. **2.** A label used in communications data frames that follows the data and might contain an end-of-message mark, a checksum, and some synchronization bits.

trailing edge \trā`lēng ej´\ *n.* The latter part of an electronic signal. When a digital signal switches from on to off, the transition is the trailing edge of the signal.

train[1] \trān\ *n.* A sequence of items or events, such as a digital pulse train consisting of transmitted binary signals.

train[2] \trān\ *vb.* To teach an end user how to use a software or hardware product.

transaction \tranz-ak´shən\ *n.* A discrete activity within a computer system, such as an entry of a customer order or an update of an inventory item. Transactions are usually associated with database management, order entry, and other online systems.

transaction file \tranz-ak´shən fīl`\ *n.* A file that contains the details of transactions, such as items and prices on invoices. It is used to update a master database file. *See also* transaction. *Compare* master file.

transaction log \tranz-ak´shən log`\ *n.* *See* change file.

transaction processing \tranz-ak´shən pros`es-ēng\ *n.* A processing method in which transactions are executed immediately after they are received by the system. *See also* transaction. *Compare* batch processing (definition 3).

Transaction Processing Council \tranz-ak`shən pros´es-ēng koun`səl\ *n.* A group of hardware and software vendors with the goal of publishing benchmark standards. *Acronym:* TPC (T`P-C´).

transaction processing monitor \tranz-ak`shən pros-es-ēng mon´ə-tər\ *n.* *See* TP monitor.

transceiver \tran`sē´vər\ *n.* Short for **trans**mitter/re**ceiver.** A device that can both transmit and receive signals. On local area networks, a transceiver is the device that connects a computer to the network.

transceiver cable \tran-sē´vər kā`bl\ *n.* A cable that is used to connect a host adapter within a computer to a local area network (LAN). *See also* AUI cable, LAN.

transducer \tranz`dōō´sər\ *n.* A device that converts one form of energy into another. Electronic transducers either convert electric energy to another form of energy or convert nonelectric to electric energy.

transfer \trans´fər\ *n.* **1.** The movement of data from one location to another. **2.** The passing of program control from one portion of code to another.

transfer rate \trans´fər rāt`\ *n.* The rate at which a circuit or a communications channel transfers information from source to destination, as over a network or to and from a disk drive. Transfer rate is measured in units of information per unit of time—for example, bits per second or characters per second—and can be measured either as a raw rate, which is the maximum transfer speed, or as an average rate, which includes gaps between blocks of data as part of the transmission time.

transfer statement \trans´fər stāt`mənt\ *n.* A statement in a programming language that transfers the flow of execution to another location in the program. *See also* branch instruction, CALL statement, GOTO statement, jump instruction.

transfer time \trans´fər tīm`\ *n.* The time elapsed between the start of a data transfer operation and its completion.

transform \trans-fōrm´\ *vb.* **1.** To change the appearance or format of data without altering its content; that is, to encode information according to predefined rules. **2.** In mathematics and computer graphics, to alter the position, size, or nature of an object by moving it to another location (translation), making it larger or smaller (scaling), turning it (rotation), changing its description from one type of coordinate system to another, and so on.

transformer \trans-fōr´mər`\ *n.* A device used to change the voltage of an alternating current signal or to change the impedance of an alternating current circuit. See the illustration.

Transformer.

transient \tran´zhənt, tran´zē-ənt\ *adj.* **1.** Fleeting, temporary, or unpredictable. **2.** Of or pertaining to the region of memory used for programs, such as applications, that are read from disk storage and that reside in memory temporarily until they are replaced by other programs. In this context, *transient* can also refer to the programs themselves. **3.** In electronics, of or pertaining to a short-lived, abnormal, and unpredictable increase in power supply, such as a voltage spike or surge. *Transient time* is the interval during which a change in current or voltage is building up or decaying.

transient suppressor \tran`zhənt su-pres´ər, tran`zē-ənt\ *n.* A circuit designed to reduce or eliminate unwanted electrical signals or voltages.

transistor \tran`zi´stər\ *n.* Short for **tran**sfer re**sistor.** A solid-state circuit component, usually with three leads, in which a voltage or a current controls the flow of another current. The transistor can serve many functions, including those of amplifier, switch, and oscillator, and is a fundamental component of almost all modern electronics. See the illustration on the next page. *See also* base (definition 3), FET, NPN transistor, PNP transistor.

transistor-transistor logic \tran-zi`stər-tran-zi´stər loj-ik\ *n.* A type of bipolar circuit design that utilizes transistors connected to each other either directly or through resistors. Transistor-transistor logic offers high speed and good noise immunity and is used in many digital circuits. A large number of transistor-transistor logic gates can be fabricated on a single integrated circuit. *Acronym:* TTL (T`T-L´).

translate \tranz´lāt\ *vb.* **1.** In programming, to convert a program from one language to another. Translation is performed by special programs such as compilers, assemblers, and interpreters. **2.** In computer graphics, to move an image in the "space" represented on the display, without turning (rotating) the image.

translated file \tranz`lā-təd fīl´\ *n.* A file containing data that has been changed from binary (8-bit) format to ASCII (7-bit) format. BinHex and uuencode both translate binary files into ASCII. Such translation is necessary to transmit data through systems (such as e-mail) that may not preserve the eighth bit of each byte. A translated file must be decoded to its binary form before being used. *See also* BinHex, uuencode.

translator \tranz´lā-tər\ *n.* A program that translates one language or data format into another.

transmission channel \tranz-mish´ən chan`əl\ *n. See* channel.

Transmission Control Protocol/Internet Protocol \tranz`mish`ən kən-trōl´ prō`tə-kol-in´tər-net prō`tə-kol\ *n. See* TCP/IP.

transmit \tranz-mit´\ *vb.* To send information over a communications line or a circuit. Computer transmissions can take place in the ways listed on the next page.

- asynchronous (variable timing) or synchronous (exact timing)
- serial (essentially, bit by bit) or parallel (byte by byte; a group of bits at once)
- duplex or full-duplex (simultaneous two-way communication), half-duplex (two-way communication in one direction at a time), or simplex (one-way communication only)
- burst (intermittent transmission of blocks of information)

Transmit Data \tranz-mit´ da`tə, dat`ə\ *n. See* TXD.

transmitter \tranz-mit´ər\ *n.* Any circuit or electronic device designed to send electrically encoded data to another location.

transparent \trans-pâr´ənt\ *adj.* **1.** In computer use, of, pertaining to, or characteristic of a device, function, or part of a program that works so smoothly and easily that it is invisible to the user. For example, the ability of one application to use files created by another is transparent if the user encounters no difficulty in opening, reading, or using the second program's files or does not even know the use is occurring. **2.** In communications, of, pertaining to, or characteristic of a mode of transmission in which data can include any characters, including device-control characters, without the possibility of misinterpretation by the

receiving station. For example, the receiving station will not end a transparent transmission until it receives a character in the data that indicates end of transmission. Thus, there is no danger of the receiving station ending communications prematurely. **3.** In computer graphics, of, pertaining to, or characteristic of the lack of color in a particular region of an image so that the background color of the display shows through.

transponder \trans´pon`dər\ *n.* A transceiver in a communications satellite that receives a signal from an earth station and retransmits it on a different frequency to one or more other earth stations.

transportable computer \trans-pōr´tə-bl kəm-pyo͞o´tər\ *n. See* portable computer.

transport layer \trans´pōrt lâr, lā`ər\ *n.* The fourth of the seven layers in the International Organization for Standardization's Open Systems Interconnection (OSI) model for standardizing computer-to-computer communications. The transport layer is one level above the network layer and is responsible for both quality of service and accurate delivery of information. Among the tasks performed on this layer are error detection and correction. *See also* ISO/OSI model.

transpose[1] \trans´pōz\ *n.* The result of rotating a matrix.

transpose[2] \trans-pōz´\ *vb.* **1.** To reverse, as the order of the letters *h* and *t* in *hte,* in correcting the

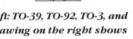

Transistor.   The photos on the left show four of several types of transistor. From left: TO-39, TO-92, TO-3, and TO-202. (The third "pin" of the TO-3 is actually the flat base of the package.) The drawing on the right shows two typical bipolar transistors.

spelling of *the;* or reversing two wires in a circuit. **2.** In mathematics and spreadsheets, to rotate a matrix (a rectangular array of numbers) about a diagonal axis.

transputer \trans`pyo͞o´tər\ *n.* Short for **trans**istor com**puter.** A complete computer on a single chip, including RAM and an FPU, designed as a building block for parallel computing systems.

trap[1] \trap\ *n. See* interrupt.

trap[2] \trap\ *vb.* To intercept an action or event before it occurs, usually in order to do something else. Trapping is commonly used by debuggers to allow interruption of program execution at a given spot. *See also* interrupt, interrupt handler.

trapdoor \trap´dōr\ *n. See* back door.

trap handler \trap´ hand`lər\ *n. See* interrupt handler.

Trash \trash\ *n.* An icon on the screen in the Macintosh Finder, resembling a garbage can. To delete a file or eject a diskette, the user drags the icon for the file or diskette to the Trash. However, until the user shuts down the system or chooses the menu option "Empty Trash," a file in the Trash is not actually deleted; the user can retrieve it by double-clicking the Trash icon and dragging the file's icon out of the resulting window. *Compare* Recycle Bin.

traverse \trə-vərs´\ *vb.* In programming, to access in a particular order all of the nodes of a tree or similar data structure.

tree \trē\ *n.* A data structure containing zero or more nodes that are linked together in a hierarchical fashion. If there are any nodes, one node is the root; each node except the root is the child of one and only one other node; and each node has zero or more nodes as children. *See also* child (definition 2), graph, leaf, node (definition 3), parent/child (definition 2), root.

tree network \trē´ net`wərk\ *n.* A topology for a local area network (LAN) in which one machine is connected to one or more other machines, each of which is connected to one or more others, and so on, so that the structure formed by the network resembles that of a tree. See the illustration. *See also* bus network, distributed network, ring network, star network, token ring network, topology.

tree search \trē´ sərch\ *n.* A search procedure performed on a tree data structure. At each step

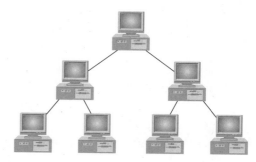

Tree network.

of the search, a tree search is able to determine, by the value in a particular node, which branches of the tree to eliminate, without searching those branches themselves. *See also* branch (definition 1), tree structure.

tree structure \trē´ struk`chur\ *n.* Any structure that has the essential organizational properties of a tree. *See also* tree.

trellis-coded modulation \trel´is-kō-dəd mo-dyə-lā´shən, moj`ə-lā´shən\ *n.* An enhanced form of quadrature amplitude modulation that is used by modems that operate at or above 9,600 bits per second and encodes information as unique sets of bits associated with changes in both the phase and amplitude of the carrier, as well as using extra signal points for error-checking bits. *Acronym:* TCM (T`C-M´). *See also* quadrature amplitude modulation.

trichromatic \trī`krə-mat´ik\ *adj.* Of, pertaining to, or characteristic of a system that uses three colors (red, green, and blue in computer graphics) to create all other colors. *See also* color model.

trigger \trig´ər\ *n.* In a database, an action that causes a procedure to be carried out automatically when a user attempts to modify data. A trigger can instruct the database system to take a specific action, depending on the particular change attempted. Incorrect, unwanted, or unauthorized changes can thereby be prevented, helping to maintain the integrity of the database.

trigonometry \trig`ə-nom´ə-trē\ *n.* The branch of mathematics dealing with arcs and angles, expressed in functions (for example, sine and cosine) that show relationships—for example, between two sides of a right triangle or between two complementary angles.

triple-pass scanner \trip`l-pas skan´ər\ *n*. A color scanner that performs one scanning pass on an image for each of the three primary colors of light (red, green, and blue). *See also* color scanner.

tristimulus values \trī-sti´myə-lus val´yōōz\ *n*. In color graphics, the varying amounts of three colors, such as red, blue, and green, that are combined to produce another color. *See also* color, color model.

troff \trof\ *n*. Short for **t**ypesetting **r**un**off**. A UNIX text formatter often used to format man pages. *See also* man pages. *Compare* TeX.

Trojan horse \trō`jən hōrs´\ *n*. A destructive program disguised as a game, utility, or application. When run, a Trojan horse does something harmful to the computer system while appearing to do something useful. *See also* virus, worm.

troll \trōl\ *vb*. To post a message in a newsgroup or other online conference in the hopes that somebody else will consider the original message so outrageous that it demands a heated reply. A classic example of trolling is an article in favor of torturing cats posted in a pet lovers' newsgroup. *See also* YHBT.

troubleshoot \trub´l-shōōt`\ *vb*. To isolate the source of a problem in a program, computer system, or network and remedy it.

trouble ticket \trəb´l tik`ət\ *n*. A report of a problem with a particular device or system that is tracked through the workflow process. Originally written on paper, electronic trouble tickets are featured by many workflow and help-desk applications. *See also* help desk (definition 2), workflow application.

True BASIC \trōō` bā´sik\ *n*. A version of Basic created in 1983 by John Kemeny and Thomas Kurtz, the creators of the original Basic, to standardize and modernize the language. True BASIC is a compiled, structured version of Basic that does not require line numbers. True BASIC includes advanced control structures that make structured programming possible. *See also* Basic, structured programming.

true color \trōō` kə´lər\ *n*. *See* 24-bit color.

true complement \trōō` kom´plə-mənt\ *n*. *See* complement.

TrueType \trōō´tīp\ *n*. An outline font technology introduced by Apple Computer, Inc., in 1991 and by Microsoft Corporation in 1992 as a means of including high-grade fonts within the Apple Macintosh and Microsoft Windows operating systems. TrueType is a WYSIWYG font technology, which means that the printed output of TrueType fonts is identical to what appears on the screen. *See also* bitmapped font, outline font, PostScript.

truncate \trun´kāt\ *vb*. To cut off the beginning or end of a series of characters or numbers; specifically, to eliminate one or more of the least significant (typically rightmost) digits. In truncation, numbers are simply eliminated, unlike rounding, in which the rightmost digit might be incremented to preserve accuracy. *Compare* round.

trunk \trunk\ *n*. In communications, a channel connecting two switching stations. A trunk usually carries a large number of calls at the same time.

truth table \trōōth´ tā`bl\ *n*. A table showing the value of a Boolean expression for each of the possible combinations of variable values in the expression. *See also* AND, Boolean operator, exclusive OR, NOT, OR.

TSAPI \T`S-A-P-I´\ *n*. Acronym for **T**elephony **S**ervices **A**pplication **P**rogramming **I**nterface. The set of standards for the interface between a large telephone system and a computer network server, developed by Novell and AT&T and supported by many telephone equipment manufacturers and software developers. *Compare* TAPI.

TSR \T`S-R´\ *n*. Acronym for **t**erminate-and-**s**tay-**r**esident. A program that remains loaded in memory even when it is not running, so that it can be quickly invoked for a specific task performed while another program is operating. Typically, these programs are used with operating systems that are not multitasking, such as MS-DOS. *See also* hot key.

.tt \dot`T-T´\ *n*. On the Internet, the major geographic domain specifying that an address is located in Trinidad and Tobago.

TTFN \T`T-F-N´\ *n*. Acronym for "**T**a **t**a **f**or **n**ow." An expression sometimes used in Internet discussion groups, such as Internet Relay Chat (IRC), to signal a participant's temporary departure from the group. *See also* IRC.

TTL \T`T-L´\ *n*. *See* Time to Live, transistor-transistor logic.

TTY \T`T-Y´\ *n*. Acronym for **t**ele**ty**pewriter. A device for low-speed communications over a telephone line, consisting of a keyboard that sends a character code for each keystroke and a printer that prints characters as their codes are received. The simplest video display interface behaves like a TTY. *See also* KSR terminal, teletype mode.

tunnel \tun´əl\ *vb.* To encapsulate or wrap a packet or a message from one protocol in the packet for another. The wrapped packet is then transmitted over a network via the protocol of the wrapper. This method of packet transmission is used to avoid protocol restrictions. *See also* communications protocol, packet (definition 2).

tuple \tup´l\ *n.* In a database table (relation), a set of related values, one for each attribute (column). A tuple is stored as a row in a relational database management system. It is the analog of a record in a nonrelational file. *See also* relation.

Turing machine \tōōr´ēng mə-shēn`, tər´ēng\ *n.* **1.** A theoretical model created by British mathematician Alan Turing in 1936 that is considered the prototype for digital computers. Described in a paper ("On Computable Numbers with an Application to the Entscheidungsproblem") published in the *Proceedings of the London Mathematical Society,* the Turing machine was a logical device that could scan one square at a time (either blank or containing a symbol) on a paper tape. Depending on the symbol read from a particular square, the machine would change its status and/or move the tape backward or forward to erase a symbol or to print a new one. *See also* status. **2.** A computer that can successfully mimic human intelligence in the Turing test.

Turing test \tōōr´ēng test`, tər´ēng\ *n.* A test of machine intelligence proposed by Alan Turing, British mathematician and developer of the Turing machine. In the Turing test, also known as the Imitation Game, a person uses any series of questions to interrogate two unseen respondents, a human and a computer, to try to determine which is the computer.

turnaround time \tur´nər-ound tīm`\ *n.* **1.** The elapsed time between submission and completion of a job. **2.** In communications, the time required to reverse the direction of transmission in half-duplex communication mode. *See also* half-duplex transmission.

turnkey system \turn´kē si`stəm\ *n.* A finished system, complete with all necessary hardware and documentation and with software installed and ready to be used.

turnpike effect \turn´pīk ə-fekt`\ *n.* The communications equivalent of gridlock; a reference to bottlenecks caused by heavy traffic over a communications system or network.

turtle \tur´tl\ *n.* A small on-screen shape, usually a triangle or a turtle shape, that acts as a drawing tool in graphics. A turtle is a friendly, easily manipulated tool designed for children learning to use computers. It takes its name from a mechanical, dome-shaped "turtle" that was developed for the Logo language and moved about the floor in response to Logo commands, raising and lowering a pen to draw lines.

turtle graphics \tur´tl graf`iks\ *n.* A simple graphics environment, present in Logo and other languages, in which a turtle is manipulated by simple commands. Some versions display the turtle and its track on screen; others use electromechanical turtles that write on paper.

tutorial \tōō-tōr´ē-əl\ *n.* A teaching aid designed to help people learn to use a product or procedure. In computer applications, a tutorial might be presented in either a book or a manual or as an interactive disk-based series of lessons provided with the program package.

.tv \dot`T-V´\ *n.* On the Internet, the major geographic domain specifying that an address is located in Tuvalu.

.tw \dot`T-W´\ *n.* On the Internet, the major geographic domain specifying that an address is located in Taiwan.

TWAIN \twān, T`W-A-I-N´\ *n.* Acronym for **t**echnology **w**ithout **an i**nteresting **n**ame. The de facto standard interface between software applications and image-capturing devices such as scanners. Nearly all scanners contain a TWAIN driver, but only TWAIN-compatible software can use the technology. *See also* scanner.

tweak \twēk\ *vb.* To make final small changes to improve hardware or software performance; to fine-tune a nearly complete product.

tween \twēn\ *vb.* In a graphics program, to calculate intermediary shapes during the metamorphosis of one shape into another.

twinaxial \twin`aks´ē-əl\ *adj.* Having two coaxial cables contained in a single insulated jacket. *See also* coaxial cable.

twisted-pair cable \twi´stəd-pâr kā`bl\ *n.* A cable made of two separately insulated strands of wire twisted together. It is used to reduce signal interference introduced by a strong radio source such as a nearby cable. One of the wires in the pair carries the sensitive signal, and the other wire is grounded.

two-dimensional \too͞o`də-men´shə-nəl\ *adj.* Existing in reference to two measures, such as height and width—for example, a two-dimensional model drawn with reference to an *x*-axis and a *y*-axis, or a two-dimensional array of numbers placed in rows and columns. *See also* Cartesian coordinates.

two-dimensional array \too͞o`də-men`shə-nəl ər-ā´\ *n.* An ordered arrangement of information in which the location of any item is described by two numbers (integers) identifying its position in a particular row and column of a matrix.

two-dimensional model \too͞o`di-men´shən-əl mod`əl, too͞o`dī-men´shən-əl\ *n.* A computer simulation of a physical object in which length and width are real attributes but depth is not; a model with *x*- and *y*-axes. *Compare* three-dimensional model.

two-out-of-five code \too͞o-out-əv-fīv´ kōd`\ *n.* An error-sensitive code for data transmission that stores each of the ten decimal digits (0 through 9) as a set of five binary digits: either two of the digits are 1s and the other three digits are 0s or two of the digits are 0s and the other three digits are 1s.

two's complement \too͞oz´ kom`plə-mənt\ *n.* A number in the base-2 system (binary system) that is the true complement of another number. A two's complement is usually derived by reversing the digits in a binary number (changing 1s to 0s and 0s to 1s) and adding 1 to the result. When two's complements are used to represent negative numbers, the most significant (leftmost) digit is always 1. *See also* complement.

two-tier client/server \too͞o`tēr klī`ənt-sər´vər\ *n.* A client/server architecture in which software systems are structured into two tiers or layers: the user interface/business logic layer and the database layer. Fourth-generation languages (4GL) have helped to popularize the two-tier client/server architecture. *Also called* 4GL architecture. *See also* 4GL, client/server architecture. *Compare* three-tier client/server.

TXD \T`X-D´\ *n.* Short for Transmit (**tx**) **D**ata. A line used to carry transmitted data from one device to another, as from computer to modem; in RS-232-C connections, pin 2. *See also* RS-232-C standard. *Compare* RXD.

.txt \dot-T`X-T´\ *n.* A file extension that identifies ASCII text files. In most cases, a document with a .txt extension does not include any formatting commands, so it is readable in any text editor or word processing program. *See also* ASCII.

Tymnet \tīm´net\ *n.* A public data network available in over 100 countries, with links to some online services and Internet service providers.

type[1] \tīp\ *n.* **1.** In programming, the nature of a variable—for example, integer, real number, text character, or floating-point number. Data types in programs are declared by the programmer and determine the range of values a variable can take as well as the operations that can be performed on it. *See also* data type. **2.** In printing, the characters that make up printed text, the design of a set of characters (typeface), or, more loosely, the complete set of characters in a given size and style (font). *See also* font, typeface.

type[2] \tīp\ *vb.* To enter information by means of the keyboard.

type-ahead buffer \tīp-ə-hed´ buf`ər\ *n.* *See* keyboard buffer.

type-ahead capability \tīp-ə-hed´ kā-pə-bil´ə-tē\ *n.* The ability of a computer program to gather incoming keystrokes in a temporary memory reservoir (buffer) before displaying them on the screen. This capability ensures that keystrokes are not lost if they are typed faster than the program can display them.

type ball \tīp´ bäl\ *n.* A small ball mounted on the print head of a printer or a typewriter (for example, the IBM Selectric) that bears all the characters in the character set on its surface. The ball rotates to align the correct character with the paper and with an inked or carbon ribbon before striking against the paper. See the illustration.

type checking \tīp´ chek`ēng\ *n.* The process performed by a compiler or interpreter to make

Type ball.

sure that when a variable is used, it is treated as having the same data type as it was declared to have. *See also* compiler (definition 2), data type, interpreter.

type declaration \tīp´ de`klər-ā-shən\ *n*. A declaration in a program that specifies the characteristics of a new data type, usually by combining more primitive existing data types.

typeface \tīp´fās\ *n*. A specific, named design of a set of printed characters, such as Helvetica Bold Oblique, that has a specified obliqueness (degree of slant) and stroke weight (thickness of line). A typeface is not the same as a *font,* which is a specific size of a specific typeface, such as 12-point Helvetica Bold Oblique. Nor is a typeface the same as a *typeface family,* which is a group of related typefaces, such as the Helvetica family including Helvetica, Helvetica Bold, Helvetica Oblique, and Helvetica Bold Oblique. *See also* font.

type font \tīp´font\ *n. See* font.

typematic \tīp-mat´ik\ *adj*. The keyboard feature that repeats a keystroke when a key is held down longer than usual. *Also called* auto-key, auto-repeat. *See also* repeat key, RepeatKeys.

typeover mode \tīp´ō-vər mōd`\ *n. See* overwrite mode.

type size \tīp´ sīz\ *n*. The size of printed characters, usually measured in points (a point is approximately $1/72$ inch). *See also* point[1] (definition 1).

type style \tīp´ stīl\ *n*. **1.** The obliqueness, or degree of slant, of a typeface. **2.** Loosely, the overall design of a typeface or a typeface family. **3.** One of the variant forms of a type character, including roman, bold, italic, and bold italic.

typography \to-po´grə-fē\ *n*. **1.** The art of font design and typesetting. *See also* computer typesetting, font. **2.** The conversion of unformatted text into camera-ready type, suitable for printing. *See also* camera-ready.

.tz \dot`T-Z´\ *n*. On the Internet, the major geographic domain specifying that an address is located in Tanzania.

u \mī´krō\ *prefix* A letter sometimes substituted for the Greek letter μ (mu), meaning micro, used as a prefix in measurements denoting one millionth, or 10^{-6}. *See also* micro- (definition 2).

.ua \dot`U-A´\ *n.* On the Internet, the major geographic domain specifying that an address is located in Ukraine.

UA \U-A´\ *n. See* user agent.

UART \U´ärt\ *n.* Acronym for **u**niversal **a**synchronous **r**eceiver-**t**ransmitter. A module, usually composed of a single integrated circuit, that contains both the receiving and transmitting circuits required for asynchronous serial communication. A UART is the most common type of circuit used in personal computer modems. *Compare* USRT.

UCSD p-System \U-C-S-D` P´si`stəm\ *n.* An operating system and development environment that was developed by Kenneth Bowles at the University of California at San Diego. The system is based on a simulated, 16-bit, stack-oriented "pseudomachine." The development environment includes a text editor and compilers for several languages, such as FORTRAN and Pascal. Programs written for a p-system are more portable than programs compiled to machine language. *See also* bytecode, pseudomachine, p-system, virtual machine.

UDP \U`D-P´\ *n.* Acronym for **U**ser **D**atagram **P**rotocol. The connectionless protocol within TCP/IP that corresponds to the transport layer in the ISO/OSI model. UDP converts data messages generated by an application into packets to be sent via IP but does not verify that messages have been delivered correctly. Therefore, UDP is more efficient than TCP, so it is used for various purposes, including SNMP; the reliability depends on the application that generates the message. *See also* communications protocol, ISO/OSI model, packet, SNMP, TCP/IP. *Compare* IP, TCP.

UDT \U`D-T´\ *n.* Acronym for **u**niform **d**ata **t**ransfer. The service used in the OLE extensions to

Microsoft Windows that allows two applications to exchange data without either program knowing the internal structure of the other.

.ug \dot`U-G´\ *n.* On the Internet, the major geographic domain specifying that an address is located in Uganda.

UI \U-I´\ *n. See* user interface.

.uk \dot`U-K´\ *n.* On the Internet, the major geographic domain specifying that an address is located in the United Kingdom.

UKnet \U-K´net`\ *n.* **1.** The University of Kentucky's campus network. **2.** In the United Kingdom, an Internet service provider (ISP) based at the University of Kent. *See also* ISP.

ULSI \U`L-S-I´\ *n. See* ultra-large-scale integration.

Ultra DMA/33 \ul`trə D-M-A` thər-tē-thrē´\ *n.* A recently developed data transfer protocol based on direct memory access. Ultra DMA/33 improves ATA/IDE performance, doubles burst transfer rates to 33 megabytes per second, and increases data transfer integrity. *See also* ATA, direct memory access, IDE (definition 1).

ultrafiche \ul´trə-fēsh`\ *n.* Microfiche with very high density. The image in ultrafiche is reduced at least 90 times from its original size. *See also* microfiche.

ultra-large-scale integration \ul`trə-lärj`skāl intə-grā´shən\ *n.* The highest currently possible density at which components (transistors and other elements) are packed onto an integrated circuit. "Ultra-large-scale" is not precisely defined but is generally considered to apply to any integrated circuit that contains more than 100,000 components. *Acronym:* ULSI (U`L-S-I´). *See also* integrated circuit. *Compare* large-scale integration, medium-scale integration, small-scale integration, super-large-scale integration, very-large-scale integration.

ultralight computer \ul`trə-līt kəm-pyoo´tər\ *n. See* portable computer.

UltraSCSI \ul´trə-skuz`ē, ul`trə-S-C-S-I´\ *n.* An extension of the SCSI-2 standard that doubles the transfer speed of Fast-SCSI to allow a transfer rate of 20 megabytes per second (MBps) on an 8-bit connection and 40 MBps on a 16-bit connection. *See also* SCSI, SCSI-2.

Ultra Wide SCSI \ul`trə wīd skuz´ē, S`C-S-I´\ *n.* *See* UltraSCSI.

UMA \U`M-A´\ *n.* Acronym for **u**pper **m**emory **a**rea. The portion of DOS memory between the first 640K and 1 megabyte. *Compare* high memory area.

UMB \U`M-B´\ *n.* Acronym for **u**pper **m**emory **b**lock. A block of memory in the UMA (upper memory area) that can be used for device drivers or TSRs. A UMB is allocated and managed by special memory manager programs such as EMM386.EXE. *See also* device driver, TSR, UMA.

unary \yoo´nər-ē\ *adj.* Of, pertaining to, or characteristic of a mathematical operation with a single operand (object); monadic. *Compare* dyadic.

unary operator \yoo`nər-ē op´ər-ā-tər\ *n.* An operator that takes only one operand—for example, unary minus (as in −2.5). *See also* operator (definition 1). *Compare* binary operator.

unbuffered \un`buf´ərd\ *adj.* Of, pertaining to, or characteristic of something that does not store data characters in memory but instead processes them as they are received. *See also* buffer[2].

unbundle \un`bun´dl\ *vb.* To separate the items of a composite sales package; for example, to sell components of a software package separately rather than as a package. *Compare* bundle.

unbundled \un-bun´dld\ *adj.* Not included as part of a complete hardware/software package; the term particularly applies to a product that was previously bundled, as opposed to one that has always been sold separately.

UNC \U`N-C´\ *n.* *See* Uniform Naming Convention.

uncompress \un`kəm-pres´\ *vb.* To restore the contents of a compressed file to its original form. *Also called* decompress. *Compare* compress[2].

unconditional branch \un-kən-dish´ə-nəl branch´\ *n.* A transfer of execution to another line of code in a program without a check for some condition being true or false. The transfer always takes place whenever such an instruction is encountered. *See*

also branch (definition 2). *Compare* conditional branch.

undelete[1] \un`də-lēt´\ *n.* The act of restoring deleted information. An undelete is comparable to (and usually included as part of) an "undo" command; it is more restricted, however, in that *undo* reverses any previous act, but *undelete* reverses only a deletion. *Undelete* generally refers only to excised text or deleted files. *See also* undo.

undelete[2] \un`də-lēt´\ *vb.* **1.** To restore deleted information, usually the last item deleted. **2.** In file storage, to restore a file's storage information so that a deleted file becomes available for access again. *Also called* unerase. *See also* file recovery.

undeliverable \un`də-liv´ər-ə-bl\ *adj.* Not able to be delivered to an intended recipient. If an e-mail message is undeliverable, it is returned to the sender with information added by the mail server explaining the problem; for example, the e-mail address may be incorrect, or the recipient's mailbox may be full.

undercolor separation \un`dər-kəl-ər sep-ər-ā´-shən\ *n.* In the CMYK color model, the process of converting equal quantities of cyan, magenta, and yellow to equivalent gray levels, which are then printed in black ink. This produces grays that are clearer and sharper than those produced by mixing colored inks. *See also* CMY, CMYK, color model.

underflow \un`dər-flō´\ *n.* A condition in which a mathematical calculation produces a result too near to zero to be represented by the range of binary digits available to the computer for holding that value in the specified precision. *See also* precision (definition 2), single-precision.

underline \un´dər-līn´\ *vb.* To format a selection of text so that the text is printed with a line slightly below it.

Undernet \un´dər-net`\ *n.* An international network of Internet Relay Chat (IRC) servers, created in 1992 as an alternative to the larger and more chaotic main IRC network. For information about connecting to Undernet, see http://www.undernet.org. *See also* IRC.

underscore \un´dər-skōr´\ *n.* An underline character often used to emphasize a letter or a word; on nongraphics displays, generally used to indicate italic characters.

undo \un-dōō´\ *vb.* To reverse the last action—for example, to undo a deletion, thus restoring deleted text to a document. Many application programs enable the user both to undo and to redo an action. *See also* undelete[2].

undock \un-dok´\ *vb.* **1.** To detach a laptop or other portable computer from a docking station. *See also* docking station, laptop. **2.** To move a toolbar from the edge of a window so that the toolbar becomes its own free-floating window. *See also* toolbar.

unerase \un-ē-rās´\ *n. See* undelete[2].

unfold \un-fōld´\ *adj. See* inline (definition 1).

unhandled exception \un-han`dld eks-ep´shən\ *n.* An error condition that an application does not internally resolve. When an unhandled exception occurs, the operating system terminates the application that caused the error.

Unibus \yōō´ni-bus`\ *n.* A bus architecture introduced by Digital Equipment Corporation in 1970.

Unicode \yōō´ni-kōd`\ *n.* A 16-bit character encoding standard developed by the Unicode Consortium between 1988 and 1991. By using two bytes to represent each character, Unicode enables almost all of the written languages of the world to be represented using a single character set. (By contrast, 8-bit ASCII is not capable of representing all of the combinations of letters and diacritical marks that are used just with the Roman alphabet.) Approximately 39,000 of the 65,536 possible Unicode character codes have been assigned to date, 21,000 of them being used for Chinese ideographs. The remaining combinations are open for expansion. *Compare* ASCII.

Uniform Data Transfer \yōō`nə-fōrm dā´tə transfər, dat´ə\ *n. See* UDT.

Uniform Naming Convention \yōō`nə-fōrm nā´mēng kən-ven`shən\ *n.* The system of naming files among computers on a network so that a file on a given computer will have the same pathname when accessed from any of the other computers on the network. For example, if the directory *c:\path1\path2\...pathn* on computer *servern* is shared under the name *pathdirs,* a user on another computer would open *\\servern\pathdirs\filename.ext* to access the file *c:\path1\path2\...pathn\filename.ext* on *servern.* *See also* URL, virtual path.

Uniform Resource Citation \yōō`nə-fōrm rē´sōrs sī-tā`shən\ *n.* A description of an object on the World Wide Web, consisting of pairs of attributes and their values, such as the Uniform Resource Identifiers` (URIs) of associated resources, author names, publisher names, dates, and prices. *Acronym:* URC (U`R-C´).

Uniform Resource Identifier \yōō`nə-fōrm rē´sōrs ī-den`tə-fī`ər\ *n.* A character string used to identify a resource (such as a file) from anywhere on the Internet by type and location. The set of Uniform Resource Identifiers includes Uniform Resource Names (URNs) and Uniform Resource Locators (URLs). *Acronym:* URI (U`R-I´). *See also* relative URL, Uniform Resource Name, URL.

Uniform Resource Locator \yōō`nə-fōrm rē´sōrs lō`kā-tər\ *n. See* URL.

Uniform Resource Name \yōō`nə-fōrm rē´sōrs nām`\ *n.* A scheme for uniquely identifying resources that may be available on the Internet by name, without regard to where they are located. The specifications for the format of Uniform Resource Names are still under development by the Internet Engineering Task Force (IETF). They include all Uniform Resource Identifiers (URIs) having the schemes urn:, fpi:, and path:; that is, those that are not Uniform Resource Locators (URLs). *Acronym:* URN (U`R-N´). *See also* IETF, Uniform Resource Identifier, URL.

UniForum \yōō´ni-fōr`um\ *n.* **1.** The International Association of Open System Professionals, an organization of UNIX users and administrators. **2.** A series of UNIX trade shows sponsored by UniForum and managed by Softbank COMDEX, Inc. *See also* COMDEX.

uninstall \un`in-stäl´\ *vb.* To remove software completely from a system, including the elimination of files and components residing in system locations such as the Registry in Windows 95 or Windows NT. Some applications have built-in uninstall utilities, and in other cases a separate uninstall program can be used. *Also called* deinstall.

uninterruptible power supply \un`in-tər-up`-tə-bl pou´ər su-plī`\ *n. See* UPS.

union \yōōn´yən\ *n.* **1.** In set theory, the smallest combination of two sets that contains all elements of both sets. **2.** In logic, an inclusive OR operation.

That is, the result, C, of any union of A and B is true (1) except when A and B are both false (0), as shown in the following truth table:

A	OR	B	=	C
1		1		1
1		0		1
0		1		1
0		0		0

3. In programming, a structure that can be used to store different types of variables (such as integer, character, or Boolean). **4.** In database management, a relational operator. Given two relations (tables), A and B, that are union-compatible (contain the same number of fields, with corresponding fields containing the same types of values), A UNION B builds a new relation containing those tuples (records) that appear either in A or B or in both. *Compare* difference, intersect.

union-compatible \yo͞on´yən-kəm-pat`i-bl\ *adj.* In database management, of, pertaining to, or characteristic of two relations (tables) that are of the same order (have the same number of attributes) and whose corresponding attributes are based on the same domain (the set of acceptable values).

unipolar \yo͞on`i-pō´lər\ *adj.* Having one state. In electronics, a unipolar device or signal is one in which the same voltage polarity (positive or negative) is used to represent binary states—on/off or true/false. *Compare* bipolar.

United States of America Standards Institute \yo͞o-nī`təd stāts` əv ə-mâr`i-kə stan´dərdz in`stə-to͞ot\ *n.* The former name of the American National Standards Institute. *See* ANSI.

unit position \yo͞o´nit pə-zish`ən\ *n.* The "one's place" in a multiple-digit number—for example, the 3 in the number 473.

UNIVAC I \yo͞o`nə-vak wən`\ *n.* Short for **Univer**sal **A**utomatic **C**alculator **I**. The first commercially available electronic computer, designed by J. Presper Eckert and John Mauchly, also the inventors of ENIAC (generally considered the first fully electronic computer). UNIVAC I was the first computer to handle both numeric and textual information.

universal asynchronous receiver-transmitter \yo͞o-ni-vər`səl ā-sin`krə-nəs rə-sē`vər-tranz´mit-ər\ *n.* See UART.

Universal Product Code \yo͞o`nə-vər-səl prod´-ukt kōd`\ *n. See* UPC.

universal serial bus \yo͞o-nə-vər`səl sēr`ē-əl bus`\ *n. See* USB.

Universal Server \yo͞o`nə-vər-səl sər´vər\ *n.* **1.** Software from Oracle Corporation that supplies information from its database in a variety of forms, such as text, sound, and video, in response to HTTP requests. **2.** Database software from Informix that works with snap-in software modules to handle user needs for specific data types and ways of processing.

universal synchronous receiver-transmitter \yo͞o-ni-vər`səl sin`krə-nəs rə-sē`vər-tranz´mit-ər\ *n. See* USRT.

Universal Time Coordinate \yo͞o-nə-vər`səl tīm´ kō-ōr`də-nət\ *n.* For all practical purposes, the same as Greenwich Mean Time, which is used for the synchronization of computers on the Internet. *Acronym:* UTC (U`T-C´). *Also called* coordinated universal time format.

UNIX \yo͞o´niks\ *n.* A multiuser, multitasking operating system originally developed by Ken Thompson and Dennis Ritchie at AT&T Bell Laboratories in 1969 for use on minicomputers. UNIX is considered a powerful operating system that, because it is written in the C language, is more portable—that is, less machine-specific—than other operating systems. UNIX is available in several related forms, including AIX (a version of UNIX adapted by IBM to run on RISC-based workstations), A/UX (a graphical version for the Apple Macintosh), and Mach (a rewritten but essentially UNIX-compatible operating system for the NeXT computer). *See also* BSD UNIX, GNU, Linux.

UNIX shell account \yo͞o´niks shel´ ə-kount`\ *n.* A shell account providing command-line access to a UNIX system. *See also* shell account.

UNIX shell scripts \yo͞o´niks shel´ skripts\ *n.* Sequences of UNIX commands stored as files that can be run as programs. In MS-DOS, batch (.bat) files provide similar capabilities. *See also* batch file, shell[1], shell script.

UNIX-to-UNIX Copy \yo͞o`niks-tə-yo͞o´niks kop`ē\ *n.* See UUCP.

UNIX wizard \yo͞o´niks wiz`ərd\ *n.* A particularly expert and helpful UNIX programmer. Some companies actually use this phrase as a job title. The newsgroup comp.unix.wizards provides answers to many user questions.

unknown host \un`nōn hōst´\ *n.* A response to a request for a connection to a server that indicates that the network is unable to find the specified address. *See also* server (definition 1).

unknown recipients \un`nōn rə-sip´ē-ənts\ *n.* A response to an e-mail message that indicates that the mail server is unable to identify one or more of the destination addresses.

unload \un-lōd´\ *vb.* **1.** To remove a storage medium, such as a tape or disk, from its drive. **2.** To remove software from system memory. *See also* memory.

unmoderated \un`mod´ər-ā-təd\ *adj.* Of, pertaining to, or characteristic of a newsgroup or mailing list in which all articles or messages received by the server are automatically available or distributed to all subscribers. *Compare* moderated.

unmount \un-mount´\ *vb.* To remove a disk or tape from active use. *Compare* mount.

unpack \un-pak´\ *vb.* To restore packed data to its original format. *Compare* pack.

unpopulated board \un-po`pyə-lā-təd bōrd´\ *n.* A circuit board whose sockets are empty. *Compare* fully populated board.

unread \un-red´\ *adj.* **1.** Of, pertaining to, or being an article in a newsgroup that a user has not yet received. Newsreader client programs distinguish between "read" and "unread" articles for each user and download only unread articles from the server. **2.** Of, pertaining to, or being an e-mail message that a user has received but has not yet opened in an e-mail program.

unrecoverable error \un-rə-kə`vər-ə-bl âr´ər\ *n.* A fatal error—one that a program is unable to recover from without the use of external recovery techniques. *Compare* recoverable error.

unroll \un-rōl´\ *adj. See* inline (definition 1).

unset \un-set´\ *vb.* To make the value of a bit position equal to 0 (zero). *Compare* set[1] (definition 1).

unshielded cable \un`shēl-dəd kā´bl\. *n.* Cable that is not surrounded with a metal shield. If the wires in an unshielded cable are not at least twisted around each other in pairs, the signals they carry have no protection from interference by external electromagnetic fields. Consequently, unshielded cable should be used only over very

short distances. *Compare* coaxial cable, ribbon cable, twisted-pair cable, UTP.

unshielded twisted pair \un´shēl-dəd   twis`təd pâr\ *n. See* UTP.

unsubscribe \un`sub-skrīb´\ *vb.* **1.** In a newsreader client program, to remove a newsgroup from the list of newsgroups to which one subscribes. *See also* newsgroup. **2.** To remove a recipient from a mailing list. *See also* mailing list.

untar[1] \un-tär´\ *n.* A utility, available for systems in addition to UNIX, for separating the individual files out of an archive assembled using the UNIX *tar* program. *Compare* tar[1].

untar[2] \un-tär´\ *vb.* To separate the individual files out of an archive assembled with the UNIX *tar* program. *Compare* tar[2].

unzip \un-zip´\ *vb.* To uncompress an archive file that has been compressed by a program such as compress, gzip, or PKZIP.

up \up\ *adj.* Functioning and available for use; used in describing computers, printers, communications lines on networks, and other such hardware.

UPC \U`P-C´\ *n.* Acronym for **U**niversal **P**roduct **C**ode. A system of numbering commercial products using bar codes. A UPC consists of 12 digits: a number system character, a five-digit number assigned to the manufacturer, a five-digit product code assigned by the manufacturer, and a modulo 10 check digit. *See also* bar code.

update[1] \up´dāt, up-dāt´\ *n.* A new release of an existing software product. A software update usually adds relatively minor new features to a product or corrects errors (bugs) found after the program was released. Updates are generally indicated by small changes in software version numbers, such as *4.0b* from *4.0*. *See also* version number. *Compare* release[1].

update[2] \up´dāt, up-dāt´\ *vb.* To change a system or a data file to make it more current.

upgrade[1] \up´grād, up-grād´\ *n.* The new or enhanced version of a product.

upgrade[2] \up´grād, up-grād´\ *vb.* To change to a newer, usually more powerful or sophisticated version.

uplink\up´lēnk\ *n.* The transmission link from an earth station to a communications satellite.

upload[1] \up´lōd\ *n.* **1.** In communications, the process of transferring a copy of a file from a local computer to a remote computer by means of a modem or network. **2.** The copy of the file that is being or has been transferred.

upload[2] \up´lōd\ *vb.* To transfer a copy of a file from a local computer to a remote computer. *Compare* download.

uppercase \up´ər-kās`\ *adj.* Of, pertaining to, or characterized by capital letters. *Compare* lowercase.

upper memory area \up`ər mem´ər-ē âr`ē-ə\ *n.* *See* UMA.

upper memory block \up`ər mem´ər-ē blok`\ *n.* *See* UMB.

UPS \U`P-S`\ *n.* Acronym for **u**ninterruptible **p**ower **s**upply. A device, connected between a computer (or other electronic equipment) and a power source (usually an outlet receptacle), that ensures that electrical flow to the computer is not interrupted because of a blackout and, in most cases, protects the computer against potentially damaging events, such as power surges and brownouts. All UPS units are equipped with a battery and a loss-of-power sensor; if the sensor detects a loss of power, it switches over to the battery so that the user has time to save his or her work and shut off the computer. *See also* blackout, brownout.

uptime \up´tīm\ *n.* The amount or percentage of time a computer system or associated hardware is functioning and available for use. *Compare* downtime.

upward-compatible \up`wərd-kəm-pat´ə-bl\ *adj.* Of, pertaining to, or characteristic of a computer product, especially software, designed to perform adequately with other products that are expected to become widely used in the foreseeable future. The use of standards and conventions makes upward compatibility easier to achieve.

urban legend \ur`bən lej´ənd\ *n.* A widely distributed story that remains in circulation in spite of the fact that it is not true. Many urban legends have been floating around the Internet and other online services for years, including the request for cards for the sick boy in England (he's long since recovered and grown up), the cookie or cake recipe that cost $250 (it's a myth), and the Good Times or Penpal Greetings virus, which will infect your computer when you read an e-mail message (it does not exist). *See also* Good Times virus.

URC \U`R-C`\ *n.* *See* Uniform Resource Citation.

URI \U`R-I`\ *n.* *See* Uniform Resource Identifier.

URL \U`R-L´, ərl\ *n.* Acronym for **U**niform **Re**source **L**ocator. An address for a resource on the Internet. URLs are used by Web browsers to locate Internet resources. A URL specifies the protocol to be used in accessing the resource (such as http: for a World Wide Web page or ftp: for an FTP site), the name of the server on which the resource resides (such as //www.whitehouse.gov), and, optionally, the path to a resource (such as an HTML document or a file on that server). *See also* FTP[1] (definition 1), HTML, HTTP, path (definition 1), server (definition 2), virtual path (definition 1), Web browser.

URN \U`R-N`\ *n.* *See* Uniform Resource Name.

.us \dot`U-S`\ *n.* On the Internet, the major geographic domain specifying that an address is located in the United States. Because the United States was the only possible location in the older ARPANET naming system, the United States can be regarded as a default location for domain name addresses ending in .com, .gov, .edu, .org, .mil, and .net. *See also* ARPANET, .com, domain name, .edu, .gov, .mil, .net, .org.

usable \yōō´zə-bl`\ *adj.* Of, pertaining to, or characteristic of the ease and adaptability with which a product can be applied to the performance of the work for which it is designed. A high degree of usability implies ease of learning, flexibility, freedom from bugs, and good design that does not involve unnecessarily complicated procedures.

USB \U`S-B`\ *n.* Acronym for **u**niversal **s**erial **b**us. A serial bus with a bandwidth of 1.5 megabits per second (Mbps) for connecting peripherals to a microcomputer. USB can connect up to 127 peripherals, such as external CD-ROM drives, printers, modems, mice, and keyboards, to the system through a single, general-purpose port. This is accomplished by daisy chaining peripherals together. USB supports hot plugging and multiple data streams. Developed by Intel, USB competes with DEC's ACCESS.bus for lower-speed applications. *See also* bus, daisy chain, hot plugging, input/output port, peripheral. *Compare* ACCESS.bus.

U.S. Department of Defense \U`S də-pärt`mənt əv də-fens´\ *n.* The military branch of the United

States government. The Department of Defense developed ARPANET, the origin of today's Internet and MILNET, through its Advanced Research Projects Agency. *See also* ARPANET, Internet, MILNET.

Usenet or **UseNet** or **USENET** \yooz´net\ *n.* A worldwide network of UNIX systems that has a decentralized administration and is used as a bulletin board system by special-interest discussion groups. Usenet, which is considered part of the Internet (although Usenet predates it), is composed of thousands of newsgroups, each devoted to a particular topic. Users can post messages and read messages from others in these newsgroups in a manner similar to users on dial-in BBSs. Usenet was originally implemented using UUCP (UNIX-to-UNIX Copy) software and telephone connections; that method remains important, although more modern methods, such as NNTP and network connections, are more commonly used. *See also* BBS (definition 1), newsgroup, newsreader, NNTP, UUCP.

Usenet User List \yooz´net yoo´zər list`\ *n.* A list maintained by the Massachusetts Institute of Technology that contains the name and e-mail address of everyone who has posted to the Usenet. *See also* Usenet.

user account \yoo´zər ə-kount`\ *n.* On a secure or multiuser computer system, an established means for an individual to gain access to the system and its resources. Usually created by the system's administrator, a user account consists of information about the user, such as password, rights, and permissions. *See also* group[1], logon, user profile.

user agent \yoo´zər ā`jənt\ *n.* In the terminology established by the ISO/OSI model for LANs, a program that helps a client connect with a server. *Acronym:* UA (U-A´). *See also* agent (definition 3), ISO/OSI model, LAN.

User Datagram Protocol \yoo`zər dā´tə-gram prō`-tə-kol, dat´ə-gram\ *n. See* UDP.

user-defined data type \yoo`zər-də-fīnd dā´tə tīp, dat´ə\ *n.* A data type defined in a program. User-defined data types are usually combinations of data types defined by the programming language being used and are often used to create data structures. *See also* data structure, data type.

user-defined function key \yoo`zər-də-fīnd funk´shən kē\ *n. See* keyboard enhancer, programmable function key.

user-friendly \yoo`zər-frend´lē\ *adj.* Easy to learn and easy to use.

user group \yoo´zər groop`\ *n.* A group of people drawn together by interest in the same computer system or software. User groups, some of which are large and influential organizations, provide support for newcomers and a forum where members can exchange ideas and information.

user interface \yoo´zər in`tər-fās\ *n.* The portion of a program with which a user interacts. Types include command-line interfaces, menu-driven interfaces, and graphical user interfaces. *Acronym:* UI (U-I´).

User Interface Toolbox \yoo`zər in`tər-fās tool´-boks\ *n. See* Toolbox.

username \yoo´zər-nām`\ *n.* The name by which a user is identified to a computer system or network. During the logon process, the user must enter the username and the correct password. If the system or network is connected to the Internet, the username generally corresponds to the leftmost part of the user's e-mail address. *See also* e-mail address, logon.

user name \yoo´zər nām`\ *n.* The name by which a person is known and addressed on a communications network. *See also* alias (definition 2).

user profile \yoo´zər prō´fīl\ *n.* A computer-based record maintained about an authorized user of a multiuser computer system. A user profile is needed for security and other reasons; it can contain such information as the person's access restrictions, mailbox location, type of terminal, and so on. *See also* user account.

user state \yoo´zər stāt`\ *n.* The least privileged of the modes in which a Motorola 680x0 microprocessor can operate. This is the mode in which application programs are run. *See also* 68000. *Compare* supervisor state.

USnail \U`S-snāl´\ *n.* **1.** Slang for the United States Postal Service. USnail, a term used on the Internet, is a reference to how slow the postal service is in comparison to e-mail. **2.** Mail delivered by the United States Postal Service. *See also* snail mail.

/usr \slash-yoo´zər, -U-S-R`\ *n.* A directory in a computer system that contains subdirectories owned or maintained by individual users of the computer system. These subdirectories can contain files and additional subdirectories. Typically, /usr directories are used in UNIX systems and can be found on many FTP sites. *See also* FTP site.

USRT \U`S-R-T´\ *n.* Acronym for **u**niversal **s**ynchronous **r**eceiver-**t**ransmitter. A module, usually composed of a single integrated circuit, that contains both the receiving and transmitting circuits required for synchronous serial communication. *Compare* UART.

UTC \U`T-C´\ *n. See* Universal Time Coordinate.

utility \yo͞o-til´ə-tē\ *n.* A program designed to perform a particular function; the term usually refers to software that solves narrowly focused problems or those related to computer system management. *See also* application.

utility program \yo͞o-til´ə-tē pro`gram\ *n.* A program designed to perform maintenance work on the system or on system components (e.g., a storage backup program, disk and file recovery program, or resource editor).

UTP \U`T-P´\ *n.* Acronym for **u**nshielded **t**wisted **p**air. A cable containing one or more twisted pairs of wires without additional shielding. UTP is more flexible and takes up less space than shielded twisted-pair (STP) cable but has less bandwidth. See the illustration. *See also* twisted-pair cable. *Compare* STP.

UTP.

.uu \dot`U-U´\ *n.* The file extension for a binary file that has been translated into ASCII format

using uuencode. *Also called* .uud. *See also* ASCII, binary file, uuencode. *Compare* .uue.

UUCP \U`U-C-P´\ *n.* Acronym for **U**NIX-to-**U**NIX **Co**py. A set of software programs that facilitate transmission of information between UNIX systems using serial data connections, primarily the public switched telephone network. *See also* uupc.

.uud \dot`U-U-D´\ *n. See* .uu.

uudecode[1] \U-U`dē-kōd´\ *n.* A UNIX program that converts a uuencoded file back into its original binary format. This program (along with uuencode) allows binary data, such as images or executable code, to be disseminated through e-mail or newsgroups. *Compare* uuencode[1].

uudecode[2] \U-U`dē-kōd´\ *vb.* To transform a uuencoded file back into its binary original using the uudecode program. *Compare* uuencode[2].

.uue \dot`U-U-E´\ *n.* The file extension for a file that has been decoded from ASCII format back into binary format using uudecode. *See also* ASCII, binary file, uudecode[1].

uuencode[1] \U-U`en-kōd´\ *n.* A UNIX program that converts a binary file, in which all 8 bits of every byte are significant, into printable 7-bit ASCII characters without loss of information. This program (along with uudecode) allows binary data, such as images or executable code, to be disseminated through e-mail or newsgroups. A file thus encoded is one-third again as long as the original. *Compare* uudecode[1].

uuencode[2] \U-U`en-kōd´\ *vb.* To transform a binary file into printable 7-bit ASCII text using the uuencode program. *Compare* uudecode[2].

uupc \U`U-P-C´\ *n.* The version of UUCP for IBM PCs and PC-compatibles running DOS, Windows, or OS/2. This version is a collection of programs for copying files to, logging in to, and running programs on remote networked computers. *See also* UUCP.

.uy \dot`U-Y´\ *n.* On the Internet, the major geographic domain specifying that an address is located in Uruguay.

.uz \dot`U-Z´\ *n.* On the Internet, the major geographic domain specifying that an address is located in Uzbekistan.

V.120 \V˘-wən-twen´tē\ *n.* An International Telecommunications Union (ITU) standard that governs serial communications over ISDN lines. Data is encapsulated using a protocol similar to the Lightweight Directory Access Protocol (LDAP), and more than one connection may be multiplexed on a communications channel. *See also* communications channel, communications protocol, International Telecommunications Union, ISDN, Lightweight Directory Access Protocol, multiplexing, standard (definition 1).

V20, V30 \V-twən´tē, V-thər´tē\ *n.* NEC microprocessors that were slight improvements on Intel's 8088 and 8086, using the same command sets but different microcode.

V.27ter \V˘twen-tē-sev`ən-T-E-R´, tər\ *n.* The CCITT (now ITU-T) recommendation that specifies the modulation scheme used in Group 3 facsimile for image transfer at 2,400 and 4,800 bits per second (bps). *See also* CCITT V series, fax, International Telecommunications Union.

V.29 \V˘twen-tē-nīn´\ *n.* The CCITT (now ITU-T) recommendation that specifies the modulation scheme used in Group 3 facsimile for image transfer at 9,600 and 7,200 bits per second (bps) over dial-up telephone lines. *See also* CCITT V series, fax, International Telecommunications Union.

V.2x, V.3x, V.4x, V.5x series \V-tōō´X, V-thrē´X, V-fōr´X, V-fīv´X sēr-ēz\ *n.* *See* CCITT V series, International Telecommunications Union.

V.32terbo \V˘thər-tē-tōō-tər´bō\ *n.* A modem protocol developed by AT&T for 19,200-bps modems, with fallback to the speeds supported by the CCITT V.32 standard. This protocol is proprietary to AT&T and was not adopted by CCITT or ITU-T. In the CCITT V series, V.34 takes the place of V.32terbo. *See also* CCITT V series, International Telecommunications Union.

V.54 \V˘fif-tē-fōr´\ *n.* The CCITT (now ITU-T) recommendation that specifies the operation of loop test devices in modems. *See also* CCITT V series, International Telecommunications Union.

V.56bis \V˘fif-tē-siks`B-I-S´, -bis\ *n.* The ITU-T recommendation that defines a network transmission model for evaluating modem performance over two-wire voice-grade connections. *See also* International Telecommunications Union.

V86 mode \V˘ā-tē-siks´\ *n.* *See* virtual real mode.

.va \dot`V-A´\ *n.* On the Internet, the major geographic domain specifying that an address is located in Vatican City.

VAB \V˘A-B´\ *n.* *See* voice answer back.

VAC \V˘A-C´\ *n.* *See* volts alternating current.

vacuum tube \vak´yōōm tōōb`\ *n.* A set of metal electrodes and intervening metal grids, contained in a glass or metal tube from which all gas has been removed. Voltages on the grids control electrical currents between the electrodes. Formerly used for amplification and switching in electronic circuits, vacuum tubes are now used in applications such as cathode-ray tubes and those requiring very high power levels. A vacuum tube is known as a *valve* in Great Britain. See the illustration.

validation suite \val-ə-dā´shən swēt`\ *n.* A set of tests that measures compliance with a standard, especially a standard definition of a programming language. *See also* standard (definition 1).

validity check \və-lid´ə-tē chek`\ *n.* The process of analyzing data to determine whether it conforms to predetermined completeness and consistency parameters.

value \val´yōō\ *n.* **1.** A quantity assigned to an element such as a variable, symbol, or label. **2.** *See* tone (definition 1).

value-added network \val´yōō-ad-əd net´wərk\ *n.* A communications network that offers additional services, such as message routing, resource management, and conversion facilities, for computers communicating at different speeds or using different protocols. *Acronym:* VAN (V˘A-N´).

Vacuum tube.   One of several types of vacuum tube.

value-added reseller \val`yŏŏ-ad-əd rē´sel-ər\ *n.* A company that buys hardware and software and resells it to the public with added services, such as user support. *Acronym:* VAR (V̄`A-R´).

value list \val´yŏŏ list`\ *n.* A list of values used by some application, such as a database, as a search string or as values for a filtered query. *See also* filter (definition 1), query (definition 1), search string.

valve \valv\ *n. See* electron tube.

VAN \V̄`A-N´\ *n. See* value-added network.

.vancouver.ca \dot-van-kŏŏ`vər-dot-C-A´\ *n.* On the Internet, the major geographic domain specifying that a particular address is located in Vancouver, Canada.

vaporware \vā´pər-wār\ *n.* Software that has been announced but not released to customers. The term implies sarcastically that the product exists only in the minds of the marketing department. *Compare* freeware, shareware.

VAR \V̄`A-R´\ *n. See* value-added reseller.

variable \vâr´ē-ə-bl\ *n.* In programming, a named storage location capable of containing data that can be modified during program execution. *See also* data structure, data type, global variable, local variable. *Compare* constant.

variable expression \vâr`ē-ə-bl eks-presh´ən\ *n.* An expression that depends on the value of at least one variable and, hence, must be evaluated during program execution. *See also* run time (definition 1), variable. *Compare* constant expression.

variable-length field \vâr`ē-ə-bl-length fēld´\ *n.* In a record, a field that can vary in length according to how much data it contains. *See also* field (definition 1).

variable-length record \vâr`ē-ə-bl-length rek´-ərd\ *n.* A record that can vary in length because it contains variable-length fields, certain fields only under certain conditions, or both of these. *See also* variable-length field.

.va.us \dot-V-A`dot-U-S´\ *n.* On the Internet, the major geographic domain specifying that an address is located in Virginia, United States.

VAX \vaks, V̄`A-X´\ *n.* Acronym for **v**irtual **a**ddress e**x**tension. A family of 32-bit minicomputers introduced by Digital Equipment Corporation in 1978. The VAX, like the later 68000 microprocessor, has a flat address space and a large instruction set. The VAX was highly favored within the hacker community but has been superseded by microprocessors and RISC workstations. *See also* flat address space, instruction set, microprocessor, minicomputer, RISC.

VBA \V̄`B-A´\ *n. See* Visual Basic for Applications.

VBScript \V-B´skript`\ *n. See* Visual Basic, Scripting Edition.

VBX \V̄`B-X´\ *n.* Short for **V**isual **B**asic custom control. A software module that, when called by a Visual Basic application, produces a control that adds some desired feature to the application. A VBX is a separate executable file, usually written in C, that is dynamically linked to the application at run time and can be used by other applications, including some applications not developed in Visual Basic. Although VBX technology was developed by Microsoft, most VBXs have been written by third-party developers. VBXs are still in use, but the technology has been superseded by OCXs and ActiveX controls. *See also* control (definition 2), Visual Basic. *Compare* ActiveX controls, dynamic-link library, OCX.

.vc \dot`V-C´\ *n.* On the Internet, the major geographic domain specifying that an address is located in Saint Vincent and the Grenadines, Windward Islands, West Indies.

VCACHE \V̄´kash\ *n.* The disk caching software used with Windows 95's VFAT driver. VCACHE uses 32-bit code, runs in protected mode, and automatically allocates space in RAM rather than requiring the user to reserve space for the cache. *See also* cache, driver, protected mode, RAM, VFAT.

VCOMM \V´kom\ *n.* The communications device driver in Windows 95 that provides the interface between Windows-based applications and drivers on one side, and port drivers and modems on the other. *See also* driver.

VCPI \V´C-P-I´\ *n. See* Virtual Control Program Interface.

VCR-style mechanism \V-C-R`-stīl mek´ə-ni-zəm\ *n.* **1.** A user interface for playing movie files that has controls similar to those on a videocassette recorder (VCR). See the illustration. **2.** A type of motorized docking mechanism in which a laptop or notebook computer is physically locked into place by the docking station. The advantage to a VCR-style mechanism is that it provides an electrically consistent, secure bus connection. *See also* docking mechanism, docking station, laptop, portable computer.

VDD \V´D-D´\ *n.* Acronym for **v**irtual **d**isplay **d**evice driver. *See* virtual device driver.

VDL \V´D-L´\ *n.* Acronym for **V**ienna **D**efinition **L**anguage. A metalanguage, containing both a syntactic and a semantic metalanguage, used to define other languages. *See also* metalanguage.

VDM \V´D-M´\ *n. See* video display metafile.

VDT \V´D-T´\ *n.* Acronym for **v**ideo **d**isplay **t**erminal. A terminal that includes a CRT (cathode-ray tube) and keyboard. *See also* CRT.

VDU \V´D-U´\ *n.* Acronym for **v**ideo **d**isplay **u**nit. A computer monitor. *See also* monitor.

.ve \dot`V-E´\ *n.* On the Internet, the major geographic domain specifying that an address is located in Venezuela.

vector \vek´tər\ *n.* **1.** In mathematics and physics, a variable that has both distance and direction. *Compare* scalar. **2.** In computer graphics, a line drawn in a certain direction from a starting point to an endpoint, both of whose locations are identified by the computer using x-y-coordinates on a grid. Vectors are used in the output of some graphics programs instead of groups of dots (on paper) or pixels (on screen). *See also* vector graphics. **3.** In data structures, a one-dimensional array—a set of items arranged in a single column or row. *See also* array, matrix.

vector display \vek´tər dis-plā´\ *n.* A CRT (cathode-ray tube), commonly used in oscilloscopes and DVST (direct view storage tube) displays, that allows the electron beam to be arbitrarily deflected, based on x-y-coordinate signals. For example, to draw a line on a vector display, the video adapter sends signals to the X and Y yokes to move the electron beam over the path of the line; there is no background composed of scan lines, so the line drawn on the screen is not constructed of pixels. *See also* CRT, yoke. *Compare* raster display.

vector font \vek´tər font`\ *n.* A font in which the characters are drawn using arrangements of line segments rather than arrangements of bits. *See also* font. *Compare* bitmapped font.

vector graphics \vek´tər graf´iks\ *n.* Images generated from mathematical descriptions that determine the position, length, and direction in which lines are drawn. Objects are created as collections

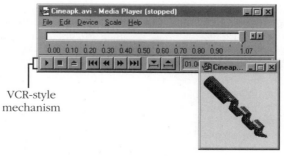

VCR-style
mechanism

VCR-style mechanism.

of lines rather than as patterns of individual dots or pixels. *Compare* raster graphics.

vector table \vek´tər tā`bl\ *n. See* dispatch table.

Venn diagram \ven´ di`ə-gram\ *n.* A type of diagram, used to express the result of operations on sets, in which a rectangle represents the universe and circles inside the rectangle represent sets of objects. Relationships between sets are indicated by the positions of the circles in relation to one another. The Venn diagram is named after John Venn (1834–1923), an English logician at Cambridge University. See the illustration.

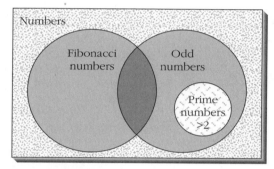

Venn diagram.

verbose \vər-bōs´\ *adj.* Displaying messages as English text rather than as concise (but cryptic) codes.

verify \vâr´ə-fī\ *vb.* To confirm either that a result is correct or that a procedure or sequence of operations has been performed.

Veronica \Vər-on´ə-ka`\ *n.* Acronym for **v**ery **e**asy **r**odent-**o**riented **N**etwide **i**ndex to **c**omputerized **a**rchives. An Internet service developed at the University of Nevada that searches for Gopher archives by keywords. Users can enter Boolean operators, such as AND, OR, or XOR, to help narrow or expand their search. If any matching archives are found, they are listed on a new Gopher menu. *See also* Boolean operator, Gopher. *Compare* Archie, Jughead.

version \vər´zhən\ *n.* A particular issue or release of a hardware product or software title.

version control \vər´zhən kən-trōl`\ *n.* The process of maintaining a database of all the source code and related files in a software development project to keep track of changes made during the project.

version number \vər´zhən num`bər\ *n.* A number assigned by a software developer to identify a particular program at a particular stage, before and after public release. Successive public releases of a program are assigned increasingly higher numbers. Version numbers usually include decimal fractions. Major changes are generally marked by a change in the whole number, whereas for minor changes only the number after the decimal point increases.

verso \vər´sō\ *adj.* The publishing term for a left-hand page, which is always even-numbered. *Compare* recto.

vertical application \vər`tə-kəl a-plə-kā´shən\ *n.* A specialized application designed to meet the unique needs of a particular business or industry—for example, an application to keep track of billing, tips, and inventory in a restaurant.

vertical bandwidth \vər`tə-kəl band´width\ *n.* The rate at which a display screen is refreshed entirely, expressed in hertz (Hz). The vertical bandwidth of display systems ranges from 45 Hz to over 100 Hz. *Also called* vertical scan rate, vertical sync, V-sync.

vertical blanking interval \vər`tə-kəl blan´kēng in`tər-vəl\ *n.* The time required for the electron beam in a raster-scan display to perform a vertical retrace. *See also* blanking, vertical retrace.

vertical recording \vər`tə-kəl rə-kōr´dēng\ *n. See* perpendicular recording.

vertical redundancy check \vər`tə-kəl rə-dun´dən-sē chek`\ *n. See* VRC.

vertical retrace \vər`tə-kəl rē´trās\ *n.* On raster-scan displays, the movement of the electron beam from the lower right corner back to the upper left corner of the screen after the beam has completed a full sweep of the screen. *See also* blanking, vertical blanking interval. *Compare* horizontal retrace.

vertical scan rate \vər`tə-kəl skan´ rāt\ *n. See* vertical bandwidth.

vertical scrolling \vər`tə-kəl skrō´lēng\ *n.* Movement up or down in a displayed document. *See also* scroll bar.

vertical sync \vər`tə-kəl sēnk`\ *n. See* vertical bandwidth.

vertical sync signal \vər`tə-kəl sēnk´ sig-nəl\ *n.* The part of a video signal to a raster display that denotes the end of the last scan line at the bottom of the display.

very-high-level language \vâr`ē-hī´ lev-əl lang´-wəj\ *n. See* 4GL.

very-high-speed integrated circuit \vâr´ē-hī-spēd in`tə-grā-təd sər`kət\ *n.* An integrated circuit that performs operations, usually logic operations, at a very high speed. *Acronym:* VHSIC (V`H-S-I-C´).

Very Large Database \vâr`ē lärj dā´tə-bās\ *n.* A database system containing volumes of data hundreds of gigabytes, or even terabytes, in size. A Very Large Database must often support thousands of users and tables with billions of rows of data, must often be able to operate across several different platforms and operating systems, and must often be able to work with many different software applications. *Acronym:* VLDB (V`L-D-B´). *See also* data warehouse.

Very Large Memory \vâr`ē lärj mem´ər-ē\ *n.* A memory system designed to handle the huge data blocks associated with a Very Large Database. Very Large Memory uses 64-bit RISC technology to allow the use of addressable main memory and file sizes larger than 2 gigabytes (GB) and to cache as much as 14 GB of memory. *Acronym:* VLM (V`L-M´). *See also* RISC, Very Large Database.

very-large-scale integration \vâr`ē-lärj-skāl in`tə-grā´shən\ *n.* A reference to the density with which transistors and other elements are packed in an integrated circuit and to the thinness of the connections between them. Very-large-scale integration is generally considered to encompass the range from 5,000 to 50,000 components. *Acronym:* VLSI (V`L-S-I´). *See also* integrated circuit. *Compare* large-scale integration, medium-scale integration, small-scale integration, super-large-scale integration, ultra-large-scale integration.

Very Long Instruction Word \vâr`ē long in-struk´shən wərd\ *n. See* VLIW.

very-low-frequency electromagnetic radiation \vâr`ē-lō-frē`kwən-sē ə-lek`trō-mag-net`ik rā-dē-ā´shən\ *n. See* VLF radiation.

VESA[1] \vē´sə, V`E-S-A´\ *adj.* Having VL bus expansion slots. *Also called* VLB. *See also* expansion slot, VL bus. *Compare* VESA/EISA, VESA/ISA.

VESA[2] \vē´sə, V`E-S-A`\ *n.* Acronym for **V**ideo **E**lectronics **S**tandards **A**ssociation. An organization of hardware manufacturers and vendors dedicated to drafting and improving standards for video and multimedia devices. Standards developed by VESA include the Display Data Channel (DDC), Display Power Management Signaling (DPMS), and VESA local bus (VL bus). *See also* DDC, DPMS, VL bus.

VESA DDC \vē`sə D-D-C´, V-E-S-A`\ *n. See* DDC.

VESA Display Data Channel \vē`sə dis-plā` dā´tə chan`əl, V-E-S-A`, dat´ə\ *n. See* DDC.

VESA Display Power Management Signaling \vē`sə dis-plā` pou`ər man`əj-mənt sig´nə-lēng, V-E-S-A`\ *n. See* DPMS.

VESA/EISA \vē`sə-ē-ī´sə, V-E-S-A`E-I-S-A´\ *adj.* Having both EISA and VL bus expansion slots. *See also* EISA, expansion slot, VESA[2], VL bus. *Compare* VESA[1], VESA/ISA.

VESA/ISA \vē`sə-ī´sə, V-E-S-A`I-S-A´\ *adj.* Having both ISA and VL bus expansion slots. *See also* expansion slot, ISA, VESA[2], VL bus. *Compare* VESA[1], VESA/EISA.

VESA local bus \vē`sə lō`kəl bus´, V`E-S-A`\ *n. See* VL bus.

vesicular film \və-si`kyə-lər film´\ *n.* A coating for optical discs that facilitates erasing and rewriting. The surface is marked by small bumps, which can be flattened and thereby erased, rather than by the pits used in standard CD-ROM discs.

V.everything \V`dot-ev´rē-thēng\ *n.* A marketing term used by some modem manufacturers to describe modems that comply with both the CCITT V.34 standard and the various proprietary protocols that were used before the standard was adopted, such as V.Fast Class. A V.everything modem should be compatible with any other modem that operates at the same speed. *See also* CCITT V series, V.Fast Class.

V.Fast Class \V`dot-fast´ klas\ *n.* A de facto modulation standard for modems implemented by Rockwell International prior to approval of the V.34 protocol, which is the standard. Although both V.Fast Class and V.34 are capable of 28.8-Kbps transmission, V.Fast Class modems cannot communicate with V.34 modems without an upgrade. *Acronym:* V.FC (V`F-C´). *See also* CCITT V series.

VFAT \V`fat, V`F-A-T´\ *n.* Acronym for **V**irtual **F**ile **A**llocation **T**able. The file system driver software used under Windows 95's Installable File System Manager (IFS) for accessing disks. VFAT is compatible with MS-DOS disks but runs more efficiently. VFAT uses 32-bit code, runs in protected mode, uses VCACHE for disk caching, and supports long filenames. *See also* Installable File System Manager, long filenames, protected mode, VCACHE, Windows 95. *Compare* file allocation table.

V.FC \V`F-C´\ *See* V.Fast Class.

.vg \dot`V-G´\ *n.* On the Internet, the major geographic domain specifying that an address is located in the U.S. Virgin Islands.

VGA \V`G-A´\ *n.* Acronym for **V**ideo **G**raphics **A**dapter. A video adapter that duplicates all the video modes of the EGA (Enhanced Graphics Adapter) and adds several more. *See also* video adapter. *Compare* EGA.

VHLL \V`H-L-L´\ *n.* Acronym for **v**ery-**h**igh-**l**evel **l**anguage. *See* 4GL.

VHSIC \V`H-S-I-C´\ *n.* *See* very-high-speed integrated circuit.

.vi \dot`V-I´\ *n.* On the Internet, the major geographic domain specifying that an address is located in the British Virgin Islands.

vi[1] \V-I´\ *n.* Short for **vi**sual. The first full-screen text editor under UNIX. The vi editor offers many powerful but not very intuitive keyboard commands. It is still in use on UNIX systems, despite the existence of other editors such as Emacs. *See also* editor, UNIX.

vi[2] \V-I´\ *vb.* To edit a file using the vi editor. *See also* vi[1].

.victoria.ca \dot-vik-tōr`ē-ə-dot-C-A´\ *n.* On the Internet, the major geographic domain specifying that an address is located in Victoria, Canada.

video \vid´ē-ō`\ *adj.* Of or pertaining to the visual component of a television signal. In relation to computers, *video* refers to the rendering of text and graphics images on displays. *Compare* audio.

video accelerator \vid´ē-ō ak-sel`ər-ā-tər\ *n.* *See* graphics engine (definition 1).

video adapter \vid´ē-ō ə-dap`tər\ *n.* The electronic components that generate the video signal sent through a cable to a video display. The video adapter is usually located on the computer's main system board or on an expansion board, but it is sometimes built into the terminal. *Also called* video adapter board, video board, video card, video controller, video display adapter.

video adapter board \vid`ē-ō ə-dap´tər bōrd`\ *n.* *See* video adapter.

video board \vid`ē-ō bōrd`\ *n.* *See* video adapter.

video buffer \vid`ē-ō buf`ər\ *n.* The memory on a video adapter that is used to store data to be shown on the display. When the video adapter is in a character mode, this data is in the form of ASCII character and attribute codes; when it is in a graphics mode, the data defines each pixel. *See also* bit image, bit plane, color bits, pixel image.

video capture board \vid`ē-ō kap´chur bōrd\ *n.* *See* video capture device.

video capture card \vid`ē-ō kap´chur kärd\ *n.* *See* video capture device.

video capture device \vid`ē-ō kap´chur də-vīs`\ *n.* An expansion board that converts analog video signals to digital form and stores them in a computer's hard disk or other mass storage device. Some video capture devices are also capable of converting digital video to analog video for use in a VCR. *Also called* video capture board, video capture card. *See also* expansion board.

video card \vid`ē-ō kärd`\ *n.* *See* video adapter.

video clip \vid`ē-ō klip`\ *n.* A file that contains a short video item, usually an excerpt from a longer recording.

video compression \vid´ē-ō kəm-presh`ən\ *n.* Reduction of the size of files containing video images stored in digital form. If no compression were done, 24-bit color video at 640×480 pixels would occupy almost one megabyte per frame, or over a gigabyte per minute. Video compression can, however, be lossy without affecting the perceived quality of the image. *See also* lossy compression, Motion JPEG, MPEG.

video conferencing \vid`ē-ō kon´frən-sēng\ *n.* Teleconferencing in which video images are transmitted among the various geographically separated participants in a meeting. Originally done using analog video and satellite links, today video conferencing uses compressed digital images transmitted over wide area networks or the Internet. A 56K communications channel supports freeze-frame video; with a 1.544-Mbps (T1) channel, full-motion video can be used. *See also* 56K, desktop conferencing, freeze-frame video, full-motion video, T1, teleconferencing. *Compare* data conferencing.

video controller \vid´ē-ō kən-trō`lər\ *n. See* video adapter.

video digitizer \vid`ē-ō dij´ə-tī-zər\ *n.* A device used in computer graphics that uses a video camera, rather than a scan head, to capture a video image and then stores it in memory with the aid of a special-purpose circuit board. *See also* digitize. *Compare* digital camera.

videodisc \vid´ē-ō-disk`\ *n.* An optical disc used to store video images and associated audio information. *See also* CD-ROM.

video display \vid´ē-ō dis-plā`\ *n.* Any device capable of displaying, but not printing, text or graphics output from a computer.

video display adapter \vid`ē-ō dis-plā ə-dap´tər\ *n. See* video adapter.

video display board \vid`ē-ō dis-plā´ bōrd\ *n.* A video adapter implementation using an expansion board rather than the computer's main system board. *See also* video adapter.

video display card \vid`ē-ō dis-plā´ kärd\ *n. See* video display board.

video display metafile \vid`ē-ō dis-plā met´ə-fīl\ *n.* A file containing video display information for the transport of images from one system to another. *Acronym:* VDM (V˘D-M´).

video display page \vid`ē-ō dis-plā´ pāj`\ *n.* A portion of a computer's video buffer that holds one complete screen image. If the buffer can hold more than one page, or frame, screen updates can be completed more rapidly because an unseen page can be filled while another is being displayed.

video display terminal \vid`ē-ō dis-plā´ tər`mə-nəl\ *n. See* VDT.

video display tube \vid`ē-ō dis-plā´ tōōb`\ *n. See* CRT.

video display unit \vid`ē-ō dis-plā´ yōō-nit\ *n. See* monitor.

video DRAM \vid`ē-ō D´ram, dram´, D-R-A-M`\ *n. See* video RAM.

video driver \vid´ē-ō drī`vər\ *n.* Software that provides the interface between the video adapter hardware and other programs, including the operating system. The user can access the video driver

to specify the resolution and color-bit depth of images on the monitor during the setup process. *See also* driver, monitor, video adapter.

video editor \vid´ē-ō ed`ə-tər\ *n.* A device or program used to modify the contents of a video file.

Video Electronics Standards Association \vid`ē-ō ə-lek-tron`iks stan`dərdz ə-sō-sē-ā`shən\ *n. See* VESA[2].

video game \vid`ē-ō gām`\ *n. See* computer game.

Video Graphics Adapter \vid`ē-ō graf`iks ə-dap´-tər\ or **Video Graphics Array** \vid`ē-ō graf`iks ər-ā`\ *n. See* VGA.

video graphics board \vid`ē-ō graf`iks bōrd`\ *n.* A video adapter that generates video signals for displaying graphical images on a video screen.

video look-up table \vid`ē-ō lōōk´up tā`bl\ *n. See* color look-up table.

video memory \vid´ē-ō mem`ər-ē\ *n.* Memory from which a display image is created, located in the video adapter or video subsystem. If both the video processor and the central processing unit (CPU) have access to video memory, images are produced by the CPU's modification of video memory. Video circuitry normally has priority over the processor when both attempt to read or write to a video memory location, so updating video memory is often slower than accessing main memory. *See also* video RAM.

video mode \vid´ē-ō mōd`\ *n.* The manner in which a computer's video adapter and monitor display on-screen images. The most common modes are text (character) mode and graphics mode. In text mode, characters include letters, numbers, and some symbols, none of which are "drawn" on screen dot by dot. In contrast, graphics mode produces all screen images, whether text or art, as patterns of pixels (dots) that are drawn one pixel at a time.

videophone \vid´ē-ō-fōn`\ *n.* A device equipped with camera and screen, as well as a microphone and speaker, capable of transmitting and receiving video signals as well as voice over a telephone line. Using conventional telephone lines, a videophone can transmit only freeze-frame video. *See also* freeze-frame video.

video port \vid´ē-ō pōrt`\ *n.* A cable connector on a computer for output of video signals to a monitor.

video RAM \vid´ē-ō ram`, R-A-M´\ *n*. A special type of dynamic RAM (DRAM) used in high-speed video applications. Video RAM uses separate pins for the processor and the video circuitry, providing the video circuitry with a "back door" to the video RAM. The video circuitry can access the video RAM serially (bit by bit), which is more appropriate for transferring pixels to the screen than is the parallel access provided by conventional DRAM. *Acronym:* VRAM (V´ram, V`R-A-M´). *See also* dynamic RAM.

video server \vid´ē-ō sər`vər\ *n*. A server designed to deliver digital video-on-demand and other broadband interactive services to the public over a wide area network.

video signal \vid´ē-ō sig`nəl\ *n*. The signal sent from a video adapter or other video source to a raster display. The signal can include horizontal and vertical synchronization signals, as well as image information. *See also* composite video display, RGB monitor.

video terminal \vid´ē-ō tər`mə-nəl\ *n*. *See* terminal (definition 1).

videotex \vid´ē-ō-teks`\ *n*. An interactive information retrieval service designed to be accessed by subscribers over telephone lines. Information can be displayed on a home television screen or a videotex terminal. Subscribers use keypads to choose from menus and to request specific screens, or pages. *Also called* videotext.

videotext \vid´ē-ō-tekst`\ *n*. *See* videotex.

Vienna Definition Language \vē-en`ə def-ə-nish`ən lang´wəj\ *n*. *See* VDL.

view[1] \vyōō\ *n*. **1.** The display of data or an image from a given perspective or location. **2.** In relational database management systems, a logical table created through the specification of one or more relational operations on one or more tables. A view is equivalent to a divided relation in the relational model. *See also* relational database, relational model.

view[2] \vyōō\ *vb*. To cause an application to display information on a computer screen.

viewer \vyōō´ər\ *n*. An application that displays or otherwise outputs a file in the same way as the application that created the file. An example of a viewer is a program to display the images stored in GIF or JPEG files. See the illustration. *See also* GIF, JPEG.

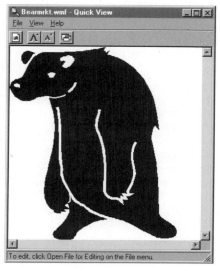

Viewer.

viewport \vyōō´pōrt\ *n*. In computer graphics, a view of a document or image. A viewport is similar to the view in a window, but usually only part of the document or graphical image is visible. *Compare* window.

vine \vīn\ *n*. A means of distributing audiotape copies that is similar to a tape tree. Because vine tapes are digital in format, there is no degradation of sound quality as tapes are copied down the vine from one participant to the next. *Compare* tape tree.

virgule \vər´gyōōl\ *n*. The forward slash (/) character. *Compare* backslash.

virtual \vər´chōō-əl\ *adj*. Of or pertaining to a device, service, or sensory input that is perceived to be what it is not in actuality, usually as more "real" or concrete than it actually is.

virtual 8086 mode \vər`chōō-əl āt`ō-āt-siks´ mōd\ *n*. *See* virtual real mode.

virtual 86 mode \vər`chōō-əl ā-tē-siks´ mōd\ *See* virtual real mode.

virtual address \vər`chōō-əl a´dres, ə-dres´\ *n*. In a virtual memory system, the address that the application uses to reference memory. The memory management unit (MMU) translates this address into a physical address before the memory is actually read or written to. *See also* physical address, virtual memory. *Compare* real address.

virtual channel \vər`chōō-əl chan´əl\ *n.* In Asynchronous Transfer Mode (ATM), the path taken by data sent from one sender to one receiver. *See also* ATM (definition 1), virtual path (definition 2).

virtual circuit \vər`chōō-əl sər´kət\ *n.* A communications link that appears to be a direct connection between sender and receiver, although physically the link can be routed through a more circuitous path.

virtual community \vər`chōō-əl kə-myōō´nə-tē\ *n. See* online community.

Virtual Control Program Interface \vər`chōō-əl kən-trōl` prō´gram in`tər-fās\ *n.* A specification for MS-DOS programs to allow access to extended memory under a multitasking environment (for example, Microsoft Windows) for 386 and higher-level processors. *Acronym:* VCPI (V`C-P-I´). *See also* 80386DX, extended memory, multitasking. *Compare* protected mode.

virtual desktop \vər`chōō-əl desk´top\ *n.* A desktop enhancement tool that provides access to the desktop when it is covered by open windows or that expands the size of the working desktop. *See also* desktop.

virtual device \vər`chōō-əl də-vīs´\ *n.* A device that can be referenced but that does not physically exist. Virtual-memory addressing, for example, uses magnetic disk storage to simulate memory larger than that physically available.

virtual device driver \vər`chōō-əl də-vīs` drī´-vər\ *n.* Software in Windows 95 that manages a hardware or software system resource. If a resource retains information from one access to the next that affects the way it behaves when accessed (for example, a disk controller with its status information and buffers), a virtual device driver must exist for it. Virtual device drivers are described using three-letter abbreviations beginning with V and ending with D; the middle letter indicates the type of device, such as D for a display, P for a printer, T for a timer, and *x* when the type of device is not under discus-

sion. *Acronym:* V.*x*D (V`-X-D´). *See also* device driver.

virtual disk \vər`chōō-əl disk´\ *n. See* RAM disk.

virtual display device driver \vər`chōō-əl dis-plā´ de-vīs` drī´vər\ *n. See* virtual device driver.

Virtual File Allocation Table \vər`chōō-əl fīl´ al-ə-kā`shən tā`bl\ *n. See* VFAT.

virtual image \vər`chōō-əl im´əj\ *n.* An image that is stored in computer memory but is too large to be shown in its entirety on the screen. Scrolling and panning are used to bring unseen portions of the image into view. *See also* virtual screen.

virtual-image file \vər`chōō-əl im´əj fīl\ *n.* A file that specifies the material to be recorded onto a CD-ROM. A virtual-image file generally contains pointers to files that are distributed across a hard disk rather than gathered in one area. Since a complete copy of the material is not assembled, problems may occur in writing the CD-ROM due to delays in assembling the material from a scattered group of files. *See also* CD-ROM. *Compare* physical-image file.

virtual LAN \vər`chōō-əl lan´, L-A-N´\ *n.* Short for **virtual l**ocal **a**rea **n**etwork. A local area network consisting of groups of hosts that are on physically different segments but that communicate as though they were on the same wire. *See also* LAN.

virtual machine \vər`chōō-əl mə-shēn´\ *n.* Software that mimics the performance of a hardware device, such as a program that allows applications written for an Intel processor to be run on a Motorola chip. *Acronym:* VM (V-M´).

virtual memory \vər`chōō-əl mem´ər-ē\ *n.* Memory that appears to an application to be larger and more uniform than it is. Virtual memory may be partially simulated by secondary storage such as a hard disk. Applications access memory through virtual addresses, which are translated (mapped) by special hardware and software onto physical addresses. *Acronym:* VM (V-M´). *Also called* disk memory. *See also* paging, segmentation.

virtual monitor \vər`chōō-əl mon´ə-tər\ *n.* An enhanced monitor viewing system for visually impaired users that uses a virtual-reality headset to move enlarged text across the screen in a direction opposite to head motion. *See also* virtual reality.

virtual name space \vər`chōō-əl nām´ spās\ *n.* The set of all hierarchical sequences of names that can be used by an application to locate objects. One such sequence of names defines a path through the virtual name space, regardless of whether the hierarchy of names reflects the actual arrangement of objects around the system. For example, the virtual name space of a Web server consists of all possible URLs on the network on which it runs. *See also* URL.

virtual network \vər`chōō-əl net´wərk\ *n.* A part of a network that appears to a user to be a network of its own. For example, an Internet service provider can set up multiple domains on a single HTTP server so that each one can be addressed with its company's registered domain name. *See also* domain name, HTTP server (definition 1), ISP.

virtual path \vər`chōō-əl path´\ *n.* **1.** A sequence of names that is used to locate a file and that has the same form as a pathname in the file system but is not necessarily the actual sequence of directory names under which the file is located. The part of a URL that follows the server name is a virtual path. For example, if the directory *c:\bar\sinister\forces\distance* on the server *miles* is shared on the local area network at *foo.com* under the name *miles**baz* and contains the file *elena.html*, that file might be returned by a Web request for *http://miles.foo.com/baz/elena.html*. **2.** In Asynchronous Transfer Mode (ATM), a set of virtual channels that are switched together as a unit through the network. *See also* ATM (definition 1), virtual channel.

virtual peripheral \vər`chōō-əl pər-if´ər-əl\ *n.* A peripheral that can be referenced but does not physically exist. For example, an application might treat a serial port through which data is being transmitted as a printer, but the device receiving the data might be another computer instead.

virtual printer \vər`chōō-əl prin´tər\ *n.* A feature in many operating systems that allows printer output to be saved to a file until a printer becomes available.

virtual printer device driver \vər`chōō-əl prin´tər de-vīs` drī´vər\ *n. See* virtual device driver.

virtual private network \vər`chōō-əl prī´vət net´wərk\ *n.* **1.** A set of nodes on a public network such as the Internet that communicate among themselves using encryption technology so that their messages are as safe from being intercepted and understood by unauthorized users as if the nodes were connected by private lines. **2.** A wide area network formed of permanent virtual circuits (PVCs) on another network, especially a network using technologies such as ATM or frame relay. *Acronym:* VPN (V`P-N´). *See also* ATM (definition 1), frame relay, PVC.

virtual reality \vər`chōō-əl rē-al´ə-tē\ *n.* A simulated 3-D environment that a user can experience and manipulate as if it were physical. The user sees the environment on display screens, possibly mounted in a special pair of goggles. Special input devices, such as gloves or suits fitted with motion sensors, detect the user's actions. *Acronym:* VR (V-R´).

Virtual Reality Modeling Language \vər`chōō-əl rē-al`ə-tē mod´ə-lēng lang`wəj\ *n. See* VRML.

virtual real mode \vər`chōō-əl rēl´ mōd´\ *n.* A feature of the Intel 80386 (SX and DX) and higher microprocessors that allows them to emulate several 8086 (real-mode) environments at the same time. The microprocessor provides a set of virtual registers and virtual memory space to each virtual 8086 environment. A program running in a virtual 8086 environment is completely protected from other virtual 8086 environments in the system and behaves as if it had control of the entire system. *Also called* V86 mode, virtual 8086 mode, virtual 86 mode. *See also* real mode.

virtual root \vər`chōō-əl rōōt´, rōōt´\ *n.* The root directory that a user sees when connected to an Internet server, such as an HTTP or FTP server. The virtual root is actually a pointer to the physical root directory, which may be in a different location, such as another server. The advantages of using a virtual root include being able to create a simple URL for the Internet site and to move the root directory without affecting the URL. *Also called* v-root. *See also* pointer (definition 1), root directory, server (definition 2), URL.

virtual route \vər`chōō-əl rōōt´, rout´\ *n. See* virtual circuit.

virtual screen \vər`chōō-əl skrēn´\ *n.* An image area that extends beyond the dimensions of the physical screen on the monitor, allowing manipulation of large documents or of multiple documents that lie partially outside the normal screen view. *See also* monitor.

virtual server \vər`chōō-əl sər´vər\ *n.* A virtual machine that resides on an HTTP server but has the appearance to the user of being a separate HTTP server. Several virtual servers can reside on one HTTP server, each capable of running its own programs and each with individualized access to input and peripheral devices. Each virtual server has its own domain name and IP address and appears to the user as an individual Web site. Some Internet service providers use virtual servers for those clients who want to use their own domain names. *See also* domain name, HTTP server (definition 2), IP address.

virtual storefront \vər`chōō-əl stōr´frənt\ *n.* A company's point of presence on the Web, providing opportunities for online sales. *Also called* electronic storefront.

virtual terminal \vər`chōō-əl tər´mə-nəl\ *n. See* terminal emulation.

virtual timer device driver \vər`chōō-əl tī´mər de-vīs` drī´vər\ *n. See* virtual device driver.

virtual world \vər`chōō-əl wərld`\ *n.* **1.** A 3-D modeled environment, often created in VRML, where a user can interact with the viewer to change variables. *See also* viewer, VRML. **2.** An electronic environment that has no basis in the physical world. Multiuser dungeons (MUDs), talkers, and chat rooms are often considered virtual worlds. *See also* chat[1] (definition 1), MUD, talker.

virus \vī´rus\ *n.* An intrusive program that infects computer files by inserting in those files copies of itself. The copies are usually executed when the file is loaded into memory, allowing them to infect still other files, and so on. Viruses often have damaging side effects—sometimes intentionally, sometimes not. For example, some viruses can destroy a computer's hard disk or take up memory space that could otherwise be used by programs. *See also* Good Times virus, Trojan horse, worm.

virus signature \vī´rus sig`nə-chur\ *n.* A portion of unique computer code contained in a virus. Antivirus programs search for known virus signatures to identify infected programs and files. *See also* virus.

visible page \viz`ə-bl pāj´\ *n.* In computer graphics, the image that is being displayed on the screen. Screen images are written into display memory in sections called pages, each of which contains one screen display.

Visual Basic \vizh`ōō-əl bā´sik\ *n.* A high-level, visual-programming version of Basic. Visual Basic was developed by Microsoft for building Windows-based applications. *See also* Basic, Visual Basic for Applications, Visual Basic, Scripting Edition, visual programming.

Visual Basic for Applications \vizh`ōō-əl bā`sik fər a`plə-kā´shənz\ *n.* A macro-language version of Visual Basic that is used to program many Windows 95 applications and is included with several Microsoft applications. *Acronym:* VBA (V`B-A´). *See also* macro language, Visual Basic.

Visual Basic Script \vizh`ōō-əl bā´sik skript\ *n. See* Visual Basic, Scripting Edition.

Visual Basic, Scripting Edition \vizh`ōō-əl bā`-sik skrip´tēng ə-dish`ən´\ *n.* A subset of the Visual Basic for Applications programming language, optimized for Web-related programming. As with JavaScript, code for Visual Basic, Scripting Edition is embedded in HTML documents. This version is included with the Internet Explorer Web browser. *Also called* VBScript, Visual Basic Script. *See also* Visual Basic for Applications.

Visual C++ \vizh`ōō-əl C`plus-plus´\ *n.* A Microsoft application development system for the programming language C++ that runs under MS-DOS and Windows. Visual C++ is a visual programming environment. *See also* visual programming. *Compare* Visual Basic, Visual J++.

visual interface \vizh`ōō-əl in´tər-fās\ *n. See* graphical user interface.

visualization \vizh`ōō-əl-ə-zā´shən\ *n.* A feature of an application that displays data in the form of a video image. For example, some databases can interpret and show data in the form of a two- or three-dimensional model.

Visual J++ \vizh`ōō-əl J`plus-plus´\ *n.* Microsoft's Java visual programming environment, which can be used to create applets and applications in the Java language. *See also* applet, Java, Java applet, visual programming.

visual programming \vizh`ōō-əl prō´gram-ēng\ *n.* A method of programming using a programming environment or language in which basic program components can be selected through menu choices, buttons, icons, and other predetermined methods.

VLAN \V´lan, V´L-A-N´\ *n. See* virtual LAN.

VLB[1] \V´L-B´\ *adj. See* VESA[1].

VLB[2] \V´L-B´\ *n. See* VL bus.

VL bus \V-L´ bus\ *n.* Short for **VESA l**ocal **b**us. A type of local bus architecture introduced by the Video Electronics Standards Association. The VL bus specification allows up to three VL bus slots to be built into a PC motherboard and allows for bus mastering (wherein "intelligent" adapter cards can do some processing independently of the CPU). A VL bus slot consists of a standard connector plus an additional 16-bit Micro Channel Architecture connector and must be built into the motherboard by the manufacturer. Standard connectors cannot simply be converted to VL bus slots. A non–VL bus adapter card can be used in a VL bus slot, but it cannot use the local bus and so performs as it normally would in a non–VL bus slot. *Also called* VL local bus. *See also* local bus, PCI local bus.

VLF radiation \V-L-F´ rā-dē-ā`shən\ *n.* Short for **very-low-f**requency **radiation.** Electromagnetic radiation (radio) at frequencies within the range of approximately 300 Hz to 30,000 Hz (30 kHz). Computer monitors emit this type of radiation. A voluntary standard, MPR II, regulates the amount of VLF radiation that a monitor can emit. *See also* MPR II.

VLIW \V´L-I-W´\ *n.* Acronym for **V**ery **L**ong **I**nstruction **W**ord. An architecture that combines many simple instructions into a single long instruction word that uses different registers.

VL local bus \V´L lō`kəl bus´\ *n. See* VL bus.

VLSI \V´L-S-I´\ *n. See* very-large-scale integration.

VM \V-M´\ *n.* **1.** Acronym for **V**irtual **M**achine. An operating system for IBM mainframes that provides virtual-machine capability. VM was developed by IBM customers and later taken over by IBM itself under the name OS/VM. **2.** *See* virtual machine, virtual memory.

.vn \dot`V-N´\ *n.* On the Internet, the major geographic domain specifying that an address is located in Vietnam.

voice answer back \vois` an´sər bak\ *n.* The use of sound-recorded messages by a computer in responding to commands or queries. *Acronym:* VAB (V`A-B´).

voice-capable modem \vois`kā-pə-bl   mō´dəm\ *n.* A modem that can support voice messaging applications along with its data-handling functions.

voice coil \vois´ koil\ *n.* A device that moves a disk drive actuator arm using electromagnetism. It works more quickly than a stepper motor. *See also* actuator. *Compare* stepper motor.

voice-grade channel \vois`grād chan´əl\ *n.* A communications channel, such as a telephone line, with an audio bandwidth of 300 to 3,000 Hz, suitable for carrying speech. A voice-grade channel can also be used for transmitting facsimile, analog, and digital information at rates up to 33 kilobits per second (Kbps).

voice input \vois´ in`po͞ot\ *n.* Spoken instructions that a computer translates into executable commands using speech recognition technology or that are embedded into documents with the aid of a microphone. *See also* speech recognition.

voice mail \vois´ māl\ *n.* A system that records and stores telephone messages in a computer's memory. Unlike a simple answering machine, a voice mail system has separate mailboxes for multiple users, each of whom can copy, store, or redistribute messages.

voice messaging \vois´ mes`ə-jēng\ *n.* A system that sends and receives messages in the form of sound recordings.

voice modem \vois´ mō`dəm\ *n.* A modulation/demodulation device that supports a switch to change between telephony and data transmission modes. Such a device might contain a built-in loudspeaker and microphone for voice communication, but more often it uses the computer's sound card. *See also* modem, sound card, telephony.

voice navigation \vois` nav-ə-gā`shən\ *n.* The use of spoken commands to control a Web browser. Voice navigation is a feature of some plug-in applications that embellish Web browsers to allow the user to navigate through the Web by means of his or her voice. *See also* Web browser.

voice-net \vois´net\ *n.* A term used on the Internet to refer to the telephone system, often preceding the user's telephone number in an e-mail signature.

voice output \vois´ out`po͞ot\ *n. See* speech synthesis.

voice recognition \vois´ rek-əg-nish`ən\ *n. See* speech recognition.

voice synthesis \vois` sin´thə-sis\ *n. See* speech synthesis.

volatile memory \vol`ə-təl mem´ər-ē, vol`ə-tīl\ *n.* **1.** Memory, such as RAM, that loses its data when the power is shut off. *Compare* nonvolatile memory. **2.** Memory used by a program that can change independently of the program, such as memory shared by another program or by an interrupt service routine.

volt \vōlt\ *n.* The unit used to measure potential difference or electromotive force. One volt is defined as the potential across which 1 coulomb of charge will do 1 joule of work, or the potential generated by 1 ampere of current flowing through 1 ohm of resistance. *See also* electromotive force.

voltage \vōl´təj\ *n. See* electromotive force.

voltage regulator \vōl´təj re`gyə-lā-tər\ *n.* A circuit or circuit component that maintains a constant output voltage despite variations in input voltage. See the illustration.

Voltage regulator.   This voltage regulator is style TO-220, one of several types available.

volts alternating current \vōltz` äl-tər-nā-tēng kur´ənt\ *n.* The measure of the peak-to-peak voltage swing of an electrical signal. *Acronym:* VAC (V´A-C´).

volume \vol´yo͞om\ *n.* **1.** A disk or tape that stores computer data. Sometimes large hard disks are divided into several volumes, each of which is treated as a separate disk. **2.** The loudness of an audio signal.

volume label \vol´yo͞om lā`bəl\ *n.* A name for a disk or tape. MS-DOS systems, which seldom use disk names except in directory listings, use the term *volume label*. Apple Macintosh systems, which often refer to disks by name, use the term *volume name*.

volume name \vol´yo͞om nām`\ *n. See* volume label.

volume reference number \vol`yo͞om ref´ər-əns num`bər, ref´rəns\ *n. See* volume serial number.

volume serial number \vol`yo͞om sēr´ē-əl num`bər\ *n.* The optional identifying volume number of a disk or tape. MS-DOS systems use the term *volume serial number*. Apple Macintosh systems use the term *volume reference number*. A volume serial number is not the same as a volume label or volume name. *Compare* volume label.

VON \V`O-N´\ *n.* Acronym for **v**oice **o**n the **n**et. A broad category of hardware and software technology for real-time voice and video transmission over the Internet. The term was coined by Jeff Pulver, who formed a group called the VON Coalition, which opposes regulation of VON technology and promotes VON to the public.

von Neumann architecture \von noi´mən är`ka-tek-chur\ *n.* The most common structure for computer systems, attributed to the mathematician John von Neumann. It uses the concept of a program that can be permanently stored in a computer and manipulated or made self-modifying through machine-based instructions. Sequential processing is characteristic of von Neumann architecture. Parallel architectures have evolved to improve on the encumbrances of sequential instructions. *See also* parallel computer.

von Neumann bottleneck \von noi`mən bot´l-nek\ *n.* Competition between data and instructions for CPU time. Mathematician John von Neumann was the first to show that a computer based on architecture linking a single processor with memory will actually spend more time retrieving data from memory than processing it. The bottleneck arises when the processor has to trade off between executing a large number of instructions per second and reading in a large amount of data in the same time. *See also* central processing unit.

VPD \V`P-D´\ *n.* Acronym for **v**irtual **p**rinter **d**evice driver. *See* virtual device driver.

VPN \V`P-N´\ *n. See* virtual private network.

VR \V-R´\ *n. See* virtual reality.

VRAM \V´ram, V`R-A-M´\ *n. See* video RAM.

VRC \V`R-C´\ *n.* Acronym for **v**ertical **r**edundancy **c**heck. A method for checking the accuracy of transmitted data. VRC generates an extra bit (parity bit) for each character transmitted. The parity bit indicates whether the character contains an odd or even number of 1 bits. If its value does not match the type of the character, that character is assumed to be incorrectly transmitted. *See also* parity. *Compare* LRC.

VRML \ver´məl, V`R-M-L´\ *n.* Acronym for **V**irtual **R**eality **M**odeling **L**anguage. A scene description language for creating 3-D interactive Web graphics similar to those found in some video games, allowing the user to "move around" within a graphic image and interact with objects. VRML, a subset of Silicon Graphics' Inventor File Format (ASCII), was created by Mark Pesce and Tony Parisi in 1994. VRML files can be created in a text editor, although CAD packages, modeling and animation packages, and VRML authoring software are the tools preferred by most VRML authors. VRML files reside on an HTTP server; links to these files can be embedded in HTML documents, or users can access the VRML files directly. To view VRML Web pages, users need a VRML-enabled browser, such as WebSpace from Silicon Graphics, or a VRML plug-in for Internet Explorer or Netscape Navigator. *See also* 3-D graphic, HTML document, HTTP server (definition 1).

v-root \V´root, root\ *n. See* virtual root.

V series \V´sēr`ēz\ *n. See* CCITT V series.

V-sync \V´sēnk\ *n. See* vertical bandwidth.

VT-52, VT-100, VT-200 \V`T´ fif-tē-too´, V`T´wən-hun´drəd, V`T´too-hun´drəd\ *n.* A popular set of control codes used in terminals with those model numbers that were originally manufactured by Digital Equipment Corporation. Appropriate software can enable a microcomputer to use these codes to emulate such terminals.

VTD \V`T-D´\ *n.* Acronym for **v**irtual **t**imer **d**evice driver. *See* virtual device driver.

.vt.us \dot-V-T`dot-U-S´\ *n.* On the Internet, the major geographic domain specifying that an address is located in Vermont, United States.

.vu \dot`V-U´\ *n.* On the Internet, the major geographic domain specifying that an address is located in Vanuatu.

V*x*D \V`-X-D´\ *n. See* virtual device driver.

w³ \W-kyō͞obd´\ *n. See* World Wide Web.

W3 \W-thrē´\ *n. See* World Wide Web.

W3C \W`thrē-C´\ *n. See* World Wide Web Consortium.

wafer \wā´fər\ *n.* A thin, flat piece of semiconductor crystal used in the fabrication of integrated circuits. Various etching, doping, and layering techniques are used to create the circuit components on the surface of the wafer. Usually multiple identical circuits are formed on a single wafer, which is then cut into sections. Each integrated circuit then has leads attached and is packaged in a holder. *See also* integrated circuit, semiconductor.

wafer-scale integration \wā`fər-skāl in-tə-grā´-shən\ *n.* The fabrication on a single wafer of different microcircuits that are then connected to form a single circuit the full size of the wafer. *See also* wafer.

WAIS \wās, W`A-I-S´\ *n.* Acronym for **W**ide **A**rea **I**nformation **S**erver. A UNIX-based document search and retrieval system on the Internet that can be used to search over 400 WAIS libraries, such as Project Gutenberg, for indexed files that match a series of keywords. WAIS can also be used on an individual Web site as a search engine. WAIS, developed by Thinking Machines Corporation, Apple Computer, and Dow Jones, uses the Z39.50 standard to process natural language queries. The list of documents returned by WAIS often contains numerous false matches. Users need a WAIS client to use a WAIS server. *See also* natural language query, Project Gutenberg, search engine, Z39.50 standard.

WAIS database \wās´ dā`tə-bās, W`A-I-S´\ *n. See* WAIS.

waisindex \wās´in`deks\ *n.* **1.** A UNIX utility for building an index to text files for access using WAIS (Wide Area Information Server) query software. **2.** A URL for accessing WAIS. The URL takes the form wais:*//hostport/database[?search]*.

WAIS server or **waisserver** \wās´ sər`vər, W`A-I-S´\ *n. See* WAIS.

wait state \wāt´ stāt\ *n.* A processing cycle of the microprocessor during which it only waits for data from an input/output device or from memory. While a single wait state is not humanly perceptible, the cumulative effect of wait states is to slow system performance. *See also* zero wait state.

wallet PC \wä`lət P-C´\ *n.* A pocket-size portable computer designed to function like a wallet, carrying "virtual" versions of one's identification, money, credit cards, and other essentials, as well as a mobile information source and communications tool. The wallet PC is still under development.

wallpaper \wäl´pā-pər`\ *n.* In a graphical user interface such as Windows, a pattern or picture in the screen background that can be chosen by the user. *See also* graphical user interface.

WAN \W`A-N´, wan\ *n. See* wide area network.

wand \wänd\ *n.* Any pen-shaped device used for data entry, such as a graphics tablet's stylus or, most commonly, the scanning instrument used with many bar code readers. *See also* optical scanner, scan head. *Compare* stylus.

wanderer \wän´dər-ər`\ *n.* A person who frequently uses the World Wide Web. Many of these people make indexes of what they find.

warm boot \wärm bōo͞t´\ *n.* The restarting of a running computer without first turning off the power. *Also called* soft boot, warm start.

warm start \wärm stärt´\ *n. See* warm boot.

watt \wät\ *n.* The unit of power equal to the expenditure of 1 joule of energy in 1 second. The power of an electrical circuit is a function of the potential across the circuit and the current flowing through the circuit. If E = potential, I = current, and R = resistance, power in watts can be calculated as $I \times E$, $I^2 \times R$, or E^2/R.

.wav \dot`W-A-V´\ *n.* The file extension that identifies sound files stored in waveform (WAV) audio format. *See also* WAV.

WAV \wāv, W`A-V´\ *n.* A file format in which Windows stores sounds as waveforms. Such files have the extension .wav. Depending on the sampling frequency, on whether the sound is monaural or stereo, and on whether 8 or 16 bits are used for each sample, one minute of sound can occupy as little as 644 kilobytes or as much as 27 megabytes of storage. *See also* sampling (definition 2), waveform.

wave \wāv\ *n.* **1.** Any disturbance or change that has an oscillatory, periodic nature, for example, a light or sound wave. *See also* waveform. **2.** In electronics, the time-amplitude profile of an electrical signal.

waveform \wāv´fōrm\ *n.* The manner in which a wave's amplitude changes over time. *See also* period, phase, wavelength.

wavelength \wāv´lenkth, wāv´length\ *n.* The distance between successive peaks or troughs in a periodic signal that is propagated through space. Wavelength is symbolized by the Greek letter lambda (λ) and can be calculated as speed divided by frequency.

wavelet \wāv´lət\ *n.* A mathematical function that varies over a limited extent of time. Wavelets are coming into increasing use for analyzing signals (such as sound). They have limited duration and sudden changes in frequency and amplitude rather than the infinite duration and constant amplitude and frequency of the sine and cosine functions. *Compare* Fourier transform.

WBEM \W`B-E-M´\ *n.* Acronym for **W**eb-**B**ased **E**nterprise **M**anagement. A protocol that links a Web browser directly to a device or application that monitors a network. *See also* communications protocol.

WDEF \W`D-E-F´\ *n. See* window definition function.

WDL \W`D-L´\ *n. See* Windows Driver Library.

weak typing \wēk` tī´pēng\ *n.* A characteristic of a programming language that allows the program to change the data type of a variable during program execution. *See also* data type, variable. *Compare* strong typing.

web \web\ *n.* A set of interlinked documents in a hypertext system. The user enters the web through a home page. *See also* World Wide Web.

Web \web\ *n. See* World Wide Web.

Web address \web´ a`dres, ə-dres`\ *n. See* URL.

Web-Based Enterprise Management \web`bāsd en`tər-prīz man´əj-mənt\ *n. See* WBEM.

Web browser \web´ brou`zər\ *n.* A client application that enables a user to view HTML documents on the World Wide Web, another network, or the user's computer; follow the hyperlinks among them; and transfer files. Text-based Web browsers, such as Lynx, can serve users with shell accounts but show only the text elements of an HTML document; most Web browsers, however, require a connection that can handle IP packets but will also display graphics that are in the document, play audio and video files, and execute small programs, such as Java applets or ActiveX controls, that can be embedded in HTML documents. Some Web browsers require helper applications or plug-ins to accomplish one or more of these tasks. In addition, most current Web browsers permit users to send and receive e-mail and to read and respond to newsgroups. *Also called* browser. *See also* ActiveX controls, helper application, hyperlink, Internet Explorer, Java applet, Lynx, Mosaic, Netscape Navigator, plug-in.

WebCrawler \web´krä`lər, krô`lər\ *n.* A World Wide Web search engine operated by America Online. *See also* search engine.

Web development \web´ de-vel`əp-mənt\ *n.* The design and coding of World Wide Web pages.

Web directory \web´ dər-ek`tər-ē\ *n.* A list of Web sites, giving the URL and a description of each. *See also* URL.

Web index \web´ in`deks\ *n.* A Web site intended to enable a user to locate other resources on the Web. The Web index may include a search facility or may merely contain individual hyperlinks to the resources indexed.

Webmaster or **webmaster** \web´ma`stər\ *n.* A person responsible for creating and maintaining a World Wide Web site. A Webmaster is often responsible for responding to e-mail, ensuring the site is operating properly, creating and updating Web pages, and maintaining the overall structure and design of the site. *Also called* webmistress, webweaver.

webmistress \web´mis-trəs\ *n. See* webmaster.

Web page \web´ pāj\ *n.* A document on the World Wide Web. A Web page consists of an HTML file, with associated files for graphics and scripts, in a particular directory on a particular machine (and thus identifiable by a URL). Usually a Web page contains links to other Web pages. *See also* URL.

Web phone \web´ fōn\ *n. See* Internet telephone.

Web server \web´ sər`vər\ *n. See* HTTP server.

Web site \web´ sīt\ *n.* A group of related HTML documents and associated files, scripts, and databases that is served up by an HTTP server on the World Wide Web. The HTML documents in a Web site generally cover one or more related topics and are interconnected through hyperlinks. Most Web sites have a home page as their starting point, which frequently functions as a table of contents for the site. Many large organizations, such as corporations, will have one or more HTTP servers dedicated to a single Web site. However, an HTTP server can also serve several small Web sites, such as those owned by individuals. Users need a Web browser and an Internet connection to access a Web site. *See also* home page, HTML, HTTP server (definition 1), Web browser.

Web terminal \web´ tər`mə-nəl\ *n.* A system containing a central processing unit (CPU), RAM, a high-speed modem or other means of connecting to the Internet, and powerful video graphics, but no hard disk, intended to be used solely as a client to the World Wide Web rather than as a general-purpose computer. *Also called* network computer.

Web TV \web` T-V´\ *n.* A system for accessing the World Wide Web and displaying Web pages on a television screen using a set-top box.

webweaver \web´wē`vər\ *n. See* webmaster.

webzine \web´zēn\ *n.* An electronic publication distributed primarily through the World Wide Web, rather than as an ink-on-paper magazine. *See also* ezine.

weighted code \wā´təd kōd´\ *n.* A data representation code in which each bit position has a specified inherent value, which might or might not be included in the interpretation of the data, depending on whether the bit is on or off.

welcome page \wel´kəm pāj` \ *n. See* home page.

WELL \wel, W-E`L-L´\ *n.* Acronym for **W**hole **E**arth 'Lectronic **L**ink. A conferencing system based in San Francisco, California, that is accessible through the Internet and through dial-up access points in many major cities. The WELL attracts many computer professionals, along with other people who enjoy participating in one of the Internet's most successful virtual communities. Because of the number of journalists and other prominent people who participate in the WELL, it has substantial influence beyond its own relatively small number of subscribers.

well-behaved \wel`bē-hāvd´\ *adj.* **1.** Of, pertaining to, or characteristic of a program that performs properly even when given extreme or erroneous input values. **2.** Obeying the rules of a particular programming environment.

well-mannered \wel`man´ərd\ *adj. See* well-behaved.

wetware \wet´wâr\ *n.* Slang for living beings and their brains, as part of the environment that also includes hardware and software.

"what-if" evaluation \hwət-if´ ē-val´yōō-ā´shən, wət-if`\ *n.* A kind of spreadsheet evaluation in which certain values in a spreadsheet are changed in order to reveal the effects of those changes. For example, a spreadsheet user can use "what-if" evaluation to try different mortgage rates and terms to see the effect on monthly payments and on total interest paid over the life of a loan.

whatis \hwət-iz´, wət-iz´\ *n.* **1.** A UNIX utility for obtaining a summary of a keyword's documentation. *See also* man pages. **2.** An Archie command for locating software whose description contains desired words.

What You See Before You Get It \hwət` yōō sē` bə-fōr` yōō get´ it, wət`\ *adj. See* WYSBYGI.

What You See Is What You Get \hwət yōō sē` iz hwət yōō get´, wət`\ *adj. See* WYSIWYG.

wheel printer \hwēl´ prin`tər, wēl´\ *n. See* daisy-wheel printer.

Whetstone \hwet´stōn, wet´stōn\ *n.* A benchmark test that attempts to measure the speed and efficiency with which a computer carries out floating-point operations. The result of the test is given in units called *whetstones*. The Whetstone benchmark has fallen out of favor because it produces inconsistent results compared with other benchmarks such as the Dhrystone and the sieve of Eratosthenes. *See also* benchmark[1], Dhrystone, sieve of Eratosthenes.

WHIRLWIND \hwərl´wind, wərl´wind\ *n.* A digital computer using vacuum tubes, developed at Massachusetts Institute of Technology in the 1940s and used during the 1950s. The innovations introduced with WHIRLWIND included CRT displays and real-time processing. WHIRLWIND project members included Kenneth H. Olsen, who later founded Digital Equipment Corporation in 1957. *See also* CRT, real-time, vacuum tube.

whiteboard \hwīt´bōrd, wīt´bōrd\ *n.* Software that allows multiple users across a network to work together on a document that is simultaneously displayed on all the users' screens, as though they are all gathered around a physical whiteboard.

white noise \hwīt noiz´, wīt\ *n.* Noise that contains components at all frequencies, at least within the frequency band of interest. It is called "white" by analogy to white light, which contains light at all the visible frequencies. In the audible spectrum, white noise is a hiss or a roar, such as that produced when a television set is tuned to a channel over which no station is broadcasting.

white pages \hwīt´ pā`jəz, wīt´\ *n. See* DIB (definition 2).

white paper \hwīt´ pā`pər, wīt´\ *n.* An informal paper stating a position or proposing a draft specification, usually on a technical topic. *See also* specification (definition 1).

whois \hōō-iz´\ *n.* **1.** An Internet service, provided by some domains, that enables a user to find e-mail addresses and other information for users listed in a database at that domain. **2.** A UNIX command to access the whois service. **3.** A command that displays a list of all users logged onto a Novell network.

whois client \hōō`iz klī´ənt\ *n.* A program (such as the UNIX whois command) that enables a user to access databases of usernames, e-mail addresses, and other information. *See also* whois.

whois server \hōō`iz sər´vər\ *n.* Software that provides the usernames and e-mail addresses from a database (often listing people who have accounts at an Internet domain) to users who request the information using whois clients. *See also* whois.

Whole Earth 'Lectronic Link \hōl` ərth` lektron`ik lēnk´\ *n. See* WELL.

whole number \hōl` num´bər\ *n.* A number without a fractional component—for example, 1 or 173; an integer.

Wide Area Information Server \wīd` âr-ē-ə infər-mā´shən sər`vər\ *n. See* WAIS.

wide area network \wīd` âr-ē-ə net´wərk\ *n.* A communications network that connects geographically separated areas. *Acronym:* WAN (W`A-N´, wan).

wideband transmission \wīd`band tranz-mish´-ən\ *n. See* broadband network.

Wide SCSI or **Wide SCSI-2** \wīd´ skuz`ē, S-C-S-I`\ *n.* A form of the SCSI-2 interface that can transfer data 16 bits at a time at up to 20 megabytes per second. The Wide SCSI connector has 68 pins. *See also* SCSI, SCSI-2. *Compare* Fast SCSI, Fast/Wide SCSI.

widow \wid´ō\ *n.* A last line of a paragraph, shorter than a full line, appearing at the top of a page. A widow is considered visually undesirable on the printed page. *Compare* orphan.

wildcard character \wīld´kärd kâr´ək-tər\ *n.* A keyboard character that can be used to represent one or many characters. The asterisk (*), for example, typically represents one or more characters, and the question mark (?) typically represents a single character. Wildcard characters are often used in operating systems as a means of specifying more than one file by name.

Win32 \win`thər-tē-tōō´\ *n.* The application programming interface in Windows 95 and Windows NT that enables applications to use the 32-bit instructions available on 80386 and higher processors. Although Windows 95 and Windows NT support 16-bit 80x86 instructions as well, Win32 offers greatly improved performance. *See also* 16-bit machine, 32-bit machine, 80386DX, 8086, application programming interface, central processing unit, Win32s.

Win32s \win`thər-tē-tōō`S´\ *n*. A subset of the Win32 application programming interface that works under Windows 3.*x*. By including the Win32s software, which is distributed as freeware, an application can gain in performance from using the 32-bit instructions available on 80386 and higher processors while running under Windows 3.*x*. *See also* 32-bit machine, 80386DX, central processing unit, Win32.

Winchester disk \win´che-stər disk`\ *n*. An early IBM name for a hard disk. The term is derived from IBM's internal code name for its first hard disk, which stored 30 megabytes (MB) and had a 30-millisecond access time, reminding its inventors of a Winchester .30-caliber rifle known as a ".30-.30."

window \win´dō\ *n*. In applications and graphical interfaces, a portion of the screen that can contain its own document or message. In window-based programs, the screen can be divided into several windows, each of which has its own boundaries and can contain a different document (or another view into the same document).

window definition function \win´dō def-ə-nish`-ən funk-shən\ *n*. A resource associated with a window in a Macintosh application. The Macintosh Window Manager calls this function to perform such actions as drawing and resizing the window. *Also called* WDEF.

windowing environment \win´dō-ēng en-vī`rən-ment, en-vī`ərn-ment\ *n*. An operating system or shell that presents the user with specially delineated areas of the screen called *windows*. Windowing environments typically allow windows to be resized and moved around on the display. The Macintosh Finder, Windows, and the OS/2 Presentation Manager are all examples of windowing environments. *See also* graphical user interface, window.

window random access memory \win`dō randəm ak`ses mem´ə-rē\ *n*. *See* WRAM.

Windows \win´dōz\ *n*. An operating system introduced by Microsoft Corporation in 1983. Windows is a multitasking graphical user interface environment that runs on both MS-DOS–based computers (Windows and Windows for Workgroups) and as a self-contained operating system (Windows 95, Windows NT). Windows provides a standard interface based on drop-down menus, windowed regions on the screen, and a pointing device such as a mouse.

Windows 95 \win`dōz nīn-tē-fīv´\ *n*. An operating system with a graphical user interface for 80386 and higher processors, released by Microsoft Corporation in August 1995. Intended to replace Windows 3.11, Windows for Workgroups 3.11, and MS-DOS, Windows 95 is a complete operating system, rather than a shell that requires MS-DOS, as does Windows 3.*x*. For backward compatibility, Windows 95 can run MS-DOS software. Under Windows 95, filenames can be up to 255 characters long and may include dots and spaces. The My Computer icon on the Windows 95 desktop provides access to the system files and resources, and the Network Neighborhood icon provides access to any network (if the computer is attached to one). See the illustration. Windows 95 supports the Plug and Play method for installing and configuring hardware and can access Windows, NetWare, and UNIX networks. The minimum configuration for Windows 95 is an 80386 processor with 4 MB of RAM, but an i486 or higher processor with at least 8 MB of RAM is recommended. *See also* MS-DOS, NetWare, Plug and Play, Windows, Windows for Workgroups.

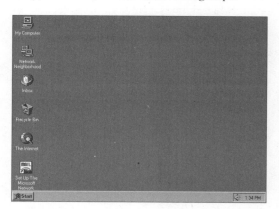

Windows 95.

Windows application \win´dōz a-plə-kā`shən\ *n*. A software application designed for use with the Microsoft Windows environment.

Windows-based accelerator \win`dōz-bāsd ək-sel´ər-ā-tər\ *n.* A type of super VGA (SVGA) video adapter designed specifically to run Windows and Windows-based applications more quickly. A Windows-based accelerator achieves performance improvements over a standard SVGA video adapter with the help of special routines built into the adapter's read-only memory. These routines relieve the Windows operating system of some of the video-related duties it must perform on a non-accelerated system. *Also called* Windows-based accelerator card. *See also* SVGA.

Windows CE \win`dōz C-E´\ *n.* A scaled-down version of the Microsoft Windows platform designed for use with handheld PCs. Windows CE includes scaled-down versions of several Microsoft application programs, including Excel, Word, Internet Explorer, Schedule+, and an e-mail client. *See also* handheld PC.

Windows Driver Library \win`dōz drī´vər lī`brâr-ē\ *n.* A collection of hardware device drivers for a Microsoft Windows operating system that were not included in the original Windows package. *Acronym:* WDL (W`D-L´). *See also* driver.

Windows Explorer \win`dōz eks-plōr´ər\ *n.* A utility in Windows 95 that enables the user to locate and open files and folders. Windows Explorer resembles the File Manager of Windows 3.1. The user can select folders from a list displayed on the left side of the screen and access files in a selected folder from a list displayed on the right side of the screen.

Windows for Workgroups \win`dōz fər wərk´groõps\ *n.* A version of Windows released in 1992 and designed to run on an Ethernet-based LAN (local area network) without the need for separate LAN software. *See also* LAN, Windows.

Windows Metafile Format \win`dōz met´ə-fīl fōr`mat\ *n.* A graphics file format used by Windows to store vector graphics in order to exchange graphics information between applications and to store information between sessions. *Acronym:* WMF (W`M-F´). *See also* vector graphics.

Windows NT \win`dōz N-T´\ *n.* An operating system released by Microsoft Corporation in 1993. The Windows NT operating system, sometimes referred to as simply NT, is the high-end member

of a family of operating systems from Microsoft. It is a completely self-contained operating system with a built-in graphical user interface. Windows NT is a 32-bit, preemptive multitasking operating system that features networking, symmetric multiprocessing, multithreading, and security. It is a portable operating system that can run on a variety of hardware platforms including those based on the Intel 80386, i486, and Pentium microprocessors and MIPS microprocessors; it can also run on multiprocessor computers. Windows NT supports up to 4 gigabytes of virtual memory and can run MS-DOS, POSIX, and OS/2 (character-mode) applications. *See also* MS-DOS, operating system, OS/2, POSIX, Windows.

Windows NT Advanced Server \win`dōz N-T´ ad-vansd sər´vər\ *n.* A superset of Windows NT that provides centralized, domain-based network management and security. Windows NT Advanced Server also offers advanced hard disk fault-tolerance features, such as mirroring and additional connectivity. *See also* Windows NT.

Windows Open System Architecture \win`dōz ō`pən si-stəm är´kə-tek-chur\ *n. See* WOSA.

Windows sockets \win´dōz sok`əts\ *n. See* Winsock.

WinG \win-G´\ *n.* Short for **Win**dows **G**ames. An application programming interface for games in the Windows 95 environment. Under WinG, games can access the video frame buffer directly for increased speed. *See also* application programming interface, buffer[1], frame buffer.

WINS \winz, W`I-N-S´\ *n.* Acronym for **W**indows **I**nternet **N**aming **S**ervice. A Windows NT Server method for associating a computer's host name with its address. *Also called* INS, Internet Naming Service. *Compare* DNS (definition 1).

Winsock \win´sok\ *n.* Short for **Win**dows **Sock**ets. An application programming interface standard for software that provides a TCP/IP interface under Windows. The Winsock standard developed out of a Birds of a Feather (BOF) discussion that arose among software vendors at a UNIX conference in 1991; it has gained the general support of software developers, including Microsoft. *See also* application programming interface, BOF, socket (definition 1), TCP/IP.

Wintel \win-tel´\ *adj.* Of, pertaining to, or characteristic of a computer that uses the Microsoft Windows operating system and an Intel central processing unit (CPU). *See also* Windows.

wired \wīrd\ *adj.* **1.** Of, pertaining to, or characteristic of an electronic circuit or hardware grouping in which the configuration is determined by the physical interconnection of the components (as opposed to being programmable in software or alterable by a switch). *See also* hardwired (definition 1). **2.** Knowledgeable about Internet resources, systems, and culture. **3.** Having access to the Internet.

wire-frame model \wīr´frām mod`əl\ *n.* In computer graphics applications such as CAD programs, a representation of a three-dimensional object using separate lines that resemble strands of wire joined to create a model. *Compare* solid model, surface modeling.

wireless \wīr´ləs\ *adj.* Of, pertaining to, or characteristic of communications that take place without the use of interconnecting wires or cables, such as by radio, microwave, or infrared.

wireless LAN \wīr`les lan´, L-A-N`\ *n.* A local area network (LAN) that sends and receives data via radio, infrared optical signaling, or some other technology that does not require a physical connection between individual nodes and the hub. Wireless LANs are often used in office or factory settings where a user must carry a portable computer from place to place.

wire-pin printer \wīr´pin prin`-tər\ *n. See* dot-matrix printer.

wire-wrapped circuits \wīr´rapd sər`kəts\ *n.* Circuits constructed on perforated boards using wire instead of the metal traces found on printed circuit boards. The stripped ends of insulated wires are wrapped around the long pins of special wire-wrap integrated circuit sockets. Wire-wrapped circuits are generally handmade, one-of-a-kind devices used for prototyping and research in electrical engineering. *Compare* printed circuit board.

wizard \wiz´ərd\ *n.* **1.** Someone who is adept at making computers perform their "magic." A wizard is an outstanding and creative programmer or a power user. *Compare* guru, UNIX wizard. **2.** A participant in a multiuser dungeon (MUD) who has permission to control the domain, even to delete other players' characters. *See also* MUD. **3.** An interactive help utility within an application that guides the user through each step of a particular task, such as starting up a word processing document in the correct format for a business letter.

wizzywig \wiz´ē-wig`\ *n. See* WYSIWYG.

.wmf \dot-W`M-F`\ *n.* A file extension that identifies a vector encoded as a Microsoft Windows Metafile.

WMF \W`M-F`\ *n. See* Windows Metafile Format.

word \wərd\ *n.* The native unit of storage on a particular machine. A word is the largest amount of data that can be handled by the microprocessor in one operation and is also, as a rule, the width of the main data bus. Word sizes of 16 bits and 32 bits are the most common. *Compare* byte, octet.

word-addressable processor \wərd`ə-dres-ə-bl pros´es-ər\ *n.* A processor that cannot access an individual byte of memory but can access a larger unit. In order to perform operations on an individual byte, the processor must read and write memory in the larger unit. *See also* central processing unit.

word processing \wərd` pros´es-ēng\ *n.* The act of entering and editing text with a word processor. *Acronym:* WP (W-P´).

word processor \wərd` pros´es-ər\ *n.* An application program for creating and manipulating text-based documents. A word processor is the electronic equivalent of paper, pen, typewriter, eraser, and, most likely, dictionary and thesaurus. Depending on the program and the equipment in use, word processors can display documents either in text mode (using highlighting, underlining, or color to represent italics, boldfacing, and other such formatting) or in graphics mode (in which formatting and, sometimes, a variety of fonts appear on the screen as they will on the printed page). All word processors offer at least limited facilities for document formatting, such as font changes, page layout, paragraph indentation, and the like. Some word processors can also check spelling, find synonyms, incorporate graphics created with another program, align mathematical formulas, create and print form letters, perform calculations, display documents in multiple on-screen windows, and enable users to record macros that simplify difficult or repetitive operations. *Compare* editor, line editor.

wordwrap or **word wrap** \wərd´rap\ *n.* The ability of a word processing program or a text-editing program to break lines of text automatically to stay within the page margins or window boundaries of a document without the user having to do so with carriage returns, as is typically necessary on a typewriter. *See also* hard return, soft return.

workaround \wərk´ə-round`\ *n.* A tactic for accomplishing a task, despite a bug or other inadequacy in software or hardware, without actually fixing the underlying problem. *See also* kludge.

workbook \wərk´boŏk\ *n.* In a spreadsheet program, a file containing a number of related worksheets. *See also* worksheet.

workflow application \wərk´flō a-plə-kā`shən\ *n.* A set of programs that aids in the tracking and management of all the activities in a project from start to finish.

workgroup \wərk´grooŏp\ *n.* A group of users working on a common project and sharing computer files, often over a local area network. *See also* groupware.

workgroup computing \wərk´grooŏp kəm-pyooŏ`-tēng\ *n.* A method of working electronically in which various individuals on the same project share resources and access to files using a network arrangement, such as a local area network, enabling them to coordinate their separate tasks. This is accomplished through using software designed for workgroup computing. *See also* groupware.

Workplace Shell \wərk´plås shel`\ *n.* The graphical user interface of OS/2. Like the Mac OS and Windows 95, the Workplace Shell is document-centric. Document files are displayed as icons; clicking on an icon starts the corresponding application, and the user can print a document by dragging the document's icon to a printer icon. The Workplace Shell uses the graphical functions of Presentation Manager. *Acronym:* WPS (W`P-S´).

worksheet \wərk´shēt\ *n.* In a spreadsheet program, a page organized into rows and columns appearing on screen and used for constructing a single table. See the illustration.

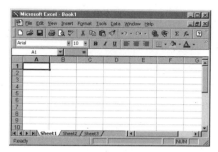

Worksheet.

workstation \wərk´stā`shən\ *n.* **1.** A combination of input, output, and computing hardware that can be used for work by an individual. **2.** A powerful stand-alone computer of the sort used in computer-aided design and other applications requiring a high-end, usually expensive, machine with considerable calculating or graphics capability. **3.** A microcomputer or terminal connected to a network.

World Wide Web or **World-Wide Web** \wərld` wīd web`\ *n.* The total set of interlinked hypertext documents residing on HTTP servers all around the world. Documents on the World Wide Web, called pages or Web pages, are written in HTML (Hypertext Markup Language), identified by URLs (Uniform Resource Locators) that specify the particular machine and pathname by which a file can be accessed, and transmitted from node to node to the end user under HTTP (Hypertext Transfer Protocol). Codes, called tags, embedded in an HTML document associate particular words and images in the document with URLs so that a user can access another file, which may be halfway around the world, at the press of a key or the click of a mouse. These files may contain text (in a variety of fonts and styles), graphics images, movie files, and sounds as well as Java applets, ActiveX controls, or other small embedded software programs that execute when the user activates them by clicking on a link. A user visiting a Web page also may be able to download files from an FTP site and send messages to other users via e-mail by using links on the Web page. The World Wide Web was developed by Timothy Berners-Lee in 1989 for the European Laboratory for Particle Physics (CERN). *Acronym:* WWW (W῾W-W´). *Also called* w³, W3, Web. *See also* ActiveX controls, HTML, HTTP, HTTP server (definition 2), Java applet, URL.

World Wide Web Consortium \wərld wīd web´ kən-sōr῾shē-əm, kən-sōr῾shəm\ *n.* A consortium of commercial and educational institutions that oversees research and promotes standards in all areas related to the World Wide Web. *Acronym:* W3C (W῾thrē-C´).

worm \wərm\ *n.* A program that propagates itself across computers, usually by creating copies of itself in each computer's memory. A worm might duplicate itself in one computer so often that it causes the computer to crash. Sometimes written in separate segments, a worm is introduced surreptitiously into a host system either as a prank or with the intent of damaging or destroying information. *See also* bacterium, Internet Worm, Trojan horse, virus.

WORM \wərm\ *n.* Acronym for "**w**rite **o**nce, **r**ead **m**any." A type of optical disc that can be read and reread but cannot be altered after it has been recorded. WORMs are high-capacity storage devices. Because they cannot be erased and rerecorded, they are suited to storing archives and other large bodies of unchanging information. *See also* compact disc.

WOSA \wō´sə, W῾O-S-A´\ *n.* Acronym for **W**indows **O**pen **S**ystem **A**rchitecture. A set of application programming interfaces from Microsoft that is intended to enable Windows-based applications from different vendors to communicate with each other, such as over a network. The interfaces within the WOSA standard include Open Database Connectivity (ODBC), the Messaging Application Programming Interface (MAPI), the Telephony Application Programming Interface (TAPI), Windows Sockets (Winsock), and Microsoft Remote Procedure Calls (RPC). *See also* MAPI, ODBC, remote procedure call, TAPI, Winsock.

.wp \dot῾W-P´\ *n.* A file extension used to identify files formatted for the WordPerfect word processor.

WP \W-P´\ *n. See* word processing.

WPS \W῾P-S´\ *n. See* Workplace Shell.

WRAM \W´ram, W῾R-A-M´\ *n.* Acronym for **w**indow **r**andom **a**ccess **m**emory. A type of RAM used in video adapters. Like video RAM (VRAM), WRAM allows the screen to be repainted while a graphical image is being written, but WRAM is faster. *Compare* video RAM.

wrap around \rap´ ər-ound´\ *vb.* To continue movement, as with the cursor or a search operation, to the beginning or to a new starting point rather than stopping when the end of a series is reached. For example, the screen cursor might wrap around to the first column of the next line rather than stopping when it reaches the last column of the current line. Likewise, a program starting a search or replace operation in the middle of a document might be instructed to wrap around to the beginning rather than stop when it reaches the end of the document.

.wri \dot῾W-R-I´\ *n.* The file format that identifies document files in the Microsoft Write format.

wrist support \rist´ su-pōrt´\ *n.* A device placed in front of a computer keyboard to support the wrists in an ergonomically neutral position, thereby safeguarding against repetitive strain injuries, such as carpal tunnel syndrome. See the illustration. *Also called* wrist rest. *See also* carpal tunnel syndrome, repetitive strain injury.

write[1] \rīt\ *n.* A transfer of information to a storage device, such as a disk, or to an output device, such as the monitor or printer. For example, a disk write means that information is transferred from memory to storage on disk. *See also* output[1]. *Compare* read[1].

write[2] \rīt\ *vb.* To transfer information either to a storage device, such as a disk, or to an output device, such as the monitor or a printer. Writing is the means by which a computer provides the results of processing. A computer can also be said to write to the screen when it displays information on the monitor. *See also* output[2]. *Compare* read[2].

write access \rīt´ ak´ses\ *n.* A privilege on a computer system that allows a user to save, change, or delete stored data. Write access is usually set by

Wrist support. One type of wrist support device.

the system administrator for a networked or server system and by the owner of the computer for a stand-alone machine. *See also* access privileges.

write-back cache \rīt´bak kash`\ *n.* A type of cache with the following feature: when changes are made to cached data, they are not simultaneously made to the original data as well. Instead, the changed data is marked, and the original data is updated when the cached data is deallocated. In a write-through cache, by contrast, changes made to cached data are simultaneously made in the original copy. A write-back cache can perform more quickly than a write-through cache. But in some contexts, differences between cached and original data could lead to problems, and write-through caches must be used. *See also* cache.

write-behind cache \rīt-bə-hīnd´ kash`\ *n.* A form of temporary storage in which data is held, or cached, for a short time in memory before being written on disk for permanent storage. Caching improves system performance in general by reducing the number of times the computer must go through the relatively slow process of reading from and writing to disk. *See also* CPU cache, disk cache.

write cache \rīt´ kash\ *n. See* write-behind cache.

write error \rīt´ âr`ər\ *n.* An error encountered while a computer is in the process of transferring information from memory to storage or to another output device. *Compare* read error.

write mode \rīt´ mōd\ *n.* In computer operation, the state in which a program can write (record) information in a file. In write mode, the program is permitted to make changes to existing information. *Compare* read-only.

write protect \rīt´ prə-tekt`\ *vb.* To prevent the writing (recording) of information, usually on a disk. Either a floppy disk or an individual file on a floppy or a hard disk can be write protected (though not necessarily infallibly). *See also* write-protect notch.

write-protect notch \rīt´prə-tekt noch`\ *n.* A small opening in the jacket of a floppy disk that can be used to make the disk unwritable. On a 5.25-inch floppy disk, the write-protect notch is a rectangular hole on the edge of the disk jacket. When this notch is covered, a computer can read from the disk but cannot record new information on it. On 3.5-inch microfloppy disks that are enclosed in plastic shells, the write-protect notch is an opening in a corner. When the sliding tab in this opening is moved to uncover a small hole, the disk is protected and cannot be written to. See the illustration. *Also called* write-protect tab. *See also* write[2].

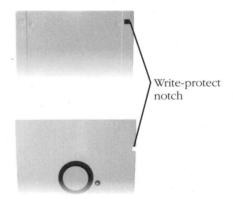

Write-protect notch

Write-protect notch. The write-protect notch on a 3.5-inch disk (top) and on a 5.25-inch disk (bottom).

write-protect tab \rīt´prə-tekt tab`\ *n. See* write-protect notch.

.ws \dot`W-S´\ *n.* On the Internet, the major geographic domain specifying that an address is located in Western Samoa.

.wv.us \dot-W-V`dot-U-S´\ *n.* On the Internet, the major geographic domain specifying that an address is located in West Virginia, United States.

WWW \W`W-W´\ *n. See* World Wide Web.

WYSBYGI \W`Y-S-B-Y-G-I´\ *adj.* Acronym for **W**hat **Y**ou **S**ee **B**efore **Y**ou **G**et **I**t. Providing a preview of the effects of the changes the user has selected before the changes are finally applied. For example, a dialog box in a word processing program might display a sample of the font a user has chosen before the font is actually changed in the document. The user can cancel any changes after previewing them, and the document will be unaffected. *See also* WYSIWYG.

WYSIWYG \wiz´ē-wig`\ *adj.* Acronym for **W**hat **Y**ou **S**ee **I**s **W**hat **Y**ou **G**et. Allowing a user to view a document as it will appear in the final product, and to directly edit the text, graphics, or other elements within that view. A WYSIWYG language is often easier to use than a markup language, which provides no immediate visual feedback regarding the changes being made. *Compare* markup language.

.wy.us \dot-W-Y`dot-U-S´\ *n.* On the Internet, the major geographic domain specifying that an address is located in Wyoming, United States.

X.21 \X̄`twen-tē-wən´\ *n. See* CCITT X series.

X.25 \X̄`twen-tē-fīv´\ *n.* A recommendation published by the ITU-T (formerly CCITT) international communications standards organization that defines the connection between a terminal and a packet-switching network. X.25 incorporates three definitions: the electrical connection between the terminal and the network, the transmission or link-access protocol, and the implementation of virtual circuits between network users. Taken together, these definitions specify a synchronous, full-duplex terminal-to-network connection. Packet format, error control, and other features are equivalent to portions of the HDLC (High-level Data Link Control) protocol defined by the International Organization for Standardization (ISO). *See also* CCITT X series, HDLC, packet switching, virtual circuit.

X.32 \X̄`thər-tē-tōō´\ *n. See* CCITT X series.

X.400 \X̄`fōr-hun´drəd\ *n. See* CCITT X series.

X.445 \X̄`fōr-fōr-fīv´\ *n. See* CCITT X series.

X.500 \X̄`fīv-hun´drəd\ *n. See* CCITT X series.

X.75 \X̄`sev-ən-tē-fīv´\ *n. See* CCITT X series.

x86 \X̄`ā-tē-siks´\ *n.* Any computer based on an 8086, 80286, 80386, 80486, or Pentium microprocessor.

x-axis \X̄´aks`is\ *n.* The horizontal reference line on a grid, chart, or graph that has horizontal and vertical dimensions. *See also* Cartesian coordinates.

Xbase \X̄´bās\ *n.* A generic name for database languages based on dBASE, a copyrighted product of Ashton-Tate Corporation. The term was originally coined to avoid litigation with Ashton-Tate. Xbase languages have since developed characteristics of their own and are now only partly compatible with the dBASE family of languages.

X button \X̄´ but`ən\ *n. See* close button.

XCMD \X̄`C-M-D´\ *n.* Acronym for e**x**ternal **com**man**d.** An external code resource used in Hyper-Card, a hypermedia program developed for the Macintosh. *See also* HyperCard, XFCN.

X Consortium \X̄´ kən-sōr`shē-əm, kən-sōr´-shəm\ *n.* The body, composed of several hardware firms, that governed the standards for the X Window System. The Open Group's X Project Team now has responsibility for the X Window System. *See also* X Window System.

XENIX \zē´niks\ *n.* A version of UNIX that was originally adapted by Microsoft for Intel-based personal computers. Although it has been sold by many vendors, including Microsoft, Intel, and the Santa Cruz Operation (SCO), it has become principally identified with SCO. *See also* UNIX.

xerography \zēr-o´grə-fē`\ *n. See* electrophotography.

Xerox PARC \zēr`oks pärk´, P-A-R-C´\ *n.* Short for **Xerox P**alo **A**lto **R**esearch **C**enter. Xerox's research and development facility in Palo Alto, California. Xerox PARC is the birthplace of such innovations as the local area network (LAN), the laser printer, and the graphical user interface (GUI).

XFCN \X̄`F-C-N´\ *n.* Acronym for e**x**ternal **f**un**c**tio**n.** An external code resource that returns a value after it has completed executing. XFCNs are used in HyperCard, a hypermedia program developed for the Macintosh. *See also* HyperCard, XCMD.

XGA \X̄`G-A´\ *n. See* Extended Graphics Array.

x-height \X̄´hīt\ *n.* In typography, the height of the lowercase letter x in a particular font. The x-height thus represents the height of the body only of a lowercase letter, excluding ascenders (such as the top of the letter b) and descenders (such as the tail on the letter g). See the illustration on the next page. *See also* ascender, descender.

Xmodem \X̄´mō`dəm\ *n.* A file transfer protocol used in asynchronous communications that transfers information in blocks of 128 bytes.

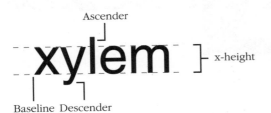

x-height.

Xmodem 1K \X`mō-dəm wən-K´\ *n.* A version of the Xmodem file transfer protocol designed for larger, longer-distance file transfers. Xmodem 1K transmits information in 1-kilobyte (1,024-byte) blocks and uses a more reliable form of error checking. *See also* Xmodem.

Xmodem-CRC \X`mō-dəm-C-R-C´\ *n.* An enhanced version of the Xmodem file transfer protocol that incorporates a 2-byte cyclical redundancy check (CRC) to detect transmission errors. *See also* CRC.

XMS \X`M-S´\ *n. See* extended memory specification.

XMT \X`M-T´\ *n.* Short for **trans**mit. A signal used in serial communications.

XON/XOFF \X-on`X-of´\ *n.* An asynchronous communications protocol in which the receiving device or computer uses special characters to control the flow of data from the transmitting device or computer. When the receiving computer cannot continue to receive data, it transmits an XOFF control character that tells the sender to stop transmitting; when transmission can resume, the computer signals the sender with an XON character. *Also called* software handshake. *See also* handshake.

XOR \X-ōr´\ *n. See* exclusive OR.

X series \X´ sēr`ēz\ *n. See* CCITT X series.

X terminal \X´ tər`mə-nəl\ *n.* An intelligent display device, connected to an Ethernet network, that performs operations on request from client applications in an X Window System. *See also* Ethernet (definition 1), X Window System.

XT keyboard \X-T´ kē´bōrd\ *n. See* PC/XT keyboard.

X Windows \X´ win`dōz\ *n. See* X Window System.

X Window System \X` win´dō si-stəm\ *n.* A nonproprietary standardized set of display-handling routines, developed at MIT. Most often encountered on UNIX workstations, the X Window System is independent of hardware and operating system. An X Window System client calls on the server, which is located on the user's workstation, to provide a window in which the client can generate a display of text or graphics. *Also called* X Windows. *See also* X Consortium.

X-Y display \X-Y´ di-splā`\ *n. See* vector display.

x-y matrix \X`Y mā´triks\ *n.* An arrangement of rows and columns with a horizontal (*x*) axis and a vertical (*y*) axis.

x-y plotter \X`Y plot´ər\ *n. See* plotter.

x-y-z coordinate system \X`Y-Z` kō-ōr´də-nət si`stəm\ *n.* A three-dimensional system of Cartesian coordinates that includes a third (*z*) axis running perpendicular to the horizontal (*x*) and vertical (*y*) axes. The *x-y-z* coordinate system is used in computer graphics for creating models with length, breadth, and depth and for moving models in three-dimensional space. See the illustration. *See also* Cartesian coordinates.

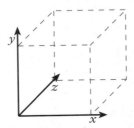

x-y-z coordinate system.

Yahoo! \yä´hōō\ *n*. The first major online Web-based directory and search engine for Internet resources, which can be found at http://www.yahoo.com. *See also* search engine (definition 2).

Yanoff list \yan´of list`\ *n*. The informal name of the Internet services list created and maintained by Scott Yanoff. The Yanoff list was one of the earliest directories of Internet services and resources. It is located at http://www.spectracom.com/islist/.

***y*-axis** \Y´aks`is\ *n*. The vertical reference line on a grid, chart, or graph that has horizontal and vertical dimensions. *See also* Cartesian coordinates.

.ye \dot`Y-E´\ *n*. On the Internet, the major geographic domain specifying that an address is located in Yemen.

Yellow Pages \yel´ō pā`jəz\ *n*. **1.** The former name of a UNIX utility, provided by SunSoft (Sun Microsystems system software), that maintains a central database of names and locations of the resources on a network. The Yellow Pages enable processes on any node to locate resources by name. This utility is now known formally as NIS (Network Information Service). **2.** InterNIC Registration Services' database of domain names and their IP addresses. *See also* domain name, IP address. **3.** Any of several Internet business directory services. Some are print publications, some are strictly electronic, and some are both.

YHBT \Y¨H-B-T´\ *n*. Acronym for **y**ou **h**ave **b**een **t**rolled. An expression used in e-mail and newsgroups to indicate that the receiver has taken a deliberately set bait. *See also* troll.

YHL \Y¨H-L´\ *n*. Acronym for **y**ou **h**ave **l**ost. An expression used in e-mail and newsgroups, often following YHBT. *See also* YHBT.

.yk.ca \dot-Y-K`dot-C-A´\ *n*. On the Internet, the major geographic domain specifying that an address is located in the Yukon, Canada.

Ymodem \Y´mō`dəm\ *n*. A variation of the Xmodem file transfer protocol that includes the following enhancements: the ability to transfer information in 1-kilobyte (1,024-byte) blocks, the ability to send multiple files (batch file transmission), cyclical redundancy checking (CRC), and the ability to abort transfer by transmitting two CAN (cancel) characters in a row. *See also* CRC, Xmodem.

yocto- \yok´tō\ *prefix* A metric prefix meaning 10^{-24} (one septillionth in the American system).

yoke \yōk\ *n*. The part of a CRT (cathode-ray tube) that deflects the electron beam, causing it to strike a specific area on the screen. *Also called* deflection coils. *See also* CRT.

yotta- \yot´ə\ *prefix* Metric prefix meaning 10^{24} (one septillion in the American system).

.yt \dot`Y-T´\ *n*. On the Internet, the major geographic domain specifying that an address is located in Mayotte.

.yu \dot`Y-U´\ *n*. On the Internet, the major geographic domain specifying that an address is located in the former Yugoslavia.

.z \dot-Z´\ *n.* The file extension identifying a UNIX file compressed using the gzip or compact utility. *See also* gzip.

.Z \dot-Z´\ *n.* The file extension for UNIX files that have been compressed using the compress utility. *See also* compress[1].

Z39.50 standard \Z`thər-tē-nīn`point-fīv-ō´ stan`-dərd\ *n.* A specification for a query language based on SQL (structured query language). It is used by WAIS, among other Internet services, to search for files through the use of keywords and is widely used for remote access to library catalogs. *See also* structured query language, WAIS.

Z80 \Z`ā´tē\ *n.* An 8-bit microprocessor from Zilog, a company founded by former Intel engineers. The Z80 has a 16-bit address bus, yielding a 64-kilobyte addressable memory space, and an 8-bit data bus. A descendant of the Intel 8080, it was the favored processor in the days of the CP/M operating system. One of the most popular computers of the early 1980s, the Radio Shack TRS-80, was based on this chip. *See also* CP/M.

.za \dot`Z-A´\ *n.* On the Internet, the major geographic domain specifying that an address is located in South Africa.

zap \zap\ *vb.* **1.** To erase permanently. For example, to zap a file means to remove it without hope of retrieval. **2.** To damage a device, usually by discharging static electricity through it.

z-axis \Z´aks`is\ *n.* The third axis in a three-dimensional coordinate system, used in computer graphics to represent depth. *See also* Cartesian coordinates, *x-y-z* coordinate system.

ZD Net \Z-D´ net`\ *n.* A Web site designed for PC users that hosts a wide range of technical special interest groups (SIGs), as well as freeware and shareware utilities. It was founded by the Ziff Davis publishing group as an online information service. *Also called* ZiffNet. *See also* SIG.

zepto- \zep´to\ *prefix* A metric prefix meaning 10^{-21} (one sextillionth in the American system).

zero[1] \zēr´ō\ *n.* The arithmetic symbol (0) representing no magnitude.

zero[2] \zēr´ō\ *vb.* To fill or replace with zeros (for example, to zero a specified portion of memory, a field, or some other limited structure).

zero divide \zēr´ō di-vīd´\ *n.* A division operation in which the divisor is zero. Division by zero is mathematically undefined, is not allowed in a program, and is considered a bug.

zero flag \zēr´ō flag`\ *n.* A flag (bit) in a microprocessor that is set (turned on), typically in a flag register, when the result of an operation is zero. *See also* flag (definition 1).

zero-insertion-force socket \zēr`ō-in-sər`shən-fōrs sok´ət\ *n. See* ZIF socket.

zero out \zēr`ō out´\ *vb.* To set a variable value or a series of bits to zero.

zero suppression \zēr`ō su-presh`ən\ *n.* The elimination of leading (nonsignificant) zeros in a number. For example, zero suppression would truncate 000123.456 to 123.456. *See also* significant digits.

zero wait state \zēr`ō wāt´ stāt\ *n.* The condition of random access memory (RAM) that is fast enough to respond to the processor without requiring wait states. *See also* wait state.

zetta- \zet´ə\ *prefix* A metric prefix meaning 10^{21} (one sextillion in the American system).

z-fold paper \Z´fōld pā`pər\ *n. See* fanfold paper.

ZiffNet \zif´net\ *n. See* ZD Net.

ZIF socket \zif´ sok`ət, Z-I-F´\ *n.* Short for **z**ero-**i**nsertion-**f**orce **socket**. A kind of socket for integrated circuits that can be opened with a lever or screw, allowing the chip to be placed in the socket without the application of pressure. The lever or screw of the socket is then closed, causing the socket contacts to grip the chip's pins. ZIF sockets facilitate frequent insertion and removal of chips, but they take up more space and are more expensive than conventional sockets.

.zip \dot-zip´, -Z`I-P´\ *n.* A file extension that identifies a compressed archive file encoded in ZIP format, as by PKZIP. *See also* compressed file, PKZIP.

Zip drive \zip´ drīv\ *n.* A disk drive developed by Iomega that uses 3.5-inch removable disks (Zip disks) capable of storing 100 megabytes of data. See the illustration. *See also* disk drive.

Zip drive.

.zm \dot`Z-M´\ *n.* On the Internet, the major geographic domain specifying that an address is located in Zambia.

Zmodem \Z´mō`dəm\ *n.* An enhancement of the Xmodem file transfer protocol that handles larger data transfers with less error. Zmodem includes a feature called checkpoint restart, which resumes transmission at the point of interruption, rather than at the beginning, if the communications link is broken during data transfer. *See also* Xmodem.

zone \zōn\ *n.* **1.** On a local area network, a subgroup of users within a larger group of interconnected networks. **2.** In Macintosh programming, a portion of memory that is allocated and reallo-

cated by the memory manager facility as memory is requested and released by applications and by other parts of the operating system. *See also* heap (definition 1).

zone header \zōn´ hed`ər\ *n.* On the Apple Macintosh, a header at the beginning of a block of memory that contains information needed by the memory management facility in order to use that memory block effectively. *See also* header (definition 2).

.zoo \dot-zoo´\ *n.* The file extension that identifies compressed archive files created with the zoo file compression utility. *See also* zoo210.

zoo210 \zoo`too-ten´\ *n.* Version 2.1 of zoo, a program for creating compressed archive files (whose names have the extension .zoo). The algorithm for zoo210 is based on that of LHARC. Implementations of zoo210 are available for UNIX and Intel systems. *See also* archive file, LHARC.

zoom \zoom\ *vb.* To enlarge a selected portion of a graphical image or document to fill a window or the screen. Zooming is a feature of many programs, including drawing, word processing, and spreadsheet programs, that allows the user to select a small part of the screen, zoom it, and make changes to the enlarged portion at a finer level of detail. *See also* window.

zoom box \zoom´boks\ *n.* A control in the upper right corner of the frame of a window on the Macintosh screen. When the user clicks on the zoom box, the window toggles between the maximum size and the size the user has set for it by dragging. *See also* window. *Compare* Maximize button.

.zr \dot`Z-R´\ *n.* On the Internet, the major geographic domain specifying that an address is located in Zaire.

Zulu time \zoo´loo tīm`\ *n.* Slang for Greenwich Mean Time.

Appendix A

ASCII Character Set

Dec	Hex	Char	Dec	Hex	Char	Dec	Hex	Char
0	00	NUL (Null)	34	22	"	68	44	D
1	01	SOH (Start of heading)	35	23	#	69	45	E
2	02	STX (Start of text)	36	24	$	70	46	F
3	03	ETX (End of text)	37	25	%	71	47	G
4	04	EOT (End of transmission)	38	26	&	72	48	H
5	05	ENQ (Enquiry)	39	27	'	73	49	I
6	06	ACK (Acknowledge)	40	28	(	74	4A	J
7	07	BEL (Bell)	41	29	)	75	4B	K
8	08	BS (Backspace)	42	2A	*	76	4C	L
9	09	HT (Horizontal tab)	43	2B	+	77	4D	M
10	0A	LF (Linefeed)	44	2C	,	78	4E	N
11	0B	VT (Vertical tab)	45	2D	–	79	4F	O
12	0C	FF (Formfeed)	46	2E	.	80	50	P
13	0D	CR (Carriage return)	47	2F	/	81	51	Q
14	0E	SO (Shift out)	48	30	0	82	52	R
15	0F	SI (Shift in)	49	31	1	83	53	S
16	10	DLE (Data link escape)	50	32	2	84	54	T
17	11	DC1 (Device control 1)	51	33	3	85	55	U
18	12	DC2 (Device control 2)	52	34	4	86	56	V
19	13	DC3 (Device control 3)	53	35	5	87	57	W
20	14	DC4 (Device control 4)	54	36	6	88	58	X
21	15	NAK (Negative acknowledge)	55	37	7	89	59	Y
22	16	SYN (Synchronous idle)	56	38	8	90	5A	Z
23	17	ETB (End transmission block)	57	39	9	91	5B	[
24	18	CAN (Cancel)	58	3A	:	92	5C	\
25	19	EM (End of medium)	59	3B	;	93	5D	]
26	1A	SUB (Substitute)	60	3C	<	94	5E	^
27	1B	ESC (Escape)	61	3D	=	95	5F	_
28	1C	FS (File separator)	62	3E	>	96	60	`
29	1D	GS (Group separator)	63	3F	?	97	61	a
30	1E	RS (Record separator)	64	40	@	98	62	b
31	1F	US (Unit separator)	65	41	A	99	63	c
32	20	<space>	66	42	B	100	64	d
33	21	!	67	43	C	101	65	e

Dec	Hex	Char	Dec	Hex	Char	Dec	Hex	Char	Dec	Hex	Char
102	66	f	110	6E	n	118	76	v	126	7E	~
103	67	g	111	6F	o	119	77	w	127	7F	DEL (Delete)
104	68	h	112	70	p	120	78	x			
105	69	i	113	71	q	121	79	y			
106	6A	j	114	72	r	122	7A	z			
107	6B	k	115	73	s	123	7B	{			
108	6C	l	116	74	t	124	7C	:			
109	6D	m	117	75	u	125	7D	}			

Appendix B

IBM Extended Character Set

Dec	Hex	Char	Dec	Hex	Char	Dec	Hex	Char	Dec	Hex	Char
128	80	Ç	156	9C	£	184	B8	⌐	212	D4	╘
129	81	ü	157	9D	¥	185	B9	╣	213	D5	╒
130	82	é	158	9E	₧	186	BA	║	214	D6	╓
131	83	â	159	9F	ƒ	187	BB	╗	215	D7	╫
132	84	ä	160	A0	á	188	BC	╝	216	D8	╪
133	85	à	161	A1	í	189	BD	╜	217	D9	┘
134	86	å	162	A2	ó	190	BE	╛	218	DA	┌
135	87	ç	163	A3	ú	191	BF	┐	219	DB	█
136	88	ê	164	A4	ñ	192	C0	└	220	DC	▄
137	89	ë	165	A5	Ñ	193	C1	┴	221	DD	▌
138	8A	è	166	A6	ª	194	C2	┬	222	DE	▐
139	8B	ï	167	A7	º	195	C3	├	223	DF	▀
140	8C	î	168	A8	¿	196	C4	─	224	E0	α
141	8D	ì	169	A9	⌐	197	C5	┼	225	E1	β
142	8E	Ä	170	AA	¬	198	C6	╞	226	E2	Γ
143	8F	Å	171	AB	½	199	C7	╟	227	E3	π
144	90	É	172	AC	¼	200	C8	╚	228	E4	Σ
145	91	æ	173	AD	¡	201	C9	╔	229	E5	σ
146	92	Æ	174	AE	«	202	CA	╩	230	E6	µ
147	93	ô	175	AF	»	203	CB	╦	231	E7	τ
148	94	ö	176	B0	░	204	CC	╠	232	E8	Φ
149	95	ò	177	B1	▒	205	CD	═	233	E9	Θ
150	96	û	178	B2	▓	206	CE	╬	234	EA	Ω
151	97	ù	179	B3	│	207	CF	╧	235	EB	δ
152	98	ÿ	180	B4	┤	208	D0	╨	236	EC	∞
153	99	Ö	181	B5	╡	209	D1	╤	237	ED	φ
154	9A	Ü	182	B6	╢	210	D2	╥	238	EE	∈
155	9B	¢	183	B7	╖	211	D3	╙	239	EF	∩

Dec	Hex	Char	Dec	Hex	Char	Dec	Hex	Char	Dec	Hex	Char
240	F0	≡	244	F4	⌠	248	F8	°	252	FC	η
241	F1	±	245	F5	⌡	249	F9	•	253	FD	²
242	F2	≥	246	F6	÷	250	FA	·	254	FE	■
243	F3	≤	247	F7	≈	251	FB	√	255	FF	

Apple Macintosh Extended Character Set

ASCII	Hex	Times	New York	Courier	Zapf Dingbats	Symbol
128	80	Ä	Ä	Ä	(	
129	81	Å	Å	Å	)	
130	82	Ç	Ç	Ç	(	
131	83	É	É	É	)	
132	84	Ñ	Ñ	Ñ	(	
133	85	Ö	Ö	Ö	)	
134	86	Ü	Ü	Ü	‹	
135	87	á	á	á	›	
136	88	à	à	à	(	
137	89	â	â	â	)	
138	8A	ä	ä	ä	(	
139	8B	ã	ã	ã	)	
140	8C	å	å	å	{	
141	8D	ç	ç	ç	}	
142	8E	é	é	é		
143	8F	è	è	è		
144	90	ê	ê	ê		
145	91	ë	ë	ë		
146	92	í	í	í		
147	93	ì	ì	ì		
148	94	î	î	î		
149	95	ï	ï	ï		
150	96	ñ	ñ	ñ		
151	97	ó	ó	ó		
152	98	ò	ò	ò		
153	99	ô	ô	ô		
154	9A	ö	ö	ö		
155	9B	õ	õ	õ		
156	9C	ú	ú	ú		
157	9D	ù	ù	ù		
158	9E	û	û	û		
159	9F	ü	ü	ü		
160	A0	†	†	†		

ASCII	Hex	Times	New York	Courier	Zapf Dingbats	Symbol
161	A1	°	°	°	✌	Υ
162	A2	¢	¢	¢	✆	′
163	A3	£	£	£	✇	≤
164	A4	§	§	§	♥	/
165	A5	•	•	•	♣	∞
166	A6	¶	¶	¶	🙋	ƒ
167	A7	ß	ß	ß	✥	♣
168	A8	®	®	®	♣	♦
169	A9	©	©	©	♦	♥
170	AA	™	™	™	♥	♠
171	AB	´	´	´	♠	↔
172	AC	¨	¨	¨	①	←
173	AD	≠	≠	≠	②	↑
174	AE	Æ	Æ	Æ	③	→
175	AF	Ø	Ø	Ø	④	↓
176	B0	∞	∞	∞	⑤	°
177	B1	±	±	±	⑥	±
178	B2	≤	≤	≤	⑦	″
179	B3	≥	≥	≥	⑧	≥
180	B4	¥	¥	¥	⑨	×
181	B5	µ	µ	µ	⑩	∝
182	B6	∂	∂	∂	❶	∂
183	B7	Σ	Σ	Σ	❷	•
184	B8	∏	∏	∏	❸	÷
185	B9	π	π	π	❹	≠
186	BA	∫	∫	∫	❺	≡
187	BB	ª	ª	ª	❻	≈
188	BC	º	º	º	❼	…
189	BD	Ω	Ω	Ω	❽	|
190	BE	æ	æ	æ	❾	—
191	BF	ø	ø	ø	❿	↵
192	C0	¿	¿	¿	①	ℵ
193	C1	¡	¡	¡	②	ℑ
194	C2	¬	¬	¬	③	ℜ
195	C3	√	√	√	④	℘
196	C4	ƒ	ƒ	ƒ	⑤	⊗
197	C5	≈	≈	≈	⑥	⊕
198	C6	Δ	Δ	Δ	⑦	∅
199	C7	«	«	«	⑧	∩
200	C8	»	»	»	⑨	∪
201	C9	…	…	…	⑩	⊃
202	CA	——NBSP (nonbreaking space)——			❶	⊇
203	CB	À	À	À	❷	⊄

ASCII	Hex	Times	New York	Courier	Zapf Dingbats	Symbol
204	CC	Ã	Ã	Ã	❸	⊂
205	CD	Õ	Õ	Õ	❹	⊆
206	CE	Œ	Œ	Œ	❺	∈
207	CF	œ	œ	œ	❻	∉
208	D0	-	-	–	❼	∠
209	D1	—	—	—	❽	∇
210	D2	"	"	"	❾	®
211	D3	"	"	"	❿	©
212	D4	'	'	'	→	™
213	D5	'	'	'	→	∏
214	D6	÷	÷	÷	↔	√
215	D7	◊	◊	◊	↕	·
216	D8	ÿ	ÿ	ÿ	↘	¬
217	D9	Ÿ	Ÿ	Ÿ	→	∧
218	DA	/	/	⁄	↗	∨
219	DB	¤	¤	¤	→	⇔
220	DC	‹	‹	‹	→	⇐
221	DD	›	›	›	→	⇑
222	DE	fi	fi	fi	→	⇒
223	DF	fl	fl	fl	→	⇓
224	E0	‡	‡	‡	→	◊
225	E1	·	·	•	→	〈
226	E2	‚	‚	‚	➢	®
227	E3	„	„	„	➢	©
228	E4	‰	‰	‰	➤	™
229	E5	Â	Â	Â	➡	Σ
230	E6	Ê	Ê	Ê	➡	⎛
231	E7	Á	Â	Á	◗	⎜
232	E8	Ë	Ë	Ë	➡	⎜
233	E9	È	È	È	⇨	⎡
234	EA	Í	Í	Í	⇨	⎜
235	EB	Î	Î	Î	⇦	⎣
236	EC	Ï	Ï	Ï	⇨	⎧
237	ED	Ì	Ì	Ì	⇨	⎨
238	EE	Ó	Ó	Ó	⇨	⎩
239	EF	Ô	Ô	Ô	⇨	⎪
240	F0			— Not Used —		
241	F1	Ò	Ò	Ò	⇨	〉
242	F2	Ú	Ú	Ú	⊃	∫
243	F3	Û	Û	Û	→+	⎰
244	F4	Ù	Ù	Ù	↘	⎪
245	F5	ı	ı	ı	→+	⎱
246	F6	ˆ	ˆ	ˆ	➹	⎠

ASCII	Hex	Times	New York	Courier	Zapf Dingbats	Symbol
247	F7	~	~	~	➴	|
248	F8	‒	‒	‒	➔	)
249	F9	˘	˘	˘	➶	]
250	FA	·	·	·	→	|
251	FB	°	°	°	➡	]
252	FC	˛	˛	˛	➤	]
253	FD	˝	˝	˝	➥	}
254	FE	˓	˓	˓	⇒	]
255	FF	ˇ	ˇ	ˇ		

Appendix D

EBCDIC Character Set

Dec	Hex	Name	Character	Meaning
0	00	NUL		Null
1	01	SOH		Start of heading
2	02	STX		Start of text
3	03	ETX		End of text
4	04	SEL		Select
5	05	HT		Horizontal tab
6	06	RNL		Required new line
7	07	DEL		Delete
8	08	GE		Graphic escape
9	09	SPS		Superscript
10	0A	RPT		Repeat
11	0B	VT		Vertical tab
12	0C	FF		Form feed
13	0D	CR		Carriage return
14	0E	SO		Shift out
15	0F	DI		Shift in
16	10	DLE		Data length escape
17	11	DC1		Device control 1
18	12	DC2		Device control 2
19	13	DC3		Device control 3
20	14	RES/ENP		Restore/enable presentation
21	15	NL		New line
22	16	BS		Backspace
23	17	POC		Program-operator communication
24	18	CAN		Cancel
25	19	EM		End of medium
26	1A	UBS		Unit backspace
27	1B	CU1		Customer use 1
28	1C	IFS		Interchange file separator
29	1D	IGS		Interchange group separator
30	1E	IRS		Interchange record separator
31	1F	IUS/ITB		Interchange unit separator/ intermediate transmission block
32	20	DS		Digit select
33	21	SOS		Start of significance
34	22	FS		Field separator
35	23	WUS		Word underscore
36	24	BYP/INP		Bypass/inhibit presentation
37	25	LF		Line feed

Dec	Hex	Name	Character	Meaning
38	26	ETB		End of transmission block
39	27	ESC		Escape
40	28	SA		Set attribute
41	29	SFE		Start field extended
42	2A	SM/SW		Set mode/switch
43	2B	CSP		Control sequence prefix
44	2C	MFA		Modify field attribute
45	2D	ENQ		Enquiry
46	2E	ACK		Acknowledge
47	2F	BEL		Bell
48	30			(not assigned)
49	31			(not assigned)
50	32	SYN		Synchronous idle
51	33	IR		Index return
52	34	PP		Presentation position
53	35	TRN		Transparent
54	36	NBS		Numeric backspace
55	37	EOT		End of transmission
56	38	SBS		Subscript
57	39	IT		Indent tab
58	3A	RFF		Required form feed
59	3B	CU3		Customer use 3
60	3C	DC4		Device control 4
61	3D	NAK		Negative acknowledgment
62	3E			(not assigned)
63	3F	SUB		Substitute
64	40	SP		Space
65	41	RSP		Required space
66	42			(not assigned)
67	43			(not assigned)
68	44			(not assigned)
69	45			(not assigned)
70	46			(not assigned)
71	47			(not assigned)
72	48			(not assigned)
73	49			(not assigned)
74	4A		¢	
75	4B		.	
76	4C		<	
77	4D		(	
78	4E		+	
79	4F		|	Logical OR
80	50		&	
81	51			(not assigned)
82	52			(not assigned)
83	53			(not assigned)
84	54			(not assigned)

Dec	Hex	Name	Character	Meaning
85	55			(not assigned)
86	56			(not assigned)
87	57			(not assigned)
88	58			(not assigned)
89	59			(not assigned)
90	5A		!	
91	5B		$	
92	5C		*	
93	5D		)	
94	5E		;	
95	5F		¬	Logical NOT
96	60		-	
97	61		/	
98	62			(not assigned)
99	63			(not assigned)
100	64			(not assigned)
101	65			(not assigned)
102	66			(not assigned)
103	67			(not assigned)
104	68			(not assigned)
105	69			(not assigned)
106	6A		¦	Broken pipe
107	6B		,	
108	6C		%	
109	6D		_	
110	6E		>	
111	6F		?	
112	70			(not assigned)
113	71			(not assigned)
114	72			(not assigned)
115	73			(not assigned)
116	74			(not assigned)
117	75			(not assigned)
118	76			(not assigned)
119	77			(not assigned)
120	78			(not assigned)
121	79		`	Grave accent
122	7A		:	
123	7B		#	
124	7C		@	
125	7D		'	
126	7E		=	
127	7F		"	
128	80			(not assigned)
129	81		a	
130	82		b	
131	83		c	

Dec	Hex	Name	Character	Meaning
132	84		d	
133	85		e	
134	86		f	
135	87		g	
136	88		h	
137	89		i	
138	8A			(not assigned)
139	8B			(not assigned)
140	8C			(not assigned)
141	8D			(not assigned)
142	8E			(not assigned)
143	8F			(not assigned)
144	90			(not assigned)
145	91		j	
146	92		k	
147	93		l	
148	94		m	
149	95		n	
150	96		o	
151	97		p	
152	98		q	
153	99		r	
154	9A			(not assigned)
155	9B			(not assigned)
156	9C			(not assigned)
157	9D			(not assigned)
158	9E			(not assigned)
159	9F			(not assigned)
160	A0			(not assigned)
161	A1		~	
162	A2		s	
163	A3		t	
164	A4		u	
165	A5		v	
166	A6		w	
167	A7		x	
168	A8		y	
169	A9		z	
170	AA			(not assigned)
171	AB			(not assigned)
172	AC			(not assigned)
173	AD			(not assigned)
174	AE			(not assigned)
175	AF			(not assigned)
176	B0			(not assigned)
177	B1			(not assigned)
178	B2			(not assigned)

Dec	Hex	Name	Character	Meaning
179	B3			(not assigned)
180	B4			(not assigned)
181	B5			(not assigned)
182	B6			(not assigned)
183	B7			(not assigned)
184	B8			(not assigned)
185	B9			(not assigned)
186	BA			(not assigned)
187	BB			(not assigned)
188	BC			(not assigned)
189	BD			(not assigned)
190	BE			(not assigned)
191	BF			(not assigned)
192	C0		{	Opening brace
193	C1		A	
194	C2		B	
195	C3		C	
196	C4		D	
197	C5		E	
198	C6		F	
199	C7		G	
200	C8		H	
201	C9		I	
202	CA	SHY		Syllable hyphen
203	CB			(not assigned)
204	CC			(not assigned)
205	CD			(not assigned)
206	CE			(not assigned)
207	CF			(not assigned)
208	D0		}	Closing brace
209	D1		J	
210	D2		K	
211	D3		L	
212	D4		M	
213	D5		N	
214	D6		O	
215	D7		P	
216	D8		Q	
217	D9		R	
218	DA			(not assigned)
219	DB			(not assigned)
220	DC			(not assigned)
221	DD			(not assigned)
222	DE			(not assigned)
223	DF			(not assigned)
224	E0		\	Reverse slash
225	E1	NSP		Numeric space

Dec	Hex	Name	Character	Meaning
226	E2		S	
227	E3		T	
228	E4		U	
229	E5		V	
230	E6		W	
231	E7		X	
232	E8		Y	
233	E9		Z	
234	EA			(not assigned)
235	EB			(not assigned)
236	EC			(not assigned)
237	ED			(not assigned)
238	EE			(not assigned)
239	EF			(not assigned)
240	F0		0	
241	F1		1	
242	F2		2	
243	F3		3	
244	F4		4	
245	F5		5	
246	F6		6	
247	F7		7	
248	F8		8	
249	F9		9	
250	FA			(not assigned)
251	FB			(not assigned)
252	FC			(not assigned)
253	FD			(not assigned)
254	FE			(not assigned)
255	FF	EO		Eight ones

Appendix E

Numeric Equivalents

Decimal (Base 10)	Hexadecimal (Base 16)	Octal (Base 8)	Binary (Base 2)
1	01	01	00000001
2	02	02	00000010
3	03	03	00000011
4	04	04	00000100
5	05	05	00000101
6	06	06	00000110
7	07	07	00000111
8	08	10	00001000
9	09	11	00001001
10	0A	12	00001010
11	0B	13	00001011
12	0C	14	00001100
13	0D	15	00001101
14	0E	16	00001110
15	0F	17	00001111
16	10	20	00010000
17	11	21	00010001
18	12	22	00010010
19	13	23	00010011
20	14	24	00010100
21	15	25	00010101
22	16	26	00010110
23	17	27	00010111
24	18	30	00011000
25	19	31	00011001
26	1A	32	00011010
27	1B	33	00011011
28	1C	34	00011100
29	1D	35	00011101
30	1E	36	00011110
31	1F	37	00011111
32	20	40	00100000
33	21	41	00100001
34	22	42	00100010
35	23	43	00100011
36	24	44	00100100
37	25	45	00100101

Decimal (Base 10)	Hexadecimal (Base 16)	Octal (Base 8)	Binary (Base 2)
38	26	46	00100110
39	27	47	00100111
40	28	50	00101000
41	29	51	00101001
42	2A	52	00101010
43	2B	53	00101011
44	2C	54	00101100
45	2D	55	00101101
46	2E	56	00101110
47	2F	57	00101111
48	30	60	00110000
49	31	61	00110001
50	32	62	00110010
51	33	63	00110011
52	34	64	00110100
53	35	65	00110101
54	36	66	00110110
55	37	67	00110111
56	38	70	00111000
57	39	71	00111001
58	3A	72	00111010
59	3B	73	00111011
60	3C	74	00111100
61	3D	75	00111101
62	3E	76	00111110
63	3F	77	00111111
64	40	100	01000000
65	41	101	01000001
66	42	102	01000010
67	43	103	01000011
68	44	104	01000100
69	45	105	01000101
70	46	106	01000110
71	47	107	01000111
72	48	110	01001000
73	49	111	01001001
74	4A	112	01001010
75	4B	113	01001011
76	4C	114	01001100
77	4D	115	01001101
78	4E	116	01001110
79	4F	117	01001111
80	50	120	01010000
81	51	121	01010001
82	52	122	01010010

Decimal (Base 10)	Hexadecimal (Base 16)	Octal (Base 8)	Binary (Base 2)
83	53	123	01010011
84	54	124	01010100
85	55	125	01010101
86	56	126	01010110
87	57	127	01010111
88	58	130	01011000
89	59	131	01011001
90	5A	132	01011010
91	5B	133	01011011
92	5C	134	01011100
93	5D	135	01011101
94	5E	136	01011110
95	5F	137	01011111
96	60	140	01100000
97	61	141	01100001
98	62	142	01100010
99	63	143	01100011
100	64	144	01100100
101	65	145	01100101
102	66	146	01100110
103	67	147	01100111
104	68	150	01101000
105	69	151	01101001
106	6A	152	01101010
107	6B	153	01101011
108	6C	154	01101100
109	6D	155	01101101
110	6E	156	01101110
111	6F	157	01101111
112	70	160	01110000
113	71	161	01110001
114	72	162	01110010
115	73	163	01110011
116	74	164	01110100
117	75	165	01110101
118	76	166	01110110
119	77	167	01110111
120	78	170	01111000
121	79	171	01111001
122	7A	172	01111010
123	7B	173	01111011
124	7C	174	01111100
125	7D	175	01111101
126	7E	176	01111110
127	7F	177	01111111

Decimal (Base 10)	Hexadecimal (Base 16)	Octal (Base 8)	Binary (Base 2)
128	80	200	10000000
129	81	201	10000001
130	82	202	10000010
131	83	203	10000011
132	84	204	10000100
133	85	205	10000101
134	86	206	10000110
135	87	207	10000111
136	88	210	10001000
137	89	211	10001001
138	8A	212	10001010
139	8B	213	10001011
140	8C	214	10001100
141	8D	215	10001101
142	8E	216	10001110
143	8F	217	10001111
144	90	220	10010000
145	91	221	10010001
146	92	222	10010010
147	93	223	10010011
148	94	224	10010100
149	95	225	10010101
150	96	226	10010110
151	97	227	10010111
152	98	230	10011000
153	99	231	10011001
154	9A	232	10011010
155	9B	233	10011011
156	9C	234	10011100
157	9D	235	10011101
158	9E	236	10011110
159	9F	237	10011111
160	A0	240	10100000
161	A1	241	10100001
162	A2	242	10100010
163	A3	243	10100011
164	A4	244	10100100
165	A5	245	10100101
166	A6	246	10100110
167	A7	247	10100111
168	A8	250	10101000
169	A9	251	10101001
170	AA	252	10101010
171	AB	253	10101011
172	AC	254	10101100

Decimal (Base 10)	Hexadecimal (Base 16)	Octal (Base 8)	Binary (Base 2)
173	AD	255	10101101
174	AE	256	10101110
175	AF	257	10101111
176	B0	260	10110000
177	B1	261	10110001
178	B2	262	10110010
179	B3	263	10110011
180	B4	264	10110100
181	B5	265	10110101
182	B6	266	10110110
183	B7	267	10110111
184	B8	270	10111000
185	B9	271	10111001
186	BA	272	10111010
187	BB	273	10111011
188	BC	274	10111100
189	BD	275	10111101
190	BE	276	10111110
191	BF	277	10111111
192	C0	300	11000000
193	C1	301	11000001
194	C2	302	11000010
195	C3	303	11000011
196	C4	304	11000100
197	C5	305	11000101
198	C6	306	11000110
199	C7	307	11000111
200	C8	310	11001000
201	C9	311	11001001
202	CA	312	11001010
203	CB	313	11001011
204	CC	314	11001100
205	CD	315	11001101
206	CE	316	11001110
207	CF	317	11001111
208	D0	320	11010000
209	D1	321	11010001
210	D2	322	11010010
211	D3	323	11010011
212	D4	324	11010100
213	D5	325	11010101
214	D6	326	11010110
215	D7	327	11010111
216	D8	330	11011000
217	D9	331	11011001

Decimal (Base 10)	Hexadecimal (Base 16)	Octal (Base 8)	Binary (Base 2)
218	DA	332	11011010
219	DB	333	11011011
220	DC	334	11011100
221	DD	335	11011101
222	DE	336	11011110
223	DF	337	11011111
224	E0	340	11100000
225	E1	341	11100001
226	E2	342	11100010
227	E3	343	11100011
228	E4	344	11100100
229	E5	345	11100101
230	E6	346	11100110
231	E7	347	11100111
232	E8	350	11101000
233	E9	351	11101001
234	EA	352	11101010
235	EB	353	11101011
236	EC	354	11101100
237	ED	355	11101101
238	EE	356	11101110
239	EF	357	11101111
240	F0	360	11110000
241	F1	361	11110001
242	F2	362	11110010
243	F3	363	11110011
244	F4	364	11110100
245	F5	365	11110101
246	F6	366	11110110
247	F7	367	11110111
248	F8	370	11111000
249	F9	371	11111001
250	FA	372	11111010
251	FB	373	11111011
252	FC	374	11111100
253	FD	375	11111101
254	FE	376	11111110
255	FF	377	11111111

The manuscript for this book was prepared and submitted to Microsoft Press in electronic form. Text files were originally prepared using Microsoft Access 95. Text composition by Publication Services in Garamond with display type in Garamond Bold, using FrameMaker 5.0 for Windows 95. Composed pages were delivered to the printer in electronic prepress files.

Lexicographer
Robert Costello

Microsoft Press

Cover Designer
Gregory Erickson

Interior Graphic Designer
Kim Eggleston

Interior Illustrator
Travis Beaven

Principal Proofreader/Copy Editor
Paula Thurman

Publication Services

Development

Text Consultants
Thomas P. Magliery
Terrence M. McLaren
Larry S. Jackson
Judson D. Weeks
Annette B. Jackson
Thomas A. Jackson
John Ross

Pronunciation Guide Consultants
Gerard Dalgish
Sharon Goldstein

Pronunciations
Julia S. Dalgish
Joel Gordon

Writers
Jerome Colburn
Robert Howecton
Ilana Kingsley
Thomas A. Long
David Mason

Production

Copy Editor
David Mason

Senior Project Coordinator
Rhonda Zachmeyer

Customer Service Representative
Karla Wright

Keep things **running** smoothly
around the **Office.**

These are *the* answer books for business users of Microsoft Office 97 applications. They are packed with everything from quick, clear instructions for new users to comprehensive answers for power users. The Microsoft Press® *Running* series features authoritative handbooks you'll keep by your computer and use every day.

Running Microsoft® Excel 97
Mark Dodge, Chris Kinata, and Craig Stinson
U.S.A. $39.95   ($54.95 Canada)
ISBN 1-57231-321-8

Running Microsoft® Word 97
Russell Borland
U.S.A. $39.95   ($53.95 Canada)
ISBN 1-57231-320-X

Running Microsoft® PowerPoint® 97
Stephen W. Sagman
U.S.A. $29.95   ($39.95 Canada)
ISBN 1-57231-324-2

Running Microsoft® Access 97
John L. Viescas
U.S.A. $39.95   ($54.95 Canada)
ISBN 1-57231-323-4

Running Microsoft® Office 97
Michael Halvorson and Michael Young
U.S.A. $39.95   ($53.95 Canada)
ISBN 1-57231-322-6

Microsoft Press

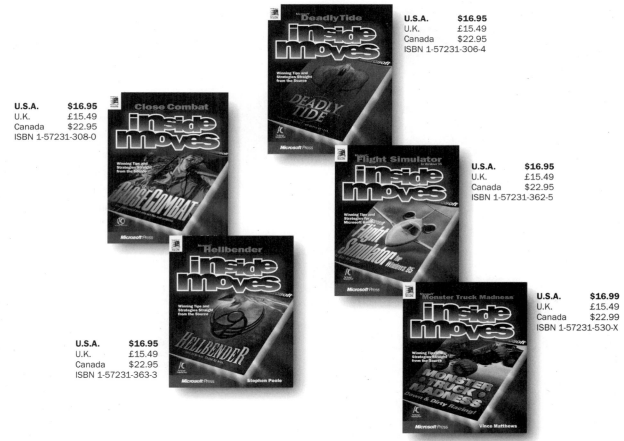

Things are looking up!

Here's the remarkable, *visual* way to quickly find answers about Microsoft applications and operating systems. Microsoft Press® *At a Glance* books let you focus on particular tasks and show you with clear, numbered steps the easiest way to get them done right now.

IMPORTANT—READ CAREFULLY BEFORE OPENING SOFTWARE PACKET(S). By opening the sealed packet(s) containing the software, you indicate your acceptance of the following Microsoft License Agreement.

MICROSOFT LICENSE AGREEMENT
(Book Companion CD)

This is a legal agreement between you (either an individual or an entity) and Microsoft Corporation. By opening the sealed software packet(s) you are agreeing to be bound by the terms of this agreement. If you do not agree to the terms of this agreement, promptly return the unopened software packet(s) and any accompanying written materials to the place you obtained them for a full refund.

MICROSOFT SOFTWARE LICENSE

1. GRANT OF LICENSE. Microsoft grants to you the right to use one copy of the Microsoft software program included with this book (the "SOFTWARE") on computers you own. The SOFTWARE is in "use" on a computer when it is loaded into the temporary memory (i.e., RAM) or installed into the permanent memory (e.g., hard disk, CD-ROM, or other storage device) of that computer.

2. COPYRIGHT. The SOFTWARE is owned by Microsoft or its suppliers and is protected by United States copyright laws and international treaty provisions. Therefore, you must treat the SOFTWARE like any other copyrighted material (e.g., a book or musical recording). You may not copy the written materials accompanying the SOFTWARE.

3. OTHER RESTRICTIONS. You may not rent or lease the SOFTWARE, but you may transfer the SOFTWARE and accompanying written materials on a permanent basis provided you retain no copies and the recipient agrees to the terms of this Agreement. You may not reverse engineer, decompile, or disassemble the SOFTWARE. If the SOFTWARE is an update or has been updated, any transfer must include the most recent update and all prior versions.

DISCLAIMER OF WARRANTY

The SOFTWARE (including instructions for its use) is provided "AS IS" WITHOUT WARRANTY OF ANY KIND. MICROSOFT FURTHER DISCLAIMS ALL IMPLIED WARRANTIES INCLUDING WITHOUT LIMITATION ANY IMPLIED WARRANTIES OF MERCHANTABILITY OR OF FITNESS FOR A PARTICULAR PURPOSE. THE ENTIRE RISK ARISING OUT OF THE USE OR PERFORMANCE OF THE SOFTWARE AND DOCUMENTATION REMAINS WITH YOU.

IN NO EVENT SHALL MICROSOFT, ITS AUTHORS, OR ANYONE ELSE INVOLVED IN THE CREATION, PRODUCTION, OR DELIVERY OF THE SOFTWARE BE LIABLE FOR ANY DAMAGES WHATSOEVER (INCLUDING, WITHOUT LIMITATION, DAMAGES FOR LOSS OF BUSINESS PROFITS, BUSINESS INTERRUPTION, LOSS OF BUSINESS INFORMATION, OR OTHER PECUNIARY LOSS) ARISING OUT OF THE USE OF OR INABILITY TO USE THE SOFTWARE OR DOCUMENTATION, EVEN IF MICROSOFT HAS BEEN ADVISED OF THE POSSIBILITY OF SUCH DAMAGES. BECAUSE SOME STATES/COUNTRIES DO NOT ALLOW THE EXCLUSION OR LIMITATION OF LIABILITY FOR CONSEQUENTIAL OR INCIDENTAL DAMAGES, THE ABOVE LIMITATION MAY NOT APPLY TO YOU.

U.S. GOVERNMENT RESTRICTED RIGHTS

The SOFTWARE and documentation are provided with RESTRICTED RIGHTS. Use, duplication, or disclosure by the Government is subject to restrictions as set forth in subparagraph (c)(1)(ii) of The Rights in Technical Data and Computer Software clause at DFARS 252.227-7013 or subparagraphs (c)(1) and (2) of the Commercial Computer Software — Restricted Rights 48 CFR 52.227-19, as applicable. Manufacturer is Microsoft Corporation, One Microsoft Way, Redmond, WA 98052-6399.

If you acquired this product in the United States, this Agreement is governed by the laws of the State of Washington.

Should you have any questions concerning this Agreement, or if you desire to contact Microsoft Press for any reason, please write: Microsoft Press, One Microsoft Way, Redmond, WA 98052-6399.

About the Compact Disc

The compact disc attached to the inside of the back cover of this book includes an electronic version of the text of the *Microsoft Computer Dictionary, Third Edition*, which you can search for specific terms. The dictionary uses some parts of Microsoft Internet Explorer to view the text. You will need to use Internet Explorer to properly view the files and use the search feature. If you do not have Internet Explorer already on your computer, this CD will install it for you.

Before using the *Microsoft Press Computer Dictionary, Third Edition* compact disc, please take a few moments to read the License Agreement on the previous page. To install the disc, follow the instructions on the CD label.

Quarterly updates and revisions will be made to the *Microsoft Press Computer Dictionary, Third Edition*, on the Microsoft Press Web site. These updates are meant to keep the content of the dictionary up to date in a field that is rapidly evolving. Click the update button in the dictionary or point your Web browser to http://mspress.microsoft.com/mspress/products/1031/ to access the update site.

Please note that these updates are meant to be viewed on the Microsoft Press Web site and cannot be automatically integrated with the contents of the CD-ROM.

If you'd like to give us feedback about this product, please send e-mail to mspcd@microsoft.com. Please note that product support is not offered through this e-mail address. For support information, please connect to the Microsoft Press Web site at http://mspress.microsoft.com/.

Register Today!

Return this
Microsoft Press® Computer Dictionary,
Third Edition
registration card for
a Microsoft Press® catalog

U.S. and Canada addresses only. Fill in information below and mail postage-free. Please mail only the bottom half of this page.

1-57231-446-XA   *MICROSOFT PRESS® COMPUTER DICTIONARY,*   *Owner Registration Card*
THIRD EDITION

NAME

INSTITUTION OR COMPANY NAME

ADDRESS

CITY   STATE   ZIP

Microsoft®Press
Quality Computer Books

**For a free catalog of
Microsoft Press® products, call
1-800-MSPRESS**

||||

NO POSTAGE
NECESSARY
IF MAILED
IN THE
UNITED STATES

BUSINESS REPLY MAIL
FIRST-CLASS MAIL   PERMIT NO. 53   BOTHELL, WA

POSTAGE WILL BE PAID BY ADDRESSEE

MICROSOFT PRESS REGISTRATION
MICROSOFT PRESS® COMPUTER DICTIONARY,
THIRD EDITION
PO BOX 3019
BOTHELL WA   98041-9946